TOTAL WAR

PETER CALVOCORESSI,
GUY WINT AND JOHN PRITCHARD

TOTAL WAR

THE CAUSES AND COURSES OF
THE SECOND WORLD WAR

REVISED SECOND EDITION

PANTHEON BOOKS · NEW YORK

We are grateful to Martin Gilbert of Merton College, Oxford, and to the
Macmillan Company for their kind permission to use the maps on
pages 116, 122, 135, 175, 187, 194, 202, 241, 245, 247, 256, 258, 360,
469, 471, 483, 496, 502, and 546, which have been adapted from the
following:

Russian History Atlas edited by Martin Gilbert. Cartography by Arthur
Banks. Copyright © 1972 by Martin Gilbert.

Recent History Atlas edited by Martin Gilbert. Cartography by John Flower.
Copyright © 1966 by Martin Gilbert.

Jewish History Atlas edited by Martin Gilbert. Cartography by Peter
Kingsland. Copyright © 1969 by Martin Gilbert.

American History Atlas edited by Martin Gilbert. Cartography by Peter
Kingsland. Copyright © 1969 by Martin Gilbert.

Library of Congress Cataloging-in-Publication Data

Calvocoressi, Peter.
Total war.

Includes bibliographies and index.
1. World War, 1939–1945.   I. Wint, Guy, 1910–1969.
II. Pritchard, John.   III. Title.
D743.C24   1989   940.53   88-43278
ISBN 0-394-57811-2

Manufactured in the United States of America

FIRST REVISED AMERICAN EDITION

Contents

The Western Hemisphere

Part I
THE SOURCES OF WAR IN EUROPE

Part II
HITLER'S WARS: 1939–41

Part III
EUROPE UNDER THE NAZIS

Part IV
THE MIDDLE GAME

Part V
THE DEFEAT OF GERMANY: 1942–5

The Greater East Asia and Pacific Conflict

Part I
ASIAN CONFLICT

Contents

List of Illustrations

List of Maps

Acknowledgements

Acknowledgement is due to Martin Gilbert of Merton College, Oxford, to
Weidenfeld & Nicolson Limited, and to the Macmillan Company for their
kind permission to use the maps on pages 116, 122, 135, 175, 187, 194, 202,
241, 245, 247, 256, 258, 360, 469, 471, 483, 496, 502 and 546, which have been
adapted from the following: *American History Atlas*, edited by Martin Gilbert,
cartography by Peter Kingsland, copyright © Martin Gilbert, 1969; *Jewish
History Atlas*, edited by Martin Gilbert, cartography by Peter Kingsland,
copyright © Martin Gilbert, 1969; *Recent History Atlas*, edited by Martin
Gilbert, cartography by John Flower, copyright © Martin Gilbert, 1966;
Russian History Atlas, edited by Martin Gilbert, cartography by Arthur Banks,
copyright © Martin Gilbert, 1972.

The maps on pages 801 and 1034 have been adapted from *History of the
Sino-Japanese War (1937–1945)* by Hsu Long-hsuen and Chang Ming-kai,
copyright © Chung Wu Publishing Co., 1971. The publishers are grateful
to Mrs George R. Lipe for permission to reproduce the maps on pp. 1202–
3. Cartography for The Greater East Asia and Pacific Conflict section by
Reginald Piggott.

Foreword to the Second Edition

WHEN this book was being written early in the seventies no governmental archives were generally open to the public. Now many are. This is the first of two important differences between the book's first edition and that which is now presented. The second is the death of Guy Wint – he died in fact before completing his work – and the new partnership of John Pritchard and myself in the preparation of this new edition.

It has frequently been observed that the opening of official archives reveals little or nothing. This sweeping judgement is a useful corrective to the view that history is enshrined, often entombed, in official papers, and it is true enough in so far as it asserts that official disclosure rarely produces revelations of major significance. But such disclosure has two important historical consequences. It exposes a mass of detail, and even if the details are in themselves mostly trivial the accumulation of them is not. In particular, the historian's ability to wallow in these details helps him to enter into the minds of those who guided, or tried to guide, or thought they were guiding, the march of events; to understand – whether sympathetically or not – why they thought as they did and acted as they did, and to readjust the impact upon them of the kaleidoscope of circumstances. Within the ambit of this book the opening of the archives compels and facilitates a reassessment of the politics of appeasement in the 1930s – to which I shall revert.

The second important consequence of the opening of the archives is that it loosens tongues and sharpens pens. It stimulates the memoir industry. This is partly a mere matter of time as men and women who have taken part in memorable events find the leisure in advancing age to recollect and write. But many hesitate to do so and they may be encouraged to put pen to paper, or to face the microphone or the camera, when the past is stirred up by official publications, whether raw materials exposed in public record offices or official histories made out of the storehouses of public papers. There is what may be called the secondary scope of disclosure: the memoirs of the people, mostly in high places, who write of themselves and their immediate experience, and also the testimony of humbler men and women who would normally remain silent but whose stories are elicited, and whose diaries are dug out, by historians anxious to put the flesh of ordinary humanity on to the skeleton of history. The non-official literature generated by official disclosure is voluminous and varied. Alongside the books by or about leading statesmen and commanders are the equally pertinent down-to-earth accounts garnered by, for example, John Keegan in his *Six Armies in Normandy* or Studs Terkel in his *The Good War*.

In reading this mass of secondary material I have gleaned suggestions and found facts which have caused me to correct or helped me to sharpen a number of episodes in this book and so, I hope, to increase its veracity and readability: for example, on the loss of Crete, the battle of the Mareth, the bombing of Monte Cassino. Other episodes have been rewritten owing to a special circumstance – the revelations about Ultra intelligence – of which I shall have more to say later in this Foreword. But I have not found myself induced to alter the principal judgements about the course of the war which were contained in the original edition.

I revert to the official archives. Their main impact – and here I refer to the British archives – is on the prewar years and appeasement. In short, the perusal of British Cabinet papers leads me to a somewhat more charitable assessment of British policy-makers but not to the belief that they were right to shirk war in 1938.

The charges against the appeasers have fallen into two main categories: that they were benighted by their ideological prejudices and therefore soft on Fascism and Nazism, and secondly that their consequent feebleness (particularly at the time of Munich) did more to endanger than to succour Great Britain, France and Hitler's other European victims. What the official records show is that the British cabinet was genuinely concerned about a factor which has not received its due prominence – the danger to British interests and British obligations from Japan. Neville Chamberlain and his colleagues may have been blinkered rightists but this was not the only or main source of their attempts to appease Mussolini and Hitler or of their shameful (and it remains shameful) betrayal of Czechoslovakia. They had worries in the Far East to which they rightly attached major importance and which to a significant extent tied their hands. Yet this is not to say that they steered a sensible course.

There is a clear distinction to be drawn between trying to detach Mussolini from Hitler (which was not only highly desirable but also well worth the effort in spite of the eventual failure) and trying to stop Hitler's expansion by throwing him chunks of Europe. If, as I still believe, the latter policy was never likely to succeed (read *Mein Kampf* and Hitler's speeches *passim*), the question that arose was how to weigh the loss of Czechoslovakia's armoury, armed forces and morale against the risk that

Japan would, in 1938, use war in Europe as an opportunity to make war against British and French possessions in South East Asia and the Pacific and against the British dominions of Australia and New Zealand. This question is not one that can be answered but it has to be put because the repute of British and French leaders of that time depends on whether they are judged in retrospect to have weighed the imponderables well or badly. Japan did go to war but not in 1938 or 1939 or even 1940 when Great Britain and France became actively engaged in war. Hitler was not deterred from war by appeasement, although his attacks on Czechoslovakia and Poland were postponed until 1939 and his attacks in the west until 1940. I still believe, as will be evident in the body of this book, that a war in 1938 would have been more easily won than the awful and chancy conflict of 1939–45, and that it would have been saner in 1938 to gamble with the Japanese threat than to eliminate Czechoslovakia from the anti-German alliance.

The principal addition to Part I of this book concerns Ultra intelligence – the decipherment, sufficiently promptly for operational use, of German high-grade Enigma ciphers used by the three armed services, the S S and certain other agencies. When I was writing the first edition of this book, which was published in 1972, I knew all about Ultra because I had worked on it at Bletchley Park during the war. The Ultra secret was about to be broken but I did not know that and I was personally bound to keep it. I made some discreet inquiries about the possibility of being released, perhaps partially, from my obligations. I was given to understand that if I broke my promise there was not much that anybody could do without looking silly, but I decided that my proper course was to observe my promise. I suspected that the continuing secrecy had become unnecessary but I could not be sure of it at that date. Later, I became convinced that the secrecy was pointless and after some discussion with persons better placed to know I tried to persuade a British Prime Minister that there was much to be said for allowing it to be known that the British Secret Service, even more renowned for its treasonable inmates than for its achievements, had in fact made an exciting and decisive contribution to winning the war. My efforts were rebuffed shortly before the secret was allowed to poke its nose out of the bag.

Part I of this book was therefore written in the full knowledge of certain things which I might neither mention nor explain. I recall in particular how my friend and editor at Penguin, Dieter Pevsner, upon reading my first version of the Battle of the Atlantic, told me that he thought it was splendid but made no sense. He was of course right since I had left out the determining factor. This was the most blatant case but there were other passages where the balance of my presentation was distorted by the suppression of the Ultra ingredient. I still, incidentally, do not know whether the Russians read Enigma ciphers. There are many reasons for supposing that they did not. Yet it remains difficult to account for the completeness of their post-Stalingrad tank victories without suspecting some element – Enigma or something else – which has not yet come to light.

In this new edition I have introduced the story of the breaking of the Enigma ciphers and its effect on the war at various times and places. As I was at pains to point out in my book *Top Secret Ultra*, this effect varied greatly: Ultra could be crucial but it never provided complete and prompt coverage of all German military activities. Besides its contribution to the defeat of the U-boats in the Atlantic it was massively useful in North Africa and copious before and after the landings in Normandy in 1944 – I have rewritten, among other things, my account of the battle of the Ardennes. Ultra shed light on such diverse corners of the war as German scientific developments and who was doing or not doing what in Yugoslavia. Most important was its cumulative and (since it came from the Germans themselves) authoritative revelation of the overall size of the German sea, air and ground forces, their capacities, equipment and dispositions, thereby giving the allied side an unprecedented familiarity with the enemy's strengths and limitations. Like so many things about the war this story is not yet fully told. Not all the relevant British documents have been released and some have been destroyed. In the pre-war story of Enigma the Poles hold pride of place for the brilliant intellectual work which enabled them, and them alone, to read Enigma ciphers before the war. Yet it is also becoming clear that a critical element in this success was presented to the Poles by the French and, furthermore, that the French got it before the Nazi seizure of power from a German working in the German cipher office.

John Pritchard's task in Part II has been the more difficult one, for unlike myself he has had to review another man's work. He has done so with a strong admiration for Guy Wint's scholarship, perceptiveness and literary style. He has also two different starting points: first, as a man of a younger generation and, secondly, as an expert primarily in Japanese matters, whereas Wint's erudition was focused on China and India, which he knew and loved well. To my mind all these points – the basic admiration, the difference in age and the diffraction of viewpoint – are manifest advantages. Much of what Guy Wint wrote is unchanged, notably in relation to China, India and Burma. But in other areas John Pritchard's contribution is decisive. Drawing largely on fourteen years' work on the documents of the Tokyo War Crimes Trial he amplifies and corrects our picture of Japan which, even in those aspects where it remains extremely unattractive, becomes historically intelligible rather than simply demoniacal. Thus he digs deep into the reasons why Japan ran amok in China and exhibited in this century a savagery untypical of Japan in the nineteenth century. He re-examines relevant features of the Japanese constitution, the nature and consequences of the factional fighting between the Japanese army and navy, and the roots of Japanese extremism. While stressing no less than Guy Wint the importance of the Manchurian Incident and the transformation of Manchukuo into an industrial and colonial powerhouse, he portrays this extraordinary achievement in terms of Japanese creativity as well as Japanese power. He brings out the significance for Japan of Russian activities in northern Asia, from the construction of the Trans-Siberian Railway a hundred years ago to the murderous Russian comeback in Manchuria in 1945. He dismisses the notion that the British were taken by surprise by the Japanese onslaught on their possessions in 1941: the British fault was not ignorance but the inability to decide what to do about a menace foreseen, alternating between the itch to dispatch the Royal Navy to teach Japan a lesson and playing it cool and hoping for the best. With the war over, the American régime of General MacArthur emerges as not merely dictatorial, which was not in the circumstances surprising, but also as flouting the terms of the Emperor's surrender.

Passing time changes more than the store of knowledge. Attitudes change too. The first readers of this book were prompted, I surmise, mainly by wonder. They wanted to know how and why this terrible war, which they had experienced and survived, had come about; and how it ran its course, with what shifts and turns, what inventions, skills and pieces of luck. This curiosity was allied with the simple convictions of right and wrong which had ruled during the war; wartime loyalties persisted for a time in post-war exhilaration and relief, equally unquestioning, providing their own scale of values. A later generation has other needs. The curiosity is still there, but an audience further removed from the intensities of war is more critical. It takes less for granted and sees no reason not to query particular reputations or general strategies, ours as much as theirs. War leaders, military and civilian, are subjected to the beady eye of posthumous inquest, which is sometimes justified by the resulting verdicts although it may in some cases smell of a distasteful iconoclasm. Strategies which, during the war, were judged purely in terms of their war-winning efficacy are reviewed and censured in moral terms which the warriors themselves would have dismissed as a luxury rightly banished from the calculation of their wartime exigencies.

War leaders inevitably loom larger than life so long as they are in charge. They become known to, and therefore misunderstood by, thousands of people who have barely heard of them before. This was particularly the case with Churchill and Roosevelt as allied leaders. For the British, Roosevelt was a towering American personality. They were oblivious of the fact that all his life Roosevelt was an object of bitter controversy in his own country. They were oblivious too of the further fact that throughout the period between the wars Anglo-American relations were normally bad. On the American side Churchill was portrayed and accepted with the lineaments of legendary and archetypal heroism, in ignorance of his record as a maverick and inconstant politician whom the electorate would dump as soon as the war was over. Wartime reputations are not made to last. Yet I would argue that these were greater men than their contemporaries and it is a mistake to disinter their evident failings if the object of doing so is to deny them this eminence.

More generally, the conduct of the war has been more critically examined. There was some criticism at the time: for example, British protests against area bombing of civilian targets and criticism in and beyond the United States of the bombing of Hiroshima and Nagasaki without at least some warning. The annihilation of these two cities and so many of their inhabitants shocked by its novelty as much as by its enormity but the first revulsion against this supreme act of destruction was confined to the few. The point is that those few have got no fewer with the passing of time, while the equally frightful bombing of Dresden has evoked, on its fortieth anniversary, passionate recrimination. (This is an instance where official disclosure and the ensuing arguments have not only left my initial judgement unchanged but have reinforced it: I find myself more than ever convinced that this operation lacked the rigorous justification which so fearful a slaughter of undefended civilians requires and – the crucial point – did require even in the press of war.)

The probing of the conduct of the war, alongside the desire to retrace its fortunes, demonstrates that the Second World War now commands attention for two distinct reasons: as a self-contained event in time, and as an example of the species war. This expanded focus of the historical viewpoint prompts two reflections. The first concerns morality and legality in war and the second concerns the status of its opposite – peace – in our post-war scale of values.

The fact that the war was fought against evil Nazis or, to be more guarded, that the war fought to curb German power incidentally entailed the destruction of Nazism – made it for many people a good war. Our side was right. The terrible suffering and devastation had to be. The Middle Ages, trying to justify wars, evolved two sets of tests called *jus ad bellum* and *jus in bello*. The first laid down rules for deciding whether the waging of a particular war was right in the first place. The second set tried to regulate behaviour once war had started. Medieval churchmen and lawyers attached much importance to *jus ad bellum*, which enabled them to distinguish legitimate wars from illicit ones and so to sanctify war on at least some occasions with a clear conscience. To *jus in bello* on the other hand they paid relatively perfunctory attention. That imbalance has been redressed in modern times and nowadays the Hague and Geneva Conventions on permissible and impermissible weaponry and on the treatment of civilians, neutrals, prisoners and others (the descendants of *jus in bello*) are taken no less seriously than restrictions on the right to make war in other international instruments. The conduct of war has become as much a matter of moral concern as its initiation. Hence the concentration in recent years, by a general public as well as lawyers, on the more dubious episodes in the Second World War and what these ready lapses into morally and legally impermissible acts may portend for the future.

Secondly, war itself – as distinct from the ways in which it may be waged – is once more a matter for debate. When the Second World War ended, the prevailing view, which amounted to an unquestioned assumption, was to the effect that nothing like it must be allowed to happen again: peace is paramount. In that spirit the victors took the lead in creating the United Nations (more or less in the image of the League of Nations) and, by Article 2 of the UN Charter, in removing from the state the right to make war except in tightly restricted circumstances. The Japanese went further still and in their post-war constitution explicitly denied the right of the state to belligerency. This novel ban on warfare, in either form, was one of the principal consequences of the Second World War and its horrors. I do not feel confident that this primacy of peace still prevails, least of all among leaders of Superpowers. The antithesis of war and peace is most blatant and compelling in the immediate aftermath of war, but gradually other values reassert themselves and people come to think, as many thought in the 1930s, that there are worse things than war: injustice, for example, or tyranny or systematic and pervasive torture. Just as medieval Christians honestly believed it right to go to war to convert pagans or kill heretics, so today, their modern counterparts have seen virtue in crusading expeditions to impose democracy (the Reagan line) or preserve communist socialism (the Brezhnev doctrine). The trouble with such notions is that they relegate peace to a subordinate place in our scale of values and, furthermore, that they are all too easily, perhaps inevitably, shaped by national self-interest rather than the disinterested virtues which they proclaim. When peace is no longer paramount, when statesmen cast casuistically about for ways of side-stepping the laws of armed conflict or reinterpreting the Charter, then the bestiality of war is that much easier on the mind and that much nearer in practice. Of such attitudes the course of the Second World War is a standing indictment, never to be forgotten.

PETER CALVOCORESSI
BATH, 1988

The Western Hemisphere

Introduction to the Second Edition

THE years 1870 to 1945 were the period in which Europe feared Germany. Before that it was France, afterwards the Soviet Union. In this perspective the Second World War is the end of an era.

In this period much was lost. The European states system disintegrated. One international economic order foundered and was not replaced by another. Concurrently with these two great dislocations Europe's primacy in the world disappeared. Given the centrality of Germany – geographical and dynamic – much retrospective attention has been focused on German responsibility, even (which is not the same thing) culpability, in this tide of events.

The European states system, which evolved and prevailed over the eighteenth and nineteenth centuries, gave priority to the state over the system – it was a system in which the whole was subordinate to the parts – but nevertheless it was a political reality recognized and used by statesmen. It rested on the proposition that where there is a plurality of states there is a community of interests; and that these common interests may be served by constant communication and mutual accommodation, even though the ultimate sovereign right to decide and act unilaterally is retained. The working of such a system required two crucial pre-conditions: that the states which mattered should be few but not too few, and that for most of the time most of them should prefer peace to war and find the system useful in keeping the peace. Its principal feature was balance. It had inherent mobility between its parts, and statesmanship was largely defined by the capacity of statesmen to manage the balancing through alliances and reversals of alliances. It was at risk whenever it became rigid through incompetent management or when any principal statesman had no use for it: that is to say, in the first case, when too many of its possible permutations were blocked or, in the second, when a man like Hitler preferred (to adapt Ludwig Dehio's phrase) *Hegemonie* to *Gleichgewicht*, empire to system. It was also at risk when the sovereign states, which were its components, became too numerous and unequal in power and resources, particularly when (as happened after 1919) the Great Powers were reduced in number and new, lesser states proliferated.

After 1870 Bismarck's new Reich was the greatest industrial and military power in Europe. Bismarck preferred *Gleichgewicht* to *Hegemonie* but he fashioned for his successors a Europe which was not only re-shaped by German victories but also systemically constricted by two fateful acts: the annexation of Alsace and Lorraine in 1871 and his treaty with Austria in 1879. The first eliminated from the system any Franco-German permutation and therefore weakened the system itself; the second tied Germany to Austria's ambitions and apprehensions in the Balkans when the last stage in the slow Ottoman retreat from Europe was setting the Habsburg against the Russian monarchy in south east Europe. Bismarck's successors, often more liberal than he but never as powerful or intelligent, failed to extricate themselves from this unnecessary strait-jacket. That is part of Germany's responsibility for the onset of the First World War. There were other parts, by no means all of them German, although two German factors contributed powerfully to the trend to war: the personality and antics of Kaiser William II, not a bad man but an uneducated one; and the post-Bismarckian attempt to challenge British naval power in the world as well as throw German weight about on the continent. These two factors put paid to another of the system's possible permutations: an Anglo-German condominium.

The two World Wars have obscured the extent to which Great Britain and Germany entertained good feelings for one another throughout most of the period from Bismarck to Hitler. Von Tirpitz and Hitler were potent destroyers of these feelings, but before the First World War there were inklings of an Anglo-German joint power structure, while after that war and the abdication of the Kaiser, British statesmen were keen to re-establish relations with Germany and restore it to the comity of European states – as France had been embraced in the Concert of Europe after the abdication of Napoleon. Great Britain even pursued this endeavour for several years after Hitler became Chancellor and then President in a Third German Reich. One of the main paradoxes of the period under discussion is the tenacity of British hostility in wartime to a country with which, for most of the time, Great Britain had no quarrel.

In the First World War Germany defeated Russia and was then defeated by a western alliance; in the second, Germany was defeated on both fronts. Among the consequences of the first war were the disappearance for ever of the Habsburg and Ottoman empires; the revolution in Russia, which removed the Tsarist monarchy and, with the aftermath of foreign invasions and civil war, removed Russia itself from European affairs for a generation; the emergence in eastern (but not western) Europe of a string of new or revived or enlarged states, all of them economic weaklings and none of them adept performers in a European states system; the reduction therefore of the managers of that system from five or six to two (or three, if Italy be accounted a competent and willing third); and the enfeeblement of Germany, prolonged until the time when it was able by its own exertions to reclaim its place in Europe on its own terms.

The instrument of the curbing of Germany was the treaty of Versailles. In 1919, as during the Second World War, plans for partitioning Germany were abandoned and its French proponents had to be content with a limited occupation of parts of the Rhineland, the emasculation of Germany's armed forces, a swingeing bill of costs and a (broken) promise of an Anglo-American guarantee against renewed German attack. Making the losers pay for a war was nothing new – after the Franco-Prussian war Bismarck imposed heavy payments on France, which paid them more than punctually – but the inclusion in the treaty of the famous 'war guilt' clause in order to justify a big bill rankled unforgettably in Germany; the haggling over the total sum went on for ten years; the American insistence on keeping inter-allied debts, the bulk of them due to the United States, distinct from reparations payments bedevilled post-war international finances, particularly in the case of France, which, owing twice what it was owed, looked to reparations from Germany to enable it to pay its debts to the United States.

The First World War was not only a huge shock. Its cost too was huge. It accelerated, if it did not cause, a breakdown in the international economic order which compounded the breakdown of the European states system. For much of the previous century relations between the (relatively few) sovereign economies were stable. The economic order was dominated by Great Britain, under the signs of free trade and gold. Their balances were measured and settled in gold, and the exchange rates of their currencies were steady. The war greatly devalued all the currencies, even more greatly disrupted the relations between them, exposed Great Britain's inability any longer to combine an international regulatory role with the pursuit of its national economic interests, and provided no alternative leadership since the United States – the world's greatest economic power – abjured any such role. (The United States gave restorative aid to Europe through investment and loans in the 1920s, but the provision of this finance made its withdrawal at the end of the decade all the more painful and disastrous. This withdrawal, beginning in 1928, had mixed causes: the failure to cut back American wartime agricultural production, leading to falling farm prices and rising farmers' indebtedness; enticing opportunities for investment at home instead of in Europe; and maniacal speculation, the stock market crash of 1929 and the consequent rush for liquidity.) So, within the very short space of a decade, the economic consequences of the war and of the Treaty of Versailles combined to create bewildering economic confusion. The Depression of 1929–31 was followed in 1933 by a world Monetary and Economic Conference whose failure – engineered by the United States – deepened the gloom, accelerated nationalist protectionism and promoted revolution.

Revolution was most feared in France but occurred in fact in Germany. Great Britain's was the first major economy to turn a corner, through a policy of substantial spending on new housing which reanimated the construction industry and associated trades. In France, by contrast, governments nailed their colours to deflation, gold and balanced budgets; lent large sums to banks and other undertakings, and lost it; and cut real wages, forced women out of jobs and so added social unrest and political instability to economic disorder. When Leon Blum's Popular Front government tried to go into reverse, it discovered that it could not do so without a coordinated international strategy which did not exist. Frenchmen talked of 1789 and threw Blum out, but although there were violent disturbances there was (as in 1968) no revolution. In Germany, however, there was. There Heinrich Brüning, hagridden by the inflation of 1922 which was ended by decreeing that 1 million million marks made 1 mark, also clung until too late to deflation in a deflating world. The moribund Nazi Party won votes and total power: twelve seats in the 1928 Reichstag elections became 107 in 1930 and the largest party block in 1932. In the next year Hitler was Chancellor.

Hitler knew what he wanted and had written a book saying what he wanted: *Lebensraum* (living space, for Germans). It could not be got without war. Hitler envisaged war and did not at all disapprove of it. Therefore Hitler's contribution to the Second World War was altogether different from any German contribution to the First. One may plausibly conclude that Germany's responsibility for the first war was greater than others, either much greater or only a little greater; but in relation to the second war Germany's responsibility is close to total. This judgement may be challenged only by disjoining a country from its rulers, by considering a term like 'Germany' to be an abstraction incapable of carrying responsibility. That within Germany many people did not want war is self-evident. But in so far as wars are waged by states, and in so far as the responsibility for a war may be apportioned between states, then German responsibility for the Second World War in Europe is in a class of its own.

The responsibility for starting the war resurrected the old charge of Germany's peculiar war guilt in the twentieth century, but in a much altered context, since it is psychologically difficult to separate Hitler's responsibility for the war from related atrocious and guilt-laden policies, particularly the killing – with the machinery of the state and for purely racial reasons – of all attainable Jews and gipsies and the design to reduce the numbers of the Slavs by 30 million. (The fact that until about 1941 Hitler still preferred to export Jews rather than kill them is relevant neither to his racialism nor to the criminality of the subsequent genocide.) Hitler's plans for Europe were not original in as much as they were an expanded version of visions of *Mitteleuropa*, which had allured an earlier generation of thrusting financiers and industrialists. If such visions lead to war the man in the street feels only a limited responsibility (at most) for the outcome. In the sixties Fritz Fischer's *Griff nach der Weltmacht* (1961) reopened the case against Germany in 1914–18 with a scrupulous and scholarly investigation of German aims, before and during the war, to seize for Germany dominion in Europe and the world. The debate which ensued became at times heated but remained essentially academic. But a later debate about German guilt in the thirties and forties went wider and deeper because it went beyond the war-making propensities of governments and ruling classes to the racial and criminal accompaniments of Hitler's conquests, which demanded widespread personal involvement in the bestialities perpetrated in death camps and in territories occupied by the German armies in the east. This later debate, although conducted mainly by historians, was not confined to academics and very many Germans felt a shame akin to guilt. The swell of disgust prompted a counter-attack which tried to explain away conduct so unbecoming a civilized people. A conservative school of writers, more nationalist than scholarly in their inspiration, argued that the mass murders of Jews and Slavs were a secondary crime, secondary because they reflected a mode of thinking and acting with which Europe had already been infected and polluted by the enormities of Stalinist communism. Others have fallen back more modestly on the argument that no man is responsible for another's crime, no generation may be saddled with moral guilt except through its own acts or connivance. But the first post-war generation acknowledged, it would seem, some guilt by association and endorsed the view that the new German state, as the successor in title of the Third Reich, was morally right to accept an obligation to Jewry and offer the sort of reparation (money) which alone can be offered after the event: an acknowledgement and a payment which lie somewhere between expiation and *ex gratia* disbursement.

These debates and their outcome are one indication among others that the Germany which emerged from its second defeat was much more radically altered than was Germany after the first war. The two other principal states of western Europe – Great Britain and France – have changed far less since 1870 than Germany appears to have done: their fundamental political and constitutional assumptions (not to mention their frontiers) have remained the same, their national temper has been, compared with Germany's, subdued, and the trend of their domestic policies has been fairly consistent and equable in a liberal direction. Germany's history in the same years has been episodic. The Second Reich began as a monarchical régime under a Kaiser who was more a military than a civilian figure; its main props, in addition to the army, were a landowning aristocracy (the Junkers of the east) and a new plutocracy (the industrialists and financiers of the west). This was something like the régime envisaged a generation earlier by John C. Calhoun of South Carolina who, before the Civil War, hoped for a partnership between the plantation society of the South and the developing industrial economy of the North, but in a very different constitutional, civilian context. The Second Reich degenerated into a monarcho–military autocracy and then, during the first war, into a military dictatorship which first overrode and then sacrificed the Kaiser. After the war the Weimar Republic, democratic and even socialist in intent, was immediately beset by armed threats from left and right which persisted to 1924 and from which the government was able to save the Republic only with the help of what was left of the army. With the revival of industry in the boom years 1924–9, Weimar governments had either to displease the military and the plutocracy or to lean on them, from which dilemma it had not extricated itself before the advent of the Great Depression and Hitler. Both the military and industry – a nationalist and protectionist combination – welcomed Hitler up to a point, and he in turn was dependent on industry for rearmament and on the army for his aggressive foreign designs. While the Nazis were in many ways repulsive and alarming to these old pillars of the state, there was enough common ground to stifle the Weimar ideals of parliamentary democracy and social responsibility. It took a second war and defeat to bring Germany into line, mentally as well as formally, with the main stream of western political and social attitudes. This alignment of the three main western European states is one of the second war's most significant consequences.

When the second war ended the European states system was left even more jejune than in 1919. In the east the Soviet conquest was a further stage in the division of the continent into east and west, an accentuation of a process already marked by the dissolution in 1919 of its old autocracies (senior members of an overall European system) and by the Treaty of Locarno in 1926 whereby a new order was established for the west from which, on British insistence, the east was excluded. With the Second

World War the Soviet Union erased the three Baltic Republics and took large bites out of Poland and Rumania and a smaller bite out of Slovakia. Otherwise the map looked in the east much the same as before the war, but a map is not the best guide to reality and the states shown on it were states only in name. In the west the map was unaltered: the causes of Hitler's war lay in eastern, not western, Europe. But the states of western Europe, although intact, had lost their confidence in their ability to construct or operate a purely European system; the old European Great Powers were no longer the top powers but were outranked by two Superpowers, and in order to safeguard themselves they prayed the United States, a geographical outsider, to become a political insider. To regulate economic affairs a new international economic order had been devised in 1944 at Bretton Woods but it lasted for less than thirty years and was followed by a fresh bout of economic instability reminiscent of the leaderless inter-war years – widely fluctuating currencies, barely controlled expansion of credit, boom and bust in stock markets, unpayable foreign debts. The new political order, resting on the mutual nuclear deterrence of the Superpower arbiters of the continent, was accepted as a fact of life for about the same span. But the régime in the east, erected by Stalin to protect his western frontiers, was a failure. Subordinate communist parties ruled in the several pre-war states. They were installed by the Soviet armies (except in Yugoslavia, which broke away from the Soviet block almost at once) and were secure so long as Soviet armies might come back in an emergency. This they did in Hungary and Poland in 1956 and in Czechoslovakia in 1968, but in Poland in 1980 the Soviet government deemed it inexpedient to intervene with force even to prevent the overthrow of the party's rule. In western Europe the alliance with the United States remained almost unchallenged. It was an insurance against Soviet hostility and, even when the Kremlin put on a more benign face with Khruschchev or Gorbachev, fear of Soviet might and distrust of Soviet intentions could not be lightly assuaged. Yet the Nato alliance, initially easy and popular, began to become irksome as commercial rivalries developed between Europeans and Americans; world policies, particularly in the Middle East, diverged; and, perhaps temporarily, Europe's assessment of United States leadership lapsed into amazed contempt and ridicule. The terms upon which a European-American alliance might endure needed to be discussed but could not be discussed so long as political leaders on both sides pretended that what was needed was maintenance and not a new model.

As the war ended all the eventual victors abandoned the idea of partitioning Germany. But Germany was partitioned. Partition was a yearning to undo Bismarck's work, a feeling that Europe might cope with pre-Bismarckian Prussia but not with Prussia-writ-large, *alias* Germany. Within a few years of the war's end two entirely new states were born: the Federal Republic of Germany and the Democratic Republic of Germany, both of them as new-fangled as the German Reich had been in 1870. But partition did not have its expected effect. The German impact on events did not evaporate. The (western) Federal Republic quickly became, at first in association with the United States but later by its own exertions, a Great Power – only half armed in as much as it might neither make nor possess nuclear weapons, but an economic giant which by the end of the eighties was the second (after Japan) provider of capital for the rest of the world. This resurgence raised once more an old question whether all, or nearly all, Germans ought not naturally to form one state, and what the power of such a state might be. The war had cut Germany in two and recreated the separate republic of Austria. Before the war and until Hitler's *Anschluss* in 1938 the separation of Austria from Germany had been maintained only because a union had been ruled out by the Geneva Protocol of 1922; but because it was maintained it came to seem proper. By analogy the separation of the two post-war German republics may also come to seem immutable. Yet these two states have long insisted that their relations with one another are not as the relations between other sovereign states, and – unlike Austrians who identify themselves as Austrians – citizens of both German republics identify themselves as Germans. A first post-war generation accepted the separation because it was clearly unable to end it without starting a war, but it will be surprising if a succeeding generation does not mate west with east as surely as the Rumanians once mated Moldavia with Wallachia.

But the future contribution of Germany to Europe's affairs does not depend on reunification. The Federal Republic is by itself strong enough to have and exercise choices, which it is beginning cautiously to consider. It is inhibited by fear of the Soviet Union and a commensurate reluctance to annoy the United States, but within the foreseeable future it may choose one or more of a number of political courses and experiment in combining them: reunion with eastern Germany; a condominium with France; substantially improved relations with the Soviet Union. The code-name for this last option is Rapallo – but with the reminder that the Treaty of Rapallo in 1922 did little for either party except enable it to thumb its nose at everybody else while they were not looking. There is once again a German power. Germany is not a Superpower or likely to become one, but there is no law in politics which says that only Superpowers count nor is there a law which says that no state may deal with a

Superpower except another Superpower. The main thrust of Superpower détente is not confined to arms deals but leads in the longer run to political debate and manoeuvre, and once the United States has given a lead in intercourse with the Soviet Union, others will not be far behind.

The only European state which won in both the World Wars was Great Britain. Except in the obvious sense – it is more agreeable to win than lose – these victories have been a mixed blessing. They have veiled and accelerated Great Britain's industrial decline, for however one may admire the economic management of the British war efforts, the wars were enormously costly and Great Britain stumbled out of them with only partial confidence and independence. A victor's natural inclination to return to what he sees as attainable normality was demonstrated in 1925 by the return to the gold standard with an overvalued pound sterling which could be maintained only by severe and damaging deflation. By reversing such policies Great Britain staged a comparatively early recovery from the Great Depression but the second war was won only at the cost of selling precious overseas assets and incurring large debts. Post-war recovery was gratifyingly swift but without a sufficiently radical transformation of industry, from those which had made fortunes in the past to the materials and methods of a new industrial revolution. With the revival of the French and west German economies Great Britain seemed once more to be flagging. Renewed international instability and inflation in the seventies propelled it, in the eighties, into a fresh bout of extravagant deflation which throttled economic activity and precipitated bankruptcies and unemployment on an unforeseen and unnecessary scale. In spite of remarkable bonanzas (North Sea oil, the collapse of world prices of raw materials, prolific proceeds of denationalization) Great Britain was forced to the bottom of the table of advanced industrial countries and forfeited unrecoverable opportunities. A half-hearted abandonment of the nostrums of the early eighties stimulated recovery, but this sad performance diminished Great Britain's standing in Europe.

The ambiguity of the British position in Europe was enhanced by a different wartime experience: the special relationship between Churchill and Roosevelt. Before the war relations between the two countries had not been close or cordial, and leaders on either side were wont to be derogatory about the other, in private sometimes very derogatory. But the war wrought a big change, not merely through the imperatives of an Anglo-American alliance and the exhilaration of a shared victory but also through the exceptional personal relations which were initiated by Churchill and welcomed by Roosevelt. With other leaders after the war this relationship became something of a fetish, but a fetish grounded in enough reality – a common experience, a common language, shared traditions –

to give substance to the magic. The relationship, however, was special in a more restricted sense than the British imagined. It made for an ease of communication at all levels which neither British nor Americans attained with others, but it could not create a special identity of interests in political or commercial matters and so far from putting American weight behind British ideas it threatened to pull British politicians into a toadying indulgence of American adventures and misadventures. On the British side the belief in this special relationship strengthened hesitations about joining the European Community (whose value and durability the British grievously underrated in the fifties and sixties) and made Great Britain, when it did join, a partner with a difference, less than fully committed to the Community's larger aims. Great Britain muffed its chances of playing a linking role between Europe and America and lapsed into a petulant limbo between the two. Where once in the community Great Britain's absence had been deplored, its presence became a matter of some indifference, even vexation. Germany's obvious European partner was no longer Great Britain but France.

The European Community was a child of war, an experiment for mustering and re-asserting Europe's diminished status and diminished economic clout in the world. Its success is problematic because it has not solved the question how much unity and central authority are necessary to make a community effective. Too much unity goes against the European grain. The Community was established in the first place by Europeans who observed Europe's economic (and therefore political) decline and wished to reverse it by joining forces and resources. The forces and resources to be joined were economic, and the Community in its first phase was an association of advanced industrial and trading states. But it failed to take a leaf out of the book of the German *Zollverein* and, instead of consolidating before expanding, it did the reverse. It did so moreover for non-economic reasons and was to that extent untrue to its first purpose. The original six members welcomed newcomers for, mainly, political reasons. They believed that membership of the Community would deter anti-democratic antics in countries like Greece and in pursuit of this implausible aim attenuated the Community's economic strength by admitting to it economic weaklings which, at this stage, it had difficulty in supporting. The political aspect of the Community has been sharpened by attempts, only half successful, to achieve common policies in extra-European affairs. What the Community most needs is not policies about other continents but a central bank and a common currency: the mobilization of resources before attempts to exert inchoate power. The untimely distension of the Community, in size and in purpose, has jeopardized it.

   To argue that the Community is ill-advised to devote its ingenuities to fabricating common external policies is not to deny that some European states have crucial external interests or that these interests are often the same. This is particularly true of the Middle East, a stamping ground for Europeans for centuries, a vital crossroads and an inescapable source of fuels. When the First World War dissolved the Ottoman empire, its Arab subjects hoped for independence but got British and French rule. This rule was eliminated by the second war which, in this area, complemented the first. The second war also gave, in the most horrible manner, a great boost to modern Zionism, which had been a not very successful Jewish minority movement originally founded to find a way to save the persecuted Jews of Russia and Rumania. The founder of this modern Zionist movement, Theodore Herzl, was an attractive but naïve Austrian Jew (Jewish by race but an atheist) who was so appalled by the pogroms of the 1880s that he devoted his life and wealth to finding somewhere – preferably in the Ottoman empire – for oppressed Jews to live a decent life. He grievously misjudged Ottoman readiness to accommodate – as opposed to listen to – his schemes, and after his death and after the First World War his successors were equally unsuccessful in getting British sympathy or support, in spite of the Balfour Declaration (1917) by which the British had promised to look favourably on the creation of a home for Jews in Palestine. (By home, the British understood a refuge for a limited number of Jews without statehood. The Zionists wanted a state.) The second war's horrors created unprecedented sympathy for Europe's surviving Jews, and by allying their own ruthlessness with this sympathy Zionists won their state, evicting all the British and half the Palestinian Arabs. Subsequently financed by the American state and by American Jewish wellwishers (who, however, did not want to go to Israel except as tourists) the new state defeated all Arab attempts to exterminate or contain it but failed to achieve a *modus vivendi* with the Arab world, with the consequence that the Middle East has been almost perpetually at war since the end of the war in Europe. Forty years on the future of the state of Israel appears a great deal less than certain.

   In the years 1870–1945 Germany lost whatever chance it may have had to dominate Europe either imperially, as Hitler wanted, or by manipulating the European states system, as Bismarck envisaged. After two catastrophic wars the western German Republic, the more important relic of the Reich, has come to terms with its western foes but is on an uneasy footing with the Soviet Union, a footing which could get better or worse as the one or the other grows richer or stronger. The eastern German Republic lacks formal relations in the one direction and satisfactory ones in the other. The prime question in eastern Europe is the degree of independence which its sovereign states may exact from the Soviet Union, which is perplexed about how to change Stalin's failed post-war settlement without reviving Stalin's fears for the Soviet Union's defences. The prime question in western Europe is whether the exceptional resources and skills of its principal national economies may be integrated to create once more a power in Europe commensurate with other world powers.

Europe's position is a double dilemma. Not only is the deployment of its resources impeded by its fragmentation into sovereign authorities – a luxury which it can hardly now afford. In addition it seems trapped in the ambiguities of power. In the first years after the Second World War power was equated with nuclear weapons. The war in Europe was the last widespread pre-nuclear war, but within a few months of its termination the concomitant war in the Pacific and East Asia saw the use of nuclear bombs. Since then wars have been divided into nuclear and non-nuclear, and states have been sharply categorized in the same way. Yet world powers are not the same as nuclear Superpowers, for the World Powers include, confusingly, Japan which has overwhelming economic power without possessing post-modern nuclear armament. Nor are all the increasingly numerous nuclear states the equals in resources of some non-nuclear ones. Western Europe, epitomized in this respect by western Germany, senses a capacity to graduate to the top level economically but feels unsafe without some kind of nuclear protection, which, however, may so mortgage its resources as to cancel its hopes of emulating Japan. After two mutually destructive wars west Germany and its associates may not do as Japan has done, because Europe's Soviet hinterland is a great deal more menacing than anything that Japan yet perceives in China. Europe therefore is constrained in a way in which Japan is not. A hundred years ago conflict between Russia, China and Japan was already a major element in world affairs, but to most Europeans it was peripheral. Now, by contrast, this continuing power dance on the other side of the globe may condition Europe's future as decisively as the material and psychological ravages of Europe's wars or the loss of Europe's worldwide empires.

Part I

THE SOURCES OF WAR IN EUROPE

CHAPTER 1
The Background

THERE are two extreme views about the European origins of the Second World War. One is that it was all Hitler's fault. The other is that it was a war in which Hitler, along with a lot of other people, and for much the same reasons, got involved. Both views stand condemned by their very simplicity. This book supports neither but it has to start somewhere, and it starts with Hitler and the Nazis.

To begin with Hitler is not to endorse the view that the war was Hitler's war. No great upheaval can plausibly be ascribed to a single individual, however extraordinary. The war that occurred in 1739 is called after a certain Captain Jenkins and his ear, but it was not much of a war and Captain Jenkins may, if a little spuriously, have it. But the conflict of 1939–45 was a World War and not one man's war. It embraced a number of originally distinct wars which merged. Some of these were, in a formal sense, started by Hitler, but the causes of this six-year compendium of fighting in Europe have to be examined in terms of much more than Hitler, or the Nazis, or Germany, or even of Europe. A World War has necessarily complex origins.

But it does not follow that Hitler was a man or a politician like any other. He was not. On the contrary, he was decidedly outside the normal run of men and of statesmen, and the things that made him different contributed to war. He saw human affairs as a conflict; he portrayed this conflict as a moral one in which he had a role which justified every means; yet morally speaking he was, by any ordinary standards, himself a criminal who used murder openly and massively. Such beliefs and such behaviour cannot fail, if allied with power, to promote war.

Hitler, however, was not the demiurge. He could not create or even destroy in a vacuum, and there were, without him, the makings of war in the world and the makings of the sort of wars which were begun like a spreading fire in the years 1939–41.

To see how Hitler and the Nazis came to power in Germany in 1933 it is necessary to understand not only Hitler and the Nazis but also Germany in 1933, and in order to understand the Germany of that time it is necessary to ask questions about the Europe of which Germany had been geographically and culturally a part centuries before Hitler was heard of.

Adolf Hitler was born in April 1889. In January 1933, at the age of forty-three, he became Chancellor of the German Reich. Six years later Germany invaded Poland and so began Europe's part of the Second World War. These are three facts among countless others which belong to the history of the sources in the Second World War. They are cardinal facts. Without them things would have been very different. But by themselves they explain nothing. The war was not the work of one man or one nation but a phenomenon which punctuated the course of Europe's history and the whole world's.

Adolf Hitler's father Alois was the illegitimate son of Maria Schicklgruber. Alois took the name of Hiedler or Hitler after Maria's husband, who may have fathered him before the marriage. Alois was a reasonably well-off minor official, inclined to be self-indulgent and quick-tempered, something of a womanizer. He died in 1903 at the age of sixty-six after having married three times. His third wife bore him six children, of whom only Adolf and a sister Paula survived beyond childhood. Adolf did poorly at school and was difficult at home. From elementary school he went to a *Realschule* and not to a *Gymnasium* which was the goal of the cleverer children or of those with the more ambitious parents. He left school at sixteen and stayed at home, spending his time drawing and making plans for buildings. He dreamed of being asked to design a new municipal theatre for the city of Linz. When he was eighteen he went to Vienna with a competence which was supplemented shortly afterwards when his mother died and he got a small pension. He also sponged on a penurious aunt. He wanted to go to the Academy of Fine Arts but failed the examination. He lived at first quite well but as his money gave out he became not only idle but increasingly lonely, shabby and bitter. He earned a little money by copying pictures; a friend hawked them for him; he was a pavement artist without a pavement. He became a middle-class misfit in a lower-class environment. He was humiliated by this decline and also shocked by what he saw. Years later in *Mein Kampf* he referred to the 'economic misery' of the companions he had at this time and to the 'crudeness of their habits and morals and the low level of their cultural development'. He also noted the fear which grips a social group when it sees itself falling down the social scale and becoming classed with the lowest workers. He looked around for someone to blame.

Vienna, in its last years as an imperial city, a polyglot centre dominated by Germans who were nevertheless fearful of losing their dominant position, was overcrowded and short of housing. The poor and destitute congregated in homes and rest-rooms. Hitler was among them. Here he picked up the common grouse that things would be much better if only Jews and foreigners – especially Czechs – were not allowed to get all the jobs. When things were specially bad this grumbling turned to hatred. Some Austrian politicians played on it and Hitler may have learned in Vienna how potent a weapon racial prejudice can be, for the forerunners of the Austrian Nazis were already at work scaring German Gentiles with the prospect of a flood of undesirable aliens who would overwhelm them economically and besmirch the purity of their race. Statistics were invoked to increase repugnance and envy. Between the middle of the nineteenth century and the outbreak of the First World War the Jewish population of the city rose from 2 per cent to nearly 9 per cent, and in Hitler's time Jews gained more than a quarter of all the places in secondary schools and university. Financial or sexual scandals were exaggerated or invented. Hitler himself swallowed the story that the city's prostitutes were run by a Jewish ring, when it is very unlikely that they were run by a ring at all. Hitler's description of Jewry in *Mein Kampf* as the 'bacillus which destroys humankind', a pestilence like the Black Death, was probably formulated during his years in Vienna, and he specifically wrote of Vienna as the 'ancient nursery of German culture' battened on by 'promiscuous swarms of foreigners'.

In 1913 Hitler left Vienna, probably in order to evade military service. He went to Munich but was traced by the Austrian authorities and summoned back to Austria, where, however, he was pronounced unfit to serve. He returned to Munich. His circumstances were still wretched and he lived the life of an urban beachcomber until war broke out and he joined a Bavarian regiment. The army and the war provided him with activity and a social framework; he became a corporal and won the Iron Cross Second Class and – a rarity for an NCO – First Class. He was in hospital after a gas attack when the Germans collapsed on the western front in 1918. He never served on the eastern front.

After the war Hitler returned once more to Munich. Bavaria had ceased to be a kingdom within the German empire and had become a province within a German republic. This change increased rather than diminished the Bavarians' dislike for Prussia and for centralized government. Moreover, after a brief communist phase, initiated and extinguished by violence, authority in Munich passed to right-wing groups which were at odds with the more left-wing government in Berlin. They were also at odds with one another. There were monarchists who wanted to restore the independent Bavaria which had existed before Bismarck's time; separatists with vaguer but similar aspirations; protagonists of a south German union between Catholic Bavaria and Catholic Austria. Hitler, while sharing the general antipathy to the central government in Berlin, wanted neither the restoration of the Bavarian royal house nor union with the Austria which he despised. He was employed in the Press and News Section of the army headquarters in Munich, was appointed a *Bildungsoffizier* (a cultural instructor or ideological education officer) and was detailed to investigate, among other things, a new political party called the German Workers' Party – DAP. He joined the party, became its star platform performer, provided it with a programme and gave it a new name – the National Socialist German Workers' Party, NSDAP. His military superiors were not only happy to see a member of their staff, still not demobilized, engaging openly in politics in this way; later they also put up some money to enable the party to buy a newspaper, the *Völkischer Beobachter*. Hitler was put on his political feet by the army and when he left the army in April 1920 he was the leader of a party which was similar to a number of other parties except that it had a startling future before it. Post-war Munich saw many parties spring up, wilt and die. They appealed to those who were afraid of Bolshevism, afflicted by defeat in war or crippled by inflation, and they offered an escape into a nationalism which dilated on the glories of the German past and the wickedness of other nations with the implication that the glories could be revived and the wicked put down. Their programmes combined this nationalism with a sort of socialism in so far as they offered the little man protection against the communist commissar on the one hand and the capitalist banker on the other.

Munich provided Hitler with a second political novitiate. Vienna had taught him to hate Jews and had given him glimpses of how to play on popular prejudices and fears. Munich added hatred of Bolshevism, further training in the uses of propaganda, the conviction that the base of political power was mass support, and the further conviction that the way to win this support was not by reasoning but by stirring up emotions. He picked up the idea that Jews and Bolsheviks were equally loathsome and so could be treated as essentially the same thing. His experiences showed him that an audience is better captured by a 'systematically one-sided approach' than by a balanced evaluation of a problem which allows the audience to wonder whether the speaker is himself really convinced of the truth of what he is preaching. This second novitiate closed with a bang and a valuable lesson. In 1923 Hitler staged a putsch. He did so in alliance with General Erich Ludendorff, one of the military heroes of the war, who suffered abnormally from the stings of defeat because his own loss of nerve in 1918 had contributed to it. The putsch was a farcical failure, but the association with Ludendorff gave Hitler the attention of the whole nation. At his trial he announced that he was a man 'born to be a dictator'. He was sentenced to prison for two years, served nine months, did some thinking and wrote *Mein Kampf*. The lesson he learned was that he should try to gain control of the state by constitutional means and not by frontal assault and never against the army.

Mein Kampf, a mixture of autobiography and political manifesto, was an immensely successful book which sold so well that Hitler eventually made a fortune out of it. It is a long book in bad German. Its author remained largely unknown until 1930 and was not taken seriously by many of those who did hear of him. This was a pity because for all its hyperbole *Mein Kampf* proclaimed much of what Hitler wanted to do and how. As a politician Hitler was an unnatural mixture of the normal and the eccentric. After the 1923 putsch he superficially adopted the normal forms of party organization, speech-making and publicity, but he also adapted them up to and beyond the point of distortion. His conformity, so far as it went, reflected his caution and shrewdness, but it was far from being a complete index to his character for his grip on his party was autocratic and intolerant, his speech-making took place in a setting of ostentatiously armed henchmen, party meetings became hierophantic rallies quite unlike the meetings of normal political parties, he was uncommonly uninhibited by scruple and an unrestrained liar (who may have believed what he said while he was saying it but who also believed that lying paid), and he was prepared to use violence whenever and however it served his purpose. In the organization of his party he insisted from the first on his personal ascendancy and refused to allow even his principal colleagues to have views of their own; in his speech-making he was conspicuously violent in what he said and how he said it; and in his propaganda, his mass meetings and the dress and deportment of his followers he deliberately gave his party the appearance, as he himself said, of 'a political fighting force and not a debating society'. If on the one hand he was using the accepted implements of politics, he was also transforming them.

Hitler did not have the mind of a statesman but rather an impresario and improviser. Where a Bismarck imposed himself on events, Hitler imposed himself on people by the fervour of his personality. He was a leader of men first and a framer of policies only a poor second. He was not an original thinker or theorizer but he was adept at picking up ideas which suited him and at taking the opportunities given him by others; he knew how to wait for his chances and how to seize them, and he was guided by certain basic preconceptions. He had a view of history. He was a Manichee, a man who sees the world and its history in terms of black

and white, good and evil, god and devil. He saw two powers face to face
in 'a world of everlasting conflict where the one creature feeds on the
other and the death of the weaker implies the life of the stronger'. For
such people the problem is to identify the good and the evil. Hitler saw no
difficulty here. He defined the party of the good as the Aryans – a 'race'
or biological group which was superior and so had to be tended, preserved
and improved by political leaders acting like farm bailiffs.

This definition of good and evil in terms of race stemmed from certain
European philosophers and historians who had, during the nineteenth
century, evolved the view that races and nations could be graded on a scale
of merit and that those lower down the scale would for ever remain below
their betters higher up. This way of thinking was fortified by Darwin's
contributions to biological science which, taken up by social scientists,
were thought to show that social groups, like natural species, evolved
to higher stages by a process of conflict involving – and justifying – the
extinction of some groups and the survival and expansion of others.
Thus backwardness, an inferior culture, was seen as a natural phenomenon
rather than as a social challenge, as something to be observed rather than
something to be changed. Hitler imbibed these ideas. Conflict, he said,
was 'the father of all things'. The German people had to be embattled and
purified, preserved from the taint of mixed blood which had caused the
downfall of the ancient civilizations; it had also to be trained in devoted
obedience to its Leader, to whom had been vouchsafed a vision and a
mission to save the world. But to save the world from what?

The party of evil was even more easily identifiable than the party of the
good. It consisted of the Jews who, ever since the time of Moses, had been
labouring with diabolical ingenuity to destroy nothing less than the human
race itself. Hitler's anti-semitism was a genuine and potent hatred. It was
sharpened by his ability to equate Jewry with communism. For him Lenin
was the latest reincarnation of Moses, Bolshevism the latest device of
Jewish malevolence and 'the most radical form of the genocide [plotted] by
the Jews'. Through Marx and Lenin and Bolshevism the Jews were repeating what they had done through St Paul and Christianity: European civilization was to be destroyed by the one as Rome had been destroyed by
the other. At one time or another Hitler conflated all his adversaries, all
those who stood for values which he despised, with the loathed Jews,
so that Jewry became a sort of cultural generic term embracing – because
it had inseminated and poisoned – not only communism but also social
democracy, liberalism, the intellectuals, aristocrats, international finance
and Christianity. Either these would be extirpated or they would extirpate
humanity. A Jewish triumph would be the 'funeral wreath of the human

race' and would leave the planet diving through space 'once again without any human life on its surface'. It was as simple and as terrible as that. The simple view, when wrong, can be the worst because it removes doubt and justifies every means. Hitler did not recoil from slaughter; it was so obviously necessary that it probably never occurred to him to consider whether it was agreeable or disagreeable. Genocide was not a moral issue but the practical application of physical means to social ends. He did not enjoy indiscriminate killing in the way that many simpler Nazis did, although he savoured personal revenge (he revelled over the films of the hangings of the conspirators of July 1944). He enjoyed secondhand descriptions of living and dying in concentration camps but was a strong anti-vivisectionist and could not stomach a demonstration of slaughter when he saw one with his own eyes.

Between the Germans or Aryans on the one hand and the Jews on the other were peoples who were neither. These peoples, of whom the Slavs were the most prominent example, did not have to be exterminated. Their function was to serve the party of the good. Their chief characteristics were their inferiority and their number. These were related terms since it is the destiny of an élite to rule over inferior hordes and use them, as for example the British did in India (Hitler admired the British empire for reasons which would have horrified the Indian Civil Service).

Nazi contempt for the Slavs merged with a far more ancient German-Slav hostility. The conflict between Germans and Slavs is a thousand years old. After the period of the great barbarian invasions and migrations in Europe the Frankish King Charles created in an era of dawning stability an empire in western Europe to match the eastern empire of Byzantium. This empire reached tentatively to the Carpathians and extinguished the alien Avar power in central Europe, but it failed to embrace the rising Slavic state of Moravia; nor did it weld the western Franks of France, still less those in Spain, to its Germanic core. This empire was shortlived. What survived was the idea of a western empire blessed by the papacy – and so essentially Italian as well as German – and distinct from Byzantium. It was revived by Charlemagne's successors in the tenth century, the Saxon emperors. By this time the place of the Avars in central Europe had been taken by the no less alien Magyars or Hungarians, whom the Saxons checked but did not exterminate. The emperors also made war on the Slavs in what is now northern Germany and on the Poles – the first Germano-Polish conflict. They made no attempt to bring the western Franks back into the empire but were even more strongly pulled towards Italy and the papacy than Charlemagne had been. This 'renovation' of the empire was clearly to include Italy but exclude the lands west of the

Rhine and Rhône. About the Slavs, however, there were doubts. Otto III (A.D. 983–1002) conceived a great western Christian empire in which other princes besides himself would have wide autonomous authority as kings. Such an empire could include non-Germans, and the Polish, Czech and Hungarian princes welcomed it and joined it. But Otto died young. His conception of the empire died with him. His successors reverted to fighting the Slavs, and the Slavs, missing an opportunity to create a countervailing empire of their own, quarrelled among themselves: the Czechs remaining in the empire, which the Poles renounced. A pattern evolved which endured, with variations, for centuries and produced in more modern times a strong German power flanked to the east by separate and weaker Polish, Czech and Hungarian ones.

By the twentieth century the opportunities created by this pattern of power were combined with racial theories and economic appetites. In the eyes of German nationalists the Slavs were biologically inferior peoples destined to become a caste of slaves; they also occupied valuable space which was needed by the Germans who, by virtue of their superiority, had every right to take it. The notion of *Lebensraum,* the idea that Germany was too small for the German race, was not invented by Hitler. It was current during the First World War and was one of the pseudo-intellectual props of the policy of *Mitteleuropa*, which aimed to establish a continental empire fit for Germans (and stretching in some versions from France into Asia Minor). Hitler appears to have been genuinely convinced of the need for *Lebensraum*, which, with his racial fantasies, constituted the basis of his foreign political attitudes. In *Mein Kampf* he wrote that National Socialism 'must attempt to remove the disproportion between our population and our living space – the latter regarded both as a source of food and as the basis of political power – between our historic past and the hopelessness of our present impotence'.

Hitler belonged to 'the race of men who dream concretely – a very dangerous breed' (the words come from Ernst Jünger's parable *The Marble Cliffs*). Taken by itself his idea that one being waxes as another declines is neither original nor startling. Goethe wrote:

> *Du musst steigen oder sinken,*
> *Du musst herrschen und gewinnen*
> *Oder dienen und verlieren,*
> *Amboss oder Hammer sein.*

> (Man must rise or fall, He must win and rule
> Or lose and serve, Be the anvil or the hammer.)

But there is a world of difference, in practice and in intent, between the figurative speech of a poet and the concrete programme of a practical politician with a literal mind and power at his command. Hitler's concrete dream envisaged a German nucleus of some hundred million people, flanked by subordinate federations colonized by other Germans. He did not think that this re-ordering of Europe could be effected without war, nor did he think that war was at all agreeable. He said that the next war would be extremely horrible and enormously destructive, but like so many of his contemporaries he believed it would be short. He also believed that too much peace was bad for a people and he took pleasure in the thought that a greater and more beautiful Germany would rise from the devastation, inhabited by survivors welded into a nation by their experiences and guided by a messianic leadership which would last a thousand years: Hitler was a chiliast as well as a Manichee. Some people have been tempted to judge that Hitler did not mean what he said when he indulged in language of this kind, that he got carried away; but it is equally possible to believe that he never spoke truer to his own nature than at these moments. Although cautious, he was not moderate.

Hitler's principal instrument was the Nazi Party, which, exploiting the circumstances of his day and age, he used to win power over the German people and the German state. Through the party he practised the violence, verbal and physical, whose effectiveness became increasingly contrasted with the ineffectiveness of his opponents and of the constitution. The Nazi Party was like the feudal system. In it a man was obligated to an immediate chief and also to the supreme Führer. There were Führers at every level but the supreme Führer was linked with all members of the movement by direct personal allegiance as well as through the hierarchy. The supreme Führer, besides being the apex of a pyramid, was also a unique being, infallible, prophetic, the incarnation of the general (Aryan) will: 'The will of the Führer is law.' His authority was not only absolute but he himself was irreplaceable: he could have no true successor. Successors of a sort – caliphs to Hitler's Mahomet – could be nominated, but this concession to human mortality did not detract from the urgency of fulfilling the Nazi mission in Hitler's own lifetime and while he was still in the prime of life.

This concept of the Führer was reflected in Hitler's relations both with his principal henchmen and with the generality of his followers. After the capture of power in 1933 the machinery of party and the machinery of state coexisted in a kind of semi-merger. The Weimar constitution was never abrogated – it was simply ignored – and the machinery of state was left largely intact, but power passed to numerous party agencies which were given overlapping functions with the result that many decisions could be made only by the Führer; the bureaucracy, reduced to a state of confusion and inefficiency, was eliminated as a barrier between Führer and *Volk*, ruler and ruled. Hitler's principal lieutenants were not men of conspicuous ability and they never constituted a team. Perhaps only Goebbels was more than ordinarily talented and even Goebbels was more marked by the extremity of his devotion to Hitler than by outstanding intellect. There was little trust or friendship in the party's higher reaches and not much cooperation. The Nazi leaders feared and intrigued against each other and, at the end, against Hitler too. Hitler seems to have been neither surprised nor dismayed by this lack of solidarity, so long as it did not affect relations with himself. A suspicious man, he expected others to be suspicious too, and he built their mutual mistrust and malice into his system of government. As a result the principal organs of the party and, after 1933, of the state, were run by feudatories, and government at the top proceeded by a series of clashes. The heads of the government did not govern by talking and working together, and the supreme chief – whether as party Führer or Reich Chancellor – was a dictator conducting a wilfully discordant band which he was not particularly anxious to orchestrate. What mattered to Hitler was the obedience of his lieutenants to himself. They did not have to agree among themselves. The party was held together by the Leader's personal magnetism and not by fellowship or community of ideas. The *Führerprinzip* was hostile to ideas, since an ideologist might find himself in a conflict between his doctrine and his Führer. Alfred Rosenberg, the party's chief racial theorist, never became a figure of the first rank and was increasingly ignored by Hitler, and the Strasser brothers, leaders of the more radical groups of the Nazi Party in northern Germany, were pressed out of the party when the Führer came to have no use for their quasi-socialist ideas.

With his remoter followers the Führer's relations were special in two ways. Without the Führer the followers were nothing, so that the Nazi Party dissolved in 1945 not merely because the Nazi Reich had been defeated but because the Nazi Führer was dead; and secondly, there was an intimacy between Führer and rank and file, a mutual dependence, which gave the movement a democratic force based, not on majorities or voting (a degrading exercise), but on the identification of the leader with the led, expressed by the former's unquestioned authority. The function of the party organization was to 'communicate a definite idea . . . to ensure its conversion from theory to reality' and to do these things with as little intervening 'machinery' as possible. This relationship between party leader and party members was repeated at second remove and transmitted from the movement to the even wider circle of the German people as a whole. While membership of the party was limited and pride (and profit) in membership preserved undiluted, the outer circle of sympathizers was progressively enlarged to create a wider mass movement which, like the party members but less intensively, was attached to Hitler personally and which, because of this emotional attachment, had a stake in his success. Hitler realized the importance of getting the masses to feel but not to think. The Führer divulged his inmost thoughts in a narrow circle whence they percolated to the Nazi élite, thence again into the party in general, beyond the party to the people and beyond the people to the outside world. At each stage they lost something in the telling and so became assimilable by people who would otherwise have rejected them as mad and bad. In such a system the élite and the leader himself could afford to propagate preposterous ideas and even to do so cynically, because the party followers and the people as a whole were blinded by their devotion and their distance from the centre. Hermann Rauschning, with whom Hitler had long and intimate talks until their breach in 1934, relates that Hitler once told him that he was well aware that there was no such thing as race, but that he needed it for his political and salvationist purposes. A saviour of the human race may well permit himself a touch of cynicism. Nor is it incompatible with fanaticism.

The Nazi party served two main purposes. Through its ideology it united the people with their leader and through its techniques it perfected the elimination of opposition. It was not a party in the ordinary sense of the word since it could never be satisfied with partial allegiance or partial dominance. It presented a comprehensive, total way of life, explaining everything, past and future, and regulating everything, public and private. Hitler did not achieve this purpose by catechizing or by arguing. He neither instructed his audiences nor explained things to them. He presented views which, half inarticulately, they were already disposed to welcome, and one reason for his success was his ability to appeal to a variety of different types of people – the disgruntled generation of the First World War, the middle classes downgraded by inflation, the deprived classes which had never played a part in German politics before, youth, the nationalism of the old order and the nationalism of the masses. But although he appealed to these classes, he did not appeal to them as classes. At a meeting addressed by Hitler the message went from Hitler to each listener separately. The audience was a crowd of distinct de-personalized objects. In the aggregate they formed not classes but a mass, 'uniform [as he said once at a marchpast] not only in ideas, but even the facial expression is almost the same . . . a hundred thousand men become

a single type'. Each man and woman, whether marching past the Führer
or standing in a packed crowd to listen to him, had his eyes and soul
focused onto a man who had placed himself in a unique position in
German political life: sufficiently remote from the normal political structure which was crumbling (Hitler never got himself elected to the Reichstag
and so never operated as a party political leader in that restricted field)
and at the same time intensely close to the magnetized individual who
wanted a Leader rather than a choice between leaders.

Hitler used fear and persuasion to an unsurpassed degree. Physical
terror was one of his principal political weapons. To quote *The Marble
Cliffs* again: 'A cloud of fear preceded the Chief Ranger like the mountain
mist that presages the storm. Fear enveloped him, and I am convinced
that therein far more than in his own person lay his power.' The Nazis
thought nothing of assaulting their opponents, torturing them and murdering them – frequently with fanatical brutality. Sadistic thugs were given a
licence instead of being shut up, and this licence was accorded to them by
Hitler not out of indifference to the finer standards of behaviour but with
the positive intention of assuring his hold over Germany in this way.
Overt opposition died and even individual thinking was stifled. The dominance of the party was rendered as nearly total as it could humanly be by
fear. Education, controlled after 1933 by the certifiable Dr Rust, became
a means for destroying the individual's capacity to form opinions and
indoctrinating the young with Nazi versions of history and ethics (and
even with German, as opposed to inferior, mathematics) through rewritten
textbooks and politically reliable teachers. Teachers who did not toe the
line were reported by the Hitler Youth, which came virtually to control the
schools. Boys and girls spent their leisure hours in uniformed youth associations where the process was continued. Books, plays, the press and broadcasting were brought under Nazi control and censorship. Justice became a
farce. It was, said Hitler, 'a means of ruling'. The courts were used to
complete the suppression of the individual; the legal profession was regimented, the Führer had the power to quash proceedings, his deputy the
power to increase inadequate sentences in cases involving offences against
the Führer, the state or the party; illegality was legalized by the invention
of the principle of 'hidden right'; an advocate who got his client acquitted
would see him being bundled into a police van as he left the court. The
whole of life was subordinated to the Nazi purpose with the concentration
camps, or the mere knowledge of their existence, in reserve to quell those
who felt like protesting openly or, given the perfection of delation within
the family, even in private.

This colossal subversion of civilized values was acquiesced in by the

German people and to some extent by Europe too. Only the war put an end to it. What permitted this acquiescence?

Hitler joined an ancient practice with a modern force – ritual with the mass meeting, mumbo-jumbo focused on the microphone. In great squares and open spaces, which he converted into cathedrals of Nazism, he filled ordinary Germans with a sense of destiny, giving them a wonderful vision of unreality as an escape from the chanciness of life and also laying bare to them, with telling candour, how much he had already achieved by violence and how much more he was going to achieve the same way. His performances were brilliantly staged but they would have remained historically inconsequential if they had not fitted the time and place of their presentation.

GERMANY

Germany had been something of an anomaly in Europe for more than a century before Hitler came to power. The Germans did not form a compact group in Europe like the French or the English, nor did they create a nation state; and they failed to find adequate outlets beyond Europe for their power, talents and ambitions. For both these reasons they were the more disposed towards expansion and conquest in Europe.

Modern Europe is a patchwork of conscious nationalisms expressed or seeking expression in statehood. Some of these have been recognizable entities for centuries but the bursting time of European nationalism came with the turn of the eighteenth into the nineteenth century. At this period the dynast, an individual with hereditary right and a personal demesne (his kingdom), came to seem old fashioned. Two changes, the one domestic and the other international, were involved: a shift of political power within the state and a redefinition of the boundaries of the state. The first of these favoured 'the people' at the expense of the dynast; the second was based on the idea of 'the nation', as opposed to history or geography or power, as the criterion for deciding where one state stopped and the next one should begin. The new ideas were most effective in western Europe, where the making of Italy was their outstanding advertisement; they were least effective in eastern Europe, where polyglot autocracies continued until well into the twentieth century. In the centre of Europe Germany looked as though it had developed into a nation state but the appearance was deceptive.

German nationalism was promoted by reaction against French cultural and military hegemony. It asserted that Germans had a separate identity and the right to mind their own affairs instead of being part of Napoleon's empire and of a French-dominated cosmopolitan culture. It aimed not only to liberate Germans but also to unite them and so helped to produce a powerful and efficient state out of an agglomeration of feeble ones. But if German nationalism looked at this stage very much like other European nationalisms, it diverged as the Germans both began to think of themselves as not only distinct but superior and at the same time failed to achieve a nation state to focus and absorb their national energies.

German writers and thinkers made much of the nation state and provided the most famous of the state's champions in the nineteenth century: the Reich created in 1870 was designed by Bismarck and regarded by almost everybody as the German nation's state. But Bismarck's Germany was incomplete. It was a federation of German-speaking states dominated by Prussia and excluding not only Austria, which was only partly German, but also numerous Germans scattered about eastern Europe; the Germans were too dispersed and too intermingled with other peoples to constitute a nation state. Bismarck's Germany was not a national gathering together, like Cavour's Italy. It was an extension of Prussian power, achieved by defeating Austria and France, and a consolidation of class power, achieved by blanketing German liberalism and passing enough social legislation to take the wind out of the German socialists' sails. It was therefore incomplete not only in the sense that many Germans were left outside it but also because whole classes of Germans within the state were excluded from effective political activity and remained subordinated to the socially superior ruling classes: it was a nation state neither in its geographical extent nor in its social cohesion. It was unstable and tense both within and at its borders. Unlike Italy, it was not even a geographical expression. If anything, it was a linguistic aspiration seeking political form and traversed by social rifts. Since it was also the most central of European states and became the most powerful, its malaise dominated European affairs for a century.

German nationalism foiled of what was, in nineteenth-century terms, its natural outcome turned to racialism. Germanism materialized as *Reich* and *Volk*, a pair of politically disruptive and often mystical concepts. A *Reich* is a claim to dominion; a *Volk* is a people linked not by habitat but by race. *Reich* and *Volk* combined imply racial dominion. (When, later, the Nazis chanted: *Ein Reich, ein Volk, ein Führer*, they were acclaiming the political activation of this dual concept.) At the same time the desire to establish a separate identity for Germans was replaced by the idea that Germans were not only distinct but superior. The line between pride and arrogance is a thin one and the assertion of an independent personality passes very easily into a claim to superiority. The Germans were neither alone nor unusual in thinking themselves better than other people, but from early in the nineteenth century Germans began to make extraordinary claims for Germanism as the embodiment of superior virtues deposited by God in people who spoke the German language. Racialists see history as a conflict between races – an alternative to Karl Marx's explanation of history as a conflict between classes – and racialists conscious of their own superiority see a world in which they are bound to do battle with other races and win. Nineteenth-century German racialist ideology postulated an Aryan race of purer, ideal human beings, the founders and custodians of all human culture. History and science were invoked to prove these unhistorical and unscientific postulates, and ancient racial gods were resuscitated to give spiritual support to this denial of the essential equality of man which had been preached for centuries in the tradition of Stoics and Christians. The pseudo-science of phrenology, which enjoyed a curious vogue in an age avid for anything which might be called scientific, measured the differences between Aryan and other skulls and when these outward signs of distinction proved disappointingly trivial, racialists fell back on inner measurements of souls which, though they were more difficult to demonstrate, were also more difficult to deny. Darwin's theories were also used. The world of men (*The Origin of Species* dealt with plants and animals) was divided into the fit and the unfit, and the survival of the fittest was taken to justify and even require the extermination of the unfit. Conflict, in any case inevitable, was the means for the improvement of the race and therefore also noble. There was no such thing as a right to live – let alone a right to liberty or the pursuit of happiness. Human rights were replaced by strife as the path of progress.

German racialism, having evolved from German nationalism, took a further step and became imperialist. Where a race and a state do not coincide the racialist may achieve his aims either by the migration of outlying members of the race into the fatherland or by the extension of the rule of the race to all parts of the world inhabited by the race or needed by it. German minorities in foreign countries were, by definition, superior people living under the rule of their inferiors. Either they must be repatriated or German rule must be extended to cover these areas. The second solution was the more appealing. Hence the notion of a Greater Germany, a German Reich extending to areas well beyond any normally accepted confines of Germany but where Germany ought to rule because some members of the German *Volk* lived there. Towards the end of the nineteenth century various Pan-German groups emerged, both in Vienna with its windows on the east and in Berlin with its consciousness of superabundant power, to advocate what was in effect a German empire in Europe. They were not inspired solely by ideology. Unlike the other great powers of Europe Germany had found no worlds to conquer outside Europe. While the western European nations conquered overseas and the Russians conquered in Asia, the Germans – partly because they were too late – conquered nowhere. Bismarck was indifferent to colonies and Germany's interest in Africa at the end of the nineteenth century was half-hearted as well as belated. So Germany's field of conquest became eastern or middle (*Mittel*) Europe. Bismarck himself preferred that Germany should live in a state of equilibrium with the Russian and Habsburg empires to the east of it, but the German-ness of the Habsburg empire was a standing invitation to call Germans to go east, to regard the Slavs as their Red Indians or 'fuzzy-wuzzies', to embark on one of the great movements of European expansion and colonization – only this time within Europe itself and at the expense of peoples whose systems were neither so alien nor so technically backward as the Asian and African societies which other Europeans subjugated. Like all imperialists the Germans easily convinced themselves that they were benefiting inferior peoples by interfering with them – until eventually the Nazis dispensed with the idea of benefiting anybody but themselves.

These racial and imperial strands in the modern German experience were picked up by the Nazis. Nazism was a product of elements in German history and elements in European history. Its peculiarly evil character was a consequence of amalgamating the worst in German public life with the worst in European public life. It was the German version of European Fascism, combining special German features with the general character-istics of the wider, European genus to which it belonged. Its outstanding special features were the demand for *Lebensraum*, which was a euphemism for imperial conquest, and its anti-semitism. Its special victims therefore were the Jews and the Slavs. These two elements were not unconnected, for the Pan-Germans of the late nineteenth century who pointed Germany towards an imperial destiny not in the sense of Bismarck's compact central European Reich but as a vast overlordship over Slav peoples and lands beyond the strictly German horizon, were also markedly anti-semitic.

During most of the nineteenth century Germans, with some reservations in regard to Austrian Germans, were not pre-eminently anti-semitic. Nor is anti-semitism a necessary ingredient of Fascism, although it has been a common one; the Italian fascists, for example, were comparatively free of anti-semitism until they imported it by a process of reverse Lend-Lease from Germany in the closing phase of the *fascismo*. German anti-semitism seems to have been mainly an indigenous growth coinciding with the growth of German political consciousness. Pan-German anti-semitism was an expression of resentment against people who insisted on being different and who refused to be assimilated to Gentile society and full participation in the German dream. (Hitler's original contribution to anti-semitism was to abandon this demand that Jews become Germans, to insist on the contrary that they could never be Germans and to emphasize the unbridgeable gap by marking each Jew with the star of David.) Although many Jews – not least in Germany in the 1920s – were assimilated into Gentile society when they themselves wished to take this course and when the surrounding circumstances favoured it, they remained liable to be singled out and attacked whenever the Gentile society had a grievance to be vented somewhere. In the latter part of the nineteenth century they were used by conservatives to pin unpopular ideas on: liberal ideas feared by the privileged classes were characterized as Jewish in order to make these classes revile the Jews. This use of racial prejudice for political purposes was begun by Bismarck and adopted and magnified by Alexander III in Russia, where anti-semitism has continued to be exploited in this way ever since. The appearance of the Jews is often markedly recognizable (though it has been embarrassingly discovered that a number of Jews have blue eyes and fair hair). They have a religion and a language which they share with nobody else. In Europe they have performed a function as useful as it is often unpopular – that of the capitalist who provides money for other people's enterprises or follies – but in the nineteenth century they preserved more of their unpopularity than their usefulness as Europe's growing Gentile bourgeoisie began to supplant them as the providers of money. The state found them less useful as it turned to financing its needs more by taxation and less by loans. Moreover, the Jews lacked two characteristics which seemed natural to everybody else: the Jew had no state and, in the state in which he lived, counted as a Jew rather than as a member of an economic or social class. In a society of classes and in a polity of nation states he was a misfit; the fact of his belonging to something which was neither state nor class fostered suspiciousness of exclusive racial loyalties and the myth of machinations behind the scenes; and his exclusion from the class structure helped his defamers to represent him as an enemy of all social structures. In the heyday of his usefulness the Jew had often been close to power and when his usefulness declined his power was thought to have become covert rather than diminished.

Racism endangered the Jews because they were the pre-eminent example of a self-chosen race. Any other self-chosen race was bound to clash with them and hate them. The Germans did so more than most and ascribed to them all the vices which were the counterparts of Aryan virtues. The German master race arraigned the Jews and the Nazi party became the principal instrument for destroying them. Again, Hitler did not invent anti-semitism; he gave it a special twist and he provided the tools and the opportunities for satisfying it. And the Nazi state did not protect these people within its borders because in the Nazi scheme of things the state was not an instrument for preserving public order or securing the rights of men but an instrument for furthering the destiny of the German *Volk*. The S A sang:

> *Erst müssen Juden bluten,*
> *Erst dann sind wir befreit.*
> (First must Jewish blood be shed,
> Only then will we be free.)

EUROPE

The ending of the old European order, by the dissolution of its economic and social foundations and consequently of its political structures, was effected by a variety of forces which together can be called democratic. Their general direction was to extend, in the name of freedom, equality and fraternity, the narrow bases of élitist societies and exclusive policies. The history of this movement, which is the stuff of the modern world, cannot be resumed here even in the briefest compass, but it is relevant to point out that it has been both divided and opposed. The division created eventually the two broad and increasingly discordant streams called liberal democracy and totalitarian democracy (that is to say, communism) – both rooted in the eighteenth-century Enlightenment but diverging over two fundamental issues, the former regarding politics as a part of human activity where the latter regards politics as comprehending the totality of human activity, the former giving a higher value than the latter to individual choice and wellbeing in the inevitable conflict between the individual and the group. The opposition to democracy has been authoritarian, the rejection of the democratic principle of extension and the reassertion of the right of special men or special groups of men to lay down the law. Where democracy diffuses power, authoritarianism concentrates it once more.

This authoritarian opposition too has been divided. It has conservative and radical branches. The conservatives have tried to arrest democratic change, or to minimize and delay it; they have been ambivalent about democracy, usually accepting for pragmatic reasons a measure of what in principle they dislike. The radical authoritarians on the other hand have been frankly anti-democratic and have set out to destroy democracy and revert to a political and social order dominated by a special caste or individual, although not necessarily by the same castes or individuals who were invested with power under the *anciens régimes*. Fascism is the outcome of this active and radical, as opposed to the passive and conservative, opposition to democracy. Mussolini defined Fascism as opposition to the principles of 1789, by which he meant opposition to what others have called the Rights of Man. It was also opposed to the Enlightenment, to reason. It preferred violence: fascists have been bent on destroying an existing democratic order and on doing so by deed and not by argument.

The politics of Europe in the last 200 years have revolved round the ideas summed up in the phrase 'the French Revolution', and the political terms in common use – such as right and left, progressive and reactionary – relate to attitudes towards those ideas. The Bolshevik Revolution of 1917 sharpened the conflict typified by 1789 and, with conservatives often passive or confused about their role, there developed in the twentieth century a triangle of forces and eventually war between the temporarily reunited streams of liberal and totalitarian democracy and their fascist foes who captured the power of the state in various parts of Europe where weak government by conservatives or democrats helped them to do so.

Modern Europe has had to digest industrial, demographic and technical revolutions and at the same time a questioning of accepted values which has amounted to a social and cultural mutation. These changes have been very unsettling. The fundamental change has been the growth of populations and the growth of towns, so that at one and the same time there were quite quickly many more people, many of them living in a completely new way. The change in the demographic and geographical patterns produced social changes. Old ties were loosened and aristocratic and paternalist structures, based mainly on land and caste, were eroded by the motor forces of the Enlightenment (emancipation from dogma and despot) and of the Revolution (power to the people). The new urban classes began to exert pressure and command sympathy. What they wanted was vague – less misery and poverty, more fairness, more self-respect – but it implied upheaval. The traditional givers of laws and *mores* (churches, kings and nobles), and the laws and *mores* themselves, lost authority under rational scrutiny and popular suspicion. It was not immediately clear what the new values were nor where they were to come from. New élites, professing a democratic instead of an aristocratic faith, emerged to take or share the power which was slipping from the exclusive grasp of the old régime and which, owing to technical revolutions in communications and manufacturing, was rapidly becoming much greater than ever before. For the most part power was shared, whether in concert or in a parliamentary system of alternating bouts between nostalgic conservatives and moderate progressives. The result was an orderly but slow development, too slow for those who maintained that no really radical social changes had yet occurred, too decided for the radical forces of the Right which were opposed, not so much to change, but to democracy. There was therefore an ever present possibility of a reversal of alliances in which the conservative opponents of change and the fascist opponents of democracy would join forces against the Left despite the fact that the one group was essentially passive and the other essentially revolutionary. The outstanding example of such a combination was the government in which the aristocratic Papen served as Vice-Chancellor under the fascist Hitler as Chancellor. As early as 1850 Palmerston, in the Don Pacifico debate in the House of Commons, recognized two varieties of radicalism, the reactionary as well as the Jacobin, but it was not until a century later that the fascist combination of reaction with violence was widely recognized as a potent and pernicious threat to European societies.

The fascist leader, like the democrat, had his ideological roots in the eighteenth century, but whereas the democrat put his faith in reason and debate the fascist believed in the power and virtue of the will. Traditionally the high road to right action has been knowledge discovered by reason; the function of reason was to uncover the knowable which, when revealed, was common property. Reason and knowledge assumed therefore universal values. The will, however, was personal. Whereas the individual impelled by reason was moving towards agreement with other individuals, the individual impelled by will was at least as likely to be moving towards a clash with other individuals. The will was subjective rather than communal, aggressive rather than irenic. The will was seen as a creative force in its own right operating in a world in which the objective reality sought by the reasonable man of the Enlightenment was an illusion. There were no external criteria of rightness, only inner promptings. Therefore the strong-willed had right on his side, and the stronger his will the more right he was. What was real was the product of each individual's inner self, and this product was *ipso facto* valid as well as real, so that the individual was entitled and indeed under some compulsion to make his will prevail. His destiny was that of a sovereign creator in a world of his own which impinged upon the personal worlds of other sovereign creators; it was not his lot, nor was it within a man's capability, to discover a single world in which all would participate, because such a world did not exist to be discovered. The world was not a semi-known and orderly system but an unknowable and anarchic non-system.

The consequences of this view were conflict and uncertainty. Both cried out for leadership. What sort of leadership? With knowledge and reason at a discount the emotions were promoted to a dominant role and the intensity of a man's feelings were rated above the soundness of his judgement: there was a deeper, inward truth in the soul by comparison with which the reason was superficial, and the leader was to be distinguished by the qualities of this ill-defined, unlocated, non-rational, even irrational soul. He was above all a doer, an activist, and whatever he wanted to do was right, including crushing weaker beings. He was unpredictable but he was to be trusted and followed none the less, since his unpredictability was only in the eye of the beholder; so long as his acts and commands issued from the dictates of his will they were not to be questioned – and it was as impossible to prove, as it was imprudent to suppose, that they issued from anywhere else. The Italian fascists summed up the position in the slogan: *Credere! Ubbedire! Combattere!* (Believe! Obey! Fight!). The fascist leader was also a saviour and redeemer, more of a superman than a man, half-way between god and man, what the ancients called a hero. By dubbing him Duce and Führer – leader in Italian and German – the fascists usurped a term to which they had no exclusive right, for Churchill and de Gaulle were leaders too. What distinguishes the fascist chief is not leadership, but the role of hero. The hero disdains reason (Homer's heroes never engage in rational debate) and prevails by the weight of authority and by killing. His criteria are quantitative – the bigger the better, whether the subject matter is the length of a speech, the volume of sound at a concert or the number of deaths in a slaughter.

His antithesis is the representative leader who derives his authority from parliaments and elections and depends on a choate body of opinion as opposed to the inchoate mass following on which fascist power is based. In countries like France and Great Britain which have had strong rationalist or parliamentary traditions fascist leaders, although they existed, made little headway. These countries did not go fascist. But their right-wing leaders felt drawn to foreign fascists and praised Mussolini and Hitler and later Franco, who were regarded by conservatives as ready helps against the extreme Left and as performing the salutary task of getting their countries out of messes into which they had fallen. Afraid of rather than familiar with Marxism, they misinterpreted Fascism. Fascist movements and fascist leaders were in truth revolutionary and dynamic, but because they had also certain characteristics which were conventionally dubbed right-wing, they were frequently mistaken for a rather uncouth kind of conservative. The characteristic British and French leaders of this period were capable rather than intelligent, well educated only in terms of an educational system designed to produce mere custodians, suspicious of and so ill equipped to understand new ideas and forces. They could see that communism aimed to subvert the existing order of which they were themselves a part – the communists themselves said so – but they failed to draw the same conclusion about the no less revolutionary fascists, whom they persisted in regarding as respectable. In some degree they were bemused by their own standards and their own democratic precepts. They could not believe that people who said such crazy things as the Nazis meant what they said; the British in particular took little account of theories which they considered to have little bearing on practical politics; they felt that a movement which attracted millions of votes could not be as bad as surface appearances sometimes suggested: thus were they able to turn a deaf ear to the very explicit statements of aims by Nazi and other fascist leaders. (In 1933 Hitler said publicly that the democracies had fortunately not understood what Nazism was about, for otherwise they could have stopped it.) In political circles Neville Chamberlain was a representative figure, hoping that Hitler and the bulk of his party were more sensible than the rowdies of the SA, hoping that they would be tamed by office and responsibility, regarding the Nazis as just another party in the twenties and then from 1930 as a necessary one for the working of government, gradually losing heart and at the end doing his best to avoid war in an impossible situation which had been created partly by his own incomprehension. Outside political circles many leaders, including in particular Roman Catholic hierarchs from the Pope downwards, were over-indulgent – to say the least – to Fascism and to atheistic Nazism because they hated communism more. The propertied classes, underrating the threat of Fascism because they compared it with communism, not expecting to be killed by fascists or even to have to surrender too much of their power and property, had no strong objection to helping fascists with their money. The march of the fascists on Rome in 1922 was a harmless parade compared with the Bolshevik Revolution of five years earlier and life in Mussolini's Italy was disagreeable only for socialists and liberals. Mussolini was appointed Prime Minister by the King in due constitutional form, as Hitler was appointed Chancellor by Hindenburg, and people who read of these appointments in newspapers without seeing for themselves what was going on in streets and prisons were confirmed in their prejudgements that these strange new groups were not revolutionaries in the accepted guillotine sense but champions of order and stability. If King Victor Emanuel of Italy and President von Hindenburg of Germany chose to act thus, what right had any foreigner to object or interfere? It was odd but not outrageous, and if socialists and Jews were having a rough time, they were probably getting no more, or not much more, than they deserved. The ruling classes of western Europe consisted on the whole of cultivated and humane men, but they were men who had also acquired a certain stolidity in the face of misfortune – their own or other people's – which could amount to callousness. They were used to ruling not only their own countries but large empires as well, populated by strange peoples to whom they owed justice and sound administration but over whom it was undesirable for practical reasons to sentimentalize. They were acquainted with 'inferior' races as well as 'inferior' classes, so that the social structure and the imperial experience of Europe combined to establish an order of values and a pragmatic indifference to inequalities which could sometimes be reconciled with ideals of justice and decency only by not inquiring too closely into what was going on. In sum the fascist attitude to socialists and Jews was not utterly different from the imperialist attitude to Blacks. The difference was one of degree, and differences of degree can be minimized or dismissed more easily than most. Hitler, in this respect as in many others, was the supremely disgusting example of something which was not so alien to the European mentality: the tendency to put different kinds of people into different sealed categories and then treat them differently. What his contemporaries, other than his victims, refused to see in time was that the degree of difference in the treatment was so extreme that it amounted to a difference in kind and went in any case far beyond the bounds of what Europe had learnt to call civilized.

CHAPTER 2

From Versailles to the Soldiers' Oath: 1919–34

THE First World War did not destroy German power. As in France after 1870 and Germany once more after 1945 recovery was swift. It was, however, punctuated by economic distress at the beginning and the end of the twenties which had profound political consequences, shaped by Germany's refusal to accept the verdict of 1918 and by resentment against the terms of the peace treaty. Nor did the war destroy much of Germany's pre-war social structure. The departure of the Hohenzollerns and other monarchs gave an appearance of political and social change which masked the fact that the rest of the ruling establishment remained in being and in power. Above all the army remained, until 1934, the arbiter of German politics.

Germany's military traditions were a legacy of its Prussian origins. The Prussian army made Prussia in the seventeenth and eighteenth centuries, and transmitted its traditions to the German Reich in the nineteenth. These traditions included the social exclusiveness of its officers as an aristocratic caste, the military virtues of rectitude and obedience, and a somewhat vague and unspecified position as the guardians of the state's wellbeing as well as its frontiers. The creation of the Reich in the nineteenth century reaffirmed the prestige of the army from the struggle against Napoleon I to the defeat of Napoleon III. The German officer was trained in the exercise of individual judgement on the grounds, elaborated by Clausewitz and other theorists, that the practice of war throws up a great variety of situations which cannot be foreseen and can best be handled by the officer who has learned to take decisions for himself. In addition the German officer had a wider education than his British or French counterpart in the sense that he was expected to concern himself with matters beyond the strictly professional. Yet, because freedom of speculation was not similarly encouraged, his actions in the wider political field were rigidly conditioned, politics were included in his province, but his political equipment was narrow. The German army was therefore significantly different from the British and French armies. The British army, from its beginnings in the time of Cromwell and his rule through Major-Generals, was more suspect as a threat to the civil power than respected as the guardian of the nation (a role reserved for the navy, which had the special advantage of all navies that it guarded the nation from outside without being able to interfere in the streets or take part in politics as easily as armies can). The British army had come to accept its place as subordinate and obedient to the civil government and was therefore denied some of the sources of esteem and self-esteem enjoyed by the German army. In France too the army was regarded since the Revolution as an instrument of civil government and not as properly a power in its own right. There was also a further difference between Great Britain and France on the one hand and Germany on the other. In all these countries the nineteenth century saw the *haute bourgeoisie* trying to get a share in political power. In Great Britain and France it did so by adopting liberal values but in Germany it opted instead for partnership with Bismarck and became a contented adjunct of a conservative oligarchy. The German *bourgeoisie*, having entered upon the political scene later than its French and British counterparts and – more important – at a stage in the evolution of Germany when military power was still actively forming the state, left power to the traditional classes and did not mediate between them and the deprived proletariat. Thus in Germany the power of the military aristocracy in affairs of state was not curbed by civilian, liberal, middle-class opinion. In Bismarck's time it was curbed by Bismarck himself, who opposed and even snubbed the army when he felt so inclined, but he did so not because he incarnated the civil power but because he was Bismarck. After his retirement the army, confronting a series of weak Chancellors, achieved a pre-eminence which culminated in the First World War when Generals von Hindenburg and Ludendorff established a military régime which not only dictated to and dismissed civilian Ministers but also invaded the prerogatives of the Kaiser. In 1918 the Kaiser went too, and the army, contemplating even weaker governments than those of the last thirty years, claimed an autonomy which was not successfully challenged by the civil power until Hitler became Chancellor. Its first post-war chief, Hans von Seeckt, a general endowed with exceptional political acumen, devoted himself to preserving what was left of the German army and its traditions and to rebuilding it. He regarded the Weimar republic as something to be survived and he was prepared to wait and survive it.

The Weimar constitution provided a framework in which Germany might evolve from an oligarchical authoritarianism to a popular democracy, but the evolution was slow to start and then struck by adversity which it was too frail to survive. The middle classes, after being blanketed by the exigencies of war, were torpedoed by the post-war inflation. During the lifetime of the Weimar republic only the Roman Catholic Centre Party maintained its strength (at about 15 per cent of votes cast). Other centre groups declined steadily until they almost vanished. Further to the Left the Social Democrats, who remained to defend the republic with the Centre Party, also lost ground, unused to the political game from which they had been excluded too long, obsessed by the communist threat on their left, and puzzled by the adaptation of Marxism to a vigorous industrial society which falsified some of its premises and drew part of its sting. They ruled Prussia, but whereas Prussia had been the decisive element in Bismarck's and William II's Reich, in Weimar Germany it was only the most important administrative unit.

Weimar Germany enjoyed a number of years of economic prosperity and a remarkable cultural outburst, but politically it remained a promise unfulfilled. It looked as though it might become a parliamentary democracy but it did not look as though it had. After the election of Field Marshal von Beneckendorf und Hindenburg (who had retired from active service in 1911) to succeed Ebert as Chancellor in 1925 it looked more like the pre-war monarchy than anything else and so long as he lived Hindenburg, himself an avowed monarchist, seemed more likely to play General Monk than General Washington. Thus Weimar Germany, besides being smaller and weaker than the old Reich, was uncertain and disunited. At first it was also turbulent. Free Corps, formed out of the disbanded army originally to guard Germany's eastern frontiers, became autonomous units owing shadowy allegiance to senior army officers but acknowledging none to the state. They assumed roving commissions to put down left-wing activities (1919 saw a rash of communist risings in large cities) and where they thought fit they organized murders. They were a throw-back to the medieval Free Knights, freebooters tricked out in romantic trappings. In 1920 the Kapp putsch in Berlin, a right-wing and pro-monarchist attempt by one of these Free Corps to overthrow the government with the open support of a part of the army, demonstrated – the more so because it was a ludicrous failure – the weakness of government and the instability of society. Kapp and his associates failed to take over the government but the government, by failing to punish them or to disband the Free Corps, showed that it was not master in its own house. A similar coup in Munich succeeded and all but withdrew southern Germany from Berlin's authority. There was a continuing struggle for power in Germany in a vacuum in which groups operating outside the law took things into their own hands by virtue only of the fact that they had arms. The atmosphere of violence was aggravated by the murder, by the Free Corps, of the moderate political leaders Matthias Erzberger and Walther Rathenau and also by the fascist march on Rome in 1922 and the Franco-Belgian occupation of the Ruhr in 1923. But the years 1924–9 (from the Dawes settlement to the Great Depression) were much less turbulent: under Stresemann's guidance Germany sought to satisfy its grievances by discussion and by entering into the comity of Europe: it joined the League of Nations in 1926 and saw the withdrawal of the victors' Military Control Commission in 1927; American loans and efficient administration combined to stabilize the currency, modernize communications, re-equip industry and reduce unemployment to (in 1928) 650,000. The army remained in the background. The more extreme parties made less noise. Germany began to look and to behave like the bourgeois politicians who were in charge of its affairs. By the end of this period it had the best roads, the fastest railways and the most modern merchant fleet in Europe. Real wages were back to what they had been before the war; industrial production was more than 20 per cent higher. But the republic was perpetually threatened by a possible alliance between the nationalist ruling classes and the nationalist masses and its governments were inevitably constricted by the aftermath of defeat.

The peace treaty had taken from Germany all its colonies, one eighth of its European territory and one tenth of its European population, and most of its iron and steel and shipping; it had placed the Rhineland and the Saar temporarily under foreign control, eliminated the German navy and air force and reduced the German army to a force of 100,000 men who were required to serve for at least twelve years in order to prevent the creation of reserves; it had extracted from Germany a written admission of war guilt and imposed an obligation to pay extensive but as yet unlimited reparations. These terms were harsh. This, however, was to be expected. They came also to be considered unjust, not only by Germans, on the pleas that the war guilt clause was a vindictive oversimplification of the causes of the war, that the reparations were excessive, that the plebiscitary principle was applied only to Germany's disadvantage and was excluded where it might have worked the other way, and that Germany had surrendered on the terms of Wilson's Fourteen Points which the peace treaty had then contravened. This last plea does not stand up to examination since no such bargain was struck, but the belief was independent of the facts – like the belief, fostered by the ruling classes, that Germany had not been defeated in the field at all but had been forced to surrender by the collapse of civilian morale.

There was nothing unusual about charging the cost of a war to the losers. Most of the war damage had been done to and not by the victors and they felt entitled to get back what they could in order to repair the damage done to their lands and buildings, their disabled soldiers and their widows and children. The obvious way to do this was to present a bill and demand payment in cash; a more sophisticated method, devised by British and French officials and welcomed by the Germans, whereby the damage in north-eastern France would have to be repaired by German labour using German materials, was blocked by French building interests. What was unusual about the bill presented to Germany after the First World War was the refusal of the victors to say how much would satisfy them. For twelve years the Germans did not know how much they might have to pay. In 1921 the Allied Reparations Commission produced the figure of 132 milliard gold marks (£6,850 million) but this amount might be increased later if the Commission decided that Germany could pay more. J. M. Keynes, whose own assessment of Germany's capacity to pay was £2,000 million, stigmatized this arrangement as morally detestable, politically foolish and economically nonsensical. Keynes also argued that all inter-allied war debts should be cancelled, since otherwise they would only be repudiated, in which prophecy only Finland proved him wrong.

This interim reparations settlement was almost immediately destroyed by the collapse of the mark which fell during 1922–3 from a par value of 4.20 to the dollar to 4,200 billion to the dollar. Germany could neither pay nor borrow. It defaulted at the end of 1922, whereupon France and Belgium exercised in January 1923 their right to reoccupy the Ruhr. Great Britain disapprovingly kept apart. A new mark, the Rentenmark, was called into existence by Hjalmar Schacht, President of the *Reichsbank*, to replace the old mark which had become a valueless string of noughts, and in 1924 a fresh attempt was made to quantify reparations. Under the Dawes Plan Germany undertook to resume payments at the rate of 1 billion new marks a year (about £50 million) rising to 2.5 billion in 1928–9. These sums were charged on the product of customs, railways and industry and were to be paid by the *Reichsbank* to Germany's creditors, who provided half the directors of the *Reichsbank* and also exercised control over the German railways. The money for the first payments was lent to Germany by the principal foreign national banks. There was still no limit fixed to Germany's total indebtedness, but Germany's more pressing worries were relieved by its creditors' willingness to lend and go on lending. In the next six years, 1924–30, they lent over 30 billion marks, enough not only to meet the Dawes outgoings but also to replace the capital destroyed by the great inflation of 1922–3, finance post-war reconstruction, pay annual deficits on foreign trade and create a gold reserve. These were good years for Germany. Then in 1929 the Young Plan reduced the Dawes payments, fixed a limit for German reparations, provided Germany with yet another loan of $300 million, removed foreign controls over the *Reichsbank* and the railways, and secured the evacuation of the Rhineland in 1930 instead of partly in 1930 and partly in 1935.

But the Young Plan still kept Germany under a heavy economic sentence. Reparations were to continue for fifty-nine years and, as *The Times* noted, Hitler was able to appeal to millions of Germans who could 'know nothing of the war but that the bill for it will outlast their lifetime'. Moreover the Young Plan, unlike the Dawes Plan, did not turn out to be a fresh start. The depression, which had started in the United States in 1928–9, was already spreading to Europe. Factories were closing, unemployment was growing and American loans were ceasing. Among the casualties was the Weimar republic and among those who gained was Hitler.

During the twenties Germany was put back on its feet by foreign governments, especially the United States, but the mere fact that Germany was once more an active competitor in the world economy revived international strains which had accompanied Germany's first advance to economic power at the end of the nineteenth century. The technically advanced countries were producing more than they themselves and the rest of the world could buy. The obvious remedy for this state of affairs – produce less – was not available since the industrial and technical revolutions which had increased the productivity of the strongest economies had also increased their need for capital accumulation and hence their appetite for higher profits and bigger markets. By the end of the twenties overproduction was creating unemployment, while in various parts of the world surplus stocks were lying unmoved and unconsumed. Germany, with its post-war neuroses and without colonial markets, was particularly vulnerable in this competition for the best slices of the international cake and its business community was looking for a government which would give priority to the requirements of its section of the nation and would secure by any means the revision of a post-war settlement which had cut down Germany's place in the world. Germany was thus predisposed to become increasingly authoritarian and revisionist.

The depression of the late twenties was virtually worldwide. It put twenty to thirty million people out of work, halved the volume of international trade, impoverished national banks and exchequers as well as families, baffled political leaders and helped men like Hitler to take power. It was dramatized, near its beginning, by the sensational collapse of the New York stock exchange in the last hour of business on 23 October 1929. On that day nearly 20 million shares were sold at lower and lower prices and by the end of that month investors were poorer by some $40 billion.

In the United States the late twenties was one of those periods of immense material optimism in which people stop thinking about limits. In a booming economy men of property believed, or acted as if they believed, that an era of richness for all had arrived and that stock prices would continue indefinitely their great leaps forward. As profits and savings satisfied and exceeded the demand for consumer goods and luxuries, they were used to create yet more monetary wealth and were re-consigned to the stock market, where they pushed stock prices up further still. Those who paused to think assumed that higher prices were being matched and justified by higher productivity. In fact, however, the great American boom had shown signs of slackening several months before the stock market's crash in October. Industrial production had taken a downward turn. This had happened before, temporarily, but in 1929 the setback was not followed by a quick recovery; it was not a pause but an about turn.

The effects of the collapse were felt over a vast area because the United States had failed to adjust to the post-war situation in the world at large. During the twenties countries all over the world were importing American goods and borrowing American money. The borrowing had two principal reasons. The first was the high tariffs which the United States maintained and which prevented its customers from selling in the United States enough goods to balance their purchases; they were forced to balance their trade either by payments in gold or by continuous American loans. The second reason was a consequence of the First World War, which created vast intergovernmental debts, partly contracted by the victors in the course of fighting the war and paying for it and partly in the form of reparations. The bulk of the inter-allied debts was owed to the United States, Great Britain and France (although France was only a net creditor if Russian debts were taken at their face value) and the bulk of the reparations payments was owed by Germany to its near neighbours. The debtors borrowed from the United States in order to discharge their obligations. After 1929, however, American loans were no longer forthcoming and at the same time the United States raised its tariffs still further, notably by the inopportune Smoot-Hawley Act of 1930. Since American lending had been financing post-war reconstruction and development in Europe as well as debt settlements and international trade, the turning off of the American tap – first because private investors preferred to play the rising markets in the United States and then because of the collapse of those markets – throttled Europe's economies.

The economic interdependence of different parts of the world was largely a consequence of the industrial and technical revolutions which had begun and flourished in western Europe and northern America. These revolutions created both a demand for primary products in places where they did not exist and speedy means of getting them there. Western Europe, with its higher standards of living and advanced skills, consumed the food and the minerals which other continents produced for its kitchens and factories. But this pattern contained the seeds of its own transformation since international trade enriched the poorer countries as well as the richer and helped the poorer to improve their own standards of living and so eat more of the food they could grow. The First World War also affected the pattern. By concentrating man's needs on munitions it boosted the demand for minerals and their price, and by disrupting communications it boosted food production for local consumption and, likewise, the farmer's profits. In the United States and other prosperous societies agriculture expanded owing to the fear that the war would prevent food from distant countries from reaching its destination. When therefore the war ended, more food was being produced than could be disposed of. Prices began to fall and continued to do so throughout the twenties with only a brief pause in 1925–8. Instead of reducing production, governments, in particular the government of the United States, subsidized the farmer's prices and so encouraged him to keep under cultivation the land which he had worked so successfully under different circumstances. Moreover, since the wartime expansion of American agriculture had been financed by credit, the farmer in the post-war world was not merely an over-producer but an indebted over-producer. From 1929 the system took perforce the violent way to solution by numerous bankruptcies.

The end of the war also brought a drop in the prices of primary products other than food. Initially this change benefited the manufacturing countries at the expense of the producers, but it soon damaged the industrial societies too by contracting their markets; the suppliers of raw materials were also the purchasers of manufactured goods, and when they no longer got good prices for their raw materials they ceased to be able to buy manufactured goods. Less was bought and sold throughout the world. There was less wealth.

By the end of the twenties there were therefore three interlocking problems: agricultural overproduction; the shrinkage of international trade, which was leading nations to protect themselves by tariffs and other barriers; and reparations and inter-allied debts which, like the reconstruction of Germany and deficits on trade between the United States and Europe, were being financed by copious but not inexhaustible American loans. At the end of the twenties the politicians who were grappling with these economic problems became overwhelmed by them.

In Europe the acute phase of the crisis began in Austria in the spring of 1931. Austria, from having been the centre of a great empire, had become a small new state athwart the division between modern industrial western Europe and the relatively backward agricultural hinterlands of south-eastern Europe. It was prohibited by the treaty of St Germain – Austria's counterpart of Versailles – from uniting with Germany and this prohibition had been reinforced by the Geneva Protocol of 1922 when economic aid had been provided for Austria in return for renewed assurances that it would not unite with Germany. Equally Austria was prevented from combining with its other neighbours in a Danubian or central European federation, because these neighbours were determined to have nothing to do with anything which looked like a revival of the Austro-Hungarian empire. Austrian independence was a shibboleth of France as the foremost champion of the post-war settlement, of Czechoslovakia as the most vigorous of the new progeny of the settlement, and of Rumania and Yugoslavia as its beneficiaries, but independence in this case did not mean the defence of Austrian independence against an aggressor but insistence on Austrian independence against, if necessary, the interests of the Austrians themselves. Since Austria was poor as well as small, those who insisted on its independence had to pay to keep it solvent or see it become a dependency of some other power.

Austria's future became an active topic of discussion and negotiation in 1930. Germany was afraid that Austria was looking to Italy for its salvation and regarded an Austro-German union as the only natural solution. Many Austrians would have preferred a wider solution in order not to become a mere province in a new German empire, but this way seemed to be blocked. France and Great Britain were at cross purposes. France was determined to prevent an Austro-German union but Great Britain was less alarmed by this prospect and wanted to patch up Franco-German differences rather than give France unequivocal support. Great Britain preferred the role of mediator to that of ally. In March 1931 Germany and Austria announced that they had agreed to form a customs union. France in particular regarded this projected union as a political scheme rather than an economic expedient. It was referred to the Permanent Court of International Justice at The Hague, which eventually declared it contrary to the Geneva Protocol but not contrary to the treaty of St Germain (in both cases by eight votes to seven). The plan was abandoned.

Meanwhile economic forces were gaining control. In May the principal Austrian bank, the *Credit-Anstalt für Handel und Gewerbe*, closed its doors. It was unable to meet its short term obligations because of the decline of Austrian industry and trade which had impoverished Austrian concerns to which the bank had lent its money. Its difficulties were accentuated when France blocked continued Austrian borrowing in the French money market. Although German banks and the Bank of England lent to the *Credit-Anstalt*, they were unable to save it and succeeded only in weakening themselves. Before the end of the month the German banks were in similar troubles from their own clients. By June the *Reichsbank* had lost over a billion marks and in July one of the leading German banks, the *Darmstadter Nazional*, also closed its doors. American banks which had lent to German banks began to feel alarmed. The Bank of England too was in trouble and borrowed from the Bank of France – France was financially the strongest country in Europe. British industrial and commercial activities were in decline. Unemployment was growing, and in June it became known that under existing arrangements the British government could meet only half of the calls on it for unemployment relief. The Labour government decided that it must balance its budget as a precondition to getting loans from American finance houses, even if part of the cost had to be paid by the unemployed. A special cabinet committee recommended cuts in public expenditure amounting to £78.5 million. The full cabinet decided that cuts of £56 million would do but it then disagreed over one item, a proposal to reduce by one tenth the dole payable to the unemployed. At Invergordon there was a mutiny when it was discovered that cuts in the pay of the lower ranks in the Royal Navy were to exceed the 10 per cent deduction required of all employees of the Crown. The government broke up and the country went off the gold standard.

Some temporary relief, psychological rather than economic, was provided by President Hoover's offer to suspend for one year the payment of debts due to the United States if other inter-governmental debts were likewise suspended. Hoover's offer anticipated an inevitable German default and shortly afterwards Germany declared that it would not resume payments after the end of the Hoover year. The Young Plan was scrapped and a conference at Lausanne in 1932 sanctioned, in camouflaged language, the abandonment of reparations. Another conference at Stresa later in the year tried to find a solution to the economic ailments of Austria and south-eastern Europe but, failing, left the area open to Germany.

The great crash and the great depression shattered more than material things. They destroyed morale. They injected a great amount of fear into ordinary people (including the ordinary people who sat in cabinets) and so turned them to an intent concern for their own affairs, present and future. The sense of community narrowed. Nation protected itself against nation, class turned against class. The millions of victims of the mysterious workings of economics looked for somewhere to lay the blame for their sufferings, and for somebody to lead them out of the mess. And nowhere were the confusion and disruption worse than in Germany, which had relied most completely on foreign loans. There too factories began to close, unemployment grew by leaps and bounds, and the cost of unemployment relief exceeded the capacity of the treasury to pay it. The resulting problem sundered the democratic parties. The Left wanted higher taxes, the Right higher unemployment contributions and lower relief; the Left, in other words, wanted the economy as a whole to subsidize the unemployment fund, while the Right wanted the fund to balance itself at whatever level was dictated by circumstances. Although both sides were prepared to temper their claims, neither would go far enough to meet the other. For two years Heinrich Brüning, who had been appointed Chancellor in March 1930, tussled with diminishing success with these economic and political storms.

Brüning was an intelligent man in his mid-forties, socially of the middle class, politically of the centre-Right, well intentioned and determined to save the republic. It was his fate to preside over the collapse of German credit and German democracy. By 1929 the steady economic expansion of 1925–8 had come to a halt and in the three ensuing years – 1930–32, the worst of the crisis – the national income was almost halved and one in three of the working population was put out of work. The Austrian crisis having triggered off a German crisis and foreigners (to whom half of all German credits were owed) having hurried to demand repayment of their short-term loans, the credit system collapsed. At the same time the problem of how to relieve the unemployed created dissensions among the centre parties of the Reichstag. Brüning, whose instinctive loyalties went not so much to democratic institutions as to the person of the chief of state, once his regimental commander, failed to hold the coalition together, a failure for which the Social Democrats share the blame. His policies were wrong enough to aggravate political dissension among the moderates and then belatedly right enough to give his ultimate successors, the Nazis, a good start. His methods – government by decree in the last resort – accustomed Germany to procedures which the Nazis turned into common form, and so accustomed foreigners to seeing Germany governed that way.

He took office with the determination not to inflate. The post-war inflation was remembered with such horror that any degree of inflation was very difficult to contemplate. A moderate or controlled inflation was not part of the German experience; inflation meant run-away inflation, a situation in which the value of a house falls to that of a box of matches between breakfast and lunch. Any inflation was a national phobia. So Brüning took the traditional, but beyond certain limits socially intolerable, course of deflation. His immediate problem was the flight of capital from Germany. Having decided against devaluation he resorted to import licensing and exchange controls (both of which were later developed by the Nazis) and to deflation, but deflation failed to boost German exports partly because the government deflated too little and partly because Germany's customers had devalued their currencies. The balance of payments grew worse and the reserves went on falling. At home the attempt to balance the budget by cutting social benefits and increasing taxes widened the rift between Right and Left. Brüning's 1930 budget had to be enacted by decree. The Social Democrats moved in the Reichstag to annul the decrees. The President dissolved the Reichstag. No parliamentary majority could be found. If Brüning hoped to gain control of the Reichstag by new elections he was disappointed, for at the elections of September 1930 the Nazis increased their seats from twelve to 107 and the communists from fifty-four to seventy-seven. The anti-parliamentary extremes were carried by the votes of the unemployed to a dominant position in the parliament and even with Social Democrat cooperation Brüning was now dependent on the President and his power to legislate by decree. By the beginning of 1931 unemployment was approaching the 5 million mark (it continued to rise until the latter part of 1932), production had declined by nearly half of what it had been in 1928, and parliament and the constitution were unworkable. Brüning's policy had failed and the failure, a product of the unenlightened economics of the time in government in Washington, Berlin and other political capitals, visited on the German populace economic hardships unparalleled in peacetime in an advanced industrial country. It also alienated an influential segment of the business class which had previously supported Brüning's Centre Party and so, indirectly, the Weimar republic. The economic crisis laid bare weaknesses in the German banking system which the government could not go on ignoring, but Brüning's attempts to correct these weaknesses – by the introduction of state supervision and inspection of banking practices – caused bankers and their associates in industry and commerce to look round for other parties to patronize. The developed world's economic ignorance and incompetence played a large part in making Germany choose Hitler.

Deflation was abandoned in 1932. It had done no good except to prove the need for something different. A new expansionist policy, based on expenditure on public works, was adopted. It was to be greatly expanded by the Nazis and to reduce unemployment – even before the impact of rearmament – from a peak of over 6 million to 2.6 million at the end of 1934. The Nazis, unafraid of state interference with private enterprise and unhampered by the trade unions, which they overpowered, pursued a policy of inflation controlled by tax increases and by wage, price and dividend restrictions. By 1937 Germany was short of labour. But a few years earlier inflation had seemed impossible. Because there had been so much of it in the early twenties, there was too little of it in the early thirties and too late. Deflation reduced Germany to something approaching despair and chaos at a time when powerful forces – the Nazis and the communists – could see that despair and chaos were what they needed.

The Nazi Party had made little impression during the years of prosperity (1924–9). It won only twelve seats in the Reichstag in 1928, but between 1929 and 1933 it grew into a mass party of the discontented. The Nazis attacked in the name of socialism the parties and policies which could produce nothing better than unemployment; they accused the entire political establishment of callousness and unimaginativeness. At the same time and in the name of nationalism they denounced the treaty of Versailles as an affront to Germany and a prime source of its economic ills. In the Reichstag elections of September 1930 they jumped from the category of a splinter party on the lunatic fringe into that of a political force which could be left out of no calculation. Six and a half million Germans voted Nazi and made the party the second biggest in the Reichstag. Newspapers abroad dug into their records to tell their readers something about its Austrian leader, Adolf Hitler, who now became world famous. Less than two years later this popular vote was more than doubled to give the Nazis 230 seats and make it the biggest in the Reichstag. But they never polled half the electorate in a free election. Even after Hitler won the chancellorship the Nazi vote in the election of March 1933 was only 43.9 per cent. But by then figures no longer meant much.

The rapid rise in Hitler's popular support created a problem for the other nationalist and right-wing parties. Either Hitler would come to power in alliance with them or he would be swept into power by the masses, with or without violence. Hitler could see this too and in the declining years of the Weimar republic he played politics in the knowledge that the German Right was in a dilemma. The Right had this much in common with the Nazis, that both were anti-republican. The Right believed, or hoped, that Hitler's wilder strains were the sort of political moonshine which can be ignored by sensible men and which is forgotten by even the worst demagogue when he gets office; Hindenburg among others seemed more put off by Corporal Hitler's social inferiority than by his manic utterances. The Nationalist Party, led by the rich industrialist and newspaper owner Alfred Hugenburg, was the first to make an alliance with the Nazis. Others waited, but when Hitler stood against Hindenburg for the presidency in 1932, the Right voted for Hitler. There were four candidates for the presidency, none of them democrats. Only Hindenburg was strong enough to beat Hitler. So the Field Marshal, receiving substantial support from an unaccustomed quarter, was re-elected, after a second poll, by the votes of the Left – to which he was now useless from senility as well as conviction.

After his re-election Hindenburg discarded Brüning and replaced him with Franz von Papen, the nominee of the anti-parliamentary forces of the Right – the army, the big landowners and big business. Papen was a member of the lesser nobility who was sufficiently insensitive to political reality to imagine that he could outwit Hitler and run a right-wing government without him. Papen fell between two stools. First he destroyed what slight chance of a centre coalition still existed when, in violation of the constitution, he dismissed the Social Democrat government of Prussia and subordinated it to the central government of the Reich. Then he changed his mind about the Nazis and offered Hitler the Vice-Chancellorship. But he was too late. His offer was not good enough for Hitler, who had meanwhile, in the elections of July 1932, become the leader of the biggest parliamentary party. Hitler asked for the Chancellorship. He was refused. Hindenburg declared that he would not give the Nazis full powers because 'they intended to use these powers to further their own ends'. Hitler was both checked and humiliated. Optimists grasped at any sign that somehow somebody was going to prevent Hitler from triumphing. But there was also a growing feeling that the Nazis would and should come to power. The more they spread chaos the more they gave the impression that they alone could allay it. Street violence was an everyday occurrence: public political murders, put at forty-two in 1929 and fifty in 1930, had quadrupled in the first half of 1931 and were still increasing. Terror and brutality, by communists as well as Nazis, sickened public opinion and alarmed the army, which shrank from the prospect of having to fight Nazis and communists at once. Hitler deliberately raised the stakes by sending a telegram of sympathy and support to some Nazis who had broken into the house of a young communist called Hans Potempa and kicked him to death before his mother's eyes. At the same time the Nazis were saying – and demonstrating – that they alone had the energy and the willpower to restore order. The public became inured to the idea that the price of order was a Nazi government.

On the parliamentary front Nazis, communists and socialists combined to defeat Papen in the Reichstag in September and in the ensuing elections in November the Nazi tide receded slightly. But Papen still commanded no majority in the Reichstag and, having failed to contain the Nazis or come to terms with them, he was no longer any use. He had been made Chancellor because the army wanted him and the President commanded him, and his failure forced the army to take the Chancellorship itself in the person of General Kurt von Schleicher. Papen had been a nominee of the army, Schleicher was its embodiment: seconds were out. Schleicher had been in favour of bringing Hitler into the government until he discovered that Hindenburg would not have Hitler. He still thought it necessary to bring Nazis into the cabinet and he proceeded to offer the Vice-Chancellorship to Gregor Strasser, the leader of the northern and more radical section of the party and the representative of what was left of socialism in National Socialism (a by-product of attempts in the twenties to woo the working classes and lesser *bourgeoisie*). Strasser was willing but stipulated that Hitler must first bless the union, which Hitler refused to do. It is difficult to understand how either Schleicher or Strasser ever imagined that he would, and Strasser merely destroyed himself by letting Schleicher use him in this way. Schleicher, who was a political neophyte, next tried an approach to the democratic Left, whereupon the financial and industrial establishment put pressure on Hindenburg to recall Papen and install a Papen–Hitler coalition. The army too failed to stand solid for its own Chancellor. Some officers, led by General von Blomberg, went over to the Nazis. Hitler now had enough backing from the conservatives, the moneyed interests and the army to make his own terms. This was the end of Schleicher, whose short period in office marked the end of the German army's exercise of political power. Out of deference to Hindenburg, who thus performed a last service by easing Hitler into power, Schleicher quietly relinquished his post. On 30 January 1933 Hitler was appointed Chancellor by Hindenburg with Papen as his Vice-Chancellor.

Hitler became Chancellor constitutionally. To say that he became Chancellor legally would be to ignore the activities of his party, which, in the preceding years, had committed countless acts of criminal violence, including murder; but technically Hitler (like Mussolini) did not seize office, it was conferred upon him. There is a difference between seizing office and assuming power. Hitler assumed power between 1929 and 1933 by violent means but he forbore to lay hands on the institutions of the state which he proposed to manipulate. Ever since his abortive putsch in 1923 Hitler had been sagacious enough to sense and insist upon the advantages of observing prescribed constitutional processes. He was a better respecter of pieces of paper than pieces of humanity, because he realized the strength of formalities and the bemusing effect of a show of continuity. He had made no secret of his intentions. In 1931, for example, he had told a German editor, a political opponent, that although he intended to come to power by winning seats in the Reichstag, after he had done so the

Reichstag might as well close its doors and be turned into a museum; and after his appointment as Chancellor it took him only a matter of months to master the whole apparatus of power and propaganda in Germany. The steps which he took were characteristic: legislation and murder.

Between 9 and 10 p.m. on 27 February 1933 the Reichstag was burnt to the ground. Hitler at once blamed the communists. He probably really thought they had done it. Others equally promptly assumed that the Nazis had burnt it with the intention of incriminating the communists and liquidating their party, and at the end of the war General Halder said that Goering had boasted in 1942 that the fire was his doing. The question remains obscure and there is much to be said for the view that the Dutch communist Marinus van der Lubbe did, as he himself claimed, conceive the conflagration and effect it on his own as a one-man protest. It is evident that the three Bulgarian communists tried with van der Lubbe (who was executed) had nothing to do with the deed. They were even acquitted. Whatever the truth the Nazis seized their opportunity with alacrity – proof either of their efficiency or their complicity. Arrests were made within a matter of hours, communist newspapers were suppressed, and an emergency decree was issued the next day overriding basic civil rights such as freedom of expression and assembly, permitting arbitrary searches and seizure of property, empowering the central government to assume the functions of local authorities and imposing severe penalties. This decree was never repealed. In March Hitler supplemented it by an Enabling Act which in effect converted him into a one-man legislature. This act, which required a two-thirds majority in the Reichstag, was passed only because the Centre Party (at the bidding of the Vatican) voted for it. A few Social Democrat voices were raised, for the last time, in courageous but futile protest. With the powers thus conferred upon him Hitler decreed all parties except his own out of existence, subordinated the federal states to the central government, and won 92 per cent of the vote in elections which he staged in November 1933. He abolished free trade unions, intimidated the churches and virtually annexed the judiciary and the educational system, thus moulding a new society in which only Nazi ideas, ethical, social and political, might be expressed and protected.

Hitler also struck down a part of his own movement, the armed S A or *Sturmabteilungen*, led by Ernst Röhm, an even earlier member of the Nazi Party than Hitler himself and one of the few men with whom he used the intimate second person singular *du*. The S A had had a job to do on the streets in the days before the Nazis came to power. They provided the rough and tough arguments for supporting the Nazis or keeping out of their way. But Hitler had had trouble with them from the start. They regarded themselves as an independent force like the Free Corps from which many of them were initially drawn and they wished to be as autonomous *vis-à-vis* the party as the German army traditionally was *vis-à-vis* the state. Hitler had been obliged in 1930 to eliminate their leader Franz Pfeffer von Salomon, an ex-Free Corps man, because he proved too independent and opposed Hitler's policy of achieving power by constitutional means. He also had to suppress an open revolt by the Berlin S A in the same year and had further trouble in the next year. Moreover the S A were growing fast. At the beginning of 1931 they were 100,000 strong, the same size as the army; at the end of that year they were 300,000 strong. By the middle of 1934, their ranks swollen particularly by unemployment and by the march-fever which swept through Germany in these troubled years, they had reached a strength of 4.5 million and were scaring the army as well as Nazi Party chiefs. The S A was the most prominent of various Nazi organizations which duplicated the organizations of the state (like a shadow cabinet duplicates a cabinet) but which had become irrelevant or embarrassing once their party had become the state. Röhm saw the S A as replacing the regular army. Politically naïve and temperamentally unbalanced, he overplayed his hand fantastically. He thoroughly alarmed the officer caste by letting it be known that in his view the armed services should be reduced to being training organizations for the S A, and he failed to see that Hitler needed the army. His ambitions contributed to the alliance which both Hitler and the army desired and provided it with a sacrificial victim. The army began at this period to dismiss its Jewish officers to please Hitler and early in 1934 Hitler forced Röhm to agree, formally and in writing, to moderate his ambitions. But rumours of an S A putsch persisted and in June Blomberg, now Minister for Defence, warned Hitler that the army would turn him out, get Hindenburg to declare martial law, hand over the government to the military and probably restore the Hohenzollerns if the S A were allowed to usurp the functions of the army; if the S A were suppressed, the army would see that Hitler got the Presidency. Hitler thereupon organized a massacre. On 30 June Röhm and about fifty other S A leaders were murdered. The opportunity was taken to murder a great many other people too; they included Schleicher and also Gregor Strasser, although there are doubts whether Hitler wanted the latter's death. But the principal beneficiaries of the destruction of the S A were not the army but Heinrich Himmler and his S S or *Schutzstaffeln*, which flourished on the ashes of the S A and became the rival military force which the army had sought to destroy with the S A.

A month later Hindenburg died. The office of President was merged with that of Chancellor. More important, the death of Hindenburg provided Hitler with the opportunity to annex the officer corps to his revolution. With some exceptions the officer corps disliked the Nazis but it shared some of Hitler's aims and was confident that its power was greater than his. From Hitler's point of view the army differed in two ways from every other institution in the state: it was too powerful to be destroyed and he needed it. Although within Germany it might challenge the power of the Nazis, externally it was essential to Hitler's purposes, especially for the conquest of *Lebensraum*. Therefore it had to be strengthened and at the same time rendered domestically harmless. On the day after Hindenburg's death every member of the armed services swore a new oath of obedience to Adolf Hitler in person as 'the Führer of the German Reich and people and Commander-in-Chief of the armed forces'. This oath was devised by General Walther von Reichenau, one of a group of officers who were at this time keenly pro-Nazi. It gave Hitler a moral authority over the officer corps which endured almost undented until the end of his life. The army, which had virtually ordered the elimination of the S A, had placed itself under the Führer's personal orders by the oath, the mystic force which bound the army together and determined its relation to the state. By this oath the army equated the guardianship of the German state with obedience to the command of Hitler, who was henceforward not only Führer but also President and Supreme War Lord.

CHAPTER 3

The Futile Opposition: 1934–8

IN external affairs Hitler's first aim was to restore German power. He intended to recover for Germany the lands and the peoples lost in Europe after the First World War and to re-establish the armed services which had been destroyed or crippled by the peace settlement. These aims were not novel but they were accompanied by another which, though likewise not novel, was rationalized by Hitler in a new way. Hitler intended that Germany should expand into non-German lands and his reason was his conviction that a people must either wax or die. He did not believe that a people could remain static and survive. So safeguarding the German people meant increasing their number (a biological rather than a military necessity) and securing somewhere for them to live. In *Mein Kampf* he had written, with a mixture of conviction and guff, of securing

... the existence and increase of our race and nation, the sustenance of its children and the purity of its blood, the freedom and independence of the fatherland, and the nation's ability to fulfil the mission appointed to it by the creator of the universe.

The British, so far as they paid any attention to this sort of thing, thought it might be met by offering Hitler colonies, a partial acceptance of the German demand to revise Versailles and a sop to assuage or eliminate his more dangerous aims in Europe; they dangled colonial carrots before Hitler up to the last months of peace. But Hitler was not to be put off in Europe by presents in Africa. He intended to colonize in Europe, not Africa. He made this clear both privately and publicly. A few days after becoming Chancellor he told his service chiefs that the restoration of German power entailed the creation of a unified German nation by converting or breaking all opposing forces and by mastering youth, the struggle against Versailles, the colonization of parts of Europe in order to gain living space, and the reinforcement of the armed services. Publicly he was no less explicit. 'The foreign policy of a nation (*völkisch*) state,' he wrote in *Mein Kampf*, 'must assure the existence on this planet of a race encompassed by the state; it must do this by creating a healthy, life-giving and natural balance between the present and future numbers of the *Volk* on the one hand and, on the other, the quantity and quality of its territory.'

In his next paragraph Hitler made it clear that the prime aim of this foreign policy was to make the *Volk* self-sufficient in food within the boundaries of its state and by extending those boundaries if necessary. This passage comes near the beginning of a chapter entitled Eastern Policy. It left therefore no doubt where Hitler coveted land. It was included in the abbreviated English translation of *Mein Kampf* which was published in 1933 – and reissued in 1935 in a cheap, paperback edition which sold nearly 50,000 copies in three years.

In 1933 he did not know how or when he was going to achieve these aims. In this sense he had no plans, but he had aims and the achievement of his aims for the German people included from the outset measures which other peoples would never willingly accept. He himself was aware of this. He did not expect to win *Lebensraum* – that is to say, other people's territories – without war.

Among the European powers Hitler distinguished between France and the USSR on the one hand and Great Britain and Italy on the other. France he regarded as an irreconcilable foe, the USSR as an inevitable one. Thus the two chief traditional opponents of the extension of German power were opponents still (although the Franco-Russian treaty of 1935 did not create so menacing a combination as the old Dual Alliance). Hitler's attitudes to these two powers were, however, very different. The irreconcilability of Germany and France came from the French side. In his view it was the French who were perpetuating the Franco-German feud; they were unbiddable, nothing could abate their animosity. At the same time Hitler despised them, so that although French hostility was a fact it was not a very serious one. French power was enough to give Hitler pause but not to thwart him – as he showed when he remilitarized the Rhineland in 1936 against the advice of his generals.

Hitler's feelings about the USSR included hatred as well as contempt. Although he despised Russians as Slavs and sub-men and lacked that respect for their tenacity which was felt by many Germans who, unlike himself, had fought on the eastern front in the First World War, the overmastering sentiment in his references to the USSR was a passionate loathing for their communism, which was for him one of the principal contemporary expressions of the age-long Jewish conspiracy against the human race. Ultimately too it was the USSR which Germany would have to fight for *Lebensraum*.

Italy and Great Britain came into a different category. They were potential allies or at least non-objectors. To begin with Hitler thought of Italy as no more than a medium power which could prove useful by engaging and distracting France and Great Britain in the Mediterranean, but the course of international politics in the mid-thirties threw Mussolini into Hitler's arms. The two dictators, though personally loyal to one another, never established a close and confidential alliance between their countries like the wartime Anglo-American alliance. Still less did they coordinate their war efforts, but the Rome-Berlin axis justified Hitler in his judgement that Italy could be brought to serve his purposes by helping to demoralize France with multiple preoccupations in the central and western Mediterranean and to convince British governments that they could not face war with Germany unless Italy were first neutralized.

Hitler's feelings about Great Britain were complex and in the end wrong. The British were Aryan and they were successful imperialists. He could respect them. Hitler must have been aware of the view current in Germany that the challenge to Great Britain in 1914 by the invasion of Belgium had been a mistake, although by the end of 1939 – after war had begun – he said that the violation of Belgian (and Dutch) neutrality was a matter of no importance. *Mein Kampf* assumed no conflict with Great Britain and a decade after he wrote his book Hitler was still pursuing the same policy of appeasement when he sent Ribbentrop to be his Ambassador in London. The Nazis avoided the Kaiser's challenge to British sea power and Hitler never had any intention of rebuilding the German High Seas Fleet. But Hitler's admiration for the British was for what they had done in the past and he thought that they had had their day. He despised Neville Chamberlain when he met him although he admired Lloyd George. The question was whether Great Britain would stand in his way. On the whole he thought not. There was, he believed, a difference between Great Britain and France: whereas France wanted to prevent Germany from becoming powerful at all, Great Britain was only concerned to prevent Germany from becoming the sort of world power which would threaten British world power. But Hitler did not want to threaten this British position. He envisaged two world powers, the one based on dominion in Europe and the other based on dominion of the seas, and he hoped that if he made this plain Great Britain would not object to German hegemony in Europe. Subsequent events seemed to show that Hitler was wrong about Great Britain and failed to gauge its inevitable and implacable opposition to his plans. But his error was pardonable. His view of Anglo-German relations was not confined to Germans. When Halifax was about to visit Hitler in 1937 Sir Nevile Henderson, the British Ambassador in Berlin, urged the Foreign Secretary to 'look facts in the face' and remember that 'the main point is that we are an *island* people and Germans a continental one. On that basis we can be friends and both go along the road of destiny without a clash of vital interests.' Further, as late as 1940, when France fell, some British political leaders gave thought and utterance to coming to terms with Hitler and letting him be. They did not prevail but their hesitations show that Hitler's error about Great Britain was only a marginal one, albeit one of those marginal errors which turn out to be fatal.

Hitler's problem in foreign affairs was to nullify international opposition to his international aims, until he was strong enough to dictate abroad as well as at home. He had to ensure that Germany's strength grew faster than fear of Germany, for if the fear grew faster then the forces which had opposed and beaten the Kaiser's Reich might together destroy the new Reich. Fortunately for Hitler this possibility was largely theoretical, for the victors of 1918 were no longer united. After that war two of them, France and the United States, had put forward entirely different solutions to the German problem and in the upshot neither scheme survived in working order. The twenties therefore had seen the elaboration of substitutes, so that when Hitler came to power the principal formalized constraints upon his freedom of action beyond his borders were, in the west, the Locarno treaties of 1925 and, in the east, a patchwork of alliances designed by France – systems which were scrappily deputizing for the treaty of Versailles and the Covenant of the League of Nations.

After victory Clemenceau's solution to the problem of what to do about a powerful Germany was to put such constraints upon it as to make it harmless for as long as possible. President Wilson's solution was to devise a system which would nullify the excesses of every state. Clemenceau was seeking a specific solution to a specific problem, Wilson a general solution to a universal ill. Clemenceau was by nature a pessimist, Wilson an optimist. Clemenceau was a Frenchman first and a European afterwards, Wilson was not a European at all.

The best that France could hope for at the Peace Conference was to dismember Germany (French policy since Richelieu), extend France and get Great Britain and the United States to promise to go to war as soon as Germany attacked France again. This programme failed completely. Great Britain and the United States offered to guarantee France's territory as part of a bargain which included, in the American case, the acceptance of the Covenant of the League and, in the British case, the formalization of the American guarantee. When the US Senate refused to endorse the Covenant, the American guarantee to France lapsed and with it the British. Nor was France allowed to annex German territory west of the Rhine. It had to be content with the demilitarization of these Rhineland areas together with their occupation by the allies until (in different zones)

1925, 1930 and 1935 and with the possibility of acquiring the small Saar territory, economically rather than strategically valuable, by plebiscite. Germany was also to be and to remain substantially disarmed, and was, as we have already seen, subjected until shortly before Hitler's accession to paying reparations designed to keeping its economy trained upon the discharge of debt instead of the creation of military might.

The collapse of the American and British guarantees was not France's only diplomatic setback. In the east Russia itself had collapsed. To most Europeans the new USSR did not look like a useful (or respectable) ally at any time between 1917 and 1941. This was to be an immensely valuable aid to the revival of Germany as a major power. France tried to replace its eastern ally by new ones – by Poland, which was re-created in 1918 and with which France made a treaty in 1921, and by making friends with Czechoslovakia, Yugoslavia and Rumania, the so-called Little Entente, all of them beneficiaries of the break-up of the Austro-Hungarian empire and so, like France, supporters of the Versailles settlement. The weaknesses of France's eastern policies became clear in the thirties. Poland was no substitute for Russia as an ally against Germany except in the limited sense that it lay at Germany's back door. Poland did not feel committed to an anti-German policy as a first priority but developed a policy of keeping its balance between Germany and the USSR. Its population was only three-quarters Polish and it was on bad terms with its neighbours. It had barely re-emerged as a state when it was launched by Pilsudski on an ambitious attempt to recreate the ancient empire of Poles, Lithuanians, White Russians and Ukrainians. It had invaded the USSR in 1920 and, as a result of securing its old 1792 borders, contained within its frontiers six million Ukrainians and White Russians; it had seized Vilna from Lithuania in 1920 and it coveted Teschen, which had been awarded to Czechoslovakia in the same year at a moment when its invasion of the USSR was going badly; it enjoyed special rights in Danzig, the port of the Vistula but demographically a German city with which it was linked by a corridor cut through Germany; and it gained much – Germans thought too much – of Upper Silesia in 1921 after a dubiously interpreted plebiscite. It was a Slav state at odds with other Slav states, a revived state with more than a touch of the intransigence which goes with the proud reconquest of independence, a new republic which (like Greece at that date) cherished tempting recollections of an ancient empire. Revived in November 1918, at war six months later, it narrowly escaped destruction in 1920 when Lenin was talking of sweeping over it into Germany. It was saved largely because its instability exacerbated European fears of spreading Bolshevism, so that France sent General Weygand to Warsaw to give expert advice on how to stop the Russian counter-attack.

Of the members of the Little Entente Czechoslovakia was the most favoured, partly because its western half lay in the technically more advanced half of Europe and partly because it inherited from Habsburg times an efficient civil service and a high level of education. It was also fortunate in its founders, T. G. Masaryk and Edvard Beneš. But these advantages and its outstanding liberal record obscured weaknesses, for Czechoslovakia was even more a medley of races than its name implied and was also the principal meeting place in Europe of the thrusting industrialism of the west and the more placid conservatism of the agricultural east. In Yugoslavia racial and religious antagonisms made this new state even less homogeneous than Czechoslovakia, while Rumania had received the uncomfortable war prize of a large Hungarian population. And throughout eastern Europe there were significant German minorities.

Furthermore, Great Britain was never happy with the new eastern Europe reorganized on Wilsonian principles. These new states were children of the United States and soon orphaned. They were also allied with France but the alliances were brittle so long as they were disliked by France's greater ally, Great Britain. They were an ingredient in a French policy which was not France's only policy. This policy was to build up a pro-French and anti-German system in the east, while retaining the power to attack Germany directly in the west. The alternative was alliance with Great Britain. This was an alternative and not a complementary policy because Great Britain did not want France to attack Germany and did not want to be entangled in eastern Europe. After the abortive occupation of the Ruhr in 1923 France never did attack Germany, even when Hitler remilitarized the Rhineland in 1936. The price of British support was, first, the surrender of the policy of a direct French threat to Germany and, later, the abandonment of France's eastern system: the first was formalized at Locarno in 1925, the latter consummated at Munich in 1938.

Neither the instability of post-imperial eastern Europe nor France's failure to get territorial safeguards or political guarantees against Germany would have mattered much if the system of collective security embodied in the Covenant of the League of Nations had been made to work. Before 1914 statesmen had tried by various means – diplomacy, conferences, the balance of power, arbitration – to prevent wars within the framework set by a multiplicity of nation states. The First World War not only signalized the failure of these techniques but was regarded as a

EUROPE IN 1914

~ARTHUR BANKS~

EUROPE IN 1923

condemnation of the multi-national system itself. A new comprehensive international system was required. President Wilson, who was among politicians the principal champion of this radical thinking, regarded a collective security system as an alternative to what had gone before, not as a supplement: the old system was bad in itself. He shared the belief that wars were caused by alliances, by armaments and by arms races; he saw the First World War as a logical consequence of the formation of the Triple Alliance and the Triple Entente and Anglo-German naval competition, and he wanted to create an international system which would make such things unnecessary and proscribe them. But the new system embodied in the League of Nations did not work in the Wilsonian way because too many important states remained outside it, because it was too new to be trusted, and ultimately because some of its more important members did not want it to work.

Between the French and American approaches to peace in Europe there emerged a distinctive British attitude which sought security by reconciling Germany with its former enemies and with the terms of the peace settlement, if necessary by modifying the latter. Champions of reconciliation argued that it was a surer safeguard of the peace than anti-German alliances, that the Germans were not after all the horde of savages portrayed by wartime propaganda but a Christian nation which had produced Goethe and Beethoven, that there was in Germany much to admire from standards of public behaviour and public administration to open-air weekends of an unimpeachably healthy nature, that the reparations demanded by the peace treaty were unfairly discriminatory. This was a laudable attempt to bury hatchets, all the more laudable since the British public continued to harbour powerful anti-German emotions. It was also firmly grounded in political calculation. The alternative to reconciliation with Germany was the prospect of a second European war against Germany and the maintenance in peacetime of a military establishment which, however natural to a Frenchman, was anathema to the British: the Dominions too disliked a view of things in which the British empire was a reserve force to be used to redeem the imbalance of power in Europe. Both as an island and as an empire Great Britain was congenitally wedded to a view of the German question which was different from the French view. The principal achievement of the British view was the Locarno treaties of 1925, a local and limited settlement which, however, bypassed the Wilsonian general approach to security and also contradicted the essential bases of French policy.

The Franco-Belgian occupation of the Ruhr in 1923 had been a failure and the tough school in Paris was eclipsed when Raymond Poincaré was succeeded by Édouard Herriot and France accepted the Dawes plan in 1924. A first attempt to reassure France focused on strengthening the League's machinery of collective security. The Covenant provided that a state must not carry a dispute to the point of war without first trying to settle it in one of a number of specified ways and accepting a cooling-off period of three months. If a signatory of the Covenant broke this rule, it was branded as an aggressor and other members would together apply sanctions against it. But the rule was a limited one. It did not apply if the Council of the League was not unanimous about the rights and wrongs of the dispute; it did not apply if the dispute was found to lie within the domestic jurisdiction of the state concerned; and it did not apply if that state observed the cooling-off rule and the dispute was still unresolved at the end of it. These exceptions were called the gaps in the Covenant and in 1924 the so-called Geneva Protocol sought to plug the gaps by providing for the compulsory arbitration of all disputes and the application of sanctions to every resort to war. The protocol was accepted by the British Labour government but the Conservatives, returning to power in 1924, refused to ratify it because Great Britain, strongly reinforced by the independent British Dominions, thought that the scope of the Covenant was already wide enough and ought not to be enlarged in such a way as to cumber members of the League with further commitments. The new British government then proposed something else – a system for keeping the peace in western Europe, based on the acceptance of Germany as a state like any other. This was the genesis of Locarno.

What France feared was a fresh German attack one day across the Rhine and through the Rhineland. Austen Chamberlain, the Foreign Secretary in Stanley Baldwin's new government, proposed that Great Britain and Italy should guarantee the Franco-German and Belgo-German frontiers without discrimination as to an aggressor; that is to say, Germany was guaranteed as much as France and Belgium. For Great Britain this reciprocity was more than a diplomatic nicety, since it ruled out a second Franco-Belgian occupation of the Ruhr, but for France reciprocity meant the end of a special advantage and a fundamental review of French strategy. It was no longer possible to hope that another war would begin beyond France's frontiers instead of with an invasion across them. The best thing now was to take steps to keep the Germans out. A few years later the Maginot Line was begun, a line of fortifications which proved useless when the Germans invaded in 1940 but which meanwhile corroded the French spirit since the obvious thing to do with a fortified line is to sit tight behind it. (The Maginot Line has been chiefly derided for its psychological effects on French military thinking and general

French morale. Tactically it was defective even on the premises of those who believed in it, since it did not cover the whole of France's eastern front – Pétain having pronounced the Ardennes to be impassable. Even had it been completed it was still an anachronism, a defensive line performing essentially the same function as a trench but ineffective in a war of movement in which no line could stop all the enemy's armour or even most of it.)

The Locarno system was also defective from the French point of view because Great Britain refused to extend it to eastern Europe. Germany did not accept its eastern frontiers. It was in fact Stresemann's intention to alter these frontiers, as well as other features of the Versailles treaty which were obnoxious to Germany, and his acceptance of a firm settlement in the west, including the demilitarization of the Rhineland, which was freely reaffirmed at Locarno, was part of the price he was willing to pay in order to separate western from eastern problems and gain a greater freedom of manoeuvre in the east. With Poland and Czechoslovakia he agreed to conclude arbitration treaties but no more. France extended guarantees to these two countries but the British refusal to do so was more significant. In the west Locarno confirmed Versailles, in the east it questioned Versailles and it did so because Great Britain, anxious to conciliate Germany, and Germany, anxious to keep a free hand in the east, prevailed over France, which would have preferred to strengthen the anti-German forces in that area. Locarno was also a principal source of the mistaken notion that Italy was a Great Power.

The Locarno settlement provided the formal basis for western European security for eleven years (1925–36). In 1926 Germany joined the League of Nations. It also took part in the Disarmament Conference which assembled at Geneva in February 1932 in a belated attempt to fix and reduce arms levels as the Covenant of the League had envisaged more than a decade earlier. But to Hitler treaties and conferences represented limitations upon his freedom of action, preventing Germany from getting strong in military muscle and breathing space. As he himself later said he had to extricate Germany from the toils of the League and the Disarmament Conference. He left both in October 1933 and in the next year he concluded a nonaggression pact with Poland, a first stab at the French system in eastern Europe. For some years Hitler managed to persuade foreigners that the sum total of his ambitions was the rectification of legitimate German grievances by negotiation. There was some nervousness about his methods but a strong tendency to credit him with the same aims as Stresemann and Brüning. Hitler achieved this chiefly by alleging it to people who wished to believe it and were in the habit of treating statements as true until they were proved to be untrue: westerners were particularly influenced by his renunciation of claims to Alsace and Lorraine (which he incorporated into Greater Germany in 1940).

Within six months of Hitler's appointment as Chancellor the four principal European Powers concluded a pact among themselves. This Four Power Pact was more important for its signatories than for what it contained, which was vague and platitudinous. It was promoted by Mussolini, who wanted to assert Italy's right to a place above the salt, welcomed by Great Britain because it accorded with the British policy of general reconciliation, accepted by Hitler because it gave him time and recognition, and signed by France because not to sign was to court isolation. It implied that the treaty of Versailles was no longer the basic factor in European affairs and that these would be regulated in future by a concert of the more powerful states, opponents of Versailles as well as its champions. The countries chiefly threatened by this prospect were the medium states of central and eastern Europe which owed their existence to Versailles and were allies of France. One of them, Poland, took the startling step of making a pact with Hitler.

But the lines were not yet drawn. An Anglo-French-Italian front against Germany seemed possible, until it was extinguished by the Ethiopian crisis, which put Italy firmly on Hitler's side. Before that Germany and Italy were at arm's length because of Austria. Austria had a Nazi Party of its own, which was subordinate to the German party. It had also a militaristic right-wing organization, the *Heimwehr* (supported by Italian funds), and a reactionary clerical government under a Chancellor, Engelbert Dollfuss, who had become Chancellor in 1932 and was secretly in league with Mussolini to crush the socialist opposition without having to ally himself either with the *Heimwehr* or, still less, the Austrian Nazis. Soon after Hitler became Chancellor in Germany Dollfuss banned the Austrian Nazi Party. Hitler had been encouraging the Austrian Nazis to make a bid for power, but he realized that he would do himself more harm than good if, with Germany still less than semi-armed and more than semi-isolated, he were to stir up so much trouble in Austria that other states would unite against him. Mussolini was at least as anxious as France to keep Austria from being annexed by Germany and he entered into agreements with Austria and Hungary, whose leaders he received in Rome in March 1934. Hitler decided therefore to hold his hand for the time being, but the Austrian Nazis were less responsive to restraint than to encouragement and in July – with the connivance of some German Nazis but perhaps not Hitler himself – they attempted a coup and assassinated Dollfuss. Mussolini staged an armed display on his frontier with Austria. Hitler did nothing and the coup was a failure. This string of incidents is revealing. Hitler did not lack political courage but he combined courage with caution. He was inclined to attend upon circumstances with the result that the timing of his principal operations was often dictated by circumstance. The later history of Austria confirms the point. At the end of 1937 Hitler was still waiting with a wary eye on France, and although he actually went into Austria in March 1938 the timing was, as we shall see, still not of his own choosing. This readiness of Hitler to bide his time can produce the misleading conclusion that Hitler's aims were never formulated so precisely in his mind as events made them appear; but it was only his timetable and not his programme which was vague. He was like those persons who love to make lists of things to do but without any clear idea when they will get them done. This does not mean that he did not intend to do them.

Austria was one of the two keys to Italian policy. The second was the Balkans. Italy looked nervously at its frontier with Austria on the Brenner and also at Albania where the eastern shore of the Adriatic comes closest to Italy. In the twenties Mussolini's policy was comparatively pacific – to secure Italian interests by treaties of mutual friendship. He wanted a government in Vienna which was neither too left-wing to make and keep bargains with fascist Italy nor too powerful to need to bother about them. In 1925 he was unenthusiastic about the Locarno plan because it created two categories of frontiers, the guaranteed and the unguaranteed, the Brenner frontier being one of the latter, and in 1934 he was alarmed by the prospect of a strong German government in Vienna in place of a more tractable Austrian one. In Albania he had rejected the policy of direct intervention advocated by nationalists like Luigi Federzoni in favour of reducing Albania to puppet status by economic domination and by marrying an Italian princess to King Zog (in the event she married another Balkan monarch, King Boris of Bulgaria, instead). Here Italy's dominant concern was not Germany but France. Albania apart, the eastern shore of the Adriatic belonged to Yugoslavia which was an ally of France and suspected Italy of coveting the Dalmatian coast. Mussolini pursued an irregular policy; Italy was not strong enough to enable him to be anything but opportunistic, especially when his European concerns became linked with ambitions in Africa. He tried to secure his two soft spots in Europe by agreement with France in Laval's time but his attempt to include in the bargain the conquest of Ethiopia caused the collapse of the Franco-Italian rapprochement and propelled him into alliance with Hitler. Then, largely at Ciano's prompting, he reverted to the policy direct intervention in Albania which he proceeded to conquer in April 1939.

Had Mussolini's ambitions been limited to Europe, a Franco-Italian alliance might have come into being, but Mussolini wanted to cut a dash in the world, especially in the Mediterranean which he regarded as an Italian lake and in Africa where, to his chagrin, France and Great Britain had acquired more prestigious empires than Italy. With a sort of Disraelian rapture Mussolini decided to conquer Ethiopia and nominate the King of Italy as emperor. He anticipated no real objections from Paris or London, which, as he correctly judged, were not really interested in Ethiopia. He had had his first encounter with Hitler in June 1934 just before the coup in Austria, but in January 1935 Pierre Laval visited Rome in an attempt to divert Mussolini to a pro-French attitude.

Laval became Foreign Minister in October 1934 in succession to Louis Barthou, who was murdered by a Croat in Marseilles along with King Alexander of Yugoslavia in what was probably an Italo-Hungarian plot to disrupt the Franco-Yugoslav alliance. Laval signed the pact with the USSR which had been negotiated by his predecessor but he did so only because this pact was in any case stillborn. France had a conservative government and the USSR a communist one. Ideological differences were not by themselves a bar to an alliance with a country which Richelieu had allied with Turks against Christians at the noontide of the Ottoman advance into Europe. But Richelieu had never feared what the Turks might do to France, whereas the politicians of the Third Republic feared very much what the USSR might do to France by means of the French Communist Party. Unlike the Sultan, Stalin had a political party inside France which was directed by the Communist International inside the USSR. Although Stalin had abandoned Trotsky's policy of permanent revolution, he had not gainsaid it and as a result an alliance between the USSR and the French Third Republic was all but impossible. For Laval the pact with the USSR which he inherited was distasteful but it was also a possible means to a different end: a rapprochement with Germany.

Laval, like a number of his contemporaries and like even more Frenchmen after the Second World War (including de Gaulle), sincerely desired to put an end to Franco-German hostility. He worked towards a rapprochement by using a Franco-Russian pact as a reserve threat and also by seeking an understanding with Italy which would still further isolate Germany. His Italian policy was dangerous because it disturbed the countries of the Little Entente. These wanted France to make an alliance with the USSR, but they distrusted Italy which was allied with Hungary—an anti-Versailles state which had lost territory to all three members of the Little Entente. So Laval risked losing his Little Entente allies unless he could reconcile them, especially Yugoslavia, with Italy. Moreover Mussolini had his price. It was a free hand for Italy in Africa. During his visit to Rome Laval at least implied that France would pay this price, although it is still open to doubt whether he was signalling to Mussolini that Italy might go ahead and attack Ethiopia or whether he meant no more than to concede to Italy an exclusive economic field in that country. The vagueness was not unintentional. Mussolini interpreted it in the most favourable light to his own ambitions and, at Stresa in April of the next year, he joined France and Great Britain in condemning breaches of the treaty of Versailles and subscribed a series of agreements whose general message was that these three powers were constituting an anti-German front. Again part of the bargain, in Mussolini's mind, was a free hand for Italy in Africa but again the understanding was so tacit that Ethiopia was not even mentioned. The Stresa front was a flimsy affair. In any case the front quickly obeyed its own nature and fell apart. In June the British government, still rather more intent on making friends with Germany than building an opposition to it, made a naval agreement with Germany in contravention not only of the treaty of Versailles but also of the declarations of the Stresa conference. France and Italy were not consulted, although France was informed at a late stage in the negotiations; its protests were ignored. This episode emphasized Great Britain's abandonment of the full letter of Versailles, but by conniving at a breach of Versailles Great Britain undermined its ability to protest against breaches of Locarno, which was its substitute for Versailles and was soon to be equally flouted by Hitler.

Although an Italian conquest of Ethiopia might endanger no vital French or British national interest, it could only be undertaken in breach of the Covenant of the League of Nations. It was therefore bound to weaken international stability by infringing the general principle of *pacta sunt servanda* as well as the precise terms of the Covenant, and a substantial body of opinion in France, Great Britain and elsewhere was not prepared to connive at Italian aggression for fear of encouraging aggression generally and weakening institutions which might be used to stop Hitler. Besides which the butchering of innocent Ethiopians to make a Roman empire was offensive on elementary human grounds. Consequently when war broke out in October, six months after the Stresa meeting, Mussolini discovered that his campaign was running up against more than a scandalized outcry. Laval discovered that his pro-Italian policy would not work so easily and he was forced to take a lead, jointly with Great Britain, in invoking sanctions against Italy.

But Great Britain and France did not persist. Torn between a policy of upholding the Covenant and the rule of law and, on the other hand, securing Italian friendship at the cost of letting Ethiopia down, they found that their zeal for sanctions stopped short of those measures which could have effectively checked Mussolini. Such measures, they feared, would force Mussolini to go to war with them. They were probably right, for Mussolini was too far committed in Africa and too vulnerable at home to refuse the challenge and survive. But by the same tokens he would not only have resorted to war; he would most probably have lost it. London and Paris were, however, not minded to bring the issue to the testing point. The British government was acutely conscious of the risks entailed, not directly from a clash with Italy but at second remove from Japan, which might turn an Anglo-Italian war into an occasion for attacking the British empire in Asia: the British cabinet was repeatedly warned by the Admiralty that the Royal Navy no longer had the capacity to wage war simultaneously in European and Pacific waters. So Great Britain and France both preferred to bluff (a threat of British naval action which had no effect on the Italian government but persuaded the Italian people that Great Britain was an enemy) and they also entered into separate manoeuvres behind the scenes to give Mussolini satisfaction in Africa. In London the Foreign Secretary, Sir Samuel Hoare, resurrected a proposal for partitioning Ethiopia which had been put to Mussolini before the fighting began and took it to Paris where Laval improved on it – from the Italian point of view. The two governments were at this point closer in their foreign policies than at most times between the wars. But this Hoare-Laval plan was then leaked to the press before it was presented to Mussolini. There was a public outcry and the plan (and Hoare) had to be dropped. But Mussolini got what he wanted anyway with the result that France and Great Britain got the worst of both worlds. The failure of sanctions discredited the League and the mechanisms of collective security and created a mood of pessimism. The Stresa front dissolved and the Rome-Berlin Axis was created – although the phrase itself, invented by Mussolini, did not appear until shortly after the outbreak of the Spanish civil war. Mussolini used force with impunity. Hitler converted a potential enemy into an ally and had a free demonstration of how boldness pays. France, estranged from Great Britain by the collapse of the Hoare-Laval plan which confirmed all the worst French suspicions about the British, was left with no entente with Italy, only an empty pact with the USSR, no rapprochement with Germany, and damaged relations with Poland and the Little Entente. The attempt to bring law and order into the international system was manifestly crippled as the League's principal members discovered that their obligations under the Covenant were incompatible with their national interests – particularly in the case of Great Britain which lacked the power to uphold both the Covenant in Europe and British imperial interests and obligations in the East.

In March 1935, just before the Stresa conference, Hitler had introduced compulsory military service in breach of the treaty of Versailles (his first breach of the treaty) and acknowledged the existence of the German air forces. In the same year he recovered the Saar by plebiscite, with nine tenths of the voters choosing reunion with Germany; concluded the Anglo-German naval treaty; promulgated the viciously anti-semitic Nuremberg decrees; recorded a 99 per cent victory in a referendum; and prepared Berlin for the oldest surviving festival of peace, the Olympic Games. In March 1936, he ordered his army to march into the Rhineland which was demilitarized not only by Versailles but also by Locarno which he had reaffirmed twelve months previously. He was copying Mussolini but was still not sure whether he could repeat in Europe the success Mussolini had had in Africa. The French government of the day was a pre-election caretaker team, divided within itself, estranged from Great Britain by the collapse of the Laval-Hoare plan, filled with fear by the gloomy and timorous advice of its own generals, and deceived by a German cover plan which induced it to believe that Hitler was using 265,000 men instead of only a few battalions backed by four divisions. Hitler assured his own generals, who feared war and defeat, that no French soldier would stir and halfway through the operation he refused a request from Blomberg for a partial withdrawal. He had the satisfaction of seeing his generals much more nervous than he was, and the success of the coup redoubled his ascendancy over them, his own self-assurance and his belief in the use of force. This was not Hitler's first challenge to the western powers – his withdrawal from the League and from the Disarmament Conference in October 1933 may be said to be the first and his acknowledgement of German rearmament the second – but it was the first in which he used his army. Yet the risks which he ran were not as great as they seemed, for three months earlier his Ambassador in Paris had passed on to him a strong hint from Laval that the French army would be used only to defend French soil and would not cross France's frontiers. Although the French Foreign Minister, Étienne Flandin, argued that a mere show of force would send the Germans scuttling back, only a minority of his cabinet supported him and it is unlikely that after the first few hours a show of force would have been enough.

By the remilitarization of the Rhineland Hitler challenged with impunity the two strongest powers in Europe, who had been also the principal champions of Versailles and were, since Locarno, Germany's allies in a comprehensive scheme for keeping the peace in western Europe. He broke France's system of alliances in the east no less than the settlement in the west by exposing the feebleness of France's will, and he implicitly asserted that Germany was a greater power in eastern Europe than either France or the USSR; thereafter nobody was prepared to put the assertion to the test. Against these gains there was only one feeble warning signal. The USSR had joined the League of Nations in 1934 and concluded a treaty of mutual assistance with France in May 1935. A similar treaty was made with Czechoslovakia and a British Minister, Anthony Eden, visited Moscow the same year. But the effectiveness of the USSR as an ally was discounted (Germany had beaten Russia in the First World War and seemed well able to do so again), the ratification of the Franco-Soviet pact was tellingly delayed for nine months and Great Britain was even further from considering such a reversal of alliances.

In July 1936 (the month in which sanctions against Italy were abandoned) a revolt broke out against the republican government of Spain. The ensuing civil war cemented the alliance between Hitler and Mussolini who recognized and helped the forces of revolutionary Fascism under General Francisco Franco; it created a new threat to France's back door; it crystallized and embittered the ideological conflict in Europe between Fascism and communism and added to the perplexities of democrats; it raised the level of violence and made it international, for in Spain battle was joined internationally as foreign volunteers and foreign governments took sides in a war which ended only six months before the beginning of the World War in Europe.

The sources and course of the Spanish civil war will not be related here but we have to consider its effects in Europe as a whole. All the principal European powers were faced with the question whether to intervene and, if so, how and how much. The insurgents appealed at once to Italy and Germany for aid. The government appealed to France. Italy and Germany responded promptly but with different motives. Mussolini, and even more so his son-in-law and Foreign Minister Galeazzo Ciano, were comparatively wholehearted in desiring Franco's victory. On the German side such a victory would bring advantages; in a future European war Germany would be entitled to expect Spanish help in the form of submarine bases and iron ore and even possibly co-belligerence, while active participation in the civil war would, as Goering pointed out and as the town of Guernica later discovered, give the Luftwaffe useful training. But Hitler did not want the civil war to turn into a general war for which he felt himself as yet unprepared and he therefore reacted with some caution and limited German aid to the insurgents until he came to feel that this risk was very small. German and Italian help to Franco were decisive on more than one occasion.

The British government was as determined as Hitler to prevent the extension of the war, and this determination overrode all other considerations. In France, Léon Blum wanted at first to help the legitimate Spanish government with arms but changed his mind owing to opposition in his cabinet and parliament: he feared civil war in France too, were he to persist in supporting a Spanish Popular Front which included communists. British opposition added to Blum's constraints. His more right-wing colleagues urged him not to get out of step with Great Britain. Thus the war in Spain intensified French dependence on Great Britain and its right-wing policies at the one moment in the thirties when France, under a socialist Prime Minister, might have been disposed to seek an opening to the Left in its foreign policy and an understanding with the USSR.

There was also a division of opinion in the United States administration where the anti-interventionists, led by the Secretary of State Cordell Hull, won the day, again partly influenced by the British decision. A Non-Intervention Committee, comprising two dozen states, was created and continued to function throughout a war in which intervention was unconcealed. The principal effects were three: first, that the continuance nonetheless of Italian and German help created profound cynicism; secondly, that the persistence of Great Britain and France nonetheless in the policy of non-intervention earned the one a reputation for hypocrisy and the other a reputation for feebleness which were equally deserved; and thirdly, that the Spanish government could get help from nowhere except the USSR which supplied it to the considerable benefit of the Spanish communists who were able greatly to enhance their initially modest position on the government side. Stalin's attitude to aid for Spain was much like Hitler's. He decided to give some aid but not too much. He too feared the extension of the war (if everybody had known of everybody else's fears, each might have been less afraid), but he also feared a Franco victory which, by further distracting and weakening France, might encourage Hitler to press his ambitions in eastern Europe.

In retrospect the Spanish civil war appears as the extreme example of a phenomenon of much wider extent in Europe. It has often been said that one of the most upsetting changes in twentieth-century Europe was the dismemberment of the Habsburg and Ottoman empires, but no less upsetting was the disintegration of apparently more coherent societies like France and Spain. In Spain, as the civil war revealed, the nation dissolved into groups which not only warred among themselves but looked beyond Spain for friends and helpers. Even in countries which did not disintegrate so spectacularly as Spain national bonds were so far enfeebled that ideological chieftains like Mussolini (a successful one) or Charles Maurras (a relatively unsuccessful one) were able to treat whole sections of their fellow-citizens – communists, socialists – as inferior parts of society, as outsiders within the walls. Social conflict was internationalized as these groups looked increasingly to their friends in other countries to help them against their own governments.

The war in Spain had a further consequence for European politics. The tactical and psychological successes of the German dive-bombers, the Stukas, created a false impression of the power of modern air forces, an impression which was immensely to Germany's advantage and played a substantial part in conditioning Anglo-French policies in the year of Munich. The Stukas in Spain spread fear far beyond it.

In November 1936 Germany and Japan signed the Anti-Comintern Pact, a short document by which the signatories undertook to exchange information and consult together about the international activities of communism and to concert counter-activities. Other countries were invited to adhere and Italy did so a year later, but the main point of the published agreement was to worry the USSR about its eastern frontiers and Great Britain about its position as an Asian power. By a secret protocol signed on the same day as the treaty Germany and Japan promised, in the event of an unprovoked attack or threat by the USSR against either of them, to do nothing which would make things easier for the USSR; each of them also promised to enter into no treaty with the USSR without the consent of the other. This secret part of the pact was not all that Hitler desired since Japan had declined to give positive help to Germany in the event of hostilities between Germany and the USSR. Japan was not to be drawn into a European war.

One of the most important pieces of evidence which we have concerning Hitler's intentions at this period is a document known as the Hossbach memorandum. This document was written by Colonel Hossbach five days after a meeting in Berlin on 5 November 1937 which he attended and at which he secretly took notes in spite of instructions by Hitler to the contrary. The meeting was attended by Hitler, his Ministers for War and Foreign Affairs (Blomberg and Neurath) and his three Commanders-in-Chief (Fritsch, Raeder and Goering), and lasted from 4.15 to 10.30 p.m. It consisted of a long statement on foreign affairs by Hitler, introduced with unusual solemnity as the fruit of four and a half years' reflection and as his political testament in the event of his death. Hitler stated, not for the first time, that the object of German policy was the security and multiplication of the German people. He repeated what he had said and written publicly on other occasions about *Lebensraum*. He rejected colonies as a solution; the necessary space had to be found in Europe, although later generations might have other problems which would force them to seek other solutions. There could be no solution without force, and this meant risks. Hitler then got nearer to details. He said that although nobody could tell what the situation would be in the years 1943–5, one thing was certain: Germany could not wait longer than that, partly because he himself would be past the peak of his powers and partly because Germany's advantages would begin to wane as its armament became obsolete and its enemies caught up. At that point he would in any event attack in order to resolve the space problem. Before it he would be guided by circumstances. He would watch his western and south-eastern flanks and he envisaged action against Austria and Czechoslovakia if France were weakened by trouble at home or by embroilments with Italy in the Mediterranean.

This document demonstrates once more Hitler's two main characteristics in external affairs: the fixity of his purpose, which was Germany's forcible territorial expansion in Europe, and the vagueness of his timing. Apart from setting an ultimate date – at least six years in the future and possibly eight – when he would definitely take the initiative, Hitler was leaving everything to opportunity, and in the event he attacked Austria and Czechoslovakia separately and not simultaneously, without the benefit of such a French crisis as he had envisaged or of a diversionary Mediterranean war. When he invaded Austria on 12 March 1938 and annexed it to the German Reich he did so because the Austrian Chancellor, Kurt von Schuschnigg, forced his hand. Schuschnigg decreed a plebiscite in order to strengthen his position in dealing with Austrian Nazi excesses – and Hitler feared Schuschnigg might succeed all too well. There were many stories at the time of the unreadiness of the German forces. Hitler had taken one of the risks which, as he had said in his lecture in the previous November, always attend the use of force. It was not a very big risk. Nobody did anything to stop him. Mussolini acquiesced. He had no choice, but Hitler's effusive thanks reflected his concern about Mussolini's reaction to the flouting of a basic precept of Italian foreign policy. Hitler's relief on this occasion may explain his loyalty to Mussolini through the next seven years.

In the eighteen months following the *Anschluss* Hitler attacked two other states, Czechoslovakia and Poland. The difference between the Austrian case and these other two does not lie in the result: all three states were eliminated. Hitler reckoned that he could have his way with them because greater states than they did not want to fight for their sake. When

THE EXPANSION OF GERMANY 1936-1939

Germany in 1936.

The 'Little Entente'.

0   100
Miles

March 1939, Germany annexes Memel.

1 September 1939, Germany invades Poland.

October 1938, Czech borderlands ceded to Germany. Remainder of Czechoslovakia dismembered March 1939.

September 1939, Germany annexes Danzig.

March 1938, Germany annexes Austria.

March 1936, Germany reoccupies Rhineland.

Shelled by German pocket-battleship *DEUTSCHLAND*, May 1937.

Germany experiments with its new bomber force in 1936.

DENMARK

Copenhagen

GREAT BRITAIN

London

Amsterdam

HOLLAND

Brussels

BELGIUM

LUXEMBURG

Paris

FRANCE

SWITZERLAND

Bern

Essen

Rhine

Nüremberg

AXIS 1936 MUSSOLINI

HITLER

Munich

Hamburg

Berlin

G E R M A N Y

SUDETENLAND

Prague

Brno

Vienna

AUSTRIA

CZECHOSLOVAKIA

Bratislava

Budapest

HUNGARY

Vistula

Warsaw

P O L A N D

EAST PRUSSIA

Danzig

Niemen

Memel

Theiss

Danube

RUMANIA

Bucharest

BULGARIA

Sofia

Belgrade

YUGOSLAVIA

ALBANIA

Adriatic Sea

Rome

I T A L Y

CORSICA

SPAIN

Madrid

Guernica

(a)Almeria

—ARTHUR BANKS—

an earlier land-grabber, Frederick the Great, had seized neighbouring territory, other European powers took up arms (whether successfully or unsuccessfully is not here the question). They did so, however, in circumstances different from those in which Hitler operated and his enemies agonized over what to do about it. Eighteenth-century monarchs had at their disposal special professional bodies maintained for the express purpose of performing or defeating such acts, but modern cabinets had to consider another kind of war. They could either call a whole nation to arms or do nothing, and so they greatly preferred to do nothing. Calling a nation to arms was a fearful and expensive way to prevent a rearrangement of the map, as Bismarck's enemies had discovered when they were beaten and as the Kaiser's enemies had discovered too, even though they won. But Hitler pressed his adversaries too far. Opposition to him stiffened with a slow desperation until, over Poland as it happened, it overbore their reluctance to go to war.

CHAPTER 4
Munich . . . Prague . . . Warsaw

CZECHOSLOVAKIA was a product of the disruption of the Austro-Hungarian monarchy. It was a sturdy democracy with natural resources, modern skills and – except on its southern or Austrian side – strong frontiers. But this promising offspring of the doctrine of self-determination was also a negation of that doctrine. It was, like Great Britain at the end of the Middle Ages, a mixture of peoples not yet congealed into a nation. It had a population of 14 to 15 million, of whom 10 million were Czechs or Slovaks, 3 million were Germans and the remainder consisted of small but self-conscious Hungarian, Ukrainian and Polish minorities. Most of the 3 million Germans lived scattered along the Bohemian and Moravian borderlands and in the principal cities. They came to be known as Sudeten Germans, but this was a deliberate misnomer. The Sudetenland, properly so called, lay north and east of their homes, but for propaganda purposes it was convenient to attach a name to them and so give the impression that they constituted a compact and detachable ethnic group.

By its nature and origins Czechoslovakia was anchored to the peace settlement which had created it, and was opposed to the reconstitution of a Danubian empire and to the resurgence of German power, especially a German power which would include Austria and so outflank it at its weakest point. Its founder and first president, T. G. Masaryk (resigned 1935, died 1937), and his successor Edvard Beneš based their policies for survival on the military strength and strategic importance of their country. They did not expect to be able to stand alone against a powerful German enemy but they aimed to make Czechoslovakia valuable and perhaps even essential to the vital interests of western states which would see to it that the Czechs and Slovaks were not once more subjected to Germans. They wanted to ensure that an armed attack on Czechoslovakia would never be a local affair; an aggressor would have to reckon with allied powers and so would think twice before beginning what was, if pledges meant anything, bound to become a general war. In 1938 Czechoslovakia had one of Europe's most noted armaments industries and an army which was almost the equal of the German army in men and equipment, though inferior in staying power because of Czechoslovakia's smaller population and human reserves. It had also an alliance with France to counter this weakness: by holding a proportion of the German army in the west the threat of a French attack would prevent a German victory.

But in 1938 the threat did not work. Hitler did not believe it. France no longer gave the Czechoslovak alliance top priority. The chink in Czechoslovakia's armour was Great Britain.

Great Britain had persistently refused to enter into commitments in eastern Europe, so that Masaryk and Beneš never succeeded in getting a British guarantee as well as a French one – until it was too late. Moreover, as the European situation got more menacing Great Britain began to work to demolish the French guarantee in the belief that it was not, as the French themselves had intended, a way of deterring Germany from going to war but had become a trap whereby a local war in central Europe would be expanded into a general European war. Great Britain hoped that the abrogation of the guarantee would remove this danger and provide a breathing space in which somehow war might be averted. The logic of British policy was to inflict the consequences of war and defeat on Czechoslovakia in the hope of saving everybody else. Czechoslovakia proved vulnerable because the French guarantee was not an Anglo-French guarantee and because, for France, the British alliance was more important than the French security system in central Europe of which the Czechoslovak alliance was a part. Since the evident revival of German power in Europe France had been on the defensive against Germany, and since the collapse of Franco-Italian relations in 1935–6 France had been left with no effective ally in the west except Great Britain. When therefore Great Britain required France to abandon Czechoslovakia, France did so.

British policy at this period has been summed up in the word appeasement. Appeasement describes a range of attitudes stretching from the desire to be fair and decent to a defeated foe to the policy of buying off a resurgent one. It covers the whole of the period between the wars, becoming more disreputable with time. The object of appeasement in the twenties was Weimar Germany, in the thirties Nazi Germany; its aim in the twenties was justice, in the thirties safety; the price in the twenties was the reduction of reparations (primarily to Great Britain) and equal rights for Germans, in the thirties the price was turning a blind eye to German ambitions and what these cost other people (primarily Czechoslovakia). Munich, where Czechoslovakia was sacrificed, became synonymous with betrayal, as Canossa with a similar kind of abasement.

The British ruling class had a propensity for seeing what was least admirable in Frenchmen and what was best in Germans, so that a subliminal distrust and dislike of France nourished pro-German sentiments which were often expressed in kith-and-kin terms – though without the excessive racialism of complementary German thinking. (There was also a number of fervent Francophiles who understood the French dilemma, but they were a minority and an increasingly lukewarm one.) This Anglo-Saxon or Anglo-Prussian kinship was reinforced after 1919 by the radical Anglo-French disagreement about the right way to behave towards Germany. Where France felt cheated at not having secured the Rhine frontier, Great Britain felt that Germany was being cheated by the special restrictions imposed on German sovereignty in the Rhineland, by inordinate reparation claims and by the limitations on German armament. Great Britain's vision was of a purged Germany playing its due part in European affairs, and too many British politicians retained this vision even when, with the Nazis, the purging ceased to be a cleansing and became an abomination. They persisted in regarding the change of régime in Germany in 1933 as something like a normal change of government in Great Britain. They were not men who found it easy to recognize abnormality and they persisted in regarding Hitler as a responsible statesman because he occupied the position of one. Even though British Ambassadors (Sir Horace Rumbold and Sir Eric Phipps) and other observers reported what was happening to the German Jews as early as 1933, they clung to a way of thinking and a way of doing business which were tragically inappropriate, to say the least. The efforts of Chamberlain and the language of a later Ambassador, Sir Nevile Henderson, betrayed an inability to understand Hitler which was based on a determination not to: Hitler's ravings were passed over and he was regarded as a man who would make bargains and stick to them because it was difficult to see what to do if he was really a totally different kind of person.

In this way men who were pro-German before Hitler found too little difficulty in going on being pro-German with Hitler. Hence the extreme ludicrousness of their comments about Hitler, when they went to visit him or simply expressed themselves about him without that effort. They believed that there was a point at which Hitler, if given enough territory round his borders and some colonies, would become 'reasonable'. They persuaded themselves that they were giving Hitler pieces of territory which Germany ought to have on the basis of the principle of national self-determination or equal rights and that, having done so, they would have turned Hitler into a man of peace. They had no objection to the absorption of Austria by Germany, and little compunction about bundling a small *parvenu* state like Czechoslovakia into the new German Reich. What they wanted was a version of the Anti-Comintern Pact, an Anglo-German understanding for which they were willing to give Hitler other people's territory in central Europe and (in the mistaken belief that Hitler's quest for living space was a hankering for lost lands overseas), British colonies and even mandated territories entrusted to Great Britain by the League, if these readjustments of real estate would remove the obstacles to a *pax Anglo-Germanica*. In the last years of peace British Ministers discussed among themselves how France might be persuaded to give some of its African territories to Germany in return for British territory in West Africa; or how the whole of tropical Africa might be re-partitioned, a throw-back to the nineteenth century's method of allaying European rivalries by removing them into another continent and buying off the more dangerous and discontented Europeans with African coin.

In May 1937 Neville Chamberlain succeeded Stanley Baldwin as Prime Minister. Chamberlain had been a highly successful provincial politician who, after being Mayor of Birmingham, had moved rather late in life into national politics and had there enhanced his reputation by his work as Minister of Health and Chancellor of the Exchequer. He had the strength, manifested in cabinet before he became Prime Minister as well as afterwards, of the man who sees one side of a case only. He was never the cleverest man in any of the cabinets in which he sat, but it so chanced that his cleverer colleagues were weaker in debate and less effective when it came to taking a decision. As Chancellor he won applause by introducing the lowest defence estimates of the inter-war years. He had the virtues and the limitations of a prosperous middle-class conservative and he had the misfortune – which was also his country's misfortune – to display his virtues in the earlier part of his career and his faults, which included stubbornness, during the last years of his life. He was a man of proven ability and impressive experience who suffered from the peculiarly English notion that there is nothing that a really intelligent man cannot tackle. It was in this spirit that he tackled foreign affairs and Hitler.

He began by getting rid of his Foreign Secretary, Anthony Eden, who was pushed into resignation in February 1938 by the Prime Minister's manners and, to a lesser extent, his policies. Chamberlain was determined to come to terms with Mussolini in spite of the conquest of Ethiopia and Italy's continuing intervention in the Spanish civil war. There was something to be said for recognizing the conquest of Ethiopia once it was an accomplished fact. (Eden himself was in favour of recognizing Franco a year later.) There was also much to be said for repairing Anglo-Italian relations if a European war seemed likely: the Italian navy was a significant factor in world politics, especially before 1939 when Roosevelt, at British request, moved American naval forces from the Atlantic to the Pacific to counter possible Japanese designs against Australia and New Zealand, which the Royal Navy was pledged to protect. Eden, however, was in no hurry to seek Italian friendship so long as Mussolini went on helping Franco. Chamberlain on the other hand regarded the matter as urgent in order to keep Mussolini at least at arm's length from Hitler. This issue – the timing of Anglo-Italian conversations – was the immediate occasion of Eden's resignation. Behind it were both a larger issue and personal pique. Chamberlain was contemptuous of American statesmanship and, like many of his class, basically anti-American. Roosevelt, like Eden but unlike Chamberlain, was opposed to *de jure* recognition of Italy's African conquests without a specific and simultaneous undertaking to take Italian forces out of Spain. Further, Roosevelt ventured to offer his services as a mediator in Europe's affairs. Chamberlain, without telling Eden or consulting the Foreign Office, brushed this offer aside. Unlike Baldwin, Chamberlain was determined to play a leading part in international affairs, as a British Prime Minister has every right to do, but Eden was irked by this incursion into his special fief. Eden's assessment of the forces which shaped European politics included not only the four powers which Chamberlain treated as the only ones that mattered, but also to some degree the USSR, the League and the United States. Yet their policies were at this time so little apart that Eden's resignation was heard by some of his cabinet colleagues with astonished incredulity. In retrospect it seems an early indication of the instability that was to ruin his career after the war.

Chamberlain's attempt to create a concert of four was in any case predoomed to failure. Mussolini privately assured Hitler that Anglo-Italian conversations and agreements would never be allowed to harm the Italo-German accord and when Chamberlain renewed his wooing of Italy after the Munich crisis neither Mussolini nor Ciano took the proceedings seriously. Chamberlain was no less anxious to come to some arrangement with Hitler. During most of 1938 the immediate obstacle to the British policy of appeasement was the so called Sudeten problem. The Nazi Party had in Czechoslovakia a counterpart called the Sudeten German Party and led by Konrad Henlein, who adopted German Nazi doctrines and behaviour and received funds and instructions from Germany. Henlein was agitating for local autonomy for the German minority. His agitation was echoed by the lesser minorities. It created confusion and disorders calculated to call in question the authority of the central government in Prague at a time when this government was engaged in discussing the rights and status of minorities. At every turn in these discussions Henlein made increasingly unacceptable claims, backed by the undefined but inescapable menace of German military action. In April he demanded not only self-government for Germans in Czechoslovakia but also the subordination of Czechoslovakia's foreign policy to Germany's interests.

In the previous November, a few weeks after the Hossbach meeting in Berlin, British and French Ministers had conferred in London about whether and how to resist German moves in central Europe. They agreed that they should do nothing about a German annexation of Austria but, largely on the insistence of the French Foreign Minister Yvon Delbos, they accepted that a German attack on Czechoslovakia would involve France in a war pursuant to its treaty obligations. Since Great Britain could not risk seeing France engaged in war with Germany and defeated, Great Britain too faced war over Czechoslovakia. The only escape lay in a German-Czech settlement acceptable to, or at any rate accepted by, both Hitler and Beneš, and this became the prime object of British policy. It entailed pressure on Prague rather than Berlin since Czechoslovakia was the weaker state, undoubtedly so if its allies could be eliminated from the equation, which Great Britain thought they could be: after the *Anschluss* France and the USSR had both reaffirmed their obligations to defend Czechoslovakia but the USSR was not judged to be in a position to do much and France was in no position to jeopardize Great Britain's friendship. In the summer of 1938 therefore Chamberlain decided to intensify British pressure on Czechoslovakia which, supplementing German pressures, Great Britain had been exerting since the previous year. After consulting the German government about his proposed intervention but without informing France, Chamberlain sent a special emissary (Lord Runciman) to Czechoslovakia to get Beneš, under the guise of mediation, to accept whatever might be necessary to keep the peace. Runciman arrived in Prague at the end of July. He subsequently reported to the cabinet that Beneš was insincere, stubborn and too clever by half.

Yet it was by this date sufficiently clear that the Sudeten problem was not the real danger to peace and that the excision of this problem would not remove the danger of war. To the accumulating evidence on Hitler's wider intentions there was added in June 1938 a specific warning. In that month Goering's adjutant, General Karl Bodenschatz, officially informed the French assistant air attaché in Berlin that Germany was preparing to build a line of defensive fortifications from the North Sea to the Swiss border, that Germany had no aggressive intentions against France or Great Britain but that, having first secured its southern flank against any threat from Czechoslovakia, it intended to eliminate the 'Soviet threat' and simultaneously secure the living space which was indispensable to Germany. Bodenschatz specifically mentioned the Ukraine and compared Germany's eastward expansion in Europe with the way in which France had secured its own needs by expanding into Africa. This was a clear enough indication of Hitler's intention to overpower Czechoslovakia, make war on the USSR and protect himself in the west by a series of fortifications which could not be completed before the middle of 1939 at the earliest. It presented France and Great Britain with a choice between keeping out of a war in eastern Europe or joining in such a war. It ruled out the possibility of preventing a war in eastern Europe by appeasement.

At the beginning of September Beneš declared himself ready to accept all the demands of the Sudeten Germans for autonomy. On 12 September Chamberlain, under pressure from many sides – the French and American governments, the Vatican, the opposition in the House of Commons, Churchill – and in the hope of inducing Hitler to be less explosive than usual in the speech which he was due to make in Nuremberg on that day, decided to go to the lengths of reminding Hitler that France was bound to fight for Czechoslovakia and that Great Britain would fight with France, but from Berlin Henderson asked the cabinet to excuse him from passing this warning on. Henderson's role in these years negates the view that Ambassadors no longer count. Whereas Chamberlain's dominant aim was to keep Great Britain out of war, Henderson had a more positive policy. He did not want Great Britain to stand in Hitler's way. It is impossible to read his statements and despatches or observe his conduct without concluding that he endorsed Hitler's aims more than he deplored Hitler's character and behaviour. He wanted an Anglo-German entente which would preserve Great Britain's imperial position in the world and license Hitler to lay the USSR low, and he made no secret of his views, either privately or publicly. He even discussed them with Goering, at which point he found that he had gone further than Chamberlain would countenance.

During the summer and autumn of 1938 a violent anti-Czech campaign was in progress in Germany. Press and radio were presenting, with the utmost emotional mendacity, a picture of persecution of Germans in Czechoslovakia and at Nuremberg on 12 September Hitler spoke with such exceptional violence that his words provoked an abortive rising by Sudeten Germans and the imposition of martial law in parts of Czechoslovakia on the 13th. Henlein fled to Germany and with his departure the situation became more manageable. But this improvement at the storm centre was lost on observers further away and two days later Chamberlain unwittingly reversed it. He resolved to put into operation a plan which he had been preparing for some time. He would go and see Hitler. This plan had been discussed only with four Ministers separately (but not in cabinet), with Nevile Henderson and with two or three other close advisers. Like Eden nearly twenty years later in the Suez crisis Chamberlain kept his cabinet very much in the dark about his plans and policies.

As with the Runciman mission France was not informed. Although he had hoped to influence Hitler's tone at Nuremberg, he was also resolved to go and talk with Hitler whatever he said at Nuremberg and however he said it. He flew to Berchtesgaden on 15 September and on the same day he agreed in principle that the Sudetenland, an area still undefined, ought to be detached from Czechoslovakia and given to Germany. At no point does the difference between these two men, now meeting *tête-à-tête* to settle the fate of Europe, appear in retrospect more glaring: Hitler humouring his distinguished guest but keeping up his preparations to use force; Chamberlain returning to London to affirm his belief that Hitler was the sort of man who would be 'rather better than his word'. The nearer the appeasers got to a settlement with Hitler the more they clung to this tattered premise – and the more they needed to still their consciences by working themselves up into a state of hatred against the Czechs as the people who might spoil the whole game.

Besides coercing the Czechs and coming to terms with Hitler, Chamberlain needed to cow France. His policy required him to scare France into dishonouring its treaty with Czechoslovakia. The British Ambassador in Paris, Sir Eric Phipps, had no great difficulty in scaring the French Foreign Minister, Georges Bonnet. He also fortified Chamberlain's views by refraining from reporting to London what Frenchmen of another stamp were saying, until ordered by the Foreign Office to do so. Yet during the September crisis of 1938 the French government and even the pessimistic General Gamelin seemed resigned to going to war for Czechoslovakia and advancing into Germany. After the robber synod at Berchtesgaden however, to which they had not been invited, French Ministers were confronted with an accomplished and perhaps not wholly unwelcome fact. After a conference in London on the 18th they accepted the Anglo-German compact and joined with Great Britain in forcing the Czechs to agree to surrender all territories where half the inhabitants were German. Beneš, who had already conceded all reasonable German demands, at first refused but he had no real choice. He was told that France refused to fight without a promise of British backing and that Great Britain refused to back France in a war begun for Czechoslovakia. All he could get, with French help, was an Anglo-French guarantee of the independence and neutrality of the new Czechoslovakia in place of the discarded French guarantee for the old one. Great Britain reluctantly agreed to give this vulnerable and enfeebled state the promises which it had refused to give to a much more worthwhile ally.

But this was not the end. So far from removing an obstacle to peace the Czechoslovak surrender brought war nearer. Hitler, baulked of the military destruction of Czechoslovakia which he had been talking about, declared that the terms forced on Beneš by Great Britain and France no longer satisfied him. Chamberlain flew back to Germany where, at Godesberg on the 22nd, he discovered that Hitler now demanded even larger stretches of Czechoslovakia, a plebiscite in other areas and the entry of German troops into Czechoslovakia before the lines of partition had been settled. This second meeting was punctuated by a stream of reports of Czech outrages which Hitler caused to be concocted and brought to him while he and Chamberlain were conferring. Chamberlain, returning to London on the 24th, told his cabinet that he believed that he had established some influence over Hitler. He was for accepting Hitler's terms and getting Beneš to accept them but the opposition within the British cabinet was hardening and was temporarily joined by Halifax. Daladier too, once more in London, was firmer; he seemed resigned to war. The Czechs had mobilized on the 23rd. Chamberlain wavered. On the 26th a last attempt by British emissaries to get Hitler to see 'reason' produced a scene of such fury that they fled without saying what they had been told to say. On the 27th Chamberlain, after some hesitation, authorized the mobilization of the British fleet which the First Lord of the Admiralty, Alfred Duff Cooper, had been urging for some days. On the 28th Chamberlain, while speaking in the House of Commons, received an invitation to go to Munich, the outcome of a British appeal to Mussolini to do something.

At Munich on the 29th the substance of the Godesberg demands was conceded – on the basis of proposals which were advanced by Mussolini as a compromise but had been drafted for him by the German Foreign Office. In substance Chamberlain and Daladier let Hitler have practically all he wanted, Mussolini being in attendance. The Russians were treated as irrelevant and neither invited nor consulted. Czechoslovakia, whose representatives came to Munich but were confined to the vestibule, chose acquiescence rather than slaughter. Beneš resigned. On the day after the conference Chamberlain, while taking leave of Hitler, produced a piece of paper on which he had drafted an Anglo-German declaration of friendship and of the determination of the two peoples never to go to war with one another. Hitler, who had no desire to fight the British, was delighted and the two leaders signed then and there. In London Duff Cooper resigned but cabinet colleagues who had talked earlier of doing so too decided not to: Chamberlain's control over his cabinet and his large and still docile majority in the House of Commons was at this time more complete than that of any British Prime Minister since the eighteenth century. In France three Ministers who had resigned before Munich withdrew their resignations after it. In December a Franco-German declaration of friendship, similar to the Chamberlain-Hitler scrap of paper, was signed. Poland took the opportunity to seize in October the area of Teschen, dubiously Polish in character but undeniably a plum.

The Munich agreement was greeted with relief by everybody except the Czechs and Slovaks. So acute had been the fear of war that this relief burst out in scenes of enthusiasm which were particularly galling to the minority whose shame or apprehension overmastered their relief. For most British and French Ministers the surrender had at least staved off war. Chamberlain had enough faith in the piece of paper which he had got Hitler to sign to talk of having secured 'peace for our time'. But some were considerably less sanguine. Soon after Munich Halifax, now Foreign Secretary in place of Eden, wanted to introduce conscription and in the following January – when there was a scare over reports that Hitler was about to invade Holland – he advocated staff talks with France and Belgium, consultation with Washington and soundings about the acceptability of British guarantees to Poland, Rumania, Greece and Turkey. Two months later, in March 1939, all lingering delusions were finally blown away when Hitler, in defiance of the Munich agreement, completed his conquest of Czechoslovakia.

The mutilated Czechoslovakia created in 1938 consisted of three federated provinces: Bohemia-Moravia, Slovakia and Ruthenia. In October Hitler directed his armed services to be ready to deal with the rest of Czechoslovakia and to seize Memel. On 14 March 1939, on orders from Berlin, Slovakia declared itself independent of Prague and asked to become a German protectorate. Hitler had a minor piece of luck over Slovakia. The union of the Slovaks with the much more numerous Czechs had not been a smooth one. When Czechoslovakia was created, Slovakia, formerly a dependency of Hungary, was much less developed than the Czech lands of Bohemia and Moravia which, under Austrian rule, had enjoyed considerable educational as well as industrial advancement. Consequently the Slovak parts of Czechoslovakia were largely administered by Czechs after independence and the Slovaks accused the Czechs with some degree of justice of being slow to remedy this imbalance. Although on nearly every occasion Slovaks gave more votes to Czechoslovak parties than to the specifically Slovak one, there was a significant autonomist movement led by Father Andrew Hlinka. In 1938 Hlinka died and his successor, Monsignor Tiso, abandoned autonomy in favour of separatism. This was a help to Hitler.

Besides turning Slovakia into a distinct German satellite Hitler completed the destruction of Czech independence. Beneš's successor, President Emil Hácha, and his Foreign Minister took the road to Berlin where both were subject to such verbal bludgeoning that Hácha fainted. German troops were already marching on Prague. Under threat of a bombing of their capital the Czech Ministers submitted and Bohemia-Moravia too was declared a German protectorate. Ruthenia was annexed by Hungary in two bites. In November 1938 Hitler, who was not particularly fond of the Hungarians but was pressed by the Italians and Poles, had allowed Hungary to seize part of Ruthenia by what was called the Vienna Award. In March 1939 Hungarian troops occupied the rest of it. Great Britain and France did nothing. Five days before Hitler seized Czechoslovakia Chamberlain told the House of Commons that Europe was settling down and the British Government was turning its attention to disarmament and to more trade with Germany. When the blow fell on Prague both its western guarantors defected on the plea that the severance of Slovakia from Czechoslovakia had nullified their guarantee: the country guaranteed had ceased to exist. A week later Hitler extorted Memel from Lithuania by an ultimatum containing false accusations of Lithuanian brutality. Memel had been renounced by Germany by the treaty of Versailles – like Danzig, which now reached the top of Hitler's agenda.

Danzig stood for different things. It was, in the first place, a largely German city to be recovered for the Reich. Secondly, as a bone of contention between Germany and Poland it was a possible cause of a German-Polish war. In that context it raised, thirdly, the two ultimate issues in Hitler's European policy – the attitude of the western democracies to a German attack on Poland and the attitude of the USSR.

Immediately after the final partition and subjugation of Czechoslovakia Hitler seems to have been in two minds over his next move. If Danzig could have been acquired as easily as Memel Hitler's obvious move was to proceed against Danzig. But Danzig could not safely be isolated in this way. So it was more than ordinarily desirable for Hitler to explore and exploit every possibility of securing Danzig, as he had secured the Sudetenland, by threats and cajolement and without war. He could, and in October 1938 did, push forward his planning for aggression in the west. He needed to be prepared for every contingency. But he also tried in the same month to do a deal with Poland: Danzig and a road across the Polish corridor to be surrendered to Germany, Poland to join the Anti-Comintern Pact. On these terms Poland could be reprieved, but this settlement could hardly be more than an interim one unless Poland were to be persuaded later, as Czechoslovakia had been constrained in its second round, to cede Polish Silesia too (Hitler had already talked of recovering the whole of Silesia) and to remain at least benevolently passive when Hitler decided that the time had come to seize his *Lebensraum* farther east.

Poland rejected the German offer and stood on its rights. It would neither endorse the incorporation of Danzig in the Reich nor would it join the Anti-Comintern Pact and so fatally embroil itself with the USSR and render itself dependent on its other neighbour, Germany.

Danzig, renounced by Germany by the treaty of Versailles but peopled chiefly by Germans, was a Free City with a government of its own under the protection of the League of Nations and with a resident League Commissioner to supervise the maintenance of its status and constitution and adjudicate disputes between the Free City and Poland. It was within the Polish customs area and Poland had rights of access to it along a route or corridor which traversed German territory. In elections in 1933 the local Nazi Party won, partly by force and fraud, just over half the votes. Thereafter it rapidly and illegally strengthened its control, while the League abdicated its responsibilities. The city was to all intents and purposes firmly under German and Nazi control for at least two years before it was forcibly incorporated in the Reich on the eve of war.

Polish foreign policy between the wars was a series of expedients designed to preserve a relatively small country from attack by stronger neighbours. It was based at first on the alliance with France. During the twenties this alliance seemed to serve its purpose but with Germany and Russia both recovering from their defeats in the First World War it was not really tested: Poland's problem was postponed until the revival of German and Russian power. When this took place the French alliance began to look undependable, which it was. Poland then adopted a policy of self-preservation by making defensive treaties with its two big neighbours (the non-aggression pacts of 1932 and 1934 with Stalin and Hitler respectively) and by refusing to be drawn into alliance with the one against the other. This policy too seemed to work for a while but although a number of Polish-German issues were resolved the intractable problem of Danzig remained and Poland was in danger as soon as Germany under Hitler became strong enough to attack the USSR. During the thirties Poland's strategic position was weakened by the declining efficacy of alliance with France and by the destruction of Austrian and Czechoslovak independence. Colonel Jozef Beck, Foreign Minister from 1932, clung to the policy of non-alignment between Germany and the USSR and also secured in 1939 a British alliance. He has been much criticized for failing to opt for the USSR against Germany. This refusal was influenced by his anti-communism, which was pronounced, and also by the fact that Poland had been at war with the USSR as recently as 1920, but alignment with the USSR would also have been a complete reversal of a policy which kept Poland reasonably safe so long as Germany and the USSR neither concluded between themselves any agreement overriding their several non-aggression pacts with Poland nor aimed to fight one another over Poland's dead body. In the end Poland was undone because Germany and the USSR did conclude such an agreement. In running the risk that they might Beck was blinded by his own over-estimate of Poland's importance and power.

According to Rauschning Hitler was thinking of partitioning Poland with the USSR even at the time of the German-Polish treaty of 1934 and regarded a German-Russian agreement as a way of safeguarding his eastern front during a war in the west which would be a necessary preliminary to a war against the USSR. Hitler's anti-communism was no bar to an ephemeral deal with Stalin. He himself said on another occasion that treaties were only meant to be kept so long as they served the purpose for which they had been made in the first place. On this thesis the German-Polish treaty could be succeeded by a German-Russian agreement for the partition of Poland, and a German-Russian agreement could be a prelude to a German attack on the USSR. These were problems in timing and tactics. But in relation to the western democracies Hitler had a problem of a different order: whether to attack them or not. He had no direct interest in doing so; there was no sense in making war on states which showed neither the will nor the capacity to thwart his plans in eastern Europe. The risk of effective French interference was a declining one, and if necessary France could be defeated. Great Britain too would probably not interfere, but if it did it could not so easily be defeated. The Luftwaffe was not suited to an attack on Great Britain and at sea Germany was a secondary power. When Hitler thought about Great Britain he preferred to dwell on the reasons why it should be willing to come to terms with him than on what he would do if it did not. He aspired to appease Great Britain, not to defeat it. *Mein Kampf* presupposed friendship with Great Britain; the dispatch of Ribbentrop to London as Ambassador was a step, however misguided, to this end; the purpose of the Anglo-German naval agreement of 1935 had been not so much to detach Great Britain from France and Italy (although it had that welcome effect) or to sanctify breaches of the naval clauses of the treaty of Versailles (which Hitler had hardly yet begun), but to reassure Great Britain that Hitler intended no threat to Great Britain's naval empire. But by 1939 it was doubtful whether Great Britain could be neutralized. It was also becoming possible that the western democracies might enter into an alliance with the USSR.

The disappearance of Czechoslovakia as an independent state automatically moved Poland and Rumania into the German firing line. Both these states had frontiers with the USSR and so in a sense Hitler's entry into Prague on 15 March 1939 brought Germany and the USSR face to face. For five and a half months between that day and the signing of the Russo-German pact during the night of 23-24 August the pattern of European politics was, on the surface at least, uncertain, as the USSR, moving to escape from an isolation which had become particularly dangerous since Munich, hesitated which side to take. At first the western democracies and the USSR seemed to be trying to overcome their mutual antipathies and draw together. Following a scare in March of imminent German action against Rumania Great Britain made an approach to the USSR. London was at this point more worried about Rumania than Poland, but the Rumanian scare subsided almost at once and when the USSR suggested a conference between itself, the two leading western democracies and the two countries threatened by Hitler, the British took evasive action, being reluctant to rub shoulders so formally with the USSR. Poland was even more reluctant. But it was also the main point of danger. It had partially mobilized on 23 March, three days before rejecting Germany's proposals for a settlement, and Chamberlain, afraid that Danzig was about to create a war at any moment, resolved to cast a British mantle over Poland. He offered it a guarantee and on 6 April, after a visit by Beck to London, the two governments publicly announced their intention to sign a treaty by which Great Britain would go to Poland's aid if it were attacked. France promised to do so too. At the beginning of May Hitler, already enraged by Beck's rejection of his proposals, secretly ordered his army to get ready to attack. Beck publicly proclaimed that peace was less precious than Poland's honour.

Great Britain and France, having committed themselves to succouring Poland, were gambling on a negotiated Danzig settlement which would once more remove a threat to peace, that is to say, give Hitler what he wanted. In default of such an agreement they would almost certainly be called upon to redeem in arms the promises which they had made. But by making these promises Great Britain in particular, which had not before been under any obligation to Poland, had forfeited the power which it had wielded in similar circumstances over Czechoslovakia. Beck was emboldened to continue to refuse to negotiate over Danzig. The guarantee given to him was a guarantee of Poland's national integrity, a guarantee therefore against attack by a dissident minority as well as from external aggression, and most exceptionally the Polish government was itself to judge if and when circumstances had called the guarantee into play. Thus Beck had a weapon which Beneš never had, although in the end it did him no good. The charge that can be made against Beck is that he did not see that the Anglo-French guarantee was worthless. Although aware of the unwillingness of his guarantors to fight for Poland, he did not believe that they would go so far as to dishonour their promises. But Great Britain and France did not mean to implement these promises. For them the guarantee was a means to gain time and to deter Hitler, while they continued to try to lever the Poles into concessions over Danzig: a military promise used as a diplomatic weapon. As such it was inept. The charge against Chamberlain, the principal author of the manoeuvre, is that by giving the guarantee he diminished the pressure that he was trying to exert on Poland over Danzig and at the same time improvidently and inopportunely deprived himself of his chance of an agreement with the USSR. Coupled with Great Britain's known determination on a peaceful settlement of the Danzig question, the guarantee was weak support for Poland and weak deterrence of Hitler.

Similar events with similar consequences occurred in south-east Europe. Ever since the disruption of the Ottoman and Austro-Hungarian empires this area had been contested between the principal land and naval powers of Europe. Most of it became in the 1930s increasingly dominated by Germany but Greece fell within the British sphere of influence and Yugoslavia proved to be a joker in the pack. (This pattern was repeated after the war with the substitution of the USSR and USA for Germany and Britain.)

Greece's principal concerns were Bulgaria and, secondarily, Italy. The Greek government wanted an alliance with Great Britain to counter the threat it perceived from Bulgaria but Great Britain, although more sympathetic to Greece than to Bulgaria, had reasons of its own for equivocation: it did not want to push Bulgaria irrevocably into the German camp. Still less did Great Britain want to offend the Duce whose neutrality in a war with Germany Great Britain hoped to secure. On the other hand Greece was not negligible in British strategic thinking since Greece would be a useful element in a war in which blockade of Germany and German-occupied Europe would play a significant part. This complex was further bedevilled by the fact that Greece had, in theory at least, an alternative policy in a revival of the Greco-Italian friendship treaty of 1928 – which was contrary to British interests since it would take Greece out of the British and into the Axis sphere of influence.

Mussolini's invasion of Albania on 7 April 1939 forced these issues. Great Britain and France gave Greece, and a little later Rumania, guarantees of their integrity and independence, but these undertakings, given in the wake of events, had little power to forestall further events. They were little more than anti-Axis slogans shouted into the wind. They did not deter Mussolini from invading Greece or Hitler from overrunning both Greece and Rumania. Like the guarantee to Poland, they had no impact on the pattern of power in Europe although they may have had some impact on how Hitler played his hand.

Hitler was a man of moods and rage was one of them. He was in a state of rage between the Berchtesgaden and Godesberg meetings in September 1938 and it seems likely that Chamberlain's guarantee to Poland affected him the same way. He riposted by denouncing not only his recently re-affirmed non-aggression pact with Poland but also the Anglo-German naval treaty. He ordered his forces to be ready to attack Poland at the end of August, and he now envisaged – although he still hoped to avoid – a war on two fronts. The essential thing was to keep the USSR out of such a war.

The Russians, like the Germans, feared a war on two fronts. Germany and Japan were allies by the Anti-Comintern Pact and there was already an undeclared war going on in Manchuria between Russian and Japanese forces. Stalin found it difficult to believe that the British and French ruling classes preferred Russian communism to European right-wing fascism. This not implausible judgement had been strengthened by the Anglo-French failure to solicit Russian support for the defence of Czechoslovakia and the transience of the British interest in cooperation for the defence of Poland and Rumania. In any case, what Great Britain and France wanted was not what the USSR needed. Great Britain and France were concerned about the independence and integrity of Poland and Rumania and might in an emergency welcome Russian help to safeguard these states, but Stalin cared nothing for the integrity of Poland or Rumania. He was worrying about the USSR and its vulnerability to German attack. He might welcome British and French aid to avert such an attack but so long as Great Britain and France wanted to strengthen Poland and Rumania and preserve their sovereignty, Stalin saw little chance of turning these states into a defensive glacis which was the only useful function that they could perform for him. Stalin needed help against Hitler and a free hand in the debatable lands between the USSR and Germany; Great Britain and France were looking for help for Poland and Rumania not for the USSR, and were unwilling to blackmail Poland into giving Stalin what he wanted in the way in which they had blackmailed Czechoslovakia into giving way to Hitler.

Stalin had made a mistake about Hitler several years earlier. He had viewed with equanimity the coalition between German conservatives, the German army and the Nazis. The conservatives and the army had a tradition of alliance with Russia, and Stalin believed that these would prove the dominating forces in a post-Weimar Germany. He regarded the

Nazis as no more than ephemeral auxiliaries in the overthrow of Weimar and so instead of impeding Hitler's rise to power by directing the German communists to make common cause with the socialists he incited the communists against the socialists and so played a part in destroying Weimar and making Hitler its heir. Stalin quickly realized his mistake and tried to rectify it. In 1934 he joined the League of Nations and in 1935 he made his ineffective alliance with France. The failure of this alliance and the obvious weaknesses of collective security forced him a couple of years later to seek with Nazi Germany the sort of accord which he would have liked to make with a military-conservative Germany. In 1937 he began the process of appeasing Hitler by dissolving the Polish Communist Party. Poland rekilled would, if necessary, seal the new compact. Stalin knew that Hitler was his enemy as much as Great Britain and France, indeed more so and more menacingly. But he also saw the basis for a business deal with Germany which could give him what he needed – time. Moreover if, like western conservatives, he too saw a world divided into communists and noncommunists, he could nevertheless draw some distinction between fascist anti-communists and democratic anti-communists. He despised and distrusted the latter and concluded in consequence that he would probably have to do a deal with the former, since the countries which had had no stomach to defend Czechoslovakia would be incapable of doing anything useful for the USSR even if they wanted to. But it is doubtful whether he finally made up his mind until August 1939. Until a few days before the signing of the Russo-German treaty he kept open the possibility of an agreement with Great Britain and France.

By their guarantees to Poland and Rumania, Great Britain and France had undertaken to help two countries whose ability to withstand Germany was clearly nil. The British estimate of Poland's capacity to resist, measured in time, was two weeks – and Poland's forty divisions constituted an army twice as large as Rumania's. If Hitler invaded Poland, France and Great Britain could invade Germany, but unless the USSR were added to the alliance the Poles would fight alone and not for long. Thus east–west negotiations were dragged onto the political scene by the logic of events. The French government and, in London, the Foreign Office but not the Prime Minister were driven to seek an alliance with the USSR despite some well-founded doubts about its political value at this date. Political missions proceeded from Paris and London to Moscow in June. They did not give an impression of enthusiasm, but the real cause of their ultimate failure was not their attitude so much as the backlog of distrust between their countries and the impossibility of agreement on the crucial issue of a Russian right of entry into Poland. By the end of July a stalemate was reached when the western powers refused to give Stalin a free hand in the Baltic states. They felt that they were being asked to connive at the suppression of the independence of these countries, which was indeed so, but was not very different from what they had done at Munich. Stalin then reanimated the talks by suggesting the dispatch of military missions. These began discussions in Moscow on 12 August. The fact that they went by ship instead of by air has been the subject of some ridicule and again there was a display of an evident lack of enthusiasm (although Daladier at least wanted an agreement at almost any price), but there was a case for the chosen method of travel since it was only on board ship that the two missions got to know each other and were able to concert their plans.

It is impossible to say whether Stalin was by now merely playing with the western powers or was hoping to do a deal with them. He had been looking both ways since April when he initiated the first in a series of moves which eventually produced the Russo-German pact, and the replacement of Maxim Litvinov by Vyacheslav Molotov as Foreign Commissar on 3 May was regarded by the French Ambassador in Moscow as a step towards a Russo-German alliance. Hitler responded with further initiatives in June and then appeared to lose interest, but serious exchanges were renewed before the end of July, at which time the German Ambassador in Moscow was forecasting a Franco-British-Russian alliance. On 12 August, the day on which the military talks began in Moscow, Hitler was telling his Italian allies of his intention to make Stalin his ally; on 20 August he sent a personal telegram to Stalin to speed things up and on the 22nd, in an address to military and civilian chiefs, he spoke as though the attack on Poland were imminent and the Russian pact assured. In the intervening week the military missions had been pressed by the chief Russian delegate, Marshal Voroshilov, to answer the question whether Russian troops would be allowed by Poland to advance into Poland to meet the German armies. The British and French missions could not give a straight answer, for although Poland (and Rumania) had withdrawn initial objections to a Franco-British-Russian alliance, the Polish government still refused to permit any entry by Russian forces except upon request to be made at the time and it assumed that the request would be for air support and not for ground units. At the last moment a member of the French mission was sent to Warsaw to press the Poles to give way, but the Poles refused and it is probable that Stalin knew on 19 August of this refusal from intercepted cipher traffic. On the 21st Daladier cabled the French mission to sign anything they could get, but on the same day a Russo-German economic agreement was signed in Berlin. This agreement was regarded as portending something more spectacular and in Moscow a visit by Ribbentrop was openly spoken of. Stalin consented to a visit by the Nazi Foreign Minister a week after the signing of the economic agreement but this was too late for Hitler. Ribbentrop arrived in the afternoon of the 23rd and a few hours later, to the amazement of the rest of the world, Germany and the USSR signed a treaty of friendship and non-aggression by which each of them abjured the use of force against the other and undertook not to help any third party in an attack on the other and not to join any group oriented directly or indirectly against the other. The treaty was to endure in the first instance for ten years. It was supplemented by a secret protocol defining spheres of interest: to the USSR, Finland, Estonia, Latvia; to Germany, Lithuania including Vilna; in Poland, the division to run along the line Narev–Vistula–San, the continuance of an independent Polish state to remain an open question; in the south-east the USSR stressed its interest, and Germany its *désinteressement*, in Bessarabia. These arrangements were later altered to give Lithuania to the USSR and the Polish provinces of Lublin and Warsaw to Germany.

One of the unwitting authors of the Hitler-Stalin pact was Neville Chamberlain. His determination to come to terms with Mussolini and secure Italy's neutrality, and his search for ways to avoid an Anglo-German war, are an example of labours which are not only in vain but carry within them the risks of multiplying misfortune. Chamberlain's motives were the reverse of dishonourable. Yet the more he laboured to find common ground with the dictators, the more did he convince Stalin that he must do so too. And Stalin, perhaps because more cynical or perhaps because harder pressed, succeeded, so that Chamberlain's diplomacy recoiled upon him. His overtures to Moscow, however distasteful to him personally, were genuine and by this date forced upon him, as they were too upon the French government.

But the deeper source of the Hitler-Stalin pact lay elsewhere. Whether or not in August 1939 Stalin was still considering an alliance with the western democracies or was merely playing for time, using the Anglo-French missions to needle Hitler into a Russo-German pact and incidentally seeing how much useful intelligence he could worm out of the British and French negotiators, it is in retrospect clear that an Anglo-French-Russian pact was of interest to Stalin only upon terms which Great Britain and France could not fulfil. These powers, having lost Czechoslovakia and a possible Russian alliance, were forced back onto a third and much weaker policy. On 25 August, the day after the Russo-German pact was made known, an Anglo-Polish treaty, implementing the Chamberlain-Beck declaration of April, was signed. It had been delayed by the Anglo-French-Russian conversations but by 22 August the British

and French governments knew that the Russo-German entente was imminent. Chamberlain was still determined to avoid any provocation of
Hitler and was hoping for a visit from Goering which would somehow
prevent war, but he could no longer delay the formalization of his earlier
undertaking, empty though it was. The treaty of August, like the declaration of April, was more an attempt to check Hitler than solid comfort for
the Poles. The earlier pledge was embodied in a formal pact of mutual
assistance against any act of aggression or any direct or indirect threat to
the independence of the signatories. An indirect threat meant in fact a
German seizure of Danzig. At the same time Great Britain both assured
Hitler through diplomatic channels that British promises to Poland meant
what they said, and intimated that Germany ought to have Danzig and
Great Britain would like to see a peaceful cession of the city. France
concluded a similar treaty with Poland, although it was not signed until
5 September, after Hitler's attack.

The only chance of averting war, so it seemed to those who wanted to
do so, was to call in Mussolini again and arrange another Munich. Great
Britain tried once more to use Mussolini as a lifebelt and a means of
appeasing Hitler with Danzig, but the French government, unaware of
what Great Britain was doing, was trying to detach Italy from Hitler by
emphasizing the dangers ahead without realizing that the Italians knew
from their contacts with London that Great Britain was hoping to remove
the dangers by giving way to Hitler. Mussolini was unwilling to lose credit
with Hitler and with himself by urging a peaceful settlement which Hitler
did not want. On the other hand he was not ready for war and knew
it, and Ciano was telling him that a German attack on Poland would
begin a general war. He told Hitler that Italy could not join in a war
which brought Poland's allies into the field unless Germany could
supply the materials of war which Italy still lacked. Asked to specify
Italy's needs he submitted a huge list. This was tantamount to asking
for the impossible. Privately Hitler accepted the conclusion that Italy
would not fight. Mussolini resigned himself to the fact that Hitler would
make war on Poland.

Hitler's Japanese ally was also proving a disappointment. After Japan
joined the Anti-Comintern Pact in November 1936 Hitler tried to get a
promise of Japanese military assistance against any enemy of Germany
and not merely against the communist USSR. By 1939 the Japanese
army was keen on an alliance with Germany and Italy against Great
Britain and France but the emperor, his Foreign Minister and the navy
opposed such a commitment. Prolonged negotiations during the early
months of 1939 ran into the sands and on 22 May Germany and Italy

signed the Pact of Steel, which marked the end of hopes for a tripartite alliance against the western democracies. Six months later Japan was the more deeply aggrieved by Hitler's pact with Stalin because Japan was actually engaged in hostilities against the USSR. Japan complained that the Russo-German pact was a breach of the Anti-Comintern Pact. A few days later its government fell and its attitude became more uncertain, but temporarily the Japanese alliance had become irrelevant for Hitler who had just given the order for the war against Poland in which the USSR was his ally.

On 25 August Hitler gave the order for Poland to be attacked before dawn the next morning. At the last moment he revoked his order – so late that one unit could not be reached in time, advanced across the frontier and was destroyed. Hitler's change of plan may have been influenced by the behaviour of his Italian and Japanese allies or by the announcement – also on the 25th – of the Anglo-Polish treaty, but the guarantee to Poland was already an established fact and Hitler was more probably hoping that Chamberlain and Daladier, if given a few extra days to reflect upon the Russo-German pact, would either coerce Poland as they had coerced Czechoslovakia or abandon it. On the 25th he assured the British and French Ambassadors that he had no designs on the British Empire and was not hankering after Alsace-Lorraine, and in the days which followed he tried to get Great Britain and France to force Poland to send a plenipotentiary to Berlin to negotiate the reversion of Danzig to Germany and a plebiscite in the Polish corridor. Given the fate which had attended other plenipotentiaries who had visited Berlin, Beck (who had already agreed in principle to negotiate with Germany) refused and his allies felt unable to press him to accept.

Germany invaded Poland on 1 September. As a prelude a small SS party entered the German radio station at Gleiwitz and announced in poor Polish that it had been seized by Poles. This futile episode, in the course of which a German policeman who was not privy to the escapade was killed, was Germany's attempt to give some colour of justification to the attack which began the Second World War. A few hours after the charade at Gleiwitz, Danzig's Nazi Gauleiter declared the city to be a part of the German Reich; there was some fighting (there is an exciting account of the fight for the Post Office in Günther Grass's novel *The Tin Drum*) but Danzig was not now what mattered. Hitler had taken a risk. He calculated, correctly, that he could dispose of Poland without fear of British or French intervention, and he was happy to know that his generals who feared a war on two fronts would again be proved wrong. But he also calculated, wrongly, that Great Britain and France would either not declare war or not fight if they did. The British and French governments hesitated, but in the House of Commons Chamberlain's reluctance to declare war in response to Great Britain's pledges and Poland's plea for action against Germany in the west, produced tense and angry scenes. Chamberlain's government, it was said, would fall if it did not declare war. On 3 September Chamberlain spoke the necessary words, but it was the Commons of England rather than the government which had taken the plunge. France followed suit.

The outbreak of war in September 1939 marked the failure of policies, for which British and French politicians have been amply criticized. The French recipe for peace and security in Europe had already broken down because it rested on incompatibles – a system of continental alliances plus an alliance with Great Britain to whom the continental alliances were obnoxious. As a result of the failure of the French recipe Great Britain came to be in a position to call the tune. It called it wrong. But why? The obtuseness of British politicians in the face of the fascist phenomenon is only a part of the answer.

It is a commonplace of history that France, denied the British and American guarantees which were its first requirement in 1919, had to fall back on second-best policies which were adequate in the twenties only because France was not then seriously threatened. The significance of Barthou and, in his different fashion, Laval was that these two Ministers tried a second time in the thirties to create an alliance system strong enough to contain Germany and that when this attempt too failed France's isolation was manifest to foe, friend and itself. Thereafter France accepted the consequences of this isolation – inability to conduct an independent foreign policy.

It is no less a commonplace that the United States kept itself aloof from European affairs between the wars. How far the United States was truly isolationist and why will be discussed in a later chapter. American isolationism, unlike the French abnegation, was a matter of choice. But it too involved withdrawal.

What has been little, if at all, noticed is that Great Britain too was isolated. The difference in the British case was that, unlike France and the United States, Great Britain refused to abnegate and continued to try to play an active role. It was, however, reduced to playing the only role possible for a state with commitments but without allies – the role of a man who gives way on one thing after another until he finds he has his back to a wall. At the turn of the century Great Britain had been committed to that search for allies which eventuated in the agreements with

Japan, Russia and France on the basis of which the First World War was fought. After that war the Japanese alliance was abandoned under American pressure, the Russian alliance disappeared with the ancient Russian state itself, and the French alliance became more of a problem than a support because of disagreements over German policy, the growing deficiencies of France as a military partner and the element of contempt and distrust in the British ruling class's attitude to France. In this situation British governments, no less than French, would have liked to believe that the new system of collective security embodied in the League of Nations was the answer to their problems and they consistently gave a high priority to support for the League for this reason, but they also believed that the collective security of their day would not work. They were not unaware of their dilemma but in the first post-war decade it did not seem a pressing one. Then, just as the world came to look more menacing, they were struck by a catastrophe of a different kind which they did not understand and which they consequently greatly exaggerated. The economic crisis of 1931 terrified the governing class, reduced Ministers to a state of helplessness and convinced them that Great Britain had been permanently and irreparably weakened. This misjudgement was a major cause of the refusal to spend money on arms in the thirties, and this failure in turn reinforced the feeling of weakness. By the mid-thirties a combination of diplomatic isolation, economic nightmare and military unpreparedness had produced political and intellectual paralysis. And this paralysis produced wrong decisions. Munich was a wrong decision.

It contained three principal elements. These were: horror of war, unmanageable imperial burdens and miscalculation of the odds in Europe.

The men who sat in British cabinets in the thirties had known the First World War – most of them had fought in it – and felt a compelling responsibility to prevent a second. Their generation had been horrified by the first war and was convinced that a second, in which they themselves would be too old to fight, would be even more frightful. They felt a compelling personal obligation to obviate war at almost any price. This motive does them nothing but credit.

Secondly, they thought in imperial terms and would have held it disgraceful not to do so: their heritage and their office constrained them to give the highest priority to the preservation of an empire whose material riches had placed Great Britain high in the world. Subconsciously too, the preservation of empire was a charge which could not be abandoned without impugning British vitality. This empire seemed to be challenged not so much by changing times as by a specific enemy – Japan – whose evident attempts to dominate China were assumed to entail similar designs in the spheres of influence established in Asia over the centuries by European powers. In 1937 the British government went to the length of giving formal undertakings at the Imperial Conference in that year to send a British fleet to the Pacific to stem or defeat Japanese ambitions. But this promise was incompatible with any policy in Europe that was likely to lead to war with Germany and Italy, since war in Europe could serve as a green light to Japan to despoil the British in Asia while conversely the dispatch of a substantial naval force to the east would negate Great Britain's capacity to make war in Europe. Great Britain's resources no longer matched its commitments as an imperial power which was also critically involved in European affairs. Short of a massive rearmament programme begun at a much earlier date (politically shunned and economically perhaps ruinous) there was no way out of this dilemma except by a retreat from empire or from Europe. The British government came near to the latter but, responding ultimately to Great Britain's inevitable embroilment in Europe, bequeathed to its successors the unenviable and, in the thirties, virtually unthinkable alternative.

The third main factor in the calculations of British foreign policy in the thirties was a misreading of the military situation, beginning with the balance and practicalities of air power. British cabinets believed that on the outbreak of war London would be immediately and catastrophically bombed and Britain forced to capitulate. This belief was absurd. The Air Staff admitted that it could not bomb Germany. This admission should have prompted the question whether the Luftwaffe could bomb England. Yet astonishingly this question seems never to have been put. Had it been the answer must have been no. When the Luftwaffe did bomb England two years later (with much less catastrophic effect than anticipated) it did so from bases in France and Belgium which it did not have in 1938 and could not have conquered so long as Czechoslovakia remained an independent, hostile and well-armed state. The destruction of Czechoslovakia at Munich, completed in April the next year, was an essential precondition for Hitler's air offensive against Great Britain. The betrayal of Czechoslovakia at Munich has been justified on the grounds that the only alternative was to fight Hitler and be defeated. This is a bad plea. In the event France was beaten anyway. Great Britain won the Battle of Britain but the correct conclusion to draw about Munich is not that Chamberlain there gained time to build up the RAF and so save his country but rather that Munich brought upon Great Britain a battle which it would not otherwise have had to fight.

In 1938 Czechoslovakia was the one country among the possible combatants which was ready for battle. Great Britain and France were not ready, nor was the USSR. More significantly, Germany was not ready. Nor of course was Italy. So any alliance with Czechoslovakia in it would have started with a peculiar advantage over its enemy. Czechoslovakia was not only ready but strong, as strong as Germany in all important departments except manpower. The Czechoslovak army of thirty-five divisions faced a German army which was about the same size or slightly larger but which, if the aggressor, needed to be twice as large as its defending antagonist. In 1938 Germany could just about match Czechoslovakia division for division with four or five regular (but imperfectly trained and incompletely officered) divisions over to guard its western front – where Czechoslovakia's ally, France, mustered seventy-six divisions. The Czechs were better equipped than the Germans in a number of ways, notably in artillery and armoured fighting vehicles. The German armoured divisions which scattered and destroyed the French army and its allies in 1940 hardly existed in 1938; even in September 1939 Hitler had only six armoured divisions in place of the ten with which he made war in the west; four of these ten had Czech tanks.

Czechoslovakia was the sixth industrial power in Europe, possessed one of Europe's most famous, extensive and efficient armaments industries and had made plans to remove it from the west to the comparative safety of Slovakia. After 1939 its output, which was roughly equivalent to Great Britain's arms output, was added to Germany's own capacity – not the least of Germany's gains at Munich. Germany also secured the existing equipment of the Czechoslovak armed forces, including 1,500 aircraft. Czechoslovak mobilization plans were excellent. The government was ready to evacuate half the population of Prague. Morale was high. All Czechoslovakia asked in return for these substantial contributions was a declaration of war by France. Confident of its ability to hold the Germans for a matter of months, it did not even depend on an immediate French offensive in strength – unlike the Poles who required, and secured from France in the following year, a promise that the French army would commit the bulk of its forces against Germany within fifteen days of French mobilization.

But there was no equivalent confidence in France or Great Britain. The pessimism of French and British staffs and politicians arose largely out of the view held in the west that, since the *Anschluss*, Czechoslovakia's soft underbelly had been exposed and its capital lay at the mercy of a German pincer attack. In fact Czechoslovakia's southern defences were far from soft and the Germans did not plan a pincer movement. Hitler and his generals had decided that an attack on Prague from the south and the northwest would be held up for too long by the Czechoslovak army and fortifications and they therefore planned a thrust from the west. When, as bloodless victors, they were able to inspect the Czech defences they were awed by the strength and depth of a system which stretched back from the frontiers almost as far as Prague. Addressing 400 journalists a few weeks after Munich Hitler told them of his feelings when he inspected these fortifications and enthused over his success in getting hold of them without firing a shot.

What Stalin would have done in the event of war in 1938 still remains an enigma. The fact that the Russian obligation to act was dependent on French action provides no clue, since this clause in the Russo-Czechoslovak treaty of 1935 was inserted not by the Russians in order to provide a let-out but by the Czechs, on French insistence, in order to discourage the Russians from acting on their own. During 1938 and before Munich the USSR delivered aircraft to the Czechs (who were short of bombers). Moscow also warned Poland not to take action against Czechoslovakia, threatening to denounce the Russo-Polish treaty if Poland attacked Czechoslovakia. Two weeks before the Munich conference Rumania lifted its embargo on Russian aircraft flying over its territory and one Russian aircraft which made a forced landing in Rumania on its way from the USSR to Czechoslovakia was not only given emergency repairs but was allowed to fly on. An airfield in Slovakia was stocked with fuel and spare parts for various types of Russian aircraft. The French Ambassador in Moscow believed that the Russians intended to go to the help of Czechoslovakia. Russian ground and air forces were moved westward in considerable numbers, although for what purpose is uncertain. They could have been used as a contribution to collective action on behalf of Czechoslovakia, or their deployment may have been no more than a defensive precaution, or Stalin may have been keeping both his options open. Furthermore the possibility of Russian action was in itself a factor since it gave Hitler not merely two fronts to worry about but three. He was risking an attack on East Prussia and had no means of meeting it. When war came a year later over Poland this threat had been eliminated. From the Anglo-French point of view Stalin was a far from certain ally in the event of war over Czechoslovakia, but he was an all but certain non-ally in a war begun anywhere else in central Europe.

Hitler's aggression against Czechoslovakia was based on a political calculation, not a military one. On a military calculation it was the lunacy which his generals held it to be. They, seeing only the military equation, were scared out of their wits and even conspired to overthrow him. Hjalmar Schacht too, the coolest of men – the financial genius who served many masters, financed German rearmament, mocked Hitler as he mocked everybody with his merciless drawing-room wit, but who did not leave the Nazi government until he was dismissed from it in January 1938 – bemoaned Chamberlain's visit to Godesberg no less than the generals: Schacht said that Chamberlain could do nothing to prevent war and that Germany was therefore lost. It follows that Czechoslovakia's allies' own calculations were, militarily, wrong. Hitler's political gamble came off not because France and Great Britain were militarily incapable but because they were strategically inept. The French army would have had little more on its hands than a *promenade militaire*, the one military performance which an out-of-date army can execute as well as an up-to-date one. In 1940 the French forces were destroyed in a few weeks by a weight of armour which in 1938 the Germans did not possess. It is moreover implausible to suppose that in 1938, with the Germans engaged in Czechoslovakia, with only five German regular divisions and seven others in the west, with the entire Luftwaffe committed in the east, with incomplete German defences described by General Jodl as a building site, and with the spur of a treaty obligation, the French army would have remained futilely static. However poor its leadership and equipment it could hardly have failed to do better than it did when war came; at least it could not have done worse.

The British case was different. The British army was irrelevant both in 1938 and 1940. Although its role in Europe's wars in the twentieth century was to send troops and not, as in the past, find the money to subsidize the armies of other countries, Great Britain did not in fact equip itself with troops to send. It was therefore unable to contribute much more than a token to continental land warfare until it had raised a wartime army in wartime, fighting meanwhile defensive battles to gain the time to do this. Consequently the crucial issue was the defence of Great Britain itself and the crucial battle was the air battle of 1940.

The British case for Munich has to be tested at two points – in 1939 when war in fact came and in 1940 when the crucial battle was fought. Rearmament was accelerated after Munich, although without much intensity until the fall of France (and Chamberlain) in 1940. Between Munich, when battle was refused, and September 1939, when it was accepted, Great Britain's expenditure on armaments was one fifth of Germany's. British fighter production was about half Germany's. There was therefore no improvement in the British position relative to the German during these twelve months; in these respects the British position actually got worse. At the time of Munich the vital radar screen was incomplete; so it was a year later. The supplementary screen against low-flying aircraft, wholly non-existent in 1938, was still wholly non-existent in 1939.

If the British government feared defeat in 1938 it had even more reason to fear it a year later when the country's defences were still ineffective against air raids and its aircraft, though more numerous and more modern, had declined in proportion to the German air force.

By the spring of 1940, on the eve of the Battle of Britain, British aircraft production had begun to overtake Germany's, so that the gap between the two forces had stopped growing and was beginning to close. In 1938 Great Britain had 600 fighter aircraft, of which 360 were immediately available for operations, but only one in five of these was modern. In 1940 all Fighter Command's forty-three squadrons had Hurricanes or Spitfires (but the squadrons overseas had not). It is therefore plausible to argue that had the Battle of Britain been fought in 1938 the result would have gone the other way. But it is implausible to assume that anything like the Battle of Britain would have been fought in a war begun in 1938 with Czechoslovakia as an ally, for the essential prerequisite to the Luftwaffe's attack on Great Britain was the possession of airfields in France and Belgium – airfields which had first to be captured by the German army which, on the 1938 hypothesis, would have been fully occupied in Czechoslovakia. Great Britain was woefully ill equipped in 1938 but it does not follow that it would have fought Germany at a greater disadvantage in that year than it did when, with Germany also better armed and above all unencumbered to the east, Great Britain was forced into war for Poland in 1939 and so forced to defend its own shores in 1940. On the contrary, there is reason to calculate that the avoidance of war in 1938 was not only a shameful act but an inexpedient and foolish one. The surrender at Munich, by postponing war, shaped its future course, ensured the defeat of France and, so far from buying time for rearmament, committed Great Britain to a battle which it nearly lost.

Munich was an over-optimistic, inadequately analysed, dubiously proper attempt to accommodate Hitler's expansive Germany in the European states system and so stave off war, but the grounds for supposing that Hitler would be satisfied with what he got at Munich were a wilful delusion and the grounds for supposing that war postponed would be more easily won were little more defensible. Chamberlain had become convinced that Czechoslovakia could not be saved. He was intent upon preventing the so-called Sudeten crisis from developing into general war. Hitler's aggressive plans were a threat to the peace, but so too – in Chamberlain's eyes – was the Franco-Czech treaty: Hitler's territorial claims might be satisfied but in order to keep the peace by satisfying them Chamberlain needed to prevent the occurrence of the *casus foederis* embodied in the treaty, or to ensure that it would be dishonoured if it did arise. This was an urgent issue since Daladier (but not all his colleagues) was prepared in the last resort to go to war if Czechoslovakia were attacked. For Chamberlain Munich was a victory because it defused the Franco-Czech treaty, but a defeat because the basis of his policy was unsound. He assumed, wrongly and implausibly, that Hitler could be satisfied by territorial concessions linked to alleged ethnic borders whereas, as the next few months showed, Hitler was determined to annex far more than the territories deemed to be German in character even by him and, ultimately, to fight the USSR for the *Lebensraum* which he had said in *Mein Kampf* Germany must have. At best Chamberlain's policy might hope to disentangle – although it did not disentangle – Great Britain and France from war. It could not prevent the war or even much delay it, and Great Britain and France were quickly involved in the war by Chamberlain's own action in guaranteeing the integrity of Poland, a complete reversal of his policy of engineering the dismemberment of Czechoslovakia in order to keep the peace. For Hitler Munich was no more than a brief, if unwelcome, check which, six months later, had cost him nothing and had incidentally stifled opposition to his expansionist adventures from those, notably in the German army, who were scared by his willingness to risk war with Czechoslovakia.

The policy of appeasement, which culminated at Munich, ensured that Czechoslovakia would be eliminated from a war with Germany. With the effortless elimination of Poland too a year later, war on Germany's eastern front was reduced to war against the USSR alone, so that Stalin, by 1945 sole combatant in the east and sole victor, became the virtually uncontrolled arbiter of the fate of central and eastern Europe.

Part II
HITLER'S WARS: 1939–41

THE European war began when the Germans invaded Poland on 1 September 1939. On 17 September the Russians did so too and Poland ceased once more to exist as an independent state. Successful in the east Hitler paused, but Stalin in November made demands on Finland which led to a war which the Russians at first bungled but eventually won in March 1940. In April Hitler conquered Denmark and Norway and in May–June the Netherlands, Belgium and France. In July–September he failed, in the Battle of Britain, to win the air superiority necessary for an invasion. Great Britain remained at war, not only in the west, but also with naval, ground and air forces in the eastern Mediterranean. Hitler toyed with the idea of a descent into the western Mediterranean through France and Spain, but the war was resumed in the eastern Mediterranean when Mussolini attacked Greece unsuccessfully in October and the British attacked the Italians successfully in North Africa in December. In 1941 Hitler consolidated his control of south-eastern Europe, including Greece, and went to the help of the Italians in Africa. On 22 June he attacked the USSR which, besides strengthening its defences in the north by the peace imposed on Finland, had annexed the three Baltic states of Estonia, Latvia and Lithuania and the Rumanian provinces of Bessarabia and Northern Bukovina. There were therefore at the end of 1941 three separate theatres of war: first, the USSR where Leningrad was invested, German forces had come within sight of Moscow, and the Ukraine had been overrun by German armies on their way into the Crimea and the Caucasus; secondly, the remnant of a war in the west maintained by the Royal Air Force in Great Britain but pushed out into the Atlantic and waged chiefly by German U-boats and their pursuers; and thirdly, the Mediterranean where the Germans and Italians were trying to win North Africa – and thence the Middle East – against the opposition of the British Mediterranean fleet and British land and air forces based in Egypt and Malta. At the end of the year this European war, begun in 1939, ceased to be purely European and merged with the wars begun before and after it by Japan – against China in 1937 and against the United States in 1941.

CHAPTER 5

From Poland to the North Cape

THE German attack on Poland was a combination of a straight punch and a pincer movement. The central German blow was delivered from Pomerania, Silesia and Moravia and was accompanied by simultaneous attacks from eastern Pomerania in the north and Slovakia in the south. All attacks were made with withering material and technical superiority, Hitler having taken the risk of committing the whole of his armoured and mechanized forces in Poland and of denuding his western fronts. The Polish forces fell back rapidly, taking the civilian authorities with them and leaving the German inhabitants exposed to the harsh vengefulness of their Polish neighbours. Fantastic rumours about the activities of a German fifth column – rumours which were to be repeated all over Europe and which were almost totally groundless – produced a panic-struck wave of summary injustice in which as many as 7,000 Germans may have been killed.

No help came to Poland from its guarantors. The French army put a symbolic toe across the German frontier but otherwise France composed itself to await the arrival of the British (that year or the next) and, when pressed by the Polish Ambassador in Paris, hedged over the promise given in May to launch an immediate major offensive. General Gamelin did not disown the promise but said, evasively and incorrectly, that French forces were engaging the enemy on the ground and in the air. Great Britain sent twenty-nine aircraft to attack German shipping (and lost seven of them) but for six months dropped nothing more serious than leaflets on German soil. The cabinet feared massive air reprisals and in Parliament the Secretary of State for Air went so far as to defend this inactivity by reminding his more bellicose critics, who wanted the RAF to attack the Ruhr which was within its bombing range, that the targets proposed were private property. The Germans in the west uneasily occupied the incomplete West Wall. They deployed thirty-three divisions, twenty-five of which were of the second grade or lower. They had no tanks, no aircraft and three days' supply of ammunition. Opposite them was the French army with over seventy divisions on the border, nearly 3,000 tanks and command of the air.

The Poles, whether from misplaced hopes or through temperamental

impetuosity or sheer desperation, had placed their forces in forward positions where they were quickly overwhelmed by an enemy who was superior
in every way. Their mobilization was slow, their leadership poor, their
communications flimsy, their reserves thin, their aircraft obsolete and
their tactics – cavalry charging tanks with the aim of dashing into Germany – hopeless. On the ground they were thrown back at all points by
the German armour and dive-bombers. In the air the rest of the Luftwaffe,
although hampered by fog on the morning and evening of the first day,
quickly forced the Poles to battle by attacking Warsaw. The Polish air
force was crippled in two days and extinguished in two weeks as a result
of air combats and the overrunning of its airfields by the German army.
The Polish army scored one noteworthy sucess by night attack southwards
across the river Bzura on 9–10 September, but this stroke was held in
check by the Luftwaffe and although one German army was temporarily
disorganized a second, which was already to the east on its way to Warsaw,
turned about and, together with a third army north of the Polish force,
encircled the Poles and inflicted fatal casualties on them. On 25 September
Warsaw was bombed all day. German command of the air was so complete
that even Ju. (Junkers) 52 transports joined in the bombing, and the city
surrendered the next day. Hitler arrived to see it on 5 October.

The German victory disconcerted the Russians both for what it was
and by its speed, and on 17 September Russian forces moved into what
the Russians called Western Belorussia and Western Ukraine on the plea
that the Polish state had disintegrated. At the cost of 734 dead the Russians
occupied half Poland (admittedly the half where Poles were in a minority).
They also, in October, took control of Estonia, Latvia and Lithuania by
exacting from their governments treaties of mutual assistance which permitted the entry of Russian troops and meant in effect that the Russians
would take over if the Germans looked like doing so. Upon Finland the
Russians had even more serious demands to make because of the vulnerability of Leningrad, situated no more than fifteen miles from the Finnish
frontier on the Karelian isthmus and close to Lake Ladoga whose shores
were partly Finnish territory. The Russians wanted to protect Leningrad
against land and sea attack by obtaining Finnish territory in the immediate
neighbourhood of the city and control of the Gulf of Finland.

The issue was one between Russian security and Finnish rights. During
October and early November Finnish delegations went three times to
Moscow. On each occasion the Russians made small concessions but
they refused to abate the substance of their demands: a lease of Hangö in
south-western Finland at the entrance to the Gulf of Finland, the cession of
a number of islands in the Gulf, a slice of territory in the Karelian isthmus

THE GERMAN AND RUSSIAN
INVASIONS OF POLAND 1939

The destruction of Poland was primarily
a German action, 1,700,000 German
troops soon defeated the 600,000 Polish
soldiers. German air attacks destroyed
the centres of the main Polish cities,
The Poles hoped to make a final stand
in the Pripet Marshes, but the USSR
advances destroyed all chance of
further Polish resistance against either
Germany or the USSR

LATVIA

LITHUANIA

Baltic Sea

Memel

Danzig

Polish corridor

EAST
PRUSSIA

Vilna

Suvalki

Minsk

Augustov

Grodno

Bialystok

Poznan

Modlin   WARSAW

Brest—Litovsk

Pinsk

Pripet
Marshes

Lodz

P   O   L   A   N   D

Lublin

Lutsk

Rovno

GREATER

Sokal

GERMANY

Tarnov

U   S   S   R

Cracow

Yaroslav   Lvov

Przemysl

SLOVAKIA

Stanislavov

HUNGARY

RUMANIA

Dividing line between the German and USSR
zones of occupation, agreed between Germany
and the USSR in August 1939.
German advances commencing 1 September 1939.
Russian advances commencing 17 September 1939.
Annexed to the USSR October 1939.
Annexed to Germany.
Annexed to Lithuania.

0   100
Miles

~ ARTHUR BANKS ~

(including the town of Viipuri) to the north-west of Leningrad and – in the far north – the Finnish half of the peninsula guarding the approaches to the Russian port of Murmansk. In exchange the Russians offered a piece of Russian Karelia twice as large as the areas demanded. They also asked for a treaty debarring each signatory from entering into agreements directed at the other. Finnish opinion was overwhelmingly against making any large cessions to an hereditary enemy, although one or two leaders argued that the Russians were not bluffing and could not in the end be denied. When the Russians saw that they could not get what they wanted by negotiation they set up a puppet Finnish government and attacked on the last day of November – for which the USSR was expelled from the League of Nations. Four Russian armies, comprising forty-five divisions, went into action, one on either side of Lake Ladoga, one directed across the waist of Finland and the fourth in the far north. The Finnish armies of 200,000 men offered magnificent resistance. They were much better clad and better shod than the ill-prepared Russians and they operated in small ski groups against inappropriately large Russian formations, but in the long term they lacked practically everything except courage and discipline. Within a short time of the opening of the campaign they were relying on teenagers to fill their fighting ranks.

The Russians began by mismanaging the campaign so thoroughly that their attacks in the south were brought to a standstill before the end of the year and they were decisively defeated in the centre in January. The Russian troops had been led to believe that they would win without serious fighting. They found themselves instead fighting unsuccessfully in a particularly cold winter in which the temperature fell below -50 degrees C. They suffered commensurately. The Finns on the other hand were so buoyed up by their initial successes that they believed that they had secured the necessary breathing space to allow foreign friends to come to their aid and complete the defeat of their enemy. (The Americans had a special regard for Finland as the only country in Europe which went on paying interest on its foreign debts in spite of the economic collapse of 1931.) But no help came. Hitler stuck to his bargain with Stalin and urged the Finns to come to terms. Sweden, Finland's nearest neighbour, was prepared to offer all aid short of war, but not fighting men. In Great Britain and France there was fervent sympathy and admiration for the Finns. Volunteers scented a cause in which they could worthily engage themselves instead of staying inactively at home watching other weak nations being bullied by Germany.

The British and French governments had more complicated reactions. Going to the help of Finland was part of a scheme for strangling Germany without having to fight it. If Germany's supplies from the USSR and Scandinavia could be stopped, Hitler would be forced to negotiate. So General Weygand, who was in Syria, would march on Baku (the Caucasian oil port) and might even link up with an Anglo-French expeditionary force starting from Finland 2,000 miles away – which would in any case meanwhile get into Scandinavia ahead of the Germans, stop Germany's supply of Swedish iron ore and, even if it could not bring the war to a halt, possibly force Hitler into a war in a northern theatre instead of the threatened attack in the west. This plan, one of the wildest surmises of the war, entailed either the cooperation of Norway and Sweden or the violation of their neutrality. Both countries refused to allow the passage of British and French troops through their territory. Plans were therefore made – or, more correctly, discussed, for nothing like a coherent plan emerged – to send four divisions to fight the Russian armies in Scandinavia. As a first step they were to invade Norway in order to prevent the Germans from getting there first, but while these measures were being discussed by cabinets and staffs in London and Paris (which had however no adequate information about the terrain or the road and rail systems which they hoped to use) the situation at the front changed. The Russians recovered themselves and launched in February a new and overwhelming attack under Marshal Timoshenko in the Karelian isthmus. The Finnish air force was reduced to one hundred aircraft against eight times that number. The Finnish line was broken. The government came to the conclusion that foreign help would be too little and too late. It decided to make peace in spite of Anglo-French – particularly French – attempts to keep Finland in the war and on 12 March Finland capitulated. At a cost of 68,000 dead the Russians secured all their original demands and a few more. Two hundred thousand Finns had to pack up and leave their homes and cross a new frontier in order to remain in their own country. Leningrad was a few degrees safer. The relations between the Soviet Union and Great Britain and France – and the United States – were several degrees colder. But Great Britain and France had been saved by the Finnish collapse from making war on the USSR while they were still at war with Germany. When, a few weeks after the end of the Russo-Finnish war, they entered Scandinavia they did so to fight the Germans and not the Russians. One consequence of this episode was the fall of Daladier. He was succeeded by Paul Reynaud who concluded with Great Britain an agreement that neither country would make a separate peace with Germany.

In February there had occurred one of those incidents which catch the imagination and help perhaps to precipitate events. The German supply ship *Altmark* was threading her way through the Leads along the coast of Norway, homeward bound from the south Atlantic. Aboard were 299 British captives, taken off ships which had been caught by the German battleship *Graf Spee*.

Graf Spee was by this time on the bottom of the sea. Like her sister ships *Scheer* and *Deutschland* (the latter renamed *Lützow* in 1940), *Graf Spee* was a pocket battleship designed to comply with the provisions of the treaty of Versailles which forbade Germany to have warships of more than 10,000 tons. In fact she slightly exceeded that limit. The pocket battleships were faster than anything which could outgun them and out-gunned in range and weight of shell anything which could catch them. On the eve of war *Graf Spee* and *Deutschland* were dispatched into the Atlantic and from October to December they harried the commerce of Germany's enemies in the southern Atlantic and Indian Oceans. Their success was moderate. *Graf Spee* claimed nine victims before the end of her career – roughly one a week. Eight groups from the British and French navies were formed to hunt the German raiders and soon after dawn on 13 December one of these – a British and New Zealand cruiser force consist-ing of *Exeter*, *Ajax* and *Achilles* under Commodore Henry Harwood – opened battle. *Exeter* was soon very badly damaged and after an hour and a half *Ajax* and *Achilles* were forced to break off the engagement and limit themselves to shadowing. The damage and casualties which they had managed to inflict on *Graf Spee* were slight, but her commander, Captain Hans Langsdorff, decided to make for harbour and shortly after nightfall she dropped anchor in Montevideo Roads in the estuary of the River Plate. The British representatives in the capital of neutral Uruguay used every device of international law to prevent her from sailing again before Commodore Harwood, waiting off shore with *Ajax* and *Achilles*, could be reinforced. During the night of the 14th–15th, the cruiser *Cumberland* joined him. On the 17th *Graf Spee* was seen to be disembarking her crew. In the afternoon she set course for the open sea, accompanied by a German merchant ship. A few miles out the remainder of her crew left her. At sunset she blew up. Captain Langsdorff had been authorized to destroy his ship if he saw no way of bringing her back home. Nevertheless two days later he shot himself.

A sea chase and a sea victory have for centuries given a special delight to the British people. The sinking of *Graf Spee* was a timely tonic during a period of mixed disaster and inactivity. It was an item in the stiffening resolve of Great Britain which was to be put to the test when France fell and the decision to fight on against Hitler rested more upon spirit than reason. More immediately there was the question of *Graf Spee*'s victims whom she had transferred to *Altmark* before being engaged by Commodore Harwood's cruisers. Two months after *Graf Spee* sank, *Altmark* and her prisoners entered Norwegian waters homeward bound. She raised a question of international law. Norway was a neutral and it was argued on the British side that it was a breach of neutrality for Norway to permit the passage of prisoners of war through neutral territorial waters. Moreover the Norwegian authorities, upon being assured by *Altmark*'s captain that she carried no prisoners, had failed to carry out an effective search. A light British force thereupon sailed into Norwegian waters on 17 February, boarded the German vessel and rescued the captives. This dashing episode was another boost to British morale, greatly irritated Hitler and brought an incidental compliment from Ciano who told the British Ambassador that it reminded him of the boldest traditions of the British navy in the time of Francis Drake. (The Italians were already annoyed with Hitler's Scandinavian policies. Hitler had refused to allow Italian aircraft, ordered by Finland before the Russian attack, to be sent via Germany. Pro-Finnish demonstrations in Rome had had a clear anti-German tone.)

The Finnish war and the *Altmark* episode showed that Norway's hopes of keeping out of the Second World War as it had kept out of the First were tenuous. Norway was too important. Its main geographical feature is its coastline of a thousand miles, guarded and punctured by islands and inlets. This coast could provide valuable bases either for a British blockade of Germany or for a German offensive against shipping in the Atlantic. It had also a second importance as an outlet for Swedish iron ore. Northern Sweden is one of Europe's principal sources of iron ore, and early in the war exaggerated hopes were attached to preventing this ore from reaching Germany. The Swedish orefields lie midway between the Swedish port of Luleå in the Gulf of Bothnia, which freezes over in winter, and the Norwegian port of Narvik, which does not. By the beginning of 1940 both sides had their eyes on Norway and when the Finnish war ended in March Churchill wanted nonetheless to proceed to secure a foothold in northern Norway. But he failed to carry the cabinet with him and it was decided instead to mine the Leads and to make preparations to land in Norway if the Germans landed or seemed clearly about to do so.

On the other side Hitler had been pressed for some time by Grand Admiral Raeder to take action against Norway before Great Britain did. By December 1939 he had made up his mind to do this and in that month Raeder introduced to him Vidkun Quisling, the only personage of the Second World War who was destined to give his name to a human type. Quisling, two years older than Hitler, was a well-educated, romantic racialist, who had had the beginnings of a brilliant army career before 1914, had helped his great compatriot Fridtjof Nansen with his humanitarian work for the League of Nations in the twenties, had gone to work and found a wife in the Ukraine, and had then turned to politics as something between a socialist and a communist. Tactless and unpopular, as well as talented, he did not fit into party life and after holding office briefly as Minister of Defence in 1931–3 he founded his own party and newspaper, both of which were complete failures. He was taken up by the Nazi ideologist and eastern specialist, Alfred Rosenberg, and a few years later was passed on to Hitler by Raeder as a useful instrument of German policy. His rewards were the post of Prime Minister during the German occupation and execution by his countrymen after the end of the war.

Hitler issued a formal directive for an invasion of Norway (plus Denmark because it was on the way) on 1 March 1940. Operations were placed under the control of the O K W – *Oberkommando der Wehrmacht*, the inter-service planning headquarters of which Hitler himself was chief with the pliant Keitel to do his bidding. The plan was a daring one. Resistance by Danes and Norwegians could not be a serious obstacle but Great Britain held command of the seas and Germany might therefore be expected – and was expected in Great Britain – to proceed by land (much as the Anglo-American armies proceeded up Italy by land three years later). Hitler chose, however, to confront British naval superiority and to seize points along the Norwegian coast as far north as Narvik, while at the same time seizing airfields by airborne troops – the first such enterprise ever attempted. The attack on Norway, from Oslo to Narvik, was launched on 9 April. In gales and snowstorms it was successful at most points, although a number of ships were lost, including the battleship *Blücher* sunk by gunnery while trying to force the passage up the Oslo fjord, and the admiral and general in command of operations were both captured. So was a Gestapo party on its way to arrest the king. The Norwegian parliament conferred full powers on the king who refused to surrender and, after escaping death in an air attack on a village where he had been located, held out in the hope of British and French help.

In London reports that the Germans had landed as far north as Narvik seemed so incredible that they were for a time believed to be a mistake for Larvik, which is near the Oslo fjord. Although Swedish sources had given warnings of the assembly of the invading forces in north German harbours, it was believed in London that these were being held ready to counter an Anglo-French invasion and not to make the first move. The British cabinet was taken by surprise, the British staffs found themselves equipped with inadequate information about harbours and airfields, plans

THE GERMAN INVASION OF NORWAY 1940

British occupied Narvik 28 May. Withdrew 8 June.

0   100
Miles

German occupied territory.

German advances from 9 April.

May Date of German occupation.

Occupied by British.

British landing 29 April. Withdrew 29 May.

British landing 14 April. Withdrew 3 May.

British landing 17 April. Withdrew 2 May.

Kirkenes
16 June

16 June

Lofoten Is.

Narvik
8 June

Bodö
1 June

Gällivare

Grong *6 May*
Namsos *6 May*

Lulea

Trondheim *16 April*

Andalsnes
2 May

GULF OF BOTHNIA

FINLAND

Icebound in winter.

Bergen

Lillehammer *22 April*

Kongsvinger
16 April

Helsinki

Oslo
9 April

Stavanger

Stockholm

ESTONIA

Kristiansand

Riga

LATVIA

North Sea

Baltic Sea

Copenhagen

LITHUANIA

DENMARK

Danzig

Hamburg

EAST PRUSSIA

USSR

HOLLAND

GERMANY

POLAND

~ARTHUR BANKS~

were made and unmade in confused succession even after operations had
been set in motion. With the Germans in occupation of all ports and
airfields the British and French were faced with the necessity of making
hazardous landings from the sea or air. They proposed at first to go
ashore near Narvik but then switched to Trondhjem fjord in central
Norway, where the Norwegians wanted to concert a combined campaign.
Next it was decided to attempt both the northern and the central ventures
but later still a direct attack up Trondhjem fjord was abandoned in favour
of two separate landings at Namsos and Andalsnes 125 and 190 miles
away. In this confusion, made worse by notably inefficient cooperation
between the army and the navy, British, French and Polish forces went
into action against heavy odds and were worsted. In Scotland troops
which had been embarked for Norway were disembarked when news of
the German attacks arrived, in order to get the ships to sea as quickly as
possible, but were then not used. At Namsos French forces were put
ashore but were without even skis or snowshoes, let alone guns and tanks,
since the ship carrying their equipment found on arrival that it was too
big to enter the harbour. For a week these men were immobile and
defenceless against air attacks. Inferior in numbers and ill supported from
the air, Anglo-French forces in the centre were withdrawn in the first
week of May, giving their Norwegian allies lamentably short notice of the
necessity to capitulate. In the north evacuation was delayed until the
beginning of June when it was harassed by the German fleet. The Royal
Navy lost the aircraft-carrier *Glorious* with two squadrons of aircraft and
failed to discover the intentions or the whereabouts of German heavy
units which were at sea in the area. The retreating transports nevertheless
escaped and reached Great Britain with the survivors of the expedition
and also the Norwegian king. The Germans were left in possession of
bases from which to operate against Atlantic traffic and, later, convoys
bound for the USSR. There would in future be no difficulties about the
transport of Swedish iron ore to Germany. Hitler's victory was won by
the imaginative use of air transport, skilful handling of naval forces, good
inter-service cooperation and a superior meteorological service – helped
by the bungling of his adversaries. The cost was borne by the German
navy which (like the German glider and parachute arms in the battle for
Crete) suffered crippling losses at the hands of the defenders in the first
phase of the operation.

The sorry Norwegian campaign was debated in the House of Commons
on 7 and 8 May. The Chamberlain government was deserted by one hundred
and one of its supporters, and although the Prime Minister still commanded
a majority of eighty-one in that solid, stolid House he no longer had the

backing needed to carry on the war. He tried to convince himself and others that mounting disaster made it desirable for him to remain at the helm, but this argument did not work. He was deposed by the Commons as a result of disorder within its Conservative ranks. There was also a growing feeling that the country needed an all-party government and the Labour Party would not serve under Chamberlain. The obvious successor in political terms was Halifax. Chamberlain himself, the Conservative Party and the king all wanted Halifax and the Labour leaders were willing to join a Halifax administration. But at a meeting between Chamberlain, Halifax and Churchill on 9 May the lot fell on Churchill. Chamberlain proposed Halifax, expecting Churchill to express his agreement, but Churchill, acting on advice given him by Brendan Bracken, stayed silent. In breaking an awkward pause to say something about the difficulties of leading a government from the House of Lords Halifax threw away his chances, and shortly afterwards Chamberlain was on his way to Buckingham Palace to tell the king that it must be Churchill, who thus assumed office and the responsibility for victory or defeat on 10 May.

When he took office in 1940 Churchill was sixty-five years old. He had been a prominent political figure for forty years and famous for most of that time. He had sat in the House of Commons since 1900 (with only a brief exclusion in 1922–4) and in cabinet on and off since 1908. He had held office as President of the Board of Trade, Home Secretary, First Lord of the Admiralty, Minister of Munitions, Secretary of State for War, Secretary of State for Air, Colonial Secretary and Chancellor of the Exchequer. He was unusually versatile. He had written over a dozen books, including a history of the First World War in five volumes, an excellent biography of his father and another in four volumes of his remoter ancestor the first Duke of Marlborough. He was a competent amateur painter and an addict of English and European history. He had been a war correspondent in Africa and India. In the variety of his aptitudes and his achievements he was matched by two only of his predecessors in the premiership, Disraeli and Balfour; he was closer to the colourful talents of the former than the philosophical intellect of the latter. He had also the vigorous and independent spirit of Palmerston, manifested in longevity and the ability to appeal to the masses. Churchill and Palmerston are the only British Prime Ministers who have been popularly referred to by friendly nicknames. As a war leader Churchill has inevitably been compared with Lloyd George but the similarities between the two men lie in their circumstances rather than their characters or tastes.

Yet in 1940 Churchill had held no office for over ten years. First a

Conservative, then a Liberal and once more a Conservative after the First World War his political career was tinged with an inconstancy which is rare in British politics and is regarded with distrust. Even after the war, when his standing was unique in British political history, he was suffered to become the leader of the Conservative Party because of his enormous popularity and not because he was regarded by Conservative leaders as one of them, and during the thirties he was to all intents and purposes a man without a party, an eccentric without an accepted place in political life. In these years he was chiefly prominent for his opposition to the Conservative government's India Bill and for his campaign in favour of rearmament. He had spent three years of his early life in India and had formed a romantic attachment to the idea of the British-in-India which penetrated his prose style and ever afterwards provided him with some of the most effective embellishments of his oratory. But he was neither much interested in the real India nor well informed about it, so that his opposition to the Bill was romantic rather than sensible and his long but ineffectual crusade against it had no effect on the history of India. It did, however, widen the gap between him and the leaders of his party, and it strengthened the view held by many in political circles that, however great his abilities, his judgement was erratic. He was more liked than listened to. This element in his reputation was not new. As against Baldwin he had been on the side of toughness in dealing with the General Strike in 1926 and he had come in for criticism because as Chancellor of the Exchequer he had accepted, against his better judgement, the arguments for a return to the gold standard in 1925 at the pre-war parity. In 1936 he made no. concealment of his sympathies with King Edward VIII during the abdication crisis – a generous attitude which may have been applauded by the people at large but greatly irritated the Baldwin government and the rest of the establishment in state and church. His campaign for rearmament won him few friends: while the left dubbed him a warmonger, Conservatives resented his opposition to their policy of appeasement and feared – especially in the light of the by-election in Fulham in 1933 where the Conservative candidate was defeated by, it was thought, pacifist sentiment – that his agitation was costing them votes.

But when war came there was an almost universal feeling that Churchill must have a big share, perhaps the biggest, in conducting it. It is easier to record this judgement than to identify its sources. There was first of all the fact that Churchill, however often he had been wrong in the past on this issue or that, had been right about Hitler's Germany. His knowledge of history was here crucial, for it was as a historian and not as a moralist that he took his stand. He had not only absorbed European history but had understood it thoroughly and acquired insights which equally well read and more intellectual observers missed. He became certain that war was coming and that Great Britain could not avoid it, for he saw the rise of Nazi Germany in terms of the classic British doctrine that no single power must be allowed to dominate the European continent. He did not suffer from the delusion that Great Britain was not a part of the continent and so could sidestep the catastrophe. Although he sensed the strategic challenge to Great Britain before the moral one to civilized behaviour – he was no quicker than most of his countrymen to react to the moral issue, commended Mussolini's rule on a number of occasions and was for a time ambivalent about Hitler – he developed also a deep and genuine loathing of Nazi brutishness and had the power to express it with peculiar sting.

This was the second source of his special position when war came. The challenge once seen, Churchill was exceptionally well equipped to expose and meet it. He was combative and patriotic in the best sense of these words and he gave the most reassuring appearance of being firm in purpose and unhesitating in action. He was not in fact a man who knew no doubts – only a singularly stupid or vain man could have avoided them and he was often fearfully worried – but he had the courage and the skill to hide his anxieties and to give the impression that he was certain of his course and applying himself undividedly to the business of doing what had to be done. He was able to communicate his attitudes to the British people and to evoke from them their latent determination to resist danger and conquer evil. The essence of his famous oratory was his ability to give voice to elemental sentiments in big words and simple phrases. He was moreover the kind of leader who suited the British people. He was both an aristocrat and a democrat, a combination which the British like and which does not strike them as a paradox. Churchill had the assurance, even something of the arrogance, of the born aristocrat, but he combined this superiority with a capacity for feeling himself a part of the people and not apart from them. For him the people meant all the people and not, as so often in British parlance, the working-class bottom half.

He possessed, finally, an abundant mental energy. This worked both ways. His habits of work sometimes irritated and exhausted his advisers who were required to consider a stream of ideas, some of which were inevitably bad ideas, and to do so at unconventional hours of the day or night. But the gain was great, for with Churchill in command there could never be any doubt about whether things were happening or not. Churchill was a leader who had no intention of allowing anybody inferior to give directions, but he was also a respecter of the people and of their principal institution, the House of Commons. Undoubted head of the executive and of the armed services, master of the bureaucracy and sometimes a rough master, he was at the same time the servant of the legislature and the electorate. He showed, because he believed, that one does not have to be a dictator to be a leader.

On the day that he became Prime Minister Hitler invaded France and the Low Countries. The so-called phoney war had come to an end. The phoney war was a period in which nothing very warlike happened (except locally, sporadically and briefly) and, more than that, in which it was possible for people who were so disposed to go on hoping that nothing very warlike would happen. It was the time in which the era of appeasement and the years of war overlapped. In May 1940 Hitler made war on the western democracies. Less obviously but no less significantly Churchill's government did something which Chamberlain's government had never done: it dropped a bomb on Germany.

CHAPTER 6

The Fall of France

HITLER had won Poland almost as easily as Austria and Czechoslovakia. Although force had to be used instead of being merely brandished and the Russians had to be allowed their share, the operation was swift and was concluded without the intervention of any other power. It might be just the latest in the series of Hitlerian conquests, more expensive and more brutal but essentially not very different. Or it might be the beginning of something much more serious. Hitherto all Hitler's victories had been in central Europe – in Germany itself (the Rhineland) and then in Austria, Czechoslovakia, Danzig, Memel and Poland. Should he now attack France, even though France had acquiesced in the Polish *fait accompli*? Hitler was for action now. In the past he had disagreed with his advisers, especially his military advisers, about the reactions and the capacities of the western powers and he had always proved his advisers wrong.

The Polish collapse could be exploited in different ways. There were those who hoped that the reluctance of the western democracies to help Poland would finally eliminate western opposition to German ambitions in central and eastern Europe without the need for a showdown; that the defeat of Poland would be accepted in the west as a defeat for the west too. On the other hand the glittering successes of the Polish campaign were an incitement to a similar campaign in the west, and so long as there was any doubt whether a war against France would have to be fought one day there was also the argument that from the German point of view the sooner it were fought the better. Before the end of September Hitler, without consulting General von Brauchitsch, the Commander-in-Chief of the army, gave the order to prepare for an attack on France that autumn and a directive was issued by OKW on 9 October. Brauchitsch swallowed this usurpation of his functions and got to work, while continuing to argue that a spring offensive would be more prudent because the army needed to train fresh units and because the autumn weather might bog down the tanks and ground the aircraft. In the event an autumn campaign was washed out by the weather and after several postponements it was cancelled. In addressing his service chiefs at the end of November, Hitler, preferring to lay the blame for his disappointment on the human factor, was so abusive about the army that Brauchitsch offered to resign. He was not allowed to – yet. The postponement of the attack had a most important consequence since it gave army leaders the time to urge changes in the German plan of campaign.

The fundamental factors in German planning were the experiences of their forerunners in 1914 and the Maginot Line. The latter was a string of fortified positions, begun in 1929 and guarding the western approaches to France between its Swiss and Belgian frontiers. This line had an awesome reputation but owing to Belgium's neutrality it stopped short at a geographical point which had little strategic significance. Its existence, however, virtually dictated a German attack through Belgium to the north of it and the question which remained open was the main objective of such an attack. Too much pondering of the campaigns of 1914 had led the German General Staff to plan an attack on a broad front stretching all the way from Luxembourg northwards, with the main weight in the north and the main objective the Channel ports which they had failed to win in the race with which the First World War had opened. This attempt to repeat and improve on the performance of August 1914 reflected a preoccupation with this failure and a special concern with Great Britain rather than France, since the principal value of the ports was their use for submarine warfare against the British Isles. This plan did not aim, primarily at any rate, to knock out the French army as the Polish army had been knocked out and it therefore admitted the prospect of a long and possibly static war. Even if the plan succeeded, the war in France would not be over; and its success was dubious since it involved a direct attack on French and British forces which, if not defeated outright, might stand on prepared lines in northern France and keep themselves supplied through the ports.

General von Manstein, the plan's most effective critic, had other ideas. He proposed that the main weight of an attack in the north should be on its left wing rather than its right and that the prime object should be the annihilation of the French capacity to resist and not the conquest of the Channel coast or any other terrain; the enemy's territory in its entirety would become a prize of war as a consequence of the defeat of his armies. Manstein proposed that German forces attacking through the Ardennes should turn southwards as well as northwards and envelop the French to the west of the Maginot Line. Manstein was Chief of Staff to Field Marshal von Rundstedt, whose Army Group A would win the chief role in the campaign if the Manstein concept were accepted. They together urged Brauchitsch, who agreed with them but did not enjoy arguments with the Führer, to press their views on Hitler; and they had a stroke of luck early in January. An officer taking the plans to a headquarters in the west fell in with some air force friends, celebrated the meeting so well that he missed his train, got his friends to fly him on his way but took a wrong course and crashed in Belgium. With the plans in enemy hands there were special grounds for changing them. (The western staffs, however, concluded that the crash had been a fake and the plans planted on them.)

Hitler was prepared to listen. A serious student of military affairs, he liked discussing military problems with those of his generals whom he respected, and Manstein was one of these for the time being. Hitler was not, as he himself imagined, a military genius, but neither was he the ignoramus and bungler that surviving generals subsequently tried to make out. From the career point of view he was an amateur and not a professional military man, but then so were Stalin and Churchill and, for good or ill, Hitler had studied the science of war at least as carefully as the first and possibly with more application than either. But his talents and inclinations were the reverse of what was needed in a supreme commander. He was strongest on detail. He knew the names of bits and pieces of military equipment and what they were for, just as he was also exceptionally well versed in the details of the architect's craft. He had the mind of a fascinated and perhaps even an inventive quartermaster, but this gift did not make him a strategist and, as a strategist, he was handicapped because his cast of mind was basically political and not military. He put political aims before military sense. His catastrophic fault as a war lord lay even more in attempting the impossible than in his strategy. On this occasion he saw the force of Manstein's arguments (he may have been thinking independently along similar lines) and accepted his plan with some modifications.

Hitler did not begin his attack in the west with any marked material superiority. The battle of France was won by superior skill and not by the crushing weight of numbers. In the vital department of tanks the Germans were numerically the weaker with some 2,700 against nearly 3,000 French and 200 British. The quality of the tanks on the two sides was about the same. But in tactics and leadership the French and British were outclassed. For many French and British officers the tank was a horseless carriage to be used in the role of a horse rather than a carriage, a mechanized charger, more expensive and less lovable than a horse but performing essentially the same function as the cavalry of a bygone age which had fought closely with the infantry arm along a defined front. But defeat in the First World War and the restrictions imposed by the treaty of Versailles had made the German army more receptive to new ideas. Under General von Seeckt, himself somewhat old-fashioned in his views but willing to encourage novel thinking in others, the German army of 100,000 was re-created on the principles, first, that compensation for small numbers lay in mobility; secondly, that armoured vehicles could provide this mobility in place of the horse; thirdly, that the armour of a tank, unlike that of a medieval knight, was even more valuable in offence than for protection; fourthly, that tanks should be used in massed cohorts – divisions, corps and even tank armies – distinct from the other arms of the service; and finally that, with this combination of speed, weight and numbers, their prime purpose was to penetrate the enemy's lines and destroy his communications.

This was the *Blitzkrieg* and it revolutionized not only the handling of armoured forces but also the whole concept of war as a face-to-face contest between rival fronts. The basic ideas were not German. They were developed in the first place by British theorists like Captain B. H. Liddell Hart, Major-General J. F. C. Fuller and Major-General G. le Q. Martel. In Germany the doctrines of these men and later the similar teaching of Charles de Gaulle, published in 1937 and better known in Germany than in France, were studied by Heinz Guderian and other young officers. Before 1933 they were tried out in practice in the USSR under arrangements made clandestinely by Seeckt with the Russian army and government, and although Hitler stopped this collaboration his special interest in armoured warfare encouraged the progressives in the German army and contributed to the formation of the first two Panzer divisions soon after the Nazis took power. In May 1940 the Germans had ten Panzer divisions. (Rather more than half of their tanks were Pkw. Is and IIs, the rest the Pkw. IIIs and IVs which were to become the mainstay of the German armour until the Panther and Tiger began to arrive at the front in 1943. Three divisions with the heaviest punch were equipped with tanks made in Czechoslovakia's captured factories.)

The *Blitzkrieg* had also a special place for airborne troops whose task was to seize key points ahead of the advancing armour. Germany's parachutists so captured the imagination by their novelty that extraordinary steps were taken to defeat them: policemen were armed and trained to deal with them, in Great Britain church bells were to be rung to give warning of their descent and the most fanciful accounts, some of them official, circulated about the guise in which they were likely to do so. But there were far fewer of them than was commonly believed. Hitler had envisaged a war of the future as a 'sky black with bombers and, leaping from them into the smoke, parachute storm troops, each grasping a machine gun', but the Germans never had more than one division of parachutists and in their most notable operation – Crete – most of them jumped with pistols or knives and had to search around afterwards for the machine guns which were dropped separately and sometimes far away.

The German attack in the west opened on 10 May simultaneously against the Netherlands, Belgium, Luxembourg and France. In the Netherlands the weight of the attack was directed against Rotterdam. Its airfield, Waalhaven, was seized by parachute troops who also captured the intervening bridges over the Maas. The main bridge in the centre of the city was seized by units which landed by it in seaplanes. A subsidiary attack on airfields near The Hague was unsuccessful. On the 14th Rotterdam was still holding out. The Germans summoned it to surrender and parleys ensued. At this point the heart of the city was heavily bombed; within a few minutes great destruction was caused and 980 were killed. Nothing like this had been seen in the war so far. Two hours later the city capitulated and on the 15th the Dutch laid down their arms everywhere. The bombing of Rotterdam has been regarded as a piece of unprincipled savagery and vandalism, but there were perhaps extenuating circumstances. The air attack seems to have been made in ignorance of the parleys which were in train and in spite of German attempts to cancel it, and when the bombers appeared German commanders on the spot tried to signal to them to desist and did succeed in making a part of the force sheer off: but doubts have more recently been cast on this attempted explanation.

In Belgium the attack began with one of the most original strokes of the war. The conquest of Belgium involved crossing a series of waterways, notably the Meuse (or Maas) and the Albert Canal which branches off the Meuse just south of Maastricht on a north-westerly course towards Antwerp. Maastricht, which is on the Dutch side of the frontier between Belgium and Holland, is only twelve miles from the German border. Just south of it and in Belgium lay the great fortress of Eben Emael, a wedge-shaped hill unassailable except from the sky and commanding the end of the Albert Canal and three vital bridges over it. In the early hours of 10 May forty-one gliders took off from German airfields with 363 men for an operation which they had rehearsed many times. Two of the gliders came to grief on the way but the rest arrived silently over Eben Emael and in the first glider-borne attack in history captured the fort and its 1,200 defenders and two of the three bridges with the loss (to the attackers) of only five lives.

As soon as the German attack in the west was known, French and British forces began to move forward to make contact with the Belgian army on the line of the River Dyle and so create an unbroken line of resistance to the Germans from the English Channel to the borders of Switzerland. Owing to Belgium's neutrality advance planning had been dangerously meagre, so much so that positions which French forces were to occupy had not been prepared for them. Almost immediately the allied line was punctured farther south. The entire British Expeditionary Force and half the French army, which had moved into Belgium, were cut off. German armour under General Erwin Rommel proved that the Ardennes were not the obstacle to tanks which had been supposed and on 12 May German units, having broken through a sector which was lightly held by second-class divisions, found themselves on French soil north of Sedan. The next day they were across the Meuse at a number of points and after only one more day they had prised open a fateful gap fifty miles wide between two French armies. General Georges, commanding the north-eastern fronts under a cumbrous arrangement as a semi-independent subordinate of the Commander-in-Chief, General Maurice Gamelin, ordered a redisposition on the basis of a false report that French forces were in flight: the general who sent the report shot himself the next day, Georges suffered a nervous collapse (he had been ill for years) and two days later a third general was dismissed for losing his nerve. The Germans advanced 200 miles in a week. One million refugees were footing it along the roads and across country.

In three days the R A F lost half of the 200 bombers which it was operating in France – the highest loss percentage which it ever suffered – and the French air force was extinguished. The French First Army, the British Expeditionary Force to its left and the Seventh French Army further north still were cut off from the rest of the French armies, and French and British reinforcements moving up to the Dyle line were ordered to suspend their advance. On the following day, 16 May, with the Dutch already out of the war, the plan for Belgium having miscarried and the Germans racing into France, Gamelin disclosed to an Anglo-French council of war in Paris that he had no reserves left. His predicament was of his own making. He had neglected to create a reserve before war began, even though one of the main objects of building a defensive position like the Maginot Line was to avoid having to string men out along a long static line and so be able to hold them in a mobile reserve instead. Gamelin had done the opposite, committing his troops to fixed positions from which he could not easily switch them when the need arose. He had compounded this basic mistake by allowing men to go on leave from 7 May in spite of accurate warnings from reliable sources of the date and place of the German attack. Three days later French soldiers hurrying to rejoin their units failed to find them before they were overwhelmed. Yet Gamelin had all the same a small reserve of eight infantry divisions; but it was behind the Lorraine and Rhine fronts.

From the Meuse the German armour pushed on for the coast with powerful and efficient air support. They reached it on 20 May. Instead of a Franco-Anglo-Belgian line containing the Germans there was a German line stretching from Germany to the sea and cutting the allied forces in two. This German line was a thin one, for the German forces which had made it were comparatively small and had advanced far ahead of their supporting formations. The problem for the German high command was to consolidate the line and produce plans for dealing with the two distinct allied forces to the north and the south of it. The problem for the allies was to try to break the line and re-establish contact between their disrupted armies.

Reynaud, who had never had confidence in Gamelin and had been on the point of dismissing him when news of the German invasion arrived, replaced him on 19 May with General Maxime Weygand, a soldier full of honour but also of years (72). Reynaud also appointed another and even older hero, Marshal Philippe Pétain (85), to be Deputy Prime Minister. Weygand's fame and barely diminished sprightliness infused some hope into headquarters staffs but he was powerless to rectify Gamelin's cardinal error. He could not in the midst of a battle create a reserve. He inherited from Gamelin a plan to attack the German corridor simultaneously from north and south but postponed its execution while he made a tour of headquarters. This tour wasted precious days (whether telephone communications were destroyed or overlooked is not clear) and largely failed to achieve its aim, since of the two principal commanders north of the corridor, one, Lord Gort, failed by accident to keep his appointment with Weygand and the other, General Billotte, was killed – also accidentally – immediately after it. But in any case Gort, acting on Gamelin's earlier orders and apparently unaware of Weygand's cancellation of them, shot his bolt prematurely and was checked by the Germans, so that by the time Weygand put the plan in motion again there was no response from the north. The effect therefore of supplanting Gamelin at this late stage was added confusion: an attack from the north at a time when the complementary attack in the south had been stayed, and consequently no possibility of an attack from the north when the new Commander-in-Chief was ready to give the signal for attack in the south. The German line became unpierceable (if it was not so already) and the Germans were able to consider in comparative leisure how they would complete the campaign. If on 20 May, when they reached the sea, there had been some doubt about whether their victories so far had been decisive, the next few days showed that no effective counter-attack could be launched against them and that, whichever way they turned first, they could outnumber the allied divisions on either front by at least two to one.

THE GERMAN INVASION OF FRANCE AND
THE LOW COUNTRIES MAY–JUNE 1940

Dunkirk 4 June – Final withdrawal 190,000 British and 140,000 French soldiers evacuated.100,000 Allied soldiers taken prisoner.

GERMANY

Rhine

Colmar

Metz

Breached 16 June

Rhine

Cologne

LUXEMBURG

Meuse

HOLLAND
Surrendered 15 May

Maastricht

Meuse

Sedan

Châlons sur Marne

Rotterdam

Antwerp

Dyle

Namur

St.Quentin

Marne

Ghent

Brussels

BELGIUM
Surrendered 28 May

Rheims

Aisne

Ypres

Lille

Arras

FRANCE

Seine

Calais

Abbeville

Somme

Amiens

Paris

Boulogne

Dunkirk

Rouen

Seine

Dieppe

Le Havre

Occupied 14 June

KEY TO GERMAN ADVANCE

10 to 14 May	on 29 May
15 to 24 May	on 30 May
25 to 27 May	31 May to 4 June
on 28 May	5 to 12 June
Siegfried Line	Maginot Line

0   50
Miles

~ARTHUR BANKS~

Yet they were undecided about how to proceed. The allied armies, although disrupted and disjointed, had fought well. The German generals hardly perceived the extent of their triumph. They were anxious to reinforce their forward units and nervous about the large French armies on their southern flank. The first thing to do was to mass their own forces once more. To the south there was need for caution. To the north there was no need for speed since the allied armies were surrounded and the idea that any great number of them could escape by sea entered nobody's head. So after covering 300 miles to reach the Channel in three days the Germans took over three weeks to go another thirty miles up the coast. Rundstedt, although delighted by the dashing successes of his younger subordinates, was taken aback by the speed of his victory, decided not to press his luck too far and ordered his Army Group to halt and regroup.

But Brauchitsch was ready to let the Panzers push on without delay and round up the allied forces to the north, while plans for the subjugation of the rest of France were being worked out. He was angered by Rundstedt's order. On the day of the order, 24 May, Hitler arrived at Rundstedt's headquarters. The plan which, at Manstein's urging, Hitler had adopted early in the year, had emphasized the prior importance of a southward rather than a northward sweep after a break-through. Presumably Hitler still had Manstein's basic reasoning in mind. He endorsed Rundstedt's order and as a result the German armour halted for three days, facing north but motionless. These days were an invaluable respite for the allied armies trapped between the Germans on the Somme and other German armies in Belgium – and the main cause of the salvation of so many men from Dunkirk.

Hitler's motives in blunting his attack on them have been one of the principal enigmas of the war. Among his motives were two different, even contradictory, considerations. Faced with a force which was now mainly British his ambivalence about Great Britain may have reasserted itself. He had no plan for continuing the war against Great Britain and expected it to make peace after France had been beaten. There was nothing to be gained by pounding the British forces on the continent and then incarcerating what was left of them. On the other hand he was under pressure from Goering to leave the rest of this battle to the Luftwaffe. Goering had taken little part in the Battle of France. The Luftwaffe was engaged in close support of the armies; the independent role of Commander-in-Chief of the Luftwaffe had, with the exception of the few days' operations against Holland, been eclipsed. Moreover Goering himself had been suffering from one of his recurrent bouts of drug-taking (to which he had become addicted since drugs had been prescribed for a painful leg wound sustained in the 1923 putsch) and upon emerging from this enforced retreat he was all the more eager for action and distinction. Like Mussolini, he figured that the time was now or never. Although Goering's pleas to leave it to the Luftwaffe and Hitler's political preoccupations with Great Britain could hardly be reconciled, they did have one thing in common: halt the Panzers. That they were stayed by Hitler out of some fellow feeling for the British is implausible and belied by the fact that, although he reined in his tanks, he gave no comparable order to restrain the Luftwaffe from strafing the cornered British.

The allied forces were in a bag round Dunkirk. Boulogne had been lost on 25 May and Calais the next day after a whole day's pounding by artillery, Stukas and tanks. At Dunkirk the evacuation and the Luftwaffe's attacks both began on 27 May. The first results were very discouraging for the beaten troops who, fiercely battered in the town and on the beaches, bitterly reproached the RAF for not protecting them. Then the weather came to their help. With rain half the day on the 29th and fog and rain all day on the 30th the Luftwaffe's onslaughts were restrained and the evacuation rate rose to eight times what it had been on the first day. But on 1 June it turned fine and evacuation by day had to be suspended. By this time the men waiting on the beaches were suffering extreme physical and nervous exhaustion and many of those who got off were sunk in the sea before they reached the other side of the Channel. But in an astonishing rescue operation by large and small craft of every description, by which the British Admiralty had hoped at the outset to save perhaps 100,000 men, more than three times that number – 338,226 – were brought away from Dunkirk.

The Belgian army was forced to lay down its arms soon after the operation began, but many French and other allied combatants escaped with the British (one third of those rescued were not British). The last British troops were taken off on 2 June but the British flotillas returned to collect Frenchmen for two more nights. The Germans were left with 40,000 prisoners. In France a further 190,000, mostly belonging to rear formations, were later evacuated from Normandy and Bordeaux, but an attempt to withdraw the British 51st Division from St Valéry failed, partly because of fog. Altogether over 558,000 (again one third non-British) were evacuated from different parts of the continent into Great Britain. This was a triumph for the British navy and a corresponding defeat for Goering, although the result might have been different if the Luftwaffe had been able to operate at full strength in the Dunkirk area on more days than the weather permitted. Significantly for the future the RAF lost over Dunkirk fewer aircraft than the Luftwaffe. British fighters, flying from bases nearer to the battle area than the German bases, took heavy toll of the Luftwaffe's bombers and Stukas.

On 5 June, the day after the close of the Dunkirk operations, the Germans launched from the Somme–Aisne line a series of attacks to the south which (together with a secondary attack through Alsace) destroyed the French army. They had spent the interval since 20 May debating whether to bring the weight of their armour to the west or east of Paris. The debate serves only to show how unsure the Germans still were about the hard facts of the situation, for in truth it did not much matter which they did. They reached the Seine at various points in three days, entered Paris on 14 June and spread rapidly into the farthest corners of France. The French army fought them – up to the bitter end French units continued to put up tough resistance in spite of the physical and psychological shocks which they had suffered – but was incapable of stopping them. The only conceivable hope of avoiding complete defeat lay with Great Britain. France, defeated and despairing, could no longer rely on itself. It turned to its ally. On the ground the British contribution had always been conceived as ancillary. The British Expeditionary Force might help the French army but could neither be a substitute for it nor rescue it. In the air, however, the British had more to offer. When the campaign opened the RAF committed thirty-nine squadrons to the battle. Ten of these were obsolescent medium bombers which were so badly mauled in daylight operations that they had to be regrouped as six squadrons within a week. The remainder were fighters (including ten Hurricane squadrons) and reconnaissance. The Hurricane force was almost doubled in the next few days but the French government appealed for still more. A first request for ten squadrons was refused. Instead heavy bombers were ordered to attack the Ruhr and then the advancing German armies. On 16 May six more fighter squadrons were detailed to the battle in France, although these aircraft had to operate from bases in Kent. Thenceforward the British squadrons engaged in France were progressively withdrawn to English bases as airfields in France were overrun. By 20 May only a token force remained. On 2 June Reynaud asked for twenty more squadrons, an impossible request. The British government provided a modest reinforcement but as the days passed and it became increasingly clear that Weygand could not turn the tide of battle, the British cabinet had to harden its heart against sending aircraft to France simply to be lost. By 11 June Weygand was himself prophesying the end at any moment. His exhausted divisions were engaged at all points, he had no reserves, and Reynaud's plea for a massive air attack to save the day was painfully unrealistic.

THE FALL OF FRANCE JUNE 1940

North Sea

GREAT BRITAIN

HOLLAND

GERMANY

BELGIUM

Dunkirk

Boulogne

Somme

English Channel

Cherbourg

Le Havre

Rouen

Aisne

Reims

Châlons

MAGINOT LINE

Brest

Seine

PARIS

Rennes

Alençon

Orléans

Belfort

Angers

Loire

Tours

Dijon

SWITZ.

Nantes

14 June German troops enter Paris.

Cher

Nevers

Saône

VICHY

Geneva

Bay of Biscay

Angoulême

Limoges

Clermont Ferrand

Lyons

Isère

Grenoble

ITALY

Bordeaux

New seat of Government.

Rhône

Garonne

Nice

Toulouse

Marseilles

Perpignan

Toulon

SPAIN

Mediterranean Sea

German advances.

Position of German armies when Armistice was signed on 22 June.

Vichy France.

0   100

Miles

~ARTHUR BANKS~

Churchill had seen for himself the writing on the wall as early as 16 May when he made the first of five visits to France during the campaign. On that first visit he heard Gamelin's gloomy assessment and observed his gloomy mien. Outside the conference room old men with wheelbarrows were burning secret papers. Churchill faced the unexpected horror of the total collapse of his only ally. A week later, on his second visit, Churchill found that the dejected Gamelin had been replaced by Weygand but only a few days later Gort abandoned all thought of an offensive and decided to withdraw the entire British Expeditionary Force to the coast; Churchill's third visit on the last day of May took place during the fighting at Dunkirk. By the time he returned again on 11 June Great Britain had no troops on the continent, Italy had entered the war, the French government had left Paris and the meeting had to take place at Briare on the Loire. Two days later the last of these meetings was held at Tours, where the government was bivouacking on its flight to the south with Ministries and Embassies dispersed in old châteaux round about.

Churchill was throughout fervently anxious to do everything possible for France and keep it in the war. Fighting the Germans without a continental ally would pose huge new problems. In addition, Churchill's generous impulses urged him now, as they urged him later on over convoys to the USSR, to go to the brink of what was wise and practicable in order to help an ally. But other voices counselled otherwise. During May and June the Air Staff became more and more alarmed about losses in France. Scarce and precious Hurricanes were being lost at the rate of twenty-five a day when the factories were delivering new ones at the rate of four a day. At one moment the Commander-in-Chief of Fighter Command, Air Marshal Sir Hugh Dowding, went so far as to say that he could not answer for the defence of Great Britain and would resign if more fighters were committed to the battle in France. By the time of Churchill's last two visits to France the real question was not how to help in that battle but what terms to try to exact before agreeing to France's inevitable surrender.

At Tours Churchill refused to release France from its promise not to make a separate peace. He promised that there would be no recrimination and that Great Britain would, in victory, see that France recovered its full dignity and greatness if it fought on. But Reynaud's cabinet reshuffle of 19 May – a move which he came to regret – had put too many doves among the hawks. Pétain, supported by Weygand and some of the civilian members of the cabinet, was in favour of giving up the fight. They had no hope for themselves and no belief that Great Britain could do anything to help them. On 15 June, with the Germans now in Paris and the French government in Bordeaux, Reynaud proposed that the French army should lay down its arms (as the Dutch had done) but that the government should remain at war and move, with the fleet and air force, to North Africa. The generals and their supporters expressed horror at this idea which would cast the whole odium of defeat on the army. Besides, the losses suffered at the beginning of the campaign made it possible to argue that there was nothing left to carry on with. The Under Secretary for War, Charles de Gaulle, supported Reynaud and those civilian members of the cabinet still anxious to fight on. De Gaulle had earlier urged Reynaud to move his government to Quimper in Brittany rather than Bordeaux in the hope that this could be a first step to a further move overseas and a refusal to surrender. Reynaud's proposal was approved by a majority of the cabinet but the Prime Minister hesitated, unwilling to insist on a course disapproved by the generals. He hoped that by the next day Pétain could be persuaded to talk Weygand round. Instead Pétain resigned.

When the cabinet met again on the 16th Reynaud had received from Churchill Great Britain's consent to Franco-German armistice negotiations on condition that the French fleet should first sail to British ports; Churchill also urged safe passage for Polish and Czechoslovak troops to Africa. But at the last moment de Gaulle telephoned to Reynaud a new proposal from Churchill for the continuation of the war on the basis of a Franco-British political union and common citizenship after the war and a pledge of total British support. This strange plan, which would have revived the abortive union effected by Henry V by the treaty of Troyes in 1420, seems to have been devised by French and British officials, notably Jean Monnet and Arnold Toynbee with the support of Lord Vansittart. It was regarded by most of the French cabinet as irrelevant to France's plight. Perhaps the British cabinet, in endorsing the plan, anticipated the French reaction, for had it been otherwise Great Britain might have found itself committed to military actions which would have lost the war as well as to a political course which would have baffled the British people. Reynaud, upon seeing that the argument among his colleagues was going against the idea, resigned that day (the 16th). Pétain took his place, formed a new government during the ensuing night and immediately sued through Spain for an armistice. But the fighting went on for another six days and so did the talk about moving to Africa. Preparations were made to transport Ministers, members of parliament and others, but nobody actually gave the word to go and so in the end nobody went – except as refugees. The opponents of the idea kept the Germans informed about what was going on and urged them to produce acceptable armistice terms as quickly as possible. After a preliminary meeting between Hitler and Mussolini at Munich terms were presented. They were accepted after what was virtually an ultimatum requiring unconditional French acceptance and on 22 June at Compiègne, surrounded by the memories and even part of the furniture of the armistice scene of 1918, France signed. Two days later a separate agreement was signed with Italy which, in one of the cheapest and least exhilarating conquests of modern times, acquired Nice and part of the Savoy.

Ten days after the signing of the armistice of Compiègne Great Britain took drastic action against the French fleet. The fall of France threatened the naval balance in the Mediterranean. Together the French and British fleets had dominated that sea. Without a French ally, and with other seas to command as well, Great Britain faced a serious Italian challenge. Although marginally superior in battleships (seven against six) and possessing two aircraft carriers against none, the British Mediterranean fleet was significantly outnumbered in cruisers and destroyers. Italy had the largest submarine fleet in the world and ten land-based aircraft for every one which the RAF could spare for the Mediterranean theatre. If, in addition, the French fleet actively joined the war on the Axis side Great Britain might well be swept from the Mediterranean.

The armistice terms originally provided for the recall of all French ships to French metropolitan ports where they were to be demobilized under German or Italian supervision – Germany undertaking not to use them except for coastal defence and mine-sweeping. The French negotiators wished to secure the right to demobilize their vessels in colonial ports and on this issue the Germans proved not unrelenting – presumably because their control over ships in distant ports was in any event limited. The armistice terms were amended to provide for demobilization in any port outside that part of France which the Germans proposed to occupy. But the fate of the French fleet was of such cardinal importance to Great Britain that the British government decided that it must be placed permanently beyond German clutches or be destroyed.

Admiral Darlan had ordered his captains on 24 June to ensure that their vessels should in no circumstances fall into German hands, but the British did not grasp the full significance of this signal, which was made available to them only in abbreviated form. Some French ships were in British ports and these were painlessly disarmed; others were in French waters; but most were in African harbours – Alexandria, Bizerta, Mers-el-Kebir (Oran), Algiers, Casablanca, Dakar. At Alexandria diplomatic interchanges between the British and French admirals resulted in the disarming of the ships by the French themselves, but in the western Mediterranean the issue was decided by gunfire. Admiral Gensoul's force at

Mers-el-Kebir included two of the most powerful capital ships afloat, *Strasbourg* and *Dunquerque*. On 3 July Admiral Somerville delivered to Gensoul an ultimatum giving him four choices: to join Great Britain in the war, to sail with reduced crews and under British control to internment in a British port, to sail under British escort for demilitarization in a French Caribbean port or to United States custody, or to scuttle within six hours. Somerville told Gensoul that if he refused all four courses the British would use whatever force might be necessary to prevent the French ships from falling into German hands. Somerville was empowered to accept a French proposal, if it were made to him, to demilitarize the ships where they were provided this could be done in six hours and under his supervision and in such a way as to keep them out of service for at least a year even at a fully equipped dockyard. This last proposition was not known to Gensoul.

When Gensoul received these terms his fleet was already almost under British fire and, affronted by this manoeuvre, he told the French Admiralty only about the fourth choice put to him. The Admiralty promised to send help. Some hours later Gensoul proposed to Somerville to demilitarize his ships at Mers-el-Kebir and, if threatened by the Germans or Italians, to sail for Martinique or the United States; he said that the disembarkation of crews had already begun. But the day was wearing on and Somerville, who had been instructed to bring matters to a conclusion before nightfall, shortly afterwards opened fire. Action was broken off but then renewed when *Strasbourg* put to sea. *Strasbourg* and twelve other vessels made good their escape to Toulon. *Dunquerque* went aground. Two other battleships were disabled. Nearly 1,300 Frenchmen were killed.

In the Caribbean French ships were damaged and put out of action for the rest of the war. At Dakar in West Africa the battleship *Richelieu* was slightly damaged but played a part in thwarting an expedition by British and Gaullist forces in September. This venture, based on faulty intelligence about the inclinations of the local French authorities who had opted for Vichy, began with an attempt by a few Gaullists who were landed in two light aircraft and one motorboat to talk the authorities into changing sides. When this mission failed the supporting British naval force began a two-day bombardment which was then abandoned because the French did not give in at once. They were, as it happened, about to do so when the attack was stopped and the attackers sailed away.

These episodes, although minor ones in the retrospect of the history of the war, planted a sting in Anglo-French relations which was to endure for a generation. Great Britain, so it seemed to many Frenchmen, acted at the time of France's abasement to take away from France all that the

Germans had left to be taken – its navy and its colonies. But for Great Britain the immobilization of the French fleet was as necessary as the evacuation from Dunkirk to enable the war to be carried on from the British Isles themselves and in the Mediterranean.

The collapse of France in 1940 was first and foremost a military defeat although, as we shall see in a later chapter, there was more to it than that. The French forces were badly equipped, badly trained and badly led. They had not been modernized after the First World War because the military and political chiefs of the Third Republic had based their policies more on hope than on preparation. They had hoped after 1919 that Germany had been as much sickened by war as France and would not start another one, and later they had postponed rearmament and re-equipment because post-depression economics gave them an added reason for doing so. In the vital sectors of tanks and aircraft, industry was producing too many types and too few machines. French tanks were too lightly armoured to survive and their tactics were obsolete. The air force had adopted a modernization plan in 1934 but four years later, when the Czech crisis came, its first line strength was below 1,400 (half the size of the Luftwaffe) and only one in ten of these aircraft belonged to the 1934 programme. Transport, clothing and light weapons were all in short supply, although nobody could say exactly how short. Commanders from Gamelin downwards were paralysed by a well-founded pessimism. In the circumstances the French forces fought surprisingly well.

The defeat of France was the high-water mark of the German army – and something more. The Germans had beaten the French as easily as they had beaten the Poles. From one angle these were two separate examples of the superiority of German arms. But the two events did not strike contemporaries that way. The defeat of Poland was no surprise. Nobody expected the Poles to hold the German army for long. Theirs was a much smaller, much less up to date and much less skilful force. But the French army was one of the great armies of the world and France itself stood – if any single country could be said so to stand – as the embodiment of western civilization. The fall of France was much more than a military decision. It was a portentous distortion of history, all the more shattering because its completeness led nearly everybody to suppose that it was final and irreversible: the post-war resurrection of France and its re-emergence as one of the few countries in the world capable of conducting an independent foreign policy and as a nuclear power were in 1940 all but inconceivable. Whereas the defeat of Poland had been a tragedy which further shifted the balance of power in Europe Hitler's way, the fall of France opened an abyss of uncertainty for the whole continent and shook the imagination as perhaps nothing had shaken it since the victory of the Turks at Mohacs in 1526.

CHAPTER 7

The Battle of Britain

THE defeat of France reduced hostilities in Europe to a single point, the Anglo-German fight. In Great Britain some people felt that the war was over, though not many cared to say so. When a French collapse began to seem inevitable the British cabinet discussed whether to invoke Mussolini as a mediator between Hitler and the two western allies. In the period between Hitler's Polish campaign and his attacks in the west, Churchill had been willing to contemplate a negotiated peace (but with a Prime Minister other than himself). Now he opposed such a move. The cabinet was divided. Chamberlain, Halifax and others favoured an appeal to Mussolini, and Halifax may have threatened to resign if Churchill insisted on obstructing a negotiated return to peace. The issue was resolved by leaving it to the French government to invoke Mussolini on its own, should it so wish. Churchill has been criticized for his obduracy at this point but it is difficult to believe that Hitler would have entertained proposals for peace when he was on the verge of a resounding triumph, or that Mussolini would have invited a snub by trying to interfere. Churchill's character and temperament told against a compromise peace and his gifts infused the British spirit and confirmed a latent feeling that, although the fighting had so far been disastrous, Hitler was so wicked an enemy that peace with him would be dishonourable. Disgust with the barbarities of Nazism kept the British at war under a new leader who was himself pugnacious enough in spirit to shoulder the miseries and scent the triumphs to come.

Hitler more than half hoped that Great Britain would make peace. On 19 July he made a speech which, in his eyes at least, amounted to a peace offer, but its tone and tenor were very ill adapted to any such purpose and it was brushed off by Churchill. As after the defeat of Poland Hitler had ready no precise plan of what to do next. He was half-hearted about attacking Great Britain. He wanted not to conquer it but to ensure that it would let him have his way on the continent. Moreover Great Britain was not only an island fortress but also a Mediterranean power, so that a continuing war could oblige Hitler to campaign against British bases and routes in the Mediterranean, to occupy or at least control the whole of France and Spain, and to put German forces into North Africa. War on this scale would be something very different from the *Blumenkriege* and *Blitzkriege* which he had fought so successfully on the continent. Great Britain was the wrong kind of enemy for the German armed forces, and Hitler, who liked short sharp operations with discernible ends, could not see where such a war might take him. On the other hand Great Britain unsubdued was a thorn in the German side, and so long as the British Isles remained in the war there was a danger that they might become a base for a new war between Germany and the United States. Although the German army could not march into England as it had marched into other countries, the German navy might blockade and starve the British, or the German air force might pound them into submission or destroy their defences and so let the army in.

A naval strategy entailed submarine warfare supplemented by commerce raiding by surface vessels and the mining of coastal waters. But Hitler had neglected his navy, partly because he was not much interested in it and partly because he never wholeheartedly faced up to the possibility of a fight to the finish with Great Britain. At the outbreak of war the German surface fleet consisted of two antiquated and Baltic-bound battleships, three pocket battleships, two battle cruisers, eight cruisers, twenty-two destroyers and as many torpedo-boats and E-boats. In the Norwegian expedition three cruisers and nine destroyers were sunk and two cruisers and one destroyer were damaged. These losses were never made good, although two new battleships and a cruiser – *Bismarck, Tirpitz* and *Prinz Eugen* – were commissioned in 1941. The submarine fleet was quite inadequate. On the outbreak of war Admiral Doenitz, the supreme U-boat commander, had only fifty-seven ocean-going boats and, although he made good use of what he had, no prospect whatever of fulfilling his hope of having 300 boats at sea at a time; normally the striking force would consist of one in three – or, at best and for short periods, one in two – of the total force. The British navy, although hardly less antiquated, was much larger.

The alternative to a naval blockade was an air offensive designed either to make Great Britain capitulate under the sheer weight and terror of bombing or to clear the way for an invasion by destroying the air defences of Great Britain, especially its fighter squadrons. This was what Hitler and Goering tried to do and, in the two months from mid-July to mid-September 1940, failed to achieve.

The renown of the Luftwaffe after the campaigns of 1939 and the first half of 1940 was prodigious and its morale was excellent. Officially it was only five years old since the treaty of Versailles had denied Germany an air force and none had been acknowledged until 1935. But the reality was different. The prohibition was evaded in a number of ways. Aircraft designers were sent to work in other countries and German aircraft types were developed in the USSR, Sweden and elsewhere. The commercial airline *Lufthansa* was used to train men, to test machines and above all to keep alive the experience and the spirit of airmanship built up during the First World War.

The principal fashioners of the Luftwaffe were Erhard Milch and Ernst Udet – together with Walther Wever, whose early death in 1936 deprived the Luftwaffe of the heavy bomber force which he alone among the three believed in. Milch was the organization man who created an aircraft industry behind the scenes, supervised the development of new types of aircraft, and used *Lufthansa* (of which he was chairman), weekend flying clubs and foreign factories and bases to make Germany a first-class air power. He became a friend of Goering, who appointed him to take charge of the Air Ministry in March 1935 when the Luftwaffe's existence was officially revealed. It was largely thanks to Milch that the Luftwaffe sprang into existence with over 1,000 aircraft, 20,000 men and the not implausible ambition of achieving parity with the Russians by growing to 4,000 aircraft by 1939–40.

But Milch and Goering fell out; probably Milch became jealous of Goering, while Goering found Milch a bore. The result was a rise in the influence of Udet and a shift in policy. Udet was lively to the point of instability – he committed suicide in 1941 – but he was no organizer and lacked Milch's capacity to get things done. He was interested in fighters and dive-bombers rather than bombers and can claim some of the credit for the appearance in 1938 of the single-seater Messerschmitt (Me.) 109E, an excellent aircraft with good manoeuvrability and an armament of four machine guns or, alternatively, two machine guns and two cannon. Udet also set his faith in the Junkers (Ju.) 87 Stuka or dive-bomber, a fearsome aircraft which dived on its target at 200 m.p.h. in order to drop its two bombs with special precision and with the added psychological effect to be derived from fitting screaming devices and painting sharks' faces on the nose of the aircraft: but it was slow and had a low ceiling and so was better at attacking refugees in open country than at surviving anti-aircraft fire or enemy fighter attacks. It was successful against shipping so long as ships' anti-aircraft guns were poor, as they tended to be at the beginning of the war, but after its successes in the continental land battles the Ju. 87 suffered severely at the hands of British ground and air defences and had to be virtually withdrawn from the battle. Udet, finally, neglected the heavy bomber. Plans for two four-engined bombers like the British Stirlings, Halifaxes and Lancasters were dropped in the mid-thirties and a third – the Heinkel (He.) 177, originally designed as a long-range reconnaissance aircraft – failed to hold Udet's interest when he discovered that this huge machine could not be made to dive. Thus Germany entered the war and fought it with fast, lightly protected medium bombers – the He. 111 and Dornier (Do.) 217, supplemented from 1940 by the Ju. 88 – which were very vulnerable in daylight unless heavily escorted by fighters. But the Me. 109E was not right for this work and had not been designed for it. It was short in range and endurance – its range was 100–125 miles and its endurance about one and a half hours – and the combination of a fighter of this kind with medium bombers was the wrong recipe for the Battle of Britain. The Luftwaffe's long-range fighter, the Me. 110, was something of a disappointment and had to be relegated to night fighting and light bombing; its failure meant that German bombers operating beyond the south-east corner of England had to do so unescorted.

In the Spanish civil war a force of 400 German aircraft – the Kondor Legion – practised bombing and mobility under war conditions and tested new types, all with gratifying results. At the time of Munich the Luftwaffe had a front line strength of 2,800 (it was believed to be stronger) and a year later, on the outbreak of the World War, its front line strength had passed the 4,000 mark. Its reserves, however, were low because the war was expected to be short. The RAF's front line strength in September 1939 was 1,660 but its reserves were proportionately more than twice as large as the Luftwaffe's and, more significant, British aircraft production was rising the faster. It did not, however, overtake German production until it passed the thousand a month mark in the spring of 1940 and so began at that point to close the gap. The French air force had, on paper, a first line strength slightly above Great Britain's but poor reserves and an even more alarming degree of obsolescence.

In the Polish campaign the Luftwaffe committed less than half its front line strength: 700 long-range bombers, 400 fighters, 150 Stukas and 350 reconnaissance aircraft. Besides bombing Warsaw, they were used chiefly to attack Polish airfields and army communications and they met little effective opposition from an enemy who had out-of-date fighters and no radar or other early warning system. The force used in Norway was less than half that used in Poland. Its tasks were to attack enemy shipping, patrol and protect German units at sea, and convey small parachute detachments to seize Norwegian airfields. These tasks were performed efficiently and, as in Poland, with very little loss in spite of atrocious weather. For the Luftwaffe the Norwegian campaign was a cross between a real war and a training exercise, and an opportunity to introduce the Ju. 88 bomber into active service for the first time. The attack on the Low

Countries and France was much more serious and varied work. Practically the whole of the Luftwaffe's front line strength was involved and for six weeks it averaged 1,500 sorties a day. In Holland parachutists were used in large numbers for the first time, capturing Rotterdam airport in the face of tough Dutch opposition. After the surrender of the Dutch the weight of the German air effort went into the support of the German army against the French army and against the British in Belgium. Airfields and factories were also attacked but the role of the Luftwaffe was first and foremost army cooperation. Only after the disintegration of the French ground forces was certain did the German bombers operate seriously against French railways, harbours and towns. The sole check to the Luftwaffe's easy superiority was in its encounters with the RAF over Dunkirk. This was symptomatic.

There was at this time still no way of measuring the effects of the heavy air bombardment of a defended target. The Germans had wiped out Guernica in Spain and had bombed Warsaw and Rotterdam, but against virtually no opposition. It appeared that the real test would come in Great Britain. In the event German bombing never came near to the point of winning the war by destroying the British economy or morale. The Second World War showed that this could not be done before the development of nuclear weapons. But air forces continued to believe that it might be. So did civilian defenders. In London committees had been set up many years before the war to estimate the probable weight and effects of bombing. They came to the conclusion that Great Britain must expect 3,500 tons of bombs in the first twenty-four hours of war, followed by a further 700 tons a day, each ton causing fifty or more casualties – that is to say, nearly two million casualties in the first two months. The material damage, which commercial insurance companies refused to underwrite on any terms, was put at £550 million in the first three weeks, and this apocalyptic vision of the triumph of Belial included the need to evacuate three quarters of the population of London and bury corpses in their thousands in quick-lime, and to witness the complete collapse of communications and other public services, panic, epidemics and three to four million cases of mental breakdown in six months. These forebodings, so unlike the contents of the usual government paper, were carefully concealed from the public. They were also very wide of the mark, for over the whole course of the war casualties per ton of bombs dropped in Great Britain were under twenty and totalled 60,000 dead and 86,000 seriously and 149,000 slightly injured.

Even had it been technically possible for an air force to inflict in 1940 the sort of damage which the planners of the thirties feared, the German air force had not been designed primarily for that function. Its heavy bombing arm was, as we have seen, the least developed and the Luftwaffe – paradoxically, in view of its status as an independent service – was built up as a partner of the army rather than as an independent force which was going to win wars on its own. The bombing of British military or civilian targets in order to wreck production or break morale was therefore only one way of approaching the problem of how to defeat Great Britain, and not the obvious way. The alternative – assuming that the slow process of blockade and starvation were rejected – was a combined operation in which the Luftwaffe would begin by nullifying the R A F and would then, with the navy, cover the transport of the German army into England. What actually happened was something between the two: a projected invasion in force preceded by an independent onslaught by the Luftwaffe which oscillated between the attempt to destroy Great Britain's Fighter Command and heavy assaults on centres of production and population. Since the Luftwaffe's attack failed, the invasion never took place.

The idea of an invasion was popular in army circles but nowhere else. The navy regarded an invasion as almost impossibly risky. Raeder's conditions were control of the air, the right weather and an attempt no later than the autumnal equinox. The navy regarded the army's requests for naval protection for its vast and lumbering armadas against the Royal Navy as grotesquely unreal, although the naval staff was not very successful in conveying this appreciation to the army staff. The Luftwaffe was not so much hostile as uninterested. Goering and his principal lieutenants hardly troubled to reply to memoranda or attend conferences about it. Hitler himself was half involved, half aloof. He so far responded to the enthusiasm generated by the army staff as to order plans and preparations and he may have hoped that the navy's precondition would be met by the Luftwaffe's separate operations. Men were assigned and trained; barges, tugs and other craft were assembled. There was a great deal of exercising and (often contradictory) paper work. Hitler kept all the options open, including retreat. He was sceptical but also serious. He would have been delighted to finish off the war in the west this way but never confident that he could do so and therefore prepared both to give it a try and to abandon it if it did not work.

The first plan for a landing, produced by the army staff in December 1939, aimed at the east coast. After cutting naval criticism this idea was abandoned in favour of landings at a series of points along almost the entire south coast. The navy consistently argued that the only feasible operation, if any, was one concentrated in the south-east where the waters were narrowest. The first directive to prepare an invasion was issued by Hitler on 17 July 1940. It prescribed that the RAF must first be reduced to insignificance, that all minefields be cleared and that the Royal Navy be kept at a distance in northern waters or the Mediterranean. If these circumstances were met the army proposed to put ashore 260,000 men in three days, assemble a force of eleven divisions in two weeks and bring Great Britain to surrender in a month. Landings would take place along three stretches of coast between Folkestone and Brighton to the accompaniment of feints against Scotland and Iceland to distract the Royal Navy. The SS would follow with a list of 2,700 persons to be incarcerated, and a special booklet was prepared for the use of the six SS commanders and their staffs who were to extinguish opposition (including the Boy Scouts who were thought to be an arm of British Intelligence). The invasion fleets moved from their assembly points to their departure stations in the first days of September, but in these same days the RAF was thwarting the Luftwaffe in what Churchill had already christened the Battle of Britain.

In July 1940 Generals Kesselring and Sperrle, commanding *Luftflotten* 2 and 3 in Belgium and northern France, and General Stumpf, commanding *Luftflotte* 5 in Denmark and Norway, had a front line strength of around 3,000 aircraft, including some 1,400 long-range bombers, 300 dive-bombers, 800 single-engined fighters and 280 twin-engined fighters or fighter bombers. Of this force 2,500 aircraft at most were serviceable and ready for action at the beginning of the battle. In the engagements which followed, Kesselring and Sperrle could on a normal day put up 800 long-range bombers and 820 fighters. On the other side the Royal Air Force had emerged from the Battle of France with less damage than might have been the case if Dowding and Churchill had not hardened their hearts against sending more fighters to help the French. (Half of those sent were lost. The RAF's losses between 10 May and 20 June were 944. They were made good by mid-July but pilot losses were not. Milch wanted to invade Great Britain on the tail of the Dunkirk retreat.) Morale was undented by the fall of France and leadership from Dowding downwards excellent. The RAF's front line strength on the eve of the Battle of Britain was 1,200. It included 800 Hurricane and Spitfire single-seater fighters, of which 660 were operational, and in this sphere the British were roughly equal in numbers to the units opposed to them. Reserves were healthy, production good and expanding but there was only a narrow margin of trained pilots. This weakness was a worrying one, for although one new aircraft was as good as the machine it replaced, a new pilot was not the equal of an experienced one. On the other hand the R A F saved many more of its pilots than did the Luftwaffe since the former could bale out over their own territory and return to the fight, whereas most of the German pilots in the like case became prisoners of war.

The Hurricane and Spitfire, with their eight guns apiece, had the best single-engined fighter armament in the world – thanks largely to Squadron Leader R. S. Sorley and to Dowding. They could destroy an enemy bomber with a two-second burst. Sorley had been so impressed by the mock-up of the Hurricane that he tried, unsuccessfully, to get it put into production before it had flown. The prototype of the Hurricane first flew in 1935 and by the outbreak of war 578 had been made (by the middle of 1940 1,747). The Spitfire, which first flew a year later than the Hurricane, began to reach the service three months before Munich and nine squadrons had been formed by the outbreak of war when 299 had been made (by the middle of 1940 809). At one point during the Battle of Britain reserves of Spitfires fell to thirty-eight but at no time did the Command ask in vain for replacements of this or any other type of aircraft. On the eve of the battle fighter production was verging on 500 a month, which was considerably higher than German fighter production or some German estimates of British production. (Goering thought that British production of all types was only 300.)

Besides this force Great Britain relied for its defence on an early warning system of revolutionary and decisive importance. It was based on radar or, as it was at first called in Great Britain, R D F – Radio Direction Finding – a method for detecting the position of distant objects by the reflection of radio rays. Without radar too many bombers would have got through. After the First World War the problem of how to stop the bomber was acute. Some despaired of solving it. Others examined desperate remedies like the death ray, an attempt to find ways of killing enemy aircrews by (for example) suddenly raising their blood to boiling point, or ways of stopping their engines by radio transmissions. No death ray was ever invented but from 1934 radar was developed by a number of men, including in particular Professors Henry Tizard, A. V. Hill and P. M. S. Blackett; H. E. Wimperis, a civilian engineer who was given a post at the Air Ministry; and Robert Watson-Watt of the Radio Research Laboratory. (Considerable discord was introduced into the research and its application when Professor F. A. Lindemann, later Lord Cherwell, was injected into the work on the insistence of Churchill who, although not in the government, had been made privy to these and other secret matters. Lindemann was neither liked nor highly regarded by many of his fellow scientists. He was wholeheartedly anxious to give of his best for the defence of the country but he tended to treat research as a branch of politics. His day came when Churchill became Prime Minister. He was one of Churchill's closest advisers.) A chain of fifty-one radar stations was built round the coast. Although still incomplete, it was brought into continuous operation in the spring of 1939 and it was later supplemented by a second chain specially designed to detect low-flying aircraft. As early as 1936 Tizard suggested that very small radar sets could be made to go into aircraft and help fighter pilots to find and destroy enemy bombers at night.

Supplementing the radar system was the Observer Corps which, armed with binoculars, manned a network of posts which spotted aircraft as soon as they came within sight or hearing. There were a thousand of these posts. They and the radar stations were connected by telephone with an operations room, to which they transmitted their estimates of the positions, speeds, heights, numbers and directions of all aircraft within their ken, and this information was plotted on large tables by counters which were moved across the table as the information came in. Orders to aircraft, whether waiting on the ground or airborne in search of the enemy, were given by Controllers watching these tables day and night. Radar and the Observer Corps relieved Fighter Command of the need to keep forces on permanent patrol in the air in order to be able to engage the enemy and avoid destruction on the ground. The Controller in the operations room, watching the plots coming in every few seconds and knowing that the aircraft represented were no more than 12–20 miles ahead of the position shown, could order his aircraft off the ground in time and direct them on the right course at the right height until the pilots could see the enemy with their own eyes (or, in later battles, with the radar devices in their cockpits). In the operations room hours of watchful, almost motionless routine would be suddenly broken when a girl in uniform placed a small arrow on the edge of the table which, if it did not turn out to be an atmospheric freak or a flock of geese, was the prelude to action – down below the drama of tenseness combined with the efficiency of techniques mastered by familiarity; up above the more fearful drama of the duel as the pilots cast around them for the enemy and then pitted against him their flying skills and their marksmanship. The Germans knew about radar but underrated its value to the defence of Great Britain.

The preliminary phase of the Battle of Britain was an attempt by the Luftwaffe, beginning on 10 July, to establish local air supremacy over the straits of Dover. Attacks on shipping still using this passage were used as a dress rehearsal to test the tactics and capacities of Fighter Command before proceeding to the main purposes of enticing it into a major battle in order to destroy it. By the end of the month the advantage lay with the RAF which had lost 150 aircraft (promptly replaced) to 286 lost by the Luftwaffe. On the other hand this initial success gave little indication of the ultimate result since the RAF had to husband its strength after its losses in France and could not afford a steady drain of aircraft, whether or not German losses were higher. In the second week of August the Luftwaffe began to attack Fighter Command's airfields and operations rooms with the intention of crippling it on the ground or provoking it into a major battle in which it would be destroyed in the air. Owing to bad weather the Luftwaffe was unable to keep up its attacks on consecutive days and again in this phase the Luftwaffe's losses were the greater – 290 aircraft to 114. In the main battle of this phase, on 15 August, the losses on the German and British sides were 75 and 34. Attacks on shipping continued, chiefly with Ju. 87s which suffered so severely that they virtually disappeared from front line operations. After a pause between 19 and 23 August the attack on Fighter Command was resumed in combination with secondary night attacks on cities. This phase, which lasted until 6 September, opened well for the Luftwaffe but was not decisive. The British suffered heavy damage on the ground. Fighter Command's No. 11 Group, covering London and south-east England, had six of its seven sector (or main control) airfields seriously damaged and five of its forward stations put out of action. One sector headquarters, Biggin Hill, had its operations room and all its communications wrecked. Further blows of this kind would have exposed London to great danger and would have forced upon Fighter Command a change in tactics (owing to the disruption of ground control) which might have overstrained its resources. But except on one day German losses of aircraft of all types exceeded British losses and by the end of this phase German losses were approaching 1,000 while Great Britain's were 550. On the other hand, in fighters alone the RAF's losses were greater and although by the end of the month the RAF was making more sorties per day than the Luftwaffe, fighter losses were beginning to exceed current production and the pilot situation was becoming a grave worry.

Although Great Britain's defences were severely tested during this phase the Luftwaffe failed to take a step which could have strained them even more severely. On direct orders from Goering it gave up attacking radar stations. Goering may have underrated the vital significance of these stations. He certainly underrated the possibility of putting them out of action. Their slim masts were not an ideal target for aircraft and nobody on the German side noticed that one of them – at Ventnor on the Isle of

Wight – had been knocked out by a raid which left delayed-action bombs lying on the site. This was one of the more notable failures of Intelligence during the whole war. The radar screen continued to function almost without interruption throughout the Battle of Britain. German attempts to jam it were too primitive to impair it to any significant degree.

A second major error on the German side occurred at the beginning of September when the mounting attack on Fighter Command was abandoned in favour of attacks on London and other cities. It is impossible to be sure of the chief reason for this switch. Both sides enormously exaggerated enemy losses and on the German side the inflated figures were taken to mean that Fighter Command and fighter production had been virtually eliminated from the battle. Kesselring, though not Sperrle, shared the view of the Air Staff that the battle was won. In addition both Hitler and Goering had been stung by British bombing raids into retaliating against British cities. On 25 August, and thereafter on a number of nights, Bomber Command raided Berlin. The first of these raids was itself a retaliation for the first German raid on London which was itself a mistake – so that the German bomber offensive which began on 7 September was in a sense a consequence of a German error. (The first raid by either side on a town had taken place on 10–11 May when the British attacked München Gladbach, a few miles west of Düsseldorf.) The British raids on Berlin did little material damage but they had enormous psychological effect. They were a great surprise. Neither the Nazi leaders nor the people of Berlin thought that Great Britain was in a position to do anything of the kind, and the former had expressly assured the latter that they could not. The answer was to attack London. An afternoon attack on 7 September was followed by another raid that night. The damage was very heavy and a thousand people were killed. This daylight raid was not repeated and the next night raid did not come until four nights later, but the attack was then renewed.

In Germany hopes rose high. The invasion craft moved to their action stations. On 11 September Churchill broadcast an invasion warning. But the day before Hitler had – for the second time – postponed the day for taking the decision whether to order the invasion or not. He would decide on the 14th. When the 14th came he postponed the date again and on the 15th – the final major engagement of the Battle of Britain took place. In the course of two battles in the morning and afternoon the German bombers suffered heavily (they lost sixty aircraft that day, the R A F lost twenty-six fighters) and the German fighters again failed to win the clear victory that they had been seeking for so many weeks. Two days later, on

17 September, Hitler called off the invasion by postponing the day of decision indefinitely. In October, when the Italians arrived to take part in the air battle, it was over. By the middle of that month the barges and other transports had all melted away. The Luftwaffe turned to night bombing of London and other cities. The famous raid on Coventry took place on 14 November. (Post-war stories to the effect that this raid was known of in advance from Ultra intelligence, and that these warnings were ignored in order not to jeopardize that source, have been scotched.) With radar not yet developed for night defence the Luftwaffe was able to cause serious damage at comparatively small cost to itself until the preparations for Barbarossa took the bulk of the bombers to the east, but once more Great Britain was able to fend off part of the attack by its technological skill. The German bombers were directed on to their targets by radio beams, flying along one beam until an intersecting beam told them that they were over the target, but British scientists quickly discovered how to jam the beacons transmitting the beams and so cause many German bombs to be dropped in the wrong place – preferably of course in open country but sometimes on an unintended target, as for instance when Dublin was bombed by a German force which had been making for Belfast.

Losses can be computed in different ways. No precise figure is unchallengeable. But, taking the Battle of Britain to have lasted from 12 August to the last day of September, the Luftwaffe may be said to have lost in operations over 1,100 aircraft of all types (not 2,698 as the British claimed at the time). The defence of Great Britain cost Fighter Command about 650 aircraft (not 3,058 as the Germans believed).

The reasons for the Luftwaffe's failure were various. Its previous triumphs were to some extent delusive. They had been won in the role of army support and not in combat with an enemy air force, and the handling of the Luftwaffe in this role had necessarily been governed in practice by the strategy of the army command. Having taken little or no part in the battles in France Goering took charge during the Battle of Britain with the enthusiasm of one who feels that his moment has come. It might have gone better for the Luftwaffe if he had not, for he must take the greater part of the blame for the Luftwaffe's ill-considered switching from one strategy and one set of targets to another. To some extent this mistake may be ascribed to bad intelligence. The gross overestimates of casualties made by both sides were more damaging to the attackers than the defenders. The German higher command, ignorant of the continuing powers of resistance of Fighter Command, made wrong decisions. Similar mistakes by the British were of less consequence, since the RAF's role was

to go on resisting in any case. But there were two other and more important reasons for the Luftwaffe's loss of the battle. The first was that it did
not have enough fighters. Of 1,050 fighters stationed in France and Belgium 800 were Me. 109s, excellent aircraft but not ideal for close escort
work and not numerous enough to provide adequate cover for bombers
on daylight missions which, ideally, required at least two fighters for every
bomber. The bomber squadrons in Norway and Denmark had no single-
engined fighter escort and only a small protecting force of twin-engined
Me. 110s. This secondary force in Scandinavia was intended by the
German Air Staff to split Fighter Command's effort by attacks on north-
eastern England, but only one such attack was made during the Battle of
Britain and the Me. 110s proved in general insufficiently manoeuvrable
for the role of bomber protection. Consequently the German commanders
found themselves in a constant dilemma, since every strengthening of the
fighter escort which they provided for their bombers reduced the number
of fighters available to engage the British fighters. In the event the bombers
failed to wreck Fighter Command on the ground and the fighters failed to
destroy it in the air.

The second principal reason for the defeat of the Luftwaffe was Fighter
Command itself – the spirit of its pilots and the quality of its machines, the
ceaseless toil in the factories where production kept ahead of losses, the
efficiency of the repair services which put damaged aircraft back into
service in the shortest possible time, and finally the higher strategy adopted
by Dowding and his principal lieutenant Air Marshal Park and persisted
in against mounting criticism which, after the battle, ensured the replacement and semi-disgrace of these two steadfast and wise commanders. The
greatest danger to Great Britain during these two months was the erosion
of its fighter force. The reserves were never exhausted but they were never
plentiful. Dowding and Park had therefore to minimize losses by cautious handling of their men and machines without thereby courting defeat
or lowering morale. They could not afford to indulge in unnecessarily
dashing tactics. They had to count the cost every day. In the end the sum
came out right.

The Battle of Britain was lost by Germany; the invasion of Great
Britain was never attempted; the blockade went on. But much was changed
that summer. Great Britain's prestige was raised high by the RAF and
Hitler was tempted into a blunder. Having failed to end the war with
Great Britain before attacking the USSR, he now proceeded to attack
the USSR none the less. He had always meant to attack the USSR at
some time in order to get *Lebensraum*. The fact that he now deluded
himself into attacking the USSR on the grounds that this was a way to

defeat Great Britain is an example of how disappointment can impair judgement. Moreover, the failure in the Battle of Britain prevented Hitler from concentrating all his strength against the USSR and eventually transformed a cloud in the west no bigger than a man's hand into the Anglo-American hurricane which, in concert with the blast from the east, was finally to devastate the Third Reich. The Battle of Britain was therefore one of the decisive events of the war.

Nevertheless Great Britain's position was still precarious and it is a measure of the continuing British crisis in this year that Churchill was prepared to contemplate two extremely un-British steps. The first, already mentioned, was the offer of a union with France – an offer so unreal that it faded almost immediately from the British consciousness. The second was even more startling and for that reason concealed. Although sceptical about the union with France, Churchill seems to have been in earnest when, in June, he offered to give Northern Ireland to the Irish Republic. The price was to be the use of Irish ports and the establishment of military and air bases in Ireland for the duration of the war, the cession of the northern counties to be effected when the war ended. De Valera countered with a proposal to permit the Americans to use Ireland in return for the immediate neutrality of a united Ireland. Churchill was ready to grant immediate unity but asked for Irish belligerence, not merely neutrality. De Valera doubted whether Churchill could deliver the unity of Ireland in the face of opposition from the Protestant rulers of the north (who got wind of the talks and were preparing to sabotage them) and of Churchill's own colleagues. So Britain forfeited a chance, albeit a slim one, to solve its Irish problem – just as, in 1915, it had proposed to trade Cyprus for Greek belligerence only to withdraw the offer within weeks and so saddle itself for half a century more with that intractable and unrewarding colony.

These two forays into the improbable did not obscure the crucial fact that from mid-1940 Great Britain was reduced to waiting for the Americans to come to Europe. Victory over Germany, as distinct from its harassment, could be achieved in no other way. Hitler's declaration of war against the United States at the end of 1941 ensured that the Americans would indeed come, but where many in Britain went wrong was in supposing that they would do so as reinforcement for Britain, ready and anxious to supplement British arms and execute British plans. This was perhaps the spirit in which Roosevelt, while his country was still at peace, proclaimed that one neighbour must lend his hosepipe to help put out another's fire, but it was not the spirit in which a great power sends millions of men and women to war. For this the Americans made their own plans. The British became the auxiliaries, occupying however an indispensable forward base.

To the Americans Germany was a great land power to be defeated by a greater land power. Stalin saw Germany the same way, but with the difference that Russians and Germans were at grips with one another from the first day of their hostilities, whereas the Americans had still to get to Europe. There must therefore be some delay during which two things must be accomplished: the Atlantic must be cleared of U-boats (Great Britain's last major contribution to victory) and a transport fleet must be built. Meanwhile American air forces would join the British and their continental and commonwealth allies in maiming German strongpoints, German industry and the German people. From the American point of view the outstanding question was not what had to be done but how long the preliminaries would take before very large, mainly armoured, land forces could be brought face to face with the German armies – in northern France.

The British contribution to the ultimate victory included one further major and peculiar achievement in the breaking of many of the Germans' most secret ciphers, the theoretically unbreakable Enigma machine keys used by all branches of the German armed services including the Abwehr (military intelligence), by the SS and police, and by the railways and certain other specialist services.

To read enciphered wireless messages of any grade, high or low, it is necessary, first, to intercept them and take down the enciphered texts and, secondly, to render these back into plain language by deciphering them. The interceptors were men and women with earphones listening in relays round the clock at various points in the British Isles and elsewhere in the world to German (and other) traffic transmitted at strengths designed to carry to other Germans but not far beyond. This gruelling and tedious work was the essential precondition. It was capped by cryptographers who, concentrated at Bletchley Park in England, achieved the intellectually remarkable and operationally crucial feat of breaking Enigma keys, often promptly enough to make the contents of the resulting intelligence (called Ultra) operationally valuable to the waging of battles in progress. Bletchley Park began as a British venture but became in 1943 an Anglo-American one.

The Enigma machine was originally a commercial machine first put on the market in Holland in 1919. It was adapted by the German armed services (who gave it its name) in the twenties and progressively developed for their most secret communications. The first breaks were made by the

Polish secret service which reconstructed the machine's internal workings, solved the problem of setting it to read a particular key on a particular day, and read Enigma traffic between 1932 and 1938; but the Poles were then foiled by the complexities continuously added by the Germans, whereupon they disclosed to the French and British secret services all they knew about Enigma and what they themselves had achieved and handed over two Enigma machines reconstructed by them. The French disappeared from the picture with their defeat in 1940 but by then the British had overcome initial scepticism about breaking Enigma (they had assigned to it only one cryptographer in 1938 and two in 1939) and were making astonishing progress in penetrating Enigma keys.

At their wartime peak the Germans used about 200 different Enigma keys simultaneously among their various higher commands and special services. All these keys were changed every twenty-four hours and in minor respects every eight hours, and even in wartime the Germans continued to add complicating elements to the machine itself. The challenge to the British cryptographers, who possessed Enigma machines thanks to the Poles, was to set the many movable parts of these machines in exactly the same way as the German operators and receivers had set their machines at the given time and for the relevant key – a formidable task. A number of keys were never broken, chiefly owing to the paucity of the traffic which they carried; others were broken irregularly or tardily; but one in particular – the principal key used by all higher formations in the Luftwaffe – was broken every day from a date (still disputed) in April or May 1940 to the end of the war, frequently on the day for which it was valid.

This intelligence had two special features. It was authentic and uniquely credible since it consisted of what the Germans were saying to one another; and it could be operationally valuable since much of what they were saying was known to the allies almost as soon as they said it. But its beginnings were not dramatic. When war began it was by no means certain that Ultra would be of much use, even if it could be got. The first fruits were meagre, scattered and unexciting. They came from breaking the key used by the German *Wehrkreise*, the static administrative regions or home commands, each corresponding to an army corps, into which Germany itself was divided. These scraps of information dealt with recruiting, training, travel arrangements and so on. The first indications of Ultra's further potentialities came during the Norwegian campaign of April 1940. The key used by the inter-service command created for the occasion was read within a week of the beginning of the operation and yielded in all about one thousand decodes. Their operational value, however, was negligible because the breaks were usually tardy and the material in them was strange and largely unintelligible in the absence of experienced intelligence officers. It was a portent but not yet a weapon.

During the campaigns of May and June in the Low Countries and France, Ultra rendered some service although again its practical application was minimal. But in, or shortly before, this period Bletchley began its uninterrupted penetration of the principal Luftwaffe key. There had been sporadic breaks of this key since the very beginning of the year but on 1 May the Germans introduced changes into the Enigma machine which countered these successes. But the difficulties created by the new obstacles were rapidly surmounted and – a fact not realized at the time – this key would never again be lost.

Two developments converted these successes into a major weapon. The first was the establishment alongside the cryptographers of intelligence staffs whose business it was to collate and interpret the scraps of information contained in the decodes. In the vast majority of cases each decode was in itself trivial and uninformative; only in association with other snippets did it become illuminating. The value of Ultra derived from the volume of stored intelligence into which each day's new items – now running into hundreds per day – fitted and from the ability of experienced intelligence officers to appreciate these items in the light of broader knowledge. Secondly, a system was elaborated from 1941 for conveying selected and paraphrased items of operationally valuable Ultra to commanders-in-chief in the field and their special intelligence staffs.

Ultra's most characteristic service was its detailed disclosure of the German order of battle: locations of units, their strengths and shortages, day by day, in men, equipment and supplies. Such intelligence became for the first time significant in the Battle of Britain. Although it did not suffice to correct exaggerated estimates of the Luftwaffe's total strength and standards of serviceability or yet provide information on the output of German factories, it gave clues to the scale of impending attacks and also details of the units stationed in northern France, Belgium and Denmark and their precise locations. It also confirmed that Hitler had abandoned his plans to invade England, at any rate for that year. In the North African campaign intelligence of this kind was supplemented by regular information on the timing and routes of tankers and other supply vessels crossing the Mediterranean from Greece to the German and Italian forces. Even more decisive was Ultra's contribution to the Battle of the Atlantic where the breaking of the U-boat key at the end of 1942 was the crucial factor in giving the victory to Britain. Ultra continued to produce copious intelligence to the end of the war. Besides its specific uses, it transformed the conduct of war on the allied side by revealing the enemy as no enemy had ever before been revealed. It created in senior staffs and at the political summit a state of mind which transformed the taking of decisions. To feel that you know your enemy is vastly comforting. It grows imperceptibly over time with the regular and intimate observance of his habits and actions. Knowledge of this kind makes counter-planning less tentative and more assured, less harrowing and more buoyant. Directing a great war is immensely tiring and good intelligence reduces the strains wonderfully. When, for example, Churchill, Roosevelt and their Chiefs of Staff met at Casablanca in January 1943 to decide what they should do after clearing North Africa and recovering control of the Mediterranean, they had been receiving a steadily increasing stream of Ultra intelligence about their enemy for three years. Without it their view of the war would have been entirely different, very much less distinct. Their decisions were still difficult, but they did not have to feel that they were planning in the dark.

The British cryptographers at Bletchley Park might have read Enigma ciphers through their own efforts but the timing of their first successes – and timing can be crucial in war – owed much to the brilliance and ultimately the generosity of the Poles. The Poles owed much to the French in their dual task of reconstructing the internal processes of the German Enigma and in breaking particular keys on particular days. And the French got the information which they gave to the Poles from a German in the German cipher service who leaked precious documents to Paris from 1931 onwards. He was at all relevant dates a member of the Nazi party and he was called Hans-Thilo Schmidt. He was a traitor and a lecher, a man whom it is impossible to admire but to whom very great thanks are due.

CHAPTER 8

The Mediterranean, North Africa and the Middle East

FOR Hitler the failure to defeat Great Britain, following the fall of France and the entry of Italy into the war, created a new range of diplomatic and strategic problems. His hopes of peace in the west had been dashed first by Great Britain's determination to fight on and then by its success in doing so. He told those round him that Great Britain was sustained by the prospect of Germany being embroiled with the Soviet Union, and this misreading of the British mood gave him a new reason – besides the quest for *Lebensraum* – to deal with the USSR. He faced a complex situation in the Mediterranean which was a theatre of war so long as Great Britain refused to make peace and where the interests of Italy, France and Spain – an ally, a vassal and a coy courtesan – collided. And thirdly, the war at sea, which became once more the chief means of reducing Great Britain, involved some risk of war with the United States.

On 27 September 1940, before the invasion of Great Britain had been officially abandoned, Hitler revived a project for a Tripartite Pact between Germany, Italy and Japan. Each of the signatories undertook to come to the aid of another in the event of an attack by any state not yet at war. The Japanese Foreign Minister, Matsuoka Yosuke, was becoming alarmed about the possibility of Japan finding itself at war with the USSR, the United States and Great Britain all at once. He was therefore willing to fall in with Hitler's plans in order to deter Washington from joining Great Britain in a war against a two-continent coalition, and in order also to put pressure on Stalin to come to terms with Japan in Manchuria. (Matsuoka's manoeuvres were stultified when Hitler abandoned his pact with Stalin and invaded the USSR.) Hitler's aims were similar. He too needed to deter the United States and intimidate Stalin – although he professed to be anxious to improve relations with the USSR and even to get it to join the pact, which would then have become an anti-American four-power club whose members divided the world into spheres of influence among themselves and collectively dared the United States not to move out of its allotted sphere in the New World. But Molotov, who visited Berlin in November, asked awkward questions about the presence of German troops in Finland and the German guarantee of Rumania and

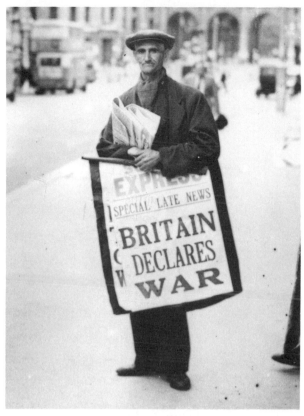

1 The first day

2 Munich: Chamberlain,
Daladier, Hitler, Mussolini,
Ciano

3 Czechoslovakia: the first
German invaders, October
1938

4 Poland: a village burns,
September 1939

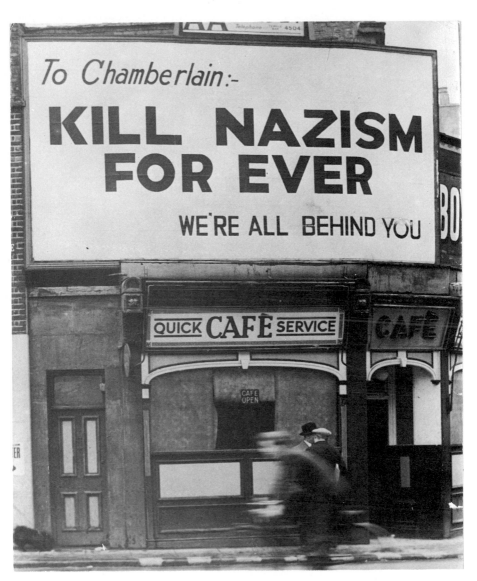

5   The voice of the people

6 *Top*: Ski troops in Finland,
1939

7 *Bottom*: German
loudspeakers patrol a Dutch
town, 1940

8 *Top*: The British
Expeditionary Force in
France, 1939

9 *Bottom*: The BEF in
retreat from France, 1940

10   *Top*: Dunkirk: makeshift
bridge

11   *Bottom*: Dunkirk: parting
shots

12 *Top*: France mobilizing

13 *Bottom*: Flight from Paris

14 *Top*: Goering and his staff
gaze across the English
Channel

15 *Bottom*: French warships
scuttled at Toulon, November
1940

observed that so long as discussion had to be conducted in an air raid shelter, there was something unrealistic about a plan for partitioning a world in which the British Empire was presumed to have ceased to exist.

Hitler's most immediate problem was the Mediterranean. This theatre was bisected by his ally Italy. At the western end were Vichy France and Spain, at the eastern end the Balkans. In France Hitler had established an occupational régime in the north and along the Atlantic coast and a satellite régime for the rest of the country. But this satellite was a satellite with a difference. Pétain had a certain number of cards in his hand – the not inconsiderable remnants of an important fleet, territories and strategic positions in North and West Africa and the Middle East, a degree of American benevolence, and a willingness to run France on lines broadly acceptable to Hitler and so relieve the Germans of administrative problems so long as they did not try to push Vichy too far. The Nazi leaders disliked the French but they could not treat France in the same way as Czechoslovakia or Poland. Therefore they could not give Italy the satisfaction, nor Spain the bribes, which these other Latin countries wanted at France's expense.

Hitler regarded Franco's Spain as a natural ally and as a debtor. A republican Spain he might have invaded without more ado but Franco's Spain he sought to bargain with. His aim was to lure Franco into active alliance in order to secure control of the western gateway into the Mediterranean and possession of one of the Canary islands as a base for the Battle of the Atlantic. The bait for Franco was Gibraltar. On his side Franco had allied Spain with the Axis by a Treaty of Friendship with Germany in March 1939 and by joining the Anti-Comintern Pact, and in June 1940 he had seemed on the verge of joining the war a few days after Mussolini did so. But there were arguments against as well as for. Hitler's attack on Roman Catholic Poland in partnership with Stalin had disconcerted the profoundly anti-communist Spanish dictator, and his innate wiliness and caution were accentuated by the need to keep Spain out of further trouble after the civil war and particularly by the need to import food. Franco, whose Ambassador in London was being cajoled by Churchill and was even given to understand that Spain might help itself to part of French North Africa, did not rise to the German bait of a joint German-Spanish attack on Gibraltar and at a long meeting with Hitler and Ribbentrop at Hendaye on 23 October he frustrated the German leaders in a bout of arguing in the course of which, besides pitching Spanish claims very high – Oran, the whole of French Morocco, large quantities of food, fuel and military equipment – he left Hitler in two minds about whether he intended to join in such an adventure at a date which he would not yet disclose or whether the securing of the western end of the Mediterranean would have to be undertaken not with him but against him. Further meetings at the end of the year between Hitler and Franco's Foreign Minister Ramón Serrano Suñer at Berchtesgaden and between Franco and Hitler's military intelligence chief Admiral Wilhelm Canaris in Madrid only increased the uncertainty. Mussolini was equally unsuccessful and Hitler toyed with the idea of a direct parachute attack on Gibraltar, which his advisers however had already considered and rejected. The German invasion of the USSR altered the atmosphere since this was something which Franco could wholeheartedly support and he sent 18,000 men to share in the anti-communist crusade of his fellow dictators. He was shocked by Churchill's prompt support for Stalin and even more by the Anglo-Russian alliance, which, Eden had assured his Ambassador in London, was unthinkable. But he continued to prevaricate over active operations in his own part of the world, so that Hitler was driven at one time to making inquiries about the chances of a coup to replace him by another general and considered as late as 1943 plans for an invasion of Spain.

If Hitler's dealings with Franco were a disappointment to the Führer, his relations with Mussolini went more seriously wrong. Mussolini's ideas were large, impracticable and not always consonant with German policy: if Hitler was to rule from the Atlantic to the Urals, Mussolini was going to rule the Mediterranean and all its circumambient lands (except presumably Spain). For Mussolini the rise of Hitler had offered a means not only of settling scores with Great Britain and France but also of winning an empire beyond Europe while Hitler kept him inviolable in Europe. The symbol of this vision was the Pact of Steel of May 1939. But at that date Mussolini was not ready for war. Like Hitler, but with more reason, he planned not to go to war until 1942 and the defeat of France in 1940 therefore upset his timetable. It did not, however, moderate his visions. At a meeting in October 1940 at the Brenner the Italian leaders made clear to their German partners that their first shopping list included not only a piece of southern France but also Corsica, Malta, Tunisia, part of Algeria, an Atlantic port in Morocco, French Somaliland and the British position in Egypt and the Sudan. Besides running counter to Hitler's plan to operate a limited accord with France, the creation of an Italian empire of this size, straddling the Mediterranean from the Atlantic to the Red Sea and marching with an equally vast German empire to the north of it, threatened to raise questions about the Middle East which Hitler was, vaguely, proposing to approach via the Caucasus and Mussolini, much more purposefully, via Suez.

Hitler had been generally content to leave Europe south of the Alps to

Mussolini. He had expected Mussolini to attack Malta in the summer of 1940 but Mussolini made no move; he was still intent on keeping out of serious wars. The Italian air force was obsolescent and the fleet, though large and in some respects first-class, was lightly armed by comparison with the British and French fleets and untrained in night operations. The army was gravely ill equipped and, although Mussolini did not know it at the time, its morale was poor: shouting fascist slogans proved a bad way of inspiring troops and the Italians were to fight badly until they were pressed back into Tunisia in 1943 and then changed sides later that year to fight the Germans on Italian soil. Mussolini's decision to go to war in 1940 was therefore the beginning of a series of disasters for Italy. Moreover, his opening of a campaign in Greece which he could not finish was seriously to distort Hitler's overall strategy.

Hitler had already in July decided to attack the USSR in the following spring and on 18 December he issued his first Barbarossa directive. In it he stated that the USSR might be invaded 'even before' the war with Great Britain was over. Since he assumed, correctly, that Great Britain could not help the USSR by opening a second front for at least eighteen months, he was not risking a war on two fronts unless the Russians held out that long. He expected to dispatch the Russians within six months and then revert to the problem of the British. But at the end of 1940 he was forced by the Italians, who attacked in Greece, and by the British, who counter-attacked the Italians in Africa, to undertake far more than he had intended in south-east Europe and eventually in Africa too. The Balkans, instead of being a flank to be secured before Barbarossa, became an independent theatre of war with extensions leading German troops and air squadrons away from the USSR into waters and sands beyond Europe's southern confines.

The Balkans and Hungary were already dominated by Germany before the war began. Annexed, by economic power, in the thirties they were to be lost in the military clash of the forties. These states had emerged as exemplars of the principle of national self-determination – which, however, they exemplified imperfectly since none of them was nationally homogeneous, although each was sufficiently a nation to have national quarrels with its neighbours. To other states they were chiefly of interest in the light of an older theory: the balance of power. Between the wars France made friends with Rumania and Yugoslavia because they stood for the maintenance of the Versailles settlement of 1919 and opposed any signs of a revival of German hegemony, but the waning of French influence in the thirties and its eclipse at Munich in 1938 forced France's friends to look elsewhere for salvation. Economically adrift and fearful of their Bulgarian and Hungarian neighbours (both of them hurt by the post-war settlement and waiting to alter the map once more), they were forced to turn to Germany. By 1939 all the states of the region, pro-Versailles or anti-Versailles, were wooing Germany with what they had – which was raw materials – in the hope either of protection or redress. To Germany they were important, as they had once been to France, not for any reasons connected with the politics of the area itself but for extrinsic reasons.

The Russo-German pact of 1939 recognized a Russian interest in the Balkans by assigning Bessarabia to the USSR. A year later Stalin, by annexing northern Bukovina as well, signalled that his interest was not limited to Bessarabia. Rumania thought of going to war but was restrained by Hitler who had other plans. Although in 1939 he had declared himself disinterested in this part of the world, he was not. Rumania's natural resources and its strategic position on the southern border of the USSR made it very important for him. In the autumn of 1940 he further partitioned Rumania by giving a piece to Hungary (the second Vienna Award, in August) and a piece to Bulgaria (the treaty of Craiova, in September). By this time King Carol was ready to throw in his hand. He had tried unsuccessfully to rule through a minor party and then through the Patriarch as Prime Minister, but after the humiliating territorial losses exacted by Hitler he abdicated and what remained of Rumania was controlled by Germany through Marshal Ion Antonescu with the title of Conducator. In November Rumania, Hungary and Slovakia – a Balkan northern tier along the Russian southern flank – all adhered to the Tripartite Pact. German troops appeared. Hitler was peacefully strengthening his control of the Balkans. He did not want it otherwise. He had no wish for a war in what was to him a storehouse and a waiting area. But on 28 October Mussolini had invaded Greece, and Hitler gradually found himself forced to make new plans and to interpose a military campaign in the Balkans before his invasion of the USSR.

Mussolini had given Hitler no proper notice of his attack on Greece. He sent a letter at the last moment and ante-dated it by five days. This was his way of retaliating against Hitler's habit of invading other countries without telling his ally in advance. In any case he knew that Hitler would object to his plans, because Hitler had been urging him to bide his time. This silly failure in cooperation was characteristic of the partnership between the Axis allies. Neither of the dictators was by nature a cooperator. They lacked – indeed despised – the habits of intercourse and interchange which are the everyday experience of democratic politicians. Moreover, by the time that their alliance had become formal on the eve of war, their relationship had begun to lose some of its strength. This was more Mussolini's fault than Hitler's, for while Hitler entertained a genuine admiration for Mussolini as his forerunner among men of iron will and retained a feeling of obligation to him, Mussolini had from the start been attracted to Hitler partly in spite of himself. He gravitated to the Axis more through repulsion from the western democracies than through any love of Hitler or of Germany, and he quickly allowed congenital jealousy to corrode an alliance which, although it had become essential for his policies, cast him as a manifestly junior, increasingly uncomfortable partner.

Jealousy and suspiciousness were strong features in Mussolini's character. He was a solitary. He had neither friends nor intimates. He had the singlemindedness and determination of the man who cares little for money or the other ordinary comforts of life (except sex), but he too often failed to relate his purposes to his resources. He was energetic without being industrious, so that his achievements were those of the gambler who leaves even the calculable to chance. His working-class origins, his poverty in early life and his consciousness of defective education and social poise made him aloof, secretive and assertive; he had neither the training nor the character to rectify his shortcomings by methodical hard work or by arguing (as Hitler sometimes did) with people who had ideas or knowledge to offer. He remained sketchily informed about public affairs and averse to listening to advisers who might be cleverer or better informed than he was; his energies, which were considerable until the last years of his life, went into posturing and rhetoric. He believed in the regenerative virtue of violence but much of the violence was, unlike Hitler's quests for *Lebensraum* and racial purity, pointless. There is something symbolic about the fact that the prelude to his rule was a spectacular event – the March on Rome – which never took place. Mussolini was appointed Prime Minister not because he advanced on the capital like a conqueror but because he outwitted rival politicians by devious scheming which he conducted at a distance in Milan and which made a grand coup unnecessary. He arrived in Rome by train.

Mussolini was a shrewd and stubborn politician who used the apparatus of tyranny because he was also a bully. Being ruthless and unprincipled he liked the short cuts which the strong arm of lawlessness provides, and very soon after becoming Prime Minister he discovered how well these methods can work in both international and domestic affairs. In 1923 General Enrico Tellini and other Italians who were members of a commission engaged in surveying the unsettled Greco-Albanian frontier were murdered on Greek soil. Mussolini bombarded and seized Corfu, berated the Greek government in extravagant style and had the satisfaction of seeing the British and French governments pressing Greece to accept Italy's humiliating and unjustifiable demands. In the following year Italy scored a substantial victory against Yugoslavia over Fiume because Yugoslavia could muster no outside support for its case. Foreign politicians were beginning to show respect for Mussolini as a statesman of consequence and were therefore contriving to turn a blind eye to such aspects of Fascism as the murder of the socialist leader Giacomo Matteotti (to which Mussolini's language certainly contributed, even though he may have given no precise order for the deed) and the suppression of personal and civil liberties in the name of efficiency and good order: they noted improvements in the public services but ignored the deterioration in manners and morals. By the time that Hitler came to power Mussolini had had a decade of experience in the techniques and fruits of brutality. He was secure at home and respected (by governments) abroad. He was ready to impress Hitler as he had impressed other leaders, but he had not bargained with the possibility that both he himself in relation to Hitler, and Italy in relation to Germany, might have to play a subordinate role in world politics. For the rest of his career he kicked ineffectually against these pricks. The invasion of Greece in the autumn of 1940 was the uncoordinated reflex of an ally who was not a good partner, of a secondary power seeking to establish parity with a first-class power by attacking a third-class one.

Mussolini wanted Italy to be a Balkan power as well as an African one. Greeks were well aware of this and Venizelos had begun in 1928 to mend Greece's relations with Yugoslavia and Turkey. He made a treaty with Italy in the same year but it became a dead letter. Venizelos wanted to end the old feud with Bulgaria too but in 1930 King Boris married an Italian princess. A Balkan pact concluded (without Bulgaria) in 1934 was mainly an anti-Italian mutual defence measure, but it lacked coherence and strength. By the summer of 1940, after Mussolini had won a little territory from France but not much glory, an Italian offensive in the Balkans seemed more than probable, the more so when the Greek cruiser *Helle* was torpedoed by an Italian submarine in the Aegean in August. The British guarantee could not be rated very high. The only hope was that Hitler would restrain his ally.

This hope was destroyed when Mussolini's Ambassador delivered an ultimatum in the middle of the night of 27–8 October. Italian troops had already crossed the Greek frontier with Albania. But the attack was a complete failure. It was undertaken against the advice of all three Italian Chiefs of Staff, who gave Mussolini accurate estimates of Greek resistance. The Duce preferred, however, to listen to his Commander-in-Chief in

Albania who promised to overrun the whole of Epirus in ten to fifteen days and secure the capitulation of the Greek army. He assured Mussolini that everything had been prepared down to the smallest detail which, since the attack had been envisaged nearly four months earlier, should have been the case. But there had in fact been little planning and the operation launched on 28 October was more like a whim than a campaign. The invading force of three divisions was totally inadequate and within a week the Greeks were counter-attacking and advancing into Albania. The Italians had attacked in three prongs. Their central prong was cut off, and the two prongs on either side had to be withdrawn. Italian casualties were heavy. Prisoners were taken by the thousand. By the third week in November there were no Italians left on Greek soil. In addition the British Fleet Air Arm damaged three Italian battleships in a night attack at Taranto on 11–12 November, as a result of which Taranto was abandoned and all Italian vessels of war were moved to harbours on the west coast. The British also moved forward into Crete and the Aegean – whence the R A F could threaten the Rumanian oilfields.

Things were also going badly for Italy on the other side of the Mediterranean. There Marshal Graziani had an army of 215,000 men in Libya. So long as France was in the war Graziani had a good case for lying low, since he was sandwiched between the French in Tunisia and Algeria and the British in Egypt, but as soon as France collapsed Mussolini began to urge him into action. Graziani was reluctant but in September, after having been ordered to fight, he began the first of the series of attacks and counterattacks which were to constitute the battle for North Africa which lasted until May 1943. In the first week of December, in a daring offensive of great political moment, the British retaliated. This move, by a force of little more than 30,000 men, was designed to show that Great Britain was still very much in the war. With remarkable daring, Churchill had sent reinforcements to the Middle East in the middle of the Battle of Britain. He hoped that a show of spirit far away from home might even get France back into the war, and although in this the desert campaign failed, it did make Hitler nervous about a rising in France and finally turned Franco against the Gibraltar plan and the entry of German troops into Spain.

Militarily the British offensive was an astonishing success. Throughout December and January the small British force under General Sir Archibald Wavell advanced from Sidi Barrani inside Egypt to Tobruk (which was captured in twenty-four hours) and then, both along the coast and across the desert, to Benghazi in the north-western corner of Cyrenaica. What had begun as a demonstration turned into a major victory. Wavell's mixed force of British, Indian, Australian, New Zealand, French and

Polish units covered 500 miles in two months and destroyed an Italian army six times its own size. This success also had wider repercussions. It forced Hitler to send help to the Italians, to revise and enlarge the scope of his contingency plans for a move into the Balkans on the basis that the British too might move into Greece in strength, and to make arrangements despite Russian objections for the entry of German troops into Bulgaria and that country's adherence to the Tripartite Pact.

But at Benghazi, which was captured on 7 February, the British advance stopped. The British cabinet had decided that it must be limited. Wavell had already been required to send four squadrons of aircraft (Blenheims and Gladiators) to help the Greeks on the Albanian front and anti-aircraft units to defend Athens; he had another war to fight in East Africa; he was responsible for the safety of Palestine and the Suez Canal, which could be threatened by an anti-British government in Iraq or by the Vichy French in Syria; and five days after the fall of Benghazi Rommel arrived in Tripoli, followed a couple of days later by the first of the German tanks which were destined to transform a desert war which now ceased to be an Anglo-Italian affair.

German intervention in North Africa had first been mooted and then dropped in October 1940. In November, during a not very amicable conference at Salzburg between Hitler and Ciano, Hitler began giving instructions and making promises. He urged the Italians to push on into Egypt and he promised air support. During that winter some 400 German aircraft operated in the Mediterranean protecting supply routes to Africa and attacking British shipping and air bases. Malta, which had been inadequately equipped to defend itself against air attack, was besieged by the German and Italian air forces which succeeded in interdicting it to the British navy and making the Mediterranean impassable by British convoys. The British continued their attacks on Italy, bombarding Genoa from the sea and bombing Spezia and Leghorn from the air in February. The Italians retaliated with hazardous but often successful attacks by small torpedo boats on British heavy units in harbour, but on 28 March British naval superiority was massively affirmed in a battle off Cape Matapan in which three Italian cruisers and two destroyers were sunk. Although the main target, the battleship *Vittorio Veneto*, got away, the Italian navy ceased to be a major factor in the war. (Italy also lost East Africa at this time. In August 1940 the Italians had forced Great Britain to leave British Somaliland and were threatening the Sudan and Kenya but the British returned in February 1941 and with the help of South African, Nigerian, Indian and French troops proceeded to invade Ethiopia and Eritrea. Addis Ababa was abandoned at the beginning of April.

Resistance continued in the north and the final, inevitable surrender did not come until November. The campaign was remarkable for the extraordinary exploits of Gideon Force which consisted of Ethiopian and Sudanese men under Lieutenant Colonel Orde Wingate and other British officers and took over 15,000 prisoners in three months.)

In the spring of 1941 the Germans attacked on the Balkan and North African fronts in campaigns which were subordinate to the attack on the USSR to come in June. Hitler had already left one front unsettled when he desisted from his attack on Great Britain in the autumn of 1940. Now, in the south, if he failed to conclude either his Balkan or his North African operations before beginning Barbarossa, he would again have multiplied his commitments. He concluded the one but not the other.

Forebodings of a German occupation of the Balkans raised forlorn hopes of a local alliance to deter it, with British support. After the Italian invasion of their country, Greeks hoped to induce the British to shift their weight in the eastern Mediterranean from Egypt to Greece, the better to attack the Italians, but the British lacked the resources for effective operations in the two theatres and were reluctant to risk what they held in the one for possible advantages in the other. The RAF gave modest aid against the Italians in Albania but although this help was increased from February 1941 it was not enough to eliminate the Italians before the advent of the Germans. There were, however, political considerations which weighed with Churchill – quite apart from the philhellene emotions roused in Great Britain by the unexpectedly successful Greek resistance. There was in the first place the British guarantee to Greece in 1939; it was time a British guarantee was honoured. Churchill hoped too that Turkey might be got into the war against the Germans; effective support for Greece would weigh with the rulers of Turkey. (Ineffectiveness did too. Turkey followed its instincts and stayed neutral.) Most importantly, Churchill had an eye on the Americans and the impact on them of the establishment of a Balkan front against the Axis. Great Britain had shown that it could win battles against Hitler but Churchill knew that Great Britain alone could never defeat Hitler on the continent. From the time he took office as Prime Minister Churchill kept his mind firmly on the big central issue of forming a coalition powerful enough to destroy Hitler's Germany, and the United States was the essential element in this design. A failure to help the Greeks, whose cause had been very popular in the United States ever since their brave riposte to the Italian invasion in the previous year, might discredit Great Britain; going to their help, even if unsuccessfully, would be accounted to Great Britain for virtue.

At the end of February 1941 Eden, now once more Foreign Secretary, went to Athens with the CIGS, Sir John Dill. By this date German intentions were apparent, Bulgarian adherence to the Tripartite Pact was clearly only a matter of time, and the chances of enlisting Yugoslavia or Turkey in joint operations with Greece and Great Britain were meagre. Bulgaria joined the Pact on 1 March and German troops began to move into that country. Yugoslavia was expected to follow suit sooner rather than later, while the Turks were refusing to join the war without assurances of British military supplies which Great Britain could not spare. Nevertheless from Athens Eden sent Churchill an optimistic assessment of the military possibilities and with this encouragement Churchill who, like Wavell, had been reluctant to prejudice the campaign in North Africa by deflecting ground and air forces to Greece, decided in favour of helping Greece and told Wavell that in the event of a German attack he would have to go to Greece's help. The Australian and New Zealand governments reluctantly agreed.

The Greek government was no less dubious. Help was welcome, but only if it were substantial. In the Greek view, token help would be worse than useless. Greek and British attitudes were now in some ways the reverse of what they had been two years earlier. Then Greece had wanted a firm British commitment in order to deter Italy while Great Britain had hesitated and recoiled for fear of provoking Italy. Now Greece was anxious not to invite a German onslaught so long as any hope of evading it remained and therefore opposed any British military involvement which would be large enough to provoke but not massive enough to deter or defeat the Germans. Greece had failed in 1940 to get enough British help against the Italians to turn their successes in the field into total victory, even though they had been willing at that stage to promise to enter Great Britain's war with Germany in return for substantial help against Italy. The Greek government feared, correctly as it turned out, that the only British help available would be inadequate to stop Hitler. Given the limits on Greek military power which remained almost entirely committed to holding the Italians in the north-west, the only possible anti-German strategy was a substantial British force in the north-east with merely token Greek support. But in spite of these doubts the Greek government agreed in principle in February 1941 to admit a British force into Greece and rejected a German offer of immunity from invasion in return for neutrality.

At this point there was a muddle. An attack through Bulgaria, Greece's traditional enemy, was taken for granted. But Yugoslavia's attitude was still uncertain. In the vortex of Balkan politics Yugoslavia and Greece had been over the years more friendly than unfriendly, and if this friendship

THE GERMAN INVASIONS OF YUGOSLAVIA
AND GREECE APRIL 1941

Legend:
- Axis Powers and Allies.
- Italian operations, October 1940.
- Italian Albania, occupied by Greece.
- German advances April 1941.
- Italian advances April 1941.
- Hungarian advances April 1941.
- British, New Zealand and Australian troop positions.

Vienna

AUSTRIA

Budapest

HUNGARY

Ljubljana

Zagreb

Fiume

RUMANIA

Belgrade

Occupied 6 April.

Bucharest

Zara

Split

Sarajevo

Y U G O S L A V I A

Nish

BULGARIA

Dubrovnik

Sofia

Occupied 10 April.

Kotor

Skopje

Occupied 7 April.

ITALY

Durazzo

Tirana

Occupied 15 April.

Klisura

Brindisi

Valona

Salonika

Corfu

Yannina

Larissa

Occupied 9 April.

Aegean

Sea

Thermopylea

Cephalonia

G R E E C E

Athens

Piraeus

Occupied by
Italy.

SICILY

Zante

Patras

Nauplia

Occupied
27 April.

Kalamata

Monemvasia

0   100

Miles

British evacuation
24-30 April.

CRETE

~ARTHUR BANKS~

held – indeed, until it was obvious that it would not hold – the Greeks wanted to keep their communications with Yugoslavia open. In order to do this, they must plan to meet the German-Bulgarian attack on a line north and east of Salonica, even though this line was unfavourable for natural reasons and harder for the British to reach. The British favoured the more southerly line along the river Aliakmon and even this position was likely to prove untenable if Yugoslavia allowed the Germans to invade through Yugoslavia as well as Bulgaria – or, as in fact happened, was unable to stop them. The situation was further complicated by the unfinished war with the Italians in the west, since a withdrawal south of the Aliakmon, without a matching retreat in the west, would expose the Greek forces facing the Italians to encirclement by the Germans – which is what happened. The Greek government hoped and expected Eden to clarify Yugoslavia's position and believed Eden to have agreed that there should be no Greek withdrawal to the Aliakmon line until this had been done. This was the first of a series of muddles for which the blame is still not clear. While the British imagined the Greeks to be regrouping on the Aliakmon line, they were in fact waiting in the north, where they were eventually caught.

In Yugoslavia the Regent Paul had hesitated about following the Rumanian and Bulgarian example and joining the Tripartite Pact. He was urged by Great Britain and the United States to resist German pressure and attack the Italians in Albania, but neither London nor Washington was able to offer any practical help, although Eden dangled territorial bribes before the Regent in return for Yugoslav belligerence against the Italians in Greece. The Regent equivocated. He was pro-British but no fool and he judged that the British wanted to pull him into the war for their own purposes and without any plan to save Yugoslavia from the Axis. In the end, impressed by the fall of France and hoping to get Salonica as his reward, he took the plunge and on 25 March joined the Pact. Two days later his government was overthrown by General Simovic, the leader of a group hostile to the Regent and supported principally by the Serb Orthodox Church. Simovic wanted to steer a neutral course by keeping clear of pacts and wars, and he continued to refuse to attack the Italians. But this was not good enough for Hitler, who was determined to scotch any possible British advance into the Aegean and Greece. He resolved to invade Yugoslavia and Greece and attacked both on 6 April, deploying against the former seven Panzer divisions and 1,000 aircraft. After heavy bombing and grievous casualties Belgrade fell on the 13th. The government capitulated four days later. Yugoslavia disintegrated. On the heels of the German conquerors Hungary, Bulgaria and Italy helped themselves to pieces of what they, wrongly, took to be a corpse; the Croat leader Anté Pavelic arrived from Rome to establish a separate Croat state; Serbia became a German puppet.

Greece was defeated only slightly less abruptly. The German attack had been preceded by a fresh Italian offensive in mid-March. Hopeful and ill-informed, Mussolini crossed to Albania, but had to go back again when his attack failed. The German attack followed. Fifty thousand British, Australian and New Zealand troops, supported by only one squadron of modern aircraft, could do little to succour the Greeks. Seven thousand Greeks were made prisoner and much valuable British material was captured. By the end of April resistance on the Greek mainland was over. Survivors from the Greek and Commonwealth forces were transported to Crete, which had been in British occupation for six months. Unfortunately for them little had been done to defend Crete in the mistaken belief that Great Britain's command of the sea made it impossible for an airborne invasion to be sustained. Churchill had urged that it be turned into a fortress bristling with everything from tanks to road blocks and defended by armed Cretans as well as British and other Commonwealth troops. He did not know that the requisite defences had not been constructed or that essential reconnaissance of the terrain had been neglected. The 3,500 Greek troops in the island had only one rifle per six men and three rounds of ammunition each; existing airstrips were not mined and proposals to build hidden airstrips in the hills not carried out; in spite of a plentiful supply of Italian prisoners of war landing stages were not constructed on the south shore nor roads to link north and south, with the result that supply ships from Egypt had to circle dangerously round the island and unload under intense enemy air attack; there were hardly any tanks and a fatal lack of radio and telegraph equipment.

The attack began on 20 May with glider and parachute landings from a fleet of 500 transport aircraft. These operations were very costly. Although air cover had been withdrawn from the defences before the invasion began, so that the approach of the air armada was unopposed, the reception was very hot and whole units were wiped out on landing or soon afterwards, many of them before they could reach the weapons which were dropped for them separately. Reinforcements were delayed because the airfields which the Germans were using in Greece were inadequately prepared dust bowls. But during the ensuing night Maleme airfield at the western end of the island was abandoned by the New Zealanders and the Germans started using it the next day. All efforts to dislodge them failed. This was a vital turn in events since, contrary to British belief, the German airborne forces were largely dependent on airfields and could not mount a concentrated attack with units dropped at random over the countryside.

A supplementary sea-borne invasion on the second night was baulked by the British navy, which suffered, however, seriously from air attacks. The defenders, believing that the main weight of the attack was bound to come from the sea, paid more attention to shore defence than to the recapture of Maleme, from which the Germans pressed eastward gradually and in increasing force. A week after the beginning of the attack it was clear that the main issues were the timing of the evacuation of the defenders and the number who would be saved. Withdrawal began on 1 June. Only half the defenders got away. The British Mediterranean fleet suffered seriously (three cruisers and six destroyers sunk, two battleships, three cruisers and an aircraft carrier damaged) in the attempt to thwart the invasion and the subsequent rescue operations and had to suspend the latter for fear of incurring further losses which would jeopardize its control of the eastern Mediterranean.

The capture from the air of an island defended by superior naval forces was a spectacular achievement but a freak. The defenders had failed to make good use of their six months' occupation of the island, denuded the island of its air fighter defences, failed with a force of 32,000 men to hold all of the three vital airfields and, having abandoned Maleme, failed to recapture it. These failures, leading to a further humiliating evacuation, blackened the reputation of the commander-in-chief, General Sir Bernard Freyberg, all the more so since he had received full and accurate intelligence from Ultra about German strengths and intentions. But the battle for Crete illustrated the limitations of Ultra as much as its value, for Freyberg had been verbally instructed by Wavell not to make tactical use of Ultra without corroborating intelligence from another source. This was standard practice and prevailed throughout the war. So important was Ultra that Churchill decreed that it was better to lose a battle than to lose this source. Consequently Freyberg was prevented from redisposing his forces on the basis of what he learned from Ultra and when he appealed to Wavell to be dispensed from the rule Wavell rejected his plea. Whether Crete would have been saved if the rules had been different it is impossible to say. But it is possible to assert that the rules were sound, since saving Crete at the cost of Ultra would probably have led in the next year to the loss of the far more crucial battle in the Atlantic.

The Germans considered themselves lucky to have won Crete so easily. They tacitly drew the conclusion that they should not have done so. Over a third of their airborne invaders were killed or wounded, the Luftwaffe lost 220 aircraft and no parachute operation of this kind was ever again attempted. Hitler, having won an extra base for helping Rommel and having driven the British beyond air range of Ploesti's oilfields, scrapped plans for a similar attack on Malta and turned his parachute units into infantry regiments.

It has been suggested that the Cretan operation delayed Barbarossa and so saved Moscow and even possibly the USSR itself in 1941. The Simovic coup in Belgrade occurred on the day, 27 March, for which Hitler had convoked a conference to discuss Barbarossa. The conference discussed Yugoslavia instead, Hitler decided to invade it as soon as possible and he postponed Barbarossa from mid-May to 22 June. Since the thaw came late that year there would have been some postponement anyway. The decision to interpose a Balkan war was chiefly important because the tanks used in it (800 of them) would need a breathing space for refitting between campaigns. This they were able to have. The further decision to take Crete caused some confusion (but nothing more serious) as the forces designated for Crete were moved south while the forces being shifted from Greece to the Russian fronts moved the other way, but the air squadrons left in Greece to cover the Cretan operation could move to their Barbarossa stations at shorter notice and the parachute troops were not intended for use in the USSR at all. Moscow was not saved by a mere alteration to the timetable of a week or two, and although the proposition cannot be incontestably proved or refuted it is very hard to see that the campaigns in Yugoslavia and Greece or the attack on Crete had any significant effect on Barbarossa. What might have helped the USSR would have been a successful defence of Crete and a prolongation of the battle there. At one time it looked to Halder as though Barbarossa would have to be further postponed but on 30 May Hitler confirmed the 22 June date.

The seizure of Crete was at the time more apparent than the cost and Cyprus seemed a possible next step. This was all the more alarming for Great Britain because the French in Syria and Lebanon recognized Vichy, in Iraq Great Britain's enemies had raised their heads and taken power, in Palestine the Mufti Haj Amin was strongly anti-British, and in Egypt King Faruq was not much less so. Consequently the whole British position in the Middle East was in jeopardy and might be scattered by a German attack.

The British position in the Middle East was anomalous. It rested on force, although with the lone exception of Aden no part of the area was constitutionally within the British Empire. During the nineteenth century the rivalries of the European powers had prevented any one of them from annexing portions of the Ottoman empire in Asia as they had annexed parts of Africa, but Great Britain had established *de facto* control over Egypt (and Cyprus). It also controlled the Persian Gulf and the lesser principalities along its western shores. The First World War produced the long-awaited withering away of the Ottoman empire and in anticipation the allied powers struck bargains for its partition in order to avoid fighting among themselves. The Russians, however, dropped out owing to the revolution of 1917 and the Italians withdrew when they scented the emergence of a Turkish national state out of the Ottoman imperial debris. Great Britain and France were left in control but the temper of the times required control to be veiled. France in Syria and Lebanon, and Great Britain in Palestine, Transjordan and Iraq established their rule under mandates. These mandates gave Great Britain a solid block of territory in the Middle East all the way from Egypt to the Persian Gulf. British forces dominated the area more effectively than Ottoman forces had ever done and this domination was practically unaffected by the grant of formal independence to Egypt in 1922 or the termination of the Iraqi mandate ten years later. Special treaties ensured the continued presence of British naval, military and air forces (although the treaty with Egypt took over ten years to negotiate) and the development of road, rail and air communications made assurance doubly sure. There was no Arab power to gainsay the British but there were Arab nationalists who, observing European politics in the thirties and remembering the interest of an earlier generation of Germans in the Middle East, hoped that Germany might come in useful to put an end to British rule over them. The German campaigns in the Balkans in the spring of 1941 stimulated these hopes, especially in Iraq.

The Arabs had also a second reason for being anti-British besides their nationalist resentment against the British imperialism which (with French imperialism) had frustrated their hopes of ruling themselves as soon as the Turks had been got rid of. In Palestine the British administration allowed a Jewish immigration which, given the background of the Zionist demand for a Jewish state, was a threat to Arab aspirations. During the First World War Great Britain endorsed the Zionist claim to a national home in Palestine (a camouflaged way of referring to the Jewish state which most Zionists wanted and which their founder, Theodore Herzl, had envisaged at the end of the previous century when he wrote his book *The Jewish State*). Under British rule the Jews in Palestine increased from less than 10 per cent of the population to nearly 30 per cent and the Arabs, who regarded the Jews as alien colonizers of Arab soil, began to look for foreign friends. The Nazis with their anti-Jewish tirades were an obvious choice for an anti-British flirtation. The Arabs were also impressed by the failure of Great Britain and France to check Mussolini in Ethiopia and encouraged by the extensive Arab revolt in Palestine in 1936. Upon the approach of war Great Britain tried to safeguard its position in the Middle East by dropping attempts, which were in any case futile, to find a way of pleasing both Arabs and Jews in Palestine and adopted instead a pro-Arab policy. In 1938 the BBC started broadcasting in Arabic, the first of its foreign language programmes. In May 1939 a British White Paper proposed severe limits on Jewish immigration (at the very moment when the case for it had been enormously enhanced by Hitler's concentration camps) and assured the Arabs that beyond these limits further immigration would be subject to Arab acquiescence. The White Paper saved Anglo-Arab relations and the British Empire in the Middle East for the war years – but not beyond.

One of the Arab politicians who wished to play the Germans off against the British and use the war to extract concessions from Great Britain about post-war Palestine was Rashid Ali el-Gailani, who became Prime Minister of Iraq in March 1940. A year later he was briefly ousted but returned with increased power. He was supported by four colonels picturesquely known as the Golden Square who were the principal spokesmen and pressure group for politically-minded army officers. The immediate question for Rashid Ali's government was whether to honour Iraq's treaty obligations to Great Britain and allow British troops to use the port of Basra at the head of the Persian Gulf on their way to reinforce the British position in Egypt. Rashid Ali and his friends, besides wanting to take a firm line with Great Britain, were afraid that the pro-British party led by Nuri es-Said would lead Iraq into the war in spite of the fact, as it seemed to them, that Great Britain was losing it. Rashid Ali therefore wanted to find out how much German help he would get if he resisted the British, but he found the Germans disappointingly vague. On the one hand Hitler was reluctant to give the Arabs what they wanted because Mussolini, who was still regarded as having at least an equal say in Middle Eastern affairs, had reservations. An Axis declaration endorsing Arab nationalistic aspirations did not square with Mussolini's intention to assume overlordship of Egypt and the Sudan in place of the British. Consequently Hitler hesitated over his Arab policy and eventually agreed to a declaration which fell short of Arab nationalist hopes. On the other hand Hitler did not want Great Britain to score a success in Iraq because such a success could swing Turkey (which had so far fallen down on obligations to Great Britain and France undertaken in a treaty of October 1939) into the British camp with embarrassing results for Germany's drive into the Caucasus and beyond. So in the end Hitler promised to give air support to Rashid Ali and to try to get Vichy to send him arms from French stores in Syria.

The British, fearful for their communications with India via Basra and their supplies of Iraqi oil, forced the pace by bringing what forces they wanted to Basra; they ignored Iraqi conditions limiting the numbers of British troops to be allowed on Iraqi soil at any one time and the length of stay of each unit in transit. On 2 May they attacked Iraq. A force from Palestine and another under Brigadier Glubb from the Arab Legion in Transjordan struck north towards Baghdad which surrendered on the last day of the month. Rashid Ali, having expected too much from the Germans, found himself a refugee in Teheran. The Germans, having expected too much from Rashid Ali and done too little for him, lost such chance as they had of taking the Middle East by frontal assault. Great Britain lost no time in making sure of Syria and Lebanon, and Iran too.

One consequence of the Rashid Ali episode had been a temporary intensification of German-French cooperation. The dominant figure at Vichy at this time was the acidly anti-British Admiral Darlan, with whom the Germans were engaged in negotiating the Paris Protocols which provided for extensive and active cooperation in the Middle East and Africa. In the Middle East Darlan agreed to give the Germans transit and landing rights for aircraft on their way to Iraq and to provide Rashid Ali with French arms, but this policy of resurrecting France through a working partnership with the Nazis was too much for Pétain who brought Weygand over from North Africa early in June in a manoeuvre to resist Darlan. The Paris Protocols thereupon lapsed but not before they had caused the British, with the Free French, to invade Syria and Lebanon.

The local French commander, General Dentz, proposed to resist with German help, but Vichy prevaricated partly through fear of British retaliation in Morocco and partly through fear of offending the Americans and so forfeiting the food and other materials which the Americans were sending to France. So Vichy attached conditions to the acceptance of German air support in Syria which caused the Germans to decline to give any help at all. They were in any case doubtful about the wisdom of helping a mandatory power which the Arabs, whom they were courting, wanted to see evicted. The British put pressure on Turkey to refuse facilities for French reinforcements and supplies (except oil which was covered by an existing agreement); Turkey refused, however, a British invitation to enter Syria from the north. General Dentz, strong in spirit and comparatively strong in numbers but weak in everything else, was forced to capitulate on 14 July after five weeks of fighting.

This British success not only extinguished Vichy's authority in Syria and Lebanon but also constrained de Gaulle to grant these two countries their independence – which was endorsed by Great Britain. But the Gaullists were not happy with the idea of recovering French territory from Vichy and then letting it go from the French empire at British behest, and no further steps were taken until 1943 when elections were held and governments installed with something less than sovereign status. In Lebanon a quarrel between the government and the French led to the arrest of the newly elected President and the dissolution of the newly elected parliament, but Anglo-American intervention forced the French to retreat and to concede real powers to the governments of both countries. Arab countries under British rule took note, waiting their turn. The United States and the USSR recognized independent Syria and Lebanon and although France tried at the end of the war to exact special privileges for itself like those enjoyed by Great Britain in Egypt, Iraq and Transjordan, and even bombed Damascus, it was frustrated by British action and forced to recognize that its defeat in 1940 had cost it its position in the Levant.

A few weeks after the capitulation of General Dentz in July 1941 Great Britain made doubly sure of its Middle Eastern position by occupying Iran in concert with the Russians. The Shah was bundled off to an island in the Indian Ocean and later to South Africa where he died.

Thus at mid-summer 1941 Germany had appropriated the Balkans and Great Britain had replied by dominating the whole of the Middle East. The first of these positions was not to be contested until the general German retreat at the end of the war, which liberated the Balkans. In the Mediterranean and North Africa the war went on. The battle for Cape Matapan in March and the withdrawal of the Luftwaffe for the Russian campaign in June eased the British position, and in July Malta welcomed the first convoy to reach port since January. Another followed in September and for a few weeks Malta became once more a naval base, but the loss of the aircraft carrier *Ark Royal* in the western Mediterranean and the battleship *Barham* in the east, and damage to Great Britain's two remaining battleships by Italian mines fixed to them in harbour at Alexandria, reasserted the challenge to British naval power.

On land Rommel advanced, retreated and survived. His first offensive, launched at the end of March 1941, carried him from Tripolitania through Cyrenaica and into Egypt. Benghazi fell but Tobruk was held by an Australian, New Zealand and Polish garrison. (The Australians were replaced by British troops during the siege. Their commander believed that their health had deteriorated so badly that they could not withstand a major attack. Also, the Australian government and commander-in-chief wanted to reassemble all Australian forces in theatre under a unified Australian command. The New Zealand troops remained. New Zealand was the only nation besides Great Britain to send fighting troops to every theatre of war.) Rommel's success offered tantalizing prospects of a German advance to Suez, Iraq and the Persian Gulf, but Hitler decided that all this must wait. The Balkans must come first because they were essential for the launching of Barbarossa before mid-summer. So Rommel had to pause. In May and June he and Wavell engaged in a series of dingdong battles for the Halfaya Pass on the borders of Egypt, and Wavell then made an attempt to relieve Tobruk which failed. In a trial of skill in armoured warfare Rommel came off best, the British suffered serious losses of newly arrived tanks, and Wavell was relieved of his command on the day of the German invasion of the USSR. He was replaced by General Auchinleck with General Cunningham in command on the desert front.

Until November Rommel remained on the Egyptian frontier, experiencing increasing difficulties with his supply lines across the Mediterranean. In that month Hitler sent Field Marshal Kesselring to Rome with the title of Supreme Commander South, reinforced the Luftwaffe's meagre strength in the Mediterranean and switched half his U-boats from the Atlantic to the Mediterranean. Generals Auchinleck and Cunningham attacked in mid-November. At the southern end of the front they defeated an Italian armoured division but in the north confused fighting, in which British and German tank formations often found themselves behind what would have been the enemy's lines if any lines had existed, produced no decisive result. At one moment the defenders of Tobruk attempted a break-out which failed. At another, Rommel, encouraged by British losses, made a dash for Egypt which also failed. Rommel's two armoured divisions were superior to the British in fire power but inferior in numbers, and in the first week of December he decided to retreat to avoid encirclement. Thus the siege of Tobruk was at last raised, but as Rommel withdrew once more into Tripolitania (his skill in withdrawal was as great as his dash in attack) leaving the British in control of Cyrenaica an acrimonious debate broke out on the British side. The main object of the campaign had not been achieved; the German Panzer army had not been destroyed. During the battle Auchinleck had dismissed Cunningham and summoned General Ritchie from Cairo to take his place. Since the battle and until the present day there has been controversy about the events of these weeks. It has been argued that if the British had waited for Rommel to attack they would have had a better chance of annihilating his forces, and it has also been argued that the retention of forces in the Middle East for this indecisive action contributed to the fall of Singapore in the following February. By this time Rommel had received new tanks via Tripoli and was planning a second eastward advance. The war in Africa was not concluded until eighteen months later and after the second front in North-west Africa, closed by the fall of France in 1940, had been reopened by the Anglo-American invasion of November 1942.

CHAPTER 9

Barbarossa

THE Russo-German treaty of August 1939 served its German purpose for almost two years. During that period Hitler made himself virtual master of the whole of continental Europe outside the borders of the USSR. A few neutrals existed on the fringes and one – Switzerland – in the middle, but nowhere was there opposition to Germany. These conquests had not been achieved without alarming Stalin. He had shared in the spoliation of Poland, annexed the three Baltic states after the fall of France and taken Bessarabia and Northern Bukovina from Rumania. Hitler then carved up Rumania and forced it, together with Hungary and Slovakia, to adhere to the Tripartite Pact. After Mussolini's unsuccessful invasion of Greece he added Bulgaria and Yugoslavia to the Tripartite Pact and moved into Bulgaria. Stalin protested – he had protested the previous year that the partition of Rumania was a breach of the Russo-German treaty of 1939 only to be met with the obvious retort that he himself had already broken it by helping himself to northern Bukovina. When the Simovic government in Belgrade repudiated the Tripartite Pact Stalin made a formal declaration of friendship with it but did not commit the USSR to go to its aid against a German attack. The two pseudo-allies were manoeuvring for positions in the one sizable undistributed area in Europe and the Germans were getting the better of the game because they did not mind provoking the Russians, whereas the Russians were still anxious not to provoke the Germans.

Stalin's agents abroad were reporting that Hitler was about to attack the USSR, the British and American governments were repeating the warnings, and German troop movements told the same tale. Most tellingly of all, German deserters were crossing what had become a Russo-German front line in Poland to give warning of the German attack. A week after the opening of the German campaign in the Balkans and on the day when Belgrade fell, Stalin concluded a neutrality pact with Japan. But he did not trust Japan to keep it and even after Hitler's attack he hesitated for some time before moving troops from his Asian to his European fronts. On 5 June he became President of the Council of Commissars or, as we would say, Prime Minister, in place of Molotov who became Deputy Prime Minister as well as Foreign Minister. (Stalin had hitherto held only

THE RUSSIAN BARRIER 1939-1940

The eastward advance of the German armies led the Soviet Union to establish a 'barrier' strip of territory between its western frontier and the potential aggressor. However, this proved of little advantage when the Germans launched their invasion in June 1941.

0   150
Miles

LATVIA
Russian before 1914
Independent 1920-1939

LITHUANIA
Russian before 1914
Independent 1919-1939

PART OF FINLAND
Russian before 1917
Finnish 1918-1939

ESTONIA
Russian before 1917
Independent 1918-1939

EASTERN POLAND
Russian before 1914
Polish 1919-1939

EASTERN GALICIA
Austrian before 1918
Polish 1918-1939

BESSARABIA
Russian before 1917
Rumanian 1918-1940

BUKOVINA
Austrian before 1918
Rumanian 1918-1940

FINLAND
Petrozavodsk
Helsinki
Viborg
Leningrad
Baltic Sea
Tallin (Reval)
Pskov
Riga
Memel
U S S R
Königsberg
EAST PRUSSIA
Vilna
Minsk
Grodno
Warsaw
Pinsk
P O L A N D
Lublin
Kiev
Tarnov
Przemysl
Lvov
Kamanets Podolsk
SLOVAKIA
Uzhgorod
Balta
HUNGARY
Iasi
R U M A N I A
Kishinev
Odessa
Black Sea

Occupied by USSR.
October 1939 to December 1940.

The German Reich by December 1939.

Under German control or influence by December 1940.

-ARTHUR BANKS-the post of Secretary General of the Communist Party.) But during these last months Stalin continued to do everything he could to avoid or postpone the German attack. The ease of the German conquest of Yugoslavia and Greece showed him that the turn of events in south-eastern Europe would do little or nothing to interfere with Hitler's plans to attack the USSR. He increased Russian supplies to Germany, promising and punctually providing special facilities for the transit of rubber from the Far East and making other economic agreements favourable to Germany; he stopped arguing about the Russo-German frontier in the Baltic area; he expunged all criticism of Germany from the Russian press; he withdrew recognition of the Norwegian and Belgian governments in exile, expelled the Yugoslav Ambassador from Moscow, refused to recognize the Greek government in exile and recognized Rashid Ali's pro-German régime in Iraq. None of these things had been asked for by Hitler and the German press was told to make no mention of them.

At home Stalin had two paramount problems. The first was the state of the Soviet armed forces and the second was strategic. The USSR's western frontier was a long one. At no great distance behind it lay Leningrad in the north and the mineral and agricultural riches of the Ukraine in the south. In the centre Moscow, although more distant, was not beyond the reach of a powerful, mechanized enemy determined to seize it within six months. This central front was bisected by the Pripet marshes which impeded switches between one sector and another. In spite of the misgivings of his professional advisers Stalin had moved forces into newly occupied territories – Bessarabia, Poland, Finland, the Baltic states – and out of the so-called Stalin Line (whose powerful guns and tangles of barbed wire in difficult forest country later impressed the Germans who overran it), until by May 1941 170 Russian divisions were stationed outside the pre-1939 frontiers of the USSR. Stalin may have been hoping that Hitler's adventures in the west would give him a chance to attack again on the Finnish front (where he had twenty-seven divisions, including five armoured) or win further ground in the Balkans but this is surmise. The fact is that well over half the Russian army was occupying new positions whose fortifications and rearward communications were incomplete.

Furthermore, the forces which would be called upon to take the shock of the German attack were still recovering from the great purges. Where Hitler had tamed his officer caste, Stalin had killed his. The purges of the armed forces were a part of the Great Purge of the civilian and military establishments which Stalin began in 1936. An officer corps constitutes by its very nature a possible alternative to civilian government and Stalin was afraid of it. The Russian army had no tradition of revolution; its sole attempt to usurp the civil power – the Decembrist coup of 1825 – had collapsed after a day; but Stalin was obsessed with the example of Bonapartism and he proceeded in the thirties to emasculate the civil war generation whose leaders, military or civilian, might conspire against him. Because of his fears he was quick to lend an ear to accusations that his officers were plotting against him. One of his agents in Paris provided false evidence against Marshal Tukhachevski, the Chief of Staff of the Army, who was alleged to be in treasonable correspondence with German officers. This evidence was planted on Beneš who guilelessly passed it on to Moscow where it was used as reliable confirmation from an untainted source of prefabricated charges. In addition Russian agents persuaded German Intelligence to forge supporting documents which were likewise sent to Moscow to build up the case against Tukhachevski even further. Tukhachevski was arrested and executed after a trial lasting one day. Six of the eight officers who constituted the court martial were also executed. The further victims of the purge embraced three of the five Marshals of the Soviet Union, all eleven deputy Commissars for Defence (that is to say, deputy Ministers), seventy-five of the eighty members of the Military Soviet, all the commanders of the military districts into which the country was divided in peacetime, thirteen of fifteen army commanders, over half the corps commanders and 20–40 per cent of all officers below brigade. They were replaced by retired stalwarts or young party enthusiasts who were either too out of touch or too unprofessional to inspire confidence or to understand the new equipment which the army was beginning to receive.

This stupendous amputation of head and members, which affected the political as much as the military side of the Soviet army's dual control, disorganized and dispirited the services more than enough to prevent them from being a threat to the régime but also almost enough to prevent them from being a threat to an enemy. The invasion of Poland in September 1939 posed no fighting problem since the Poles had already been beaten by the Germans (it did, however, disclose organizational and logistic inefficiency), but the Finnish war was an inglorious shock, forcing the Russians to employ one and a half million men and to take three months over the sort of operation to which Hitler would have allotted a week or two. But this shock was also perhaps a boon. It forced Stalin to accelerate the reorganization of his defences. In May 1940 S. K. Timoshenko was made a Marshal and Defence Commissar at the age of forty-five, replacing the veteran Bolshevik K. E. Voroshilov. New training programmes were introduced. So were professional titles for ranks. Military commissars were abolished (they were reintroduced in 1941 and abolished again in 1942) and steps were taken to boost the prestige of the armed services. In February 1941 G. K. Zhukov, who had recently concluded a successful campaign against the Japanese in contrast to the deplorable performance of some of his colleagues on the Finnish front, was promoted full general and Chief of Staff of the Army; he became the pre-eminent figure among Stalin's Marshals but, like Marshal Soult whom he in some ways resembled (including the possession of a political temperament), was as heartily disliked by some of his fellows as he was lauded by others.

In the field, however, only a few of the army's new leaders had emerged, its divisions were below strength and its preparations – especially in frontier districts – had been impeded up to the last moment by Stalin's continuing obsession with avoiding provoking the Germans and so prolonging the respite. By ill chance the Russian forces were caught in the process of changing over to the T 34 tank which was only beginning to emerge from the factories. In addition they were, not for the first time, changing their tank tactics. In earlier years the Russians, like the Germans, had imbibed some of the new ideas about tank warfare propounded by Liddell Hart, Fuller and Martel, but in the thirties Stalin had changed his mind. The defeat of the Italians at the battle of Guadalajara in the Spanish civil war, perhaps also Marshal Tukhachevski's support for the new doctrine, and Russian experience in Mongolia and Finland, all undermined Stalin's faith in large tank formations and he decided that tanks should not be concentrated in tank corps and tank armies but should be spread through other formations in accordance with an older doctrine. Then the German successes in France made him change his mind again, although not in time to enable the Russian forces to be regrouped before suffering severe defeats.

Hitler's attack was launched on 22 June, two days earlier than the date on which Napoleon had led the Grand Army across the Niemen in 1812. It was the biggest military operation ever mounted. Although Hitler believed that the USSR would collapse, he was taking no chances and in any case he loved sheer size. His hosts, which included contingents of a dozen nationalities, attacked in three directions. Northern and Central Army Groups under Field Marshals von Leeb and von Bock headed towards the cities of Leningrad and Moscow, Southern Army Group under Field Marshal von Rundstedt for the Ukraine, the Don basin, the Crimea and the Caucasus with their wealth of grain, coal and oil. Their main objective was to surround and destroy the Russian forces in western Russia and prevent any 'battleworthy elements' from escaping into the interior: the capture of cities and provinces would then follow automatically. Surprise was complete: psychological surprise, because the Russian public had been allowed no hint of what was in store; tactical surprise, because the Russian forces in western areas were not forewarned. So began the most appalling, devastating and savage conflict in the history of warfare.

It was conducted on both sides by obsessively ruthless tyrants, battering one another like a pair of rabid rhinoceroses – with this difference that they used not their own bodies but those of millions of men whom, by the exercise of will, they committed to every kind of suffering, mutilation and death. Until nearly the end of its four years this fearful contest was remote from the other theatres of war, so that when it ended its impact on the rest of the world – on those who were neither Russian nor German – was incommensurate with its hideous actuality.

Stalin has been heavily blamed for his inept dispositions in the face of an invasion which was easily foreseeable. Apologists have suggested that he believed American and British warnings to be a ruse to induce him to mobilize and so provoke Hitler much as the Kaiser had been provoked to attack in 1914 by Russian mobilization. But this argument discounts the warnings received by Stalin from other quarters. While the timing of Hitler's invasion was a matter for conjecture until almost the last moment, it was virtually inevitable and, from several months earlier, imminent. Hitler had himself proclaimed his intention to annex parts of the Soviet Union as living space for the German race and he was deflected neither by his pact with Stalin in 1939 nor by his failure in the Battle of Britain to secure peace in the west before attacking in the east. For Stalin the pact of 1939 was never more than a means to a respite, a way to gain time not peace. The charge against him is that he made such poor use of the time he bought. He was already suffering from the two great diseases of the autocrat: vanity and isolation. His brutal domination over colleagues in the Communist party and the armed services deprived him of honest deliberation and advice; absurdly confident of his ability to fend off Hitler he was prone to play down warnings which clashed with his preconceptions, while some intelligence never reached him from subordinates who were too scared to tell him things likely to be unwelcome. From the winter of 1940–41 his own agents (notably Richard Sorge working in Japan for Red Army Intelligence) were reinforcing the warnings conveyed by the American and British governments but apart from his neutrality pact with Japan in April 1941 Stalin's attitude was almost entirely passive. Delay was his tactic and it was ineffectual.

Stalin's armed forces and his frontier defences, although in the process of reorganization and re-equipment, were hopelessly and chaotically inadequate when Hitler sent four fifths of his armies – three million men – across the dividing line in Poland, confident of making mincemeat of his enemy and of capturing Moscow, Leningrad and the Caucasus before the end of the year. Hitler was to be proved nearly right but yet disastrously wrong. The Russian fronts were broken in several places within hours of the opening attack. Whole armies and Fronts (the Russian equivalent of Army Groups) were annihilated in spite of desperate, if ill coordinated, resistance and suicidal counter-attacks. Stunned by the magnitude of disaster on every front, and perhaps fearful for his own life, Stalin stayed silent until 3 July but on that day he took control of the war. In a broadcast speech he appealed to Russian patriotism; in the field he dismissed generals and had them shot. From this point onward he functioned as supreme war lord. Although often suspicious of his generals he did not make Hitler's mistake of dismissing the best of them. At the end of July he removed Zhukov from the post of Chief of Staff and recalled the aged, infirm and only dubiously competent Marshal Shaposhnikov who might be expected, like Keitel on the German side, to do his master's bidding; but Zhukov, having been sent to take charge of the defence of Leningrad, was brought back in October to save Moscow and was thereafter uninterruptedly at the centre of war planning until the capture of Berlin.

The main weight of the German attack was in the centre. The striking power of each Army Group was concentrated in Panzer Groups. Army Group Centre had two of these; each of its neighbours one. The Panzer Groups struck swiftly and directly, disrupting the enemy front and outdistancing the rest of the German forces which advanced as a second wave in encircling movements to trap the Russian forces which had been severed from each other by the slicing Panzers. In this way the Russians were cut up into sections and surrounded in pockets, and the speed and success of the German Panzer Groups were so great that the pockets were very large. Some of them contained up to fifteen Russian divisions. Huge numbers of prisoners were taken. On the Russian side there was almost total disorganization. Roads and railways were made unusable by the Luftwaffe. Every kind of communication failed. Frantic reports from the front and appeals for instructions, sent *en clair* for want of time to encipher them, dismayed incredulous staffs at higher echelons which retorted that the reports must be wrong and reprimanded the senders for not using their codes. But amid this confusion the Russians faced forward and even counter-attacked, driving their tanks suicidally into German artillery fire and pouring uncoordinated masses of men into the path of the unstoppable Germans. Others retreated or fled, destroying such installations and livestock as they could, often themselves destroyed either by the Luftwaffe or by the machine guns of the N K V D. Their officers were summoned back to Moscow to be shot there. The Germans, advancing up to fifty miles a day, were equally amazed by their own success and by the violent, valiant and often ferocious resistance of men who should have been totally demoralized. They began from the start to perceive that the war in the east was going to be different from the other campaigns of the past two years.

In mere numbers the Russians could match the Germans at many points. They had more men and more tanks, field artillery and aircraft. They had about 20,000 tanks, of which some 7,000 were in forward areas, but most of them were obsolescent and according to Marshal Konev, writing after the war was over, losses were so heavy that by September there were only forty-five serviceable modern tanks between the Germans and Moscow. Konev, one of Stalin's outstanding tank commanders, regarded the Russian T 34 as the best tank in any army during the entire war, but it did not become the mainstay of the Russian forces until 1943. Russian manpower was immense but infantry divisions were still not motorized and shortages ranging from radio equipment to medical supplies were crippling. Large areas of the U S S R passed into German hands. Goebbels proclaimed on 10 July: 'The eastern continent lies like a limp virgin in the mighty arms of the German Mars.' As whole armies surrendered and cities fell (Minsk 28 June, Smolensk 16 July) the German victory in the field seemed complete. But the Russians were not quite overwhelmed. Their armies were not destroyed. Nor were their air forces.

The Russian air forces (the largest in the world) and Russian aircraft production were, like the Russian army, in a stage of re-equipment and expansion in the years immediately before war came. Although markedly inferior to the German and British air forces – in machines, output, design, technical equipment, training, maintenance, ground organization and airfield construction – the Russian air forces had reached a point where improvement in all these departments could be rapid. The most important feature of the air war in the east after 1941 was that this improvement was not only astonishingly rapid but far more so than the Germans or anybody else had believed possible. In the first half of the war the Russians were able to offset their all-round inferiority by superiority in one thing – numbers. In the second half of the war they had air forces which were not only bigger but better than the Luftwaffe.

Russian aircraft production passed German production about the end of 1937, that is to say, before Munich. It then rose steadily from around 800 a month to 900 in 1939 and 1,000 by the time of Barbarossa. The first deliveries from new factories built in the Urals in the early thirties began

OPERATION 'BARBAROSSA'
22 JUNE 1941

Under German rule or influence by June 1941.

General direction of the German advance.

Occupied by German forces between June and December 1941.

Cities besieged by Germans 1941.

NORWAY

SWEDEN

FINLAND

Murmansk

Kandalaksha

Archangel

BALTIC SEA

Helsinki

Leningrad

Tikhvin

Vologda

Novgorod

Pskov

Gorki

Riga

Moscow

Danzig

Smolensk

Riazan

GREATER

Minsk

Tula

S

S

R

Warsaw

Pripet Marshes

U

Orel

Kursk

Voronezh

GERMANY

Kiev

HUNGARY

Lyov

Kharkov

Stalingrad

RUMANIA

Rostov

YUGOSLAVIA

Odessa

BULGARIA

Sevastopol

BLACK SEA

GREECE

0   200
Miles

~ARTHUR BANKS~

to reach units in 1939, but when production and assembly plants in the west were overrun by the German armies total output was halved. It recovered by the middle of 1942 and then rose remorselessly to a peak of 3,000 a month. First line strength was 3,000–3,500 at the beginning of 1938, 4,000–5,000 a year later; after surmounting the crisis of 1941–2 it reached 10,000 by mid-1943, 15,000 by mid-1944 and over 20,000 before the war ended. But when war began reserves were poor. There was no pool of aircraft on which operational units could draw in order to replace their losses; new aircraft had to go straight from factory to units, so that the operational strength of units depended directly on the irregular factory flow and was sometimes down to half the prescribed establishment – with depressing effects on morale as well as on strengths. There were acute shortages of high-octane fuel at the front and essential raw materials for the factories. The Russian air forces had no radar, no ground control, not enough fighters and very few night fighters. Such fighters as could be spared from the fighting at the front were concentrated on airfields round Moscow for the defence of the capital. Strategic bombing of targets in the enemy's rear was impossible in 1941 and hardly developed at any time. Russian long-range bombers, unequipped with radar, engaged in danger-ous and largely ineffective missions in which a half to three quarters of modest forces of about one hundred aircraft failed to find their targets. Bomb loads never exceeded two tons, a light load compared with the ten tons carried by the British Lancaster. Finally, the Russian air forces were still divided in 1941 between a western front against the Germans and an eastern front against the Japanese, and in spite of Stalin's growing assur-ance that he had nothing to fear in the east he hesitated to denude his eastern front until the threat to Moscow forced him to transfer 1,000 fighters and fighter bombers westward in the autumn of 1941.

The first three months of the campaigns of 1941 were catastrophic but just not fatal. The Russian air forces, attacked by an enemy who was technically much superior, were caught by surprise, inadequately camou-flaged, undispersed, unsure of their supplies and communications: Russian fighters, 20–100 m.p.h. slower than the German Me. 109s, were outfought, frequently in the course of retreating from one airfield to another further back. Great numbers were destroyed on the ground, either by surprise attack or because they had to be left behind owing to shortages of fuel or spare parts. The Luftwaffe claimed to have destroyed 1,489 aircraft on the ground on the first day; a first attempt to retaliate by bombing German targets cost the Russians 500 aircraft. On the day after the battle opened one commander of a Russian bomber group committed suicide after losing 600 aircraft against only twelve German. Russian losses by the end of August probably amounted to more than 5,000 aircraft. A month later their front line strength in the west had been halved and the Germans believed that the Russian air force had ceased to exist. Significantly, they were puzzled by the continued arrival of reinforcements. They were handicapped by their inability to reach and bomb the factories in the east where many of these aircraft were being turned out. They continued to shoot down the new aircraft which were thrown by the Russians desperately into the battle as soon as they arrived, but the flow never ceased and the Luftwaffe itself began to feel the strain.

German front line strengths shrank too, sometimes to half establishment. Space and snow came to the help of the Russians. The Luftwaffe, however excellent, was too small for a 2,000-mile front. As units were switched from Leningrad in the far north to the Ukrainian or central front, operational efficiency declined. The Luftwaffe could not keep up its initial effort of 1,500–2,000 sorties a day. It was farther away from its bases at home than it had ever been, its communications longer and more precarious, its flying conditions more testing. Once again it was short of fighters, and although the Stukas made their final onslaught of the war they too were too few to deliver along this huge front the series of packed punches which had drilled holes in the armies on the western fronts. When the snow came and the airfields froze, the High Command of the Luftwaffe failed to provide its men with the right clothing or its machines with anti-freeze. Its difficulties were accentuated by the makeshift nature of some of the airstrips which it was obliged to use and which were inferior to the airfields round Moscow being used by the Russians. By the end of the year German operational strength along the whole front had fallen to 1,500 and in the Moscow sector the Russians had assembled twice as many aircraft as the Luftwaffe.

But this capacity of the Russian air forces to survive was secondary. The decisive fact was the survival of the Russian ground forces. At the end of the first four weeks of the campaign the Germans paused for breath – and for argument. The Panzer units were farther ahead of the infantry than had been expected and some of them were 200 miles from their depots in eastern Poland; spare parts had to be flown to them since many roads were only unsurfaced tracks and there were hundreds of thousands of armed Russians behind the German lines. How many it is impossible to say: certainly 250,000, perhaps twice that number, whole armies cut up and disoriented but not eliminated. Guderian and other tank commanders wanted to resume their advances as soon and as fast as possible in order to keep on hammering the Russians, prevent the consolidation of a new line of Russian defence, exterminate the enemy's fighting capacity and capture Moscow. Hitler on the other hand wanted to hold in the centre, strengthen his northern and southern Army Groups, bypass and isolate Leningrad with the one, and push south with the other until he was in a position to sweep round behind Moscow and the Russian armies to the west of it. Besides this strategic problem Hitler and his generals were worried by the gap which had already developed between the Panzers and the rest of the army and would be yet further increased if the Panzers were given their head, and they were worried because their advance not only extended their lines from west to east but also, fanwise, on a north-south axis – owing to the fact that the starting line of June had been considerably shorter than the line along which they were forced by geography to operate by the end of July.

The German forces were becoming stretched in all directions and it was not impossible to envisage the Russians inserting unused reinforcements between the Panzers and their supporting units, while at the same time breaking out of one or two pockets farther west and starting effective guerilla action against the German lines of communication. To give point to their fears several thousand Russian troops did break out of the Smolensk pocket. So from mid-July to mid-August the debate went on; the Germans failed to make the best of some of the most favourable weather of the summer or to exploit the chaos reigning in western Russia where local commanders and local party officials tussled with problems of discipline and administration and no firm directives reached them from the top (except simply to attack Germans whenever they were seen); the battered Russians had time to breathe, to re-group and to rush reserve divisions into the gaps. These divisions were half-trained, poorly equipped, sometimes still in civilian clothes, but they arrived and played their part; the Germans had not thought that they could be brought into the line so quickly. So great was the urgency on the Russian side that when trains reached their destinations the locomotives were uncoupled and sent back post haste without waiting for the rolling stock.

During these weeks Stalin's authority became assured. It is not certain that it was so in the first disastrous weeks of war, or that he believed it to be so. A few days after the German invasion a defence committee to run the war was established under his chairmanship. The other members were Molotov, Voroshilov, Malenkov and Beria. Below this committee was the *Stavka*, a supreme planning staff which controlled the Fronts. The *Stavka* consisted originally of a dozen senior officers but Stalin, Molotov and Voroshilov were added to it soon after the outbreak of war. In July Stalin became, like Churchill, Defence Minister as well as Prime Minister; in August, like Hitler, Commander-in-Chief too. But titles do not make victories and his plight, as he himself saw it in this month, is revealed by his avowal to Harry Hopkins, Roosevelt's special emissary, that he would welcome American troops on any part of Russian soil under unrestricted American command. But by the autumn, he, like Russia, had weathered the first storm and was ready to face the next. He reorganized the higher commands and imposed his will on his commanders. The system of dual military and party control in the armed services, abolished shortly before the war began, had been reintroduced a few weeks after the German attack and command of three Fronts entrusted to Voroshilov and Zhdanov in the north, Timoshenko and Bulganin in the centre and Budyenny and Kruschchev in the south. Budyenny, a dashing hero with a big moustache but a little brain, was later relieved and succeeded by Timoshenko, who was replaced in the vital central sector first by Konev and then by Zhukov.

On 23 August the pause on the German side ended. The attack was resumed – in the south Guderian's armour was switched from Bock's Army Group Centre to Rundstedt's Army Group South. Two days later Dnepropetrovsk fell and the Russians blew up the great dam at Zaporozhe which supplied the power for the mass of industries in the Dnieper bend, a self-mutilation which proclaimed that they had little hope of recapturing lost territory in the near future. Kiev was now at the western tip of a Russian salient, half encircled and urgently threatened. To Budyenny and Kruschchev its loss seemed certain and its abandonment a strategic necessity, but Stalin insisted on a fight to the finish. This was not pure stubbornness. Stalin may have reasoned that Budyenny, whose forces were larger than those facing him, ought to be able to hold Kiev; that in any case any delay was worth while in order to check an advance which threatened to envelop Moscow; and that the retreat of so large a force at this juncture would be psychologically disastrous. Kiev had to pay the price, which turned out to be very high. Four Russian armies were surrounded and when they surrendered on 17 September the number of prisoners who fell into the German bag (even if they were fewer than the German claim of 665,000) was immense. Here, as elsewhere in this savage war, the prisoners were worse off than the dead, for the Germans frequently failed to give them medical assistance or to feed them properly. From Kiev the Germans swept on over the Ukraine; Odessa was abandoned, Kharkov taken; Rostov was lost but recovered.

In the centre Guderian's armour, switched back to this sector after a mere couple of weeks in the Ukraine, prepared for its last thrust of the year, the drive for Moscow. It was launched at the beginning of October. Again the Russians were taken by surprise – their air reconnaissance and their wireless intelligence were poor – and they suffered enormous losses. Something like panic developed in Moscow, accentuated by reports of how the Germans were treating prisoners and civilians and the NKVD shooting deserters. Some two million Muscovites were evacuated in due order and others simply fled. But Stalin and his principal military advisers and civilian subordinates remained. Reinforcements were rushed up from Mongolia – a switch which was less of a gamble than it appeared on the surface because Stalin had been told by the spy Richard Sorge in Tokyo that Japan had decided to attack in the Pacific and not in north Asia.

After the first week of the German October offensive the weather broke and converted the battlefields into mud swamps so thick that tanks and vehicles struggled in them in vain. The Germans slithered and stuck and prayed for frost to harden the going again. But they were unlucky once more. The mud was late in freezing over, and when it did in November the temperature fell not only late but sharply, causing them terrible suffering. In December came blizzards which reduced visibility to fifty yards. Clothing was inadequate. A request by Guderian for winter supplies had earned him a rebuke for implying that they might be needed. The men stuffed their clothes with paper to keep warm, often with leaflets sent to the front to be showered upon the enemy and tell him that surrender was his only sane course. By Christmas the Germans had 100,000 cases of frostbite. Dysentery was rife. Like their comrades in the Luftwaffe the army had no anti-freeze. Their guns would not fire. Yet they were constantly harassed, usually by small parties of Russians at night. The intense cold and snow also prevented supplies of food from reaching them. What food they had often had to be cut with axes or saws. Soup froze if a man paused for a minute in getting it into his mouth. The medal earned by these afflicted men was nicknamed the Order of Frozen Flesh. Some committed suicide. Looking back over the war when he came to write about this time Guderian recalled 'the endless expanse of Russian snow during this winter of our misery . . . the icy wind that blew across it . . . too thin shelter . . . insufficiently clothed, half-starved men'.

By the first week in November the Germans were within fifty miles of Moscow; by the end of the month twenty miles. The final German assault came on 1 December and failed. Stalin had already decided to counter-attack before the year ended. Local and limited counter-attacks during November had not been able to stem the German advance but a stronger and more coordinated attack launched on 5 December pushed the Germans back as Stalin harried his generals and these in turn drove their men forward. This was the first appreciable Russian victory and there were more crumbs of comfort in the south where the Kertch peninsula was recaptured and Sebastopol held. Hitler failed to emulate Napoleon's feat – in 1941 or ever. Perhaps if he had taken Guderian's advice to concentrate on Moscow he might have succeeded; and perhaps he would then have won his war in the east. But neither of these propositions is certain. What is certain is that in the first week of December 1941 one of the most precarious moments of the war was reached and passed.

Leningrad too survived, although threatened by famine as well as arms. The siege of Leningrad became one of the epic events of the war. The magnificent capital of Peter the Great, built on either side of the Neva and on the islands in its estuary, contained three million inhabitants, of whom close on one million died in the siege. When the German invasion was launched desperate but belated preparations were made to withstand an assault and the Russian forces renewed their attack on the Finns, who, despite protestations of neutrality, were expected to make common cause with the Germans. Finnish forces re-occupied territory lost in the war of 1939–40 but Field Marshal Mannerheim was unwilling to overstep the 1939 frontiers (which his troops reached in August) and, partly in response to American pressure, refused persistent German requests for an alliance and joint operations against Leningrad.

The northern group of German armies advanced rapidly. It reached the river Drina in four days, pressed on to Pskov after a short pause and might perhaps have captured Leningrad before the end of July. Its leading units, which had covered 470 miles in three weeks, were only sixty miles from the city but at this point they halted and did not resume the advance until 8 August. Hitler – in a mood not unlike the one which had allowed the British to escape from Dunkirk – wanted to nurse his armour and reduce the city by siege and air attack, after which it was to be razed to the ground as a symbolic extirpation of its eponymous guardian, the founder of the bolshevist state. He seems always to have been in two minds about Leningrad. On the one hand he willed its obliteration, but when he was thinking in broad strategic terms he did not want to waste before it large forces which should be advancing into the heart of Russia. The first shells fell on it in the first days of September. Zhukov arrived to direct the defences on the 11th. The city had been all but completely invested a few days earlier.

Leningrad had been the scene of the most celebrated episodes in the overthrow of the Tsars (whose capital it had been) and the jealous defender ever since that date of all that was purest in communist tradition and doctrine. Inside this city men, women and children now laboured ceaselessly on civil defence and emergency fortifications; to seaward the Russian Baltic fleet, whether riding the waters or imprisoned in the ice, provided an extra ring of guns; even the guns of the ancient cruiser *Aurora* which had been turned into a museum were removed and put into the first line; industries and population were evacuated to the east; patriotic enthusiasm was fanned by propaganda lectures. Leningrad was besieged from September 1941 to January 1944. It had at the outset only one to two months' supply of basic foods, much of which was then destroyed by air attack. Unlikely substitutes were turned into eatables. Uneatables were eaten. Equally catastrophic was the shortage of water for elementary cleansing and of medicines. Deaths from hunger began to occur before the end of 1941 and the monthly rate soon reached the annual average; deaths from privation ran at the rate of several thousands a day and created a serious threat to the morale as well as the health of the survivors, who were already exhausted by extreme cold, hard work, hunger, disease, and the collapse of public services. On Christmas Day 1941 about 4,000 died. The most serious threat came in November 1941 when Tikhvin was taken by the Germans. This town, due east of Leningrad, was on the railway by which the Russians hoped to keep the city supplied, and when it was lost the Russians were compelled to begin the construction of a road from a point safely east of Tikhvin to the eastern shore of Lake Ladoga, whence supplies would be taken across the water or the ice to the south-western corner of the lake thirty-five miles from the city. The first plan was to build a railway line across the ice but a large frozen lake is far from being a flat surface and the first train left its rails near the beginning of its journey. Next came a plan to tear up the city's tramlines and re-lay them on the lake but this scheme was abandoned almost as soon as it was thought of. Finally, the Russians began to build a road and collect lorries – from Moscow and from the American and British vehicles arriving in the far north – to make the passage by night, in the bitter cold of an exceptionally bitter winter (the temperature averaged twenty degrees below freezing over a whole month) and against the fierce north-east winds which constantly swept the surface of the lake. Some supplies got in this way but it was a desperate expedient which could hardly have saved the city. Fortunately the Russians recaptured Tikhvin in December. The encirclement of Leningrad was never complete because the Russians kept possession of the south-western corner of Lake Ladoga. Nevertheless starvation was sometimes only one or two days off during this first and most exacting winter of the war. In Berlin invitations to a reception in Leningrad to be attended by Hitler were printed but never sent out.

Leningrad won a further reprieve in 1942 owing to the resistance of Sebastopol where the German 11th Army, which was designated to switch to Leningrad after the fall of Sebastopol, was not freed from its southern

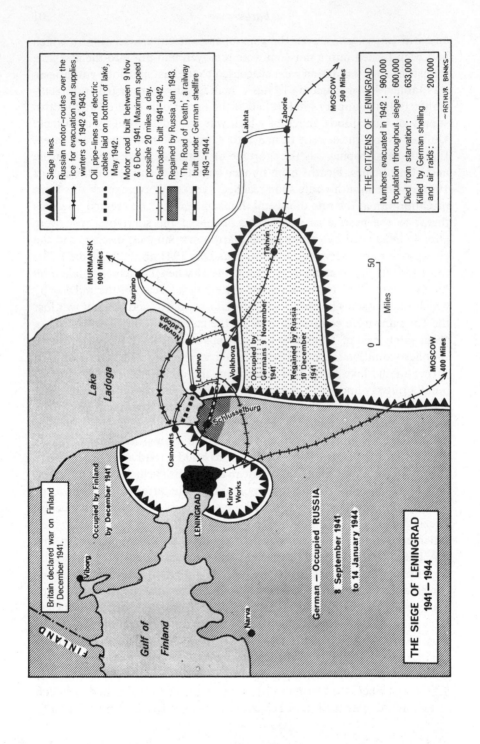

THE SIEGE OF LENINGRAD
1941 – 1944

German – Occupied RUSSIA
8 September 1941
to 14 January 1944

Britain declared war on Finland
7 December 1941.

Occupied by Finland
by December 1941

THE CITIZENS OF LENINGRAD

Numbers evacuated in 1942 :	960,000
Population throughout siege:	600,000
Died from starvation :	633,000
Killed by German shelling and air raids:	200,000

— ARTHUR BANKS —

Siege lines.

Russian motor-routes over the ice for evacuation and supplies, winters of 1942 & 1943.

Oil pipe-lines and electric cables laid on bottom of lake, May 1942.

Motor road built between 9 Nov & 6 Dec 1941. Maximum speed possible 20 miles a day.

Railroads built 1941-1942.

Regained by Russia Jan 1943.

'The Road of Death', a railway built under German shellfire 1943-1944.

FINLAND

Gulf of Finland

Viborg

Narva

LENINGRAD

Kirov Works

Osinovets

Lake Ladoga

Novaya Ladoga

Karpino

MURMANSK
900 Miles

Lednevo

Volkhova

Schlusselburg

Occupied by Germans 9 November 1941

Regained by Russia 10 December 1941

Tikhvin

Lakhta

Zaborie

MOSCOW
500 Miles

MOSCOW
400 Miles

0   50
Miles

task until July and then only moved north partially. A German attack on Leningrad in the autumn of 1942 was forestalled and nipped in the bud by a Russian counter-offensive and shortly afterwards 11th Army was again concentrated in the south. A Russian operation at the beginning of 1943 eased, though it did not remove, the German blockade by opening a new corridor for supplies from across the lake but complete relief had to await the general collapse of the Germans. Leningrad was not freed from attack until January 1944. It received the Order of Lenin. Its endurance and its sufferings and triumph have been immortalized in Shostakovich's seventh symphony, not the greatest work of that great composer, but written and first performed in the most extraordinary circumstances – in the city during the siege. (The most poignant musical cries of the war are Richard Strauss's lament over the destruction of Munich, *Metamorphosen*, the thrilling pathos of the middle movement of Bela Bartók's Concerto for Orchestra, and Britten's setting of poems by Wilfred Owen in his *War Requiem*.)

At the end of 1941 the German conquests in the USSR were vast, but Hitler had not defeated the Russians. He had failed to take Moscow or Leningrad, had taken Rostov and lost it again, had overrun the Crimea but been baulked before Sebastopol, and had suffered in the USSR casualties of about three quarters of a million, of whom one in four were dead. The very arguments about priorities Moscow or Leningrad, Leningrad or the Ukraine, Sebastopol or Leningrad – prove that from the very beginning the German forces were stretched. Once Russian resistance was not wholly broken within weeks, the German command faced choices because the tasks were too many. The same applied to the Luftwaffe. In the first four weeks of the campaign a force of 3,000 aircraft averaged 2,500 sorties a day and thereafter 1,500–2,000 a day for the rest of the year. Their performance was excellent (the Me. 109F, faster but less heavily armed than the Me. 109E, was making its first operational appearance) but in spite of this remarkable effort the force was too thinly spread for its commitments and again switches told the tale – to Leningrad at one moment and then back again to the central front for the main assault on Moscow. Air raids on Moscow were hardly more than token gestures. The city was attacked seventy-six times between the beginning of the campaign and the end of 1941 but the weight of the attack was often trivial. The largest force employed in a single night was 127 and in far more cases than not the bombers could be counted in single figures. The Luftwaffe's reserves were sometimes worryingly low and at the end of the year the mercurial Udet committed suicide. Thus the startling achievements of 1941 on the ground and in the air had by December essentially failed, and a fresh advance in 1942 was to culminate in the disaster of Stalingrad, whereafter the two great land powers of Europe were measured against one another until the Germans were utterly repulsed.

On the Russian side crippling casualties – at least three million men and probably 18,000 tanks in the first disastrous three months – were offset by patriotic determination and furious despair which mounted as the Germans resorted to monstrous cruelties. Sadistic and debauched proconsuls and their henchmen were invested with authority in the rear of the advancing armies (whose commanders preferred to turn a blind eye to proceedings which disgusted them – within limits). Mass executions and the deliberate burying alive of half killed victims united and fired all Russians who escaped this appalling demonstration of the dark side of human nature. At the top Stalin's nerve held, a new layer of brilliant field commanders was moving into the crucial positions and Soviet Intelligence from agents in Switzerland and Germany itself as well as Tokyo was providing a reliable basis for the conduct of the war. One of these agents was Richard Sorge in Tokyo, a handsome and talented German in Russian pay who had become a personal friend and confidant of the German Ambassador and had the almost incredible experience of discovering the answer to one of Stalin's most vital questions on the very eve of Barbarossa and on the day before the Japanese police arrested him as a spy. From his contacts with the Japanese cabinet Sorge was able to tell Stalin that the Japanese were not going to attack the Russians in Mongolia, but the Americans in the Pacific. When Sorge's information was confirmed by Japanese inactivity, Stalin began to nerve himself to denude his eastern frontiers. He did so just in time, although he still hesitated until he was within sight of the end of the short Siberian campaigning season. Reinforcements from the east, including 1,700 tanks and 1,500 aircraft, reached Zhukov on the Moscow front at the beginning of November at the point when the Russians had drained the last reserves from their training schools and the Germans thought that the Russians were finished.

The German failure to defeat the Russians in 1941 was the second and greatest turning point in the war in Europe. If Hitler could not beat the Russians in six months he could not beat them at all. He had prepared for a short war. He had not prepared for and he could not win a long one. Nor could his relations with his generals survive a long one. At the end of 1941 he took over command of the army himself from Brauchitsch and nine months later he would dismiss Halder, his Chief of Staff. More important perhaps, the handling of the 1941 campaign had produced quarrels with more highly respected field commanders and had deepened the mutual distrust between Hitler and the officer corps. By the end of the year Guderian, Rundstedt and Hoepner had all been dismissed. Others would follow later. In assuming personal command in the war in the east Hitler jettisoned his ablest generals.

It was at this point – the end of 1941 – that the European war begun in Poland in September 1939 was converted into a world war. On 7 December the Japanese attack on the American fleet at Pearl Harbor opened the war in the Pacific and made the United States a belligerent in that theatre. With one of the most startling gestures of the whole war Hitler immediately made the Americans belligerents in the Atlantic and Europe as well by a declaration of war. Germany was thenceforward engaged in a war that had spread right round the world.

CHAPTER 10

War with America

ON 11 December 1941 Hitler declared war on the United States of America. In retrospect the actual participation of the United States in the war in Europe and the hugeness of its contribution to victory obscure the fact that, all through 1941, the United States was still largely unwilling to become a belligerent. Many Americans felt that the war was not theirs, in the sense that it could affect no vital American interest; and those who nevertheless felt emotionally involved hoped that they could contribute to the defeat of the dictators without having to send their own sons to be killed.

Europeans have become used, during the twentieth century, to describing their wars as World wars, the implication being that everybody of any consequence automatically gets involved once Europeans start fighting. To many Europeans in both World wars American participation took the form of a belated recognition of the obvious. But it was not obvious that a European war must become a World war or that the United States must send fighting men to Europe. Even after the United States became a belligerent Americans regarded their country's intervention as assistance to friends in need rather than as the defence of essential American interests. There was a lot to be said for this view. The American continent was a long way from Europe. It could not be hit or invaded by German air or land forces and could only be marginally harassed by naval ones. Hitler showed in any case no desire to do any of these things. There was (save from Japan) no external threat to the United States, no enemy within sight. Moreover this commonsensical geographical view of the matter fitted comfortably into American history and mythology – the creation of the United States as a society detached from Europe and its ills, a community which had better things to do than get involved in the deceits and squabbles which constituted European politics.

Not that the United States had in fact been as isolationist as it believed itself, and was believed by others, to be. In the famous debates in the Senate after the end of the First World War about adopting the Treaty of Versailles and joining the League of Nations there had at no time been a majority against the new internationalism. Debate had been about the conditions to be attached to ratifying the treaty, and the combined forces of those who wanted unconditional acceptance and those who wanted conditional acceptance decisively outnumbered the isolationists who wanted no acceptance at all. The entry of the United States into the League was vetoed by the Senate only because the compact body of Wilsonian internationalist Senators joined forces with the small band of isolationists to defeat the amendments proposed by Republican internationalists. The event was decided by Wilson's determination to have all or nothing. The Senate's action was nevertheless interpreted as a signal of American withdrawal. Nor was this interpretation altogether wrong, for the League became the principal outward and visible sign and the principal organ of international involvement, and it never had the United States among its members. Yet the United States was willy-nilly enmeshed in European affairs because of the war debts owed to it by its recent allies, debts which these allies could not pay unless they in their turn were paid the war reparations owed to them by Germany. Consequently the United States took an active part in the attempts to sort out these problems, so much so that the two main plans for settling the German debt – the Dawes Plan and the Young Plan – were named after the American members of the teams which produced them. But this special kind of involvement, backward looking to the last war, was no pointer to a wider international involvement. On the contrary, it kept alive memories of the unpleasantness of war and added to them resentments about allies who, after the war, defaulted on their financial engagements.

Further than that, there grew up in the United States a suspicion that the American declaration of war in April 1917 had been engineered by chicanery. Catastrophic events tend to breed, a generation later, a critique which probes for hidden, and perhaps disreputable, motives. Americans were perturbed by the notion that the arms industry – the merchants of death as they were more picturesquely called before the invention of the sterner term military-industrial complex   had promoted belligerence for the profits to be made out of it, while yet other Americans blamed Wilson for feebly succumbing to cunning allied propaganda about the wickedness of U-boats. Criticisms of this nature became so strong that they were investigated, and given added circulation, by a committee of the Senate – the Nye Committee – between 1934 and 1936. This scrutiny contributed to the mood which induced Congress to pass the Neutrality Acts of 1935, 1936 and 1937. These Acts were intended to make clear the American resolve to keep out of another war and to prevent a President from leading the nation into one. Neutrality, a posture usually adopted by small states to avoid getting hurt in the quarrels of the great, became paradoxically the statutory refuge of the greatest power on earth. In order to give body to this general policy the Congress decreed that American arms were not to be delivered to belligerents or to be carried in American ships (but belligerents might buy non-military goods provided they paid cash for them and carried them away in non-American vessels); further, the President was empowered to take other precautionary measures by, for example, forbidding American citizens to travel in belligerent ships. It was in implementation of these Acts that Roosevelt issued in September 1939 a declaration of American neutrality.

There has been much debate over the attitudes of the American people towards external affairs, and even more about President Roosevelt's role in leading his country towards war. American isolationism was, as already noted, rooted in history and plausibility. The United States came into existence as a result of war against a European power and was peopled by migrants who left Europe out of distaste or discomfort. With an enormous and comparatively empty country to explore and exploit they concluded, as well they might, that other people's affairs were of no account and that they themselves had no vital interests beyond their own bounds (with the exception of the central American and Caribbean lands to the south which were not so distant as not to matter). The threat to the Union in the 1860s and the problems of reconstruction after the Civil War intensified the tendency to introspection, but two forces in particular were working against it. The first was the diversification of American economic interests and their consequent expansion overseas, coupled with a growth in American power which both tempted and enabled the United States to scan larger horizons. These material considerations were reinforced by the moralistic ingredient in American society, a factor in the American make-up which derived partly from the puritan origins of many of its communities and partly from that remoteness from events which allowed Americans to think of external politics in general terms of right and wrong instead of the more pragmatic categories of expediency and prudence to which Europeans, with their eyes on close neighbours and sensitive frontiers, were more prone.

This moralistic trend found expression, in political affairs, in a self-dedication to freedom and democracy, and this dedication made nonsense of isolationism. The isolationist attitude had found expression in neutrality, which is the formal expression of the emotion of isolationism. Covertly, however, neutrality negated isolationism, for whereas isolationism asserted that other people's conflicts could be overlooked, neutrality could mean that they were looked at and found to be equally lacking in merit on both sides. Thus neutrality was a Trojan horse in the isolationist camp, since Europe between the wars proved on inspection not to be an arena where unregenerate Europeans were simply tangling over issues of no significance. On the contrary, Fascism threatened democracy, Nazism threatened even more basic human norms; there were fights abroad in which all good men must join to put down brutality and faithlessness and uphold democracy and civilized manners. So a conflict developed within the United States. As the troubles of Europe and Asia became more troubled (by, for example, the Japanese attacks on Manchuria and China and the Spanish civil war), there was an atavistic and very powerful resolve to keep all the clearer of them, but at the same time a minority which concerned itself with foreign affairs developed a strong reprobation of the aggressive and fascist powers. Being neutral turned out to be more difficult than it used to be. To most Americans neutrality meant keeping out of wars, but to some Americans it began to appear that neutrality in Hitler's wars meant keeping out of a just war. Keeping out of wars was self-evidently sensible, but keeping out of a just war was not so clearly right.

The debate over Roosevelt's personal responsibility in bringing the United States into war has been not untinged by the emotions roused by Roosevelt in issues which have nothing to do with the war. Roosevelt was one of those men who can instil passionate enthusiasms and also intense hostility, even hatred. By his keenest admirers he has been credited with the foresight of genius; to his bitter enemies he was little better than a charlatan. The only common ground here is the acknowledgement that he had uncommon influence over the course of events. This is not the place for a complete assessment of Roosevelt as President, but we have to inquire into the nature of his influence, the use he made of it and the evolution of his policy in relation to international crises and to war.

Roosevelt was elected President in 1932 in the wake of exceptional turmoil in the United States. Although Americans had no external enemy to fear, they had experienced another kind of fear and disaster. The economic collapse which began so dramatically on Wall Street on 23 October 1929 took away from millions the basic material conditions of their lives and left them feeling helpless, bewildered and scared. The shock to morale was all the greater because, unlike the soldier who in some sense covenants with death, the brusquely impoverished father of a family had not contemplated this material bereavement, had done nothing to deserve it and scarcely understood it. There was more panic in the face of this economic blast than in the face of rifle fire or bombs. It was up to Roosevelt to do something about it and he did do, and was seen to do, lots of things. Not all these things were useful or even sensible but all of them, the failures as well as the successes, were activities and activity was a large part of what was needed. One can argue about the value of planting thousands of trees or of creating new government agencies, but it is impossible to doubt that the sum total of sheer activity by government became transmuted into a bank of popular confidence on which Roosevelt was ever afterwards able to draw. He became at once a strong President, capable of weathering storms and of giving a lead, the more so because the strength of his political position was buttressed by exceptional (though not infallible) political skill, superior intelligence and eloquence. But Roosevelt was no revolutionary or visionary innovator, either domestically or in foreign affairs. At home he was a compassionate, managerial conservative whose New Deal meant some change in the distribution of power, little change in the direction of policy. In external affairs his attitudes were at first no different from those of millions of Americans. He was an isolationist in the sense of wanting to keep out of foreign affairs on the assumption that these spelt trouble, but he was not opposed to playing a part where no trouble seemed to brew. Thus, he proposed in 1935 that the United States join the Permanent Court of International Justice, but was defeated by the Senate. He not only took an interest in disarmament but offered to join a European collective security system if the Europeans would first disarm. He was riled by the failure of the Disarmament Conference in 1933 and blamed Germany, which was seeking to increase its armament, rather than France or Great Britain, which were simply declining to reduce theirs. On the other hand he allowed Hitler's introduction of con- scription in 1935 to pass without protest even though it was a breach of the American-German peace treaty of 1921 (the treaty concluded by the United States in place of the Treaty of Versailles). Again like millions of Americans, Roosevelt, disposed though he was to criticize the fumbling policies and imperial philosophies of France and Great Britain, was coming to regard Nazi Germany as nastier and more dangerous – though not in the same devilish category as the USSR. The remilitarization of the Rhineland in 1936 added to the general uneasiness and to the share of blame to be attributed to Germany. Nazi anti-semitism also began to have its effect. It offended decent Gentiles as well as American Jewry (which counted for more than something in Roosevelt's own state of New York), but on the other hand there was good business to be done with Germany and it entered nobody's head in Washington that government could or should interfere with business. Roosevelt and the American people, like European leaders and peoples, were divided and unclear about trends in Europe during the thirties and about what initiatives, if any, to take in respect of them. But they were becoming increasingly anti-Nazi and so anti-German, and this trend was fed by the association of Japan with Germany. Both countries came to be seen as cruel and power-hungry, associated moreover not only by their domestic oppressiveness and external aggressiveness but also in their economic policies which were imposing a blatant economic hegemony in their respective spheres of influence in place of the American ethos of the Open Door which was not only more subtle and more amiable but also calculated to serve American commercial interests.

In November 1936 Roosevelt was re-elected President by a margin of 11 million votes (as against 7 million in 1932). Foreign affairs played little part in the electioneering and what Roosevelt had to say was along conventional keep-out-of-trouble lines. During his second term Roosevelt suffered a decline in popularity which was to be marked by the reduction of his majority to 5 million votes in 1940. The New Deal was not wholly successful and very far from being universally popular. The President's tussle with the Supreme Court and the manoeuvres by which he tried to pack it lost him the support and respect of many who had been among his warmest admirers. Moreover, if tradition was anything to go by, he would cease to be President in 1940 because no President had ever tried to serve more than two terms. He was still a strong President and an intelligent and eloquent one, but his strength was flecked by failures and by the running out of his time. He was not well placed to innovate in foreign affairs, especially if innovation meant running a risk of war. But foreign affairs imposed themselves on his attention. The Japanese attack on China in 1937 with its reminder of the growth of Japanese power and the consequent threat to American power in the Pacific posed for Americans a problem of a special kind. In Great Britain, where it was axiomatic that a war against Germany, Italy and Japan at once would be suicidal, the question debated was whom to conciliate: many people's first choice, notably in the Foreign Office, was Italy, but others, notably in the Treasury and in the services (the pledge that Australia and New Zealand would be protected from Japan by the Royal Navy was a constant consideration and was reaffirmed at the Imperial Conference of 1937) argued that the growth of Japanese power meant that Great Britain should revert to the alliance with Japan which had been abandoned after the First World War under American pressure. But Americans did not see Japan that way. An American-Japanese alliance was an impossibility and so American-Japanese rivalry created an external threat such as Hitler never posed. It was in the context of the Pacific and East Asia that the United States began to evolve a policy of meeting a threat by extending to an ally – in this case

China – all aid short of war and within the Neutrality Act. Moreover, Japanese aggression affected American public opinion owing to the extent of pro-Chinese feeling in the United States.

Partly in response to these worries on his eastern flank and partly because he wanted to be useful, Roosevelt tried in the last two years of peace to mediate in European affairs. He thought of meeting Hitler (as, later, he would hope to resolve other problems by personal contact with Stalin). He proposed a conference of neutrals to discuss modes of international behaviour, disarmament and access to raw materials. Although offended by the manners and behaviour of the dictators, he thought of himself at this time as one of the neutrals rather than as one of the democrats. Nor did the leading democrats do much to swing him to their side. Chamberlain, deep in his ineffective attempts to make friends with Italy and Germany, did his best to head off the American President. He wanted no joint Anglo-American initiative and preferably no American initiative at all – at this point; for it is only fair to add that, under some pressure from cabinet colleagues and the British Ambassador in Washington, he kept up his correspondence with Roosevelt and left a way open for an American initiative later on. Roosevelt might have overridden these obstacles if he had had any clear idea of what to do, but beyond offering his good offices in a vague and general way he was essentially without a European policy. It was hardly possible for him to have such a policy so long as the precondition of all American activity in Europe was to minimize involvement. He did not intend to fight the dictators and there was at this time no government in Europe which wanted him to. He was reduced to following events – in both senses of that phrase. He had little faith in Chamberlain's manoeuvring to avoid war over Czechoslovakia, but privately supported Chamberlain in the absence of anything else to do and publicly stated that the United States would not fight if France and Great Britain went to war for Czechoslovakia. Like most people he was relieved when war was avoided at Munich; like many people he was shocked by Hitler's breach of the Munich agreement and the annihilation of Czechoslovakia in March 1939. By this time his ineffectiveness in European affairs had strengthened Hitler's view that he did not have to worry about the United States, but round about this same time Roosevelt was becoming convinced that war was certain and American involvement at least a possibility. Within six months war had started.

Whereas Churchill was temperamentally a man of action upon whom full responsibility fell after war had begun, Roosevelt was an intellectual in a situation of half-peace half-war. His country was not equipped for war militarily or industrially and his fellow citizens were not ready for it psychologically. His nature and his circumstances alike made him gingerly in pace, and it was only as circumstances developed that he was able to resolve his hesitations about what American opinion would endorse and what he himself ought to do. To Americans the war in Europe presented itself as a contest between Germany on the one hand and Great Britain and France on the other. The question was who would win. A second question was whether it mattered to the United States who won. At the outset Roosevelt established a distinction: the United States was formally a neutral but it cared about the result of the war and, since it cared, it should use 'all methods short of war' to help Great Britain and France to defeat Hitler. This position did not go unchallenged. A not inconsiderable part of the American press and a number of influential public figures were either hostile to Great Britain or entranced with Nazi ideas or genuinely indifferent. Anti-British and anti-imperial groups were, if limited, vocal. There was no surge of pro-British feeling until the Battle of Britain (in which a number of American volunteers took part in defiance of the laws of their country), and even the Battle of Britain had only moderate effect in the western United States and less still in the psychologically more remote Middle West. On the other hand pro-German propaganda was an almost complete failure. The German-American Bund never had more than 6,000 members and could not efface the image of the Nazi as a bully.

But however partisan Americans might become it still did not follow that they could see the war as one which affected American national interests. It was difficult to believe that the United States, bounded by the Atlantic and Pacific Oceans, was not also protected by them. To the ordinary American it appeared that, although there might be a moral case for helping the democracies to defeat Nazism, there were no strategic issues of self-interest which required the United States to make war. The argument, a familiar commonplace in Great Britain, that no state must be allowed to become all-powerful in Europe did not make sense to a people separated from Europe by the Atlantic Ocean and not merely by the English Channel. In the thirties the speeds which were to be reached within a generation and the weapons which were to annihilate distances as well as cities were undreamt of by all save a few.

If there was a danger it seemed more likely to emerge from Latin America. Recollecting perhaps German attempts in the First World War to get Mexico, in alliance with Japan, to make war on the United States, and greatly exaggerating the potential threat from the Germans settled in the southern parts of the American continent, the United States turned immediately on the outbreak of war to the problem of immunizing the

New World from it. In October 1939 the American states met at Panama in an inter-American conference and agreed to quarantine the New World by proscribing transfers of territory within it from one European power to another and by designating a security zone extending 300–1,000 miles seaward from its eastern shores. Belligerents were required to abjure naval operations in this area. Great Britain, France and Germany contested the legality of this declaration but the British soon ceased to complain when they discovered that the United States was prepared to connive at infractions of the ban, even to the extent of helping to detect and locate German vessels.

Latin American attitudes to the war were compounded of three main strands. Through the historical Spanish connection and indigenous anti-communism there was sympathy for Franco and, by extension, for his fellow dictators in Europe. There was antipathy to the British blockade of European markets and, among the wealthier classes, grousing about the reduction in imported luxuries. Thirdly and perhaps most pertinently, all eyes were on Roosevelt and his manoeuvres between the traditional neutrality of the New World and his partiality for the democratic (if not the imperial) character of the anti-Axis allies. Pearl Harbor was therefore a climactic event since it precipitated the United States into open belligerence. Furthermore, many Latin Americans, while perceiving little real threat to their region from Germany, saw Japan as a more credible enemy. Within weeks of Pearl Harbor, all Latin America except Argentine and Chile broke off relations with Japan, Germany and Italy. Parts of Central America and the Caribbean were overrun by the United States in return for Lend-Lease and promises of financial and technical aid to sugar the pill of United States domination. Since Washington felt that this was no time for concern over the internal affairs of its neighbours, governments were strengthened by Washington's benevolence and liberal and revolutionary aspirations were stifled even more effectively than in German-occupied Europe.

In Mexico – the most delicate area because of its border with the United States, its nationalization of foreign oil companies in 1938 and memories of Japanese meddling in the First World War – ingrained antipathies were overridden by the exigencies and opportunities of war (some Mexicans did well out of exports of gold and other minerals to the United States) and Mexico took the extreme step of declaring war in May 1942 after U-boat attacks which sank Mexican vessels, drowned Mexican citizens and created popular outcry and a rare party political unity. A Mexican air unit was sent to the Pacific in the last year of the war – in order, like Cavour's dispatch of Sardinian troops to the Crimea, to raise Mexico's international standing. Only Brazil, which declared war on the Axis powers in August 1942 and on Japan in May 1945, sent a force to Europe (to Italy in 1944). It emerged from the war with the largest slice of Lend-Lease to Latin America and the strongest armed forces. The other major South American countries, Argentina and Chile, were the least keen to declare war, partly because of their mutual quarrel over the islands off the southern tip of the continent. They became nominal belligerents in 1945 under the threat of exclusion from the conference convened at San Francisco to create the United Nations. In Argentina a by-product of the war was the overthrow in 1943 of civilian rule, an event which led eventually to the elevation to the presidency in 1946 of Colonel Juan Domingo Perón. Washington regarded the post-1943 military régime as fascist and pro-German and attacked it with an outspoken vigour which was unusual among sovereign states and seriously alarmed the British who, besides stigmatizing Washington's handling of the situation as crude and crass, were nervous about the considerable British investments in Argentina and Great Britain's dependence on it for the meat ration.

The dangers from the German population of Latin America were largely a product of war nerves. There were 300,000 German nationals (*Reichs-deutsche*) and 1.75 million persons of German extraction (*Volksdeutsche*) in the sub-continent, and Nazi propaganda and German trade had both been intensified in the thirties, but the likelihood and consequences of pro-German coups were alike exaggerated. Here, as in other parts of the world, the *Reichsdeutsche* in particular were regarded as a disciplined fifth column which had been prepared by the External Affairs Department of the Nazi Party to play an active role in war. But out of about three million *Reichsdeutsche* living outside the Reich only 30,000 had been enrolled by the party by 1939, and the belief in the sinister efficiency of these people was a myth, a projection of the German reputation for thoroughness coupled with the glamorous novelty of the idea of the fifth column, a term coined during the Spanish civil war. (Absurd stories were spread with hysterical waywardness in many countries, particularly in Europe; these stories were reported by most of the world's leading news-papers and treated as undeniable by parliamentarians and others who raised a patriotic clamour for indiscriminate arrests; nobody was allowed to be what he seemed to be; thousands of innocent persons, including Jewish refugees from Germany, were seized and many of them were shot.)

In the two years and a bit which elapsed between Munich and the American elections of 1940 Roosevelt rearmed, tried to restore peace by diplomacy and gave what aid he could to the western allies. He had asked Congress in January 1938 for a 20 per cent increase in the navy allocations; his request had created an uproar but been granted. The same thing happened a year later when he asked for more money for the army and air forces. Early in 1940 he sent Under Secretary Sumner Welles on a tour of European capitals, sent a special emissary to the Vatican to initiate American-Papal mediation and tried to keep Italy out of the war. All these efforts were failures. The war went on and Ribbentrop, visiting Rome on the heels of Welles, extracted from Mussolini a promise to enter it at some unspecified date. The fall of France shifted American opinion, official and unofficial. After that catastrophe there was no significant opposition to huge and rapid rearmament, and a Selective Service Act was passed in September. The elimination of French power and the probable elimination (as it seemed) of British power too forced Americans to think about the consequences to themselves of the disappearance of two great friendly navies and the emergence of a new German-Italian naval power which had also annexed the French fleet. The United States made unconventionally strong representations to Pétain and his Navy Minister, Admiral Darlan, in order to prevent the French government from surrendering its fleet to Germany in the armistice negotiations. Here was a visible external threat similar to the growth of Japanese power in the Pacific. Roosevelt strengthened his cabinet by inviting two eminent Republicans, Henry L. Stimson (a former Secretary of State) and Frank Knox, to become his Secretaries of War and the Navy: unlike Churchill Roosevelt looked to the Right rather than the Left in constructing a war coalition.

When in 1940 it seemed that Hitler was winning the war rather easily Roosevelt still could do little to stop him. He had refused a request from the French government to send troops to Europe. But it was becoming plainer than ever that if Hitler was to be denied a complete victory more would be required of the United States than methods short of war. Helping the western allies meant ensuring the flow of traffic across the Atlantic against U-boats and German surface raiders. It meant supplies and protection; later it was to mean credit too. A first attempt to amend the Neutrality Act failed but Congress soon relented so far as to permit belligerents to buy military as well as non-military goods on a cash-and-carry basis. For the moment cash was not an immediate problem, but carrying was. Then, if the United States was to help protect the carriage, it would have to risk its own vessels and invite German retaliation, engaging in unneutral activities which might lead to war. Non-belligerence, which was essentially an attempt to get the best of two incompatible worlds – those of neutrality and partisanship – would be put at risk and would prove to be no more than the transitional stage from the one world to a full role in the other.

Roosevelt both saw and accepted the risks rather sooner than most people. Since the American people later proved by their actions that they accepted the consequences, Roosevelt might justly claim that his leadership had been endorsed and any deviousness which might have been involved condoned. But to some extent too his leadership determined the course. His simple presentation of the issues, his patience in unfolding his policies, his readiness to accept responsibility, and his calm handling of critical national decisions – for all the superficial detachment which he sometimes displayed as he turned from affairs of state to his stamp collection – these qualities inevitably led him to form and not merely observe the popular will. In which exercise of power he was giving an example of democratic leadership.

During 1940 Roosevelt resolved to seek a third term in the Presidency, an event not only unprecedented in American history but so obnoxious to American instincts that after the war it was prohibited by constitutional amendment. The war was not the only reason for this decision. He was deeply concerned to preserve the social innovations of the New Deal and he saw among leading figures in his own party no liberal Democrat upon whom he could rely to do this. But the conviction that the United States was going to become more deeply involved in war and that he should guide it also played a major part in his decision. At this stage Roosevelt developed the idea that the United States was in substance, if not formally, already under attack. He was a master of the art of democratic communication, and his regular fireside chats – one of the adroitest political uses of radio, which had at this period only been used effectively by politicians of a different stamp, Hitler and Mussolini – gave him the ear and the confidence of the people. They trusted him and when in 1940 they were asked to give him a third term 27 million of them decided to do so: his attractively unusual Republican opponent Wendell Wilkie (with whom in later years Roosevelt thought of making a progressive alliance and a new party) received 22 million votes, a big gap in a modern American presidential election. But it would be wrong to conclude that the 27 million who voted for Roosevelt did so because they were ready to fight against Hitler. They were with Roosevelt in wanting Hitler to be beaten – as were the great bulk of the 22 million who voted for Wilkie – but they wanted Hitler to be beaten by the British and were not yet convinced that the British could not do this without the United States as a fighting ally. Roosevelt himself still clung to the hope that the American role need not be a fighting one or that, if it came to fighting, the American share could be limited to sea and air and would not involve sending army conscripts overseas. During his campaign he promised again and again not to send Americans to fight in foreign lands 'except in case of attack' (on one occasion, subsequently much quoted against him, he left out the proviso) and there must have been many who voted for Roosevelt because he had kept the country out of war and who would have refused him a third term had they supposed that he would not continue to find ways of doing so. No opinion poll during the year before Pearl Harbor showed more than one in five Americans opting for war.

If in 1940 the defeat of France had been offset by the British success in the Battle of Britain, in 1941 the defeat of Great Britain became once more a possibility to be reckoned with. The threat to Great Britain at sea, which had come near to success in the First World War, was manifested on the first day of the Second when the German U-30 sank the British passenger ship *Athenia* (the victims included twenty-eight Americans). The threat at sea was posed by mines (laid by surface vessels, submarines or aircraft), surface raiders and U-boats. At the beginning of the war the magnetic mine did much damage to British shipping in coastal waters, but it was quickly mastered by technical counter-measures. Surface raiders, such as the pocket battleships *Graf Spee* and *Deutschland* whose exploits have already been narrated, caused much concern but comparatively little damage. The enduring enemy was the U-boat. Fortunately for the British, Doenitz's fleet was a small one. He divided his boats between Atlantic and North Sea raiding and mine-laying and in 1939 his operations were not too alarmingly successful: 114 merchantmen sunk, but at a cost of nine U-boats. (U-boats also sank the aircraft carrier *Courageous* in September and the battleship *Royal Oak* in Scapa Flow in October.) In 1940, however, the U-boat fleet, reinforced by a production drive, began to score abundantly. One convoy lost thirty-two ships in an attack which continued through four consecutive nights, and Hitler's new conquests gave him bases in Norway for U-boats and armed merchant raiders, bases for E-boats along the entire length of the English Channel, and bases for long-range aircraft – the F.W. 200 or Condor – which flew from Bordeaux over wide spaces of the western Atlantic and landed at Trondhjem in Norway, flying back the next day. Great Britain occupied the Faroes and Iceland when Denmark was overrun, but losses in this year mounted at an intolerable rate and Doenitz lost only twenty-two of his rapidly growing force.

Churchill turned to Roosevelt. A week after the British declaration of war in 1939 Churchill had begun, as First Lord of the Admiralty, an intimate correspondence with the President. He continued it when he became Prime Minister. The two men developed a very special relationship which was of incalculable benefit to Great Britain. This personal partnership, and its post-war institutionalization in the continuing Anglo-American alliance, appear so solid a part of the international scene that they have come to be regarded as a natural by-product of a common language and common traditions. In fact, however, Anglo-American relations were bad throughout the twenties and despite an improvement at the time of the London Conference in 1930 politicians on both sides continued to refer to each other privately in scathing, sometimes almost scurrilous, terms. There was neither trust nor liking between them. Their two countries were in the process of exchanging roles, particularly on the high seas where Great Britain's cherished naval supremacy was passing away, and against this background politicians sparred with conscious and unconscious jealousy. In constructing their alliance Churchill and Roosevelt had to work with a mixed legacy.

One of the first fruits of their special relationship was the destroyer-bases deal of September 1940 which placed in British hands fifty extra ships with which to prosecute the war against the U-boats. (A few weeks earlier Roosevelt, by the Ogdensburg agreement, had established a Joint Defence Board with belligerent Canada.) At this time Churchill was at least as worried about the war at sea as he was elated by victory in the Battle of Britain. Roosevelt, after lengthy study and intricate legal argument, agreed to transfer these fifty old but serviceable American destroyers to Great Britain in return for a promise never to surrender the British fleet and for the lease to the United States for ninety-nine years of six bases in the western Atlantic. (Two other bases were accepted as a gift. Churchill had wanted the two deals to be wholly distinct gifts but Roosevelt's advisers, already in difficulties about deciding whether the President could effect the exchange without recourse to Congress, insisted that there must be a substantial, related *quid pro quo*.) But by the end of 1940 British shipping losses were running at the rate of 300,000 tons a month and were destined to rise in February, March and April 1941 to 400,000, 500,000 and 600,000 tons. Great Britain was running out of cash too. The timing of American aid had become vital.

Roosevelt's policy was to aid Great Britain by all means short of war. So much was clear. What was unclear was how and how quickly aid could be made available and, more distantly, whether aid short of war was going to be enough. Soon after his re-election Roosevelt received an

urgent plea from Churchill. In reply he moved to depart from all semblance of neutrality in order to ensure that Great Britain should receive
the tools it needed to survive. The device was Lend-Lease. He told the
American people that if a neighbour's house was on fire it was only
common sense and self-protection to lend him a hosepipe. The necessary
Bill, which the President always referred to as the Aid to Democracies
Bill, was introduced early in January 1941 and signed by the President on
11 March. Thereafter Great Britain placed orders for American materials
with the American government which purchased what was required from
American firms and paid them. The materials were then lent or leased to
the British in return for a promise of payment after the war: the United
States agreed to accept post-dated cheques in lieu of cash when there
was no cash left.

Lend-Lease was a gesture of very great moral significance. It buoyed
Great Britain up by promising to bring nearer the day when it would no
longer be fighting virtually alone. Churchill wanted American belligerence
even more than he wanted American aid, and to him, as to most people in
Great Britain, financial aid was the prelude to co-belligerence, not an
alternative. The material benefits of Lend-Lease were at first limited.
Until some months after Pearl Harbor and Hitler had forced the United
States into war on two fronts American industry was largely on a peacetime basis, the main exception being the Liberty ship programme which
launched its first ship in September 1941; Great Britain's own war production was greater than that of the United States. During 1941 Great Britain
got little more from the United States than it had imported in 1940 and
continued to pay cash for most of it. But what did come was important:
for example, in 1941 a million tons of food (a fifteenth of British imports
of food) and enough fuel oil to raise stocks from a danger point of 4.5
million tons to 7 million tons, which was maximum storage capacity.

The Lend-Lease Act was followed a few months later by an equally
significant act, drawing the United States closer to war. When Hitler
attacked the USSR, Roosevelt, following Churchill, promised aid to
Stalin. The attack was no surprise to Roosevelt and his advisers who had
known from secret sources from early in 1941 that Hitler had signed his
first directive for the campaign. Roosevelt and his Secretary of State,
Cordell Hull, had been doing their best to keep on reasonably good terms
with the USSR, but the anti-Soviet voices in the United States were
much more numerous than the anti-British ones had been. Anti-communism was a powerful emotion, especially among Roman Catholics.
Stalin's seizure of half Poland, his war on Finland and his annexation of

Estonia, Latvia and Lithuania caused bitter anger, which was not confined to the émigré communities from these countries. The time would come when admiration for Russian resistance to Hitler, especially during the battles for Stalingrad, would raise a tide of pro-Russian feeling, while at other levels and later in the war Churchill was to be criticized for being too anti-Russian, but American sympathy for the Russians never sufficed to efface underlying emotions of an opposite order and even at the fearful juncture of Stalingrad's agony – when Americans watched with genuinely bated breath and, perhaps, with less mixed emotions about the Russians than for many years before or after – there was (as too in the Battle of Britain) no plan to do anything to save the city if the last hour should strike. Roosevelt's promise of aid in 1941, therefore, was an act of leadership from which another President, heeding the cross-currents within his country, might have refrained.

Whatever the value of this act in time to come, when it was translated into $11.3 billions' worth of supplies, the immediate effect was slight and could not be otherwise. Even in relation to Great Britain Roosevelt was still treading warily. The Lend-Lease Act itself underlined the peculiar posture of the United States by once more expressly prohibiting the entry of American vessels into combat areas and the use of the US navy for convoy duties. But less than four weeks later the sinking in a single night of ten ships in a British convoy of twenty-one showed that further steps were necessary if the United States set more store by the defeat of Hitler than keeping out of a shooting war. Roosevelt ordered the occupation of Greenland and contemplated occupying the Azores. A force of three battleships with an aircraft carrier, cruisers and destroyers was transferred in May from the Pacific to the Atlantic. In the same month Roosevelt declared an unlimited national emergency. American shipyards were opened to British ships in need of repair. American ocean patrols were extended, shadowed Axis vessels and reported their positions to British units every few hours. A number of coastal cutters were transferred to the British flag. Roosevelt adopted and popularized a phrase of Jean Monnet dubbing the United States 'the arsenal of democracy'. But the United States remained officially non-belligerent and even the sinking of the *Robin Moor* by the Germans provoked no declaration of war.

In May the British scored a ringing success at sea. Raeder, who had more faith in capital ships than Doenitz and was continuously frustrated by Hitler's refusal to allow the indiscriminate use of submarines, renewed his surface challenge. Attempts to do this in 1940 had proved abortive, but in 1941 two new ships, the battleship *Bismarck* and the cruiser *Prinz*

Eugen, were ready. Raeder planned a great offensive with them in conjunction with *Scharnhorst* and *Gneisenau*, which had been at Brest since March. But these two battle cruisers had suffered damage and had not recovered by the time that *Bismarck* and *Prinz Eugen* were ready to sail from Gdynia on 18 May: they never sailed the high seas again.

Bismarck was sighted by a Swedish ship soon after she left her German berth, and London was quickly informed. From Bergen she proceeded with *Prinz Eugen* north-westward, passing north of Iceland and thence into the Denmark Strait between Iceland and Greenland. Emerging from the Strait into the Atlantic the two ships were spotted and shadowed. Battle was joined west of Iceland soon after dawn on 24 May by the battleship *Prince of Wales*, also newly commissioned, and the twenty-year-old battle-cruiser *Hood*. *Hood* was sunk within minutes by a shell which pierced her decks, and all but three of her complement of 1,419 died. Half an hour later *Prince of Wales*, also hit, was forced to break away, but the aircraft carrier *Victorious* came up and delivered a first attack before the end of the day. *Bismarck* managed to shake off her pursuers, turned for Brest, but then incomprehensibly gave away her position by breaking wireless silence with a long message to the German Admiralty. Even then she might have escaped – as her instructions required her to do – for the bearings obtained by shore stations from her intercepted wireless transmission were wrongly interpreted when relayed to Admiral Sir Francis Tovey's flagship *King George V* which led the chase in the wrong direction. The British Admiralty, however, correctly divined *Bismarck*'s intentions and early on the 26th an aircraft of RAF Coastal Command sighted her. A separate naval force which included the aircraft carrier *Ark Royal* intercepted her and *Ark Royal*'s aircraft, having first attacked but missed one of their own attendant cruisers, so wounded *Bismarck* that she became a sitting target for the British ships converging on her from all quarters. Encircled and doomed, she was sunk by torpedoes early in the morning of the 27th. One hundred and fifteen of her complement of about 2,400 were saved.

This German challenge on the surface was never to be renewed (although – with *Scharnhorst* and *Gneisenau* only damaged and *Tirpitz* about to come into service – the British Admiralty could not know this) and the Battle of the Atlantic was once more left to Doenitz, who built up his U-boat force to 120 during 1941 and was contriving to keep as many as half of them at sea at once. Although the pressure from the U-boats was relaxed when half of them were diverted to the Mediterranean at the end of the year, the newer boats were operating at longer ranges and the Atlantic crossing was as hazardous as ever. On the other side Roosevelt took yet further measures. The second half of 1941 was the period in which the Russians were now fighting but the Americans were not. In July Roosevelt nevertheless sent US marines to Iceland to join the British troops who had been stationed there since May 1940. This extension of American arms entailed supply and escort duties by the US navy in an operational zone. In August British and allied shipping was allowed to join American convoys and sail in them. American vessels of war were, without the knowledge of the public or the Congress, fighting an undeclared war farther and farther away from the shores of the American continent. Inevitably the German navy was in fact retaliating, although Hitler kept up the appearance and even the substance of restraint. He authorized in July attacks on American merchantmen but only in a restricted zone in the eastern Atlantic and not on the approach routes to Iceland.

In August, at Placentia Bay in Newfoundland, Roosevelt and Churchill held their first wartime meeting. It had been planned as early as January when Roosevelt's unconventional personal emissary, Harry Hopkins, paid his first wartime visit to London. Attended as it was by the Chiefs of Staff of both countries, the Placentia Bay conference looked like a joint council of war and many on the British side hoped that it was the curtain-raiser for an American declaration of war. Stalin too wanted such a declaration and had made his wishes and his plight clear to Hopkins in Moscow a week earlier. But Roosevelt was not yet ready to take that plunge, perhaps not convinced that he would have to, and the conference's main product was the Atlantic Charter, which many of the British participants regarded as a gust of high-sounding irrelevance. But the Atlantic Charter was more important than that. If the Americans were to go to war they must know why and wherefore, and the Charter set out war aims which would be worth fighting for. Merely contemplating war aims is a step towards war, while in the absence of war aims a democratic leader can hardly ask a people not under attack to start fighting. The Atlantic Charter was a part of the preparation of the American people for war, even though it turned out not to be strictly necessary since the issue of war or peace was decided by Hitler's act and not by the choice of Americans. The Placentia Bay conference was also a prelude to war in another sense, for after it the President ordered an inquiry into what the United States would require if war should come – a pre-war war plan. And thirdly, the conference inaugurated the personal acquaintance between service chiefs which was to grow much closer and be formalized by the creation of the Anglo-American Combined Chiefs of Staff Committee.

At sea the war continued to suck at the American resolve to avoid it. In

September, following an astutely publicized encounter between a U-boat and the USS *Greer* – an inconclusive engagement described by Roosevelt as an attack on an American vessel – the President announced that the United States would protect non-American as well as American shipping in the Atlantic security zone and would fire at sight on all German and Italian warships seen there. Incidents multiplied. American opinion was growing more anti-German than anti-war. In October and November 1941 the neutrality legislation was being progressively eroded by Congress. American merchantmen were armed and the President was empowered to send American ships into British ports. The United States was virtually making war in defiance of the rules. But it showed no sign of actually declaring war: undeclared war was serving the dual purpose of helping the democracies and keeping the bulk of Americans out of the firing line (those who wanted to go and fight were tacitly allowed to join the British or Canadian forces). When the United States was attacked at Pearl Harbor the President only asked Congress to declare war on Japan. Then, four days later, Germany declared war on the United States.

This act by Hitler has been described as one of gratuitous folly. It is certain that, by adding the United States to his overt enemies at a time when Germany was fighting both the British Empire and the USSR, Hitler sealed his doom. But the die was cast before December 1941. By the time Hitler declared war the United States was already an active ally of the British and the Russians. Up to the middle of 1941 Hitler had every reason to keep the United States out of the war at almost any cost and he did, as we shall see, set himself firmly not only to avoid provoking Roosevelt but also to ignore Roosevelt's provocations of him. After the turn of the year, however, the situation changed. With the launching of Barbarossa, Hitler was involved in the dreaded war on two fronts, while the United States was, though neutral in name, already decreasingly so in substance. Hitler therefore embarked on the policy of goading the Japanese into war partly in order to distract the Americans from Europe and the Atlantic and partly also because, obsessed with the British, whose survival forced him to fight the USSR with half a hand tied behind his back, he wanted Japan to deal Great Britain a knock-out blow in Singapore and India. In pursuance of this complicated aim he was forced, in November 1941, to promise Japan that Germany would declare war on the United States if Japan did. This policy failed because the Japanese blows at Pearl Harbor and Singapore were not knockouts and because of the unforeseen capacity of the Americans to fight, uniquely, a war in every quarter of the world.

Hitler badly misjudged the Americans, partly because of his preconceptions and partly because he was badly served. He entertained fantastically wrong notions of American society and politics. He believed that the masses of decent Americans (whose ancestors, he incorrectly recalled, had failed by only one congressional vote to adopt German as their national language) were on the verge of revolt against a dominant Jewish ruling class and that the United States, so far from being a bastion of democracy, was a corrupt and demoralized country fit and eager for the reception of Nazi ideas. To Hitler, Roosevelt, especially in his 1940 election campaign, was a desperate trickster clutching at any opportunity to win votes and retain power in defiance of a groundswell of popular enlightenment. On this view the United States was not nearly such a formidable enemy as its material power might make it appear. Besides being blinded by his prejudices Hitler was misled by exceptionally inept reporting by his emissaries in Washington, especially his service attachés who, pandering to these prejudices, devoted more ink to political nonsense than to technical reports. He overrated and misjudged the pro-Nazi German-American Bund; failed to appreciate the distaste of Americans for his racialism; overestimated the addiction of Americans to a comfortable neutrality; and mistook the prominence of men like Colonels Charles Lindbergh and Robert R. MacCormick, Senators Burton K. Wheeler and Gerald P. Nye and the 'radio priest' Father Charles E. Coughlin for real political influence.

He was also, and more pardonably, misled by the American record in the thirties. The economic crisis and isolationism prevented the United States from playing an effective role in world affairs in that decade. Hitler understood this, but he did not understand how far war would change American attitudes and policies. When Japan invaded Manchuria in 1931 (partly to forestall a possible Russian move which could precipitate a new Russo-Japanese war) the Secretary of State, Henry L. Stimson, had toyed with the idea of intervention. He was well aware of the force of isolationism in the United States but he hoped that by a show of determination he might influence the political balance in Tokyo where a civilian cabinet was at odds with the army factions which had provoked the fighting in Manchuria. This cabinet had no desire to begin a war with China in order to stave off a war with the USSR, but it fell. Stimson thereupon proposed economic sanctions against Japan but President Herbert Hoover did not like the idea (nor did the British government). Stimson pressed his interventionist policy again a few months later when Japanese troops were landed at Shanghai, but the President remained opposed to it and Stimson knew that American opinion would not tolerate it: he was using the prospect of sanctions as a counter, but in the knowledge that he could not play it. In the Ethiopian crisis Stimson's successor, Cordell Hull, instituted voluntary sanctions against Italy but there was little cooperation between the United States and the leading members of the League and Hull's initiative merely associated the United States with a failure. The remilitarization of the Rhineland, the Spanish civil war, the conclusion of the Axis and Anti-Comintern Pacts, the extension of the war in the east to China itself in the summer of 1937, the sinking of the American gunboat *Panay* and three tankers on the Yangtse in December all reinforced the American desire to keep clear of wars; and were seen to. Moreover, Roosevelt's unhappy attempts to intervene diplomatically in European politics in the late thirties, revealing his own hesitations and the hiatus between the American and British governments, roused only Hitler's scorn, and his attempts to avert war at the last moment were brushed off by Hitler. The war was going to be short. Either Great Britain and France would do nothing to help Poland or they would intervene and be quickly subdued. On this basis there was no American problem. But the basis was wrong. The war was not short and the Americans soon began to take a menacing hand in it.

The six months which embraced Hitler's invasion of the USSR and his declaration of war against the United States marked also the destruction, by his own acts, of his power of initiative in world affairs. The failure of Barbarossa was crucial, for had he defeated the USSR before the end of the year he would have been supreme in the European continent and either he would have issued no declaration of war against the United States or he could have done so without involving himself in the pincer movement which finally crushed him. It was the burden of Barbarossa which led him from a European to a world strategy, from a league in which he could certainly play and possibly win to a league in which he must lose.

But, secondly, the survival of Great Britain was also crucial because, without it, it is unlikely that the United States would have joined the war as an ally of the USSR against Germany.

Hitler's failures in Barbarossa and the Battle of Britain were both narrow ones. Something has already been said about both these engagements and more will be said later in this book about the sources of Russian endurance and victory. If Hitler had lived (as Napoleon did) to ponder his mistakes and failures in tranquillity, he would no doubt have fought the battles of the autumn of 1940 and the autumn of 1941 over and over again. He might also have puzzled no less over the incomprehensibility of the Americans and the British, who behaved in these critical years 1939–41 with what, to an outsider, could only seem perverse inconsequence. If Hitler made mistakes about the Anglo-Saxon peoples, whom in some moods he judged to be not much inferior to the German, he could claim that he was to some degree misled by their illogicality as well as by his own preconceptions and advisers.

He could hark back to the British declaration of war at the very beginning. This declaration, which was a formal consequence of the German attack on Poland two days earlier, had no discernible practical results at the time. If it was anything more than an empty formality it implied a determination to attack Germany. But neither Great Britain nor France had forces or plans for doing so, nor did they do so. (The only plans extant were for air operations in response to full-scale German action in the west.) In the event it was Hitler who attacked them and not the other way round. Seven months later he defeated France and prepared to defeat Great Britain. His plans posed a threat to American security which the Americans could, by the use of naval and air forces, have helped to defeat. Yet they too declined, as the British had declined in 1939, to take any direct action, and if they abstained at this critical point they might be counted most unlikely to intervene in a European war at any other. On this premise Hitler's own declaration of war at the end of 1941 was a formal act without practical consequences like the British declaration in 1939; the practical consequences, if any, would be in the Pacific where the Americans were already embroiled with the Japanese. But the Americans, who had abstained from direct action in the face of the threat in 1940, were ready by 1941 to throw themselves into the European war and even give it priority over a Pacific war. The intervention which had seemed politically impossible in 1940 became automatic in 1941. To Hitler it might have appeared that the British and Americans had leaders who did not understand power. The British had ostensibly engaged themselves in 1939 to do something which they had not the power to do; the Americans in 1940 had the power to intervene in a situation of critical importance to themselves but abstained from doing so. But in this assessment of the seeming political ineptitude of his adversaries Hitler failed to take account of Aristotle's diagnosis of the nature of the commercial state, slow to action but rich in the capacity to procrastinate and then triumph – not to mention Bernard Shaw's analysis of the Englishman's genius for triumphing through an insensitivity to the dangers of his own position amounting to a kind of sublime arrogance.

Hitler had for years intended to make war on the USSR but he never wanted a war against either Great Britain or the United States. These wars he merely accepted when they came. He tried to come to terms with Great Britain and then to defeat it, and when both these efforts failed he turned away. He tried for a time to avoid war with the United States. On the outbreak of war in 1939 he forbade attacks on passenger ships, and when the *Athenia* was sunk with its twenty-eight American passengers he had the crew of U-30 sworn to secrecy on their return to port and tried to persuade the world that the sinking was a British stunt to drag the United States into war. In October he permitted attacks on enemy merchant ships without warning and on enemy passenger ships after warning (the need for this warning was lifted at the beginning of November), but he still refused to sanction attacks on neutrals. He allowed the *City of Flint*, which had been captured, taken to Norway and there released by the Norwegians (who interned the German boarders), to proceed without further molestation and he kept to this reticent policy despite the insistent pleas of his naval advisers. If Roosevelt's only concern had been to avoid incidents in the Atlantic he would have had no great problem, for Hitler wanted to avoid such incidents too. As late as the summer of 1941 Hitler was still turning a deaf ear to Raeder's pleas to sanction indiscriminate retaliation in the undeclared war which the Americans were waging in the Atlantic.

Thus Hitler had pursued in the Atlantic a policy of avoiding conflict with the United States up to the last months before he declared war. But in the Pacific, where he operated at second remove through his Japanese allies, he had the choice between restraining Japan in order to prolong American non-belligerency and, alternatively, egging Japan on. He chose the latter course. Engaged in a war on two fronts in which the Americans were becoming unofficially or even formally involved, he wanted to create a second front for the Americans too. Japan could open this front and at the same time attack the British Empire which had so sadly failed to respond to Hitler's offer of an honourable place in a world partitioned on Hitlerian lines. Hitler knew from his agents that Japan had decided not to attack the USSR and, by relaying to Tokyo his own version of Great Britain's helpless plight and his contemptuous estimate of American valour, he encouraged the more bellicose members of the Japanese cabinet. Discussions in Washington between the Americans and the Japanese during the autumn puzzled and worried Ribbentrop and his Ambassador in Tokyo, who could not make out whether they represented a genuine attempt to avoid war. Even after the fall of the comparatively moderate Konoye cabinet and the appointment of General Tojo as Prime Minister on 18 October the Germans were afraid that the Japanese might fail them, and so in November Ribbentrop went so far as to promise to help Japan in a war against the United States and not to make a separate peace. On 11 December Hitler fulfilled this promise. Italy declared war too.

After 1941 Hitler started no more wars. He gradually lost those he had started.

Every war plan has two main elements: the instruments with which to wage it and the right time to begin it. On both counts Hitler's war on the USSR was not merely a conspicuous failure but also mismanaged and mistaken. Although his armies came within an ace of capturing Moscow and so perhaps of victory, they were inadequately equipped to pursue it after the first six months and 1941 was the wrong date, since Hitler, on his own statement of 1937 which there is no reason to disbelieve, intended to win *Lebensraum* in the east in 1943–5. It was furthermore no part of any plan of his to make war on the USSR when engaged in other wars elsewhere. In attacking Czechoslovakia and Poland, Hitler gambled on getting what he wanted without war. In the first case the gamble came off but in the second it failed and produced war not only with Poland but a war in the west which he could neither win nor conclude. By 1941, elated perhaps by his continental successes in the west, he gambled again by advancing the date for his war in the east and by discounting the significance of continuing British belligerence. By the end of that year his most serious purpose – the winning of *Lebensraum* – was in jeopardy; and his declaration of war on the United States further exposed his maladroitness, for it converted Great Britain from a relatively minor offshore enemy into an assembly area for the legions of a vastly more dangerous foe.

In retrospect it is clear that Hitler could no longer win the war after this date. But Germany was not yet doomed to the unconditional surrender which the allies were to exact, for the German U-boats might starve Great Britain of food and arms and prevent American armies from crossing the ocean, and German V weapons might force the western allies, if not to surrender, at least to negotiate a separate peace in the west.

Part III

EUROPE UNDER THE NAZIS

CHAPTER 11
The New Order

FOR four years Germany dominated the greater part of Europe more completely than it had ever been dominated before. How far was this domination also purposeful? Every conqueror sets out with a complex of aims. On the one hand he has ideas, more or less precise, about what he wants to do with the lands he intends to conquer. On the other hand his attitude will be to conquer first and leave the rest till afterwards. Among the Nazis there were some who regarded the conquests of 1939–41 as a prelude and an opportunity: they had a Grand Design, even though this design was more of a vision than a plan and even though they could not always agree among themselves about what they wanted or how to achieve it. There were also others, more pragmatic, who treated the gains of these years as assets to be exploited in the war that was still going on: in so far as they had a Grand Design, it was one with a low priority for the time being. Hitler himself belonged rather to the pragmatic school. He was concerned first and foremost with winning the war and one of his keenest interests – perhaps his main interest – was in military equipment and military tactics. But he was hardly less preoccupied with the two great questions of *Lebensraum* and race, and his ideas and writing were the stuff out of which men like Alfred Rosenberg and Heinrich Himmler, although often with different interpretations and opposing aims, began to create a New Order for Europe during the war years.

Politically the New Order was simple. German hegemony was to be extended by German arms and accepted by everybody else. Nazi values were to be exported from their German centre and the pattern of Nazi revolution and Nazi life repeated in other lands. The first pre-condition of the New Order was conquest: land had to be got. How much land was left vague. It adapted itself to circumstances. At the high tide of German successes the concept of the *Grossraum*, or Greater Germanic Estate, embraced Europe from the Atlantic to the Urals, although a little earlier it had seemed to make do with rather less of Russia. The determining features of the *Grossraum* were not its borders but its nature. Instead of finding where people lived and then drawing permanent or semi-permanent frontiers to fit the ethnic facts, the Nazis began by designating an area and then moved people around in order to make demography fit the facts of power. The *Grossraum* therefore might be any size and in 1942 one writer envisaged it as covering one sixth of the globe. It was not a fixed area but a biological habitat like a nature reserve. It was where the German family lived.

The Germans themselves were to be the proprietors and directors of the *Grossraum* but not its only inhabitants. It would also contain the other Nordic races, who were only a little inferior to the Germans but would have no effective political or economic power; and non-Nordic peoples who, suitably regrouped and assigned to their economic functions, would be the helots of the *Grossraum*. (Hitler liked reading history books and admired Sparta.) These sub-human varieties would be kept in subjection by, among other devices, depriving them of education. As Hitler himself put it, they were to 'know just enough to understand road signs, so as not to get themselves run over by our vehicles. For them the word "liberty" must mean the right to wash on holidays.' His aim in the USSR was to 'Germanize the country by the settlement of Germans and treat the natives as redskins'. An even more inferior variety of human being, too vicious to be allowed any place however menial, would be eliminated. Thus re-ordered, the *Grossraum* would be made economically self-sufficient, in-dependent of the other major areas in the world although specially linked, in some versions, with Africa in a Eurafrican super *Grossraum* which was partly just an even more grandiose vision, partly an extension designed to furnish Europe with the raw materials of which it had not got enough, and partly a way of finding an exciting but peripheral role for the Italians, whose position in a purely European *Grossraum* was, for obvious reasons, never spelled out.

Given these imaginings there were two main fields for action, the demographic and the economic. People had to be moved or removed; the work they did had to be reorganized to fit the plan for a Germano-centric autarkic Europe. During the war quite a lot was undertaken demographically, but the economic planning of the New Order was overshadowed by the exigencies of war economics.

The economic aspects of the New Order were never condensed into a single document or plan and it is to some extent misleading to propound any such plan by piecing together what was said about it by different people at different times. Nevertheless a general outline existed.

The Nazis were centralizers, but half-hearted ones. At one level they believed in the concentration of power. They converted federal Weimar Germany into a unitary state and they would have carried this centralizing process beyond Germany into Europe, making Berlin the political, econ-omic and cultural – in sum, the totalitarian – capital of a super-state.

But although they focused power on a single central capital, they also diffused it among the departments and agencies which were centred in the capital. This fragmentation was partly a reflection of Hitler's policy and his character: he was not an administrator and he ruled by dividing. It was also a consequence of lack of foresight. Especially during the war new problems thrust themselves upon Germany's rulers and the Nazi way of dealing with them was to create new agencies. In this respect they acted more like the Americans with their similar propensity for bureaucratic proliferation than like the British or French, who have characteristically preferred to accommodate new problems and new functions within the settled framework of the existing civil service and the existing machinery of government. The New Order, had it come into being, would have been controlled by a single but fissiparous and philoprogenitive machine.

This machine would have existed to serve Germany's interests but it would have claimed incidentally to serve other interests too. The core of the *Grossraum* – a Germany which had engulfed Alsace-Lorraine, Luxembourg, parts of Belgium and Silesia – would be to Europe what the Ruhr was to Germany. Here would be most of Europe's heavy industry and all its arms industries. Beyond it industries would exist on sufferance only and their primary purpose would be the production of consumer goods for Germans. Each conquered area would be a tributary, judged and regulated in terms of the needs of Germany. Besides consumer goods these areas would produce food, and their agriculture would be re-planned to suit Germany: more arable in Denmark, for example, and less dairy farming. In return Germany would provide a guaranteed market for all Europe's food production and abolish unemployment. The countries beyond the central core would, by virtue of centralized planning, become specialized producers knowing what they could export, how much credit they could have and how much labour they would need; an international labour pool would enable the planners to operate an effective international division of labour. This picture was neither entirely unfamiliar nor entirely unattractive to Europe. The notion of an economic entity larger than any existing political unity, and of the need for Europe to organize economically on a wider scale, had been propagated by various champions of European unity ranging from men in official positions like Aristide Briand in France and Paul van Zeeland in Belgium to the League of Nation's Inquiry for European Union and private enthusiasts like Count Richard Coudenhove-Kalergi. Europe moreover had had more than its fair share of economic instability between the wars and might therefore be persuaded that it was worth forgoing the freedom to choose for itself what it would

make or grow if it could buy stability in exchange for economic sovereignty.

The German New Order was in this sense an attempt to construct an
economy broader than a national economy and it suffered from the basic
defect of most such schemes attempted in a nationalist world. Its scope
was international but its purpose was national. Long-range planning, long-
term agreements, guaranteed markets, fixed exchange rates, a European
clearing system – plans to link the Baltic and the Black Seas by an Oder–
Danube canal, the Rhine and the Po by another, plans to dam the Straits
of Gibraltar in order to endow all Europe with cheap power – all these
things could not conceal the fact that the basis of the New Order was
German power and German requirements and not a European cooperative. The benefits to everybody else would be the crumbs from the
rich man's table. It could hardly look otherwise during a war.

Ideas of this kind were peace aims rather than war aims and when the
war turned into a long war and a losing war they were inevitably submerged. Up to 1942 the New Order was proffered with a kind of open-
handed exultation and in the belief that it would strike some response, but
from 1942 onwards the voice of Germany turned from allurements to
warnings, prophesying communist horrors to come rather than a new
Eden. At the same time the New Order, such as it was, had to be applied
to keeping Germany going in a painfully immediate present. Instead of
enlarging and fertilizing Europe's economy, it had to nourish Germany's
war effort.

The lengthening war also held up the demographic planning of the New
Order but it did not do so entirely. Some movements of population were
undertaken and horribly much was achieved in the way of extermination.
Both these aspects of the matter fell primarily, though not entirely, within
the province of the SS and they acquired from the SS their overriding
characteristic of ferocious brutality.

The SS grew out of a small blackshirted bodyguard originally called
the *Stosstrupp Hitler* and renamed *Schutzstaffeln* (SS) in 1925. Even more
than the Nazi Party itself they were the instrument of Hitler's personal
will. They were drenched in Nazi ideology and they enjoyed a life of
special licence which was nowhere better illustrated than on the very
slopes of Hitler's own Bavarian eyrie where they could revel off-duty in
an efficiently organized orgiastic hedonism calculatingly and cynically
proffered to them by their non-alcoholic and near-chaste Führer. They
were the principal beneficiaries of the destruction of the SA in 1934 and
from that time their power expanded as they absorbed the police forces of
Germany, built up a well-equipped private army of thirty divisions,

became an economic force in control of a large part of the Reich's labour and of extensive factories, and duplicated their German functions and powers in occupied Europe. The SS became the rulers of Germany, the effective core within the amorphous mass of the Nazi Party. Their chief from 1929 (when their strength was under 300 men) was Heinrich Himmler, a man pre-eminent among the senior Nazi leaders for his mediocrity, a quality which ensured Hitler's confidence almost – but not quite – to the end. He was said to be so obsessed by blondness that he could not bear to have dark-haired people around. He had a little knowledge of Germanic origins and runic inscriptions which he pursued with the unintelligent concentration of a man whose hobby is his life, but paradoxically he was also a visionary with ambition who throve in the struggle for power because of his enthusiasm for a purer Germanic world on Nazi principles – which he accepted wholesale and uncritically without any of the cynical reservations of the sharper-minded Hitler or the softer-living Goering. Himmler was also acute enough and lucky enough to rise to the top in the Nazi jungle and stay there. Before the war ended he was not only *Reichsführer SS*, Chief of the German Police and Minister of the Interior but also Commander-in-Chief of the Home Army and he had twice – on each occasion briefly, ineptly and for the most part at a distance – held command of an Army Group in the field. He had become a contender for supreme power in succession to Hitler, although Hitler himself said in 1945 that Himmler would not do as his successor because he had no culture.

The annexation of the police by the SS was the vital step in the transformation of the SS from its modest beginnings within the Nazi machine into the power which ruled Germany and terrorized a continent. In Weimar Germany each province had its own government and its own police force. The most important of these forces was the Prussian police controlled by the Prussian Minister of the Interior, who was a more influential personage than the shadowy Reich Minister of the Interior. As Minister of the Interior and then Prime Minister in Prussia, Goering was, before he exchanged cruelty for easefulness, the most powerful policeman in Germany. Himmler was chief of the Bavarian police in Munich. But Himmler also got himself a subordinate post in the Prussian system.

The Prussian police was a rambling system whose branches included the Schupo (traffic police and men on the beat), the Orpo (*gendarmerie* living in barracks), the Kripo or criminal detectives, the Gestapo or secret state security service, and special services like the fire brigades and railway police. Himmler became deputy head of the Prussian Gestapo and he also became Chief of Police in various other provinces besides Bavaria. In

1936 a unified German police force was created with Himmler at its head, and in 1943 he became also Reich Minister of the Interior, an office which, with the centralizing tendencies of the Third Reich, had by then outstripped its Prussian counterpart in importance.

After 1936 the next step was to incorporate the detective and intelligence functions of the police into the SS. The new German police was divided into two main branches, the Orpo on the one hand and on the other the Sipo or Security Police embracing the Kripo and the Gestapo. As head of the Sipo Himmler appointed Reinhardt Heydrich who was already head of the *Sicherheitsdienst* (SD) or security services of the SS. For a short time the Sipo under Heydrich remained with the rest of the police within the Ministry of the Interior, but shortly before the outbreak of war it was transferred to one of the main branches of the SS, the newly created RSHA – *Reichssicherheitshauptamt* or Reich Security Division. Departments III and VI of the RSHA were the SD (Home) and SD (Foreign); Department IV was the Gestapo and its sub-department IV 4b meant Jews. In personal terms the RSHA was Heydrich until his assassination in Prague in May 1942, when he was succeeded by Ernst Kaltenbrunner; Department IV was Heinrich Müller; IV 4b was Karl Adolf Eichmann.

The chain of command Heydrich–Müller–Eichmann exhibits the variety of the SS. Müller, the head of the Gestapo, was the type of the faceless professional policeman who knew his job and did it; he was for a long time not a member of the Nazi Party; his origins were obscure and probably lowly and he had a chip on his shoulder. It was in a sense fitting that in April 1945 he simply vanished after walking out of Hitler's bunker to go back to his office and has never been heard of since. He has been suspected of being in Russian pay and of taking refuge in Moscow at the end of the war, where he is said to have died in 1948. Heydrich and Eichmann, his immediate superior and subordinate, were very different. Both had goals rather than jobs. Heydrich's driving force came from ambition, Eichmann's from obsession. Both were virulent anti-semites. Eichmann became in practice the principal agent in the destruction of the Jews, supervising and directing the application of Nazi racial policies first in Bohemia and Moravia and then in Poland and ultimately in Hungary. After the war he escaped to South America but in 1960 he was traced and kidnapped by a Jewish organization and delivered to Israel where he was tried, condemned and executed. Heydrich, a failed naval officer, was Hitler's right-hand man in the massacre of June 1934 and it was he rather than Himmler who ensured that the victors should be the SS and not the army. He pursued his course by vigour harnessed to ability and by intrigue served by his intimate knowledge of the personal weaknesses of the senior Nazi chiefs and the skeletons in their cupboards. As head of the RSHA he was one of the most powerful men in Germany, although not in the top rank, and it has been conjectured that when he took the office of Protector of Bohemia and Moravia in 1941 he did so with an eye to climbing higher by this circuitous route. He was as ruthless and violent as any of his colleagues and much more intelligent. (He also played the violin and at his funeral the cultivated, anti-Nazi Admiral Canaris wept.) His death removed Himmler's most formidable rival.

Heydrich was still a little-known figure in the thirties. Müller and Eichmann were even less well known, and comparatively few members of the general public would have recognized them. But the SS itself was not difficult to recognize. First in Germany and then throughout Europe its members strode along the streets or hurtled along the roads in cars in the special costumes designed to make them look as terrifying as possible – the sinister uniformity of the black shirt, no jacket to impede the swing of the arm, the expensive breeches and the hard shiny boots, and on every cap the head of death as a *memento mori* to every living citizen. The complexity of the German SS and police added to the terror. In occupied Europe the men of the Orpo were the visible intimation of police rule and police brutality. They were the men who could be seen rounding up one's neighbours and who might at any time of day or night come for oneself, while behind them in the recesses of buildings whose whispered addresses became household fears were the men of the Gestapo and the SD.

Himmler's long-term plans for the re-ordering of Europe were based on reducing the Slavs by 30 million and planting a German upper crust in selected parts of Poland, the Baltic states and the USSR. In 1942 the SS produced a blueprint or Eastern Plan covering the next twenty-five years. It involved the establishment of temporary German strongpoints, partly garrisons and partly colonies, peopled by peasants under arms. These settlements would be at central points. At the same time permanent settlements were to be planted at the extreme edge of the *Grossraum*, where, at first under SS control, they would shield the *Grossraum* like the marcher principalities of feudal times. This Germanic population would reach 3.5 million at the end of twenty-five years. Among them would be a local population of landless poor. The plan was revised and re-issued but at the beginning of 1943 Hitler decreed that all these schemes must await the end of the war and so stopped Himmler from putting it into operation. At about the same time some Americans, including the Secretary of the Treasury Henry Morgenthau, were evolving a similar plan for turning Germany into an agricultural zone after the war.

Himmler was concerned not only to dispatch Reich Germans out into the *Grossraum* but also – and not without a degree of contradiction – to gather *Volksdeutsche* back into the Reich. (Hitler was more interested in the latter than the former programme.) As a first step *Volksdeutsche* in occupied territories were treated as a privileged class, given positions of minor authority where possible, allowed to use special shops and so on, but this policy, first adopted in Czechoslovakia and Poland, sharpened the Russians' natural distrust of *Volksdeutsche* and led to large numbers of them being deported to the east before the Germans could reach them. Himmler's plans were further confounded by disputes among the Germans themselves. While the S S started registering the *Volksdeutsche* whom they found round the Black Sea and elsewhere with a view to resettlement, for diverse reasons the army commanders, Rosenberg and Goering all wanted them left where they were. It also transpired that fewer of them still spoke German than had been expected. The only transfer of any consequence effected by the SS in the USSR was the eviction of a number of Ukrainians from the neighbourhood of Zhitomir and Kalinovka to make way for Volhynian Germans who did not want to go there. Significantly perhaps this single practical example had not been envisaged by the Eastern Plan. It created trouble in the German administration of the Ukraine and squabbling in Berlin and had no sensible purpose. Apart from this there was no considerable displacement of the *Volksdeutsche* of the USSR until the tide of war turned and about 300,000 of them were swept westward not as settlers but as refugees.

In other areas Himmler was less obstructed by rival authorities. One hundred and thirty-two thousand *Volksdeutsche* from Bessarabia and northern Bukovina and another 32,000 from southern Bukovina and the Dobrudja were earmarked for Germany and about 46,000 of them were settled in annexed territories; the rest probably spent the war in transit camps. Another 9,000 Germans from Warsaw and 14,000 from Slovenia had a similar fate. Poland was to be sorted out by moving 164,000 Germans westward from what had been the Russian zone in 1939 and an equivalent number of Ukrainians and White Russians from the original German zones eastwards. In addition 80,000 Baltic Germans were to find new homes in Poland. In the west Alsace-Lorraine and Luxembourg were prepared for Germanization by removing 105,000 inhabitants ('foreign elements') from the former and 7,000 from the latter. In practice these schemes produced chaos and a degree of incidental economic disruption which led to complaints about the damage done to the war effort by the SS. Some of the Baltic Germans found themselves moved back to where they had come from after only a few months, while the fate of the German-speaking Tyrolese was like a scene from Dante. In a plebiscite in

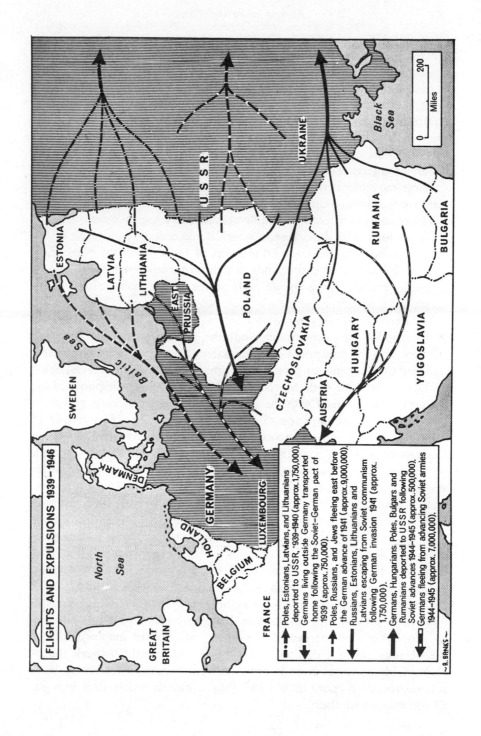

FLIGHTS AND EXPULSIONS 1939 – 1946

Poles, Estonians, Latvians, and Lithuanians
deported to USSR, 1939–1940 (approx.1,750,000).

Germans living outside Germany transported
home following the Soviet:–German pact of
1939 (approx.750,000).

Poles, Russians, and Jews fleeing east before
the German advance of 1941 (approx.9,000,000).

Russians, Estonians, Lithuanians and
Latvians escaping from Soviet communism
following German invasion 1941 (approx.
1,750,000).

Germans, Hungarians Poles, Bulgars and
Rumanians deported to USSR following
Soviet advances 1944–1945 (approx.500,000).

Germans fleeing from advancing Soviet armies
1944–1945 (approx. 7,000,000).

~ R. BANKS ~

1939, 185,365 opted for the Reich; by 1941 this figure had somehow grown to 220,000 and the next year it was even bigger; but while somebody was apparently persuading more and more Tyrolese to ask to be moved to the Reich, nobody was making adequate arrangements for them to get there and it seems unlikely that more than 80,000 did so. At one time Himmler toyed with the idea of sending them all to the Crimea and many spent the war in camps waiting to be moved to nobody quite knew where. Few *Volksdeutsche* actually reached the Reich. A number were settled in the annexed territories and a greater number simply got lost.

These movements of population were only a part of the plan. There was also the elimination of undesirables, notably Jews and Slavs.

The attempt to exterminate whole peoples was a logical consequence of Nazi ideology, and the degree to which it succeeded was a result of the military conquests which placed millions of Jews within the Nazi grasp and of the reiterated propaganda which so transformed thousands of Germans that they were able to perform the cruellest obscenities. Many thousands more witnessed them or were otherwise aware of them.

The purity of the Aryan race did not require mass murder. It required the prevention of inter-breeding, but the prevention of inter-breeding required also the prevention of all human contact since even the strictest laws and the most intense propaganda cannot guarantee correct responses of the heart and the flesh. Moreover, in Nazi mythology the purity of the Aryan race was linked with the salvation of the human race, and since both doctrines posited a Jewish enemy, they together bred a hatred of Jewry and a determination to exterminate it. The discrimination against Jews, which was first prescribed by law immediately after the Nazis took power, led on to degradation, outlawry, pillage and murder; mass murder was methodically organized after the war began. By the laws of the first phase, culminating in the Nuremberg decrees of September 1935, not only were marriage and fornication between Jews and Gentiles condemned but also the slightest physical touch. Yet the accompanying pathological ravings of some Nazi zealots and a part of the press were not seen as a prelude to anything worse. There was some emigration and a few suicides, but even when a special Jewish Bureau was established without any concealment in 1936 (Eichmann was its chief) hope and incredulity were still allowed to prevail over desperation. Emigration moreover was baulked by prohibitions on the export of property and by the inaccessibility of the obvious haven, Palestine, where the British, caught between the irreconcilable promises given to Jews and Arabs in the First World War, refused to admit more than 1,500 Jews a month unless they brought £1,000 apiece with them.

But persecution was already grievous and in November 1938 a young seventeen-year-old Jew called Herschel Grynszpan decided to force it upon the attention of an unwilling world by a desperate deed. He murdered a German diplomat in the Paris embassy, Ernst vom Rath (whom he mistook for the Ambassador). Retaliation took the form of a pogrom which the Nazis were able to organize in advance because vom Rath lingered in hospital before dying. News of his death reached Hitler in Munich where he had gone to celebrate the fifteenth anniversary of his 1923 putsch. Local party and SS authorities had already been warned of what was coming and of the need to conceal the fact that it was pre-arranged. Traffic in selected areas was diverted, the telephone lines of Jewish subscribers were cut and at 2 a.m. organized squads wrecked 200 synagogues and other Jewish property (including a Jewish sanatorium), murdered seventy Jews in the Buchenwald concentration camp and arrested 20,000 Jews. So much plate glass was broken that the outburst of this one night was given the name of the *Kristallnacht*. In addition the Jewish community was collectively condemned to pay twenty-five million marks for the repair of damaged property and also a fine of one billion marks – which practically dispossessed it of the goods and enterprises which had not already been taken from it. Jews were expelled from hospitals, old folks' homes and schools, and public places were put out of bounds to them. A proposal to take away their driving licences was discussed but dropped. No foreign government protested. The British Foreign Secretary, Lord Halifax, ruled that a protest would constitute unjustifiable interference in the internal affairs of another state and warned his subordinates against giving unnecessary offence to Hitler. In this last year before the war the German Jews began to flee their fate, but the acquisition of Austria and Bohemia and Moravia added to the Reich as many Jews as left it. From the Nazi point of view the problem remained the same size – about 357,000. Then the conquest of Poland enormously increased that number, multiplying it by ten.

In 1938 Hitler discussed with Himmler the killing of whole sections of the population of Czechoslovakia and a year later similar discussions took place as a prelude to the Polish campaign. SS chiefs conferred with army chiefs about the modalities of this first instalment of the New Order. The ruling class, the intelligentsia, the Jews were to be collected and killed. The German Jews were not thrown into the programme at this stage partly because the Nazis had not finally made up their minds between deportation and extermination, and partly for logistical reasons: there was so much to be done first in Poland and later in the USSR that the mills of destruction could not grind fast enough.

The last serious attempt to purge Germany of Jews without killing them was the Madagascar plan. This plan had been adumbrated before the war and was revived after the fall of France, whose colony Madagascar was. The plan was to send all European Jews to this island in the Indian Ocean where they could be autonomous under German sovereignty and would, as Hitler put it, be hostages against the 'good behaviour of their co-racialists in America'. Problems of transport and the like were examined in some detail but the war did not end with the fall of France and so the Germans could not get hold of Madagascar or send Jews there. Instead they kept the German Jews in Germany until they could be sent to Poland to be killed along with Jews from other parts of Europe.

In the interval between the defeat of Poland and the attack on the USSR, Hitler set up a new agency, Operations Staff Rosenberg, which began as a research body for the collection of material about Jews, communists and Freemasons and the formulation of a policy for combating these pests. With a hideous simulation of scholarly application it assembled a huge library and, by combining pillage with study, amassed incidentally a fabulous art collection. It was expanded into a Ministry for the East, in which thousands of industrious, ingenious and even learned Germans worked away at schemes which had no relevance to the war going on around them; their activities were viewed with irritated scorn by the professional staff of the German Foreign Ministry and with even more irritated jealousy by Ribbentrop who considered that Rosenberg was being allowed to poach on his own preserves as Foreign Minister. Since the East meant the Baltic states and the USSR, Rosenberg became on paper the potential disposer of the Russian empire. His aim was to destroy the Russian state in perpetuity by fragmenting and pastoralizing it and by creating new separatist states out of the debris. Hitler had decided to give Leningrad to Finland and Bessarabia and Odessa to Rumania. From what remained Rosenberg intended to fashion at least four states: a Russian rump, renamed Muscovy, stretching from the Arctic to Turkestan and containing 60 million inhabitants; a Caucasian state; the Ukraine; and the *Ostland*, consisting of the three Baltic states and White Russia. All these states would be ruled by German Commissioners of proconsular dignity and two of them actually began to take shape in the *Ostland* and the Ukraine under Commissioners whose functions were similar *in partibus infidelium* to those of the Gauleiters of the Reich.

The *Ostland* was a hybrid. White Russia's function was to be a dump for undesirables who had not been murdered and could not yet be transported to Siberia. The fate of the three Baltic states was peculiarly poignant. These singularly well governed and civilized communities were first

THE ROSENBERG PLAN 1941

■ Germany before the invasion of the U S S R in 1941.

▨ Territory to be annexed to Germany and controlled by Berlin.

▨ Independent states to be under close German control.

▨ Proposed Soviet national territory.

Proposed administrative centre for the entire eastern region.

CHINA

0   500
Miles

~ARTHUR BANKS~

SIBERIA

Krasnoyarsk
Tomsk
Barnaul
Novosibirsk
Omsk
Alma Ata
Lake Balkhash
Karaganda
Samarkand
Tashkent
TURKESTAN
Aral Sea
Svedlovsk
URAL
Vorkuta
Kazan
Ufa
Magnitogorsk
Krasnovodsk
Archangel
Koltas
MUSCOVY
Murmansk
Astrakhan
CASPIAN SEA
Vologda
Moscow
Ryazan
Stalingrad
Tiflis
GREATER FINLAND
Leningrad
Kharkov
Rostov
Novorossisk
GREATER CAUCASIA
Helsinki
Kiev
GREATER UKRAINE
Batum
AFGHANISTAN
Minsk
GREATER BERUSSIA
BALTIC SEA
GREATER GEORGIA
BLACK SEA
FERSIA
Riga
BALTUM
CRIMEA
TURKEY
POLAND
BESSARABIA
Odessa
Berlin
GERMANY
Warsaw

shackled by the USSR in 1939 and then absorbed in the next year. On the approach of war in 1941 the Russians started deporting and massacring the inhabitants, and they continued to do so as they slowly retreated before the Germans. The Germans began by treating the three states comparatively lightly and even accorded them a degree of administrative autonomy, but in 1942–3 they introduced their full programme of concentration camps, slave labour and the murder of Jews – to the accompaniment of public lectures on the superiority of German culture. (When the Germans were again evicted by the Russians, the killings went on none the less. A number of refugees, mainly Estonians, escaped to Sweden, though many died on the way. Depopulation was continued by deportations into the USSR after the war.)

In the Ukraine Rosenberg was encouraged by signs of welcome for the Germans (an autonomist, anti-Soviet movement raised false German hopes) and by the surrenders of Russian troops in the first weeks of the campaign (which he exaggeratedly ascribed solely to political rather than military causes). But his schemes never came to anything. Hitler was not interested in separatist vassal states. He told Rosenberg that the Baltic states, the Crimea, Baku and its neighbourhood, the Volga region and the Kola peninsula in the far north were to be entirely German. Erich Koch too, Rosenberg's Commissioner in the Ukraine, regarded his bailiwick simply as a source of food and labour for the Reich and derided his chief's political vision of a Ukrainian state as a stepping stone on the way to the Caucasus and a fender hung out to keep Russians and Poles at a safe remove. For Koch, as for Hitler, the Commissariat was a prelude to colonization. But Koch was a cleverer man than his chief Rosenberg. He soon sensed that this prelude had no sequel and he rarely visited the Ukraine. Rosenberg himself had to witness all his plans set on one side even before the turn of the military tide extinguished them. He experienced complete failure earlier than his equals in the Nazi hierarchy.

Rosenberg's activities provided a cloak for the operations of the SS. Although Rosenberg's Ministry, like the government of Hans Frank in Poland, was regarded by the SS as a nuisance and there was a good deal of friction between these different authorities, they became in effect collaborators in measures designed to kill even more people than the regular armed forces. They dealt death in the open and death in the camp.

Death on a grand scale by one or other of these methods was resolved upon in 1941 before the invasion of the USSR. A massacre programme was discussed between SS and army chiefs in May and four special squads or *Einsatzgruppen* were formed by the SS to round up and kill ideological opponents such as communist officials, political commissars

GERMAN RULE IN THE EAST 1941-1944

Six million Jews were murdered in the concentration camps and cities plus an equal number of non-Jewish Russians and Poles, two million of whom were children. Two million Soviet prisoners of war also were starved or beaten to death, and this policy of mass-murder led to partisan activity behind the German front line.

Baltic Sea

Reval
Novgorod
Pskov
Riga
Volokolamsk
Dvinsk
OSTLAND
Kovno
Vitebsk
Danzig
STUTTHOF
Vilna
GREATER
GERMANY
TREBLINKA
Bialystok
Minsk
Orel
Kalisz
CHELMNO
Warsaw
Lublin
SOBIBOR
Gomel
Kursk
MAJDANEK
BELZEC
Rovno
Chernigov
Cracow
Kiev
AUSCHWITZ
Lvov
Zhitomir
SLOVAKIA

UNOCCUPIED
TERRITORY

UKRAINE

HUNGARY

RUMANIAN MILITARY GOVERNMENT

Nikopol
Rostov

Melitopol
Stavropol
Krasnodar

RUMANIA

Odessa

Sevastopol
Yalta

Black Sea

	Areas ruled by the German military.
	Administered by the General-Government of Poland.
	Administered by the Ostland and Ukraine Reichskommissariats.
	Annexed by Germany.
□	Main concentration camps.
★	Partisans active in these areas.

0   200
Miles

~ARTHUR BANKS~

and Jews. A special order for the murder of political commissars was issued by Hitler and transmitted through army channels at the beginning of June. A commissar was not defined, and, whether or not the vagueness was intentional, its effect was to license indiscriminate killing. Not only were suspected commissars shot out of hand or delivered by the army to the SD (which came to much the same thing): in addition recalcitrant or awkwardly sick prisoners could be dubbed commissars and summarily disposed of. The trigger-happiness of army officers and other ranks was encouraged by a further order, issued on the eve of the invasion, which did away with judicial proceedings in the military area and empowered battalion commanders and upwards to hear cases and impose penalties (including death) without the formality of assembling a court.

The four *Einsatzgruppen* were quite small – each was 500–800 strong – but their importance was shown by the choice of their commanders, who included the heads of Departments III, V and VIa of the RSHA. These men expected to end up in the four principal cities of the USSR where they would blossom into the local tsars of the New Order. Meanwhile their business was simply to kill. They began by inciting pogroms but were disappointed by the unenthusiastic response and were obliged to set to work more systematically. Leading Jews were required to assemble their fellows at given points, whereupon all were driven off to a nearby open space, stripped and shot. The dead and half dead were tumbled into trenches. Others were drowned or burned alive wholesale. No concealment was attempted or possible. The razzias were witnessed by thousands, talked about and even photographed. The executioners had to be kept up to their task by being made half drunk (which did not improve their aim), by treble pay and long holidays. A typical operation involved several hundred victims and took several hours. The largest single operation was the killing of over 33,000 Kievan Jews in two days in September 1941 as a reprisal for the blowing up of a hotel – the fearful inspiration of Yevtushenko's poem *Babi Yar* and the basis for Anatoly Kuznetsov's novel of the same name; the mass grave of these dead and dying Jews continued to be used as a dump for what the Nazis regarded as human refuse until it contained at least 100,000 corpses. A year later about 16,000 Jews were killed in a single day at Pinsk with the help of grenades, axes, dogs and SS cavalry. On the only occasion on which Himmler attended a massacre, it turned his stomach and made him order a change in technique: there was to be less shooting and more gassing.

Each of the *Einsatzgruppen* tended to magnify its achievements, so that it is impossible to take at its face value the boast by one commander, Erich Ohlendorf, that he had been personally responsible for the death of

90,000 people, most of them Jews, before he relinquished his command in June 1942, but it is probable that the number of Jews killed by Germans in the east was about two million. The disposal of the bodies was so rudimentary that the gases generated by decomposition betrayed the places of burial by a continuous barrage of small explosions, and a special squad had to be formed to open the graves and lay this ghastly evidence by chemical action, bonfires or mechanical pulverization.

The Jews of the rest of Europe were meanwhile being driven to their principal graveyard, the extermination camps of Poland. These camps were a specialized variety of the concentration camps which the Nazis had established in Germany immediately after coming to power.

A concentration camp is essentially a guarded area where people are sent and kept against their will, as though in prison. But a concentration camp is something different from a prison. A camp may be established because the prisons are full, but this is not why the Nazi camps were established. A man is sent to prison because he has been accused and convicted of a crime, and he is sent by a court. The men and women who were sent to the concentration camps were not accused or convicted of crimes; they were simply obnoxious to the régime, either because they were opposed to it or because they were – like the Jews – obnoxious by definition. And they were not committed to the camps by a court. They were sent there by party functionaries exercising a whim like an absolute monarch signing *lettres de cachet*. Further, the men and women in the camps were not meant to come out again. They were meant to rot and die there, and usually they did. Finally, the concentration camps were not created, like prisons, to hold men in durance and no more. They were also intended to intimidate those who remained outside them, and they did so by the cruelty of those who ran them and whose behaviour was no secret, and by the doubts which were allowed to circulate about citizens who abruptly disappeared from normal life.

The first concentration camp was established in March 1933, within a few weeks of the Nazis taking power. It was at Dachau, near Munich. Others were established in the years that followed, and the camp business received a boost when the *Anschluss* with Austria and the subjection of Bohemia-Moravia opened up new areas for the Nazi press gangs. With the beginning of the war the nature of the camps as well as their scale changed, for they became the scene of the Nazi policy of mass extermination. In the next few years millions were killed in them, perhaps seven millions – by hard labour, privation, epidemics, medical experiments on their bodies, fusillade, bastinado or asphyxiation.

During this period the camps were divided into two main categories.

Most of them were labour camps, in which people from all over Europe toiled for Germany for a certain number of months until they dropped dead or were killed off because they had become useless. Some of these camps were near important factories and were run by the captains of big industry. In a different category were the death camps, whose business was extermination. There were five of these, all of them in Poland. The first was established at Auschwitz (Oswiecim), near Katowice in Silesia, soon after the defeat of Poland in 1939. Auschwitz developed into a complex of camps, one of which was the showpiece of modern technical killing by means of the gas called Cyclon B (guaranteed to kill within ten minutes) and of modern technical disposal in the ovens of its crematorium. After the invasion of the USSR four more extermination camps were established in Poland at Chelmno, Treblinka, Sobibor and Belsec (not to be confused with Bergen-Belsen which was partly a Wehrmacht hospital camp and partly an SS internment camp near Hanover in Germany).

The Polish Jews had priority because they were on the spot. There were in Poland in 1939 over three million Jews. Their numbers made them a special case. Nowhere except in Palestine did Jews constitute so large a proportion of the population. Nowhere except in the United States were so many Jews to be found. Nowhere at all, probably, was anti-semitism so potent or the extermination of Jews so readily acceptable to Gentiles. The first German plan was to concentrate all Jews from the German zone of Poland in an area in the east of the zone, but the attempt to do this created such chaos on the railways that the plan had to be abandoned. Instead ghettos were established in the principal towns. A Jew found outside a ghetto could be executed. Those inside were starved and over-crowded. Epidemics developed fast. Jew-baiting was encouraged with the inevitable results of torture and private-enterprise murder. The Warsaw ghetto, whose sealing walls were completed in October 1940, contained about half a million Jews. The extermination camps began functioning at the end of 1941 with Chelmno destroying about a thousand human beings a day, and during 1942 the Polish ghettos were gradually emptied into them. At one time Treblinka alone was taking 6,000 a day, and Auschwitz, which killed well over one million people in less than three years, could take twice as many in its stride. The disposal of the Warsaw ghetto began in July 1942 when there were probably still about 380,000 Jews in it. By the beginning of October there remained only 50–60,000 hiding and starving in insanitary cellars and sewers (built to British design in the previous century). They were governed by a suborned Jewish police and a half honest *Judenrat* until, driven beyond the limits of endurance and faced with the extinction of all hope, an enfeebled residue staged in April 1943 a desperate and doomed rising. They fought alone: most Polish Gentiles were indifferent to their fate or worse. Yet their struggle lasted seven weeks before all were either killed or taken and shipped to the gas chambers. Their enduring memorial is Schoenberg's threnody for speaker, chorus and orchestra, *A Survivor from Warsaw*. A commemorative volume with some fifty illustrations was prepared by the SS and presented to Himmler.

By this time the stench of the camps had become so horrible and the danger of epidemics so great that mass burials and mass pyres had been largely superseded by cremation in specially designed ovens which would take half a dozen bodies at a time. The congestion in the extermination camps (sometimes aggravated by technical breakdowns which obliged trainloads of living victims to wait unloaded in sidings for several days) was caused by the international character of the Polish camps. Deportations from Germany itself and occupied countries swelled the traffic from the end of 1941.

In this year the Nazis finally decided to rid Germany of all its Jews. A plan to deposit them in the USSR having been frustrated by transport difficulties, they were routed instead to Auschwitz and eastern Poland for extermination. A conference on the Wannsee in January 1942 decided also to kill all Croat, Slovak and Rumanian Jews in occupied territory and to inform the governments of Croatia, Slovakia, Hungary and Bulgaria that the Germans were ready to deal with their Jews too. Jews from Austria and Bohemia-Moravia were treated as German Jews. Technically this extermination programme was based on an earlier programme for the 'euthanasia' of alleged incurables which accounted for some 90,000 victims of Nazi distemper before unwelcome disclosures in 1941 brought it to a halt and subsequently transferred its apparatus outside the Reich where its catchment was extended from 'incurables' to Jews, gipsies and Russian prisoners of war. (Of the many millions of Russian war victims two million were murdered prisoners of war.) The Wannsee conference made concrete Hitler's proclaimed aim to destroy the Jews, but action had already begun in the previous year when the *Einsatzkommandos* killed a million Jews.

The Wannsee conference came up against the problem which had been worrying Nazi racists for years: what to do about Germany's half-Jews and quarter-Jews. Heydrich proposed that the former should be sterilized instead of being deported, but Hitler objected, mainly because at bottom he opposed any solution except their removal from German soil. The problem of the half-Jew continued to be debated but was never settled one way or another. Quarter-Jews, who were exempt from the

Nuremberg laws, were to remain unmolested unless they were too obviously Jewish in appearance or – sinister opening for blackmail – there were special circumstances. There was a special category of privileged Jews. These included war veterans, Jews over sixty-five, holders of the Iron Cross First Class, senior civil servants, Jews with foreign connections or an international reputation, and others who still had the means to bribe the police. Their fate depended very much on the personal whim of the local Gauleiter and other officials. Privileged Jews remained subject to blackmail, often crudely expressed in such terms as 'going up the chimney' or 'making compost'. They had no legal status or redress and might suddenly find themselves dispatched to a concentration camp for talking in a tram or smoking in the street or receiving a food parcel. The camp at Theresienstadt (Terezin) in Czechoslovakia was reserved for them and was from time to time opened to representatives of the Red Cross. Privileged Jews died in Theresienstadt instead of in other camps, until the confusion of the last stages of the war caused them to be dispersed for extermination. When the war ended Theresienstadt had a residue of 20,000 inmates, one third of them not Jews.

The Greater German Reich was declared purged of Jews in November 1943. This was not strictly true. Many Jews who had married Gentiles, as well as half-Jews and quarter-Jews, survived. There were about 33,000 of them in Germany at the end of the war.

In western occupied countries Jews were removed immediately from public office and subjected to petty inhumanities such as being forbidden to eat in cafés or restaurants, use public transport or (in Holland) ride a bicycle. Next a census would be taken, property confiscated, segregation enforced. During 1942 many western Jews were driven into labour camps in their own countries and in the following year deportation began. It was substantially completed before the end of 1943. At first certain categories were exempted – for example, childless Jews married to Gentiles were given the alternative of sterilization – but these were administrative measures designed to ease the logistics of mass transport and mass murder and keep sections of Jewry quiet until their turn came. In 1943 Auschwitz was so busy that Jews from Holland and Luxembourg had to be sent all the way to Sobibor and Treblinka respectively. French Jews on the other hand went mainly to Auschwitz. Preparations for their deportation began in March 1942 and were extended in June to include the unoccupied zone: 100,000 Jews were to be collected and sent east. After the biggest single round-up – in July when 13,000 men, women and children were crammed into the concentration camp at Drancy and the Vélodrome d'Hiver in hideous conditions – French Jews were being transported to Poland at the rate of a thousand a day. The total was aggravated by Switzerland's refusal to admit or harbour Jewish fugitives. By a curious twist, however, a number of French Jews were saved by French anti-semitism. France had an anti-semitic strain of its own hardly less pronounced than Germany's. Even today, after the Nazi holocaust, no Jew has replaced the French Jew Alfred Dreyfus as the principal symbol of European anti-semitism. French anti-semites were given their heads by Vichy and at Laval's direction the French police helped the S D to round up the Jews in France, but Laval's perverted nationalism insisted that French Jews, as opposed to Jews of different nationality who had fled to France, should be dealt with by the French authorities instead of being sent to Germany or Poland. Some of them survived and after the extension of the German occupation to the whole country in November many escaped to the Italian zone and Monaco. Thus the Germans contrived to kill only about a quarter of French Jewry as compared with half the Belgian Jews and over three quarters of the Dutch. (The last were specially vulnerable in a small country in which it was difficult to hide. They had nowhere like the Ardennes, where many Belgian Jews and other refugees congregated, and as a community they had had little contact with the Gentiles who alone could have concealed large numbers of them.) In the west as a whole the 7,500 Danish Jews fared least badly. An attempt was made to round them up after the Germans took over in 1943, but all save a few hundred were saved. A German official leaked a warning of the plan and practically the entire Jewish community was first hidden and then transported in small vessels to Sweden, where they were looked after until the end of the war. When the Germans came to round up their victims, they found that the birds had flown. Of Norway's small Jewish community of about 2,000 some 750 were caught. Italian Jews were deported to Auschwitz and other camps by the Germans after the fall of Mussolini.

South-eastern Europe also provided its share of victims – about one million. In Rumania, with its large Jewish community of nearly three quarters of a million, pogroms were initiated without German encouragement and two thirds of Rumanian Jewry perished during the war in one way or another. In Bulgaria on the other hand the government's agreement to fall in with German plans by surrendering its Jews for deportation was thwarted by demonstrations of public disgust. In Serbia and Croatia most Jews were killed without being deported. A number of Croatian Jews escaped from the German to the Italian zone of occupation and thence later to the partisans. Of the 75,000 Greek Jews in Salonica at least two thirds were sent to Auschwitz in 1943.

In Slovakia the work of deportation and extermination was begun in

1942 with the cooperation of the puppet government but then suspended; it was resumed and completed after the Slovak rising of 1944. The Hungarian Jews were the last to go. Up to July 1944 they were persecuted but not exported for extinction. They numbered at this date about 440,000 of whom nearly half were in the Hungarian capital. The arrival of Eichmann heralded a grim turn but the Regent Hörthy (until the abolition of his régime by the Germans in October) was willing to offer an escape route and after some hesitations the American and British governments consented to discuss ways and means. A section at least of the SS seemed to be privy to these manoeuvres and two Hungarian Jews (Joel Brand and another) who arrived in Istanbul in July were thought to be instruments of an SS plan to secure from the allies food, soap and 10,000 lorries – the last for use on Russian fronts only – in return for allowing Hungarian Jews to escape their coming fate. Although Jewish leaders realized that western belligerents would not agree to help the German effort against the Russians, some of them hoped that the negotiations might be spun out in such a way as to stave off the killing of surviving Jews or to organize their ransom for money instead of lorries. But the offer was not taken seriously by the outside world and Brand was even put in prison by the British in the Middle East with whom he was supposed to negotiate. The Hungarian Jews were pawns whom the allies refused to buy on the terms proposed, while in Hungary Eichmann, more intent on the genocide of the Jews than on the provision of food and transport for the German armies, proceeded to round up and dispatch for extermination those Jews whom the fanatics of the post-Hörthy régime did not shoot, club or starve to death. Discussions with the Americans and British dragged on unrealistically until February 1945 when Hitler, perhaps previously unaware of them, put an end to them.

The separateness of the Jews militated against their survival. Cut off and marked out by their history and their circumstances, they were exposed to separate destruction in a way in which no other groups were exposed. Their alternatives were to resist in isolation or just wait. They did both: many waited but others, belying the passivity which had marked their people between their risings against the Romans and the outrages of the twentieth century, rebelled in arms as well as in spirit. Flight from the community was inhibited by family loyalties. It tended to be postponed from month to month in the desperate hope that, as in the past, the Jew would be saved because he was useful: in the *Ostland* a Jew's most precious document was his work certificate. In Germany a number of Jews passed themselves off as bombed-out refugees, resorting to every kind of disguise and desperate expedient to save themselves and their families; in

Vienna this was called 'doing a U-boat' – that is to say submerging. Gentiles were sometimes faced with the harrowing dilemma of taking them in or turning them away for fear that they might, by giving asylum to the outcasts, be consigning themselves and their own children to torture and death.

Many Jews resisted. In France Jews amounted to about a quarter of active resisters, many of them being Polish Jews who had left Poland during the pre-war period of anti-semitic, right-wing rule. In Poland several thousands of Jews took to the woods, formed bands of their own and fought, often in cooperation with escaped Russian prisoners. In Galicia they bought or took weapons from Italians who had been fighting on the Russian front but were on their way back to Italy. There were even risings inside the concentration camps, which were all the more remarkable in view of the utter exhaustion of most of the inmates. (Russian prisoners, for example, were driven on foot for hundreds of miles after the commissars among them had been shot and arrived in no condition to do anything except fall down.) The end of the extermination camp at Sobibor was highly dramatic. In September 1943 a first contingent of 1,750 Russian Jews arrived there, some of them former soldiers of the Russian army. All but eighty were immediately gassed but these eighty were kept alive to help build an extension of the camp and a few weeks after their arrival these and other Jews rose and attacked their guards with axes, knives and their bare hands. After ten SS guards had been killed about 400 prisoners escaped from the compound. Many of them ran into minefields and were killed. Others were rounded up again during the next few days in a hunt organized by the local SS command and yet others were killed by anti-semitic members of Polish right-wing bands. A few joined partisan groups and some eventually rejoined the Russian army. But Sobibor itself was destroyed by this act. Himmler ordered it to be abandoned and all traces of it to be expunged.

There were risings at Auschwitz too. The first, by a handful of surviving Russian prisoners of war in the summer of 1942, was largely a failure. Some were shot trying to escape, others were recaptured later; a few got away. Two years later a second attempt, organized by Jews in the Auschwitz extermination camp, was also unsuccessful. Four SS guards were killed but so were 455 prisoners.

As the war neared its end and the Russian armies approached Poland the surviving inmates of the extermination and labour camps were hurriedly destroyed by lethal injections or by being mowed down by gunfire. Some were removed to camps farther west, but although Himmler ordered the killing to stop in October 1944, a mere two or three per cent of all the

JEWISH EXTERMINATION
1941 – 1945

◉ German concentration camps and extermination camps.

□ Approximate Jewish population 1941. (total: 8,500,000).

■ Number of Jews exterminated by 1945 (total: 5,400,000).

RUSSIA (German occupied)
□ 2,500,000
■ 750,000

TURKEY

Black Sea

0   200
Miles

—ARTHUR BANKS—

LITHUANIA
□ 140,000
■ 104,000

TREBLINKA 1942

POLAND
□ 3,000,000
■ 2,600,000

SOBIBOR 1942

STUTTHOF 1942

WARSAW GHETTO

CHELMO 1941

MAJDENEK 1943

BELZEK 1942

RUMANIA
□ 750,000
■ 500,000

BULGARIA
□ 48,000
■ 40,000

GREECE
□ 80,000
■ 60,000

GROSSROSEN

AUSCHWITZ 1940

HUNGARY
□ 800,000
■ 700,000

ALBANIA

LATVIA
□ 100,000
■ 70,000

Baltic Sea

RAVENSBRÜCK 1942

SACHSENHAUSEN 1936

THERESIENSTADT

CZECHOSLOVAKIA
□ 810,000
■ 60,000

MAUTHAUSEN 1938

AUSTRIA
□ 70,000
■ 60,000

YUGOSLAVIA
□ 70,000
■ 58,000

Adriatic Sea

NEUENGAMME 1940

DENMARK
□ 6,000
■ 100

BELSEN 1943

GERMANY
□ 250,000
■ 180,000

FLOSSENBERG

DACHAU 1933

HOLLAND
□ 140,000
■ 104,000

VUGHT 1940

MITTELBAU–DORA 1943

BUCHENWALD 1937

SWITZ.

ITALY
□ 120,000
■ 9,000

BELGIUM
□ 85,000
■ 40,000

GREAT BRITAIN

NATWEILER

FRANCE
□ 300,000
■ 65,000

From Europe 280,000 Jewish refugees to U.S.A., South America, Great Britain, and Japan 1933-1940.

Jews abducted during the war survived it. The number of deaths is incalculable. It lies somewhere between four and six million. The gipsies, who
were also marked down for total destruction, lost perhaps 200,000 lives;
the evidence about their sufferings is vague, but on one occasion at Auschwitz 4,000 of them seem to have been gassed in a single, if prolonged,
operation. Gentiles too were killed in droves, including Germans for
whom the first concentration camps were originally instituted: at least
half a million men and women died in the German concentration camps
during the war from illness and ill-treatment. Himmler's aim of reducing
the world's Slav population by 30 million was not attained, although the
losses suffered by the Russians in battle and at the hands of the SS went
some way towards realizing this abominable ambition. The apostles of
the New Order showed that, given time, their destructive plans were not
beyond the compass of human techniques and human will.

The massacre of millions of European Jews was a culminating act in the
history of the relations between Jew and Gentile. Hitler did not invent
anti-semitism. It was wrapped up in Europe's inheritance from Christendom. It lay ready to Hitler's hand and he used it with a pitiless thoroughness which made him a special kind of anti-semite. The myth of a
Jewish conspiracy to pervert the world is a Christian myth which has been
propagated by Christian writers of eminence and authority almost as far
back as the origins of their religion and right up to the present century,
and the same writers have also been responsible for the odious slanders
against the character and practices of the Jew which Hitler and other
modern anti-semites were able to cite and endorse. (One of the com-
monest of these myths is the charge that Jews murdered non-Jewish
children for ritual purposes. The first child alleged to have been killed in
this way, William of Norwich, who died in 1144, is still officially venerated
by Roman Catholics as a saint and martyr although there is no particle of
evidence about the manner of his death. Nor is there any better evidence
about any of the other cases of this kind.)

In the eighteenth century opponents of Christianity, such as the leaders
of the Enlightenment, who might have been expected to defend the Jews,
had their own kind of anti-semitism since they reprobated Jewry as the
forerunner of Christianity, while in the nineteenth century racist theories
sharpened the persecution of the Jews by making their offence inexpiable.
So long as the Jew was persecuted on account of his religion he might
escape its worst consequences by baptism, but when he was persecuted on
account of his race he had no way out except death. Whether Hitler, who
called himself a Roman Catholic, believed Christianity's anti-semitic
inventions or those of the racists is a question which he himself would

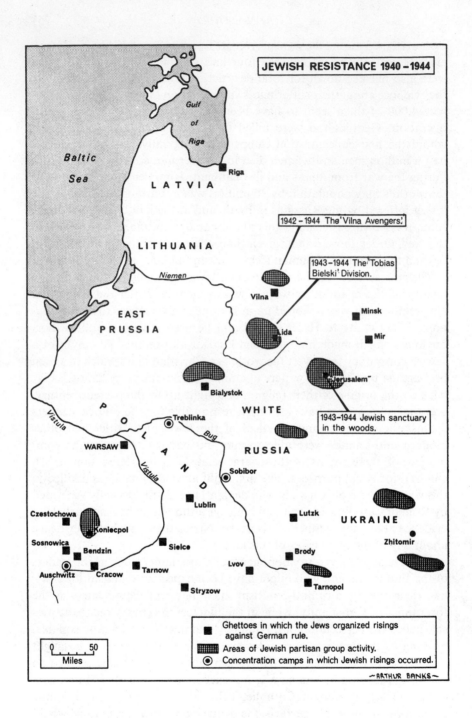

JEWISH RESISTANCE 1940–1944

Baltic Sea

Gulf of Riga

Riga

LATVIA

LITHUANIA

Niemen

1942–1944 The 'Vilna Avengers'.

1943–1944 The 'Tobias Bielski' Division.

Vilna

EAST PRUSSIA

Minsk

Lida

Mir

Bialystok

WHITE

'Jerusalem'

1943–1944 Jewish sanctuary in the woods.

Vistula

POLAND

Treblinka

Bug

WARSAW

RUSSIA

Vistula

Sobibor

Lublin

Lutzk

UKRAINE

Czestochowa

Koniecpol

Zhitomir

Sosnowica

Bendzin

Sielce

Brody

Auschwitz

Cracow

Tarnow

Lvov

Tarnopol

Stryzow

■	Ghettoes in which the Jews organized risings against German rule.
▦	Areas of Jewish partisan group activity.
◉	Concentration camps in which Jewish risings occurred.

0   50
Miles

~ARTHUR BANKS~

have regarded as senseless. The point was not whether they were true but whether they were useful, and, as he once said to Rauschning, anti-semitism was an essential tool for spreading Nazism in Germany and beyond. On this issue his political cynicism fitted nicely with his deeper emotions, since besides using anti-semitism he hated Jews.

The enormity of what was done in the forties has led to a search for an explanation: what are the origins of this conflict and its Hitlerian solution? This is one of the most complex problems in the history of Europe, to which much learning and ingenuity have been devoted. Certain general factors appear at first sight: the religious differences, accentuated by Christendom's condemnation of the Jewish race for deicide; the recognizable physical features of many Jews; their own insistence on their religious and national identity, accentuated by their dispersal; the special functions which, historically, they filled in European societies, often unpopular ones such as money lending. At a deeper level theories about the vulnerability of the Jews have been advanced. One of the more interesting of these attaches importance to the fact that the special services which they once provided came to be no longer needed; for example, their function as the financiers of the state was essential so long as the state was financed through personal borrowing by monarchs but became otiose when this method was replaced by government taxation of the whole community. But the more that Jewish-Gentile relations are probed the more dangerous does it appear to generalize beyond a certain point, for it becomes clear that the position of the Jews in Christendom has varied greatly from time to time and from place to place, so that an explanation of the plight of the Jews in Poland in the twentieth century, for example, will not – except superficially – fit their circumstances in France at the same or any other date.

The premeditated execution of five to six million people by methods of singular barbarity should, one hopes, be difficult to explain. Part of the explanation is to be found in the fact that anti-semitism is ancient, widespread and irrational; yet this is no explanation, since it merely shifts the question back into the past and, by raising it again in a remoter historical context, makes it even more difficult to answer. The emotions which anti-semitism produces are fierce, and the ends which these emotions have compassed have been tacitly approved by thousands or millions of people who would themselves recoil from the methods used. Schemes for saving Jews from Nazi Germany were half-hearted at best. Before the war the Nazis would promise only a small annual exodus of workers without families or capital and tried to link this exodus with a boost to German exports by getting the receiving countries to undertake to increase their purchases of German goods. No country could be found willing to take substantial numbers of Jews; the British barred Palestine to them except in small numbers and on stringent terms; the Americans were so unimaginative as to require certificates of birth which few German Jews possessed and none could ask for from a German official (but a number of Christian priests forged baptismal certificates for them); a Bill to permit 20,000 Jewish children to enter the United States was killed by a 'patriotic' lobby in the Congress on the grounds that it offended against the sanctity of family ties and in spite of the fact that the immigration quotas from Germany were regularly underfilled. Hitler was able to exult that nobody wanted the Jews and so, since there was nowhere for them to go, he had no option but to destroy them.

Hitler's personal commitment to the wholesale murder of the Jews is incontrovertible. He himself proclaimed it more than once. He believed in it; he devoted considerable resources to its accomplishment in the middle of war; and Himmler, Canaris and others stated that it was ordered by Hitler and was therefore not to be questioned. The lack of any written order signed by Hitler is neither weighty nor surprising.

Allied leaders have not escaped some share of the responsibility for these terrible murders. Their culpability is at an altogether lower level but by the winter of 1942 – 3 at the latest the purpose of Auschwitz and its four companion outfits in Poland was known and published. The facts were so appalling and so unwelcome that most of those who became aware of them contrived to disbelieve or dismiss them. But in 1944 the truth became inescapable when two Jews who had escaped from Auschwitz arrived in the west to tell their tale. Jewish organizations pressed for action such as the bombing of access routes or the bombing of the gas chambers themselves. Allied governments tried to sidestep the issue, alleging that the camps were beyond acceptable bombing range. Yet Auschwitz was within range by August 1944 since a synthetic oil plant, adjacent to the camp and revealed by photographic reconnaissance in April, was bombed in that month and the camp itself was accidentally bombed in September in the course of an American raid on a target a few miles further east. One excuse for inaction against the camps – that the inmates might get killed or be put the more quickly into the gas chambers – seems peculiarly inappropriate in the light of the knowledge that 12,000 were being gassed daily at Auschwitz alone. While the greater number of the victims had been killed by this time, the minority who died later were nevertheless very many. The charge of moral myopia will not go away.

The Roman Catholic church had, it may be thought, a special obligation to do something for the Jews both because of its special contribution to

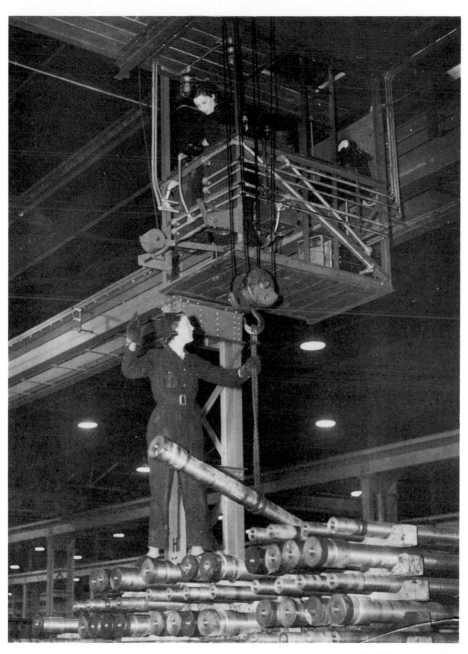

16 Women's work: 'somewhere in Wales'

17 *Top*: The latest in air raid
shelters: South Wales, 1938

18 *Bottom*: The London
blitz: nightly scene in Holborn
tube station

19 The London blitz:
Smithfield

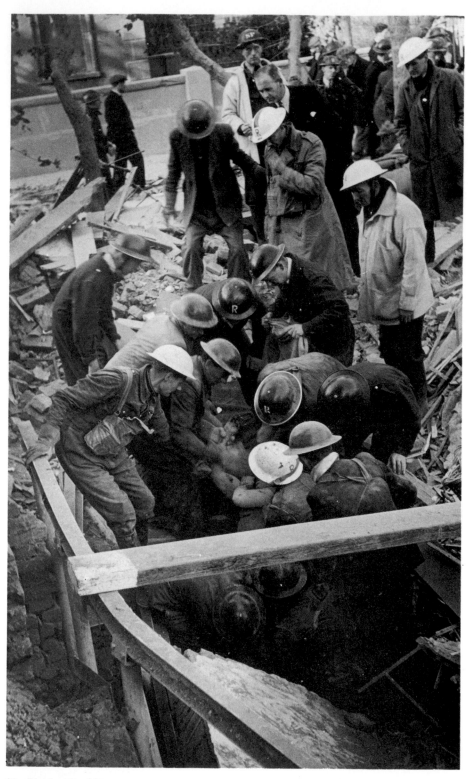

20   The London blitz:
retrieving the dead and dying

21 Join the Wrens

22 All for the front, all for
victory!

23 *Top*: The Ukraine
welcomes Germans, summer
1941

24 *Bottom*: German defeat
before Moscow, winter 1941

25 Stalingrad: winter 1942–3

26 Stalingrad, 1943

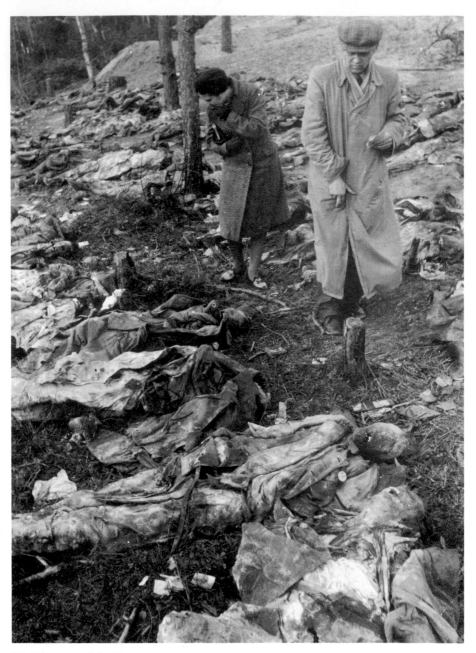

27 Discovery of the Katyn
massacre

anti-semitism over nearly 2,000 years and because of its own teaching on brotherly love. Very many churchmen were compassionate men horrified by Nazi crimes but the church as a body was caught in the toils of its own propaganda, old and new. In modern times Jewry, besides being collectively charged with the judicial murder of Jesus, was associated with a special kind of ungodliness. The French Revolution and the Bolshevik Revolution were both blamed, again by professed Christian writers, on the Jews, who were made the scapegoats for whatever was alarming to the established order, and especially to the established ecclesiastical order, in a world which had begun to change faster than seemed desirable to those who were used to running it. Again, Hitler did not invent the equation of communism with Jewry; but he was able to profit from it. The more sophisticated and honest enemies of communism knew that the government of the USSR was very far from being run by Jews, but, because they detested and feared communism, they hesitated to speak out against Nazism for fear of undermining the German state and so helping Russian communism to advance into the centre of Europe and join hands with powerful communist parties in the west. The Jews – and the Christian conscience – were sacrificed to this dilemma.

The Roman Catholic church in Germany was persecuted by Hitler. It also came to terms with him and in 1933, on orders from the Vatican, the Centre Party, which was the political face of the church, voted for the Enabling Act which gave Hitler full authority to destroy the German constitution and society. Most of the Roman Catholic bishops then made haste to take back all that they had been saying about the beastliness of the Nazis, Roman Catholic theologians set themselves the task of demonstrating the essential compatibility of Christian and Nazi doctrine, and pulpits which had been used to denounce the latter emitted a new view of the Führer as a man of God. The church so far attuned itself to Nazism as to overlook the concentration camps and endorse Hitler's foreign policy. When war came the German Roman Catholic clergy broadly supported it and continued to do so in spite of the murder of their Polish colleagues, officially reported, and in spite of Hitler's unwarranted attacks on small, helpless neutrals; his attack on the USSR evoked a crusading enthusiasm. But many Christians, priests and laymen, exerted themselves and risked their lives to succour Jews. The Dominican and Jesuit orders were specially mindful of their Christian duty.

In the Vatican two Popes, Pius XI and Pius XII, had to contend with the spiritual and practical crises occasioned by the rise of Fascism and Nazism. Pius XI, who became Pope in 1922, was faced with the problem of the relations between the Vatican and first Italy and then Germany.

Pius VIII had faced a similar problem in his dealings with Napoleon. Mussolini and Hitler, like Napoleon, wished to establish treaty relations with the Vatican and both succeeded. In the case of Hitler, Pius XI and his nuncio in Berlin and eventual successor, Eugenio Pacelli, believed that a concordat with Hitler would do more good than harm because it would give the Vatican a stronger claim to interfere on behalf of persecuted priests. A concordat was concluded in July 1933. Its effects were disappointing since Hitler persecuted the German clergy more than ever once he had got it, but the motives of Pius and Pacelli were sincere and their reasoning could not be definitely condemned before the event. Both men were disgusted by the Nazis and by anti-semitism. In March 1937 Pius XI issued, in German, the encyclical *Mit brennender Sorge*, which was read from all Roman Catholic pulpits in Germany and, although it contained no explicit reference to anti-semitism, was understood as a clear and sharp, if belated, attack on Nazi policies; but again the effects were very limited. Pacelli, who was consulted by the Pope before the encyclical was issued, toned up its language. He himself more anti-Nazi than many western conservatives and diplomats, delivered in the same year an openly anti-Nazi speech at Lisieux and upon his accession to the Papacy was condemned by the Nazis as even worse than his predecessor.

Despite the ritual mystery surrounding the election of a Pope the elevation of Pacelli to the Papal see on the death of Pius XI in 1939 was a foregone conclusion. Pius XI, departing from all precedent, had practically designated Pacelli as his successor, and one of the shortest conclaves on record sufficed to fill the vacancy. Pius XII had served as nuncio in Munich and then in Berlin and had other special connections with Germany, but he was also at that date the most widely travelled Cardinal in Europe and beyond ever to become Pope. The breadth of his experience and of his intelligence were alike unusual. His opposition to inhumanity and aggression were beyond question. Yet he has been assailed for failing in his human and Christian duty. This supreme accusation against a supreme pontiff relates to his conduct in relation to both Christians and Jews. Directly and by his example he did much for thousands of Jews who were saved from death and given money, food, clothing and even employment in Roman Catholic institutions. But he made no public protest against the murders of Jews, did not use his awful weapon of excommunication against the murderers, refused to speak out against Vichy's anti-semitic laws (even when the French bishops did) and refused to intervene when, in October 1943, the Germans carried off over a thousand Jews from Rome itself to be gassed.

The Pope adopted one standard when he protested against the Russian invasion of Finland and another when he failed to protest against the German invasion of Poland. Although copiously informed about the Germans' treatment of the Poles he kept silent. He was chided by Cardinal Tisserant for even more unbecoming reticence over the misdeeds performed in his name by the *ustachi* in Croatia. This new state, which emerged from the dismemberment of Yugoslavia in 1941, was placed under the rule of Ante Pavelič, an Italian protégé since the twenties and a rabid Roman Catholic who was intent on destroying the two million Orthodox Christian Serbs in Croatia and on reviving the temporal sovereignty of the Papacy. Pavelič introduced a religious reign of terror, demanding wholesale conversions to Roman Catholicism, perpetrating atrocities which were ghastly even by the standards of these ghastly years, and encouraging his *ustachi* bands (often led by priests) to run amok. Roman Catholic bishops were appalled by his barbarity but judged it wiser to say little and accept compensation for their injured feelings in redeemed souls and enhanced church property. The Pope himself said nothing in public.

Pius XII could have argued, and perhaps did, that he must avoid the charge levelled against Benedict XV in the First World War of taking sides against Germany, that excommunication was no longer an incisive weapon (though he used it against communists after the war) and that public protest could do the victims more harm than good, but his posture in his dilemma was an unheroic one and contrasted unfavourably with that of some of his own nuncios and other Roman Catholic notabilities who were stirred to an open opposition which was often effective. He was in the uncomfortable dilemma of occupying an office whose pretensions were greater than its capacities and, in preferring the cautious to the outspoken course, he seemed to neglect his obligation to re-state the violated canons of human behaviour. Although he might not be able to save the victims, he could have pointed the finger of divine anger against the criminals. By keeping silent, he sanctioned the unheroic frailty of all those lesser men who prefer, unless exhorted and inspired, to pass by on the other side. He invited the charge of failing to keep the Christian conscience sharp and clean. That charge has since been laid. The record is mixed.

CHAPTER 12

Exploitation

THE pattern of German power in Europe was a patchwork. Very little territory was formally annexed to the Reich: Danzig, large slices of Poland and smaller ones of Belgium. Other areas were intended and prepared for annexation although not formally annexed and even formally assured of their continuing integrity and independence: Alsace and Lorraine, Luxembourg, parts of Slovenia. In these areas compulsory military service was introduced and the Reich Ministry of the Interior set about imposing German law and the German legal system, integrating postal, railway and customs services, changing place names and even personal names, adjusting citizenship rights and constraining the population to speak German. Formal annexation was only a matter of time. These were, from the practical point of view, districts which were contiguous with the Reich and had special strategic or economic value; from another point of view they were districts which had once been part of a medieval Germanic empire or were peopled by kinsmen of the German race.

Three other territories which were distinct from the Reich were nevertheless completely subordinated to it through a Governor General, a Protector and a Reich Minister. These territories, all of which lay to the east of Germany, were brought within the German customs area; their separate existence in international law was barely conceded; and various overlords within the Reich such as Goering as Commissioner for the Five Year Plan and Sauckel as Plenipotentiary for Labour were entitled to direct demands to their rulers. They were the Government General of Poland, ruled by Hans Frank with the status of a head of government but not a head of state; the Protectorate of Bohemia and Moravia, in which parts of the administration (justice, for example) were placed under Reich Ministries in Berlin but which had also a nominally autonomous administration in pseudo-diplomatic relations with Berlin and a Protector (first Neurath, then Heydrich and ultimately Frick) who advised this administration what to do and saw that it did it; and the Baltic and Russian territories which came under Rosenberg, who had theoretically the same executive and legislative powers as Hans Frank in Poland and exercised them through his Ministry for the East and its Reich Commissioners in Riga and Rovno for the *Ostland* and the Ukraine respectively.

GERMAN CONTROL IN EUROPE 1942

~ARTHUR BANKS~

Germany and her allies.

Annexed areas and areas scheduled for annexation.

Areas completely subordinated to Germany.

Areas under military government.

Areas under Reichkommissars.

Independent (in theory) until 1943.

Unoccupied France (until Nov 1942).

Neutrals.

The rest of occupied Europe was governed by military or civilian governors according to its continuing strategic importance. Greece, Yugoslavia, Belgium and occupied France were under military government. These areas were subject to decrees promulgated by the military authorities of the Reich and applied by the local military governor, who was in addition usually helped by civilian advisers posted to his staff to guide him in all but purely military affairs. The government of Belgium and north-eastern France, which formed a single administrative zone, was transferred to a civilian Reich Commissioner in July 1944 for the better supervision and regimentation of the local population. Greece and Yugoslavia both saw Italian and Bulgarian occupiers as well as German. The native government of Greece was put in the hands of a puppet government in Athens, that of Yugoslavia was divided between a puppet government in Belgrade and the separatist Croat state established under Ante Pavelič. This state comprised not only Croatia but also Bosnia and Herzegovina and part of the Dalmatian coast and was roughly co-terminous with the eleventh-century kingdom of the same name. Pavelič was a rabidly anti-Serb Croat who had curried favour with the Italians before the war as an enemy of the Yugoslav state and was then pressed on an unenthusiastic Hitler by Mussolini. After May 1941 Pavelič, who had had to cede most of the Adriatic islands and Dalmatian coast to Italy and accept a prince of the Italian royal house as king in Croatia, turned against the Italians. The king never visited his kingdom.

Norway and the Netherlands were placed under civilian Reich Commissioners – Josef Terboven and Artur Seyss-Inquart – who were directly responsible to Hitler and were empowered to legislate by decree and review all existing laws. The powers of crown and government were transferred to them, and each appointed deputies to overlord sections of the central administration and its regional offshoots. Obnoxious or potentially subversive elements in public life, such as parliaments and other elective bodies, the press and broadcasting, were abolished or brought under control, and the national police was subordinated to the German police and SS. Denmark was exceptional in that its head of state, the king, remained in the country throughout the war and in the exercise of his functions for most of it; the Danish cabinet continued to look to the sovereign and the Danish army remained in being in designated zones. There was no formal agreement but the military capitulation was made and accepted in return for recognition of Denmark's continuing independence and neutrality. Until 1943 relations between Germany and Denmark were conducted through diplomatic channels, although German officials had to be reminded from time to time that they must not treat Denmark as just another occupied country. In 1943 the Germans took over the country, the king was closely confined, the army was disbanded, the navy scuttled itself, and the government and parliament were dissolved. Thereafter Denmark was run by the S S.

If Germany had won the war Denmark and the Netherlands would probably have been annexed despite explicit assurances to the contrary. In both countries, although earlier in the Netherlands than in Denmark, political forms and economic activities were adjusted to German patterns and needs. Political parties – other than the local Nazi variant – were extinguished, Nazi laws introduced, production and labour treated as segments of the German economy. In the Netherlands trade-union leaders began by cooperating with the Germans in the hope of preserving their various auxiliary institutions and activities, but membership of unions dropped sharply and the creation of a labour front in 1942 caused union officials to resign too. Some unions were dissolved by decree when their officials resigned in protest against the appointment of pro-German overseers; one Roman Catholic union was dissolved when the Roman Catholic hierarchy ordered members to leave it on pain of being denied the sacraments. Dutch S S were formed as early as the autumn of 1940 (from candidates with untarnished ancestry back to 1800), took a personal oath to Hitler as the Greater German Führer and provided fighting units for the eastern front. Himmler planned to plant Nordic settlers from these countries in various parts of the U S S R, whether they wanted to go there or not.

France, unlike every other defeated country, was run from two different capitals, Paris and Vichy. From Vichy Marshal Pétain's government exercised authority over the whole country except Alsace-Lorraine, virtually annexed to the Reich, and the zone in the south-east ceded to Italy by the armistice. From Paris Hitler's plenipotentiary, Otto Abetz, also exercised functions which covered occupied and unoccupied France: he was a career diplomat whose tasks were to advise the military commander in the occupied zone on political matters, to maintain permanent contact with the French government in Vichy and its representatives in the occupied zone, and generally to influence French politicians, the press and broadcasting. He straddled France, advising the German rulers in the north and bringing pressure to bear on Pétain and his ministers in the south. But in practice France was partitioned. As a defeated country waiting for a peace settlement it was subject to the interim arrangements accepted with the armistice. The Germans exacted the right to occupy the north with military and police forces, detached the north-east which, in terms of military government but not of civil administration, was controlled with Belgium from

Brussels, and created a prohibited zone running along the north and west coasts under strict military control. Abetz ruled indirectly in the unoccupied zone by addressing representations to Vichy, and Vichy's subservience to German power was never in doubt; although there was no outward German presence in the unoccupied zone until it too was occupied in November 1942, the S D operated there on a restricted scale from the beginning (for example, in tracking down wireless transmitters and operators).

In all these countries the pattern of German control at the top was invisible to most people who never had or were never given any clear picture of what role the Germans had assumed. What people saw was not a new pattern imposed by the conqueror but a series of random consequences of the impact of German rule on local administration. At the centre the Germans kept and even enlarged the powers of civil servants whom they converted from administrators into ministers-to-the-Germans with power to issue decrees, a form of indirect rule in which the Germans directed the civil service and the civil service directed everybody else. Local government bodies also remained in being, often with familiar faces in the same offices, but this reassuring continuity was contradicted by uncharacteristic behaviour on the part of mayors and other office-holders. Disturbingly these no longer did what they were expected to do. Nor did one mayor behave like the next one, for each reacted differently, the one more obediently, the other more defiantly or more slyly, to the directions of his superiors. Mayors whom the Germans regarded as satisfactory remained in office and were given enhanced authority, but since unsatisfactory mayors were replaced, those who survived became in effect appointees holding office during good behaviour. German observers were inserted into the machinery of government at the centre and also to some extent lower down – for example, on the governing boards of French *lycées*; Labour Offices were put under undisguised German control, so that an unemployed worker coming in to register even in a comparatively small town would find himself face to face with a German official who might direct him to work in Germany or in some occupied country other than his own. But for the most part the general public continued to deal with local authorities whom it knew, and was unaware of the extent to which or the methods by which they were subjected to German regulation. In fact German control, even where it was not obtrusive, was thorough and pervasive. Courts, like the administration, continued to function outwardly much as before, but the German police kept a watch on the sentences given in criminal courts and might override them, with the result that criminal justice became something of a lottery in which sentences differed widely from court to court and the accused did not know whether his sentence would stand. He even had reason to fear a light sentence since the Germans were more likely to step in and increase it.

In all occupied countries, whether under military or civilian rule, a great deal went on which did not meet the eye and was not meant to, and in particular Himmler's Higher SS and Police Führers were a law unto themselves. They normally held SS rank equivalent to that of the military governor or local troop commander and, *de jure* or *de facto*, circumvented the German military and civil power in implementing policies determined by Himmler. In the inevitable quarrels with local governors the SS had the advantage of knowing exactly where they stood, since the SS and police authorities in conquered areas were replicas by extension of the system familiar in the Reich. Most other offices were *ad hoc* creations in which a good deal of confusion prevailed.

The Germans turned out to be much less fond of local Nazis and pro-German parties than vice versa. They used such parties but felt no call to support them. In Belgium, for example, they made use of various collaborationist groups until these cancelled each other out by their competitive jealousies. In the Netherlands Seyss-Inquart paid very little attention to Adrian Mussert and the Dutch Nazis although some individuals were given minor administrative office. The Danish Nazi Party also proved valueless. In Norway a rather different situation arose because the German Commissioner Terboven was determined to retain power in his own hands, governing through a council in Oslo and regional deputies appointed by himself until ordered by Hitler to acknowledge Quisling and make him Prime Minister; Quisling's original role had been to subvert Norway in the German interest but this plan had been abandoned in favour of the military conquest of the country with the result that it was not clear to the new rulers sent by Hitler whether Quisling still counted or not. Only in France, under the aegis of Vichy, did native fascists flourish for a while. For day-to-day administration the Germans relied, where they could, on the existing machinery of government and its existing staff, supplemented by an injection of German officials at key points with the title but more than the status of observers. In the east, where the machinery was less good, the reliance impracticable and Slav sub-men by definition unemployable, they had to take over themselves except at levels or in matters which did not interest them.

One country escaped: Switzerland. In 1940 the general Swiss view was that Germany had won the war. The question was whether it would pay the Swiss better to be tough in this situation or pliant. They knew before the war that the Nazis treated Switzerland in their training manuals as part of the Reich and showed it as such in official maps, and they also knew that the German army had plans for an attack on Switzerland. These plans were never put into operation but they nearly were on more than one occasion.

Swiss planning for defence against Germany began in the mid-thirties, ostensibly within the constraints of Swiss neutrality. In fact a very small number of Swiss leaders deliberately transgressed this neutrality by entering into secret military discussions with France. They went so far as to conclude, at the military but not the political level, plans for the entry of French forces into Switzerland at the request of the Swiss government. Documents captured by the Germans in France in 1940 gave Germany grounds for invading Switzerland but they never did so.

Swiss airspace was infringed by both sides from 1940, for the most part accidentally. The Swiss defences engaged aircraft, inflicting and suffering casualties. A blackout was imposed in November 1940 in response to German pressure when British bombers used Switzerland as a navigational aid. As the air war grew fiercer but not much more accurate Switzerland suffered increasing damage, for which it received reparation after the war from the United States. It was blockaded by both sides and so forced to introduce rationing of food and fuel. It was specially vulnerable on two counts. Spies proliferated, and any undue toleration of their activities could be dangerous: about 1,400 Swiss citizens and foreigners were arrested during the war years by a Swiss police determined to give the belligerents no excuse to denounce Swiss neutrality. (But the famous Lucy ring, frequently alleged to have been a British device for conveying Ultra and other special intelligence to Moscow, was no such thing.) Secondly, geography had set Switzerland in the eye of the hurricane – to quote the phrase used by a post-war Swiss historian. Under a multilateral treaty of 1909 Switzerland was obliged to allow the passage in wartime of all non-military material over its Alpine railways. This right was most valuable to the Germans and Italians since the use of the Swiss route freed others for military traffic, and there was therefore a corresponding fear that the railways would either be seized by the Axis or sabotaged by their foes.

That Switzerland remained in spite of these hazards immune from direct attack was primarily the reward of determination. The Swiss constitution provides for the appointment of a military, as opposed to a civilian, commander-in-chief in times of emergency. On 30 August 1939 the Swiss parliament gave the cabinet emergency powers and on the same day General Henri Guisan was named commander-in-chief. The appointment was controversial and contested and Guisan had to be on his guard throughout the war against the intrigues of civilian and military personages who held that Switzerland's only chance of escaping a German invasion lay in a scrupulous emphasis on the Swiss tradition of neutrality: they believed that Switzerland must aim above all at avoiding any provocation of Hitler. General Guisan argued otherwise. He said that independence was even more important than neutrality, since without independence there would be no neutrality to protect; that the only threat to independence came from Germany; and that preparations must be made to meet this threat. On his orders a thousand factories, public works and public services, and Switzerland's numerous tunnels were prepared for demolition. In a dramatic, secret scene on the historic Rütli (where the Swiss confederation was inaugurated in 1291) 650 officers of the army took an oath to resist. A mountain redoubt was fortified where fighting would go on even if Switzerland's borders were forced and its frontier cities taken. Justified by results, Guisan lived to receive the acclaim of even the most timorous of his fellow citizens.

Germany's European allies complete the picture. They were Italy, Slovakia, Hungary, Rumania and Bulgaria. Slovakia was a puppet from the moment of its creation in 1939. In south-east Europe Hitler was prepared to let Rumania down as much and as often as it suited him, give Hungary most of what it wanted, enlarge Bulgaria to the dimensions tantalizingly glimpsed at San Stefano in 1877, and let Greece become an Italian province. If Hitler anticipated squabbles between Italians and Slavs he did so without distaste. Thus Bulgaria and Hungary were uneasy allies who made hay while the sun shone – Bulgaria at the expense of Rumania, Yugoslavia and Greece, and Hungary at the expense of the first two of these. When the sun stopped shining for the Germans in the middle of the war all these countries began to try to change sides. Rumania, which had tried to avoid taking sides between Germany and the western democracies, slid into alliance with Germany through fear of the Soviet Union but not without being forced by Hitler to yield territory to its neighbours and, indirectly, to evict its king. After being forced to cede Bessarabia and Northern Bukovina to the USSR King Carol sought territorial guarantees for the rest of his state from Hitler, but Hitler refused. The king, whose weak position was threatened not only by the loss of national territory but also by the hostility of the fascist Iron Guard (whose temper had not been improved by the murder in 1938 of its leader Corneliu Codreanu), tried to save himself by inviting the army leader Marshal Ion Antonescu and the Iron Guard to join his government, but they were advised by Germany not to. The loss of more territory by the second Vienna Award and the Treaty of Craiova (by which Hitler allotted parts of Rumania to Hungary and Bulgaria) made Carol's position impossible and he abdicated. Antonescu, a stupid rather than a sinister man, with a pushing wife, joined the government of the new King Michael and so too did the Iron Guard, but the mutual antipathy of the army and the Iron Guard produced a threat of civil war. The Iron Guard attempted a coup but Hitler, who wanted no trouble in Rumania and who had formed a favourable impression of Antonescu in the course of two visits by the Marshal to the Führer, decided to back the army which, with the help of German tanks, smashed the Iron Guard. Its leaders were lodged in internment camps until 1944 when, Antonescu having been overthrown by the tides of war, they were extracted to form a phantom Rumanian government in Vienna.

Italy was an ally of a different sort and its collapse in 1943 caused the biggest alteration to the pattern of German occupation before the retreat of the Germans themselves. The Germans were obliged to occupy those areas in south-eastern Europe which had been left to the Italians and to worry about the quantities of Italian arms which passed into the hands of Yugoslav and Greek partisans. Even more serious was the problem of Italy itself. Hitler was ill-informed about Italy. He had forbidden secret service activities there and the reporting of his civilian and service emissaries was deplorably poor. His belief in Mussolini made him reject warnings of the coming collapse. He helped Mussolini, rescued from captivity on the Gran Sasso by a spectacular piece of kidnapping in a small aircraft, to create a new Italian republic in the north, whose unreality and incapacity merely confused the picture but were not allowed by the German military and police commanders in the field to interfere with their respective businesses. Italy north of the allied line of advance became German occupied territory under military rule.

This patchwork of alliance and domination arose out of the needs and fortunes of war. It was not meant to endure. While it did, its function was to secure obedience to German wishes and, increasingly, to supply the German war machine with materials, goods, food and labour. As German needs became more urgent, German methods became harsher and resistance grew.

The German armies were accompanied in their invasions by special economic squads, whose first tasks were to seize what Germany wanted by way of pillage – raw materials and manufactured goods, gold and foreign currencies, machinery and rolling stock – and to protect valuable installations and essential factories, which were to be exploited as going concerns. Once these immediate aims had been achieved, the Germans began to look further ahead, but because they looked to an early peace and not to a long war they made mistakes. In either event the industries of non-German lands were to supplement the German economy, but expectations of an easy war led the economic planners to plan initially in terms of the New Order and, particularly in the east, to neglect or dismantle heavy industry: for over a year no attempt was made to repair factories and plants damaged by the retreating Russians, so that these were back in working order only shortly before the retreating Germans had to blow them up again.

The German economy had not been prepared for a long war. Hitler expected the war to be short and the German economy to take it in its stride. Production was adapted to the needs of the moment but not at first expanded. Thus in 1940 aircraft production was reduced (by 40 per cent) because the army needed more tanks and the navy more submarines, while in the next year factories which had made this switch were required to revert to aircraft because the Luftwaffe regained priority over the army and the navy in the light of its need to repair before Barbarossa the damage it had suffered in the Battle of Britain. But with the failure of Barbarossa to achieve its objectives by the end of the year it became inescapably clear that Germany needed a greatly expanded arms base and must also exploit the industrial potential of conquered countries both to contribute to Germany's arms production and to manufacture those other goods which Germany was ceasing to make for itself as its industry was converted to materials of war.

In areas formally or virtually annexed to the Reich, where there was no collision between short-term and long-term aims, industries were incorporated into German industry in order to enlarge its capacity. In Silesia, for example, coal production was very greatly expanded, synthetic oil refineries were built, and heavy engineering and arms production were developed. To the east of the areas which were treated as part of the Reich Goering ordered the transfer to Germany of all enterprises 'not absolutely essential for the maintenance of the bare existence of the inhabitants at a low level', unless transport difficulties made it more practicable to keep them at work on German orders where they were. In general, industry in the east was limited to producing goods and services required by Germany's armed forces and administrators, satisfying what Goering considered to be the bare needs of the local population and processing raw materials. In the west, after an initial few months of looting stocks and equipment, the policy was to exploit industrial capacity by nurturing and milking useful enterprises and to close down the rest by depriving them of raw materials. Factories which went on working had to deliver a high proportion of their output to the Germans; in some cases these levies reached 100 per cent (for example, of magnesium, heavy castings, industrial precision parts). The equipment of factories which closed was either taken to Germany or left to rot, while their labour was transferred to war work in Germany or occupied countries or assigned to the Todt Organization, which constructed the defences, installations and buildings needed by the armed forces outside Germany. Production of non-military goods was increased as German industry became more exclusively concentrated on war production, and towards the end of the war there was some dispersal of war production from Germany as a result of bombing.

The German apparatus of control was very powerful. Allocations of fuel and raw materials were regulated by licences issued by special agencies which were either German or under close German supervision. German specialists were often attached to industrial concerns. All contracts above a certain value had to be reported to the authorities and any firm attempting to do business without such notification lost its allocations. This relatively negative kind of control was supplemented by the active desire of collaborationist governments to keep their industries going and to maintain employment and the capital resources of the country. They therefore welcomed German orders. In some cases the German authorities placed orders with particular firms for goods which went straight to Germany and were paid for either through a clearing system or by being set against the occupation costs which the Germans charged for their presence and sustenance in occupied countries. (These occupation costs were far higher than the real costs of occupation. They were in fact huge, continuing fines.) In other cases general agreements were made covering whole industries, for example textiles, automobiles. In these cases the type of the product was fixed to suit the Germans, who took what they needed but set aside a proportion for the producing country: the Germans were also able to fix prices since they were the principal purchasers. Thus subordinate governments and foreign industrialists were largely in German hands. Either they worked for the Germans or they were forced to close, and if they were forced to close their employees would probably be sent to do forced labour in Germany. By August 1942 it was estimated that firms could only survive if at least three quarters of their output was for the Germans. The firms which remained in operation lost their independence. If the directors collaborated they had to allow German observers into their plants; if they refused, they were evicted and replaced by German managers and technicians.

Besides this subjection of industry by official processes, businesses in occupied countries were taken over either by confiscation or by purchase. Jewish property was confiscated without compensation. So, later, was the property of enemies of the Reich, a category which was interpreted by

Seyss-Inquart to include those who had assisted, were assisting or might be expected to assist anti-German activities. In the USSR, where the German state was declared to be the successor in title of the Soviet state, property of the Communist Party or any political association was, together with state property strictly so called, transferred into German state ownership. The same rules were applied to the Baltic states even though property had only been transferred to state ownership in 1939 and the population was markedly pro-German. In Poland an organization was established to confiscate land without compensation and re-sell it to Germans at nominal rates. The German banks extended German control by buying shares in foreign enterprises or in foreign banks which themselves had substantial holdings in such enterprises. In these ways the commanding heights of the economies of conquered countries were captured at practically no cost either by the German state or by major German industrial and financial groups. If this dual approach to expropriation contained within it the seeds of a conflict in Germany between state control and private control, the conflict itself was averted, or postponed, by the loss of the war.

Control was likewise imposed on agriculture. Again, the annexed areas were integrated with the Reich. In western and south-eastern Europe the Germans preferred to exercise control indirectly by strengthening the powers of local Ministries of Agriculture and forcing them to use their powers to implement the requirements of the Reich's Food Office, which prescribed production and delivery quotas, prices, subsidies, and feeding and seeding rates. Germany looked to these territories for much of its food and so kept them at first well equipped with farm machinery and fertilizers – many eastern districts were better supplied than before the war – but from 1941– 2 the exigencies of the Russian campaign disrupted this policy. Before the war ended food production in occupied Europe fell by about a quarter and much of it was requisitioned. The requisitions were generally addressed to the individual farmer, who was required to deliver up his produce in return for a claim slip with which he was left to get what compensation he could from his government. Other materials, such as coal, were requisitioned in the same way.

The food left over for civilian consumption became increasingly hard to move as the transport system failed. As a result of shortages of fuel, rubber and rolling stock, food was either not distributed at all or went bad during interminable waits at sidings. The use of canals and barges, where these existed, provided a partial alleviation, but shortages and distribution bottlenecks operating upon each other caused prices to rise steeply. Black markets flourished. Some governments tried to beat them by fixing prices and buying in essential products in order to regulate supply. They were unsuccessful: at one time it was estimated that nine out of every ten eggs marketed in the *département* of the Seine were being sold on the black market. Rations, which were introduced all over occupied Europe at a lower level (Denmark alone excepted) than in Germany, were frequently not honoured. Diets became increasingly vegetarian, and while country people often managed to live well enough half the population was required to exist on two thirds or a half of the pre-war normal.

Epidemics developed – tuberculosis, diphtheria, polio – and were made worse by a shortage of medicines. One of the by-products of undernourishment was an increase in industrial accidents which probably damaged production more than sabotage did. In particular areas at particular times the daily diet sank catastrophically. The worst examples were Athens and some of the Greek islands where it was 600–800 calories in the winter of 1941–2 and some Dutch cities where it fell to 500 calories in the winter of 1944–5. Hunger was made all the more insupportable by cold. Clothing and fuel both became desperately hard to get and – between the drop in real wages and the black market – impossibly expensive. Dutch city-dwellers were reduced to cutting down trees in parks and stealing any scrap which they could find to burn to keep their enfeebled bodies warm. In the east the situation became a tragic farce. The produce of the great granary of the Ukraine was garnered for the Reich but then left to rot because there were not enough trains to move it, until the Reich Commissar, Erich Koch, hit on the idea of doling out surplus stocks to service men going on leave in the form of 'Führer food parcels'. Germany got less out of the USSR after invading it than before. But occupied Europe was forced to yield 25 million tons of food to Germany, most of it requisitioned. During 1941 – 3 these supplies increased Germany's civilian ration by something between a fifth and a quarter.

It is difficult to give a picture of life in occupied Europe in terms of individuals as opposed to statistics because conditions varied enormously from place to place and from month to month. The constant factor was uncertainty – uncertainty about what could be got and, if it could, what it would cost. Necessities were frequently unobtainable and then suddenly on the market – the black market – at impossible prices. In France, for which reliable figures are easier to come by, the official cost of a kilo of butter rose from forty to sixty-one francs during 1941–3 but this price was entirely unreal, for when butter was available in, say, Paris it fetched by 1943 600– 800 francs. Tobacco and wine were rationed to a packet of the one and a litre of the other per adult per week but the rations were notional and black market prices were ten to twelve times the official price. Meat was frequently unobtainable for a month at a time. Meals could be got in subsidized works canteens or restaurants, but each lunch might cost a fifth of a weekly wage, so that a lunch a day more than consumed an entire pay packet. Shoes and clothes were already scarce and expensive by the winter of 1940 when a yard of woollen fabric or a pair of shoes cost the equivalent of half a weekly wage; by 1943 a pair of shoes absorbed six weeks' wages, a suit four to five months'. Coal and electricity were so rigorously restricted that the fuel ration was not enough to cook with, especially as the inferior food available could only be made edible by slow cooking. In Paris a ton of coal rose to the equivalent of two to four months' wages.

The most important of all the commodities which the Germans had to regulate was labour. Germany was short of labour before the war, while in a number of European countries there was appreciable unemployment. This imbalance was accentuated by the call-up of men for the German armed services and by the dislocations of war which put men and women out of work in conquered countries. The *Anschluss* with Austria and the annexation of the Sudetenland had automatically increased the Reich's labour force and there were in addition about 300,000 foreign workers in Germany in 1939 as a result of the operation of the law of supply and demand. During the war this force was enormously increased by three main methods: encouragement of more or less voluntary migration, the use of prisoners of war, and forcible recruitment.

In western and southern countries the Germans advertised the advantages of going to Germany for jobs: sure employment, good conditions, good pay, good holidays. Germany also made agreements with a number of satellite and allied governments, including Italy and Spain, for the supply of permanent and seasonal workers. The response was, however, inadequate, especially when reports of actual conditions in Germany filtered through and showed up the fraudulence of German enticements. Although a foreign worker from the west or south (as distinct from an eastern worker whose wage was derisory) was entitled to the same wage as a German worker, he was often put to less skilled work than he had been doing and so found himself earning less than he had expected. He had to pay German taxes and contribute to social insurance schemes from which he was not likely to benefit, since he did not expect to remain in Germany; and when inflation took hold of his home country without any corresponding increase in his German wage, he and his family found that the real return for his labours was drastically cut.

The Germans had therefore to stimulate volunteering by making work in occupied countries more difficult to come by and more unpleasant.

Men who were physically fit but who declined to volunteer to go to Germany lost unemployment pay; men in prison for civil offences were released if they promised to go; managements were forced to dismiss entire categories of workers needed in Germany; factories were closed; normal working hours were extended to a seventy-two-hour week or a thirteen-hour day; ration cards were withheld. These measures were the bridge between voluntary recruitment and the use of physical force. Between May 1940 and May 1941 the foreign labour force in the Reich rose by almost two million, the percentage of foreign labour from 3.2 to 8.4. By mid-1944 the percentage was 19.7. The voluntary element became very thin, the more so after allied bombing added to the discomforts of working in Germany. Sauckel estimated in 1944 that out of five million foreigners working in Germany fewer than 200,000 had come voluntarily.

The first prisoners put to work were some two to three hundred thousand Poles captured in the 1939 campaign and this number was greatly increased by the German victories in west and east in 1940 and 1941. Thereafter there were close on two million prisoners working for Germany until the war ended. The rules of war which Germany had accepted permitted the employment of prisoners other than officers, but the conditions which Germany's prisoners – most of them captured in the east – were forced to put up with during the Second World War contravened all the rules of war and of human decency. By 1944 about 40 per cent of them were, according to Albert Speer at Nuremberg, being used directly or indirectly in arms production. Non-commissioned officers were generally required to work and so too were Russian commissioned officers: the Nazis in effect did not recognize the validity of a Russian commission. Russian prisoners were paid half wages.

The German attitude to Russian combatants was one of calculated callousness. Since they regarded Slavs and communists as hardly better than Jews, the Germans killed them or allowed them to die with similar cruelty and, likewise, in millions. The total number of prisoners taken by the German armies in the USSR was in the region of 5.5 million. Of these the astounding number of 3.5 million or more had been lost by the middle of 1944 and the assumption must be that they were either deliberately killed or done to death by criminal negligence. Nearly two million of them died in camps and close on another million disappeared while in military custody either in the USSR or in rear areas; a further quarter of a million disappeared or died in transit between the front and destinations in the rear; another 473,000 died or were killed in military custody in Germany or Poland. (About 800,000 were released either on the grounds that they were not Russians or for volunteering to serve against the

Russians, leaving therefore about one million, of whom 875,000 were, by German standards, fit for work.) This slaughter of prisoners cannot be accounted for by the peculiar chaos of the war in the east. In such a war some prisoners will die through insufficient attention, but not millions of them. The true cause was the inhuman policy of the Nazis towards the Russians as a people and the acquiescence of army commanders in attitudes and conditions which amounted to a sentence of death on their prisoners. The Nazis encouraged barbarity against Russians by warning German troops to expect barbarity from them. The Russians were portrayed as uncivilized hordes. In addition the Germans made play with the fact that the USSR had not adhered to the Geneva Convention of 1929 on the treatment of prisoners of war, although it was known in Germany that the Russian armies had been ordered to observe the Geneva rules and the USSR had formally through Sweden requested reciprocal observance. In practice the Germans refused. Goering told Ciano that Russian prisoners of war, having eaten everything possible including the soles of their boots, had begun to eat each other and, 'which is more serious, had also eaten a German sentry . . . some nations must be decimated . . . there is nothing to be done about it'.

As the war went on forced labour became the only possible answer to Germany's problems. It was in addition sanctioned by ideology. On the day of the inauguration of Hans Frank's régime in Poland all Jews were formally condemned to forced labour and all other Poles were equally formally deprived of any right to leisure. The obligation to work included the liability to be sent to work in Germany. These regulations were copied by Rosenberg in 1941 for the Baltic states and the USSR. They were enforced by terror. Any person resisting recruitment was likely to see his house burned down and his family seized as hostages and sent to a labour camp. One of Rosenberg's principal officials compared the proceedings to the blackest days of the slave trade. He recorded that people were rounded up and shipped to Germany without any regard to health or age and that by 1942 over 100,000 had had to be sent back because they were utterly useless. Many of them died on the way and the next contingent of westbound workers would have to wait until the dead bodies of their rejected compatriots had been thrown out of the windows in order to make room for them in the disgusting trains (which incidentally were badly needed by the army). Women gave birth in the trains and the babies were thrown out onto the embankment. One German official charged with the provision of skilled Ukrainian labour for the Reich complained that his trains were held up by returning transports filled with discarded persons packed fifty or sixty to a truck and that eastward and westward bound trains stood motionless alongside each other for long periods; he added that his recruits often went hungry in these circumstances and that even the German Red Cross refused to feed them on the grounds that they were Russian swine. Another official complained of the propaganda effects when 400,000 Ukrainian domestic helps were being sent to Germany and before they arrived the German press announced that they would have no free time, would not be allowed to go to cinemas, theatres or restaurants, and might only be absent from the house where they worked for three hours a week at the most. His memorandum denounced the political ineptitude of treating eastern Europeans as second class whites in the sight of the whole coloured world and reminded his colleagues that the Russians were fighting 'with exceptional bravery and sacrifice for nothing more nor less than the recognition of their human dignity'. But the mixture of incompetence and callousness went on. By the end of the war the age limit for labour recruitment in the east had been lowered to ten.

The influx of foreign workers enabled Germany to shift labour from civilian to military employment – nearly six million by May 1941, nearly eight million a year later – without introducing compulsory service for women. In 1942 the number of women in civilian employment in Germany was lower by 189,000 than in 1939. But in 1942 the situation was radically altered by the failure to defeat the Russian armies in the field. In 1941 the German army had suffered heavy casualties for the first time and became a competitor with industry for men. In the autumn of 1942 Himmler concluded formal agreements with the Minister of Justice, Otto Thierack, and the Minister for Armaments, Albert Speer, by which the inmates of concentration camps and prisoners of war were released for work in factories in return for the allocation to the SS of a percentage of their output of weapons. The hours of work of the concentration camp victims were unlimited and the Himmler-Thierack agreement provided that 'antisocial' persons might be worked to death.

Forcible recruitment of labour was introduced in the west and southeast as well as in the east. Stricter controls were imposed in the Reich and in March 1942 Fritz Sauckel was appointed Plenipotentiary for the Deployment of Labour with extensive powers over the recruitment, use and distribution of German and foreign labour. Sauckel, whose appointment was part of no plan but a reaction to external events, collected over two million more foreign workers by May 1943 and increased the total labour force in Germany by just under two million in one year in spite of the drain caused by the demands of the fighting services. But his field for recruitment was narrowing. Poland had already been forced to contribute to the limit of its capacity. South-eastern Europe could not be denuded without imperilling the supplies of food which it provided for the Reich. In the USSR skilled labour had retreated eastward with the Russian armies and unskilled labour was largely required by the military and civilian authorities in the German occupied zones. In western Europe unemployment had been eliminated by earlier labour drives and by the demands of factories which were working for the Reich. From 1943 the difficulties became even acuter in both east and west – in the east because the advancing Russian armies reduced the area from which labour might be drawn, and in the west because labour was needed locally to make good the shortfall in German factories occasioned by bottlenecks and bombing. Moreover the machinery of German control was breaking down. Even in the west the Germans ceased to operate through local governments and began to round up labour in the streets of big cities – in one operation in Marseilles they kidnapped 1,000 French police by forcing them into lorries while they were on an exercise – and to seize the fathers of men who took to the woods and hills. Yet in Belgium 23,000 men evaded compulsory labour service by escaping to the Ardennes and in one area of France 95 per cent of those called for labour service during the winter of 1943–4 got away. Metaphorically Sauckel was being required to squeeze blood from a stone. In practice his minions squeezed it from human beings as they combed Europe for workers. Until the last year of the war Sauckel produced enough manpower to keep war production going and even to increase it, but after the middle of 1944 the economy began to crumble and not even the appointment of yet another plenipotentiary – this time Goebbels as Plenipotentiary for Total War – could keep the factories going.

The conditions of the millions of foreigners who worked for Nazi Germany varied according to their skills and racial ratings, but even the most favoured were shockingly treated. Jews as a rule were exterminated even if capable of working. Eastern workers fared worse than western or southern ones, Russians worse than Poles, Poles worse than the Baltic nations. The best treated were the skilled Danes, Flemings, Swiss and Hungarians, after them the French and Dutch, further down the scale the less skilled and racially inferior Balkan and Mediterranean peoples, including Italians and Spaniards, for whom the Germans had little respect even though they did not inspire the loathing directed against Slavs. For all of them Sauckel decreed that they should be fed, housed and treated in such a way as to ensure maximum production at minimum cost, and eastern workers in particular were kept in conditions which, besides being horridly inhumane, were also inefficient since they made them unfit for work and so reduced their output unnecessarily quickly. Agricultural workers were mostly housed and fed by their employers, but factory workers lived in barracks or in camps where they were segregated in huts by nationality. The camps, which were for western workers, were guarded by men and barbed wire; the inmates were not allowed out except to work. The huts were badly built, scantily furnished and scandalously lacking in sanitation. They were overcrowded, unheated and, as the war went on, unrepaired. Rations were in theory the same as those of German civilians, although in the case of eastern workers there was not even a pretence that they were: Goering ordered Russians to be fed lightly and without seriously interfering with German rations. In the camps ration cards were surrendered to the commandant who was free to provide what he thought fit in exchange. The diet of an eastern worker in a German labour camp was never within 1,000 calories of the lowest German ration, and the quality of the food was so poor that disease and mortality rates were preternaturally high. Concentration-camp workers received a diet roughly equivalent to the 1941–2 Athens famine rate.

But from the German point of view these miserable victims served their purpose. They constituted a fifth of Germany's wartime labour force; in 1944 there were seven million of them in the Reich. According to Albert Speer the western and Italian workers among them were at this date responsible for 25–30 per cent of the German effort. In addition Europe made, over the whole period of Germany's dominion from 1940 to 1944, contributions in kind equivalent to 14 per cent of Germany's own gross product and so increased by rather more than 50 per cent the resources available to Germany for the purchase of arms and equipment. No slave-driver could have hoped for more.

CHAPTER 13
Resistance

CONSCRIPTED labourers, prisoners of war, Jews, communists and gipsies were all minority groups. Even together they were still a minority of the peoples who came under German rule. The great majority stayed where they were or returned to their homes after having been temporarily scattered by the German advances. Some experienced life in a battle zone and in an army rear area; most of them a much longer spell under some form of occupational régime while the great bulk of Germany's front-line fighting forces was engaged on Russian soil. Only in the east, and to a lesser degree in Italy, did civilian populations live through protracted fighting.

The first shock left little room for anything except the sheer facts of defeat and abandonment. Those in the path of the *Blitzkrieg* were left dazed as the Germans swept away the familiar things of daily life from goods and houses to the governments and officials to whom a settled people is wont to turn for guidance or instruction in a crisis. Communities were atomized. The individual's first thought was to find his family, recover his belongings and get himself a job and a livelihood. The job became all important, first as a means for securing the necessities of life in a strange world and later in order to qualify for exemption from forced labour; a job meant also a renewal of contact with familiar routines, an assurance that some things remained the same. But jobs were scarce and in the immediate wake of defeat there was widespread unemployment. Many factories were reduced to a ten-hour week and earnings sagged until labour began to be required again for reconstruction and the occupiers' needs (building airfields, for example). Some employers paid reduced wages to help and keep their workers during temporary stoppages caused by lack of materials or power, but poverty spread alarmingly as the gap between earnings and prices widened at both ends and large quantities of food, clothing and other necessities disappeared into expensive black markets. Poverty caused neglect of children, social divisions and crime. The towns became resentful of the comparatively better-fed countryside; the law-abiding resented the profits made by black marketeers who, since they sold mostly to Germans, were beyond the reach of the law; the poor looked with rising anger at the advantages of the rich (in

Paris, to take an extreme case, the six most famous restaurants were exempt from all restrictions until 1943). Crimes such as theft, whether committed by adults or juveniles, multiplied and became respectable; in the Netherlands the crime rate almost trebled; stealing was both a symptom of poverty and a form of protest. Scruples of all kinds wilted in the face of need, and the hostility of the have-nots against the haves quickened. Prostitution increased by as much as tenfold as a result of financial hardship and the break-up of family life; women with no previous police records traded themselves to German soldiers in spite of the hostility which their conduct provoked among their more forbearing compatriots.

As a general rule everybody over fifteen had to have an identity card, observe a curfew and expect to have his movements restricted. The police state arrived on the heels of the German army. Jews had to produce baptismal certificates of grandparents or lose their citizenship. Few people possessed such documents but a number were forged by Christian clergymen. Freedom of movement was curtailed by the virtual elimination of private transport and severe limitations on public transport. Bicycle-taxis appeared in towns. Mail was censored and in some cases prohibited: between the zones of France the only kind of mail allowed was printed postcards with simple messages of the 'we are well/ill . . .' type, from which the sender could choose one by crossing out the rest. Newspapers either became pro-German and sparse of news or disappeared; about half of the national and local press ceased publication and the circulation of the survivors dropped sharply. Radio programmes continued under German control. The Germans offered good pay to well-known broadcasters, kept favourite programmes on the air and tried to use radio to propagate their views, but the nature of radio prevented them from securing a monopoly, and although they penalized listeners to enemy broadcasts they could not proscribe transmissions from neutral Switzerland, whose broadcasts became an important item in preserving for the conquered a window on the world. But life narrowed and this spiritual retrenchment was reflected in swelling attendances at cinemas and sporting events – even when, later, the Resistance admonished people to stay away. It also threw families together and sharpened the demand for books, including serious books about national history and culture.

Immediately after the end of the fighting there was a marked difference between those parts of a country which had seen the war at first hand in the form either of enemy armies or of refugees, and other parts which had learned of it by hearsay. Soon, however, all parts faced the same question: attitudes to the victors; to which was added the secondary question of attitudes to collaborators, which were often more bitterly intense. As people recovered they tended to divide into two groups, those who on the whole accepted the new world in which they had woken up again and those who felt too angry or too ashamed to do so. Although ultimately the Germans earned widespread hate, at first their coming raised more questioning than clear-cut emotions. The behaviour of the occupying forces in the west was for the most part correct and even affable and it was some time before their habit of strolling around singly in villages and towns was replaced by more circumspect promenading in pairs or groups and the abandonment of attempts at social intercourse with the natives; even where there was from the beginning a wall of silence, there was also that mutual respect which has been most tellingly portrayed in Vercors' *Le silence de la mer*. Some countries had an anti-German tradition but others – Greece, for example, which was anti-Italian but not initially anti-German – had not. The Germans were given the benefit of the doubt. Attitudes crystallized slowly in societies which had been atomized and people were thrown back on local or personal motives in deciding what to think and how to conduct themselves. There was something of a psychological vacuum in which the Germans had, and lost, their chances. There was no overall pattern. In a country like France, where the Third Republic had failed to command wide enough allegiance, the new order benefited at the start from adventitious aids such as the countervailing respect for Pétain (especially in the lower reaches of the social scale), an intensification of anti-British feelings among the bourgeoisie and a reinforcement of anti-radicalism. But these were not inherently pro-German feelings. They only gave a conditioned blessing to the German presence and perpetuated for a while after the armistice the confusion created by war. Only in the east did it swiftly become clear that the German occupation was a threat to the entire population and that the choice lay between resistance and extermination.

In most places there was a case for collaboration, for lying low for the time being. Moreover the disruptions of war and the contradictions of the occupation made it difficult for ordinary people to get a lead from their traditional mentors. In Belgium the king had declared himself a prisoner while his government had fled to London to continue the fight. In Denmark the king and government were undisguisedly anti-German. The king ignored German salutations on his daily rides through his capital, sent telegrams of sympathy to police wounded in a fight in which 300 Danish Nazis were arrested, gave an audience to a well-known historian just before he was arrested for spreading anti-German propaganda, and eventually threatened to abdicate if anti-semitic legislation were introduced, but he and his government also officially discouraged anti-German activities and recommended a policy of acquiescence for a considerable time.

Two things in particular resolved this ambivalence: the course of the war and the behaviour of the Germans. A numb acceptance of Germany's victories sprang not only from the shock of defeat but also from the conviction that defeat was complete and final. Men like de Gaulle who never accepted defeat at any moment were rare and had the logic of events against them. But even before the end of 1940 doubt began to spread. The failure of the Luftwaffe in the Battle of Britain and the British initiative in Africa at the end of the year showed that the war was not over. The entry of the Russians and then the Americans into the war in 1941 showed that the Germans were going to lose it. These events became well-known throughout occupied Europe through broadcasting and a clandestine press which became amazingly extensive. One of the most important facts about occupied Europe was that people in it knew what was going on. This knowledge was due to radio which prevented Europe from being totally cut off. The BBC's news services were widely heard and believed; Swiss radio, with its built-in reputation for neutral impartiality, played a similar role; communists, who took after June 1941 an exceptionally important part in Resistance, listened to broadcasts from the USSR, which possessed the most powerful transmitter in the world and the longest experience in broadcasting propaganda; governments-in-exile in London reached their compatriots with news and exhortation and gave them a factual and legal basis for opposing the Germans and their satellite regimes.

Foreign broadcasts nourished indigenous clandestine newspapers. The clandestine press became an industry of great potency in forming the will to resist. In Belgium about 12,000 persons came to be engaged in it and published 300 papers; in France underground presses produced books in fine editions as well as over 1,000 papers and pamphlets (this figure included regional editions of the same paper); in Denmark the number of papers published rose from 222 in the whole of 1943 to 315 in the first four months of 1945 and by the end of 1944 over 10 million copies of these papers and pamphlets had been printed and distributed; in the Netherlands some papers appeared three times a week after the confiscation of radio sets in 1943 and the five principal left-wing papers attained a combined circulation of 450,000. The distribution of this quantity of material was a well-organized and yet highly risky business, handled by members of small local groups who took their lives in their hands with every sheet which they delivered to a neighbour. These groups and their newspapers recall the secret societies which carried on the revolution in France underground after the restoration of the *ancien régime* in 1814. Through their efforts the underground in Europe was in general better informed about the war than the regular combatants were about the underground. The flow of information was an essential factor in rebuilding the societies which had been smitten by the German victories and in stimulating opposition to a no longer invincible victor. It restored to the defeated a sense of coherence and a sense of purpose, and the clandestine press which raised the morale of Resisters likewise demoralized an enemy who, having thought that he had finished off the opposition, was presented with evidence of its persistence and even began to exaggerate it. The activities of the clandestine press led to other forms of resistance, as the confidence of these groups expanded and with their confidence their aims. Many active Resisters served an apprenticeship by helping to run a clandestine paper.

The German contribution to anti-Germanism was no less substantial. The natural nationalist opposition to the presence of Germans was swollen by opposition to their behaviour. Besides being aliens, they showed themselves inhumane: Jews were segregated, deported and killed – the round-up of Jews in the Vélodrome d'Hiver shocked Parisian opinion even more than the taking of hostages; human rights and freedoms were trampled on far beyond the necessities of war and occupation; the new rulers pillaged the material resources of the defeated, failed to provide them with enough food and conscripted them for labour in appalling conditions; prisoners of war did not come back; all in all the non-German individual was degraded body and soul. This inhumanity converted the resentment of the subject populations into hatred – which in Norway was given an edge of a very special kind, for in the First World War Norwegians had looked after German children, and they were filled with disgust at the thought that the invading armies of 1940 probably contained some of these very children grown to be violators of the charity shown to them twenty-five years earlier. Hatred of the Germans fostered various forms of opposition such as networks for helping fugitive allied servicemen who had been shot down or had escaped from prison camps; the collection and forwarding of military intelligence; the clandestine press; industrial sabotage, go-slows and strikes; and eventually the beginnings of organized and active armed resistance.

But the Germans went even further. Confronted with this opposition they took the iron fist right out of its velvet glove and began to use terror as a principal means of government. Hostages were taken and shot, concentration camps established, stunning reprisals exacted and picked areas devastated. Although the details varied in practice from country to country the overall pattern was uniform because it reflected not individual initiative or local eccentricity but a policy devised and commanded at the highest level in the German state, the Nazi Party and the armed services. Thus in December 1941 Keitel, as Chief of Staff of the Armed Forces, issued the *Nacht und Nebel* (Night and Fog) order which was designed to strike fear into whole populations. Hitler, he said, was interested in no penalty except death; no other deterrent seemed to him effective; even a sentence of hard labour for life struck him as a sign of weakness. Consequently the *Nacht und Nebel* order decreed that in cases where the death penalty was unlikely to be imposed by a court in an occupied country, offences against the Reich were to be visited with a substitute death. The offender was to be secretly spirited away to the Reich without trial, leaving friends and relations to tremble in suspense for his fate – and theirs.

The distinction between guilt and innocence had already been virtually abolished, for as early as September 1941 Keitel had instructed commanders on all fronts to ascribe all acts of resistance to communists and to execute batches of so-called communists for every German soldier killed: fifty to a hundred communists was the number recommended. A few weeks later fifty hostages were executed in France as a reprisal for the death of a German officer, and a further fifty a few days later when another officer was killed; the executions would have been twice as many but for strenuous intervention by Vichy. By the end of the war about 30,000 French hostages had been shot and the toll was comparable all over occupied Europe. In the Netherlands Seyss-Inquart revealed in May 1942 that 480 prominent Dutch personages were being held and that many had already been shot in retaliation for breaches of public order; on another occasion the village of Putten was burned down and all its males deported (very few ever returned) after a German motorcar had been attacked in the neighbourhood and one German wounded. In Poland a tally was established of one hundred Resisters to be killed for the death of every one German, and at Palmiry, a village near Warsaw, several thousand deaths were in fact exacted in revenge for a single attack. At Televaag in Norway 300 houses were burned down, 76 persons deported and a further 260 interned in April 1942 in an attempt to intimidate and quell Norwegian resistance. The first case of devastation and mass executions in Italy occurred at Boves in Piedmont in September 1943, while in Rome 330 people picked at random were executed in March 1944 after thirty-two German soldiers had been killed by a bomb. At Oradour-sur-Glane, selected by a mistake instead of a place of the same name a few kilometres away, only ten persons out of a population of 652 survived the calculated fury of the Germans, the men being shot and the women and children being locked into the church and burned to death. This last enormity occurred in July 1944.

The most famous of these razzias befell the village of Lidiče in Czechoslovakia where the entire population was killed or sent to concentration camps with a horrifying sort of nonchalance in revenge for the assassination of Heydrich. At the end of 1941 two men from the Czechoslovak army in England, one a Czech and the other a Slovak, had arrived by parachute, with British assistance, in order to do this deed, which was undertaken in the belief that Heydrich and his police chief, Karl Hans Frank, were planning to destroy the entire Czech people. It was achieved in the following May when the two executioners threw a bomb into Heydrich's open car. He took a week to die. About 1,500 Czechs were immediately killed, including the executioners and another 120 members of the Resistance who had escaped into a church. In addition, 3,000 Jews were removed from the concentration camp at Terezin (Theresienstadt) and sent to Poland to be killed. But this was not the end. A few days after Heydrich's death, Lidiče, apparently selected at random, was sealed off by the S D. That day nothing much happened, although a woman and a small boy were shot and killed for trying to escape. The next day the entire male population over sixteen years of age was shot in batches – 172 of them in a leisurely massacre which took ten hours; the women were sent to Ravensbrueck concentration camp and the children to a different camp; pregnant women were first allowed to give birth to their children in hospital and then joined their friends in Ravensbrueck, their babies having been killed. Lidiče itself was razed to the ground. Lezaky, another small village near Prague, was treated in the same way a few days later. These savage reprisals were supplemented by some 10,000 arrests. The Czech composer Martinů, who had fled from Paris to the United States in 1940, composed an orchestral 'Memorial to Lidiče'.

As things got worse for the Germans, so did their behaviour. In July 1944 Hitler ordered all saboteurs to be executed on the spot and all suspects to be handed over to the S D (which was worse). This decree, called the *Kugelerlass* or Bullet Decree, was a form of words for transferring wide categories of prisoners to the S D for execution. It did not apply to British or American combatants unless they were commandos (in which case they were already covered by the Commando Order of 1942 requiring them to be summarily slaughtered to the last man, even if they surrendered). The *Kugelerlass* was extended two months after its promulgation to prisoners under sentence and to those whose cases were still pending. Keitel explained that there was to be no compunction about innocent persons who might accidentally get killed in the course of the measures needed to eliminate what he called dissidents. The response to these foul and frantic measures was active armed resistance on a militarily significant scale and, complementarily, a dwindling of the numbers of collaborators and *attentistes* as the complicity involved in siding with the Germans or even doing nothing amounted to condoning the unforgivable.

Such were the cumulative sources of Resistance. The word itself did not make its appearance at once. In France it does not seem to have been in general use before 1943, although Gaullism had by that time become a well-known term. The phenomenon of Resistance, however, appeared immediately after defeat, if only in modest, disconnected and often unsuccessful forms, spontaneous expressions of spirit by disbanded officers and men of the fighting forces which the Germans were usually able to master without much difficulty. Most people remained, then and for some time thereafter, very vague about their neighbours' activities and about Resistance movements, and also ignorant (as they were meant to be) about the separate intelligence and escapers' networks. People heard that something was going on without knowing what it was. The development of Resistance was to some extent dependent on growing awareness of its existence and endorsement of its aims and methods, and this interacting process took time. It was not until the butcher, the baker and the candlestick-maker felt moved to join active Resistance groups that there could be active Resistance groups for them to join. The process was one of awareness leading to complicity, and complicity leading to activity. Movements grew as householders sheltered Resisters, fed them, lent rooms for radio transmissions, failed to report raids on their farms by gangs who might be Resisters (though sometimes they were not), and so gradually became more deeply and sometimes more actively involved.

In point of time the earliest forms of opposition were intelligence networks which had in some cases been formed before the war began – in Czechoslovakia, for instance, in 1938. Some of these became so extensive that they were able to shadow and report on the entirety of the official administrative machine. Besides spying on German activities and installations they recruited their own agents and helped agents who arrived from outside (mostly by parachute). Belgium, partly because of its proximity to England, was specially active in this work, providing some 5,000 agents, supported by another 13,000 helpers. Czechoslovakia, to which aircraft from England could safely make the return flight only on moonless nights, was less closely linked but provided valuable information both to Great

Britain and, before Barbarossa, to the Russians, to whom it supplied detailed warnings of the impending German attack, including the names of the airfields which the Luftwaffe intended to attack; Czech Intelligence also unmasked a German sabotage group working beyond the Urals. In Poland an underground organization operated throughout the country, reporting on German troop movements, following the Germans as far as the Volga and the Caucasus and dispatching in 1942–4 some 300 reports to the west by radio or by courier via Hungary, Sweden and Switzerland. In Greece, to take a further example from another quarter, 1,072 agents – Greek, British, American and Polish – were dropped during 1941–4 and stayed in the country for varying lengths of time, usually a few months.

Similar to the intelligence networks were the escape routes along which escaped prisoners or airmen who had been shot down (and who, especially in England in 1940, were urgently needed back with their units) or Europeans seeking a way to re-enter the fight by getting to England were passed from hand to hand, sometimes by men and women who had performed the same service in the First World War or by their children. These routes were often long and intricate, running from Belgium or northern France or Germany itself through Switzerland and unoccupied France to Spain, Portugal or Africa; or from Poland through Czechoslovakia, Hungary, Yugoslavia and Italy; or northwards to Sweden. In Belgium alone some thirty-five groups were engaged in this work at one time or another, employing 10,000 persons and using their own teleprinter communications.

These were examples of the more obviously useful services which Resisters could render. They were of their nature clandestine. But Resistance was also effective in more open, if less concrete, ways. People came to realize that it was worth showing how they felt, and that strong feelings did not have to find vent in such dangerous activities as spying or such violent ones as guerrilla warfare. They used symbols and badges, like the red, white and blue knitted caps with which Danish students paraded their affinity with the R A F; or the Dutch habit of raising their hats when the traffic lights turned to the symbolic orange colour; or the Parisian students' mimicry of Germans, especially German airmen whose dress they copied by sporting their biros in the way that the Luftwaffe wore daggers. They even used silence, abruptly terminating all conversation if a German entered a shop or, again in Paris, rising and leaving university lectures if Germans came in to attend them. (The Germans closed the Sorbonne after a demonstration at the tomb of the unknown soldier at the Arc de Triomphe in November 1940.) Anti-German leaflets were slipped into licensed newspapers before distribution, a simple way of getting a large circulation. University laboratories were used to make bombs for the Resistance. Post-office workers intercepted denunciatory letters addressed to the SD by opening all SD mail and significantly impeded the activities of the SD which depended on a network of correspondents – amounting in Paris alone to eight to ten thousand persons. Police went into the business of forging false identity papers, a contribution which they were specially equipped to make owing to their familiarity with the genuine articles and their possession of genuine official stamps. Administrators turned their talents to losing dossiers and protracting discussions with the occupiers. A peculiar form of patriotic self-denial practised in France was hoarding instead of spending coins containing nickel and bronze in order to deny the metals to the Germans; this ingenious tactic not only created an embarrassing shortage of small change but also represented a considerable sacrifice by the poor, who had to go without the things which their coins could have bought.

From these non-violent declarations of hostility Resisters passed to equally non-violent but more positive protests, such as the resignation of the Norwegian bishops and nearly all the judges of the Norwegian High Court and the almost unanimous refusal of Norwegian teachers to sign an undertaking to teach in accordance with Quisling's party line, a protest which was backed up by hundreds of thousands of signed letters from parents. But moral resistance of this kind was possible only in countries where the Germans were, at least comparatively, lenient. In the east spiritual resistance could not be overt, but it occurred none the less, as witness the clandestine education of two to three thousand students in Poland and the continuance of scientific work and the secret publication of its results.

Economic resistance occurred everywhere. The methods were sometimes almost trivial but the results were considerable. Germany was denied the fruits of European labour and skill which, in an atmosphere less poisoned by hate, could have contributed extensively to Germany's war effort and home comforts. The means included going to work regularly a quarter of an hour late, mixing labels on packages so that they went to the wrong destination, more serious sabotage in factories and on railways, and strikes. Polish economic sabotage affected the delivery of Russian goods to Germany before Barbarossa and the supplying of the German armies on the eastern fronts after it, in both cases on a large scale. Sabotage in Czechoslovakia had become a serious worry to Heydrich before his assassination, and Czechs conscripted into the German army also engaged in sabotage. Strikes in Italy were the precursors of the fall of Mussolini and were repeated against the Germans when they occupied the northern half of the country. There were a number of extensive strikes in the Netherlands. But the strike was a dangerous weapon, which many workers were unwilling to use. It entailed not only loss of job and pay but, consequently, liability for deportation to compulsory labour service in Germany; and the leaders of the Dutch strikes were executed.

The more spectacular operations included two Anglo-Norwegian raids on the Lofoten Islands in 1941, when several thousand tons of shipping and eighteen cold-liver-oil factories were destroyed. These raids were a good example of the hazards of Resistance. Besides the material damage inflicted, they gave a boost to British and perhaps to Norwegian morale and kept Hitler guessing about his enemies' intentions, but they also provoked heavy reprisals and, when the British withdrew without warning on the second occasion after a week's stay which the local inhabitants had expected to be permanent, bitter resentment among the Norwegians left behind and an official protest from the Norwegian government in London. The reprisals severely damaged the Resistance movement in the same way, although not quite to the same extent, as the Czech Resistance movement which was virtually destroyed by the reprisals exacted after the death of Heydrich.

Limited operations could, however, be extremely valuable as well as less costly. The British were worried about German nuclear research. They wished to destroy the plant at Vemork in Ryukan in Norway where heavy water was being produced by electrolysis, and early in 1942 a first group of Norwegians from England was dropped in the region to spy out the land. In November a first attempt, by glider attack, to destroy the plant failed but in the following February a party of Norwegians succeeded in putting it out of action for five months. Later in 1943 it was bombed and partially destroyed by the Americans. The allies also wished to destroy the entire stock of heavy water. This involved the sinking of a ferry on which innocent Norwegians would be bound to be travelling. The Norwegian government in London was asked to decide whether this should be done. The government hardened its heart and gave the order to proceed. In similar limited operations valuable stocks of pyrites, iron ore and ball bearings were destroyed. Towards the end of the war sabotage groups were converted into anti-sabotage groups. One of their most notable achievements was the preservation by the Belgians of the port of Antwerp which was placed intact into the hands of the allies immediately they entered the city.

A large part of the Danish Resistance effort was directed to sabotaging Germany's exploitation of Denmark's food and strategic position. The Danish government refrained at first from encouraging sabotage for fear of reprisals, but the British pressed for more activity and got their way towards the end of 1942. The anomalies in the Danish situation were largely removed by the German take-over in 1943, when the official government ceased to function and a less inhibited, undercover government was formed under the name of the Freedom Council. From 1943 sabotage, and especially railway sabotage, increased: there were nearly 2,000 separate incidents in the first four months of 1945. At the other end of Europe the Greek Resistance, by blowing up the Gorgopotamos viaduct in November 1942, interrupted for six weeks the main route by which German supplies were going to Rommel in Africa and brought the port of Piraeus to a standstill. Subsequently Greek sabotage parties derailed 117 trains, destroyed 209 locomotives and 1,544 wagons, cut telephone wires and wrecked various tunnels, bridges and motor vehicles. Similar damage was inflicted on communications all over Europe. Much of it was quickly repaired by the Germans.

Economic sabotage merged into military action. The essential requirements were suitable terrain and climate and the support of the population. Without places to hide and people to help the dice were too heavily loaded in favour of the regular military and police forces of the occupiers. The Netherlands and Denmark, flat and bare, could not support a powerful militant movement, even with massive popular sympathy (in Denmark in elections in 1943 97 per cent of the votes cast were given to democratic parties and the Danish Nazis won only one seat out of 150); in the USSR partisan activity was impossible in the north and difficult in the Ukraine. Next, the Resistance forces needed training and organization which were to some extent of an orthodox military nature but also markedly unorthodox; and they needed arms. Secret armies had to operate on a cut-and-run basis until their German enemies were demoralized and themselves on the run. Attempts by partisans to fight pitched battles often led to disaster (as for example in the Vercors and at Montmouchet, as will be related in a later chapter). Active Resistance groups tended to form in the first place round regular officers adrift from defeated armies, but these first leaders were as a general rule superseded by new men who rose to command by proving their aptitude for the new kinds of warfare prescribed by circumstances. These leaders had to strike a balance between the need for caution in the face of a superior enemy – the need to score points but also to survive to carry on the fight – and on the other hand the need to engage the enemy frequently and effectively enough to satisfy their followers. Arms were not less important than tactics and there was a constant tug of war between the accumulation of arms (by raids or by parachute drops from outside) and the loss of arms through discovery of dumps by German Intelligence: this last danger put pressure on Resistance leaders to use arms when they had them instead of waiting for a more propitious moment.

Active Resistance contributed to the tribulations and ultimately to the defeat of the Germans by tying down units or preventing their orderly transfer from one front to another and by engaging them in battle. The threat of an armed rising in Norway by the Resistance movement called Milorg in cooperation with allied forces constrained Hitler to detail thirteen army divisions, 90,000 naval personnel, 6,000 SS men and 12,000 paramilitary troops to watch and control a country with a total population of only three million, and at the end of the war Milorg received the surrender of 400,000 Germans (ten times Milorg's own strength) and liberated over 90,000 prisoners of war, nearly all of them Russians. When the Anglo-American armies landed in Normandy in July 1944 French Resistance forces delayed the reinforcement of the crucial sector: the SS division *Das Reich* took nine days to get from south-western France to the battle area. In September the Dutch paralysed the railways at the time of the allied advance towards Nijmegen and Arnhem. The Danes harassed and impeded the withdrawal of German forces from Norway to the defence of Germany itself. National armies were reborn and rejoined the war: 120,000 Belgians were fighting as regular units by the end of the war, the Danish secret army was 45,000 strong, 60,000 Czechs fought with the Russian army in addition to the units which had been serving with British forces since the beginning. In France the Alpine departments and the Massif Central were liberated by the French Resistance, whose total contribution at the time of the re-invasion of Europe was put by Eisenhower – with perhaps a degree of pardonable exaggeration – at the equivalent of fifteen divisions.

This impressive resurgence of European nationalism in arms helped to salve the humiliation of the defeats in 1940–41 and by doing so contributed more to the spiritual rehabilitation of Europe, which was in the balance, than to the defeat of Germany, which was assured by other forces. It also emphasized the national character of European policies since the Resistance movements were nationalist not only in the sense of being anti-German but also in the almost complete absence of any contacts among themselves. At one point Resistance leaders met at a conference in Switzerland and discussed a new and less nationally divided Europe, harking back to Mazzinian ideas of a confraternity of nationalisms, looking forward to a *Europe des patries*, echoing ideas which were being discussed at the same time by anti-Nazi conspirators inside Germany; but so long as the war continued there was little opportunity for common action. At-

tempts to concert French and Belgian, Yugoslav and Italian Resistance
came to little. A Resistance movement had to be ultra careful about its
security and it was often suspicious of its neighbour's politics or ideology.
So the international character of the external attack on Germany by the
Anglo-American-Russian coalition could not be matched by any corresponding internationalism on the continent. Communism, which might
have served as a link between Resistance movements, did not do so during
the war because communist resisters were no more able than non-
communist resisters to make effective contacts beyond the bounds of their
local field of operations. Thirdly, the patriotic aims of Resistance were
yoked with objectives of national regeneration and revolution which will
be more closely examined in the next chapters. Although Resistance movements began without any definite political purpose and were often anti-
political in the sense that they distrusted the political parties and institutions
which had failed them before the war, yet at the same time these movements
were obliged to be political in another sense. They responded to prevailing
popular emotions and aspirations which were of a political nature and,
because they were constructive and not merely hostile to occupiers or pre-
war régimes, imposed on the Resistance movements a distinctive blend of
moral-political programme which was characteristically left-wing.

As Resistance developed it involved not only the Resistance movements
themselves inside occupied countries but also governments in exile (all of
them in London except the Greek government which was in Cairo) and
the organizations established with similar aims by the British and American governments. The first of these in point of time, and for some time the
most active, was the British Special Operations Executive (SOE) which
was created in July 1940 as a department in the Ministry of Economic
Warfare. The date indicated the need: to preserve or renew contacts with
a continent from which Great Britain had been expelled and cut off. The
Ministry indicated the prime aim: to injure Germany's war-making capacity by sabotage. The two together prescribed the method: to find, train
and dispatch small groups of technically equipped demolitionists. At the
beginning of the war the British government had made plans for interfer-
ring with Germany's supplies of iron ore from Sweden and oil from
Rumania and although these had been attended by no success the notion
of economic warfare had been embodied in a Department of State, and
after Dunkirk Great Britain's inability to do much else in Europe, combined with the emergence of Resistance in the following year and Churchill's decision to foster it, focused attention on the possibilities of sabotage. SOE set to work to find saboteurs with the right aptitudes and
languages (they were recruited in French-speaking Canada and polyglot

South America as well as among the refugees from Hitler's Europe) and it eventually established sixty training schools for operations in Europe besides others for Asia. These schools sent 7,500 agents, mostly nationals of the countries concerned, to western Europe and 4,000, mostly British agents and military liaison parties, to Italy and south-eastern Europe.

Almost at the outset these operations were extended from sabotage to intelligence. Many intelligence contacts had been broken by the retreat from the continent. In addition, military intelligence networks had been penetrated by the Germans before the war: in Holland, for example, the British headquarters, which was next door to the house made famous in the First World War by Mata Hari, had been under surveillance since 1935 and all visitors to it had been regularly photographed as they went in and out. There was therefore something of an intelligence vacuum and it seemed natural to ask SOE, which was organizing sabotage trips, to get its agents to do some intelligence work too. Unfortunately agents of the one kind are not necessarily the right people for work of the other kind, nor had they been trained for it, and the confusion of the two functions endangered SOE's work. It also endangered Resistance groups, since there were more agents around who had contacts with these groups and were at the same time liable to be picked up by German counter-intelligence or to become unsuspectingly involved with double agents.

A further extension of SOE's work occurred when subversion and insurrection were added to its brief. Churchill told Hugh Dalton, the Minister of Economic Warfare, that it was his business to 'set Europe ablaze'. Prizing variety and unconventionality for their own sake, and stirred perhaps by the historical recollections of chouans, carbonari and klephts, Churchill welcomed the chance to revive the fighting spirit and fighting forces of Europe's nations. He wanted to summon them to make life hell for the Germans and, ultimately, to cooperate with the allies' regular armies when the time should come to return to the continent. But this part of the programme raised unforeseen political complications. SOE's emissaries became charged with diplomatic tasks: persuading Resistance groups to adopt certain policies or tactics, reconciling them with one another for the good of the common cause, reporting on them and advising which were more worthy of support than others. Supplying one organization with arms in preference to another was a political act. The British tried to operate on the principle that the only thing that mattered was harassing the Germans and the only touchstone for deciding between competing groups was this anti-German fervour. But this simple rule of thumb ignored the facts. The Resistance movements were not simply, sometimes not primarily, anti-German. They represented for the time being the domestic politics of their countries. Some of them were fighting against the pre-war order and distrusted or opposed their governments in exile with which the British government was in alliance; and they became more definitely left-wing after Hitler's invasion of the USSR unshackled the communists and set them free to join and try to dominate the Resistance.

To a man with Churchill's uncomplicated sense of purpose these were secondary matters so long as the Germans had to be beaten. He knew that war and politics could not be separated but he also knew which he was going to subordinate to the other. The political issues would have to be dealt with later, by which time they would doubtless present themselves in a new context and a new light. Meanwhile he pledged Great Britain to the restoration of the independence of Europe. He became a European leader. The V sign for victory which he coined and its aural equivalent · · · –, tapped out in Morse or played by the BBC to all Europe in the familiar phrase from Beethoven's fifth symphony, were symbols of an intimate link between Great Britain and the subject peoples of the continent without distinction between political creeds. Although a conservative and a monarchist, Churchill discarded all tests except that of anti-Germanism. Only when the war was manifestly won but not concluded did he turn from battling to politics and set himself, unsuccessfully in the one case, successfully in the other, to baulk the republicans in Italy and Greece.

The Americans saw things otherwise. They were quicker to see the communists than the klephts in the Resistance ranks. They were even inclined to suspect all Resistance movements, including Gaullism, of being either communist or stalking horses for communism. They appreciated the political implications of helping the Resistance. They fell into a different kind of unreality from the British. Traditionally wary of European politics and less well versed in them because of their distance from the scene, they sought to separate strategic from political issues, to avoid giving blank cheques to exiles and to get on with the war in the expectation that victory would produce a return to stability in Europe, a withdrawal of American intervention and a settlement of political problems by Europeans through the magic of free elections. But this expectation was wishful thinking. It is almost true to say of Roosevelt that he substituted a talisman for political analysis and had no political aim in Europe during these years other than getting agreement, particularly from Stalin but also from everybody else, on the holding of free elections all over Europe (except in Germany) as quickly as possible after the end of the war. On this basis it might be safe to help the Resistance. The Office of Strategic Services (OSS) was created to emulate and in many instances surpass

SOE. American aid was lavish. It was given without acknowledging that this kind of intervention had political as well as military implications: whereas the British, in helping Tito for example, gave aid on the deliberate basis that military considerations overrode all others and that the obvious political implications must of necessity be subordinated, the Americans tended wishfully to believe that military and political considerations were so far distinct that military aid had insignificant political consequences.

Resistance created difficulties between the allied governments – in this case mainly the British – and governments-in-exile. Supporting governments-in-exile was not always compatible with the aid given by the British to armies-not-in-exile. The governments suspected the British of trying to dominate and direct a part of their national activity. They also protested on behalf of their nationals against what they regarded as foolish British tactics or serious British mistakes. There was an acrimonious feud between French and British authorities over which of them should employ French citizens as agents. The Norwegians and the British tussled ill-naturedly for control of Milorg and, as already mentioned, the Norwegian government protested sharply against experimental British coastal raids in 1940 which seemed to the unfortunate Norwegians in the places raided to achieve nothing beyond provoking frightful German reprisals. Relations with the Dutch were even worse and led to allegations that the British wanted to destroy the Resistance and that a senior SOE officer was a German agent. These accusations were the outcome of the so-called *Englandspiel*, the penetration by German Intelligence of SOE's networks in the Netherlands. An SOE agent was captured. He sent a pre-arranged coded signal to warn his headquarters in London of his capture and the vulnerability of his communications but London, in breach of its own rules, decided to ignore this warning and assume that the agent had made a mistake and could still be treated as secure. This basic error was repeated and was observed by the Germans who confirmed the illusion by staging bogus acts of sabotage to persuade SOE that its plans were working as intended. As a result all but two of sixty agents sent to the Netherlands were caught and sent to die in concentration camps, enough British equipment to train and arm 10,000 men was intercepted by the Germans, and many arms dumps and agents' networks were uncovered not only in the Netherlands but also in France where brave men and women fell into the hands of the SD.

Disgruntlement arose also from lack of communication and so lack of understanding on both sides. Resistance leaders did not realize that SOE and OSS were the poor relations of the traditional armed services, which tended to regard Resistance movements as amateur sideshows, a drain on

their material and planning resources, an impediment to the more serious
business of conventional campaigning and a distasteful adulteration of
honest fighting with dubious politics. Resistance commanders complained
of being undervalued and undersupplied. They asked in vain to be given
the jobs which Bomber Command thought it could do better, felt bitter
when innocent civilians were killed because a factory which could have
been more easily and more cheaply disrupted by sabotage was attacked
by hundreds of bombers, and blamed the allied organizations with which
they were in touch. They did not know that SOE and OSS frequently
shared their views, nor did they know how limited resources were (for a
year SOE had only two aircraft) nor perhaps how difficult they themselves
were to reach. To take an extreme case: at the beginning of the war Great
Britain had no aircraft with the range necessary to fly to Poland and back
without landing and but for the invention of wireless the Poles' feeling of
abandonment would have been complete. The situation improved with
the arrival in service of the Lancaster and Liberator and the conquest of
air bases in Italy, but even then not many of the latest types of four-
engined bomber could be spared for liaison with the Polish underground,
eastern Poland remained out of reach of the western allies throughout the
war, and Poles never felt satisfied that the British were doing enough to
sustain what they regarded as a substantial arm of the general allied war
effort. Of the operations attempted – 858 in all – only a little over half
were successful. Polish complaints about the scale and purposefulness of
British aid have to be judged against the Poles' own uniquely dangerous
position. Caught in the German-Russian crossfire – and not for the first
time in their history – they witnessed the fearful German onslaught on the
Polish intelligentsia, were vaguely aware of a Nazi plan to deport 16–20
million Poles to Siberia after the war and judged from their experiences in
1939–41 that their treatment at Russian hands would be little less painful.
Their appeals were attuned to their desperation.

Yet despite the mistakes and misunderstandings great and small, and
despite the activities of double agents who were more numerous and more
successful in their special brand of perfidy than the romantic would like
to believe, the combination of Resistance and allied governments was an
appreciable factor in winning the war and is not diminished by the fact
that collaborators were more numerous than resisters. Men and women
of many nations worked together with thrilling trust and courage even
during the periods when the organizations to which they belonged happened to be quarrelling. SOE and OSS provided arms, wireless sets and a
great range of ingenious equipment, invented new weapons and new gad-
gets, found, trained and dispatched thousands of remarkable men and

women. The contribution to Europe's morale was also great. The B BC in particular not only linked the Resistance with Great Britain by providing news, encouragement and coded instructions but also created an *esprit de corps*. The Resistance could have become a separate war, but it did not. It has a special history and a special pride but they are part of the shared experience of the Second World War.

Sharing and cooperating imply communication. By the mid-twentieth century radio had put millions of people in direct touch with one another. In spite of prohibitions on listening, confiscations of radio receivers and jamming, a government could not prevent its people or its conquered subjects from hearing something of what other governments had to say. Radio propaganda became one of the most effective subsidiary weapons of the war. It was used for communicating with friends, keeping their spirits up and concerting active operations against the enemy. It created a sense of presence, or impending presence, which was invaluable between Great Britain and the continent after other normal links had been broken. It also enabled belligerent governments to address each other's peoples in attempts to shake their steadfastness, undermine their morale and generally sow doubt and unease. It was a difficult weapon to use because it was relatively untried and two-edged. On the one hand it provided, like the activities of S O E and O S S, an extra means to attack the enemy's military efficiency. From this point of view any statement which upset the combatants on the other side was useful and it did not essentially matter whether the statement was true or false. Lies, forgeries and rumours were all used in the course of what came to be called black propaganda. Radio programmes supposed to emanate from secret stations in enemy territory – the most famous was *Soldatensender Calais* – spread stories about, for example, how top Nazi bosses were enjoying themselves with blondes and plenty of food and spending more time in specially safe air raid shelters than in visits to the front. Leaflets and forged copies of well-known German newspapers were used in the same way. But the basis of black propaganda was nevertheless credibility, and credibility required a substantial degree of truth. Therefore black propaganda, however much it might embroider the facts, could not do without them. Its basic technique was to retail facts and insert among them one or two tendentious and alarming items. The tricks of the black propagandists (which make particularly entertaining reading in retrospect) were unfailingly ingenious but no more than marginally instrumental in directing the fortunes of war.

For white propaganda on the other hand truth was all important. White propaganda was directed against the enemy's civilian morale rather than his military efficacy. The distinction could on occasions be a fine one, but even in modern warfare there is a dividing line between the civilian and the military factors in the total war effort: white propaganda, like the mass bombing of civilian housing to which we shall come in a later chapter, was an attempt to destroy the enemy's will to fight as opposed to destroying his fighting forces. White propaganda also aimed to swing opinion in occupied Europe.

Neither side was very effective when it tried to subvert the other. German broadcasts to Great Britain were almost entirely ineffectual. British broadcasts to Germany, although much better informed and more imaginative, did not achieve their main object and Goebbels was able, as we shall see, to maintain German morale right to the end and against fearful odds. Suffice it to say here that the BBC's broadcasts to Germany, in which there was an almost dogmatic addiction to truth, were hampered because Goebbels could argue that they were not true. He repeated British bombing claims which the Germans themselves and neutrals could see to be greatly exaggerated and he was able for a time to decry BBC statements by recalling discredited accounts of German atrocities in the First World War and saying that the British were at it again. The BBC was also hampered by mass bombing which, although it had the same aim, proved to be counterproductive in the sphere of morale.

In their propaganda to occupied Europe the British and the Germans had opposite problems. The Germans, who were in occupation, cajoled, impressed and bullied. Their principal advantage was their monopoly of public entertainment and their principal instrument was the film. The British and the Americans, physically at a distance, exploited radio. Their principal advantage was that their audience wanted to believe what they were saying. Fostering and satisfying this desire required them to tell the truth and as the war progressed allied propagandists were in the happy position of having the truth working for them. It remains an open question, debated by psychologists, how far one man can make another act contrary to his basic wishes or instincts. Anti-German propaganda during the war had little effect on Germans for, although it may have penetrated their minds, it did not stir them to action against their leaders. But anti-German propaganda to non-Germans proved its worth.

CHAPTER 14

Revolution in the South-East

NONE of Hitler's European victims fought the war solely with the idea of defeating Germany and getting back to their pre-war circumstances. Even Great Britain, the most conservative of the countries involved, by turning massively to the Labour Party at the end of the war in spite of the risk of seeming ungrateful to an extremely popular national leader, recorded its dissatisfaction with the past. On the continent similar feelings were universal, but they differed greatly from place to place. Broadly speaking there were peoples who wanted to change the institutions under which they lived, if need be by force, and peoples who were content to retain their institutions but wanted to improve what went on within them. Again broadly speaking, it was in eastern Europe that the revolutionary current was strongest, while western Europeans aimed rather at reform – excepting perhaps the French (a case specially difficult to categorize and best considered separately). Thus the war against the Germans and Italians was crossed with civil wars, actual or incipient, whose roots lay in the pre-war past but which developed during the war because wars make men look more critically at their state and accustom them to action in pursuit of political goals.

Norway, Denmark and the Netherlands were relatively stable and united countries. They looked forward to the full restoration of their monarchies and parliamentary institutions. They participated in the war beyond their borders as well as by resistance at home. The Norwegian government had commandeered the Norwegian merchant fleet, 85 per cent of which was outside Norwegian waters at the time of the German invasion; it thus became the largest merchant shipping concern in the world. It was very much in the fight and also comfortably in funds. Contact with Norway was maintained by the so-called Shetland bus which conveyed persons to and from Norway and also several hundred tons of war supplies. Of the smaller but nevertheless appreciable Danish merchant navy over 60 per cent served with the allies. The Dutch also provided fighting men for the allied forces, and the Queen of the Netherlands, who escaped like the King of Norway to London, contributed to the unity and steadfastness of her occupied country by her broadcasts to them.

Belgium's case was superficially different because of its linguistic and racial divisions and because the king became an object of controversy. He was criticized for surrendering himself into captivity instead of accompanying his government to London, he was suspected (unfairly) of undue partiality for the Germans, and his re-marriage during the war was unpopular. The Germans exploited the differences between Flemings and Walloons (as they had done in the First World War) and exacerbated the social tensions in a country in which the monarchy had become a reflection of division instead of a symbol of unity. After the war the king obtained a popular vote of confidence but by so narrow a margin that he found himself obliged to abdicate within a few days of the resumption of his full functions. Yet here too there was no serious challenge to the country's political institutions, other than the monarchy. There was, however, in all four of these countries an intensified concern with social questions. The discussion of such questions was a long-established feature of western European political life, but during the war they became more real when different sorts and conditions of men shared their experiences – in fighting the enemy and helping one another, in receiving the same food rations and facing the same firing squads. War made Europe more egalitarian and more leftward inclined.

In eastern Europe this shift to the left occurred in situations in which social reform was barely conceivable, or at any rate not at all likely, without political revolution. Hence the special importance of the communists with their uninhibited attitude to violent revolution, an importance which is in the first instance distinct from the proximity of these countries to the Soviet Union. In the countries which were allied with Germany – the central strip comprising Hungary, Rumania and Bulgaria – opportunity did not present itself until the Germans and the governments under their protection began to fail, and when the opportunity came it came not to reformist or revolutionary groups but to the Russian conquerors and the account of what happened belongs to the story of the defeat of Germany and not of European Resistance. In Poland and Czechoslovakia too the decisive factor proved to be not an indigenous Resistance movement but Russian power. Czechoslovakia, less in need of reform than Poland and the other countries of eastern Europe, had a moderate government under Beneš which aimed to pursue a broadly based, middle-of-the-road policy in post-war Czechoslovakia and to maintain friendly relations with both Moscow and the western democracies; it succeeded only up to 1948.

The Polish government, established in exile in London, was a right-wing government which feared popular revolution and had every reason to fear the Russians as much as it hated the Germans. Its policy was to wait. It hoped, not unnaturally from its point of view, that the Russians and the Germans would exhaust and maim one another. It aimed therefore to build up a secret army in Poland but not to use it until German and Russian strength had been sapped and the pre-war régime could be restored with British and American help. Still less did it wish to provoke a national rising which would develop on similar lines to Tito's and leave the London government in exile for ever. Resistance to the Germans was therefore discouraged and until mid-point in the war was conducted almost entirely by Polish Jews and escaped Russian prisoners of war.

The secret army, or Home Army (A K), built up by the London government, was an amalgam of remnants of the old Polish army with bands which came into existence under German rule. Some of these bands were socialist, others consisted of right-wing Nationalists, yet others were affiliated to the Peasant Party. The socialists agreed in 1942 to become part of the A K, and the Peasant Party groups, although on the whole more hostile to the A K than friendly to it, accepted its authority the next year. Not all the Nationalist bands joined the A K. Some did so in 1944 after prolonged negotiation; others collaborated with the Germans. There were also left-wing groups which remained separate from the A K. Most of them were socialist and they created a small army of their own in 1944. The Communist Party, which had been harried by pre-war Polish governments and dissolved by Stalin before the war began, was being re-formed by Wladislaw Gomulka but it remained weak until the Russians began to send it arms at the end of 1943. In that year the London government's waiting policy was upset by the military successes of the Russian armies which destroyed the prospect of a long Russo-German bloodletting and also by a peasant rising in eastern Poland where Himmler, having discovered here the homeland of the ancient Burgundians, was creating a pure German colony – with *Volksdeutsche* from Rumania who had forgotten the German language. Owing to the A K's disinclination for risings the credit for supporting this rising against the S S went to the Peasant battalions and also to the communists who were able to score some anti-German successes in one or two areas including the country round Lublin. (Hitler's idea of reviving a Burgundian kingdom for Himmler was a typical piece of Nazi medievalism. Such schemes, although they may be dismissed as ridiculous extravaganzas, testify also to the hold of the romantic past on the German imagination. Historians – specially Treitschke who was as eloquent as he was eminent – had written excitingly about the way the Teutonic Knights had colonized and controlled eastern lands and had fired a new generation with the zeal to go out and do likewise. But Hitler was not unique in his historical romanticism. Roosevelt toyed with the idea of creating 'Wallonia' by putting together parts of Belgium and northern France, Luxembourg, Alsace and Lorraine.)

In south-eastern Europe revolution had freer play. In Greece and Yugoslavia civil war in fact occurred, in Greece hesitantly and ultimately unsuccessfully for the insurgents, in Yugoslavia on a full scale and successfully; in neither with Russian help. Albania, where various Resistance groups united against the Italians but then fell out and started a civil war from which the communists ultimately profited, was shifted from the Italian to the Yugoslav sphere of influence.

In Greece, General Ioannis Metaxas, who had been appointed Prime Minister by the king in 1936 and quickly converted his power into a dictatorship, had been placed in a dilemma by the unsolicited British guarantee of 1939. This guarantee, a promise of aid against Italo-German aggressiveness, ran counter to Metaxas' policy of relying on Hitler to keep Mussolini away. This policy failed when Mussolini attacked without telling Hitler and so forced Metaxas into a fight which he had neither wanted nor foreseen. By responding stoutly to Mussolini's ultimatum he made himself a national hero and temporarily united Greek monarchists and republicans, whose feud was the mainspring of Greek politics. But he was slow to accept British aid, which he did not relish, and his sudden death in January 1941 did not entirely remove the obstacles to British collaboration first against the Italians and subsequently against the Germans.

When the brief German campaigns against Greece and Crete ended, the king and his government had disappeared to Egypt leaving behind a political void which was filled by a pro-Axis puppet government, consisting mostly of generals who not implausibly believed that the war was over and won by the Germans. This government had little authority. The country was divided and roughly, sometimes very roughly, administered by German, Italian and Bulgarian occupiers. Away from the towns guerrilla bands began to form in the hills which constitute so much of Greece and make it unattractive to regular military formations. These bands were all predominantly left-wing and republican. Their members were largely uninterested in or contemptuous of the old struggle between royalists and Venizelist republicans and saw in the exile of its protagonists an opportunity to refashion Greek politics on less sterile lines. Few of them were communists, and at first they gave communism little thought, for it seemed hardly conceivable that the Greek Communist Party could play a leading part in Greek affairs.

Founded shortly after the First World War the Communist Party had

had a difficult row to hoe. It could make little appeal to the peasants, who formed the bulk of the population, because Venizelos had broken up big estates and given the peasants land of their own. Its anti-clericalism was equally lacking in appeal. Even more damning was its advocacy of separate Macedonian and Thracian states, which it had been forced to adopt by the international communist movement and which was regarded by practically all Greeks as the purest treason. After 1936 it was virtually destroyed by one of the few intelligent and sophisticated policemen to be produced by twentieth-century authoritarianism, Constantine Maniadakis, Minister of the Interior under Metaxas. Maniadakis' devices included the creation of a bogus Communist Party under his own wing and the publication of his own edition of the communist newspaper *Rizospastis* to the confusion of all concerned, especially communists. When the war came the party's principal leaders were either in prison or exile. But in the next three years they prepared to take over the country and came within measurable distance of success.

They did this in disguise. They created the National Liberation Front (EAM) which, with its armed bands (ELAS), became the principal symbol of Greek resistance to the occupiers and, carefully suppressing regular communist propaganda, provided the communist leaders with broad popular support on a basis of patriotic nationalism, calls for unity against the enemy and hopes of social reform after the war. Their aim was to establish their organization as the natural successor to the occupiers and the government of post-liberation Greece. There were three threats to this programme: the legitimate government which would try to return from exile; other patriotic Resistance movements which might thrive sufficiently to challenge EAM; and the British who appeared on the scene unexpectedly in order to organize sabotage of Axis lines of supply to North Africa.

The British military mission (it later became Anglo-American) was both an embarrassment and an opportunity. The leaders of EAM and other Resistance groups were ambivalent about waging war on the occupiers. Many of their followers were filled with a patriotic fury which they wanted to vent in action, but harrying the occupiers meant bringing down reprisals on the innocent country people upon whose goodwill the bands relied for sustenance and who were in any case their compatriots. Reprisals were exceedingly fierce. Hostages were taken and executed and whole villages were wiped out; 1,000 people were killed in a single incident at Kalavryta, 250 women and children were burned to death at Klisura. The total number of hostages executed in Greece has been put at 45,000.

In addition the Germans, Italians and Bulgarians executed another 68,000. (But the greatest killer in Greece was famine. Nearly half of the Greeks who died in the war starved.)

The bands had moreover a further reason for avoiding engagements with the occupiers. Each band was suspicious of its neighbours, usually rightly, and did not want to waste its energies and endanger its survival before the day of reckoning which would come when the occupiers withdrew. On the other hand the British mission had arms and golden sovereigns to give away and these precious supplies had to be earned. The price was cooperation with the British against the occupiers. The principal military result was the destruction of the Gorgopotamos railway viaduct, already mentioned – a feat of diplomacy as well as daring, since ELAS and its chief rival EDES were persuaded to work together for the first, and last, time. A joint band of 150 Greeks engaged and destroyed an Italian force while British saboteurs blew up the bridge. Its destruction and the consequent interruption of the German supply line to Africa for a few weeks may have been militarily marginal. On the other hand an accumulation of marginals may be greater than the sum of the parts. Politically the operation had consequences that are easier to define, if contradictory. Its success heartened the Greek communists who began in the next year to construct a major movement of their own. Equally, however, their opponents derived from the same success an assurance of their continued separate existence, thus ensuring that the Greek resistance would not be unified under communist control.

The Anglo-American mission contrived to enlist the bands in further, if separate, activities in 1943 when an extensive railway sabotage plan was put into execution in order to deceive the Germans into expecting an allied landing in Greece rather than Sicily. This plan caused the diversion to Greece of a Panzer division and hampered its return. The Greek communists were also deceived. Thinking that the allies were about to arrive in Greece and that the war was ending, they attacked the anti-communist resistance and so started the first civil war which during the winter of 1943–4 they lost. But their miscalculation was not fatal to them owing to the fortuitous gains which they had already reaped from the Italian surrender to the allies in September 1943. This event gave ELAS all the arms it needed and so made it independent of the Anglo-American mission. It so happened that ELAS predominated in the areas of Italian occupation, and although captured Italian arms were meant to be allocated between all the bands, ELAS was able – as a result of this piece of luck and of some high-paced intrigue – to keep the lot. It became an armed force of about 19,000 effectives, ten times the size of EDES. It had already attacked and destroyed some smaller bands and earlier in 1943 it had captured Colonel Stephanos Saraphis, one of the ablest non-communist leaders, and had persuaded him to become commander-in-chief of ELAS. Saraphis' ready acceptance, which surprised the communists, showed how far ELAS had established itself as the only band worth belonging to. Its most serious rival was EDES, a group formed by the republican Colonel Napoleon Zervas (its repute was later tarnished when it was joined by some shady right-wing characters seeking to escape the stigma of collaboration with the occupiers, and Zervas himself modified his republicanism partly to please Churchill); but EDES was confined to a small region in the west and as early as July 1943, when the allied mission persuaded the bands to sign an agreement establishing a joint headquarters, this was located at ELAS headquarters. From this year onwards the communists were less concerned with their rivals inside Greece than with the Greek government in exile and its army and navy.

The leaders of EAM aimed to sow division in the military and political ranks of the exiles and above all to delay the king's return until they could make it impossible. First mutinies in the Greek army occurred in February 1943. The king broadened his government (in Egypt) to the Left, whereupon a number of royalist officers resigned their commissions in protest. In order to assert its authority the Greek government asked the British to arrest these officers. The net result was a diminution of right-wing influence in the army. The king agreed in July to submit the issue of the monarchy to a referendum after the war but, when pressed also to undertake not to return to Greece before the question had been put to the vote, he refused. In this he was strongly supported by Churchill and Roosevelt. Churchill further advised him to refuse a request from EAM for seats in the government. EAM, influenced perhaps by the news that Great Britain had decided to back Tito and his communists in Yugoslavia and by the false hope that the Italian surrender heralded a general Axis collapse, made its first bid for power and opened operations against rival bands. But EDES survived, the war went on and this premature bid contributed to the ultimate defeat of ELAS by sowing dissension in its own ranks and stimulating the puppet government in Athens to recruit anti-communist security forces.

In March 1944 EAM established a provisional government inside Greece and so formally set up a challenge to the government in exile. In April more mutinies – this time in the navy as well as the army in Egypt – occurred and the conservative Prime Minister, Emmanuel Tsouderos, resigned under pressure from his left-wing colleagues. But his successors were no more able than he had been to control the situation and the

British had to intervene again. Thus the government in exile disintegrated at the same time as EAM had set up a rival to it. But EAM now changed its tactics and instead of insisting on its own creation as the only legitimate government it entered into negotiations for a share in the government in exile which had again been reconstituted under a new Prime Minister, George Papandreou, the political heir of Eleutherios Venizelos. After murdering Colonel Psaros, the leader of a smaller but not inconsiderable band, EAM sent representatives to a conference in Lebanon convoked by Papandreou in order to form a coalition between the exiles and the Resistance organizations. The upshot was a new government which included communists, but some of these feared that Papandreou had outsmarted them and reduced them to a subordinate role instead of the dominant one which they might attain by steering clear of all the politicians in exile. They were, however, under pressure from the Russians to put national and anti-fascist unity before communist power and they even agreed in September that all the bands should be subordinated to the new government and placed under the command of a British general. A few weeks later, in October, when Papandreou and his colleagues moved to Athens on the heels of the retreating Germans, it looked as though he and the British had pre-empted a communist take-over. A small British force followed in December.

But EAM controlled most of Greece outside the capital and in December, very probably on Tito's advice, it reversed its policy and made a second bid for power. (An alternative but less easily acceptable version is that EAM was provoked into hostilities by the British, so that it might be destroyed. There is evidence for the proposition that the shooting in the main square of Athens which opened the fighting was not begun by EAM.) EAM was without outside help. A Russian mission had gone to Greece in 1944 but reported that the Greek communists were not worth helping. In any case Stalin, as he told the Yugoslav communist Edvard Kardelj at the time, was convinced that the Americans would not allow Greece to be taken over by communists. Accordingly he had agreed to allot Greece to Churchill in return for a free hand in Rumania, a bargain which was sealed when the two of them drew up spheres of influence at Moscow in October 1944. EAM was therefore trying to emulate Tito's success in winning power for communists without external aid. It began by attacking EDES, whose forces had to be evacuated by the British to Corfu, and openly assumed control of all Greece except a few islands and a small area in the centre of Athens from which the British could not be dislodged. The British, with tacit Russian support (evinced by the appointment of an Ambassador to the Papandreou government) and in spite of

fierce criticism in the United States and in Great Britain itself, sent reinforcements and defeated the insurrection after six weeks' fighting. ELAS
was not trained for regular as opposed to guerrilla fighting and its political
leaders were probably divided: in some parts of Greece ELAS did not go
over to the offensive and there were still those who preferred the tactics of
coalition to a coup. The failure of the insurrection was accompanied by
communist atrocities which left an indelible mark on a whole generation
of Greeks.

In the face of these events Churchill compelled the king to delay his
return until it could be legitimated *de novo* by a plebiscite. The archbishop
of Athens was appointed regent while the British defeated EAM and
negotiated a truce. A year later, in March 1946, the royalists scored
heavily in elections and six months afterwards King George II was summoned back by a popular vote of more than two to one in his favour. The
communists then renewed their insurrection with help from Yugoslavia,
Bulgaria and Albania. They were not defeated until 1949 when the re-
equipment and training of the Greek army by the Americans and the
defection of Yugoslavia from the communist block sealed their fate. The
communist domination of EAM and ELAS, the bitterness engendered
by the atrocities of 1944 and the subsequent onset of the Cold War altered
the nature of the political and social struggle which many Greeks had
taken to the hills to prosecute in the early days of the war. For Greece the
Second World War was an opportunity for change which came and went.
Greeks who wanted social change but not communism discovered that
they could have both or neither.

One of the many differences between the Greek and Yugoslav Resistance movements was the appearance in Yugoslavia of a commanding
figure, Josip Broz, later known to all the world as Tito. No national
Resistance fighter inside occupied Europe achieved anything approaching
his eminence; outside it only de Gaulle surpassed him. He possessed
courage, tenacity, intelligence, personal authority, and organizing experience gained in Moscow and the Spanish civil war (though he did not
actually go to Spain). He created the independent communist state of
Yugoslavia. He was helped by the divisions and weaknesses of his political
adversaries at home, by the disorders of the times, by the terrain of his
country and by outsiders – notably the British and Americans and to a
small extent the Russians – but of all the elements in his victory his own
personality was the outstanding one.

A second major difference between Yugoslavia and Greece was the fact
that Tito fought his enemies during the war instead of waiting. This policy
brought him into conflict with the other principal Resistance figure, Draza

Mihailovič, and eventually earned him the support of the western allies who had begun by backing Mihailovič.

Mihailovič was the accredited representative in Yugoslavia of the government in exile, which conferred on him the rank of general and the titles of Commander-in-Chief and Minister for War. He was also early in the field. But he failed to become a national leader for two main reasons: he was not truly national and he refused to lead. He was an impassioned Serb rather than a Yugoslav, as compared with Tito who, although half Croat and half Slovene, insisted on Serb-Croat cooperation and a federated Yugoslav state. Mihailovič too was reluctant to court disaster for his movement and reprisals for his compatriots by embarking on large-scale operations before the Germans were weakened by outside events. He and his followers, who were called *četniks* and were mainly former Serb army officers, were ready to undertake limited daring exploits but they had no thought of starting a national rising such as was in the minds and in the teaching of communist leaders. Mihailovič aimed to re-create a regular army against the day of German withdrawal and meanwhile, isolated exploits apart, to wait. In the course of waiting his hostility to Tito and to communism developed to the point where he opted for collaboration with Yugoslavia's national enemies in order to save it from communism. And in so adjusting his priorities, he destroyed himself.

The beginnings of the communist Resistance movement were small but professional and immediate. Tito began to organize resistance as soon as the Germans invaded Yugoslavia and in spite of the fact that Stalin was at that time still one of Hitler's allies. He himself moved from Zagreb to Belgrade in May 1941 and was ready with a call for action by the end of June when the German armies attacked the USSR. He had the beginnings of regional organizations, sabotage plans and groups of followers who, although critically short of arms, included some three hundred veterans of the war in Spain. They inherited the traditions of the *hajduks*, heroes like the pig-breeder Karadjordje who had become the leader of the Serb revolt of 1804 against the Turks and the founder of the modern Serbian state. Although the Communist Party was small (it had about 12,000 full members in 1941) it had non-communist contacts and sympathizers as a result of following the Popular Front policy adopted by the Comintern in 1935. By the autumn of 1941 these partisan groups had grown strong enough to undertake operations in Serbia and establish a headquarters at Užice where they ran an arms factory and a printing press. These successes led to discussions for joint operations with the *četniks* (some of whom were being attracted to the communist side), and until attacked by the *četniks* the partisans supplied the *četniks* with arms from their Užice factory. Mihailovič, however, had been directed by the government in exile, whose grasp of the situation was naturally imperfect, to assume command over the communist partisans. This Tito was neither prepared nor obliged to accept in spite of chidings from Moscow whence Stalin, anxious above all for allied cooperation, was urging him to forget about communist revolution for the time being and concentrate on a common anti-Axis front with all friends of the western allies. Fighting broke out between *četniks* and partisans. The *četniks* tried but failed to evict the partisans from Užice and suffered a series of defeats. These events eliminated all possibility of cooperation and induced Mihailovič to accept arms from the Italians to continue the struggle. The immediate gain went to the Germans who took the opportunity to clear Serbia of all Resistance groups.

In the following year the partisans were hard pressed by the Germans and Italians. Hitler had become aware of their potential danger, and they were forced to suspend operations and seek refuge in the mountains of Bosnia and Montenegro. A number defected. But thanks to Tito's leadership, reinforced by the professionalism of the Spanish war veterans and of former officers of the Yugoslav army who joined the partisans, the movement survived, recuperated and re-emerged as a well-ordered army of four brigades. It also began to assume the functions of a civil administration in the areas which it controlled, fixing prices and decreeing social changes as well as keeping order. In November 1942 an Assembly at Bihac foreshadowed the partisans' claim to become the government of Yugoslavia.

In 1943, when their strength had risen to about 20,000, they were attacked by forces about six times as large, lost half their equipment and a quarter of their men killed in battle or massacred afterwards, but they escaped once more from Bosnia to Montenegro in the spring and back from Montenegro to Bosnia in the summer. Their losses were all the more grievous because the wounded either died or had to be shot until this grim and tragic burden was relieved by British medical supplies and a medical airlift to British hospitals in Italy. Their enemies in these operations were a combination of Germans, Italians, Bulgarians, *četniks* and *ustachi*. (The last were organized brigades of toughs who clustered round Pavelič's court in Croatia in an atmosphere described by Ciano as 'cowboy'. They massacred Serbs and Jews on a scale which horrified most other Croats; hated the Orthodox church and the Cyrillic alphabet with pathological intensity; and became so corrupt that even Pavelič felt constrained to have two of their leaders shot.)

A few months after their defeat in Montenegro the fortunes of the partisans were transformed by the general Italian collapse. They gained control of most of Croatia including the Dalmatian coast and islands, seized large quantities of Italian arms and were able to recruit and equip an army of 250,000. They were now a formidable force, a nation in arms, and at the end of the year Tito was proclaimed Marshal of Yugoslavia and President of the Council for the Liberation, which was in effect an interim government. The king's return was to be conditional on a plebiscite in his favour.

For much of this time the outside world knew little about what was going on in Yugoslavia. A first British mission arrived in Montenegro in September 1941 with the dual purpose of getting information and giving such help as could be spared from the scant resources available in North Africa. It was assumed that help would go to Mihailović, for although the British were already aware of the country's internal dissensions, they clung to the hope that Mihailović could unite all opposition to Germans and Italians. Towards the end of the year a British officer who had visited the headquarters of both Mihailović and Tito advised that no help should be delivered to the former pending the outcome of talks which were then going on between the two (Tito was receiving no aid at this date), but this advice was not followed and Great Britain, partly out of loyalty to the Yugoslav government in London which was an ally, decided to build up Mihailović by broadcast propaganda and military aid. Then for a year all communication between the British authorities and their man in Yugoslavia was cut by Mihailović. Among the British counsels were divided, as SOE in London continued to repose in Mihailović a faith which SOE in Cairo no longer held, but by the end of 1942 Ultra revealed (to the select few entitled to see it) that the two leaders were fighting one another and, during 1943, that Mihailović was collaborating with the Italians and then with the Germans also. Further emissaries sent to Yugoslavia, owing to the growing importance of the Balkans in overall strategy, told the same story and when the reconciliation which the British (and the Russians) desired was shown to be plainly impossible Great Britain decided to drop Mihailović and his friends in London (who did not disown him until August 1944) and support Tito. This reversal of policy was influenced by the delayed discovery that Tito could be much more useful than Mihailović (thus confirming simultaneous Russian arguments that Mihailović had become no better than a collaborationist) and by the coincidence that a British mission to Tito in May 1943 arrived during a great battle in which 20,000 partisans, although defeated, proved that they were a disciplined army under skilled command and not a random collection of guerrilla bands. This engagement also provided first hand proof of the *četniks'* collaboration with the Germans as well as the Italians.

From this point aid to Tito became the largest item in the Anglo-American aid programme. A naval and air base was established on the island of Vis with a small naval detachment and a squadron of Hurricanes. Another air base was opened at Bari for operations in the Balkans. Yugoslav pilots and tank crews were trained in Egypt, and Yugoslav prisoners in Italy were collected and formed into a Yugoslav legion. Yugoslav wounded were flown to hospitals in Italy. Great quantities of equipment were sent to Tito, mainly by the Americans – 100,000 rifles, 50,000 machine and sub-machine guns, 1,380 mortars, 630,000 grenades, 700 wireless sets, 175,000 uniforms, 260,000 pairs of shoes. (The first Russian supplies did not arrive until April 1944.) When the Germans launched another major offensive against the partisans in May 1944, allied air forces came to their support, flying 1,000 sorties a day. Later in the year these air forces cooperated with the partisans in attacks on the Germans' lines of communication and harassed their retreat – in spite of Tito's suspicions that this cooperation was intended to pave the way for an allied occupation of the Balkans. In London King Peter dismissed Mihailovič and instructed the *četniks* to put themselves under Tito's command, but Tito made it clear to Churchill that the king could not return unless recalled by a plebiscite. Mihailovič made a final bid to retrieve his fortunes by an understanding with Pavelič, but the partisans engulfed all opposition and on 20 October 1944 they entered Belgrade. The Russians who had entered the country as allies from the north-east departed again (in accordance with a prior agreement between Stalin and Tito) and Tito ruled unchallenged. For nearly four years the Germans had been obliged to hold down Yugoslavia by force of arms instead of ruling it indirectly through complacent nominees. After the Italian collapse this necessity had cost them a standing force of fifteen divisions. Most of these were German, although they had some help from Bulgarians, *četniks* and the puppet régime in Belgrade. As the Russians advanced in central Europe the main concern of the Germans was the Russian front bearing down on Yugoslavia from the north-east but their troubles were increased and their forces distracted by the guerrilla fighters who had engineered a national uprising. The human cost to Yugoslavia was a population almost precisely decimated.

The final stage in the transfer of power to the communists was accompanied by some transient formalities. In an attempt to save the monarchy Great Britain forced King Peter to appoint a new Prime Minister, Dr Ivan Subasič, who went to Yugoslavia and concluded in December 1944 an agreement with Tito which provided for an interim regency and a parliament containing pre-1941 parliamentarians (provided they had not collaborated with the enemy) as well as members of the wartime communist assembly. A provisional government, formed in March with Tito at its head, included leaders of other parties, but they did not last long and before the end of the year the monarchy too was formally abolished after elections which the communists could hardly fail to win and did win. Yugoslavia had become a communist state and an independent one, the first since 1917. In this its war fortunes were unique, although the establishment of other communist states in eastern Europe at this time led many people to confound Yugoslavia with these under the generic name of satellites.

CHAPTER 15
France

FRANCE suffered during the decade which ended in 1940 two collapses which opened two debates. The spectacular collapse of France as a fighting force in 1940 was preceded by the collapse of the Republic itself, a collapse as complete as the collapse of the Weimar republic but unperceived; for although the symptoms of political and social disintegration were apparent and discussed, their full import did not become clear until the catastrophe of 1940 tore away the veil of illusion and showed that the Third Republic was no longer there. At this point Vichy took, temporarily, the place of the Republic. In the years before, France had become a vacuum governed by a *vis inertiae* deputizing for political institutions.

The failure of these institutions in the thirties was marked by parliamentary instability, by the growth of anti-parliamentary forces and by one significant but abortive attempt to arrest the drift of governmental incapacity. The political parties in the Third Republic were numerous, weak, young (none was as old as the republic itself or could even boast a foundation date earlier than the twentieth century) and usually unable to combine to produce positive programmes or policies. They combined in narcissistic and unproductive unions whose main effect was to keep Ministers in Ministries. This vacuity brought parliamentary democracy into contempt and encouraged the anti-parliamentarianism of those still unreconciled to the revolution of 1789 and of a more modern fascist brand, so that the republic was assailed from without at the same time as it was decomposing within. Both menaces were laid bare by a scandal which began, within a year of Hitler's seizure of power, with the suicide of a financial crook called Stavisky in January 1934. It continued with accusations against Ministers of complicity in Stavisky's swindles and against the police of hushing up the scandals and murdering witnesses, and it culminated in anti-government demonstrations which turned into drilled fascist riots. At this time various fascist and other right-wing leagues had a combined enrolled membership of about half a million and the sympathies of many times that number. At the centre of the storm was the Radical Socialist Party which was the pivot about which French politics turned.

The destruction of the Radicals would mean the destruction of the parliamentary system because the Radicals, as the centre party, were a *sine qua non* of any parliamentary coalition and because the party had personified the Third Republic almost from its inception. The Radicals were now, in the 1930s, the chief targets for charges of corruption and incompetence. Their lack of competence was partly a result of their position. They never won enough seats to form a stable one-party government and they found it difficult to make up their minds between alliance with socialists or conservatives. They had inherited a left-wing tradition of which they remained conscious and proud, but they had been moving steadily to the Right in their social outlook and their political programmes. Their inclination was to prefer the socialists, but the socialists were reluctant to join in government for fear of being outbid in the constituencies by the communists, from whom they had split off as a minority group in 1919. The socialists therefore resorted to the common but pernicious device of French parties of pledging support to another party but refusing to share office and responsibility – and then withdrawing their support, often sooner rather than later. These tactics, which the communists were to use against the socialists and Radicals in 1936, exposed all Left-inclined Radical governments to impermanence and eventually split the socialists themselves between those who wanted to give more support to the Radicals or less. The Radicals too were split between left- and right-wing groups, each hankering after a different kind of coalition. Further to the Right were a number of conservative parties, some more parliamentary and others more authoritarian.

The riots of 1934 had some cathartic effect and after an interlude of emergency 'national' government under Gaston Doumergue the socialist leader Léon Blum succeeded in creating a Popular Front stretching from communists to Radicals which, after an electoral victory in May 1935, took over the government with the hope of achieving parliamentary stability and social and economic reform. But the communists refused to join the government and displayed a chequered loyalty to it. A number of social reforms were introduced but Blum's administration was never able to concentrate attention, as its chief would have liked, on these overdue matters. The need to rearm absorbed funds required for social improvement and in 1936 the outbreak of civil war in Spain placed Blum in a dilemma from which he was unable to escape.

The Spanish government, also a Popular Front, appealed for help and Blum at first promised to give it, but his Radical colleagues represented middle-class Frenchmen who were afraid of the communist element on the government side in Spain and did not want to help it. Blum also feared that he could not count on the civil service or the armed forces and that, at the worst, he might even be risking civil war in France if he took sides actively in the civil war in Spain. Furthermore, the British government wanted to keep out and so Blum was forced by the balance of political power within France and by his principal ally to refuse help to the Spanish Popular Front. In June 1937, after little more than a year in office, his government was ousted by the Senate which had little liking for the Prime Minister's reforms and what they would cost the more prosperous sections of the bourgeoisie. A second Popular Front government was formed under a Radical Prime Minister with Blum as his deputy and the communists in undisguised opposition. This government was a Popular Front only in name. In substance it was a return to the old Radical-dominated merry-go-round and it was not long before the socialists quitted it. Blum did not so much fail to give France government and reform as demonstrate the impossibility of doing so. Long before 1936 the opposition to reform had become too strong to beat. His administration also gave a sharper edge to the danger of civil war in France as people gathered in the streets to shout: Better Hitler than Blum; and meant it. For Blum, personally an exceptionally generous as well as an exceptionally clear-minded man, was hated for what he stood for – social justice – and for what he was – a Jew.

The collapse of the political fabric of the Third Republic was not unwelcome to many Frenchmen but the collapse of its armies was a shock to all. There had been a feeling of weakness in France for a decade, but few had realized the closeness of the connection between social malaise and military impotence. The weakness of France was in any case puzzling. It was not the natural weakness of a small country like Denmark, but weakness embedded in strength. France continued to manifest, throughout the period between the wars, a vigorous artistic, scientific and cultural life, nationally and internationally renowned, and possessed not only one of the largest armies in the world but also one of the largest bank balances. Yet France was uneasy and pessimistic. The pessimism went deep. It came from the feeling that there were not enough Frenchmen. Between Waterloo (1815) and Sedan (1870) the population of France had risen from 30 to 36 million, while that of the hereditary enemy, Great Britain, had doubled from 13 to 26 million and the Prussia of 11 million had become the Germany of 41 million. During the 1930s the marriage rate in France was halved and the death rate overtook the birth rate. The annual call-up, which had produced 600,000 men in 1914, produced only 240,000 in 1936 and was then again halved in the next four years. The economic scene was as dismal as the demographic. The French theory of government required the National Assembly, as the embodiment of the sovereignty of the people, to be master of the executive, and the French political system

contributed to the relative weakness of the executive power by proliferat-
ing numerous and undisciplined parties, none of which was capable of
forming a government on its own. The resulting coalitions did not dare to
affront the voters and since France was still a country of small farmers
and small businessmen the voters to whom governments kowtowed were
principally this section of the community. The kowtowing took the form
of not imposing unpopular taxes and trying to find alternative sources
of money for state expenditure. French insistence on war reparations from
Germany was partly a consequence of this search, and when the reparations did not materialize governments resorted instead to unbalanced
budgets and borrowing, devices which undermined confidence at home
and abroad in the French economy and the capacity of the politicians to
run it. In universities and schools the prevailing tone of the twenties and
thirties was cynical – and the influence of intellectuals was in France
pronounced. No less pervasive was the attitude of the lesser bourgeoisie,
which noted with alarm the fact that production was static. In external
affairs the bloodiest war ever fought on French soil had been followed by
disenchantment and disillusion. The attitudes represented by the massive
figure of Clemenceau and the forceful policy of the Ruhr occupation of
1923 passed away. They were succeeded by disinvolvement and pacifism,
especially among ex-combatants and those who might be expected to
continue the warrior caste, with the result that the Munich settlement of
1938 was greeted with relief and the mobilization of 1939 accepted with
reluctance. But the ignominious collapse of 1940 was nevertheless an
unforeseen humiliation.

Hence arose the two questions which occupied Frenchmen during the
next few years. Who was to blame for these collapses, and what was to
take the place of what had collapsed?

The first answers were provided by Vichy because Vichy was, at first,
a fact in a country where most facts seemed to have vanished. Vichy
answered that it was all the fault of the parliamentarians of the Third
Republic, especially the left wing, and that their place was now filled by
Vichy. The history of France in the next few years is the story of the
rejection of these answers.

The Vichy régime was the parent and the child of the armistice. The
armistice was demanded by the generals, Weygand and Pétain, who dominated the last days and the last cabinets of the Third Republic and who
showed themselves less stout than some of their civilian colleagues. The
last President of the Republic, Albert Lebrun, appointed Pétain Prime
Minister on the advice of his predecessor Paul Reynaud, who resigned
because there was nothing else he could do. Pétain and Weygand, who

notoriously had never agreed about anything else in the course of their long lives, insisted on an armistice for political as well as military reasons, and Vichy was therefore from the start a politically defined and not a national régime. The military reasons were no doubt compelling, for the army had been defeated, but the defeat of the army was something more than a military event. It raised also the spectre of revolution, and the generals felt it their duty to preserve the army to prevent revolution. Nor were they eccentric in taking this view. Vichy may not have represented the broadest national consensus but its aims were widely sensed as sound preservative medicine: to retain the French empire by abandoning the fight, to gain for France an independent place in the German New Order, to mitigate and survive enemy occupation by judicious collaboration and to safeguard the traditions of France by firmly suppressing the degenerative forces of internal change. In order to achieve these aims the generals capitulated and agreed to set up a new government covering in effect only one third of France and to pay German occupation costs (which initially were nine times as much as the sums required of Germany under the Dawes Plan). Vichy left vague for the time being the extent of military, economic and political collaboration which would be needed in order to secure these aims. Like Hitler, Vichy did not foresee a long war or the demands that such a war would make.

The head of the new régime, and its symbol, was Pétain. Born during the Crimean War and taught his catechism by a veteran of Napoleon's *Grande Armée*, Pétain had been on the verge of retirement with the rank of colonel after a career that had been neither distinguished nor undistinguished, when the outbreak of the First World War opened the doors of immortality to him. At the end of that war he was one of half a dozen Marshals of France who were world famous – all of whom he then proceeded comfortably to outlive. His particular fame rested on two things: he had saved France at Verdun in 1916 and he had shown an unaccustomed humanity in the face of mutiny, preferring to decorate soldiers who had done well than shoot those who had failed. In person he was dignified, calm, unpretentious; in politics, so far as was known, he was detached, so much so that the Left trusted him as the sort of general who would not lend himself to coups; in religion he was a Roman Catholic but not a pronounced one like Weygand, a poor church-goer and married (at sixty-five) to a divorcée. He seemed the type of figure who could be relied on to do the right thing in a crisis.

From 1921 to 1931 he was vice-chairman of the Council of War and so Commander-in-Chief designate if war came, and he remained a member of the Council after 1931 because in France, as elsewhere, old Marshals never died professionally so long as there was breath in their bodies. Although succeeded in the vice-chairmanship by Weygand and, after 1935, by Gamelin he remained a potent figure and his continuing availability was emphasized when, after the fascist riots in Paris in 1934, he was made Minister of War in the Doumergue government at the age of seventy-eight – a military dugout called in to support a political back number. After a brief spell as Ambassador in Madrid, to which post he was appointed at the age of eighty-one, he returned to the centre of things in time to be present at the culminating crisis of 1940. In retrospect there is an element of slyness in the way he managed to be half a spectator and half a participant in the fall of France, observing in private conversation that Gamelin was incapable but refusing to give his opinion to the Prime Minister who, for all Pétain cared, might find out for himself. When the crash came he was stationed somewhere between the centre of the stage and the wings, so that only half a step was needed to carry him to the leadership of the nation.

At first the nation was on the whole relieved to have him. He was old but he had extraordinary physical fitness. He carried round with him a part of the glory of France at a time when this commodity was in short supply, especially in political circles. He was respected, if not vociferously popular; he was liked by the poorer people because he had been a soldiers' soldier as well as a Marshal of France. He had stood firm once before – *ils ne passeront pas* – and standing firm was again the vital need. He had never done anything blatantly wrong. What was wrong was concealed. He was vain as well as old and his physical fitness was beginning to be offset by declining mental powers. He was a narrow-minded, authoritarian reactionary and although his inertia created the impression that the sins of Vichy should be attributed to his entourage rather than to himself the pattern of Vichy was a reflection and emanation of his own ideas.

Vichy did not regard itself as a merely passive régime guarding France from its external enemies so long as the war lasted. No less than the Resistance movements, which opposed and eventually defeated it, Vichy had positive and revolutionary policies which were intended to transform France lastingly. The only thing that Vichy regarded as temporary about itself was its capital, which it had chosen in preference to Paris in order to keep a certain distance between itself and German headquarters (and possibly the Parisians too). This spa of 25,000 inhabitants in the Auvergne, famous for repairing the stomachs and livers of those who had lived too long or too hard in the colonies, could serve as a capital because the government would soon move back to Paris. But the government's work need not wait upon its move. Laws and decrees poured out. Besides dealing with the immediate post-defeat problems of refugees, unemployment and rationing, Vichy charted what it called a National Revolution. Full powers to govern by decree – powers more ample than those possessed by Louis XIV but, in the eyes of reactionaries, none the worse for that – were bestowed on Pétain as head of state, and the sufferings and humiliations of France were declared to be the essential pre-condition for national regeneration through the cultivation of the basic virtues and values of labour, family life and patriotism. This, the conservative in contradistinction to the radical way to salvation, was the core of Vichy's ideology. (But Vichy did not succeed in monopolizing it. Gaullism heeded it too: after the liberation a film by Marcel Pagnol, *La Fille du Puisatier*, made to extol Pétain and Vichy's cultural revolution, continued to be shown with little alteration to extol the spirit of Gaullism.)

Vichy's constitutional revolution was the work chiefly of Pierre Laval who was ultimately to be the principal scapegoat for the Vichy régime. Laval was an ex-socialist, an ex-parliamentarian, many times a Minister of the Third Republic, a man of humble origins and markedly un-aristocratic appearance, a decidedly clever man but not a broadly intelligent one, a political manipulator of the first rank but one inclined to mistake his own astuteness for achievement. When Pétain, Weygand and their supporters in Reynaud's cabinet brought the war to a stop, Laval appeared to talk deputies into giving the new government legitimacy and plenary powers and so changed the nature of the state which Pétain was to guide. By assiduous and insidious lobbying among the flotsam and jetsam of the Third Republic which accumulated at Bordeaux and then at Vichy, Laval got these representatives of legitimacy to turn Pétain, whom he mistook for a mere figurehead, into an autocrat. The state still contained a Senate and a Chamber of Deputies but they could only meet upon being summoned by Pétain and Pétain had no intention of convoking them. The Vichy government operated through a series of committees whose activities contrasted with the impassivity of the Marshal and so gave the erroneous impression that Pétain reigned but did not rule and ought therefore not to be blamed for all the enormities committed in his name. Thus arose the Vichy myth of the martyr Pétain, beset by the conquerors of France on the one side and its political riffraff on the other, but preserving its dignity and its honour by his personal bearing.

Democracy and civil liberties were quickly abolished. Besides suppressing parliamentary rule at the centre Vichy decreed that local councils should be appointed and not elected except in communes with fewer than 2,000 inhabitants. Trade unions were disbanded and political parties forbidden. The judiciary lost its independence. Public officials became liable to arbitrary dismissal by the head of state and 2,000 were purged in Vichy's first six months. Those who remained in office had to take an oath of personal loyalty to Pétain. New laws were given retroactive effect so that people could be tried and condemned for doing things which had been lawful when done. They could also be tried and condemned for their opinions or for merely associating with persons who had fallen foul of the authorities. Prefects were empowered to arrest, without charge, anybody whom they judged to be imperilling the security of the state. By 1942 there were 80,000 in prisons or concentration camps. Their conditions were so appalling that some prisoners were reduced to eating the straw in their palliasses and in some prisons there were a hundred deaths for every one that had occurred before the war. Certain categories of person were deprived of the protection of the law. Vichy was profoundly anti-semitic and defined a Jew more strictly even than the Nuremberg decrees of the Third Reich: a woman with only two Jewish grandparents became a Jew if she married a Jew. Vichy's anti-semitism was more national and religious and less racial than Hitler's. It asserted the unassimilability of the Jew to French society and regarded him therefore as a threat to the coherence of that society, but it admitted that French-born Jews who had fought for France had become, by the baptism of blood, French rather than Jewish. The first anti-semitic laws were promulgated in October 1940. All Jews were excluded from the public service, from teaching and from positions of authority in industry and the press, radio and cinema. Foreign Jews – including Algerian Jews who were deprived of their French nationality – became liable to internment. Existing laws against libelling racial and religious minorities were repealed. A second batch of anti-semitic laws in June 1941 aryanized Jewish businesses. The owners, who had been promised in 1940 that they would not be deprived of their possessions, received inadequate compensation or none.

Vichy's national mystique did not stop at Jews. All foreigners and all persons with foreign fathers were made ineligible for the public service, and all naturalizations since 1927 became subject to review. This cleansing of the nation was reinforced by educational reform. Pétain was almost obsessively interested in education and had aspired at one time to become Minister of Education. He regarded education as a branch of morals rather than learning and he regarded physical exercises as the basis of sound morality. The body took precedence over the mind; sound thinking, as opposed to dangerous thinking, could be induced by setting all French children on the road to that physical fitness which characterized the Marshal himself; loose thinking meant morally faulty rather than intellectually untidy thinking. Therefore every child in a primary school had to do ten hours of physical training a week and this quota was reduced by only one hour in the secondary school. The rest of education consisted preponderantly of instruction about God and patriotic duties and Greek and Latin. In line with conventional Roman Catholic teaching Pétain, like Hitler, believed that woman's place was in the home and her purpose childbearing. Divorce was made more difficult, large families were encouraged, women could only get marriage grants upon undertaking not to go out to work, and abortion became not only a criminal but a capital offence. The family was the elemental institution in a collectivist scheme of things which denied the value of the individual. Pétain himself said that there was 'no creative virtue' in individualism and he regarded French society as a large family to be ruled firmly by himself and to some extent by God.

Pétain's Vichy was a reactionary, authoritarian, Roman Catholic, chauvinist, corporatist state, but it was other things as well. Pétain was both a comfort to conservatives of all kinds in need of a father figure and a gift to an assortment of extremists who were looking for a stalking horse. Consequently Vichy became an *omnium gatherum* of anti-republican and anti-progressive forces which attracted pro-German and pro-Nazi Frenchmen and uncommitted opportunists. It gave scope to the most diverse personages. There was Jacques Doriot, the ex-communist bully who had been in German pay for a number of years before the war; Joseph Darnand, whose followers were required to swear an oath to fight 'democracy, Gaullist dissidence and the leprosy of Jewry', whose *milice* was merged with the *Waffen SS*, who commanded a French SS expeditionary force on the Russian front in 1943 and who returned as Secretary-General for the Maintenance of Order, in which capacity he made the *milice* even more feared and hated than the SD; the anti-German, monarchist publicist Charles Maurras who set up as a sort of ideologist for Vichy; and, from 1943, the Bourbon claimant, the Comte de Paris, who went to Vichy with an eye perhaps to Pétain's job but was fobbed off by Laval with an offer of a minor post and later declared himself a Gaullist. The most pro-German of French right-wing leaders, Marcel Déat, preferred Paris to Vichy, against which he kept up a steady flow of criticism. Many French fascists disliked Pétain.

In external affairs Vichy had no choice. It was compelled to collaborate with Germany. Its options were limited to the degree and manner of collaboration, and within this narrow field the most important person was Laval. On 11 June 1940, Pétain issued the first of his Constitutional Acts which, with the disdain of grammar characteristic of monarchs, opened with the words '*Nous, Philippe Pétain . . .*' and appointed him

Chief of State. The office of President was by implication abolished. By succeeding Constitutional Acts, issued on the same day, Pétain gave himself plenary powers in the appointment of Ministers and civil servants, in legislation, budgeting and finance, in the control of the armed forces, and in the making of treaties. He might also declare a state of emergency but he might not declare war. The Senate and Chamber remained in being but were prorogued and might be recalled only by Pétain. By a further Act on the next day Pétain nominated Laval as his successor. Laval became therefore the Caliph to Pétain's Mahomet, and since Pétain was much older than Mahomet had ever been, Laval might regard himself as the real manipulator of the totalitarian powers with which, largely by his own efforts, Pétain was invested.

To Laval there was nothing shocking about the idea of collaborating with Germany. He had long been a champion of a Franco-German entente. He had been in politics since before the First World War, had been Prime Minister of France before Hitler came to power in Germany, and like many Frenchmen of his generation he saw European politics in terms of Franco-German conflict or agreement; and he preferred the latter. He observed the American disengagement from Europe after 1919 and he regarded the British with their extra-European empire as but dubious partners in Europe. He was not pro-German in the enthusiastic way in which some Frenchmen admired German achievements in the arts and politics, but as a political realist he desired a Franco-German understanding and wished to promote it sooner rather than later because he accepted the general view that, in relation to Germany, France would continue to become demographically and industrially the weaker. Italy he regarded as a natural and useful third member of the entente. As Prime Minister in 1931 he wished to settle the issues of reparations and disarmament in order to clear the way for a triple entente which, had he achieved it, would have anticipated the post-war cooperation of Robert Schuman, Konrad Adenauer and Alcide de Gasperi.

He was out of office from the beginning of 1932 until October 1934 when he succeeded Barthou as Foreign Minister. During this interval Hitler had become Chancellor in Germany. Laval had therefore a choice between persevering with his German policy or dropping it and reverting to the classical French policy of alliance with Russia against Germany which Barthou had been pursuing. Laval chose to persevere because his Franco-German vision of Europe still made sense to him – as it still did after 1940. His anti-communism, which was pronounced, pointed in the same direction and although he continued his predecessor's negotiations with Moscow he did so only in order to have an alternative policy to fall back on – and he even told the German Ambassador in Paris that this was his reason. The Ethiopian crisis wrecked his policy but did nothing to alter his belief in it.

In the summer of 1940 France, although decisively and humiliatingly defeated, still counted in the European balance, the more so because of its overseas colonies. Hitler had a vague plan for an anti-British, continental block which would include France as well as Italy and Spain; in such a block the French colonies could be strategically more useful to him than anything which Mussolini or Franco had to offer. German and French military chiefs seriously debated joint operations in Africa for the recovery of colonies which defected to de Gaulle and the transfer of British colonies to France. But Hitler was indecisive and half-hearted about cooperation with France. He himself and a number of his principal colleagues disliked the French and distrusted Laval personally. At Vichy the men round Pétain were also divided and uncertain; some agreed with Laval's policy of making the best obtainable bargain with a securely dominant Germany, while others cherished a lingering hope that Germany might fail to defeat Great Britain and believed that a British victory was not only possible but also better for France. Laval moreover discovered that Pétain was no mere puppet. This was not only a surprise and a disappointment but also a severe handicap since the two men had very little in common. There was life in the old Marshal yet and in December 1940 he showed it by dismissing Laval.

Laval's fall did not mean an end to the collaborationist policy. Pétain disliked Laval's pretensions rather than his policies. The Marshal's distrust of his deputy was also exploited by some of Laval's colleagues who were afraid that Laval might worm his way into the Marshal's confidence to their own discomfiture. For a couple of months it was not clear who was Laval's successor. It might be Pierre-Étienne Flandin, another leading politician of the Third Republic and a sincere admirer of much that Germany had produced through the ages, or it might be Jean Darlan, the anti-British admiral who was moved less by respect for Germany than by anger over the British attack on his ships at Mers-el-Kebir. In February Darlan was appointed Deputy Prime Minister and Foreign Minister and, the next day, Pétain's successor; a few days later he was Minister of the Interior too, and a week later still a cabinet reshuffle which excluded Flandin and other Vichy notables confirmed Darlan's pre-eminence. But Darlan's collaboration soon went too far for Pétain who, having got France out of the war on one side, was determined not to re-enter it on the other. In May 1941 Darlan negotiated with the Germans a series of protocols by which France would provide extensive facilities and war material in the Middle East in connection with the revolt of Rashid Ali in Iraq and would give the Germans free harbour and railway facilities in Tunisia and permit the harbour and airfield at Dakar to become German bases. Since the routes between Bizerta and Europe were to be protected by the French navy, Darlan was not only sanctioning active military cooperation in the Middle East but also upsetting the most delicate and contentious element in the French surrender: the undertaking to Great Britain not to allow the French fleet to join the Axis. Pétain refused to endorse Darlan's policy and demoted the admiral from his high position in the state.

Equally, however, Pétain refused to be lured back into the war on the allied side. From January 1941 Roosevelt had in Vichy as his Ambassador and personal representative Admiral William D. Leahy, whose task was at first to keep French aid to Germany down to a minimum by arguing that the war was far from over and that Hitler was going to lose it, and by supplying France with food and other necessaries. In 1942 Roosevelt went further and sent a secret emissary to entice Weygand into bringing the French in North Africa over to the allies in conjunction with the planned Anglo-American invasion. Weygand was not to be drawn and reported the conversations to Pétain whence they were conveyed to Berlin; and Pétain instructed Weygand to reply that an Anglo-American landing would be opposed by the (very numerous) French forces in Algeria and Morocco. In April Leahy's recall marked the end of this abortive American attempt to deal with Vichy.

A few weeks later Great Britain's seizure of the French colony of Madagascar to prevent it from falling into Japanese hands embittered Vichy and during the rest of the year the possibility of Vichy making common cause with the Germans was again mooted. When the Anglo-American invasion took place in November Hitler asked Vichy to declare war. Pétain refused but broke off diplomatic relations with the United States. The Germans occupied the whole of France and seized the use of French ports in eastern Algeria and Tunisia. At this point some Vichy leaders revolted: Darlan ordered French naval vessels in metropolitan France to sail for Africa and the French Commander-in-Chief in North Africa, General Alphonse Juin, ordered resistance to the Germans and Italians who were occupying Tunisia. Pétain himself, at the head of a government becoming increasingly irrelevant to the practical course of events, began to play a less effective part in it. He retained the allegiance of some of his compatriots and when dispatched to Paris by the Germans in April 1944 to attend a memorial service for victims of allied bombing he was so warmly received that the Germans themselves felt that their attempt to make use of the Marshal in this way had been a mistake. For the most part he lived secluded at Vichy or near Rambouillet. The composition of his cabinet was increasingly determined by the Germans and after he had been forced to accept Déat as a member in 1944 he ceased to attend its meetings. Four years earlier he had been the strong silent soldier who had sat in Reynaud's government until he undermined it. At the beginning of the occupation his *silences* were taken to be a guarantee of the honour of France. They were found to be a guarantee of nothing.

Laval had been restored to power in April 1942 with the title of Prime Minister which he kept until August 1944 along with the posts of Foreign Minister and Minister of the Interior. He still thought that France could bargain with Hitler and when the Germans sought French cooperation against the allies in North Africa he tried to get a German-Italian guarantee of the French empire. But Hitler, who had less than no use for Laval personally and was no longer as interested as he had been two years earlier in France's colonial assets, saw no reason to bargain with France. Germany was now more interested in French labour and Laval was caught up in the satisfaction of German economic demands. He became in the process so identified with the machinery of German exploitation that he was, by the end of the war, the principal scapegoat for all the crimes of Vichy and was subjected to a disgracefully unfair trial before a singularly ugly execution.

By the armistice agreement France was required to pay 300 million francs for every day that the occupation lasted. This sum was supposed to represent the cost to Germany of occupying the northern zone and when therefore the occupation was extended the daily price was raised to 500 million in token of Germany's new obligation to defend southern France and Tunisia. After the allied landings in Normandy in July 1944 the price went up to 700 million, the surcharge representing France's contribution to the general defence of Europe. All these sums greatly exceeded the cost of occupation and were used by Germany for general purposes, including the purchase of French natural resources and industrial enterprises. (The Germans kept the value of the franc high, since they were being paid in francs and were using them to buy up valuable properties.) Thus the armistice payments went much further than reparations, for which in any case the Germans, having suffered practically no damage, had no claim. The payments were a levy fixed by a victor who was using this method to appropriate the capital assets of the vanquished. In addition the Germans requisitioned, and Vichy ceded, supplies of food and other raw materials to which the former were not entitled under the armistice agreement, while even in the southern zone French factories worked for the German war effort, producing aircraft engines and other indubitably military equipment.

These exactions, which began immediately after the capitulation in 1940, were compounded and transformed in 1942 when the Germans began to press for labour. Laval hoped to satisfy the Germans and pacify his compatriots by a deal by which France would supply labour in exchange for the release of prisoners of war (the *relève*). At the same time, in June 1942, he revealed the depth of the anti-communism which was absorbing him more and more as the German campaigns in the east went wrong, by exclaiming that he desired a German victory since otherwise Bolshevism would triumph everywhere. Fulfilling Germany's need for labour became the measure of his commitment to Germany's victory, but at the time when he was coming to see the Germans exclusively as a defence against communism, his compatriots were increasingly concerned with their reprisals against the Resistance and their drive for forced labour. A first labour plan, negotiated between Laval and Sauckel and covering the second half of 1942, provided for the delivery of 250,000 men. It was almost precisely fulfilled. So was a second plan covering the first quarter of 1943. Thereafter Laval tried to apply a brake, offering to transfer French labour to German war work in France but objecting to sending Frenchmen to Germany. Frenchmen themselves took to the woods to avoid compulsory labour service, but a total of 641,000 workers was sent to Germany under the Sauckel programmes and in 1943 the French forced labourers in Germany outnumbered even the Russian conscripted and prisoner labour force – 1.7 million against 1.3 million. The French contingent included prisoners of war, workers enticed to Germany before the Sauckel programmes began and workers from Alsace-Lorraine and north-eastern France which were outside the Laval-Sauckel agreements. Vichy also shipped off to Germany thousands of Spanish refugees from the lost civil war. (Others, escaping Vichy's net and Hitler's camps, fought in various parts of Europe and some, flying their own flag, marched into Paris with Leclercq in August 1944.) France's sacrifice in labour lost to Germany during the war has been computed as the equivalent of the total output of the French labour force in a normal year. It was as if no work was done in France for a whole year. The value to Germany of the work done by French workers, including prisoners of war, has been estimated at 200 billion (1938) francs.

Laval's attempts to reconcile his countrymen to Sauckel's demands by securing the repatriation of prisoners of war failed. Between two and three million Frenchmen had been taken prisoner in 1940. Vichy's efforts to secure the return of these men were neither effective nor, in the eyes of many, wholehearted: returning prisoners might include obstreperous critics of pre-war and Vichyite policies and too high a percentage of communists. (To some extent the return of prisoners was feared by ordinary Frenchmen too because there were not enough jobs or food to go round.) During the Sauckel programmes prisoners were repatriated at the rate of about one prisoner for every six forced labourers. They returned to a country where production had been cut by a third since 1938, most foods had to be bought in a black market where they cost anything from twice to five times the official price, coal could only be had at ten to twenty or even thirty times the official price, rations were providing 1,200 calories a day or less than half the normal needs of an adult, and mortality was rising rapidly – especially among infants.

These conditions showed that at the most elementary level of material life Vichy had failed. It had also failed in three other respects. It had failed to lay the blame for the collapse of 1940 on its political enemies; it had failed to protect its own citizens; and it had failed to preserve the decencies of public behaviour upon which a conservative régime is wont to insist with special eloquence. Accordingly, even though no alternative French government was in the making, Vichy forfeited its own title to rule France.

The centrepiece of the attempt to lay the blame for France's disasters on the republican régime was the trial at Riom of Daladier, Blum and Gamelin. This trial, which opened on 19 February 1942, was meant to be a demonstration of treason in high places but became instead a counter-attack by the accused civilians on the criminal negligence of the French military establishment – which included Pétain himself, who had been Minister for War in the Doumergue government of 1934 and had stated, among other things, that it was impossible for an enemy to cross the Meuse at Sedan. (Because of Pétain's embarrassing involvement in the story of French inefficiency the scope of the trial was limited to the events of 1936 and later.) The principal issues were the extent of French unpreparedness for war, the failure of the army to use the credits allocated to it, and its inefficiency in the use of such weapons as it did have. In a welter of widely differing statistics the prosecution alleged material deficiencies of scandalous proportions while the accused (other than Gamelin who remained silent throughout) produced figures to show that the weapons had been made available in reasonable numbers but had then either been stored away by the military or so ineptly distributed that some formations had too much and others too little, while large stocks fell unused into German hands. The Riom trial was as unedifying a national *post mortem* as could be conceived and although the Vichy government was able to show that

France had been materially ill-prepared for a war against the modern German armies – a fact well known to everybody – it was unable to prevent the accused from retorting that the defeat must also be attributed to bad military planning and coordination before and after the outbreak of war. Since Vichy represented the military establishment which was the target of this counterattack, the trial was a failure – all the more important in that it left in possession of the field the rival view that Vichy, so far from being the high road to national salvation, was but the last refuge of those responsible for the republic's military ineptitude, political defeatism and moral unpreparedness, a cul-de-sac containing surviving specimens of the *deux cents familles* who were supposed, however exaggeratedly, to have dominated French industrial and social life for their own selfish ends. The trial was abruptly suspended after two months and was never resumed.

The authority of Vichy as a government was further eroded by the fact that on the one hand it lacked the power to protect French citizens against the Germans, while on the other it abetted German excesses. Some 30,000 French hostages were shot during the occupation, while countless other French men and women suffered transportation or mental anguish through the operation of *Nacht und Nebel*. France became a police state as well as an occupied country; Vichy's police assisted the German police and Vichy's administration and courts were progressively adapted to the requirements of the occupiers. Vichy's first anti-semitic law was passed in 1940, Darlan established a special Jewish office in 1941 and deportation of Jews began in 1942. With the increasing strength of Resistance movements all male relatives over eighteen of any Resister were made liable to the death penalty, his female relatives to forced labour and his younger relatives to detention in reformatories. Vichy fell back, in company with the Germans, on intimidation as a means of government, coupled with a proliferation of petty regulations enforceable by heavy fines (for example, the offence of carrying chickens to market with their legs tied together). But gradually, and without destroying the appearances of administrative propriety, local authorities, the police and the magistrature ceased to comply. Local officials either delayed or sabotaged instructions. The police, who frequently became covert allies of the Resistance, gave opportune warnings. Sentences passed by magistrates for breaches of occupation laws revealed so consistent a pattern of extreme lenience that the Germans protested to Vichy.

Public opinion began to manifest itself against Vichy at an early stage. Newspapers protested against increasing concessions to the Germans, applauded the Yugoslav revolution of 1941 and promoted a dialogue with their readers on such questions as censorship and the thinness of public information. Officials considered too zealous in their cooperation received miniature coffins as a warning. When Vichy broke off relations with the USSR in June 1941 popular reaction was so outspoken that Pétain felt obliged to broadcast – *c'est de vous-mêmes que je veux vous sauver* – and to double the police.

The ultimate condemnation of Vichy lies in the fact that for each Frenchman killed in the fighting in 1940 another died later as a civilian victim of the war. Vichy functioned as a satellite in Germany's New Order and was doomed to become nothing else, to sterility and transience. Neither its own roots in French society nor the shortcomings of previous governments were adequate to give it the credentials or the lifeblood of an independent French régime. Movements formed to sustain it showed by their wilting that it could not be sustained. *Les Amis du Maréchal* and, still more so, *Les Jeunes du Maréchal* were exposures of the barrenness of their own titles, while *Le Francisme* failed entirely in its functions as an anti-Resistance movement. Under Vichy the unity of France was a slogan which was belied not only by the physical disunity of the country but also by moral disunity. At the very best Vichy exercised a limited control over a minority; one third of the population lived in the non-occupied zone, while two thirds of France's home-grown food was produced in the north and so laid Vichy under the necessity to bargain with the Germans in order to secure fair shares for the south.

And Vichy was resisted from the start. Men demobilized from the defeated French forces did not cease to regard Germany as the enemy. Laying the blame for France's defeat on Great Britain – as Vichy tried to do but with only moderate effect – did not alter this fact, and Vichy was obviously Germany's creature: the hectic note of treason appeared from the first in the rejection of Vichy. Although there was at first little that they could do about the situation, the attitude of Resisters was clear to themselves and their friends and they took what opportunities they had of proclaiming and spreading it by such acts as scribbling slogans on walls or defacing propaganda posters. More purposeful sabotage was already in evidence by the autumn of that year. Personal and local protests of this kind provided the basis from which a mood might develop into a movement with nationwide organization and purpose. This development occurred along two lines which had, at a point, to be merged. Within France local groups formed and came into touch with nearby local groups. Beyond France de Gaulle used the remnants of an army, the undecided loyalties of the French overseas empire and the force of his own personality and his own faith to create a new French régime whose authority would be accepted by all who were fighting against Germany – by French Resistance groups of all kinds and by the British, American and Russian governments.

When de Gaulle made his first broadcast to the French people from London on 18 June 1940 he was almost unknown. He was a general and he had been a junior Minister in Reynaud's last government owing to the accident of personal acquaintance with the Prime Minister. Within his profession he was noted for his intelligence and clarity of thought and for unorthodox ideas on tank warfare; he had also a reputation for incommunicativeness and intractability (he learned later how to communicate). Beyond the profession he was barely known, even by name. Among parliamentarians, for example, most of the members of the Committee on National Defence would have known something of him, but perhaps only a dozen other members of the Senate and the Chamber could have said who he was. When he began to be talked about, it was only with difficulty that a photograph could be found and for some months the face and figure which were to be so well known were only to be picked out in the back row of a formal photograph of Reynaud's last administration. There was no very strong reason why anybody listening to him on 18 June should imagine that this was a saviour and future President of France. He said that the war was not over and France not finished. Unlike many other Frenchmen at this time he did not argue about Great Britain's powers of resistance but about France itself: not about whether Great Britain could fight on but whether France could. And he did not so much argue as affirm. To argue about the fate of France at this point was almost certain to lead to a pessimistic conclusion. De Gaulle's resistance rested therefore on faith and action and he relied on these two forces to change the argument. He was able to do this because, besides being a patriot, he had in his bearing and his intelligence an authority which gave substance to his call for faith and action.

He was in this respect very like Churchill without Churchill's extraversion. Both men appealed dramatically to a people for sacrifices and in both cases the success of the appeal lay in the personality of the appealer, but whereas Churchill used words to make personal contact with his compatriots, de Gaulle used them in order to make himself not so much their leader as their symbol. To some extent the distinction was one of circumstances, for Churchill was among his people and was clothed with the legitimacy of office whereas de Gaulle was an exile without official standing of any kind (later in life he was to prove that he too knew how to move about among crowds); but the difference was even more a difference in character. De Gaulle's strength was that of the strong silent man of the English stereotype. His passions were under powerful control and during the early years of exile his natural reticence was reinforced by the fact that he was playing his hand from weakness. The poverty of his resources imposed on him the need to say as little as possible in order to reveal as little as possible. He was not interested in becoming a platoon commander in the Anglo-American host, for by doing so he might perhaps contribute to the defeat of Germany but without displacing Vichy and all it stood for. If as a Frenchman he was concerned to defeat the Germans, he was no less concerned, as a republican, to overthrow Vichy and restore and refine the post-revolutionary tradition of French republicanism. As a soldier from within this tradition he accepted the subordination of the military to the civil power but equally he wanted the wielders of civil power to behave better in future than they had behaved in the past. He was impatient of excessive parliamentary interference in the business of government and contemptuous of the past performance of political parties, but he wished to curb rather than abolish parliament and parties.

Consequently the simple solutions of the military dictator were not open to him. He wished neither to destroy the institutions of the republic nor to ignore the people, to whom on the contrary he appealed. But his respect for these institutions derived at least as much from his conservative temper as from any democratic conviction and his attachment to republic and people was long suspect in Resistance circles, especially on the Left where his sympathy and support for the Russians were as much a surprise as Churchill's. Like Churchill he envisaged a partnership between the populace and himself, but unlike Churchill he cultivated this union not only to win the war but also to restore and purge and to some extent refashion the republic. Unlike Churchill again, he was not a democrat in the Anglo-Saxon sense: he never used the word democracy and when he spoke of the republic he did so in the old Roman sense of the common weal. With regard to the war the movement which he set out to build was a military one, but with regard to *l'après-guerre* it was a civil movement which required the unification of all Resistance groups inside France with, and under, his own group in London and the empire. Gaullism was therefore *la France combattante* and also the next French republic. Since the Americans and, to a lesser extent, the British underrated the value of the first and refused for a long time to acknowledge the second, de Gaulle's role in exile became one of stubborn self-inflation.

De Gaulle's first task was to command the allegiance of as much as possible of the French empire, his second to command the attention of everybody else. Indo-China, the Middle East and North Africa had declared for Vichy, while in West Africa the attempt to acquire a foothold at

Dakar was a failure. In general too little was known about the Gaullist group in London and its prospects to tempt distant proconsuls into rejecting the armistice and Vichy's claim to legitimacy. De Gaulle had first to build up his own forces, create a following in France itself and show that Hitler's principal enemies accepted him as an ally. However, Félix Eboué, the governor of Chad in French Equatorial Africa, chose the Gaullist side and was followed by other African colonies, by Tahiti, the Marquesas Islands and New Caledonia, and by the French colonies in India. One other colony, the oldest, was seized by de Gaulle, who thereby earned lasting hostility in Washington.

St Pierre et Miquelon had been divided since the fall of France between a Vichyite minority which was in control and a Gaullist majority. The colony consisted of a group of islands a dozen miles off the south coast of Newfoundland. It had some strategic importance, for it lay off the mouth of the St Lawrence and could be used against convoys by harbouring U-boats and reporting the movements of shipping. Atlantic cables passed through its waters and after these had been cut the colony remained in close contact with Vichy by means of a radio station which, besides transmitting weather reports and Vichyite propaganda, reported on shipping and gave instructions to agents. Both Newfoundland (then a British Crown Colony) and Canada were suspected of designs against the islands, and the United States warmly advocated Canadian annexation. Great Britain, however, and also Canada after some wavering, preferred a Gaullist coup and were embarrassed by American schemes. The Canadian cabinet settled on a compromise whereby Canada would, by threats of economic sanctions and in the last resort by force, seize the radio station but not remove the Vichyite governor or overthrow his régime.

In October 1941 de Gaulle broached with Eden the question of a Gaullist coup. Eden, although sympathetic, felt obliged to refer to Ottawa and Washington. De Gaulle dispatched Admiral Émile Muselier to end the discussions by taking the islands; the coup was not difficult since the population was largely pro-Gaullist. But Muselier decided to go to Ottawa first. There he found the government undecided between its own plan to seize the radio station and the Gaullist plan to seize the colony. The Canadian government consulted Washington which objected strongly to a Gaullist coup, largely because it had just negotiated a general agreement about all the French possessions in the western hemisphere with Vichy's representative, Admiral Robert. Roosevelt was ill informed and badly advised on French affairs; he refused to regard Vichy as fascist or de Gaulle as a democrat, he was partly right in both cases, but he was wrong in imagining that this simple categorization was all that mattered; he exaggerated American influence at Vichy and tended to be combatively uneasy about his pro-Vichy policy which he knew to be regarded with scepticism by his British allies and with distaste by his own press and public. Roosevelt was therefore all the more hostile to de Gaulle who represented an additional challenge to his Vichy policy and whom he in return represented as no more than a fringe military figure. His objections to the St Pierre adventure prevailed. The British and Canadian governments gave way with reluctance and so did de Gaulle and Muselier. But in almost the same breath de Gaulle ordered Muselier to go ahead and take the islands.

This Muselier, with three corvettes, a submarine and grave misgivings about the probity of his undertaking, did. Great Britain and Canada were privately pleased but officially reticent; the American press and public were enthusiastically in favour of this first stroke against European dictatorship in the American continent; but in Washington Roosevelt and his Secretary of State Cordell Hull, who was more convinced than the President that Gaullism was insignificant, were so infuriated that they issued unnecessarily offensive statements about the Gaullists and tried to get the Canadians to mount an expedition to recapture the colony – a project which only incensed Ottawa against Washington. The rights and wrongs of this episode are still not entirely clear. The overthrow of Vichy's authority in the colony was in the allied interest. Roosevelt and Hull were wrong in their estimates of Vichy and de Gaulle and their reactions to the event were out of proportion to its significance. Roosevelt would probably have been glad to treat the affair as an irritating episode and forget it – he called it a 'teapot tempest', which is presumably something not much bigger than a storm in a tea-cup but Hull took it to heart to such a degree that he lost his judgement, nourished a personal animosity against de Gaulle and accused Great Britain of conspiring with de Gaulle against the United States. On the French side de Gaulle's action, of which Muselier disapproved, is less easy to assess. It is at least possible that, after accepting Washington's veto on his plan, he learned for the first time of the Canadian plan and thereupon, imagining himself deceived, reversed his decision. The most important consequence of the coup was to give de Gaulle and Gaullism great prestige throughout the French empire and in France.

For about a year the Gaullists were ill informed about happenings inside France itself. Resistance groups seemed to be small and uncoordinated. They might one day be useful adjuncts of a Gaullist army. For the time being their sabotage activities were good for French morale and good practice for the day when sabotage would help an invading force.

Activities on a larger scale raised problems. They were for the moment premature; they might do more harm than good; they might tend towards the emergence of a separate centre of authority in competition with the Gaullists and, after 1941, increasingly under communist control. Guerrilla operations did not seem to be a good idea. De Gaulle's headquarters, predominantly military and right wing, discounted the value of large-scale populist resistance and viewed it without enthusiasm. But this attitude changed during 1942, by which time Gaullism as a whole had edged leftward in reaction to Vichyite positions and in sympathy with the Russian stand against Germany, and had learned more about the Resistance movements inside France.

The main concern of the Resistance was the revival and consolidation of all that was best in the French spirit as a necessary precondition to action against the enemy. It was therefore at least as much concerned with Frenchmen as with Germans, for the defeat of the Germans was to be only an intermediate operation between a revolution in French public feeling and – the ultimate end – a revolution in the structure of French society and politics. When the Germans first entered Paris and other French cities their reception was far from universally hostile. Fraternization was common not only in shops and restaurants but in casual encounters on streets and squares where crowds gathered to listen to news broadcasts or concerts and rubbed shoulders with Germans, whom they were ready to treat as ordinary human beings. Resistance-minded Frenchmen regarded all this as a dangerous, even disgusting, self-deception. They were also concerned to combat Vichy's implicit claim to provide the right answers for France, and to demonstrate that Vichy, so far from serving France, was putting German interests before French ones. Vichy started with a major advantage since there was widespread acceptance of the view that France's disasters should all be blamed on the parliamentarians whom Vichy was attacking and displacing, so that the Resistance, which also accepted this view, was forced into the awkward position of damning political parties but at the same time advocating a restored, if regenerated, political system. Essentially, as postwar events proved, this was an illogical position, for the system demanded parties by whatever name they might be called (movements, rallies and so on became in fact parties as soon as they moved into action). But the Resistance contrived to evade the illogicality. It was joined by men of different parties and different social backgrounds. It did not at first look to de Gaulle nor know much about his movement except that it was a long way away in London and possibly under British control. In the south men of right-wing temperament often dropped out in the early days and accepted Vichy, so that southern Resistance movements had begun to wear a left-wing air even before they were joined by communists after the German invasion of the USSR. This ideological colouring of the Resistance was increased by the hostility or ambivalence of the ecclesiastical establishment: in general the Roman Catholic episcopacy had an outstandingly poor Resistance record, redeemed only partially by the heroism of a minority of the lesser clergy. Political parties continued throughout the war to be regarded in the Resistance with some distaste and there was a vague hope (except among the communists) that the unity forged during the Resistance would somehow dispense with the need to resuscitate the old parties after liberation. Postwar problems were, however, subordinated to the needs of the present, and old political leaders worked alongside new non-political chieftains to create forces which would cause real embarrassment and damage to the German occupiers.

Their efforts were aided by the revulsion against Vichy. This was at first gradual and patchy. Its principal sources were Vichy's own actions, the behaviour of the Germans coupled with Vichy's failure to take even a moral stand against it, and the recovery of courage effected by time, nationalism and the growth of the clandestine press from amateurish hand-outs to real newspapers. Particular events accelerated the general trend: the introduction of forced labour, which transformed the scale of the Resistance by hitting the middle classes as well as the working classes (comparatively well represented in the Resistance from the start); and the raids on the continent at St Nazaire and Dieppe which confirmed what people were hearing on the radio about the progress of the war (although the Germans decreed the confiscation of private radios, they were unable to confiscate enough of them to stop people knowing about the war).

The rejection of Vichy automatically turned attention to de Gaulle as an alternative government and by the beginning of 1942 a number of Resistance groups had decided to accept de Gaulle's leadership. In the south the principal Resistance movements were the *Francs-Tireurs et Partisans* (FTP), *Combat* and *Libération*, all of them active by the end of 1941 and all in contact with de Gaulle. In the occupied zone, where Resistance was in the nature of things more difficult and dangerous, *Libération-Nord* and *Organisation Civile et Militaire* (OCM) played the leading part, became effective in 1942 and also established contacts with the Gaullists in London. Although the Communist Party denounced the war until Hitler invaded the USSR, many individual communists joined Resistance movements before that date. After June 1941 the *Front National*, which covered the whole country and embraced diverse opinions under communist leadership, pursued a policy of cooperation between all Resistance movements and advocated extensive and immediate action, even courting reprisals in order to intensify anti-German feeling. Its object was to harass and kill the occupiers in order not only to end the occupation but also to transform French politics. To the rank and file of Resisters, and even to their regional leaders, the politics of the movement to which they belonged were very often unknown.

At the end of 1941 de Gaulle sent one of his principal lieutenants, Jean Moulin, to France. Moulin began by uniting the movements in the south, thus completing the elimination of Vichy as a force for the future. The further work of combining Resistance movements in northern and southern France, and uniting the Resistance with Gaullism, was facilitated by the German occupation of the whole country in November 1942 and by the consolidation of de Gaulle's position as the unrivalled chief of French forces overseas in spite of American attempts to prefer Giraud or Darlan. The communists accepted de Gaulle's leadership at the end of 1942. In March 1943 Resistance movements from all parts of the country combined in the *Mouvements Unis de la Résistance*, which gave birth to the *Comité National de la Résistance* (CNR) which first met in Paris in May under Moulin's chairmanship and recognized de Gaulle as the national leader of France. A few weeks after this meeting Moulin and other French leaders were picked up by the Gestapo, tortured and killed, but during his last months in his native country Moulin had created the organs with which France would re-enter the war. (The CNR did not meet again until after the liberation. Owing to the activities of the German police it was forced to operate regionally.) The recognition extended to de Gaulle by the entire Resistance put him for the first time in command of considerable forces and greatly increased his political standing with his western and eastern allies.

Relations between the French Resistance and the western allies were uneven. Resistance leaders inside France (as elsewhere) suspected the British and American governments of not taking them seriously enough, of regarding them as a sideshow, and of sending fewer arms and other supplies than they could afford. They protested against the bombing of targets in France which they themselves could sabotage with much less loss of innocent civilian lives – although not, owing to the nature of sabotage, with lasting effect. Being in a position to observe the inaccuracy of strategic bombing they continually urged, without carrying conviction, that they had a better way of doing the job. Raids on Nantes from 16 to 23 September 1943 were a particularly grave example of the futility of the policy of total air warfare which the British and Americans had uncritically taken over from the Germans. Senseless destruction threatened to alienate the population not only from the perpetrators but also from the Resistance which was in a sense allied with them. On the other side the British and American governments, besides underestimating the effectiveness of the Resistance, exaggerated the tensions within it and, the Americans especially, were afraid that a civil war would break out in France before the Germans were defeated and that the communists would win it. With more justice they regarded the Resistance movements as insecure and not to be trusted with information of value. In fact Anglo-American assistance to France was very great but it was of a kind not always visible to Resistance leaders. While these anxiously awaited parachute drops which never came or seemed (until the eve of invasion) disappointingly meagre, Great Britain lent France £30 million and the United States gave de Gaulle all the facilities of Lend-Lease from November 1941 and helped to equip and maintain large French forces in Africa from the time of the Casablanca conference and in France itself in 1944, particularly after the Ardennes offensive at the end of that year when eight new divisions were formed out of Resistance units. But politically Roosevelt continued to drag his feet. In July 1944, when the CNR declared itself the provisional government of France, Washington recognized it as a *de facto* government, delaying until October the further step of recognizing it as the *de jure*, though provisional, government; and Roosevelt opposed de Gaulle's presence at Yalta.

Within France Resistance of a quasi-military kind was intensified from 1943 and organized in regions under the aegis of a three-man directorate which was established by the CNR and coordinated the efforts of the various military bodies in the field. Bands were mostly fifty to a hundred strong, although some were as large as 500–1,000. Nearly all their arms came from the Americans and British who supplied 1,000 tons of equipment by March 1944 (of which the Germans seized a third) and 8,000 tons in the next six months, the period spanning the invasion of France. Early in 1944 the movements joined forces as the *Forces Françaises de l'Intérieur* (FFI), by which time their combined field strength had reached about 30,000 and it was commonly assumed that an allied return to the continent was not far distant. Increasing strength meant increasing temptation to use it and sometimes action was premature and tragic.

At Glières for example, in Haute Savoie, a band of 500 men organized during 1943 by a former lieutenant in the *Chasseurs Alpins* attacked a considerable force of heavily armed Germans in February 1944 and lost half its men. Such incidents became more frequent as the great moment of liberation approached and misunderstandings over the role of the FFI and cooperation with the invading forces took their toll. Thus at

Montmouchet the Resistance, mistakenly believing that allied troops would arrive to join forces in an attack on the Germans simultaneously with the landings in the north, assembled a strength of 3,000–4,000 men and opened battle. Fighting went on for a week. The Germans suffered to begin with ten casualties for every one among their enemies but in the end they won a complete victory. A similar misunderstanding produced a similar tragedy in the Vercors. The Vercors, a natural fortress south-west of Grenoble, was occupied by Resistance units in the winter of 1942–3. From small beginnings – a group of local men in a small way of business, most of them socialists – the Vercors redoubt grew into an assembly centre and refuge of considerable importance, but it was not meant to be a stronghold to be defended in battle against regular German forces. Nevertheless such a battle took place. Again there were false expectations of outside help. Resistance leaders believed that plans for a joint operation had been endorsed by the French and allied authorities in London and Algiers when in fact these plans were, owing to administrative incompetence, not even known to many of the people who would have been involved. A few days before the landings in Normandy the Vercors Resistance mobilized and serious fighting began on 13 June. It continued for forty-one days, the Resistance force of 3,500 men holding an area where they expected allied reinforcements to land by air and so condemning themselves to static defence against two German divisions which eventually surrounded and liquidated most of them. This episode produced the sharpest disagreement between de Gaulle and his communist associates in the Provisional Government; the communists, who held among other posts the air portfolio, pressed for air support for the rising (which was rejected as impracticable) and accused de Gaulle of betraying the Resistance, in return for which de Gaulle dismissed the air member of his government.

But these episodes were not typical. Elsewhere the Resistance played a successful part in the defeat of the Germans. On a signal from the BBC the FFI mobilized 200,000 (lightly) armed troops and as many ancillaries in support. According to Eisenhower they were worth fifteen divisions and shortened the campaign by two months. They denied the French rail system to the Germans; disrupted road communications by felling trees and other devices; destroyed German minefields; cut down hedges in order to help the operations of allied tactical air squadrons; spread rumours of parachute landings which distracted the German command; obstructed the transfer of the German SS division *Das Reich* from the south-west so that it took nine days to reach the battle area in Normandy; forced 20,000 Germans to surrender to the Americans at Issoudun (and were very annoyed when the Americans gave their captives oranges, which no Frenchman had seen for years); successfully blocked off Brittany and then cleared it after the Americans had broken out of their Normandy beach-heads; took thousands of prisoners; protected works of art.

De Gaulle arrived in Paris on 25 August, the day after the surrender of the German military governor to General Jacques Leclercq of the revived French army and Colonel Rol-Tanguy of the Resistance as representatives of the French republic (the rising of the Parisians is narrated below in the context of the allied victories in France). He had already made careful preparations to assume the government of the country. The adherence of the Resistance to the Gaullist movement enabled him to do so by general consent. He was, however, apprehensive lest the communists might make a bid for power, using the local Liberation Committees which had been set up in each *département* and were mostly under communist control. Further, Roosevelt's hostility to him and the United States' continued refusal to recognize the CNR as a government or to come out against Vichy made him fear that the allies intended to impose a military government on France as they had on Sicily. He therefore chose and appointed *préfets* who were to be ready to assume authority as soon as invasion or Resistance had swept away Vichy's local government officials.

De Gaulle was also greatly concerned about the unity of the French people. He opposed the view, strongly held in the Resistance, that French society could be made healthy by a surgical purge of malign elements. The conflict between the Resistance and Vichy had generated much bitterness, which found vent during the occupation in the publication of lists of collaborators, the marking of their houses, summary executions (possibly 5,000 instances, plus another 5,000 in the throes and immediate aftermath of liberation) and an increasingly vocal determination to bring to trial and exact retribution from men and women of all ranks who had helped the enemy or served Vichy. In March 1944 a first Vichy Minister, Pierre Pucheu, was tried for treason and executed and a few months later another, Philippe Henriot, was assassinated in public and in daylight. Judicial and extra-judicial punishment of this kind was regarded by many in the Resistance and in de Gaulle's entourage as both inevitable and excusable, but de Gaulle himself deplored vengeance and regarded a purge, however conducted, as impracticable and likely to poison rather than heal French society. Some retribution was, however, inevitable and a special High Court was created to hear the principal cases. Fifty-eight cases were brought before this court, which passed eighteen death sentences (ten of them *in absentia*); three of the eighteen were executed. Altogether nearly 125,000 cases were heard by other courts and nearly 7,000 death sentences pronounced, of which 767 were carried out. Pétain was among those

sentenced to death by the High Court. De Gaulle had hoped that Pétain
would not be captured by French troops, nor return, and he was relieved
when the death sentence on the Marshal was accompanied by a recom-
mendation to mercy which he accepted. Pétain was consigned to a fortress
on the Île d'Yeu off the west coast of France where he read de Gaulle's
memoirs and remained until a few weeks before his death in 1951, when
he was removed from the fortress but not from the island.

As Head of the Provisional Government of France de Gaulle saw his
task in the same terms as he had seen it in 1940 as a junior minister and
then as a refugee: to ensure and assert France's position as a major power.
Although he might and did toy with the idea of presenting France as the
champion of smaller powers or medium powers (the latter was a category
which was recognized by the practice of the League of Nations and which
France tried unsuccessfully to introduce into the structure of the United
Nations), his basic aim was to range France unequivocally with the Big
Three. He rejected the idea that France was a western equivalent of
Poland or a power of the same consequence as Yugoslavia. This aim was
formally achieved when France was accorded equal status with the Big
Three in the administration of Germany and a permanent seat in the U N
Security Council, but France still needed a special role to sustain this
equal status. De Gaulle hoped that France might mediate between Anglo-
Saxons and Russians and at the same time create and lead a western
European group embracing the Low Countries, Spain, Italy and part of
Germany as well as France itself – the countries touched by the Rhine, the
Alps or the Pyrenees. In both these notions he was echoing Resistance
aspirations for Great Power harmony and a European federation. But the
harmony of the Resistance itself began to disintegrate under the pressures
of peacetime politics and when the communists tried to refashion the
post-war all-party government by forming an alliance and excluding the
new Roman Catholic party, the M R P, de Gaulle decided to retire and
leave the parties to conduct their despised manoeuvres without him. He
announced his decision in January 1946. By the end of the next year the
communists too were out of office. For a decade the government of
France reverted to the political forces of the Third Republic until revolt in
Algeria and a threat of a military coup in Paris itself drove them in 1958
to abdicate in favour of de Gaulle, who returned to save France once
more and to pursue his interrupted task.

Part IV

THE MIDDLE GAME

CHAPTER 16
The Muster against the Axis

THE alliance which confronted Hitler in 1939 was a Franco-British one. When France fell Great Britain had to consider whether to carry on the fight. In retrospect it is easy to conclude that there was never any doubt about the answer to this question. It was never directly put, but there was a question all the same and there was a case for answering it in the negative. The defeat of France seemed to put Great Britain in a hopeless position, safe perhaps from military invasion but incapable of beating Germany and doubtfully capable of warding off intolerable air attacks. To the staid man of cool mind who was trained to assess a situation and then ask what was the most sensible thing to do about it – to the typical British statesman – the conclusion could well be that a government's job was to make the best of a bad business or, in other words, come to terms with fate in the person of Hitler. Some members of the British government reasoned this way. The historical importance of Churchill is that he did not. Having assessed the situation he refused to deduce his own course from it; he determined rather to alter it. He treated the concept of peace offers from Hitler as a contradiction in terms and ignored them. Moreover his famous speech on 4 June – 'we shall fight on the beaches, we shall fight on the landing-grounds, we shall fight in the fields and in the streets, we shall fight in the hills; we shall never surrender . . .' – gave the lead that the country wanted. Its reception showed how far the British mood had cleared since 1938. Then the question had been whether the British should fight, but now it was whether they should fight on.

But Churchill had been Prime Minister for only a few weeks. He was not the entire master of his cabinet, still less so of the Conservative Party, and both were substantially what they had been in the last years of appeasement. Official as well as popular feeling had changed since Munich, but it had not changed out of all recognition. Two weeks after Churchill's no-surrender speech his Under-Secretary of State at the Foreign Office, R. A. Butler, was telling the Swedish Minister that the Prime Minister's voice was not necessarily decisive, that the war might not have to be fought to a finish and that an opportunity to make a reasonable compromise peace would not be missed in spite of the 'diehards' in the cabinet. It is unlikely that Butler, a junior minister, was acting on his own. The Foreign

Secretary, Halifax, himself reinforced this appraisal by telling the same
Minister that commonsense would prevail over bravado. (The Swedish
government thereupon gave in to German pressure and allowed German
soldiers going home on leave from Norway to travel through Sweden.)
Another member of the old team, Hoare, who had wavered in the late
thirties into toying with the idea of a Russian alliance and had then been
relegated to the right wing as Ambassador in Madrid, was being similarly
propitiatory. It was as a result of consorting too exclusively with people
of this kind that the United States Ambassador in London, Joseph P.
Kennedy, reported that Great Britain was finished – a judgement at vari-
ance not only with the facts but also with that of the Russian Ambassador,
Ivan Maisky, who was assuring Stalin that the British would fight on
despite the fall of France. (A year later Maisky found an ingenious solution to the reverse problem of persuading the British that the Russians
would fight on and win in spite of Hitler's first victories in the USSR: he
persuaded a British publishing firm to issue a cheap edition of Tolstoy's
War and Peace.)

The question of a negotiated peace had been broached in the British
Cabinet before the French capitulation, when some Ministers proposed
invoking once more the good offices of Mussolini. Churchill was inflexibly
hostile to any such move, even when faced with a threat of resignation by
Halifax who argued that this was no time for obduracy. Yet Churchill's
stance was not simply emotional bravado. Hitler was not likely to want to
talk peace with the fall of France within his grasp, and Mussolini was even
less likely to court a snub by making an inopportune and unwelcome
approach to the lord of the continent.

Hints of peace in the summer of 1940 could have had two differing
purposes. The more obvious purpose was to indicate that Great Britain
was prepared to follow France in the acknowledgement of defeat: Lloyd
George, who was known to be pessimistic about any other course, might
play the role of Pétain and Churchill would leave the stage like Reynaud.
Alternatively, defeatist talk might be a mere manoeuvre to gain time
while British forces were evacuated from the continent. Although Churchill was anxious to get Lloyd George to join his government, there is no
evidence that Churchill believed that the war should no longer be carried
on, and his repeated overtures to Lloyd George are as consonant with a
wish to muffle his old comrade-in-arms as to be supplanted by him. In the
event there was no Pétainist peace. Butler and Halifax both left the Foreign
Office before the end of the year and Churchill, more dogged and more
passionate than the common run of politicians, became greatly more
assured in his control of the government and his identification with the

popular mood. But wars are not won by spirit alone. The British determination embodied in Churchill could hardly have prevailed against Hitler but
for Great Britain's insular geography and its imperial past. As an island
state Great Britain could parry and gain time. But this was only a negative
advantage. It might enable Great Britain to get left out of Europe's
catastrophic affairs but it could not directly affect them. As an island
Great Britain was an anti-German perch, but there was in 1940 nobody to
perch on it, for the Americans were unlikely to join a war which had
dwindled to a formal state of belligerence and no more. But Great Britain
was also an empire and it was the combination of British Empire and
British Isles which kept the war alive: the American armies first joined this
war not in Europe but in Africa.

Great Britain's imperial past had two major consequences. First, it
provided a base in the Middle East to serve as an alternative point for
accumulating forces and launching them against the European continent
and, secondly, it provided the men and materials which India, the Dominions and the colonies contributed to the war. When Great Britain declared war in 1939 the Dominions did so too – in the case of South Africa
by a vote of eighty to sixty-seven in Parliament, in the other cases wholeheartedly. This response was not the automatic reaction which it had been
in 1914 but a freely formed resolve based on the close links of kinship and
imperial solidarity and on revulsion against Nazi enormities. In India the
Viceroy, acting with complete constitutional propriety but almost equally
complete obtuseness, declared war without consulting any Indian leader.
In spite of this tactless insensitivity Indians fought once more in Europe's
wars at Great Britain's behest – to such good measure that Wavell felt
bound to complain to Churchill in 1942 that the Indian army had the
equivalent of seven divisions in the Middle East (more than it had in
India) at a time when the country was dangerously threatened by the
Japanese. Throughout the war there was never any shortage of volunteers
for the Indian armed services. The Indian princes also pledged all their
resources to the British cause and the independent kingdom of Nepal, the
home of the Gurkhas, maintained its distinctive fighting reputation.

By mid-1941 the British Chiefs of Staff were making plans for the
following year on the basis that they would be able to deploy about sixty
divisions, of which slightly over one third would come from India and the
Dominions (India eight, Australia five and a third, Canada four and a
third, South Africa two, New Zealand one). The bulk of the armour, the
equivalent of twelve divisions out of fifteen, would be British, but otherwise the imperial contribution was striking. Some Canadian units reached
Great Britain as early as 1939 and took part in the battle for France next

year; Australia and New Zealand agreed in January 1940 to the dispatch of a division each to the Middle East. Similar contributions were made to naval and air forces. The Commonwealth Air Training Scheme, established by the British, Canadian, Australian and New Zealand governments, trained tens of thousands of pilots, radio operators, gunners and observers annually at elementary and advanced schools in the various countries, and South Africa and Rhodesia set up schemes of their own, the latter with British instructors and aircraft. All this help was given with little restriction. South Africa did not allow service outside the African continent and restricted service outside the Union itself to volunteers: they served in North and East Africa. All the Dominion governments tried, as they were bound to do, to secure some say in broad strategic decisions and the right to be consulted on operational decisions of special moment to themselves. Australia and New Zealand complained about the dispatch of their units to Greece without adequate consultation, Canada showed concern about plans to commit Canadians to an assault on Trondhjem without express Canadian consent. But in general the Commonwealth commitment was unfettered as well as generous.

Thus, whether he fully realized it or not, Hitler was already in 1940 threatened from many quarters and by many peoples. The focus for this threat was the Middle East and it is conceivable that the threat to Hitler would not have materialized if Mussolini had not stirred it up by urging Graziani to attack in the desert and by invading Greece towards the end of 1940. By doing these things Mussolini opened a second front within range of British imperial power. He unshackled the British strategic initiative which had been neutralized when Great Britain lost in France its only fighting ally.

Churchill's problem after the defeat of France was how and with whom to get back to the continent. There were two possible ways of doing this. The one was to bring France back into the fight and the other was to make the journey back to within striking distance of Germany by way of the Balkans. A view of Europe from the south-east had been familiar to Englishmen since Egypt became to all intents and purposes a part of the British Empire and the Mediterranean, if not a British lake, at least a British highway signposted by Gibraltar, Malta, Alexandria and Suez.

Until the spring of 1941 the Balkans were debatable ground. Churchill built up British forces across the water in Egypt. But then Hitler conquered south-east Europe too, and the British in Egypt, their forces (mostly Australians and New Zealanders) thrown out of Greece and Crete, had to give up thinking of engaging the Germans anywhere on the continent; they were confined to the subsidiary problems of Libya and the Horn of

Africa. At this point Hitler himself again reopened the war in Europe and created for the German army an enemy who was to engage it until it was destroyed. His attack on the USSR in June 1941 transformed the war by carrying the bulk of Germany's ground forces to the east and out of occupied Europe, thereby making Resistance a serious practical possibility and opening for the British the prospect of returning to the continent either by assault on its weakened western defences or through ports captured by a French Resistance movement. Six months later Hitler's declaration of war against the United States ensured that this re-entry would be immensely massive. Hitler had dissolved the Anglo-French alliance only to create a convergence of British, Indian, Dominion, Russian and American forces against him. From 1942 onwards, the muster of these diverse enemies, joined by contingents from Hitler's victims, were on their several ways into Germany. But these had to be concerted.

The principal allies – the United States, the USSR and Great Britain – were united in their primary war aim but often divided about how to achieve it. Between the Americans and the British there was an accumulation of trust and fellowship which produced, for all its occasional rubs, an exceptionally efficient and harmonious alliance, but between them and the Russians there stood a generation of mistrust, thousands of miles and ineradicable divergences on post-war aims. There was also much mutual ignorance about attitudes and intentions, notably on post-war issues over which there was little meeting of minds, if only because – very often – minds were not yet made up.

The Grand Alliance which defeated Germany was fashioned by circumstances rather than by men. In the thirties the western European democracies had shunned the USSR because in a number of ways their rulers preferred Hitler to communism: either the USSR was weak, in which case it was no use as an ally, or it was strong, in which case it might dominate central Europe – an eventuality to be avoided at almost any cost. Stalin had no more liking for them than they for him and, concerned about how to keep out of trouble for as long as possible, he too had opted for Hitler in 1939: the victor in the ensuing war between Germany and the west would confront the USSR and probably be happy to attack it. But when in 1941, with that war still undecided, Germany invaded the USSR, an alliance between the west and the USSR became a natural sequel which imposed itself, or interposed itself, on the current of history. Although there was some surprise at the immediacy and wholeheartedness of Churchill's and Roosevelt's response, there was nothing surprising about the event itself. Hitler's decision to attack the USSR while he was still at war with Great Britain meant that an east–west alliance against him would precede the east–west conflict which he in effect postponed to 1945.

So long as the war lasted the maintenance of this anti-German alliance was a cardinal aim of the leaders on both sides of Germany. The war on two fronts was the war which Hitler could not win. A separate peace in west or east spelt danger for the other half of the alliance. For Great Britain the German attack on the USSR, because it came before Churchill had achieved his aim of seeing the Americans join the fighting, was an immense relief in a year of critical strain, and even after Hitler's declaration of war against the United States, six months after Barbarossa was launched, the maintenance of the Russian capacity and will to fight was essential to a western victory. Not until 1943 at the earliest were the German armies so mauled by the Russians that the western allies might hope to put their own great armies onto the continent without intolerable losses. Yet these forces must make their invasion not long after 1943 in order to be certain that new German weapons, such as chemical weapons, would not render it impossible. As late as the autumn of 1944 they were sharply reminded in the Ardennes that the Germans, even in a war on two fronts which they were clearly losing, remained dangerous foes.

On the Russian side Stalin, by his appeals for material aid and for the reopening of a front in France, proved his urgent fear of defeat in single combat with the Germans. He asked for British divisions to be sent to fight on Russian soil and for a no-separate-peace agreement, which was concluded between Molotov and the British Ambassador (Cripps) in October. His fears were allayed by the survival of Moscow at the end of 1941 and still more by the endurance of Stalingrad at the end of 1942 and were all but completely removed by the Russian victories in the summer of 1943. But the preservation of 'anti-fascist solidarity' remained a cardinal principle of Stalin's war policy, even to the extent of restraining communists like Tito and Togliatti, lecturing the one on the need to conciliate and collaborate with anti-fascists of all kinds and telling the other to mute anti-monarchism until the war was over. It is arguable that, if forced to a choice, Stalin might have put the control over eastern Europe above the preservation of the alliance once the USSR's moment of vital danger had passed, and that he never regarded eastern Europe as negotiable during the last two years of war; but he was never called upon to make that choice, an escape for which he could claim some personal credit since it was partly due to his refusal to confabulate with Roosevelt and Churchill until the end of 1943.

But although the overriding needs of the partners ensured its maintenance, the alliance was neither deep nor harmonious. Evidence to the contrary is to be found only in communiqués, notoriously misleading, and in descriptions of banquet scenes, traditionally unbuttoned. The persistent reality was a background of mistrustful manoeuvre and speculation. Although anti-Germanism was strong enough to hold the alliance together, it was – apart from a certain mutual martial admiration – just about the allies' only bond. Churchill and Stalin might admire as well as need one another but Stalin could remember the Churchill who had advocated the overthrow of the new Bolshevik régime not only by backing Russian Whites and enlisting British volunteers but also by using German troops, while Churchill could remember that one of the first acts of the Bolshevik government had been to desert the allied cause and make a separate peace with Germany. Difficulties appeared at once and were thereafter never absent. Churchill's declaration of sympathy and solidarity, made within hours of Hitler's attack, was followed by negotiations for an Anglo-Russian treaty which laid bare one of the problems which was never resolved until the Russians were strong enough completely to override their allies' views – the problem of the Soviet Union's European frontiers. What Stalin had got in his treaty with Hitler in 1939 he wanted his new allies to recognize and endorse – in the Baltic, Poland and the Balkans.

Churchill's general inclination was to mollify Stalin without entering into specific undertakings governing the shape of post-war Europe; in particular he could not concede Stalin's claims against Poland without flagrantly violating the Anglo-Polish treaty of 1939 and forgetting that Great Britain had gone to war in 1939 on behalf of Poland and was still host to a Polish government in exile. If Bessarabia presented no such problem (Rumania had joined in the attack on the USSR) the extinction of the three Baltic states raised political and moral principles which Great Britain did not care to flout in a formal diplomatic document.

In August 1941, on a battleship off the coast of Newfoundland, Roosevelt and Churchill had signed the document which became known as the Atlantic Charter and which was intended as a declaration of general war aims. For Roosevelt the Atlantic Charter was the equivalent of Wilson's Fourteen Points, a working paper setting out the basis on which a new and fairer world would be constructed. For Churchill it was less a document than a call or proclamation to stir the world. For Americans it was the equivalent of the Constitution, for the British of the Magna Carta – the one a document with continuing practical effects, the other a piece of secular religion. By the Atlantic Charter Roosevelt and Churchill renounced territorial aggrandizement, asserted the right of all peoples to choose how they should be governed, condemned territorial changes contrary to the wishes of the inhabitants of the territory and looked forward to an equitable distribution of raw materials, fair trading practices, freedom of the seas, disarmament and an international security system. They hoped to get Stalin to endorse this declaration but they got no further than a vague statement of approval from the Russian Ambassador in London, Ivan Maisky. At the end of 1941 Eden, on a mission to Moscow, discovered that Stalin's post-war aims included not only the recognition of the fruits of his pact with Hitler, but also fragments of Germany and the transfer to Turkey of the Dodecanese (which Great Britain's other ally, Greece, was expecting to be given as soon as Italy was defeated). But Stalin was not at this stage in a position to insist. Eden became privately convinced that it would be politic to concede Stalin's claims in the Baltic, but Churchill (and the Conservative Party) were not so minded, unmoved by Eden's arguments that when the war ended Stalin would take the republics anyway. The Anglo-Russian treaty, eventually concluded in May 1942, contained no undertakings about post-war frontiers and Stalin let the matter rest until the Teheran conference in November 1943, by which time his military position had greatly changed.

As important as Poland and more urgent was the question of a second front. Stalin pressed for one in July 1941 and again in September. Churchill's desire to help was genuine but he and many of his advisers were for a time sceptical about the value of the new ally which looked like being defeated and bundled out of the war almost as easily as France had been – in which event aid would have been wasted and Great Britain, once more alone, that much worse off. Churchill's spirit responded to the Russian needs but his strategic senses were more alert to the battles in the Middle East, the defence of the British Empire and the fear of a junction between the Germans and the Japanese. He had to count the cost of promises very carefully. Great Britain was a fighting ally of the USSR for six months before the United States too came into the war and the brunt of military aid to the USSR and the delivery of war material by the Arctic route must fall on Great Britain.

Roosevelt was less cautious. When, after the American entry into the war, Molotov visited London and Washington in the hope of getting more and quicker western aid, Roosevelt allowed himself to be less guarded than Churchill and half-promised a second front that year (1942). Churchill, who envisaged raids on the French coast in 1942 and a major invasion in 1943 at the earliest, felt obliged to record in writing his opposition to Roosevelt's imprudent engagement, and from this time the

Russians regarded Great Britain as a drag on more purposeful and generous American policies. In April 1942 the American planners produced, and the Chiefs of Staff adopted, proposals for an invasion of France by a million American troops in the spring of 1943 and for a smaller attack in the autumn of 1942 if either the Russians or the Germans showed signs of collapsing. The British did not object to this programme although they were convinced that any invasion in 1942 was out of the question. Churchill did not believe that so huge an American force could be assembled in England in time for a major invasion in 1943, especially if the war in the Atlantic had not first been won. Great Britain moreover was committed to the North African campaign, which could not on the most favourable estimates be completed in time to permit the opening of a new campaign thousands of miles away before the end of 1942; it was in fearful difficulties in the Far East, exemplified by the fall of Singapore and the Australian government's insistence on recalling troops from abroad for the defence of their homeland; and Churchill and his advisers were ceaselessly aware of their limited resources in men and materials.

In Great Britain Churchill's views prevailed, if not without question, yet without serious challenge. On the issue of the second front Lord Beaverbrook alone raised a voice of eminence and influence in favour of an immediate landing in France. Early in 1942 Beaverbrook had resigned from the government, which he believed to be crumbling, and had gone to the United States where he made a public appeal for the opening of a second front, recklessly if necessary. On his return to London he established an organization to campaign for a second front and lent himself for a while to anti-Churchill manoeuvres, but these came to nothing in spite of a certain amount of intrigue and gossip on the political fringes in which Beaverbrook's name was freely used. Beaverbrook then rallied to his old and loyal friend and found himself back in the government before the year was out.

Despite the loss of Singapore in February and Tobruk in June, Churchill's position was never threatened as Asquith had been threatened by the reverses of 1916. Public opinion saw no alternative to Churchill and wished for none. The Conservative Party, as a whole, having made Churchill its leader in 1940, knew that it could not prosper without him, while the Labour Party never aspired to the leading place. Churchill was master of his cabinet and of Parliament as neither Asquith nor Lloyd George (the latter dependent in 1917–18 on the votes of a party not his own) had ever been. He was also in undoubted control of his service chiefs whom he could dismiss if he chose – again unlike Lloyd George, who distrusted Haig but dared not dismiss him. As Minister of Defence and chairman of the Chiefs of Staff Committee Churchill was a civilian warlord who had no cause to fear military intrigues against him; no British general in the Second World War complained to the king about civilian incompetence and interference as Haig did in the first war; in his relations with the military Churchill had an authority which no British Prime Minister – and, in France, only Clemenceau – had ever had before. Churchill's conduct of the war remained therefore remarkably uninhibited until it was curtailed by Great Britain's declining share in the total allied war effort. But this did not happen until there were more Americans than British under arms in the European theatre and up to 1943 it was still difficult to ship American forces to Europe owing to U-boats, shortage of transports and the competing claims of the war in the Pacific. At the end of 1942 there were only 170,000 American troops in Europe (and 140,000 in North Africa) out of 500,000 planned earlier in the year.

Roosevelt, as Commander-in-Chief as well as President, was confronted throughout the war with two series of strategic problems: the claims of the Pacific theatre against the European, and the alternative uses to which American power could be put within a theatre. Until Munich the United States had no plans for fighting Germany. It had plans of a vague and general kind for a war against Japan. Munich stimulated thinking about new problems and new theatres and in April 1939 the Chiefs of Staff, faced with the possibility of a war on two fronts, provisionally recommended that Europe should come first. At the end of 1940, with war palpably nearer, the Chief of Naval Operations, Admiral Harold R. Stark, recommended a policy of attack in the Atlantic and defence in the Pacific, which he was prepared to subordinate to the war against Germany and the Anglo-American alliance. This policy had been affirmed at a joint Anglo-American staff conference in March 1941 which hoped that war in the Pacific might be avoided but recommended that, if it came, it be subordinated to the war in Europe; but there were always dissentients on the American side. In his State of the Union address to Congress at the beginning of 1942 Roosevelt said that Hitler came first. By this time the United States was actively involved in hostilities in the Atlantic, and Hitler's declaration of war three days after Pearl Harbor had removed any need to reconsider, in the light of Pearl Harbor, the priorities which had governed American planning for the past few years: Hitler made the Americans' war a war on two fronts from its first week.

But although American priorities were never reversed, they were inevitably questioned from time to time. At the beginning of 1942 American strategy in the Pacific was largely dictated by the requirements of the defensive, but the United States recovered from the blow at Pearl Harbor with astonishing rapidity and was able after the naval victories of the

28   Sisters in a Polish field

29 *Top*: Rounding up
Warsaw Jews for the death
camp

30 *Bottom*: Polish hostages
hanging

31 A search in the Warsaw
ghetto

32 Russian partisans near
Minsk, 1941

33   Berlin: recovering in the
open after being bombed out

34   A Russian partisan about
to be executed, 1941

35 *Top*: Berlin: women and children take refuge in a hotel

36 *Bottom*: Berlin: the Tauentzienstrasse

37 *Top*: Stuttgart: the city
centre

38 *Bottom*: France, 1944: a
Frenchman kills a German
oppressor and welcomes
American liberators

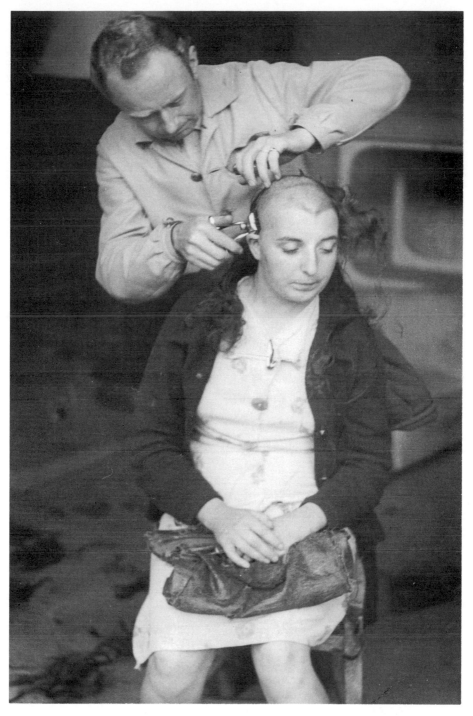

39 France, 1944: the
collaborator's fate

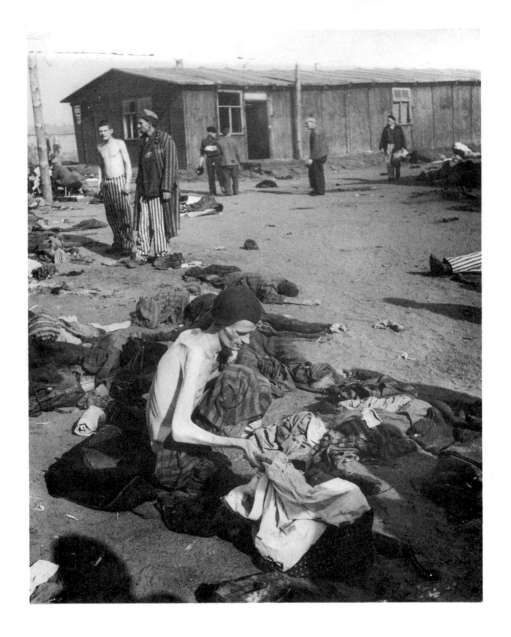

40   Belsen, 1945

Coral Sea and Midway in May and June to go over to the offensive sooner than had been expected. This turn of fortune lent strength to the pleas of the Pacific commanders, Admiral Chester W. Nimitz and General Douglas MacArthur, who were authorized to take the offensive and who therefore succeeded in altering to some extent the division of forces between the theatres. At the end of 1942 there were more Americans in the Pacific than in Europe.

In the European theatre Churchill dominated the strategic debate on the western side during 1942. Although he did not convince the American, or British, Chiefs of Staff he won a wavering Roosevelt over to his plan for a major Anglo-American landing in North-west Africa (Torch) which would join forces with the British army in the Western Desert, bring the North African campaign to a close and make the Mediterranean safe for the allies. Roosevelt was the more easily won over because he saw action in North Africa in 1942 as a partial redemption of the half-promise which he had given to Molotov of action in France in 1942, but to Stalin a second front in Africa was not the second front he wanted and in August Churchill set out for Moscow for his first meeting with Stalin in order to explain and justify this strategy. The meeting was boisterous but not disastrous and it formed Stalin's view of Churchill: he liked the man but not his plans. How far the two leaders ever understood one another is debatable, but so long as their common and overriding anti-German aim subsisted they preserved a mutual respect and did business with one another.

When the Grand Alliance came into being in 1941 the war in Africa was for the British, the senior combatants, nearly the whole of the war, but both the Americans and the Russians were dubious about it and regarded it as a sideshow. The Americans regarded battles in the eastern Mediterranean as battles to salvage the British Empire, battles in the western Mediterranean as battles to salvage the French Empire; and they had not entered the war to save or restore empires. The Americans, and the Russians too, thought of battles as much bigger affairs than anything that had occurred in Africa and could conceive of no vitally significant operation except the biggest possible battle in Europe at the earliest possible moment. Again, the Americans and Russians looked to a victory to be achieved preponderantly by ground forces, whereas Churchill clung to the belief in victory by air bombardments. (If he had been right, Great Britain would not have become so junior a partner in the Anglo-American effort.) In the final analysis Churchill and the British Chiefs of Staff did not question the paramount importance of an invasion of France and they agreed that other operations had to be justified by their contribution to the re-opening of a western front. Where they disagreed was in their assessment of the relevance of operations in the Mediterranean to this overriding aim. They were also more impressed than the Russians by the difficulties of landing in France (they seem to have given up the notion that the French Resistance would capture French harbours for them) and their hesitations on this score were increased in August 1942 by the costliness of the experimental raid on Dieppe.

In this atmosphere every British argument in favour of exploiting success in Africa by expanding the campaign in the Mediterranean was interpreted by the Americans as an attempt to turn this campaign into an alternative way of defeating the Germans without the necessity for a frontal assault in the west, and American suspiciousness was increased by the realization that Torch would rule out an invasion of France not only in 1942 but in 1943 too. On the American side there was a feeling of having been tricked by crafty British with ulterior motives. Churchill's strategic agility – his addiction to a strategy of ingenious pinpricks at spots as remote from a decisive theatre as northern Norway or Rhodes, which were the products of his lively sense of opportunity and often disconcerted his own advisers as much as his allies – was interpreted, wrongly, as unwillingness to face up to the serious business and daunting casualties of a landing in France.

Torch developed into an open-ended temptation. While the fighting in North-west Africa was still going on Roosevelt and Churchill met in January 1943 at Casablanca. They accepted the premise that for the time being their primary weapon against Germany was not direct invasion but air bombardment, and they sanctioned an invasion of Sicily as soon as possible after the defeat of the Germans and Italians in Africa, which was not completed until May. In that month they met again in Washington and decided to do something more in the western Mediterranean after taking Sicily, but what this was to be – an attack on Sardinia and Corsica or in Calabria or somewhere else – was left undecided and was still undecided when Sicily was invaded in July. This invasion, which caused the fall of Mussolini, led the allies on to an invasion of the Italian mainland but did not deliver Italy into their hands and effectively removed all prospect of a landing in France (Overlord) before 1944.

For twelve months therefore – from the end in Tunisia to Overlord – the three allies went their separate and barely coordinated ways towards Germany. The Russians won in July 1943 the battles in the Kursk salient which, even more than Stalingrad, spelt the end of Hitler's bid to subjugate the USSR. The western allies conquered Sicily in the same month, and then, landing at Salerno, set out in September for Rome, which, however, they did not reach for nine months because Hitler, after some hesitation, reinforced his armies in Italy and built them up by the end of the year to twenty-five divisions by withdrawals from both the Russian and western fronts. These latter operations involved the western allies in further disputes which were not without interest to Stalin both for their bearing on Overlord and their wider political import.

In the year before Overlord the western allies had in mind three principal operations. They could not, however, attempt all three because all of them required landing craft and there were not enough landing craft to go round. The first of the three possibilities was a second landing on the Italian coast to supplement the landing at Salerno and expedite the capture of Rome; this was effected in January 1944 at Anzio. The second was a landing in the Andaman Islands in the Bay of Bengal intended to lead to the recovery of Sumatra and Malaya; this was promised to Chiang Kai-shek by Roosevelt in Cairo in December 1943 but subsequently cancelled. The reason for the cancellation was the third operation – a landing in the Dodecanese. This was one of Churchill's pet plans and his strategic objective was the same as that of the Italian campaign: to win air bases (in the Aegean case, for attacks on the Rumanian oilfields) and to create a threat which would force Hitler either to evacuate the Balkans or reinforce them at the expense of more vital fronts (Hitler in fact built up his forces in south-eastern Europe to twenty divisions). Churchill was also keen to bring Turkey into the war. He argued that the Anzio and Dodecanese operations could be effected with the landing craft which were later to be used in support of Overlord by an invasion of southern France (Anvil), but that landing craft sent to the Indian Ocean could not be brought back to the Mediterranean in time. This argument won the day. (But the Dodecanese venture was a failure. Designed to coincide with the surrender of Italy, it was first postponed and then undertaken belatedly and with greatly reduced forces. An attempt to get the Italian garrison on Rhodes to change sides failed and the Germans put in troops of their own. The British nevertheless sent small detachments to take Kos, Leros, Samos and other nearby points. They were driven out of Kos after twenty days and out of Leros a month later and abandoned their remaining toeholds. The Germans made 900 allied and 3,000 Italian prisoners on Kos and shot Italian officers who had sided with the British. No attack was made on Rhodes. Turkey stayed neutral until the last week of February 1945.)

A successful British return to Greece, like the plan later proposed for an advance from Italy over the Brenner or through the Ljubljana Gap to Vienna, could have had political implications for the balance of power in central Europe after the war. But it does not follow that in 1943 Churchill sponsored his Dodecanese adventure for political reasons. It has been

ALLIED ADVANCES 1942–1945

November 1943 Russians begin westward advance reaching Berlin in May 1945

October 1942 British advance

Stalingrad

Black Sea

Danube

Cyprus (British)

El Alamein

Mediterranean Sea

Warsaw

Baltic Sea

Budapest

Berlin

Vienna

Leipzig

Dresden

Danube

Rhine

Munich

Milan

Rome

Malta (British)

German counter-attack at the Ardennes

Paris

Rhône

Loire

Brest

Algiers

Oran

Gibraltar (British)

Ft Lyautey
Casablanca

Safi

'D' Day 6 June 1944

Allied advance held up for a week by Falaise pocket

8 November 1942, First US landings of the war

0   250
Miles

→ Advance of the Allies

~ARTHUR BANKS~

assumed on too little evidence that Churchill was attracted to the Dodecanese by his memories of the First World War when he was deeply enmeshed in the Gallipoli campaign and by a desire to establish a military
presence in eastern Europe which would limit Stalin's post-war hegemony,
but Churchill's concern about the position of the Russians in Europe does
not seem to have been aroused before 1944 – and then chiefly by events in
Poland – nor does he seem to have imagined that a minor British operation
in the Balkans was the right way to limit Russian power. His attempt to
regain a foothold in the Aegean was an aspect of exploiting the collapse
of Italian Fascism by reaching out a hand to the Greek and Yugoslav
partisans who had captured his imagination as doughty allies in the
common cause. It was opposed by the Americans and the Russians as an
unnecessary and perhaps harmful distraction from the engaging of the
German armies in the west.

Nevertheless Churchill's strategies did acquire a political element which
became increasingly evident as the war went on. He was proud of British
achievements in Africa and the Mediterranean, aware that the victories to
come in western Europe would be more American than British, subconsciously anxious to make the most of what was, in Italy, still at least as much
a British as an American show. Like every great patriot he was a bit of a
chauvinist. He was also a European, whereas Roosevelt, like Woodrow
Wilson before him, was not a European and did not have the European's
sensitivity to the balance of power in Europe. Churchill, largely because
of his special interest in history, had this sensitivity to an unusual degree.
In the last year of the war the coming domination of Europe by the
Russians worried him quite apart from the fact that the government of the
USSR was a communist autocracy, and he was also worried by his inability
to get Roosevelt worried too. Roosevelt, again like Wilson, looked askance
at power political issues and attached more importance to the creation of
a new world organization which would impose universal harmony upon
particular disharmonies. For this purpose Russo-American cordiality was
all important and Roosevelt seized on the chance of wartime cooperation
as a means to establishing a more enduring entente. Everybody else's
salvation would flow from such an entente – a view of international order
which died with Roosevelt and the Cold War but revived with mutual
nuclear deterrence, the thaw of the 1960s and the fear of China to take the
place of fear of Germany. But Churchill, like Clemenceau *vis-à-vis* Wilson
in 1919, was more sceptical. In the heat of war Stalin might be pictured
as the benevolent Uncle Joe projected by wartime emotions; with the
approach of peace he could be looked at more coldly.

The first meeting of the three leaders of the Grand Alliance did not take place until the Russian victory in the east had been assured and the preponderance of American over British might in the west had been made manifest. There were only two such meetings during the war in Europe: the first, which lasted four days, at Teheran in November 1943 and a second, which lasted eight days, at Yalta in February 1945.

Before Teheran Roosevelt and Churchill had had a series of meetings as well as a continuous and intimate correspondence. Churchill had met Stalin once, and Roosevelt and Stalin had met not at all. During 1943 distrust within the alliance had become serious. In the United States the view that Stalin was no better than Hitler was being freely expressed in the press and elsewhere; it was reinforced by the revelation in April 1943 of the Katyn massacre in Poland and by the constitution in Moscow in July of a Free German Committee which was taken as evidence of Russian flirting with Germany. From Stockholm came reports of Russian feelers, designed either to end the war in the east by a separate peace or to scare the western allies into thinking that Stalin was about to do so. The western allies feared that Stalin might be content to push the Germans back into Germany and then leave the Nazi régime intact. On his side Stalin, besides being embarrassed and angered by the publicity given to Katyn, feared that the Americans might divert most of their strength to the Pacific and resented, unreasonably, the suspension of the Arctic convoys for three months after disasters suffered in June 1942. Above all Stalin was trying to hold his allies to their promises to open a second front in 1943. By a second front he meant a landing in strength on the continent which would draw off great numbers of German divisions from the east. In the crisis of 1941 he had specified thirty to forty divisions. He accepted as adequate neither the western air offensive which engaged the best of the Luftwaffe's aircraft and aircrews (to the considerable advantage of the Russian armies) nor the operations in the Mediterranean which tied down a number of German divisions in the Balkans and diverted twenty-five to Italy. Although Churchill had given no promise of a cross-Channel invasion in 1943 he seems to have felt that, when in Moscow in August 1942, he had given Stalin grounds for expecting one; and Roosevelt had been much more explicit. Both western leaders had a feeling of unease about postponing the big assault to 1944.

Roosevelt and Churchill liked meeting for the sake of meeting. They believed in the value of man-to-man talks of a general nature, informal and on an assumption of shared aims and proved comradeship. Such meetings must, they felt, generate understanding and trust, eliminate the rubs in the alliance and so accelerate victory and lay a sure basis for post-war harmony. They envisaged not so much a diplomatic conference as a council of war. Stalin took a more professional view of summit meetings. He wanted a regular conference or nothing. He had exercised power and responsibility unremittingly for twenty years, during which he had got his way by always doing his homework more thoroughly than his adversaries, by never taking decisions in anybody's time but his own, by knowing how far to go at any given moment (unlike Hitler but not unlike Bismarck) – in short by arming an unusually clear mind and unusually ruthless character with the most rigorous professional techniques of the statesman and negotiator. Whereas Roosevelt and Churchill looked to their subordinates to supply these technical assets as required, Stalin embodied them in himself. He had neither the gifts nor the weaknesses of the amateur. He may have been a repulsive man but he was an exceptionally gifted and experienced master of his craft.

Roosevelt and Churchill, desiring a meeting on general grounds, thought that the sooner it took place the better. They pressed for it on and off throughout 1943. Stalin on the other hand had no use for a conference which was unlikely to further specific or particular objectives and he therefore blew hot and cold, favouring a conference when his fortunes and his bargaining power were in the ascendant, putting it off when they waned or when he was vexed. Early in 1943 he seemed willing to meet his associates. By this time the three great crises of the war, from the Russian point of view, were behind him: Moscow had been saved in 1941, Japan had not attacked when Germany did, Stalingrad had not fallen. Yet he still prevaricated, probably on account of the Anglo-American conference of May which resolved on further operations against Italy, and it was not until after the spectacular Russian victories on his central front in the summer which finally eliminated all prospect of a German victory over the USSR that he again reversed his position and agreed to a meeting in Teheran at the end of the year. The second front was no longer a condition of Russian survival. Rather the failure to open a second front could be used as a lever politically against the western allies. And the Polish problem had also been transformed by the certainty that Russian armies would soon be on Polish soil once more.

During 1943 Stalin broke with the provisional Polish government which had its headquarters in London. Relations with this government had been established after Hitler invaded the USSR by an agreement signed in London by General Wladislaw Sikorski, the head of the government, and Ivan Maisky; the agreement provided for an 'amnesty' for all Poles in the USSR and the raising of a Polish army on Russian soil. This was the season of Stalin's direst need. He was prepared not only to see American troops in the USSR but a Polish army too and General Anders, captured in the war of 1939, was disinterred from the Lubianka prison in Moscow to command it. The Poles in the USSR, however, were not enthusiastic about fighting alongside their hereditary and recent Russian enemies. Trouble soon came. The Russians accused the Poles of breaking the Sikorski-Maisky agreement by not committing their divisions to the front as quickly as they were formed. The Poles were probably reluctant to use up their fighting power in the defence of the USSR against the Germans, and as the pressure on the Russians eased, Stalin's priorities changed and he became more wary about a scheme which would take a Polish army, commanded by anti-Russian and anti-communist officers, into territories which he had recently seized from Poland and intended to keep.

Eventually, on Churchill's suggestion and with Stalin's consent, Anders's divisions left for Italy via Iran, thus incidentally ensuring that the liberation of Poland from the Germans would be accomplished by the Russians alone. Churchill, who established a personal friendship with Sikorski, hoped to be able to resolve the differences between his Polish and Russian allies by persuading Sikorski, who was in turn to persuade his compatriots, to cede territory in eastern Poland to the USSR in return for equivalent territory in the west to be taken from Germany: Poland was to be shifted westward. The Poles did not want to be shifted; they wanted the cancellation of the Russo-German deal of 1939 and the restoration of Poland's 1939 frontiers. But Stalin was determined not to give up what he had won before the German and Russian invasions of 1939, and talked of a new 'ethnic' Poland to the west of the Russo-German partition line. He was prepared to accept the somewhat less favourable 'Curzon Line' invented in 1920 by Lord Curzon and opportunely dug out by Eden, but he did not intend that the new Poland should have its old government, and in 1943 events enabled him to begin the process of displacing it.

During the short war of 1939 a great many Polish officers disappeared. They were believed to be in Russian captivity but they failed to reappear after the amnesty proclaimed in accordance with the Sikorski–Maisky agreement of 1941. They were in fact dead and in April 1943 thousands of bodies were found in pits in the forest of Katyn. They had been murdered. The temper of the times inclined western opinion to the belief that they had been murdered by the Germans and when Goebbels proclaimed that they had been murdered by the Russians few people in the west believed him. Yet it gradually became obvious that this was the case and that a massacre of some 10–14,000 prisoners had been perpetrated. The Polish government in London asked for an investigation by the Red Cross, whereupon Stalin seized the occasion to sever relations. A few months later, in September 1943, the death of Sikorski in an aircraft accident at Gibraltar removed from the scene the one Polish leader who, because he was a man of singular ability and vision, enjoyed the friendship of Churchill and had some personal credit with Stalin, might have been able to repair the breach between Moscow and the London Poles and implement Churchill's policy of making territorial but not political concessions to the USSR.

After Sikorski's death Churchill was virtually without any cards to play against Stalin on the Polish question. Sikorski's successor as head of the government in exile, Stanislaw Mikolajczyk, saw the need for an understanding with the Russians but he lacked Sikorski's authority and both his Minister of War, General Kasimierz Sosnkowski, and General Tadeusz Bor-Komarowski who succeeded to the command of the Polish Home Army (AK) when its first commander fell into German hands, were strongly anti-Russian. (They were also anti-semitic.) But Stalin, following his military successes of the summer, was about to take possession of the contested field, having turned Katyn to good account by divesting himself of the commitments in the Sikorski-Maisky agreement. At Teheran he was in a position to urge Churchill to acknowledge that Poland was his to dispose of, and Churchill, being already sufficiently in agreement with Stalin's case for securer frontiers in areas through which Hitler had attacked, went far towards doing so. He even took the lead in the discussions on Poland, leaving Stalin to concur. It was agreed that the Poles should be left out of the discussions until later. (About the three Baltic states nothing was said; the silence proclaimed their coming fate.)

Stalin had at Teheran other demands too: half East Prussia, a third of the Italian fleet (to be delivered in January 1944), the Kuriles, the southern half of Sakhalin and a free port at Dairen. In return he accepted an abortive plan propounded by Roosevelt for emasculating Germany by dividing it into five segments and putting the Ruhr, the Saar, Hamburg and the Kiel Canal under international control; agreed to join a world organization and to collaborate in a European Advisory Commission for the discussion of German problems; and repeated the promise already made by Molotov a few weeks earlier to join in the war against Japan as soon as Germany was defeated.

All these matters were dealt with in a single day. The other three days were devoted to military rather than political business. The principal outcome was a promise by the western allies to invade France in May 1944.

The comparatively long list of matters agreed at Teheran can be accounted for less by supposing a basic identity of views than by the fact that both Roosevelt and Stalin attached comparatively little importance to what the other most desired. Roosevelt was chiefly interested in establishing a personal relationship with Stalin, ensuring his entry into the war against Japan and enlisting his participation in the new organization which was to replace the League of Nations. Stalin had no objection to any of these things. For him the real importance of the conference lay in the territorial and political settlements which it might help to ensure in eastern and central Europe and to a lesser extent in the Far East: he intended to keep what he had won before Hitler's invasion from Finland, the Baltic states, Poland and Rumania and to round off these acquisitions by establishing a primary Russian influence in Bulgaria and the Straits. These were matters to which Roosevelt was much less alert than Churchill. How Roosevelt would have reacted to Russian meddling in western Europe it is impossible to say because Stalin showed no interest in western Europe. Beyond his immediate sphere of interest he postulated only the restoration of an independent Czechoslovakia and Austria and he talked vaguely about partitioning Italy. Churchill continued to have forebodings, but his objections carried in 1943 less weight than they would have done if the conference had been held at an earlier date, partly because of the turn of the military tide in the USSR and partly because the preponderant voice in the western alliance was no longer British but American. Stalin even allowed himself to make during the conference half bantering, half barbed attacks on Churchill which he would hardly have been likely to make a year earlier; he treated Roosevelt with immaculate respect and condescension. Roosevelt responded with what his detractors have called naïvety.

The charge is in part valid not because Roosevelt was a foolishly vain man, as lesser men have argued, but in the sense that Roosevelt seems to have overestimated his superabundant political gifts. He had wanted to meet Stalin without Churchill being present and had sent a personal emissary, Joseph E. Davies, a former Ambassador in Moscow, to prepare a *tête-à-tête*. He argued against the British that it was impolitic to engage in a conference at which Stalin might feel himself outmatched by two to one, but Roosevelt's deepest motive was his determination to talk Stalin into a personal friendship which would be the counterpart of his special relationship with Churchill. His own career had been based on his special gifts as a manager of men, and he seems to have thought that he could manage Stalin too in much the same way as he had managed American politicians of varying degree and varying views. It is said that old and sick men fall into the error of exaggerating their principal talents. Roosevelt, long a cripple, had held one of the most arduous offices in the world for an unprecedented number of years of unparalleled domestic complexity and external stress. Although at Teheran he seemed still to retain his extraordinary powers, at Yalta only fifteen months later he was dying. His mistake at the end of his life – if one can speak of a mistake in the case of a man whose faculties are deserting him – was to imagine that he could captivate a man like Stalin, a man of a kind uncommon even in American politics and placed in circumstances utterly remote from the imagination of any person raised in the American tradition. Roosevelt was the youngest of the three leaders – three years younger than Stalin, eight years younger than Churchill – but at Teheran and Yalta Stalin was the fittest of the three, not only fitter than Roosevelt but probably also fitter than Churchill, who succumbed to pneumonia after Teheran for the second time that year. It is not unnatural that Stalin had the best reason to be pleased with the way the conference went.

On the immediate strategic issue the Teheran conference agreed that the Anglo-American armies in Italy should advance to Hitler's Gothic Line (which ran from Pisa to Rimini). If necessary, Overlord might be postponed for a month, but once the Gothic Line was reached further operations in Italy would be entirely subordinated to the requirements of Overlord. This proviso meant in practice that the Supreme Commander in the Mediterranean, now Field Marshal Sir Harold Alexander, would have to relinquish a number of divisions for Anvil which was to take place simultaneously with Overlord. No thought was given to what would be done if the Gothic Line was not reached before the Anvil divisions had to leave the theatre to keep to the Overlord timetable. Yet this is what happened. The Anglo-American advance was so retarded by the Germans that Alexander had to request the cancellation of Anvil. The British Chiefs of Staff supported him; the American Chiefs were very angry but agreed to let him keep his divisions until after the capture of Rome. But Rome was not taken until two days before D-day for Overlord on 6 June with the result that Anvil, postponed until the middle of August, contributed nothing to Overlord and was proved by Overlord's success to be unnecessary before it took place. Alexander was denied the chance to press forward to the Danube, a plan of his which was warmly espoused by Churchill although regarded as over-optimistic by his military advisers, and the Mediterranean strategy petered out in the autumn rains of the Po valley.

On the eastern fronts the Russians gained in 1944 a series of military victories over the Germans and their allies which they were able to convert without impediment into political advantage. In the west the immense accumulation of American men and material for the invasion of France was accomplished without serious opposition from the German U-boats, and the invasion itself was successfully effected in June and equally successfully exploited until the German counter-attack in the Ardennes in November temporarily delayed the last stages of the overthrow of German power. These operations in east and west were affected by Germany's continuing need to defend itself on more than one front but otherwise the campaigns of the eastern and western allies owed little to one another. They were independent operations, usefully coincidental but only very loosely coordinated. In these circumstances allied cooperation became even more political and less military, more concerned with the post-war settlement and less with the conduct of the war.

In October 1944 Churchill went again to Moscow for his third meeting with Stalin (the second without Roosevelt who was campaigning for election for a fourth term as President). Churchill had now become much more worried about the fate of eastern and central Europe and the inability of the western allies to prevent the Russians from imposing communist rule in the countries which their armies were overrunning. He tried to strike a bargain with Stalin but since he was bargaining only about eastern territories, without being willing or indeed entitled to concede anything in the west in return, his position was not a strong one except in relation to Greece which, as a Mediterranean country, was more accessible to Anglo-American sea power than to Russian land power.

Stalin and Churchill agreed that all countries would be subject to the joint control of all three allies but that the degrees of interest of each of the three might be unequal and would vary from state to state. In a curiously offhand way in the course of one of their conversations they attempted to represent this idea arithmetically: the Russian interest in Rumania was put at ninety, the western at ten; the same interests in Hungary and Bulgaria were defined as eighty and twenty respectively, in Yugoslavia as fifty-fifty; Greece was rated 90 per cent a western sphere, 10 per cent Russian. This somewhat crude calculation gave offence to the Americans in particular who regarded it as a reversion to the worst practices of spheres of influence. It represented, however, certain realities, whether it was wise or not to put them down on paper. A mark of ninety or seventy-five to the one side acknowledged the impossibility of thwarting that side's wishes in that area; a fifty-fifty mark recorded uncertainty or a desire not to come to grips there for the time being. In central Europe it recognized what Stalin's armies had already ensured. In the Mediterranean it gave the British a free hand in Greece.

Poland was not in the list. Both leaders probably thought that, so far as frontiers were concerned, the Polish question had been settled at Teheran.

When Mikolajczyk, still apparently ignorant of what had passed at Teheran, flew to Moscow to try to get Stalin to accept Poland's pre-war frontiers, he failed and the Warsaw rising and its defeat by the Germans (described in a later chapter) eliminated the armed forces in Poland on which the London Poles were relying. Poland's fate had become settled, and both in Moscow and in London Mikolajczyk found himself treated as a wrecker whose inconvenient demands were imperilling the peace of Europe. He was even upbraided by Churchill in much the same terms as the Czechs had been chided by the appeasers of 1938.

The three leaders met again at Yalta on 4 February 1945. As at Teheran there was no formal agenda; each was free to raise or try to keep out whatever topic he wished to air or to pigeonhole. Since the Teheran conference Russian forces had entered Poland (and the Baltic States) and Stalin had allowed the Polish National Liberation Committee (communist and pro-communist Poles with headquarters in Lublin) to call itself a government. At Yalta Churchill tried to commit Stalin to early and free elections in Poland, but Stalin sidestepped these points by concentrating on frontiers. Poland was discussed briefly. Its frontier with the USSR was fixed and the city of Lvov was decreed to fall on the Russian side of it, but the western and northern frontiers were not agreed. Stalin, having discovered that there were two Neisses, tried to get his allies to agree to the western one but Churchill, arguing that the new Poland would have too many Germans in it, refused and Stalin had to wait for his armies to do the job. The government of Poland was to be reorganized under the direction of Molotov and the American and British Ambassadors in Moscow; it was to have an infusion of Poles from London to leaven the Lublin Committee and after the reorganization free elections were to be held with universal suffrage and a secret ballot. Thus what was left of the Polish issue was shifted out of the conference and onto a committee of three which was to meet later – in Moscow.

The conference was no more precise about the rest of liberated Europe. It adopted a general declaration promising free elections. Stalin agreed that France should have a zone of occupation in Germany and (after much argument) a place on the Allied Control Commission which was to administer Germany. He also conceded everything that Roosevelt wanted in relation to the United Nations: having asked for sixteen seats he accepted three without any fuss and even agreed to support an American demand for three seats if Roosevelt should consider that American public opinion demanded them. In separate Russo-American discussion on the Far East he sought and obtained reaffirmation of the promises already made to him together with an American undertaking to force Chiang

Kai-shek to accept them and a further American undertaking not to tell Chiang what was afoot until Stalin was ready for this disclosure. Stalin succeeded in other words in making Roosevelt his accomplice in imposing, at a moment of his own choosing, conditions on Chiang which included recognition of the independence of Outer Mongolia (and its virtual dependence on the USSR), a Russian share in the running of the Manchurian railways, and a Russian naval base in China. A vague notion of sweetening this large pill by getting Great Britain to transfer Hong Kong to China never came to anything. At first sight Stalin's gains over Roosevelt at Teheran and Yalta over the Far East are surprising, but they have to be seen against Roosevelt's growing awareness of the uselessness of Chiang as an ally against Japan and his need therefore for Russian help at a time when the coming nuclear weapon was still too mysterious to be relied upon.

With Poland on the way to the solution desired by Stalin and with these considerable Far Eastern advantages underwritten by the United States the only remaining item of real interest to Stalin was reparations. On this issue Stalin got much of what he wanted but not all. Roosevelt took comparatively little part in the reparations discussions. Although the American position was virtually the same as the British, the arguing was left to the latter. Whereas the Russians wished to impose reparations as a penalty, the Americans and British regarded them as restitution only for civilian damage. They considered that reparations should be paid only out of current German production and only after securing to the German people a minimum standard of living. They were opposed to the removal of capital assets and to the pauperization of Germany. Stalin on the other hand hoped to secure, besides regular reparations, payments spread over ten years, a German labour force to work in Russian devastated areas for ten years and something like 80 per cent of Germany's surviving heavy industrial plant. He proposed that the USSR's share of reparations payments in cash should be $10 billion and that the apportionment of the total sum should be made on the basis of the contribution which each of Germany's victims had made to the German defeat and not on the basis of its losses – a method which could have operated to give very little to countries which had been quickly defeated, however much they had suffered afterwards. Although the conference reached no final decisions on reparations Stalin succeeded in stamping the figure of $10 billion on future discussions. Most tellingly, Stalin abandoned at Yalta the policy of dismembering Germany. The simplest explanation of this change is that, confident of the departure of American troops from Europe, he thought he had a chance to dominate all Germany.

When the Yalta conference broke up, the Russian armies were on the Oder and the Danube and the western armies on the Rhine. The Grand Alliance had won the war in Europe. One of its leaders did not live to see the end: Roosevelt died on 12 April. His successor, Harry S. Truman, joined Churchill and Stalin at one more conference, at Potsdam in July. Its discussions were about war in Asia, but peace in Europe. But the shape of the new Europe was settled neither at Yalta nor at Potsdam, meetings which affected no more than the marginal details of the march of armed events. In earlier years Stalin had pleaded with Roosevelt and Churchill to open a second front in 1943, for want of which he feared defeat. Having survived and won, he benefited from the delay, for it gave him a mastery which he would not have enjoyed if the western armies had been able to begin their advances into central Europe a year earlier.

CHAPTER 17

The Clearing of North Africa

THERE is at first sight no obvious reason why a European war should be fought in Africa. The short reason why the Second World War spread from Europe to Africa was that the British and Italians were already there. The British had been the overlords of Egypt for sixty years and kept considerable military forces and military installations in Egypt. The Italians had begun to acquire an empire in East Africa at about the same time as the British occupation of Egypt in the 1880s and had extended it by taking Libya and Cyrenaica from the Turks on the eve of the First World War and by the conquest of Ethiopia in the 1930s. The campaigns of the Second World War in Africa were a consequence of these imperial positions, and the failures of the Italians in 1940–41 brought, as we have seen, the Germans into this field too. Nor was this all. France too had an empire in North Africa, exercising direct rule in Algeria which was juridically a part of France and indirect rule in the two flanking monarchies of Morocco and Tunisia which had been reduced to protectorates and where the French had steadily encroached on the authority of the native administration. This empire was preserved after the French collapse of 1940 so that the whole of North Africa from the Atlantic to the Red Sea was under European dominion throughout the Second World War. It was treated by Europeans as a campaign ground in their essentially European conflicts.

But these were not the only conflicts. North Africa was not a sand table. The military campaigns of 1940–43 were superimposed upon a further conflict between rulers and ruled, between imperial power and nationalist aspirations. The war provided nationalists with new opportunities in an old cause. The Americans, whom the war brought into the western end of this increasingly crowded scene in 1942, sympathized with the nationalists' hope of turning the evils of war to some good by accelerating the liberation of their homelands from foreign domination. To Europeans therefore Africa was one of the places where they vied among themselves, but to non-Europeans – whether African or American – one European was in this context much the same as another and none of them belonged there.

The system of government in Egypt was a three-cornered game between the British, the king and the Wafd. The British had been the real rulers of Egypt since 1882 and still had the ultimate power since, in spite of conceding formal independence after the First World War, they retained by treaty the right to station considerable forces in the country. King Faruq, the last descendant of the Albanian line of Mehemet Ali, wished to rule as well as reign but was hedged in by the British on one side and the Wafd on the other. The Wafd, founded by Zaghlul Pasha and led since 1927 by Nahas Pasha, was an upper-class nationalist movement which wanted to be rid of the British and the king. On coming of age Faruq had dismissed a Wafd government but kept the apparatus of parliament in spite of the fact that there was no political party of consequence except the Wafd; every other party was no more than the *clientela* of notabilities, incapable of giving the king cnough backing against the Wafd or the British, let alone both. The Wafd, smarting under its treatment by the king, was inclined to ally itself with the British against the king and justify this policy *ex post facto* by getting true independence for Egypt by agreement with the British, but it was on delicate ground since too much friendliness between it and the British caused some nationalists to defect, Egyptians being divided among themselves about whether to get independence from the British by helping them to win the war in the expectation of later reward or by siding with their enemies.

When the war began, Egypt had at once broken off diplomatic relations with Germany and taken further pro-British steps such as handing over control of Egyptian ports and imposing a censorship, but the German victories in Europe in 1940 and the entry into the war of Italy, which had a much larger army in North Africa than the British, raised the question whether a more ambiguous policy would not be wiser. Egypt severed diplomatic relations with Italy but declared that it would not go to war unless the Italians invaded Egypt or bombed towns or military targets in it; Egyptian troops were withdrawn from the western frontiers to avoid incidents; and the Egyptian government refused to act as severely against the large Italian population (60,000) as the British authorities would have liked.

But the British were still powerful on the spot and were not willing to tolerate a government which hedged in this way. It was forced to resign and was replaced by a more pro-British one. The British also obtained other changes, including the retirement of the Chief of Staff of the Egyptian army, at the price of promising to buy considerable quantities of Egyptian cotton which they did not want. When the Italian advance into Egypt was repulsed by Wavell at the end of 1940 the pro-British policy was hailed as a success, but in April of the following year the Italians, now accompanied by the Germans, re-crossed the frontier and the champions of a stricter non-belligerence raised their voices once more. There were demands for the withdrawal of British troops and stores from Cairo and Alexandria. The Egyptian government was also beset by the economic problems created by its inability to buy and sell in foreign markets, by inflation and by the refusal of parties outside the government to join in forming a national coalition. In February 1942, following popular demonstrations in Cairo and a tiff with the king, it resigned.

The British Ambassador had already tried to persuade Faruq to retain his pro-British government. When it fell the Ambassador returned to the palace to demand the appointment of Nahas – by six o'clock that evening. The king refused. Three hours later British tanks and infantry entered the palace grounds. The king gave way. Afraid of retaining a mildly pro-British government when Rommel's star was in the ascendant, he was forced to accept Nahas, who was both more pro-British and a personal enemy, because that star was still at a distance. The drama at the palace when Faruq was forced to yield was a re-enactment of similar scenes in the past: not long after the British bombardment of Alexandria and the occupation of Egypt in 1882, Sir Evelyn Baring (later Lord Cromer) initiated the full British raj in Egypt by conveying to the Khedive Tawfiq (Faruq's uncle) the British cabinet's decision that the Khedive's government must either toe the British line or be evicted; and Tawfiq's son Abbas had been forced on his accession in 1892 to dismiss his chosen Prime Minister. Faruq in his turn was obliged to keep Nahas in office until nearly the end of the war, although Nahas was then dismissed as he was preparing to present to Great Britain his account for services rendered. After the war the Wafd blocked British attempts to re-negotiate the Anglo-Egyptian alliance with a non-Wafd government along lines which would have preserved some of Great Britain's favoured status, but its triumph was short-lived for after 1952 the more radical nationalist movement of Naguib and Nasser extinguished the Wafd as well as getting rid of both the king and the British.

By its show of power at the beginning of 1942 Great Britain had secured its base for the campaigns of the coming year. The first to move was Rommel. He entered Cyrenaica from Tripolitania in the first days of the year and so opened a series of campaigns in the North African deserts which took him almost to the Nile and the Suez Canal before the German and Italian forces were thrown back all the way to Tunisia and he himself, ill and defeated, laid down his command and returned to Germany to rest, to recover, to resume great responsibilities, to rebel against Hitler's judgement and ultimately to kill himself on Hitler's orders.

Rommel was the dominating figure in the desert war. There were exceptional commanders on the British side too – Wavell, Auchinleck, Alexander, Montgomery – but they were many and on the Axis side there was only one such figure of fame. Rommel, unlike most German officers, had been not merely an acquiescent Nazi but a keen one and his unconcealed enthusiasm for the new régime probably played some part in furthering his career in the years immediately before the war. But it was by his talents rather than his opportunities that he became famous. He was a first-class divisional commander and he proved his worth in the campaign in France in 1940 when he led an armoured division from the Meuse to the English Channel with all the personal dash and professional skill expected of the new wave of German tank commanders. When the time came for his promotion to a different type of command he was fortunate in finding, in North Africa, the one higher command of the whole war which required many of the aptitudes of the divisional commander. On the British side Wavell, Auchinleck and Alexander all at one time or another exercised tactical control of their forces to a degree unusual in a supreme commander. Rommel did so continuously and his fame as a desert general rests not so much on his exercise of his higher army command as on the flexibility, improvisation and quickness of judgement which he displayed in battle. Later in the war he was to command army groups, but never with that outstanding success which, as commander of the German Afrika Corps and the German-Italian Panzer Army, singled him out from his brother generals and field marshals.

The distinctive character of the desert war derived from the terrain as well as the personalities involved. The distances were great, the forces small. At Alamein the opposed armies deployed between them only 1,500 tanks and 1,500 aircraft, and in that battle the full tally of men on the Axis side was no more than a fifth of the German casualties in the battles in the Kursk salient the next year. The desert war was a war of movement and supply. The men on the ground were tormented by the heat and by the sandstorms which were the mechanics' worst enemies, while the men at sea, hazarding the passage in the Mediterranean, lived in constant expectation of a submarine or air torpedo. Each time the British advanced westward the Royal Navy was set a hard task in maintaining the supply route along the coast against Axis submarine and air attacks. The Axis armies were dependent on supplies from Europe which were intercepted in crippling quantities by British naval and air patrols acting on precise Ultra intelligence about the sailing of tankers and other vessels from Greek and Italian ports.

After Rommel re-entered the lists at the beginning of 1942 both sides

THE NORTH AFRICAN THEATRE

1 Mersa Breda
2 Agedabia
3 Beda Fomm
4 Msus
5 El Adem
6 Bir Hacheim
7 Fort Capuzzo
8 Halfaya Pass

~ARTHUR BANKS~

0   200
Miles

were preparing for a major effort. Churchill was urging Auchinleck to attack first. Great Britain needed a victory to offset disasters in the Far East. Singapore had fallen in February; the Japanese were occupying Burma; the War Cabinet ordered preparations for the destruction of the oil refinery at Abadan in western Iran and sent an expedition to take Madagascar before the Japanese did. The position of Great Britain again seemed critical. No American divisions could be expected to reach European or African theatres of war before the end of the year, while the Russians, although they had saved Moscow in 1941, could well lose the Caucasus in 1942. If they did, the British forces in the Middle East might have to face three ways: against Rommel advancing on Egypt, against new German armies descending from the north through Iran, and against the Japanese to the east. India too might be threatened from two sides – through Burma and through Afghanistan and Iran – in which event the Middle East command would lose its Indian divisions and all further hope of reinforcement from the Indian army. Hitler, who still regarded the Russians as mincemeat in the making, was not only dreaming of conquests of this kind but planning them. A special unit under General Helmuth Felmy (an exceptionally able army officer who had risen to the command of an Air Fleet but had been sacked after the episode of the crashed aircraft which gave away Hitler's plans for invading the Low Countries) had been formed with agreeable headquarters at Cape Sunion near Athens where it collected intelligence about the Middle East and trained Arabs for subversion. In 1942 it was moved to the Caucasus and began to take an interest in India too (although by the autumn it was back at Sunion with waning prospects).

Churchill's anxiety for an early victory in the desert was therefore not just a piece of impetuosity but a consequence of the disquieting view of the war seen as a whole from London. In the event Rommel attacked first and scored a great victory which carried him over the Egyptian border and produced the only occasion during the war on which Churchill is known to have allowed the strains to get the better of his emotions.

General Ritchie's Eighth Army was holding a series of positions stretching from Gazala, some thirty-five miles west of Tobruk, southward into the desert as far as Bir Hacheim which was garrisoned by a French force under General Pierre Koenig. These positions consisted of a number of strongpoints or boxes (not unlike the mile castles on a Roman wall) linked by minefields. They were meant to serve both as a shield for Tobruk and as a springboard for a British offensive. For this reason – and also because the longer the British line the farther would Rommel have to extend his supply lines if he planned to circumvent it – the British armour was dispersed, whereas Rommel's was concentrated for the attack which he launched on 26 May. Rommel moreover attacked in the south, whereas Ritchie had stationed the bulk of his forces at the northern or coastal end of the line. While the Eighth Army had the advantage in manpower and in tanks, the Luftwaffe was more than a match for the Desert Air Force.

Rommel's attack began with a feint in the north to distract attention from his main thrust which was made in the ensuing night by German and Italian armour in the south. Bir Hacheim held firm and Rommel fell into a dangerous trap which made his position desperate, exposed one Panzer division to air attack as it lay stranded for want of fuel, and brought a substantial part of his forces to within a few hours of surrender from thirst; but he was saved by his own resourcefulness and by the tentativeness of his opponent who failed to seize his opportunities. Bir Hacheim continued to hold out for two valuable weeks, at the end of which Koenig made good his escape with two thirds of his men. By this time the southern half of the Eighth Army's positions had been dissolved and Ritchie and Auchinleck were faced with the alternatives of a bold total withdrawal to the Egyptian frontier or a qualified withdrawal leaving a substantial force in Tobruk which, besides its considerable strategic importance, had acquired emotional and symbolic significance.

Neither British commander had intended Tobruk to stand a second siege and its defences were in no fit state to do so. There was a severe shortage of anti-tank weapons. Nevertheless Auchinleck decided to try to hold it and left a garrison of 35,000 which, misinterpreting or disregarding Ultra intelligence, he disposed ill-advisedly. Rommel attacked on 20 June. Tobruk fell to him in a day. Practically the entire garrison was taken prisoner, including one third of all South Africans on active fighting service. Rommel captured invaluable supplies, fuel, vehicles and other provisions without which he would not have been able to remain on the offensive. Churchill, who received the news at the White House in Washington, gave way under his emotions. He called the loss of Tobruk a disgrace second only to the loss of Singapore. Less than a month after launching his attack Rommel, promoted Field Marshal, entered Egypt on the heels of the Eighth Army. Cairo and Alexandria were seized with panic. Mussolini went to Africa where a white horse was waiting to carry him into the Egyptian capital.

Auchinleck took personal command of the Eighth Army in place of its defeated and dismissed commander and in a limited but nevertheless decisive duel in the first week of July, known as the First Battle of Alamein, he defeated the German and Italian forces opposing him so severely that the Axis command had to commit parachute troops (as ground troops) in order to save Rommel from having to retreat once more. Auchinleck's victory owed much to the picture of the enemy which he got from Y service intercepts and from Ultra.

The appearance on the borders of Egypt of these troops, which could more appropriately have been used in an attack on Malta, symbolized a strategic choice which the German and Italian staffs had to make in the first half of 1942. They lacked the resources to take Cairo and Malta at once. Voices were raised in favour of reducing Malta first in order to secure complete control of the supply routes through and across the Mediterranean. From the narrowness of their lucky victory in Crete the Germans had concluded that Malta could not be taken by airborne landing alone, but it might be battered and starved until ripe for capture by combined seaborne and airborne assaults: a force of 1,000 aircraft (mostly from the Russian front) was assembled at the beginning of the year under the supreme command of Field Marshal Albert Kesselring, who set up his headquarters in Rome.

Great Britain's position in the Mediterranean had been endangered by serious naval losses inflicted at the end of the previous year by U-boats in both the western and eastern basins, by minefields and by the 'human torpedoes' with which the Italians penetrated the defences of Alexandria in order to fix explosives to the hulls of warships. During the short period at the turn of the year when Rommel had been driven out of Cyrenaica five supply ships reached Malta, but with Rommel's first forward moves at the beginning of 1942 the Luftwaffe was able to reoccupy North African airfields which, together with its bases in Crete, were used to interdict the passage of east–west convoys. In February an entire convoy, attempting to make this passage, was destroyed; its last surviving ship was scuttled in desperation. In March a convoy of four vessels, attacked from the air and by the Italian surface fleet, managed to get two ships through, but in the ensuing months this attack on Malta's lifelines was redoubled by fierce air attacks on the island itself. These occurred several times every day. In the harbour repair soon ceased to keep pace with destruction. All ships which could be removed sailed away and the rest were scuttled. Without shipping and without labour – the population took to living underground during daylight – the docks became a silent testimony to the triumph of air power. The air defences were too feeble to interrupt the work of destruction. Reinforcements of Spitfires, flown in from an American aircraft carrier in April, were destroyed on their airfields before they had had time to engage the enemy. Further reinforcements in May fared better owing to the frantic efficiency of the ground crews which serviced them and got them into the air again within a few minutes of their arrival, but by the middle of May Malta was holding out with little hope of survival against the bombing and the blockade. At this point Hitler, hesitatingly, agreed to divert the Luftwaffe and give priority to the attack on Egypt which Rommel and Mussolini were urging upon him – Rommel because he wanted to attack Ritchie before Ritchie attacked him, Mussolini because he was enticed by the prospect of entering Cairo and adding Egypt to the Italian empire.

The blockade of Malta continued while Rommel fought his battles with Ritchie and Auchinleck. In June an attempt was made to run convoys simultaneously from east and west. Of the eastern convoy no ship reached the island but from the west two out of seventeen merchantmen made port. In August a further convoy of fourteen merchantmen sailed from the west. Five of its ships reached Malta; one of them, the American tanker *Ohio*, torpedoed on two successive days, arrived lashed between two destroyers. In both these operations the escort fleets suffered very heavily. The losses included the British aircraft carrier *Eagle* which went down with a squadron of Spitfires on board. Over Malta itself the air fighting became fiercer both in intensity and in temper. The chivalry of the desert war was notably absent. With the arrival of another convoy in November the situation of the defenders was eased. The siege was raised by events in Africa.

These events were the final defeat of the German-Italian Panzer Army, of which the battle of El Alamein was the centrepiece. Before that battle Churchill had drastically changed the structure of command in the Middle East.

After Auchinleck's victory in July Churchill urged a further attack to destroy the Axis forces in North Africa once and for all, thereby eliminating the possibility of a war in the Middle East on two or three fronts and setting the Eighth Army in motion to the west before the Anglo-American invasion of North-west Africa which was in preparation for the late autumn. From the purely local point of view the better strategy was to wait and then launch an attack with far better prospects of success – which was what Auchinleck preferred to do and his successors in fact did. But Auchinleck, yielding to superior orders and wider arguments, attacked again in the summer and failed. This failure confronted Churchill at a time of peculiar stress, for he was about to go to Moscow to tell Stalin that there would be no Anglo-American invasion of Europe in 1942 since the western allies had concluded that the African campaign must be finished off first. Churchill knew that an invasion of North-west Africa would be a poor substitute for an invasion of Europe in the eyes of the hard-pressed Russians, and he knew too that however sound his strategic reasoning his political good faith was bound to be distrusted by Stalin. But he had made up his mind, and had persuaded Roosevelt, that the sensible thing to do was to concentrate force in Africa before Europe and persuade Stalin that this strategic plan was conceived in the general allied interest and not in disregard of the Russian predicament. It would help him if he were able to show that success in North Africa was assured and likely to be prompt. He therefore decided to visit the African front on his way to his difficult assignment in Moscow and he arrived there in no halcyon mood.

It was clear that Auchinleck could not remain personally in command of the Eighth Army but Churchill was not satisfied that he should merely revert to his supreme command in Cairo. He had decided that Auchinleck's inability to pick the right commanders and the breakdown of morale in the Eighth Army after its defeats in the desert and the last failure in Egypt required dramatic changes, including the replacement of Auchinleck himself. He proposed to divide the cumbersome Middle East command, putting Auchinleck in charge of Iraq and Iran, and the Chief of the Imperial General Staff, General Sir Alan Brooke, in Cairo. For the Eighth Army Churchill wanted General Gott, one of its corps commanders, as opposed to General Montgomery, the choice of the CIGS. Auchinleck and Brooke both refused the proffered appointments. Churchill got his way over Gott but a few days later Gott was killed in an aircraft accident and the army command went to Montgomery after all. The higher appointments in Cairo and Baghdad went to Generals Harold Alexander and Henry Maitland Wilson. Auchinleck returned to India where he was re-appointed to his old post of Commander-in-Chief when Wavell became Viceroy in the following year. Both these men were great soldiers whose careers became tinged with sadness instead of the glory which their gifts might so easily have commanded. Many of their contemporaries felt that they were shabbily, perhaps even unjustly, treated.

At the end of August Rommel made a last and desperate bid to reach the Nile but was checked by Montgomery in two days of fighting in the battle of Alam Halfa. This was the first step in Montgomery's rise to a fame greater than that of any other British general in the Second World War. He had inherited from Auchinleck a battle plan but he introduced crucial changes into it: the victory was his.

Rommel's supplies were now down to 6,000 tons a month and only a quarter of the shipping attempting to reach him across the Mediterranean was getting through. In the air the Axis dominance had ended and the Luftwaffe and the Desert Air Force were now equals. On the ground the German and Italian tanks and motorized units were in constant danger of being halted by lack of fuel. After their failure at Alam Halfa the German-Italian armies had no choice but to await the attack of a stronger enemy who was able to pick his own time. Rommel himself was invalided home.

Montgomery had no intention of being hustled. When pressed to advance the date of his attack he threatened to resign. He was determined fully to repair the morale and the material of the Eighth Army before engaging the enemy and he had Alexander's full support. He won the confidence of his subordinates by the professional rigour of his training schemes and his (less professional) public relations encounters with all units under his command. He became personally known throughout his army and he was seen to be above all a commander who neglected no necessary detail in preparation and would know no hesitations in battle. His caution was not of the depressing kind: if he delayed giving battle, it was not because he was undecided but because he knew how he meant to win and was not to be deflected from his plan. In addition to his qualities as an excellent tactical commander and leader of men he had certain advantages denied to his predecessors. British industry was now in a state to meet the material needs of the fighting services. American Sherman tanks and Flying Fortresses added weight to the attack. Roosevelt had offered Shermans to Churchill as soon as the fall of Tobruk became known; 300 were dispatched at once; their engines, shipped separately, were lost at sea but promptly replaced. Roosevelt decided also to send complete formations of fighters and heavy and medium bombers to the Middle East and so made the coming battle the first Anglo-American engagement of the war (though not by any means the first in which American airmen had flown against the Luftwaffe). Last but not least, Ultra was giving British field commanders unparalleled assistance. Montgomery was a general who knew how to use it. The general who receives better intelligence than any of his predecessors has ever had does not cease to need generalship. He is not reduced to being an automaton. He is required to be tested in new circumstances, in which he may either fail or triumph. It is one of Montgomery's claims to fame that he was extraordinarily quick to weigh up, appreciate and act upon intelligence received, so that the campaigns which he fought provide an excellent illustration of generalship and intelligence in partnership in action.

When the (second) battle of El Alamein began on 24 October the German and Italian forces were outnumbered by about two to one in

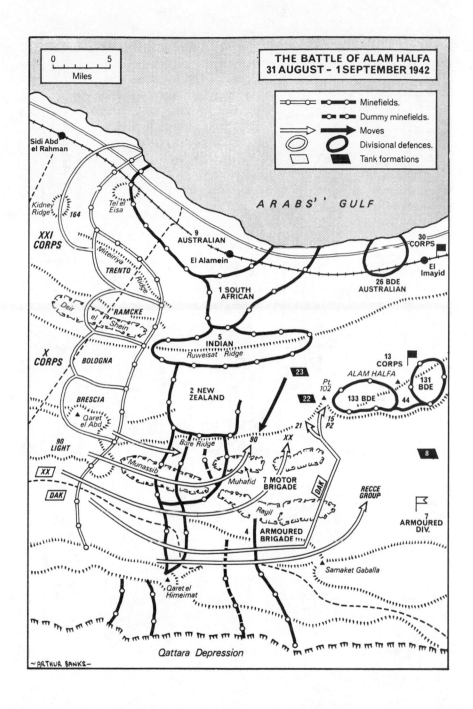

THE BATTLE OF ALAM HALFA
31 AUGUST – 1 SEPTEMBER 1942

Minefields.
Dummy minefields.
Moves
Divisional defences.
Tank formations

0 — 5
Miles

Sidi Abd
el Rahman

Kidney
Ridge   164

Tel el
Eisa

ARABS' GULF

XXI
CORPS

Miteiriya
Ridge

TRENTO

9
AUSTRALIAN

El Alamein

30
CORPS

El
Imayid

26 BDE
AUSTRALIAN

Deir
el
Shein

RAMCKE

1 SOUTH
AFRICAN

X
CORPS

BOLOGNA

5
INDIAN
Ruweisat Ridge

13
CORPS

ALAM HALFA

133 BDE

131
BDE

44

BRESCIA

Qaret
el Abd

2 NEW
ZEALAND

23

Pt.
102

22

90
LIGHT

Bare Ridge

90

21
XX

15
PZ

8

XX

Munassib

Muhafid

7 MOTOR
BRIGADE

DAK

RECCE
GROUP

DAK

Ragil

4   ARMOURED
BRIGADE

7
ARMOURED
DIV.

Samaket Gaballa

Qaret el
Himeimat

Qattara Depression

~ARTHUR BANKS~

THE BATTLE OF EL ALAMEIN
23 OCTOBER 1942

Mediterranean Sea

El Hamman

1 ARMD DIV
ASSEMBLY AREA

El Amayid

10 ARMD DIV
ASSEMBLY AREA

Alam el Halfa Ridge

13 CORPS

HQ 8 ARMY
HQ 30 CORPS

30 CORPS

El Alamein

Meteirya Ridge

4 IND DIV

Ruweisat Ridge

50 DIV

44 DIV

7 ARMD DIV

HQ 13 CORPS

9 AUST DIV
51 (H) DIV
NZ DIV
1 SA DIV

Tell el Eisa

Sidi Abd el Rahman

HQ PZA AFRICA

Ghazal

LITTORIO ARMD DIV

15 PZ DIV

Qaret el Himeimat

El Taqa Plateau

ARIETE ARMD DIV

21 PZ DIV

HQ 10 CORPS

El Daba

90 LIT DIV

HQ 21 CORPS

21 CORPS

HQ DAK

HQ 20 CORPS

10 CORPS

Qattara Depression

10
Miles
0

○ German troop positions.

◎ Italian troop positions.

Enemy minefields (perimeter and main lines).

Forward line of British minefields.

~ARTHUR BANKS~

men, guns and tanks. In the air the British advantage was narrower but the Axis unserviceability ratio was exceptionally high. Montgomery commanded an army of 195,000 men with over 1,000 tanks against a combined German-Italian army of 104,000 men with 500 tanks. The disposition of his enemies were known to Montgomery in great detail. So were their shortages of fuel and ammunition. Their supplies, particularly their supplies of petrol, were precarious and the intelligence available to Rommel (who was posted back to the front at once) about his enemy's strengths and intentions was of a completely different and inferior order to Montgomery's. The tide had turned against Rommel and the issue in the last week of October was not defeat or victory but the nature and extent of the defeat. Both issues were decided in little more than a week. Montgomery, using a brilliantly elaborate deception plan, took his enemy by surprise and scored a skilfully designed and executed victory. But in spite of fuel shortages and in spite of a final attempt to obey an order from Hitler to stand firm, Rommel got away with an army which remained a force in being for several months more. Montgomery has been criticized for not annihilating as well as defeating Rommel, but Montgomery's own resources were limited and he was determined to put an end once and for all to the see-saw character of the desert war. Fresh Anglo-American armies under Eisenhower had landed in North-west Africa three days after Rommel began his retreat and Montgomery followed Rommel westward through Cyrenaica and Tripolitania in order to join up with Eisenhower and finish off Rommel by trapping him in Tunisia between his Eighth Army and Eisenhower's First. But Hitler too put fresh forces into Africa and the first junction was not between Eighth and First Armies but between Rommel retreating from Egypt and a new German-Italian force put into Tunisia in order to hold at least a part of Africa and prevent the British and Americans from closing this theatre of war.

The Anglo-American invasion of North-west Africa (Torch) was originally proposed by Churchill to Roosevelt at their meeting in August 1941. Roosevelt at first fell in with the scheme, but he later inclined to prefer the unrealistic alternative of a landing in Europe in 1942, partly in order to succour the Russians and partly because the British retreats in the early part of 1942 had made an African venture less attractive. But Great Britain's further defeats in the summer of 1942 caused him to revert to Torch, largely in order to succour the British. On the military side, however, neither the American nor the British service chiefs (except the British Admiralty) were enthusiastic about a second front in Africa, and the American chiefs went so far as to try to force Roosevelt and Churchill into a European landing by proposing to give priority to the Pacific theatre if a European campaign were postponed.

The strategy of the invasion of North-west Africa, which was finally accepted by all concerned in July 1942, was British and naval. The idea was to clear the Mediterranean. To the British naval staff the need to do this was self-evident. The other services were slow to respond, especially the air staff which was concentrating on how to smash Germany on its own by air bombardment. The American staffs were largely unaware of what was going on until the early summer when they woke up to it and precipitately concluded that it was all a ruse to forestall an invasion of France in the near future. This was a misinterpretation, for the British regarded an early invasion of France as impossible anyway and never intended operations in northern Africa or southern Europe to supplant that ultimately essential operation. The naval strategy of clearing the Mediterranean did not necessarily imply a campaign in Italy or even Sicily, and the naval staff in fact preferred the occupation of Sardinia, Corsica and the Dodecanese as threats to the Germans in southern Europe, threats to be posed by occupying these islands without using them as springboards for more ambitious land operations. There were no long term plans or even blueprints, no conferences to take the big decisions about the future which, if books about strategy and policies are to be believed, have to be taken by identifiable groups of decision-makers. Subsequent events – the invasion of Sicily and then the landings on the Italian mainland – followed pragmatically, each born out of the success of its predecessor, links in a chain which grew but was never preconceived.

The invasion of North-west Africa was an essay in military cooperation with political complications. The political complications were provided by the existence of rival French authorities and American misreading of their comparative values. France's North African possessions had been made safe for Vichy by Weygand, the first High Commissioner appointed by Pétain, and by General Alphonse Juin who was made Commander-in-Chief in North Africa in 1941 after being released from German imprisonment. For both these generals and many of their colleagues the task of a patriotic Frenchman was to preserve French territory from Germany and also from any other aggressor – which, after the affairs at Mers-el-Kebir and Dakar in 1940, meant for the time being Great Britain. Gaullism, owing to de Gaulle's links with Great Britain, was therefore not much in evidence and was thought to be even weaker than it was, especially in the United States where Roosevelt's dislike of de Gaulle encouraged underestimates of both the man and his movement.

In April 1942 General Henri Giraud escaped from the prison in Germany where he had been kept for two years. He was sixty-three years old and his escape created a sensation which led the western allies to ascribe to him virtues which he never possessed. The Americans saw in Giraud an instrument for undoing de Gaulle. They smuggled him out of France to serve as an anti-Gaullist as much as an anti-Vichy rallying point but Giraud had neither the political sense, the intelligence nor the appeal of de Gaulle and he was a failure in the role for which the Americans cast him on the too slender grounds of being a senior general and a brave escaper. It was not long before the Americans wrote him off and reverted to their pro-Vichy stance. On the eve of the landings in Morocco and Algeria – whose precise date was not imparted to him – Giraud was taken by submarine and flying boat from France to Gibraltar and Roosevelt entered into an agreement with him placing all French forces in Morocco and Algeria under his command – apparently without properly informing Eisenhower, who believed that he had been given supreme authority over all forces, French as well as American and British. Meanwhile Eisenhower's deputy, General Mark Clark, had already been dispatched to Algeria by submarine to persuade the French political and military chiefs to collaborate with the coming invasion. Since the French forces in North-west Africa (about 120,000) outnumbered the Anglo-American assault forces, it was important to secure at least the neutrality of the French if the landings were to be successful and promptly followed by an eastward advance along the coast into Tunisia. Roosevelt was so apprehensive about the French reaction that he asked Churchill to keep the British fighting component out of action for at least a week. His policy was to win over Vichy's representatives in Algeria by keeping the British temporarily in the background and the Gaullists permanently out of the picture (a manoeuvre which de Gaulle never forgot).

Clark found that the senior French commanders, with the exception of Juin, were willing to accept Giraud as Commander-in-Chief but his limited time and limited instructions prevented him from probing the relative strengths of Vichyite and Gaullist sentiment. Had he done so, he would have found that the American partiality for Vichy did not correspond with the flow of French patriotism which Roosevelt and Churchill were seeking to re-engage in hostilities. Nor could he or anybody else on the allied side foresee that Darlan would be in Algiers on the day of the landings. This chance – Darlan had flown to Algiers to see his son, who was ill – capped all the existing confusions and misconceptions, since it gave the Americans the opportunity to do a deal with a senior representative of Vichy and so to outrage anti-Vichy feeling more completely.

The American and British armadas sailed from their home countries

ALLIED LANDINGS IN NORTH AFRICA
8 NOVEMBER 1942

0   100
Miles

Mediterranean   Sea

Balearic Islands

Algiers

Oran

A L G E R I A

S P A I N

P O R T U G A L

Gibraltar

SPANISH
MOROCCO

Tangier

F R E N C H

M O R O C C O

Mehdia

Rabat

Fedela

Casablanca

NORTHERN
ATTACK

CENTRE
ATTACK

Safi

SOUTHERN ATTACK

Convoys pass
Gibraltar from
5-7 November 1942.

Cape
St Vincent

Atlantic

Ocean

NAVAL FORCES

from BRITAIN

ASSAULT CONVOYS

CONVOY SL 125

1/11

31/10

30/10

U-boat attacks
27-31 October 1942.

ASSAULT CONVOYS
from USA

~ARTHUR BANKS~

direct to their landing places on the Atlantic and Mediterranean coasts of Morocco and in Algeria. Their most easterly landing point was fifteen miles east of Algiers. The advantages and the hazards of landing farther east in order to make sure of Tunisia as well had been debated and the hazards were held to outweigh the advantages. Roosevelt's political representative, Robert Murphy, informed Juin of the landings on the evening before, but when they took place on 8 November the chosen date had been revealed to no other Frenchman. This precaution precluded assistance by well-disposed French commanders and occasioned some resistance, but surprise was justified in military terms and opposition was soon rendered manifestly pointless. On the 9th Darlan ordered a cease-fire. The political confusion was, however, ludicrously complete and in the course of the day almost every senior Frenchman was arrested by one or other of his compatriots. Darlan's readiness to change sides was at first suspect to the Americans and British, the more so since the depth of his anti-British feelings was well known, but he was a more useful counter than the disappointing Giraud since, unlike Giraud, he was in a position to give orders to Vichy's proconsuls – Juin, the Commander-in-Chief in North Africa, and Noguès and Estéva, the Residents-General in Morocco and Tunisia – who were showing regrettably little disposition to depart from their allegiance. The Americans – though not the British – had no basic objection to dealing with a Vichy Minister and were as willing to work with Darlan on this occasion as they – and the British – were willing to accept Badoglio as an ally against the Germans in the next year. Aware that they were giving serious offence to anti-Vichy feeling they tried to limit their commitment to Darlan but only succeeded in offending him as well. This tangle was only resolved on Christmas Eve when Darlan was assassinated by a fanatical Gaullist. The Americans fell back on Giraud who stepped temporarily into Darlan's shoes, which had already been adjudged too big for him, but Giraud had meanwhile displayed a considerable ineptitude for the role thrust upon him. At Casablanca in January de Gaulle and Giraud were persuaded to cooperate in the Committee of National Liberation established in Algiers, but Giraud gradually faded out of the picture. He later resigned from the Committee, leaving de Gaulle triumphant and resentful.

The invasion of North-west Africa introduced to the general public one of the major figures of the war, Dwight D. Eisenhower. General Eisenhower has too often been written down as a man who was lucky enough to rise to an eminence beyond his talents and there to contrive to make no disastrous mistakes. This judgement is wrong on both counts, for Eisenhower did make mistakes and yet he was bigger than this grudging estimate makes out. If he is not among the great captains, he was an exceptionally well-trained, methodical and unself-centred commander with in addition a humanity, perhaps unexciting but on occasions crucial, which enabled him to get on well with other people and also to help them get on well with each other. Few in 1943 expected him to go on from his North African command to even higher things, but his military and human competence so recommended him to his superiors that he was chosen to lead the allied invasion of France in the next year.

The German reaction to the invasion of North-west Africa was to occupy southern France and Tunisia and try to seize the French fleet at Toulon. This last endeavour failed. The fleet disregarded an order from Darlan to sail for Africa but it scuttled itself rather than fall into German hands. In Tunisia the Germans seized the opportunities presented to them by Anglo-American caution in making no landing east of Algiers. German and Italian troops occupied Tunisia and when the German commander, General Jürgen von Arnim, sent Kesselring pessimistic appreciations of the situation, Kesselring told him that he was not interested in appreciations and ordered him to hang on – an outstanding contravention of the Tolstoyan norm that supreme commanders are not the masters of events in battle. American and British forces occupied Bône in Algeria, near the Tunisian border, on 12 November and crossed the border four days later, but by the end of the year the Anglo-American attempt to secure Tunis had petered out and the Germans were pouring troops in by sea and air. In the east the Eighth Army had recovered Tobruk on 13 November and reached Benghazi on the 20th, while Rommel was retreating comparatively unmolested to join Arnim. Together their forces would outnumber their American, British and French adversaries and thwart them for six months.

Rommel had to strike before Eisenhower's and Montgomery's forces closed in on him. In mid-February he attacked the (mainly British) First Army under Eisenhower's command. Eisenhower was deceived by the excellence of his own intelligence. He knew from Ultra decodes that Kesselring in Rome had ordered Rommel to detach some of his units to Arnim for an attack in northern Tunisia. He did not know that Rommel preferred to attack further south and was prepared to disobey Kesselring rather than abandon his plans. So when Rommel attacked at the Kasserine Pass the allied command was divided, some (relying on Ultra) regarding this attack as no more than a feint in aid of Arnim; Rommel inflicted and even humiliated the American corps holding this sector. But First Army was not driven back and Rommel was obliged to disengage from his Tunisian front in order to counter the approach of Eighth Army from the east. On 6 March he attacked south-eastwards from the Mareth Line towards Medenine. Montgomery had only one corps approaching Tunisia, his second still east of Tripoli. Rommel's plan was to annihilate the forward corps and so send Montgomery's whole army reeling back once more into Cyrenaica or even Egypt and his reputation out of the history books. Rommel issued his orders but a few hours later, thanks to Ultra, they were in Montgomery's hands. Dropping all normal security precautions Montgomery drove his forces through the night with their lights full on. They arrived in time to thwart Rommel.

The battle of Medenine did not end the war in North Africa but it decided the issue. On 9 March Rommel left Africa never to return; at the end of the month Montgomery took the Mareth positions (which had been built in the thirties by the French to keep the Italians away from Tunisia); in the first days of April Eighth and First Armies joined hands; and on 12 May the Tunisian bridgehead, which the Germans and Italians had held for six months, was eliminated by a final capitulation. Almost three years after Mussolini had goaded the reluctant Graziani into action against a British Empire lying naked in the Middle East after the fall of France the last Italian and German combatants – 150,000 of them – were prisoners of war.

The end of the fighting left a more complex pattern in North-west Africa than in the territories farther east. The former Italian colonies were under British military occupation and Egypt was for the time being under British politico-military control, but in North-west Africa there were, first, French authority; secondly, the American and British military commands and their civilian representatives; and thirdly, the Sultan of Morocco and Bey of Tunis and the nationalist movements in their countries and in Algeria as well.

French authority had been unbroken, even by the collapse of 1940. Allowed by the armistice agreements with Germany and Italy to keep 120,000 troops in North Africa, the French had no difficulty in maintaining their control, particularly since nationalist leaders still at large had been picked up and put away just before the war began (the principal Moroccan leaders had been in prison since 1937). The humiliation of France was not unequivocally welcome to Arab opinion. The French empire had been a mixed experiment. On the one hand it represented the domination of one nation over another, a degradation and a denial of political rights and human values, but on the other hand it was a relationship between two cultures, a developing association which was prized so long as its fruits counterbalanced the thorns of unequal political dualism. Between the wars this balance had swung more and more the wrong way. The cultural association needed by its very nature to be an expanding one, but in France conservative views predominated, there was little awareness that the empire might be coming to a dead end and no willingness to grant more than minimal reforms. When the Popular Front produced a plan to extend the franchise and citizenship rights in Algeria – the *projet Violette*, so called after the Governor-General of Algeria – it was first blocked and then destroyed by the politically dominant and economically favoured white settlers or *colons* who threatened to disrupt the entire administration of Algeria if the plan were brought to the floor of the National Assembly. This rigidity sharpened nationalist animosities, and French governments were trapped between two increasingly hostile forces. But the nationalist movements were still weak. It took time for people at large to conclude that the nationalists might achieve more than abortive demonstrations and neither the bulk of the population nor, in Morocco and Tunisia, the sovereigns considered that conditions were ripe for a challenge to the power of France.

The defeat of France in 1940 changed this attitude only fractionally. That defeat was a shock which pained the Arab élite in spite of their quarrels with the French state. It also had unpleasant possibilities: Tunisia, for example, was immediately exposed to Italian covetousness and feared attack by land and sea. The Tunisian nationalist leader Habib Bourguiba, imprisoned at Marseilles, insisted that Tunisian nationalism must be anti-Axis. From the Vichy régime nationalists had nothing to hope for (Vichy's reaction was to apprehend any prominent nationalists still at large) and Bourguiba declared himself for de Gaulle and for the western allies. In Morocco, where General Noguès had established good relations with the Sultan after considerable disturbances in the early thirties, the Sultan had promised in 1939 to support the French war effort and the nationalists had promised not to impede it. The collapse of 1940 did not at first disturb these tolerances.

The year 1942 had profounder consequences, for in that year France suffered a second defeat when the Americans and the British landed in Morocco and Algeria without prior agreement with the French and opened fire on them. Moreover this second defeat was inflicted on France within the sight and hearing of the Arabs, it was followed by the quarrels between de Gaulle and Giraud which greatly harmed French prestige and it was accompanied by overt and covert American support for independence movements. In Tunisia, occupied by the Germans, there was the additional coincidence that a new Bey, more sympathetic to the nationalists than his predecessor, had just succeeded to the throne.

With the allied armies arrived thousands of copies of the Atlantic Charter which the Arabs had heard about and could now read for themselves. They concluded that the whole power of the invincible United States was now behind the independence movements. In Algeria Murphy, Roosevelt's political representative, encouraged nationalists to make claims designed to secure American and British pledges about the post-war government of Algeria. Algerian leaders offered their cooperation during the war in return for the immediate convening of a conference at which Algerians would draw up a new constitution for Algeria. The aims were unexceptionable but the tactics were dubious, since the French authorities were incensed by what they regarded as undercover blackmail and reacted indignantly not only against American interference but also against Algerian demands which otherwise they were not far from accepting – and went some way towards accepting once de Gaulle had established his authority over Vichy's minions and Washington's protégés.

In Morocco Roosevelt intervened personally. He had never made any secret of his detestation of imperialism in principle and his condemnation of the niggardliness of the French, British and other European empires in relation to their dependants, and during his stay at Casablanca in January 1943 he had a meeting with Sultan Mohammed V ben Yusuf, who came away from it with the belief that the United States would provide the political pressures and the economic aid needed to restore full Moroccan independence. The Sultan was already half-way inclined to make common cause with the Moroccan nationalists and his encounters with Americans encouraged him to lean still further that way. A year later the Istiqlal or Independence Party, formed by the merger in this climate of separate existing bodies, issued a declaration of independence which sought unilaterally to abrogate the treaty upon which Franco-Moroccan relations rested. It was followed by demonstrations which showed how the populace as well as the sovereign rated the French connection and France's ability to maintain it. Towards the end of the war the French arrested – but never charged or tried – nationalist leaders whom they accused of complicity in German plotting. There were more riots and Frenchmen were massacred. The French reacted with too much counter-violence and talk of too little reform. The war boosted nationalist hopes and activity and at the same time set an example of violence which was to be followed on both sides as the nationalists proceeded to their goals after the war was over.

In Tunisia the new ruler, Bey Moncef, was more than half a nationalist. He succeeded unexpectedly in 1942 and decided that his best policy was to take the leadership of the nationalist forces. Since the principal nationalist leaders were in French prisons this was not too difficult but it led to

strained relations and ugly scenes with Vichy's Resident-General, Admiral
Jean Pierre Estéva. Before the conflict could be resolved the Germans
arrived in order to stop the Anglo-Americans from seizing Tunisia as well
as Algeria and Morocco. For six uneasy months the German command
and the French administration coexisted (Estéva was later condemned to
life imprisonment for this collaboration), while Tunisian towns and villages were bombed in a war which Tunisians could not by any stretch of
the imagination regard as their own. Some Tunisians collaborated with
the Germans and some with the allies; most, including the Bey, waited as
equivocally as possible.

A few weeks before the final defeat of the Germans, Bourguiba was
released from prison, sent to Rome to be brainwashed with Axis seduce-
ments and then forwarded to Tunis. His policy was unchanged: independence and a treaty with France. But too many Frenchmen had come to
regard him as an enemy of France and in addition Giraud, whom the
allies had elevated to High Commissioner in North Africa, needlessly
affronted Tunisians by deposing Moncef as soon as the Germans had
been ousted. This tactless and illegal action – the Franco-Tunisian treaty
gave the French government no power to appoint or depose a Bey – compromised the French at the moment when they were trying to re-establish
their authority. Giraud shortly afterwards disappeared from the scene
and the Gaullist régime in Algeria proposed some cautious reforms which,
though they might have been acceptable before the war, no longer sufficed
after the French setbacks of 1940–42. In March 1945 Bourguiba, concluding that discussions in Tunis would get nowhere, left secretly for Cairo
where he established a Committee for the Liberation of the Maghrib with
himself as secretary-general and the veteran Moroccan rebel Abd el-Krim
as president. He did not return to Tunis for over four years.

In both Morocco and Tunisia the conflict was about the distribution of
power between the French and native governments. Under the protectorate treaties the French had gradually assumed more power and more
responsibilities and the nationalists were seeking to reverse the process by
securing elected central and local councils with native majorities, freer
access for Arabs to the upper reaches of the public services, equal pay for
Arab and French employees and a strict application of the treaty provisions governing the role of French officials in the administration of the
protectorates. These were questions of adjustment. What transpired
during the war and immediately after it was that the adjustments would
not be made. Each side calculated its position in such a way as to make it
refuse to go near enough to the other side's position to effect agreement.
The French calculation was a miscalculation, since in the end France had

to concede complete independence and the ending of the protectorate status. The main source of this miscalculation was the blindness of pre-war and post-war French conservative governments which first failed to see the need for changes and then failed to see that changes which might have sufficed before the war did not meet the case after it. The brief Gaullist interlude of 1942–6 might have set a more generous course and so have reached the inevitable dénouement more quickly and less painfully, but it was constricted by American intervention and was impelled into an anti-Americanism which tainted its attitudes towards the nationalists, who were in turn tempted into believing that what they could not extract from France by themselves they could get by playing the American card. Gaullism, moreover, was a strange mixture of radicalism and conservatism. At Brazzaville in 1941 de Gaulle promised the Africans of France's sub-Saharan empire a bigger share in government, a wider franchise and more decentralization of public business, and in Algeria in 1943 de Gaulle and his chosen Governor, General Georges Catroux (who had been born in Algiers), showed that they appreciated the need for a new start. Yet the changes which were then proposed turned out to be disappointingly meagre and in Algeria, as in Tunis, the opportunity for an amicable and progressive re-ordering of relations passed sourly away.

On the last day of the war in Europe the inhabitants of the Algerian town of Sétif proposed to hold a procession distinct from the official one. They were given permission to do so provided no banners were displayed. The provision was ignored. Somebody started shooting. Twenty-one Frenchmen were killed. The affair developed into a revolt involving troops, air bombing and naval gunnery. Thousands more people were killed, mostly Algerians. Violence begot bestial ferocity on the one side which begot excessive reprisals and summary executions on the other. The established authorities prevailed but a number of the malcontents fled to the hills to carry on the fight. Although one war had ended in North Africa in 1943, two years later another and longer one had grown out of it, not to be ended until de Gaulle was brought back to power in 1958 to do so.

CHAPTER 18

The End of Fascism

THE allied victory in North Africa was only the half close of the Mediterranean campaign. Africa was not an end in itself but a part of a struggle for control of the Mediterranean and one way of getting back onto European soil. An invasion of Sicily was a logical sequel, for it could be argued that without Sicily and its airfields the free passage of the Mediterranean had not been unquestionably secured. At Casablanca in January 1943 Roosevelt and Churchill agreed that the forces which they had assembled in North Africa should be used to invade Sicily and so re-open the Mediterranean. They had not, however, taken any further decision. Whether Sicily, besides being a sequel to Africa, was also to be a prelude to mainland Italy was as yet unresolved, although studies were put in hand for crossing the Straits of Messina, landing in the heel of Italy as well as the toe, and taking Sardinia and Corsica. Nor was the purpose of a possible landing in Italy settled. If it led to the fall of Mussolini and the end of Italy's part in the war, the allied armies might either press northwards in a major attack into Austria or even Germany itself, or alternatively their task might be to draw German forces into Italy in order to weaken German resistance to an allied invasion of northern France. These two strategies were incompatible since the second would be best served if the allied armies made no rapid progress up the peninsula. On the whole the Americans (and Montgomery) saw Italy in this second light, whereas the British – or at least Churchill and Alexander – were intermittently seduced by the prospect of a major rather than an ancillary campaign in Italy.

The invasion of Sicily was launched on 10 July. The small island of Pantellaria had been easily captured a month earlier, but in spite of this pointer the Germans were preoccupied by a cover plan designed to make them fear a landing in Greece and wholly taken in by a piece of deception indicating an attack on Sardinia: a dead body with bogus plans was put in the sea in such a way that it would be washed up in Spain and in the justified belief that the Spanish authorities would hand the papers to the Germans. A genuine attack on Sardinia had been vetoed by Eisenhower.

Mussolini had no faith in the Sicilians. He did not dare to arm them and he had long since ordered all Sicilian-born officials to be transferred from the island to the mainland. The allies had command of the air. They landed at half a dozen points along the eastern half of the southern coast and along the east coast below Syracuse. An American plan for additional landings at Palermo and Catania was abandoned, largely at the instance of Montgomery, who had been impressed by the quality of German and Italian resistance in Tunisia and did not in any case want to see the allied forces spread too widely. The allied force, which sailed from American and British ports as well as North Africa and Egypt, consisted of a modest invasion force with very powerful naval and air cover. One hundred and sixty thousand men were put ashore in the first wave, with 600 tanks and 14,000 vehicles. They were supported by a fleet of 750 vessels and by over 4,000 aircraft. The British landings were completely unopposed and the Americans almost so, although there were 230,000 Italian and 40,000 German troops in the island. The first counter-attacks, which were directed against the Americans and almost dislodged them, were broken with the help of naval gunfire, and thereafter victory was swift. General George Patton's Third US Army, which had landed on the left flank of the combined force, reached Messina on 17 August by a round-about route which took his men swiftly across the centre of the island to the north coast and then eastward. They arrived just ahead of the British coming up by the shorter but more difficult east coast route. This was the end of an operation which, although successful, had again – as in Tunisia – been rendered costly and protracted by determined German intervention. It had also generated some blatant Anglo-American ill-will in the field. The Germans got away.

A military government was established in Sicily. In practice the island fell once more into the clutches of the Mafia. Mussolini, who understood gangsterism, had been the one ruler of Italy to get the better of the Mafia. His disappearance was the signal for its revival. *Mafiosi* from the United States, where they had been keeping their hands in, got themselves attached to the American forces because they could speak Italian and soon, partly by graft and partly from the need to fill local posts vacated by refugees, occupied most of the positions that mattered. Within a few months they were the government of Sicily. Later on, after toying briefly with Sicilian separatism, they entered into an alliance with right-wing politicians in Rome to defeat the Left and keep Sicily corrupt and miserable.

The conquest of Sicily spelt defeat for Italy but did not give the allies victory over the Germans in Italy. So far as it represented a way of defeating the Germans it left open the question whether a campaign in Italy was a worthwhile adjunct of the campaign in northern France which, everybody agreed, was to be the main blow. Italy itself, as a fighting force and as an independent sovereign state, was finished for the duration. It had undertaken a war for which it was neither equipped to fight nor willing to fight. Mussolini's Italy was hardly ready for any war in 1940, certainly not for a long one in two continents, but after attacking France and Greece it had become involved in wars in North Africa and East Africa and in the USSR. By the beginning of 1943 the Italians were not only dismayed and angered by the consequences of these gigantic miscalculations but were saying so. Strikes, beginning at the Fiat works in Turin, protested against rising prices and harsh working conditions and disclosed the workers' basic demand for peace. These strikes succeeded the defeats of the Italian armies on the Stalingrad front and were followed by the defeats in Sicily. Mussolini had already realized in 1942 that the war could only be won by negotiating a peace in the east but Hitler refused to consider such a thing. In February 1943 Mussolini in a general re-shuffle hedged his bets by demoting Ciano and Grandi, who were anti-German (and credibly rumoured to be plotting against him); he also appointed a new Army Chief of Staff who was suspected by Kesselring and Hitler of being ready to switch sides at the first opportunity. Ten days before the Sicilian landings Mussolini received Mihai Antonescu, who had come to suggest that Italy, Rumania and Hungary should all leave the war together and hoped that Mussolini would give the lead. After the Sicilian invasion he found himself compelled to fight on Italian soil with a million Italian servicemen engaged outside the country – 580,000 in the Balkans, 217,000 on the Russian front and 200,000 in France, not to mention those killed or taken prisoner in the Western Desert and Tunisia, who numbered at least 200,000 more. The defence of Italy required not only the recall of the Italian troops in the USSR (for which the landings in Sicily provided a welcome excuse) but also German reinforcements which would turn Italy into an occupied country.

   Mussolini had no doubt what he ought to do but he did not dare to do it. In order to spur him on to ask for an armistice his advisers grossly exaggerated the size of the invading armies, which they represented as initially twenty-five divisions when they knew it to be eight. On 19 July Hitler and Mussolini met at Feltre, but Hitler did not allow Mussolini to get a word in and Mussolini's nerve, none too good by now even when Hitler was not around, failed him. After listening to one of Hitler's long disquisitions on the way the war was going, which included some very rude remarks about the Italians, he took refuge in silence. This failure sealed his fate.

   The fascist chieftains or *gerarchi* feared for themselves and their régime. Mussolini's alliance with Hitler had proved a disaster. It had led to war, humiliation and defeat which, by 1942, were threatening the survival of Fascism. To save Fascism the alliance had to be broken. But Mussolini, who had made the alliance, was incapable of unmaking it. Moreover Italy was in no position simply to back out of the alliance unaided. It must change sides and make a new alliance in order to be rid of the old. There was no reason to think that this could not be done, although there was a question whether Mussolini himself might not have to be jettisoned in the process. The king might, if pressed by the anti-fascist members of the royal family, demand in a crisis the Duce's removal but he was very unlikely to insist on forming a government without any fascists at all. Similarly the allies would probably accept a partly fascist government. During the war they had made statements about the total overthrow of Fascism, but Churchill had also said that Mussolini was personally to blame for everything and until 1940 neither he nor Roosevelt had been notably anti-fascist. Both Great Britain and the United States had lived with Fascism for twenty years, for much of that time amicably enough.

The *gerarchi* therefore wanted a reversal of alliances, by and with Mussolini if possible, without and against him if necessary. After the Feltre meeting they knew that they must proceed the second way. On 24 July the Fascist Grand Council met for the first time since the outbreak of war. Twenty-eight men attended. Grandi proposed that the king should be restored to his post (taken from him in 1940) as Commander-in-Chief. He delivered a strong attack on Mussolini's conduct of the war. He spoke for over an hour and so impressed wavering members of the Council that when a pro-Mussolini resolution to adjourn was moved it was lost. There was a short pause during which Grandi and others moved around taking soundings. Mussolini himself seemed listless. Although only sixty, he was a sick man, his mind sluggish and his judgement gone. Upon the resumption Grandi's proposal was approved by nineteen votes to nine. It was a vote of no confidence in the Duce. It was now two o'clock in the morning. The members of the Council dispersed without any very clear notion of what their vote portended. During the morning of the 25th Mussolini worked as usual in his office. In the afternoon he went to the Villa Savoia for a private talk with the king whom he still regarded as an obedient puppet. But, if only out of self-interest, the king had become as dissatisfied with Mussolini as the fascist *gerarchi* and when Mussolini arrived the king dismissed him from the office to which he had appointed him over twenty years earlier. It is not known whether Mussolini argued in his own defence. The interview lasted only twenty minutes. As the ex-Prime Minister emerged he was politely arrested and driven away in an ambulance. He showed no fight and seemed to have no stomach for the stirring events which lay ahead.

Mussolini was succeeded as Prime Minister by Marshal Pietro Badoglio, a soldier who for twenty years had lent his prestige to the fascists in return for places and titles but had been dismissed in 1940 during the fiasco of the Italian attack on Greece. Upon succeeding Mussolini, Badoglio played an inglorious role, swearing loyalty to the Germans while negotiating with the allies. He and the king wanted to get out of the war but they did not see how to do it without turning Italy into one more German-occupied country, unless the allies could be persuaded to cut off and overwhelm the Germans. Badoglio was willing to capitulate to the allies but he wanted to make conditions: he would capitulate if the allies landed on the mainland, the farther north the better. He tried to persuade them to land at Genoa. If they would not venture so far he argued for a parachute operation to seize Rome; all the airfields round Rome were held by the one Italian division indubitably loyal to the House of Savoy, the Piedmontese Grenadiers. In addition Badoglio, while publicly professing loyalty to the German alliance, had circulated instructions for action against an assumed communist plot which he intended to put into operation by a pre-arranged code word, accompanied by the simple instruction to substitute 'Germans' where the original plan said 'communists'.

The discussions between Badoglio and the allies were protracted. They were conducted in secrecy in Lisbon and then Madrid and were complicated by the fact that the allies conceived themselves to be negotiating a surrender whereas the Italian emissaries considered that they were discussing joint action against the Germans in Italy. The Casablanca declaration had expressly committed the allies to demanding the unconditional surrender of Italy as well as Germany with the result that much time was spent in negotiating the conditions of a surrender which was none the less to be made to appear unconditional. Moreover the allies were divided about undertaking a major campaign on the mainland. They were tempted by the ease of their conquest of Sicily and by Mussolini's fall. An occupation of southern Italy would give them air bases for bombing Germany and would force Hitler to choose between abandoning Italy altogether or reinforcing it at the expense of the western front which the allies were about to attack. Naples, with its prestige and its capacious port, was a prize worth having and, unlike Rome or Genoa, was within the range of allied air cover. The Americans, in accordance with their broader strategy, had been reluctant to lodge large armies in a new Italian theatre but an attack towards Naples could be represented as no more than a variation on the operations which were in the planning stage and so half-way to being acceptable. They overcame their hesitations. The allies decided to cross from Sicily into Calabria, to land in the heel as well as the toe of

Italy and to mount a third operation to land at Salerno, thirty-five miles short of Naples. From there, in some as yet undefined way, a road to Rome would be opened.

As the first troops were crossing into Calabria the negotiations with Badoglio were finally concluded. An act of surrender was signed on 3 September. It was to be disclosed on the 8th, the day the allies landed at Salerno. Badoglio asked that publication should be delayed to enable him to redispose his forces. Eisenhower, who distrusted Badoglio, refused and had the news of the surrender broadcast on the appointed day. Badoglio was obliged to follow suit and later accused Eisenhower, incorrectly, of having promised not to invade before 19 September. The Italians were caught unprepared, the Germans immediately occupied Rome and its airfields, and a promised allied airborne coup against these airfields had to be cancelled. The king and his government fled to Brindisi. The Italian fleet, which put to sea and made for Malta, lost the battleship *Roma* – sunk by a new kind of bomb, controlled after release by radio by the pilot who dropped it. The formal Italian surrender was completed at Malta on 29 September and a month later, on 13 October, Italy declared war on Germany. Badoglio's flight from Rome to Brindisi committed Italy to civil war.

The Germans had expected an allied landing from the sea near Rome combined with a parachute operation and they proposed to withdraw all their forces south of Rome. This strategy was that of Rommel, who had been put in command in northern Italy. But Kesselring, who commanded in Rome and southwards, had other ideas. Decisive as ever, he believed that more of Italy could be held than the Lombard plain and circumstances helped him to wean Hitler away from Rommel's plan. For a time Rommel's plan prevailed and the Eighth Army was unopposed when it began to cross from Sicily into Calabria on 3 September. Montgomery proceeded sedately northward, the Germans withdrawing with equal circumspection. A separate landing at Taranto was similarly unopposed. In the early hours of 9 September the main assault on the Italian mainland was made at Salerno by an Anglo-American force of three divisions under the command of General Mark Clark which had sailed from ports in Algeria, Tunisia and Tripolitania. This landing was not unopposed. The defences, which had been manned by Italians, were in the process of being taken over by the Germans, who had just learnt of the Italian capitulation, and as they moved into their new positions they found themselves immediately in the path of the allied invasion. Their commander had no instructions covering this situation and he took it upon himself to resist. He was aware that the Eighth Army was advancing up the coast from

Messina and he planned to throw the main invading force back into the sea before the Eighth Army could arrive. He nearly succeeded. After initial successes in getting ashore the invading force was thrown onto the defensive and Clark took preliminary steps for an evacuation. But the allied units held their ground and by skilful use of parachute units Clark was able to check his antagonist, who broke off the engagement and withdrew northwards upon the approach of the Eighth Army.

While the invaders were struggling to keep their grip on the beaches at Salerno the people of Naples rose against the Germans and fought them savagely for three days, suffering terrible reprisals before the allies reached Naples on 1 October, their first staging point in a long slog to the north.

Hitler was now converted to the strategy of holding central Italy as well as the north. A new German line was formed along the Volturno thirty miles beyond Naples. The allies had added southern Italy, Sardinia and Corsica to their conquest of Sicily (but allowed the Germans to remove all their troops from Sardinia and Corsica); for anything more they would have to fight. Hopes of easy victories in Italy were becoming dampened. The allied armies moved from their landing places into the mountains and valleys where they were to spend long months toiling, fighting and sitting in the rain with the occasional respite provided by leave in towns where they could rest and revel and where – as Curzio Malaparte's *La Pelle* (*The Skin*) has most dramatically recorded – liberation became shoddily confused with corruption.

Hitler made political as well as strategic redispositions. Perhaps he had never intended to allow Mussolini to be kept in prison. He retained some respect for his fellow dictator and forerunner and he hoped that, with Mussolini as a mascot, he could re-establish a fascist régime, keep Italy true to the Axis and so protect his southern flank. After his arrest in July Mussolini had first been held for ten days on the island of Ponza in the Gulf of Gaeta and then for three weeks on the island of La Maddalena between Sardinia and Corsica where he passed the time translating Carducci into German; but in neither was he judged secure from a possible attempt at rescue. At the end of August he was moved to the Gran Sasso, where he was considered entirely safe. But two weeks later, on 12 September when the battle on the Salerno beaches was still undecided, he was kidnapped in an operation of uncommon skill and daring by the German SS officer Otto Skorzeny and flown in a small aircraft into which he barely fitted to Germany and thence to northern Italy where he was established as the head of a new government which never attained either power or dignity.

The restoration of Mussolini to the political stage and the flight of the

THE INVASION OF ITALY
JULY 1943

Allied advances.

0 ——— 100
Miles

Taken 26 April 1945

Entered May 1945

Milan
Turin
Verona
Venice
Trieste
Genoa
Bologna
Ravenna
Leghorn
Adriatic

Liberated by
Free French
Sept 1943.

GOTHIC LINE

Finally taken
18 May after
five months.

CORSICA

Sea

ROME
Monte Casino
Termoli

Entered
4 June 1944

Anzio
GUSTAV LINE
Sangro

SARDINIA

Bari

Beachhead
22 January–
22 May 1944

Naples
Salerno

Taranto

Mainland
landings
9 September

BRITISH

Occupied by Anglo-
American troops
Autumn 1943.

Palermo
Messina

SICILY
Catania

Tunis
Licata
Syracuse

BRITISH

AMERICANS

Sousse

~ARTHUR BANKS~

king and Badoglio to Brindisi were minor episodes in the campaign joined in Italy between the western allies and Germany, but in the history of Italy they had greater significance for there were many Italians who wanted neither Mussolini nor the king and Badoglio. The appointment of Badoglio to succeed Mussolini sufficed the allies, who had no particular animus against the monarchy and were well enough suited by any government which was prepared to turn against the Germans. Churchill was by temperament a monarchist of a traditional and sentimental kind; like most conservatives he tended to think of society as a number of applecarts which must not be upset; he had not been among Mussolini's enemies until Mussolini attacked France and declared war on Great Britain, he was prepared to see some fascists in Badoglio's cabinet, he believed that Italy's choice lay between king and communism, and he feared a second E L A S in Italy if anti-fascist elements forced the pace of political and social change. But Italians wanted change, more change than was involved in a palace revolution effected by the Fascist Grand Council and the king and his entourage. If and so far as Italy in 1943 could be likened to an applecart, the apples in it were rotten. Italians were not concerned, as Churchill was, simply to undo what had happened since 1940 and chase the Germans out of Italy; they wanted to undo everything that had happened since 1922 and destroy Fascism. Anti-fascists had existed in Italy before Nazis had been heard of. To them Mussolini's dismissal was no more than a cabinet re-shuffle, an acknowledgement that his foreign policy had failed and been discarded. But they were more concerned with internal than external affairs.

The anti-fascists were the inheritors from the Risorgimento of a successful tradition of resistance and conspiracy within the country and by exiles. Both the exodus and internal resistance had begun immediately after the March on Rome, exiles and anti-fascists in Italy regarding themselves as true Italians whose mission it was to destroy Fascism in the same way as their grandfathers had been dedicated to the destruction of Austrian, Papal and Bourbon tyranny. Inside Italy anti-fascist groups formed, notably in universities. A clandestine press flourished as it had in the days of the *carbonari*. So did mural graffiti – slogans on walls played a prominent part in the struggle between fascists and anti-fascists. The Communist Party, well organized, covering the whole country and driven underground, managed to preserve some of the structure of the banned trade unions, organized strikes and other demonstrations (on May Day for example), displayed red flags and maintained active contacts with Italians and other sympathizers beyond the frontiers. Outside Italy the exiles spread over many countries from France, Switzerland and Belgium to Latin America and the United States. Many of them were comparatively humble people who were used to seeking seasonal work in other parts of Europe or who maybe had relatives more permanently settled in the New World, but they included also men who had made names for themselves in politics or the literary world. They too formed groups, issued newspapers and kept resistance alive.

In 1929 Carlo Rosselli made a dramatic escape from prison on the Lipari Islands and formed in Paris a movement called Justice and Liberty (with a paper of the same name) which brought anti-fascists of different political persuasions together and gave the anti-fascist crusade a distinctive flavour. For Rosselli and his friends it was not enough to be anti-fascist or to put the clock back to 1922. There must be a positive programme for putting the clock forward. These men not only hated Mussolini for his brutalities, especially after the murder of the socialist leader Giacomo Matteotti in 1924; they also regarded the Risorgimento as unfinished business and proclaimed once more the Mazzinian aims of democracy and a republic which had been submerged in Cavour's monarchist, bourgeois and capitalist Italy; and they added socialism to democracy and republicanism. They did not win the adherence of all anti-fascists. The more conservative of these formed a National Alliance which hoped to persuade the monarchy and the papacy to turn against Mussolini – but the Duce kept the king securely by his side and negotiated in 1929 a concordat with the Pope. The National Alliance issued pamphlets and disseminated them by getting each recipient to make six copies, of which at least two were to be sent to fascists. Its most famous exploit occurred in 1931 when the young poet Lauro De Bosis, taking off in an aircraft from the south of France, circled Rome for half an hour at dusk on an October evening and scattered 400,000 leaflets from 1,000 feet over the centre of the city before setting course for the sea, where, having run out of petrol or lost control of the aircraft which he had only just learnt to fly, he died.

Repression became severer as opposition persisted. Something like a small war developed between the fascist police and their enemies. Police agents followed the exiles abroad and this Italian civil war spilled over into foreign territory, particularly France and then Spain, where another civil war gave the anti-fascist exiles a chance to fight against Mussolini's fascist troops. In France consulates and other public buildings belonging to the Italian state were attacked. Men were killed on both sides. In 1937, on the thirteenth anniversary of Matteotti's murder, Carlo Rosselli and his brother Nello were murdered near Paris at Mussolini's bidding. When war came in 1940 the struggle, nearly twenty years old but still alive, was intensified. Mussolini now had fresh enemies and was beginning to lose some of his friends. The German alliance was unpopular; the Roman Catholic church was shifting away from Fascism. In August 1942 a conference of free Italians at Montevideo, presided over by the pre-fascist statesman Count Carlo Sforza, drew up a programme for a democratic and social republic of Italy. The next year the allied invasion of Sicily was regarded not as a conquest but as the beginning of liberation.

For thousands of Italians therefore, with all this behind them and within them, the Badoglio government was unacceptable. The government itself realized the precarious nature of its authority. It equivocated. It freed political prisoners and banned the Fascist Party, but it retained the censorship and the black-shirted fascist militia. Party politics were not resumed and all party politicians were kept out of the government. The war went on. Ordinary people were confused and then became angry. German troops began to pour in – and were resisted by Italians at three or four points along the frontier. Rome was hit by the allies from the air and suffered 1,000 casualties and the king's car was stoned when he visited the scene. Outside Italy local commanders and troops did not know whom to fight, if anybody; some of them turned against the Germans and on Cephallonia in the Ionian Islands 8,400 Italians were killed. By September when the king and Badoglio fled from the capital and Mussolini was carried off by the Germans to create a second fascist state in the north and two thirds of the country was under German occupation, the new government had disappointed the hopes and forfeited the respect of a great part of the population and was only sustained by the allies, particularly the British.

This period of uncertainty and disenchantment between July and September 1943 was followed by a second period, stretching from the events of the latter month to the German evacuation of Rome in June 1944. After its declaration of war against Germany in October 1943 the Badoglio government devoted much of its constricted energies to re-orienting the Italian army; by the end of the year regular Italian units were fighting in the Anglo-American forces, which also included French, Polish, Greek, Indian and New Zealand contingents and even Japanese from California. Allied generals were not enthusiastic about Italian help, but after Montgomery's departure the Eighth Army helped to train and equip a number of volunteer brigades which showed that Italians could fight as well as anybody when they wanted to. The Americans refused to copy the Eighth Army's example and the war ended before it got very far. Had the war gone on longer the Eighth Army would have fathered a first-class Italian army – composed chiefly of communists.

Owing to the slowness of the allied advance up Italy most Italians found themselves in German-occupied territory. They could not join Badoglio's forces even if they wanted to. Disbanded soldiers and released prisoners-of-war – impelled by anti-German patriotism or fearful of being put to work or thrown into prison by the Germans or of being transported to forced labour in Germany – took to the hills. These men had not for the most part been anti-fascist but their defeats had caused a revulsion of feeling against Mussolini's senseless policies and a certain sympathy therefore for Mussolini's domestic enemies. These groups were at first small and basically anti-German; they were aware of the existence of other similar groups but not coordinated with them; they had no doctrine or political aims. But they grew. Where Germans were present in ordered strength and fixed positions they were obliged to coordinate their ventures in order to survive (many of them did not) and be effective. They needed the support and cooperation of the settled population and gradually became an adjunct of something quite different, the anti-fascist popular movement which had a political, as opposed to a merely anti-German, purpose and was planning a national uprising.

The term Resistance was not used in Italy during the war. (It was adopted after the war by extension from other parts of Europe.) This is indicative, because Resistance implied resistance to the occupier; the Italian movement which developed from 1943 was not primarily concerned with the occupation. It was an attempt, which ultimately failed, to make a revolution and take over the government of the country. It included republicans, socialists, communists, liberals and those left-wing Roman Catholics who looked backwards to pre-fascist Christian Populism and subsequently became a section of the Democratic Christian Party. Their common watchword was Renewal. They created a joint committee – the Committee of National Liberation (C L N) – which they regarded as the future government of Italy and, like Charles Albert of Savoy one hundred years earlier, they relied on themselves and not on foreigners: *l'Italia farà da se*. Two groups were particularly prominent: the communists with their Garibaldi brigades and the Action Party, the heir of Justice and Liberty, with similar brigades.

On the political front old parties reappeared and new ones were formed. Exiles returned. Barred from the government by the king and Churchill, they held a congress at Bari in January 1944 which demanded the immediate abdication of the king. Publicly and privately Churchill resisted them, speaking in the House of Commons against any change in the Italian government and instructing his representatives in Italy to support the king and Badoglio; but the British on the spot, more alive than Churchill to the trend of events, fostered the revival of democratic politics. Ironically the monarchy owed its reprieve not to the British but to the communists against whom Churchill was trying to protect it. The communist leader Palmiro Togliatti, returning from eighteen years in the USSR, joined in the demand for a new government but argued, on Stalin's instructions, that the fate of the monarchy should be deferred until the end of the war. The upshot was the withdrawal of the king from public life with a promise to instal his son Umberto as Lieutenant-Governor of the realm as soon as Rome was recovered. Badoglio remained Prime Minister but took representatives of six anti-fascist parties into his government. For the first time in history socialists and communists joined an Italian government.

When Rome fell the king transferred his powers to his son and Badoglio resigned. (The king still did not abdicate. He did so, belatedly, in 1946 when Umberto became king for a month. A plebiscite then abolished the monarchy by 12 million votes to 10 million.) The new Prime Minister was Ivanoe Bonomi, the penultimate pre-fascist Prime Minister and a respected figure acceptable to all anti-fascists in the short run. His government lasted until the end of the year when it was replaced by a narrower coalition, still under Bonomi. Another transient anti-fascist coalition was formed before the end of the war and lasted a few months after it. It was followed over the next twenty years by an unbroken series of Right-Centre governments. It is, however, tempting to see some consequences of the partisan movement in the post-war politics of north central Italy where much of the partisan activity took place. This part of the country has a tradition of opposition dating from at least the anti-Papalism of the Risorgimento; it has also a significant proportion of landless rural labourers. Since the war Emilia at its northern and Umbria at its southern end have given the communists their strongest base and their only popular majorities over the Christian Democrats, and between these two extremes the area, if less 'red', has still been consistently red with the exception only of a dent in Romagna where the radical but anti-communist Republican Party has been traditionally strong.

The attitude of the allies to the partisans was mixed. Churchill was in favour of guerrillas who harassed Germans. Most professional generals were hardly even that and all of them – generals, Churchill and other political leaders – were opposed to a national rising amounting to a civil war. Even in the midst of a Great War the idea of civil war was peculiarly repugnant with its moral implications of fratricidal strife and the special degree of unregulated cruelty which civil wars have evoked from early times down to the war in Spain still vivid in many minds. The allies looked with a favour which was exceptional on the national rising in Yugoslavia because it was successful and directed against their enemies and because they themselves were not there; but in Italy it was not so clear to the allies that the partisans were fighting against a common enemy and, besides, their activities might get in the way of allied military operations. The allies also, perhaps consequently, underrated the Italian effort. They were used to thinking of the Italian army as bad fighters and could hardly imagine that guerrilla forces might fight better than regular ones. Nevertheless allied aid, mainly British, was bountiful. It included 3,000 tons of supplies dropped by parachute – about half the partisans' total requirements.

After the fall of Rome partisan warfare in the countryside was intensified. So was sabotage by special action groups in towns. A series of strikes in northern cities in 1943 was capped in March 1944 by a general strike called by the C L N throughout the north. A million men and women responded and the strike lasted eight days. The Italian partisans became as numerous as any Resistance movement in Europe. By mid-1944 they numbered about 100,000 and were on their way to double or treble that strength before the war ended. Partisans killed, wounded or captured at least 50,000 Germans. Their own losses were heavy, particularly in areas where they assembled in large numbers and exposed themselves to organized German attack and also when the allied pressure was taken off the Germans and their northward advance blocked after the withdrawal of forces to France. Thirty-five thousand partisans lost their lives and another 20,000 were wounded. Another 10,000 civilians were killed in fights with the Germans or in reprisals. In addition 9,000 Italians were deported during the two years of direct German occupation, very few of whom were ever seen again.

As the winter of 1944 approached it became clear that the war would last into 1945. When General Alexander decided in November that he could undertake no further operations that year he advised the partisans too to suspend operations and go home. His message was broadcast *en clair,* so that it was received and read by German commanders who happened to be engaged at the time by substantial bodies of partisans. The partisans were infuriated by the message for many reasons. In the first place they could hardly go home without being arrested and shot. Further, they suspected that the allies wanted to deprive them of any share in the ultimate German collapse and make sure that the Germans should surrender to the Anglo-American command and not to any representatives of democratic Italy; they regarded the allied command as covert allies of the Right and knew that the popular rising with which they were preparing to end the war and inaugurate the new Italy was feared by the allies as a bloody communist revolution. They also resented the tone of the advice, which seemed to them too close to an order, and they had occasion to rue its consequences when the Germans, relieved of the necessity to bother about the allied armies, concentrated on the partisans and succeeded in killing thousands of them. Even Mussolini took heart and appeared in Milan and made a speech there.

The weather added to the stock of partisan troubles. The winter of 1944–5 was severe and the partisans suffered from it more than the German regular troops. But they were determined not to cease from their operations or to forgo their claim to be the liberators of Italy. They survived and, as the overall position of the Germans became more and more hopeless, they were able to renew the offensive in the spring. In April, when the Fifth and Eighth Armies launched their final attack, the northern cities rose; in Genoa 9,000 Germans surrendered to Italians and other great cities were captured by partisans. So was Mussolini who, politically, had survived the king after all and was trying in these last days to come to terms with the allies behind the backs of the Germans and through Cardinal Ildefonso Schuster, the Archbishop of Milan. At a meeting in the archiepiscopal palace of Milan on 25 April Mussolini learned that the Germans in Italy were negotiating with the allies behind his back and he thereupon dropped his own negotiations and set off for the Swiss border. He was captured and then recognized by partisans on 27 April and was shot the next day with his mistress Clara Petacci outside a small village. Their bodies with those of other fascists were displayed a day later upside down in front of a filling station in a square in Milan. They were suspended by meat hooks.

CHAPTER 19

Hitler's German Enemies

HITLER was hated by many Germans before the war began and, like Mussolini, he acquired fresh enemies when his wars turned to failures. There were plots against him before the war and more plots during the war. At first the conspirators aimed to displace him; later they came to believe that assassination was the only way to get rid of him. At first they were anti-Nazis of one kind or another; later they included Nazis who wanted to take his place or simply to save their own skins. The plots usually involved the army, since only the army had the organized power needed for a successful coup, but towards the end they involved also the SS which had grown into a separate and considerable armed force (the Waffen SS). Others, anti-Nazis or Nazis, might intrigue but only the leaders of the army or the SS had any hope of overthrowing Hitler's régime and taking control of the state.

Hitler's alliance with the army was crucial to his capture of power and to the prosecution of his external policies. He devoted a great deal of his political skill and his personal charm to this alliance. He was successful in the short run but even before war broke out he had become disappointed with the officer corps and distrustful of it; the build-up of the Waffen SS was a consequence of this disappointment and distrust. In its early days the Nazi Party had appealed to a number of German officers because they despised the civilian Weimar republic or were bored by it and were attracted by Hitler's promises of a better place for the army in a Nazi Germany and by Hitler's genuine personal interest in military matters. Hitler took care to moderate the radical strains in the Nazi Party which were likely to antagonize the preponderantly conservative officer corps and he traded on the political simplicity of a class which saw politics in black and white terms and was looking only for the most suitable partners with whom to fight socialism and communism. Field Marshal Werner von Blomberg, who became Minister for War when Hitler became Chancellor, had deluded himself into thinking that the Nazi Party was based on military virtues and military values and he saw no danger in letting Hitler gradually extend his influence by indoctrinating the services with Nazi propaganda. A handful of officers, notably General von Reichenau and Rommel, were openly enthusiastic about the party and its leader, although this enthusiasm began very soon to turn to disenchantment and then hostility. Others, like the Commander-in-Chief, Werner Freiherr von Fritsch, had reservations. Fritsch was appointed Commander-in-Chief by Hindenburg in 1934. He came from a civilian, not an army, background, but he had proved to be a brilliant officer. In character he was extremely reserved, inclined to self-doubt and – adopting the army tradition – non-political in the sense of not wanting to have anything to do with politics and not understanding much about it. He was not Hitler's choice for the post and he made Hitler uneasy.

Hitler's alliance with the army had been cemented in 1934 by the destruction of the SA and by the Soldiers' Oath but it was not followed by the wholehearted partnership which Hitler had hoped for. The army played along with Hitler without letting him feel that he was one of them. Hitler explained his aims and attitudes to selected groups of officers on more than one occasion and at great length, but their response was not enthusiastic. The more he made it clear to them that the army's role was to conquer *Lebensraum* in the east, the more sceptical and chilling did they become. Hitler did not understand that, like most professionals, the generals were conservative and cautious, nor did he appreciate the persistence of pro-Russian feeling inculcated by Seeckt's post-war policy of collaboration and by the respect learned on the eastern front in the First World War. By 1938, having sacrificed the SA to the army, he was finding the army an unsatisfactory tool. He decided to change its leadership and an outlook which seemed to him altogether too defensive and spiritless.

Two years earlier the SS had tried to tempt him into a plot against the army but he had refused to be drawn. Now, tempted a second time, he accepted the bait. Blomberg had just married a second wife. Hitler himself attended the wedding although the new Marschallin had been only a secretary. After the marriage the SS informed him that she had a police record as a prostitute. Hitler, who was easily shocked about some things as well as easily angered, agreed that Blomberg must go. He resigned, recommending Goering (as Commander-in-Chief of the Luftwaffe) as his successor, but Hitler dismissed the idea with the offhand remark that Goering was too lazy and abolished Blomberg's post. In its place he created a new Combined Services Staff (OKW) under General Keitel, weak in character and not particularly strong in intellect, through whom he proposed to exercise closer personal control over the services. This step was unpopular with the army.

Hitler also got rid of Fritsch. Fritsch was framed by the SS. He was accused of being a homosexual, which he was not. The SS dug out some police files concerning a certain Frisch who was. Fritsch resigned but his brother officers insisted that he should be given a trial. The case collapsed; the SS had to spirit away the now inconvenient Frisch who would have given the game away under cross-examination; and Fritsch was acquitted.

He was, however, only partially rehabilitated. In September 1939 he was wounded in the course of a patrol near Warsaw and died, apparently not unwillingly. The army was perturbed by the Blomberg episode and revolted by the Fritsch case but it did nothing beyond presenting a memorandum to Hitler against the creation of the OKW. Fritsch was succeeded by General Walther von Brauchitsch, an officer with a high professional reputation but only moderate strength of character: his wife, who nagged him, was a fervent Nazi.

By this time the officer corps as a whole had seen more of Hitler and the Nazis and come to like them much less. The army had acquiesced in and to some extent welcomed Hitler's rise to power because it was right-wing and anti-communist and looked forward to certain professional advantages from the new régime. It was also anti-semitic, though not so obscenely so as the Nazis; it wanted to be decently anti-semitic. But Nazi behaviour in power and the Nazi programme, especially Hitler's readiness to risk wars which the generals thought they could not win, disgusted and alarmed many officers who had not thought overmuch about the sort of people the Nazis were. By 1938 this was clear to all but the most determinedly blind. But it was not clear what should be done about it. The German army had no tradition of coups and did not know how to set about them. Its officers had exacting moral standards and a high sense of their duty to their country and they had come to believe that Hitler was a disaster. But they were by temperament neither political activists nor conspirators and they continued to serve Hitler while hating him. Hitler had every reason to distrust them but equally he had much reason not to fear them. They abhorred treason, particularly the graver form of treason which action against the head of state entailed. (Treason had two forms in Germany: the lesser *Landesverrat*, the betrayal of state secrets, and high treason or *Hochverrat*, involving action against an individual or a group.) Given their training and upper-class origins it is not surprising that few of them reached the conviction that treason was right; or that those who did so reached it only with extreme difficulty. They hated Hitler for being a murderer but did not want to be murderers themselves.

There were, however, exceptions and one of them was the Chief of Staff of the army, General Ludwig Beck. Beck was a quiet and industrious officer, a man with a wider culture than most of his fellows, much respected, perceptive and high-principled. He lacked, however, the talents of the successful man of action. In August 1938 he was retired by Hitler who may or may not have known that Beck was plotting against him. Beck had concluded that Hitler's foreign policies were insane and were leading to a war for which Germany was unprepared. Hitler must therefore be removed. As Chief of Staff Beck had ready access to all senior officers and he was also in touch with a number of civilians who thought like he did – including Ulrich von Hassell, an aristocrat and former Ambassador in Rome who was dismissed by Ribbentrop in 1937, and Carl Goerdeler, a former mayor of Leipzig. Admiral Wilhelm Canaris, the chief of the Armed Forces Intelligence Service (the Abwehr), Major-General Hans Oster, one of Canaris' principal subordinates, and other members of his department were also in the plot. This group tried in the summer of 1938 to get the British government to make an outspoken attack on Hitler whereupon army officers would arrest him on the grounds that he was leading his country into a suicidal war. But the British government did not speak out and Chamberlain's policies seemed to show that Hitler was running no risk of war and was far from insanely endangering Germany. Beck and his friends, appalled by Chamberlain's visit to the Führer at Berchtesgaden and conscious that German opinion after Munich was more likely to support Hitler than a group of conservative generals and diplomats, half of them retired, relapsed into impotence. This episode is characteristic. The British government believed that the foreign policies of the Beck group would not be very different from Hitler's (a judgement with some degree of truth in it) and concluded that there was therefore little to choose between it and Hitler (a wildly false conclusion). The conspirators' argument was that a British move would make all the difference, while the British response was to ask why the conspirators could not get on with the job without it. Even the more resolute army officers such as Beck looked for a first move by somebody else.

This military–civilian conservative opposition to Hitler was not the only one. There was intense and sometimes vocal opposition by students and among the clergy: many hundreds of priests, Roman Catholic and Protestant, were sent to concentration camps and killed. There was also opposition among former politicians from the middle-class world of the Weimar republic and among socialists from its dissolved trade-unions. Communist opposition was mostly of a different kind and consisted of spying for the USSR. The Rote Kapelle, a widespread, if overrated, communist network which penetrated even the Foreign Ministry in Berlin, succeeded in circulating an anti-Nazi periodical in six languages among foreign workers in Germany and later operated throughout much of occupied and neutral Europe. But the value of the information which it provided was not great, and it was destroyed in 1942 by the combined resources of the Abwehr, the SD, the Gestapo and the Chi-Stelle (the German code and cipher establishment at Potsdam).

Finally, there were groups of younger men, mostly belonging to the upper classes but radical or socialist rather than conservative and actively inspired by Christianity. They too objected to assassination on principle and toyed at first with schemes for arresting Hitler and putting him on trial. But they were more adept in conference than in conspiracy and their scruples complemented the efficiency of the secret police. Their interests were diffuse. They discussed plans for a post-war federation of European nations under an elective, revolving European presidency, as well as debating the removal or murder of Hitler. They took enormous personal risks which led many of them to the torture chamber and the scaffold. Although they shared the primary aim of the Beck group – getting rid of Hitler – they did not want the same kind of post-Nazi Germany. They distrusted Goerdeler, who was the conservatives' first choice for Chancellor but who appeared to them reactionary, incautious and over sanguine, and they proposed instead Martin Niemöller, an eminent Protestant divine and ex-naval officer who was in a concentration camp. Prominent in this set were Count Helmuth von Moltke, the pivot of the Kreisau circle, which was a small discussion and action group; Count Claus Schenk von Stauffenberg, an exuberant, widely travelled and widely read young Roman Catholic; Fabian von Schlabrendorff, a mildly conservative Prussian lawyer serving in a staff post in the army; and Adam von Trott zu Solz, a man of unusual physical and intellectual distinction, a socialist and a Christian with special links with Great Britain from his years at Oxford as a Rhodes Scholar. Trott's dilemma and fate were characteristic of his time. Deeply troubled about the right course for a patriotic and democratic Germany he decided, upon leaving Oxford, to temporize and postpone a decision between self-exile and returning to Germany to fight tyranny. After a spell as a lawyer in Germany he obtained, with the help of the chairman of the Rhodes Trustees, Lord Lothian, a semi-academic post in China. In order to secure the chance to return to Germany and enter the public service (which he ultimately did) he sent a number of reports containing anti-British judgements, but in the course of reinsuring his position on the German side he forfeited the trust of many of his British friends, who concluded that they had been duped. When therefore, after the outbreak of war, Trott tried to use his British and American connections in order to get allied support for anti-Nazi plots inside Germany he failed; so strong was the prejudice against him that even Sir Stafford Cripps, a friend who knew his true worth and had become a senior Minister in the British government, was forced by Eden (relying on reports in the Foreign Office about Trott's activities and on statements by some of his erstwhile friends) to desist from attempts to get his colleagues to take the German opposition groups seriously.

These groups were in truth relatively ineffective, although they were not, as many people in London believed, spurious, more German than anti-Nazi and so not to be trusted. Within Germany the Gestapo probably knew a great deal about their various activities but did not think it necessary to do much more than keep an eye on them, at any rate until after the attempted assassination of Hitler on 20 July 1944. In 1941 General von Witzleben, one of the more determined anti-Nazis, was dismissed from his post as Commander-in-Chief in the west on the eve of Barbarossa – possibly a precautionary move. In November 1939 two British Intelligence officers in Holland who believed that they were in touch with plotters in the German army were lured across the German border and seized. These officers, Captain S. Payne Best and Major R. H. Stevens, had been outwitted by the S D and had been having interviews with an S D officer, Walter Schellenberg, who was posing as an emissary of a group of disgruntled German officers. Schellenberg had had four meetings with Best and Stevens in Holland and had established a regular radio link with them and he was preparing to go to London to pursue his game there when he was ordered, much to his annoyance, to go instead back to Holland and kidnap Best and Stevens. On 8 November, the anniversary of the 1923 putsch, there had been a bomb incident in Munich and Hitler may have believed that this incident, although probably arranged by the Gestapo in order to enable it to spring a few traps, was a genuine attempt on his life in which British Intelligence was involved.

With the outbreak of hostilities plotting within the army became more difficult. The army officer's congenital reluctance to plot was greatly strengthened by war, which made treason peculiarly heinous, and the worse the war went – the nearer the dreaded Russians came – the more untimely did revolt seem. In addition war scattered the officers who might have concerted effective action. Brauchitsch and Beck's successor as Chief of Staff, Franz Halder, a capable but stolid Bavarian, listened to plotters, swayed this way and that, but could not bring themselves to do more than not give them away. The plotters hoped for a military reverse which would serve as a prelude to overthrowing Hitler. The Abwehr tipped off the Danes and the Dutch about the impending invasions of their countries, and others hoped that something would go wrong with the campaign in France. There were attempts to suborn senior commanders – Bock, Rundstedt, Kluge, Manstein, Guderian – who showed where their sympathies lay by not reporting these moves and showed also their own temper and perplexities by doing nothing else. Goerdeler displayed his lack of judgement by persisting in his belief that the generals could be made to act, and the Beck group discussed whether to try to rope some senior Nazis into an anti-Hitler conspiracy. Goerdeler was prepared to accept Goering as an interim Chancellor but Beck did not like the idea. At this time the group's aim was to get rid of Hitler, open negotiations with Great Britain and France and end the war. The emphasis was on the restoration of peace and Christian morality – but without the restoration of Czechoslovakia; parts of Hitler's conquests in Czechoslovakia and Poland were to be retained and the *Anschluss* was to be undisturbed.

The war made cracks in the Nazi Party. The first to show were in the troubled mind of Rudolf Hess who, on 10 May 1941, arrived in Scotland out of the blue. He had flown from Munich in a Me. 110 fitted with extra tanks and after failing to find the landing ground he was looking for had parachuted to earth and twisted his ankle. He was rescued by a farmer to whom he gave a false name and he asked to be taken to the Duke of Hamilton, whom he had met when the Olympic Games were held in Germany in 1936 and whom he knew to be commanding a Fighter Command sector in southern Scotland. Hess was, like a number of Nazi leaders from Hitler downwards, an *Auslandsdeutscher* or expatriate German. He had been born in Alexandria, where he lived until he was fourteen. As a young man of twenty he had served in the First World War and at the end of it, unemployed and somewhat feckless although anything but destitute, he ran into Hitler and was immediately enthralled. He took part in Hitler's Munich putsch and shared Hitler's cell after the fiasco, thus earning a minor part in the composition of the most celebrated prison book since Boethius and Bunyan – Hitler's *Mein Kampf*. Shortly after becoming Chancellor, Hitler nominated Hess as his deputy in the Nazi Party and in March 1939 he was declared second in line of succession to the chancellorship (Goering came first). He was therefore a very elevated Nazi, close to Hitler and intimately involved over many years in the enormities of the Nazis within Germany. He was also a hypochondriac and a devotee of astrology and his wife was a member of the miscalled Oxford Group – later renamed Moral Rearmament – founded and led by Dr Frank Buchman, who had on one occasion thanked God for Adolf Hitler.

Hess was not clever like Goebbels or devious like his party successor Martin Bormann, no heavyweight but entirely loyal to Hitler. Like too many of the senior Nazis Hess liked to try his hand at foreign policy, a pastime which provoked angry scenes with Ribbentrop (whom later he had to sit next to in the dock at Nuremberg), and in 1941 he evolved a plan for getting Great Britain to make common cause with Germany against the USSR. He tried to get in touch with Hoare in Madrid and with the Governor of Gibraltar, and after failing in these endeavours he decided to go himself to Great Britain, where he imagined there to be an alternative anti-communist and anti-Churchill government waiting to come into existence. Since he left a letter explaining his motives to Hitler it is reasonable to assume that Hitler, who flew into a rage on learning of his flight, had no foreknowledge of it, but it is not possible entirely to discount the view that Hess was the bearer of an official peace proposal. In Great Britain Hess's arrival was treated as a bizarre phenomenon and a propagandist opportunity (reduced, however, by Goebbels' promptness in giving the news of the flight before the British did) but not as a serious political event; the Russians on the other hand may have taken Hess's escapade more seriously, given their abiding fears of a western alliance (including Germany) against the USSR. Hess's position as deputy to the Führer was filled by Bormann, a protégé of Hitler who made himself indispensable by being always around, a mean-spirited man who came to be specially feared and disliked by the other party chiefs. Hess remained in detention in Great Britain until he was taken to Nuremberg at the end of the war to stand his trial on charges of complicity in murder and other crimes. There was some doubt about his sanity, but doctors in Great Britain and at Nuremberg declared him to be sane enough to stand trial (although an amnesiac) and he was sentenced to life imprisonment. The doubts about his mental state saved him from being hanged and his lingering longevity – he lived until 1987 as the sole prisoner of Spandau gaol in Berlin – gave him fame of a different sort.

More significant was the discontent of Himmler, who began to see the writing on the wall after the failure of the Russian campaigns of 1941. Goering's star had fallen with the defeat of the Luftwaffe in the Battle of Britain and the bombing of German cities, but Himmler's was rising with the wartime expansion of the Waffen SS into a considerable pretorian army. This expansion got under way in 1942 as Hitler's distrust of the regular army grew. The Waffen SS, so named in 1940, had grown out of the small but independent SS *Verfügungstruppe* which Hitler had created as a military (not a police) force as early as 1935. He had shown his affection for it by donning its uniform when he appeared before the Reichstag in 1939 to tell Germany and the world that Germany and Poland were at war and he had given it special tasks and opportunities in one campaign after another. He also gave it the best equipment, but its expansion from 1942 onwards perforce diluted its ethnic and ideological purity and even its prized standards of physical aptness and it became a mixed force which included even Slavs and Indians. Himmler, who thus found himself at the head of a personal army of eventually thirty divisions and so a power in his own right, began about 1942 to weigh the advantages of negotiating with the western powers instead of pursuing a war on two fronts which was coming to look more and more like defeat on two fronts. (Later on Himmler's doubts were greatly stiffened by the disclosures of Cicero, a German spy who, for £20,000, stole secret documents from a safe in the bedroom of the British Ambassador in Ankara. At the time of the Teheran conference these documents showed, among many other things, that Hitler's and Ribbentrop's reliance on the collapse of the East–West alliance was unfounded.)

In May 1942 the Bishop of Chichester, Dr George Bell, who happened to be in Stockholm on ecumenical business, was approached by German Christians who asked him to impress on the British government the reality of German resistance to Hitler. Their plans envisaged the overthrow of Hitler by the SS, followed by the overthrow of the SS by the army. The Bishop reported these matters to Eden at the Foreign Office but without effect. The approaches in Stockholm coincided with other feelers put out in Spain and Turkey and the British government suspected that, wittingly or unwittingly, the Bishop's Christian friends were being used by the Nazis to initiate discussions designed to lead to a compromise peace which would leave the Nazis in power in Germany and in possession of much of their ill-gotten gains – or at least designed to sow discord between the western allies and the USSR.

In January 1943 at Casablanca Roosevelt suggested and Churchill hesitantly agreed that they should declare that the only acceptable conclusion of the war was the unconditional surrender of Germany, Italy and Japan. Roosevelt got this idea from the State Department (which later became lukewarm or cooler towards it). He wanted at first to leave out Italy but it seemed simpler to include it. The phrase 'unconditional surrender', with its echoes of General Grant's ultimatum to General Buckner in Fort Donelson in 1862, sprang readily to the mind of every American but there were also more immediate reasons for adopting it: memories of the end of the First World War and of Germany's later claim that it had never really been defeated; the need of the two western leaders to find something ringing to proclaim at a moment when they could not foresee any very powerful military action against Germany for the immediate future; and their need to assure Stalin that they would negotiate no separate peace with Germany and to prevent him from doing so.

The most pressing aim of the declaration was to hold the Grand Alliance together at a time when Stalin was disappointed and angry and when

both Japan and Italy were working for a separate peace between Germany
and the USSR — a policy which Ribbentrop was known to favour. In
retrospect the overriding importance of this aim still cannot be gainsaid.
To risk letting the alliance fall apart implied either that the western allies
could win on their own or that they could find another ally. Neither
during the war nor since has it been seriously argued that the western
allies could defeat Germany if the German armies were released from
their commitments in the east. The only alternative ally that has been
suggested is the anti-Nazi Germans. But there was too little reason to
suppose that Hitler was going to be overthrown by an internal revolt or
that Nazism would be eliminated if Hitler were murdered. The anti-Nazi
Germans were no substitute for the USSR. Nor would a victory over the
Nazis with the help of the German army cut down the disturbing power
of the German state and the German threat to European stability and
freedom which had been among the causes of the war.

The declaration on unconditional surrender, whatever its strategic
necessities, may nonetheless have done something to consolidate German
opinion and discourage Hitler's enemies at home. Although it was intended to proclaim an uncompromising opposition to Nazism, Fascism
and Japanese militarism and not any intention to eliminate the German,
Italian or Japanese states, still less their peoples, it inevitably acquired
wider and fiercer connotation. Yet in fact the declaration did not quench
German opposition to Hitler. The army plotters were becoming convinced
of the necessity for Hitler's assassination rather than a coup aimed at no
more than his removal from office. First in a senior staff post at army
headquarters and then as Chief of Staff at Army Group Centre on the
Russian front General Henning von Tresckow was working to put conspirators in key positions. He also tried to win the active support of the
Commander-in Chief of the Army Group, Field Marshal von Kluge, but
Kluge could not make up his mind and consequently a plan to shoot
Hitler when he visited the headquarters in March 1943 had to be abandoned. Instead a bomb, secreted in a bottle of Cointreau, was put on
board the aircraft carrying Hitler back from Smolensk to Germany. But
the bomb failed to go off. At least five more attempts on Hitler's life were
made in the latter months of 1943, all of them equally unsuccessful because
the determination and daring of the conspirators were not matched by
technical efficiency.

There was then a pause before the famous and nearly successful attempt
on 20 July 1944, when Colonel Count Claus von Stauffenberg carried a
bomb in a briefcase into the Führer's conference room in his headquarters
in East Prussia, placed it beneath the table and left to fly to Berlin where

Beck, Witzleben and other officers were waiting to take over the capital and the government. But Hitler had not been killed – he was only slightly hurt and was able to show Mussolini the workings of Providence a few hours later – and the group in Berlin, who might have achieved something all the same, did nothing for the two hours during which Stauffenberg's aircraft was in the air and out of contact. On landing, Stauffenberg announced that Hitler was dead but a few telephone calls proved that he was not. The telephone lines between Berlin and East Prussia had not been cut – a vital slip on the part of the conspirators. There was confusion in Berlin, arrests and counter-arrests, with the established order quickly coming out on top. Beck shot himself. Stauffenberg and three others were executed at once. Then the shootings stopped and a longer and more comprehensive hunt began. In the east Tresckow committed suicide by walking east into no man's land. In Germany the principal result of this ill-fated scheme was the slaughter by the SD over the next six months of many fine men whom post-war Germany could ill afford to lose.

From 1938 to 1944 the conspirators against Hitler had sought outside help, especially from Great Britain, because they believed that without it they must fail. Denied it in 1938 they desisted for a while. Later, driven by a desperate patriotism, they acted without it and failed. By 1944 the worst horrors of the war had been perpetrated and, had they succeeded then, they would have done no more to it than shorten its final phase. Some uneasy questions remain. Were they right in their belief that outside help was essential? Probably they were, for they were never more than a small band attacking the centres of power of an exceptionally well-armed, well-disciplined and well-informed organization – the Nazi Party and police at the controls of the German state. Potentially the conspirators represented a powerful counterforce, for they had brains and devotion and the concurrence of some men in positions of power. But they failed to make the all-important step from conspiracy to success in action and there is something to be said for the argument that the missing additive could have been supplied by the British. This is a very serious argument, for it amounts to saying that the British missed a chance, first, of averting war and then of shortening it. To this argument there is no certain conclusion. What is certain is that the conspirators failed to impress the outside allies whom they needed. For this they were, partly and negatively, themselves to blame. They were a diverse group, at times a number of groups, and their schemes seemed imprecise and variable, their effectiveness doubtful. It was not always clear what sort of help they wanted. But there was failure on the other side too. Plotters start at a disadvantage because most governments, even governments which share their aims, are congenitally opposed to plotting. The characteristic members of a British or American government have some difficulty in making mentally common cause with conspirators of any kind and are inclined to underrate them. There was a lack of imagination, a failure to understand the drive which animated the conspirators, the counterpart of the failure of conservative ruling classes to understand Fascism.

And finally there was an aversion not only to plotters but also to Germans. Many of those caught up in the war fought it with good spirit and a clear conscience because they hated Nazism and wanted to destroy it, but anti-Nazism would never have started the war. In order for there to be a war for the destruction of Nazism there had to be a war about something else. The signal to start a war, or to accept a war challenge by an enemy, is given by governments and no government in the thirties asked itself whether it should go to war to destroy Nazism. What governments did ask themselves was whether they would have to go to war to stop Hitler – by which they meant stopping the territorial expansion of the German state. So the war, when it came, was a war against Germany. The part of Hitler's programme which provoked it was not the beliefs and practices of Nazism but the infringement of frontiers by Germany. The German conspirators against Hitler were the natural allies of anybody fighting Nazism but they were not the natural allies of a state at war with – or contemplating having to fight – Germany. The common ground between the German anti-Nazis and the enemies of the German state was not as large or as open as it seemed to those for whom the struggle was about righteousness rather than territory. In the last analysis the conspirators failed to find outside allies because, besides being anti-Nazi, they were also German. They were therefore doomed to be the bravest but the least effective of Hitler's serious enemies.

Hitler died in the end by nobody's hand but his own. From 1943 all his principal subordinates were thinking of how to end a war which could not be won. He himself was not. Once he had lost all chance of ending it on his own terms he gave little thought to ending it at all. He became obsessed with continuing it and, regardless of the true state of affairs, conducted increasingly hopeless operations by issuing nonsensical orders to armies which were shrinking to the size of divisions. His principal associates did not share his monomaniacal delusions. They tried, first by persuasion and then by conspiracy, to make peace with one part of the Grand Alliance or another. To a man like Ribbentrop who had signed the Russo-German treaty of 1939 a second essay in *Realpolitik* on these lines was tempting; he was supported by professional diplomats who had favoured such an alignment since the early 1920s and by the Japanese who tried in September 1943 (on the eve of the fall of Mussolini) and again in the spring and autumn of 1944 to end the Russo-German conflict. (But Ribbentrop later became disenchanted with the Russians and offered to arrange a conference with Stalin at which he would shoot Stalin with a specially designed fountain pen.) From the German point of view a peace or truce on the eastern front would release all Germany's forces for new victories in the west and re-open the flow of food and other materials with which the (then unravaged) U S S R had supplied Germany before Barbarossa. During the winter of 1943–4 German emissaries were taking soundings in Stockholm, probably with the knowledge but not necessarily with the endorsement of Himmler, but such prospects as they might have had were eliminated by the German belief that Germany was still successful enough to lay down conditions, such as the establishment of an independent Ukraine.

But if Ribbentrop wanted to make peace with the U S S R Goebbels, who neglected no opportunity to denigrate Ribbentrop, took the opposite view and developed a lively concern for the preservation of western civilization against the barbarous east – at the same time equating the Nazi with the Anglo-American view of what that civilization stood for. The invasion of Normandy strengthened the ranks of those who wanted a separate peace in the west, since they saw the impossibility of fighting on two fronts and the certainty of defeat in the east unless they surrendered in the west. The success of Overlord meant that Germany no longer had the slightest hope, without western help, of preventing the Russians from doing to Germany what the Germans had done to them. To prevent this retribution even Hitler should be discarded. Himmler, who had been fully informed about anti-Nazi plotting from 1943 at the latest but preferred not to take action, was toying with the idea of an alliance between the army and the S S for the removal of Hitler and the installation of himself as Chancellor in a new government consisting of a few Nazis and representatives of the military and the civilian oppositions to Hitler. His Waffen S S had grown to a force of a million men with the best equipment. (The other irregular army, Goering's twenty-two Luftwaffe Field Divisions, was of poor quality; its failures hastened Goering's decline.) Himmler wrongly supposed that the western allies would accept the substitution of himself for Hitler as an adequate consummation of the war in the face of the Russian menace and he entered into clandestine correspondence with the western allies through intermediaries in Sweden, Switzerland and Italy. These schemings played a minor part in the surrender of the German forces in Italy and in Hitler's barren last-minute switches of posts in the Third Reich.

Judgement on the German opposition to Hitler is not easy. Before the war, and during it, this opposition was ineffectual but it has been argued that the allies, Great Britain in particular, were partly to blame. Anti-Nazi conspirators existed in influential positions in the armed forces and the secret services and by September 1938 they had brought themselves to accept that Hitler's intention to conquer the whole of Czechoslovakia constituted a sufficient threat to German interests to warrant a coup against him and the dishonouring of their oaths of loyalty to him. A day for a putsch was fixed but one condition remained to be fulfilled. The conspirators wanted some assurance that the western powers would applaud and, if necessary, intervene. But the signal that they got was the wrong one: at Munich, Great Britain and France proclaimed in effect that they preferred to deal with Hitler and try to restrain him. This is not surprising, since governments are conditioned to deal with other governments, not with private plotters. Their appraisal of the effectiveness of the anti-Nazi activists was low, even scornful, and in looking for ways to avert war they put no faith in the hazards of a domestic German coup. What is surprising is that they found, and apparently sought, no way of encouraging the putsch without aborting the meeting at Munich in which their hopes for preserving peace principally reposed. Doing one thing with the right hand and another with the left is a common diplomatic technique. In this instance the western allies did not think it worthwhile.

After war had broken out only mutiny at high levels in the armed forces or the assassination of the Führer could have altered the course of events but the psychological and practical obstacles to either coup were formidable. There was plotting by some generals but it amounted to little more than risky talk. There were a number of assassination plans but not even Count Claus von Stauffenberg's attempt on 20 July 1944 came to anything. Again it has been argued that, particularly after the German disaster at Stalingrad, leading figures in the Abwehr made potentially fruitful overtures to the western allies who refused to take them seriously. These overtures were intended to elicit western support for a military coup against Hitler and his régime, leading to a separate peace with the west which would scupper both Nazism and a Russian victory over Germany. Alternatively it has been alleged that these approaches were not so much ignored as sabotaged within the British secret services, so that they never reached the right ears. That Admiral Canaris, General Oster and others in the Abwehr and elsewhere hated Hitler and desired a separate peace is evident enough. How far they disclosed their hopes to western contacts is less clear and what is not clear at all is how the British and American governments would have reacted if they had formally debated the conspirators' intentions. There is no evidence that they ever did so. The prevailing mood was deeply sceptical about all anti-Nazi Germans, and even had they felt it expedient – and found a way – to support such plots they were, to say the least, ambivalent about a separate peace involving the betrayal of their eastern ally. The anti-Nazi Germans wanted to save Germany, the allies to vanquish it.

CHAPTER 20
Great Britain at War

THE British experience of war between 1939 and 1945 was unique in that Great Britain was assailed and blockaded without having any of its home territory overrun and that its war effort was accompanied by changes in society and in the scope and structure of government which were presided over and directed by an established and virtually unchallenged government. In meeting their emergency the British were not able to superimpose a war economy on their existing peacetime economy, as the Americans did in the comparatively unruffled circumstances vouchsafed to them by physical inviolability and economic elbow room; nor could they, as the Russians did, fall back on the vastness of space and the rigours of autocratic rule to get the most in human labour and human endurance out of a patriotic people fighting against an enemy within the gates; nor, finally, were they left, as many continental Europeans were left, to face the present and shape a post-war future in the absence of a native government or in defiance of it.

To the question why Great Britain fought on in 1940 only an impressionistic answer can be given. It would take in an accumulation of factors, of which the most important are these. The Munich agreement of 1938 was a relief to a great many people who sensed the onset of a war which was never represented to them as a national or patriotic necessity. But Munich was also felt as a disgrace, and the sense of shame was compounded six months later when Hitler tore up the Munich agreement and completed his annexation of Czechoslovakia. That action finally revealed to the British that they had had enough of Hitler. The full story of the concentration camps was still to come but revulsion was now pressing hard against the dam of incomprehension. Moreover when war came, it came with a weird slowness, so that for nearly a year the British watched the approach of the storm; and all they saw nerved them for a fight where others had been unnerved. When prognostications of an unimaginable rain of death proved ill founded, the British found themselves spectators in a phoney, unnatural and yet humiliating war: no help was given to the Poles; no help reached the Finns, whose gallantry was at least equal to that of the Poles and more effective; Norway, a much respected country, was occupied by the Germans under the British nose. When the campaign in the west opened, the bombing of Rotterdam revived the German reputation for Hunnish atrocities in the First World War. France collapsed – a shock but in a sense also a release, since the British as a nation had no great opinion of the French and were as happy to fight, if need be, without a French ally as with one. Whereas Munich and the occupation of Prague and the growing evidence of Nazi barbarity had braced the younger generation for a fight, the bombing of Rotterdam stirred an older stratum of anti-German patriotism which, inclined also to be contemptuous of France, was undismayed by the prospect of single combat. And old and young were equally fortified by the retreat from Dunkirk which with a glorious perversity they regarded as a victory.

Something must be said too about British society. Although socially stratified to an extraordinary degree, this society was ideologically more coherent than most in Europe, less distraught by fascist or communist fissures, readier to respond unitedly to the generous humanity, the aristocratic chauvinism and the courage of a Winston Churchill. Furthermore, Great Britain was a singularly law-abiding, government-conscious and well-governed country. It was well governed not in the sense that the government was good for the people as a whole, but in the sense that government worked well within the limits set for it by the people who did the governing. Great Britain between the wars was not an agreeable place to live in. It was crowded with misery and injustice: estimates of the underfed in the worst years in the thirties go as high as twenty million. Little was done by government to help this large section of the nation and much of what was done was silly, for the governors were for the most part men of limited awareness and only moderate intelligence. Yet the temper of Great Britain did not become revolutionary. Rather did it become resigned in the face of chronic unemployment, killing poverty and the obscene slums which were among the most frightful places in which Europeans had ever been expected to live; and one of the main reasons for this resignation may be found in the fact that Great Britain had strong government. Strong government does not in this case mean repressive government but a government which never looked like breaking down or running down and which remained fully competent to perform its allotted tasks and preserve the formal framework of the nation's life. Although government was bad in the sense that it was inadequate in conception and in performance, it worked. It accepted a deplorably narrow view of its functions, but this view was traditional and excited little rebellion (except of the intellectual kind) with the result that the machinery of government did not become discredited. There was in 1940 in Great Britain neither a feeling of disintegration nor a movement to take the opportunity to alter the system of government. The British did not rebel against inequality and injustice because on the whole they did not believe in equality or expect justice. These things were too abstract or remote to be pursued or regarded as ingredients in real life: real life in Great Britain was steeply graded, material goods and opportunities were seen to be unfairly distributed, and even the law was accepted as one thing for the rich and another for the poor. But this did not mean that the British were supine. It meant that their demands were peculiar. What they did require of their rulers was freedom for themselves – the note which was struck in the seventeenth century and has dominated all others ever since in English history – and financial honesty at the top, and because they got these things in large measure Great Britain was, despite blatant social inadequacies, law-abiding. Freedom and incorruption were the secular religion of Great Britain (religion in its essential Latin sense of something that binds together), and *in hoc signo* the British engaged the enemy as a united people. At Mons in 1914 desperate men had seen angels in the sky; at Dunkirk in 1940 they saw German aircraft; but what mattered on both occasions was not in the sky but in tradition.

For the British the crisis of the war came with the fall of France. This event left Great Britain alone, exposed to direct attack, committed to a vast industrial effort to re-equip its armed forces, and uncertain about its food supplies. Alongside the military problems of survival and riposte was a twofold problem of government. First, the direction of the war consisted in a series of choices. Great Britain could not simply do what it had not done earlier. Doing some things meant not doing others. Men, women and materials were needed in more places and for more purposes than they could fill and somebody had to decide which came first. Only the government could take such decisions and so the government found itself involved in a range of activities which it had not undertaken in peacetime. Secondly, the direction of the war had to command popular approval. This was to some extent assured by the very nature of the emergency and by the confidence inspired by Churchill personally, but British society was sufficiently sophisticated and emancipated to require to feel in broad terms that the conduct of the war was efficient and to see that it was fair. The military front was left by the public and also by Ministers themselves very much to Churchill and his professional advisers, but on the home front the government acknowledged the need to assume new responsibilities for an equitable distribution of the burdens of war and for post-war reforms. Churchill promised blood, toil, tears and sweat. But his government had to do more than promise what Clemenceau had called the grandeurs and miseries of war.

Social awareness and a social conscience were not a product of the Second World War. They can be glimpsed in British history in the earlier part of the century and indeed much earlier than that. In the thirties unemployment had thrust itself, with the help of the press, on public attention. Most people knew that slums existed, even if they had no idea what they were like. But the depression between the wars frightened members of the ruling class even more than it touched their consciences. They feared for their own standard of living (which they were apt to confuse with the wealth of the nation) and they were as much afraid of the poor as sorry for them. So they nailed their slogans to the mast of orthodox economics, demanded reduced expenditure even if it meant wage cuts, imposed heavy import duties to keep prices up and opposed schemes for the relief of poverty as utopian and a threat to the value of sterling which, by inverting their priorities, they regarded as more vital than finding work for the unemployed. The war, like previous wars, affected this emotional muddle in two ways. By throwing people together, whether in the armed forces or in fire-watching posts or in civilian billets or in the reception areas where urban evacuees migrated, it forced people to become rather less ignorant of each other's circumstances than they had been, or had preferred to be, before. Shock, shame and comradeship created a positive desire for reform for idealistic reasons. Secondly, by creating an emergency which required the mobilization of the whole nation, war forced government to take note of the whole nation, to make it fit for the fight in body and spirit and to cater for its basic needs. The health and morale of the entire population became, in the Second World War, a matter of the first concern in the same way as the stamina of professional armies and their loyalty to their princes had been the essence of warmaking in earlier times. Looking after the whole population, in and out of uniform, became a function of government for practical reasons. On the material side it included the provision of food, accommodation, medical services, adequate working conditions, fair wages; on the spiritual side it involved justifying the war morally (not difficult with the Nazis as enemies), making people feel that their hardships were being equitably shared and assuring them a better society when the war was over and not merely a return to things as they had been.

The relief of poverty, however poverty may be defined, had long been regarded as a proper function of government, as witness a series of acts from the Elizabethan poor law to industrial insurance. During the war government came to provide for people for other reasons too: because they were pregnant or because they were old (even if they were not necessitous) or because they were very young. Therefore the war became a stepping stone in the slow and piecemeal progress from the concept of relief to the concept of welfare. Further, attitudes to poverty itself changed too. The old poor law had been administered locally; the right to relief existed only within the parish. But many people no longer lived all their lives in the places where they were born, and the increased mobility of the population in wartime finally destroyed a basis for poor relief which had long been out of date as well as inhuman. The poor became a charge on the nation instead of a charge on the parish, and local authorities ceased to have an interest in chasing away poor people who might by tarrying acquire claims on the local budget.

The immediate need in the early summer of 1940 was to re-equip the armed forces and survive the air bombardment which was bound to come. This meant specially hard work in specially difficult conditions. Many basic pre-requisites were missing. British industry was short of equipment, notably machine tools, and of certain raw materials, notably steel, rubber and aluminium. It was also short of factory space and of statistics about factory space: neither industry itself nor government knew how much space there was or how it was being used or how it might be adapted for war. Much effort was put into new building when it could more economically have been employed in conversion. There was not a serious overall shortage of manpower but there was a shortage of some special skills. There was also a ludicrous and throttling lack of statistical information about manpower – information about how many people were doing what where, for example, how many people were employed in the building industry. The first wartime government had done little to remedy these deficiencies and the second, taking office on the day when Hitler attacked in the west, still did not know what was scarce and what was not: it assumed, for example, that there could be no shortage of coal or shipping. Its difficulties were compounded by the losses of men and material in France, by the primitive inefficiency of much of British industrial management, and by unforeseen shortages of foreign currency. Required to build and equip new factories, to replace lost weapons and design and produce new ones, to feed the population, ensure a bearable standard of living and bearable working conditions, and to import essential minima of overseas raw materials, it was forced to plan in a time of unprecedented stringencies and turmoil.

There were three principal domestic upheavals during the war. They were caused by evacuations, the blitz and the break-up of families through the direction of men into the armed forces or to industrial work away from home and the flow of women into factories, agriculture and the services. The government assumed the task of regulating these changes and mitigating their unwelcome consequences. The complex series of measures introduced for these purposes covered the provision and rationing of food and other goods, the control of manpower and the regulation of working conditions, the control of prices, the provision of new social services for all classes of the population and the preparation of social reforms for post-war Great Britain.

Because the damage which the Luftwaffe would do to London and other big cities had been greatly exaggerated, the government had prepared, among other things, a plan for moving several million people out of the main target areas. The general principles, adopted in 1938, were: the designation of evacuation, reception and neutral areas; no compulsory removal, except from special areas where national security rather than personal security so required; schoolchildren to be moved *en masse* with their teachers; and the government to take compulsory billeting powers. When war came, close on 1.75 million people were moved by train and boat under the government's scheme. They included very young children with their mothers, pregnant women, the blind and crippled, inmates of hospitals and prisons, and government departments. In addition two million people moved themselves (and over 8,000 went to the United States and Canada, one quarter of them with government aid). This migration of close on four million persons was smaller than had been expected, but the private enterprise element was larger: in some specially attractive areas official immigrants were outnumbered by eight to one. In general the arrangements at the points of departure were fair to good, the arrangements in the reception areas fair to bad. Owing partly to official parsimony and partly to the filling of prospective billets by unofficial, and usually more welcome, refugees the accommodation of the government's charges sometimes verged on the chaotic, and the refugees were made to perceive the distaste of country people for what were called, and sometimes were, urban dregs. Elsewhere their reception was all that generosity could desire. But everywhere there was a bit of a shock. Town children were not only put out by the change of scene, they were also disturbed by being separated from their families and became the more prone to obstreperousness by day and bedwetting at night. The hosts looked with horror and for the first time at children whose clothes were thin and dirty and torn and whose hair had lice in it; some of them began to feel that much was being asked of them, even if there was a war on, others that not enough had been asked of them in peacetime to remedy the social ills of slum life which had never before been brought home to them. Such encounters may be salutary but they are hardly ever easy for either side. By the end of the year a million of the evacuees had decided that they would rather go back to the cities again. The discomforts of social adjustment, and the false sense of security engendered by the phoney war, repopulated the target areas. In 1940 a second evacuation took place when, after the fall of France, 200,000 schoolchildren were moved from London and other cities and some of the more exposed coastal zones were redesignated evacuation areas, but the partial failure of the first wave of evacuation caused a number of people to opt for bombing and death.

A secondary consequence of evacuation was an enormous increase in the mobility of the population. Military service and compulsory direction of labour had the same effect, and over the whole period of the war the number of moves made from one home to another inside Great Britain exceeded the total number of the population.

The London blitz, which began on 7 September 1940 and continued for seventy-six consecutive nights with only one intermission, caused great dislocation and some discontent, which were countered by solidarity and comradeship in adversity, by the efficiency of voluntary bodies and by the active sympathy and interest of superior beings like Churchill and the king and queen. Although the weight of the attack had been so far over-estimated that the tonnage of bombs dropped on London in the whole war was less than what had been expected in the first two weeks, the damage per ton was higher and the trouble and danger caused by un-exploded bombs (5–10 per cent of the total) unforeseen. Casualties per ton on the other hand were lighter – fifteen to twenty per ton in place of the estimated fifty to seventy, a reflection not only of happily inaccurate forecasting but also of the effectiveness of precautions ranging from shelters in basements, gardens and subways to rescue, ambulance and hospital services. On the other hand victims often did not know what relief services existed or where they were to be found. There was much improvisation, for the homeless turned out to be a bigger problem than the dead, and the raids came by night instead of by day. Sleeping facilities had to be provided in underground railways and other public places, and rest centres – mostly provided at this stage by private effort – were initially too few, under-equipped and overcrowded. At one point in 1940 there were about 25,000 homeless people in London and, in addition to death and destruction, human beings had to contend with lack of sleep, more dirt and more broken glass than most people had thought about, the blackout, sirens (reduced on Churchill's command from a two-minute to a one-minute wail), an increase in the accident rate especially among children, queues, and a continuous strain which was not totally lifted until the war ended. Outside London air raids were less concentrated. In the attacks on cities and ports which began at Coventry on 14 November 1940, when 554 people were killed and much of the city including its cathedral destroyed, the dispersion of the effort over two dozen major targets lessened the impact on each. The renewed attack in 1942 – the so-called Baedeker raids – was a tip-and-run operation which did comparatively little damage, and the V weapons, arriving only in the summer of 1944, were too late to be a prolonged menace. Air raids killed 60,000 people, seriously injured 86,000 and slightly injured 149,000. Half these casualties occurred in London and two thirds of them while Great Britain was fighting alone.

The evacuation and the blitz were the two sides of a single coin depicting the parrying and withstanding of the enemy's attack. In this attack the family, the basic unit in British society, was buffeted in its two vital parts: the link between the spouses and the care of the children within the family group. The British family had become smaller since the First World War, more compact perhaps but also more vulnerable. It no longer had so many older children to look after the babies; the older children were fewer and not enough older. With the father away and the mother perhaps doing part-time work there was no reserve for emergencies. Older relatives and friends, who might have been expected to lend a hand, were also more likely to be out at work and when the bombing began there were soon many houses with a room or two damaged and so without the extra space for taking somebody in for a night or a week. People who had moved might not have got to know their neighbours well enough to ask for the little services of neighbourliness. Looking after a family with these traditional longstops gone became a constant worry.

The separation of the spouses was another worry. Husbands and wives do not normally want to live apart. During the war one or both of the separated spouses was often in danger. Sometimes neither knew for certain where the other was. Letters took a long time and in any case not everybody was used to conveying feelings by letter; many letters were awkward, stilted compositions which said nothing of consequence except that the writer was alive and well, or alive and recovering from something or other; they were, as Wilfred Owen wrote in the earlier war,

> ... the sighs of men, that have no skill
> To speak of their distress ...

Many separations began on the morrow of marriage, and many of the married were unusually young. Although the marriage rate fell during 1942–4 (it had been abnormally high in 1939–40), there was an increase in the proportion of marriages contracted by persons between twenty and twenty-four and a very notable increase in the number of persons marrying under twenty-one – nearly one third of the women who married for the first time during the war were under twenty-one. The birth rate, which fell in 1941 to its lowest recorded level, rose sharply from 1942 onward.

The number of illegitimate births rose dramatically – from 26,574 in 1940 to 64,743 in 1945; the percentage of single and widowed women bearing children rose from a pre-war average of 0.55 per cent to 1.04 per cent. Separation was one cause: the number of husbands separated from their wives by military service may have reached 2.5 million at its peak, about a quarter of a million men served overseas continuously for the full five years of war, and very many more were absent long enough to promote the conception of bastards on one side of the family or the other. Civilian husbands too were separated from their families when they were sent to work in distant factories or their offices were moved wholesale from one place to another. Although attempts were made to keep families together, it was impossible in wartime to provide the necessary accommodation. The number of foreign servicemen in Great Britain varied between a quarter and half a million and rose to 1.5 million before the invasion of Normandy. Many of them contributed to the illegitimate birth rate along with the relaxation of moral conventions occasioned by war, separation and the shortened expectation of life.

But although the number of illegitimate births rose so that something like 100,000 children were born illegitimate during the war who would otherwise have been born in wedlock, there is no evidence of an increase in extra-marital sexual intercourse and the proportion of extra-marital conceptions in fact fell. One seventh of all children born in the last year before the war had been conceived extra-maritally, and nearly 30 per cent of mothers had conceived their first child out of wedlock. During the years 1940–47 one eighth of children were so conceived. The war affected what happened after conception. Whereas before the war 70 per cent of the parents who procreated before marriage got married before the child was born, during the war they did so less and less until in 1945 only 37 per cent married in these circumstances. In sum, the rise in the number of illegitimate births in wartime betokens no change in sexual behaviour but a decline in the opportunities available to couples to regularize the status of their misconceived offspring. The result was a magnified social problem, often misinterpreted as a moral one. The percentage of unmarried mothers under twenty-five dropped during the war, although in the higher age groups it increased. The biggest increase (41 per cent) occurred among the thirty to thirty-fives.

There were more divorces. The grounds for divorce had been extended by statute in 1937 and a number of men and women found in the services advice about divorce and a cheaper way of getting one, but the increase from 10,000 petitions a year just before the war to nearly 25,000 in 1945 reflected also a general loosening of family ties. Juvenile delinquency also increased, although it still concerned only a small proportion (between 1 and 2 per cent) of the young. Cruelty to children and neglect increased. So did truancy from school. But drunkenness was halved.

The government had to take cognizance of these social trends. The armed services adopted a liberal attitude towards applications for compassionate leave or compassionate postings by anxious husbands or fathers. By the end of the war requests in these categories were being made at the rate of 200–300 a day and about half of them were being granted. At home the government established and paid for services for pregnant women, young children, old people and even, with some reluctance and a good deal of secrecy, unmarried mothers. State care for pregnant women was a new idea. Before the war local authorities had been empowered – but not, except in the case of midwives, obliged – to provide services, but where they did so the quality varied extensively, some were very bad and the death rate was shockingly high. There was little comprehensive care embracing pre-natal, midwifery and hospital services because these services often came under different authorities. The war exacerbated the problem since displaced mothers were seldom able to have their babies in billets and there was an acute shortage of maternity beds in hospitals. The government therefore established emergency maternity homes, which had high standards and a low death rate and which proved to be one of the most successful of the government's wartime incursions into the field of social welfare.

The unmarried mother remained a being apart. Practically her only recourse was to the old poor law and the workhouse; when she left the workhouse, even to go to work, she had to carry her baby with her in order to satisfy the authorities that she was not running away and abandoning it. She could get no public assistance outside the area to which she belonged owing to the rigid administration of the poor law by districts and the determination of each district to guard its territory against trouble and expense from beyond its borders; she was, for these as well as other reasons, unwelcome as an evacuee in a reception area. Apart from the workhouses there were in 1939 only four publicly assisted homes for unmarried mothers in the whole of England and Wales and further accommodation provided by voluntary organizations for 3,000–4,000 mothers per year – against a total of illegitimate births which, as already mentioned, passed 25,000 before the war began and then rose steeply. The death rate for illegitimate babies was twice the normal. The armed services assumed during the war some responsibility for the illegitimate children and so-- called unmarried wives of servicemen, and the government, with a similar eye on morale, gave some niggardly assistance to those similarly situated in war industries, but for moral and financial reasons the government's scheme was run in such a hole-and-corner way that many possible beneficiaries never got to hear about it. The war dented attitudes to the livelier consequences of adultery and fornication, but not much.

The government was bolder in grasping the nettle of venereal diseases, whose incidence roughly doubled during the war. New centres for treatment were established (some existed before the war) and considerable publicity was given to the dangers, causes and cures. Some newspapers, putting prudery before health, refused to accept the government's advertisements. Doctors were given power to order patients to submit to treatment for venereal disease, as also for scabies, which, according to the Ministry of Health, was developing into a threat to the war effort. At one point the Rubber Control stopped the manufacture of contraceptives but this particular exercise of administrative discrimination in relation to a scarce commodity had to be reversed as a result of representations by interested parties – an example of the power of the consumer.

The care of children under five presented special problems since they were not evacuated with their schools like their older brothers and sisters and many of the mothers who had been expected to stay at home and mind them went out to work. The call-up of women was one of the more contested and controversial decisions of the war on the home front. It was foreshadowed early in 1941 when women were required to register on a limited scale. This step was partly a precaution and partly an appeal. It was hoped that women who had neither jobs nor household duties would go to work, but the number of such women turned out to be small and when industry, notably the aircraft industry, began to run into serious labour shortages the net was extended and the power to direct women to work was used. The lower age limit was eighteen and a half and the upper, fixed in October 1942 at forty-five and a half, was raised by steps to fifty. Women with husbands at home or children under fourteen were exempt, but they were nevertheless asked to work and 13 per cent of those with young children did so. Older women also volunteered for work. By the end of 1943 the female labour force had increased by over two million, half of whom were working voluntarily and for no pay. The consequences, during the war and afterwards, were considerable. Women undertook work which they had not done before and persisted in it after the war: the diversity of female labour was greatly increased (the main cause, together with higher taxation, of the decline in domestic service – from 5 per cent of households to 1 per cent). Women also became more accustomed to working after marriage, another change which stuck. It was discovered, to the surprise of some men, that in most jobs undertaken by women a woman was the equal of a man except when she came to be paid.

Day nurseries for very young children had first been established in 1880. They were expanded during the First World War but allowed to dwindle and in 1938 there were only 104 in existence. In addition there were nursery schools and classes, mostly in very poor districts, taking about 185,000 children, that is to say, one in ten of all children under five. There were also a number of children in workhouses. Voluntary and official bodies supported welfare centres, health visitors, medical attention and free meals. These services were cut when war began owing to a complete failure to foresee the problems which would arise when labour became scarce and even women with young children would be exhorted to go to work. Despite anxious prodding by the Ministry of Labour little was done for two years but thereafter the exigencies of the situation – and demonstrations in London and elsewhere – caused the government to pay more attention to this section of the population and before the war ended there were over 200,000 children in day nurseries or nursery schools. They were mostly run by voluntary organizations and paid for by the state. A small number of residential nurseries was also established, largely through American and Canadian generosity although the government ultimately agreed to foot the bill; they accommodated about 20,000 children. Finding premises, equipment and toys for all these establishments proved difficult; it so happened that the makers of cots had been specially unlucky in the blitz and at one point there was a shortage of rubber teats which had to be imported from the United States owing to a shortsighted prohibition on their manufacture in Great Britain; toys were made by air raid wardens waiting for raids and by prisoners, as well as being sent by sympathetic foreigners. Finding staff was also difficult and the number of mothers released for industry was not very much greater than the number of women employed to mind their babies, although it does not follow that the scheme was of minimal value since many of the child-minders could not have been usefully employed in anything except child-minding. The standards prevailing in the nurseries were high, epidemics very few and the idea of nursery schools caught on and survived the war.

In making provision for young children and pregnant mothers the government was extending to whole categories services which it had previously supplied only to the indigent, thus removing the stigma of poverty which had inhibited people from asking for what they needed. It had also to provide certain necessities for the whole population without distinction of class or category. The most important of these necessities was food.

Much of Great Britain's food came from overseas. Enemy action and shortage of shipping endangered the nation's food supply and created a corresponding need to produce more food at home. But Great Britain had very little surplus land to bring into cultivation. Therefore more food involved changes in uses of existing agricultural land and greater productivity per acre. This in turn meant more machinery, especially more tractors, and the modernization of agriculture which had been neglected during the pre-war years. Imports could be cut by increasing arable farming at the expense of livestock since feeding stuffs were largely imported. At the beginning of the Second World War Great Britain's arable acreage was smaller than it had been in 1914 by 2.75 million acres. The government therefore gave generous grants for ploughing up unploughed land and for improvements such as drainage. It also helped marginal farmers – a policy which was continued after the war. In the course of the war ploughland expanded from under 13 million acres to over 19 million and tillage from nearly 9 million to 14.5 million. The number of tractors rose from 52,000 just before the war to around 200,000 at the end. Cereal crops increased by 50 per cent and so did potatoes. Milk production was maintained but the country's population of pigs, poultry and sheep contracted sharply as imports of feeding stuffs fell from 8.75 million tons to 1.25 million. Yet the food value of this diminished animal population was considerably increased by more intelligent farming and its money value rose by 30 per cent at constant prices.

The needs of war changed both the structure of farming and even the landscape itself. In some areas small farmers retreated before the economics of a machine age until the average size of a farm was ten times what it had been. Much ploughed land did not return to pasture after the war. The Wiltshire downs, for example, which had been pasture land since neolithic times, were ploughed and have continued to be ploughed.

Local War Agricultural Committees were established to give advice (which was not always well received) on such comparatively new subjects as chemical weed control and soil analysis, to chide and if necessary evict bad farmers and to reclaim and work any derelict land that could be found. They had considerable powers and they used them. They also owned and hired out machinery. These committees consisted of unpaid local people assisted by paid officials, one of many examples of the blending of the voluntary system with the new expertise and the new concept of central direction. Although they were regarded by a conservative countryside as a regrettable and temporary necessity, their effects were salutary: output per acre was increased by 10–15 per cent, total production rose by 35 per cent with only a comparatively small increase in the labour force, neglected land was restored, finance became available and profits were made. The farmers with the most and best land did best, but all did better than before. After the war the powers of the wartime committees were perpetuated by statute (in more circumspect language) but the new committees used their powers much less.

Hardly less important than the production of food was its equitable distribution. Great Britain's wartime rationing system was almost a work of art. The simplest form of rationing is to assign to every individual a given quantity of a limited number of specified substances. This system becomes somewhat less simple when the quantities assigned vary according to categories of consumers – infants, pensioners, heavy industrial workers, diabetics, etc. Furthermore even a comparatively simple system of this kind will not work unless the authorities can ensure the continuous provision of adequate stocks of the rationed goods at all places and times, a task which was particularly difficult in Great Britain's case owing to the uncertainties of imports. But the British system was far more extensive and flexible than specific rationing of this kind. It embraced foods beyond the basic necessities and gave the consumer a certain range of choice. The system was tripartite: first, it specified precise rations of some foods, for example, butter. Secondly, it rationed meat by price instead of by quantity, so that a family might either pool its rations to buy a good joint once in a way or choose to have less good stewing meat more often. (Offal, rabbit and chickens were off ration.) Thirdly, the system imposed a general limit on purchases in a wider area – biscuits, jam, oranges, sweets were examples – within which, however, the purchaser was free to choose. This was achieved by a brilliant, if simple, device called the points system. Every individual was allotted a certain number of points, represented in his ration book by tokens of varying point-value which he could exchange for rationed foods at any time in a prescribed period. The goods which fell within this scheme were graded so that, for example, a packet of biscuits or a tin of sardines cost so many points. The gradings were altered from time to time, upwards or downwards, in accordance with the availability of stocks, and the individual's aggregate number of points in a quarter was also varied in order to increase or restrain his overall demand on rationed goods (other than specifically rationed ones). The points system introduced administrative difficulties since the consumer's freedom of choice made it impossible precisely to predict the demands which were likely to be made in a given period in different parts of the country – people in the south-west might develop a marked taste for biscuits while people in the north-east were making a run on sardines – but the flexibility in demand and consequent alleviation of the monotony of wartime diet were worth the extra effort, and the scheme as a whole was a major success for government planning as well as a triumph for fairness. The opulent could not (in theory – though appearances sometimes seemed otherwise) get unfair advantages by eating large meals in restaurants because for any meal costing more than 5s. (25p) coupons had to be surrendered. No coupons were required in works canteens but these meals were limited to a value of 5s. – and usually to baked beans and a mass-produced wartime invention called, after the Minister of Food, a Woolton pie. There was little cheating or black marketeering. Besides food, clothes and household goods were similarly rationed. Each individual had a separate book of coupons for these goods. Overall purchasing power was restricted but within this general limitation the purchaser could choose whether to buy half a dozen yards of cloth or a pair of sheets or a new dress.

Food and household goods were also cheap. The government's policy was to keep people healthy and vigorous by keeping the price of food down. Price controls were introduced in stages until by the end of 1942 they covered all goods in general demand. Special attention was paid to children, who, in this and other respects, were exceptionally well looked after during the war. They had different ration books and were provided gratis with milk, orange juice and cod liver oil (for vitamins) and meals in school. Standard – 'utility' – clothing and furniture were introduced, and utility clothing was exempted from purchase tax. These controls brought the cost of living down and, since wages were not brought down too, many people were financially better off during the war than they had been before it – a particularly grim commentary on the social outlook of pre-war governments. Average personal expenditure on food rose from 10s. 8d. (53p) to 14s. 6d. (72½p): that is to say, people continued to spend roughly between a quarter and a third of their net income on food, although by the end of the war they were buying at 14s. 6d. slightly less than they could have got for their 10s. 8d. at the beginning of the war. This stability was remarkable in view of the great increase in the cost of food. Home-produced food doubled in cost; imports, although reduced in volume (by 25 per cent), also doubled their cost. All in all the annual cost of food rose by £726 million, of which £472 million was paid directly by the consumer and £254 million was met by government subsidies. The extent of government intervention is shown by comparing this last figure with the pre-war cost of food subsidies – £72 million.

By this combination of measures – food production, rationing and price control – the government succeeded in ensuring an adequate, if monotonous, diet and an adequate, if uninspiring, supply of other basic goods. The first two years of war, with meat severely rationed and all imports of fruit discontinued, were a period of shortage but no danger to health. Civilian consumption was rather restricted by the shortage of steel, timber and aluminium, of which there was little left over for such things as kitchen utensils, furniture or sports goods. Textiles were also reduced by the transfer of labour from the textile industry to more urgent war production; part of the textile industry never recovered the labour and the markets which they lost. These were the years of the biggest cuts in civilian standards, personal expenditure on food dropping by 20 per cent during 1941, on other household goods by more than 40 per cent and on clothes by 38 per cent. There was, however, a compensating gain. The quality of what was available improved. The government imposed minimum standards on such goods as 'utility' furniture and fabrics, so that although richer people had to make do with goods inferior to what they had been used to, most people were getting a better buy than before the war. Design too, as well as the material itself and the workmanship, improved over a whole range of goods which had previously been turned out tastelessly for a public which was supposed not to care. Cheapness was no longer synonymous with shoddiness.

From 1942 life continued on a reduced plateau, which people at large accepted and the government maintained with such variations as it might introduce when supplies could be improved and the balance between military requirements and the demands of civilian morale could be adjusted. Housing began to present a bigger problem than food or goods. By the end of 1941 300,000 families were living in sub-standard houses and no fewer than 2.5 million persons in houses which had suffered bomb damage of varying degree. There was overcrowding and discontent, but the building industry was using the bulk of its depleted labour force (reduced by two thirds by July 1944) to build airfields and camps and to repair factories, railways and docks. From 1943, however, some of this labour had to be diverted to repairing domestic housing and converting large houses to accommodate more families. This work was given a high priority and in 1944 nearly 3.5 million men were engaged in repairing houses and maintaining and renewing industrial plant. They themselves created a lodging problem when they were drafted into cities in large numbers and their work was offset by the arrival of the V weapons but by the end of the war 40,000 houses were being repaired per week. Nevertheless the war left a massive housing problem which was only partially and temporarily eased by spending £150 million on 'pre-fabs'.

Although enough food of the right sort is the basis of fitness, diet is not the answer to everything. People still get sick or tired or bored. The government was therefore obliged to assume responsibility for hospital services, to intervene in the regulation of working conditions and even to provide entertainment and other resources for filling in time.

Great Britain's pre-war hospital services were an uncoordinated muddle, partially masked by the excellent and devoted work which went on in some sections of what could hardly be called a system. Hospitals included over a thousand voluntary hospitals which were unrelated to each other, many of them in shocking condition, short of equipment, antiquated and bankrupt

The War Office had its own hospitals; local authorities, of whom the independent voluntary hospitals were inherently suspicious, ran others. Apart from London and a few other rich areas there was a serious shortage of doctors and nurses. Plans had been discussed before the war for a comprehensive state hospital service but they made little headway against the rivalries of the different hospital bodies. Estimates of likely civilian casualties produced an irremediable problem: about 250,000 beds could be made available by cramping patients and staff and lowering standards of care and hygiene as against an anticipated need for 1 million to 2.8 million beds. Fortunately the problem never materialized and the government was granted the right combination of breathing space and exigency to impose (against the protests of the War Office and by overriding the independence of local authorities) a regional system in which new hospital boards, covering wide areas, allotted varying functions to hospitals of all kinds in their areas. The coming of war was an accelerator which forced a highly unsatisfactory state of affairs on the attention of government, provided an excuse for the beginnings of action and laid the basis for a new system in which the distinctions between the different kinds of hospital would be eliminated by overall state control, and a more sensible area of management – the region – would replace both the single voluntary hospital and the variety of local authorities which were often too small or too poor to do the job properly.

Hospitals clearly existed to perform a public service. In 1939 this was not true of the railways, which were generally considered to exist to make a profit. They were also unprepared for war and barely fulfilled their function in it. Before the war it was assumed that there would be no lack of carrying capacity on the railways and that they could cope with twice the amount of normal goods traffic provided the turn-around of wagons was accelerated and passenger travel drastically curtailed. But curtailing passenger facilities has psychological, not merely statistical, consequences and there were in any case no solid statistical grounds for this optimism, the main effect of which was to absolve the government from making any overall plans for war transport. The first winter of war exposed the fallacy.

The distribution of coal was held up to such an extent that a quantity had to be diverted to coastal shipping and for several weeks coal was given absolute priority on the railways in order to prevent a national outcry. This was only the foretaste of a crisis which was compounded by the strains of a population on the move, by bombing and by the closure of ports, which forced traffic away from the coastal and into the inland system. During 1940 deliveries of coal to London, to take a single example, were all but halved and the points of intersection of the main railway lines nearly quivered to a standstill; cooperation between the different railway companies was far from good. In the next two years, with less bombing and more planning, more coordination between the Ministries of Transport, Supply, Food and Mines, the institution of central control over rolling stock and road transport, and the loan of 400 locomotives from the United States and the War Department, things improved. By 1943 the government had established effective control over inland transport but it could not in wartime remedy the capital depreciation and mismanagement of the pre-war years and even as late as the penultimate winter of war about a hundred factories stopped work because they were short of coal. At this time the railways had increased by 50 per cent their capacity in terms of tons of goods carried per mile but they were also on the verge of collapse: government intervention and regulation were a salvage operation which averted disaster but could do no more.

Few things so frustrate industrial effort and fray tempers as traffic failures, and the railway failure during the war not only hampered production but also exasperated individuals who were kept waiting for trains (and buses) after long stints of overtime. Workers who had been moved some distance from their homes became specially disgruntled. Train fares were higher than corresponding bus fares with the result that trains were not used to full effect until fares were reduced and travel allowances given to the less well-paid workers. Transport was beginning to be regarded, at least in wartime, as a public service run for people and not as a commercial enterprise run for profit.

The government greatly extended its supervision of industrial life. Ernest Bevin secured the transfer of the Factory Inspectorate and the administration of the Factory Acts from the Home Office to the Ministry of Labour and expanded the whole concept of government intervention from safety in factories to welfare in industry. One of his first steps as Minister of Labour was the creation of a Factory and Welfare Division in his Department. All factories employing 250 people or more could be directed to install amenities such as canteens and to appoint welfare officers. Bevin considered that adequate transport for workers, day nurseries for their infants and the rehabilitation of the disabled all fell within the scope of government responsibility. The numbers of factory doctors and industrial nurses were increased; when the war began there were only thirty-five full-time and seventy part-time factory doctors in the whole country but by the time it ended there were 181 and 890. On the lighter side the B B C introduced 'music while you work' and outside working hours the government encouraged entertainers to make life as normal as possible. On the outbreak of war places of entertainment had been closed, but it was soon perceived that this mood was unhelpful and dance halls, cinemas, theatres and dog tracks were quickly re-opened and football matches resumed. Museums too re-opened, although their most precious possessions were removed from danger and stored in caves, country houses and other refuges.

The main tool for the regulation of the pre-war economy, in so far as it had been regulated and not left to sort itself out, was monetary – the budget. The main tool in wartime was, however, not monetary but human – the allocation of manpower. The armed services, which employed fewer than 500,000 men and women before the war, topped 5 million before it ended. If civil defence and munitions workers are added to the armed services the total number required in these occupations of first importance was 8 million in 1941 and 10 million by the middle of 1942. The civilian labour force remained roughly static but had to be considerably re-deployed. On the one hand a manpower budget was introduced. All users of manpower, military and civilian, were required to assess their future needs. These assessments were always excessive, sometimes falsified, and they always added up to a total that was not available. The reconciling of these competing claims was a cabinet matter. Secondly, in the civilian sector sweeping powers were given to the Minister of Labour and National Service (Ernest Bevin from May 1940 to July 1945) to direct labour from one occupation and one place to another and to forbid workers to leave specified kinds of employment. Bevin was at first slow to use the powers given to him because he was so short of accurate statistics that he did not know what directions he ought to give. He was also careful not to introduce compulsion until the need for it had become evident to those who were to be compelled. He himself gave much thought and personal energy to explaining the needs, thereby creating a sense of participation and comprehension without which direction of labour would have been exceedingly unpalatable. There was virtually no hostility to the idea that certain categories of persons having special manual or intellectual skills should be exempted from military service if they could make a better contribution to the war effort in some other way. The basic criterion was no longer the equal exposure of all to the dangers of the enemy's bullets but the graded contribution of each to a complicated mesh of national services. In one much debated instance Bevin directed young men away from military service not because they were specially skilful or specially clever but because a civilian service, coal getting, was desperately short of labour. At the beginning of the war, when there was unemployment in the coalfields, miners had been allowed to join the forces and the labour force had declined by 10 per cent before the government began to suspect that it might face a shortage of miners. Shortages of coal in the winter of 1940–41 were due to transport difficulties and not to supply. Coal was not rationed, but consumption was kept down by restricting the supplies allocated to coal merchants, and steps were taken to ensure that householders with storage space might not build up stocks in cellars at the expense of their less favoured neighbours. By 1942 it was clear that a serious crisis was at hand. With an ageing labour force, ailing machinery, incompetent planning or none, and a heritage of exceptionally bad labour relations the industry was unable to deliver the coal and the government created a new Ministry as a way of asserting central control. It also expedited and paid for the installation of modern machinery and decreed a national minimum wage – an important step in view of the low scale of pre-war wages in an industry noted for its insecurity and risks to health and life. In October 1943 Bevin directed that a proportion of the young men being called up for national service should be selected by lot for work in the mines instead of joining the armed forces – a direction which was popular neither with the recruits nor with the miners but which was necessitated by the decline of the industry and worked well enough to stem a further drop in the labour force and production in the mines. In the last eighteen months of war 21,800 'Bevin Boys' were directed into the mines. In 1945 175 million tons of coal were mined, 56 million less than in 1939.

Control over labour was matched by control of industrial materials (through a Production Executive established in 1942 and later expanded into a Department of State) for the purpose of keeping a just balance between production for the armed forces and production for civilian consumption and morale. By these two main instruments the government indirectly controlled British industry and sought to make the wisest allocation of the nation's resources in men and materials. Until the last year of war British industry produced 60 per cent of the munitions and weapons of war needed by British and Commonwealth forces, the United States contributing 25 per cent and the Commonwealth the remaining 15 per cent.

The manufacture and purchase of all these war materials and of essential

civilian requirements had to be paid for. In financing a war a government
has few options in the area of military supplies. It must buy or make all it
can and pay for them by taxation and borrowing. Its choice is restricted to
adjusting the balance between taxation and borrowing (when it does not
have to do both to the hilt) and to spreading the burden of taxation in one
way rather than another. In the area of civilian supplies, however, a
government may feel less constrained. Subject to the obvious limitation of
not calamitously underfeeding or overstraining its own people it may
control the volume of goods supplied and their price with some regard to
the financial implications. In other words it may screw down the level of
privation more or less, and the less it does so – the more, that is, it eases
the living and working conditions of the population – the more financial
problems it creates for itself. In particular, a policy of cheap food and
cheap household goods unaccompanied by wage control produces inflation. Great Britain did not abandon during the war the principle that
wage rates ought to be fixed by bargaining and not by edict, the government accepted the principle that wages ought to be increased where they
were particularly low or where productivity was boosted, and a steep rise
in the cost of living early in the war produced inevitable wage claims.
When these claims were met the working population had more money
with which to buy cheapened goods. Wage rates were kept in check by
voluntary restraint and a readiness to accept sacrifices, but nevertheless
they rose substantially: between 1939 and 1945 money earnings increased
overall by 81 per cent from a variety of causes, including wage increases
(32 per cent) and overtime (20 per cent). Earnings rose faster than the cost
of living index. (The figures were as follows. The rise in the cost of living
index in 1939–41 was 26 per cent. Thereafter it rose only 3 per cent more.
Since the index was an antiquated one it did not accurately reflect the real
rise, which was somewhat greater. Given a pre-war base of 100, wage rates
rose by the end of the war to 150, earnings to 180. The size of the civilian
working population remained static.) But the gains of the working classes
did not greatly disturb the economic gradation of British society. The rich
and the very rich, although hard hit by direct taxation, found their compensations – the rich recovering after the war their ease and affluence
through expense accounts and capital gains, and the middling and professional classes finding, somewhat to their surprise, that they were the
principal beneficiaries of new social services such as subsidized further
education of which the poor were often still too poor to avail themselves.
Within the working classes the average wage of the unskilled worker rose
from 70 per cent to 80 per cent of the basic wage of the skilled worker.

To contain inflation and keep borrowing within manageable proportions the government relied primarily on big increases in direct taxation:
income tax, which stood at 7s. 6d. (37½p) when war began, was up to 10s.
(50p) less than two years later. Purchase tax was introduced in 1940 – in
two grades, 16.6 per cent and 33.3 per cent. An excess profits tax, designed
to forestall complaints of war profiteering, was introduced at 60 per cent
in 1939 and raised in 1940 to 100 per cent. The government laid down
how much profit was too much – excess meant any increase over a specified
pre-war standard and this incursion into the operation of a market
economy was accepted as not only inevitable but, in the circumstances,
proper. But purchase tax was to a large extent a concession to popular
feelings against war profiteering and economically a disincentive to production, and in 1941 the government tried to resolve this dilemma between
social and fiscal policy by promising to repay 20 per cent of the tax after
the war. Revenue from direct taxation was trebled. Indirect taxation rose
by 160 per cent. But the government still had to borrow. Half of all
national expenditure during the war (other than purchases covered by
Lend-Lease and similar credits) was met by borrowing, at home or abroad.
The government introduced a variety of savings certificates and defence
bonds to attract the pennies and the pounds of different classes of person.
The bulk of the national deficit was met by home borrowing.

The country's external debt rose by £3,500 million and a quarter of its
overseas assets were sold. The United States government supplied Great
Britain with materials to the value of $27,025 million under the terms of
Lend-Lease (the pound sterling being at that time worth $5.00); taking into
account goods and services rendered to the United States to the value of
$5,667 million (in, for example, building camps and airfields for American
forces in Great Britain) the net British debt to the United States was
$21,358 million. Canada made a loan of $700 million free of interest in
1942 when Great Britain's liquid resources in Canada ran out. This loan
was followed by a gift of $1,000 million and by further loans totalling
$1,800 million. Great Britain's total bill for Canadian goods and services
was $7,441 million, of which rather more than half was paid in cash.
The United States and Canada were much the most important of Great
Britain's suppliers and creditors, but non-dollar aid from various other
sources amounted to £4,000 million, that is to say an addition of nearly
half the total of North American aid.

American Lend-Lease was a blessing but a mixed one. It became available when Great Britain was left with no other way to pay for American
goods, and all British dollar holdings and other assets in the United States

had first to be sold, sometimes at considerable loss. For more than two years after the passing of the Lend-Lease Act the value of the goods paid for in the United States in cash exceeded the value of the goods acquired on deferred credit under Lend-Lease. The conditions attached to the loans were stringent. No British goods manufactured even in part with raw materials supplied under Lend-Lease might be exported; goods for civilian consumption were excluded, so that Great Britain had to use gold or hard currencies to buy such things as tobacco, thus depleting its dollar reserves, which the United States had (privately) resolved ought to be allowed to stand no higher than $1,000 million; and Great Britain had to undertake to eliminate discrimination from its post-war trading system and therefore to abolish imperial preferences. Reverse Lend-Lease was given to the United States without any strings. In 1944 Lord Keynes led a mission to Washington to salvage Great Britain's export business by persuading the American administration that exports were so vital to Great Britain that some conversion of industry to exports must be permitted during the war. Predicting a complete British collapse after the war, he was largely successful in his mission but in August 1945 Lend-Lease stopped in peculiarly damaging circumstances: goods to the value of $650 million which had either arrived in Great Britain or were on their way had to be paid for in cash. Great Britain, being completely incapable of earning dollars in this quantity immediately after the end of the war, had to borrow $3,750 million from the United States and accept burdensome conditions including a promise to make the pound convertible within a year of the ratification of the agreement by Congress. Until the end of the war Great Britain, like the United States, was in favour of free trade as the basis of the international post-war economy and had expressed this view in the Atlantic Charter (which declared that all states should have access on equal terms to the world's trade and raw materials) and at the Bretton Woods conference which evolved the International Monetary Fund. The convertibility of currencies was an important element in this scheme of things and the British government was sufficiently optimistic to imagine that the pound could be made convertible within five years of the end of the war. It was shocked by the American demand for convertibility within one year and unable to persuade the United States that this was impossible – as it proved to be when the free convertibility of sterling in July 1947 caused such a rush for Great Britain's reserves that it had to be discontinued after five weeks.

The purchase of war equipment in the United States was forced on the British government by the inadequacy of its own resources. American industry was not only bigger than British industry and immune from war damage but also more efficient technically and managerially and so quicker. By buying in the United States instead of at home the British government forfeited a measure of control over the nature of the product. It had, especially after Pearl Harbor, to persuade the Americans to part with materials and weapons which they needed for themselves and it had also to argue for designs which, although they were to be produced in the United States, were to be used by British troops and had to be as nearly as possible what British commanders wanted. These matters were handled through joint boards in Washington and by constant coming and going between the two capitals. Inevitably there were disagreements about weapon design and for the most part American rather than British designs were put into production. When placing orders with industry the American administration would order more than it needed for itself in order to cover possible, but not yet precisely ascertained, British requirements. What the British did not eventually want was sold on Lend-Lease terms to the Free French.

It remains to consider the post-war measures adopted in Great Britain while the war was still being fought, and here a *caveat* is needed. It is temptingly easy to see in the conduct of the war on the home front a compact in which people agreed to work and endure, to postpone attempts to better themselves and even forego some hard-won gains in return for promises of post-war reform. This is, however, a misleading analysis if it implies that the work and endurance were conditional on the promises. Post-war reforms were not needed as a bait nor were they offered as a reward. They were worked out – in the exceptionally difficult circumstances of war – as an instalment of something due, to which the accident of war and the ferment created by it in Great Britain contributed.

The impulse came from the Labour Party, which was the more insistent on wartime action because it did not expect to win the first post-war election. It was supported by Liberals and Tory reformers with similar aims and ideals, but opposed by the larger part of the Conservative Party and press which denounced social inquiry as a diversion from the war effort and, in extreme cases, as opening the door to communism. Churchill himself was hostile but consented under pressure to the setting-up of an interdepartmental committee of civil servants with Sir William Beveridge as chairman to consider Social Insurance and Allied Services. The first initiative had come from the TUC, and the appointment of the Beveridge committee was partly a way of fending it off. But the committee came to life in an unusual way. Beveridge was not only an exceptionally well-equipped civil servant but a much less retiring one than most with a keen desire for radical reform and a no less keen political sense. He perceived that a report of the usual kind signed by the whole committee would be too tame and he got everybody concerned to agree that it should carry his own signature alone. The report, published in November 1942, was a closely reasoned and numerate technical document but its main lines were clear enough and radical enough to evoke great enthusiasm and great hostility. Beveridge proposed the extension of social insurance to the entire population on a compulsory contributory basis by which the cost would be shared between employers, employed and the Exchequer. He also declared that social insurance required new policies in relation to health, education, housing and unemployment. The opponents of welfare on this scale, reading the signs rightly, had begun attacking the report even before it was published. Alarmed by the spectre of continuing high taxation, which they regarded as a temporary war phenomenon not to be sanctioned for fighting any evils save those of Nazism, they denounced Beveridge's proposals as sapping the spirit and health of the nation. They were at the same time heatedly opposing Bevin's Catering Wages Bill which was designed to prevent employers from taking advantage of employees in a notably disorganized and therefore ill-paid industry. This opposition ultimately failed but Conservative hostility to Beveridge succeeded in preventing him from being invited to pursue his work. He thereupon produced on his own a second report on Full Employment in a Free Society which placed the prevention of mass unemployment at the centre of politics, argued that a return to mass unemployment after the war was immoral, uneconomic and avoidable, and attacked the view that government intervention in social policy must lead to an unacceptable destruction of freedom. The government so far accepted the paramount duty of maintaining employment as to issue its own White Paper on Employment Policy. These documents ensured that post-war governments for at least a generation would at the very least pay lip service to the doctrine that a government should plan to prevent unemployment instead of hoping not to be plagued by it; they asserted, even though without gaining universal assent for it, the proposition that a high level of employment (rather misleadingly called full employment) might be a prior aim to the maintenance of a particular ruling exchange value for the pound.

In 1943 a Ministry of Reconstruction was set up to think about post-war problems. These included the control of the environment and land use, about which three reports were issued during the war; a Town and Country Planning Act was passed in 1944. New Education Acts were also passed for England and Wales (1944) and Scotland (1945). They extended free education to children beyond the elementary stage. They also introduced a test to be taken at the age of '11 plus' in order, by dividing children into a clever minority and an ordinary majority, to enable the grammar schools to survive as separate and superior establishments. In terms of Great Britain's past achievements in providing education for all these Acts were a definite step forward. They were comparatively uncontroversial since the need for better education was evident on material as well as social grounds; the country needed more and better education in order to prosper and it had been shocked by the degree of ignorance and illiteracy revealed by the call-up of the nation to the armed forces. More controversial was the question of health and who should pay for it. A White Paper in 1944 on a National Health Service, raising the issue of a free and full medical (not merely hospital) service, was vague. It was welcomed by doctors as well as the general public but there was significant opposition to the idea of a salaried service and to the extinction of a private medical sector. It was, however, the precursor of the National Health Act which was introduced after the war by the Labour government along with a Family Allowance Act, a New Towns Act and a National Insurance Act.

The extension of the scope of government, whether to fight a war or to undertake a social transformation, affected the structure of government. Early in the war the Chamberlain government took sweeping powers by a series of legislative enactments, but it made sparing use of these powers and remained fundamentally a peacetime administration grappling with war problems rather than a war directorate prepared to accept and use the huge concentration of power foisted upon it by the nature of its responsibilities. The British system was government by the executive tempered by the executive's own distrust of power; the executive could do pretty much what it wanted but was traditionally shy of straying far outside the tracks delineated by *laissez-faire* dogma. This reluctance to take and use power was fortified by British belief in the value of voluntary effort, a belief grounded in experience and justified in war when voluntary organizations old and new played a highly important role in conjunction with officialdom. Nevertheless the business of war required the creation of nearly a dozen new Ministries, an expansion of the central government and a complication of the machinery of coordination in Whitehall which accustomed Ministers, civil servants and the public to think of government in widening terms. War also raised questions about government away from the centre. During 1937–9 the country was divided into a number of regions under Regional Commissioners, appointed, not elected – prefects, in the continental vocabulary – whose functions extended beyond the strict problems of civil defence. The Regional Commissioners were general factotums of the central government. As such they could be expected to be suspect, but they became in fact popular owing to the manifest inadequacy of the existing patchwork of elected local governments, which were very uneven in size, financially weak and endowed with only partial authority in a number of fields. There developed a popular demand for increasing the powers of the Regional Commissioners and so an opportunity to reform the geography and structure of local government by combining the old elective principle with the new pattern, but this opportunity was missed and the regions were allowed to expire. A unified fire service and regional hospital boards were the principal survivors of a reorganization which was otherwise expunged because, war being regarded as an ephemeral and malevolent phenomenon, most of its products were so regarded too.

More specialized but more enduring was the acclimatization of science and scientists in the machinery of government and the processes of decision-making. This was another pre-war trend accelerated by war. It belied the view often expressed that modern science had become a world unto itself, inaccessible to non-scientists, however clever they might be. The Second World War saw – not of course in Great Britain alone – a revival of the term military science in the broad sense in which it had once been used to designate a partnership between the field commander-staff officer and the inventor-designer, of whom Archimedes and Leonardo da Vinci were the archetypes. This partnership had been broken in the post-Clausewitz age when war became a profession for professional soldiers (notwithstanding that many nineteenth-century commanders were very amateurish indeed), but it was reconstituted in the twentieth century for two main reasons. First, new weapons became increasingly complicated. The tank, the aircraft and the submarine were already very different from the rifle even before radio and radar made them more different still. Designing them, and thinking of defences against them, were highly technical matters. The purely professional soldier could no longer tell the expert what he wanted because he did not know. He had to rely on the expert to diagnose his problem and find an answer to it. This was how the scientists came to present the air force with radar as the answer to the problem of how to stop the bomber. The scientist, tackling problems instead of waiting to be given specifications, acquired an initiative in war, which however he could only exercise in close consultation with the non-scientist. Secondly, scientists developed a new role called operational research. In cooperation with the fighting services they watched the battle and evaluated results with their analytical tools. Having invented new weapons they did not merely hand them over but took part in a continuing debate about the most effective way to use them. Thus hard tests of the effects of

41 The Arab Legion

42 *Top*: Kismayu, Ethiopia:
the British evict the Italians,
February 1941

43 *Bottom*: Malta: a crippled
tanker in harbour

44 *Top*: Tobruk: January 1941

45 *Bottom*: Libya: the British advance, November 1941

46 *Top*: Briefing Mustang
aircrews, 1943

47 *Bottom*: Sicily, July 1943:
invasion

48 *Top*: Sicily, July 1943:
Militello turns out for the
British

49 *Bottom*: Italy: Americans
land at Salerno, September
1943

50   *Top*: Italy: Anzio,
February 1944

51   *Bottom*: Monte Cassino:
May 1944

52 *Top*: General Mark Clark
ascends the Capitol, Rome,
June 1944

53 *Bottom*: Americans on
their way to France through
an English village, 1944

54 *Top*: D-day in Normandy,
6 June 1944

55 *Bottom*: The Battle of the
Bulge: identifying civilian
victims at Malmédy, Belgium,
December 1944

bombing during the German-Italian retreat in North Africa and in the capture of the island of Pantellaria before the invasion of Sicily served to build up the case for using bombs in tactical attacks on rail and road communications rather than in the mass bombing of civilians, housing and factories. The debate on this particular issue was protracted and bitter, but the significant thing is not that this was so but that scientists took part in it at the highest and most intimate levels.

These activities – together with the less ferocious aspects of science such as the uses of penicillin, the development of sulphonamides, skin-graft surgery and shock therapy – altered the popular conception of the scientist as a special kind of being who resided somewhere in the wings. Science acquired a place at the heart of the machinery of government, in the practical business of the conduct of war and, by analogy and under the name of technology, in the development of industry. In addition people began to recall that science simply meant knowledge. They felt that they ought to have more of it, even if its arcaner specialities were beyond them. Hence the debate on Two Cultures in which educated people lamented their inability to understand what other educated people were talking about and deplored the division of their culture into parts. They raised their voices against this estrangement partly because it was intellectually unhealthy and partly, whether they perceived it or not, because the war had shown that the gap was not unbridgeable. Hence too the growing suspicion that a system of government by men and women versed in only half a culture might not suffice to keep the country abreast of the times.

When the war ended the cost had to be counted. There had been much death and destruction. Damage to life and property had been less than anticipated and less than in the First World War; deaths in action, including the merchant navy, were 380,000, half the total for the earlier war, to which had to be added another 60,000 who lost their lives as civilians. But the blitz had been short as well as sharp, the V weapons had arrived mercifully late and the battles which were specially British – the Battle of Britain, the Battle of the Atlantic and the North African campaigns were all fought by quite small bodies of men. Industrially there had been overstrain in some places. Inferior labour and materials had had to be used. The retail and distributive trades, the textile and clothing industries, building and pottery had all lost 50 per cent or more of their labour. Timber had been over-felled. There was a permanent loss of some craft skills. Some overseas investments had been sold and the reserves had been depleted; Great Britain parted with a third in value of its foreign investments and a third of its gold reserve. But the investments were recovered or replaced within a few years of the end of the war, and exports, cut by more than 60 per cent during the war, were restored to their pre-war level by the end of 1946. Here was vigour. The government was itself spending three quarters of the country's gross national product in place of one quarter before the war. It was doing so because its military expenditure had been doubled and it had undertaken expensive social obligations. The latter held promise for the future. It had constructed buildings and plant, much of it transferred to private industry when the war ended. It had trained more skilled workers than the country had ever had before and spent more in scientific research and development. All major industries except the clothing industry were producing more than before the war despite bombing and other tribulations, and Great Britain emerged from the war as a pioneer in nuclear technology and with an electronics industry stimulated by wartime investment. It had the makings of a more sensible control of economic policy in the practice, initiated during the war, of making estimates of the national income and expenditure – a practice which was unheard of in pre-war Great Britain and which amounted to a revolution in budgeting. The foundations had been laid for radical reform after a generation and more of economic and social failures. Even the arts were recognized as something more than a peripheral eccentricity; a Council for the Encouragement of Music and the Arts, created in 1939 with the help of the Pilgrim Trust, was later given a government subsidy and was preserved after the war under the name of the Arts Council. The strain and the achievement had been tremendous; there had been irreparable pain; the prospect was inspiriting.

War intensifies and simplifies emotions. Because of the pressures of an enemy at the gates the British people experienced a sense of community which loosened its class structure. Before the war the rulers saw their main enemy in Bolshevism, which was a threat to their class rather than to the state. During the war the threat was Nazism, which was hateful to all, and Germany, which was challenging the existence of the European nation state. Nazism enslaved human beings, Germany enslaved states, and both reminded the British of all classes that they were determined never to be slaves. The enemy therefore stimulated national unity – as Napoleon and other conquerors had done. In Great Britain this national unity was further fed by a new richness of communication between governors and governed. On the military side Churchill's personality and talents not only inspired confidence but gave people the feeling that they were all in it together. On the social side – and it became more accurate to refer to non-military affairs as social rather than civilian – wartime planning and post-war planning added to the sense that the nation was one and that post-war Great Britain would be a better place than pre-war Great Britain had been. In terms of institutions war menaces democracy by requiring the suspension of democratic safeguards and processes, but in terms of popular participation and involvement in affairs war may – and in Great Britain did – nourish the substance of democracy even when it was temporarily dismantling some of its trappings. It gave more of the people more concern for and knowledge of affairs of state. They became, if not insiders, at any rate less outside than they had been. There was an enlargement of the body politic to something nearer the bounds of British society as a whole. The governors who had to look to the safety of the state and to the welfare of society were to that extent distracted from their pre-war preoccupations with the class interests and the imperial interests which had seemed to be their natural and proper business but which had either alienated or failed to stir the mass of their fellow citizens. The war made the British state more national and less imperial, more democratic and less oligarchic. It produced more social change than had ever been compassed anywhere in so few years, save only by revolution – and not often then. The ruling class abandoned the resistance of a generation to reform and therewith its own integrity. Society was no longer the same and the ruling class was no longer the same. The question for the future was whether, how far and for how long this impetus would be maintained; or how soon an enlarged ruling class would revert to the traditional role of ruling classes to keep things pretty much as they are, to institutionalize, to put a brake on change for fear of putting the skids under themselves. In July 1945 the British people manifested in a general election an uncommon seriousness and optimism about their common future. The main source of these feelings, and the main condition of their survival, was not simply the baneful fact of war but the clearing by war of the channels of com- munication within the nation. Soon after the end of the war these channels began to silt up again.

Part V

THE DEFEAT OF GERMANY: 1942–5

CHAPTER 21

The Battle of the Seas

GREAT BRITAIN's survival in 1940 did not remove the danger of defeat. The U-boat might still succeed where the Luftwaffe had failed. The crisis of 1940 was followed by the crises of 1941 and 1942, when Great Britain's imports of food, weapons and materials for industry dropped to within sight of a war-losing level.

The essence of the crisis was shortage of shipping. Ships were needed for many purposes and all over the world. Supplies had to be brought to Great Britain across the Atlantic and from many distant sources of vital raw materials; troops and their equipment had to be moved to different battle-fronts, including the Middle East, East Africa and the Far East; the blockade of Germany had to be maintained around the coasts of Europe, a task which was magnified every time the Germans won control of a fresh country; and there were special obligations like the dispatch of aid to the Russians by convoys which gathered in Scotland and Iceland to make the passage to Murmansk or Archangel. The fulfilling of these tasks against the U-boats, the German high seas fleet and the Luftwaffe entailed a battle which lasted several years and cost many lives.

The idea of a shipping shortage did not come naturally to the British. It seemed almost as absurd to suppose that Great Britain would lack ships as to suppose that it might run short of coal. In fact it did both and the reasons were similar. The neglect and mismanagement of the coalfields by their owners had become proverbial and had created so much ill will that it smouldered on and produced strikes even in the all-forgiving and all-compelling atmosphere of war. The shipyards were in not much better case. They were antiquated and inefficient, but such is the force of habit that the government did not wake up to the consequent dangers until some time after the war began. The provision of ships seemed to be one thing that Great Britain did not need to worry about. This complacency was fostered by the months of phoney war which were nowhere more deceptive than at sea. Great Britain lost 150 dry cargo ships in the first nine months of war and made good the loss by new building or capture. But this simple sum told only part of the story. Imports were affected by many factors: few foreign ships ventured to British ports; British ships had to take roundabout routes which delayed them (carrying capacity cannot be measured simply in numbers of vessels); at home, when the east coast ports had to be closed, unloading facilities elsewhere became over-burdened; there was a shortage of hard currency to buy goods with; the fall of France increased voyage times by 30–40 per cent; the convoy system reduced the speed of all but the slower ships.

Imports began to sink rapidly. In 1941 they were 30.5 million tons of dry cargo against a peacetime norm of about 50 million. This was only very slightly more than in 1917 when population and industry were ap-preciably smaller, and yet the ports which were still working had difficulty in handling even this limited volume. 1942 was worse again – 22.9 million tons. Throughout this period cargo space declined. But in 1942 consump-tion at home was exceeding imports by the alarming amount of 2.45 million tons and half the imported raw materials consumed by industry had had to be drawn from stocks. Running down stocks at this rate was potentially catastrophic because stocks had not been built up before the war (wheat stocks at the beginning of the war were for three weeks, for example) owing to a facile and false view in the Admiralty that the inven-tion of radar had put paid to the U-boat. The exploding of this view turned complacency into something like panic, aggravated by gross exag-gerations of needs by the Ministries of Supply and Food and by the absence of any reliable statistics. Consumption was screwed down so that, until 1942, it was even lower than imports, but the corollary of this rigour was that rations could hardly be further reduced, or imported raw mater-ials economized, without direct danger to the war effort, the creation of unemployment and a possibly lethal blow to morale.

In 1943 the decline was checked and stocks were replenished as imports topped consumption by 2.8 million tons. The balance swung into deficit once more in 1944 when imports fell by 1.3 million tons and consumption rose by 3.4 million, but by this date the U-boat had been beaten, the pattern of imports had been altered by Lend-Lease which enabled goods to be imported manufactured or semi-manufactured instead of in bulkier raw forms, and the government had learned by experience at what point it need get alarmed. But these figures tell the gravity of a situation which gave Germany its one chance of a substantial victory after the failure of its air forces over Great Britain and its armies before Moscow. For three years Great Britain was closely beleaguered and Hitler could entertain some hope of reconverting the war to a war on one front. Great Britain's survival at sea, which could never be confidently predicted in these years, saved the United States from the predicament posed for Great Britain by the collapse of France in 1940: whether to carry on or call it defeat.

There were two critical phases in this battle. The first followed the conquest of western Europe by Hitler and the second followed Pearl Harbor. Both events made Great Britain's position worse. The first cut Great Britain off from sources of supply, especially food. It put the Germans in possession of bases for submarines and long-range reconnaissance aircraft on the Atlantic coasts of Norway and France; U-boats took up new stations in concrete pens in Atlantic harbours and the long-range F.W. 200s began making wide sweeps over the ocean, flying from Bordeaux to Trondhjem one day and back another. From this time all traffic to London had to go north of Scotland (the trip round Scotland to London and back took more than half the time required to cross the Atlantic) and many ships were routed into ports unaccustomed to handling the cargoes they were carrying; there was much confusion in these ports. Finally, by closing the Mediterranean, Hitler's continental victories doubled the distance between Great Britain and Bombay and more than quadrupled the distance to Suez. Great Britain obtained some compensation in the muster of European shipping which took refuge in British ports and took service alongside the British merchant navy as one European country after another was overrun. Largely as a result of appeals and veiled threats put out by the BBC no ship at sea at the time of the conquest of its home port returned there, although not all of them went to British ports. Neutral shipping too carried goods for Great Britain. More than four fifths of Sweden's dry cargo shipping outside the Baltic did so. Not all of this can be ascribed to sentiment. Great Britain invented a warrant scheme and refused to issue warrants to ships sailing in conditions or under contracts which were damaging to the allies. Ships sailing without such warrants were denied facilities in ports under British control and in American and some other neutral ports, and found it almost impossible to get insurance.

Pearl Harbor inaugurated a second crisis by multiplying the calls on American shipping and unleashing a successful U-boat campaign against it. South African ports became so crowded with ships in search of asylum or in need of repair or on their way to the Middle East that by mid-1942 nearly eighty vessels at a time could be found waiting to berth or go into dry dock. The advance of the Japanese overland and at sea disrupted the economies of southern Asia by stopping the export of Burma's rice, oil and rubber and Bengal's coal: India's east coast ports were closed, the feeding of India, Ceylon and parts of east Africa became an allied responsibility, and countries round the Indian Ocean faced starvation and a general breakdown of public services. In Bengal in the summer of 1943 1.5 million people died of hunger. Thus commitments increased as carrying capacity was once more drastically reduced. It was at sea, much more than on land, that the several wars which together made a world war interacted.

The British government, besides welcoming the merchant fleets of its continental friends, bought second-hand vessels in any part of the world where they could be found, but this source was exhausted by the end of 1940. There remained the United States. But the American shipbuilding industry was in no better shape than the British. It had been allowed to atrophy after the First World War and in the years 1921–36 it constructed, tankers apart, only two ocean-going freighters. In 1941 total construction was under 1 million tons (lower than Great Britain's) as against an assessed need of 8 million tons for the war in Europe, excluding tankers and troopships and quite apart from whatever the United States might want for itself elsewhere. In May Roosevelt ordered 2 million dry weight tons, including tankers, to be found for Great Britain and other democracies at war. The British had hoped that it would be 2 million gross tons, excluding tankers, and all of it for Great Britain alone. (Two million d.w. tons equal 1.3 million gross tons.) So there was some disappointment as well as relief. Later in the year Roosevelt gave more help by sanctioning American escorts for allied vessels, by opening American ports to allied ships in need of repair and by Lend-Lease; but substantially Great Britain had to get through 1941 on its own. Rations were severely cut and some foods, including fresh vegetables and fruit, were deleted from overseas cargoes. The government budgeted on imports of 30 million tons, half in food and half in arms and industrial raw materials, and Churchill ruled that any reduction below 30 million tons must be borne by the Ministries of Supply and Food in the proportion of two to one. In the same year shipping was also needed to move an average of 29,000 men by sea per month, and it was estimated that the figure would rise to 70,000 a month in 1942. (The latter figure was almost reached. It included the transport of 16,500 men a month to the Far East in January–March 1942. The situation was eased by commandeering six large passenger liners which sailed fast enough to dispense with escorts and were refashioned to carry up to 15,000 men at a time.)

At the end of 1941 Pearl Harbor dashed hopes of increased American assistance. American construction was immensely increased in 1942 – to the 8 million tons prescribed a year earlier and then to 13.5 million in the following years, tankers and naval construction excluded – but these astonishing achievements hardly sufficed to keep pace with the American need. The ships sunk by the Japanese at Pearl Harbor had to be replaced, while on the east coast the German U-boats, whose successes against British shipping were doubled in the first months of the new year, sailed zestfully into American territorial waters where the Americans, disdaining Great Britain's experiences in two wars, refused for several months to introduce a convoy system and lost in consequence a disabling number of vessels. In response to the crisis in the Pacific the great bulk of civil shipping requisitioned by the Administration after Pearl Harbor was committed to the Pacific theatre, and when the Anglo-American invasion of North Africa took place at the end of the year, Great Britain had to lend the United States troopships, dry cargo ships and practically all the tankers used in that operation.

Moreover, the estimates of the number of ships needed, and the time for which they would be needed, were both misjudged. For four months North Africa absorbed 106 ships a month in place of an anticipated sixty-six, and instead of going over to a maintenance basis in February 1943 the armies had to be kept supplied on a fully operational basis until May – the most serious consequence of the decision not to attempt any landing east of Algiers. These operations coincided with the U-boats' record month – 729,160 tons sunk in November 1942. In the second half of 1942 the United States was lending shipping to Great Britain but only on a modest scale, on a short-term basis and in smaller quantity than reverse British lendings to the United States: each American vessel was made available for a single voyage at a time. American aid increased Great Britain's carrying capacity by 7.5 per cent to 10 per cent in the second half of 1942, but British loans to the United States over the period of the North African campaign ran at the rate of 17 per cent of all the dry cargo tonnage sailing on British account (net of American loaned shipping) during the seven months October 1942 to April 1943. Great Britain's total dry tonnage cargo committed wholly or primarily to the needs of the armed services was greater than the total of American shipping committed in the same way – 8.5 million tons against 6 million. British requirements were at this time also greater since British troops overseas were more than twice as many as American troops overseas, British theatres of war were about twice as distant from their principal bases as American theatres, and the concurrent British civilian needs had no American counterpart since the United States did not have to import food or, to the same extent, raw materials. During 1942 Great Britain lost on balance 1.4 million gross tons while the United States merchant fleet rose by 2.7 million gross tons. By and large Great Britain's basic problem was its inability to match sinkings with new building. The United States built in most periods more than it lost, but the net increase in its fleet did not keep pace with the increase in its needs, so that there was a continuing conflict between satisfying the expanding needs of the US armed services and helping Great Britain and other allies.

The turning point in the Battle of the Seas came in the winter of 1942–3. In that period the U-boat was defeated. The Luftwaffe had been eliminated from this battle in 1942. Its anti-shipping force, though skilled, was always small. Its torpedo-carriers were a neglected and minor branch of the service; its long-range F.W. 200s were reduced by bombing of the Bremen factory where they were made; it was too deeply absorbed by prior commitments on the eastern front and in the Mediterranean. The U-boat was the weapon which threatened to turn the allied shipping shortage into an allied defeat, for the U-boat accounted for two thirds of all British, allied and neutral shipping losses during the war – 14.7 million gross tons out of a total of 21.6 million. Aircraft accounted for 13.4 per cent. Surface raiders came third. Of the tonnage sunk by U-boats nearly half – 6.3 million tons – went to the bottom in the year 1942. Over half of all these sinkings were in the North Atlantic.

The U-boats of the First World War had come so close to victory that Great Britain tried after the war to get submarines abolished by international agreement. Yet Germany began the second war with very few. Admiral Karl Doenitz, the commander of the U-boats, had argued in the thirties against the building of capital ships on the grounds that they would not be ready in time and that the space and effort could more profitably be used to build the fleet of 300 submarines with which he reckoned that he could starve Great Britain into surrender. Essentially Doenitz's argument was the same as that used by the champions of strategic bombing (whom we shall come to in a later chapter): he said that his weapon was a war-winning one on its own. It is not clear whether the verdict of history is that no single weapon can ever do the trick or that no government can ever be persuaded that it will. In any case Doenitz failed to convince Hitler and Germany began the war with fifty-seven submarines, of which thirty-nine were operational when war broke out but only twenty-three were capable of ocean-going operations. With such small numbers Doenitz could not essay the pack tactics which he had been elaborating and the first months of the war produced, as we saw in Part II of this book, no sensational results at sea. Then for eighteen months Germany's operational submarine force declined and it was not until the summer of 1941 that new construction so far outpaced losses as to give the force a real boost.

The task of defeating Doenitz and assuring Great Britain's sea-borne supplies fell first and foremost on the Royal Navy. But this was not its only task. It had also to secure its own bases, not one of which at home or overseas – even Scapa Flow – was adequately defended against air and submarine attack at the outbreak of war. It had, until 1940, to be ready to foil an invasion of the British Isles and it had to maintain – and, when lost, re-establish – important strategic routes in the Mediterranean. It had to nullify the German surface fleet. It possessed an impressive number of battleships: *Iron Duke*, a solitary survivor of the days before the First World War which spent the second war at anchor; ten survivors of the First World War of the *Queen Elizabeth* and *Royal Sovereign* classes; and *Nelson* and *Rodney*, both launched in 1925. The tally of capital ships was raised to sixteen by three battle cruisers, also survivors of the First World War. In addition a new class of battleships – *King George V* and her four sister-ships – had been laid down and the first of these were about to be commissioned. The decision to build these ships has been criticized as an obtuse failure to see that the battleship had had its day and that the money could more profitably have been spent on aircraft carriers, but it has also been pertinently argued that it was impossible in the radarless mid-thirties to foresee that an aircraft carrier and its aircraft could be any use except by day and when there was no fog.

From cruisers downwards the Royal Navy was uncomfortably short of modern vessels. It had sixty-one cruisers, but a third of them had been launched in 1919 or earlier. It had to obtain fifty old destroyers from the United States. Six of its ten aircraft carriers were old or converted, and it lost three soon after the war began. It was primarily designed to fight big fleet actions in which heavy capital ships would be ranged against each other and would prevail through the weight and accuracy of their gunnery; but so far as fleet actions were fought at all in the Second World War they were won by aircraft. It had paid too little attention to the design of aircraft suited for operations at sea – partly because it did not secure full control of its own air arm until 1937 – and it could call on very few long-range reconnaissance aircraft. The weakness in both these categories was not cured until the Americans remedied it. Between the wars it had, unlike the German navy, neglected the magnetic mine which both sides had used successfully in the First World War. It found that the Germans could lay mines faster than it could sweep them. During the crucial years to 1943 it was short of torpedoes, although the torpedo was the most destructive of all the weapons used at sea in the second war. But in spite of this backlog of deficiencies it prevailed because it was a highly professional and valiant force, because its adversaries had even more serious deficiencies and because it was seconded in its tasks by the R A F.

The lesson of the First World War on the protection of merchant shipping was clear: convoys and close escorts. This lesson had, however, been learned late in the war and after Churchill had left the cabinet. The problem was debated again intermittently during the thirties and the convoy system was adopted, hesitantly and conditionally, shortly before the second war broke out. But Churchill did not like close escort work. His conception of the war at sea was a series of sweeps, which he likened to cavalry sweeps. He believed that the emphasis should be at least as much on seeking out and destroying the enemy as on guarding the merchant ships. So the escort vessels available were split between close escort and wide forays. These tactics consumed fuel and wasted bombs and depth charges for comparatively little return, while the merchantmen plied their course at unnecessary risk. They were based on two false assumptions: first, that a convoy was more easily spotted by enemy forces and so more vulnerable than single ships and, secondly, that single ships could fight back successfully if attacked. Not until 1942 did the figures and arguments of operational research convince Churchill that he was wrong, as the British cabinet had been wrong at the beginning of the first war and the Americans continued to be wrong in the second even later than the British.

The risks run by the merchant ships were accentuated by two other factors. Up to mid-1943 the Germans were able to read British naval ciphers which gave them the positions of British surface and submarine vessels and convoys. Secondly, the Royal Navy had been unable before the war to come to any arrangement with the RAF for operational control over the squadrons of Coastal Command, and even when it did so in 1941 that Command was still kept short of modern long-range aircraft which were allotted in priority to Bomber Command. Bomber Command undertook (among its many missions) bombing raids on U-boat bases and building-yards but the effects of these raids were disappointment and some of the aircraft employed in them could have been used to better purpose on Atlantic patrol.

The Battle of the Seas began in earnest after the fall of France. To defend their precious merchantmen the allies had insufficient escort vessels, insufficient reconnaissance aircraft, inadequate intelligence and inadequate gear for detecting submarines and destroying them. The German occupation of French and Norwegian Atlantic ports laid shipping under an aerial surveillance which forced it to take long and devious routes: an average crossing of the north Atlantic took fifteen days, a southerly crossing by way of Freetown in Sierra Leone twenty-one days. Great Britain lacked not only enough escorts to cover the convoys constantly at sea for this length of time but also escorts with enough range to accompany the merchantmen the whole way. At first close escorts accompanied convoys only as far as 15° west longitude – about 200 miles beyond the west coast of Ireland. This limit was gradually extended during 1940 to 19° west. At this point the escorts halted and made rendezvous with an eastbound convoy, which had been escorted by Canadian destroyers for the first 300–400 miles of its journey. But there was a gap in the middle and after the fall of France even short-range German surface forces could operate as far as 25° west. This gap could only be closed by providing escort vessels with a wider radius of action and by routing convoys farther north and giving air cover from Iceland and refuelling facilities there. The sloop, the only escort vessel which could go all the way across the Atlantic, eventually provided continuous protection but sloops were few when war began. Iceland, although occupied in 1940 when Hitler invaded Denmark, was not brought into the Battle of the Atlantic until 1941. Coastal Command was kept busy looking for invasion barges in the North Sea throughout most of 1940, and a request by the Admiralty for a reconnaissance squadron to be stationed in Iceland was not granted until early the next year.

From this date, however, things began to improve. Close escorts were provided up to 35° west, more than halfway from east to west, and from July 1941 convoys were given continuous protection in three stages, covered by groups based in the Western Approaches, Iceland and Newfoundland. But the cover, though continuous, was still thin. Up to the end of 1941 the average number of escorts per convoy was only two. At the same time the continuing lack of long-range reconnaissance aircraft enabled U-boats to patrol on the surface with fair immunity. The older boats took the risk of being spotted, and the newer ones which came into service in 1941 were able to operate beyond the range of British aircraft.

Losses at sea in 1941 of ships sailing on British account totalled 4.3 million gross tons (1,299 vessels). Losses of this order were not replaceable. In 1942 they were much worse: 7.8 million tons (1,664 vessels). The share of the U-boats in the latter year rose to four fifths and the U-boat fleet was growing. A force of ninety-one boats at the beginning of 1942 had grown to 212 by the end of the year despite the loss of eighty-seven boats during the year. In one battle in March 1942 U-boats caught two convoys at once and sank twenty-one out of ninety-eight vessels with the loss of only one U-boat. An action of this kind, which sent over 140,000 tons of shipping to the bottom, went a long way towards giving Doenitz the 800,000 tons a month which he was aiming at. A few months later, when American escort vessels were almost completely withdrawn from the regular Atlantic convoy service for tasks in the Pacific or to support the coming landings in North Africa, the U-boats scored heavily and consistently. They developed new tactics whereby one boat acted as a tracker which signalled the position of a convoy to other boats which then assembled for a surface attack by night. The weakness of these tactics was the need to break wireless silence and so reveal the position of the tracker to the allied listening services, but the risks proved worthwhile and Doenitz was not far wrong when he concluded that he was achieving his monthly target and his Führer's aim. But the sinkings of March 1942 – 273 ships totalling 834,164 tons – were only once exceeded – in June when 173 ships totalling 834,196 tons were lost. These were sinkings from all causes. In November exceptional successes by U-boats pushed the total above 800,000 once more and for the last time.

The Atlantic was the one place where Great Britain could still lose the war. The U-boats might starve Britain of food and weapons of war and prevent the Americans from assembling in Great Britain the vast strengths needed to force a re-entry into France and so beat Hitler. In London an anti-U-boat committee was formed, consisting of British and American brass and boffins under the chairmanship of Churchill himself. During 1942 new radar detectors and new offensive weapons, such as new kinds of depth charge, were introduced; at the end of the year the strategic bombers of both nations were directed to attack, as first priority, U-boat construction yards in Germany and U-boat bases in France; and in December the Ultra cryptographers delivered a critical blow by breaking the new U-boat Enigma key.

Bletchley had been reading the German navy's principal cipher from March 1941. This cipher was used by the Atlantic U-boats until early in 1942, when these boats were given a new cipher of their own, thus blotting out for an unforeseeable period the British Admiralty's chief source of information about the movements and intentions of the U-boats. Naval Enigma was always more difficult to break than other keys because the machines used by the German navy were the most complex. Nevertheless the new key was broken in December and the U-boat threat began immediately to fade. In March 1943 the boats scored their last major victory when they sank thirty-two vessels for the loss of only one boat (they had at this time over one hundred boats at sea at a time) but a few weeks later they broke off an engagement in which they had lost six boats, and after further defeats of this kind they completely withdrew for a time from the Atlantic. New boats continued to be commissioned, but the rate of sinkings began to catch up with the rate of production and by 1944, when the Atlantic became a highway crowded with men and munitions making for France and Germany itself, U-boat sinkings exceeded in tonnage the allies,

BATTLE OF THE ATLANTIC
1939-1942

GREENLAND

ICELAND

Reykjavik

Julianehaab

CANADA

Murmansk

Belfast

GERMAN
OCCUPIED OR
CONTROLLED

St Johns

New York

North

CONVOY ROUTE FROM MAY 1941

UNITED
STATES

Bermuda
(GB)

Atlantic

Azores
(Portuguese)

Gibraltar

Casablanca

Ocean

WEST INDIES
Puerto Rico (USA)
Virgin Is (USA)
Antigua (GB)
St Lucia (GB)
Trinidad (GB)
(GB)
Georgetown
Paramaribo
(Dutch)
GUIANA

Dakar
(French)

AFRICA

Freetown
(GB)

CONVOY ROUTE
FROM JULY 1942

CONVOY ROUTE

Recife
(Pernambuco)

SOUTH
AMERICA

South

Rio de
Janiero

Atlantic

Ocean

Cape
Town

to EGYPT, MIDDLE EAST
& RUSSIA

Montevideo
(Uruguay)

Battle of the River Plate
14 December 1939.

0   1000

Miles

~ARTHUR BANKS~

⊙ US & British bases.	▫ Main U-boat bases.
▨ Occupied by Britain 1940.	▨ U-boat activities Sept 1939 - March 1941.
▥ US Protectorate 1941 - 1945.	▤ U-boat activities April 1941 - July 1942.
● Limit of Allied air patrols.	Areas not possible to patrol
Ⓡ Allied coastal convoy system established July 1942.	by Allied land based bombers.

losses in merchant shipping. Altogether 1,162 U-boats were built and commissioned during the war and 941 of them were sunk or surrendered in the course of it. One of these was captured by an aircraft.

The latter phase of the war against the U-boats was waged simultaneously with the battle in Arctic waters in which the German surface fleet and the Luftwaffe joined to prevent the dispatch of allied aid to the Russians and to sink the allied vessels carrying it. After the loss of *Bismarck* in 1941 Hitler had little use for his capital ships but during 1942 he concentrated them in Norway, chiefly because he was afraid that the allies intended to invade that country. *Bismarck*'s sister-ship *Tirpitz* was moved to Trondhjem in January. The battle cruisers *Scharnhorst* and *Gneisenau* and the cruiser *Prinz Eugen* were recalled in February from Brest on Hitler's direct order (once again he had to override his professional advisers, Raeder considering the order so crazy that he refused to take responsibility for it). They succeeded in running the gauntlet of the English Channel by day to reach home ports, whence *Prinz Eugen* was directed to Norway. She was damaged by a torpedo on her way and had to turn back but Germany's strength in northern waters was further increased by the dispatch of the cruiser *Admiral Hipper* and the two battleships *Scheer* and *Lützow* and, in the following winter, two more cruisers and *Scharnhorst* and – once again – *Prinz Eugen*. Although *Lützow* ran aground and was out of action for several months, this build-up was alarming for the British Admiralty, the more so since attempts to cripple ships by air attack in harbour had proved disappointing. *Scharnhorst*, *Gneisenau* and *Prinz Eugen* had survived a winter's battering in Brest before making their successful dash up the Channel and it was proving impossible to do any real damage to *Tirpitz* in her narrow anchorage up the Trondhjem fjord.

Tirpitz, like *Bismarck* before her, was the most powerful vessel on either side in the Atlantic war. Yet she took part in no battle. Launched in April 1939, she did her trials in the Baltic during 1941 and was dispatched to Norwegian waters at the beginning of 1942. The British Admiralty feared another sortie into the Atlantic, like *Bismarck*'s the year before, and these fears gave rise to one of the most brilliantly daring ventures of the war. If *Tirpitz* made for the Atlantic, she would probably sooner or later need to put in at St Nazaire. An old American destroyer, *Campbeltown*, disguised as a German ship and filled with explosives, was sailed up the Loire estuary to St Nazaire, deceiving the German gunners defending the harbour until the last few minutes. Her captain and crew sailed her straight at the dock gates and rammed them, while commandos landed to destroy other selected installations. The next day *Campbeltown* blew up. The dock at St Nazaire was never repaired by the Germans.

BATTLE OF THE ATLANTIC
1942 - 1945

0 — 1000
Miles

SUBMARINE WAR 1939-1945
1,200 U-boats involved
700 U-boats sunk
32,000 German sailors drowned
2,700 Allied ships sunk.
30,000 British merchant seamen
drowned.
36% of the total British merchant
Fleet was sunk between June 1940-
December 1945.

GREENLAND

Reykjavik
ICELAND

Julianehaab

CANADA

Belfast

GERMAN
OCCUPIED OR
CONTROLLED

St
Johns

Halifax

New York

North

Azores from
Oct 1943

Gibraltar

UNITED
STATES

Bermuda
(GB)

Atlantic

Casablanca

Key
West
USA

Exuma (GB)

Ocean

Guatanamo

Jamaica

Puerto Rico (USA)
Virgin Is (USA)
Antigua
St Lucia (GB)
Trinidad

Dakar from Nov 1942

Freetown (GB)
Monrovia (Liberia)

AFRICA

Panama
Canal

(GB)
Georgetown
Paramaribo (Dutch)
Cayenne (French)

Belem

Takoradi
(GB)

EXTRA CONVOY ROUTE

Recife
(Pernambuco)
Salvador
(Bahia)

Ascension Is
(GB)

SOUTH
AMERICA

FROM

Rio de
Janeiro

South

Cape
Town

Montevideo
(Uruguay)

Atlantic

1943

Ocean

⊚ U S & British bases.	▦ U-boat activities August 1942 - May 1943
● Limit of Allied air patrols.	▨ U-boat activities June 1943 - April 1945
◻ Main U-boat bases.	▢ Areas not possible to patrol by Allied land-based bombers.

~ARTHUR BANKS~

But although *Tirpitz* never attempted a foray like *Bismarck*'s she indirectly inflicted grievous losses on allied shipping in Arctic waters. Churchill's response to Stalin's request for help in 1941 had been not merely generous in spirit but incautious in degree. He promised a convoy every ten days, to the dismay of the Admiralty which was thinking in terms of one every forty days – if it had to run any at all against such suicidal odds. The run of 1,500–2,000 miles lay through seas made dangerous by icebergs, tempests, fogs and interference to radar by natural causes. It was almost entirely within the range of the Luftwaffe, to which the interminable daylight of the summer months was an extra boon. The convoys could not sail eastward beyond a certain point without courting the risks of attack by shore-based German bombers and of a major fleet action should German capital ships put to sea. It was therefore necessary to consider in advance which mattered more, the merchantmen or the escorts. If the merchantmen, then the escorts must be committed to the risk of heavy losses. If the escorts, then the merchantmen must in a crisis be abandoned. The Admiralty, faced with this predicament by Churchill's insistence on the overriding need to get supplies to the USSR by this route, decided that if and when a choice had to be made the merchantmen would be abandoned.

The first convoy sailed from Iceland in September 1941 and was followed by others at the rate of one about every two weeks. Their destination was Archangel or Murmansk, the former being seasonally, and the latter permanently, ice free. Murmansk's more temperate clime was offset by the fact that in 1941 it was only thirty miles from the front, and the Russians therefore preferred Archangel and undertook to keep it open with eight to ten icebreakers. But only two of these materialized and after one had been hit by a bomb in January 1942 five British ships were frozen into the ice for the rest of the winter. The principal problems of these early convoys were the shortage of escort vessels, the natural hazards of the journey, the inadequacy of ice-breaking and unloading facilities at the Russian end and the failure of the Russians to provide coal, ballast, stores or fresh water for the return journeys. The ships employed on this task, which were among Great Britain's newest and best, had to be specially fitted to withstand the climate. Once so equipped they were virtually restricted to the Arctic run, and the tying up of six or seven merchant ships a month was an appreciable drain on Great Britain's hard-pressed merchant fleet.

German opposition did not at first make itself felt. Twelve convoys reached their destinations intact. But PQ 12 was the last to do so. Goods were piling up in Iceland and with the knowledge of this situation Stalin

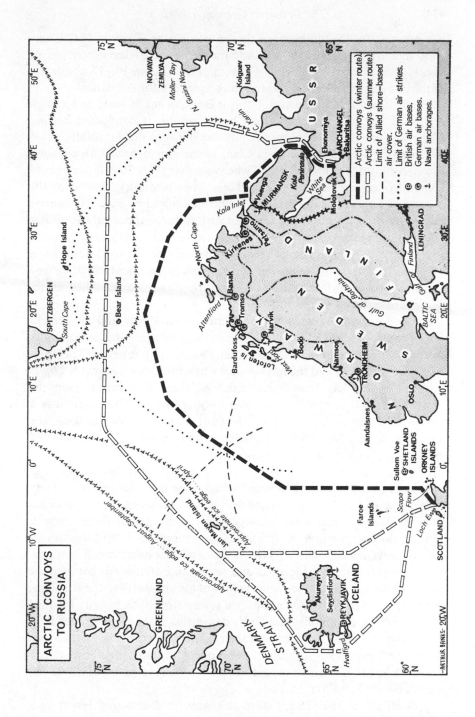

ARCTIC CONVOYS
TO RUSSIA

Arctic convoys (winter route).
Arctic convoys (summer route).
Limit of Allied shore–based
air cover.
Limit of German air strikes.
British air bases.
German air bases.
Naval anchorages.

—ARTHUR BANKS—

GREENLAND

DENMARK STRAIT

Approximate ice edge ....August—September

Jan Mayen Island

Approximate ice edge .... April

ICELAND

Akureyri
Seydisfiord
REYKJAVIK
Hvalfiord

SCOTLAND
Loch Ewe
Scapa Flow
ORKNEY ISLANDS
SHETLAND ISLANDS
Sullom Voe
Faroe Islands

Aandalsnes

NORWAY
OSLO
TRONDHEIM
Namsos
Bodö
Narvik
Vest Fiord
Lofoten Is
Bardufoss
Tromsö
Banak
Altenfiord
North Cape
Kirkenes
Petsamo
Vaenga
MURMANSK
Kola Inlet

SWEDEN
FINLAND
Gulf of Bothnia
Gulf of Finland
BALTIC SEA
LENINGRAD

U.S.S.R.
Kola Peninsula
White Sea
Molotovsk
Ekonomiya
ARCHANGEL
Bakaritsa

C. Kanin
R. Gusini Nos
Moller Bay
NOVAYA ZEMLYA
Kolguev Island

SPITZBERGEN
South Cape
Bear Island
Hope Island

20°W
10°W
0°
10°E
20°E
30°E
40°E
50°E
40°E

75°N
70°N
65°N
60°N
75°N
70°N
65°N

was pressing for the fulfilment of the ten-day pledge. Early in 1942 Churchill, against the advice of the Admiralty, promised three convoys of twenty-five to thirty-five ships every two months. In June PQ 17, consisting of thirty-five merchantmen and one tanker, set sail for Archangel.

The British Admiralty was not only a Department of State and a General Staff but also an operational headquarters. It conducted battles. There was therefore a division of authority between the Admiralty and – in this case – the Commander-in-Chief of the Anglo-American covering force, Admiral Sir John Tovey, who was flying his flag in the newly commissioned battleship *Duke of York*. The Admiralty, fearful of the powers of *Tirpitz* and mindful of the dilemma posed by each PQ convoy in turn, had decided that if a German surface force appeared the cruiser and destroyer escort force was to be ordered to withdraw and the convoy to scatter, each merchant vessel being left to make its way to its destination as best it could on its own; the convoy was to be dissolved upon any threat of hostile surface action; an attack by *Tirpitz* on the allied navies was not to be faced.

The convoy was spotted by the Germans on 1 July and air attacks began on the 4th, when four ships were sunk. Before this attack Admiralty intelligence gave strong indications that *Tirpitz* had put to sea. The order to scatter was given and the naval escort was withdrawn westward. *Tirpitz* had not in fact left Trondhjem (although she did so later). Thus the convoy was left exposed to air and U-boat attack. The result was a massacre. Twenty-four of the thirty-five ships went to the bottom. The German surface forces did not need to join in the action. They had achieved their object without doing so.

This catastrophe dictated a pause. PQ 18, sailing in September, was escorted by an aircraft carrier and lost no more than thirteen of its forty ships, and PQ 19 was not dispatched until December. Between-whiles thirteen ships attempted the passage singly. Only five of them made it. During 1943 no convoys sailed in the light months. But the pressures on the Russians had been eased by the victories of their own arms. The northern convoys caused hard feelings and produced bitter words between the allies so long as allied aid seemed a matter of life and death to the Russians, while the carrying of it was not only a severe strain on specially strained shipping resources but also peculiarly dangerous to the men engaged in it. These convoys lost 7.5 per cent of their cargoes, as compared with losses of 0.7 per cent in the Atlantic. Forty convoys in all sailed east, thirty-seven back; 811 merchantmen set out on the passage east, 715 back; 100 ships were sunk, 2,800 men died.

Not all aid to the USSR went this way. In fact rather less than a

ALLIED CONVOY PQ17 JULY 1942

0 __ 200 Miles

75°N

70°N

60°E

50°E

40°E

30°E

20°E

~ARTHUR BANKS~

Spitzbergen

Bear I.

Hope I.

ICE

WASHINGTON
BOLTON CASTLE
PAULUS POTTER

EARLSTON

EMPIRE BYRON

PANKRAFT

RIVER AFTON

Trawler AYRSHIRE with SILVER SWORD
TROUBADOUR
IRONCLAD

ALDERSDALE

DANIEL MORGAN

HONOMU

ZAAFRAN

Track of PALOMARES

FAIRFIELD CITY

PETER KERR

Position of PQ17
on scattering
4 July 1942.

TIRPITZ, SCHEER,
HIPPER, 8 destroyers,
sailed 1145, 5 July.

2130
5 July

North Cape

Altenfiord

Banak

Ki-Kenes

Petsamo

Vola Inlet

Murmansk

Vaenga

Iokanka

Goulo

C. Kanin

Kolguev I.

ICE

HOOSIER

EL CAPITAN

PAN
ATLANTIC

WINSTON SALEM (ashore)

EMPIRE TIDE

HARTLEBURY

OLOPANA

ALCOA
RANGER

JOHN WITHERSPOON

Sukhoi
Nos

NOVAYA

ZEMLYA

Matochkin
Str.

Kara Str.

75°N

70°N

20°E

30°E

40°E

50°E

60°E

quarter of it did, the principal route being through Iran. After the war the Russian economist N. A. Voznesenski estimated allied aid at 4 per cent of the USSR's own production; western estimates range a little higher. In figures the United States delivered supplies to the value of $11.3 billion, Great Britain £428 millions' worth. In retrospect the lists are long, dry sets of figures which are difficult to take in: 22,000 aircraft, 13,000 tanks, 2.7 million tons of petrol, 15 million pairs of boots, 2,000 telephones and a million miles of field telephone cable; but while the war was being fought these shipments were very much more than sets of figures, especially in 1941–2 when the Russians were recovering from the first shocks and, as we shall see in the next chapter, struggling to salvage and move factories and get industrial production going again. One tenth (in value) of American supplies consisted of food and this, together with the miscellaneous deliveries of vehicles, chemicals, clothing, tents, blankets, leather goods, radio equipment and medicine were probably even more welcome than the tanks and aircraft which the Russians soon began to turn out for themselves, of excellent quality and in huge numbers.

The harassing of the northern convoys was the last exploit of the German high seas fleet. In September 1943 British midget submarines – craft of fifty feet manned by specially intrepid crews of four – attacked *Tirpitz* at her anchorage up Trondhjem fjord and put her out of action for six months. But the British Admiralty dared not let this powerful vessel remain in being. Her very existence was a threat, even though she remained inactive. Aircraft of the Fleet Air Arm, flying off aircraft carriers, inflicted further blows on her in April 1944 but the damage was comparatively light and further attacks failed. Then Bomber Command was called upon. A first attack by Lancasters operating with 12,000 lb. bombs from Russian airfields crippled her in September but left her afloat. A second attack by Lancasters in November sank her. *Scharnhorst* had been sunk a year earlier and the German surface fleet had long since ceased to play the role which Grand Admiral Raeder had looked forward to. He had resigned his command at the beginning of 1943 when his fleet was already crippled by fuel shortages and the loss of the Führer's confidence. Hitler felt that the men could be better used in other ways and talked of de-commissioning all capital ships. Above and below the waters the command of the seas was no longer disputed anywhere except between the Americans and the Japanese in the Pacific.

The high seas and the ships sailing upon them had been used to ensure or interdict supplies, not to stage major naval battles. There was nothing like the Battle of Jutland, let alone Trafalgar. The vital issues in the Battle of the Seas were, first, whether the British people should get enough to eat, British factories get enough to keep going and the British armed services get enough to fight on; and secondly, the movement of troops across the seas. The worst months of the blockade were also the months in which command of the seas was an issue all over the world – in the Pacific and Indian Oceans as well as the Atlantic – and all the active theatres of war depended on the movement of tens of thousands of men and their equipment every month. The Americans, unaided, were fully committed in the Pacific, so that the armies which they had promised to send eastward in fulfilment of their pledge to put Europe first had to be transported largely in non-American vessels. The major role in keeping the routes open was played by the British with material help from some of their European allies. The British merchant service was maintained throughout the war at a strength of about 145,000 men. Volunteers could and did enter it at the age of sixteen. Employment was traditionally by the voyage, that is to say, any seaman could leave his ship upon his return from any voyage; but none did so. After March 1941 the government had the power to prevent seamen from leaving the service and to direct former seamen back to it, but the flow of volunteers was such that it never had to worry about the manning of the ships. Thirty-two thousand died directly or indirectly through enemy action and many more were disabled.

The defeat of the U-boat was, like the Battle of Waterloo, a 'damned nice thing – the nearest run thing'. The Germans came closer to victory at sea than anywhere else after 1941, and at the time of their defeat in 1943 they had not exhausted their capabilities. They lost, not because they had no more cards to play, but because they played them just too late. They had a new long-range torpedo which could be fired from ranges outside the scanning range of the victim's detecting apparatus; with this torpedo they could strike before being seen. They also had a faster U-boat equipped with the new device called Schnorkel. Thanks to its speed this boat could overtake and then outdistance vessels previously immune and thanks to its Schnorkel, a tube which just broke surface and enabled it to breathe without surfacing, it could remain virtually concealed from sight and from radar. These innovations did not have the chance to take effect in the battle because allied skills had beaten the U-boat back to a position of no recovery.

The U-boat had started the war in a theoretically winning position because it was too difficult to detect and destroy. Sailing faster and deeper than the submarines of the First World War and more strongly built it was almost out of sight and, except when directly hit, it was impervious to depth charges which had improved little over twenty years. Yet, fortunately for Great Britain, it was still essentially what it had been in the First World War – a submersible surface craft and not one which could live permanently beneath the waters. It had to surface to live and it was therefore still vulnerable to detection and destruction by an enemy who knew where it was and had good enough weapons. Its main weaknesses were its inescapable need to surface to recharge its batteries and the practice, enforced by the German High Command, of maintaining contact with home and so betraying its position from time to time by breaking wireless silence. These weaknesses, coupled with the small number of available U-boats in the first two years of war, enabled the allies to turn the tables. As in the air, Great Britain's lead in radar was crucial. Radar was used to find the U-boats when they were forced to surface and a variant of radar – asdic or sonar, developed in both Great Britain and the United States – probed beneath the seas to find submerged boats. The Ultra breakthrough robbed the unwitting U-boat of its invisibility, and as Coastal Command acquired aircraft which could fly farther, detect at great ranges and with greater accuracy and carry more lethal weapons than the pre-war depth charges, so the U-boat was forced from the offensive to the defensive. It did not recover in time to stage another round. Its reverses in 1943 added up to final defeat.

CHAPTER 22

The Victory of the USSR

THE USSR presented Hitler with a problem which was not only different in scale from his British problem but, militarily, diametrically opposite to it. Stalin had resources – of manpower, raw materials and space – which were greatly superior to Germany's. Against them Hitler had to pit superior skill and superior organization in a bid to win a quick victory. He had to break the USSR, not wear it down. In the west he could lose the Battle of Britain but still hope to win the long-drawn-out Battle of the Seas. In the east time was not on his side. He not only hoped to win in six months but needed to win in not much more. He threw the immensely efficient armed forces of a thoroughly modern industrial power against a colossus which had not reached the same stage of industrial sophistication and was, in addition, weakened both materially and psychologically by a generation of turmoil: revolution and civil war, followed by ostracism, the destruction of the peasantry, political and military purges, and a police tyranny and an inquisitorial system of government extremely ill calculated to elicit loyalty. Hitler relied on his military engine to destroy the enemy's power to resist and, at second remove, to encourage the peoples of the USSR to turn against their own government. Although at the end of 1941 he had failed to achieve the decisive victory which he had hoped for, the successes of German arms had been so great that the USSR was like a man who has had his weapon dashed from his hand and does not know where to turn to get himself another. A third of the USSR's industrial capacity had been overrun and another third was under fire from the German armies and air forces, its output gravely cut. The next three years produced fighting more ferocious and devastating than any experienced by man. Both in scale and temper and therefore in its consequences the war in the USSR was altogether different from any of the other campaigns embraced by the Second World War.

Although Stalin had played every available political card in order to fend off a war with Germany and although his military dispositions could be criticized for unpreparedness, he had taken a number of steps to prepare the USSR for war on the industrial front. He introduced measures at the end of 1938 to curb absenteeism in factories and restrict the excessive movement of labour which were a debilitating feature of the Soviet economy: absenteeism became grounds for dismissal and eleven months' employment in one job a prerequisite for two weeks' holiday. In 1940 new measures punished slacking and forbade certain changes of job without permission. In the same year the government took power to direct workers from one place to another. The costs of transporting and re-housing the worker and his family were to be paid by the state; he was to receive six days' pay on arrival at his destination; and he was promised that his wages would not fall. The government also tackled the problem of training. It had an alarming shortage of technicians, especially below the top ranges. It established vocational schools to take nearly a million trainees a year who were then assigned to jobs and were required, military service apart, to stay in them for four years. Young people who were not exceptionally clever or exceptionally privileged were diverted into these schools and away from high schools and universities, where fees were introduced for all but the favoured few; in the face of the emergency created by the threat of war higher education was denied to all but a small élite.

With the advent of war the armed services made big demands on man-power and their losses were so heavy that they continued to do so to the end. The population of the USSR in 1941 was about 200 million but at least one in ten of these died, in uniform or out of it, before the war was over. The territories annexed by the USSR in 1939–40 – an area larger than the United Kingdom – added to its population a million Poles and perhaps half a million Balts, but the total labour force fell from a pre-war total of 28 million to below 20 million by 1943. Half the workers in war industry were women and the proportion of women in agriculture was much higher. Something like half the male peasantry was conscripted into the army, leaving the fields to be worked by women, children and old men, or not worked at all. Millions of these peasants never returned to the countryside, for when the war ended the survivors among them were needed in the towns and factories and for many years after 1945 women continued to provide two thirds of agricultural labour.

The labour available for war industries was not only reduced by the needs of the fighting services and, by western standards, inadequately trained; it was also in the wrong places because industry itself was to a very large extent in the wrong places for a war which began with a German invasion. The removal of industry from threatened areas under the stress of war and the expansion of production in eastern regions of the USSR became a crucial factor in the USSR's victory – the most crucial factor after the Soviet armies had survived the first six months of war. This effect has been presented as nearly a miracle. Like all miracles it had a basis in hard fact.

The USSR was not in 1941 an industrial power like Germany or Great Britain or, least of all, the United States, but it was in process of becoming one. The industrialization of Russia had begun in the nineteenth century, albeit patchily, later than in western Europe and under the heavy disabilities of an ailing political and social system. The revolutionary régime which came to power in 1917 had ambitious ideas about modernizing and urbanizing the USSR and making it self-sufficient but the government's plans were severely hampered by the destruction caused by the First World War and the ensuing civil war and by its own political and economic isolation. The conditions were harsh and the base low. Capital was scarce; communications were poor; technical skills, even secondary education, were thinly spread; the USSR was rich in natural resources but they had never been properly surveyed. But a poor beginning makes for (statistically) impressive achievements, and during the first Five Year Plan (1928–32) and again during the second Plan capital investment, industrial output and gross national product were all doubled and transport facilities increased in even greater proportion. Education was extended and the shift of the population as a whole rose by a third between 1914 and 1940, the urban population from the country to the towns was accelerated while the population was multiplied by 2.4. There was therefore a considerable alteration not only in the number of people at work but even more so in what they were doing.

The main industrial effort remained where it had been – in the areas round Moscow and Leningrad, in the Ukraine and the Don basin. The development of existing facilities had first priority. Nowhere else was there an adequate supply of skilled labour. But the development of other areas – the Urals, western Siberia and Kazakhstan – was a theme which appealed to communist propagandists as well as to the romantic imagination. These areas were known to be rich in minerals. The pre-revolutionary regime could be blamed for doing too little about them. Lenin had said that the right thing to do was to create industries where raw materials were to be got. Consequently the repair and extension of industry in the traditional centres in European Russia was to be matched by exciting new schemes farther east. This eastward trend was gradually intensified. Up to 1930 the traditional centres absorbed the bulk of the effort. During the thirties they still retained their primacy but at the same time vast sums began to be lavished on other areas, particularly the Urals and the Siberian district round Kuznetsk (the Kuzbas), and under the third Five Year Plan, which began in 1939, other areas in western Siberia and central Asia were promised increased attention of the same kind. Railways were built, electric power provided, resources surveyed and populations moved to where labour was required. In the new development areas there was not only a total lack of skilled labour but a considerable shortage of any labour at all, to remedy which the government compelled migrations and used convicts and political prisoners ruthlessly. (In 1941 the NKVD was responsible for a sixth of all new construction in the USSR.)

This relocation of industry, which was to prove strategically vital, was at first economically irrational. Thus coal was mined in the Kuzbas in Siberia and iron ore round Magnitogorsk in the Urals, but there was no iron ore near Kuznetsk or coal near Magnitogorsk and the two centres were well over a thousand miles apart. This situation was, however, later redeemed by supplying Magnitogorsk with coal by rail from Karaganda in Kazakhstan (half the distance away) and by opening up the new iron-fields of Gornaya Shoriya in Siberia to be fed with Kuzbas coal. Thus nature justified the huge expenditure of capital and labour and the USSR found itself endowed with two new industrial complexes in place of one barely cohesive one. (The development of the Kuzbas illustrates the pace of expansion. In the decade 1928–38 its production of coal rose from 2 million to 16 million tons a year.) As the production of iron and coal rose upon the basis of improved communications and technology, more power and more labour, so the USSR began to be supplied with the quantities and the varieties of steel to sustain its expanding industries and, an increasingly more urgent preoccupation, its armament as well.

This wider distribution of the steel industry was the most important single element in the development of the eastern regions, but not the only one. Western Russia is poor in non-ferrous metals, which Tsarist Russia had imported on a significant scale. But copper had been mined in the Urals and the Caucasus since the seventeenth century, and the USSR planned to exploit the copper, lead and zinc of Kazakhstan. This work was put in hand before the war and greatly developed during it, so that Kazakhstan became second only to the Urals in sustaining the Russian war effort. The chemical industry was also diffused, although it remained preponderantly European, and was so severely damaged that American, British and Canadian imports were required to make good the losses. The radio industry was also expanded. Besides 120 large broadcasting stations the USSR was operating 2,000 local stations before the war and had begun a public television service in 1938 (discontinued during the war).

In sum, the Ural, Siberian and central Asian areas, which had been opened up as ancillary industrial enterprises primarily in order to modernize the USSR and make it economically independent of capitalist countries, had become in addition an alternative arms base. Without this

SOVIET INDUSTRIAL RESOURCES
1941 – 1945

German–occupied territory by December 1943.

Soviet–occupied centres throughout the war.

OIL Soviet–controlled materials 1941–1945.

Soviet–controlled railways 1941–1945.

Routes of Allied aid 1941–1945.

Scapa Flow

GREAT BRITAIN

North Cape

Berlin

Murmansk

Kandalaksha
COPPER
IRON

Warsaw

Leningrad

Archangel

IRON

Vologda

Moscow

Kotlas

COPPER

Kirov

PLATINUM

COPPER

Odessa

OIL

Saratov

Kuibyshev

COAL

Sverdlov

IRON

Tobolsk

MANGANESE

BAUXITE

Orsk

COPPER

Omsk

From the Pacific Coast of the USA via Vladivostok

Black Sea

Astrakhan

OIL

Novosibirsk
IRON
TIN

Barnaul

COPPER

ZINC

LEAD

MERCURY

TURKEY
Neutral

OIL

Caspian Sea

Aral Sea

COPPER

COPPER

OIL

Krasnovodsk

OIL

Lake Balkhash

ZINC

Ashkhabad

COPPER

Bukhara

Begovat

Tashkent

Alma Ata

IRAN

Joint Anglo–Soviet Occupation

LEAD
MERCURY

CHINA

Persian Gulf

AFGHANISTAN
Neutral

0   300
Miles

~ARTHUR BANKS~

alternative the USSR might well have collapsed at the beginning of 1942. The German victories of the previous year had eliminated much of the fruits of the Russian industrial effort of the thirties: between a half and two thirds of its productive capacity in coal, pig iron, steel and aluminium, a quarter of its engineering output. Over 300 ammunition factories had been put out of action. By November 1941 the USSR's overall industrial output had been halved, and during November and December no coal whatever was delivered from the Moscow or the Donets minefields. Industry in the Urals and eastward could not immediately fill the gap but it supplied a base.

A gigantic movement of people and plants took place. The number of people involved may have been as high as 12 million. From Leningrad more than two thirds of the city's capital equipment, building excepted, were conveyed away. According to N. A. Voznesenski, the head of Gosplan (the State Planning Commission), these movements involved 'millions of people . . . hundreds of enterprises, tens of thousands of machine tools, rolling mills, presses, hammers, turbines and motors . . . 1,360 large enterprises – mostly war enterprises – were evacuated to the eastern regions of the USSR.' The impressive aspect of this undertaking was its hugeness, not its organization. The railways, although they had been singled out for improvement under the third Five Year Plan, were reduced to chaos as west-bound trains carried men to the armies at the front while east-bound trains, loaded with machinery, workers and deported Volga Germans and Polish prisoners of war, were pushed into sidings where some of the equipment stayed to rot and men and women to die. At the new sites wooden structures were thrown up to house machinery, but there was often neither time nor materials to build houses for the workers. They sometimes set to work, in temperatures below zero, before the roof was on their makeshift factory and they slept on the floor among the machines. Their privations were terrible. Food was scarce, hospitals (and schools) non-existent. They just worked as long as they could. Mortality was high, output per head poor. The wonder was that they were not worse. By their efforts war industry kept going. But the early months of 1942 were critical. Thereafter production in these regions expanded dramatically until their aggregate war production reached 2.5 times the total pre-war production of the entire USSR. Labour, while it declined overall, rose in 1940–43 from 1 million to 1.5 million in the Urals and by similar degrees in western Siberia and Kazakhstan, each of which had employed nearly half a million in industry on the eve of war.

The principal features of this victory on the home front were two: the rigours which an authoritarian government (aided by the appeal to patriotism) could impose on the people, and the adaptability of the Soviet economy, which partly made up for its technical weaknesses by its ready response to central planning and direction. Once the corner was turned and production resumed, expansion was astonishingly rapid. By the middle of 1942 arms production exceeded its pre-war level. In the next years output in the east continued to rise, while industry in the occupied western areas was rehabilitated with amazing vigour as fast as they were liberated. The Moscow coalfields, for example, whose pre-war production was 35,000 tons a day, resumed output in January 1942 at the rate of 590 tons a day, increased it to 22,000 tons by May and were back to normal by October 1942. Electrical generating capacity, nearly half of which was physically destroyed by the Germans, was also back to its pre-war volume before the war ended. Russian production of tanks and aircraft surpassed German production in 1943. At their peak they reached 40,000 aircraft and 30,000 tanks and other armoured fighting vehicles a year – alongside an output of 150,000 pieces of artillery, 500,000 machine guns and at least 2 million sub-machine guns and 3 million rifles. Stalin had won, by however narrow a margin, the fight for the material resources of war; but there was also the question of human responses.

The response of the people of the USSR depended not only on how they were treated during the war but also on how they had been treated before it. Wartime privations, however severe, were expected and attributable to the enemy, but the history of pre-war relations between government and governed gave rise on the German side to hopes of rebellion and, one may suppose, to equivalent fears on the Russian side.

The intensive industrialization of the thirties was Stalin's special contribution to the evolution of Soviet society. Through it he established his totalitarian authority and because of it he waged a savage fight against the peasantry which had been one of the protagonists in the revolution of 1917. The question of the peasants is the question of food. The food which peasants produce can either be bought or seized. During the confused years of revolution and civil war after 1917 it was most frequently seized but seized with some justification and consent, since the struggling revolution – to which the peasants adhered – had no money to pay for it and no means to produce the goods which the peasants might have taken in exchange for their produce. The peasants understood this, but they also learned the strength of their position and when the civil war ended they in effect bargained with the central government and forced it to reward them for their labours instead of merely appropriating its fruits.

For the next six years (1921–7) the New Economic Policy sought to provide goods to satisfy and stimulate the peasants, but some of the richer peasants continued to demonstrate their power by keeping food off the market when they were dissatisfied with the returns offered to them. A series of good harvests increased their power and the temptation to hold back supplies for the towns and play the markets, so much so that the government had to import grain to save the towns from starvation. The New Economic Policy not only derogated from the basic principles of the Bolshevik Party by making concessions to private operators and to the profit motive, so that bolsheviks like Stalin came increasingly to resent the power of the peasants and to determine to destroy it, even at the cost of another revolution; it also made the peasantry a rising power opposed to the party and opposed to the towns. So instead of running consumer industries to pay for peasant produce the government would force the peasants to pay for heavy industry by reverting once more to the civil war practices of exploiting their labour and taking their produce on the state's own terms. There was in fact no other way of paying for industrialization, since the USSR was neither forming the needful capital within its borders nor able to borrow it abroad. Peasants had paid for industrialization before – for example, in the Industrial Revolution in western Europe – but not nearly so harshly or so fast as Stalin made the Russian peasants pay.

They paid for internal reasons, but the way they were forced to pay was largely dictated by failures in foreign policy, in particular the rupture with Great Britain and the collapse of the attempt to foster communism in China. These failures were all the more dangerous, given the failure to promote communism in Europe a decade earlier. Industrialization could no longer wait and so with the first Five Year Plan the peasants were brigaded into collectives in order the better to be coerced. In the course of his war on the peasantry Stalin sharpened the totalitarian machinery and police terror of the state and converted the Bolshevik Party from a policy-making organization, which to some extent it still was in the twenties, into an apparatus of arbitrary power to be used not only against the peasants but also against townspeople and enemies or imagined enemies of all kinds. The more prosperous peasants were ruined, great numbers of peasants were killed and agricultural production was disastrously reduced. The horrors of these years made their contribution to the industrialization which Stalin had resolved to effect, but at a price which raised the question of how far the peoples of the USSR could be counted loyal to it in war. Unable to pay the Russians to work harder or inspire them to do so as perhaps Lenin or Trotsky might have done, Stalin had been left with only the modern equivalent of flogging them – a police régime in which the workers, trapped by informers and false accusations, were consigned whole-sale to hard labour camps. Stalin was not blind to the risks inherent in this ferocity. His first wartime speech on 3 July 1941 appealed, in terms unwontedly similar to the appeals to patriotism made by democratic leaders, for sacrifices, ruthlessness and unity, for a scorched earth policy and guerrilla warfare to help the desperately struggling armed forces.

The sacrifices which the peoples of the USSR may have braced themselves to make in 1941 can hardly have been as gruelling as they turned out to be in fact. Life in the USSR during the war became not only grim but so difficult to sustain that about a million people died of starvation. The armed services and workers in war industry got enough to eat. By and large other people did not. The total amount of food provided and purchased was almost halved. Personal consumption fell below that of the frightful famine year in 1932. The sugar ration, to take an extreme example, was reduced to half a pound a year. The supply of vegetables was cut by nearly two thirds, of meat by more than half, of flour by nearly half. There was no attempt to keep up tobacco stocks, which fell by three quarters, nor the flow of vodka, which was halved. Production of consumer goods was not much more than adequate for the needs of the armed services. Real earnings were cut by a half or more. Compulsory saving was increased by contributions to war bonds which were to be redeemed after the war – but lost nine tenths of their value when the currency was reformed in 1947. Prices had begun to rise with fear of war in 1939 and rose sharply during 1940. After the outbreak of war in 1941 prices of rationed foods and goods were pegged at their, already enhanced, pre-war levels, but they were scarce in the state shops which sold rationed and price-controlled commodities, while in other shops prices rocketed upwards and reached by 1943 about fourteen times their 1940 levels. (After the war the prices of price-controlled commodities were re-adjusted, in a number of cases by trebling them. When rationing ended in 1947 basic prices were about three times what they had been in 1940. But vodka had gone up ten times.)

Hours of work were lengthened. Holidays, other than the weekly day of rest, were cancelled. The seven day week was reintroduced in 1940 – that is to say, one rest day in seven instead of one in six or (before 1929) one in five. The normal working day was extended from seven hours to eight, but plant managers could extend it up to eleven hours, for extra pay at higher rates. The state offered some palliatives. The USSR had a well-established, comprehensive social insurance scheme which worked on a non-contributory basis, was financed by central and local government authorities and the state's business enterprises, provided sickness and other benefits graded according to wages and length of service, and gave pensions to men at sixty and women at fifty-five: pensions ranged from 50 per cent to 100 per cent of the basic wage (the latter for the lower paid), but there was a ceiling which, although not ungenerous in the thirties, became niggardly with wartime inflation. The state also recognized the need for solace of a different kind. From the outbreak of war, churches became packed with people praying that their country would be saved from its enemies and that they themselves would have the fortitude to bear their increasingly intolerable burdens of mental anguish and physical pain. In 1943 Stalin re-established the Holy Synod of the Russian Orthodox church and allowed it to elect a patriarch and re-open seminaries.

A large proportion of the population of the USSR lived outside big towns and their attitudes were specially difficult to control or predict. While Stalin appealed to them from the one side, the Germans were hoping to find among them a substantial number of disaffected who would take the first opportunity to turn against their government. Both sides wanted them to take an active part in the war, the one as guerrilla partisans against the invaders, the other as auxiliaries on the German side.

Stalin seems to have envisaged guerrilla resistance before the German invasion took place, for instructions for it were issued within a few days. The civil wars after 1917, still a living memory in the USSR, had made partisan warfare less esoteric than it was in the west, and communist doctrine tended to blur the sharper distinction made in more traditionalist societies between professional and popular campaigning. The rapid advances made by the Germans in 1941 placed them in control of large areas from which the inhabitants had not had time to flee. German control was unevenly spread and Stalin could have ordered the civilian population to escape eastward; broad corridors, more or less unpoliced by the Germans, could be traversed without much danger. But no such withdrawals were made. Many of the inhabitants may have been unwilling to leave their homes, even though they were in enemy occupied territory, in order to be drafted into Stalin's armies, but it seems that Stalin did not in any case want to use them that way. They could be more useful as guerrilla fighters within the enemy's lines.

Bands were quickly formed to harass German units and communications, to collect intelligence and to exact vengeance upon anybody who collaborated with the enemy. From these beginnings a considerable force grew, although not without some initial setbacks. Moscow's first plan was to provide a core of organizers, with some elementary training in partisan warfare and of indubitable party loyalty, who would be reinforced by local anti-German patriotism and enthusiasm. This plan was not at first very successful. Local enthusiasm was not as marked as had been hoped and the first groups had to contend with some pro-German attitudes as well as the attentions of the SD. Problems of supply and communication were extremely severe during 1941 and these first groups achieved little beyond a few hit-and-run raids and enough reprisals against collaborationists to make people think twice before helping the Germans. A number of these bands were completely eliminated. In the same period other bands came spontaneously and haphazardly into existence. Out of the flotsam and jetsam of the defeated Russian armies, groups 300–1,000 strong formed, but their first aim was survival rather than further action against the Germans who, until the end of 1942, still looked like the winning side. During 1942, however, the government was able to impose a degree of organization and direction on the bands and began to draft the local peasantry into an effective, if subordinate and ancillary, fighting force.

The Germans employed around 250,000 security troops (usually substandard or foreign conscripts) in the USSR, partly in response to this activity, but shortages of men and materials limited their anti-partisan operations. The partisans harassed German communications and retarded reinforcements, notably in conjunction with the Kursk offensive in 1943 and before the Russian attacks in White Russia in the summer of 1944; they also inflicted about 35,000 casualties. They were helped from the start by the Germans themselves. The horrors, already related, perpetrated by the SD and the *Einsatzkommandos*, the destruction of over three million prisoners of war, the deportations to extermination camps and forced labour, the killing of a further million partisans and civilians in the USSR, the burning of villages and shooting of villagers by way of reprisal – on one occasion 158 villages were burned down as a single act of reprisal – all these things inflamed anti-German hatred and made villagers think that they might as well join the partisans instead of waiting to be killed or enslaved by the Germans. Thus, although the Germans sent agents (operation Zeppelin) to infiltrate the bands and the *Volksdeutsche*; although the Ukraine contained the seeds of a separatist and anti-Soviet movement; although the Germans appointed a Russian civilian governor of Bryansk as an experiment; and although they captured a potential anti-Soviet leader in General A. A. Vlasov, their excesses (like those of the Poles in the same parts in 1920) ruined whatever chances they may have had of subverting any appreciable number of Soviet citizens and swelled the active ranks of their adversaries.

By mid-1942 the partisans probably numbered about 150,000. Their strongest ground was White Russia, where wooded country provided the best terrain; Bryansk became a principal base and from it they extended their operations into the Ukraine. But the government still could not spare them much in the way of up-to-date equipment. A year later the Germans put their strength at 200,000 and eventually they may have reached half a million. From 1943 they received new equipment from the USSR's reorganized factories, including mortars and artillery, special anti-tank guns for attacking locomotives, radios which kept them in touch with one another and with the Russian High Command, and medical supplies which had been almost totally lacking. They were supplied by air and constructed and maintained airfields for this purpose. Most of them were between seventeen and thirty-five years old, conscripted peasants with a sprinkling of army officers and other ranks and party officials. Whereas in the early days the emphasis was on reliable party members, the proportion of these inevitably fell as the movement became bigger; the consciously and actively political element may have been around one tenth in the later years. Towards the end of the war partisan brigades moved into other countries as an advance guard of Russian retribution and in order to help form local committees of reliable residents. In Poland they fought some minor engagements against the Polish Home Army and in Slovakia some 3,000 of them joined with Slovaks parachuted from the USSR in the Slovak rising against the Germans at the end of 1944, but in Rumania and Hungary their activities were insignificant and in Latvia they were driven out again.

The partisan movement had also a political purpose. The Germans occupied areas of the USSR containing a population of 70 million. These areas included large tracts, with a population of 20 million, which had only very recently come under Russian rule, and where anti-Russian feeling was intense. In all these areas, temporarily lost, Stalin was concerned to preserve some vestiges of the presence of the Soviet state. He had no reason to assume that the peasantry of the USSR would remain loyal to his régime and even less reason to suppose that the population of the Baltic states and eastern Poland would not jump at any chance, even a chance presented to them by the Germans, to repudiate it. The destruction by the Germans of the apparatus of government was a threat to the communist system, especially in areas where local separatism – political as in the Ukraine or religious as among the USSR's Muslim peoples – reinforced dislike of Stalin's communist autocracy and police rule, dislike of forced collectivization and dislike of war. The partisan movement was a reminder, if necessary a forcible one, that the government of the USSR was still in being and still in the fight. The partisans actively combated German attempts to subvert local leaders. Village elders appointed by the Germans were killed, so that fear of the German conqueror was more than offset by fear of the continuing capacity and omniscience of the central government of the USSR and its servants.

Yet a number of Soviet citizens did collaborate with the Germans or take service with them. There is more than a suggestion of severe disaffection in the fate of the Tartars, Kalmucks, Chechens and other minorities, about a million of whom were deported from the Caucasus in the winter of 1943–4, charged with collaborating with the Germans. The brutality with which they were treated (later acknowledged by Khrushchev), the thoroughness with which all traces of their homes and even their cemeteries were obliterated, and above all the date, betray a grim punitive intent persisting after all need for precautions had disappeared. In more lastingly occupied territories perhaps half a million or a million Russians, the so-called *Osttruppen*, took German pay. Their main reason was not a desire to serve against their own country but the appalling way in which the Germans behaved in the areas which they occupied. Joining the *Osttruppen* was a way out. Most of the *Osttruppen* were used as rear units in various parts of Europe but the Germans also made some attempts to form more active Russian fighting forces. In 1941 they established a Russian National Liberation Army (RONA) for anti-partisan warfare. It was later converted into the SS Division Kaminsky. In 1944 it participated in the suppression of the Warsaw rising where, even by current SS standards, its barbarous behaviour was outstanding and caused Guderian to protest to Hitler himself; its commander, Kaminsky, was killed by the SS themselves. There were one or two other formations of this nature, such as the XXSS Cossack Cavalry Corps. The SS overcame their prejudices against Slav sub-men by dubbing any Slavs who came over to their side Cossacks and pretending that Cossacks were not Slavs.

Another Russian formation on the German side was the Russian Liberation Army (ROA), which is connected with the name of General Vlasov. Vlasov began the war by deserving well of his country. Like Zhukov he had seen service in the Far East. After commanding a corps on the southern front in 1941 he was posted to the Moscow front as commander of the Twentieth Army at the age of forty-one and had a share with Zhukov in saving the capital. He became appalled by Stalin's ruthlessness in the sacrifice of lives and when, in the following summer, he was captured by the Germans on the Leningrad front he was ready to be transformed into an anti-communist leader.

The ROA was more of a scheme than an army. Hitler was afraid of creating a substantial all-Russian force and he refused to incorporate the *Osttruppen* in the ROA. He preferred to use it in non-combatant, para-military roles; it was a piece of window-dressing which was meant to imply massive Russian disaffection within the USSR, serving Goebbels's anti-Russian propaganda and helping to keep up the morale of the *Osttruppen* who might begin to wonder how prudent it was to go on working for the Germans. Late in 1944, however, Hitler toyed with the idea of assembling all his Russian bits and pieces into an army under Vlasov and recognizing Vlasov as the head of a Russian government in exile. As a result Vlasov found himself in 1945 in command of two divisions totalling about 50,000 men. A part of this force was sent into action on the eastern front in March. Whether designedly or not, it suffered very heavy casualties. In May further units under Vlasov himself went to the Prague front where they joined the Czechs and turned against the Germans. The commander of a Russian force moving south from Berlin towards Prague proposed joint action with a neighbouring American force, but the American commander refused, and when it became clear that Prague was about to fall to the Russians alone, Vlasov tried to escape to the west. He was caught and hanged by the Russians with nine of his associates. Several thousand of his army were turned over to the Russians by the Americans.

Vlasov was one of those Russians who had imagined that nothing could be worse than Stalin's rule. Before the Germans undeceived him on this point by their own bestialities he and others who thought like him had welcomed and incited desertions from the Russian forces to the German side. His supreme aim was another Russian revolution, to be achieved if necessary with the help of the Germans (he was never interested in cooperation with the Americans or British who were Stalin's allies). His crime and ultimately his fate lay in continuing to hold to this course after the Germans had displayed their own beastliness and had moreover become the losing side. He regarded Stalingrad as a defeat. He was therefore a traitor in the strict sense of the word. He was moreover a traitor who found in the end that he had misplaced his trust, so that he had doomed himself to a death without compensations. Like a number of traitors with a cause he is entitled to be remembered as a tragic figure. He was a premature anti-Stalinist whose anti-Stalinism involved aiding the invaders of his country.

In the field the decisive events, after Hitler's failure to score a knockout victory in 1941, were the bitter, yard by yard struggle for Stalingrad in the following winter and then the huge tank battles of the Kursk salient in July 1943.

Stalin's aims for 1942 were to repel Hitler's central Army Group, relieve Leningrad and recover the Ukraine. These plans, which probably assumed a second front to be opened by his allies in the west that year, were not fulfilled. In January the Russians attacked with determination on all fronts against an enemy who was pitifully ill-equipped for the Russian winter, but Stalin was so over-ambitious that these attacks were damaging without being decisive, and so ruthless that they inflicted on his own armies losses as heavy as those suffered by the Germans. As in the previous year large Russian formations were often surrounded and had to be rescued (or not) by further attacks which detracted from Stalin's main aim of inflicting a major defeat on the Germans in the central sector. The German armies, although badly battered, remained in being and in March Stalin was compelled to desist. The rest of the year was coloured by the ill-directed exertions of the first quarter which left Stalin without the men or munitions needed for anything but defensive operations. In addition Stalin made a series of serious mistakes. He refused to allow Timoshenko to break off his offensive towards Kharkov in May although it was evident that the Russian attack had been forestalled. Large Russian losses included the capture of 200,000 men. Furthermore, and in spite of convincing evidence to the contrary, Stalin insisted on believing that major German preparations in the southern sector were merely a feint to cover a second attack on Moscow.

This was a complete misreading of Hitler's intentions, all the more fateful since Hitler, in spite of his disappointments the year before, still held the initiative. His plan was to clean up the Crimea, capture Stalingrad and occupy the Caucasus up to the Turkish border. Thus the main weight of the renewed German attack was to be in the north and south, with the centre remaining relatively static. In the south the programme – the Crimea, Stalingrad, the Caucasus – entailed a number of differing and ultimately diverging operations. The whole of the Crimea was overrun by May except Sebastopol which, having heroically sustained a siege of 250 days, did not fall until July. Manstein's Eleventh Army, which had won these victories, was then switched to the Leningrad front although Manstein himself would have preferred to cross the straits of Kerch (which run along the eastern shore of the Crimea), strike northward with the sea of Azov on his left, make contact with the forces designated for the capture of Stalingrad and preserve the contacts between these forces (Army Group B) and others (Army Group A) which were heading south-eastward into the Caucasus.

In July 1942 Hitler moved his headquarters to Vinnitsa in the Ukraine, whence he had the satisfaction of seeing his armies advance without serious check across the Don to the Volga and to the Caucasus mountains. But these favourable beginnings were the end of Hitler's joy. Very unwisely Hitler had succumbed to the temptation to attempt simultaneously two operations which he had originally planned to put in motion one after the other and which, the more either of them succeeded, were bound to open a gap between Army Groups B and A, the one making for Stalingrad and the other disappearing right-handed into the Caucasus.

In the air the Luftwaffe was still supreme. Although the Russians had two or three times as many aircraft as the Germans (and four or five times as many fighters), and although they were also receiving American Toma-hawks and British Hurricanes, and although the Germans had re-linquished some squadrons for the Mediterranean, the Luftwaffe was able, when called on to make a maximum effort, to fly as many as 3,000 sorties a day – ten times as many as the larger Russian forces. But on the ground the Russian armies, reorganized, backed by reorganized industries and enjoined by Stalin in an order of the day of 1 July to yield no more ground, met their enemies with a new effectiveness and a new confidence. The German advances slowed down. Army Group A failed to reach the Caucasian oilfields before it had to turn round and fight its way back again. Army Group B crossed the Don, won a series of engagements in the narrow zone between the easternmost sweep of the Don and the Volga, and reached the Volga in the last days of August. But the capture of Stalingrad, which would put Hitler in command of one of the most important points in the rail and waterways system of the USSR, proved just too much for it.

The battle for Stalingrad has become one of the most celebrated epi-sodes of the war. Its importance was realized at the time. In the summer, as the Germans approached, Stalin relieved Timoshenko who commanded what had become the South-west Front and appointed General V. N. Gordov in his place. In August Zhukov was dispatched to the Front with special powers – which caused, among other things, jealousies and disputes which had to be referred to Stalin. Stalin may have recalled how he had himself been a commissar on this front in 1919 and had attached to himself a group of officers and commissars antagonistic to the supreme warlord, Trotsky: Khruschchev was now unwittingly building a similar group of loyal friends who would stand by him in the decade after Stalin's death. As German pressure increased the South-west Front was divided into two, confusingly named, new Fronts: the Stalingrad Front, sub-sequently renamed the Don Front, and the South-east Front, sub-sequently Stalingrad Front, the latter commanded in turn by Generals A. I. Eremenko and K. K. Rokossovski. But the most famous name on the Russian side was to be that of General V. I. Chuikov, second in command of the Sixty-fourth Army and then picked by Khrushchev on 12 Septem-ber to command the Sixty-second Army. Chuikov had been an army commander before the war began. He was relegated early in the war but was soon reinstated. He was still an army commander when the war ended. He was ready in criticism of his superiors and sometimes unfair, and like a number of Stalingrad heroes he fancied that too much of the credit for that famous victory was taken after the event by Stalin, Zhukov and to a lesser extent Rokossovski.

Chuikov and the Sixty-second Army were penned into a city which was in the grip of the Germans; all industry within it and all traffic along the Volga were stopped. From the middle of September the city itself was the battleground and its principal buildings, which sometimes changed hands as many as five times in a day, the tactical objectives. The German Sixth Army under General Friedrich Paulus occupied seven eighths of it and twice – in the third week of October and again on 11 November – almost succeeded in overrunning the defenders. The Germans still had a definite superiority in the air. Although their sorties dropped from about 2,000 a day during the autumn to half that figure during the height of the siege, and although the Russian effort was growing, the Luftwaffe was flying about twice as many sorties as the Russians. The Sixty-second Army, inspired by its commander who was always in the thick of the battle, maintained itself by winning back by night ground lost during the day. It was never completely cut off, for it had its back to the river which the Germans failed to control at every point and beyond which was sited all the Russian artillery.

In November the Sixth Army was itself surrounded, when the Russians attacked and defeated the armies on its left and right. This stroke had been planned by the Russian command in September and nervously anticipated by the German generals, but they had been unable to get Hitler to guard against it and when it happened they were taken by surprise. Hitler had dismissed the Chief of Staff of the Army, General Franz Halder (he also took over personal command of Army Group A in the Caucasus from Field Marshal List, who was also dismissed), and replaced him by General Kurt Zeitzler who – although not noted for disagreeing with Hitler – warned him that his forces were dangerously strung out, especially in the Stalingrad sector where the Sixth Army, the spearhead of Army Group B, was worried about its flanks. Hitler refused to withdraw the Sixth Army and abandon the attack in Stalingrad. Instead he tried to buttress it by sending the Rumanian Third and Fourth Armies into positions to the left and right of the Sixth Army and by putting in some Luftwaffe Field Divisions, of whose value the army generals were rightly dubious. Army Group B consisted therefore of the Sixth Army with a Panzer army (Fourth Panzer) on its right, this German core being flanked on either side by the two Rumanian armies and, on the left, by Italian and Hungarian forces. The Army Group's contacts with Army Group A to

THE BATTLE FOR STALINGRAD SEPTEMBER 1942 - FEBRUARY 1943

Built-up areas of Stalingrad and its suburbs.

German forces, 13 September 1942.

Lines of German advance, involving street fighting and hand to hand fights.

Sole part of the city in Soviet hands on 12 November.

ORLOVKA

Orlovka

RYNOK

Volga

GORODISCHE

Mokraya Mechetka

MATVEEV KURGAN

'Important factories'

Tsaritsa

Sta.

Sta.

STALINGRAD

MININA SUBURB

Volga

| 0 | 1 | 2 | 3 | 4 |

Miles

The Germans planned to capture Stalingrad followed by a northward advance along the Volga. This operation was frustrated by the Soviet defence which endured for five months.

~ARTHUR BANKS~

the south were very tenuous. This was the position when the Russians attacked on 19 November (twelve days after the Anglo-American landings in Morocco and Algeria). The Rumanian Third Army was routed at once. So was the Rumanian Fourth Army the next day. There was now a gap between the Sixth Army and the Italians and Hungarians further to the left and a wider gap than ever between Army Groups B and A. And the Sixth Army, which consisted of twenty-two divisions and 220,000 men, had to be supplied by air or extricated.

The strains of the autumn months of 1942 made Hitler singularly moody and intractable. He stayed at his headquarters conducting the war on paper, refusing to allow his plans and his hopes to be upset by reports of what was actually happening in the field. The German staffs had good intelligence about the Russian forces and their dispositions; their intentions were not difficult to guess. But Hitler, pitting his will against the Russians' resources, continued to believe that he could prevail by insisting that that was how it was to be. The arguments of his generals failed to persuade him that he must give up the idea of taking Stalingrad and concentrate on saving the Sixth Army. By November the generals, now deeply pessimistic, were reduced to hoping that something would happen to change Hitler's mind before it was too late, but even after Paulus had been surrounded Hitler found arguments for sticking to his guns: the new Tiger tank would do the trick and meanwhile the Luftwaffe would keep the Sixth Army supplied.

But the Tiger was not yet in service and the Luftwaffe could do nothing of the sort. Goering, confronted with the question whether he could deliver 700 tons a day to the Sixth Army, declared that he could. This irresponsible pledge was partly the result of a successful supply operation earlier in the year to other forces surrounded on the Russian front. This operation, however, had been conducted in much better weather and before the Luftwaffe had had to send squadrons (including Ju. 52 squadrons) from Russia to Africa; and it had cost crippling losses. But Goering preferred to undertake, however vainly, to save the Sixth Army than to incur reproaches for not stepping forward to say he could. The generals at Hitler's headquarters knew that Goering's promise was absurd but their protests, muted by fear of the Führer, were passed over. The daily target of 700 tons was reduced to 300, but the Luftwaffe never came anywhere near it. It had no adequate landing grounds near the Sixth Army or within its shrinking perimeter, and the cold, which set in early in November and was accompanied by thick fogs from the middle of the month, made flying extremely hazardous when at all possible and the servicing of aircraft on the ground a torture for frozen mechanics. The lift began on 25 November. On that day and the next sixty-five tons were delivered, on the third nothing. A big effort was made in mid-December but the fog came down again and although a few F.W. 200s continued to drop a few tons on most days until the end, the Luftwaffe's contribution was wholly ineffectual. The total supplied by drops and landings was 3,295 tons. The Luftwaffe lost 488 machines and 1,000 men.

At the end of November Manstein was given command of Army Group B (renamed Army Group Don) but it was still not clear whether he was to save the Sixth Army by opening an escape route for it to the west or by breaking the Russian ring round it and so enabling it to remain on the Volga. Hitler equivocated. Manstein's own plan was twofold: an eastward offensive by the Fourth Panzer Army and a simultaneous westward attack by a part of the Sixth Army, leaving however the rest of the Sixth Army still on the Volga; and, at a later stage, a breakout by the whole of the Sixth Army to the west. The operation began on 12 December and the German armour advancing from the west got to within forty miles of the Sixth Army's position, but nine days later it was halted. Neither Manstein nor – still less, since he was Manstein's subordinate – Paulus was willing to give the order to the Sixth Army to break out without Hitler's approval, which they could not get. Without it the first part of Manstein's plan was pointless and, as the events showed, also impracticable. By mid-December therefore the fate of the Sixth Army was sealed. The Russians, after inflicting further defeats on Italian, Hungarian and German armies north-west of Stalingrad, offered Paulus on 8 January honourable terms of surrender. Hitler made Paulus a Field Marshall and told him to stand his ground.

By this time the city had been turned into something which none of those who fought there had ever imagined and none who survived could ever forget. The closest and bloodiest battle of the war was fought among the stumps of buildings burnt or burning. From afar Stalingrad looked like a furnace and yet inside it men froze. Dogs rushed into the Volga, to drown, rather than endure any longer the perils of the shore. The no less desperate men were reduced to automatons, obeying orders until it came to their turn to die, human only in their suffering. The Germans were on half rations from the end of November. By the middle of January the German zone, which had measured twenty-five miles by twelve when Paulus was first surrounded in November, had been halved. A little later it was cut in two. Again the Russians called for surrender and again Hitler refused to permit it. The final capitulation came on 2 February. Ninety-one thousand survivors, including a Field Marshal and twenty-four generals, were taken captive. The Russians had already taken 16,700 prisoners during the last weeks of the fighting. Some 70,000 Germans died during the siege, many of them from exposure or starvation, some by suicide.

At Stalingrad the Russians first demonstrated the material strength which was to overwhelm the German armies in 1943 and 1944. They concentrated over a million men against German armies which were numerically slightly stronger and, although still inferior in aircraft, they had the measure of the Germans in tanks and guns. Even in aircraft the balance was shifting. A new Russian fighter, the La. 5, made (like the British Mosquito) of wood, came into service and helped the Russians to achieve local air superiority. Although at Stalingrad the Luftwaffe committed 1,000 aircraft – about half its strength in the Russian theatre but diminished in October when Hitler ordered some squadrons to Leningrad – its numerical superiority was beginning to be offset by growing experience, skill and morale on the Russian side and by anxieties about repairs, reserves and replacements on its own. From 1943 onwards the Germans continued to keep between a half and two thirds of the Luftwaffe in the east, but some of its best pilots, newest aircraft and latest equipment were reserved for the defence of the Reich and for other theatres, and the shortage of pilots and aircraft gradually increased to the point where at times new aircraft, even new types, were given to the Rumanian and Hungarian air forces, which had pilots to fly them, while at other times German squadrons were obliged to make do with obsolescent machines. The Russian air force on the other hand was not only growing in quantity and quality but, since it undertook very little strategic long range bombing, was able to devote almost its entire strength to attacking the German armies and their installations and communications.

There was after Stalingrad also a qualitative change in the war in the USSR. The importance of Stalingrad was much more than statistical. This battle destroyed the idea that the German army could not be beaten: here, on the contrary, was defeat unmistakable. The surrender of the Sixth Army was a tremendous psychological as well as military blow to the Germans and an equally powerful boost to Russian morale and to Stalin's campaign to show that Russia's great patriotic war could be won. The effect on Hitler was to accelerate his physical and mental decline. In 1942 his speech and handwriting began to show the effects of Parkinson's disease, a general decay of the nervous system which destroys a man's coordination and eventually his understanding. A year later he had become a shambling, shaking wreck, pathologically suspicious of his generals, contemptuous of the qualities of his fighting men, driven increasingly to substitute his personal stubbornness for the divisions which he pretended to direct but which were often not really there. He showed at

Stalingrad, in catastrophic degree, his inability to accept even the concept of defeat. His astonishing memory and grasp of detail, his energy and quickness, his serious application to the art of war and the way with men which he sometimes displayed – all these things were destroyed, first, by the distortions induced by failure in a mind of terrifying rigidity and irrationality, and then by disease. The nemesis of will was upon him and his people.

The defeats of Army Group B in the winter of 1942–3 exposed Army Group A to the risk of being bottled up entire in the Caucasus. The Russians planned to advance from the Don to the Donets and then turn about and capture Rostov at the mouth of the Don from the west. This manoeuvre would have established a Russian line from Stalingrad to Rostov, cutting off Army Group A's line of retreat. The Russian plan was, however, frustrated and the Fourth Panzer Army succeeded in making contact with Army Group A and opened an escape for it, thereby enabling its forces to survive and fight another day. The thaw in March eased the pressure on the Germans who recaptured Kharkov which they had lost a few weeks earlier. Thus the Russian victories, although massive, were not decisive and the Germans were able to regain the initiative and hold much of the Donets basin. This, if anything, was the Sixth Army's posthumous reward. But the losses of the German armies could not be replaced; after the middle of 1943 the eastern fronts had even to surrender units for Italy, the Balkans and the west, and by the end of that year thirty divisions – 15 per cent of those on the Russian fronts – had been disbanded for want of replacements to fill the gaps in their ranks.

As a result of the fighting in February and March 1943 the Russians held Kursk, a hundred miles south of Orel and a hundred miles north of Kharkov, both of which cities remained in German hands. The Russian position was therefore a huge bulge extending westward from Kursk for seventy miles and measuring some hundred miles from north to south at its eastern end. After some hesitation Stalin decided to wait for Hitler to attack first. By this time his air reconnaissance had greatly improved his intelligence about German dispositions and he was also receiving valuable information from an infiltrator in German headquarters and from the spy ring in Switzerland called Lucy which had excellent contacts in Berlin and elsewhere and provided him with the date chosen by Hitler for his attack.

Hitler's aim was to re-establish German mastery and morale by eliminating the Kursk salient. The German attack was launched on 5 July by Kluge in the north and Manstein in the south with a combined force of a million men and 2,700 tanks. The Luftwaffe, despite its commitments in other theatres, was able to fly 3,000 sorties a day and Hitler hoped that after cutting off the Russian armies in the bulge he would be able to turn about and dash for Moscow, 200 miles north-east of Orel. On the Russian side two Fronts, commanded by Rokossovski and Vatutin, were backed by a reserve Front under Konev which had been constituted in their rear. The Russian armies were plentifully supplied by Russian industry, and although the Russian Marshals had somewhat fewer tanks than their opponents, the Russian air forces were for the first time able to put many more aircraft into the air than the Luftwaffe. Russian field intelligence was detailed and accurate.

The ensuing battles in the Kursk salient were the main encounter of the war between the Russian and German armies and they were astonishingly short. The German attack in the north was held from the beginning and by 10 July Kluge was forced onto the defensive, partly by the weight of Rokossovski's artillery and the effectiveness of his anti-tank weapons, and partly in anticipation of a Russian counter-attack on his left flank. The Russians also used air to ground rockets which, although not much more destructive than other weapons, were more demoralizing. In the south Manstein was initially more successful and Konev's reserves had to be called upon to help Vatutin. The result was the biggest tank battle of the war. By 12 July it was a clear Russian victory. The German offensive had failed. The Russians counter-attacked, took Orel and Kharkov and extended the fighting along the whole front from the Baltic to the Black Sea. Their gains included Kiev which fell to them in November.

The battles for the Kursk salient cost Hitler half a million men and when they failed, all possibility of avoiding total defeat had gone. The rest was retreat. The Russian armies, under the meticulously competent overall direction of Stalin (who achieved a more effective relationship with his generals than Hitler did) now outnumbered the Germans. The German Tiger tank, which had appeared in the previous autumn, and the Panther, which made its first appearance in these battles, failed to give Hitler the decisive superiority in the tank war which he had hoped for and which had been eluding him ever since 1941. His Tiger II, first used in 1944, was too late to affect the issue. The Russians, with the heavy Joseph Stalin tank, the medium T 34 (which had reached units just in time in 1941) and the light T 70, proved themselves at least the equals of the Germans in quality, and in 1942 Russian production outstripped German. The Russians were great war builders, the peers – given the circumstances – of the Americans. From 1943 their annual production of armoured fighting vehicles (that is to say, tanks, armoured vehicles and assault guns) was around 30,000. In Germany, where after Stalingrad Hitler had charged

SOVIET ADVANCES 1942–1944

Soviet – German Frontier October 1939.
Front line November 1942.
Soviet gains to April 1943.
Retaken by Germans June–July 1943.
Soviet gains July 1943 – April 1944.
German-controlled territory
April 1944.

—ARTHUR BANKS.

Guderian and Speer jointly to overhaul and increase the output of armoured fighting vehicles, production reached a peak of 19,000 in 1944.

Despite defeat Hitler maintained his refusal to sanction any withdrawal, rationalizing his stubborn strategy by his need to keep Rumania, Bulgaria and Hungary in the war and Turkey from joining his enemies – none of which he succeeded in doing as he was pushed back from the Dnieper to the Bug to the Dniester. A fresh Russian winter offensive, beginning in December, relieved Leningrad early in 1944, cut off a German army in the Crimea and brought the Russians to the Carpathians and into Rumania. As his entire southern front collapsed Hitler dismissed Manstein and other senior commanders.

The Russians paused before beginning a new series of attacks in the summer. These began on 22 June – the third anniversary of the launching of Barbarossa – in White Russia where the German Army Group Centre had been instructed to hold and protect Lithuania, East Prussia and northern Poland. Hitler was deceived into expecting that the main Russian attacks would be in the north and south rather than the centre. Army Group Centre was first split into two and then destroyed in a couple of weeks. The German losses were around 400,000 and this huge defeat left Poland and eventually Germany itself defenceless. In the north Army Group North, defending Latvia and Estonia, was cut off as the Russians advanced to the sea west of Riga. In the autumn it was pressed back into the Courland peninsula where it survived until the general capitulation. In Finland a Russian attack in June led to an attempt by the Finns to negotiate peace and a visit by Ribbentrop to Helsinki to stop them. President Ryti gave Ribbentrop his personal promise not to make peace but this was a trick to enable Finland to get German aid for a few more weeks and then come to terms with the Russians, as occasion served, by changing president. In August President Ryti was replaced by Field Marshal Mannerheim and an armistice was signed in September. Finland had to pay an indemnity, lease the naval base of Porkkala, ten miles from Helsinki, to the USSR for fifty years, and provide the Russians with other military facilities so long as the war against Germany lasted. In the farthest north the Russians forced back German troops until they crossed into Norway and operations were suspended by the weather.

The Russian victories in the summer of 1944 posed a grim problem for the Polish government in exile in London and its forces in Poland, the Home Army (AK). They regarded the advancing Russians with at least as much dread and hatred as the defeated Germans. The Russians' winter offensive of 1943–4 had carried them across Poland's pre-war frontier and the ensuing summer offensive across the dividing line fixed by the

Ribbentrop-Molotov pact. The commander of the A K, General Tadeusz Bor-Komorowski, first instructed his men to harass the Germans and neither attack the Russians nor be drawn into the Russian army. He later ordered them to occupy towns abandoned by the Germans and, if absolutely necessary, to defend themselves against the Russians rather than allow themselves to be evicted from their positions. These later instructions amounted to a recognition of the fact that the Polish army might be required to fight the Russian army in order to assert the Polishness of Poland's eastern territories. The Russians for their part declared these territories to be Russian, refused to recognize the A K as a regular combatant force (as the United States and Great Britain did), arrested A K commanders in their westward progress and sponsored in July the Polish Committee of National Liberation (the Lublin Committee) which at the end of the year they recognized as the provisional government of Poland. In this situation the London government decided to play a major card. In order to gain control of the Polish capital before the Russians, and to prevent its rivals within Poland from taking the lead in opposing the enemy, it ordered Warsaw to rise. In doing so it gravely underestimated the German opposition. It also failed to notify either its western allies or the Russians, from all of whom it would quickly be obliged to beg desperately for help. Its 20,000 armed insurgents had ammunition for only seven days. When the battle ended half of them had been killed as well as some 200,000 of Warsaw's population of one million. The survivors were transported to the extermination camps. Nine tenths of the city itself was destroyed.

Preliminary signals for the rising were sent out by radio in the last week of July and the rising began on 1 August. It lasted two months. It was met and defeated by the Germans with an appalling barbarity, particularly on the part of the S S which used half-crazed gangs of criminals and prisoners of war (notably the S S Kaminski brigade) to gas whole clutches of people trapped in the city's underground workings and to burn others alive after sousing them with petrol.

At Teheran in the previous November Roosevelt and Churchill had tacitly accepted that the imminent invasion of Poland by the Red Army left them with few weapons to gainsay Stalin's plans for post-war Poland. The Poles' hope that Churchill would send a British army to Poland was no more than a measure of their political incomprehension and Churchill, with mounting irritation, failed repeatedly both before and after the rising to get the London Poles to see that they must take the Russian victories into account. At Teheran the three leaders agreed in imprecise terms that Poland should be shifted westward to an area between the Curzon line in the east and the river Oder in the west (but with the city of Lvov switched to the Russian side of the Curzon line). At this time Stalin was, if only for tactical reasons, willing to arrange some cooperation within Poland with the AK and to allow the London Poles a minor position in the new embryonic Polish government; but he was plainly determined not to allow the London Poles, whom he rootedly distrusted, to restore pre-war Poland and become its government, nor could he be forced to do so except possibly by an extreme Anglo-American threat tantamount to the determination of the anti-German alliance.

The stronger Stalin's military position became, the weaker was his need to cooperate with the AK or accommodate the London Poles, while his distrust was accentuated by Polish attempts to get arms by air from the west – arms which, in Stalin's view, were designed for use against his forces rather than Hitler's. On 21 July he unveiled the Polish National Committee (the Lublin Committee) which was to be as subservient to him as the London Poles were hostile. At Churchill's prompting Mikolajczyk flew to Moscow where he found Stalin obdurate and engaged in fruitless wrangles with the Lublin Poles as Warsaw's sacrifice began.

That the London Poles should have failed to take Moscow into their confidence about the rising is hardly surprising since it was in large part an anti-Russian venture. That Stalin should prove unhelpful is no more surprising. He disliked most Poles and most distrusted the London Poles and the AK. He was certainly irritated and possibly embarrassed by their sudden and unheralded initiative which happened to come at a moment of strategic debate about the next phase of his general offensive. He had some justification for his repeated accusation that the rising was reckless. He may have been expecting to take Warsaw himself by the end of the first week in August but he was disconcerted by local German successes which dislocated his planning. General V. I. Chuikov, the hero of Stalingrad and now serving on the central front under Marshal Rokossovski, later testified that German air attacks were intense in the Warsaw area, that the Russians lacked bridging equipment vital for forcing the passage of the Vistula and that Rokossovski believed (erroneously, as it turned out) that the Germans had an armoured force east of the Vistula which might attack southward and endanger any Russian positions established across the river. Finally, Stalin may be credited with some ignorance of the barbarous nature of the German suppression of the rising. Nevertheless his refusal to help or to facilitate Anglo-American aid is one of the grisliest examples of the triumph of calculation over humanity in the history of *Realpolitik*. Stalin had some excuse for some inactivity at the beginning of the rising, but thereafter it is impossible to avoid the judgement that

Stalin saw the rising as an opportunity and took it. The rising played into his hands. The responsibility of the London Poles for what happened to Warsaw is great. So is Stalin's.

The London Poles had asked for and been refused Anglo-American air and parachutist support before the rising began. Such aid, they were told, would be too costly without Russian cooperation. This judgement was proved correct. From Italy Air Marshal Sir John Slessor reported that, in the absence of permission to land in Russian-held territory and refuel (which was not granted), operations to Poland were so impossibly dangerous and comparatively useless that he would not undertake them unless ordered to. He made, however, an exception in favour of a Polish squadron under his command. It suffered very heavy losses. The RAF and South African Air Force later joined in a desperate attempt to supply the insurgents and, with the Poles, dropped 233 tons. When the Poles pleaded for direct and massive American air drops to supplement this inevitably meagre effort, the Russians refused (15 August) to allow the aircraft to land at Russian airfields before returning to base. At one point Churchill suggested to Roosevelt that aircraft should land on Russian airfields without Russian permission and see what happened, but Roosevelt was not willing to go as far as that. On 10 September Russian ground forces made a successful attack on the suburb of Praga. They then began an attempt to cross the Vistula, established a number of bridgeheads but were forced by the Germans to retreat. On 13 September Russian aircraft began dropping food and ammunition to the Poles in Warsaw. At least fifty tons – perhaps considerably more – were dropped, most of it accurately but in damaged condition because parachutes were not used. At the same time Stalin lifted his veto on the use of Russian airfields by the Americans and on 18 September the US Air Force undertook a single daylight operation with 110 Flying Fortresses, most of whose drops fell wide of the mark. By 2 October there was nobody left in the city to save or help.

Later that month, in Moscow, Churchill tried to persuade Stalin to accept the revised Curzon line as a *de facto* arrangement to be reviewed at a peace conference but Stalin would have none of it. His armies were now not merely in Poland but, since mid-August, on German soil too, and Finland and Rumania were suing for armistices. Churchill's efforts to persuade Mikolajczyk that all these things were part and parcel of Poland's future fate led to angry scenes between the two men, as the one berated the other for betraying the undertakings given by Great Britain to Poland in 1939. By the time the three leaders met for the second and last time at Yalta in February 1945 Poland was completely occupied by Stalin's forces. Warsaw, held by the Germans for three months after the defeat of the rising, had just been entered by the Russians, Polish contingents under their command leading the way. At Yalta Churchill and Roosevelt continued their expostulations about the composition of the new Polish government but they held even fewer cards than they had held at Teheran: Stalin was in Poland and they were not. The AK had been dissolved by the Russian winter offensive and in March seventeen non-communist Polish leaders, proceeding under safe conduct and at Russian invitation to meet a Russian general, were dispatched to Moscow where all were imprisoned and some died.

Upon recovering the Ukraine the Russians entered Rumania as well as Poland and posed an increasingly awkward problem for Germany's other allies: Bulgaria, Slovakia and Hungary. These allies had already seen the writing on the wall. The German defeats in 1943 and the capitulation of Italy in the same year had set them thinking about how to secure their future in a Europe which was going to be dominated by the USSR in place of Germany.

In Rumania Ion Antonescu's attempt to concert action with Mussolini in 1943 was fruitless. He was then recaptivated by Hitler and his talk of secret weapons but in August 1944 he was dismissed by King Michael after a stormy interview. Attempts to secure western help against the Russian wrath to come were fruitless, for there was nothing the western allies could do for the Rumanians and they were left to make the best terms they could. The king broke off relations with Germany and made contact with the Communist Party (which had been outlawed before the war). After a short period of confusion, during which Bucharest was bombed by the Germans and the German Ambassador committed suicide and his colleagues disappeared for good into the Soviet Union, a new and essentially communist government was installed under Petru Groza. Rumania was required to ratify its territorial losses to the USSR in 1940 but was promised the return of what it had lost to Hungary (but not what it had lost to Bulgaria); it was also required to pay an indemnity to the USSR and fight against Germany.

In Bulgaria, which was at war with Great Britain and the United States but not with the Soviet Union, the government declared itself neutral but failed none the less to stave off a Russian invasion and declaration of war. Bulgaria, under a new government, was compelled in September to declare war on Germany. In the same month Russian troops entered Yugoslavia. They shared with Tito's partisans in the capture of Belgrade in October and then retired a few days later.

The Slovaks, like the Poles, rose against the Germans as the Russian armies approached. Slovakia was an ally of Germany and a co-belligerent but in October 1943 an entire Slovak division had come over to the Russians and in the same period partisan warfare flared up inside eastern Slovakia. In 1944 the country was in a state of general revolt. National committees emerged and commandeered factories and the property of collaborators. An army 65,000 strong engaged the Germans. It hoped to be joined by the Russian army and there is still controversy about why it was not. Marshal Konev seems to have been approached by Slovak officers with a plan for a rising in conjunction with a Russian attack, and to have recommended Stalin to adopt this plan. A Russian advance began early in September. But the Russians had to cross the formidable Carpathians against stiff German opposition and it was the middle of October before they set foot on Slovak soil. By this time the Germans, who had been forewarned of the rising, had defeated it and burned sixty villages and filled at least 200 mass graves with slaughtered Slovaks. The Russians later complained that they had been given too little advance notice of the actual date fixed for the rising. They may also have been sceptical about Slovak estimates of the importance of the operation.

In Hungary the Regent, Admiral Horthy, Europe's senior head of state (he had been one of the leaders of the movement which overthrew Bela Kun's communist regime in 1919), was forced by events to try to abandon the German alliance which had served him well for a number of years. He had joined it because he belonged to a small, nostalgic and illiberal ruling caste for whom anti-Bolshevism was an overriding issue. He had benefited from the two awards of 1939 and 1940 which had given him chunks of his neighbours' territories, he had been happy to help Hitler invade Yugoslavia and the Soviet Union in 1941 and he had been gratified to find that Hitler did not want to oust him in favour of the leader of the local equivalent of the Nazi Party – Ferenc Szalasi of the Arrow Cross (who wanted even more of his neighbours' territories than Hitler was prepared to concede). Up to 1944 Horthy tried to persuade himself that Hitler, after abandoning the Balkans, might succeed in holding the Carpathians and Transylvania and so keep the Russians away from central Europe, but the impending collapse of Rumania showed him that he had no choice and he prepared – too late – to make his escape from the war, even at the price of turning to the communist USSR.

For Hitler, however, Hungary had exceptional strategic significance. He had to hold it so long as he had troops in south-eastern Europe and even if these were safely withdrawn the loss of Hungary would set the Russians well on the way into Vienna. He therefore took over Hungary (thereby initiating anti-Jewish razzias) and sent Otto Skorzeny, the saviour

SOVIET ADVANCES
IN SOUTH-EAST
EUROPE 1944

Front line 20 August 1944.
Soviet advances 20 August – 20 October 1944.
German withdrawals.
British attacks October 1944.
British paratroops land 13 October 1944.
Tito's partisans.
Albanian partisans.

—ARTHUR BANKS—

Black Sea

USSR

Odessa

Jassy

RUMANIA

Bucharest

Danube

Sofia BULGARIA

Istanbul

TURKEY

GREECE

Belgrade

YUGOSLAVIA

ALBANIA

Tirana

CZECHOSLOVAKIA

HUNGARY

Budapest

Vienna

AUSTRIA

Danube

Drava

Sava

Adriatic
Sea

BULGARIA

YUGO.

ALBANIA

GREECE

Athens
Piraeus

Patrai
Corinth

of Mussolini, to kidnap Horthy. Skorzeny first kidnapped the Regent's son and then, in a singularly bold escapade, seized the citadel of Budapest with one car and four tanks. The Regent escaped but immediately afterwards resigned and was taken to Germany under guard. The Germans installed an Arrow Cross government under Szalasi, who was however an incompetent visionary and was hated by the Hungarian army. At the end of 1944 Budapest was beleaguered by Marshal Malinovski. The Germans tried to relieve it but failed, and the city surrendered on 12 February 1945. In this case the Russians made no effort to restrain their troops, who proceeded to eliminate the *ancien régime* in the most direct and gruesome manner. Horthy's long reign ended, as it had begun, with terror and bloodshed, and Hungary virtually lost its independence too.

The Russo-German campaigns were the most terrible war that has ever been waged. The numbers of the dead were huge. The great sieges of Leningrad, Stalingrad and Sebastopol recalled the war-making of other times but the field campaigns were something new. They were the acme of (pre-nuclear) industrial warfare. The mechanized armies of tanks and workshops were industrial plants in motion attended by hundreds of thousands of technicians. These ponderous devastators, made of steel and moved by oil, churned up the countryside and at intervals blazed away at each other, leaving the land covered with warped steel, stinking oil and corpses. In between these armadas men in various kinds of armoured or unarmoured transport, and sometimes still on foot, covered great distances because they were winning or losing or simply because they were required to shift themselves laterally from one part of the front to another. Sometimes there were long lulls, passages of normalcy embedded in senselessness and horror, and if the weather was fine, men might go through the motions of ordinary life and, with their singing and their horseplay, behave as though they were on an excursion rather than a highly organized killing. But then for many months there would be slush and mud and clothes never really dry, or the intense cold which made it dangerous to take off a glove. The most remarkable thing about this war was that, on both sides, men went on fighting it for nearly four years.

Part of the price demanded by Stalin was the repatriation to the USSR, after the war, of all those who had given aid to the Germans and were captured, or could be tracked down and apprehended, in the allied sphere of operations. That deserters and persons who had served the enemy should be tried and sentenced by the state which they had betrayed was nothing new. What was new was a situation in which such traitors should be apprehended not by their own state but by an allied state. This situation raised questions, juridical and political, which gave rise to embarrassment and heartsearching when the war ended and, a generation later, to bitter controversy. The surrender to the Russians of Soviet citizens who had put on German uniforms did not, during the war, seem outrageous or even unusual, and the case for doing so was fortified by two things: many of the persons concerned were known to have behaved with a brutality exceptional even in so awful a war, and there was on the British side an awareness that the advancing Russian armies would soon have in their power British citizens liberated from German prisoner-of-war camps. All these circumstances contributed to the agreement, finally concluded in 1944 and affirmed at Yalta, to exchange all nationals accused of desertion or treason. It was obvious that the Soviet victims of this agreement would receive harsher treatment than their western counterparts and might well be shot without trial, but these surmises were deemed to be irrelevant (as pertaining to the internal jurisdiction of another state) or, if not irrelevant because outrageous, then so impossible to reconcile with the political imperatives of the alliance as to be best forgotten. What was overlooked at the time was that the captured Soviet citizens were in law the nationals of a state with which neither Great Britain nor the United States had an extradition treaty, so that there was no sound juridical basis for their repatriation, however justified the USSR might be in treating them as criminals once they were within its jurisdiction. (Persons who had not become legally Soviet citizens after 1917 were not covered by the agreement.)

Decades later attempts were made to stigmatize this agreement as a piece of political cynicism or disgraceful kowtowing to Stalin. When the war ended British and American tribunals lent over backwards to rule that individuals sought by the Soviet authorities were not liable to repatriation because they were not Soviet citizens as defined by the agreement, while in the field many fingered for repatriation to the USSR were encouraged to jump off the backs of lorries or trains and take to the woods. Nevertheless appalling scenes took place as those destined for repatriation, aware of what was in store for them, committed or tried to commit suicide; and in the general post-war chaos some persons not covered by the agreement (mostly Ukrainians) were wrongly included among the repatriated and so presumably consigned to penal settlements or death.

CHAPTER 23

Mass Bombing

FRIGHTENING your enemy is the fundamental and presumably the oldest weapon of war. Starving him – hitting him where it hurts most – cannot be much less old. Mass bombing is the most modern way of trying to destroy both his morale and his economy at one and the same time. Where earlier warriors rushed upon their foes with painted bodies and hideous screams, or poisoned wells and beleaguered towns, their more sophisticated though hardly more civilized successors rain high explosives on factories and homes and set fire to whole cities. Only the techniques and the scale are new.

Perhaps the hallowed antiquity of the aim explains the fact that these new and fearful means were generally accepted in the Second World War. Air raids involving the indiscriminate killing of enormous numbers of civilians were the current step in the natural evolution of the art of war. The very concept of the civilian hardly remained valid. The traditional distinction between men setting forth to risk their lives and those who stayed behind out of range of death disappeared in the first half of the twentieth century. All were now combatants in their several ways. A civilian was a combatant who did not happen to be enrolled in the traditionally recognized fighting services; he was constantly proclaimed to be in the front line, a description implying that he was risking his life as much as anybody and would not think to complain about staking it. Even the deaths of children were accepted as, if not legitimate, yet logical consequences of war, occasioning special grief no doubt but relatively little indignation: that was the way things were.

At the beginning of the war Great Britain and France had promised, in response to a plea by Roosevelt, to confine bombing to strictly military targets provided the Germans did so too, but what was a military target was unclear and changeable. Yet there seemed to be one rule which still survived. There was still a sense of proportion and a feeling of uneasiness if it were disregarded, an acceptance of the ancient Greek tag that means must bear some relation to ends. To destroy factories or the people who worked in them, or the homes of people who worked in them, was perhaps legitimate; but to do these things – as for instance in the bombing of Dresden – without being able to point to a commensurate strategic advan-

tage was not just a sad necessity but also uncomfortably hard to justify –
either in general moral terms or in the strict application of the medieval
doctrine of Just War.

But if a majority acquiesced in what seemed to be the inevitability of
the deplorable, a minority clung to an older teaching. This minority,
trying to bend modern capabilities to the Christian faith instead of adapting the latter to the former, said that since all killing was wrong in the
absence of special justifying circumstances, indiscriminate mass killing
needed to be very meticulously justified indeed – and was not. Champions
of this tradition such as Dr George Bell, Bishop of Chichester, accepted
that the nature and context of war had so changed that many deaths,
hitherto regarded as unjustifiable, must be accepted, but they alleged that
there was still a line to be drawn somewhere and that the destruction
of closely packed residential areas, because they were closely packed residential areas, was a sin and – even in the absence of any international
convention on air warfare – a crime. Even if it was permissible to kill men
and women at work in factories, it was not permissible to kill men,
women and children in their homes. For keeping these Christian ideas
before men's minds in spite of the clatter of arms the Bishop of Chichester
was not elevated to the highest Christian office in England when the see
of Canterbury, for which many inside the church and out considered him
pre-eminently qualified, fell vacant at the end of 1944. He was even denied
the lesser see of York many years after the war was over and after it had
virtually been promised to him.

The advent of air power had brought with it a school of theorists who
alleged that this new weapon could contribute to war-making by doing
something that had never been done before, and could do this independently and without the help of the older sea and land forces. The Second
World War put this theory to the test and (with air power as it was before
the introduction of nuclear weapons) found it wanting. The prime aim of
assailing industry, communications and morale was to compel the surrender of the enemy even though his armed forces had suffered no irreversible defeat in the field. Defeat in workshop and homestead was to
take the place of defeat in the field as the first aim of strategy. This had
been the aim of naval blockade, but no navy had ever succeeded in
making a blockade more than an ancillary element in war-making. It had
neither broken morale nor brought the machinery of war to a halt. If air
power could succeed in these tasks, then the bomber aircraft would prove
a truly revolutionary weapon, more revolutionary than either the submarine which upset a number of military concepts in the First World War or
the tank which did the same in the Second.

Although aircraft had appeared in time to take part in the First World War, their role had been too limited and tentative for any settled conclusions to be drawn about the nature of air power. Consequently the question was much debated, *a priori* and often acrimoniously, between the wars. The importance of air power was conceded, but the best way to use an air force was hotly contested between those who thought of aircraft as a sort of extended artillery operating in conjunction with and under the control of army commanders and, on the other hand, those who held that air power had superseded land power. There were no even approximately accepted estimates of the amount of damage which a bomber force could inflict and most estimates were wildly excessive, largely owing to the unjustified assumption that if a bomber could reach its target, it would have relatively little difficulty in hitting it.

In 1917 Churchill, then Minister of Munitions, said:

It is improbable that any terrorization of the civil population which could be achieved by air attack would compel ... surrender ... we have seen the combative spirit of the people roused, and not quelled, by the German air raids. Nothing that we have learned of the capacity of the German population to endure suffering justifies us in assuming that they could be cowed into submission by such methods, or ... not be rendered more desperately resolved by them.

But in 1940 he thought that 'only the Air Force' could win the war. It is not clear what changed his mind, but it is probable that the champions of bombing had succeeded between the wars in implanting in many minds the belief that precision bombing could win a war. This involved considerable loss of life in the factories hit, but it did not envisage the mass bombing of civilians in their homes as well as their factories. But when it came to the test, precision bombing failed to be precise and area bombing was substituted for it as a means whereby an air force could live up to its claim to win a war.

The weightiest of the early champions of the independent role of the bomber were to be found in Italy and the United States – in particular General Giulio Douhet and General William Mitchell – but its most effective protagonist between the wars was the Royal Air Force under Air Marshal Sir Hugh Trenchard. The US Air Force was the most powerful of all bomber forces before the war ended, but the RAF was the first to acquire and operate a heavily armoured four-engined bomber; the Luftwaffe never had one in any number which counted. In spite of the urgent need to equip Fighter Command with modern fighters, the Air Council decided simultaneously to provide Bomber Command with four-engined bombers, ordered prototypes of the Stirling, Halifax and Manchester (later redesigned as the Lancaster) in 1937 and placed an order for 3,500 heavy bombers in October 1938 for delivery in the spring of 1942. Although these aircraft were not available as early as the Hurricane and Spitfire (with the result that Bomber Command's best crews had to fly antiquated Blenheims and die in them) they were brought into service in 1940–41. This decision by the Air Council, like the decision to build the eight-gun fighter, was undoubtedly justified, although it was partly the outcome of a conflict of views which was resolved by adopting both – by allowing Dowding to have his eight-gun fighter while at the same time going part of the way with the opposition to Dowding which decried the fighter arm and wanted to concentrate on a smashing bomber force, the symbol and justification of an independent air force.

In Germany a similar conflict was resolved in a different way. The accidental death of the protagonist of the heavy bomber, General Walther Wever, led to the cancellation of plans for such an aircraft, to a decision to rely on speed rather than armour, and to a disproportionate concentration on fighters, dive bombers and the role of army cooperation. The bomber became the Cinderella of the Luftwaffe. The Battle of Britain showed how ill judged this policy was. The Luftwaffe's relatively fast but lightly armed and lightly armoured medium bombers were defeated – as the RAF's obsolescent Blenheims had been over France a year earlier. For a time both sides were restricted to operations under the cover of darkness which were clearly not a war-winning effort. But although both sides were thus reduced to similar tactics, their circumstances were very different. The RAF's Bomber Command was conserving its strength, making few sorties in mass, keeping its losses down to about 3 per cent and awaiting the early delivery of the four-engined aircraft which were to take over from the two-engined Wellington, Whitley and Hampden; between the outbreak of war and the end of 1941 it increased its strength from 200 to 500 and the latter figure included the first few dozen Stirlings and Halifaxes. The Luftwaffe had nothing of the kind in view.

On the British side a further consequence was the evolution of a singularly independent Bomber Command under a Commander-in-Chief less amenable than his fellows to the overall strategic control of the Chief of the Air Staff and dedicated to proving the proposition that his force could win the war independently and was doing so and ought not to be impeded by diverting new bombers to Coastal Command's war against the U-boats. This position was further enhanced when the heavy bombers reached the Command in strength in 1943, their radar aids became increasingly precise and the invasion of France was postponed to 1944. Moreover by this time Bomber Command's pertinacious activity had won for it a position of independence from the Americans which the British army, preparing for the role of minor partner in Overlord, could never claim. British independence, which had been saved by Fighter Command in 1940, was symbolized thereafter by Bomber Command.

The first test of air power as an independent war winner as distinct from the army support provided by the Luftwaffe in Hitler's land campaigns in the west in 1940 came with the Battle of Britain. From the Luftwaffe's point of view this battle had two entirely different phases. The aim of the first was to destroy the Royal Air Force as a prelude to invasion. This attempt failed. It was succeeded by the attempt to destroy from the air British installations, homes and people, and in this phase the Luftwaffe operated wholly independently of the other two services and its bomber arm came into its own.

London and the industrial midlands were the principal targets in night-time attacks of which the most celebrated was the raid on Coventry on 14 November. Decades later a sinister myth about this raid arose, when it was put about that Churchill and others were forewarned about it by Ultra but failed to take steps to prevent or mitigate the deaths and destruction on the grounds that the safeguarding of the Ultra source was paramount. None of this is true. Ultra did not mention Coventry and the question of securing the Ultra secret did not arise.

Three days before the raid a decoded procedural Enigma message gave a list of frequencies and other directions for a German operation called Moonlight Sonata. It was evident from the message that the operation involved an exceptional effort. No date was given. No target was specified but broad target areas were referred to by code names. From other available evidence these were believed to be areas in and near London. In a separate part of the message appeared the word Korn. In retrospect it has been suggested that Korn stood for Coventry – on the grounds that the initial letters were the same, a common German practice with cover names. A day or two later another routine message set out bearings from a series of beam emplacements in northern France used by the Luftwaffe to direct its bomber raids. The bearings intersected at Birmingham, Coventry and Wolverhampton. These targetings indicated that, at some unspecified future date, these cities were likely to be bombed (which was probable in any case). At almost the same time a prisoner stated that Birmingham and Coventry were shortly to be bombed. His was the only specific reference to Coventry by name. These pieces of information were taken to portend a major raid at the full moon (15 November) with London as the main target and the west midlands the most likely alternative. Certainty would have to await the activation of the beams which could be relied upon to point to the night's target a few hours before sunset. Between 3 and 4 p.m. on 14 November monitoring of the beams' frequencies showed that Coventry would be the main target that night. The usual counter-measures were put in hand, including special precautions prescribed some weeks earlier, although one of these – the jamming of the beams – was rendered largely ineffective by a mathematical error. In addition 'intruder' operations were flown that night against German targets all the way from Berlin to the west coast of Brittany. Churchill, so far from pondering whether to save Coventry or safeguard Ultra, was under the impression that the raid was going to be on London and ordered the car that was taking him to the country to turn back to the capital.

Throughout the winter the Luftwaffe's bombers wrought a vast amount of destruction but with no strategic gains. If day bombing was too costly, night bombing was too inaccurate. In the first year of the war the British discovered that even fair-sized towns were missed by two thirds of the then inexperienced crews; during the winter of 1940–41 photographic reconnaissance and other intelligence revealed that results were not much better at night even though the enemy's night fighters (not yet equipped for night fighting) were virtually impotent. Bomber Command's claims, advanced with partisan fervour and, some thought, with a degree of partisan recklessness, were shown to be very wide of the mark. One solution was to choose larger targets. Attacks on oil refineries were abandoned but attacks on rail centres continued, because these could be significantly damaged even if the bombs fell as much as 1,000 yards wide of the aiming point. But even rail targets could not be usefully attacked without the help of the moon and rather than do nothing on moonless nights Bomber Command began raiding areas of population and hoping for the best. Intelligence continued to report a significant number of misses by miles. This combination of operational imprecision and reliable intelligence drove the Command, under the forceful leadership of Air Marshal Sir Arthur Harris, increasingly to area bombing. It was powerfully supported by Churchill's fiercely singleminded Principal Scientific Adviser, Professor Frederick Lindemann (Lord Cherwell), who believed that it was both possible and legitimate to destroy half the working-class houses in all the larger German cities, but was strongly contested by other eminent scientists, notably Professors Henry Tizard and P. M. S. Blackett, who alleged (correctly, as it turned out) that expectations were greatly exaggerated and argued for more selective operations such as the war against the U-boats. The policy in action cost the lives of over 55,000 aircrew in Bomber Command – and twice as many in the American air forces in Europe.

When Harris assumed command in February 1942 his force was ready to make massive attacks within a restricted radius and in March Bomber Command's main campaign of the war opened with a raid on the ancient and inflammable city of Lübeck which was chosen because it was lightly defended and easily accessible from the sea. This was the first operational appearance of the Lancaster. Four raids on Rostock, east of Lübeck and also on the Baltic, followed in April. These raids were experiments and demonstrations. They provoked a German counter-attack on cities in England which were also lightly defended and historically and artistically noteworthy – the so-called Baedeker raids on places like Bristol and Exeter. In May Bomber Command hit back with the 1,000-bomber raid on Cologne, for which training machines and crews were pressed into temporary service. The material damage was not great, but the boost to morale in the force and among civilians, the shock to the Germans and the impression made on allies, Resistance movements and neutrals may be thought to have justified the effort and the cost. German retaliation was ineffective.

In the latter part of this same year Bomber Command's effectiveness was increased by the formation of a corps of specially equipped and trained Pathfinders, which preceded the main body of aircraft to locate and mark their targets. Other technical aids to navigation and aiming followed. The ground operated Gee was supplemented by Oboe, which helped pilots to keep to the right course but had limited range and was subject to jamming, and from 1943 by the airborne radar H2S which enabled the bomb aimer to 'see' his target in spite of poor weather and the heights to which he might be forced by anti-aircraft guns and searchlights. Nevertheless precision bombing remained impossible except at ruinous cost. When in May 1943 the Möhne, Eder and Sorpe Dams were breached in an attempt to immobilize industry in the Ruhr (by dispersing the waters stored to provide energy for industries), the attack was made from the perilous height of sixty feet by a select band of nineteen Lancasters carrying a specially designed mine and crews who had been trained for months over replicas of the target area. On the night of the raid bad weather added to the perils: one aircraft and its crew made ten runs over the target before releasing its mine. Eight of the nineteen aircraft were lost, fifty-four of 133 men killed. This extremely heroic operation had been conceived before the war but rejected, and its outcome justified that rejection inasmuch as it proved to be horribly costly and only moderately successful. Six dams were attacked, two were breached; a number of German workers were drowned but the German grid was able to prevent serious industrial disruption. The air weapon was still at the stage of the bludgeon; precision bombing was suicidal. No comparable raid was ever carried out. The bombing of cities remained Bomber Command's main way of proving the claim of air power to be a war-winner, the civilian population being the principal target with factories as, in the words of a Bomber Command directive, a bonus.

In this context the Ruhr was marked out as the Command's main target. But it was very heavily defended. Essen and Düsseldorf were both attacked in the summer of 1942. In retrospect these raids underline how far Bomber Command was and remained an élite force. Essen was attacked by 1,000 aircraft but this was the last time that Bomber Command put 1,000 aircraft into the air for a single raid before 1944. During 1943 it gradually intensified its campaign against the Ruhr and extended it to more distant targets such as Hamburg and Berlin. Its strength in aircraft was not much greater at the beginning of 1943 than it had been a year earlier, but half of these were four-engined aircraft. In addition the Mosquito, one of the outstanding aircraft of the war, designed in the mid-thirties but comparatively unnoticed until now, had the range and speed to enable it to brave the German defences all the way to Berlin with a 4,000 lb. bomb. On the other hand the Luftwaffe's early warning system, ground controls and night fighter tactics were being greatly improved. When the war began Germany had radar which was more accurate than British radar but of shorter range and not linked with a ground control system of the same complexity and sophistication. As a result the bombing operations of 1942 defeated the German night defences, but in 1943 the tables were turned and the German night fighters began to strike almost as freely as though they were operating by day. Bomber losses rose to over 5 per cent of the attacking force. For several months it was not clear who was winning. Nerves were taut on both sides and in August 1943 the Chief of Staff of the Luftwaffe, General Hans Jeschonnek, committed suicide.

In Berlin, which suffered sixteen major night raids spread over four months in the winter of 1942–3 as well as additional American daylight raids in the latter part of this period, the damage was severe enough to cause a considerable exodus and close all schools, but even in the immediate aftermath of the raids less than half of the city's industries stopped work and many of the stoppages were brief. Hamburg on the other hand, which was attacked by night and day seven times in nine days in July and August 1942, was savagely and to some degree permanently wrecked with the assistance of two new techniques: the dropping of strips of tinfoil called Window which so confused the defence's radar scanners that bomber losses on the first night were only twelve out of 800; and the raising of fire storms by incendiary bombs which created fierce currents of flame rushing at temperatures of 1,000° centigrade to the centre of the storm at speeds of 100–150 m.p.h. and incinerating people above and below ground. At least 50,000 were killed in this way and a million more fled from the city: half the houses were destroyed and more than half the remainder damaged.

Yet morale broke in neither city. Bomber Command failed to bring German industry to a halt and the German defences pushed bomber losses up beyond 5 per cent and, early in 1944, even to 10 per cent. A new German airborne radar called Lichtenstein gave the night fighters longer range and a wider angle of vision and also enabled them to overcome Window. In an attack on Nuremberg in March the Command lost ninety-four aircraft out of 791 (12.5 per cent). In four and a half months 1,000 aircraft were totally lost and 1,682 more seriously damaged. Such losses were not tolerable. The Command's onslaught had been parried. No other arm suffered such casualties during the Second World War. The cost and the results were horribly reminiscent of Passchendaele. The only consolation was that German counter-attacks on London and elsewhere in the early months of 1944 had been thwarted by the defences, and the Luftwaffe could no longer even carry out reconnaissance flights over Great Britain.

The American strategic bombing offensive was showing the same pattern of destruction at great cost and without commensurate results. At the Casablanca conference of January 1943 Roosevelt and Churchill had agreed that strategic bombing was for the time being their principal weapon against Hitler and their principal way of helping Stalin. At that time, however, the US air forces were comparatively small and stretched over many theatres (the Pacific and Atlantic, North Africa and the Middle East), and it was not until the second half of that year that the US Eighth and Fifteenth Air Forces were able to add significantly to the British effort: the first American raid on Germany was made on 17 August 1942 by eighteen aircraft of which twelve found their target.

The Americans entered the battle with the conviction that area bombing was useless and precision bombing possible. The main instrument of American bombing was the four-engined B17 or Flying Fortress, an aircraft bristling with guns and designed to fight off any enemy's daylight fighter attacks. But the B17s were badly mauled by the German fighters and the American commanders drew the conclusion that effective precision bombing of the German economy as a whole must be preceded by the destruction of German fighter production – by precision bombing. The duel which followed was weighted against the Americans because the

ALLIED BOMBING OF GERMANY

Main centres of civilian casualties
Main areas of bombing
Industrial areas
Aircraft industry factories
Main railways
Canals
International boundaries

~ARTHUR BANKS~

EAST PRUSSIA

POLAND

Baltic Sea

North Sea

HOLLAND

BELGIUM

LUX

FRANCE

CZECHOSLOVAKIA

AUSTRIA

Breslau
Rostock
Tutow
Berlin
Dresden
Magdeburg
Bernberg
Leipzig
Chemnitz
Halle
Hamburg
Kiel
Lübeck
Hannover
Brunswick
Halberstadt
Aschersleben
Gotha
Kassel
Frankfurt
Schweinfurt
Regensburg
Nürnberg
Fürth
Munich
Augsburg
Stuttgart
Darmstadt
Wiesbaden
Coblenz
Cologne
Wuppertal
Dortmund
Essen
Duisburg
Düsseldorf
Bremen
Bremerhaven

Oder
Elbe
Weser
Ems
Rhine
Danube

May 1942
First 1,000 bomber raid

0   100
Miles

fighter factories were not only specially well defended but numerous, dispersed and far away. An attack in August 1943 on the Messerschmitt factory at Regensburg coupled with an attack on ball-bearing factories in Schweinfurt came to grief with excessive losses. A further attack on Schweinfurt two months later caused the loss of more than a quarter of the attacking force. The conclusion drawn this time was that successful precision bombing at tolerable cost was impossible without a fighter escort capable of going all the way with the bombers. The right aircraft happened to be at hand. The American P51 (Mustang), already in service with the RAF in a modest way, was chosen for the job and equipped with long-range tanks which enabled it to cover the required distances without losing too much speed or its capacity to outmanoeuvre the German fighters. This aircraft played a role as remarkable in its way as the Spitfire or the Mosquito, for after it had been put into production with the intensity for which American manufacturers were famous, it enabled the B17s, withdrawn from the battle in the autumn of 1943, to resume their offensive, and this combination overcame the German defences. The German fighters were eliminated from the battle by their fighter foes and the American and British bombers were together able to undertake round-the-clock bombing of Germany and, from the summer of 1944, to pound an economy which had abruptly begun to disintegrate irretrievably fast.

Hitler had not prepared his economy for a long war and Germany was not ready for one when it came. In 1939–41 Germany was able to fight and win a series of campaigns on a half-stretched economy, but it could not overrun the whole continent on this basis, and after 1941 it had to convert to a war economy in the face of the crippling campaigns in the east and the increasingly severe bombardment from the west. Germany was not short of equipment or factory space; it started the war with twice as many machine tools, and multipurpose ones, than Great Britain and probably still had more than the United States half-way through the war. Its vital industries were as efficient as any in Great Britain or France and its output of coal and steel was greater than the combined British and French output; but it was economically inferior to the United States and the USSR, it was short of practically all minerals, and its steel and aluminium industries were dependent on imported iron ore and bauxite until sources had been overrun by the German armies. Stocks of some raw materials were low when the war began but they were replenished for a time by the bonuses of conquest. Germany's greatest economic weakness was the inefficiency of its administrative machine. Hitler's government was ill adapted to make the huge adjustments required in order to fight and beat the Russians and the Americans at one and the same time. Nazi Germany had no single central administrative authority; it was run by discordant authorities dominated by potentates more attuned to mutual in-fighting than to working together against outside enemies; its industries as well as its administration were a tangle. Hitler himself was in no sense a planner or an organizer. He seems to have regarded talk as a substitute for planning and, from the records that have been left behind of his sessions with his favourite associates, it would appear that the talk, which was of a miserably low intellectual order, was intended less for use than for ostentation. Nevertheless Germany was astonishingly successful for two years in sustaining an enormous war effort and expanding its war production.

The conquests of 1939–41 were regarded, from the economic point of view, as bonuses which enabled the government to fight wars and increase the German standard of living at the same time. Domestic consumption in Germany rose to the end of 1941. More significant, however, in the longer run were the failures of 1939–41; the failure to finish off Great Britain and, more serious still, the failure to defeat the Russians before the first winter of the war in the east. These failures forced Hitler to expand his arms base, his labour force and also his armed forces. The latter, which stood at 5.6 million in May 1940, expanded voraciously and, at the same date in the next three years, reached 7.2, 8.6 and 9.5 million; the rise of nearly a million in 1942–3 was achieved despite losses of the same extent in the same period, and with further losses of 1.6 million in 1943–4 the total armed manpower began to fall. In October 1944 all available males between sixteen and sixty were mobilized in the *Volkssturm*, to fight and not to labour.

During these same years the German labour force had dwindled steadily, until by the end of the war it had been reduced by a quarter. This decline was not made good by the conscription of women (as was done in the much more tightly regimented British war economy), and although the proportion of German women at work in wartime Germany rose, their numbers did not, partly because of the Nazi doctrine that woman's place was in the home and partly owing to the afflux of foreign labour which obscured the need for a more extensive conscription of German labour. During the war the numbers of Germans at work increased by no more than the natural increase of the population, whereas in Great Britain and the United States the number of workers rose by 15 per cent over and above natural increase. (If, on the other hand, the significant manpower figures should embrace the armed services as well as industry, then Germany was using in these joint occupations a smaller proportion of its population than Great Britain.) As we have seen in an earlier part of this book, the German labour shortage was met by putting prisoners of war onto war production and raiding conquered countries for slavelike labour, but although the labour so acquired ran into millions of men (three million by May 1941, over four million a year later and over six million from May 1943), foreign labour was no substitute for German labour, especially in skilled jobs.

The re-orientation of German industry was begun by Fritz Todt, a brilliant technician who created at short notice an organization which stood up to unparalleled enemy bombardment for nearly three years after his death in an aircraft accident in February 1942. He was succeeded by Albert Speer, an indifferent architect with an aesthetic taste akin to Hitler's but also a gifted and versatile amateur with a flair for organization and an excellent sense for capturing and retaining Hitler's trust and friendship. Like Schacht, Speer has been judged, not without equivocation, to have been a non-Nazi technocrat who served the Nazi government in spite of his better nature and his better intelligence. Again like Schacht, he escaped the death penalty at the Nuremberg trial, where he was sentenced to twenty years' imprisonment for crimes against humanity (Schacht was acquitted on all counts), and he has since been treated by historians with some leniency, partly owing to his courage in refusing at the end to obey the (now decrepit) Führer's orders to lay Germany waste and partly because he survived the Nazi era to talk and write about it with some intelligence and show himself decent after the event. Speer's wartime achievement was considerable but not perhaps as remarkable as has been made out. He kept the German aircraft industry going in spite of crippling shortages and furious bombing, but what he and it produced was quantity rather than quality and the last aircraft of the Third Reich were inferior replicas of finer models. He believed in centralized capitalist control with the emphasis on the large leading industrial concerns as opposed to the Nazi partiality for the little man and the regionalism embodied in the local boss-rule of the Gauleiters. He kept the conveyor belts moving. Hitler backed him for three years, made him Minister for Armaments and Munitions (later Minister for Armaments and War Production) and defended him against satraps like Goering (as head of the Four Year Plan) and Funk (at the Ministry of Economics) and also against the army's own Office of War Production in his efforts to rationalize the German economy in terms of the overriding need for weapons. But Speer never won a completely dominant position. Goering and Milch managed to exclude aircraft production from his empire (except partially in 1944–5), and the odious and jealous Sauckel retained the control and procurement of labour to the end. Nevertheless Speer succeeded in more than doubling Germany's war production by the middle of 1943 and more than trebling it by the middle of 1944. Under his direction Germany produced arms in great quantities; in the latter part of the period it produced more weapons than the available divisions could use.

The areas of principal concern in the defence of Germany's war machine against air attack were the aircraft industry, the synthetic fuel plants, the Ruhr's coal and steel production and the rail, road and water services which linked these activities and distributed their output. In the end the interdependence of the different parts of the German economy proved to be its Achilles' heel. This was shown most clearly by the experiences of the aircraft and fuel industries.

Aircraft production, which reached a first wartime peak in the middle of 1943 and then fell back, rose again in 1944 and surpassed all previous records in the autumn of that year. But the squadrons had by then no fuel for their aircraft, because for a time there had been too few aircraft to defend the fuel plants. The pre-war target for the German aircraft industry was 2,000 a month, increased to 2,300 shortly after the war began. Actual production was 700–800 a month from 1935 to 1940. During the first part of this period the types which played the biggest part in the war were being evolved. During the first two years of war Hitler, still planning on a short war, was not worried about production or interested in the development of further new types since he believed that the war would be over before they could be brought into service. In 1941 there was a modest increase in production and in 1942 a well-organized expansion in Germany and occupied Europe which raised production from 1,000 to 1,600 a month. In the summer of 1943 the damage inflicted by allied bombing – although it was repaired before the end of the year – forced the German Air Ministry, which still had more than thirty different types in production, to streamline the industry. Production, which had risen by June 1943 to 2,316 and had been set a new target of 3,000, was cut back by the raids to below 1,900.

In 1944 the industry was put under new management. Speer and Milch severely cut back the production of bombers, introduced a seventy-two hour week with high wages and improved working conditions, created new factories underground and provided the older ones with better defences, improved the repair services and raised the target first to 6,400 a month and then to 7,400. As a result production, which had again fallen at the beginning of the year to 1,369, rose in September to 3,538 new aircraft, while damaged aircraft returning to squadrons provided another 776, almost twice as many as in January; the production of single-engined fighters was more than doubled between February and June. Of a total of 113,514 aircraft produced during the war 40,593 were produced in 1944. The annual production of fighter aircraft in 1939–44 inclusive was 605: 2,746: 3,744: 5,515: 10,898: 25,285. Even in 1945 production of fighters almost reached a total of 5,000 for the four months before the war stopped. But this astonishing riposte to the bombing of the aircraft industry was in vain.

Until the end of 1943 Speer had been able to answer the allied bombing offensive. Reconstruction kept pace with destruction, stocks of vital materials (mostly large at the beginning of the war) were not dangerously run down and essential imports were maintained in spite of damage to railways and rolling stock. In 1944 the allied air forces were required to combine their attack on Germany with preliminary operations in aid of Overlord, but their own resources in the production of aircraft and the training of pilots enabled them, ominously for Germany, to fulfil both roles; the weight of the American attack was enormously increased, so much so that in one month in 1944 more American bombs were dropped than during the whole of 1942. Bomber Command similarly dropped in the last quarter of 1944 a bomb load four times as heavy as in the same part of 1943 and twenty times as heavy as in the same part of 1942. The synthetic oil industry, which was singled out for special attention in 1943–4, began to falter. Although the damage inflicted by a first series of raids was repaired, Speer's miraculous reconstruction services did not manage to cope so fully with a second series, stocks began to be drawn down alarmingly and production fell below demand. During nine consecutive days in September 1944 no aviation fuel whatever was produced except on one day, and production for the month was the hopelessly inadequate total of 9,400 tons. A pause in the bombing owing to bad weather gave some respite, but Germany's air defences were, if not totally eliminated, at least rendered negligible for the last six months of the war. When Dresden was bombed in February 1945, there was no defence of the city. Yet the aircraft industry was still producing 1,000–2,000 aircraft a month when the war ended.

This critical interdependence of aircraft and fuel production was made the more acute by the concentration of German heavy industry in the Ruhr and the dependence of industry outside the Ruhr on coal from the Ruhr. Germany was never short of coal but the damage done to communications in and around the Ruhr prevented Ruhr coal (80 per cent of Germany's output) from being moved to where it was needed. At the end of 1944 coal was being transported out of the Ruhr at one quarter of the normal rate and a few months later, after the winter's respite, this traffic was again halved. This dislocation of the Ruhr, combined with the conquest of Silesia and Lorraine by the Russians and Americans, strangled the steel industry which produced in the last quarter of 1944 less than 4 million tons in place of a projected 37.2 million. Other sectors of the economy collapsed with equal or greater suddenness in a chain reaction. At the end all fronts, except one, collapsed together – the fronts where the armies were still fighting and the economic front which finally succumbed under air attack.

The one front which held out with incredible tenacity was morale at home. This was the achievement of Joseph Goebbels, Minister of Propaganda and one of the few masters of his craft among the Nazi chieftains. What Speer did for Germany's war industry Goebbels did for its morale. Ultimately Hitler's greatest debt was to Goebbels whom he had once described – in an interview with a right-wing editor as early as 1931 – as his Field Marshal on the spiritual front, the man whom he would make Minister of Propaganda when he came to power and who would occupy a post as important as that of Foreign Minister or Chief of the General Staff.

Propaganda – the attempt to make an impact on large numbers of people in order to affect their mood and their actions, to get them to change their minds or not to change their minds, to get them to act in a certain way or not to – is an ancient instrument. It was modernized and immensely extended in the twentieth century by the invention of radio, and Goebbels was one of its master practitioners. He was not universally successful. In addressing himself to foreigners he was less adept than some British propagandists who had a better understanding of the society – and the language – of their enemy than Goebbels ever had. Also, like all propagandists, he found there was a limit to the extent to which he could affect people who basically did not want to believe what he had to say. But with German audiences he was very successful not only before the war but even in the face of the horrors of the Russian campaigns and mass bombing. He was appointed to his post a few weeks after Hitler became Chancellor and he held it until he and his entire family died with Hitler in Berlin.

He staffed the executive side of his Ministry with bright young men, half of them with a university education, and he taught them how to appeal to the emotions and the reason of the masses at one and the same time, so that an audience which had had its feelings roused would be captured not merely for the moment but also enduringly because a message had lodged in their minds. There were no limits to Goebbels's emotive appeals. He set out to intoxicate audiences and throw them into hysteria. The most rabble-rousing speeches of western politicians were by his standards sedate. In the years before and after the Nazi capture of power in 1933 Germany was in a state of crisis and Goebbels's techniques were designed to benefit from this feeling of crisis and to perpetuate it. People were screwed up, perils and evils were emphasized, the situation was presented as one which called above all for action – and for a man who could lead into action and must therefore be followed. From 1933 to 1939 German opinion was never allowed to let up, still less when war came. Goebbels could not make the Germans want war – there was a wild outburst of joyful relief in Berlin in October 1939 upon a false report that the British government had fallen and the war was over – but he created a mentality of endeavour and was able during the war to foster, against the odds, a solid mood of endurance. A crucial element in his technique was simplicity. Even in the most febrile and far-ranging tirades Nazi orators pinpointed and repeated one or two essential facts or arguments, eschewing generalization, representing issues as conflicts between good and evil, making them concrete and personal. While hammering away at favourite themes like the wickedness of Jews, the ill treatment of the Sudeten Germans, the need for *Lebensraum*, the western democracies' sinister but feeble attempts to encircle Germany, atrocity stories from the republican side in the civil war in Spain or, after the war began, successes in the field, Goebbels and his disciples held their audiences by the actuality of specific illustrations, true or false, which went home.

Goebbels made great use of shows: sporting events, funerals, festivals of every kind. Using entertainment to capture the public was not new – Thomas Cromwell had subsidized plays which were performed in town squares and on village greens throughout England in order to rub in Henry VIII's case against the papacy – but Goebbels made the most of its vastly increased scope. The Olympic Games of 1936 were turned into a propaganda event of the first magnitude. Goebbels also realized the importance of films, commissioning documentaries and newsreels and bringing pressure to bear on the film industry (which was not brought wholly under government control until it was nationalized in 1943) to make the sort of films he wanted. War films were used to impress neutrals as well as to fortify morale at home, where newsreels were compulsorily shown in all cinemas. These films, like Nazi oratory, were simple and repetitive. The press was not only regimented and bullied, but overwhelmed by official hand-outs, press conferences and special briefings. The number of newspapers in Germany sank during the Nazi period from 4,700 to fewer than 1,000. Uniformity, imposed by decree and by fear, produced dullness but once again it simplified the issues. The reader did not get the impression that one paper was saying one thing and another another, so that it was impossible to know what to think.

In the first years of war Goebbels's task was made comparatively easy by the turn of events. He extolled Hitler as the infallible leader who told his people what he was going to do and did it. A cheap radio set (with a limited range) had been marketed just before the war and about 70 per cent of German households had a radio. Goebbels made play with the taunt that the British were fighting to the last Frenchman and ascribed the collapse of France to racial miscegenation, but by July he was restraining overconfidence about the collapse of Great Britain and was soon advising editors not to tell their readers that London was a heap of ruins: British resistance was futile but it might go on for a time.

The invasion of the USSR gave him a new line. He represented the German attack as pre-emptive, alleging that Hitler had certain intelligence of a Russian attack, and he plugged the theme of the brutal and subhuman Slav. He did not minimize the rigours of the new war. After a calculated pause of a week came twelve special announcements (*Sondermeldungen*), all issued on the same day – a Sunday – and taking up practically the whole of the day. This battery of victory communiqués created an overwhelming effect commensurate with the scale of operations in the east and gave anxious Germans, who had been struggling to make sense of unfamiliar names scattered about their maps, the assurance that details did not matter. But Goebbels was careful not to commit himself to the statement that the war was won and he was therefore all the more horrified when Hitler and his press chief, Otto Dietrich, declared in October with premature exuberance that it was. Goebbels had already foreseen that his theme was as likely to be the preaching of total war as the proclaiming of total victory, and as winter came on he reverted to his sober warnings, started a campaign to collect clothes for the men freezing at the front and made regular reports on the response to this appeal. On the more optimistic side he could at least claim that Hitler had done better than Napoleon in spite of General Winter and the brutish tenacity of the Russian soldier, and that the gains in oil, grain, iron ore and other materials were considerable. Rommel's victories also provided good cheer.

From 1942 Goebbels, as the chief upholder of the home front, had to counter the general decline in Germany's fortunes and two major catastrophes in the defeats of the German armies in Russia and the heavy bombing of German cities. At first the army's communiqués about Stalingrad had been optimistic, the strategic importance of the city was underlined and its capture was to be the climax of the war in the east. The capitulation of the Sixth Army was a tremendous blow and Goebbels, not without courage, took the unique step of issuing a *Sondermeldung* about a defeat instead of a victory. It was accompanied by muffled drums, the

national anthem and a three-minute silence, and all places of entertainment were closed for three days. Two weeks later a vast – and picked –
audience was assembled in the *Sportpalast* in Berlin. Ten questions were
put and answered to counter enemy propaganda that Germany had had
enough and to pledge total war. In the shadow of Stalingrad this demonstration probably stiffened morale but it also made people think that
total catastrophe might be on the way.

The tenth anniversary of Hitler's coming to power was marked by the
first assertion that capitulation was out of the question: it was also the
first mention of capitulation. The eastern battles in 1943 and 1944 increased the foreboding. There were only three *Sondermeldungen* in 1943;
there had been sixty-five in 1941. The fall of Mussolini did not help.
Hitler himself became remote, seldom appearing or speaking. Allied propaganda suggested that he had been driven to silence by his own mistakes;
he had no words to explain what had gone wrong. Goebbels countered
with a new image of Hitler as the supreme sufferer, stoically enduring like
Frederick the Great in adversity, shunning the limelight unlike his flashy
and temporarily successful opponents. At the same time, as disaster threatened, Goebbels worked to inculcate the feeling that the only way to avert
it was to stick by Hitler.

Mass bombing was Goebbels's biggest problem. When bombing first
began, Goebbels had repeated with sarcastic comment the exaggerated
claims made by the British Air Ministry on the basis of aircrews' instant
reports, but these tactics no longer sufficed when the destruction became
heavy. Goebbels did not seek to deny it. He used it to stir up hatred
against the enemy. He also showed himself all over Berlin, inspecting raid
damage, showing that a Minister cared and was in control, and so forestalling panic and a break in morale. He initiated an anti-defeatist campaign
(strengthened by a few death sentences) and although he could not prevent
the German mood from drooping he succeeded in preventing it from
turning into action against the government. His plea that this was the
time for government and people to hang together was sufficiently widely
accepted. Appointed Plenipotentiary for Total War in 1944 he extended
normal working hours, conscripted women up to the age of fifty, cut
entertainment, schooling and university courses and by these and other
means ensured that Germans should go on fighting not just because they
were afraid of the Gestapo but also because they were persuaded that this
was the right thing to do. With a part of their minds they knew that they
were defeated and that fighting on meant postponing the end without
altering the outcome. But because Goebbels spoke to them straight, they
took what he said as straight. By telling them, as one adult to another,

that things were bad, he dissuaded them from facing the fact that they were hopeless. They behaved like a man who knows that he is condemned to death with cancer but prefers to believe the doctor who tells him that he has appendicitis. At the same time Goebbels piled on the horror of Slavic hordes about to sweep over Germany devastating the land and debauching its maidens. The nearer it came, the worse did Goebbels make fate sound, so that there seemed to be no purpose in doing anything except go through the motions of warding off the inescapable.

In the final assessment the bombers' contribution to the defeat of Germany must be judged a weighty one in the final stages of the war. In the light of the pretensions of the Douhet-Mitchell school of air strategists two questions arise: Did the bombers win the war? If they did not, could they have done? The answer to the first question is no. The German armies were fatally defeated by the Russians in July 1943 and at that point the bomber onslaught had barely begun and had caused no decisive damage; it did not do so for another year. The second question is hypothetical. Air power equipped with nuclear weapons may be a war-winning weapon in the sense that it can compel the surrender of an enemy whose armed forces in the field are undefeated. There was, however, no such air power in the European theatre in the Second World War. On the other hand it can be plausibly argued that the surrender of Japan after two nuclear bombs was a consequence of the overwhelming superiority of American air power over Japan's total defences. It is all a question of degree and there is nothing to prove that the fatal imbalance between attack and defence could be achieved by nuclear weapons alone. If the allied air forces had been even stronger than they were, and if allied air policy had not wavered between general attacks on population and morale and selective attacks on economic nerve centres and bottlenecks, then Germany might have been brought to surrender without the necessity for a major invasion and the hard-fought campaigns from Normandy to the heart of Europe. Such a possibility cannot be disproved, but the experiences of the American and British air commands show that this strategy would have been exceptionally costly in lives. It is moreover all but certain that, in a war in which Germany was being attacked by the USSR as well as by themselves, the western allies would never willingly have confined themselves to strategic bombing or have delayed their invasion in such a way as to allow the Russians to occupy the whole of Germany.

Leaving aside the inadmissible claim that bombing did win, or could have won, the war on its own, there emerges a different question: how far bombing, judged as a contributory instead of an independent factor, shortened the war. No precise answer to such a question is possible, but in general it is pertinent to recall that allied bombing diverted German air power from the offensive fronts to the defence of the Reich and diverted German labour – 1–1.5 million men, many of them skilled – to repair and reconstruction works. Perhaps these contributions should be adjudged significant subsidiary sources of Germany's defeat. They cannot be held to be decisive but they must have made the allied victory somewhat easier and somewhat quicker. Both area bombing and precision bombing made this kind of contribution, for even if a government at war is more intent on protecting its factories than its industrial proletariat, there is nevertheless a point beyond which it cannot leave its people undefended and unhoused. Speer's evidence after the war was that precision bombing could do crucial damage; but until the last phase the allies were not able to carry out effective precision bombing operations. Area bombing, to which they resorted instead, paid only a small dividend and one which those who bring ethics into the equation may well regard as too small.

CHAPTER 24
The Western Fronts

AMERICAN and British armies set foot on the mainland of Europe in Italy in September 1943 and in France in the following June. The armies in Italy reached Rome two days before the invasion of France. They had spent over eight months fighting their way up the peninsula against tough German opposition in harsh mountain country and horrible weather.

When they landed in Italy the allies hoped to be in Rome before the end of that year. Hopes in the Italian theatre were apt to be exaggerated. Churchill in particular had got into the habit of regarding anything to do with Italy as soft. The Americans were more sceptical. The opposition was German, not Italian, and it was commanded by Kesselring, who had prepared three defensive positions south of Rome. The allies' best hope was to strike rapidly northward with Clark's US Fifth Army, while Montgomery supported his advance on the eastern side of the peninsula. But both Clark and Montgomery made slow progress. Heavy rains helped the defenders. Both armies gained ground but no road to Rome was opened. For the Germans the worst consequence of the landings in Italy was the establishment of the US Fifteenth Air Force on Italian airfields whence it could attack targets in Germany, northern Italy, Austria and Rumania.

At the beginning of 1944 the attack towards Rome was renewed with a frontal attack in the centre and a simultaneous landing at Anzio forty miles south of Rome on the west coast – the place where Nero was born and the Apollo Belvedere found. The Germans, crediting the allies with an adventurousness which they did not display, believed that they would land north of Rome at some place like Leghorn. The Anzio landing was hurriedly planned and timidly directed. The initial landings on 22 January were practically unopposed and a daring commander might have made a dash for Rome and got there, but General Lucas, the commander of the expedition and a man of basically pessimistic temperament, on discovering that there were no Germans in his path behaved as though there were. Kesselring was given time to organize a defence and seized it. He disposed of reserves which his opponents, ignoring intelligence assessments, had underrated. By the end of a week the expedition was in trouble and when the Anglo-American force made a bid to advance from its carefully consolidated beachhead on 30 January, it incurred savage losses (one unit lost 761 men out of 767). The Germans counter-attacked in the first week in February; allied losses mounted, morale and confidence sank; the allies were all but evicted; the German attack was renewed in mid-February and after four days of heavy fighting the allies were again on the brink of total defeat when they saw to their surprise that the Germans, unaware how close they were to victory, were drawing off. The Anzio venture had failed to achieve its purpose but the Germans had failed to eliminate the beachhead.

In the centre of the peninsula the allies were equally frustrated. The two sides were roughly equal in numbers on the ground but the Germans were more easily reinforced, as well as exceptionally well equipped; the allies offsetting these German advantages by superiority in the air, in intelligence and in deception. The main allied thrust was not successful until the middle of May and then only after one of the more questionable actions of the war – the destruction from the air of the abbey of Monte Cassino.

Of Kesselring's three defensive positions the strongest – the Gustav line – contained the famous Benedictine abbey, founded in 524 by the creator of western monasticism and the repository of one of Europe's most prized libraries. Although it no longer held the bones of the saint, which had been removed to the banks of the Loire thirteen centuries earlier in order to save them from the Lombards, the abbey had been temporarily enriched with pictures and other works of art removed from Naples to escape the war. The Germans supervised the removal to Rome of the abbey's treasures and most of its monks in October 1943 when the US Fifth Army, by crossing the Volturno and then the Sangro rivers, threatened the Gustav line. Monte Cassino, although an obstacle to allied progress, was not of prime military importance since it was surrounded by higher peaks and the combatants were understood to have assured the Pope that the abbey would be neither fortified by the one side nor attacked from the air by the other.

At the outset of 1944 the allies were moving arduously towards the town and abbey. A British corps under Clark's command crossed the Garigliano and French troops under Juin (campaigning with Chateaubriand in his pocket) crossed the Rapido north of Monte Cassino. The abbey, in which the abbot and five monks still remained, was hit for the first time in January but a first allied attack on the town failed after three weeks of heavy losses in foul weather. Although American and French forces got to within striking distance of both town and abbey they could not cover the last thousand yards and a final assault by New Zealand and Indian units was thrown back by superior German numbers and artillery fire.

On the allied side opinions differed about whether this artillery fire came from the abbey. The Germans denied that the abbey was being used for military purposes but their enemies were not prepared to believe anything they said and General Ira C. Eaker, who was one of a number of senior commanders to make a personal air reconnaissance, reported that he had seen German troops in the abbey. The allied command declared that the abbey would no longer be spared and although American, British and French generals opposed its bombardment it was attacked on 15 February by 142 Flying Fortresses and destroyed.

This operation was, however, fruitless. The town and hill were not taken and the battle was resumed a month later with a heavy air and artillery bombardment which reduced the town of Monte Cassino to a shambles. The New Zealanders went in again, only to be checked by German resistance and uncleared rubble. They failed to reach the heart of the town. A complementary attack by the Indians on the monastery likewise failed after getting within 400 yards. A week later both town and monastery were still in German hands and the attack was called off after a final New Zealand attempt to dislodge the defenders. The road to Rome remained blocked. The best that the allies could claim was that they were holding twenty-two German divisions out of some other battle. The strategy of the Italian campaign had postulated the surrender of Italy and the creation of fresh options leading the allies to the Balkans or the Danube or into Germany itself. The collapse of Italian resistance had, however, produced a German resistance stout enough to bar all these routes, and the longer the campaign lasted the more pointless it became. Its object had been to give the allies useful victories in the interval between the re-conquest of the Mediterranean and the re-conquest of France, but the nearer the French invasion approached the more the Italian campaign became a sideshow producing nothing important which could not be obtained by invasion in the west.

But Kesselring's position was never more than a defensive one in a theatre of secondary importance. He could expect little in the way of reinforcements and in May he was finally forced to abandon all his positions south of Rome. British and Polish units of the Eighth Army opened a new attack which was at first held but French forces then executed a spectacular turning movement in almost impossibly difficult mountain country and forced the Germans to evacuate Monte Cassino at last on 17 May. On the next day the Poles entered the ruined abbey and the British the town, and the Germans began to retreat all along the line. The forces in the Anzio bridgehead broke out but were too slow to cut off the Germans who retired north of Rome in good order. Kesselring abandoned the Italian capital after declaring it an open city and established a fresh holding line through Lake Trasimene and a stronger one, the Gothic line, in Tuscany.

Clark entered Rome two days before Overlord, not six months as Churchill had hoped. General Sir Harold Alexander, the overall commander of the Fifth and Eighth Armies, was now in a position to exploit their successes, but the timing was wrong. Alexander's dual purpose was to entice German divisions into the Italian theatre and then keep them there or cut them off. He wanted to maintain both his armies at full strength, force the Gothic line and then move either left into France or right into Austria, sucking more German troops into the theatre as he intensified the threat to Germany itself. Although the soft underbelly of the Axis had proved less soft than Churchill had imagined, it was now pierced and the Italian campaign was on the verge of justification. On the last day of May Churchill promised Alexander his full support for keeping his armies up to strength, but Churchill's was no longer the deciding voice and Alexander was obliged to relinquish part of his forces for an invasion of southern France (operation Anvil or Dragoon) complementary to Overlord. The Americans, supported at first by Maitland Wilson and believing that Kesselring was more likely to be milked than reinforced, wanted to make a bigger thrust up the Rhône valley than up Italy, and after bitter argument they prevailed. Anvil turned out to be an unnecessary reinforcement of Overlord but Alexander lost seven divisions and part of his air strength and was told to go ahead with this reduced force; Kesselring on the other hand got four extra divisions.

Retreating in his own time, Kesselring reached the Gothic line in August and then held up the allies long enough for the autumn rains and mud to come to his assistance. Churchill and Alexander were still hoping to make for Vienna, but the Americans refused to reinforce a theatre which had become decidedly secondary, and after a limited German counter-attack in the last week of the year operations were suspended and more allied troops were withdrawn from Italy. The last hope of staking a claim to be heard in the post-war settlement of central Europe by effecting a junction with the Russians in Vienna had gone.

It had never been a realistic one. Victory in Italy in 1943 was beyond the allies' grasp and victory in 1944 was pointless because there was never any thought of making the winning thrust anywhere but in France. By 1944 no other front could hope for the men and material needed for so decisive a role.

In November 1943 Rommel was sent from a semi-active command in northern Italy to inspect the coastal defences of the western front from Dunkirk to Brittany. He found them rusty, uncoordinated and manned by second- or third-rate divisions which were well below strength. By this date the allies had already chosen the general area in which they would land but their decision was not known to the Germans. The alternatives were obvious. Either they might cross the Channel at its narrowest point and make their landings east of the Somme, or they might land in Normandy west of the Somme. The principal argument in favour of this latter plan was the unsuitability of south-east England for the accumulation of the vast quantities of men and stores which were to be put into the invasion and above all the meagre capacity of the Kentish ports compared with the Portsmouth-Southampton area. In addition the latter was less vulnerable to attack and less open to reconnaissance; and on the other side the strongest German defences were in the Pas de Calais. These considerations outweighed the disadvantages of the longer sea passage and the opening of the new front further away from the frontiers of Germany, and the allies settled without much debate on the bay of the Seine.

When Rommel arrived in France he found that the Commander-in-Chief West, Field Marshal von Rundstedt, inclined to the view that the invasion would come in the Pas de Calais. OKW took the same view. Rommel, however, queried it and as the months went by the pattern of allied air activities and the absence of mining in the bay of the Seine strongly supported him. By the spring the Germans were nine tenths convinced that the main attack would be delivered in Normandy but some of them, Hitler in particular, expected either diversionary or follow-up operations in the Pas de Calais: they were deceived by spoof radio activity simulating the presence of large forces in south-east England and their inferiority in the air was by now so marked that they could not survey even Kent accurately enough to establish that there were no armies there.

More important than this initial divergence about where the invasion was to be expected was the dispute about how to meet it. Rundstedt saw no hope of preventing a landing. His strategy was to accept it and then throw the enemy back into the sea by a counter-attack. Rommel on the other hand believed that, in France as in North Africa, Sicily and Italy, once the allies had gained a foothold they could not be forced off it again. He proposed therefore to deny rather than repel the invasion, by mining the shore and the beaches and by engaging the enemy before he could cross the vital hundreds of yards between the water's edge and the first natural cover beyond the open sands and rocks. Hitler decided in favour of Rommel and appointed him to command, under Rundstedt, the group of armies deployed from Holland to Brittany, but insisted with characteristic caution on retaining large forces east of the Somme after as well as before the invasion and with characteristic indecision on holding much of the armour in reserve outside Rommel's immediate command and immediate operational area. These prevarications proved specially perilous because allied air supremacy, and the extensive destruction of communications in the weeks before the battle began, immobilized German forces caught in the wrong place. On the eve of the invasion Rundstedt had sixty divisions, of which forty-three were available to Rommel (the remaining seventeen were south of the Loire), but of these forty-three only eighteen were in Normandy; five were in Holland, one in the Channel Islands and no fewer than nineteen in Belgium and France east of the Somme.

The preparations on the allied side were of the utmost thoroughness and ingenuity. There had been disputes about the timing of this operation but none about whether or not to launch it. Preliminary planning had been put formally in hand after the Casablanca conference of January 1943 and before that raids on the continent – at St Nazaire, for example, in March 1942 and at Dieppe in August – had been undertaken with an eye to gaining information and experience which would be valuable for a full scale invasion. Detailed and daring reconnaissances of the landing beaches were carried out in order to establish the lie of the land, the obstacles below and above the water line, the state of the going for tracked and other vehicles and a thousand and one other pieces of information. Elaborate feints were devised to keep the defenders guessing and dispersed. Entirely new accessories of war were designed and constructed, from the two artificial harbours (Mulberries) as large as medium-sized ports which were towed across the Channel in sections (beginning on D-day) and the oil pipelines (Pluto – eventually twenty came into use) which were laid under it, to a variety of strange adaptations of tracked vehicles for carrying prefabricated bridges, laying carpets on the sand and destroying land mines.

The principal commanders had been designated in 1943 and had been working together and training their subordinates for much longer than is usually possible in war: General Dwight D. Eisenhower in supreme command with Air Marshal Sir Arthur Tedder as his deputy and General Walter Bedell Smith as Chief of Staff; Vice-Admiral Bertram Ramsay, General Bernard Montgomery and Air Vice-Marshal Trafford Leigh-Mallory in command of the three services in the assault phase; Generals Omar N. Bradley and Miles Dempsey commanding the two invading armies, the former destined to command an Army Group after the build-up. One and a half million Americans were transported across the Atlantic with all their own equipment and food and crammed into southern England. Unprecedented and often very irritating new security measures were introduced, affecting even the embassies of neutrals and allies. A fleet of over 5,000 vessels was assembled for the initial phase: 1,200 naval vessels, including seven battleships, to bombard the coastal defences, sweep mines, escort the invaders and tackle enemy sea- and air-craft; and 4,000 transports, barges, tugs and other sea-going and amphibious craft for the conveyance of the armies with their tanks, armoured cars, guns, vehicles, ammunition and the lavish variety of modern fighting gear. In the air the allies mustered 7,500 aircraft in direct support of the invasion and 3,500 bombers which could be and were used in this battle as well as for the continued strategic bombing of Germany. Eisenhower failed to get the heavy bombers included in his command but succeeded in getting them used for the destruction of German communications to the battle area (in accordance with a plan worked out in great detail by a civilian professor of anatomy). Naval and air supremacy ensured the passage of the thirty-seven divisions assembled to strike the decisive blow in the west.

Two hazards remained: the weather and the issue of the first engagements. The invasion was once postponed by twenty-four hours and Eisenhower seriously pondered a second postponement which would not only have been a much longer one but by ill chance would have re-timed the operation to coincide with a serious and unseasonable storm which blew up on 19 June. In the event the first invaders crossed the Channel by air at two o'clock in the morning of 6 June to be dropped some miles behind the five landing beaches, and at dawn five separate groups approached these beaches from the sea. These men – 20,000 airborne and 70,000 seaborne – were the advance guard of a force of two million drawn from a dozen nations which was to be set ashore in France within the next two months. Their first objectives lay along a line which stretched for forty miles from the eastern base of the Cotentin peninsula eastward to the mouth of the river Orne which flows into the sea eight miles northeast of the town of Caen. The task of the first invaders was to get onto the beaches and then get off them again as quickly as possible.

The first day's objectives included Caen. Fortunes were mixed. At the westernmost beach the Americans secured their first objectives with the loss of only twelve men before the end of the day. At the next beach, however, the second American landing was an almost complete disaster and, after suffering 3,000 casualties, was saved only by the successes in neighbouring sectors. At the remaining three beaches British and

THE PRE-INVASION SCENE MAY-JUNE 1944

ALLIED PRE-INVASION CONSIDERATIONS

0 — 50 Miles

The longer route across Channel, but further from German aircraft. Also, German defences weaker in Normandy than in the Pas de Calais.

The shorter route across Channel, but German forces heaviest in Pas de Calais. Also Kentish ports unsuitable for large ship and troop concentrations.

E N G L A N D

Weymouth
Southampton
Portsmouth
Dover
Strait of Dover
Calais
PAS DE CALAIS
Boulogne

ENGLISH CHANNEL

Dieppe

Cherbourg

Rouen

Caen
Seine
Paris

St. Malo

N O R M A N D Y

GERMAN PRE-INVASION CONSIDERATIONS

0 — 50 Miles

ENGLAND   Allied bogus radio activity

KENT
Dover
Strait of Dover Calais
PAS DE CALAIS
Boulogne

Southampton
Weymouth
Portsmouth

ENGLISH CHANNEL

Cherbourg

Dieppe

Rouen
Seine
Paris

Caen

N O R M A N D Y

Rommel (and later, Hitler) believes the invasion will occur here and, thus he strengthens beach defences. He is anxious that the Allies do not achieve a foothold.

Von Runstedt and OKW expect invasion to occur here. German strategy accepts the initial landings but envisages a counter-attack will dislodge the invaders.

ALLIED PRE-INVASION BOMBING

+++++ Railways.
★ Targets destroyed.
☆ Targets heavily damaged.

E N G L A N D

Southampton
Weymouth
Portsmouth
Dover

ENGLISH CHANNEL

Ostend
Dunkirk
Ghent
Cologne
Calais
Lille
Brussels
BELGIUM
Rhine
GERMANY
Abbeville
LUX.
Moselle
Trèves

Cherbourg
Dieppe
Le Havre
Rouen
Amiens
Laon
Metz

Caen
Seine
Soissons
Reims
Nancy

St Lô
Falaise
Chartres
Paris
Strasbourg

St Malo

Rennes
F   R   A   N   C   E
Troyes
Chaumont
Belfort

Le Mans
Orleans
Loire
Rhine

Nantes
Tours
Dijon

0 — 50 Miles

~ARTHUR BANKS~

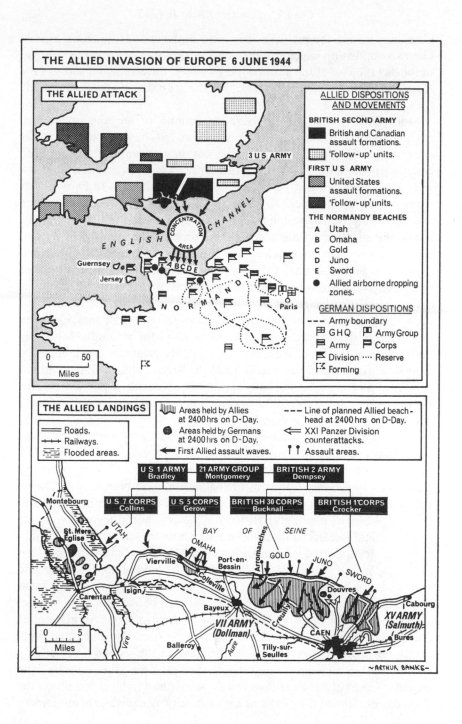

THE ALLIED INVASION OF EUROPE 6 JUNE 1944

THE ALLIED ATTACK

3 US ARMY

ENGLISH CHANNEL

CONCENTRATION AREA

Guernsey

Jersey

A B C D E

NORMANDY

Paris

0   50
Miles

ALLIED DISPOSITIONS AND MOVEMENTS

BRITISH SECOND ARMY

■ British and Canadian assault formations.

▥ 'Follow-up' units.

FIRST U S ARMY

▨ United States assault formations.

▨ 'Follow-up' units.

THE NORMANDY BEACHES

A Utah
B Omaha
C Gold
D Juno
E Sword
● Allied airborne dropping zones.

GERMAN DISPOSITIONS

--- Army boundary
⊞ GHQ   🏴 Army Group
🏳 Army   🏳 Corps
🏴 Division   ···· Reserve
⚑ Forming

THE ALLIED LANDINGS

▥ Areas held by Allies at 2400 hrs on D-Day.
● Areas held by Germans at 2400 hrs on D-Day.
← First Allied assault waves.

--- Line of planned Allied beach-head at 2400 hrs on D-Day.
⇐ XXI Panzer Division counterattacks.
↑↑ Assault areas.

═ Roads.
+++ Railways.
▭ Flooded areas.

US 1 ARMY Bradley	21 ARMY GROUP Montgomery	BRITISH 2 ARMY Dempsey

US 7 CORPS Collins	US 5 CORPS Gerow	BRITISH 30 CORPS Bucknall	BRITISH 1 CORPS Crocker

Montebourg

St. Mere Eglise

UTAH

BAY   OF   SEINE

OMAHA

Vierville

Port-en-Bessin

Arromanches

GOLD

JUNO

SWORD

Douvres

Cabourg

Colleville

Carentan

Isigny

Bayeux

Creully

CAEN

XV ARMY (Salmuth)

Bures

VII ARMY (Dollman)

Balleroy

Vire

Aure

Tilly-sur-Seulles

0   5
Miles

~ARTHUR BANKS~

Canadian troops fought their way onto and beyond the shore against German opposition which stiffened uncomfortably after noon. At the end of the day the fate of the paratroopers was still uncertain and some of the Americans were in serious trouble, but the seaborne invaders had made their lodgements.

Montgomery, who was in overall command of all land operations, aimed to take Caen with his British-Canadian left, but although his forces came within four miles of it they did not enter it until 10 July or gain complete possession of it for another week. This was a serious setback since Montgomery's first plan was to drive through Caen to Paris. It was compounded by bad luck. By 18 June 629,000 men had been put ashore and the Mulberries, although not yet completed, were handling 6,000 tons a day. But on the next day a strong and unseasonable gale blew up and lasted for five days. It wrecked one Mulberry, damaged the other and blew about 800 craft onto the shore. Supplies directed onto the beaches and through the Mulberries, which had reached an average of 22,570 tons a day, were drastically cut and when the gale abated the armies had 20,000 vehicles and over 100,000 tons of stores less than they had been counting on. This shortfall was not made good for a month. Moreover Cherbourg, at the tip of the Cotentin, was only belatedly captured on 26 June with its port facilities wrecked and the harbour blocked; it could not be used at all for weeks, not fully for months. Nevertheless a million men were in France at the end of the first week in July and over a million and a half before the end of the month.

Once they had got ashore the allies' principal fears were stalemate in Normandy and the imminent threat of Hitler's V weapons. Their principal uncovenanted advantage was the persistent success of their deception plan which kept Hitler from reinforcing his armies in Normandy from his substantial forces east of the Seine. Combined, a stalemate and the arrival of the V weapons might give Hitler, not victory, but a negotiated peace; but stalemate became impossible as the German armies in Normandy remained unsupported from outside. Nevertheless the failure to take Caen and so open the short and direct route to the Seine and Paris kept the issue in doubt from mid-June to mid-August. A series of costly attacks on Caen failed. In mid-June a British corps suffered defeat at Villers-Bocage, a battle which coincided with the release of the first V 1s. An attempt at the end of the month to outflank Caen to the west also failed. A direct attack, preceded by heavy air bombardment, in the second week of July caused terrible casualties on both sides but gave the allies only half the city. A renewal of these tactics a few days later had to be called off on the third day but forced the Germans out of the city. Meanwhile Montgomery and Bradley (who was still subordinated to Montgomery and not directly to Eisenhower) planned to end the battle for Normandy by breaking westward into Brittany and then encircling the Germans to the south. Although still plagued by the tardy capture of Cherbourg and by continuing bad weather, Bradley launched his forces out of the Cotentin peninsula on 25 July and, having defeated a German spoiling attack across the base of the peninsula, sent Patton's US Third Army into Brittany and so round to Argentan, which it reached the day after the Canadians, coming south from Caen, reached Falaise (16 August), thus trapping the Germans in a bag with an escape route only fifteen miles wide. This gap was closed on the 19th when American and Polish units joined hands. About 60,000 Germans were killed or captured and huge quantities of arms and vehicles lost in the Normandy pocket.

On the German side these battles were fought by Field Marshal von Kluge who succeeded both Rundstedt, dismissed by Hitler on 1 July, and Rommel, accidentally put out of action when his car was hit by an aircraft on 17 July. Kluge was in turn dismissed on 17 August. He committed suicide, probably because he knew that Hitler knew that he had been cognizant of the plot to kill Hitler on 20 July. For the same reason the convalescent Rommel was forced by the SD, acting on Hitler's orders, to kill himself.

The new Commander-in-Chief, Field Marshal Model, managed to extract a not negligible number of the encircled troops in Normandy, but two days before his appointment fresh American and French armies under General Devers landed in the south of France (15 August) and two days after it Patton reached the Seine north-west and south-east of Paris. On the 19th Paris rose. Within the Paris Liberation Committee there were differences about whether to wait for the nearer approach of the regular armies or not, the communists being for action now, the non-communists for delay. The pressures for action became irresistible and the order was given for the liberation of the capital by its own people. There was fighting in the streets between the Germans and the Resistance. A truce was arranged but Hitler would have none of it and ordered the destruction of the city, if necessary by bombing. The truce degenerated into confusion and fighting started again. At one time the bells were ringing for victory while the guns were still firing as the last of the SS and their French accomplices defended all that remained to them: their lives. De Gaulle urged that General Jacques Leclercq's Second French Division be sent forward since, left to themselves, the Parisians could be overwhelmed by the Germans and their city destroyed: 1,500 of them were killed in the rising and twice as many were wounded. After some hesitation de Gaulle's

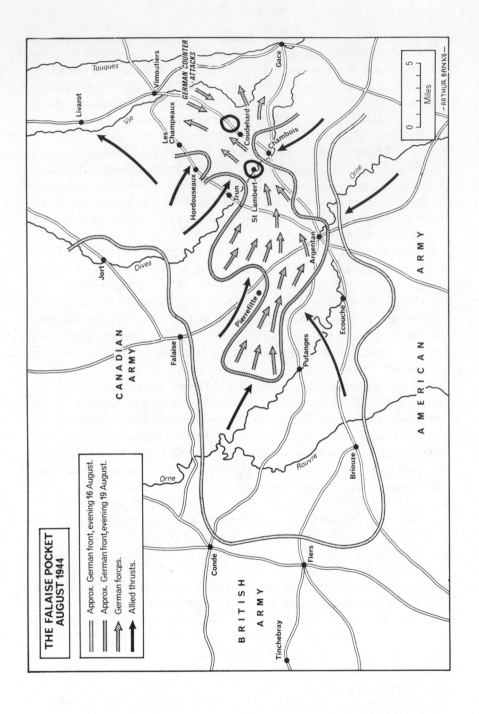

THE FALAISE POCKET
AUGUST 1944

Approx. German front, evening 16 August.
Approx. German front, evening 19 August.
German forces.
Allied thrusts.

CANADIAN ARMY

BRITISH ARMY

AMERICAN ARMY

GERMAN COUNTER ATTACKS

Touques
Vimoutiers
Livarot
Vie
Les Champeaux
Coudehard
Gace
Chambois
Hordouseaux
Trun
St Lambert
Orne
Jort
Dives
Argentan
Falaise
Pierrefitte
Ecouche
Putanges
Rouvre
Conde
Orne
Briouze
Flers
Tinchebray

Miles
5
0

— ARTHUR BANKS —

request was granted and Leclercq entered Paris on 25 August (the British tactfully declining an American suggestion that a token British contingent with a Union Jack should accompany Leclercq). The German military governor, General Dietrich von Choltitz, who had disregarded and defeated Hitler's orders, surrendered to Leclercq and to Colonel Rol, alias Tanguy, one of the military leaders of the Resistance and a communist veteran of the Spanish civil war. Choltitz surrendered to the French Republic and not to the allied command, an action which the Americans, though riled, took in good part. The allies had already discovered that they could not get away with their facile assumption that upon the defeat of the Germans France would be provisionally administered by them. (They had prepared an occupation currency but de Gaulle's indignation on learning of its existence had blown it away.) De Gaulle arrived in Paris and proclaimed a provisional government of France at the Hôtel de Ville on 30 August.

After the end of August the allied advance slowed down. Hitler had ordered the German garrisons, which still held a string of ports, to resist to the last man in the hope that the allies would divert forces to invest these places and so be delayed. For the most part the allies ignored the garrisons which were therefore simply isolated and kept out of battles farther east until they were obliged by events to surrender, but in one or two cases German stubbornness paid off, notably at Brest which did not surrender until 18 September and so could not be used to supply the increasingly large and increasingly distant allied armies. On 1 September, the initial phase being completed, Eisenhower assumed command in the field in northern France and thenceforward exercised it to the end through his two Army Group Commanders, Bradley and Montgomery. Eisenhower's principal concern was the supply of his large and rapidly moving armies. He himself, underrating the Germans' capacity to pull themselves together for a last round, seems to have thought that he could keep up the pace along his whole front with the resources available to him. Montgomery was the most eloquent of those who said that this was impossible. He argued that the logistical problems produced by the unexpectedly swift advances after the break-out at Caen had made it essential to concentrate a punch either on the left or the right, and he naturally made the most of the case in favour of the left. He wanted all the support that the Supreme Commander could give him for a drive across the Somme, through Belgium, into the Ruhr and on to Berlin. This way, he believed, he could finish the war before the end of the year.

Montgomery may have been right but neither then nor in retrospect was he obviously so and he pressed his point of view regardless of the

THE ALLIED ADVANCE FROM NORMANDY TO THE RHINE 6 JUNE 1944 – 7 MARCH 1945

D-DAY 6 JUNE 1944

SWITZERLAND

0   50
Miles

A.BANKS

American armies from Southern France.

German held until 8 May 1945

Channel Islands

Cherbourg 22 June

Le Havre

Rouen 30 Aug

Calais 30 Sept

Amiens 31 Aug

Antwerp 4 Sept

Brussels 3 Sept

BRITISH & CANADIANS

ARDENNES

16 Dec

Cologne 6 Mar
Remagen 7 Mar 1945

Aachen 21 Oct

Rhine

Rhine

AMERICANS

Metz 18 Nov

Nancy 16 Sept

Epinal 15 Sept

FRENCH

Dijon 11 Sept

Yonne

Paris 25 Aug

Orleans 17 Aug

Seine

Tours 26 Aug

Loire

Falaise 23 Aug

St Malo

Rennes

Nantes 6 Aug

St Nazaire

Lorient

Brest 19 Sept

Allied line December 1944.

Last German counter attack.

German border and Siegfried Line.

D-day + 49 (13 July).

D-day + 68 (24 August).

D-day + 81 (26 August).

Falaise pocket.

political pressures on Eisenhower and even beyond the limits prescribed to a loyal or considerate subordinate. Eisenhower was sceptical of Montgomery's strategy and, although an exceptionally honest and fair man, he could not avoid giving weight to a political problem. He was an American general in command of a preponderantly American force, and giving preference to Montgomery meant favouring a British general whom the American public and many American senior officers disliked. Not only Eisenhower himself but also Marshall felt that the voice of Congress and the voice of the American press had to have some weight in these strategic decisions. Their sensitivity on this score was the more acute because the commanders on the American side included in Patton a soldier who was no less colourful than Montgomery and readier to resort to insubordination if he did not get the orders he wanted. Holding back Patton's drive from the Seine to the Saar in order to enable Montgomery to knock out the German army somewhere else was something that Eisenhower was not prepared to attempt.

On the last day of August Montgomery took Amiens, due north of Paris, and crossed the Somme and less than a week later he had taken Brussels and Antwerp and developed a bold plan for a further advance. The obstacles to continuing eastward into the Ruhr, apart from his difficulty in getting the undivided support of the Supreme Commander, were stiffening German resistance and the prepared defences of the Siegfried line (the West Wall) which guarded the German frontier from Switzerland up to and including Belgium – but excluding Holland. Montgomery proposed to strike north instead of east, advancing from Belgium into Holland instead of the Ruhr. By doing this he would cut across the German supply lines in Holland, isolate and surround the remaining German forces in Belgium and western Holland by extending his own lines to the coast at the Zuider Zee, get beyond the northern end of the Siegfried line and then turn east into the north German plain. He might also catch the Germans where they would least expect a major blow.

The operation was to be a dual one. Airborne troops would seize a series of bridges over the principal waterways in Holland and so gain control of key points along the north–south line Arnhem–Nijmegen–Eindhoven. At the same time ground troops would advance from the south to Eindhoven, thence to Nijmegen and finally – the crucial link – to Arnhem. Eisenhower approved the plan and gave Montgomery the Hundred-and-first and the Eighty-second US Airborne Divisions for the Eindhoven and Nijmegen drops. The bridge over the Lower Rhine at Arnhem was to be captured by the British Airborne Division. But there remained some misunderstanding about how far Eisenhower had decided to give Montgomery all the material support he needed, even at the cost of staying Patton's advance.

This operation, which was launched on 17 September, was intended to revitalize the allied advance which had been petering out since the beginning of the month. It came to grief after a week's bitter fighting, one of those failures which nearly succeed but are turned into disaster by the chances of war and by muddle – but not, as has sometimes been supposed, by betrayal. The two American divisions accomplished their tasks, the Hundred-and-first Division comparatively smoothly and the Eighty-second Division on the fourth day after one of the most dashing exploits of the war in the west. The British ground forces (XXX Corps under General Horrocks) made punctual contact with the Hundred-and-first Division and then sent forward armoured units in time to follow up and consolidate the Eighty-second Division's successful capture of the bridge over the Waal at Nijmegen. But XXX Corps' further advance towards Arnhem was impeded by mines and the skilful and vigorous recovery of the Germans, and meanwhile the British Airborne Division had got into trouble.

The airborne drops were spread over three days and the defences of the bridge at Arnhem were reputedly so fierce that it had been decided to drop the British division about eight miles from the bridge. In this way the division could expect to find itself on Dutch soil more or less intact and would then proceed to attack the bridge like an ordinary ground formation. In other words the defences at the bridge had persuaded the British, before a shot was fired, not to attempt a direct airborne *coup de main* but to mount a hybrid attack which was part airborne and, in the second and decisive part, a straight fight through fields and villages. Given these tactics it was peculiarly unfortunate that German strength in the area had been seriously underestimated. Ultra intelligence pointed with some but not complete certainty to the presence within striking distance of the German II SS Panzer Corps comprising the Ninth and Tenth Panzer Divisions, but this intelligence was poorly evaluated. These divisions were in the area for refitting, had been excellently equipped and were ably commanded. Moreover, by a piece of grave misfortune, the British orders for the entire operation were captured on the first day off an American soldier whose glider crashed.

Nevertheless the first day's operations were everywhere successful and on the Arnhem sector the British units began their advance towards the town through a friendly population anxious to show their delight by hospitality of every kind. On the second day, however, German opposition surprised the British and the situation began to get confused. Poor weather intervened and airborne supplies to the units which had already been dropped miscarried to such an extent that most of them were collected by the Germans. Aircraft losses were heavy. From the third day the British were being forced to make local withdrawals and it soon became clear that the fate of the Airborne Division depended on what speed XXX Corps could make to its relief. As hope faded, the story became one of endurance, heroism and the gradual strangulation of the perimeter, while the prematurely exuberant Dutch awaited the return of the Germans in the cellars of houses where they had been dispensing good cheer to the British but which were now being wrecked above their heads. The attackers' losses were 1,200 dead and over 3,000 taken prisoner. The Arnhem bridge remained in German hands until the middle of April 1945. The Arnhem operation, the last major parachute operation of the war, summed up the experiences of four years which had begun with the successful German operation which opened the campaign in the Low Countries in May 1940. These experiences showed that parachutists could play an important role as the advance guard of a main force which was not too far away and was advancing rapidly, but that they could not yet take an independent giant stride ahead on their own.

The failure at Arnhem gave the Germans a last chance to consolidate a line beyond Germany's own borders. On 5 September – the day after Antwerp had fallen in the north and Lyons to the Americans advancing from Toulon in the south, and two weeks before the Arnhem operation – Hitler had recalled Rundstedt once more and had given him the task of holding what was left of Belgium, Holland and the Siegfried line. But Hitler also intended Rundstedt to do more than that. He would take advantage of a lull on the eastern front to switch troops to the west for an offensive in the Ardennes at the end of November from the Meuse to the sea. His main target was Antwerp, captured by the allies on 4 September. For it he assembled twenty-five divisions grouped in three Armies, including the newly created Sixth SS Panzer Army commanded by General Sepp Dietrich. Hitler did not, however, tell his principal commanders in the west of the plans which they were to execute and it was not until the end of October that they were informed. Rundstedt, Model and their senior commanders and staff officers immediately objected that the plans were too ambitious. They proposed a watered-down version designed to encircle a part of the American forces west of Aachen with the option, in the event of speedy success, of going on to Antwerp at a second stage, but Hitler refused to consider any alterations to the plans which his own staff had already worked out in detail. All he would grant, under pressure of circumstances, was the postponement of D-day to 16 December.

The last German offensive of the war of any note was accordingly launched on that day. It caused immense perturbation because it came as a complete surprise to allied commanders. This should not have been so. Ultra intelligence, which was copious from start to finish of the campaigns of 1944–5, gave numerous indications of a substantial offensive in the offing and in the general area of the Ardennes (but, as usual, no date). It had reported in September the creation of Sixth SS Panzer Army and, early in November, the reinforcement of the Luftwaffe in the relevant sector by units switched from further north and from the Russian fronts. German railway ciphers, which were being read at Bletchley Park, gave detailed information of movements of men and material, and orders to Luftwaffe reconnaissance units showed that the Germans were specially anxious to conceal something that was going on to the east of the Ardennes. In addition signals intelligence, monitoring German army traffic, noted the appearance of new formations which had been ordered to keep radio silence – itself a significant order but one that could not be completely obeyed since the units had to break it once or twice a day in order to make sure that they were still in proper touch with one another. Why these pointers were missed is still unclear but it has been surmised that allied staffs were so convinced (and in fact correctly) that Hitler could no longer launch such a venture successfully that they overlooked the fact that he might nevertheless try. With their minds concentrated on how best to cross the Rhine they had become immune to the notion that the Germans might re-cross the Meuse.

But not even the element of surprise could give Hitler's gamble any chance of success. After four days it had failed. Eisenhower placed all troops north of the German thrust – including two American armies – under Montgomery's command, a redisposition of some courage in view of the prevalent American animus against Montgomery and the contrary advice of Bradley who underrated the gravity of the situation. The Germans were lucky with the weather at the outset, for fog in England for the first three days, followed by fog on the continent, prevented the allied air force from taking part in the battle. Yet the German advances were not as great as had been planned and an order by Patton (who feared that the Germans might break left rather than right and so cut across his rear) to withdraw was not executed, so that the town of Bastogne was held and became an American strongpoint, brilliantly defended by the US Tenth Armoured and the Hundred-and-first Airborne Divisions and supplied by air. By the 22nd Rundstedt, under pressure on both flanks, was counselling the abandonment of the attack. The Fifth Panzer Division under General Hasso von Manteuffel continued to advance until Christmas Eve but was then diverted to Bastogne. From this point the Germans were forced onto the defensive and began to suffer increasing casualties. The battle of the Ardennes was substantially an American victory under a British commander. The German thrust failed, but it was a nasty shock to the allied commanders and publics because of the surprise which cast doubt on allied intelligence, its initial successes, and Eisenhower's alteration in the command which stirred up national animosities.

In January Hitler abandoned his offensive in the west. He had hoped for a quick victory, to be followed by a massive counter-attack on the Russians in the east. He had been defeated by allied air superiority, by the defenders of Bastogne, by poor cooperation among his own forces (especially between the Fifth and Sixth Panzer Divisions) and by a new weapon, the proximity fuse. This fuse contained a tiny radar which, in conjunction with radio waves and their echoes, made a shell go off at a distance from its target. It was estimated to increase the effectiveness of artillery tenfold. Although used against Japanese aircraft in 1943 it was not used in the European theatre before the emergencies of the V1 and Ardennes offensives.

The end of the attack on the Ardennes coincided with a lesser attack in Alsace begun on the last day of the year, although originally conceived as a move to cover the left flank of the Ardennes offensive. This operation gave rise to a major row between Eisenhower and de Gaulle, about which there are many accounts, including accounts by Eisenhower, de Gaulle and Churchill. These accounts cannot be reconciled and so it is still impossible to produce an unassailable version. By the time the attack in Alsace came it was – whatever the original German plan – distinct from the flagging Ardennes offensive and a comparatively minor affair. But Eisenhower may not have seen it that way. Rundstedt's attack had forced him to contemplate a major switch of Patton's forces northward and a consequent re-deployment of his southern Army Group which, under Devers, had come up into the line from the south of France: Devers's forces might have to take over part of Patton's front and perhaps even withdraw from the Rhine to the Vosges. Such a withdrawal meant abandoning Strasbourg.

Devers's Army Group included a French army under General de Lattre de Tassigny, but Devers did not tell de Lattre, and Eisenhower did not tell de Gaulle, that a withdrawal was anything but a hypothetical contingency. Their reticence was no doubt due to their knowledge that a withdrawal, exposing Strasbourg to recapture and reprisals by the Germans, would be strenuously resisted by the French. De Gaulle meanwhile had instructed de Lattre to defend Strasbourg, the arch-symbol of Franco-German rivalry ever since 1870. In doing so he was ignorant of Eisenhower's instructions to Devers and convinced, correctly as it happened, that a withdrawal was unnecessary. The upshot was that Eisenhower and Devers got themselves into a position where they were trying to outwit de Gaulle and de Lattre by putting into execution a plan which had been represented as something less than a plan, while the French commanders were taking decisions into their own hands to the extent of denying the superior command powers of the American commanders. Upon discovering what was afoot de Gaulle sent Juin to Eisenhower's headquarters where a battle of threats developed between him and Bedell Smith, and sent a signal to Churchill who flew at once to France to smooth over the controversy. Strasbourg was not evacuated.

On 12 January a new Russian offensive opened. Hitler had already begun to switch part of his armour in the west back to the east in order to meet it. Since 6 June the Germans had lost three quarters of a million men in France. They were now defending the Rhine.

The imminence of victory cast a number of shadows before. The anti-German alliance was a military combination created by, and unlikely to survive without, German aggressiveness. So long as the war lasted the allies' reciprocal needs overbore their mutual distrust but the evaporation of the German threat twitched aside this cloak of common concern. Months before the end of the war both the Anglo-Americans and the Russians were preparing to forestall one another in a dash to seize secret German installations and valuable German scientists. Both sides had been manoeuvring to set battle lines, which might later become political lines, separating their respective zones of operations and occupation in Germany. And both were uneasy about the fate of their citizens in German captivity or German employ who would be found in areas which they did not control.

Some of these persons were prisoners of war taken by the Germans on their western or eastern fronts. But prisoners of war were a relatively small category; prisoners from the west were not very numerous, while prisoners from the east had been comprehensively murdered. Much the largest number of non-Germans in Germany were Russian and other citizens of the USSR who had been overrun by the German victories of 1941–2 or had defected to the German side. When the war ended over two and a half million of them were sent back to the USSR from the American, British and French zones of occupation in Germany and Italy and years later it was alleged that they had been forcibly returned in defiance of the most basic rules of humanity. The great majority – about nine out of ten – were Displaced Persons who returned voluntarily; probably it never occurred to them to do otherwise. The bulk of them were back in the USSR within three months of the end of the war. They may have been hideously disillusioned when they got there but nobody forced them to return.

Of the remaining quarter million about 200,000 were Soviet citizens who had been captured in German uniforms which they had donned for a variety of reasons. Some did so in order to survive, others because they hated the USSR. They had given aid to the enemy, although mostly in humble capacities and simply to save their skins. They too expected to be able to return to their homes unnoticed and unpunished, even if technically they were deserters or traitors. They went back of their own accord. But a residue of about 50,000 did not. They were forcibly repatriated and paid, presumably atrociously, for what they had done. They comprised three main groups: some 10,000 survivors of the Ukrainian SS Division; some 5,000 survivors of the two Vlasov divisions; and about 25,000 Cossacks, including 5,000 women and children. There were also, in Italy, remnants of the Turkestan Division, central Asian and Azerbaijani Muslims who had served in the Wehrmacht and had exhibited appalling ferocity to men, women and children. All these groups consisted of Soviet citizens who had fought for the Germans against the USSR and had committed dreadful atrocities which made them war criminals as well as deserters and traitors. They were liable to forcible repatriation under agreements made in 1944 (and confirmed at Yalta) – agreements which applied to citizens of all the anti-German allies and were in line with commonly accepted rules of international law. Given the large numbers involved, and given post-war chaos, it is impossible to show or even to suppose that no mistakes were made. In particular a number of Ukrainians not covered by the agreements because they were not Soviet citizens at the prescribed date were nevertheless delivered to the Russian authorities and barbarously treated. Chaos also worked the other way. Guards of camps and convoys allowed or encouraged their charges to disappear into the woods to escape a fate which they expected to be worse than death, and the most culpable groups evaded retribution in substantial numbers: many members of the Ukrainian SS Division claimed, successfully if falsely, that they were not Soviet but Polish citizens, and more than half the Vlasov survivors did the same, thus escaping not only the net prepared for deserters and traitors but also arraignment for war crimes. In Italy, where a first trawl through the Displaced Persons camps had yielded 2,000 Soviet citizens taken in German uniforms, further investigations carried out by special tribunals with painstaking thoroughness condemned to forcible repatriation only 264 men out of a much larger number of grave suspects whom the tribunals exonerated, since by this time (1947) they were looking for any excuse to save the accused from Russian vengeance. The tragedy of the 264 was not that they were innocent victims but that they encountered a fate out of proportion to their offences.

CHAPTER 25

Disintegration

BY the beginning of 1945 the accumulation of Germany's reverses had produced disintegration. It is surprising that the war lasted into May. Even in the previous summer Montgomery had believed that Berlin could be reached before the end of 1944, and on the other front Chuikov, the defender of Stalingrad and ultimately the conqueror of Berlin, chafed at his superiors for not allowing him to make straight for the city at the beginning of the new year. Hitler no longer had an army capable of sustaining the fight, he had so little fuel that his soldiers had standing orders to siphon off the fuel in a disabled tank before abandoning it, he scarcely had an air force at all, his anti-aircraft units were manned by a mixture of regulars, prisoners of war and teenagers down to sixteen, and his secret weapons had not worked the miracles that were expected of them.

After 1942 the Luftwaffe had performed one function brilliantly at the cost of relinquishing all others. It had created a fighter defence of Germany which defeated American and British strategic bombing until the final phase of cumulative disintegration was reached. But otherwise – apart from limited local successes, as when it drove the British out of the Dodecanese in 1943 – it ceased to count in one theatre after another. Its formations were outnumbered, its airfields bombed and its new types and new weapons failed it. In 1943 the Do. 217 was equipped with a 1,000 lb. radio-controlled glider bomb (Hs. 293 – first used against the Italian fleet as it escaped from Italy to Malta upon the Italian surrender) and also with a 3,000 lb. radio-controlled anti-personnel bomb (FX), but these were primitive prototypes of things to come and neither was successful. The He. 177 four-engined bomber appeared in 1943, but in small numbers only and after Germany's chance to affect the issue by heavy bombing had passed; the Luftwaffe was never able to drop the super-bombs which were dropped by its enemies on German cities (the heaviest bomb used against Germany was 22,000 lbs.).

The Me. 262 jet fighter and the Me. 163 rocket-propelled fighter appeared towards the end of 1944, but by then it was too late. Both these aircraft were the successors of earlier models which had flown before the war began and in both Germany was the pioneer, but their champions had been unable to persuade Hitler or Goering to adopt them because it was assumed that the war would be finished and won without them. The Me. 262 was, however, put into series production half way through the war (1,294 were made) because Hitler mistakenly supposed that this 500 m.p.h. fighter could be usefully converted into a bomber.

During 1942–3 the Luftwaffe had been called upon to fight on four fronts. It was not strong enough to do so. Its own bomber offensive was defeated, it failed to succour the German armies in the east or in the Mediterranean, and it was squeezed out of the Battle of the High Seas. The Russian campaigns acted like a magnet and a churn. Great numbers of aircraft were drawn into battles in which the Luftwaffe was gradually ground out of existence. In 1944 a new front was added in the west. This was the last straw. The destruction of the Luftwaffe was accelerated by a training crisis, a fuel crisis and a breakdown in its intelligence. By 1945 it was out of the fight.

Germany did not manage to produce the Second World War's most startling new weapon – the nuclear bomb. In the aftermath of defeat some German writers and scientists sought to ascribe this failure to the reluctance of German science to place so terrifying a weapon in the hands of so terrifying a man as Hitler, but the truth seems to be that the Germans failed to produce nuclear weapons because they took a wrong turning. They did, however, produce at the end of the war special weapons which, had they been brought into service earlier, might have had a considerable effect. These were the V weapons, V standing for *Vergeltung* or retribution. With them Hitler hoped to flatten London and force Britain to capitulate by the end of 1943, while Churchill was so alarmed that he considered using gas in retaliation.

There were three V weapons. The V 1 was a jet-propelled pilotless aircraft twenty-five feet long with a ceiling of 2,000– 3,000 feet, a range of 200–250 miles, a speed of 470 m.p.h. and a one-ton warhead. It cost only £125 and consumed in flight only 150 gallons of low-grade fuel. Beginning in June 1944 2,448 of these weapons hit Antwerp, 2,419 London (out of 10,492 aimed at it) and 3,132 hit other parts of England. The V 2 was a rocket. It was fifty feet long and six feet in circumference and carried a one-ton warhead. It rose into the air for fifty to seventy-five miles and could reach a speed of 3,600 m.p.h. Its range was 220 miles. Its motor, controlled from the ground, was cut at the crucial moment, thus setting it on course. It was impossible to intercept and arrived without warning since it travelled faster than sound. The V 2 was therefore a more terrifying weapon than the V 1, but each V 2 cost about £6,000, exclusive of research and development costs. Again Antwerp was the chief sufferer, receiving 1,265 hits. London received 517 and other parts of England 537.

The V 3 was a long-range gun. One weapon of this kind – originally there were to be two – was installed at Mimoyecques, near Calais. It had twenty-five barrels, each of them 416 feet long, entirely embedded in limestone and concrete, and the whole weapon was serviced and controlled by an extremely elaborate underground network. Its construction absorbed 1,000 tons of steel. It was to fire one shell on London every twelve seconds, but although the site was well prepared the components did not start arriving until early in June 1944. Allied bombing first severed its electricity supply and then scored a direct hit with a heavy bomb. In any case trials in the Baltic had not been completed when the site at Mimoyecques was overrun by the allied armies.

Development and production of the V 1 and V 2 were held up by rivalries between the army, which was in charge of the V 2, and the Luftwaffe, which was responsible for the V 1. These jealousies were accentuated when the S S tried to get control of the whole programme and at one point in March 1944 arrested the brilliant young researcher Werner von Braun and other key scientists. Allied Intelligence had wind of these inventions from November 1939 when the 'Oslo Report', a comprehensive report on German war science, was received in London from an agent or well-wisher (who is still anonymous). A year later Peenemünde was identified as the experimental area for these weapons by an agent who appears to have been in or near German military intelligence under Admiral Canaris. No further clues became available for over two years but early in 1943 prisoners of war (including two generals) were overheard talking about Peenemünde and photographic reconnaissance began to disclose some of the test station's activities. In August of the same year Peenemünde was bombed for the first time and Ultra began to provide information about the nature and capabilities of the V 1 and V 2. Ultra put an end to a debate about whether Hitler was counting on a pilotless aircraft or a rocket by showing that he meant to have both but conflict and confusion persisted on the allied side, particularly over the size of the warheads which the new weapons might carry. These doubts arose chiefly from ignorance about the fuel used, there being a correlation between bulk of fuel, range and size of warhead. In London these differences caused some of the bitterest quarrelling of the war because Lord Cherwell – who was not only an exceptionally stubborn and often ill-mannered man who allowed scientific disagreement to invade personal relations, but who also resented the fact that the coordination of intelligence about Hitler's secret weapons had been assigned to a committee under Duncan Sandys, Churchill's son-in-law, whom he did not like – pooh-poohed the existence of any threat from rockets or pilotless aircraft.

The first V 2 was launched at the experimental station on Peenemünde in the Baltic in October 1942 after three earlier failures, and a first V 1 a few weeks later. Attempts were made to cripple the programme by bombing Peenemünde and other places where parts of the apparatus were being manufactured but most of these targets were at long range. On the night of 17–18 August 1943 600 bombers of Bomber Command attacked Peenemünde in three waves in the hope of interrupting research and killing key scientists. As a result of a successful feint towards Berlin the first and second waves suffered only slight losses in spite of a full moon, but fighter attacks on the third wave brought the total loss to forty-one aircraft. At Peenemünde 732 people, mostly non-Germans, were killed, some projects were abandoned or moved elsewhere, but work on the V 1 and V 2 was only interrupted for a short time. The attack on Peenemünde itself and related industrial targets was supplemented from December 1943 by attacks on sites along the north coast of France which had been identified by photographic and other intelligence as launching sites for the V 1. There were about a hundred of these sites known, from their appearance, as ski sites. These attacks were moderately successful but they were countered by swift repair and then by a German ruse. The Germans pretended to be repairing the sites when they were in fact abandoning them, using them as dummies and constructing new sites by a new method which enabled them to build a site in a matter of days. This deception was not discovered until May 1944 and during the first half of the year the allies wasted more bombs on these abandoned sites than the Germans had aimed at London during the eight months of the 1940–41 blitz.

The German failure to bring the V 1 and V 2 into operation before the summer and autumn of 1944 respectively, by which time allied armies were approaching, was largely due to teething troubles. British estimates of the production and effects of these new weapons were unduly pessimistic. Plans were made to evacuate the population and the government from London on the assumption that V 1s would arrive at the rate of 45,000 a month, and that the V 2s, arriving at the rate of one an hour and carrying a ten-ton warhead, would cause 108,000 casualties a month. At the beginning of the war the German production targets for the V 1 and the V 2 were 3,000 and 900 a month. In 1944 the former target was raised to 8,000. This figure was never reached but the earlier one was passed in 1945. Altogether 32,000 V 1s were produced. Production of the V 2 rose from fifty in January 1944 to 253 in April when it fell back because priority was given to the V 1. It picked up again later in the year, was steady at around 630–60 in the last four months and reached 690 in

January 1945. Nearly 6,000 were produced in all. These figures were creditable to the Germans and would, timing apart, have been alarming for the British.

Hitler's plan of attack on England was to fire a salvo of V 1s at dawn and dusk every day with intermediate single launchings every twenty to thirty minutes, but when the attack began on 12 June from fifty-five sites it was a rushed fiasco. On the first day ten V 1s were launched, of which four arrived. Appreciable damage was caused to rail traffic, factories, hospitals and housing, mostly south of the Thames. There was then a pause of three days but in the ensuing two weeks 2,000 were launched. At first spotter aircraft gave warnings but the number of V 1s destroyed was small. Anti-aircraft guns in the London area had to cease firing after the first two days because they were bringing the V 1s down in the city. Batteries were re-deployed along the south coast and, with the help of radar and proximity fuses, gradually succeeded in hitting half and then three quarters of their incoming targets. Some V 1s were destroyed by aircraft. The attack on London was suspended in September (Antwerp and Brussels came under fire a few weeks later) but it was followed by the V 2 attack.

There was still much doubt about the potency of this weapon. In June parts of a V 2 fired from Peenemünde had come down in Sweden and valuable information about it had come into allied possession. Another came down in Poland without exploding; it was hidden, dismantled and secretly conveyed to England. But there were still controversies about the size of the warhead; estimates varied between ten tons and one ton (the latter being correct). On 6 September two V 2s were aimed at Paris but the firings were a failure. On that day Duncan Sandys announced in London that 'except possibly for a few last shots, the Battle of London is over'. Two days later the first V 2s struck London. They were fired from Holland. The worst aspect of the attack was the number of men, women and children who were blinded by flying glass before they knew that anything had struck. In spite of doctors working round the clock on delicate eye operations many lost their sight for life. There was also severe material damage, but the firing sites were already threatened and had to be removed as the British armies approached them. The weight of the attack was diverted to Antwerp which was more seriously damaged than London and did not get relief until March 1945.

There has been a tendency to laugh at Hitler's V weapons. This is partly because it seemed in 1944 the best thing to do. But the weapons were not negligible and would have been extremely dangerous if they had been available earlier. In the first two weeks the V 1s killed 1,600 people, seriously injured another 4,500 and damaged 200,000 houses; the casualty rate in England in June 1944 was as heavy as it had been in September 1940, although the weight of attack measured in tons of explosives was much lighter. Over the whole period of the V 1 and V 2 attacks 29,400 houses were completely destroyed in London and over a quarter of a million damaged. It may be argued that Hitler could have used to better purpose the 200,000 persons engaged in the development and production of the V 2 – he might, for example, have got more from their brains and their labour if they had worked on defensive projects – but against this must be set not only the chance that the V weapons might have been ready sooner, but also the hard facts that the British had to increase their fighter, anti-aircraft and balloon defences, suffer appreciable material damage and divert a significant air effort to Peenemünde and the launching sites. The V weapons failed but their failure does not prove that they were ridiculous. They were the forerunners of much that has been developed since the war. They may not have been the weapons that Hitler hoped for to settle the result of the war, but if their appearance had not been delayed by allied bombing by a few months, they could hardly have failed to affect its course.

The V weapons were Hitler's last offensive expedients. After their failure he continued to produce expedients but they were defensive. In October 1944 he called into existence a new force, the *Volkssturm*, a Home Guard of last resort under Himmler's command and consisting of all available men between the ages of sixteen and sixty. The Werewolves, another desperate expedient, were to constitute armed bands operating like marauding partisans after the defeat of Germany. The Alpine redoubt, where Hitler said he would make his last stand, was even more phantasmal. It never existed, it had no men in it or prepared defences, and the Führer himself did not go there.

The first front to go was the Italian. Early in 1945 senior SS figures in Italy made approaches to Swiss contacts and indirectly to the head of the American intelligence services in Switzerland, Allen W. Dulles. These SS officers wanted to negotiate a separate surrender to the western allies of the entire Italian front. Dulles was not interested in a partial surrender, but he was concerned to keep the discussions alive in the hope that they would contribute to a total and unconditional surrender on all fronts. In March the German Supreme Commander in Italy, Kesselring, the Luftwaffe commander, Pohl, and Hitler's Ambassador in Italy, Rudolf Rahn who was in command of Mussolini and his government, were all brought into the discussions. Although they thought at first that they were discussing a negotiated and partial surrender, they quickly came to realize that what was in train was capitulation on all fronts and that the western allies would neither accept any vestige of Nazism in a new German government nor envisage any split between themselves and the Russians. The Russians, however, who knew that Himmler was trying to do a deal with the west via Stockholm, not unnaturally assumed (as for a while did some in the west) that the talks initiated by the S S in Switzerland were part of an anti-Russian venture. After a delay caused by the transfer of Kesselring to the western front and the need to initiate his successor, Vietinghoff, a surrender of all the German forces in Italy was made on 1 May by the army and air commanders acting on their own authority. It was botched by a farcical succession of arrests and counter-arrests among the Germans themselves but clinched when the news of Hitler's suicide reached Italy on the next day.

On the main fronts the German armies were overwhelmed by superior numbers and material. After the retreats of 1944 Hitler hoped to hold the line of the Vistula in the east (where Himmler was appointed to command an Army Group) and the Rhine in the west. The Russians, opening a new campaign in mid-January, crossed the Vistula, turned northwards to the sea to envelop the German forces in East Prussia and overran Pomerania and Silesia up to the Oder and Neisse rivers which they reached at the beginning of February. In the south they captured Budapest on the 12th. In the west German commanders tried vainly to obey Hitler's orders to give no ground and transport neither men nor material eastward across the Rhine. They were weakened by the transfer of a Panzer division to the east after the failure of the Ardennes offensive. This German armour, which was to defend the Hungarian oilfields, was believed to be routed through Dresden but when Ultra revealed the division's orders this belief was found to be wrong. The mistake was pointed out to the British and American bomber headquarters concerned; the latter expressed willingness to cancel the raid if the other would do so too but the former saw no reason to alter its plans. The presumed passage of the German armour through Dresden was only an ostensible reason for the operation. Equally dubious is the plea that the raid was executed in aid of the advancing Russians. There was no Russian request for a raid on Dresden although the western allies had been asked to attack Leipzig (a request which was taken to be a pointer to Stalin's plans for his line of advance on Berlin, about which he gave his allies no direct information). Dresden, so far barely damaged, was chosen because it was big, famous and crowded, so that its destruction might stampede the enemy towards surrender. So on 13 and 14 February one of Europe's most splendid cities was recklessly destroyed. Industrial targets were barely hit and the rail services were put out of action for only three days. The number of people killed has been estimated at 135,000, although the true figure may be half or even less than that huge total. The slaughter was in any case immense, most of it by burning people to death in buildings or in the streets. All this destruction was done in two night raids lasting an hour each, and a third raid of ten minutes at midday on the next day. One thousand two hundred and twenty-three aircraft dropped bombs. They faced no opposition.

On 7 March an American unit, seeing to its surprise that a bridge at Remagen, south of Bonn, had not been destroyed, crossed the Rhine and in the next weeks large forces followed at several points. Three of the western armies hoped and believed that they were on their way to Berlin. In addition there existed a plan for airborne attacks on key points in Berlin by a force of 20,000 paratroopers. But in the event the western allies made no attempt to reach the German capital. The reasons for this abnegation were two: Eisenhower's strategic decisions and the existence of an agreed division of Germany into separate administrative zones, with Berlin inside the Russian zone.

The zonal agreement grew out of administrative planning which had not been intended to have – but did have – political consequences. At their conference in Teheran in November 1943 Roosevelt, Churchill and Stalin agreed to create a European Advisory Commission which, sitting in London, would produce preliminary plans for the occupation of Germany. This Commission inherited a plan prepared in London by the Anglo-American planning staff which subsequently became part of Eisenhower's headquarters. This plan divided Germany into three zones – a British one in the north-west, an American in the south-west and a Russian in the east: Berlin was inside the Russian zone. Roosevelt had indicated to his own officials before Teheran that he did not like the arrangements proposed for the American and British zones and wanted them the other way round. But the dispositions had evolved logically from the planning for Overlord which always put the American armies on the right of the allied forces and the British (and Canadian) armies on the left, and in addition Roosevelt's reservations and objections got lost in Washington and were not conveyed to the American member of the European Advisory Commission until too late. A separate American proposal for a corridor linking Berlin with the north-western zone also got overlooked. The Russians were well satisfied with an arrangement which gave them 40 per cent of Germany and its capital (subject though the capital would itself be to tripartite division and control), while the western allies, who continued to be afraid that Stalin might run out of the European war or refuse to join the war against Japan, were loath to suggest amendments of any kind. The plan was therefore adopted by the Commission in March 1944 and confirmed at Yalta in February 1945.

It was not meant to settle anything more than immediate military and administrative matters. The future of Germany in a larger sense was left vague. Germany was *tabula rasa* with no agreement about what to inscribe there. At Casablanca Roosevelt had enunciated his demand for unconditional surrender and Churchill had fallen in with a design which was at once bold in outline and entirely imprecise in everything else. Stalin too endorsed unconditional surrender later in the war. Churchill was disposed to curb and isolate Prussia, thus implying decentralization or perhaps partition, but he gave relatively little attention during the war to post-war problems. At Quebec Roosevelt and Churchill, to the horror of their principal political advisers, Hull and Eden, endorsed the Morgenthau plan for constraining Germany by converting it from an industrial to an agricultural economy, but this vision quickly evaporated. At Teheran the three leaders were in favour of some kind of partition, which Churchill opposed at Yalta and the new trio all rejected at Potsdam. Events, not plans, eventually reshaped Germany.

It did not, however, follow that western forces were not to advance to Berlin or anywhere else so long as the war lasted. The plan only bound them to observe fixed lines of demarcation when the war was over and the occupation had begun. Stalin expected the Americans and British to race him for Berlin and the western allies had strong motives for doing so as they speculated about the future of an alliance which was about to pass from military cooperation to political manoeuvre.

Montgomery's and Bradley's Army Groups both crossed the Rhine in the third week of March. Montgomery, commanding Canadian, British and American armies — the last was the Ninth US Army under General William H. Simpson which had been subordinated to him during the Ardennes offensive – was heading across northern Germany for Berlin; Bradley with three US armies under command was heading across central Germany. Further south the American-French Army Group under Devers was making equally rapid progress. A few days earlier Hitler had signed the first of a number of orders for the total destruction of everything. On the 28th the Russians made their first air attacks on Berlin. At this time Eisenhower, to the dismay of his subordinates and still more of Churchill, took his eyes off Berlin. Although there were no longer any meaningful German armies in the field Eisenhower clung to the view that his task was to seek out and destroy the enemy's forces rather than seize his capital and he held to this resolve even after the US Ninth Army crossed the Elbe on 12 April. He instructed Bradley, reinforced by the re-allocation to him of Ninth Army at Montgomery's expense, to push eastward towards Erfurt, Leipzig and Dresden – on a line, that is, running well south of Berlin, which he declared to be irrelevant, and through Saxony, which was. He now adopted the policy of the concentrated thrust which Montgomery had urged upon him in the previous summer but he had chosen the wrong thrust. Further, in an unprecedented message to Stalin – which was probably dictated by anxiety to avoid an unpleasant clash between American and Russian forces and partly also by a genuine belief in the importance and practicability of post-war Russo-American cooperation – he disclosed his intention not to go for Berlin and gave Stalin a detailed account of the allied order of battle. Stalin was so surprised that he thought the message was a trick, did not send the equivalent information on Russian plans and dispositions which Eisenhower had asked for, and immediately accelerated his own measures to take Berlin. Churchill was not only surprised but appalled at this assumption of politico-strategic authority and by the revelation that the Supreme Commander had so little notion of the political importance of Berlin. To his own Army Group commanders Eisenhower remained for a time vague, so that when the first Anglo-American crossings of the Elbe were made the troops were still under the impression that they were on the last lap to Berlin. On 15 April, however, Simpson received a precise order to go no further. He was expecting to be in Berlin two days later. Thus it was at Torgau on the Elbe, on 25 April, that Americans and Russians first exchanged salutations.

Farther south too the Americans, spurting across Germany to Czechoslovakia, were reined back by punctilio. A line of demarcation had been agreed on 30 April. On 4 May, with German resistance vanishing, Eisenhower asked Moscow to let him keep up his momentum. He was only fifty miles from Prague and in a position to reach it before the Russians. Stalin, who had conceded to Eisenhower the right to advance as far as Pilsen, was not prepared to see him advance farther, and when Bradley offered at a meeting with Konev on the 5th to cooperate in the taking of Prague Konev declined. On that day Prague rose against the Germans. But the Americans neither advanced to their assistance nor felt able to send supplies by air. Eisenhower and Truman felt that they had done their best; Truman had already told Eisenhower at the end of April that he was 'loath to hazard American lives' for what he described as 'political purposes', and neither leader saw much point in taking a city which would then be immediately turned over to the Russians. Konev began to move towards Prague from Saxony to the north-west on the 6th and Malinovski and Eremenko from the south-east and east respectively a day later. The first Russians entered Prague on the 9th. But by then the 30,000 insurgents had been overpowered by the Germans and 8,000 of them killed.

For his main central thrust in 1945 Stalin had grouped his armies in three fronts under the overall direction of his Supreme Headquarters in Moscow. These fronts were commanded, from north to south, by Rokossovski, Zhukov and Konev. D-day, originally fixed at 20 January, was advanced to the 12th at the request of the western leaders when hard pressed in the Ardennes. Rokossovski was directed north of Warsaw to Danzig and then westward. Zhukov, who relinquished his senior staff appointment in Moscow in order to become the captor of Berlin, struck straight towards the German capital from south of Warsaw. Konev, moving further south through Silesia, also had Berlin in his sights. The last barrier of any consequence was the river Oder, especially the fortress of Küstrin (which, bypassed, did not surrender until the end of March) at the junction of the Oder with the Warthe due east of Berlin. Chuikov's Eighth Guards Army reached the Oder on 1 February and began to cross the next day. Chuikov wanted to press on despite logistic difficulties and the risks, which he rightly discounted, of a last German stand. But Stalin, like Eisenhower, was wary. He ordered Zhukov to consolidate on the Oder and turn northwards into Pomerania and clean it up. Stalin overestimated German strength in Pomerania as well as the opposition lying between Zhukov and Konev and Berlin. Chuikov fumed against the restraints imposed on him and after the war he complained that Zhukov had failed in his duty by not urging a more adventurous strategy on the overcautious Stalin. He was probably right since Guderian had already expressed the opinion at the end of January that Berlin would fall in a few days and Hitler was sending such reinforcements as he could muster not to eastern Germany but to Hungary. But Stalin may have had a political motive when he reined Zhukov in. By doing so he enabled Konev to draw up. The two Marshals were rivals and it suited Stalin to promote compepition between them and let them both share the glory of taking Berlin rather than let one of them garner too many laurels singlehanded.

Stalin's delaying has also been explained in other terms. It can be argued that in the opening weeks of 1945 he was anxious not to take Berlin too soon. Chuikov crossed the Oder on the eve of the Yalta conference and Stalin had no wish to disrupt the conference or the Grand Alliance. Berlin was doomed, its fate only a matter of time, and it was more important for him to safeguard the ravaged USSR against western hostility than to deliver the *coup de grâce* to Germany in one week rather than another. So long as Roosevelt lived Stalin probably felt that the American President's determination to remain on good terms with the USSR was a cardinal factor in his own foreign policies, but Stalin knew enough about western democracy to understand that Roosevelt was not the sole maker of policy and that there were significant anti-communist and anti-Russian forces in the United States and Great Britain. To take Berlin, assuming that he could have done so, while his western allies were still on the wrong side of the Rhine involved ending the war in a way which would have given him so dominant a position in Germany as to alarm the western powers and even revive visions of an anti-Russian alliance between them and the still not totally inconsiderable remnants of German military power. A dominant position in Germany could be more of a hazard than an asset so long as the war-weary USSR had not the strength to sustain it against a western coalition, and although Stalin banked on Roosevelt's determination to withdraw from Europe, he must also have recalled that Churchill had in 1919 not only supported western intervention in the USSR but had advocated the use of the German army to effect it. Whether such fanciful calculations did or did not pass through Stalin's mind remains unknown. The final onslaught was in fact delayed until April.

It was then mounted at short notice and, in the belief of Stalin's Marshals, under the impression that Montgomery had been ordered to get to Berlin before them. At a conference on 3 April Zhukov and Konev told Stalin that they could beat Montgomery and were told to produce their plans in forty-eight hours. Stalin drew a line on a map from east to west, dividing their zones of operations but stopping fifty miles east of Berlin with the implication that beyond that point the leading Marshal might be free to move on the German capital by any route he chose. The attack was launched on 16 April with 2.5 million men, 6,250 tanks and 7,500 aircraft against one million men, 1,500 tanks and 3,300 aircraft. Prolonged resistance by the Germans was impossible and by the 22nd the Russians were fighting in the streets of the capital. Konev's men had a slight lead over Zhukov's and there was some confusion as the two Fronts converged, but the suburbs were gradually reduced and in the early hours of 1 May General Krebs, Hitler's last Army Chief of Staff, acting under instructions from Goebbels and Bormann, sought out Chuikov to ask for an armistice. He told Chuikov that Hitler was dead and that he had come to negotiate with the Russians on behalf of a new German government which had been formed in compliance with Hitler's will and in which neither Goering, Ribbentrop nor Himmler had any part. Chuikov telephoned Zhukov. He was told that Stalin refused to negotiate. The Germans must surrender unconditionally on all fronts. Shortly after midday Krebs went back to the centre of Berlin where he shot himself. The next day, 2 May, the commander of the garrison capitulated.

Hitler had been dead two days. He spent the last weeks of his life underground in Berlin. By the Chancellery in the middle of the city was a complex of heavily protected underground shelters arranged in two floors. Hitler and his mistress Eva Braun had a set of rooms in what was called the Führer's Bunker at the deeper level. With them were Goebbels, his wife and five children, a doctor, a cook, a valet, a couple of secretaries and an Alsatian bitch which had just pupped. Nearby, in similar shelters, were Bormann, Artur Axmann, the Hitler Youth leader, and an assortment of adjutants, guards and so on. Other people came and went. Ten days before his end Hitler emerged from his delusion that the war could still be won and told Keitel that he accepted the fact of defeat and would shoot himself. He told Speer the same thing the next day. But from time to time hope still flickered and every day the increasingly senseless conferences took place in the war room. Goering had gone south but he quickly learned of Hitler's decision and sent him a signal proposing that he should immediately take over as though Hitler was dead. Since Goering was officially Hitler's successor there was nothing very odd about this proposal but it infuriated Hitler who ordered Goering's arrest and dismissed him from his command of the Luftwaffe.

A few days later Hitler was still further incensed on learning that Himmler, at a personal meeting with the Swedish Count Folke Bernadotte, had taken it upon himself to propose capitulation. (Since he proposed to capitulate in the west but not in the east the western allies rejected his advances.) Hitler ordered Himmler's arrest and had his SS adjutant, Hermann Fegelein, who was in the Bunker, shot there and then. That same night, 28–9 April, he married Eva Braun. After the ceremony and a wedding meal Hitler retired to write his two last documents. His will dealt with personal matters. It contained nothing particularly unusual except the gift of his pictures to found a picture gallery in Linz. His political testament, a much longer document, rehearsed all his old attacks on the Jewish race and reaffirmed his belief in the German need for *Lebensraum* in the east. Next to the Jews he blamed the German officer corps for all that had gone wrong. Having dismissed Goering and Himmler, he appointed Doenitz President and Commander-in-Chief of the Armed Forces and Goebbels Chancellor. He also appointed a number of other Ministers and a new Commander-in-Chief of the Army to succeed himself. On the afternoon of the 30th Hitler said his good-byes. He then poisoned the dog and Eva and shot (or possibly poisoned) himself. Their bodies were burned

THE SOVIET DRIVE TO BERLIN 1945

0   20
       Miles

GERMAN UNITS

PZA Panzer Armies.

A Armies.

PZD Panzer Divisions.

ID Infantry Divisions.

2nd White Russian Front

1st White Russian Front

1st Ukrainian Front

To Rostock

To Stralsund

Karow

STETTIN

To Hamburg

Starsow

Wittenberge

Gransee

Army Group Vistula

3 PZA

3 PZA   9A

Hohenzollern Canal

US UNITS

Fehrbellin

Havel

Stendal

Elbe

Nauen

Lanke

Bernau

Buckow

9A

Küstrin

Warte

BERLIN

Spree

Fürstenwalde

Frankfurt

remnants

9A   4 PZA

(13 Divisions in all)

Oder

Möckern

12A

Treuenbrietzen

Army Group Centre

4 PZA   17A

Cottbus

Wittenberg

To Leipzig

Dessau

Schlieben

US UNITS

Torgau

Ruhland

4 PZA

Neisse

Elbe

Diesa

DRESDEN

2 PZD

2 ID

17A

To Prague

OPERATIONS APRIL–MAY, 1945

Front line 16 April.

Soviet thrusts 16–20 April.

Front line 19 April.

Soviet thrusts 20–26 April.

Front line 25 April.

Soviet thrusts 26 April–9 May.

Front line 8 May.

German counter-attacks.

~ARTHUR BANKS~

outside in accordance with instructions which had already been given. That night the surviving inhabitants of the Bunker made their escapes, but not the Goebbels family. After the failure of the Krebs mission to Chuikov Goebbels gave poison to his children and either shot or poisoned his wife and himself – the second Chancellor of the Third Reich.

Doenitz, its President for a week, was also its undertaker. On 2 May he sent Admiral Wilhelm Friedeburg to Montgomery to negotiate a surrender in the west. Montgomery refused to negotiate. On 7 May representatives of all three of the Reich's fighting services arrived at Eisenhower's headquarters at Reims and there, in the presence of senior American, Russian, British and French officers (but not of Eisenhower himself) surrendered unconditionally to the western and Russian commands. After the formal act there was a brief encounter between Jodl and Eisenhower at which Eisenhower asked Jodl whether he fully comprehended what had been done and Jodl said he had. On the next day, towards midnight, and again in the presence of senior officers of the four principal victors, the act of surrender was ratified at Russian headquarters in the German capital, Berlin.

Epilogue

THE Second World War was fought to a finish in Europe and had to be. Hitler could have ended it by negotiation because he was fighting for material things and might have decided at some moment or other that he had won enough of them. He wished to do so after the defeat of Poland and again after the defeat of France, although with the reservation that making peace on either occasion was only a prelude to a fresh bid for *Lebensraum* in the east. There was no lack of peace-makers: the Pope, Mussolini, the massed sovereigns of the Low Countries and Scandinavia, the King of Rumania, all tried to mediate in various ways and at various dates in the closing months of 1939. The inactivity of France and Great Britain during the obliteration of Poland gave Hitler and others grounds for believing that their declarations of war had been retractable formalities. Hitler could hardly conceive how, although they had been silly enough to go to war on behalf of Poland, they would continue at war on behalf of what had become non-Poland. With the Right preponderantly and the communists wholly for peace and with the knowledge, leaked by German counter-intelligence, that Hitler had given orders for an attack in the west in November, France and Great Britain could logically be expected to give up. But 1939 brought neither peace nor war. Hitler had to postpone his attack in the west and the peace offensive continued in 1940 up to and again after the German campaigns in Scandinavia and the west. Roosevelt sent his Under-Secretary of State, Sumner Welles, on a long exploration in European capitals in February and March, and the Pope and Mussolini kept up their feelers. After the fall of France Hitler tried again to secure his gains and close the account but Churchill refused.

The hesitations in London about whether to seek terms or not in 1940 reveal the differences between Hitler's war aims and those of his enemies. Great Britain, the sole effective combatant at this point, was fighting for no specific or material gain. It was fighting against Hitler and Nazi Germany. On the British side therefore negotiation meant not compromise but the abandonment of British war aims, which, in so far as they could be rationalized at all, were the surrender of Germany and the collapse of Nazism. Unconditional surrender was implicit in the nature of the war long before it was proclaimed at Casablanca. The alternative, for Great

Britain, was to acknowledge that it had no war aims and had got into war by a mistake; but, once in, it could get out in this way only with the utmost difficulty, for a declaration of war is so weighty a pronouncement that it is intolerable to regard it as meaningless. To retire from a war with nothing accomplished and without being beaten requires a very unusual psychological effort. In this particular case it entailed also a sense of shame, for the evils of Nazi Germany had sunk in and making peace with Hitler seemed iniquitous. Although fearful of war in 1938 and glad to be spared it, the British were by 1940 determined to see it through.

So the war went on and the aim of surrender was achieved, although at great cost. Fighting on had not only a certain inevitability nor was it only the fulfilment of a praiseworthy obligation. It involved the deaths of millions of people, including victims of Nazism – like the Jews – who might have been killed anyway but might not, and countless other civilians who certainly would not have died the premature and often horrible deaths which came to them. To ask whether the frightful cost was worth it is to ask an exceptionally painful question, but Hitler's régime was as horrible as any that Europe had ever seen and more horribly well equipped to pursue its fearful ends, and it may be thought that hardly any price could have been too high to pay for the elimination of the German Nazis. The tragedy was that the price had to be paid by so many people and so innocent.

As the Nazis recede into history they become objects of interest to historians, sociologists and psychologists, but they were in their own generation objects of pure horror. This horror can be expressed by saying that they represented a threat to civilized values and standards of behaviour; it can only be conveyed by recalling, with increasing effort over receding time, the things which they did to individual human beings. The battered but living skeletons found in the stinking degradation of the torture camps in 1945 are Hitler's truest memorial.

Hitler was many things, including an archcriminal, a criminal over and above criminals. His principal surviving accomplices were arraigned and tried in a series of trials in which they were charged with violations of the laws or customs of war, with 'crimes against humanity' and with 'crimes against peace'. The first of these categories includes offences such as the refusal to give quarter, the use of certain proscribed weapons (for example gas, expanding bullets) and the execution of prisoners of war, that is to say, acts which have become illegal by custom or have been declared illegal by international conventions. The most flagrant violations of these agreements during the Second World War were the execution of commandos after they had surrendered and the execution of commissars, or anybody said to be a commissar, among captured Russian soldiers. The expression 'crimes against humanity' was coined to designate acts which, although not explicitly proscribed by international pronouncement, are clearly contrary to law in civilized states independently of the existence of a state of war, such as the killing of men and women simply because they belong in certain categories and without any allegation of criminal acts committed by them; or forced labour. 'Crimes against peace' denoted the preparation and waging of aggressive war in contravention of international law.

War crimes trials are not new. The notion that wars have rules which must be observed is at least as old as classical antiquity. It was reasserted by such eminent Renaissance jurists as Vitoria, Suarez and Grotius, and the first adequately recorded war crimes trial in Europe took place nearly 500 years ago. During the Second World War Germany's enemies and victims gave early warning of their intention to bring war criminals to justice. At the beginning of 1942 nine countries jointly declared that the punishment of war criminals by judicial process was one of their war aims, and shortly afterwards a War Crimes Commission was established to collect and sift evidence and consider what should be done about it. In November 1943 Germany's three principal enemies declared that when the war was over criminals would be handed over to the governments of the countries where their crimes had been committed and that major criminals, whose crimes could not be attached to specific areas, would be tried by an international tribunal.

This tribunal, the International Military Tribunal, was formally constituted by an agreement signed in London in August 1945 on behalf of the American, British, Russian and (provisional) French governments and it subsequently conducted the most famous of all war crimes trials at Nuremberg in 1946. In addition the American authorities conducted twelve trials in their zone of Germany during 1946–9 under the provisions of a four-power ordinance (Control Council Law No. Ten) and the French held a smaller number of similar trials. The British, more tardily, put Manstein on trial on seventeen charges on nine of which he was found guilty, but dropped a plan to try Rundstedt, who had issued the commando order, on the grounds that he had become too old and feeble. The Russians held no trial under Control Council Law No. Ten. In Italy Kesselring was among the accused in trials held by the British. He was sentenced to death but this sentence was commuted to imprisonment, first for life and then for twenty-one years; and he was released on medical grounds in 1952. All over the rest of what had been occupied Europe, Germans from the SS, the armed services and the civilian administration had to face charges of murder, plunder and offences against the person of varying magnitude. Finally, the Germans themselves instituted similar proceedings when they recovered their juridical independence. Such trials were still occurring over twenty-five years after the end of the war as fresh facts came to light and criminals who had successfully lain low for years were discovered.

The first protests against war crimes in the Second World War and the first enunciation of a determination to prosecute the criminals were attempts to put a curb on the atrocities which were being perpetrated in Europe, by reminding people at all levels that even in war certain things were not permitted and that those who ignored the law might be brought to account. Further, there developed during the war a desire to assert both the existence of international penal law and the practicability of enforcing it by judicial process. And if the perpetrators of local crimes were to be indicted and perhaps executed, it seemed right and necessary to indict also those at the top who had either inspired or commanded these crimes. Hence the trial at Nuremberg in which twenty-two men who had wielded exceptional power and authority were put in the dock. (The indictment named twenty-four but one, Robert Ley, committed suicide in prison and a second, the industrialist Gustav Krupp von Bohlen, was found unfit to plead because of age and infirmity.) The Nuremberg defendants included the principal surviving political figures of the Third Reich but this and later trials were not confined to Nazi Party leaders since the prosecutors wanted to establish also the accountability of all, irrespective of party affiliation, who had wielded and abused power: service chiefs, police chiefs, industrial chiefs, holders of high judicial office, scientists and doctors who had used human bodies for inhumane experiments, etc. Twelve of the twenty-two accused were sentenced to death, three to life imprisonment, four to terms of ten to twenty years and three were acquitted. All the death sentences were carried out except that on Goering, who committed suicide after he had been sentenced, and Bormann who was either dead or in hiding and was convicted and sentenced *in absentia*. In the next most important trials – the twelve American trials under Control Council Law No. Ten – 185 defendants were indicted. Of these 177 stood trial, twenty-six were sentenced to death (but two of these sentences were remitted), thirty-five were acquitted and the remainder received sentences ranging from life to small terms which in fact resulted in their immediate release.

These proceedings commanded something less than universal approval among the general public and in the legal profession. The general public was worried by the appearance of unfairness resulting from the fact that

the defeated were tried by their conquerors. Even though the trials were
not unfairly conducted they were, from this point of view, not unassailable. Alternatives had been considered but rejected as impracticable. A
trial by Germans was ruled out by the farcical outcome of the attempt to
get the Germans to do the same job after the First World War, and a trial
or trials by selected neutrals offered complications of procedure and language even more daunting than those involved in the solution adopted –
quite apart from the fact that there were few neutrals and they did not
want to assume the required role. (There was at least one trial in the
French zone of Germany at which French judges were joined by one
Belgian and one Dutch judge.)

From the legal point of view the principal objection to the trials was the
argument that, since there existed no international legislature to make
international law, there was no offence of which the accused could be
guilty or with which they could be charged. This argument raises a fundamental question about the nature of law: is it made by enactment, so that
without enactment it does not exist; or can it evolve from some other
source, so that it may be valid without enactment, in which case the
enactment is not creative but declaratory? Murder, to take a simple example, has been regarded as a crime and punished in certain states before
any legislative act declaring it to be a crime and saying how it would be
punished. War crimes, properly so called, have existed independently of
the Hague and Geneva conventions which regulate conduct in war.
Neither in the case of crimes against humanity nor in the case of war
crimes could the criminals of the Third Reich claim that they did not
know that the actions which were subsequently held against them were
criminal. Nor, given the warnings issued by their adversaries from 1940
onwards, could they claim that they had not been warned that they would
be tried. Many of the offences laid to their charge were committed after
this date.

The category of crimes against peace is not so clear cut, but the International Military Tribunal, presided over by a Lord Justice of Appeal
from Great Britain sitting with eminent judges and jurists from other
countries, held that preparing and waging aggressive war had been a
crime at least since the conclusion of the Kellogg-Briand Pact of 1928;
that it was a crime which could be committed by an individual; that
although it might be difficult to define aggression in general it was possible
to recognize it in particular cases; and that eight of the accused had
committed this crime.

Some of the Tribunal's negative decisions were as striking as its positive
conclusions. It refused to make any pronouncement on genocide in peace-

time within a state's legitimate boundaries. After the war a convention banning genocide was adopted by the United Nations and ratified by a number of states but this convention contains no adequate provisions for enforcement. The Tribunal also refused belligerent rights to non-uniformed partisans and held that there is nothing in international law to prohibit in all circumstances the execution of hostages. Finally, the Tribunal did nothing – because it was not asked to – to adapt the laws of war to the age of mass bombing. Since the international code of war had not been revised since the Hague Convention of 1907, throwing a bomb from a balloon was expressly prohibited but dropping one from an aircraft was not (unless the target were totally undefended) and it appeared that, although gassing people was clearly unlawful in the same way as poisoning wells was clearly unlawful, the unlawfulness of indiscriminate bombing remained open to debate.

As a normative body the International Military Tribunal had serious limitations. It was an international body created by agreement among only a few nations. Even though the laws which it applied were not new, their codification was *ad hoc* and *post hoc*; its Charter was devised for the specific purpose of trying individuals who, however much they deserved to be tried and condemned, were in everybody's mind before the Charter or the indictment was drawn up. None but losers were tried. The judges, however fairly they discharged their judicial office, were provided by the victorious prosecutors from among their own nationals. There was therefore a risk that the principles enunciated at Nuremberg would lack moral backing and legal endorsement and that the trial itself would become a piece of history without contributing to international law.

In order to give them a wider sanction the General Assembly of the United Nations in 1946 unanimously affirmed the principles recognized by the Charter and by the Tribunal's judgement and asked the International Law Commission to re-formulate them. The Commission formulated in 1950 seven principles which have therefore, as a result of the war, become part of the corpus of international law. They proclaim: that a person who commits an act which is a crime under international law may be punished for it; that this liability is not avoided merely because the internal law of the accused's country provides no penalty for the criminal act, or because the accused was acting as a head of state or government official, or because he was following an order from his government or a superior (provided, in this last case, that he had a moral choice); that any person charged with a crime under international law has the right to a fair trial on the facts and the law. The principles also defined three kinds of crime: crimes against peace, war crimes and crimes against humanity; and stated that complicity in any such crime was itself a crime under international law.

Crimes against peace are defined as planning, preparing, initiating or waging a war of aggression or a war in violation of international compacts, or participating in a conspiracy to do any of these things. War crimes consist (as they have done since ancient times) of violations of the laws or customs of war: examples given include the murder, ill-treatment or deportation – for slave labour or any other purpose – of civilians, the murder or ill-treatment of prisoners of war or persons on the seas, the killing of hostages, plunder of public or private property, wanton destruction of cities, towns or villages, or devastation not justified by military necessity. These definitions leave a lot of things open to argument, but they assert that it is proper to open the argument, to bring it before a judicial tribunal and to demand punishment. Finally, crimes against humanity are defined as certain acts against the civilian population when these acts are done in connection with any crime against peace or war crime. The acts are: murder, extermination, enslavement, deportation and other inhuman acts, and persecution on political, racial or religious grounds.

The Nuremberg trial and its aftermath were an attempt to establish that war is not so much a visitation like a plague or an act of state like a treaty of alliance, nor even a duty like a just war, but pre-eminently a crime and a punishable one.

The prime cost of war is measured in death and destruction. By this reckoning the cost fell most heavily on the USSR. Perhaps 20 million died – more than all the dead of all nations in the First World War and a staggering death roll for the short period of four years. Another twenty-eight million were made homeless. In the territories which they had occupied the Germans (whose scorched earth policy in retreat was much more efficient than the Russians' own destructiveness in 1941) destroyed half the living quarters in the towns and three quarters of it in the countryside. Two thirds of the wealth of these areas was extinguished. Over thousands of square miles the land was bared, neglected and almost uninhabited: no towns, no villages, no buildings to shelter man or even beast, hardly any beasts, hardly any people. There was one cow where there had been ten, one sheep or one goat where there had been four, one pig in place of two. Crops had to be sown by hand. Such machinery as could be seen was unusable rusting monuments to war but no longer aids to livelihood. The unoccupied areas had suffered too from neglect: in the oil industry, for example, technicians had had to go away and fight, leaving their machinery and installations to fall into shocking condition.

Recovery was at first slow. Communications had been wrecked or worn out – 40,000 miles of rail track and a vast quantity of rolling stock destroyed. Production of many peacetime necessities had been all but abandoned – the output of tractors reduced from 116,000 a year to 8,000. Political conditions prohibited a quick reconversion of the economy – the American nuclear bomb had to be countered by a Russian one. So when in 1946 two thirds of the inhabitants of Stalingrad had returned to the city, only one sixth of its buildings had been patched up. Many of the rigours of war continued. There was little real improvement in living conditions for a decade. The memories of war were ineradicable and its consequences were prolonged with deep, if incalculable, effects on post-war domestic and international politics.

The next heaviest burden fell on the Germans. At least four and a half million of them died, including about a million civilians; their military dead were twice as numerous as in the first war. In Germany as well as the USSR material damage was very heavy. These two peoples – the Russian and the German – were the chief victims not only in the European war but also in the World War, since Japanese casualties were around two million. The one possible exception is the Chinese whose death roll, peculiarly difficult to assess, has been put as low as 2.5 million and as high as 13.5 million. Great Britain, France and Italy all suffered fewer deaths than in the first war. British fatal casualties, including civilians, were 450,000 with another 120,000 from the British Empire; in the first war the imperial total was nearly a million. France lost 200,000–250,000 in action and about as many civilians, as against nearly a million and a half in 1914–18. Italy, whose loss of life was greater than the French and not far short of the British, sacrificed 410,000 (one in every five a civilian) as against its earlier total of 615,000. Belgium's military casualties were approximately the same in both wars but in the second it lost more civilians than servicemen. Norway, Denmark and Holland had been spared the first war. Their losses in the second were small by comparison with the figures already quoted but sizable in relation to their own populations and Holland had the highest number of civilian deaths (200,000 or more) of any country in western Europe other than Germany itself. In central and eastern Europe the civilian deaths were very heavy indeed, since they included 5 million Jews, another 4 million non-Jewish civilians and a further million Yugoslav Resisters. In their regular armies the chief sufferers were Yugoslavia and Hungary, which lost some 400,000 each, and Poland and Rumania, which lost 300,000 each. The price paid by Austria was also around 300,000. Bulgaria escaped comparatively lightly with 20,000 deaths, half of them civilians, but in Greece the dead exceeded

250,000, two thirds of them civilians. American casualties on all fronts, Pacific as well as European, were 290,000, nearly six times as many as in the First World War. These casualties would have been higher if the Americans had not had the best medical services among the combatants. All these figures are, in the nature of the case, not only approximate but disputable. They add up to something like 50 million.

No great European war since the Seven Years War has so little changed the map of Europe or so much changed the map of the rest of the world. If Hitler had won, his New Order would have transformed Europe, but since he did not win states and frontiers were more restored than altered. Estonia, Latvia and Lithuania were the principal victims, engulfed in the USSR, their populations removed wholesale. Parts of Finland, Czechoslovakia and Rumania (and Afghanistan) were also annexed to the USSR. Poland had to submit to being shifted, partly because the boundaries which it had won after the First World War were not ethnically easy to justify. In eastern Europe a few provinces changed hands. But there was no post-war conference to allocate real estate, as after the defeat of Napoleon. The reason was not merely the fact that territorial annexation was out of favour (although this was so) but also the fact that real estate was ceasing to be an index of power. Stalin, who was an expansionist and was in a position to incorporate large areas in the USSR, did not do so because he did not need to. Communists believed that new Soviet Republics would be created; that Yugoslavia, for example, would become one of the Republics of the USSR. But Stalin decreed otherwise. He told Tito that Yugoslavia and other nearby countries were to become People's Democracies, juridically outside the USSR. He may have been deterred by the fear that the Americans would not tolerate the territorial expansion of the USSR but he did not need to put the issue to the test because Russian power sufficed to establish a new kind of Russian empire in central and eastern Europe – extending over much of the old Habsburg and Ottoman lands in Europe as well as those of the Tsars. Its authority could be assured by indirect rule through obedient communist cliques. It did not work in Yugoslavia but it worked everywhere else for the rest of Stalin's life and many years beyond. Where the First World War had dissolved Europe's empires, the Second resuscitated one of them and vastly enlarged it – in modern dress. The main thing for Stalin was to implant a particular social system where he could: annexation was not necessary for this purpose, occupation sufficed and occupation could be vicarious. He said to Djilas in 1944: 'This war is not as in the past: whoever occupies a territory also imposes on it his own social system.

Everyone imposes his own system as far as his armies can reach. It cannot be otherwise . . .' But the determining factor was the radius of power of the army and not the legally established frontiers of states.

This new Russian empire was the product of circumstances and not of compact. The western leaders have been accused of handing over half Europe at Yalta to Stalin – as they have likewise been accused of cheating China at Teheran of its rightful claims in Asia. But Stalin would have established his empire even if there had been no Yalta conference. In the war on Hitler's eastern front, which was largely independent of the land, sea and air campaigns in the west, the Russian armies beat the German armies. Power in central Europe passed therefore by conquest from Germany to the USSR. What Roosevelt and Churchill tried to do at Yalta was to prescribe limits within which Russian power would be exercised. They have been criticized for not doing more to shackle that power. It is conceivable that, at Teheran fourteen months earlier, they could have driven a different bargain but it is unrealistic to forget that the circumstances of 1943 were inappropriate for driving post-war bargains at all. The Teheran conference was a war conference between partners intent on keeping each other in the war. Post-war problems – which is a euphemism for foreseeable and foreseen post-war disagreements – could only be raised at Teheran at some risk to the common war effort. Yalta was a different kind of conference, but by February 1945 Stalin's local power in eastern Europe could not be gainsaid. Roosevelt and Churchill extracted from him the declaration on liberated territories which was intended to assure basic democratic rights and procedures, but when Stalin disregarded this declaration there was nothing that any western power could do in the Russian sphere of influence created by Russian arms. All they could do was retaliate elsewhere. The creation in 1949 of the German Federal Republic and of Nato was a kind of retaliation against Stalin's exclusive and authoritarian hold over eastern Europe.

The biggest changes occurred in Germany. Since Hitler was not displaced by his army or his people, the surrender of Germany and the collapse of Nazism occurred simultaneously. They were a single event. Germany therefore was laid completely low. This had been envisaged: German power would disappear at the end of the war, in some versions for ever. There would of course be Germans and they would inhabit a place called Germany but this Germany would not exist as an independent unit in the power political structure. It was easy to see that this would be a fact immediately after the war. Less thought was given to how it would be perpetuated. Germany might be deprived of its industry, pastoralized, occupied, but the essential requirement for its indefinite subordination was the maintenance of an invincible alliance against its resurrection. This was assumed, if only superficially, and did not turn out to be so.

One of the main reasons why it did not turn out to be so was that Germany ceased to exist as such. Instead of persisting as a unit reduced to insignificance, it became divided into two units which rapidly became politically and militarily significant. This consequence of the war was entirely unforeseen and by removing Germany as a unit from the political scene it removed also the allies' main incentive to maintain their alliance. There was no Germany for them to keep down: the alliance brought about in 1941 for a limited purpose had achieved that purpose with the surrender of Germany and its subsequent partition. There were instead two Germanies to be kept up, each appropriated by the one side or the other. The Cold War might have developed in any case. Probably it would, but the division of Germany fundamentally impelled and shaped it. To some extent a consequence of the Cold War, this division was also – more perhaps than has been appreciated – a major formative factor. Moreover the division of Germany, besides dividing the allies, did more than anything else to keep the Americans in Europe. They stayed, first, to administer Germany and argue about its future; later to defend Western Germany and their own positions in it. When the anti-Nazi alliance was converted into a duel between the victors, the Americans were still in Europe and acquired new reasons for staying there.

The Nazis and their fascist like had been defeated by the combined forces of liberal democracy and totalitarian democracy. In the exuberance of victory there were those who hoped that the alliance of the anti-fascists would endure, but soon these two traditional streams – the sources, as noted earlier in this book, of the collapse of Europe's *anciens régimes* – found themselves no longer side by side but face to face. Europe's triangle of forces resolved itself into the duel called the Cold War.

In terms of Europe the Cold War was an ideological contest between liberal democracy and totalitarian democracy; the simpler description of it as a contest between communists and anti-communists is misleading since not all anti-communists are liberal democrats. The Cold War was at the same time a power struggle between the United States and the USSR. Had this contest remained European the principal issue would have been the possible revival of Fascism, the reconstitution of the triangle of forces, and the manoeuvres of its three elements to make a pattern of two against one either in the same way as during the war or in some other way. War, being by its nature dual, had forced the triangle to conform for a few years (1941–5) to its law which says that there can be only two sides.

56 *Top*: Paratroopers landing
in southern France, 1944

57 *Bottom*: British units
arrive in Bayeux, June 1944

58 *Top*: De Gaulle at the Arc
de Triomphe, 24 August 1944

59 *Bottom*: Paris 1944: a last
sniper causes an alarm

60 Churchill and de Gaulle
in Paris, 11 November 1944

61 *Top*: Americans in what is
left of Saarbrücken, March
1945

62 *Bottom*: Americans cross
the Rhine, 26 March 1945

63 *Top*: Field Marshals
Montgomery and Rokossovski
take a salute from Cossacks
on the Elbe

64 *Bottom*: Eisenhower and
Montgomery

65   Franz von Papen, captive,
April 1945

66   Pierre Laval, captive in
Lins, Austria

67 Berlin, the Reich
Chancellery: Hitler's office

68 Berlin, the Reich
Chancellery: the reception hall

69   Red Flag over the
Reichstag, Berlin: May 1945

After the war and the elimination of the one side the surviving forces moved from identity to opposition and so formed a new pattern, rigid until the appearance of some third element to give it mobility.

In the late forties and fifties this third element was neither European nor fascist. The Second World War, as has already been said, changed the map of the rest of the world as markedly as it left the outlines of the map of Europe recognizably familiar. The Seven Years War had decided that Great Britain and not France should have the lion's share of the dark continents in which Europeans had been seeking profit and adventure. North America and much of southern Asia were secured for Great Britain. France, the Netherlands and Portugal retained positions in Asia and, with Belgium, Germany and Italy, also shared in the later partition of Africa. The nineteenth and early twentieth centuries were the heyday of these European empires. The Second World War was the centrepiece of the last act of the story; the generation after the war was kept busy with the epilogue. As a result the nature of world conflict changed. This conflict had been a dispute centred in Europe, a dispute over political forms coupled with a struggle for power. It became a worldwide contest, still ideological and strategic, but one in which the third element was the significantly dubbed Third World which ceased on decolonization to be part of the Western World.

The new states which emerged from the dissolution of Europe's overseas empires, in far greater number than those which had emerged from the dissolution of its continental empires after the First World War, decided for the most part not to attach themselves to either side in the Cold War but to take up a distinct, non-aligned position. So far as the Cold War was ideological they sensed, correctly, that the ideological issue was a European one and had little to do with their immediate needs. Further, they diagnosed the Cold War as essentially a struggle for power which was bound to hurt them and which they must therefore try to stop. They rejected neutrality – opting out – as neither possible nor desirable. The Second World War had shown how little a neutral could rely on having his neutrality respected; the changes in the nature of war suggested that neutrality was a thing of the past. The neutral's claim to stay out of a war required certain conditions which were disappearing. It rested upon the assumptions that a state of war was clearly distinguishable from peace and that a given war could be restricted to certain areas and prevented from leaking through the frontiers of the neutral state. But the very expression Cold War showed that the concept of war as something overtly declared and conducted with lethal weapons against proclaimed opponents no longer sufficed; guerrilla and subversive wars, whose tech-

niques had been expanded in many parts of the world during the Second
World War, also increased the uncertainty about what was a war and
who was a belligerent. Air warfare eroded the significance of frontiers;
nuclear fall-out abolished it.

For all these reasons attempts to keep out of war by choosing the
classic posture of neutrality seemed to make little sense. Keeping out was
no longer a guarantee of safety. Those who wanted to fend off war could
no longer seek to barricade themselves against it; they must actively try to
prevent or extinguish it. Thus third parties came to believe that they must
in their own interests – to which it was easy to add the moral imperatives
of the peacekeeper – play a part in international affairs rather than abstract themselves from the scene. Leaders of new states were in any case
inclined towards a negative non-alignment: their consuming preoccupation with independence made them eschew alliance with a dominant
power, their pressing economic needs made them seek trade and aid in all
quarters, their concern for the cohesion of their new and often divided
societies counselled them against a foreign alliance which would offend a
particular domestic faction of the Left or the Right. But their non-
alignment was not merely negative. Despite their weaknesses, of which
they were only too well aware, they adopted a policy of positive non-
alignment, that is to say intervention, in order to ensure the survival and
independence which other states had tried in the past to safeguard by
going into political purdah. And because they mattered to the protagonists
in the Cold War, at least to the extent that each of these wanted to stand
no less well than the other with the non-aligned, their emergence from
European dominion into statehood after the war altered the terms and
area of international politics.

Yet important though they were this widening of the scene and multiplication of the cast were almost trivial beside the irrefragable involvement
of the United States in the world's proceedings. This involvement after
the Second World War has become as much a commonplace as American
isolationism after the First, and at times pushed to equally questionable
limits. It was the war which marked the change.

The American experience of war was different from all others. First,
the United States had war aims, in the sense of purposes to be accomplished by going to war as opposed to the bare winning of a war that
had happened. Taking part in a European war which they did not feel
obliged to fight in response to an external threat, the Americans needed
war aims. A people which is not forced to fight must have a reason for
doing so. A people which has no choice needs no aims, but a people which

has a choice must have aims. To Europeans the American preoccupation with war aims seemed either unreal or hypocritical. Europeans had no war aims except the aim first to survive and then to win, and these were not aims freely considered and adopted but simply a formulation of the force of circumstances. (The Resistance did develop war aims, but these were adopted in the course of the war and not as a reason for going to war; and they touched only a proportion of Resisters and a very small proportion of the whole people, which is one reason why they were so thinly attained.) But Americans, who had not been attacked and were not fighting for survival, could not be led into war without some explanation of why they should do any such thing, and the simplest way of satisfying this natural requirement was to present a statement of what the war was about and how the world could be made better by helping the right side to win it. Such statements are necessarily vague and often grandiose. Therefore they are easy to contemn. But for a people not under compulsion they are a necessity.

They also colour that people's outlook after the war is over. If a war is fought and suffered for certain purposes, there is a duty – not least to the dead – to see that the purposes are achieved. Where victory is the end of war, the war ends with the victory. But Americans believed that there were other ends and that the war had been fought to rescue and restore values such as freedom and justice, which Nazis and fascists had scorned and destroyed (and imperialists, in their less brutal ways, were also ignoring). Americans were not more devoted to these values than good men elsewhere but they were more committed to doing something to secure them. The sins of communist governments could not be overlooked. Therefore the war spirit which had animated the United States in the war was not assuaged when the fighting – against the dictators – ceased but oppression and injustice did not; and Americans carried into the more complicated world of peace politics the guiding principles which had sufficed in the simpler world of war. They remained campaign-minded.

Secondly, the American homeland remained inviolate. Although the American contribution in manpower and materials was enormous, the men and women with their equipment went out of the United States to battle and never imagined doing battle in it. Nor did those left behind know, at first hand, anything of bombardment or the fear of bombs, resistance, evacuation or privation. At second hand, through press and radio, they knew more about distant events than a people at war had ever known before, but the events themselves remained distant. It was the kind of war which had once been familiar to Europeans but had ceased to be so. Although in material terms the American war effort was the most up-to-date imaginable, in social terms it belonged still to an era in which combatants set sail while non-combatants stayed safely behind. War fosters and sanctifies material effort: in the United States the materialism promoted by military exigencies was not countered, as in Europe, by the social emollients produced by shared dangers. In this respect the American experience of war brought changes which were comparatively less abrupt during the war but, as with the effects of war aims, comparatively more potent after it. The United States took the war in its giant stride but did not afterwards look nearly as much the same as Europe did ten to twenty years after the war ended.

Thirdly, there was the sheer size of the achievement. Over 15 million men and women were summoned to do services of one kind or another – as compared with 22 million mobilized by the USSR, 17 million by Germany and 12 million by Great Britain, the Dominions and colonies. Gross national product was nearly doubled, rising from $91 billion to $166 billion. Overall industrial output was doubled, while at the same time agricultural output also increased by more than a fifth. New industries were created (synthetic rubber) or given an enormous boost (electronics). The expansion of American shipbuilding from one to 19 million tons a year has already been mentioned. Such efforts were common. Aircraft production rose from below 6,000 a year on the eve of war to more than 96,000, the numbers employed in the aircraft industry from 46,000 to more than 2 million. Altogether the Americans made 275,000 aircraft, of which 40,000 went to their allies. American aircraft provided the RAF with an increment of 20–25 per cent over and above what it obtained from the British aircraft industry.

So too with tanks. American tank production, negligible in 1941, rose to 14,000 and 21,000 in the next two years. The American Sherman became the mainstay of the western allies. The British army possessed 3,300 Shermans on the day when it returned to France in 1944. The Sherman did not give the western allies the superiority over German models which they were looking for, but the Pershing, which came into service in 1944, proved a match for the last German tanks, the Tiger and Panther. British industry, obliged after Dunkirk to replace losses as quickly as possible, began by supplying current obsolescent models and the newer Churchill and then developed the Cromwell and the Comet which reached fighting units towards the end of 1942 and 1944 respectively, but tank design and production were, by agreement, primarily an American commitment and the resulting models were American designs with the incorporation of as many British ideas as fitted them. In addition to the first essentials of aircraft, tanks and shipping the United States produced a total of 64,000 landing craft (to Great Britain's 4,300) and equipped its allies as well as itself with practically all the transport aircraft, self-propelled artillery, amphibian vehicles and heavy trucks which they required. That remarkable vehicle the jeep was produced in such quantities that the Americans were able to spare 86,000 for the British. (The Germans had a jeep too, which was water and sand proof.) As a result of this war effort the United States, uniquely among the combatants, began the next phase of its history materially better equipped than before.

Fourthly, the war altered the distribution of power in the United States geographically and politically. It accelerated the shift of money and people from the east to the west coast and gave the south the boost which it had never had since the Civil War. Industry invaded the west where it had been relatively inconspicuous and the south where – outside Texas, already well supplied with capital from oil – it had hardly been at home at all. As the aircraft and telecommunications industries expanded into the south, employment and communications boomed. Atlanta, for example – designed by geography to be as much a natural centre in the age of aircraft as in the age of rail – a city where the complete devastation of the Civil War had opened the way for a *post bellum* entrepreneurial class to supplant the old upper class which had remained sufficiently dominant elsewhere (in Mississippi for example) to impede rejuvenation – had at last the opportunity to join the mainstream of American modernization and prosperity. The demands of war gave a new mobility both to southern whites who moved to the nearest city and to negroes who, whether through the calls of economic expansion or through conscription, moved to all parts of the country, including parts where they had been little seen before. These shifts and needs helped the anti-discrimination cause. Roosevelt gave a pledge of no discrimination in industry, wrote non-discrimination clauses into the government contracts upon which industry increasingly lived during the war and created a Fair Employment Practices Commission. (But the pledge was widely evaded and the Commission harassed. In the armed services negroes continued to be relegated to subordinate positions. Secretary Stimson debarred them from equal opportunities on the grounds that they were incapable of learning the necessary skills. Secretary Knox was even firmer. The negro was not integrated in the armed services until the Korean War.) Thus the primacy of the old centres of wealth (and liberalism) in the north-east was eroded and movements of population, begun in the First World War but arrested by the great depression, were resumed. The consequences of these economic and social movements began to become apparent only in the generation which followed the war years.

The balance of political power was affected by more than geographical shifts. As the British and the Germans both discovered, war is a mighty centralizer. For the United States too the same proposition held good. War necessitated an immense increase in federal budgets and federal spending. The proportion of federal to other taxes grew. This centralization of authority accelerated a constitutional trend, as between the federal government and the states, but did not inaugurate any economic or social revolution, as between government and private interests. Roosevelt had to combat the marked reluctance of American society to entrust the government with regulating powers. His administration had at first no adequate control either over the estimates made by the armed services of their requirements and so of their demands on industry, or of industry itself, and it was not until 1943 that Roosevelt succeeded in imposing centralized government control over activities traditionally jealous of government interference. American capitalism produced the goods but it wanted also to remain sovereign in its own house, and resisted government direction until complaints of the monopolization of government contracts by the bigger corporations and rumours of scandals gave Roosevelt the opportunity and the necessary backing to create new government agencies to fix priorities, allocate orders and at the same time check inflation by price, wage and rent control. The Congress mistrusted the vast increase in the government's powers which accompanied the vast increase in the nation's efforts. It was only with difficulty persuaded that the one required the other. The unions too bridled against the shift which the war imposed on the balance of power between government and unions, and at one point Roosevelt was forced to nationalize the coal mines in the face of strike threats from John L. Lewis, the leader of the mineworkers. Roosevelt eventually secured control over the economy through the Office of Economic Stabilization, the Office of Price Control and his annual Finance Acts. The latter raised the income tax and extended it to whole classes which had never had to pay it before; federal income tax rose, at the top level, to 94 per cent. A corporation tax rising to 50 per cent was imposed and an excess profits tax was introduced which rose by stages to 95 per cent of the excess. Yet government expenditure on the war grew so fast that during the four war years only 41 per cent of it was covered by taxation. For the rest the government had to borrow and to control the consequent inflation by the statutory regulation of wages and prices.

The war finally brought the great depression to an end, but at the same time the semi-socialist New Deal gave way to a fully capitalist war economy. This war economy performed prodigies of productive valour in the service of the military. The achievements of the partnership were miraculous, so much so that they stamped a pattern on the further development of the American economy and American society in the nuclear age.

Fifthly and finally, the United States was not only transformed domestically but also was seen to have become to an unprecedented degree the world's most mighty power. This power, however reluctantly acknowledged, had played some part in propelling the United States into war. Even before the mobilization of its resources in manpower and production the United States possessed enormous industrial and military might. Its low posture in the twenties and thirties was out of line with its capacities and Americans were perhaps readier than appeared at first sight to be up and doing – preferably with a good cause – because the sense of power possessed is itself an incentive to the use of power. The war destroyed reticence. Victory destroyed bashfulness, since victory was seen as a triumphant use of power for good ends. Then the power itself was vastly accentuated by the American monopoly of the nuclear bomb, but neither victory nor the bomb was the source of American power. They were on the contrary among its consequences. Yet the bomb created a new situation since it made the United States more powerful than all other states put together, not merely more powerful than any other state or any conceivable coalition of states. It could impose its will universally, should it be prepared to threaten and resort to nuclear war. And, so it seemed in 1945, it might maintain this position indefinitely since it was widely, if wrongly, assumed that no other state would be able to make nuclear weapons for a long time to come.

The appearance of nuclear power as a military factor coincided with the disappearance of a system of international politics in which several states of roughly equal strength predominated. Although this system left its mark on the nascent United Nations, where five states were held to be superior and were given a permanent place and a veto in the Security Council, the new reality was a bipolar system in which predominant power belonged to the United States and the USSR, each of whom was accepted as markedly superior to everybody else. Since these two powers were presented and accepted as the protagonists of two opposed ways of life, the bipolarity was also inherently an actively hostile confrontation. Europe was the chief object of this ideological and power conflict.

Yet the universality of American power was, despite first appearances, limited. The Americans recoiled from the use of nuclear weapons. The novelty of these weapons made them more awful than anything that had gone before, even though the two occasions on which they had been used (described in the ensuing part of this book) had not caused as many deaths as some more conventional instances of slaughter. Their continuing toxic effect, vaguely apprehended, added to the revulsion. There was widespread feeling in the United States that nuclear weapons should not be uscd again. But if this were so, the threat to use them was not a threat but a bluff. Thus, even before the USSR itself constructed a nuclear bomb, the American monopoly had been negated and the American omnipotence converted into a predominance paralleled by Russian power. The American monopoly was both a fact and a myth.

In Europe in particular, American power was countered by Russian power. The Russians occupied half Europe and maintained very large armed forces within and beyond their borders after the war ended; Stalin, with a ruthlessness reminiscent of his war on the peasants in the thirties, gave an absolute priority to war industries and war research, in particular to discovering the scientific and technological secrets of nuclear power which Russian experts were already close to mastering. By postponing for a generation the amelioration of the quality of life in the USSR Stalin ensured that power in Europe should be shared.

The Cold War, which is the name for the rather novel way by which this contest for power was initiated and then conducted, was something that Roosevelt certainly, and Stalin probably, would have wished to avoid. It represented Europe's continuing claim on the attentions of the world's two super-powers and it was the principal outward and visible sign of the post-war involvement of the United States in international affairs. This involvement would probably have come about in any case, but historically it followed from the recognition of the facts of power and geopolitics, brought about by war and Roosevelt. The direction of the involvement, on the other hand, was determined by pre-war concepts and Truman. Shortly after Hitler's invasion of the USSR Truman, then a Senator, said that the United States ought to help the Russians so long as they were being beaten by the Germans but that, if the Russians began to win, then the United States should help the Germans, so that as many as possible of both might be killed. This was a denial of the thesis that the war was a war against Fascism and a reassertion of the thesis that liberal democrats and communists could not live together amicably. Truman, like Stalin, belonged emphatically to the pre-war generation. He was also, unlike Roosevelt, relatively inexperienced in international affairs and so more dependent on the State Department and more receptive to an official line on the USSR which was harder than Roosevelt's had been. Those who believe that men make history will say that two men in particular, Truman and Stalin, made the Cold War. Those who believe that men operate only on the surface of deeper currents will point to Truman and Stalin as examples of the strength and direction of those forces which, having been driven underground for a space like the fountain of Arethusa, re-emerged after the defeat of Fascism to take control once more of men's conflicting destinies and destinations.

How events were shaped is a matter for debate. The events themselves are clearer. In June 1948 the United States formally abjured isolationism by the Vandenberg resolution adopted by the Senate, and ten months later it signed the North Atlantic Treaty in company with Canada and ten European states. These two events marked the end of isolationism – with a particular intent.

The cost of a war in men and materials, and the redistribution of territory and power which it brings about, are only two parts of the consequences of war. There is a third, less tangible but at least as important.

Wars intensify simple emotions and they also create opportunities and heighten expectations. Wars are horrible and bearing them is only made possible by hating one's enemy and by believing in a better future for one's self.

The hatred cannot be switched off. It may abate, though slowly, but since the Second World War the hatred felt for Germans in those years among Russians, Jews and others who suffered terribly has remained a factor in European affairs. It may be exaggerated for purposes of propaganda but it exists to be exaggerated and is easily rekindled. One of the war's many causes was the madness which took hold of Germany and one of the war's effects was to spread this madness and fill all Europe with violence and with the toleration, even the applause, of violence. There was in this respect a difference between the war in eastern Europe and the war in the west, and this difference has affected post-war emotions and therefore post-war political attitudes. The German onslaught in the west was less savage than in the east and German barbarity in western occupied territories was episodic whereas in the east it was planned and persistent. Consequently the western response was less vicious too. It is difficult to gauge the feelings of those who rejoiced, in Great Britain for example, at the news of the destruction of German cities. There was a certain grim Old Testament satisfaction, but there was little exultation and the dominant feeling was probably the thought that such blows must hasten the end of the war. There was much bitterness but little of the sheer hatred which disfigured the First World War, and although the two catastrophes were only a quarter of a century apart the generation of the second war would have considered it absurd to boo dachshunds in the London streets as their fathers had done. There was a certain sobriety.

There were also expectations and, after the war ended, a balance to be struck between satisfied and unsatisfied expectations. Making the world a better place to live in meant, in Europe, political, economic and social changes, a further instalment of the long-drawn-out revolution promising freedom, equality and brotherhood; outside Europe it meant, in the first place, the end of foreign and colonial rule. Of these twin aspirations the second was substantially satisfied in less than a generation after the end of the war and in some places within a few years. The British, French, Dutch and Belgian empires in Africa and Asia (but not yet the Portuguese) dissolved. They were doubtless already dissolving but the war accelerated the process by weakening the resources and the nerve of the metropolitan powers and by a revolution in thought which made empire seem in 1945 much more old-fashioned and dubious, as well as impermanent, than it had seemed six years earlier. By 1960 these empires were extinct or vestigial. Their demise constituted the greatest change ever made in a short space to the map of the world and to the mechanisms of international relations.

Within Europe the revolutionary current stimulated by the war was less successful. The old order proved remarkably tenacious, perhaps because the economic stringencies of the aftermath of war, on top of the strains of the war itself, drained the life out of reform movements. There were gains. In Great Britain, for example, the creation of a free public health service transformed the lives of millions of people not only by relieving or preventing sickness but also by removing the hideous worries of those who had had to endure illness or watch it in their children without being able to pay to do anything about it. In other countries too social services and social experiment received a fillip and even right-wing parties and governments took to thinking and acting in terms which they would have abhorred before the war. In eastern Europe civil liberties were obliterated by the political repression and economic obscurantism, worthy of Tsar Nicholas I, which Stalin and his successors in Moscow felt impelled to adopt, but in the USSR itself the government was the legatee of its own wartime promises of a better life and of wartime measures of toleration – such as the toleration of religion, the reappearance of priests, more freedom for writers, the appeal to popular sentiments in place of the use of disciplinary threats. Post-war stringencies produced a retreat from this tentative liberalization but did not altogether kill its seeds. War, it has been said, is the midwife of revolution. But nobody has said what is the period of gestation. The revolutions of 1848 occurred thirty-three years after the end of Napoleon's wars.

Finally there is the Middle East. Hitler's climax to Gentile persecution of the Jews – a drama unequalled for shame in the history of European civilization except by the slave trade – was effected with horrors even more appalling than the pogroms in Russia and Roumania in 1881 and 1905. It piercingly and urgently sharpened the desire of the survivors to depart to Zion. It probably also sharpened the desire of guilt-laden Europeans to see them go and it certainly accentuated the sympathies of some Gentiles for a people whom they had too often and now too fatally reviled. But Zion was no empty haven waiting to receive them. For half a century Zionists had been resolved to find a home in Palestine for the Jews and to create a Jewish state there. Some of them had imagined a state under Ottoman suzerainty and later some of their successors thought of an autonomous dominion within the British Empire, but most Zionist leaders realized from the first that what they sought must be an independent sovereign state. They also realized that it would be impolitic to say so, since the creation of this new state would entail the dispossession, or at least the subjection, of the existing Arab inhabitants of the lands for which Zionists yearned as a refuge and a religious fulfilment.

When the war ended, the Zionists, who had refrained from harassing the British in Palestine so long as the war lasted, resorted to violence in their turn. They took up arms and drove the British out. They then defeated the Arabs who came against them, jointly but hardly unitedly, and so won their state and enlarged it by provoking the Palestinians by terror into flight. Zionism was not only rendered more urgent by Nazi brutality; it was also itself brutalized. Israel's doors were, as a matter of principle, open to all Jews whencesoever, and the Jews of Europe hurried to it – except those in the west who were too comfortable to move and some in the east who were not allowed to. This migration, which was supplemented by similar migrations of non-European Jews, opened a new chapter in the history of the Middle East by implanting the state of Israel in a part of the world which Arabs regarded as theirs, which they had hoped to inherit from the Turks with British help in 1919, which they had seen the British take for themselves, and from which they were now not only debarred but actually – by arms or by fear – evicted. The Jewish problem had been off-loaded by Christendom onto Islam. But it did not cease to concern Europe: for the Middle East remained what it had been for centuries – one of the world's most convenient highways – and what it had become in the twentieth century – one of the world's primary sources of mineral wealth – so that the world's Great Powers could not ignore it.

But their continued intervention took new shapes. The Second World War destroyed the pattern imposed after the First. Then the British and French had established a post-Ottoman condominium, in despite of the

Arabs and to the exclusion of the Russians. But the Second World War
eliminated first the French and then, more gradually, the British and so
created new opportunities for Arabs – and Russians. These new opportunities coincided with swelling revolutionary and nationalist currents
in the Arab world which offered Arabs a new Arab-Russian alliance in
place of the Arab-British association which had governed Middle Eastern
politics during the First World War and after it. Against this potential
Arab-Russian entente Israel and the United States constituted, however
loosely, a counter-system. Thus the Superpowers who, in Europe, were the
protagonists in the Cold War were, in the Middle East, antagonists in an
area where keeping the peace would require them to restrain not themselves but others.

It has been said that wars settle nothing. This is too caustic a dismissal
of human endurance and human striving. At the end of this great war in
Europe the Nazis and their fascist allies were beaten. Things would have
been very different had they not been. Fascism, perhaps not irretrievably
but yet at this point decisively, was defeated.

A famous Russian historian of classical antiquity has judged that Greece
declined because men came to distrust reason and Rome fell because it
tried to maintain an exclusively privileged society wherein the rich were
enervated and the poor alienated. If these judgements on the ancestors of
Europe's civilization have any bearing on its own fate, then the Fascism
of the twentieth century begotten of anti-rational and anti-democratic
authoritarianism was a malign cancer and its defeat in 1945 at least a
reprieve.

The Greater East Asia and Pacific Conflict

If you say which ruler possesses moral influence, which commander is the more able, which army obtains the advantages of nature and the terrain, in which regulations and instructions are better carried out, which troops are the stronger, which has the better trained officers and men, and which administers rewards and punishments in a more enlightened manner – I will be able to forecast which side will be victorious and which defeated.

Sun Tzu, *The Art of War*, fourth century B C

Part I
ASIAN CONFLICT

CHAPTER 1

China and Japan

THERE are two principal countries of the Far East with an ancient civilization, China and Japan: and the war in the Far East had its origin in the quarrel between them. This developed gradually out of events which began about a century earlier and set afoot historical processes which were seemingly uncheckable. With apparent fatalism inflammable materials were stacked.

Ultimately, the fire started and flames enfolded the two countries in a most bitter war of survival. This in turn caused a wider blaze in the Pacific; and the fire in the East coincided with Hitler's fire in Europe. The conflagrations merged, and the wars became one. Almost all the peoples of East Asia and South Asia were engaged.

The start of this great drama came with the different ways that China and Japan responded to the unfamiliar intrusion of the West into Asian affairs.

In East Asia China, even in its decadence, has always been a most absorbing topic. It has lain across the map of Asia, establishing standards and precedents, rather as the Roman Empire dominated the ancient western world. Traditionally, East Asia had no system of international relations in which independent countries coexist with one another, such as was known from the earliest times in Europe, but was a system in which all the lesser countries revolved like satellites around the great central structure, which was regarded by all men as central, necessary and almost unchanging. In the middle of the nineteenth century, this was still true, even though China was standing on the verge of one of the most calamitous periods of its history that was to cause its very name to be a reproach. It still dominated the political imagination, both of its inhabitants, and of visitors to East Asia. So much history had gone into its making, and so revered was Chinese civilization in Asia, that traces of mortal disease did not at first cause extreme alarm. Nevertheless China belonged to the ancient world, which, in 1850, was passing rapidly away.

What was threatening China was the impact of the western world. China was known as the Middle Kingdom for it seemed the centre round which all things revolved and it had flourished through so many ages because it was unique. Now, for the first time in its history, it was coming

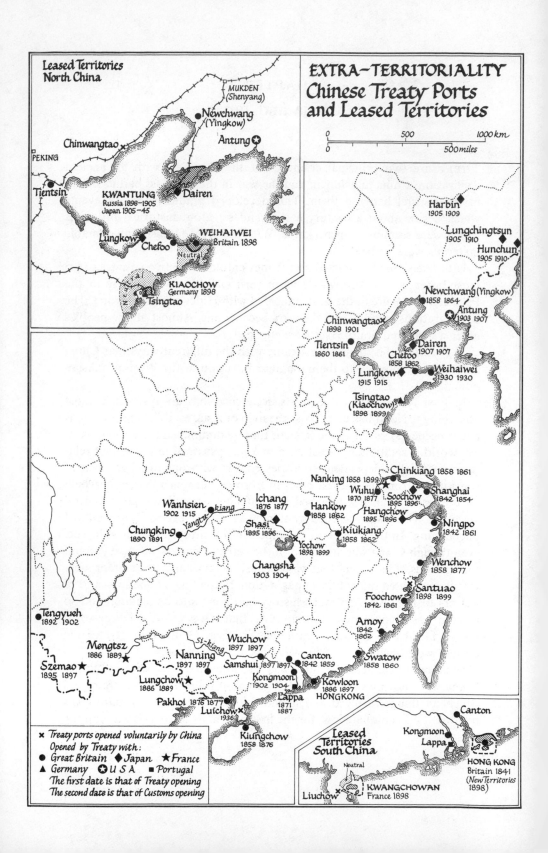

into contact with Powers which had totally different traditions and which were totally ruthless. They came from the other side of the world, but, from the alarm they caused, and from the absence of normal human rapport, they might have come from Mars. These Powers, well organized politically, were not inclined to concede to China a moral superiority.

The history of China and the West is chequered. The record of the foreign Powers is not so black as it is painted, whether by Chinese communists or by liberal western historians, who are overwhelmed, often quite unreasonably, by guilt. In some ways China's suffering was inevitable. It was the necessary result of the unavoidable process of a withdrawn state being thrust upon the world. Many of its experiences can be seen today to have been renascent; they conferred new and valuable matter upon an ancient civilization. The version put about by the communists is exaggerated, perverted and untrue. But something like their view is held by most of the Chinese people. The myth has been agreed upon. It must be attended to in any account of what really happened.

China, according to this view, was, for nearly a hundred years, harried by several foreign Powers which had projected themselves into East Asia by their navies and their fleets of merchantmen; and for most of the time it fought a losing battle against them.

The agony of China began in the middle of the last century. It was compelled by foreign governments to open itself for trade, which meant consenting to having its tariffs fixed by these agents; to accord to foreigners extra-territorial rights, which rendered them immune from Chinese law; and to permit them to set up in some of the choicest parts of the Empire small foreign communities which were thereafter protected from Chinese jurisdiction by warships and small bodies of troops. These were the famous Treaty Ports, now of dolorous memory. In addition, the same rights were exacted for Christian missionaries, who were let loose to subvert the ancient Confucian system. The Chinese Government was powerless to resist. It had neither the technical means (in arms and warships), nor the political stamina, nor the control of its own people, nor the ability to organize them.

Externally nothing had changed except for the establishment of neat, well-ordered townships side by side with the sprawling cities of China. They were clean; they appeared innocent. In this innocuous guise, imperialism came to China and soon began its work without anybody recognizing that it was initiating a new age. The first trade treaty, the Treaty of Nanking of 1842, which opened the five ports to British trade and residence, contained crippling restraints on China's sovereignty, but at the time was regarded as relatively innocuous. The Treaty provided that foreigners should administer their own justice to aliens and so appeared to be relieving the Chinese of a vexatious duty and to be keeping the foreigner at arm's length, which was very much the Chinese desire.

Moreover, by specifying areas where foreigners could live, it appeared to have spared the Chinese demands for the sale of land elsewhere. The foreigner was generally prohibited from acquiring real estate in China – a kind of apartheid set-up. But the foreigner had been given the means to enforce his will, and used it ruthlessly. He partly got round the rule that he should not own land by inducing the Christian missionaries, specifically exempt from the prohibition which applied to foreign businessmen, to hold the land in their name.

At first the Chinese did not understand what was being done to them, or how serious was the damage done to them in the Treaty Ports. But the misdeeds of the imperialists slowly became clear to everyone, and gradually produced a mood of terrible baffled rage.

China had not only to fear imperialism when it was seaborne. Before the coming of the foreign ships, it had been conscious of the land threat from its neighbour, Russia. This threat endured without interruption and in varying degrees of intensity. By land or sea China was surrounded by adversaries. It was still the Middle Kingdom, but no longer the axis round which the world turned; rather it could boast the name because it was the centre against which the spoliative instincts of the world were directed.

China was, it is true, saved from conquest and annexation. This was because the foreign Powers arrived not alone, but in multiplicity, because each was jealous of the other, because each realized that its trading rights depended on none achieving full political control of China. The Chinese Empire was thus permitted to continue.

It is important not to overstate the case. There were many personalities among the foreigners in China who bore nothing but goodwill to the country. There were institutions which were actively philanthropic. Foreign influence often brought about great changes, almost by accident. The Treaty Ports were often impressive for their neatness of construction and they disseminated new standards of public administration over a limited area. But the Chinese argued that this kind of imperialism did the maximum harm to China while ensuring that the imperialist Powers conferred no countervailing benefits.

Thus, groups of foreigners – nearly all businessmen – lived in China, organized entirely according to the customs and conventions of their homeland and subject to their own laws, in juxtaposition to the Chinese who were still subject to their ancient form of government. Most of the foreigners had only one interest: to make money through trade. Inevitably, even if the foreign communities had had no intention to influence Chinese society, the free action of the foreign groups deeply modified the Chinese society all around them, especially because the Chinese Government was unable to place limits on their activities. The operations of buying and selling, the freedom to conduct almost all forms of enterprise which private initiative could suggest, the freedom of money and its free use – all tended to erode the old Chinese civilization, which the Chinese, bound by treaty, were unable to safeguard.

The Chinese were in the position of a man bound hand and foot, watching the activities of an assailant who was openly plotting his ruin. As a result of the unwelcome guests, Chinese society was changing; but China could do nothing about it. Chinese anger mounted against the foreign communities, but China was impotent.

The Chinese feeling raged more strongly against the Chinese who collaborated with foreigners than against the foreigners themselves. The Chinese who showed himself unduly obliging to the foreigner, who set himself to make money by taking advantage of the conditions of foreign business, who was willing to act as the agent of the foreign business community and performed the indispensable role of interpreter and middleman, roused angry resentment. This class was called the compradors, from the Portuguese word meaning 'to provide': they were China's universal agents, at the disposal of the foreigner. Without the compradors, the pattern of the new type of imperialism would never have come into being.

The comprador class became extremely rich and prosperous. Eventually many of the Chinese Nationalists came from this class. So did many people who contributed in various ways to the new China: in arts, in science, in medicine. For many decades the Chinese creative energies seemed to be located in this class. The fact that it was hated was never sufficiently appreciated by foreigners, whose needs had called it into being.

The principal state in the hostile group ringing China was Great Britain, but there was one foreign country which behaved in a way unlike the others, the United States of America, which had a different history and different traditions from those of the European nation-states like Great Britain.

The United States, which came into being as the result of rebellion against Britain, did not form a new national state of its own, but was, rather, a repository of the elements of the western world which showed, by emigrating to America, that they desired to have a new political civilization. The United States did not altogether escape the nineteenth-century trend of western countries to be aggressive and self-assertive, but was distinctly less predatory, less remorseless, than others.

Thus in its relations with China the United States pursued a milder course than its western peers. True, it was drawn into the harrying. When the other states took the extra-territorial privileges, for the protection of their nationals, the United States joined in; and it took its share among the other powers in setting up the International Settlement at Shanghai. But its pursuit of China was not relentless, and it did not demand exclusive concessions of its own, which were the aim of other governments and which came to be dotted all over China like so many colonies. The United States' interest was in international trade – in contrast to Britain whose special concern was with the investment of capital in China – and in promoting it the United States was no more scrupulous than other states in forcing its activities upon China, which, officially, did not welcome them. But in this international trade the American concern was more with the attitude of other Western Powers than with that of China. The United States had always the fear that these would end in a policy of splitting up China into various spheres of interest, from which American interests would be excluded or discriminated against.

Hence the United States' aim of preserving the open door into China. On this principle American official policy turned. It sought to establish a system by which all the Powers voluntarily restricted the use of political influence to secure for themselves an economic privilege such as was not enjoyed equally by other Powers. The American activity on these lines culminated in securing in 1900 the assent of Powers interested in the China trade to this 'Open Door doctrine' and in guaranteeing American support for China's territorial integrity. The United States regarded this as a pro-Chinese policy, anti-imperialist, and in fact it was more so than suited the habits and interests of the other Powers. But it is understandable that later generations of Chinese should have pointed to the solid gains which it was the United States' intention to gain from it. They were not impressed by the advantages that this non-cooperation of the United States with the other Powers undoubtedly brought to China, and regarded these as incidental and not philanthropic.

Nevertheless, the United States was philanthropic. From the 1870s a section of the American public became aware of China as a great Asiatic people which might with justice call upon the United States for aid. This was the United States' first public response to the needs of a section of the world community; a response which afterwards became progressively wider, and embraced successively Japan, the states in Europe assisted by the Marshall Plan, and states of Latin America. They had no legal or other claim on the United States; the United States had no obligation to them. It responded in their cases to the simple fact that they had needs which the United States could fill, and the United States did not pass them by on the other side. Often, of course, there was, mixed with the practical philanthropy, a great deal of hypocrisy, of unscrupulous dealing, of serving a concealed interest, of power hunger only a little better than Europe's because it was veiled; but, though these existed, it was a remarkable fact that there was a genuinely philanthropic policy in which these found a place.

The initiators of the wave of goodwill were the American missionaries. Thousands of these were active in China and, through them, links were forged between innumerable small towns in the United States and similar units in China. To a remarkable extent the American people actually took the Chinese people by the hand, and led them over the first stages of their modernization. Politically, the organs of government in the United States impressed the Chinese people, many of whom recognized the remarkable behaviour of the US, even though their vast pride suffered from the American patronage. It was natural for the descendants of two thousand years of mandarins to feel disgust at becoming pupils of such a commercial people, lacking a long history, as the Americans. Relations were therefore not easy. But Chinese, in a more judicious mood, had to admit that this relationship was the most satisfactory that China had experienced in modern history.

This adventure in philanthropy was a part of the history of the American people, not the American Government. It was not officially inspired. The thousands of American missionaries, the vast expenditure, the use of skill and manpower, were all of them privately directed. So also American businessmen for the most part took their own risks and reaped their return, and largely did not employ American organized public force. The interplay of the missionary and the businessman, the clash between disinterest and the long-term interest which American activity promoted, was of course one of the principal themes for the historian of the time to savour. And in the United States the widespread goodwill to China set up currents which, in a society as democratic as that of the United States, were bound to influence the state and produce subtle changes in its policy towards China. So intertwined were most of the impulses of the United States.

Confronted with such acute danger, China made sporadic efforts to modernize itself and to generate a counteractive power; this should have been possible by reason of its size, its population and the reasonableness of its people. But for a long while its governing class was so set in conservative ways – as an essential part of their Confucian civilization – that the efforts failed. To reform and reorganize, China had to go through a shattering revolution, leave its ancient political civilization and venture out on ways new and untested. It had to experience a slow rebirth.

For a time the Chinese mandarins, the higher civil servants of the Confucian bureaucracy, had supposed that the secret of the terribly formidable strength of the West lay in some technical devices which had been added to the instruments of government. If they could discover what these were, the Government of the ancient Empire would be rejuvenated, and able to stand up for itself. Steam power, explosives, modern weapons were all of them the candidates for the shattering secret of western power. But the Empire's attempt to purchase these devices from the West left it no better off. It was clear that the Chinese Government lacked the talent to reorganize its society so that it might adapt itself to make proper use of these. It could not mobilize China. It remained inert, and a powerless victim to those who chose to victimize it.

Under constant strain, the old system of government was ceasing to act. The old régime had been based on the principle that a harmony had to be imposed on the disharmonious elements of which society consists. The policy was largely based on government by exhortation, and by displaying the example (at least in theory) of universal benevolence; and this proved workable because of the Confucian ideas which prevailed in all areas under Chinese rule. Confucianism, as much as the secular institutions of the old China, held the state together. But the old Confucian philosophy was being undermined as Chinese society, for the first time in two thousand years, began to change fundamentally. In the rough world which had developed, China had to discover new principles on which to base its government.

Some Chinese looked abroad at the new system of parliamentary democracy which was becoming so fashionable. Could this be the secret which made the West so strong, and could its institutions not be taken over by China? For a time there was enthusiasm and hope about these ideas. But it should have been clear that they were not likely to be a helpful model to China, which had its own powerful political traditions, built by more than two thousand years of history, and not readily set aside. Nor could a system of government be easily imported and acclimatized, which had been built up so painfully in Europe, which was the product of so many attitudes of action and habit, themselves born of wars, revolution, and the slow work of many centuries. China was too unlike Europe, and China was made a dangerous gift by its friends who intemperately supported this nostrum.

The course which China took was therefore quite unpredictable; it was empirical and, even today, with hindsight, it is hard to trace out what experiments it made, and how much China suffered.

One of the reforms which it made apparently without realizing the profound consequences which it had, was to abolish the Civil Service. This it did in 1905; the examinations by which it was recruited were suspended. Earlier, the existence of this college of administrators, chosen to serve the Empire by competitive public examinations, had been regarded, with some justification, as one of the strong points of Chinese civilization. But in the first decade of this century, the Chinese Civil Service was held to be old-fashioned and conservative. It was selected from among the classes which were steeped in Confucianism, and this made it the enemy of reform. The classes in favour of modernization all combined their resentment against it as constricting the development of the country. It was supposed that by striking it away, China would release forces which would transform it. That the mandarinate preserved standards of government and maintained the unity of the country was totally ignored. A great blow was struck at public order by its abolition, but the country thought that it was a blow in the cause of progress and liberation.

The Manchu Empire survived the sacrifice of the mandarins by only six years. The Empire and its outworn apparatus were discarded in 1911: it had stood in the way of reform; probably a revolution was the necessary prelude to recovery. But the first results of the fall were catastrophic. The power of the Empire was divided between war-lords, who commanded their own provinces. This was the worst and most helpless period of Chinese history up to that time. Chinese politics seemed to be without rhyme or reason. Power drifted from one war-lord to another with no meaningful result. The rise or fall of one provincial satrap or another brought no lightening of the gloom. There was no change, no regeneration, no significance.

The dawn for which men hoped first became visible with the rule at Canton, a city in the south of China, of the group called the *Kuomintang*, which had emerged from a revolutionary party of the last days of the Manchus. This group proclaimed itself the Nationalist Party of China and held its first National Congress in 1924. It was at first primitive, overlaid with the colour of circumambient war-lord governments, incompetent, corrupt, and very weak. But it was in certain aspects new, and had, at least in form, a modern party organization which was in part borrowed from western countries, though the methods of its operations were mainly drawn from China itself. It functioned in an authoritarian way, owing its power to its Army and police, but it claimed that this method of government was a transitory one. After a period during which it held the nation in tutelage, it would transfer the basis of government, and would become liberal and democratic. In after years, the length of this period of tutelage, the holding of the Kuomintang to its promise of democratization, became one of the principal questions of Chinese politics.

The Kuomintang slowly widened its authority; and came to be looked on as the party of national regeneration. It was a focus which attracted the support of all Chinese everywhere, who longed for a sign that China was at last reasserting its national strength.

It was the turning of the tide. Nationalism, with all the social and political reorganization which that connoted, began to do its work upon the Chinese people. The leader of the Kuomintang, Dr Sun Yat-sen (1866–1925), had described the great weakness of China, in its enforced competition with the Western Powers, as the absence of any cohesive power which could hold the people together. China, he said, was like a tray of sand: shake it and it fell apart. But, in China as in other parts of the world, the power of nationalism was to introduce a new faculty of maintaining social unity. How and why is one of the *arcana imperii* of the time. But it was abundantly clear that, as the movement proceeded and gathered strength, China was behaving quite differently from the recent past. The tray of sand was shaken; and the grains now tended to cohere in patterns which promised well for the future.

A fact which should have recommended the Kuomintang of the 1920s to serious attention by the outside observer was that in its organization and spirit it was not a copy of the western parliamentary parties. It was something devised for China, produced by Chinese thought to meet specific Chinese needs. It owed something to Soviet practice – many of the features in the organization of the party being borrowed from Russia at a time when Sun Yat-sen was enthusiastic, but had little understanding of Communism – and, with a rosy eye-wash, it professed to look forward to a time of universal democratic rights. But the Kuomintang – as it was to function in the 1930s – was a party of nationalist authoritarianism.

Cutting across the political vicissitudes of the times was a social crisis. In a sense China was doomed to experience disorders in any case. China has a long history, and has endured a time of acute crisis once in every three or four hundred years which is marked by troubles, the fall of a dynasty, civil commotion of a prolonged and hopeless kind. Various causes have been suggested for this clearly marked cyclical course of

Chinese history, but the most probable is that it is caused by pressure of population.

In the time of prosperity – when a dynasty is at the peak of its fortunes – the population is within manageable limits. The prosperity continues; the population grows; it becomes too large; there is intense pressure on the land; there are rising rents, and a diminishing food surplus for the towns; there are social distress, outbreaks of civil war and banditry, reverses in the struggle to maintain the frontier; there are corruption and extraordinary administrative decadence. After a time there comes the near or total collapse of government. China enters on a nadir of its history, from which there comes eventual recovery as the population regulates itself. Malthusian checks come into play, the extreme pressures are relaxed, the natural Chinese civilization reasserts itself.

There can be no doubt that China had entered on one of those adverse phases in the latter part of the eighteenth century. The Manchu dynasty ended its golden age in the unnaturally long reign of the Emperor Chien Lung (who reigned from 1736–96), and the population increased ominously. In the nineteenth century it would have been due for its time of troubles, regardless of the troubles brought on it by its new problems of foreign relations. The middle years of the century saw the Taiping rebellion and the revolt of the Chinese Muslims against the Government, both classic cases of a population explosion, both resulting in a very great slaughter. The two political maladies came together – the troubles from the cyclical character of Chinese history and the troubles from the totally new and exceptional strain of encountering its rivals in the world. Each set of troubles complicated the other; each intensified the other; recovery became ever more difficult.

The Kuomintang, and Chinese nationalism, promised to bring relief to the political problems of China in the 1930s. At the same time there were signs that the social causes which had brought political collapse were about to be ameliorated by process of time, and it seemed likely that the efforts of the Kuomintang at social and economic improvement would not continue to be dogged with adversity. These signs, however, were hard to read correctly, and may have been misconstrued.

For the relative slowness of China's regeneration there are a number of reasons. The rebirth of a nation – it was nothing less – takes time, which cannot be cut short beyond a certain measure. It is a natural process, not entirely controllable by political or human means. But China's peculiar and horrifying experience of the last century remains to some extent a mystery. China's progress in our day has been so rapid, so revolutionary, that it is hard to understand why in the fairly recent past it took so long to get off the ground. In the last resort one is left with the bare statement – that a crisis of population coincided with a crisis of foreign relations, that the results of both became merged, and that it took more than a century to work out the consequences.

The other country, Japan, had an altogether different experience and its past must also be studied if Japan's place in the world cataclysm is to be understood. Japan was a lesser country than China. Generally its population was only about one sixth of China's. But it was inhabited by a people, which, by vigour, by a genius for imitation and adaptation, and by artistic and warlike qualities, had made itself unique in the history of Asia. Japan had built up a civilization in many respects peculiar and outstanding. It responded to the stimulus of the coming of the westerners in a way which transformed the history of the region.

Since the beginning of the seventeenth century Japan had been exercised by the problem of relations with the West. It read the writing on the wall in the shadow cast by the Portuguese and Spanish galleons which at this time used to visit Japanese ports. Should Japan encourage them or should it deter them? After a brief period of cultivating their friendship it withdrew itself into seclusion. It persecuted mercilessly, as possible enemies of Japanese security, the missionaries about whom at first it had been enthusiastic. It cut all ties with the external world, diplomatic, cultural and, as far as this was possible, economic. It was the classic case of a hermit kingdom. This policy of exclusiveness preserved Japan intact until the United States, in the year 1853 and again in 1854, dispatched a naval squadron under the command of Commodore Perry and compelled it to resume normal intercourse and foreign trade.

Thereupon Japan was in danger of being reduced to a colony by the imperialist Powers. For its escape it had to thank the diplomatic adroitness, the skilful reasonableness of a few leading Japanese statesmen during the first years of the 1870s while Japan was renewing its contacts with the world. Once they had lost their first instinctive anti-foreignness they exposed themselves with zeal to all western influences. Japan's survival beyond this critical interval is owed to the remarkable changes which were brought about in Japanese society as a result of contact with western countries. From a militarily weak country, with a contemptible technology, Japan in a few years became like a hedgehog, which the imperial Powers, even at the height of their aggressiveness, thought twice about mauling.

Japan's history, which made this national strength possible, has been one of social change – a marked contrast to the sluggish conservatism of

China's official social history. Japan was able to accept change because the Japanese were born relatively free of an overpowering tradition. Its governing circles were able, in contrast to the Chinese, to produce men who were imaginative, forceful, and free of the deadening desire that life should be preserved exactly as it had been known in previous centuries. They were daring and iconoclastic. They were not bound by a thwarting public opinion, as was the mandarinate in China.

In China, the society, the civilization, took precedence over the Government. It was a civilization not disposed for change. But in Japan the Government was not held in invisible fetters by public opinion and by the past.

Furthermore a Japanese Government which desired to make changes was more likely to be able to implement them. Society was more responsive to governmental direction: it was more at its mercy. For this the main reason was geography. Japan consisted of a chain of islands, all of them comparatively small, all of them accessible by sea. Thus a fairly good system of communication could be established. This alone made it very different from China: in China there were, by the standards of that day, majestic roads, but, even so, the population in the outer provinces was at three months distance from the seat of central government. In consequence the ability of the centre to regulate the affairs of a large part of China was much reduced. But in Japan, no such inhibition palsied the national administration. Its efforts did not peter out in vast distances which separated it from its subjects.

The progress of Japan was rapid and, to the Western Powers spreading their influence through the world, unprecedented. In 1868 occurred the so-called Meiji Restoration. This was a revolution, not a restoration, although this great political change in Japan was dressed up as a revival of things past. An old, vestigial system of an Emperor, long confined to a kind of museum existence, and preserved partly for religious reasons, was called into employment; the existing system of government, a highly traditional one presided over by hereditary prime ministers or *Shōguns*, was suppressed. The new system was organized by the *Samurai*, the ex-feudatories of Japan's feudal past which it was abandoning. Exercising their remarkable talent for mimesis, they copied from what their intelligence judged to be the essentials of the formidable western system.

The Japanese surprised themselves by the ease with which they were able to reproduce in Japan most of what went into the making of western civilization. From Britain they copied the organization of the navy; from France the army structure, the nucleus of an educational system and hybrid neo-Napoleonic codes of criminal and civil law; from Germany the

Army General Staff organization, certain legal principles and commercial practices, modern medical training and some political institutions. Subsequently, the influence of the American educational system supplanted that of the French. Western-style agriculture, forestry and mining, the rapid expansion and efficient use of new railways, and phenomenal growth in the textile industry transformed the life of most Japanese, helping to provide sustenance for the engineering, shipbuilding and manufacturing industries which took somewhat longer to enter the modern era. The degree of Japan's modernization was often even greater in its appearance than in reality, for the old, and essentially Japanese, institutions and modes continued behind a façade of reform. Nevertheless, reform there was, and a purposeful – if eccentric – resolve to modernize. Soon Japan began to operate with a revolutionary change in efficiency.

For the European onlooker, the spectacle of Japan at this time was of remarkable fascination. For him it was a new experience to kick an ancient civilization, and to find that it did not crumble. It was bracing and fascinating. Enough of the old, graceful, picturesque, fragile civilization of old Japan still survived to make the process of the metamorphosis of Japan of almost incredible interest; and, in addition, of poignant pathos. American, British and French men of letters grasped the occasion of describing what was happening before their eyes, and the result was a series of books describing the topography, anthropology, ethics and aesthetics of Japan in transition. Among them Redesdale's *Tales of Ancient Japan* is especially valuable for the picture which it gives of the national ethos, and of the reaction to it of a civilized and imaginative westerner.

This was the elegiac tribute of the West to a country which showed spirit in resistance. It was quite different from the contemptuous tone and temper of the writings about India and China at the time. And for the foreigners who were blind to the more subtle qualities of a nation's progress, the rapid expansion of trade and of the whole economy were impressive and sobering.

By 1890 it was plain that the once real threat that Japan would fall a victim to straightforward western imperialism was ebbing. Instead, Japan shocked the Western Powers by joining with them in harrying and nibbling at China, whose disorders invited pressure.

The Japanese designs upon China cannot be explained by greed alone. British, and afterwards French, commercial penetration of China had been accompanied by the effective exercise of military power. United States interests in the area had grown, although more fitfully in response to the vagaries of American politics. Russian exploits, however, provided the immediate catalyst for Japanese expansion onto the Asian mainland.

When Tsar Alexander III's engineers began construction of the Trans-Siberian Railway in 1891, their picks and rails foretold the doom of an enfeebled China – and fatefully strengthened the influence of Japanese visionaries who sought a foothold on the Asiatic continent in the interests of self-defence but who also dreamt of Japan's development into a first-rate Imperial Power. Thus Count Yamagata Aritomo, principal architect of the modern Japanese Army and perhaps the most important Japanese oligarch of his era, advised the Emperor Meiji in October 1893 that the Russian railway 'poses an immediate threat to the Far East', predicting that within a decade the Tsar would snatch Mongolia, gain control of Manchuria and advance against Peking: 'the completion of the Trans-Siberian will sharply alter the situation in the Orient and exert a strong influence on our nation. It is not only for this reason that we must prepare adequate military power within the next eight or nine years; we must also be prepared to grasp any opportunity which may present advantages. This is a truly critical juncture in the fortunes of our nation.'*

Japanese concern over Russia's advance into the Great Power stakes of East Asia did not blind the Japanese to developments in other quarters, and Japanese eyes also fastened onto Korea, Japan's hereditary enemy. It was conventional military wisdom – in which the teachings of the ancients harmonized with advice tendered by a forceful imperial German general staff officer assigned to help educate the Japanese officer corps – that Korea, a 'dagger at the heart of Japan', must not fall under the sway of any third power. The Japanese had engaged in Korean political intrigues for almost a generation, and when the vassal Korean King turned to his suzerain, China, for military support to help subdue local uprisings fomented by the anti-western Tonghak Tong (Eastern Learning Society), the Dowager Empress of China quickly sent in a small armed force. This violated the spirit of the Kanghwa Treaty of 1876, signed by Japan and Korea, and the Sino-Japanese Treaty of Tientsin of 1885, which taken together bound China and Japan to refrain from (open) interference in Korean domestic and external affairs. The Japanese feared that this would lead to replacement of Korean independence or autonomy by the re-imposition of Chinese hegemony over the peninsula and the extinction of Japanese influence in Korea. Resorting to their rights under the Chemulpo Treaty of 1882, the Japanese responded by dispatching a mixed brigade of

---

* R. F. Hackett, *Yamagata Aritomo in the Rise of Modern Japan, 1838–1922*, Harvard University Press, Cambridge, Massachusetts, 1971, p. 157.

their own, deploying some seven thousand men ostensibly for the protection of Japanese diplomats, residents and property interests. The Tonghak Rebellion was short-lived, but in the aftermath of French and British encroachment during the past half-century into Chinese tributary states (which China had been powerless to prevent in Indo-China, Tibet and Burma), the Chinese were determined to suffer no such humiliation at the hands of the Japanese. The Japanese demands were treated with ill-concealed contempt. Western offers of mediation were rejected. Fighting soon developed. Japanese troops seized the Korean royal palace on 23 July, and two days later, following a brief naval engagement off P'ung Island (in which the Japanese routed a squadron of Chinese warships), a Japanese cruiser intercepted and sank a solitary British-registered steamship, the *Kowshing*, which was ferrying 1,100 Chinese troops, a German military adviser and a large quantity of weaponry to Korea. Following these developments, China and Japan formally exchanged declarations of war on 1 August 1894. Within six weeks, the Japanese Army won control of most of Korea through a succession of uninterrupted victories. The Japanese Navy proved equally adept in a sea battle off the mouth of the Yalu River which left it in command of the Yellow Sea. In October, two Japanese divisions crossed into South Manchuria and three more advanced upon Liaotung. Port Arthur fell to the Japanese on 21 November, and Wei-hai-wei on the Shantung Peninsula surrendered on 12 February 1895. As seven Japanese divisions prepared to march against Peking, the Chinese sued for peace.

After difficult negotiations, the Treaty of Shimonoseki was signed on 7 April 1895. The jubilant Japanese equated its harshness with the requirements of moral justice. Others viewed the outcome with alarm. By its provisions, China recognized the complete independence of Korea; ceded to Japan the Liaotung Peninsula (including Port Arthur), Formosa (Taiwan) and the Pescadore Islands; agreed to pay Japan a punitive indemnity that recovered two thirds of the military expenses incurred by Japan during the war; opened up portions of the Yangtze River to Japanese commerce; gave Japan trade concessions at Shasi, Chungking, Soochow and Hangchow; granted the Japanese highly prized most-favoured-nation privileges, and, to guarantee compliance with these provisions, sanctioned a temporary Japanese military occupation of Wei-hai-wei to be paid for out of the Chinese exchequer.

Japan had won a spectacular victory over China, but Japanese exhilaration was short-lived. The Shimonoseki Treaty proved to produce a Pyrrhic peace, as hard-hearted settlements are wont to do. Within China, demands for reform and a national re-awakening became irresistible.

Abroad, not for the last time, Chinese diplomats combined with western geopolitical schemers to deprive Japan of the fruits of conquest. Kaiser Wilhelm II of Germany, seeking better relations with Russia and hoping to stimulate even greater Russian attention to East Asia at the expense of the Franco-Russian Alliance in Europe, persuaded the impressionable Tsar Nicholas II, who had just succeeded to the Russian imperial throne, that Japan should be induced to retrocede the Liaotung Peninsula to China in consideration of a relative pittance. In any case, the Russians had a palpable fear that *any* Japanese presence on the Asiatic continent would spread, in the memorable phrase of Prince Lobanov, like 'a drop of oil on a sheet of blotting paper'.* Unwilling to see the European balance of power undermined by bilateral Russo-German collaboration, the French joined the Russians and Germans in this famous 'Triple Intervention', which their respective Ministers in Tokyo put to the Japanese Government on 23 April 1895. The Japanese were aghast: their Government hesitated, canvassing for support from the other Great Powers. The British Foreign Secretary expressed 'some doubts as to whether it would be prudent in the interests of Japan's future for her to acquire a toe-hold on the mainland. Not only would Japan have to increase her military expenditures to maintain such a possession, but she might also incur the potential danger of China and Russia embarking upon a war of revenge. In these circumstances, it might be more judicious for Japan to adopt a conciliatory attitude.' The United States took a similar view. Only Italy declared a willingness to support Japan.

With the Russian fleet now standing at Vladivostok, the Japanese Government yielded up southern Manchuria and with it Port Arthur. The Japanese public was outraged. In an Imperial Rescript issued to his people, the Emperor Meiji counselled his subjects to 'endure the unendurable', a phrase to which his descendant Hirohito would return in August 1945. A sense of bitter humiliation and a thirst for satisfaction penetrated deeply into the nation's consciousness, recalled thereafter whenever foreign Powers sought to deprive Japan of the fruits of military accomplishment.

The hypocrisy of the Western Powers was all too evident. Within three years, German troops had landed at Kiaochow Bay, occupied Tsingtao and extorted a ninety-nine-year lease on both. Then Germany obtained rights to construct two railways across Shantung Province and won important mining concessions. The Russians, meanwhile, concluded a secret

* Quoted by G. M. Berger (ed. and trans.) in Mutsu Munemitsu, *Kenkenroku: A Diplomatic Record of the Sino-Japanese War, 1894–1895*, Tokyo University Press, Tokyo, 1982, p. 282. Prince Lobanov had become Foreign Minister of Imperial Russia in March 1895.

alliance with China in 1896, aimed against Japan, in consideration for which China gave Russia rights to construct the so-called Chinese Eastern Railway 925 miles across North Manchuria, cutting 600 miles off the Trans-Siberian line to Vladivostok and making possible Russian economic domination of northern Manchuria. Then the Russians demanded and obtained mining rights and the huge Yalu timber concession in Korea, installed Russian military and financial 'advisers' and sought a naval base at Masanpo, directly opposite the Japanese island of Tsushima. The Russian battlefleet was sent to occupy Port Arthur and Dairen (Talien-wan/ Dalny) in December 1897 and extorted twenty-five-year leaseholds which provided the Tsar with his first ice-free ports in East Asia. In March 1898 the Russians obtained the right to build a branch railway from Harbin to Port Arthur and a leasehold on the entire Liaotung Peninsula so recently retroceded by Japan to China. The whole of these railway zones were aggressively patrolled by Russian gendarmerie. It was plain beyond contradiction that the Tsar contemplated nothing less than the virtual annexation of Korea and Manchuria, which were to be secured by the iron rails to Vladivostok and European Russia. Far to the south, the French, too, were carving out their pound of flesh, winning a ninety-nine-year leasehold on Kwang-chow Bay together with railway rights for a line to run between French Indo-China and Yunnan-fu. Britain obtained a ninety-nine-year lease on the New Territories at Hong Kong. A host of other projects and proposals appeared: the 'Celestial Kingdom' was disintegrating, unequal to the western onslaught, and on the horizon, half-way across the Pacific, the United States annexed Hawaii and took possession of the Philippines, raising the prospect of American imperial designs in East Asia.

While Japan redoubled its efforts to build up its military and naval resources and its domestic economy, the Japanese Government also strove to reach some kind of accommodation with the Western Powers. Seeking first to protect its interests in Korea, an agreement was concluded with Russia which on the face of it recognized Korean independence and safeguarded the Japanese commercial and industrial foothold in Korea. Both signatories promised to refrain from interference in the domestic affairs of Korea. Neither side was to send military or economic missions to Korea, and the two sides were to abandon any plans to construct defence facilities on Korean soil. Nevertheless, given the fact that China was now in no position to contest the issue, the Russo-Japanese agreement had the effect of establishing Korea as a condominium of the two contracting parties, neither of whom expected to abide by its provisions for long.

U S S R

MONGOLIA

Harbin

MANCHURIA
(MANCHUKUO) 1932

Mukden

Pailingmiao

Peking

Tsinan

Tsingtao

Hwang-ho

KOREA
(CHŌSEN)
1910

Nanking

Hankow

Shanghai

Yangtze-kiang

C H I N A

Amoy

Swatow

Canton

Hong Kong

Haiphong

HAINAN
1939

Kuril Is
(Chishima)
1875

KARAFUTO
1905

HOKKAIDO

HONSHŪ

Tōkyō

SHIKOKU

KYŪSHŪ

J A P A N

Bonin Is · · 1876

· 1891

Ryūkyū Is
1874–9

TAIWAN
(FORMOSA)
1895

PHILIPPINE IS
(USA)

Mandates 1919
Marianas Is
Caroline. Is
Marshall Is

P A C I F I C

O C E A N

IMPERIAL EXPANSION OF JAPAN 1875–1939

Japanese Empire 1870   Manchuria (1932)
Japanese expansion to 1932
Additional extent of occupation to 1939

0   300 km
0   200 miles

Meanwhile, Chinese popular outrage over the nation's devastating defeat by Japan and over the ensuing western scramble for the spoils reached boiling-point. An uprising, known to history as the Boxer Rebellion, broke out in Shantung in 1898 and soon threatened to engulf the Manchu dynasty. However, the imperial régime skilfully deflected the public's anger away from itself and against the outside Powers. The unrest grew in seriousness and intensity under banners reading 'protect China, exterminate foreigners'. A number of missionaries and Chinese Christian converts were murdered, churches and warehouses were destroyed and European residences in Tientsin and elsewhere were attacked. Finally, the riots reached a climax in June 1900 after the German Minister to China was murdered. Chinese government troops joined the mobs and attacked the foreign legations in Peking with the apparent aim of annihilating the 'foreign devils'. A siege ensued in which a small force of only 458 legation guards and assorted foreign volunteers narrowly prevented the legation quarter from being overrun.

An international expedition, spearheaded by 12,000 Japanese troops, who made up more than half of the total force, was hurriedly assembled, captured Tientsin on 14 July and fought its way to relieve the foreign legations in Peking on 14 August 1900. The Chinese surrendered, agreed to punish those held to be responsible for the outbreak, permitted the foreign Powers to establish strong garrison forces along the railway to Shanhaikwan, and consented to pay the victors an indemnity twice the size of that imposed by the hated Shimonoseki Treaty. The conduct of the Japanese contingent was remarked upon by observers as being especially praiseworthy and well-disciplined, in sharp contrast to the deplorable inhumanity displayed by all of the other foreign forces, who engaged in widespread rape and looting. The German contingent, however, conducted itself with particular bestiality surpassed only by the Russians, who, while showing reluctance to participate in the relief of the legations, took independent action elsewhere, murdering thousands of civilians and, under the pretext of protecting the Chinese Eastern Railway, pouring an estimated 100,000 Russian troops into Manchuria, thereby occupying virtually the whole country. While the other international expeditionary contingents departed after the conclusion of a general settlement with the Dowager Empress, the Russians remained firmly in possession of Manchuria and demanded Chinese recognition of its status as a Russian protectorate. The other Powers prevailed upon China to reject these demands, but Russian forces continued to infiltrate into North China in large numbers. St Petersburg strongly resisted international appeals to follow the example of the other Powers by effecting a rapid withdrawal:

thus hatched the *casus belli* of the Russo-Japanese War which followed in 1904–5.

In these incidents nearly all the ingredients of international politics in East Asia up to 1945 (and even beyond) are already plain. Japan perceived that events were presenting it with an extraordinary opportunity: Japanese were to speak, until their final defeat in 1945, of 'Japan's hour of destiny', the fleeting opportunity of which they must take advantage. In East Asia, in the Japanese view, any further advance of the Western Powers into East Asia must be checked: in the long run, there must emerge a hegemony of either Japan or China, and the concept of co-existence seemed to have no place.

In general, in the comparison between the two, Japan was the weaker Power. The immense size of China, the antiquity and impressiveness of its civilization, its latent economic superiority, must in the end prove decisive – or be harnessed by the alien intelligence of the West. All the warlike qualities of the Japanese people and the advantages of geographical position could not prevail against such illimitable potential. But over the short period, in a time of instability and of unnatural weakness of China, Japan would have the advantage of stealing a march on China, of becoming, despite the historical disparity between the two, the stronger partner (if only some compromise could be reached with the Western Powers); and then, if Japan was willing to rely on its will and on the use of force, it could count on maintaining for an indefinite period the advantage which it had. Japan would stake all upon its ability to repress by force the natural event of a revival of Chinese power – or its obvious alternative, the military and economic consolidation and re-extension of western imperial interests throughout East Asia.

From that determination came the events which led Japan to its fateful participation in the Second World War. Japan's resolution to stake all its future upon the employment of force came to determine most things in the life and domestic achievements of its gifted people.

It was an audacious resolution, and a rather horrifying one. It meant choosing to act against what many abroad regarded as the progressive forces of the age, and allying with the darker tendencies, which were never far below the surface. It involved Japan in courses of action which gradually led to its having a reputation for cruelty and insensitivity, and it coarsened the emotional life. Inevitably Japan turned away from the more delicate things in its civilization. Japan had chosen to follow *Bushidō*, 'The Way of the Warrior' (of which more anon) and to concentrate its interests on making itself feared as the ogre of the Far East. Japan was dazzled by its feudal past, and did not sufficiently take note of the fact that military effort in the new conditions of industrialism was quite unlike that of Japanese tradition. Bushidō in the twentieth century was to be unlike that of the days of the Samurai and feudal lords (*Daimyō*). With fevered resolution Japan found itself impelled on the road of national brutality, and this was hard because in a part of their minds, the Japanese, like the Germans and Americans, desire to be loved, and find it difficult to understand when their actions make them monstrously unlovable.

The contrast between this alarming and determined imperialism, and the natural diffidence of a great many Japanese, perhaps the majority, has often been commented on. The Japanese have a tendency to be abnormally apologetic for themselves and unassertive. As a people, they reprobate individualism. It strikes the Japanese as selfish. This trait is one of the most pronounced in the Japanese character, and is at the root of much that is peculiar in politics, in ethics, in Japanese tradition. It explains why they have rarely produced great assertive figures to take charge of the affairs of the nation individually.

But the very modesty of individual Japanese explains much of what was horrible in recent Japanese history. When the fashion for national aggressiveness set in, few people had the decisiveness, the resolution and the courage to oppose it. What was the individual Japanese doing in taking it on himself to resist the rush of the whole people, even if their direction was to the Gadarene lake? This artistic people, when its emotions were touched, was capable of a national behaviour which was arrogant, demanding, fierce and sinister in the extreme. A naturally diffident people became ready to sweep aside all the restraints which stood in its way. But the fact that there was another side to Japan, another aspect to the machine of conquest, needs to be kept constantly in mind if Japanese action is not to be a continuous puzzle.

It was some time before this hardening of the Japanese attitude towards China became plain. This is often forgotten: it is wrongly assumed that the Japanese hostility became rigid much earlier than in fact it did. For a long while Chinese and Japanese had viewed each other with natural affection. Japan remained, in a peculiar way, tied to China by linguistic, cultural and religious connections. The two languages were distinct from one another, but the Japanese had borrowed thousands of Chinese characters, could write Japanese in these and incidentally found them exceptionally valuable in rapidly assimilating complex scientific and technical innovations imported from the West in recent times. This proved a powerful bond of attachment. In the modern period many of the leaders of Chinese nationalism had been inspired by modern ideas by residence as students in Japan. They looked back on that period with nostalgia. Japan, where the conditions of life were not so very different from China's, was for these young men the convenient forcing house and museum of western attitudes, the place where western institutions were on show but had not become too uncomfortable, and where life was not a leap in the dark. Moreover in Japan there still survived, by habit and as the result of conviction, the consoling sense that China was a land with a magnificent past.

A belief that Japan could be the natural protector of Chinese nationalism, and that together the Chinese and Japanese peoples might discomfort the western world; the fascination of the Chinese at discerning the Japanese methods of surviving in the dangerous world and getting level terms with its horrific visitors: these facts tended to postpone an inexorable break between China and Japan. The Chinese and Japanese still preserved a special feeling for each other, even when the Japanese were behaving most brutally and insensitively. For a long while the Chinese had the instinct that they should be patient, and that the day might come when the temporary clouds between the two countries would disappear and that Japan would become useful to them. They cherished Japan's successes, as, for example, its victory in 1905 in the Russo-Japanese War, as a matter for the common pride of Asians.

In the end, the relations between China and Japan took a turn for the worse, and became cooler. Events on both sides contributed to this. Chinese nationalism became more unrestrained and irresponsible: it revealed more clearly its ultimate goal. Japan set itself with more determination to thwart reviving Chinese ambition; and the internal events in Japan had rendered inactive the groups which fostered understanding and indulgence. Relations became colder; but only disastrously so during the 1930s. When this happened, much of the warm regard of each country for the other, especially among the more traditional classes, still continued in latent form. It was suppressed, but it was always there just below the surface, an imponderable factor in the situation of East Asia.

While this national resolution was slowly forming as the response to the circumstances of the time, it should be remembered that the circumstances were different from those of today. Japan made a disastrous choice, which was to lead to untold retribution and havoc, but at the time of its first moves toward empire building its decisions did not appear so eccentric. In the later part of the nineteenth century, force was still the final tool in the conduct of international relations; all countries accepted this, and Japan was not peculiar. Britain's conquest of India still stood out as the brazen example of what imperialism might succeed in doing. The only deterrent was in the calculation of consequences, and these were at that time clear of such devastating things as the atom bombs, or even, for the most part, of the horrors of wars of attrition.

For all its apparent modernization, many features of the Japanese state continued to be very different from those of the West. In contrast with the Western Powers, Japan, though it wore the trappings of a modern state, continued to be at least mentally attached to the Middle Ages. This accounted for its often bewildering reaction to the situation in which it found itself. It explains frequently surprising recourses to the methods of the past. They did not represent an abrupt move to reaction by the Japanese, as they were apt to be interpreted by the West. Rather they were the intrusion into modern ways of the instinct of an earlier day, which had never died completely in Japan. Japan, though suitably made up for the part of a contemporary Power, was never quite at home in the modern world; it was wearing a kind of fancy dress, and the West dimly recognized the fact. The West was never entirely at home with Japan, for it sensed a certain eerie mystery, as of a survivor from a past civilization.

The psychological drama behind Japan's attempt to prevail by force, and especially behind the attempt to prevail over China, is exceedingly interesting.

Throughout their history the Japanese have always exhibited symptoms of schizophrenia, exemplified in their attitude towards China. Japan admired China, and simultaneously it despised it; it was tied to China and yet yearned to be free. Its attitude combined the pious reverence of a child towards a grandparent with the disrespect which eventually led to war with its cultural ancestor. For the civilization of Japan, though ultimately it was due to the Japanese spirit playing upon the various influences which went into its making, was, in its remote origin, derived from China. From China came the initial impulse, and the Japanese could never put this out of their minds. On one hand they accepted, in an excess of self-abasement, the traditional Chinese view of the Japanese as being a race of 'deformed dwarfs'; on the other, they felt themselves superior, and proclaimed themselves with neurotic insistence to be the children of the Sun Goddess – 'the race of Yamato' – and destined to rule the entire world, even a world as powerful, rich and wide as their extended knowledge of the nineteenth and twentieth centuries proved it to be. This ambivalence and the unreality behind so much of Japanese action – together with the extremes of violence alternating with extremes of self-control – are the key to understanding a great deal of East Asian history.

The relations with China always preoccupied the Japanese. Even when Japan was led, via China, into war (which few people in Japan really desired) against the United States, Britain and finally Russia, it was essentially a by-product of this great absorbing interest. When Japan went to war against the US and Britain, it was because the West intervened between Japan and its victim China. In a sense, Japan was perfectly sincere in claiming that it wished to protect China: it was protecting it from the western aggressors so that it could be preserved intact for Japan's benefit.

However, it must not be supposed from this description that Japan acted monolithically. For a country as consensus-orientated as was Japan, there were always surprising divergencies from the norm. From time to time there rose movements which altered the policy of the Government, and even at times seemed to offer the prospect of a reversal of policy. But, seen in perspective, Japan's drive on China continued with little interruption throughout the period.

CHAPTER 2

Japan in International Affairs

JAPAN followed this resolute policy of establishing its ascendancy over China for half a century down to 1945. It was hampered in its execution by the jealousy of the Western Powers, which believed that they had a monopoly in exploiting China. In asserting itself in China and the Pacific Ocean, Japan ran the risk of increasing opposition from these Powers. It had discovered early that they would not willingly leave it in peace to bully China: not because they were sympathetic to China, but because they objected to Japan's rise.

In pursuit of its purpose, Japan had to resort to one of the oldest devices of diplomacy. Ringed by a group of unsympathetic powers, Japan set itself to split their united front, to woo one of them as its ally and advertise its useful role in return for patronage. If it could enlist the friendship of one of the larger Powers, for which it was prepared to pay a price, it reckoned on being able to hold in check the others, and to avoid being compelled by them to forgo advantages at China's expense (as had happened in 1895).

Where could it find the friendly patronage? Which Great Powers could it woo away from the conventional attitude of suspicion of Japan as an upstart? Above all, how could Japan supply a Great Power with an inducement to take certain risks to gain its friendship? These problems exercised Japanese statesmen at the turn of the century.

Opinion was divided. It was generally agreed that the extreme enemy of Japan, the frustrator of all its schemes of advance, was its immediate neighbour, Russia. Nevertheless one school favoured an apparently direct appeasement of Russia, and, when it had the upper hand, began negotiations which might have found a way for Japan and Russia to co-exist. Another school wanted an alliance with Germany. Already Japan felt the attraction of Germany; in its programme of modernization it had borrowed from Germany the outline of its Constitution, and also it had copied much in the organization of its Army. In the formative years of Japan's foreign policy Japan had soundings with Germany which looked towards a much closer link.

But eventually another school prevailed. It was the group which was inclined to rely on the Japanese Navy. Japan was a group of islands; it was a maritime Power; it felt that it was obeying its predestined fate in accepting a maritime solution of its problems. It did so by throwing in its lot with Britain. Japan, perched offshore of the land mass of Asia, was aware that its conditions of life were very much the same as those of Britain, which was similarly an island nation offshore of the land mass of Europe. The geopolitical attractions of an alliance with Britain were re-inforced by a strong emotional reaction in Japan. The political attitudes of the Western Powers since the enforced opening up of Japan to foreign trade in the middle of the nineteenth century had been marked by galling restraints on its mainland explorations, for instance, in the restriction of its spoliation in China in the war of 1894–5, and in some quarters by a cultural insensitivity, of which the term 'yellow peril' was an example. The British readiness to come to an understanding not only promised a politi-cal alliance of real value but also wiped out a sense of previous humilia-tions and produced a response of warm friendship in Japan. Thus in 1902, there was concluded the Anglo-Japanese Alliance, which gave Japan the partner which it sought.

The Alliance was an event of fundamental importance in Japanese history. The complicated diplomacy which preceded and followed it are a clue to all that happened in East Asia. History had taken hold of Japan, and placed the Japanese eventually in a position from which their nation drove on, blindly, but with a certain exhilaration, to its fated part in the Second World War, and to doom. Too much attention cannot be given to these events by anybody wishing to find out what really happened. With one eye turned towards Pearl Harbor, and, what lay beyond, to Hiroshima, the complexities of these years must be unravelled.

From the Japanese point of view, the desire for an Anglo-Japanese Alliance sprang from the expectation that the final disintegration of China was imminent and that a major conflict between Japan and Russia must ensue from Russia's ever-increasing military and political power in the region. Still impressed by the vigour and resourcefulness of British imperialism, which the whole world regarded as the most highly evolved imperial system in history, a powerful faction within the ruling Japanese oligarchy came to believe that Japan's only means of protecting its own security and achieving relatively modest objectives on its own East Asian doorstep lay in reaching an effective military and political alignment with Britain. This view, in the end, prevailed against others who regarded such steps as premature, or who instead perceived that the British Empire was passing into a period of appeasement and decline rather than of driving ambition, and who therefore desired that Japan should avoid hazarding all on an alliance with an irresolute, diffident Power but rather seek a rapprochement with Russia aimed at establishing an East Asian condominium between just the two of them. The Russophils had been more influential than those who pressed for an alliance with Britain during the decade that followed the Triple Intervention, but the impetuosity and aggressiveness which characterized Russian penetration into Manchuria, Korea and North China gradually tipped the balance.

At the same time, the British, feeling the harsh condemnation of the world over the Boer War, and fearing any potentially hostile combination of the European states in a world of uncertainties, began to seek alliances: the time had come to choose sides. Approaches were made to Russia in hopes of detaching it from an alliance with France: the British proposed what would have amounted to an Anglo-Russian condominium that would take in most of China, the Balkans and the Middle East. These breathtaking overtures were misunderstood by the Russians, however, and so the moment was lost. Britain then turned to Japan, the sole remaining rising military Power in East Asia. At first it seemed that a Triple Alliance might be possible between Britain, Japan and Germany to further their individual interests in East Asia. This prospect faded as the Germans neglected to pursue the matter, and in January 1902 the first Anglo-Japanese Alliance was concluded.

That Alliance was in effect a neutralizing arrangement so far as Japan was concerned. The two Powers declared that their motives were to maintain the status quo and general peace of 'the Extreme East', particularly with reference to 'the Empire of China and the Empire of Korea', and in securing 'equal opportunities in those countries for the commerce and industry of all nations'. It went on to acknowledge Britain and Japan's special interests in China and, revealingly, recognized that Japan 'is interested in a peculiar degree politically as well as commercially and industrially in Korea'. They agreed that 'it will be admissible for either of them to take such measures as may be indispensable in order to safeguard those interests if threatened either by the aggressive action of any other Power, or by disturbances arising in China or Korea' – which in other words gave them a free hand to do what they liked within their respective spheres of influence. The Treaty next provided that if either of the two partners became involved in war with a Third Power, the other partner would remain strictly neutral and endeavour to dissuade other states from joining in the fray against its ally. However, if these efforts proved unavailing and 'any other Power or Powers should join in hostilities against that ally, the other High Contracting Party will come to its assistance, and will conduct the war in common, and make peace in mutual agreement with it'.* The Treaty had a nominal five-year term but with provision for its indefinite extension in the absence of any notification to the contrary.

The effect of this upon Japan was that probably it would be relieved of the prospect of war with more than one adversary. The Treaty virtually guaranteed that the neutrality of the other Powers was likely to be assured. For example, under the protection of the Treaty, Japan could safely make war on Russia, being reasonably assured that it would not be assailed by any Power which otherwise might be inclined to come to the aid of Russia. British power, promising war against any ally of Russia, or any combatant of Japan, was enough to secure the neutrality of all other Powers. So, by a minimum use of actual force, the danger of war against several countries simultaneously was very much reduced.

The Russians and French were outraged by the Anglo-Japanese Alliance and in March 1902 issued a joint declaration opposing it. But some vestiges of caution remained intact in St Petersburg, and in April 1902 the first positive result of the Alliance could be perceived when a Russo-Chinese Accord was announced which provided for a staged withdrawal of Russian troops from Manchuria. Its first phase was concluded without difficulty a month later. But the Russians soon appeared to have had second thoughts about continuing with the process. Fresh Russian units flooded into southern Manchuria to areas where no Russian forces had penetrated before, and the Russians began to establish themselves in strength near the mouth of the Yalu River, directly across the Korean frontier.

The British, United States and Japanese Governments protested. They were unavailing. A diplomatic resolution of the crisis was sought in vain. Finally, Japan gave Russia a deadline. It expired, unheeded.

Seen from the Russian perspective, there was a ghastly inevitability in the progression of events leading to the Russo-Japanese War. Once the Maritime Provinces had been acquired, it seemed a natural step to build a railway to bind the ends of the Empire together. That in turn produced demands for concessions in Manchuria and Korea and, then, led to attempts to seek ice-free naval and commercial ports in the East. All of this required huge investments of capital, and that in turn had to be protected. Japan stood in the way: her opposition could not be tolerated. The Anglo-Japanese Alliance brought matters to a head. Those who advocated conciliation were overborne by jingoistic voices on both sides. War, finally, appeared to become inescapable.

* International Military Tribunal for the Far East (IMTFE), Defence Exhibit 2292, Text of Anglo-Japanese Alliance, 30 January 1902.

On 6 February 1904 Japan severed diplomatic relations with Russia and launched a surprise attack upon the Russian Far Eastern Fleet two days later. A number of Russian warships were sunk, scuttled or badly damaged at Chemulpo (the port of Seoul, capital of Korea) and at Port Arthur. The remainder fled back to harbour and were bottled up in Port Arthur.

This first of Japan's great wars also set what many have regarded as a precedent of undiplomatic conduct. Japan began it by a surprise attack on the Russian Navy: it dispensed with a declaration of war. This point has been exaggerated beyond all proportion by virtually all commentators, but it is not difficult to place within its proper context: when a British survey* conducted in 1883 reviewed 'all the circumstances under which hostilities have been commenced by different countries against others, prior to a declaration of war, from the year 1700 to 1871', it could enumerate fewer than ten conflicts where hostilities had been preceded by a declaration of war during that period compared with 107 cases where no such declaration had been pronounced. Every one of the European Great Powers – and the United States – had 'engaged in such transactions again and again'. Even where there had been declarations of war in the past, it had been exceptional for a state to declare war with the intention of preventing its enemy from being taken by surprise (a point to which we shall return later). Thus Japan's freedom to launch a surprise attack against the Tsar was not fettered by customary international law, and no international agreements to refrain from undeclared war existed until a convention was signed at The Hague in 1907 (where it would evolve as a direct result of the Russo-Japanese War). Moreover, even those who framed the 1907 Convention did not intend to prohibit surprise attacks but merely to clarify a sense of the seriousness, justification and responsibility for such a conflict.

In view of the appalling record of barbarism which the Japanese soldier so richly came to deserve in later years, it is also worth pausing to reflect that in this war, as in the Boxer Rebellion a decade earlier, Japan's treatment of prisoners and scrupulous regard for international conventions on clemency were exemplary. Foreign observers attached to the two opposing sides in considerable numbers likewise remarked upon the high standard of medical services and hygiene that they found on the Japanese side compared to the Russian side's deplorable neglect of such matters. Given the ferocity of the fighting, the inhospitable climate, and the ap-

* J. F. Maurice, *Hostilities without Declaration of War: An Historical Abstract of the Cases in Which Hostilities have Occurred between Civilized Powers Prior to Declaration or Warning from 1700 to 1870*, H.M. Stationery Office, London, 1883.

palling losses suffered by both sides, Japan went to extraordinary lengths in caring for the wounded and ill, and for captives for whom it was responsible. Japanese and western commentators alike comprehended that there was a considerable difference between the humane and civilized conduct of the Japanese and that of other peoples.

The watching world was surprised at Japan's temerity in challenging such a mighty antagonist, and was astonished at Japan's survival. The Russians, handicapped by the Trans-Siberian Railway's single track and scarcity of rolling stock, strove to bring up fresh troop reinforcements, munitions and supplies while trying desperately to complete the final hundred miles of track round the southern shores of Lake Baikal. The Russians began the conflict with 110,000 regular troops and 30,000 railway guards in the war zone. The Japanese began with 180,000 men in the field and dispatched another 30,000 to Korea with the outbreak of hostilities. As the war progressed, these large opposing forces were heavily reinforced. The Russians transported a further 210,000 troops out to the operational theatres of the war (which still left Russia with more than four million trained soldiers and militiamen in reserve or deployed elsewhere within the Russian Empire). The Japanese Army comprised fewer than 250,000 men under arms at the beginning of the conflict and had only 400,000 in reserves, but Japan threw its full weight into the war as it developed, managing to maintain a local superiority in forces throughout the conflict. The campaign was characterized by gross incompetence within the Russian command and by brilliant recklessness on the part of the Japanese (who showed a breathtaking disregard for the expenditure of human life, repeatedly launching massed assaults against heavily fortified and entrenched positions). The besieged Russian garrison at Port Arthur finally surrendered in January 1905. Elsewhere, a succession of mammoth battles, involving more than a quarter of a million men on each side, culminated in a final battle which took place in March for possession of Mukden. It ended with a shattering defeat for the Russian forces, which then withdrew northwards in disarray. The Japanese by now were too exhausted to pursue their enemy and so let them go.

Several weeks later, a classic victory by Admiral Tōgō over the Russian Baltic Fleet in the Straits of Tsushima annihilated what was left of the Russian Navy. Ten years before, Tōgō had captained the man-of-war which sank the British merchant ship *Kowshing* at the beginning of the Sino-Japanese War. Now he confirmed his position in the pantheon of Japanese naval heroes. In the greatest naval battle fought since Trafalgar, four Russian battleships were lost and four captured out of a total complement of eight; seven cruisers out of twelve were sunk; five destroyers out of nine were sent to the bottom; one cruiser and two destroyers reached the safety of Vladivostok, and several other vessels fled to the safety of foreign ports where they were promptly interned. The only losses sustained by the Japanese during the battle were three torpedo boats. It was a victory almost beyond comprehension, and it led the Russians to accept the good offices of the United States (extended by President 'Teddy' Roosevelt following a secret approach to him by the Japanese Government). An armistice was agreed and serious peace negotiations were opened. All of this was to be recollected by the Japanese as they calculated their chances of following up the projected attack on Pearl Harbor in 1941 – or the Battle of Midway in 1942 – with a negotiated peace settlement.

The world was astonished at Japan's survival. The Russians had lost every engagement of the war and yet Japan's victory was less complete than popular legend might suggest. Japan was exhausted and grasped at peace after eighteen months of war. The conflict cost Japan more than 86,000 dead and an additional 6,700 reported missing or taken prisoner by the Russians, who in turn suffered 43,300 dead and 39,500 missing or taken captive. Japan was in no position either to sustain such losses in future or to carry the financial burden of continuing such a war.

Although the Japanese military and naval victories were spectacular, the Russians had time on their side. In the peace negotiations conducted at Portsmouth, New Hampshire, the Russians proved effective negotiators and stoutly resisted a number of the Japanese demands. Russia finally agreed to acknowledge 'the paramount political, military and economic interests of Japan in Korea', and transferred to Japan Russia's Kwantung Leased Territory on the Liaotung Peninsula, including Port Arthur and Darien, together with a railway zone extending along part of the Russian-built Harbin to the Port Arthur branch of the Chinese Eastern Railway from Changchun ('Hsinking') to the sea. The Japanese failed in their efforts to acquire the whole of Sakhalin Island, which had served as a remote Russian penal colony, but secured possession of special fishing rights and its southern half (land which Japan had occupied following the battle of Tsushima). Title to all Russian property and interests within these territories passed to Japan, but the Japanese were unable to extract a separate indemnity to offset their war expenditure. Japan was in no position to demand to annex Manchuria, though it might seem to have gained the right to do so. The two sides agreed to restore Manchuria to Chinese sovereignty and administration. But Japan was given the right to safeguard the South Manchurian Railway zone with Japanese troops. This was fateful. From this military base, the power of Japan was to spread over to the mainland and came to menace all China. As a first step, taken in December 1905, Japan and China concluded a separate Treaty of Peking by which the Empire of China reluctantly consented to the terms of the Treaty of Portsmouth and at the same time agreed to permit Japan to extend the railway network eastwards to Korea.

The Japanese public, however, long remained unaware of how near Japan had come to exhaustion and ultimate collapse during the war against Russia: that is not the sort of information any nation reveals at such times. Accordingly, the terms of the Treaty of Portsmouth fell far short of what the nation had expected. The political parties in the Imperial Diet reacted with bitterness and consternation. Riots broke out on the streets of Tokyo, suppressed by armed troops at the cost of a thousand casualties. Martial law had to be declared, there was a general curtailment of such tender liberties as the Japanese public had come to enjoy, and the Government finally had to resign.

The second Anglo-Japanese Alliance, concluded secretly in London a month before the restoration of peace with Russia, was in some sense a compensation for the disappointments clearly pending for Japan at Portsmouth. The new Alliance was not announced until after the Treaty of Portsmouth was signed in September 1905. One obvious departure from the terms of the 1902 Treaty was the new Agreement's recognition of Japan's paramount position and right of control over Korea (with the rather cynical proviso 'always that such measures are not contrary to the principle of equal opportunities for the commerce and industry of all nations').* The new Alliance also differed from the old in placing the protection of India on an equal footing to the defence of the special interests of the respective powers in 'the Extreme East'. It was a potent warning against any Russian threat to the British Raj in India. The most critical difference of all was that the two parties now determined that an 'unprovoked attack or aggressive action, wherever arising' from even a single enemy state upon either of the two signatories would bring the other signatory into the conflict. Another indication of the trust which both sides reposed in their relationship was that they doubled its term to ten years (or longer, should neither side give notice of its abrogation).

The British public received word of the new Anglo-Japanese Alliance with delight. The Government and Opposition parties alike committed themselves to dependence upon three cardinal principles which would

---

* IMTFE, Defence Exhibit 2293, Text of Second Anglo-Japanese Alliance, 12 August 1905.

henceforth underpin the defence of the British Empire: establishment of a close harmony with the United States, improvement of relations with France, and a confident trust in the extended Alliance with Japan. These were popular policies.

Within Japan, however, the mood was different. The spectre of the Triple Alliance had risen from the past: news of the extended Alliance could not wash away a sense of grievance and shame. Once again the nation seemed to have been deprived of the fruits of Japan's military and naval exploits through a combination of the ineptitude of her civilian bureaucrats and a conspiracy of the foreign Powers. The truth, however, was that the execrated bureaucrats had done all that was humanly possible – and that the goodwill of the Americans and the British saved Japan from far greater humiliations and the spectre of a war of attrition that Japan could never win.

Meanwhile, at the outbreak of the Russo-Japanese War, Japanese troops had moved rapidly to occupy Seoul and spread across Korea. Afterwards, Korean independence was all but erased, and the concessions which the Tsar's agents so audaciously had secured were cancelled at a stroke by the Korean Government to appease the Japanese. Over the next three years, the Japanese occupation authorities tightened their stranglehold upon the country as the Japanese made effective use of that freedom of action which they had secured in their treaties with Great Britain, Russia and China. Finally, during July 1907, Japan decreed the disbandment of the Korean Army. In violent revolt, the Koreans rose up in the name of their lost autonomy, if not for their independence. The Korean régime had been arbitrary, tyrannical and corrupt, but this was a rising against a totally alien foe, a national rather than a factional cause. Yet it was a hopeless struggle. Well-seasoned Japanese troops fought back with ferocity and after a vicious struggle emerged victorious. A purposeful, forcible attempt to assimilate the country began, lasting until 1945. In August 1910 Korea was annexed to the Japanese Empire, which suffered only occasional pangs of indigestion afterwards.

The arrogance and roughness of the Japanese occupying authorities multiplied the pre-existing fear and hatred which the Chinese, Taiwanese, Manchurian, Korean and Sakhalinese indigenous populations already felt towards their new masters. As Japanese immigrants arrived to assume the functions of bureaucrats, managers, entrepreneurs and colonists, Japanese control, relentless and thorough, was exerted throughout their new domains. There was little if any hope that the Japanese would be content with a temporary occupation of alien soil: they dreamt of eternity and called it 'cooperation'. It left a legacy still palpable today.

The demands of life within the modern world were vastly greater than this formerly self-sufficient island race appeared able to sustain without exploiting the resources of its newly acquired imperial outposts on the Asiatic mainland and on islands beyond the horizon. Security and hubris required vastly increased military expenditure. Foreign markets were beginning to close to Japanese manufactured goods, but the Japanese people were developing an appetite for overseas trade and western consumer products.

The extent of this economic, colonial and military transformation was beyond the expectation of the British statesmen and officials who had negotiated the terms of the first or even second Anglo-Japanese Alliance. By 1911 Russia had restored good relations with both Japan and the British Empire. In a sense, the Anglo-Japanese Alliance coupled with the outcome of the Russo-Japanese War had forced the Tsar to abandon any dreams of establishing his hegemony over East Asia. At the same time, trouble was brewing just beyond his European borders. There were war scares and unrest in the Balkans and in North Africa. Anglo-German naval rivalry had reached such a pitch that it seemed most unlikely that either of those two Powers could afford the expense of a protracted stalemate. The temper of public opinion, the inability of nations to increase their expenditure on armaments indefinitely, and the rigidity imposed upon mobilization plans circumscribed by the manpower, munitions, provisions and railways that now were regarded as essential in modern warfare all contributed to a chilling certainty that a second European War of some dimension was bound to occur sooner rather than later. Meanwhile, considered from the point of view of naval relations between the Great Powers, it had become a basic principle of naval strategy that a 'fleet in being' seeking command of the sea should be concentrated against its principal enemy rather than allow itself to be divided (a lesson taught by the popular American naval theorist Alfred T. Mahan and reinforced by the recent Russo-Japanese War). Conditions in Europe required the British fleet to concentrate in Home Waters during peace as well as in war. Protection of British imperial interests in East Asia now appeared to depend upon support from Japan.

At the same time, American concern was hardening into opposition as Japan endeavoured to squeeze the Western Powers out of all of Japan's recent territorial acquisitions in the process of assimilating colonial domains encompassing some ·3 million square kilometres (an area more than three quarters the size of Japan Proper). Under the terms of the second Anglo-Japanese Treaty, Japan was entitled to expect backing from the British Empire if any serious conflict with the United States should develop (as might happen, for instance, if the United States Fleet ever backed up American diplomatic protests by staging a naval demonstration in the Western Pacific). Moreover, at this moment British and American negotiators were seeking to formulate an Anglo-United States Treaty of General Arbitration. There seemed very real justification for hope that far from aggravating relations between Japan and the United States, a new Anglo-Japanese Alliance would help to prevent serious trouble from arising between them.

Thus the Anglo-Japanese Alliance was revised in 1911 * and effectively became redirected to meet the threat of war against Germany and its allies while underscoring the happier relations which both signatories now enjoyed with Russia and their desire for harmony with the United States. It was not a charter for aggression.

Despite the unpleasant side of Japan's increasing strength, the Alliance served Britain in the same way that it served Japan. In effect, it provided that the British interest in East Asia would be protected in case Britain became involved in war in Europe. If that happened, Britain would rely on Japan to keep the British Empire and its interests intact in the Pacific. And so it happened when Britain had to fight the first European War. The Treaty was not quite perfectly observed, at least in spirit. Some Japanese, influential ones, could not help speculating on what Japan might do if Britain should lose the war, a possibility which they did not seem to see with regret; and the positive aid Japan gave was less than might have been expected of an honourable ally had Britain, in fact, not asked her to do less still. But concerning the effect of the Treaty as a whole, Britain was content: in the years ahead, British admirals, treasury officers and cabinet ministers often lamented its demise.

When the European Powers initiated the Great War, Japan declared war on Germany. Its action in doing so was prompted by loyalty to its ally but also by an expectation that the War would offer opportunities to strengthen Japan's position in East Asia and to avenge losses imposed upon Japan at the time of the Triple Intervention. Although the Chinese had declared their neutrality at the outbreak of the War, the Japanese launched a land offensive across Shantung Province and, with British naval support, laid siege to the German port of Tsingtao, which finally capitulated in early November. The Japanese forces then established control over the remainder of Germany's Shantung Leased Territory. In doing so, they seized the railway zones that traversed the Province from

* IMTFE, Defence Exhibit 2294, Text of Third Anglo-Japanese Alliance, 13 July 1911.

Tsingtao to Tsinan, the Chinese provincial capital, and gained Japan the distinction of employing military aircraft for the first time in the history of warfare. After the campaign ended, Japanese security forces were left to police the railway zones. Peking sought the return of these railways to Chinese administration and, when its efforts failed, unilaterally announced the abolition of the Shantung war zone and requested the withdrawal of all foreign troops from China.

The balance of forces in the East was disturbed by the Western Powers being engaged in war in Europe – which for the western countries was a kind of civil war. The eastern countries made their calculations accordingly. China's audacity would have seemed unthinkable in previous years, and in the short term it misfired badly. Japan, in turn, seized its opportunity and secretly presented China with virtually an ultimatum, the notorious Twenty-One Demands, a document prepared in advance by the Japanese Foreign Minister in consultation with junior officials and sanctioned by other Cabinet Ministers for use on the first such occasion that might present itself.

Acceptance of the Twenty-One Demands would have ended even the circumscribed independence of North China: it would have transformed it into a Japanese protectorate. The pattern of probable events had been made clear in Korea. China was saved when both the scheme and the methods adopted by the Japanese Government came under sustained attack from all sides but especially from three distinct directions: a diplomatic intervention by the United States; apprehension expressed in Japanese military circles (particularly when it was proposed to dispatch further military forces to China in order to secure Peking's compliance), and condemnation by three of the *Genrō*, the last surviving oligarchs of the Meiji Era, who emerged from the shadows to curb what they regarded as a gross abuse of power and trust by the Foreign Minister and the Prime Minister. It is not likely that any one of these sources of pressure was strong enough on its own to force the Japanese Government to water down the Twenty-One Demands. As matters stood, however, the Japanese Government was compelled to drop its most objectionable terms, which would have granted Tokyo an exclusive right to select military, economic and political advisers to 'assist' the fledgling Chinese Republic; obliged China to purchase more than half of her munitions from Japan; established Japanese control over Chinese arsenals; authorized Japan to build more railways on Chinese soil, and even provided for the creation of a joint police command within areas designated by Japan. There were other demands which the Japanese Government was unwilling to abandon.

Helpless still, China was forced to acquiesce in four other sets of

'Demands', which conferred upon Japan control of the extra-territorial rights in Shantung formerly extorted by Germany; extended Japan's leaseholds in Manchuria from twenty-five years to a period of ninety-nine years and guaranteed Japanese subjects the right to own land; gave Japan a foothold in Inner Mongolia; forced China to concede Japan control over the exploitation of iron and coal resources in Central China, and barred China from ever again ceding any island, harbour or bay along her coast to any Third Power.

At a stroke, these concessions endowed Japan with rights and interests in China which were in no way inferior to those acquired piecemeal by all of the other foreign Powers who had enforced their claims there during the past three quarters of a century. The Japanese Government felt, indeed, that the Twenty-One Demands would open a new era of 'cooperation' with China that ultimately would free both of them from interference by the Western Powers: Japan was giving China the 'freedom to say yes' in what promised to be a unique scheme for the future interdependence and mutual advancement of the two countries. Seen from the Chinese side, of course, the Twenty-One Demands excited the just wrath of every Chinese, who already regarded Japan as their most loathsome foreign enemy. Efforts were made by later Japanese Governments to appease China by extending huge loans and bribes to the Chinese authorities, and these had some effect. But Japan's inept mishandling of the Twenty-One Demands thoroughly discredited her in the eyes of the world. Above all, it strengthened American opposition to Japan, attracted great sympathy for China (which had been noticeably rare in previous decades), and was one instrumental factor in Britain's subsequent decision to abandon the Anglo-Japanese Alliance.

Meanwhile, Japanese naval forces had moved swiftly at the outbreak of the First World War and established their control over the German island territories in the Pacific Ocean, including the Marshalls, the Marianas, Palau and the Carolines. Japanese naval escorts protected ships carrying troops and supplies bound for the European War and the Japanese main fleet acted as a deterrent that shielded Australia and New Zealand from enemy attack. As the War developed, Japanese cruisers and destroyers were sent into the Mediterranean and were assigned to the exceptionally arduous and dangerous escort and patrol duties necessary to combat the menace of German submarines there.

Japan more than met its obligations to its ally during the First World War. Strictly speaking, Japan had no duty to take part in the War. The Anglo-Japanese Alliance of 1911 specifically applied only to 'the consolidation and maintenance of the general peace in the regions of Eastern

Asia and of India', not to what might have been limited to a European War. No precise military obligations had been spelt out in the Anglo-Japanese Alliance anyway, but it had never been anticipated that Japanese forces would serve in any European theatre of operations.

The Japanese felt, indeed, that they did everything which could be asked of the Anglo-Japanese Alliance, given the constraints placed upon them. Throughout the two decades which it lasted, that Alliance stood as the cornerstone of Japanese policy. Upon that rock, Japan safely took the first steps to the establishment of its Empire. The irony was that the extension of this Empire was to lead Japan into the most disastrous war of the 1940s, and war with its former ally. It pressed ahead with imperial enterprises when jangled events had deprived Japan of the British alliance and had transformed Britain into an enemy, or a wished-for victim. It is no wonder that the Anglo-Japanese Alliance was, by old-fashioned and conservative Japanese, looked back upon with melancholy regret. It represented the time of safety. It was an instrument which had brought Japan respect, growing power and few doubts or perplexities. It was a tower of strength to Japan psychologically. It had been the dependable way, felt the solider elements in Japanese society, amid other kalaeidoscopic attractions, and Japan had been wise not to forsake it.

The issues in East Asia grew more complex and divided. One of the most serious problems to arise was the Siberian Intervention, which grew out of the chaos of the Russian Revolution of 1917. For a time it appeared that the Revolution might spill over into Manchuria and Korea. At an Allied conference meeting in December 1917, General Foch pressed for an invasion of Siberia. The idea met with a cool response from Britain and the United States. The Japanese, however, began to study the respective advantages and disadvantages of intervening on their own. In the following month, the British came round to the French idea and suggested the possibility of seizing Vladivostok in order to safeguard the huge Allied war supplies – some 600,000 tons – that lay stockpiled there. Within a fortnight, two Japanese cruisers and a British cruiser reached Vladivostok harbour and dropped anchor to await developments.

The British asked the United States to reconsider the French proposal and suggested Japanese occupation of the Trans-Siberian Railway. President Wilson flatly rejected the idea. Even ruling circles in Japan, however, were divided on how far they should venture in attempting to halt the advance of bolshevism: it was arguable that direct intervention might prolong the war or lead to an Anglo-Russian reconciliation and possibly provoke further trouble after the eventual restoration of peace. On the other hand, Japanese occupation of Eastern Siberia and the Maritime Provinces was an attractive notion in its own right.

Eventually the arguments in favour of military intervention became irresistible after the Czech Legion, striving to escape from Russia in a mass exodus via the Trans-Siberian Railway, was caught up in a hopeless tangle of international (dis)agreements, orders and counter-orders. The trains were stopped: time passed, and the 70,000 Czechs gradually lost patience, strung out in troop trains over a distance of 6,000 miles of track from beyond the Volga to Vladivostok. Trotsky ordered his Red Army to disarm the Czechs and utilize them as conscript labour battalions. The Czechs intercepted his messages and fought their way out, capturing the great port of Vladivostok and holding the eastern sections of the Trans-Siberian Railway. As fighting continued, the Czechs moved back into the interior and allied themselves with the White Russian and Cossack armies operating right across Siberia to the Urals. It was their military effectiveness more than their predicament which persuaded the Western Powers and Japan to act in 'support' of the Czechs.

In July 1918 British, Chinese, Czech, French, Japanese and United States representatives at Vladivostok declared that the Allied Powers would henceforth assume responsibility for the safety of the area. British troops began coming ashore on 3 August, followed a week later by the Japanese. An American division arrived and so did smaller French and Canadian contingents. Although the British troops soon made their way as far westwards as Irkutsk, the other Western forces scarcely made their presence felt. The Japanese, however, dispatched some 70,000 troops, a force vastly greater in number than the other Powers had sent: it was more than a little reminiscent of the Boxer Rebellion except that on this occasion the barbaric behaviour of the Japanese troops is said to have been indistinguishable at times from that of their adversary. After extraordinary adventures, the Czechs finally extricated themselves from Russia in good order and in April 1920 embarked on their evacuation ships at Vladivostok. All of the national contingents of the Allied Expeditionary Force then withdrew except for the Japanese, who stayed.

The Japanese Government endeavoured to recall its troops from Russia but the Japanese Army refused to concede. The Japanese Cabinet found itself unable to prevent the Army from extending its military operations into northern Sakhalin. Eventually, however, the Japanese contingent bowed to the inevitable and returned home in October 1922. Nothing could turn the episode into a triumph. On the contrary, the disobedience of the Army set an evil precedent. The Japanese public, far from rejoicing in the achievements of its forces, distanced itself from the Siberian campaign. Militarism, until the outbreak of the Manchurian Incident a decade later, had become thoroughly unpopular in Japan for the first time in the nation's modern history.

Meanwhile, at the Paris Peace Conference which had opened in January 1919, Japan's standing as a Great Power was confirmed when it took part as one of the 'Big Five' nations who arrogated to themselves the overall design of the post-war settlement. In the main, the Japanese delegation emerged from the Peace Conference having achieved most of its demands, including succession to the rights formerly held by Germany in Shantung and a South Seas Mandate to administer the islands north of the Equator which Japan had seized from Germany during the war. All of these gains were achieved in the teeth of efforts to prevent them. Japan also won one of the coveted permanent seats on the Council of the League of Nations. However, Japan signally failed in its attempt to persuade the Powers to add a clause to the League of Nations Charter establishing the principle of racial equality in the affairs of member states. The proposal attracted the support of China, Czechoslovakia, France, Greece, Italy and Poland but was defeated after it was strongly attacked by Australia and the United States (in the end, Britain, too, sided with the antipodean representatives notwithstanding its affectionate regard for the Anglo-Japanese Alliance). Voices in Japan had prophesied that rivalry between the 'white' and 'coloured' races of the world would escalate into a struggle for world domination following the Great War. The portentousness of Japan's failure to gain acceptance of the racial equality clause was not lost upon the Japanese. Nevertheless, it has to be said that the matter was considered a relatively minor and mischievous distraction by the four other Great Powers, who no doubt were prompted by domestic racial prejudice but also had regard for the discrimination and prejudice to which the Koreans, Taiwanese and Manchurians were subjected under Japanese rule.

The Treaty of Versailles did not silence those who opposed Japan's continental ambitions. Japan had taken the precaution of securing an agreement with Russia in July 1916 sanctioning Russian domination of Outer Mongolia in exchange for formal Russian recognition of Japanese influence in China, but that achievement was nullified by the Russian Revolution. Similarly, Japan had signed the Ishii-Lansing Agreement of November 1917 which seemed to give recognition to Japan's claims on mainland China, though in vague form. However, the Chinese kept the Shantung issue alive, steadfastly refusing to sign the Treaty of Versailles on the grounds that China had conceded to Japan's wartime demands only under duress. This line of reasoning had little to commend itself to foreign governments. It is difficult to think of more than half a dozen territorial disputes or border adjustments resolved by any means other than 'unequal' treaty or conquest to the disadvantage of one side or another: these are practices in which all states have engaged, and, as the reader will agree, there were abundant local precedents for Japan's extra-territorial demands upon China. Yet in this instance the Chinese complaint enjoyed a sympathetic reception in countries such as the United States, where popular sentiment was already aroused against Japan's aggressive behaviour.

The mood of the American public was growing increasingly hostile towards Japan and antagonistic towards the European Powers, too. The first phase of American antagonism towards Japan had coincided with the racial tensions which erupted in California at the turn of the century and from thence spread to every state westwards of the Rocky Mountains by the time of the First World War: it is impossible to exaggerate the outrageousness and popularity of the xenophobia and race hatred so manifest on the Pacific slopes during that period. The second phase took account of Japanese subjugation of Korea, Taiwan and 'Karafuto' (Southern Sakhalin) but mainly developed out of the earlier phase and in response to the Twenty-One Demands. When the Koreans rose again in revolt during 1919 and the Japanese acted promptly in restoring order, the violent measures adopted by the Japanese Army to suppress the rebellion further weakened Japan's position abroad.

However, an entirely new phase of bitterness and rivalry had already become apparent during the first European War. The United States Navy had felt its own strength, and with this development America became less inclined than formerly to share the seas with other Powers. The United States Government declared its policy to build the most powerful fleet afloat, and the United States Navy Department unveiled a programme capable of achieving that objective by construction of a navy both numerically and qualitatively superior to any of its rivals. The British Admiralty showed its determination to keep ahead of the Americans (or at least its resolve not to be left behind). This state of affairs posed a more pressing threat to Japanese independence and development than anything which had occurred since the Meiji Restoration. Japan turned its hand to the construction of warships which arguably were the most sophisticated designs in the world. Complex naval arms rivalries between many of the Powers were threatening to run out of control, but nowhere was this more likely to give rise to another world war than in the Pacific. The costs of naval rearmament on this scale were astronomical: each of the Powers began to reflect that it might be cheaper to reach a naval accord with its chief rivals than to risk financial ruin.

Great changes were coming over the whole world. The instincts of imperialism had begun to subside in all the countries involved, Japan excepted; the climate of opinion was changing, and there was a reconsideration in many countries of their long-term objectives. In all lands, the doubts of the liberal intelligentsia were undermining the former certainties. It was even asked whether it was certain that imperialism in certain countries really paid; whether the profit from the economic rampage over China was equal to the costs and dangers of keeping China down. There was an unfamiliar readiness to receive politely the advances of Chinese nationalism. Above all, the instinctive resort to force showed signs of waning; there was more readiness to treat China as other countries were treated.

In these new circumstances the British decided to terminate their Japanese Alliance; and thereby struck a heavy blow at Japan's sentiment and security. On balance Britain considered that the Treaty had come to have disadvantages which outweighed its attractions. The immediate motive for not renewing it was pressure from the Canadian Government, which in turn reflected opinion in the United States. The chief reason for Britain's acquiescence to American pressure to break the Anglo-Japanese Alliance was the belief that, if Britain was faced with a choice between American goodwill and that of Japan, the decision must go in favour of Anglo-Saxon solidarity. Every aspect of the issue was meticulously analysed in Whitehall and in consultation between the Prime Ministers of the British Dominions. Far more careful consideration of what was involved took place behind closed doors in London than anywhere else in the world: that was an inevitable result of the unequalled governmental efficiency of Great Britain. Yet perhaps few such fateful decisions have been made with so little national debate, and with such small public realization of what had been done, and what it meant for the future.

The ending of the Treaty confirmed that the world was to divide upon racial lines. By rebuffing Japan, this event compelled Japan to recognize itself as being on the Asian side. It confirmed the tendency of Japanese and westerners to see the tensions of this part of the world as consisting in the polar opposition of the white and the yellow races. Japan, cast out again from the inner ring of Powers which had the last word in world affairs, would in the end seek to overthrow this same inner ring. It would do so in the name of the equality of races. In its manoeuvres it could no longer be assured of the neutralization of most of the Western Powers; and undoubtedly it would make a commotion in seeking to forward its interest in a world grown more hostile to it.

As a compensation for the old Anglo-Japanese Alliance, Japan had to content itself with an agreement for limitation of naval power, in which Japan's status as one of the greatest naval powers in the world was recognized. The Japanese Government, weakest of the three, appreciated that Japan had little option but to do everything possible to restore a semblance of international goodwill. Thus Japan suffered the mortifying experience of coming to the Washington Conference, convened by President Harding a few months after his inauguration, and of being obliged to sign a series of interlocking agreements that gave away a good deal of what the Japanese people believed they had earned during the recent Great War.

In a Four Power Treaty with Britain and the United States (joined by France at the last minute after pressure by the American Secretary of State), Japan was compelled to give up the protection of the Anglo-Japanese Alliance in favour of what amounted to a quadruple non-aggression pact respecting one another's 'rights in relation to their insular possessions and insular dominions in the region of the Pacific Ocean'. This Treaty also vaguely provided for mutual consultation – but not arbitration – in the event of any of the signatories finding themselves in a dispute that seemed insoluble by normal bilateral diplomacy.

In a separate Washington Five Power Treaty with Great Britain, the United States, France and Italy, Japan undertook to abandon its own naval expansion programme and to accept an inferiority of six tenths of the tonnage permitted to the British or Americans in capital ship and aircraft-carrier displacement. At the same time delegates also established limitations on the size and armament of capital ships and aircraft-carriers and agreed to observe a ten-year 'building holiday' during which no new capital ships would be laid down. In naval arithmetic, that left the Japanese Navy no margin of superiority against either of its two foremost potential enemies in its own home waters.

The one major concession which the Japanese delegation wrung from the other representatives was a promise to maintain the present balance of power by refraining from the construction of new naval bases and fortifications in the Western Pacific and by renouncing the right to increase their existing naval repair and maintenance facilities in the region. The United States only accepted this proposal on the understanding that it did not extend to Hawaii and islands contiguous to the Western Hemisphere, but Guam, Midway, Western Samoa, the Philippines and the Aleutians were effectively condemned to helplessness and lost much of their potential value as staging areas or main fleet bases. Britain excluded the Canadian offshore islands, Australia and its dependencies, New Zealand, and above all Singapore. Hong Kong, however, was left unprotected. The British also agreed to surrender their leasehold on the Shantung port of Wei-hai-wei to China as an inducement to the Japanese to do likewise with Japan's special interests elsewhere in that Province. Japan promised to demilitarize the Kurile Islands, 'Karafuto', Formosa, the Pescadores and the Japanese Mandated Islands. The whole of French Indo-China was excluded from the Treaty (not that France ever seriously contemplated its defence). These voluntary undertakings were intended to reduce the risk of conflict in the Pacific. If it ever became necessary for Japan to defend herself against an attack by either one of the Anglo-Saxon naval powers, any fleet hostile to Japan would have to leave secure fleet repair and revictualling facilities thousands of miles behind. This arrangement compensated the Japanese to a considerable degree for the inferiority which she had to accept in relation to the size of her fleet compared to that of the United States or Great Britain.

The Japanese Navy had hoped to establish its right to indisputable mastery of the Western Pacific and so free Japan to reconstruct East Asia with little regard for either British or American sensitivities. The Japanese delegation at Washington had the wisdom to leave such schoolboy dreams behind, but the Naval Treaty did force the Japanese Navy to revise its strategic thinking and fatally compromised the design of its heavy war-ships: emphasis was placed upon their speed and armament with little attention to cruising range and crew accommodation. The same defects also became evident in some other classes of ships as well. This in time – as we shall see – was to lead to their comparatively early exhaustion and inefficiency when deployed in the punishingly long and far-flung naval campaigns of the Pacific War.

The Washington Conference contemplated a period in which Treaty Ports and extra-territoriality in China would be no more. The Powers professed to be willing that China should eventually be admitted to the comity of states as an equal, and welcomed the signs of modernization. The instrument embodying these agreements, called the Nine Power Treaty, was for twenty years a memorial of the limitations put upon Japan from having a free hand to decide the shape of the Far East. Japan joined with all of the remaining Powers interested in the Pacific (apart from Russia who bitterly objected to being excluded) in pledging itself to respect China's integrity and independence. The principle of the Open Door, which the Americans regarded as holy writ and others privately regarded as sanctimonious nonsense, was endorsed by China for the first time and publicly reaffirmed by all of the other Powers, who also denied that any of them would henceforth seek special rights, privileges, monopolies or preferences in China 'which would abridge the rights of subjects or citizens of friendly states' there. Although there were provisions for mutual consultation in the event of breaches of these undertakings, the Nine Power Treaty had no specific provision for 'collective security' or for mutual guarantees. In Japan the change of mood in the Powers who were party to the Treaty was received with consternation, which would have been greater if most Japanese had not regarded it as hypocrisy. Nevertheless, Japan did agree to withdraw its garrison from Hankow and, in a separate Sino-Japanese Treaty, restored Shantung to China (while retaining a short-term interest in the Shantung railway zone which would ensure that Japan did not suffer any financial losses from the reversion). Sino-American efforts to restore China's position in Manchuria were blocked by Britain and Japan, but the Powers agreed to terminate the Allied Intervention in the Russian Civil War. There were many other achievements during the Washington Conference: we need not consider them in detail.

All in all, there was a remarkable blend of *realpolitik*, self-sacrifice and compromise at the Washington Conference. It produced nine treaties and twelve international resolutions. The nations represented there seemed determined to avoid a repetition of the events which had culminated in the calamity of the Great War: they gave expression to a common desire to mark the end of an epoch and the beginning of a better, more peaceful world. For a time it appeared that the 'Washington Treaty System' would operate in the way its authors had hoped. The Washington Conference itself had a profound moral influence everywhere, established a precedent in successful arms control negotiations, curbed Great Power rivalries in East Asia and resolved a number of troublesome issues. Nevertheless, it dissatisfied the naval advisers of each of the Governments concerned and effectively concentrated those Governments' attentions upon their unremitting conflicts over other matters affecting peace and stability in East Asia.

Within the admiralties, treasuries, foreign ministries and cabinets of nations, the processes of administration continued much as before. The Washington System fell far short of satisfying those unreconstructed ultra-nationalists of every hue and country whose exaggerated visions of manifest destiny always seem to be intertwined with paranoiac apprehension. It is this which finally led to the downfall of the Washington System.

Scarcely before delegates returning from the Washington Conference had unpacked their bags and souvenirs, the United States Supreme Court pandered to public prejudice and shamelessly ruled in November 1922 that Japanese were ineligible for United States citizenship through naturalization. One year later, the Court also ruled that the States of California and Washington were entitled under the Federal Constitution to deny Japanese the rights to own or lease land. A further step embittering relations took place in 1924 when the United States Congress smashed the 'Gentleman's Agreement' that had underpinned Japanese-American relations since 1907, and passed an Exclusion Act which barred Asiatics, including Japanese, from any hope of being accepted as immigrants. About the same time Australia became notorious for a White Australia Policy. Canadian hostility against Japanese immigration was no less vocal. These developments, more than any others, convinced the Japanese that, whether they wished it or not, the great world of contemporary history insisted that they were to be Asian; Japan would take them at their word and would seize the Asian leadership.

Japan, having been disowned by its partner among the Great Powers, was thereafter condemned to a restless search for an ally which would offer her the same security as Britain had done. Although Japan persisted in efforts to revive Anglo-Saxon goodwill towards Japan, it was an exercise in futility. Many Japanese continued to believe that cooperation with China was not only possible but offered East Asia's ancient civilizations their only hope for survival against the onslaught of western wealth and technology. Japanese efforts to supervise the recovery of China had been thwarted by China's unwillingness to cooperate and by the intervention of other Powers. Japan was induced to retreat. It was still lacking in self-confidence. It had not yet developed the willingness to outrage the rest of the world. But the stage was being set for the more determined confrontation from which Japan would not back down so easily. The Chinese would be goaded into stubborn effort to defend their revolution and the recovery of their vital power. Japan would be lured by the attractions of a dangerous new ally in the West which some factions would calculate would give Japan the security which its Government and people had sought. Others imagined that an alliance with Russia offered Japan better protection than no alliance at all. Japanese decision-makers indeed responded to this impulse, overcame their animosity towards the Soviet Union sufficiently to recognize the régime in 1925, and sought to explore opportunities for closer economic relations. But communist agitation within Japan, Korea, Manchuria and China made the Japanese shy away from more intimate political connections with Russia. As Japan cast around during the first decade after the Great War, its neuroses of alarm and resentment deepened and became always more dangerous. Far more was at stake than a struggle for the mastery of China, but nevertheless in a sense it was true that all the Powers concerned would drift in the end into a war that came from the complications arising out of this fatal competition.

CHAPTER 3

The Japan Which Struck

AT the start of hostilities between two countries it is customary to take stock of their rival strength. Japan, both in its own eyes and in the eyes of the rest of the world, began the conflict, of which the first phase opened in 1931, with overwhelming advantages. Most eye-witnesses to the initial clash would have been astonished if they had had a glimpse of what it would eventually grow into. It was expected that Japan would settle the quarrel in a small-scale colonial war, such as the world had been accustomed to in the recent past.

Japan had reason for its confidence. It was a modern state, recognizably like the states of the western world. It had a formal constitution like a western country. It was indeed a copy of these, and it included such institutions as a constitutional monarchy, a cabinet, a civil service, and two houses of parliament with rather more than consultative powers. It had, moreover, a modern industrial structure. Its achievements in making a success of a western-style economic system is one of the wonders of East Asian history, the more remarkable because the traditions of Japan had appeared to tell against commercial success. The ethos of Japan remained unbusinesslike. There was, fairly widespread, a deep contempt for money. But this had not prevented the Japanese from setting money to do its work.

The state machinery was strong. Its administration, even if there was much corruption, was reasonably well organized. Though Japanese institutions were apt to strike the westerner as being odd and haphazard in the way they were run, they produced the result intended: they had the secret of effectiveness.

The national unity, which had been so conspicuous in the war with Russia nearly three decades earlier, had not been undermined as Japan entered on a more sophisticated life in the 1930s. Its people, in spite of an increase in wealth, continued to be easily regimented. The success of the Government in doing this was due to the extraordinary competence and ubiquitousness of the police, which was one of the traditional features of administration in Japan. For centuries the police had been harrying the Japanese people. One of the victims of modern extremism was the curious, nonconformist cults of Japanese Buddhism. The police seemed to be infuriated by their existence, and persecuted them severely.

Though there were the beginnings of social unrest and of a Communist Party, this was as yet scarcely reflected in Japan's political life. Dangerous ways of thought were appearing among students – in themselves a surprisingly large class – and there was a dedicated, but very small and ineffective left-wing movement: but though this was enough to give nightmares to the police, and to the Army which played a special part in keeping the morale of the nation untainted, they could console themselves that they were dealing with an eccentricity rather than a serious threat.

Though Japanese is an exceptionally difficult language to learn, the population was almost entirely literate. Knowledge, especially technical knowledge, was advanced. The newly literate populace, which was so different from other populaces in Asia, did not band against the Government. Indeed, the Japanese people, though hardy and enterprising, remained extraordinarily docile to govern. They had an ancient tradition of turbulence, upheaval, and a readiness to make civil war: but these had become only a distant memory. Their martial quality had been mobilized, exclusively and entirely, in the national interest, and was embodied in the Japanese Army.

For the result of the war, much would naturally depend on the capability of the Army. The Japanese Army had had a various history, and had passed through changes since the days of the Meiji Restoration, during which it had been organized. In the 1930s it was a National Army, the product of universal military service. But though this was its origin, it stood apart from the nation in a rather sinister way.

The young men of the Army, when called to the colours, were trained in a manner which was calculated to ensure their obedience, to brutalize them, to make them unlikely to act like the rest of the Japanese people. They became docile instruments of the officer corps. Extraordinary stories leaked out of the barbarity of the system of military training. The Japanese Army was not the nation in arms – since it rejected much in Japanese life which might have made it more capable of self-control in the aftermath of battle – but it was the Japanese peasantry in arms. Such a force was dangerous because it was liable to be swayed by terrible spasms of inane and savage barbarism. The rigid discipline under which it was kept in Japan was suddenly set aside when it found itself under foreign skies and in different surroundings. The woes of the Asian continent wherever the Japanese soldier was to tread were to be proof of this.

The corps of professional officers, the centre of this military system, was drawn from the entire nation and, at least in theory, was not limited to certain parts of the country or certain social classes. In practice, the vast majority of soldiers sprang from rural peasant stock. In a sense most never left behind the poverty and deprivation of their backgrounds, living a Spartan existence throughout their years of service. Yet it did offer a unique escape from the rigid stratification of Japanese society outside. Boys who chose the Army as their career joined at the age of fourteen or upon completion of their compulsory primary education. Few would have been able to afford further schooling but for the Army. There they were trained in the numerous military schools. The most capable of them were selected through competitive examinations as officer candidates at the Japanese Military Academy. After some experience as junior officers, the brightest attended the Army War College and then graduated into the true élite of the Army as staff officers. With factionalism playing its peculiar part in Japanese affairs, their subsequent careers depended on the clique in the Army to which they attached themselves (a matter often predetermined by the geographical regions from which they originated).

Soldiers followed a certain conventional pattern in their lives, with somewhat different aims, interests and ethics from those of the majority of the Japanese people. They were less liable to be swayed by ordinarily changing ideas because their education had been distorted. The common soldier had no human rights and was subject to incessant oppression, brutality and cruelty from his superiors. Nevertheless, his was a better lot and an incalculably more interesting life than that of his family back home, where the struggle for daily existence made military life far more of an attraction or matter of the family's economic survival than it was for urban youth. The better sort of officers, having come mainly from much the same background or from military families, had a deep-felt sympathy for the plight of their men and an intimate knowledge of the conditions of privation which they had left behind. Likewise, conservative country folk who deplored the percolation of western influences into the lives of the young and into the policies of their Government, looked to the Army for reinstatement of the values of old Japan. At any rate, it was widely appreciated that the strength of the Army lay in the strength of the peasantry, in the strength of equal opportunity for advancement through ability, and in the strength (and weaknesses) of an army educational system that had to carry an enormous burden further and wider than in other advanced countries. From thence there was a natural tendency for the War Ministry and for the Army's powerful Inspectorate-General of Military Education to interest themselves in the indoctrination of youth throughout the nation – and in what Allied post-war prosecutors later termed 'the preparation of public opinion for war'.

The Japanese educational system, founded on liberal principles, became a tool for ultra-nationalist and militaristic indoctrination at about the time of the First World War. This was possible only because more than 90 per cent of the population had achieved literacy by the turn of the century, a lasting tribute to the Meiji educational system. Military training was made compulsory in schools, and by 1925 military officers were assigned to all middle and upper schools and to universities. Arrangements were made for local military education centres to cater for the majority of the populace who could not afford to continue their education past the minimum of primary school. Thus by the end of the so-called liberal decade of the twenties, an effective system for national indoctrination had been implanted and was in use.

This was particularly obnoxious because of the peculiar quality of Japanese militarism. This derived from the fact that, in traditional Japan, the use of arms had been a monopoly of a military caste called the *Samurai*. Officially the Samurai had been brought to an end soon after the Meiji Restoration. Nevertheless, the tradition which animated these professional soldiers continued to prevail in the modern Army, and became dominant in the period of national assertiveness which prevailed in the thirties. By and large, the Japanese Army officers of the professional, thorough-going kind guided themselves by a code of ethics called Bushidō, the Way of the Warrior. Bushidō prescribed the life of the soldier at all points. It proclaimed that his ultimate fate was to serve his master, and as the Imperial Institution had divine status, the valiant death of a soldier in the service of his Emperor was a kind of sublime super-nova of his bodily existence in which the fulfilment of perfect service was consubstantial with eternal righteousness and truth.

Bushidō laid down everything that was possible in the relation of one Samurai with another, the mutual obligations of paternalistic absolute lords and the total obedience of loyal knights. That same mantle of benevolence was to protect the weak and vanquished, and there was great concern that unfortunates and the wayward should be restored to paths of righteousness appropriate to their proper status. This should not be confused with tolerance, forbearance or respect for human rights. These liberal values were poles apart. Harshness, endurance, the carrying out ruthlessly of impossible orders, vengeance and the duty in circumstances of disgrace to commit *seppaku* – more vulgarly known as *hara-kiri* (self-slaughter by a peculiarly courageous and painful method of dis-embowelment) – were its subjects: it is helpful to appreciate that the Japanese regarded neither the heart nor the intellect but the bowel as the seat of the soul. The Way of the Warrior demanded intense self-control and preparation, a process which alone permitted the fusion of a spiritual ideal with human flesh and will-power to produce a mystical energy offered in the service of one's lord. It did not glorify unnecessary violence or mayhem but comprehended that the victims of either could find transcendence in death. Leadership, on the other hand, was both an instrument and function of the force of the code, produced out of an iron discipline and the effusion of a kind of tyrannical, overbearing love that did not admit of the vulnerability of the warrior. Not surprisingly, such esoteric teachings were corrupted and completely failed to meet the challenges of universal conscription and Total War against alien foes in the modern world.

Bushidō was a deeply fatalistic cult. Its parallels are perhaps to be found in old German sagas with their compounds of horror and doom, honour and absolutism. It is significant that the revival of the typical Bushidō outlook was associated with a type of politics such as that which prevailed amid the Nazis. The gloom and grimness of this tradition of Japanese militarism were symbolized in the deliberate drabness of the Japanese uniform. The Army was taut but without glitter. Alone among military Powers, Japan exhibited no military panache. Bushidō painted the heroic life as one which excluded frailty and which was directed to perfect service and success. This produced an 'attack spirit' which led to recklessness in rushing into conflict and to savagery in battle and afterwards. Surrender was punishable by death, and it was a disgrace to be taken prisoner alive. Nevertheless, most internecine Japanese civil wars – and they had been interminable until the twentieth century – had ended in a negotiated capitulation by the vanquished to the victor. It was the demonstration of superior force which imposed its own logic; it was not mass slaughter. Honour, then, was preserved on both sides. The reader may wish to recall these facts when contemplating the justifications commonly put forward for the use of atomic bombs at Hiroshima and Nagasaki in 1945.

Bushidō was a remarkably compelling code, abhorrent although aspects of it are when judged in terms of western values. It differed but was not incompatible with the fabric of mainstream Japanese culture. Honour, self-respect, the marriage of beauty and utility, and the avoidance of shame were of vital importance to Japanese in every walk of life, not merely ideals to which they paid little more than lip-service. Japanese traditionally loathe ostentation and regard egotistical self-advertisement as both despicable and unworthy: those who yield to such impulses incur scorn and ostracism. Simplicity and economy, on the other hand, are admired. Combining these factors, we begin to appreciate why Japanese militarism seems so curiously anonymous at a distance. It did not carry any 'cult of personality', as did most European and American brands of militarism. A consequence was that Japanese generals, interesting personalities though many of them were upon closer acquaintance, seldom attracted public adulation or popular glorification. The national heart neither venerated nor reviled them for their deeds. The public might feel pride, respect or satisfaction but rarely affection for them. Only within individual military units did loyalty, devotion and charisma find full expression – with the result that they often became the fiefdoms of gifted commanders.

The tragedy of Japan happened in dangerous ideas becoming so influential when, in the twentieth century, Japan possessed the power to make itself so formidable internationally. Japan's modern military machine was administered by men who took as serious guides to conduct a rigid social and ethical tradition quite out of date and barbaric. Of course, not all the officer corps lived by this code. Some were as civilized as the most progressive civilians – or as susceptible to blandishment and self-gratification. Many Japanese regarded the ideas of the Samurai as absurd, medieval, deeply irrational, frightening and frightful. It was not uncommon to regard the cult of Bushidō (if not the Samurai caste) as a plague in Japanese civilization which must be eradicated. But the fact that it was really an eccentricity made Japanese militarism the more difficult to keep under control, and it attached itself easily to wild and irresponsible aims.

Japan was strengthened for war by a peculiar psychology of its people: so strange and well-marked that the study of its evolution has become one of the standard exercises of East Asian history. This psychology proceeded from certain moral conflicts which the Japanese, almost to a man, accepted as axiomatic. A Japanese longs, before all other things, for a world organized on the principles of harmony. Harmony is only to be achieved when everyone fills his predestined place, and asks for himself neither too much honour, dignities and awards, nor too little. It is an outlook curiously like that of the European Middle Ages, at least in its theory. It is worship of 'degree, priority and place'. Above all, it is an outlook which detests anarchy. The simple fact which the Anglo-American democracies found hard to understand was the horror which the Japanese felt at an individual or group which had a clear conception of its own interests, as distinct and separate from those of the community, and which set out to realize them. In fact, that very idea was all but incomprehensible.

The state, to a Japanese, was itself a moral entity. The notion of *Kokutai*, the national essence or polity, is complicated but embraces absolute righteousness, truth and beauty – in short, all national virtue. It was inseparable from the Emperor-system. Private interests had no legitimacy except in the context of Kokutai. On the other hand, this also ensured that private interests, where they did exist, intruded into national concerns. Japanese ultra-nationalism, although it did not admit of private interests, derived its authority from an appeal to the internal moral fortitude of each individual and his inseparable identification with the national virtue. Resting upon a consensus of devotion to the Emperor and to the Kokutai, therefore, ultra-nationalism escaped the censorship of common sense in society as a whole. Little by little, this insane part of Japan succeeded in becoming dominant.

There was no sudden or diabolical transition from enlightenment to despotism. It is tempting to suggest that military, archaic Japan took captive twentieth-century, ingenious, civilian Japan, and swept it along towards the challenge to other civilizations of the world, which was the principal history of Japan in this time. Many historians have characterized the 1920s as liberal and democratic, and have condemned the thirties as a period of unmitigated terror and depravity. But the elements of modernity and reaction continued to exist side by side as they always had done; first one, then the other, moving back and forth into prominence. The images conjured up by Hugh Byas in a brilliant wartime book, *Government by Assassination*, are graphic, helpful and have proved durable, but recent investigators have struck a better balance between those who felt that only the *Sturm und Drang* of dark terror and brutality held centre-stage in Japan during the thirties and those, principally in Japan, who have been swayed by the romantic apologists of the period.

It is true that the period did produce violent domestic outbursts which appeared to threaten the social order of Japan. Assassination attempts cut down no fewer than three Prime Ministers and a host of other prominent officials and public figures. A number of revolutionary plots were exposed or briefly erupted into murder, melodrama and farce, but the scope of violence was strictly confined both by those who perpetrated such deeds and by those who apprehended them. Every one of the attempted *coups d'état* failed to achieve its ends. The plans of the conspirators, indeed, are remarkable not only for their boldness but for their deficiency in anticipating the consequences which would follow either from success or failure. They had not worked out detailed political programmes for change. They simply seem to have felt that the violence of their insurgency would itself provide an all-compelling logic for change to which the nation would respond satisfactorily.

The culprits, when caught, were regarded as misguided patriots, not traitors. It was recognized that they generally sought no personal gain, and indeed their heroic idealism and self-sacrifice attracted genuine public sympathy if not support. They were handled gingerly by the authorities. Some escaped punishment altogether, a few subsequently rose to higher command within the armed services, and others received light penal sentences. Yet all of the assassins and most of the other principals appear to have been dealt with severely by the courts, and some were executed. It is, perhaps, revealing that the greatest censure was reserved for those who had harmed the innocent, failed to act in a respectful manner towards victims and bystanders alike, or refused to do the decent thing by committing suicide afterwards. In these matters such terrorists had transgressed the code of Bushidō.

The Japanese nation was shaken by the terrorist crimes, some of which were appallingly bloody, but there was neither mass intimidation nor any sign of panic by people in authority. Paranoia did not affect the workings of the state, and attempts were made to accommodate or re-absorb rebels who atoned – although not necessarily the causes they espoused – within the political system. The broad political objectives of the terrorists were recognized as fundamentally revolutionary, not reformist. Yet there was no mass murder, no official or secret campaign of counter-terror mounted by the organs of the state, no private civil war between rival factions, no 'outlaw' category of 'non-persons', no exile system. The effect of the disorders was less than is commonly supposed.

A democratic state has the right to defend itself: whether it has the right to commit suicide is a question which arises from the history of Japan as well as that of Germany in the twentieth century. The Japanese Diet passed a peace preservation law in 1925. This was designed to combat the spread of communism, anarchism and other subversive doctrines after the First World War. The law attracted strong political support from the major parties and evidently met with a good deal of public satisfaction. A repressive 'Thought Police', the *Tokubetsu Kōtō Keisatsu*, or Special Higher Police, was created to enforce the law. It is tempting to regard such Orwellian developments as proof of tyranny. Yet these measures were the creation of a widely admired and democratic system, not the trappings of a police state. Later, it is true, the military gendarmerie (*Kenpeitai*) played an increasingly important role towards the same end. Both of these police forces struck terror into the hearts of their enemies and were not averse to employing beatings and other forms of torture. Yet the remarkable fact is that the Japanese always preferred to rely upon conversion (*tenkō*) rather than penal sanctions. They had inquisitors but no fiery *auto-da-fé*. Although tens of thousands of people were arrested on suspicion of harbouring or promoting 'improper thoughts' between 1925 and 1945, only one Japanese was executed for such crimes (late in the Pacific War). Westerners in Japan were terrified by ugly street demonstrations against them, which often were known to have been deliberately incited by the police, yet not one foreigner was killed during these incidents. Japanese communists were jailed, but, even during the most militaristic period, liberals and western-style internationalists suffered no more than denunciation and censorship. The mainstream political parties themselves went into eclipse from the middle of the 1930s, but the civil and court bureaucracies and their institutions remained in place and were not simply replaced by military absolutism or fascism.

The Japanese also had a sense of being under an immense obligation, which any amount of altruistic behaviour could never requite, to their family predecessors, to the Japanese Emperor as embodying the Japanese state, and to the Government of the day for making life tolerable. It was possible for a Japanese Government to make extreme drafts upon this sense of obligation, and a diffused sense of responsibility in general among its people, and to do so almost without limit.

In organization for war, the Japanese system was the stronger because of the Emperor-system with which the whole was covered. Though in actual fact the Emperor had, or at least exercised, little political power, as a figure-head he was of the utmost possible importance. The Emperor, as an institution, has now undergone change, probably permanent. It is true that the Emperor survived the war; but he was to lose, by contact with the realities of the modern world, so much of the mystique which at this period continued to surround the office that today some careful inquiry is necessary to recapture it. The Japanese Emperor is no longer regarded as a divine person. But in the 1930s it was widely accepted as axiomatic that he was of different stuff from ordinary humanity.

Immensely awe-inspiring, extremely sacred, the incarnation of all that was meant by the Japanese national spirit, remote, mysterious, never criticized in press or parliament – the Emperor Hirohito obviously possessed qualities which made him the ideal mascot for war. In fact the role of the Japanese Emperor, at least in its remoter origin, was as much sacerdotal and magical as it was governmental. It is significant that the Japanese word meaning to observe a religious rite is radically connected with the word meaning government. Simply to dwell in the same country as the Emperor conferred felicity, and laid on his subjects a readiness to endure sacrifice which recognized no limit.

The court of the Japanese Emperor was not notably military in its atmosphere. He existed as a man, as well as an idea, and it was hard for

him to live up to the position required of him by the theorists of the
Japanese state. It was strange to find that the Emperor Hirohito was a
mild-mannered, courteous prince, and that he lived in a court which was a
museum of venerated or picturesque objects. It was rather like the
entourage of a British monarch. It was decorous and somewhat dull: but
it was colourful – and was much more strongly marked by fragile aestheticism than is ordinary life in Japan. This was not really surprising,
because, in the long history of the Japanese monarchy, it had seldom been
associated with military leadership. Though in theory the Japanese
monarch was the supreme commander, in military matters as in civilian,
only the Emperor Meiji had taken this at all seriously. His successors,
including Hirohito, reverted easily to the more ancient attitude. Emperor
Hirohito was head of the state, he received reports from ministers, and
advised but played a strictly constitutional part. He did not sully the
office with politics. The court class clearly did not want war.

A basic cause of all the misfortunes in East Asian politics was the
fundamentally precarious state of the Japanese economy. Japan had
built up, especially during this century, an impressive industry, but was
at bottom a poor country. It lacked raw materials. Its chief asset was
its manpower, and it owed its economic advance to the organization of
this. Its people were strenuous, punctual, persevering, disciplined, adapt-
able: out of these talents, combined with a leadership capable of
putting these to use, there was constructed one of the most thriving
economies of the world. Japan threw itself with zest into imitating the
western countries.

Starting in the early days of the Meiji Restoration, Japan built up its
industry, and the rest of its economy, systematically. Its constant impediment was that it had to build bricks without straw. But it succeeded.
The result was that the Japanese economy followed a particular pattern.
It imported almost all the raw materials for industrial use: iron, the rare
metals, coal, oil and, in the early days, machinery; it exported many of
the products of industry. The raw materials were sent to Japan, and the
Japanese people, organized in a great productive machine, processed these
and marketed the product. It lived thus upon the proceeds of being the
workshop of the East, but one to which the raw materials were delivered
from abroad, and one which was kept going by orders from abroad. This
was the basic pattern which shone through, although of course much in
the economy was exceptional to the system.

The broad lines of the Japanese economy were thus very similar to
those of the British economy in Europe. There were differences: Japan

never allowed its agriculture to become so small a part of the economy as did Britain when Britain concentrated on being the workshop of the world. Japan, unlike Britain, never took the decisive step towards *laissez-faire*, and never abandoned the direction of its economic destinies to blind economic laws. It never, to the same extent, was confident, as Britain was at the time, that the economic machine, if left to itself, would automatically right itself, whatever the predicaments to which it was exposed by adverse political circumstance. The Japanese Government had constantly in mind that Japan's prosperity was at the mercy of other countries allowing it unimpeded access to raw materials, and unimpeded access to markets for the sale of its products; and it sought, by countless means, to remedy this. Japan, like Britain and most other countries at the present time, had a continual anxiety from its balance of payments. It lived dangerously. It knew that it must export or die.

Its great industrial machine, and along with this, the remarkable nexus of mercantile institutions which it built up, all depended on the inward flow of raw materials, and on being able to find a foreign market for the finished products. If ever this process was interrupted, or seriously dislocated, Japan would be halted, its national talents would be wasted, its prosperity disappear, its nakedness be exposed.

Such a restless, dynamic society, explosive and always ready to seek new opportunities, uneasily aware of the narrow conditions for its survival, was not easy to fit into the world around it. It was constantly producing new situations: its nature, and its indispensable quality, was to be at home in constant vicissitudes. Though, as a military empire, Japan stood for a certain stability, it was really, though it would have denied this, the force making for constant instability in East Asia.

Arrogant although Japanese seemed to foreigners, there was nothing acutely xenophobic about either Bushidō or the civil structures of Japan. Quite the contrary. Nevertheless, these institutions could not fail to be affected by the intense international pressures upon Japan. Even the anti-foreignism of the Tokugawa period was no less adopted as an expedient than the borrowing of western technology, education and institutions which prevailed in Japan after the Meiji Restoration. In each case, these were responses to what were perceived as threats from outside (and who is to say that they were disproportionate to the degree of danger). In reacting against these alien threats, the Samurai tradition became subverted into a pessimistic militarism that was an amalgam of reactionary national politics and an inherent belief in the spiritual dignity of the Japanese race and cultural traditions. It found itself a rival to the civil apparatus of a modern state in seeking to protect and act on behalf of the Imperial System.

The civilian bureaucracy and the economic infrastructure of Japan were not consumed by the coercive forces and atavistic spiritualism of militarism. They continued to operate side by side, each harnessed and constrained by one another. Policy did not evolve from tyranny. It evolved from a consensus of opinion, part of Japan's historical sense of community, which took into account pressures for radical action, the perils of insubordination and *faits accomplis*. The need and desire to achieve an orderly consensus were profoundly felt by the public at large and by all decision-makers in particular. Their problem was that efforts to compromise with extremists could not produce policies which any external observer would regard as 'moderate'. Astonishing although it may seem, Japan did remain a land of law and order throughout the years leading up to the Pacific War. Nevertheless, the processes of cause and effect in international relations guaranteed that Japanese policies tended progressively to become more and more outrageous. When the democratic institutions of Japan finally failed, it came about neither as a concession to indigenous terrorism nor even to institutionalized military indoctrination and subversion: it came about as a direct response to the emergency of war.

As the twentieth century proceeded, it became a fixed idea in Japan that the country was in great peril, and the Japanese felt their economy to be ever more insecure. They had had the experience of entrusting themselves to be carried forward by the great expansion of world trade, and had been taught by successive trade cycles to fear disaster. The grave effect of the world depression on Japan after 1929 strengthened the case of the Army for finding a military solution to economic dangers. Japanese exports were halved within the space of two years. While industrial wages declined by nearly a third, rural incomes dropped by two thirds. The price of raw silk fell by 65 per cent within a year of the Wall Street crash. This deprived the agricultural class of its second main source of income and caused widespread distress in the countryside. As banks foreclosed on the small farms and businesses in rural areas, the Army, with its intimate connection with the Japanese peasantry, was greatly concerned. The younger Army officers were frequently drawn from the class of small landowners and viewed affairs accordingly. Big business, banking interests and the new political order of post-war Japan were blamed for their avarice, for their over-dependence upon foreign nations, and for the calamitous effects of this reversal in the country's fortunes. Steps were taken by the nation's civilian leadership which headed Japan back towards economic recovery more rapidly than any of her trading partners: given the nation's paucity of national resources, this was a considerable achievement.

Nevertheless, ideas of expansion through foreign conquest were gaining in popularity. Right-wing propagandists found a sympathetic response in meetings of patriotic groups, veterans' associations, chambers of commerce, farmers and even in the judiciary. In an early sign indicative of this change of mood, a former Chief Justice of the Supreme Court, Baron Hiranuma Kiichirō, who had served as a Minister of Justice shortly after the Washington Conference, founded one of the most powerful of all the extreme right-wing pressure groups, the *Kokuhonsha*, or National Foundation Society, as early as 1924, serving as its President between 1926 and 1936 (during the whole of which time he held office as Vice-President of the Privy Council): this particular society was dissolved when he became President of the Privy Council in 1936. Eventually he went on to become Prime Minister of Japan in 1939. Another example was Ōkawa Shūmei, one of the most notorious of all the ultra-nationalist propagandists, an intellectual who had specialized in Marxism and Indian philosophy after graduating from Tokyo Imperial University. Later, he headed the South Manchurian Railway Company's influential East Asia Economic Research Bureau, then became a professor with particular expertise in colonial economic enterprises. He was a money-spinning rabble-rouser. Many of his political books and pamphlets today might appear to be the ravings of a lunatic, but they were taken seriously enough by many of his countrymen at the time. He became one of the arch-terrorists of the thirties, and his association with other conspiratorial figures of the day runs like a thread through the decades. One cannot escape the fact that there was a great deal of continuity in these affairs. It was not simply a question of an old guard giving way to brash new men who were more inclined than their elders to seek violent solutions. Not surprisingly, however, there was an answering response from the Army, where ideas of expansion through foreign conquest began to be heard once again, not now primarily from the generals but from the young officers. The militaristic dragons within Japan had awakened from their slumbers.

If Japan were able to conquer the adjacent territory from which raw materials could be produced – such as Manchuria – and if it should obtain military control of some of the markets for buying Japanese exports, it could breathe at peace. It could have the assurance of maintaining its industrial greatness, of safeguarding the livelihood of the countryside and of solving problems of over-population. The peace, prosperity and

progress of all Asia, as well as Japan itself, depended on this consummation. The Japanese military were able to argue that they supported not
only a narrow national cause, but that they were crusaders for the whole
of Asia. The well-being of the entire continent depended on the safeguarding of the Japanese economy. Only the western countries could
think it an advantage that the Japanese talent should be thwarted.

This was the frame of mind behind the Japanese attempt to gain absolute control of China, and later, of South-East Asia. The Japanese believed
themselves to be economically propelled. This does not mean that the war
was an economic necessity, or that the Japanese soldiers who made it
were economic puppets. But they made Japan's economic problems the
justification of their military action, and, not insincerely, supposed themselves driven on by economic forces which compelled them to act as they
did.

The Army's emergent views on economics became a matter of
concern to the large mercantile institutions which dominated the economy
of the country. These institutions, with plenty of money to spare, found
that, in the condition of Japanese politics of the day, it was prudent to
buy support wherever possible – not only from politicians in the
Diet, but from soldiers and from the cliques involved in canvassing the
plans of the Army. Whether this was *real* corruption or should be
seen as merely betokening the close harmony desired by commerce, the
fighting services and government in Japan is a point where many Japanese
observers feel westerners misinterpret Japan. It was certainly less crude
than the relationship between, say, American big business and government
has tended to be. Undoubtedly the degree of corruption can easily be
exaggerated: there were many honest senior Army officers, just as there
were many incorruptible Cabinet Ministers, bureaucrats and Diet members. But the links between the Army, with its economic fixation, and the
opportunist commercial interests, were well-established, widely ramified,
and liable to influence Japan's politics in an irregular manner.

The gathering public discontent, which is inevitable in a difficult economic situation, expressed itself in growing criticism of the established
organs of government, and of the regular methods of doing public business. The forces of radicalism became more insistent, and membership of
extremist societies began to expand alarmingly. The famous 'Shidehara
Diplomacy' of the later half of the 1920s had been little more than a re-
articulation of the principles set forth in the Nine Power Treaty of
Washington. But the post-war attitude of appeasement adopted by the
Western Powers – of spinning out for as long as possible their period of
privilege while eventually coming to terms with the changed world –

seemed hardly comprehensible in Japan. The harsh facts of the economic depression supplied the country with arguments for a 'forward policy' of expansionism.

In the late twenties a document called the Tanaka Memorial was in fairly wide circulation in Tokyo. It was a forgery, published by the Chinese in 1927, but like any successful forgery it had credibility. Baron Tanaka Giichi had served as War Minister at the time of the Washington Conference and more recently at the end of 1923. He became leader of one of the two main political parties of Japan in 1925 and, after a banking crisis and financial scandal in 1927 lost a rival three-party coalition a general election, he took office both as Prime Minister and Foreign Minister of Japan until July 1929. The document with which his name will always be associated purported to be a memorandum to the Throne presented by General Tanaka shortly after he became Prime Minister, and it outlined a plan to take military possession of all North China. It also proclaimed that 'In the future if we want to control China, our primary aim must be to crush the United States, just as in the past we had to fight in the Russo-Japanese War. But in order to conquer China, we must first conquer Manchuria and Mongolia. In order to conquer Europe and Asia, Japan must conquer China, and in order to conquer the world, we must first conquer Europe and Asia.' The document went on to declare that Japan must throw off the shackles of the Nine Power Treaty. Under the pretext of trade and commerce, the Japanese would spread their influence from Manchuria and Mongolia into the remainder of China. 'Armed by the rights already secured, we shall seize the resources all over the country. Having China's entire resources at our disposal, we shall proceed to conquer India, the Archipelago, Asia Minor, Central Asia and even Europe. But to get control of Manchuria and Mongolia is the first step if the Yamato race wishes to distinguish itself in Continental Asia.' What a mad adventure!

In truth, however, the 'Positive Policy' adopted by Baron Tanaka's Government bore very little relation to the so-called 'Memorial'. It was characterized by a somewhat bellicose style of 'military diplomacy', but it differed little in practice from the objectives pursued by Baron Shidehara and other 'moderates'. It did not include any blueprint for aggression. In fact, Tanaka did no more than deflect a military advance northwards by Kuomintang troops, who, preceded by a vanguard of propaganda agents, were seeking to crush the war-lords of North China and so round off China's political and administrative reunification. The result was an experience which boded ill for the future.

Within a year of coming to office, Prime Minister Tanaka had reached an informal understanding with Chiang Kai-shek which appeared to guarantee an acceptable standard of protection for Japanese residents in North China and scrupulous respect for Japanese rights in Manchuria. Although the Chinese were in a belligerent and confident mood, making no secret of their intention to re-establish a tight control over North China, they had their hands full in conducting their own private war: the Japanese position in Manchuria did not seem imperilled. Tanaka, who relied heavily upon Japanese financiers and industrialists to preserve himself and his party in power, was keenly aware that they strongly opposed any measures that would harm Japanese trade with China. The Army General Staff, for reasons of caution, also opposed any intervention in China. Thus Tanaka and the Army were inclined to feel that Chiang Kai-shek and his moderates ought to be given the opportunity to demonstrate that they could indeed be relied upon to protect Japanese residents and their interests in North China. This, it was hoped, would create stronger bonds of mutual trust and goodwill. Although there were dissenting voices on the sidelines, the Governments of both nations, in short, wished to avoid any conflict.

The War Ministry, unwisely, favoured intervention, and there was foolhardy political pressure upon the Cabinet from its party supporters in the Diet, who reminded the Government of its election promises to extend any protection necessary to ensure the safety of Japanese residents in China during time of trouble. Finally, reluctantly, the Japanese Government sent out an expeditionary force to Shantung and appear to have intended to withdraw it as soon as it had served its purpose by demonstrating that the Japanese were sincere in their determination to protect Japanese citizens in China. There was no intention of using this force in large-scale combat operations. It was simply a token force, and in fact its size made it something of a hostage to the well-disciplined armies which China then had so close at hand. It was a mistake. As that ancient seer Sun Tzu had warned, 'If not in the interests of the state, do not act. If you cannot succeed, do not use troops. If you are not in danger, do not fight.'

Unfortunately, the Commander of the Japanese division which landed in Shantung failed to resist the temptation to exceed his instructions. Seeking glory for himself – or more charitably for his Army – he proceeded to enter Tsinan, the provincial capital of Shantung, where there were more than two thousand Japanese residents. At the same time, a Kuomintang force also entered the city, possibly in ignorance or defiance of Chiang Kai-shek's orders. Both sides maintained strict military discipline and, their honour having been upheld, the Japanese decided to trust to the promises of the Chinese forces and began to withdraw. However, a purely accidental clash then occurred, frantic efforts by both sides to disengage proved unavailing, and fighting gradually spread across the city. A temporary ceasefire finally took hold, and the bulk of the Chinese forces departed, leaving only a comparatively small holding-force behind to maintain order. But the Japanese Commander and his staff felt that the inconclusive result of the fighting had undermined Japanese military prestige. The Army General Staff in Tokyo, abandoning their earlier caution, took the same view. Both were determined to resume fighting. The Japanese Cabinet caved in under the pressure, and reinforcements were ordered to the area. The result was that the Japanese gained the military victory they craved and won control of the city and surrounding countryside, subjecting the unfortunate Chinese inhabitants to a terrible occupation which lasted into the following year.

Japan's actions, of course, won for Chiang Kai-shek's forces a propaganda victory of incalculable value which far outweighed his temporary loss of territory. The whole episode, however, was designed as a limited operation and, though bungled from start to finish, it was defensive, not aggressive, in intent. It was certainly true that a rough and ready faction within the Japanese Kwantung Army, guardians of the South Manchurian Railway zone, wanted to seize North China once and for all. At that time, however, neither the Army General Staff in Tokyo nor the Japanese War Ministry supported such a scheme.

The events at Tsinan are especially significant for three reasons. It serves to remind us that the Japanese soldier yielded to no one in foolishness and was second to none in vanity. Although acting in defiance of superior orders has always been a characteristic of the Chinese way of warfare, this was the first occasion on which insubordination by Japanese troops deliberately invited war with a foreign Power. It was the first example of any Japanese Cabinet's acquiescence in pursuing a military adventure which it knew to be foolhardy. Although the Japanese commander at Tsinan was prematurely retired shortly after the Japanese forces were withdrawn, nothing constructive was done to prevent such a deplorable incident from happening again.

Always it was the northern part of the country which interested Japan. Though the nationalist ferment was happening in the south, and from South China came the impulses which were making China a revived power in world politics and a danger to countries such as Japan, even the forward bloc of Japanese imperialists was at first content that this should be left alone if Japan could cooperate with China in controlling the vast resources of manpower and potential economic wealth in the north. All the while, Japanese diplomacy and semi-secret organizations were busy spreading Japanese influence in China, softening up the Governors of the Chinese provinces where the Japanese sought to protect their own interests, and making propaganda to counter the effects of the nationalist ideas spreading from South China.

Many political groups in Japan, even those which declared themselves activated by generally liberal principles, found themselves in sympathy with the policy of containing Chinese nationalism. At least, few strongly resisted it; many, however, were inclined to regard a decisive countermove by Japan as being more of a dream than practical politics. But, as the country moved towards what was to be its great expansionist adventure in Asia, there began to appear sharp differences between the different sections of opinion. These were over the extent to which Japan should press China; over tactics, methods and timetables; over whether Japan should aim at direct conquest of Chinese territory, or some form of indirect control. As the critical period came nearer, the danger of collision with other Powers grew increasingly plain, and there was disagreement about how they should be confronted. In particular the Army and the Navy came into conflict. The Navy had favoured the old plan of advance behind the umbrella of good relations with the Anglo-Saxon naval Powers, and for long was cool or hostile towards Asiatic adventures. But the Navy fiercely resented what seemed to be the pusillanimity of the civilian Cabinets in tamely agreeing with the United States and Britain to Japanese naval limitation. It supported conspiratorial sorties which resorted to assassinations as a protest; and in this set the Army a fatal example to follow. The right wing in politics was also divided. There were differences between cautious conservatives and wild visionaries: between those who were carried away by a mythical view of Japanese history and those who interpreted the realities of the day with cool realism.

These differences became increasingly expressed in struggles between organized factions. In these, there took place the real conflict over the path which Japanese affairs were to take. In Japanese politics during these years the great decisions were not fought out in the formal seat of national debate, in the Japanese Parliament, but were made as the result of fierce factional dispute. There were factions within the Army, factions within the different sections of business, factions of the Navy.

Political life of this kind – a tussle between factions fought in a jungle fashion – proved very congenial to Japan. It was more comfortably Japanese than was the contest between political parties carried on according to rules in the Japanese Diet. It was natural for a Japanese to look to a faction and its fortunes for forwarding his interests. The faction was organized in such a way as to give free play to Japanese paternalism. In Japan there is a disposition to see all problems in terms of personal relationships rather than great political principles. This was more compatible with the breakdown of society into competing factions than it was with the struggle of political parties.

After the Russo-Japanese War, the Army had estimated that twenty-five divisions would be required to guarantee the Empire's safety. Subsequent events placed a severe strain upon the Army's strength, and during the First World War it had lagged well behind the military efficiency of other major Powers. After the Siberian Intervention, the critical number was reduced to twenty-one divisions. The comparative liberalism of the twenties led to a growing assertion of civilian dominance over military affairs. Financial considerations led the Government to cut back military spending from 49 per cent of its budget in 1921 to 28 per cent in 1927, a drastic reduction by any standards. Such a dramatic decline graphically mirrored the declining influence of the fighting services during the period. The Navy, of course, bore the brunt of much of the cut-back and accordingly the Washington Naval Treaty spared a large part of Japan's financial assets. At the same time, the Army perceived its need to effect a modernization programme to improve its efficiency in modern warfare. Four Army divisions were axed, and some of the money saved by demobilizing no fewer than 38,000 troops was spent on mechanization, Army aviation, an anti-aircraft regiment and specialist communications training establishments.

These developments, however, were accompanied by a shift in underlying assumptions, within the Army in particular, which ultimately played a crucial role in reversing the trend of civilian dominance. The War Ministry appreciated that the recent European War had shown that in any future hostilities, Japan would have to depend upon the 'total mobilization' of the nation's economic, political and military resources. In a sense there was a convergence in doctrine between the European and Japanese defence staffs. By 1929 the Japanese Army had worked out the apparatus and at least an outline of contingency plans required for coordination of all the civil, military and economic strength of the nation in an emergency. Although resisted by some Army and reservist die-hards, these arrangements and doctrines received widespread support within the Army, and in time they became an administrative basis for authoritarian control over the civil power during the period which lay to the future. Whether this should be regarded as a process achieved by usurpation rather than by mutual consent is a moot question to which we

can supply no definitive answer. Nevertheless, it is clear that the civil
power felt itself under compulsion to comply with what the Army
demanded and that the Army seized almost every opportunity open to it
to extend its grasp over the machinery of politics.

In 1931 Japan's conviction of its manifest destiny, its need for economic
recovery, the restlessness and ambition of its political leaders, especially
of the Army, converged. The year seemed to be the predestined time for
action. The place for action was Manchuria.

Manchuria consisted of three provinces which were an integral part of
China, but were not part of old China. It lay to the north of the Great
Wall which had been built to shelter China from barbarian raids. It was
the home of the Manchus, which had been the barbarian tribe which in
1664 had penetrated the defences, overthrown the Ming dynasty, and
substituted for it the Manchu dynasty which had continued until 1911.
Towards the end of its life, this dynasty nearly lost its original homeland
to tzarist Russia. It had the mortification of proving powerless to protect
it, and of seeing Japan wage the Russo-Japanese War to put an end to
Russia's penetration of Manchuria instead of protecting it itself. As the
result of that war, Japan did not annex Manchuria, but China did not
recover its full and unconditional control of it, and Japan enjoyed special
privileges.

The South Manchurian Railway Company, a corporation owned by the
Japanese, had much authority and excessive control in the region. The
railway company was operated by the Japanese in an expansive mood,
and was used by them to build Japanese political power. It grew from
being simply a railroad undertaking, operating the line which ran from
north to south as the spine which held Manchuria together, into a general
trading organization with vast interests in the development of the country:
and it took on political functions which in turn led to Japan having to
maintain a force for the defence of its employees.

In the civil war in China which followed the fall of the Manchu Empire
in 1911, Manchuria suffered rather less than the rest of the country. A
gifted common labourer turned bandit, named Chang Tso-lin, was able to
build up power with which he took over the territories. He recognized
that in these provinces he could survive only if he had the protection of the
Japanese, or, at least, that he could not flourish against Japanese wishes.
He chafed at Japanese interference, but he submitted, and governed
Manchuria, in all that was essential, as a Japanese puppet. In his maturity,
and perhaps in response to stirrings in China, he became restive.

He also had held a part of China south of the Great Wall. From there, in 1927, he was driven out by the expansion of the Kuomintang. The Chinese Nationalist challenge had come in that part of China where Japan had become dominant. In Manchuria, Japanese capital was making very substantial profits, and it had become the lodestar for Japanese economic expansion. Manchuria itself scarcely resembled the primitive and neglected hinterland which the Japanese and Russians had coveted since the beginning of the century. Japan was faced with the decision whether to acquiesce in China's re-establishment of its control – in which case the Chinese pronouncements and record left no reasonable doubt that they would terminate Japan's privileged position, at once or after a few years – or would stand and fight.

Chang Tso-lin himself was at first determined to resist. He tried to rally the people to join him in his struggle to exterminate the communist-tainted Nationalists. The Japanese Foreign Ministry wanted to warn both sides that Japan wished to remain neutral but must insist that no armed soldiers would be permitted to cross the Manchurian frontier. The 'Old Marshal' should be advised privately that it was time for him to retire (he was, in fact, only fifty-five years old). Prime Minister Tanaka, however, took the view that both peace and Japanese interests in Manchuria would be best protected by a continuation of Chang's rule north of the Great Wall.

In a crucial Japanese Cabinet debate, the Prime Minister's arguments prevailed. The Government decided to advise Chang to withdraw into Manchuria and issued instructions for the Kuomintang to be assured that Japan would forestall any attempt by Chang to interfere in China's affairs again. At the same time, Japanese military authorities were given to understand that they should turn something of a blind eye towards attempts by Chang's forces to smuggle their weapons back into Manchuria: they might well be necessary to contain any disruption by anti-Chang forces in Manchuria. This was to prove a fateful decision.

The Chinese Nationalists accepted the solution offered by the Japanese, but Chang, foolishly, for some months clung to a vain hope that he might be able to work out something better. In the end, perceiving the morale of his forces fast crumbling and that he could not block the Nationalist Armies from seizing control of North China, Chang agreed to the Japanese Government's plan and ordered his troops to retreat into Manchuria. The Japanese Government's plan appeared to be working.

In the course of his evacuation of his southern territory in 1928, the train in which Chang was travelling was blown up, and Chang Tso-lin perished. It was widely supposed at the time that the Japanese had found him unsatisfactory as the Japanese agent for resisting the Kuomintang and had murdered him. This does the Japanese Government less than justice. The truth was, if anything, more disturbing to the few who knew it. A small cabal of Kwantung Army officers, none above the rank of colonel, took strong exception to Prime Minister Tanaka's instructions that Chang's forces need not be disarmed at the frontier. They had plotted the assassination in hopes that it would provide an excuse to impose Japan's direct rule over the whole of Manchuria by force. Neither the Army General Staff nor the Kwantung Army's top brass knew anything about the plot in advance. Rather more surprisingly, even the hawk-eyed Kenpeitai surveillance officers appear to have been ignorant of it beforehand.

The murder of Chang Tso-lin failed to bring about the immediate military and political transformation which its authors desired, nor were they more successful in other bombings which they perpetrated afterwards in hopes of achieving the same ends: neither the Chinese nor the Japanese were prepared to embroil themselves in a wider conflict. The Japanese Government made an endeavour to discover who had been responsible for these outrages. A secret report was prepared by the Kenpeitai, named the guilty men and demanded their punishment. The Emperor wanted them severely punished, too, and went to unusual lengths to make his wishes known. The Government, embarrassed by the affair, also wanted to put the culprits on trial. The Army General Staff, however, took the view that full disclosure of the facts would tarnish the prestige of the Army to an unacceptable degree. Moreover, no one could doubt that the villains of the piece had been motivated by a sincere sense of patriotism. The Army connived with right-wing elements of Tanaka's own political party in the Imperial Diet while at the same time the Government came under fire from the Opposition benches. Powerless to take any constructive action, Tanaka and his Government were forced to resign. Accordingly, the Kenpeitai Report was suppressed, the insubordination went unpunished, and, officially at least, the facts surrounding Chang Tso-lin's death remained mysterious. Thus, although Tanaka showed considerable moral courage in striving to effect a genuine reconciliation with China during the last remaining months of his premiership, the Chang Tso-lin Incident became another of the stepping stones leading the Japanese Army into chronic instability and disorder: one conspiracy was following another, each designed to force the hand of successive governments and to present them with *faits accomplis.*

Chang Tso-lin was succeeded by his thirty-year-old son, Chang Hsueh-liang, a golf-playing, self-cured opium addict whose engaging personality disguised his huge will-power and immense intellect. He was much closer in touch with the mood of China south of the Wall than his father had been. To what extent was not realized by outside observers (although the Japanese Government was well aware of it): most people were astonished when he formally accepted the sovereignty of the Kuomintang over Manchuria. It was a recognition of the power of the national idea. Chang Hsueh-liang appeared to have admitted that the day of the war-lord was passing. Chinese nationalism had coerced him into accepting its claims to dispose of Manchuria as Chinese soil, and of himself as a Chinese subject. But the 'Young Marshal' also had to contend with attempts by the Japanese Government to dissuade him from siding with the Nationalists. Using their threats and fair words (knowing also that Japanese troops had murdered his father), he appeared to be tempted by the promises of Japanese emissaries, buying time to secure the best possible terms from the Kuomintang. He described his aims as 'autonomy and compromise'. He achieved both. But though Chang himself submitted to the pretensions of the Kuomintang when he had wrung as many concessions from them as his position allowed, the Japanese did not fail to notice that Chang's apparent acquiescence to his enemies firmly buttressed his personal authority in Manchuria (in much the same way as King John's feudal submission of England to the Pope was a supremely astute move calculated to confound enemies moving in for the kill).

It was a challenge to Japan, which successive Japanese Governments were obliged to resist but could not be seen to do so directly. Accordingly, the Tanaka Government, while still clinging to power but irreparably damaged by the shockwaves from Chang Tso-lin's murder, made no protest when the Kuomintang flag was unfurled in Manchuria. Yet the Japanese made it perfectly clear that they would brook neither interference nor disregard for their treaty rights in Manchuria, and in this determination the Japanese civil and military authorities were united but only in this.

The incoming Japanese Government, under the direction of Prime Minister Baron Hamaguchi Osachi and Foreign Minister Shidehara Kijūrō, altered the emphasis of Japan's foreign policy from one of bilateral Sino-Japanese rapprochement to a wider design of multi-lateral cooperation in which not only Japan and China but the Western Powers would work together to create new conditions for peace, development and prosperity in East Asia. This strategy, known to history as the 'Shidehara Policy', was given a boost by renewed civil strife in China during 1930, which led to a number of atrocities against foreign residents. For a short time the Western Powers turned away from their individual efforts to seek better relations with China and decided that to dispel the chronic disorder in their relations with China, the foreigners must sink their differences and endeavour to achieve solutions based upon their common interests.

The Army in its entirety mistrusted the Shidehara diplomacy in relation to China. As we shall see in the next chapter, such policies opened deep ideological chasms within the Japanese naval establishment when the Government accepted appalling risks to her security for the sake of an international accord on naval arms limitations. That kind of split and the grave constitutional crisis which it provoked did not occur in the Army. The Shidehara Policy was regarded as particularly woolly-minded and abhorrent by the men who fancied themselves as the well-honed cutting-edge of the Japanese Army, the Kwantung Army Headquarters staff, who evolved a final blueprint for the military conquest of the whole of Manchuria.

The Japanese War Ministry, too, made contingency plans to ensure that Manchuria did not slip from Japan's control. As the Tanaka Memorial had anticipated, the War Ministry's prime consideration was the importance of Manchuria in the event of any future war against the Soviet Union or, come to that, against the United States. There was nothing especially sinister in this: such ideas were no more than the common currency of Japanese ultra-nationalists in those days. The War Ministry conceived a three-step plan to deal with the Manchurian situation. In the first instance, it was not proposed to go beyond the Japanese Government's existing policy of insisting that the Manchurian authorities must have scrupulous regard for the holy writ of Japan's treaty rights and interests. If this policy failed, however, the next step would be to install a régime favourable to Japan. If this did not produce the desired result, then the ultimate solution would be the military conquest of Manchuria (and possibly its incorporation into the Japanese Empire). While this may seem to differ little from run-of-the-mill contingency plans routinely produced by the military planning staffs of other nations, even without benefit of hindsight this particular draft plan could be regarded as a fairly bald scheme for aggressive imperial expansion, for in every important aspect the War Ministry's plan conformed to the pattern of Japan's handling of the Korean problem years before. That is scarcely surprising. Japan had few other precedents to draw upon from her own direct experience, and many senior officials within the War Ministry and Army General Staff had been involved personally in the subjugation of Korea during their careers. Indeed, the two successive Chiefs of the Army General Staff during this period each came directly from previous postings as Commanders-in-Chief of the Korean Army. The likelihood of the military taking independent action unauthorized by the Cabinet developed almost into a certainty when the Army General Staff, having already established a broad measure of agreement with the War Ministry, sent a senior emissary to Manchuria in November 1930 for a meeting of minds with key staff officers of the Kwantung Army Headquarters.

By August 1931 the Army General Staff, the War Ministry and the Kwantung Army's strategists all knew more or less what they were prepared to do, but they spent the whole of that month seeking to agree on the details and timing of their plans for solving the Manchurian problem by direct military action. The War Ministry and Army General Staff in Tokyo wanted to delay matters until the spring or summer of 1932, not only to ensure that they would have time to complete all necessary preparations but also because it seemed prudent to await the inevitable downfall of the Wakatsuki Cabinet before embarking upon such an ambitious campaign, especially since the Opposition Party and the press were becoming increasingly demonstrative against the Shidehara Policy in relation to China and Manchuria. The Kwantung Army, however, or rather the small clique within it who were privy to the plot, were determined to take action in September 1931.

The general political blood pressure was rising fast. The Japanese were particularly bellicose following an outbreak of trouble at Wanpaoshan, west of Changchun (Hsinking), where antagonism between about 400 Korean immigrant farmers and local Chinese peasants bred violence for which the Chinese authorities refused to accept responsibility. This incident in turn produced a chain reaction of anti-Chinese riots within Korea itself, resulting in death and injury to several hundred Chinese. In a further incident that also took place during June 1931, a Japanese Army Intelligence officer, Captain Nakamura Shintarō, was murdered together with his three aides while on a secret foray into northern Manchuria: while the circumstances remained mysterious, it was widely conjectured during the summer that Chang Hsueh-liang's men were responsible (indeed, a regimental commander of Chang's Reclamation Army was arrested and charged with the offence a few days before the Mukden Incident which began the Manchurian Affair). The Wanpaoshan and Nakamura Incidents stiffened the resolve of those who were predisposed to seek a military solution of the Manchurian problem. Yet by September 1931 it was plain that a diplomatic resolution for each of these problems was in prospect. That scandalized those who aspired to a forceful, 'forward' policy, men who saw no other remedy to the underlying malady of Sino-Japanese rivalry in Manchuria.

The precise timing of the Mukden Incident, however, was decided by a handful of perhaps half a dozen Kwantung Army hot-heads who were fearful that their own immediate superiors as well as the desk-bound Army bureaucrats of the Army General Staff and War Ministry were now at best half-hearted and at worst positively hostile towards the plot. These fears were amply justified. What they did not know was that War Minister Minami Jirō had been called to the Imperial Palace for an audience with Emperor Hirohito on 11 September and was told by Hirohito in no uncertain terms that Army discipline – particularly in the Kwantung Army – *must* be restored. The newly appointed Commander-in-Chief of the Kwantung Army, Lieutenant-General Honjō Shigeru, was a solid, highly respected soldier who previously had kept his political opinions to himself. But during the informal inspection tours which he undertook immediately after his arrival in August, he had lost no opportunity to lecture his officers and men against rash actions. His chief of staff, Major-General Miyake Mitsuharu, who had been impressed for some months by the Army General Staff's determination to avoid trouble in Manchuria for the time being at least, learned that the conspirators wanted to act in late September and tried to nip the matter in the bud: Miyake forthrightly refused to authorize any provocative actions and secretly cabled Army authorities in Tokyo that 'the present situation was becoming very delicate' and required 'extensive personal talks'.

Tokyo caught Miyake's meaning and an emergency conference was convened, attended by the top generals of the War Ministry and Army General Staff. Bearing in mind the Emperor's attitude, and strong warnings given to Minami even more recently by Foreign Minister Shidehara, the generals decided that the Chief of the Army General Staff's Operations Division, Major-General Tatekawa Yoshitsugu (who had attended the meeting), should proceed at once to Manchuria bearing personal letters to Honjō from Minami and the Chief of the Army General Staff, informing Honjō of the Emperor's wishes and instructing Honjō to prevent any unauthorized incident. Tatekawa, however, secretly let it be known to the conspirators what his mission was designed to achieve – and that he intended to take a roundabout route which would give the conspirators a few days' grace before he would see Honjō and Miyake. Upon receiving this news, the conspirators promptly moved the date of their plans forward by ten days.

A Kwantung Army officer of the Special Services ordered a Japanese railway maintenance worker at swordpoint to set and explode small explosive charges which blew up 31 inches of the South Manchurian Railway downline just north of Mukden at about ten o'clock on the night of 18 September 1931. So little damage was caused that the speeding southbound express from Changchun, approaching the site a few minutes later, was seen to sway and lurch sideways over the gap but carried on without halting and reached Mukden Station punctually at 10.30 p.m. Nevertheless, this small blast, which the instigators of the plot and the Japanese Government afterwards blamed upon Chinese saboteurs, led within hours to the Japanese military occupation of Mukden and to the outbreak of full-scale military operations elsewhere.

Major-General Tatekawa, having arrived in Mukden dressed in civilian attire in the late afternoon before the Incident began, claimed to be 'worn out' from his journey, and dined with several of the leaders of the plot. Their ringleader, Colonel Itagaki Seishirō, the Senior Staff Officer of the Kwantung Army, takes up the story:

He did not incline to mention his business immediately, except a few words to the effect that the superiors were worrying about the careless and unscrupulous conduct of the young officers. I answered that there was no need of worrying if that was the business, and remarked that I would hear him at leisure the next day, because he seemed tired out.*

Tatekawa took his ease that night at a geisha house, passing out from rather too much sake. He awakened to the sounds of gunfire as Japanese soldiers swarmed across Mukden. He staggered to the door and into the waiting arms of military guards, who took him back inside, admonishing him that it was dangerous outside and they were there to see that he came to no harm.

Meanwhile, Major-General Miyake, hearing news of the Mukden Incident shortly before midnight, called together his staff and rang Honjō, who had retired for the evening (he was then in his bath). Among those who hurriedly gathered at the Kwantung Army's Headquarters that night was another one of the principal architects of the plot, Lieutenant-Colonel Ishiwara Kanji, the Kwantung Army's brilliant and sardonic Operations Chief, who tells us:

Then appeared the Commander of the Army, after a careful study the whole staff arrived at the following conclusion: 'The expected worst has unfortunately come owing to outrageous acts on the part of China; the limit of patience is reached. There is no knowing how the situation may aggravate even during this night unless we take a resolute measure to chastise the enemy. There is no time to lose. We must resolutely mobilize the whole strength of our military might to seal the fate of the enemy within the shortest possible time.'

* R. J. Pritchard and S. M. Zaide (eds.), *The Tokyo War Crimes Trial*, 12: *Transcript of the Proceedings in Open Session*, Garland Publishing, New York, 1981, p. 30261.

When I expressed my opinion as the operational officer to General Honjō to that effect, he meditated a few minutes with his eyes closed, and then, judging from the general situation, he made a final decision, saying resolutely, 'Yes, let it be done on my own responsibility.' We were all silent with deep emotion . . .*

Honjō and his staff then briefed themselves as well as possible. Honjō issued fresh orders and counter-orders, deploying his forces throughout Manchuria: Ishiwara had his hands full trying to keep the old general in line without disclosing the true nature of the plot (which aimed at nothing less than committing Japanese forces to such an extent that there could be no turning back). Finally, Honjō left Port Arthur with most of his staff shortly after 3 a.m., reaching Mukden in time for lunch. It was all a bit late by the time Major-General Tatekawa finally handed over his messages to Honjō on the night of 19 September.

Long before that, Consul-General Morishima Morito was summoned to the headquarters of the Japanese Military Special Services Mission in Mukden barely forty-five minutes after the outbreak of the Incident. When he began to remonstrate with Colonel Itagaki and his officers, it was soon clear what the Japanese Government was up against, as Mori-shima told the International Military Tribunal for the Far East fifteen year later:

I insisted that there was no question involved of interference with the right of military command but rather that I was certain the matter could be adjusted amicably through normal negotiations and that the latter course would be advis-able from the viewpoint of the interests of the Japanese Government. At this point in the conversation, Major Hanaya† unsheathed his sword in an angry gesture and stated that if I insisted upon interference with the right of military command, I should be prepared to suffer the consequences. He stated further that he would kill anyone who endeavoured to so interfere. This outburst on the part of Major Hanaya broke up the conversation, and I returned to my headquarters to make a full report, which I did.‡

As it happened, the West was dealing with a British financial crisis, which led among other things to the British naval mutiny at Invergordon. That in turn drove Britain from gold and prompted the devaluation of the pound. But that did not influence the Japanese: it would have run against

* ibid., 9, p. 22119.
† Major Hanaya Tadashi was Acting Head of the Japanese Army's Special Services Organi-zation in Mukden during the absence of his chief, the 'Lawrence of Manchuria', Colonel Doihara Kenji (who was then in Tokyo receiving fresh orders to reach a settlement of the Nakamura Case on terms which had dismayed the Kwantung Army's young dissidents). Hanaya was another one of the key figures behind the Mukden Incident.
‡ ibid., 2, pp. 3020–22.

the entire history of Manchuria for Britain or any of the other Western Powers to mobilize naval forces against Japan in opposition to actions ostensibly taken in defence of treaty rights and interests. The Japanese Army stood forward as the undisguised makers of its policy towards China and sent units throughout southern and central Manchuria. The Japanese Government, with obvious misgivings by some of its members, was dragged along in its wake.

While Japanese diplomats assured foreign statesmen that the military operations were only a temporary expedient to restore peace and order and that Japanese troops would be withdrawn at the earliest possible moment, the advance of Japanese military forces in Manchuria continued scarcely without pause. Most international observers simply concluded that the Japanese Government was cloaking its naked aggression with sweet words that only compounded the sense of treachery and deceit, but in fact the Japanese civil authorities were striving desperately to restrain the Army. The War Ministry and Army General Staff were divided among themselves and unable to regain control of the Kwantung Army machine. Many senior officers were unwilling or unable to intervene. Some, like Major-General Tatekawa, had always been sympathetic to the conspirators. Others, including War Minister Minami, regarded this unauthorized military adventure with grave misgivings and alarm but felt obliged to support their men while military operations continued in the field. It seemed scarcely possible for them to do otherwise since the Kwantung Army, joined by forces of the Korean Army, defied orders from Tokyo and advanced inexorably from victory to victory.

The Japanese public, conscious of the strength of modern armaments, and for a long time inclined by the experience of their early victories to underrate China's power of resistance, put their complete confidence in the use of force: they regarded the war light-heartedly and with rejoicing. Their levity recalls the comment in *Coriolanus* of the Volsces greeting war:

> Let me have war, say I. It exceeds peace as far as day does night:
> it is sprightly, waiting, audible, and full of event: peace is a very
> apoplexy, a lethargy, deaf, mulled, sleepy, insensible.

They would have been wiser to reflect on the comments of Thucydides at the beginning of the Peloponnesian War in ancient Greece. He makes a wise envoy argue that war is so full of accident and so difficult to control that one should always embark on it with deep anxiety, even if the results seem assured. Thucydides writes: 'Consider the vast influence of accident in war before you are engaged in it. As it continues it generally becomes an affair of chances, chances from which neither of us is exempt, and whose event we must risk in the dark.' But Thucydides was a Greek, no Tatekawa, and not much read in Tokyo.

CHAPTER 4

The China Which Was Struck At

THE notable advantage of Japan in the 1930s was that it was a relatively well-organized and modern state attacking, in China, a society which was still in the early stages of adopting modern institutions. At the time, Japan's resolve to subdue China did not seem absurd or incredible. It faced, it is true, a huge adversary. That China was immense, and had unlimited manpower, might well have daunted it. Japan had only one fifth of China's population. But there were many factors which told against China's deployment of its potential strength, and which made Japan's ambition seem less absurd.

There was the economic position. China had a totally inadequate industry for making war. Except for coal, with which China was bursting, it was generally short of accessible raw materials. Initially it had a pitifully small steel industry. Its equipment for generating power was completely insufficient. Its railway system had great gaps. Its roads, for modern needs, were, for the most part, terrible. It had no system for enlisting its scientists, who were produced in some quantity in the gifted Chinese race, in its war effort. Its population contained far too many illiterate peasants, far too small a middle class, for its economy to be properly organized. Such was the technical side of China's capacity for war-making. The facts encouraged aggressors against it.

In China the state did not have the same reality as it had come to have in Japan. China, in spite of chaos, held together as a society, but this was because of the natural cohesiveness of families and clans. The principles of its unity were of very ancient origin. The family, and not the state, was the centre of loyalty. In a day when the Japanese were becoming, in form at least, more and more like the typical nation-states of the West, the Chinese continued to be rather archaic, to breathe the air of the ancient world, to be sceptical of the overriding claims of the state upon the individual. It is true that, from these very qualities, China drew on a massive strength – something primeval – with which it could confront Japan. But, equally, it was at a deep disadvantage.

In an effort to redress this weakness China put its faith in nationalism. In doing this, it followed the pattern of all the peoples of Asia. Nationalism was their support. Peoples responded to it, and it gave them an impetus which propelled them past crises which would otherwise have overthrown them.

Nationalism was an astonishingly simple force. For all its surprising lack of intellectual content, it produced in country after country the same result. Nationalism brought in new considerations, and a man was given by it new motives by which to govern his conduct. It burst the narrow confines in which men had been content to see the affairs of the world. It made a man feel that he belonged to and had objectives in common with the whole community, and not simply his own family. The majority of the Chinese people espoused nationalism with passion. Few were untouched by it. Its wings beat strongly in all recent history. It was the central, compelling force of the times. It was the root of the war, just as religion was the base of events in the Thirty Years War in Europe.

Of course it happened that nationalism, great as was the stir which it made, loudly as it raised its voice, often had to compromise. Too often it came off second best in China at this time in a struggle with the quiet voice of family obligation. It was seldom that the claims of the nation would totally prevail over the more ancient social ties. Throughout the period, this was true of China, as it was also of most other agrarian societies. All men, or nearly all men, acted in ways which proved that the family was still the centre of their interest. Society was simply a federation of families. To keep this in mind is to understand many things about the modern history of Asia. Yet, by and large, nationalism prevailed in China in the 1930s. It was the force which animated politicians, and gave them the power to make China perform tasks which would otherwise have seemed impossible.

At the start of the war with Japan, China was governed by the quintessential national party, the Kuomintang. The Kuomintang had its origin in a number of societies, more or less secret, which had worked to overthrow the Manchus. As a single party it dates from 1912. When the old régime fell, the Kuomintang was not yet strong enough to claim the succession. It came, however, to power in Canton, and raised an army. With this, and with the support of the relics of the old system of government, it had made good its authority, subduing the warlords who had divided up the inheritance from the Manchus. It gradually became the dominant power throughout the country. But in doing so, it compromised, abandoned large parts of its revolutionary programme, and took care to make itself acceptable to the social classes which had great traditional authority in Chinese society. It took in tens of thousands of

CHINA : POPULATION DENSITY and DISTRIBUTION

PEKING
Tientsin
Nanking
Shanghai
Wuhan
Chungking
Canton

0   500 km
0   300 miles

Approximate Population Density
(Based on hsien estimates, 1934)

Per sq. km	Per sq. mile
>400	>1024
250—400	640—1024
150—250	384—640
100—150	256—384
25—100	64—256
1—25	2—64
<1	<2

Urban Population Centres

- ■ > 1,000,000
- ◧ 500,000 — 1,000,000
- ● 200,000 — 500,000
- • 100,000 — 200,000
- △ 50,000 — 100,000

PEKING
Chingyuan
Tientsin
Lanchow
Tsinan
Tsingtao
Sian
Nanking
Shanghai
Chengtu
Wanhsien Wuhu
Wuhan
Soochow
Hangchow
Ningpo
Chungking
Nanchang
Changsha
Wenchow
Kunming
Kweiyang
Foochow
Mengtsz
Yungning
Canton
Amoy
Swatow
Hong Kong

CHINA : AGRICULTURE

0   500 km
0   300 miles

(C)

(C)

NORTH CHINA
1 or 2 crops per year

(C)

1242 (3.1)

1427 (2.6)

978 (3.9)

(A)

1277 (2.1)

1930 (1.9)

1468 (2.6)

(a)

2244 (1.7)

2684 (1.4)

(b)

4189 (0.9)

(B)

3495 (1.1)

SOUTH CHINA
2 or 3 crops
each year

Density of population per square mile and name of region

- 897 Yangtze Plain
- 647 North China Plain
- 581 Red Basin of Szechwan
- 421 South Yangtze Hills (a)   417 South-Eastern Coast (b)
- 290 Central mountain belt (A)   285 Hills of Liangkwang (B)
  286 Mountains of Shantung, Jehol, Liaotung (C)
- 211 Loess Highlands
- 157 South-Western Tableland

Cultivated Land

■□ Percentage of cultivated land (black squares)
to total area of the region (white squares)

1427 Density of population per square mile
on cultivated land only

(2.6) Area of cultivated land per person
(in mow ; 100 mow = 16.47 acres)

Figures used to make this map are taken from
G.F. Cressey (Geographical Foundations of China).
Areas of regions correspond to planometer reading
and are adapted from the same publication.

CHINA: COAL RESERVES

0 ——————— 500 km
0 ——————— 300 miles

HEILUNG-KIANG

KIRIN

CHAHAR   JEHOL
                    LIAONING

2%
SINKIANG   KANSU   NINGHSIA   SUIYUAN   1%
                                    HOPEI
                            52%
                            SHANSI   SHANTUNG

TSINGHAI   SHENSI   29%   HONAN   KIANGSU
                            3%

                    HUPEH   ANHWEI

4%   CHEKIANG
SZECHWAN   KIANGSI

            KWEICHOW   HUNAN   FUKIEN

YUNNAN   KWANGSI   KWANGTUNG

CHAHAR

■ Coal production 1936
≡ Iron production 1936

SHANSI   HOPEI
            SHANTUNG

HONAN
        ANHWEI
    HUPEH

COAL and IRON PRODUCTION

members who would have been shocked at the modernizing radical programme of the original founders. By the time Japan struck, it would have
been hard to say exactly what the Kuomintang stood for. It was a purely
national party. It was dedicated to advancing China's interests, and to
protecting these against the foreigner, Japan included, and in this it was
ferocious. But beyond that, it was hard to see any principles which it
followed, except feathering the nests of its many members. Its Government
had to rule over a hotch-potch of interests, and for this a succession of
compromises was necessary.

The party brought together the rural gentry and urban bankers and
merchants, bosses of secret societies and trade unionists, brokers, soldiers
and bandit leaders. Its attitude to the particular questions it faced was
determined by expediency. Some classes, for example landlords and
bankers, were more powerful socially than others, and the party mirrored,
instead of trying to modify, the existing social system. The Kuomintang
was a comprehensive party, never a party of genuine revolutionaries. In
general the party had become more conservative the older and larger it
grew, because each group that it included strove, before all else, for its own
survival.

The Kuomintang liked to represent itself as a progressive, avant-garde
party. The westernized and sophisticated classes, which made up one of its
influential parts, advertised it as being democratic. Certainly it was, in the
intention of this wing, to be aligned with the progressive forces of mankind. But the enlightened part of the party leadership was all too aware
that it sat with colleagues who were anything but liberal and democratic.
They also had to reconcile their claim with the blatant fact that the
Kuomintang operated a single-party system of government, that (with
one temporary exception to be described later) it did not tolerate the
existence of rival parties, and that it carried on government – if only as a
temporary measure – as a Kuomintang dictatorship. It announced that it
would become democratic in future but it fixed no date for this transition.
The dictatorship aspect of the Kuomintang was to give many of its leaders
a sense of unity with the Axis countries of Europe. It embarrassed greatly
the pro-American and pro-British circles, which were very powerful
among the Shanghai businessmen who formed the support of the Kuomintang with which westerners came most readily in touch. But they did
not count in the party for as much as was supposed.

The Kuomintang, from its earliest days, owed its strength to the Army.
In fact the Kuomintang was the Army. Its being, ethos, performance, all
depended on the military. This was the outstanding fact about it, and the

paradox is that this fact was never grasped by western observers. The westerners in China, in dealing with the rise of nationalism, commonly met and negotiated with the middle-class and civilian members of the party. Chinese militarism had a bad name, and the middle class, who struggled against it, were ready to assure the foreigner that their party – the Kuomintang – stood for the complete supremacy of the civilian element, which was what the West desired to hear. The westerner, in this and other matters in which the Kuomintang was interested in misleading him, too easily accepted the expurgated version of Chinese reality. After all, the civilians were often highly articulate and convincing. By contrast, the generals were for the most part ill-educated, and even the best of them trained in very poor military academies. The westerner seldom understood how the decisions as to power were taken in the Kuomintang; he did not understand how the mind of the generals moved. And yet for a true appreciation of Chinese history at the time, the politics of the generals were the essential study.

The Chinese war-lords never stopped being war-lords. Republicanism was to that extent a veneer, democracy a debased and irrelevant concept in the day-to-day existence of peasant, landlord and soldier. National identity, however, was a mystical concept – xenophobic, utopian, mercenary and feudal all alike.

How, then, was the Kuomintang 'Army' made up?

The Kuomintang Army was a painful thing to contemplate, especially in the early days of the Chinese revolution. The southern forces had a far better reputation than those of the north. From the late 1920s, the Kuomintang hired several bands of gifted German military advisers, led first by the redoubtable Max Bauer, Ludendorf's right-hand man during the First World War; then successively by Hans von Seeckt, architect of Germany's post-war *Wehrmacht*, and by Alexander von Falkenhausen, perhaps the most courageous of them all. They sought to improve the equipment and organization of the Chinese Nationalist Army and, above all, to create cadres of the type that made both the *Wehrmacht* and the professional British Indian Army so effective when it became necessary first to train and afterwards to lead vast conscript armies into battle. But the situation in China was not exactly comparable. The few smart, well-drilled regiments which the Germans brought into being scarcely concealed that the dedication of the German instructors and their herculean labours were not equal to the politics, corruption and social upheaval of China. Organization of the whole Army continued to be dreadfully poor. The Kuomintang Army generally appeared as much a rabble as did the army of the Revolution in France in the years which followed 1793. But for a time that had incarnated the spirit of the Revolution. In the same way, in an oriental and haphazard fashion, these soldiers were the true spirit of the Chinese revolution.

The Chinese Army was an army of mercenaries. The leaders of the Kuomintang were content, unlike the Japanese, with raising an army by payment, as China had always done. This was peculiar for an army which was the instrument of revolution: a political force is more usually raised by making service compulsory. But China could raise a force of millions, at incredibly little expense, so overcrowded was the land. There were far more men than there was equipment. There was a rudimentary general staff. The financial administration of the Army opened the door to corruption: the pay for whole regiments was made to colonels, who were left to fix the pay scales and conditions of service with their men. They were divided in their allegiance between the central and the provincial authorities, and between the centre and local generals, who were little more than respectable bandits. A Japanese, taking note of their indiscipline, had little cause to be anxious about them.

The weakness of the Chinese Army reflected the essential backwardness of the social system. It was an army which was raised from the peasantry. This peasantry had so many just causes of grievance against the holders of power in China that it could not be relied upon to fight with any tenacity. Here is the key to the life of the country, here the explanation of all the events which have since followed.

The Kuomintang could not trust the rank and file of the Army, and this lay at the core of the frustration of Chinese nationalism. The party, which claimed essentially to be the party of the nation, evolved a policy for which it could not expect the support of a sufficient part of the Chinese nation.

This was the most important fact about China in 1931. It leads to an examination of the realities of Chinese society.

The trouble of China at this period was that it was virtually without an effective administration. From this proceeded many of the peculiarities of Chinese society.

The Government issued enlightened decrees – hence the good reputation internationally of the Kuomintang. But there was no civil service to give effect to them; no government with an effective will; almost anarchy. The apparatus of the Chinese administration was adequate when it was worked by educated and dedicated men; but the spirit of the times had forced these into retreat. A rapid and appalling worsening took place. The machinery of government fell into decay. There was an abundance of officials, but these were not bound together in any articulated system. They stood out, but each acted on his own, without giving the impression of orderly administration. Most offices became objects for purchase. The magistrates and assistant magistrates, having bought their posts, set themselves to exploit their office to recoup themselves. They taxed remorselessly, and they sold justice. They were venal and incompetent in the performance of their principal functions which should have been to protect the people against those who always appeared to prey on them in the times of decay of government. In the atmosphere of general decline, the elements of society which felt themselves naturally strong organized themselves and usurped the functions of government. Usually this meant groups of landlords: in many areas they raised an unofficial militia, which terrorized the countryside and ran the locality: it seized grain from the peasants at low prices, intervened to back up the money-lender in exploiting the farmer, carried out a forced loan on the people to meet the Government's demand for troops, put down forcibly the resistance of the bolder spirits, supported all kinds of obnoxious practices, such as protecting the opium trade, and gave more or less open protection to bandits. Sometimes the local bosses found themselves on different sides in support of different claimants on governmental power; and the pressures on the rank and file of society were thus doubled.

In spite of all this, it is important to remember that the Chinese peasant, if the whole circumstances of his life are considered, still probably enjoyed, at least at the start of this period, the best life of any peasant in any country in the world. China was in decay politically; it was in mortal danger from the Powers around it; but for a long while the degree to which this affected the peasant, and the number of peasants whose lives felt the consequences, can be exaggerated. China had begun to fall to pieces, but this process had not yet reached a stage where, for the mass of the people, it discounted the other advantages of Chinese civilization. If the miseries over so large a part of the rest of the world are borne in mind, if the misfortunes and the quality of life caused by creeping industrialization are weighed up by the observer, the balance is tilted and the virtues of Chinese life appear very shining. The worst man-made calamities which the Chinese had to fear were famine and the insecurity of life due to there being no adequate rule of law. On the other side, he enjoyed the protection of the family, of public opinion, and the many things which are summed up in the term 'Chinese civilization'. At any rate, the peasant was not dissatisfied with his lot.

He would have been surprised to learn that he was pitied. The decay of

China he regarded as a passing phenomenon: he must wait, be patient, and all would come well again. Misery was to break over him, but civil war, its root cause, did not become endemic until the middle of the second decade of this century. The checks and balances which limited arbitrary powers, the pressure of public opinion, still operated, and did not cease to do so until the break-up of society had proceeded a long way.

At the centre of life in China, there was, like a canker, the question of the ownership of the land. China had always been rent by a great schism. It was divided between the peasants who owned some land and the peasants who were landless. The schism was the fundamental one in Chinese life: from this division of the population, and all the facts incidental to it, there have followed, almost from the beginnings of Chinese history, many of the characteristic trends of its society and politics.

In 1931 five out of every six Chinese lived by agriculture: and the proportion had remained more or less constant throughout history. From his relation to the land depended most of what was significant to the status, to the life itself, of the typical inhabitant of the country. Land ownership gave a man the entitlement to a share in the good things of civilization. Without land he was virtually an outlaw. Education, which was the key to social advance and to status, was firmly in the hands of the landed. They controlled the village school. Without going to the school, there was no way of progressing upward on the educational ladder, and of taking advantage of the opening of careers to talent, which should otherwise have been a unique benefit of the Chinese social order.

A peculiarity of the Chinese agrarian system was that in spite of the social importance of land ownership, there was no rich landed class. There was nothing comparable to the Junkers, or to the landlords of eighteenth-century England or Ireland. There were a few excessively rich landlords, usually the product of families which had recently done extremely well in state service: but these were the exception, and were like fish out of water in the rural society. The landowners in China were very numerous, but each possessed land on a scale grotesquely small, and did nothing to make these privileges less painful to the landless labourers, and to the masses in the country districts who were totally unprivileged.

The division between the rural gentry and rural proletariat was exceedingly sharp and brutal. The landless were powerless: they were at the mercy of the landowners, who were also local officials, money-lenders, or merchants. (The only alleviation of their position was that if, by a miracle, they chanced to prosper economically, society put no obstacles in the way, legal or otherwise, of their acceptance.) The situation is now the constant theme of Chinese communist propaganda. Its contention is that in Chinese society one part has lived off and mercilessly exploited the other part. The classic film *The White-headed Girl* represents very well the plight of the exploited class. Possibly their state of wretchedness is exaggerated, but not very much. In all China's long dynastic history, behind all the civilization and elegance of life, the reality was that it was the arena of a permanent class war. China has been permanently divided between two classes, one of whom has had nothing to lose but its chains, and has, through the centuries, sat down constantly with appalling insecurity. The Chinese landowners bled white the masses of the people. As it had been since the beginnings of time, so it was still in 1931.

This tension was reflected in the politics of the period. The Kuomintang, as it developed, came to be completely monopolized by the landowning class. Though it had originally had place for eccentrics, for deracinated Chinese, for émigrés who were the product of a different social system, it underwent a change as it spread widely throughout China, and was adapted for purposes of the class struggle. The landless were denied membership, or at least denied any office of power. The Kuomintang régime was essentially a landlord régime. The Kuomintang official or politician was bound together in a kind of freemasonry with most of the Army officers. They all belonged to the exploiting class; they banded together against the landless. Any threat to the landed interest and the landlords closed their ranks, however much they might struggle and be divided over other matters; and as a result the landless mass had no escape, except to contract out of society, and take to a bandit life. Brigandage was thus endemic over every province of China; in China, alone among civilized countries, banditry was talked of as an everyday condition of life, to which the poor might resort from time to time as a matter of course. The provinces never had a police force which could cope with this stream of malcontents.

The nature of the Kuomintang had grave consequences in the organization of the Army. Most of its rank and file were drawn from the landless class: on the other hand, all of the officers were from the landed. The officers were well enough contented with the policy of the party. The rank and file could not be. Thus there was always a sense of grievance in the Army, and a sense of incipient revolt. The Army might for a time be made loyal – by occasional bounties, by the popularity of some local commander. But over the long run the Army remained sullen and of uncertain temper. It saw no reason to fight wars, or to incur danger, and found the lure of military life to lie in the plunder which was traditionally the reward of its exertions.

Here the contradiction at the centre of the Kuomintang – to use a
Marxist phrase – became obvious. It was a party which, born out of
revolutionary civil war, should have been carried forward by the Army.
But its leadership, after the early years, took fright, and did not countenance the Army playing with revolutionary ideas such as the expropriation
of the landlords. The Army ceased to be revolutionary. Discipline was
called in against radical sentiment. By this action, the Kuomintang ceased
to be a genuine revolutionary force in Asia.

The social disruptiveness, which was the inevitable result of such a
social system, was increased by a tendency which has always existed in
Chinese society and which from time to time in Chinese history bursts out
and determines the affairs of the country. This is a very deep sentiment
among the Chinese people towards anarchy. This is found among all
classes, landed and landless, and goes with Taoism and Buddhism, two
religions which have always been popular in China. There is a deep distrust
of government as such: the typical Chinese has an insuperable scepticism
about its benefits, and a temperamental optimism about the chances of
regulating life without the recourse to official paraphernalia. For the
three decades after the fall of the Manchus, this instinctive trend in the
country was powerful, especially among the landless. The rise of the
Kuomintang happened essentially as a reaction to this, and was marked
by a revival of Confucian ideas and the notions of the more realist figures
of Chinese civilization. But at this time, the natural and amiable inclination of the Chinese towards anarchy was not yet passed. It weakened
considerably the reformist aims of the Kuomintang.

The inclination of the Kuomintang rank and file to mutiny, and the
dissent of much of the country from a social order dominated by the rural
gentry, were expressed in the rise of a rival nationalist party and
government, that of the Chinese communists. From the early 1920s, China
had seen both the nationalist Kuomintang, and, though it was at first
very weak, a Communist Party which also appealed to nationalism,
though it claimed to be internationalist. The Chinese Communist Party
was founded in 1922 by members of the intelligentsia. In its first months it
had been a study centre for fostering the readings of Marxist writings.
These had had a great boom in interest due to the revolution in Russia;
before that, Marxism had been practically unknown. The achievements of
communist government in Russia gave Communism a great prestige in
China: and Communism in China also began to receive direct aid from
Russia: Moscow began to direct its disciples. The doctrine spread widely,
and the Communist Party began to be of some consequence. At this time

the Kuomintang still retained some of the radicalism of its early days, and a section of the party was not averse to some of the communist ideas. It looked with envy upon the support which Communism was gaining, and was prepared to collaborate with the communists in return for the accession of strength which this might bring to a coalition. In the mid-twenties, the two parties collaborated in advancing their common cause against the war-lords. Together they established the Kuomintang power, sketchily it is true, throughout China.

But the communists, with their Marxist beliefs, were not a safe ally for such a party as the Kuomintang. The communists were real revolutionaries, determined that one branch of political thought alone should prevail. The Kuomintang was a comprehensive party. Though it was itself a dictatorship, it was in reality much more a federation of parties, and it attempted nothing like the rigid thought control of Communism. Gradually it became clear to the Kuomintang that, by the understanding with the communists, it was nursing a viper in its bosom. It drove them out of the alliance.

The breach occurred in 1927, at the moment when the great port of Shanghai fell to the Kuomintang. This brought the vast accession of the economic backing of bankers and great commercial interests. The Kuomintang judged that its strength from this was worth much more than the strength which an alliance with Communism could bring it. It was willing to sacrifice the former association, which brought it a certain mass backing, to the new partnership, which brought it the immediate, tangible economic strength. It seized, shot and arrested as many of the communist leaders as it could lay hands upon. In Shanghai it used the secret societies, which were its habitual allies, for rounding up the known organizers of the Communist Party. It included in this purge a number of radical Kuomintang members of whose sympathies it felt unsure. Radicalism withdrew from the Kuomintang. From the time of the coup in Shanghai, the Kuomintang was definitely a conservative and right-wing party.

In retrospect it is obvious that these events in Shanghai were of great importance for Chinese history. But at the time they were not appreciated fully. The western observers, in particular, saw them as a blood-letting which strengthened the Kuomintang. The Kuomintang was, at this period, in the ascendant, and there was no comparison between it, and its sudden great prestige – its recognition as the legitimate government of China, and the millions of dollars with which it was watered by Shanghai business – and the communists, who led a hunted life, and who only appeared in the news as the comrades of China's notorious bandits.

The Communist Party took years to recover from this blow. In the interval the Kuomintang appeared supreme. But the communists survived, and reorganized. Their earliest actions, on recovering the zest for a campaign, had been frittered away in trying to organize secret anti-Kuomintang centres in the towns. They were under the influence of the Russians, and the Russians, from the experience of the October Revolution, considered that the only way of making revolution was by inducing the industrial proletariat to take action. But such a tactic was entirely impossible in China: the towns did not dominate political life, industry was too small, the powerful armies could move in to suppress them. From the futility of these tactics, they were saved by the genius of several rising young figures, one of whom was Mao Tse-tung. He was the discoverer of the way to make Communism an effective power in China. From 1928 he had shifted the effort to the rural areas. He laid claim to have discovered the power of the peasantry. He used the slogans of land reform to raise revolutionary armies. Through Mao Tse-tung the communists became again a power in China, however modest was their strength at first in comparison with that of the Kuomintang.

The communists, by making alliance with local bandit chiefs, managed to organize a small opposition government in the heart of the Chinese countryside. This was the famous Kiangsi Soviet, the first communist government in China. It owed its being and its survival to the general disorder sweeping China. But their ability to create a government was to have vast consequences in the direction of Chinese affairs. It meant that the radicalism which was endemic in China was being provided with a practical programme. It is true that in the past there had often been a ferment of desperation in the country, but it had remained always without an effective organization and effective ideas to attach itself to. The masses were ripe for revolution, but their emotions were never attached to some cause worthy of them. For example, the Taiping Rebellion, in the middle of the last century, was a far more significant revolt than is today in general understood, and came near to overthrowing the Manchu Government: but the Taiping acted under an ideology which was unworthy of their rebellion. It was a half-crazy messianic movement, which borrowed most of its ideas from the corrupted teaching of Christian missions. The movement failed because the Taiping did not offer a régime which, in the country's judgement, was comparable to that of the imperial régime.

It was now different. In Kiangsi, the communists had set up an actual government. It had teachings, organization, slogans, all of which attracted classes which were deeply hostile to the Kuomintang. It provided the standard round which they could rally. They had been able to set up on Chinese soil a soviet government which had become the centre of revolutionary action.

At first the Kiangsi Soviet had simply the sympathy of the dispossessed and alienated masses elsewhere in rural China. It was conscious of waves of sympathy which washed round it, but it was unable to bear any effective support to its well-wishers. Other soviets were established, too, but they had a more ephemeral existence. Over vast areas of the country, the Kuomintang was still unchallenged. Nevertheless, by founding the Kiangsi Soviet, and keeping it alive, the communists had kept open the possibility that one day they would eclipse the Kuomintang, and that, one day, the support of the country, still given to the Kuomintang, would be transferred in bulk to them.

At first, the significance of these events was overlooked by the outside world. Very little was known about them; the communists were underrated as a danger to the Kuomintang. The Japanese had a livelier appreciation than the westerners, but it was supposed that they were so much interested in blackening the face of the Kuomintang, as a disorderly, untrustworthy government, that their concern could be regarded as routine propaganda. Chiang Kai-shek, the military leader of the Kuomintang, judged however – rightly as events were to make clear – that the danger was acute and deadly. He threw a cordon round the communist district, and kept up a constant pressure upon it. He proclaimed that, if the communists were not extirpated, they might grow into a force which would eventually overwhelm the Kuomintang. They might transform all the existing politics in the Far East.

All this was eventually to prove a correct forecast. Chiang Kai-shek, who had received a very limited education, who was the product of rural China and who was obviously outshone in intellect by the *haute bourgeoisie* of the Kuomintang to which he had been linked, was found to have perceived the realities of China more correctly than did his more sophisticated colleagues, trained in the universities and banking houses.

Chiang not only judged events. He set himself to try to influence how these would move. It was his will which determined that at first the threat from Japan should be given less weight than the threat from the Chinese communists. As a result, the head-on clash between Japan and China was delayed for some years. He had a civil war on his hands, whose issue would be of greater consequence than that of any war between China and Japan. Therefore the civil war loomed far larger in his mind than a national war. The civil war came first.

Chiang Kai-shek was therefore in the unpopular position of demanding that Chinese should concentrate on fighting Chinese. He neglected to take account of the fact that Chinese national feeling demanded that Chinese should fight Japanese. Even though there were plenty of wealthy and propertied Chinese, who saw that Communism was a real threat to their interests, they were held back and checked by nationalism from whole-heartedly acting upon calculation. The majority were ashamed to do what calculation directed.

CHAPTER 5

Naval Conflict by Methods Short of War

A T the Washington Conference, Japan had refused to entertain the idea of accepting a 10:10:6 ratio on any categories of naval vessels apart from capital ships and aircraft-carriers. Japan took the position that any agreement as to other classes would have to concede to Japan at least 70 per cent of whatever number the British and United States insisted upon maintaining, especially in heavy armoured cruisers (regarded as the most powerful of the unregulated classes of warships). This determination, together with a protracted dispute between Britain and America over the tonnage and calibre of cruisers which they wanted, unfortunately scuppered any chance of reaching a comprehensive régime of naval arms limitations or reductions – extending to all classes of ships – as part of the Washington Naval Treaty.

In fact, Britain continued to boast the most powerful fleet afloat. The United States Navy failed to achieve its dream of a 'navy second to none' because the American taxpayer and United States Congress refused to pay for it. The elected representatives of the American people found better things to do with money than build warships. They nevertheless saw nothing wrong with striving for naval dominance in international relations. American statesmen scarcely would admit it, but the two reasons underlying their demands were first of all an overweening national vanity and, secondly, a strong expectation that there was more likelihood of war against Japan than against any other Power. Thus the United States wanted to reconstruct its Navy with that specific contingency in mind. Having enshrined the Washington standard of naval strength in capital ships and aircraft-carriers, the United States was determined to compel Britain and Japan to accept the same 10:10:6 ratio as a general rule and particularly intended to concentrate upon the construction of a cost-effective number of heavy cruisers designed for fleet work (it had very little interest in routine trade protection duties).

Britain's Royal Navy, too, regarded the contingency of war against Japan as 'the general basis on which preparations are made'. War against the United States was ruled out by successive governments as a matter of national policy simply because there was no longer even the remotest chance of British victory in such a war. A war against Japan, however, could be waged and won. No other potential antagonist posed any serious threat to Britain's mastery of the seas. Thus it was that even before the more turbulent era of the 1930s, the United States and Britain had each examined every aspect of the eventuality of war against Japan in studies which were protracted in length and, one should say, refined to the point of exhaustion, in fleet exercises and war plans.

The British saw the primacy of Japan's threat to their Imperial security in the context of Britain's unique dependence upon the preservation of safe sea communications between those constituent parts of the Empire which were its vitals. For this purpose, light cruisers were perfectly adequate to form the connective tissues for imperial defence – and were also the only affordable means for achieving that end, given the large number of vessels (seventy) which the Royal Navy claimed to be necessary. Even that figure of seventy light cruisers related solely to the hypothesis of a single-handed war against Japan, one in which neither side had the benefit of allied naval support. Unfortunately, since light cruisers were no match for heavy cruisers in offensive armament and armour protection, it was plain that the Japanese would require vessels to meet the threat of any new heavy cruisers built by the United States, thereby outclassing the vessels which the Royal Navy wanted to build instead. The only one of the three Powers in a position to give way without compromising genuine national security was therefore the United States.

The Japanese had not neglected their naval reconstruction in the aftermath of the Washington Naval Treaty. Japanese naval construction in the aftermath of the Washington Conference had but one prime objective: Japan's total ascendency over the United States Fleet in any future contest that might be fought in the waters of the Western Pacific. This was purely a regional, not a trans-oceanic, policy. And so successful were the Japanese naval construction programmes that by the late 1920s, Japanese naval experts recognized that they could afford even to reduce their naval strength for the sake of an agreement with the United States and still retain a modest margin of safety, provided that Britain and the United States did not ask for too much.

At the Geneva Naval Conference of 1927 the United States took the view that 'Equality with Britain is the sole basis on which a just treaty limitation can be imposed.' Having said that, they reiterated their demand for the construction of a new generation of heavy cruisers rather than light ones, a position which the Royal Navy was bound to regard as unfriendly if not antagonistic. The Americans' apparent hostility to Britain was to some extent in surrogation for the thinly disguised paranoia which the United States harboured against Japan. Japan, genuinely desiring international arms reduction, strove mightily to prevent a breakdown between Britain and the United States and did her best to seek a compromise which would benefit all. Unfortunately, the United States remained obdurate and American press reports of private Anglo-Japanese conversations revived all the old paranoia which the United States had exhibited in the run-up to the Washington Naval Conference seven years before. The British and Japanese did succeed in reaching accord, but their efforts to bring the United States into a rational frame of mind proved totally unavailing. It was an experience which embittered naval relations between the British and United States navies for years afterwards.

These things develop a momentum of their own. The apparently irreconcilable objectives of the United States and British delegations contributed to what the chief British delegate deplored as 'mischief, friction and ill-will'. The 1927 Geneva Conference – which like all such so-called 'disarmament' or 'international arms limitations' negotiations belong to a special category of 'war by other means' – produced fresh anxieties and engendered animosity through the very processes of addressing hopes and needs. In this case emotions became so over-wrought in the conflict between naval delegations that certain key officials, admirals and government ministers on both sides began to regard the development of actual hostilities between Britain and the United States as a serious possibility. The Japanese public were pleasantly surprised by reports of this Anglo-United States rivalry at Geneva, for it seemed to lift the threat of Anglo-American collusion against Japan. Their rejoicing turned to dismay a few months later, when the United States announced plans for a huge naval expansion programme.

This came about partly due to the fact that Anglo-American rivalry and antagonism actually worsened still further during the year following the collapse of the Geneva Naval Conference. The immediate occasion was a clash between the two nations during deliberations of the League of Nations Preparatory Commission for the forthcoming General Disarmament Conference scheduled to take place at Geneva. The Americans believed – quite wrongly – that 'perfidious Albion' was seeking arrangements with the French against the United States. The Americans, not for the first time, were exceptionally ill-informed and misled by half-baked and malicious press reports, and by efforts of the United States naval establishment to manipulate the zephyrs as well as the prevailing winds of American public opinion. No democratic government finds it easy to separate 'arms control' from 'military appropriations' and 'economic priorities'. In naval arms negotiations foreign offices tend to aim at an agreement, any agreement. Admiralties want a limitation but insist upon maximizing their special requirements. Treasuries are invariably interested in economies in naval strength. Nevertheless, the American budget process and military procurement interests are singularly complicated if not ungovernable, and that, perhaps, was the root of the problem.

In fact, there had been nothing underhand in Britain's negotiations with the French, nor in the earlier discussions with the Japanese. Yet as a result of these affairs, the American and European Governments were driven further apart. Such was the seriousness of the rift and exchange of recriminations that only the exercise of considerable efforts by President Coolidge and Prime Minister Baldwin halted the downhill slide of Anglo-American relations by snatching the issues from the hands of the feuding naval experts and rebuilding political common sense.

By 1930 the Japanese Naval General Staff had good reason to be content with the Washington Treaty system, which had enabled them to concentrate their relatively slender resources on heavy cruiser and submarine development. Thus, unknown to the United States Navy, Japan achieved a qualitative superiority over the United States in these classes of ships and a *de facto* numerical ratio considerably in excess of that for which they asked at the bargaining table.

Matsudaira Tsuneo, the Japanese Ambassador in London, welcomed Prime Minister Ramsay MacDonald's suggestion of a new naval arms limitation conference and, as a contribution towards ensuring its ultimate success, proposed that it be preceded by a settlement of the parity dispute between Britain and the United States and by agreement between Britain and Japan concerning Japan's strategic requirements. The need for greater moderation in the American demands was acutely felt, both by Britain and Japan. The United States had eighteen heavy cruisers, and Japan had twelve. Britain had fifteen and wanted no more. But if the United States insisted on increasing her heavy cruiser strength to twenty-one or even twenty-three (as she showed every sign of doing), then Japan would certainly insist on a 70 per cent ratio, thus increasing her number to fourteen. That would leave the Royal Navy dangerously insecure in Far Eastern waters. Accordingly, it was all too clear that unless the Japanese could reach some understanding with Britain beforehand, the British were likely to have no option but to side with the Americans in denying the Japanese the 70 per cent figure which they were so convinced was essential to Japan's security.

Seeking to strengthen his hand, Prime Minister Hamaguchi arranged for a review of Japanese defence policy at the official residence of the Navy Minister, attended not only by his entire Cabinet but also by leaders of the less liberal opposition *Seiyū-kai* (literally, the 'Party of Political Friends') and members of the Privy Council. Even some of his friends, however, had serious misgivings about the extent to which the 70 per cent ratio had become non-negotiable. When Navy Minister Takarabe suggested that an Imperial Conference be called to decide upon Japan's aims and then unite public opinion, Court circles initially favoured the idea. But the last of the *Genrō*, wise old Prince Saionji Kinmochi, succeeded in quashing it: 'Do nothing of the kind,' he told Takarabe. 'In diplomacy, one does not burn his bridges or show his hand.' Nevertheless, Hamaguchi won a great deal of credit at the time when he held a press conference and revealed his Government's determination to adhere to the 70 per cent ratio in heavy cruisers at the very least. Addressing the Diet, he declared:

Our claim ... is based upon the practical necessity to make our defence secure against foreign invasion. We offer no menace to any nation, we submit to menace from none. On that fundamental principle, it is our desire to seek a naval agreement satisfactory to all the parties concerned.*

This was not hyperbole. It was pre-eminently sane, the minimum to which any nation aspires if it possesses the wit and means to survive as an independent state. It did not go down well in Washington, D C, however, where the United States Government was equally determined that the Japanese must submit to an extension of the Washington Conference's 60 per cent ratio in all classes of warship. What the United States feared was that it might someday find itself unable to enforce its will upon Japan if the Japanese were to run amok in China (or even the Philippines). The American position, as Gregory Bienstock pointed out in the mid-thirties, was that 'unless America is able to carry the war into Japanese waters, she will lose it'.† But to put it another way, unless America could carry the war into Japanese waters, there was most unlikely to be any resort to war in the first place.

At the London Naval Conference of 1930, Britain and the United States finally found ways to overcome their most serious difficulties. They then joined in common cause against Japan. Although Britain did induce the United States to moderate the xenophobic and unreasonable attitude of the United States to a slight degree, the Japanese were the only participants who, for a second time, sought a reduction rather than merely a limitation in naval armaments. Moreover, as Captain C. Varyl Robinson,

* Speech before the Imperial Diet, 21 January 1930, as quoted in Takeuchu, *War and Diplomacy in the Japanese Empire*, Chicago, 1935, pp. 289–90, and cited in J. B. Crowley, *Japan's Quest for Autonomy*, Princeton University Press, Princeton, 1966, p. 44.

† G. Bienstock, *The Struggle for the Pacific*, Kennikat Press, Port Washington, New York (reprint of 1937 edition), 1970, p. 242.

the British Naval Attaché assigned both to Tokyo and to Peking, privately observed shortly before his return to England, Japan alone among the naval powers had based her policy solely on her minimum defensive requirements rather than leaving a margin sufficient to pursue a successful naval offensive. Baron Shidehara, confirmed internationalist though he was, reportedly likened America's behaviour to that of a rich 'spoilt child', who could afford to squander unlimited resources on armaments if it should please it to do so. Nevertheless, once the British and American delegations had reached agreement, the Japanese could make little headway in protecting their own interests. Prime Minister Ramsay MacDonald afterwards reported to King George V that 'From beginning to end, the two delegations [Britain and the United States] worked in complete harmony. To all intents and purposes they were one team.'* Even allowing for exaggeration, this nevertheless shows the very real dangers to which the Conference exposed the Japanese. When a compromise was reached in the end, it therefore came as a relief to the Japanese as well as to the British and American delegations – and privately most circles within the Japanese Government admitted that they had achieved more than for a time had seemed possible.

In some respects it can be argued that the 1930 London Naval Conference actually reduced the real security of each of the major naval Powers. France, who attended the Conference but tried to wreck it, and Italy, who also found herself in an untenable position, both refused to sign the Treaty. So far as Britain was concerned, the effect of the Treaty was that she was able to adhere to her present strength of fifteen eight-inch calibre cruisers while building an additional 90,000 tons (fourteen ships) of light cruisers and at the same time increasing her strength in auxiliaries and conducting an extensive modernization programme for her existing fleet. The United States increased its strength by three eight-inch gun cruisers and five light cruisers, although it was agreed that construction of these vessels would be deferred until the mid-thirties. More importantly, the Americans became entitled to construct 346,811 tons of new vessels, including seventeen heavy cruisers, to replace older ships. Japan, by contrast, was not permitted to construct a single new heavy cruiser and was permitted only 50,769 tons of new construction in all other categories of warship put together. Thus although Japan gained a 70 per cent ratio in six-inch calibre (light) cruisers and in destroyers together with parity in submarines, she was restricted to 60.02 per cent of the American heavy

* S. Roskill, *Naval Policy between the Wars: II, The Period of Reluctant Rearmament, 1930–1939*, Cassell, London, 1976, pp. 65–6.

cruiser strength. These figures gave Japan an overall entitlement to 69.75 per cent of the American gross tonnage figure but the appearance of an improvement in ratios over Washington Conference levels was illusory. The real effect of the London Naval Treaty was that Japan had to concede in principle her right to a hegemony in the Western Pacific which she had enjoyed in practice since 1905. After agreement was reached, the Head of the Japanese Delegation, Wakatsuki Reijirō, sadly but soberly remarked, 'Suspicions and misunderstandings will only be deepened. This is what the Japanese Government views with the most serious concern.'* Indeed, the bullying tactics of the American Secretary of State, Henry L. Stimson, towards the Japanese during the Conference begs comparison to that of Adolf Hitler towards the Austrian Chancellor, Dr Kurt Schuschnigg, on the eve of the Austro-German *Anschluss*.

All of this contributed to the gradual determination of Japanese ruling circles to turn away from such negotiations in future, or at least not to subject themselves to the likelihood of such humiliating consequences. At the same time, the London Naval Treaty had left the British and United States navies inadequately prepared to meet their very real national defence requirements in the decade ahead. In the short term, however, the worst effects of the Treaty were visited upon Japan. In particular it brought about the resignation of the Chief and Vice-Chief of the Naval General Staff, the retirement of the Navy Minister and Vice-Minister, an assassination attempt upon the life of Prime Minister Hamaguchi (who suffered a lingering death as a result of wounds inflicted by a right-wing fanatic) and the political ruination of his *Minseitō* (Democratic Party). These events all cast a shadow over the ensuing years. As the gifted Admiral Katō Kanji told Prince Saionji's ubiquitous secretary, Baron Harada Kumao:

It's as if we had been roped up and cast into prison by Britain and America. When I and my kind have gone, it will be you [Harada] and your kind who must bear the brunt of it. Since there's no fixed national policy, it follows that the programme for national defence will also vacillate. This is indeed disturbing . . . What has caused me the gravest concern recently has been the activity of those about the Throne.†

At this point we must digress momentarily to explain that the Japanese Navy had become a house divided against itself. In Japan, the Emperor exercised 'Supreme Command' (*Tōsui*) through the Army and Naval General Staffs together with the Supreme War Council (a kind of panel of

---

* Crowley, op. cit., p. 65.
† Harada Diary entry for 28 April 1930, as translated in T. F. Mayer-Oakes, *Fragile Victory*, Wayne State University Press, Detroit, 1968, p. 111.

elderly umpires who, when requested to do so by the Army or Naval General Staffs, advised the Emperor on important military and naval policy issues). On the other hand, the Emperor exercised his organization and administration (*Hensei*) of national defence through the War and Navy Ministries. The Army and Naval General Staffs, according to Dr Minobe, the distinguished Japanese constitutional scholar to whom the ruling élite now turned for guidance, were entitled to *participate* in defence planning and rightly 'should be given every serious consideration by the Government'.* Nevertheless, Dr Minobe continued, the General Staffs 'do not at all have the right of decision'. Traditionally, the Naval General Staff had far less power than the Army General Staff. Executive power in the Navy rested almost exclusively with the Navy Minister in time of peace. Senior members of the Naval General Staff chafed at being condemned to a position of perpetual inferiority to the 'prima donnas' of the Navy Ministry. They envied the far greater power of their Army counterparts. Thus while the Navy Ministry had broad powers as the 'administrative' side of the Navy, the Naval General Staff was confined to 'operational' or 'staff' duties defined in the narrowest possible sense. The Naval General Staff tended to be less moderate than the Navy Ministry, just as the Army General Staff was more imbued with an offensive spirit than the War Ministry. All of these organs experienced difficulty in resisting the influence of more radical elements within the officer corps, but clearly the Navy Ministry was far more fortunate in this respect than the others.

The Navy as a whole was a much more moderate service than the Army. On most issues even the Navy General Staff felt some temptation to seek a form of compromise. It did not really identify itself with the arcane feudalistic ethic which had proved so attractive to the Army. At one time the Navy had been administratively subordinate to the Army. In ancient times its prime functions were to transport the Army, to maintain the Army's lines of communication, and to preserve the Army's freedom of manoeuvre. But the modern Japanese Navy cherished its independence from the Army. It had adopted western values as well as European practices with far less modification than its elder brother service. It was also much more élitist. It drew its officer corps not from poorly educated peasant youth but from upper- and middle-class young men straight from the universities, and it was susceptible to the same kind of class consciousness as that which afflicted the officer corps of the United States Navy and Royal Navy. The naval officer was typically far more familiar with international affairs, more technologically sophisticated and, generally

* Mayer-Oakes, op. cit., pp. 112–15.

speaking, more cosmopolitan than his Army compatriots. At the same time, the Navy was much smaller. Its officer corps was only a fifth the size of the Army's, and its political influence, rarely more than, say, a third of the Army's, shrank further still during the London Naval Treaty controversy. In the past, the Navy had prided itself on its internal cohesion. The disciplines of life at sea helped to preserve the Navy from the ravages of political storms and social upheaval ashore. In any case the Navy lacked traditional ties with the agrarian-cum-revolutionary radicalism so deeply implanted within the Army. And looking across the horizon and in foreign ports of call, the Navy had reason to know and greatly respect the strength of the Royal Navy and United States Navy, understood the economic capacity of their respective countries and saw little advantage in entangling Japan in China at the expense of good relations with the western democracies. Perhaps equally significant, there were as yet no foreign naval Powers towards whom any Japanese naval officer could look for assistance if unbridled national passions should erupt into war.

These considerations particularly affected the older generation of naval officers: Admiral Ōkada Keisuke, Navy Minister in the preceding Cabinet and a future Prime Minister; Admiral Count Yamamoto Gonbei, also a former Navy Minister, who had twice been Prime Minister; Admiral Saitō Makoto, three times Navy Minister, now Governor-General of Korea for the second time, subsequently another Prime Minister: all of these and others were strong supporters of the Treaty faction. The talents of men like these were considerable, and so was the esteem in which they were held by the Genrō and palace officials. Yet the fact remains that the most able men of the Naval General Staff were bitterly resentful of their continuing subordination to the Navy Ministry, and in that sense the London Naval Treaty came as merely the last straw. As Katō Kanji complained:

Before the Government dispatched the instructions to the delegation in London, they ought to have listened to our views on this matter; and yet when I wanted to present explanations at meetings of the Cabinet, I was prevented from attending . . . They are altogether defiant of the General Staff. It would have been acceptable if they had allowed me to have my say and then had given me to understand before the instructions were sent that there was no alternative after considering the matter from various angles. But they didn't even do that. The very issuance of the instructions shows a disregard for the Navy General Staff and is equivalent to ignoring the prerogative of Supreme Command. Can I stand by and allow decisions on the national defence to be made in this way?*

It is scarcely surprising that this sense of genuine grievance struck a

* Harada Diary entry for 5 May 1930, as translated in Mayer-Oakes, op. cit., p. 121.

responsive chord outside the confines of the Navy. The main parliamentary opposition party (*Seiyū-kai*), Hiranuma's *Kokuhonsha*, the Naval Reservist Organization and the combined services' Military Club, all joined the band-wagon. This mésalliance could not stop the Treaty but it forced the 'moderates' into adopting means which only reinforced the determination of the dissidents to redress the balance.

It is within this context, then, that we may note the sentiments expressed by one of 'those about the Throne' in reply to the efforts by the Navy's diehards, Admiral Katō Kanji in particular, to throttle the London Naval Treaty before it could be ratified: the venerable Grand Chamberlain, Admiral Suzuki Kantarō, drily commented,

It behoves the Chief of the Naval General Staff as the Emperor's chief staff officer to be more discreet and circumspect. It is highly reprehensible to drum up popular support for his own notions and then to try to push them through because of the public opinion thus aroused. Only the mediocre could clamour for 70 per cent or nothing. He who is Chief of the Naval General Staff must be able to utilize whatever strength is allotted to him; whether it be 60 or even 50 per cent that may be decided upon. It may be that Katō is too obstinate and emotional. So it seems to me.*

Prime Minister Hamaguchi's successors, alas, were not nearly so prepared to brave the demands of Japan's fighting services. Baron Wakatsuki, who took charge after a short caretaker period during which Baron Shidehara was Prime Minister *pro tempore*, had to yield to the expedient of promising to consult more closely with the Army and Navy General Staffs in any future matters affecting national security. After the London Treaty crisis, the right of 'supreme command' was much more jealously guarded than before – and was upheld by the preponderance of Japanese public opinion. Moreover, the Naval General Staff had learned the lesson that it would need to maintain the support of public opinion against the bureaucrats and officials who, having outmanoeuvred them in securing ratification of the Treaty, could no longer be trusted. Meanwhile the Japanese, like other top-class naval Powers, secretly bent their backs to the task of planning ways of circumventing the régime of naval limitation treaties to prepare for the likelihood that no satisfactory arrangements would be achieved by the time that all the existing agreements were due to expire at the end of December 1936.

There were many within the Army as well as the Naval General Staffs who were alarmed by the success of the bureaucrats and party politicians in railroading the London Naval Treaty through the Supreme War

* Harada Diary entry for 28 March 1930, as translated in Mayer-Oakes, op. cit., p. 103.

Council, the Cabinet, the Privy Council and the Imperial Diet. The whole affair had raised constitutional issues of the gravest importance, unresolved issues which struck at the heart of the military's independence and direct responsibility to the Throne on matters relating to Army as well as Navy control over the means available to them in the execution of national defence policies in the widest sense. When Prime Minister Hamaguchi had advised the Emperor to sign the Treaty against the wishes of his Naval General Staff, he tugged at the lynchpin which enabled the military and civil arms of government to work together, and his actions were thus contributory to a natural reaction, the sabre politics of the 1930s. Nor can one overlook the significance of the fact that the political ferment surrounding the London Naval Conference had coincided with the world depression. This increased pressure on governments to find solutions but it also added to the xenophobic sense of grievance which the ignorant, foolish and mad felt against foreign Powers.

Finally, it is worth stealing a last look at the Army's key role during these 'disarmament' controversies, for it not only helps to illuminate the constitutional relationship between the defence services but also may help to dispel the common misapprehension that the Japanese Army was invariably hamfisted in relation to the affairs of other government departments which affected the 'national polity'. Had the Army taken strong exception to the London Naval Treaty, it lay within the power of both War Minister Ugaki Kazushige and the Army General Staff to force the issue by his resignation, at one stroke bringing down the Cabinet and the Treaty. At the time, Ugaki was seriously ill in hospital. The pressures exerted upon him to resign were great. For a very long time, he stoutly resisted these pressures, confiding to Navy Minister Takarabe (another courageous man), 'This disarmament is a Navy matter and the Army has no share in or knowledge of it. A joint Army-Navy meeting would be quite superfluous. The Navy alone must handle it.' * As the matter dragged on for months, it began to appear that Ugaki would have to yield to the mental and physical strains. His Cabinet colleagues and Prince Saionji then prevailed upon him to appoint his Vice-Minister to deputize for him as War Minister *ad interim*. Constitutionally, this was another unprecedented step, but another hurdle had been surmounted. Whatever may have been Ugaki's motives (and there were many who felt that he would one day make a first-class premier), the Japanese Army General Staff as well as Ugaki had resisted a marvellous opportunity to join forces with the rank and file of the Naval General Staff in seeking to bring about

* Harada Diary entry for 9 June 1930, as translated in Mayer-Oakes, op. cit., p. 147.

the collapse of the Government and possibly to establish in its stead a new political order based upon the apocalyptic and hyper-nationalistic authoritarian principles which Katō Kanji and many of his adherents held dear. Whatever the dangers on the horizon (and they were manifold) Prince Saionji's voice tells us how determined were those who struggled against the rising tide of pessimism: while ratification of the London Naval Treaty was still far from assured, he declared:

Today, when new impetus has been given to peace through the new agencies devised after the Paris Peace Conference, agencies based on a spirit of peace for the promotion of human welfare, no nation should have offensive armaments. In a word, then, may we talk of weapons for defence, but nowhere can anyone today talk of weapons for aggression. These may seem to be wholly new schemes and principles, but if we go back a little further, we find they have a long and splendid history. This is what Jean Jacques Rousseau advocated so long ago. Men are not beasts; hence they should cease chewing each other up. For the welfare of mankind, let us preserve peace: this is the spirit that has come forth as the new principle today since the Peace Conference. Both the disarmament treaties and the Anti-War [Kellogg-Briand] Pact stem from a fine long-developing tradition. There's no intention of using treaties to threaten or reduce a particular nation's armaments. On the contrary, these treaties should be considered as undertaken for the sake of human happiness which can come from a spirit of the love for peace.*

His words express the well-nigh universal aspirations of the human race, but the tensions and accidents of history are no illusion, and the breadth of his vision is mocked by the horror and torment of the years that were still to come.

* Harada Diary entry for 13 June 1930, as translated in Mayer-Oakes, op. cit., pp. 158–9.

CHAPTER 6

The Great Manchurian Adventure

IN September 1931 the Japanese Army operations in Manchuria rapidly developed beyond the South Manchurian Railway zone. The movements of the Kwantung Army after the bomb incident (which the Chinese were not slow to accuse them of contriving) were so systematic, orderly and comprehensive that they obviously had been considered long in advance. Army field commanders were openly flouting normal civilian controls, and the Japanese Government floundered in the wake of events, responding sluggishly to news from the front.

The Japanese quickly overran Manchuria. Efforts both by the Japanese Government and Lieutenant-General Honjō, Commander-in-Chief of the Kwantung Army, to contain the affair and to restrain the advocates of a 'forward policy' were unavailing, and as Honjō's own orders were disregarded and his officers led their forces across Manchuria, the private doubts in Japanese official circles were laid aside amid scenes of public jubilation. Although vastly outnumbered 20:1 by Chang Hsueh-liang, the Manchurian armies were routed by the Japanese. In the fighting, only one of Chang's generals, Ma Chan-shan, resisted skilfully. Originally he seems to have been relatively well-disposed towards the Japanese until it became obvious that the Japanese wanted him to step down for another Manchurian war-lord, Chang Hai-peng, to become the provincial governor of Heilungkiang. Ma showed, by his field tactics, that he had studied the teaching of the old Chinese military texts on how to feign and double-cross. He won momentarily a great deal of popularity in the national press of China by the 'successful' action which he fought on the Nonni River. The importance of his actions was exaggerated. It was a campaign of delay. There was precious little fighting. He received no support, either from other Manchurian generals or from the Chinese central Government, which did not use its forces to support him. This is far from difficult to understand. Ma had regular forces twice as numerous as the total numerical strength of the Japanese troops then in the whole of Manchuria, his tactical position was more secure than his ability to seize the offensive, and the main struggle at the Nonni River bridges was anyway not a direct contest between 'the Chinese' and 'the Japanese' but between the assembled forces of two rival Manchurian generals, one of whom was favoured by the Japanese. As the subsequent report of the League of Nations Commission of Enquiry pointed out, the feuds between rival generals and their gangs were a critical factor in the unfolding of these and other events.

The complete evacuation of Manchuria by the troops of Marshal Chang Hsueh-liang, practically without striking a blow, was not unconnected with the internal conditions of China south of the Wall.*

A full appreciation of the Japanese achievement in Manchuria can be approached only through an understanding of the immense geographical obstacles which had to be overcome by the Japanese forces. Chang Hsueh-liang not only had governed the whole of Manchuria, a country extending 900 miles in length and the same in breadth (encompassing some 380,000 square miles of territory, much of it mountainous, equivalent in size to the combined area of Germany and France). His rule also extended to control of the province of Jehol, an adjacent fiefdom which added a further 60,000 square miles to his domains and which left him in military command of the northern approaches to Peking beyond the Great Wall. While it is true that railway construction in Manchuria was far more developed than that of China Proper in 1931, communications were difficult and depended chiefly upon river and road traffic. Many of the rivers in Manchuria were navigable only by small craft at the best of times and all were generally frozen between October and March each year. With winter temperatures well below freezing throughout the land for six to eight months of the year, followed by summer temperatures rising to 38° C (100° F) in conjunction with widespread monsoon floods over many parts of the country, the climatic environment of Manchuria varied from bad to intolerable, certainly utterly inhospitable to the alien Japanese invaders.

By January 1932, however, the Kwantung Army, exploiting the divisions between Chang Hsueh-liang's lieutenants and supported by units of the Korean Army, had established a complete mastery over the whole of South Manchuria and had made serious inroads into Russian-dominated North Manchuria, too. Most of the time the Kwantung Army struck first and informed Tokyo afterwards. As Prime Minister Wakatsuki recalled afterwards:

It was the unanimous sense of the Cabinet that these operations in Manchuria must cease immediately and War Minister Minami agreed to put this Cabinet policy into effect with the Army at once. However day after day expansion con-

* *The Report of the Commission of Enquiry into the Sino-Japanese Dispute*, Chūō Korou, Tokyo, n.d. [October 1932], p. 100.

MANCHURIA
Economic and Strategic Significance

+++ Railways built 1932 ++ 1932–45
— Roads in use/under construction

0 _____ 300 km
0 _____ 200 miles

U S S R

Chita
TRANS-SIBERIAN RLY.
Amur
International boundary
Provincial boundary
Argun
Heiho — Blagoveshchensk
Khabarovsk
Manchouli
Hailar
Nunchiang
Birobidzhan
Dailai Nor (L.Hulun)
K H I N G A N
Pei-An
HEILUNGKIANG
Buir Nor (L.Peir)
Tsitsihar
Angangki
Hailun
Chiamussu
MONGOLIA
Nonni
Tailai
CHINESE
Sungari
Harbin
L.Hanka
C H A H A R
EASTERN RLY
Suifenho
Voroshiloy (Ussuriysk)
Tungliao
Hsinking (Changchun)
Kirin
K I R I N
Liaoyuan
Tunhua
Hunchun
Vladivostok
Laoha
Sungari Res.
J E H O L
Liao
Tumen
Chihfeng
Mukden (Fengtien)
Yalu
Jehol (Chengteh)
Liaoyang
FENGTIEN
Peking
KOREA (CHŌSEN)
Sea of Japan
Tientsin
Antung
SOUTH MANCHURIA
Port Arthur (Ryojun)
Dairen

Industrial Resources and Centres

● Coalfields
▲ Iron Ore
■ Aluminium shale
◆ Magnesite
○ Molybdenum
✕ Hydro-electricity

Tsitsihar
Hokang
Fuchin
Chiamussu
Sungari
Paichengtzu
Harbin
Mishan
Hsinking
Kirin
Ssupingkai
Tunhua
Tumen
Sungari Res.
Vladivostok
Fuhsin
Pepiao
Fushun
Erhtaochiang
Chihchou
Anshan
Niusintai
Yalu
Hulatao
Penhsihu
Chitaokou
Tapeiling
Antung
Yellow Sea
Port Arthur
Dairen

0 _____ 300 km
0 _____ 200 miles

Human Resources

◆ Main areas of Japanese Agrarian Colonies

Population density per square mile

280	75–150
225	50–75
	12–25
	<12

◯ Areas of Korean Agricultural Settlement

tinued and I, the Prime Minister, had various conferences with General Minami. I was shown maps daily on which Minami would show by a line a boundary which the Army in Manchuria would not go beyond, and almost daily this boundary was ignored and further expansion reported, but always with assurances that this was the final move.*

War Minister Minami strove to make excuses for the continuing disobedience of the Kwantung Army. He also strove, in vain, to reason with that Army's headquarters. The Army General Staff, meanwhile, may have had an underlying sympathy for the objectives of the Kwantung Army, but it issued a stream of orders intended to bring operations to a halt. There was some discussion as to the feasibility of cutting off military expenditure on the Kwantung Army, but this came to nothing when it was pointed out that such a course would produce an extremely dangerous situation for all concerned. The efforts of the authorities in Tokyo to stem the tide of the Japanese advance continued up to the end of 1931. The Kwantung Army was outraged, for instance, when the Army General Staff took exceptional steps to order the immediate evacuation of Tsitsihar, lynchpin for the control of the whole of North Manchuria, in mid-November 1931. Later still in November, after riots broke out in the northern Chinese city of Tientsin in the wake of political activities fomented by the Kwantung Army's ubiquitous secret service agents, the Army General Staff in Tokyo not only refused a request by the North China Garrison Army for reinforcements but also demanded that the Kwantung Army withdraw 150 miles back from the Chinchow area on the alluvial plains of south-eastern Jehol (where it had planned to advance on the pretext of seeking to relieve the garrison forces at Tientsin). That was about as much as any Japanese central authorities could have done towards reimposing control upon the troops in the field, for it was appreciated that all moves of this kind not only undermined military discipline in Manchuria but provoked extreme political unrest at home.

Caught in this cleft stick, the Wakatsuki Cabinet finally collapsed in mid-December 1931, at which time the moderate General Minami was put out to pasture and replaced as War Minister by the much more charismatic figure of Lieutenant-General Araki Sadao, who recognized together with Prime Minister Inukai Tsuyoshi and the Ministers of Finance and Foreign Affairs that in the absence of a 'fixed policy' by the new Government it would be powerless to prevent the further spread of hostilities in Manchuria. Araki convinced first his senior

---

* Pritchard and Zaide, op. cit., 1, pp. 1556–72, *passim*, and 1592.

ministerial colleagues and then the rest of the Cabinet that the only practical alternative to a drift into chaos was for the Government itself to resolve to occupy the whole of Manchuria together with Jehol, Chang Hsueh-liang's last foothold north of the Great Wall. As the Imperial Diet was not in session, the matter was submitted directly to the Privy Council which reluctantly consented to the plan and approved the necessary expenditure.

The first experience of Japan's adventure in the conquest of mainland China did not impress much of the outside world. What the Japanese would do in Manchuria had been awaited with some curiosity. Some countries had been ready to be tolerant. The development of Manchuria under Chang Hsueh-liang and his father before him had been arbitrary and exploitative. The Changs were reported to have kept a standing army of 300,000 men, greater than the regular forces of the Japanese Empire. They had created a huge munitions factory 1½ miles long by half a mile wide, said to be the largest arsenal in the world after the old Krupp complex in Germany. Some foreign experts estimated that more than 85 per cent of Manchuria's state revenue of 133 million Chinese dollars for the fiscal year 1930 was spent on Chang Hsueh-liang's brand of militarism. The exploitation of Manchuria's rich natural resources had been devoid of imagination or enterprise. It would not have needed any exceptional skill in administration for the Japanese to do better. What they achieved, however, was little short of miraculous.

Japan decided to govern indirectly through friendly Manchurians rather than to establish direct administration. Thus far the choice was wise. We must not underestimate the change of attitudes which the Japanese had to undergo as they moved from being a mainly introspective, homogeneous race and culture to become the guiding spirit of a polyglot empire, from thence establishing a wholly new regional system. There were several mechanisms which effected these changes. We have seen how Japan after the Meiji Revolution had adopted and adapted western ideas and technology with quite extraordinary vigour and discernment. This was but one mechanism. Another mechanism by which the transformation was accomplished has been seen by some oriental observers to be little more than an exaggeration and adaptation of traditional Buddhist religious precepts that were held in common in nearly every territory that came under Japanese sway until 1945.

The concept of 'racial harmony' (*minzoku kyōwa*) between the Japanese and other Asiatic peoples first attracted attention in the late 1920s, when it was nurtured in Japanese intellectual circles in Manchuria and Mongolia. It was soon a topic for animated discussion everywhere among the Japanese settlers, and it became especially fashionable among second-generation Japanese residents in Manchuria who had known no life outside that of their adopted country. It was rather a natural expression of the attempts of these Japanese pioneers to achieve some enduring balance and stability in their relationship with the Mongolian, Manchurian, Chinese, Korean and White Russian populations that were more firmly ensconced in the area. At the root of the doctrine was a notion that bears a passing resemblance to that of the brotherhood of man in that it was certainly predicated upon a thirst for peaceful co-existence and co-prosperity. It was not, however, a doctrine indistinguishable from that preached by the Author of the Sermon on the Mount. It was no programme for racial equality nor for racial integration. On the contrary, it soon developed into a self-conscious programme for a social and economic re-stratification of Asian society by race. From the beginning, the Japanese in Manchuria perceived that their own special rights and privileges could not be preserved, much less extended, if Manchuria and Mongolia were subducted into the turmoil of Chinese politics. Yet there was ample scope for enlarging upon Japan's share in the development and exploitation of Manchuria and Mongolia if the region could be made a 'floating world', regulated by its own autonomous government yet responsive to pressure waves generated by Tokyo and by local Japanese special interests as well as by legitimate Chinese interests. This was not only a political and cultural imperative for the many Japanese who embraced such ideas. It was above all a question of their economic survival.*

Even at the earliest stage in the evolution of the idea of *minzoku kyōwa*, Japanese residents in Manchuria and Mongolia were thinking in terms of severing the ties that bound *Manmō* (Manchuria and Mongolia) to China Proper. But at that stage a purely Sino-Japanese 'racial harmony', nothing that need embrace other races, too, was favoured as the proper means to attain that end without recourse to military force. That soon changed. By 1930, as the effects of the world depression were felt in the region, a new sense of urgency was imparted as acutely vulnerable Japanese enterprises found themselves subjected to especially severe attacks. The anti-Japanese movement as a whole (to which nearly all the indigenous peoples of China, Manchuria and Mongolia responded wholeheartedly) and the discriminatory economic policies of Chang Hsueh-liang's régime in particular, gravely prejudiced the Japanese communities notwithstanding

* Hirano Ken'ichirō, 'Racial Harmony: A "Cover-Up" Ideology for a Puppet State', in *Proceedings of the British Association for Japanese Studies*, VI:1, *History & International Relations*, Sheffield University Press, Sheffield, 1981, pp. 92–7.

70   *Top left*: The Shōwa
Emperor of Japan, Hirohito,
riding his favourite white
horse

71   *Top right*: The railway
carriage in which the 'Old
Marshal' of Manchuria,
Chang Tso-lin, was killed by a
bomb in 1928

72   *Bottom*: The assassination
of Prime Minister Hamaguchi
Osachi at Tokyo Central
Railway Station in 1930

73 Japanese terrorists in
court *Top*: Members of the
'Ketsumeidan' (Blood
Brotherhood)

74 *Bottom*: Army cadets
involved in the 15 May
Incident

75 The Manchurian Incident (1931–4) *Top left*: Site of the explosion outside Mukden that signalled the start of the Manchurian Incident in September 1931

76 *Top right*: Warlord Chang Hsueh-liang, the 'Young Marshal' of Manchuria

77 *Bottom*: A star witness for the prosecution: 'Mr Henry Pu-Yi', last Emperor of China and ex-'Emperor of Manchukuo', stands with the Chief Prosecutor of the IMTFE, Joseph Keenan

78   The 26 February Incident,
1936 *Top*: Japanese Army
rebel troops occupy the
grounds of Tokyo's
Metropolitan Police
Headquarters

79   *Bottom*: Rebel troops
cover the approach to the
Hibiya Crossing, near the
Imperial Palace, Tokyo

80 *Top*: Japanese marines,
landed from the fleet to quell
the Army rebels, advance
through a waterside district of
Tokyo, 27 February 1936

81 *Bottom*: Lukouchiao, the
'Marco Polo Bridge'

82 The China Incident,
1937–45 *Top*: Horse-drawn
artillery

83 *Bottom*: Japanese artillery
in the battle for possession of
the Chinese quarter of Tientsin
in August 1937

84 *Top*: The great North Gate of Taiyuan, capital of Shansi Province in North China

85 *Bottom*: Japanese forces enter Nanking, led by their triumphant Commander-in-Chief, General Matsui Iwane

86 *Top left*: A not
uncommon scene from China's
'Middle Kingdom' in those
days

87 *Top right*: Japanese
soldiers are photographed
using bound Chinese prisoners
of war for bayonet practice

88 *Bottom*: A column of
Japanese troops belonging to
the Kwantung Army

the latent strength of the South Manchurian Railway and of the Japanese military forces garrisoned in the vicinity.

Many of those who could afford to do so left the Asiatic mainland and returned home to Japan. Others less fortunate found the attitude of the Japanese Government singularly unhelpful. As one spokesman for the Manchurian Youth League poignantly observed, 'With the basis of our life destroyed by lawless Chinese officials and with no place to return to, we are treated like enemies by the so-called sovereign of Manchuria and like stepchildren by Japanese statesmen.'* Some form of self-reliance and unity obviously was required, and Japanese residents in Manchuria and Mongolia began to contemplate the creation of a Manchurian state genuinely independent of Japan, if that should be the only way to protect their persons and livelihoods. 'In this way,' as Hirano Ken'ichirō has pointed out, 'the Japanese residents in Manchuria separated themselves from Japanese imperialism, the main target of Chinese nationalism, and at the same time identified themselves with the other racial groups living in Manchuria.'†

By the following year, 1931, the sense of abandonment which Japanese residents in Manchuria felt towards their motherland had become more acute. When the South Manchurian Railway announced plans to close its central teachers' training college, the plight of the Japanese expatriate community became desperate. In short, the idea of racial harmony had gained a widespread popularity among Japanese residents in Manchuria over the course of several years before the outbreak of the Manchurian Incident. Thus came to hand, ready-made, a fit instrument for the purposes of the Kwantung Army. It gave the militarists within that Army a blueprint for the political mastery of an entire country. It was a concept within the capabilities of the comparatively small military force under their command. And it was familiar to the tens of thousands of Japanese civilians who regarded that country as their own. Manchurian politicians and generals could be bought and sold by the sackful. By accumulating such sackfuls, Manchurian political institutions, internal allegiances and external relations could be transformed, and when they were transformed, the Japanese would emerge as a race of managers.

The structural side of the concept of 'racial harmony', indeed, was no less important. From the early years of the century, successive Japanese governments and private venture capitalists had promoted the commercial and industrial development of Manchuria and had used the influence

* ibid., p. 93.
† ibid., p. 95.

which their economic success brought them in seeking a special, and
rather corrupt, relationship with the Manchurian civil bureaucracy. It
was a relationship neither so very different from that which had existed in
Korea prior to its incorporation into the Japanese Empire, nor in any way
superior to the practices of the European merchant adventurers who had
sapped the native energies of half a dozen continents during the previous
half-millennium. Now the Japanese came to believe that it was imperative
that the lingering apathy of the rural masses in Manchuria should be
preserved. It was noted that the Manchurian peasantry traditionally were
unmoved by affairs of state and by international relations. What mattered
to them more were family, clan and local interests, which in turn were
bound up in autonomous feudal relationships between landlords and
tenants which had survived for centuries. So long as these traditional
cultural values and constraints could be preserved intact, the indigenous
population would pose no threat to Japanese economic or political
enterprise.

Accordingly, it seemed to be in Japan's interests to cultivate relations
with the Manchurian landlord class and for this purpose to stress their
common interest in Manchurian autonomy. It must be remarked upon
that though thinly populated overall, the country did include nearly $34\frac{1}{2}$
million inhabitants. Fewer than 3 per cent of the population consisted of
Manchus by race. Fully 90 per cent were Chinese. That formed a not
inconsiderable number of potential antagonists to pacify and police.
Fortunately for the Japanese, the bulk of the Chinese were recent immigrants from North China with little love for the southern-dominated
Kuomintang, so the Japanese cultivated local and particularist sentiment
on fallow ground. Since direct imperialism had acquired a bad name even
in these remote regions by 1931, even the most ardently imperialistic
Japanese could not hope to overcome this unless they succeeded in
wrapping up reality in some more acceptable political form. Aside from
the influential Japanese circles in Manchuria to whom the authorities
looked for guidance, there were many in Japan who strongly believed in
Pan-Asian ideals. For these and other reasons which we shall probe
shortly, the thrust of Japanese policies towards Manchuria in the period
following the military conquest of the country made a direct appeal to the
sentiment of 'Manchurians' in general and especially of those conservative
or reactionary elements within the country who inevitably possessed great
power and influence in such a society.

Thus, in 1932, the Kwantung Army unwrapped its own plan for the
creation of a radical state which was designed to secure the political
autonomy of the Kwantung Army within all of the domains it now

controlled and also to give comfort to the Chinese of the old days of the Empire. It was called 'Manchukuo', the state of the Manchus. To administer it, there were invited a number of families of the old régime, especially those who had been identified by the Kwantung Army's secret service as friendly to Japan. The Kwantung Army's 'Lawrence of Manchuria', Colonel Doihara Kenji, went south to discuss the situation with Aisin-Gioro Pu-Yi, known universally by his nickname of 'Henry', conferred upon him by his English tutor. Pu-Yi, who in infancy had been deposed by the Chinese Revolution of 1911 as the last Manchu Emperor of China, was persuaded to become the titular head of this new state as a willing tool of the Japanese. No doubt the two sides had differing expectations regarding the true meaning of 'cooperation'.

'Henry' Pu-Yi was an extraordinary creature, undeflected by thought but not by ambition, whose admirable personal traits are difficult to discover. When he was brought before the International Military Tribunal for the Far East by hulking Soviet guards to stand as a star witness for the Prosecution in the early weeks of the Tokyo Trial, Pu-Yi wildly accused the Japanese of attempting 'to enslave the people of the whole world, and they started it with their experience in Manchuria'.* He seemed notably short of gratitude for the favours that the Japanese had bestowed upon him. From the witness-box he recalled his visit to meet Emperor Hirohito in Tokyo during 1940, long after Japanese military, political and economic authority had been established in Manchuria, and however much the seriously discombobulated Pu-Yi sought afterwards to distort the facts, what he conveyed to listeners spoke volumes about the harmony which the Japanese had hoped to establish with Manchukuo. Accompanied by his Japanese military aide-de-camp, the Manchu Emperor had been received by Emperor Hirohito with every sign of goodwill. As a token of his esteem, Hirohito gave him two of the three treasures vouchsafed as sacred to the Japanese throne (a sword, a piece of jade and a mirror). Young Pu-Yi received the sword and the mirror. According to ancient Japanese legends, the magical sword had been discovered by the brother of the Sun Goddess, Amaterasu Omikami, who had descended to earth to hack to death an eight-tailed serpent. The sword, found inside the monster's eighth tail, was thereafter renowned as the Excalibur of Japan. According to Pu-Yi, Hirohito also related how Amaterasu Omikami had given the sacred mirror to her grandson, the first Emperor of Japan, and his heirs, 'and told them that when you see this mirror, it is the same as when you see me'.† Pu-Yi took the two symbolic treasures back to

* Pritchard and Zaide, op. cit., 2, pp. 4005–7, 4011.
† ibid., p. 4010.

Manchuria. He told the post-war Allied court, 'That was the worst humiliation that I have ever faced.' * The Prosecution, although it never disputed the authenticity of the divine talismans, chose to regard this episode as evidence of a plot by Japanese war leaders to impose Japanese state shintoism upon Manchuria, and from thence throughout China and beyond, 'to control the minds, the souls, the wishes, the movements of the people'.† In fact there was no such grand design, no such uniformity of ambition, and years after the trial Pu-Yi confessed that he had lied during his testimony to save his own skin. Nevertheless, the anecdotal story just described does betoken the Japanese Empire's conception of the seriousness of its commitment to the struggle in which it was engaged on the continent. The sacred insignia offered to him by Hirohito effectively elevated Pu-Yi to a transcendental brotherhood between the two rulers and their realms, and it is therefore quite wrong to suppose that the Japanese conceived that Pu-Yi regarded the episode as symbolic of Japan's subjugation of Manchukuo into slavery.

Meanwhile the Chinese Government, from its capital in distant Nanking, had reacted to the Mukden Incident and its aftermath by playing the card which it hoped would relieve it of danger without its being driven to resolute action. It appealed to the League of Nations. The League's prestige as a peacekeeping machine had been growing in Europe. During minor European disputes in the previous dozen years, the Council of the League had at times intervened when peace was threatened. China was led to think that it might do so over Manchuria, too. The League had never yet been engaged in restraining a Great Power, and this was the task it was now set. Undoubtedly the Kuomintang leaders, though realist enough in home affairs, showed themselves surprisingly ingenuous in supposing that textbook methods of collective security could be followed, with effective results, in checking Japan.

Possibly the Kuomintang politicians were misled by a number of western enthusiasts who abounded in Nanking and Shanghai, and who were later to be joined by refugees from the rising storm in Europe. It had become a matter of prestige among the Chinese to become the patrons of expatriate dilettantes. A great (and venal) banker like T. V. Soong derived face from their permanent employment on his staff. This was reminiscent of a classical period in Chinese history; in the days before the establishment of the stable military empire, when China consisted of a group of

* ibid., pp. 4010, 4174.
† ibid., pp. 4006–7. The words are those of the Chief Prosecutor, Joseph Keenan.

warring feudal kingdoms, roving scholars offered themselves to the Chinese kings, who gladly employed them. Now, as then, the scholars, though cosmopolitan, had more influence on policy-making than most of the regular politicians. They were often dangerous or erratic advisers. Disillusioned by the western record, many of them made a cult of the Kuomintang because it was an apparently revolutionary power which was willing to experiment with new methods. They urged China to attach its fortunes to League procedures.

The League was embarrassed by the confidence shown in it. The skies were darkening over the world: the economic crisis had set in, and the Great Powers looked with alarm at being called to do anything which could further unsettle the world's economy and might even lead to military conflict between themselves and the Japanese. Faced with awkward problems from the rise of Germany, and yielding to the advice tendered by their general staffs, Intelligence experts and economists, the Governments of the leading Powers were more concerned with what they could do to take the danger out of these problems by diplomatic fiddles than they were ready to risk ships, troops and treasure on some quixotic and hazardous experiment in a course so doubtful (and possibly misbegotten) as that of protecting China. The Foreign Ministers who composed the League Council therefore agreed that the situation was far too dangerous for them to gamble by a concerted resort to armed intervention against one of the Great Powers. They used the customary expedient. They appointed that international Commission of Enquiry to which reference has already been made. It was presided over by an Englishman, Lord Lytton, who had been Governor of Bengal and was the grandson of the Victorian historical novelist, Bulwer Lytton.

The Japanese military and the Japanese civil service, although often at cross-purposes and mutually antagonistic, worked uneasily with the tentacles of the South Manchurian Railway which were everywhere. Together they were supreme in Manchukuo. The Japanese, though they had little racial feeling compared to Europeans, were very arrogant: peoples who were subject to them saw their follies, feared their excesses, but secretly tended to despise them. Many Japanese showed their worst qualities in the lands they ruled. In Japan itself there were people of intellectual and moral distinction: but the Empire had proved a catalyst, sifting out men of coarser fibre from the finer sorts.

There was so much to be done. Since its inception the South Manchurian Railway had constructed no fewer than twenty-five company towns, complete with district steam-heating schemes, together with scores of schools, colleges, technical institutes, a university, hospitals and a public health system second to none. By 1931, largely due to the enterprise of the SMR, there were 240,000 Japanese residents in Manchuria. Now ambitious efforts were rekindled in Japan to attract Japanese settlers from farming districts on the Japanese mainland. The cost of this programme was shared between the SMR and the Japanese and Manchukuoan Governments. The scheme was administered initially by the East Asian Industrial Development Company and then successively by the Manchurian Colonization Company and the Manchurian Colonial Development Company established specially for this grand purpose. The Kwantung Army drew up plans for settling five million colonists within twenty years, but between 1932, when the programme began, and 1937 fewer than 5,000 braved the hardships in the five isolated settlements chosen for the first experiment: fewer than 70 per cent of them overcame homesickness, endured the harsh climate and survived the fearful toll taken by infectious diseases and Manchurian bandits. It was a complicated scheme, however, and much progress was made. The infrastructure of training centres, land development, road construction, sanitation and hydro-electric power was ambitious in the extreme. By the outbreak of the Pacific War in December 1941, more than 100,000 new Japanese settlers, including women and children, lived in some 200 agricultural communities scattered over the Manchurian hinterland. One unforeseen consequence of this rapid development was that a marked labour shortage resulted in the rural communities of Japan Proper. Had the twenty-year programme developed as originally planned, it has been estimated that it would have cost Japan and Manchukuo ¥10 billion in treasure to complete. Small wonder that the Japanese Ministry of Finance and the Manchurian authorities were reluctant to proceed.

Meanwhile, other Japanese came out to Manchukuo as managers or trained technologists. Many of them were prepared to spend the balance of their careers in the service of the new state. Less admirable were many of the floating population of leech-like personalities who came to get rich quick. These camp-followers were the worst exploiters. One way or another, by 1939, the total Japanese population of Manchukuo had climbed to 837,000.

The dross found its way into many of the agencies of Japan's foreign ventures. Soon they began to make a reputation which was to be a lasting impediment to the further spread of their rule. There were complaints of arbitrary actions, arrests, executions. Notwithstanding pledges in 1932 by the Manchurian puppet régime and by the Japanese authorities in Tokyo promising to respect the Open Door principle, occidental investors and trading concerns found themselves tied down under masses of Japanese red tape and pettifoggery or were squeezed out altogether.

One Japanese publicist for the new régime wrote with greater candour than one might suppose he intended: 'The Open Door, as a practical matter, can be enforced only where law and order are maintained by stable and honest government.'* Western diplomatic protests met with indifference and inactivity. Manchukuo became a closed market for Japanese manufactures. And so whereas at one time all of the SMR's rolling stock had been American made, now the SMR relied upon its own workshops at Dairen, Mukden, Hsinking, Harbin and Tsitsihar to manufacture and repair the equipment it required. Meanwhile other branches of the SMR concentrated upon the creation of integrated traffic systems involving port development, inland waterways, road networks, even shipbuilding. The machinery of government was used to promote the interests of the SMR and fostered a multitude of subordinate economic enterprises. Working together, the Japanese and Manchurian authorities built up an impressive road system in a country that in 1932 was conspicuously lacking in motor transport. In the nine years between 1932 and the Pacific War, Manchukuo doubled its road mileage to 70,000 km. At the same time military and civil airfields were constructed throughout the country and regular airline services developed between all of its principal cities. Telecommunications developed with similar speed: the size of the telegraph network trebled in the six years between 1933 and 1939. All of this was achieved while other experts unified the currency, reorganized customs collection, reformed and centralized the internal revenue services, and modernized the banking system. Conservative monetary policies were instituted by the Government of Manchukuo acting in concert with gifted Japanese economists. It was an intrinsically competent and efficient system which they devised, far more equitable than that which it replaced, but it fell hard upon the entire population.

Above all, it depended upon continuing Japanese capital investment and purchasing power. Japan became increasingly dependent upon Manchuria for basic raw materials. Gold mines opened up. Forests covered 36 per cent of the country and the timber industry thrived as never before. New coal and iron ore finds all helped to buoy up Japan during a period of increasing adversity. Japanese investment mounted. It came to more than ¥4 billion between 1931 and 1940. After a time, surplus Japanese capital began to dry up as Japan became enmeshed in the China Incident and slowly drifted towards the Pacific War from which there

* Kawakami Kiyoshi, quoted in James A. B. Scherer, *Manchukuo: A Bird's-Eye View*, Hokuseidō Press, Tokyo, 1933, p. 117.

would be no turning back. Inflation began to bite as the Government of Manchukuo became obliged to borrow in order to meet current expenditure. Nevertheless, inflation never approached the levels that it did in unoccupied China. Japanese investment in Manchukuo during the whole period between 1931 and 1945 has been estimated at no less than ¥9 billion – an astonishing figure. That quite transformed a country of which it truthfully had been said for centuries: 'Manchuria produces two crops, soybeans and bandits.' *

Japan created in Manchukuo a state welfare system of a type never before seen in East Asia. Nevertheless, there were huge social costs in producing the economic miracle of Manchukuo, costs which beggar any attempt to describe the depravity underlying official policy.

Throughout Manchuria, Inner Mongolia and North China, Japan used its political influence and financial muscle to further all kinds of economic activity, some very detrimental to the indigenous populations. In particular it fostered the opium trade.

Opium had first become an issue in East Asia at the beginning of the previous century. The British, in forcing the trade upon China, had sought to counter the fact that China bought too little from the West, and thereby caused an adverse balance of trade, by creating a new Chinese want, opium. It was grown in great quantities in India, and could easily be shipped to Canton. The Chinese Government protested, and pointed to its duty to protect the Chinese people from the effects of the drug. Two wars had to be fought to overcome its moral objections.

The subsequent history of opium contains a number of unexplained matters. Why did the country as a whole take to opium smoking? What were the effects of the drug upon people's efficiency? Why was the habit, which had been so widespread a few years earlier, checked so completely and with such ease when China eventually had its communist revolution? In the 1930s this ultimate solution of the problem was still far off. Opium had long ceased to be an article of western import: it had become instead a major Chinese product, and though it was not legalized, it was consumed everywhere throughout East Asia. The Kuomintang régime in China and the Manchurian warlords in their domains to the north drew from its trade a revenue which was outside the ordinary state budget, which was unpublished, but which was the most important item in the financing of their respective armies. The Japanese systematically set about cornering this market.

The evidence must speak for itself. According to reports by United

* ibid., p. 93. Manchukuo produced 60 per cent of the world's soybean supplies.

States customs officers, amply confirmed by Japanese and Chinese witnesses at the Tokyo Trial, narcotics abuse in Manchukuo was used to stabilize the national budget, support the Kwantung Army's swollen establishment and maintain 'law and order'. It was an extraordinarily cynical process. The practice of opium smoking, previously encountered mainly among the business and professional classes, saw a meteoric rise. Whereas less than twenty opium dens operated in the Chinese quarter of Antung, for example, prior to the Mukden Incident no less than five hundred were in business within the Japanese Concession there. By July 1932 the number of these establishments in the Chinese city had increased to more than eighty while 684 were licensed in the Japanese Concession. Out of a population of 130,000, over 20,000 had become addicts, and with profits at more than 600 per cent, it was estimated that the revenue derived from this traffic was worth $6.48 million* that year for this one city alone. Even in the surrounding rural areas, the number of addicts rose to approximately 15 per cent of the population. Networks of Japanese and Korean houses of prostitution and bars of every description were augmented by retail opium shops, smoking dens, heroin dens, even pawn shops which exchanged opium for clothing and other personal property.

Opium, as it was usually taken in China and Manchuria, is a comparatively mild drug, and the Chinese addiction to it probably did them no great harm. A quite different effect, however, is produced by the derivatives of opium: heroin and morphine.

The Japanese set themselves to flood the provinces of North China and the lands beyond the Great Wall with heroin and morphine. Partly they did so because of the very high profits obtainable, partly they had in mind the destructive effects of these two drugs. Their use would corrupt the population, cause them to become apathetic, and weaken their will to resist.

One Japanese agency alone was discovered to be dealing with 200 lb of morphine a day in the early part of 1932. This explosive growth continued. The number of opium addicts in Antung and its environs doubled to 40,000, 25 per cent of the population, in the single year of 1933. Unofficial estimates suggested that $19 million was wasted on drugs in that one small locality in that year. Much of that was 'illegal' rather than licensed, yet the total sold by the state Opium Monopoly Bureau in its first year of operation amounted to $33 million, a mighty surplus over the $5 million in receipts estimated in the Manchukuo national budget for the fiscal year

---

* For all practical purposes, the Manchukuoan yuan or dollar was at parity with the Japanese yen, worth more or less 28.6 US cents apiece.

1932–3. The scourge continued to grow. So did the population of Antung and similar areas. The number of addicts there increased to 340,000, a third of the total population, by December 1934.

Farmers were encouraged to grow opium as part of the Kwantung Army's pacification programme in the countryside. While farmers who grew food crops were eligible for state loans of 5 cents an acre at 7 per cent interest per annum, those who grew poppies could borrow up to 33 cents an acre at 2.3 per cent interest. The poppy tax set at $1.66 to $2.32 in Chang Tso-lin's day was reduced to 83 cents an acre in 1934. But even as the farmers stampeded to produce poppies, the state monopoly purchasing officials cut the producers' profits so savagely each year that many of the farmers found themselves unable to repay their loans and so had their lands confiscated by the Japanese. Still, legal and illegal cultivation of poppies continued to spread as the years passed. Legal cultivation increased by 17 per cent from 133,333 acres in 1936 to 156,061 acres in the following year as demand continued to outstrip supply despite an officially admitted importation of a further 41,335 lb of opium into Manchukuo from the Korean Monopoly Bureau in 1936. Annual opium production in Korea was stepped up to meet that demand: in February 1937, the Director of the Korean Monopoly Bureau declared that it would increase from 57,870 lb to 82,670 lb per annum: 70 per cent of that would go to Manchukuo. Other imports came in from Turkey, Persia and elsewhere.

In mid-1937 the League of Nations Advisory Committee on Traffic in Opium and Other Dangerous Drugs focused the world's attention upon what was happening. As one speaker declared:

We should not be far short of the mark if we said that 90 per cent of all the illicit white drugs of the world are of Japanese origin, manufactured in the Japanese Concession of Tientsin, around Tientsin, in or around Dairen or in other cities of Manchuria, Jehol and China, and this always by Japanese or under Japanese supervision.*

For a time the press was full of stories of the trade, of the protection illegally given the traders by the Japanese Army and Navy, and of the unfortunate inhabitants reduced to fawning submission to morphine and its paraphernalia. The world, startled by Japanese cynicism, reacted more deeply against it than Japan perhaps foresaw. The West, which had the opium wars on its conscience, was more scandalized by the Japanese re-enacting the events of the buried past than prepared to hail them as brothers in crime.

By the end of the 1937 season the Japanese were driven to promise

* Pritchard and Zaide, op. cit., 3, pp. 4697–8.

reforms. They were heartless, empty promises. The harvest in Manchukuo alone that year amounted to a staggering 2,800,000 lb of raw opium. In 1937 the state monopoly budgeted $29,025,000 for the purchase of raw opium and recorded sales of $47,850,000. In 1938 it authorized an expenditure of $32,653,000 on raw opium and received $71,045,200 in revenue. By 1939 the cost rose to $43,470,000 and sales reached $90,908,400. The scope for racketeering in such a climate was virtually unlimited. This was an entirely new instrument of Total War, and it set the pattern for Japanese occupation forces elsewhere. Most disturbing of all, however, is the well-documented fact that this policy was approved and promoted not only by the Kwantung Army, by the Japanese Army General Staff and by the Japanese War Ministry but by the Japanese Cabinet as well.

Meanwhile, a handful of rogue Japanese industrialists began to pour capital into the exploitation of huge, newly discovered coal and iron ore reserves and then into prodigiously profitable investment in virtually monopolistic enterprises, keenly monitored and sheltered by the Kwantung Army, such as Ayukawa Gisuke's *Nihon Sangyō* Company (better known as Nissan) and the great Manchurian Heavy Industries Company which he founded in 1937. The latter became all-powerful within its sphere of activities, hiving off interests which had formerly been the exclusive preserve of the far more paternalistic SMR. All of this greatly worried many of the giant financial and industrial combines on the Japanese mainland, such as the colossal family firms of Mitsui, Mitsubishi and Sumitomo, who not only showed a marked reluctance to invest in Manchuria but feared the emergence of potential competitors and tried in vain to persuade successive Japanese Governments to seek the orderly development of a purely complementary Manchurian economy under totally civilian direction.

The close collaboration between Japan and Manchuria, without doubt oppressive to its opponents, was welcomed in many quarters as an alternative to political disorder and economic instability. There had been an amazing drive towards modernization affecting one of the most backward frontiers on earth. The huge importation of Japanese capital and entrepreneurs had made it possible. The thousands of Japanese 'advisers' who forced themselves into every nook and cranny of the land guaranteed that there could be no resistance. These developments and the cost of the expanded military appropriations necessary to underwrite the whole endeavour increased the burden of defence expenditure to which the Japanese nation was already committed in the naval rearmament programme which successive Japanese Governments all regarded as an

essential defence requirement in an uncertain world. The inevitable result
of all of these commitments was to force the Japanese Government and
taxpayer into an economy geared for war production. This in turn led
Japan to reconsider its trading relationship with the rest of the world.
Non-essential trade was sharply curtailed and strong preference for home-
produced goods instead of the allure of foreign manufactures took root in
the hearts of Japanese consumers and traders: it has remained a marked
characteristic of Japanese society to the present day.

These new economic practices rapidly improved Japan's balance of
payments notwithstanding the depths of the great depression in the world
at large. By as early as 1933 Japanese expenditure on armaments produced
a boom economy in which most Japanese rejoiced. Japanese exports cut
through the international economic doldrums and by 1936 had surpassed
the record levels of 1929 by 60 per cent. Japan soon dominated the world
market in cheap textiles of good quality, undercutting not only the recovery and historical ascendency of Britain's Lancashire cotton mills but
also the emergent textile industrial exports of India which on the eve of
the depression had risen to prominence in the market stalls of Africa,
Asia and South America.

The true cost of Japan's military adventures on the Asiatic mainland,
however, worried Japanese economists from the beginning. As a number
of them foresaw, Japan found itself unable to escape a progressive dependence not merely upon the territories which it had conquered but also
upon war materials imported from the United States. As imports of non-
essential goods declined, strategically important commodities became an
increasingly high percentage of Japanese imports. They were also politically sensitive. For the time being, this proved to be little problem.
Isolationist sentiment in the United States counteracted the influence of
those Americans who sought to intervene in the relations between Japan
and her continental neighbours. The United States Secretary of State's
proclamation of the 'Stimson Doctrine' of 'non-recognition' of territorial
changes achieved by the use of force failed to move that pragmatic economist President Herbert Hoover during the nightmare of the great depression, and after 1932, when Franklin D. Roosevelt occupied the White
House, the attention of the United States administration was at the very
least distracted by events in Europe, by his grand strategy aimed at improving relations with Latin America, and by efforts to effect an economic
and political transformation within the United States itself. The United
States had its finger on the jugular vein of Japanese military expansion so
long as Japan had no other source for vital strategical commodities.
Given the disparity in economic and material resources of the Japanese

Empire compared with those of the United States, the Japanese Army appreciated that means should be sought to neutralize or to woo the United States away from its moral support for the Kuomintang. Since it appeared highly improbable that Japanese reassurances or efforts to appease the Americans would suffice so long as Japanese ambitions on the continent were unfulfilled, diplomatic and even military links with Nazi Germany and fascist Italy became increasingly attractive means of holding off the threat of intervention by the Anglo-Saxon Powers.

A particularly nauseating sanctimoniousness did arise in certain American and European political circles. Stripped to essentials, the cry was in support of 'Collective Security and the League'. It depended upon a willingness by powerful states to hazard their own forces in support of economic and diplomatic pressure upon aggressor states. However, the human, material and financial costs of any such actions inherently bite back hardest at those Powers whose unswerving devotion to the cause is essential if success is to be achieved. Selflessness of that kind, always a rare commodity, generally disappears from the scene when the aggressor is a first-class Power and the issues are 'exceedingly complicated' – as they plainly were in this case.

A policy of forceful intervention commanded too little support to become a realizable possibility. The United Kingdom alone among members of the League of Nations possessed in the Royal Navy the means to enforce whatever sanctions might have been instituted, and there were good reasons to doubt suggestions by the American Secretary of State, Henry L. Stimson, that the United States stood ready to share the burden of any concerted sanctions to force Japan out of Manchuria. How would such sanctions be enforced? In this instance they could be made effective only by interposing naval forces between Japan and the Asian mainland or between Japan and her outside sources of supplies. What would any self-respecting nation do to defend itself against the first (or only) ships that might be mustered against it? The choice for such a nation was stark. It could lie low and wait for the tempest to subside, leaving the supporters of 'Collective Security' with egg on their faces and with no stomach for another such venture if further steps should be taken by the aggressor following the inevitable disbanding of such an expensive naval operation. Alternatively, it could sink or damage the interfering vessels, at the besieged nation's selected moment, close to that nation's own repair and supply depots, and far – very far – from the white knights' bases.

Thus it was that British public and official opinion about the Manchurian Incident mattered more than the views of any other Third Power including the United States. The *Manchester Guardian* alone among prominent British newspapers argued that Japanese complaints in Manchuria were entirely unjustified. Most of the press held the contrary view, believing that the Japanese had a strong case against the Chinese. Wags among old China hands declared that the only thing worse than a Japanese victory would be a Chinese victory. Such attitudes remained prevalent throughout the crisis and were not confined to conservative press and political circles. The former Liberal Foreign Secretary Lord Grey, for instance, told an audience at the Central Hall, Westminster, on 11 December 1931, 'Japan had a strong case in Manchuria, where her interests were being threatened by lawlessness, and if Japan had submitted her case to the signatories of the Covenant and the Pact [of Paris], it would have been the business of those signatories to see how the remedy could be applied.'* Even Lord Lytton long shared the same view, at least until February 1933. He then told an audience in Manchester, 'Let me say to the partisans of China that the case of Japan *vis-à-vis* the League may be a weak one, but the case of Japan *vis-à-vis* China is a strong one.' He developed this theme in an interview with the *Daily Herald* a few days later: 'Japan has a case. She has a very strong case on merits. But she has no case at all for the action she has taken.' While the Pact of Paris may have been violated, as all conceded, that was not yet regarded as tantamount to law-breaking. More importantly, it was far from clear that Japanese actions were in breach of the Covenant of the League of Nations. The Japanese Government had been trying for months to gain redress for its grievances from the Chinese central Government at Nanking and had shown great patience in the face of long-continued provocation. The *Daily Telegraph* in London, for one, suggested in October 1931 that 'The right of a government to protect its interests against barbarism and anarchy is a well-recognized one, and if Japan is studious to keep within it, her position is a strong one.'

Thus when the League of Nations Council demanded the total withdrawal of all Japanese troops as a precondition to negotiations for the settlement of the dispute, many people in Britain – and virtually everyone in Japan – felt that this was to ignore reality and to prejudge the Japanese case. Moreover, when the League Council decided to affix a deadline for that withdrawal, that was seen – quite rightly – as a new obstacle to the resolution of the dispute, and as an insufferable slap in the face for the Japanese, who were already exceedingly resentful and irritated by the

---

* R. Bassett, *Democracy and Foreign Policy: A Case History, The Sino-Japanese Dispute, 1931–33*, Frank Cass & Co., London, 1968, p. 32.

double standards of certain Western Powers. Mindful of the history of the area, this reaction by the Japanese was entirely appropriate. In a sense, therefore, League interference actually helped deliver the Japanese nation into the hands of hotheads who had no time or thoughts save for action.

The Army's Manchurian adventure proved far from disappointing. The Japanese, despite their excesses, were slow to abandon the hope of sincere or large-scale cooperation with the Chinese. The Japanese embraced the idea of Sino-Japanese cooperation with such fervour that it seemed only logical to crush the influence of those that opposed it. The driving spirits of the Kwantung Army and kindred forces within the Army General Staff and War Ministry, far from meditating upon means of ending Japanese control over Manchuria, became increasingly interested in the provinces of China itself south of the Wall, at least in the provinces of the northern half of the country. The grass may not have seemed greener in that valley than it had turned out to be north of the Wall, but it was nevertheless green. It became fashionable in Japan for ambitious young officers to seek service in the Kwantung Army. Others of the same stamp chose to seek their future in the much smaller China Garrison Army and to build up their military experience while acquiring detailed local knowledge from the vantage points of places such as Peking, Tientsin and Shanghai, which were certain to acquire a critical importance if relations between the Japanese Empire and China were to degenerate into Total War. The hopes of these military adventurers grew, and it was in the nature of things that they were not deterred by the unfortunate end to which some of their colleagues came simply because the Chinese had grown anxious about the Japanese Army's secret service.

While the Lytton Commission was preparing its report, the crisis took a new turn. The shock to China had been deeper, spread quicker and produced more results than many in Japan had expected. Events passed out of control. A commotion among the Chinese people, not any specific action by the Chinese Government, was the unexpected factor. A boycott of Japanese goods took place, which was partly spontaneous, partly organized by Chinese secret societies, and fully exploited by the competing political activists of rival Kuomintang and communist factions. Violence broke out in Shanghai as a result of the boycott and in consequence of street demonstrations that grew out of a curious mésalliance between religious extremists belonging to the Japanese *Nichi-ren* Buddhist sect and a few Kwantung Army *agents provocateurs* sent there to distract attention from events in Manchuria. Large-scale riots soon developed. Terror was met by counter-terror.

All of this provoked Japan to land a token force of about 700 marines on 28 January 1932 with the task of doing no more than protect the city's 30,000 Japanese residents and the large commercial stake which they had built there over the decades. They met with something like the resistance of a Popular Front. Panic spread through the Japanese community. The Japanese Minister in China was Shigemitsu Mamoru. In all but name he was Ambassador: as befitted China's third-rate status in the international world, few countries dignified their chief representatives in China with the rank of Ambassador, and Japan was no exception to this practice. Shigemitsu came to the conclusion that the only way to save Japanese residents and the beleaguered marines from annihilation from the now frenzied mobs was to request his Government to call up large-scale re-inforcements. Even the post-war Tokyo War Crimes Tribunal absolved him of any guilt for his part in the affair. The Japanese Cabinet agreed with Shigemitsu's assessment, and a marine brigade of 10,000 men hur-riedly embarked the next day on a squadron of fast destroyers which set sail from Japan under the command of Vice-Admiral Nomura Kichisa-burō, a man later fated to serve briefly as Foreign Minister of Japan in the critical months following the outbreak of the European War in 1939, later still as Japan's forlorn Ambassador to the United States between November 1940 and the Japanese attack on Pearl Harbor. The marine reinforcements rapidly found themselves unable to cope with the situation despite gunnery support at point-blank range from Japanese warships which had steamed up the Wangpoo from the Yangtze fifteen miles downstream. Lieutenant-General Ueda Kenkichi, until recently Com-mander of the China Garrison Army maintained by Japan in North China in conformity with the old 'Unequal Treaties', was ordered by the Army to proceed from Japan with the Ninth Infantry Division to rescue the marines. Unexpectedly, even Ueda's division proved unable to tip the balance. Two more divisions had to be sent from Japan, this time under the overall military command of ex-War Minister General Shirakawa Yoshinori.

The Chinese 'defence' of Shanghai, improvised on the spur of the moment, was impressive. This was one of the first demonstrations in modern times of which the world took effective notice, that the Chinese, or some of them, were a martial people. Hitherto the Chinese had fought their wars by often incompetent professional armies or under bandit chieftains, operating from books of rules which, though they might give occasional apt counsel as they had done on the Nonni River, were hope-lessly out-of-date. The people, who were sceptics by tradition, expressed their contempt for all things military. But in this, as in so much else,

China was changing, and the Powers in contact with it grudgingly took notice of the fact.

The resistance was at first hampered by the ambivalent, cautious, luke-warm attitude of the Chinese Government. Perhaps by accident, there happened to be garrisoned, on the outskirts of Shanghai, a rather wayward left-wing unit of the Chinese Army known as the Nineteenth Route Army. This force was commanded by Tsai Ting-kan, an ingenuous, simple-minded man who had breathed in the simple slogans of the nationalists (and also, it appeared, of the communists). This officer, whose military training had been elementary, and who had received no indoctrination politically, and his troops, simple peasants with the most ordinary equipment, stiffened the resistance of the rest of the Chinese. As two more Chinese divisions, the 'China Bodyguard Army', joined the struggle for control of Shanghai, the significance of the fighting increased. Large parts of the International Settlement were destroyed and the Chinese suburbs beyond were ravaged.

It must be stressed that the initial Japanese military aims were modest, and operations in Shanghai were conducted in the early stages with relative self-restraint. Japan was doing no more than acting fully in conformity with the old extra-territorial rights which Japan as well as the British Empire, France, Italy and the United States possessed in the International Settlement. In the beginning, Admiral Nomura even anticipated that a restoration of orderly conditions in Shanghai by his marines would be welcomed by the other international contingents in the city: the British had sent in their own troops to quell similar disturbances as recently as 1926. Whatever the moral issues underlying the whole affair, and not-withstanding the activities of provocateurs on both sides, there was certainly no intention on the part either of the Japanese Government or of the Army General Staff to 'punish China'. Except within the headquarters of the Kwantung Army, the issue was seen in Japanese high circles as entirely one of 'self-defence'. As the struggle continued, however, each side inflicted hideous atrocities upon their enemies. Japanese conduct especially became remarkable for its extreme cruelty. The dispassionate historian must reject the judgement of the Tokyo Tribunal 'that the real purpose of the Japanese attack was to alarm the Chinese by indication of what would follow if their attitude toward Japan continued, and thus break down resistance to future operations. The Incident was part of the general plan.'* It is nevertheless indisputably correct that:

The needless bombing of Chapei [a squalid Chinese suburb tucked in a corner between the western edge of the International Settlement and the northern bounds

* Pritchard and Zaide, op. cit., 20: *Judgment and Annexes*, p. 49106.

of the separate French Concession], the ruthless bombardment by naval vessels, and the massacre of the helpless Chinese farmers whose bodies were later found with their hands tied behind their backs, are examples of the method of warfare waged at Shanghai.*

The fighting lasted until 3 March when the Japanese at last broke through to the open country beyond the city. The confidence of the Japanese military received a setback from the unexpected resistance, and from the international stir which the crisis had provoked. The good offices of the United States, Britain, France, Italy and officials of the League of Nations helped to effect an armistice. Chief credit for the settlement, however, properly belongs to the British Minister, Sir Miles Lampson, and to Minister Shigemitsu, the very man who had called for the marines at the end of January. It was he who persuaded the Japanese Commander-in-Chief at Shanghai, General Shirakawa, to order a ceasefire on 3 March, on the very eve of a meeting by the General Assembly of the League of Nations which was due to consider the crisis. Negotiations to achieve a lasting peace were fraught with difficulties, but the final breakthrough sprang from the personal courage of Shigemitsu. As he and other Japanese dignitaries stood on a reviewing stand at a parade to mark the Emperor's birthday on 29 April, a Korean nationalist threw a bomb which killed General Shirakawa, tore off part of General Ueda's foot, blinded Admiral Nomura in one eye, and killed the chairman of the local Japanese residents' association. Shigemitsu, too, was caught in the blast but refused to undergo life-saving surgery until a peace agreement was reached on 5 May. His own account of what happened was confirmed after the war by western diplomats and foreign correspondents who rallied to Shigemitsu's defence during the Tokyo Trial proceedings:

The text of the agreement having been drawn up at the British Consulate-General, the scene of the negotiations, the document was brought round to my bed in the hospital, where, racked with pain and in danger of my life, I managed to complete the numerous signatures required. I said then to Chang the Chinese Secretary: 'Relations between Japan and China must now enter a state of amity. I pray that this document may be the starting-point of future good relations between our two countries.' At that moment it was a question whether my life could be saved. The Chinese Secretary returned to the council chamber and in impressive tones disclosed my message. When all the signatures were completed, the operating table was wheeled in and one leg was amputated.

Peace having been restored, the Japanese forces were withdrawn from the Shanghai area and conditions returned to normal.†

* ibid., p. 49105.
† M. Shigemitsu, *Japan and her Destiny*, Hutchinson, London, 1958, pp. 78–9.

In fact, of course, conditions did not quite return to normal. Chinese morale everywhere was recharged by the stout resistance which their compatriots at Shanghai had maintained against crack Japanese troops for more than six weeks. It did not affect the outcome there or anywhere, but it gave the Chinese hope and gladdened the hearts of their friends.

Finally, the League of Nations Commission of Enquiry made known its findings, and as the British historian of Japan, Richard Storry, later remarked, these 'included a sympathetic explanation of Japanese grievances that was more compelling than anything put out by Tokyo'.* The Report by Lord Lytton's Commission was a thoughtful document. It cautioned that '[the] issues involved in this conflict are not as simple as they are often represented to be. They are, on the contrary, exceedingly complicated, and only an intimate knowledge of all the facts, as well as of their historical background, should entitle anyone to express a definite opinion upon them.'† After such a shot across the bows of public opinion, it is tempting to alter course, or heave to, for a discourse on the minutiae of the Japanese, Manchurian and Chinese claims and counter-claims. Happily, however, we need not dwell on the rights and wrongs that bemused contemporary observers were obliged to consider. It is sufficient to note that as a case study in international politics and in the misconduct of civil/military affairs, the period encompassing the Manchurian Incident and the foundation of Manchukuo is so rich, fascinating and, indeed, thought-provoking that we must regret the usual knee-jerk conclusion that Japan and its leadership were intent from the beginning upon nothing less than the complete subjugation of Manchuria and its incorporation into the Japanese Empire with as little fuss as possible. This is belied by the cracks that the crisis produced within the Japanese Government and its armed forces. It was understood, as articulated in the words of the Report of the League of Nations Assembly, adopted on 24 February 1933 (a month after Hitler's rise to power), that 'Past experience shows that those who control Manchuria exercise a considerable influence on the affairs of the rest of China – at least of North China – and possess unquestionable strategic and political advantages. To cut off these provinces from the rest of China cannot but create a serious irredentist problem likely to endanger peace.'‡ Nevertheless, the habit of disparaging the

* 'The English-language Presentation of Japan's Case during the China Emergency of the Late Nineteen-thirties', in *European Studies on Japan*, Paul Norbury Publications, Tenterden, Kent, 1979, p. 146.
† *The Report of the Commission of Enquiry into the Sino-Japanese Dispute*, op. cit., p. 166.
‡ *Sino-Japanese Dispute: Report adopted on February 24, 1933, by the Assembly of the League of Nations*, United States Government Printing Office, Washington, DC, 1933, p. 16.

military prowess of all oriental races died hard. From a sociological as well as from a military point of view, the most curious fact remains that western observers generally failed to appreciate the magnitude of Japan's feats of arms. There was still an inclination in many quarters to regard the Japanese as only marginally more civilized than the Chinese.

The Lytton Commission did not scruple to say that Japan had been an aggressor, though in polite and reasoned language, and though it held that China had itself been provocative, and was therefore in part guilty. The Report was accepted by the League Council by a vote of forty-two to one, unanimously but for the dissenting voice of Japan. It was too much for Japan to swallow. It may be uncharitable if not inaccurate to say that Japan objected to China, the parvenu, being treated as equal with Japan, which thought of itself as one of the established imperialist Powers of the world. Nevertheless, its reply was to resign from the League of Nations in March 1933.

The final scene was enacted at Geneva by the Japanese Ambassador, Matsuoka Yōsuke, a graduate of the University of Oregon, who was later to serve as President of the South Manchurian Railway between 1935 and 1939 and would thereafter reappear on the international stage as Foreign Minister of Japan. The drama was described as follows in *The Times*:

> Mr Matsuoka announced immediately after the vote that his Government found themselves compelled to conclude that Japan and the other members of the League entertained different views of the manner to achieve peace in the Far East, and were obliged to feel that they had now reached the limit of their endeavours to cooperate with the League with regard to Sino-Japanese differences. The Japanese then walked out in a body. They maintained the self-possession of their race to the last, but many of them are known to have been cleft in their emotions.

Their departure was seen with ruffled feelings by some of the officials of the League of Nations, who, while they recognized that Japan was aggressive, felt themselves obliged to state that, on the various international committees and agencies which the League promoted, Japan had been a most valuable member. The hearts of some of them were heavy at what they felt had been the driving out of Japan from associating with enlightened governments, and at the increased opportunity which this gave to all the darker forces at work in Japan.

The Manchurian Incident, or rather the failure of the League of Nations to find an effective means of enforcing the moral precepts professed by the majority of states, seriously handicapped the League's efforts to resolve subsequent international disputes elsewhere. No attempt was made by the League Council to organize sanctions against Japan, although

Japan's actions did not technically relieve it of the threat: but it is obvious that the Powers snatched at excuses eagerly. Also, by withdrawing from the comity of nations, Japan relieved the League of the effort to regulate internationally the privileged position of Japan in Manchuria, which the Lytton Commission had agreed that it should have. In fact, there was precious little that the League or any of its member states could have done to wrest the initiative from the hands of the Kwantung Army. Any economic, military or naval demonstration in support of China would only have undermined still further the efforts of moderate Japanese statesmen to bring the Japanese militarist factions under control. Moreover, China's domestic upheavals and disregard for the 'extra-territorial' rights of Western Powers had aroused considerable apprehensions among many foreign governments in the years preceding the Manchurian Incident. Small wonder, then, that a fatal inertia overcame international outrage particularly in those countries where the initial response of public opinion had been favourable to Japan, especially since Japan at first did not seem intent upon displacing western investment and commercial interests whether in North China or Manchuria. The protection of that investment and those interests had always been a matter of great concern to western governments and was one of the principal objects of their policies towards China and Japan. Now those governments perceived that a major change was taking place in the relations between Japan and the outer world. It was not so much a change in Japanese aims as in the preparedness of the Japanese to defy western opinion in seeking the furtherance of those aims. And so while the personal integrity of Japanese diplomats abroad remained in high esteem, the opinion spread throughout the democratic nations of the world that the Japanese Government was itself out of control or that it was content to carry out its true predatory plans behind honourable professions which it intended to breach. European dictatorships, by and large little involved in the East Asian crisis, nevertheless drew the lesson that the use of force could pay considerable dividends for 'have not' nations who possessed the will to grasp the meat they craved.

Robert Osgood, in a book entitled *Problems of Modern Strategy*, defined Limited War as a conflict 'fought for ends far short of the complete subordination of one state's will to another's and by means involving far less than the total military resources of the belligerents, leaving the civilian life and the armed forces of the belligerents largely intact and leading to a bargained determination'.* Berenice Carroll, another student of the

---

* 'The Reappraisal of Limited War', in *Problems of Modern Strategy*, ed. A. Buchan, Praeger Press, London, 1970, p. 92.

subject, observed that a war regarded by the aggressor as a limited campaign may seem to be a Total War to the power upon whose soil it is waged, especially if the defending power succumbs to the invading forces.* Still another expert, Arthur Marwick, suggests four tests by which Total War may be identified: it must involve whole populations; the organization of the home front is as critical an influence as that of the military front; it shall mobilize all of the resources of science, technology and propaganda available to each side, and it shall be an 'all out' and 'all-embracing' struggle.† Looking back over the development of the Manchurian Incident and its aftermath, it becomes evident that these events involved the whole populations of Manchuria and Japan. Japan as well as Manchuria was thrown into immense upheaval. This has been under-appreciated in most western historical accounts of the Greater East Asia or Pacific War, yet it is essential to grasp the fact that the Manchurian Incident marked not simply a military signpost pointing to a providential turn of fortune in a backwater territory encountered along Japan's road to Hiroshima. It was that but more. It changed the political and social geography of both countries, creating a political and economic breakwater in the historical evolution of East Asia which only the unprecedented tide of changes endured in 1945 would sweep away. Japanese historians have long recognized this. So should we. As Kipling reminds us:

> The toad beneath the harrow knows
> Exactly where each tooth-point goes;
> The butterfly upon the road
> Preaches contentment to that toad.‡

The Manchurian Incident and the transformation of Manchukuo into an industrial and colonial powerhouse had no real precedent in contemporary history. This experiment in colonial government by proxy deeply affected the Japanese, and it is instructive to link events there first with the China Incident and afterwards with the conduct and expectations of Japanese forces during the Pacific War. The Japanese were conscious of the fact that the Second World War, if it came, would be a Total War. They were keenly aware of their industrial and material shortcomings in comparison to the Western Powers. The Japanese counterpart of the 'Yellow Peril' was a nightmare in which the barbarian western hordes,

---

* *Design for Total War: Arms and Economics in the Third Reich*, Mouton, The Hague, 1968, pp. 9–36.
† *Britain in the Century of Total War*, Bodley Head, London, 1968, *passim*.
‡ R. Kipling, *Rudyard Kipling's Verse: Definitive Edition*, Doubleday, Garden City, New York, 1942, p. 26.

possessed of unlimited money and manpower, would inexorably sweep across Asia and the Pacific. The Japanese knew that they must rely upon their own mental fortitude, physical self-sacrifice and traditional values embodied in their 'national polity' to escape defeat (indeed, this helps us to explain the tenacity of Japanese resistance – and suicides – during the war). For many decades there had been a wide measure of agreement, one certainly not confined to political extremists, that in the event of hostilities with any Third Power, it would be vital to harness all of the energies of Manchuria as well as of the Japanese Empire.

In Manchukuo the Japanese developed the first economy anywhere since the end of the First World War to be mobilized and dedicated to Total War. By the same token, the scale of Japan's achievements in Manchuria went largely unnoticed abroad. The partnership, whatever its strains (and they were considerable), between the Kwantung Army and the South Manchurian Railway and its Research Department, technical institutes and training establishments, was hugely important in setting a pattern for the future both in Japan Proper and throughout Greater East Asia. Like some latter-day East India Company, the S M R possessed incalculable prestige and not inconsiderable influence. Yet there were other forces at work as well. It was a time of five-year plans and huge monopolistic enterprises, state-controlled in theory but run by highly entrepreneurial venture capitalists. One can find similar partnerships and attendant strains manifest in the South Seas Mandated Islands, in Japanese-occupied territories everywhere, in the Asian Development Board's activities in China and beyond, in the evolving relationship between the *zaibatsu* and the Japanese political parties, and in the emergence of what is often regarded as a kind of totalitarian, non-party police state (in imitation, so it is said, of European fascist systems). It is true that many Japanese felt attracted by foreign political systems – although whether by democratic or totalitarian solutions depended upon the taste of the individual. Yet to dismiss the Japanese as imitators is to underrate the far greater importance of Japan's own creativity and dynamism. Overriding all calculation, however, was a sense that the modern history of Japan inspired faith that somehow the Japanese would muddle through, and that their cause was just.

CHAPTER 7

China: Internal Revolutions and Foreign Policy

CHINA made a great impression upon the foreigners who came to assist in its modernization. Following his return from a period of service with the Chinese Government, one young Englishman wrote a long private report on the relations between China's internal affairs and foreign policy. The Head of the Far Eastern Department of the British Foreign Office read it and minuted, 'It tells one more about the subject than anything I have seen.'* In his opening remarks the reporter had observed:

In the nation as a whole, the proportion of persons with high natural gifts is at least as large as, perhaps larger than, that of other eastern or western peoples. It is true that, owing to poverty and to the social structure, the greater part of this talent is never brought to fruition: nevertheless changes in social institutions may well put China once again in the forefront of civilized nations. The developments in the Far East ought therefore to be of first-class interest to the rest of the world.†

The prime characteristic of modern China was the importance of the farmer and the rural situation. This did not mean that farmers governed the country or that the Government was in their interest. On the contrary, as we shall see later, there were few countries in the world where the farmer had less to say in the conduct of affairs: and this was one of the causes of China's troubles during this time. Nevertheless, it was, broadly speaking, true that though China was governed almost exclusively by townsmen, it was not events in the cities – for example, the sentiments of the town proletariat – which made China strong or weak: it was the events in the countryside. An overwhelming proportion, perhaps 85 per cent, of the Chinese population lived upon farms. If this peasantry were reasonably satisfied, the Government would be powerful: when the peasantry was against the Government, the Government, *vis-à-vis* its neighbours, was half-paralysed.

The second most noticeable feature was the high density of population in certain areas. To a perceptive observer at the time, Chinese history –

---

* F 7911/166/10, minute by C. W. Orde, 4 January 1937, F O 371/20252, preserved at the British Public Record Office, Kew.
† ibid., memorandum by Guy Wint, 15 December 1936.

though this is subject to controversy – could perhaps be given a cyclical interpretation in terms of cyclical changes in the size of population, bearing in mind that every such simplified interpretation can be only partially true, and that a full analysis would require many factors besides population to be taken into account. With increasing population there was increased pressure on the land; as a result farms would become smaller, rents, and the number of tenant farmers, would increase. Finally, the standard of living would sink so low that banditry would break out on a nationwide scale. In the confusion which resulted, a dynasty would fall, either from pressure outside or from internal weakness; there would follow prolonged civil war; eventually, as a result of violence, pestilence and starvation, the population would reduce to limits which would permit the majority of farmers to win such a living from the land as to place the attractions of peace and order above the more adventurous and uncertain life of banditry. This would enable the political power which happened at that time to be in the ascendant, to consolidate itself and to found a new dynasty; and with peace re-established, China would enter upon one of its periods of great literary, artistic and cultural productivity. Later on the population once more would increase, pressure upon the land grow, and revolt break out afresh. That was how things appeared to stand in the years which preceded the outbreak of Total War between Republican China and Imperial Japan.*

In spite of its apparently easy defeats, and in spite of its disappointments at Geneva, China did not lose face. In this Japan was disappointed. It had counted on its action being regarded in the public opinion of the world as an old-fashioned colonial operation, which, in the atmosphere of 1931, was still condonable. China, a manifestly unequal Power, was to be put in its place. But the world, to Japan's surprise, was not inclined to revise its previous impression that China was genuinely in revival, and to write it off as now discredited.

As soon as the fighting in China was checked by a truce, China resumed its continuous, painful steps towards recovery as a Power in world affairs. The Japanese became conscious, though at first they could scarcely credit it, that this Chinese ambition was now fostered by the former imperialists who had once treated it with so much contempt. In fact, Japan's determination to rise had now become so evident, and was seen with so much misgiving by other Powers, that it was natural for its rivals to

---

* Adapted from the private memorandum submitted by Guy Wint to the British Foreign Office, 15 December 1936: see above.

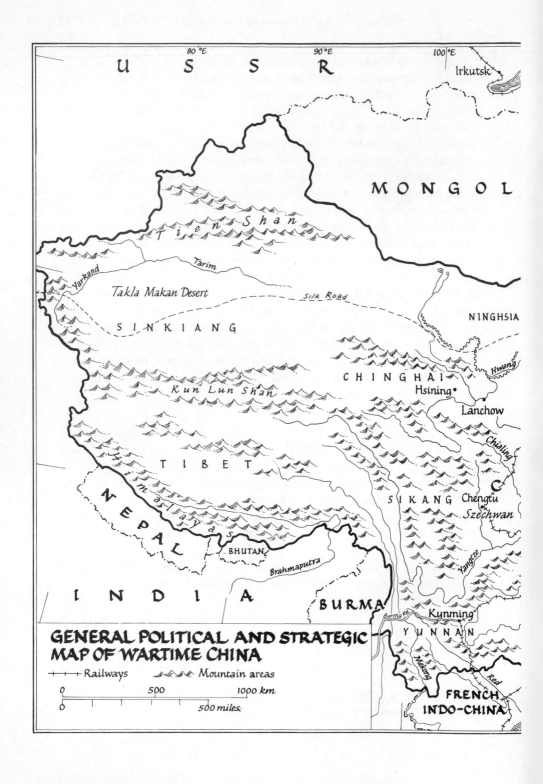

GENERAL POLITICAL AND STRATEGIC
MAP OF WARTIME CHINA

+——+—— Railways · ⌃⌃⌃ Mountain areas

0 · · · · · 500 · · · · · 1000 km
0 · · · · · 500 miles

110°E   120°E   130°E   50°N

Chita

Khabarovsk

Little Khingan Mts.

KHINGAN   HEILUNKIANG

Great Khingan Mountains

Tsitsihar

Harbin

•Ulan Bator

I A

MANCHURIA

Sungari

Hsingkiung
(Changchun)

K I R I N

Vladivostok

INNER MONGOLIA

JEHOL

Mukden

Sea of   40°N

Liaoyang

Liao

FENGTIEN

Japan

Paotow

Great   Wall

Peking

KOREA
(CHOSEN)

Ordos
Desert

Tatung

HOPEI

Tientsin

Dairen

Pt Arthur

Chefoo

JAPAN

Taiyuan

Hwang

SHANSI

Tsingtao

Yenan•

SHENSI

Loyang

Kaifeng

Tsinan

SHANTUNG

Yellow
Sea

Wei

Sian   HONAN

KIANGSU

Han

Huai

Chinkiang

East

Nanking

Shanghai

30°N

H   I   N   A

Yangtze

ANHWEI

Basin

Ichang

Hankow

Hangchow•

Han

Ningpo

China

Chungking

Nanchang

CHEKIANG

Changsha•

KIANGSI

Wenchow•

Sea

HUNAN

Kan

Kweiyang

Nan   Ling

Foochow•

Okinawa

FUKIEN

Hsi

Amoy

Canton

KWANGTUNG

FORMOSA
(TAIWAN)

•Nanning

Hong Kong

South
China Sea

20°N

HAINAN

switch their interest benevolently to Japan's enemy. This slow, but lasting change was more evident in Governments than in the sentiments of western businessmen, who, by the old habit of consorting with the Japanese, for a long while had found the change in their Governments nearly as puzzling as did the Japanese.

In the next six years, from 1931–7, this progress continued. Domestically, for China, they were dominated by one man, Chiang Kai-shek. He drew ahead of his civilian colleagues in the Government and came to hold in the public mind of China a position very much like that of the emperors of old. By foreigners he was equated with Chinese Nationalism, its embodiment and its principal agent. Chiang was the dominant figure in China until the end of the Second World War. Many people forwarded the drama but their personalities remain shrouded. In China, however, it is possible to tell what sort of man Chiang Kai-shek was. An attempt to analyse and assess his personality is necessary, for, in understanding what qualities he had and why they established his supremacy in Chinese government, many of the obscure facts about China's régime may be made plain.

Chiang was the successful general of the Kuomintang. He had mounted on the shoulders of the party and come to dominate it. His special characteristic was will-power. He knew just what he wanted, and was never idle in his pursuit of it. This gave him an advantage over most of his rivals and competitors in Nanking. He was gifted with a great self-confidence, which probably meant that he despised most of the other leaders of the party.

Devious, subtle, resourceful – these he had to be if he was to hold his position among the shifting sands of Nanking. His outstanding quality was an exceptional tenacity: he got his way through single-minded persistence. His mind being made up, he would never change. In this, but not in other ways, he was like Shakespeare's Julius Caesar:

> But I am constant as the northern star
> Of whose true-fixed and resting quality
> There is no fellow in the firmament.
> The skies are painted with unnumbered sparks,
> They are all fire, and every one doth shine,
> But there's but one in all doth hold his place.
> So in the world: 'tis furnished well with men
> And men are flesh and blood, and apprehensive,
> Yet in the number I do know but one,
> That unassailable holds on his rank
> Unshaked of motion: and that I am he.

He had a chilling attitude to the issues of life and death. If an object could be obtained with comparatively little sacrifice, so much the better. But if its purchase should cost 100,000 lives, he was willing, with scarcely any hesitation, to pay the price. He would have regarded this attitude as realistic.

He was not especially clever, inspiring, good, proficient at public speaking or public appearance. He was the product of a provincial military college in China, and of a rather inferior Japanese education. With this background he was neither so well educated as to have eccentric views, nor so badly as to appear scandalously ignorant. Accordingly the middle ranks, the mediocre, served him well as the medium out of which he rose to fame. He had a poor imagination, but, as against this, an exceptionally good memory. He dissimulated, and always held back his real thoughts. His suspiciousness was boundless. But if he did not check this, he could point to it having served him well. He was habitually surrounded by so much deceit that only a carefully nurtured suspicion kept him aware of the plots of remarkable complexity which were the stuff of Chinese politics.

He had a flair for political manoeuvre, and was excellent at manipulating his colleagues. He knew, and was at home in, the labyrinth of Chinese affairs – in the secret societies, in knowing how to use money to build a personal empire, in knowing how to operate a front in politics, and what to say in public through that front. He had the political talent, which comes near political mysticism, for nearly always foreseeing how things would fall out, and for knowing what needed to be done in particular circumstances. This flair, which included judging a situation correctly – and not with the distraction of moral considerations – was perhaps the key to his success in politics.

He preferred to rule through the ubiquitous secret societies which were always one of the chief characteristics of China. Some of these societies were of ancient origin, had existed originally for respectable purposes, but had degenerated. Chiang took steps to bind the societies to himself. They secured discipline among their members by strong-arm methods, always secret. Chiang, being fundamentally uninterested in ideas, jumped at the opportunity of gaining China by means of authority in this twilight world, twitching a string here, a string there. The extent to which China, before the Communist Revolution, was a rabbit warren of secret societies, ramified with weird ceremonies and tied up at distant removes to Confucianism, cannot be exaggerated. They caught in their net all who mattered in the Government – bureaucrats, soldiers, businessmen. Because of these societies, Chinese public life was always shrouded in a certain mystery. Nothing happened in a quite straightforward way. In any transaction the trail at some stage went underground. Things could not be done without recourse to the secret society. And, more probably than not, Chiang would be involved.

If he never pursued lofty or exceptional aims, that meant he would be set on nothing he could not achieve. He kept his nose to the ground, and pursued ends which were strictly practical. He was cautious and did not expose himself recklessly to danger: but when danger found him, he could call forth the stoic courage of the better type of army officer to sustain him in it. Science and all the arts did not interest him. He became a Christian, and he used to read, and read again, familiar books: but he had no taste for new books. He was not speculative. He had no particular ideas about the way the world was changing, and probably was never in a position to understand this. When he did not understand a point, he was unwilling to speak, and became inscrutable.

He had the natural xenophobia of the uneducated man; but he had the wit to conceal this in his necessary dealings with foreigners. These found him puzzling, and they never established complete rapport with him. But some of them were very much impressed by the man, and agreed that he was dignified, not garrulous, and reserved. He had a cynical view of human nature. But by natural instinct he tended to consort with the type of man who was foreign to exceptional virtue. His cynical views thus proved correct, as far as those with whom he came into contact were concerned. His rancour and vindictiveness against his enemies were constantly spoken of. But probably this rancour proceeded from considerations of prudence, which taught him that a man who was once his enemy was likely to remain so, and that generosity had few conquests, rather than from bitterness of mind.

In private life he was rather dull, faithful by routine to his intimates, determinedly egotistical. In the wider circles of life, he had no friends. Those who knew him well agreed that he was neither particularly wicked nor noticeably squeamish. A study of the countless crises he survived, and his way of dealing with them, might be added as an appendix to Machiavelli's book.

He was not magnetic and not lovable, though he was sometimes loyal to his colleagues and was admired for this. To outer show, he appeared ascetic, and if, as his enemies alleged, this was a pose, it did not appear so to the mass of the people. His family were venal, but he himself was probably not open to accepting bribes: he more than tolerated such practices in others, especially as a means of exerting political control. He felt the pull of the past and he played round with Confucian ideas, and the somewhat austere and chilly teaching of Chinese conservatives, which ceased to be revolutionary and swung to the Right, was his guiding thought.

Yet that Chiang was in many respects a remarkable man cannot be denied; otherwise he could not have battled on, receiving countless checks, seldom achieving total success. Only his will and obstinacy were indomitable.

The interest of the nation was in reconstruction. The prime concern of Chiang Kai-shek was in fighting the communists.

Chiang was obsessed with the civil war. So were his principal bankers and backers within the Chinese oligarchy, right down to village level. The first shots of the communist wars were fired in Nanchang, the capital of Kiangsi. In August 1927 the garrison commander, Chu Teh, had revolted and declared for the communists. How many soldiers were involved in that rebellion is doubtful, but the number was probably not more than 5,000. Defeated, they retired to the south, met a powerful Government force, and, reduced to a tenth of their former strength, scattered.

Thus, almost unnoticed, began a war which, by the eve of China's life and death struggles with Japan, devastated great areas in one third of the provinces of China and cost the Central Government over a billion dollars. Hundreds of thousands of lives were lost, and the issue remained in doubt.

As we have seen, the communists occupied, and maintained, a soviet Government in part of the Kiangsi province and neighbouring territory. Between 1930 and 1934 they resisted five successive so-called bandit-suppression expeditions, each of them more elaborate than the last. For a time, the heavy losses sustained by the Red Army were offset by new recruits inducted into their ranks in large numbers. Some came from the local farming communities, some from deserters from the Kuomintang forces. In 1930, when the communists made their first big gains, their armed forces do not seem to have numbered more than 20–30,000 men. Between 1931 and 1934, their number increased to 120,000 regular troops. In addition to their regular army, the communists also disposed of large numbers of militia men, not so well trained or equipped but playing an important part in guerrilla warfare.

The communists promised the expropriation of the gentry and the redistribution of land. The only experiment with communal ownership of land was made upon a small scale, persisted in for one year, and officially declared a failure. On the whole, there can be no doubt that, as a device for enlisting the support of the masses, the policy pursued was shrewd and

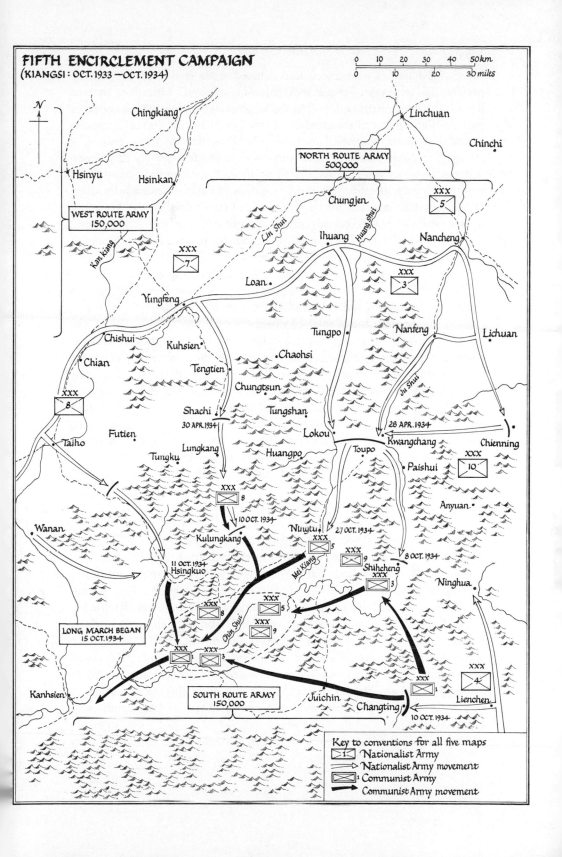

FIFTH ENCIRCLEMENT CAMPAIGN
(KIANGSI : OCT. 1933 — OCT. 1934)

0   10   20   30   40   50km
0   10   20   30 miles

N

Chingkiang

Linchuan

Chinchi

Hsinyu

Hsinkan

NORTH ROUTE ARMY
500,000

WEST ROUTE ARMY
150,000

Kan kiang

XXX
5

Lin Shui

Chungjen

Ihuang

Huang shui

Nancheng

XXX
7

Loan

XXX
3

Yungfeng

Tungpo

Nanfeng

Lichuan

Chishui

Kuhsien

Chaohsi

Chian

Tengtien

Chungtsun

Ju Shui

Futien

Shachi

30 APR.1934

Tungshan

Lokou

28 APR.1934

Kwangchang

Chienning

XXX
8

Taiho

Tungku

Lungkang

Huangpo

Toupo

Paishui

XXX
10

Anyuan

XXX
8

Wanan

Kulungkang

10 OCT.1934

Niuytu

27 OCT.1934

XXX
5

8 OCT.1934

XXX
9

Mei Kiang

Shihcheng

XXX
3

Ninghua

11 OCT.1934

Hsingkuo

XXX
8

Chin Shui

XXX
5

XXX
9

LONG MARCH BEGAN
15 OCT.1934

XXX
1

XXX
5

XXX
1

XXX
4

Lienchen

Kanhsien

SOUTH ROUTE ARMY
150,000

Juichin

Changting

10 OCT.1934

Key to conventions for all five maps

XXX ⌐1 Nationalist Army
───▷ Nationalist Army movement
XXX ⌐1 Communist Army
━━▶ Communist Army movement

successful. Families whose sons had enlisted in the Red Army were given preferential treatment in the redistribution of land. Moreover, it was linked with a tax reform effort that did not merely replace one tax collector with another and produce greater income but rather led to real increases in the disposable income of most people. The effect of these policies – strange for a communist programme – was to create a society of yeomen farmers, small capitalists. At the same time, the communists instituted compulsory education for the indoctrination of children and adults alike. Other activities included the organization of credit cooperative societies, the provision of health services (greatly handicapped by the lack of drugs, instruments and modern, trained physicians) and an attempted socialization of trade. Added to this was a cry for the expulsion of the Japanese – a sure-fire formula for winning massive popular support.

The foregoing is the bright side of the picture. On the debit side must be put the restriction of individual liberties – though it may be questioned whether the poorer classes enjoyed much liberty under the old régime; the arbitrary system of government; a large element of confusion and incompetence in the administration; the ruthless destruction of property and of monuments of ancient China; and – the most discreditable part of the soviet record – the massacres and persecutions. These atrocities are well attested. In many villages of Kiangsi there was a field left uncultivated and shunned by the inhabitants: this was the execution ground. It is, however, fair to add that the war against the gentry, although in no way restrained by the soviet Governments, was rather willed by the people than dictated by communist officials. Behind the slaughter lay centuries of oppression and pent-up bitterness. Significantly, recruits were attracted by the Red Army rather than by the politics of the Communist Party.

As is common in revolutions, the terror was directed as much against those within the ranks of the revolutionaries as against their enemies. The death penalty was imposed, and in the majority of cases carried out, upon officials detected in corruption; disobedient soldiers of the Red Army, soldiers who looted, minor intrigants. Death was even the penalty for lax work. For example, during a time of flood, labourers engaged in dyke building were warned twice for idleness, and on the third offence were shot. The ruthless proscription of supporters diverging from the party line recalls, and during those years surpassed, the achievement of Adolf Hitler. In 1934 an internal political crisis was ended by the execution in one week of 4,300 persons, most of them members of the Communist Party.

Some of the leaders enjoyed a special pre-eminence, especially Chu

Teh, the Commander-in-Chief, and a political organizer named Mao Tse-tung. Chu Teh appeared to be of a type not unfamiliar in Chinese history: born into a wealthy landlord family, by the time he had reached middle age he had shown an aptitude for life as a successful war-lord, enjoying the pleasures of corruption, the dissipations of opium-smoking and responsibilities which are said to have included nine wives and concubines. An admirer wrote:

One might have thought he had everything he desired: wealth, power, love, descendants, poppy dreams, eminent respectability, and a comfortable future in which to preach the proprieties of Confucianism. He had, in fact, only one really bad habit, but it was to prove his downfall. He liked to read books.*

Chu underwent the first of several conversion experiences: 'Disembarrassing himself of his previous encumbrances, he went to Shanghai and joined the extremist wing of the Kuomintang.'† He then left the country to take up political studies among Chinese students in Hanover, Paris and Moscow. While in Germany he became a member of the Communist Party. He returned home late in 1925 and was appointed Chief of the Bureau of Public Safety in the provincial capital of Kiangsi. After raising the communist rebellion against the Kuomintang in Kiangsi, he became a man of a somewhat Rabelaisian turn, living in a very democratic way, and receiving from his followers unbounded devotion, both because his picturesque character appealed to their imagination and because of his genuine care for their well-being. So much legend grew up round him that it is hard to sort out true from false. He was said to be a man of quickly changing moods. Like King Saul, he was given to fits of extreme depression; at other times, like Cromwell, he was inclined to play the buffoon. He was known to order massacres on the grand scale. He was said to live in one room, eat the same food as the common soldier, and drew the regulation wage of a private – $3 a month. Alone among the important figures in China, he is said to have refused the protection of a bodyguard. Chu Teh, though sympathetic to the farmer and the grievances of the poor, did not belong to the doctrinaire wing of the party. Leadership there fell to Mao Tse-tung, an ex-schoolmaster, around whom as much legend grew as round Chu Teh.

Mao came from Hunan, a province noted for the energy and fiery temper of its inhabitants. Son of a poor peasant family, his early career need not detain us. In many characteristics – in his secrecy, and in a

---

* Edgar Snow, *Red Star over China*, Gollancz, London, 1937, p. 355.
† F 1113/1113/10, China Personalities Report by Sir A. Clark Kerr, 19 December 1940, FO 371/24699, British Public Record Office, Kew.

certain indirectness – he was typically Chinese; it was said that he took none of his collaborators into full confidence, and was unwilling that they should be in too close touch with one another. When confronted with opposition, he rarely compromised, but veiled his opinion and, in the end, by subtle manipulation, usually carried his point. He was an orator. His characteristics, which were of significance for the fortunes of the Kiangsi Soviet and the travails of his movement thereafter, were an inflexible attachment to principle and a talent for organization. The first of these qualities kept the agrarian rebellion upon communist lines and caused its leaders to pursue something like a consistent policy; the second ensured that an administration, a more or less ordered community, emerged from the storm of revolution, and that the Red Army was fed and supported from the civilian side in such a way as to make it the formidable power which it became.

These and one or two others were the great names among the communists, but in Kiangsi Chu and Mao were certainly not dictators. Not only did they have to give way to each other, but frequently also to other members of the Central Committee of the Chinese Communist Party. It was the Committee which governed; Chu and Mao were the most prominent of its members, but they were not all-powerful.

During most of the time they were in Kiangsi, the communists were able to import supplies from the outside world. The territory between Kiangsi and the sea was held for some time by the Nineteenth Route Army, the force which distinguished itself in the defence of Shanghai against the Japanese. Somewhat radical in its leanings, the Nineteenth Route Army adopted towards the communists a neutrality which was distinctly benevolent, and made no difficulty about the passage of arms and ammunition from the ports of Swatow and Amoy. But the principal source of ammunition was the Government forces. Until the traffic was detected, large quantities could be purchased from corrupt junior officers in the Government Army; moreover, deserters from the Government side usually brought their equipment with them; and the Red troops referred to Government soldiers as 'our ammunition carriers'.

Nevertheless, the communists never obtained heavy armaments such as big guns or tanks; for a time they possessed two aircraft, but they were not extensively used. The weapon on which they most relied was the machine-gun. Operating on interior lines in the early years, their tactics then were those of guerrilla war. Its elements were ambushes, sniping, surprise attacks at the hour when the morale of their opponents was lowest, and propaganda among the enemy forces (perhaps the most formidable of all their weapons). One of their chief assets was the support received from the population; in many recaptured districts the Government troops were received with a hostility suitable only to a foreign invader, spied on, harried and delayed in every possible way. Another was the speed of movement of the communist forces. Marching as a rule by night, and maintaining contact by means of radio, they would arrive in over-whelming force against an objective, before the Government, infinitely better supplied and much superior in numbers, knew that it was even threatened. As time passed, the communist forces became increasingly professional in their training, and guerrilla warfare gave way to the tactical deployment of the Red forces in large conventional formations.

In fact the communists proved to be far more successful than the Kuomintang in the mobile warfare which characterized the earlier ex-peditions, but inexorably the tactical skill of the Red forces was overcome by the immense firepower and numerical strength of Chiang's armies.

As is the way in warfare, the communist tactics eventually called forth new tactics on the other side which checked them. It was not, as might have been expected, the employment of aircraft which defeated them. Aircraft, though they played some part in the Government campaigns, never proved a decisive weapon. Since the Red troops moved by night, it was difficult to detect and bomb their columns, and the Government was unwilling to drop bombs upon civilian villages. The weapon which the Government and its German advisers discovered to be a deadly one was the blockhouse. Fortified by machine-guns, these were able to command the surrounding countryside and were practically invulnerable to any force which, like the communists, lacked artillery and suitable aircraft. The communists, in their turn, attempted to erect their own blockhouses to stem the Government advance, but their constructions were easily destroyed by gunfire. Guided by his German military advisers, and backed up by artillery and air support, Chiang's armies systematically advanced, carving up the countryside with a new road network, protected by chains of thousands of blockhouses in ever-decreasing circles, depriving the communist leadership of any hope of maintaining its grip on its soviet base. From that time on, communist raids into Government territory became almost impossible: the ground which the Government recovered was held effectively, and little by little the national troops pressed forward until finally the communists gave up the fight.

In the Fourth Encirclement Campaign during 1932, the Hupeh-Honan-Anhwei Soviet was forced to evacuate through the mountains, fleeing west-ward in disorder to the comparative safety of Szechwan, where they made the best of a temporary respite. Finally, in October 1934, the Central (Kiangsi) Soviet was squeezed out by the Kuomintang. Exhausted, squabbling among themselves, the communists had no option but to take flight or face annihilation. In more attractive terms, the time had come for a move in a way which has become classic in Chinese communist strategy: one step back in order to prepare for two steps forward. It was regarded at the time, however, not as a moment of impending victory or grand strategic opportunity but rather as a desperate struggle for day-to-day survival:

The Central Committee of the CCP, the Government, the Red Army, their personnel and dependants fled, with the Kuomintang forces on their heels. This was only the beginning of the worst disaster in the history of the Chinese communist movement. The Red political power which controlled some 300 *hsien* (counties) at one time in Kiangsi, Hupeh, Honan, Hunan, Anhwei, and Fukien, was almost totally wiped out. The revolutionary movement appeared to be on the verge of extinction. The defeat split the Chinese communist leadership both in China and Moscow and gave rise to serious internal disputes.*

Ninety thousand survivors broke through Chiang's lines and made an astonishing march, in which their columns again and again repelled or evaded the troops sent to block their way, from Fukien and Kiangsi to the Tibetan borderlands in the far west of China. Chased by Chiang's forces, the communists then made their way northward and up to the remote and mountainous province of Shensi at the north-west frontier between China Proper and Inner Mongolia, on the northernmost approaches of China to the Soviet Union. The Long March covered a distance of 6,000 miles and virtually wiped out the Red Army. The number which reached the relative safety of the north-west a year later was 20,000.

By this fantastic march the communists associated themselves with all that was remarkable in Chinese military history. Out of their struggles emerged a cohesive party leadership and an exceptional sense of political and social unity. They captured the imagination of the country in a way that was quite disproportionate to their size and their real importance. Arrived in Shensi, they set themselves to build a new soviet Government, as they had had before in Kiangsi, one which was milder than the Kiangsi model and which did not automatically frighten off all the propertied class of peasants. It made more appeal than had the Kiangsi model to rational feeling, less to class warfare. Moreover, it was hallowed by the record of legendary deeds of the communists in the transit force which had crossed eighteen mountain ranges and forded twenty-four rivers from Fukien and

* Kataoka Tetsuya, *Resistance and Revolution in China: The Communists and the Second United Front*, University of California Press, Berkeley, 1974, p. 12.

Kiangsi to their new home. When they took up the cry for war against Japan, they were heard with increased respect throughout China.

It must not be supposed that the communists had a monopoly of reform activities. The National Government, in fact, embarked upon a plan of economic development which, though on a small scale compared with the effort in such countries as Soviet Russia, nevertheless, both by its scope and success in execution, surprised many experienced observers. The programme covered the whole country, and it was therefore much more difficult to carry out than that of the communists, which was confined to a relatively small area. Moreover, in judging the results, it must be remembered that the greater part of the resources intended for reconstruction were swallowed up in the civil war.

The National Government postulated that, without law and order, economic development was impossible and that the first use of its resources must be the creation of an efficient police system. This involved many difficulties, one of the chief of which was the problem of identifying persons in country districts. To all inquiries from outside, villagers presented an unhelpful and united front. To remedy this state of affairs, the Government revived a part of the ancient administrative machinery of China, first invented eight centuries before but allowed to fall into disuse during the past hundred years. This was called the *pao chia*. Every ten families were grouped into a unit called the *pao*; every ten paos formed a *chia*. All members of the pao must be registered, and every person in the province must wear on his clothes a label showing to which pao he belonged. Each pao and each chia had a headman, appointed by the Government. When any person was wanted by the police, the pao to which he belonged had to produce him, otherwise the members were held, in theory, collectively responsible for his misdeeds. It was a far from perfect system of control but it was on the whole very serviceable as a police measure. It also made the creation of an efficient militia possible and that, in turn, was frequently employed in public works construction such as the creation of motor roads, dyke building and irrigation projects. At the same time, improvements in medical services, agricultural methods, free education, the revival of the silk, cotton and tea industries, the creation of a cooperative movement, and a genuine opium-suppression campaign were all given enormous attention by both the military and civil authorities. Western observers noted that the principal defect in this reconstruction effort was that it did not include a drastic reform of land ownership and tenure. The second defect in the programme was its rigidly authoritarian structure. The third defect was the inability of the National

Government to override the reluctance of the gentry to carry out the redistribution of power and influence rapidly and efficiently. These defects, of course, were intertwined with each other.

Meanwhile, Chiang Kai-shek himself had grown in strength, consolidating his executive control over the political forces of the Kuomintang. Of the four groups which combined to make the Kuomintang revolution, the communists and farmers had been eliminated from a share in the Government; the educated, bourgeois group was relegated to a very inferior position: left to administer national finance in the interest of the Army but otherwise disposed to ignore constitutional principles, checks and balances, and confined to commerce, industry and learning, and the Army, under General Chiang, was really supreme. His Army was master of nearly all China.

Chiang Kai-shek, indeed, did not consider that he had suffered a setback. Militarily, he had won. His reconquest of the Kiangsi soviets had taken four years. It is, however, necessary to be very cautious in interpreting this as a reflection upon the national armies. It is not only that, in guerrilla warfare, the regular forces tend to be at a disadvantage, nor that the Government was distracted by the Japanese question. There were also matters of policy involved. For it is easy to understand that the communist war gave to the military authorities the opportunity to build up, test and experiment with, a national well-equipped Army upon a modern basis. The years 1932 and 1933 were spent in this undertaking, and operations were carried out with only a fraction of the national forces. When the whole might of Chiang's Army was turned against the communists in 1934, the result was a foregone conclusion.

The military cohesiveness of Chiang's nationalist forces depended upon his ability to command and enforce the personal allegiance of the warlords who fought under the nationalist banner. It was on this that his political and military authority ultimately rested, but he also attended to building up an élite section of the national army to set an example under his direct control. This was the section which had been trained by German military advisers since the expulsion of a Russian advisory team in 1927. These advisers, with establishment levels of around forty to seventy men, were led by men such as Colonel Max Bauer (1927–9), Colonel Hermann Kriebel (1929–30), Lieutenant-General Georg Wetzell (1930–34), General Hans von Seeckt (1934–5) and General Alexander von Falkenhausen – some of the most illustrious and experienced military officers of the time. They succeeded in adapting themselves to the manners of the more military Chinese, and spoke significantly about the warlike qualities of the Chinese under proper leadership. In startling contrast with the hordes of ragged Chinese troops in their tattered uniforms which were all too familiar in China, occasional khaki-clad regiments were now to be seen, very smart, alert, marching with precision: the élite of the Kuomintang. Its numbers were to rise to 300,000 men. Eventually the German military advisory group, acting with remarkable independence from Berlin but strengthened by a treaty which Chiang had negotiated with the German Government, began pressing Chiang to break off his campaigns against the Chinese communists and to march against the Japanese instead.

Throughout this period, German armaments manufacturers eagerly shipped up-to-date weaponry to Chiang Kai-shek's forces. As time wore on, this was subject to countervailing political pressures within the Third Reich and compromised German-Japanese relations, but the fact remains that in the year preceding the Anti-Comintern Pact, for instance, almost 60 per cent of German arms exports went to China (20 million Reichsmarks, 113 times the value of German exports to Japan). The Chinese contracts therefore became important in building up the military production of Nazi Germany.

The British and Americans had no doubts that they were being made scapegoats by the Japanese, whom they found entirely unreceptive to suggestions that the Japanese should address their complaints to their German allies. The discomforture of the Japanese was acute, but they were unable to accept the loss of face that would have resulted from any loud objections to Berlin. They did make their displeasure known, but for a prolonged period little notice was taken by the German arms exporters and their governmental patrons. As the disparity between German military exports to China and Japan became increasingly embarrassing, efforts were made by the Germans to adopt a 'policy of balance' between the two sides. This compromise solution proved to be unstable. Eventually Joachim von Ribbentrop and his cronies, who opposed the Chinese connection, overcame those who wished its continuance, ordered the German military mission to return home and forced German arms suppliers to tear up their Chinese orderbooks. Nevertheless, according to British and American Intelligence estimates, German and German-occupied Austrian and Czech arms factories continued to supply up to 75 per cent, and even more, of all foreign military equipment and ammunition sent to China from abroad throughout the first two years of the China Incident. When the decision to stop this traffic was taken in April 1938, the Reich Ministry of Economics calculated that the loss sustained by the German armaments industry from cancellation of contracts already signed amounted to 282 million Reichsmarks. Nevertheless, reliable reports indicated that a significant quantity of military supplies continued to flow from Germany and its satellites to China. It is indicative of the importance of this connection that in the first shipment of war materials to pass all the way up the fabled Burma Road into Free China in December 1938, there was German and Czechoslovak machine-gun ammunition valued at $112,000. At the same time a Norwegian steamer unloaded 1,300 tons of Italian arms and ammunition at Rangoon. These were by no means isolated instances. So much for the solidarity of Axis collaboration with Japan. The British Cabinet even took the extraordinary step of instructing British naval and customs authorities to turn a blind eye towards a German freighter due to unload a contraband shipment of arms at Hong Kong in the week following the outbreak of the European War.*

In everything, things began to go well for China. Its great weakness had been disunity, and the lack of a modern political structure. Now, very slowly, and largely by means of the tortuous, devious policies of Chiang Kai-shek, which he pursued with resolution, China's political unification made progress. The Kuomintang prevailed in new provinces: the warlords who survived had their powers reduced: the central Government of Nanking found new ways of undermining them, and of making new contact with the people by new institutions. Chiang Kai-shek, alert, like the Japanese of the earlier generation, to take advantage of borrowing what seemed to him relevant from abroad, took over various devices from the contemporary example of Hitler for reinforcing his personal ascendancy. The country began to be studded by a secret organization called the Blue Shirts, whose members were pledged to advance his interest: this included thugs, but also highly respected professors from Peking University, who felt that the desperate needs of the country required that Chiang should be supreme. During this period there was only one retrograde moment when a nationwide unrest among Chiang's opponents led to an outbreak of civil war on the old pattern: but this was soon stopped by diplomacy.

In 1935 the Kuomintang, advised and assisted by experts lent to it by the League of Nations, France, the United States and the Bank of England, greatly enhanced its prestige when it introduced a new currency throughout the whole country: and held it more or less stable for the first time in the history of China. The new system replaced the silver standard which had been made unworkable by the financial policy of the United States. Franklin D. Roosevelt's Government, under pressure from senators advancing the interests of silver producers, had raised the price of silver,

---

* R. J. Pritchard, *Far Eastern Influences upon British Strategy towards the Great Powers, 1937–1939*, Garland Publishing, New York, 1987, pp. 96–8; J. P. Fox, *Germany and the Far Eastern Crisis, 1931–1938*, Clarendon/LSE, Oxford, 1982, *passim*.

and, ignoring Chinese protests, created a deflationary spiral of about 30 per cent between 1931 and 1935 which drove China to seek another basis for its currency. The success of the Kuomintang in bringing a fiat currency into areas which it had previously occupied by military means alone was the best sign of the consolidation of its authority. It gave both the Kuomintang and China a fillip: and braced it to face the approaching war. Britain, by giving aid in this reform, had shown that it considered the new China worth taking risks for, and that it was willing to develop its East Asian policy on the hypothesis that China was becoming stable.

In these years an additional person of the drama was beginning to play an interesting and much publicized part. This was Madame Chiang, whom Chiang had married, as his second wife, in 1927. She was one of three ambitious and remarkable sisters, one of whom was the widow of Sun Yat-sen, the leading spirit among the founders of the Kuomintang, who had died in 1924 and was revered as a national hero. One of her brothers was T. V. Soong, the banker, Kuomintang politician and Minister of Finance between 1928 and 1933. Her other sister married the fabulously wealthy H. H. Kung, seventy-fifth lineal descendant of Confucius and Minister of Finance from 1933 to 1938. Madame Chiang supplied the female influence, which recalled to Chinese, who are extremely historically minded, many parallels in the dynastic histories of the past. In a way this increased their tendency to see Chiang as being like one of the founders of past dynasties. But, though her influence on Chiang was considerable, it must be seen for what it was, and not misinterpreted. She was not responsible for developing any new qualities in him: the stubborn will, which had made his place initially in the Kuomintang, was all his own. Madame Chiang, who was American-educated (as were all five of her brothers and sisters) and in temperament had become more American than Chinese, was his window on the United States. Through her, the relations of China and the United States became closer than they would have been without her. Madame Chiang gave her husband a glamour, an interest, which he could not have hoped for himself in American eyes. She was a forceful personality, wilful and dogmatic, and, though she lacked great political wisdom, she had an intelligence which made her a useful intermediary with foreigners. Some observers regarded her as a very wicked lady, misguided, corrupt and selfish in the extreme. Others, such as Sir Stafford Cripps, saw more wholesome qualities. Chiang's use of his wife was skilful, and she, in turn, probably possessed more power and influence than anyone else of her sex in the world at that time, apart, perhaps, from Eleanor Roosevelt.

In 1934 Chiang Kai-shek, assisted by his wife, launched what was called a 'new life movement'. This was not very popular: it was the subject of mirth among foreigners and the sophisticated classes of urban China. It was an attempt to revive the ancient Confucian virtues as the spiritual basis of the new state. Confucianism had been repudiated soon after the revolution which overthrew the Manchus; but a void had been left, and the Kuomintang lacked a spiritual basis on which to build the new order. Confucianism was not really a religion; it was a code of ethics which from earliest times had been accepted as the ideal of the Chinese people: it served throughout history as the powerful pillar of the state, and the fact that in China this role was performed by ethics, which in other states was performed by the great organized religions, has been one of the characteristics and fateful elements of Chinese civilization. Confucianism performed the unlikely part of presenting in a fossilized form the ethical outlook and views of the feudal society which was the state of China two thousand years ago. Attitudes which would have been appropriate in a good Chinese feudatory continued to be advocated, though the society which gave rise to them had long since changed. Confucianism urges submissiveness, demands reverence to the old, deplores a headstrong attitude in individuals, prizes the rites of courtesy, assumes that the business of women is to obey in all things. The task which the Chinese set themselves was to reinstate Confucianism, without allowing a too evident Confucian control of all the institutions of public life.

The new life was to be puritanical. A gloom settled over Chinese society. Nevertheless, by dint of propaganda, by the use of all the Government machinery for indoctrination, by the use of various Army bureaux for its propagation, and by manipulation of all the Government powers of patronage, a not unimpressive Confucian revival began to make headway in China. The change in the intellectual climate of China, with the substitution of a rather narrow Confucian dogma for bland scepticism, was one of the notable features of the time.

In the middle thirties the sense that China was recovering, which increased Chinese self-confidence at home as well as affecting the policies of all the powers concerned in the region, caused the Chinese to feel an increasing resentment at Japan's constant pressure upon them. In 1934 Japan, its ambitions enlarging after the conquest of Manchuria, was demanding that an area, carved out of China's northern provinces, should be declared autonomous, and that the writ of the Government of Nanking should cease to run there. Obviously the calculation was that in a short time it would pass under the control of Japan. The activities of Japanese agents caused a wave of indignation, and this was particularly strong among the students of Peking. Peking was always the seat of three or four universities, and their pupils, partly because of the regard which China traditionally paid to scholarship and to the learned life, enjoyed peculiar prestige. They were buoyed up by memory of the great demonstration which they had made fifteen years earlier against a particularly corrupt Government because of its craven acceptance of foreign demands; this had never been forgotten by the Government or by the students themselves; they had come to think of themselves as the custodian of the nation's conscience; they felt themselves morally obliged to be the nation's barometer. The Japanese overstepped the limit. Pressed too hard, the students erupted, in December 1935, in a great demonstration against the Chinese officials who were subservient towards the Japanese.

Those who had the good fortune to be present on this occasion felt, even if obscurely, that they were taking part in a historic action. The beauty of Peking in the freezing mid-winter, the sense of great issues happening which could only be dimly seen, the foreboding and the excitement, the sense of returning power and rising might in the Chinese people – of a people long oppressed feeling strength to quell the brute and boisterous force of the oppressor – all this made a memorable event in the history of China's ancient imperial city. Even though Peking at this time was demoted, and had temporarily ceased to be the capital city, the students must have sensed the drama of its being the setting for this great demonstration that marked China's national resurgence.

The growing nationalist temper was directed in part against Japan: in part against Chiang Kai-shek, because, though he was the military leader of China, he declined to act as its champion. Instead of calling China to arms he continued to sit in Central China, and called for the national attention to be riveted there, to wars for the eradication of communism. In doing this, Chiang began to be regarded as almost a traitor to the Chinese nation. China, or at least its intelligentsia, was ready to go to war, but it felt that one hand was tied behind its back by the Generalissimo of its own armies, or at least was engaged in keeping down the peasantry – an action which the younger, generous section of the nation did not desire at all, and was only necessitated because the landed interests of the Kuomintang required it. How long would these interests continue to control Chiang? When would he become responsive to the will of the younger and more virile section of the nation?

One point stands out sharply. That is, that China, being preoccupied with so many domestic problems, was very ill-placed to deal with foreign aggression. The conflict in the countryside between the gentry and the peasants, which is a normal occurrence in Chinese history at periods of two or three centuries, was then in an acute phase. It was made more bitter because of the distress of the farmers due to the dislocation of the rural economy which resulted from the increased trade with western nations. The contact with the West had led also to the emergence of new classes, the commercial plutocracy and the urban proletariat. The conflict between them increased the social tension; and it introduced to China a medley of new ideas and new conceptions, which profoundly influenced the behaviour of the intelligentsia and began also to influence the behaviour of the masses which, since they were in many cases conflicting, added to the confusion of affairs, caused divided aims and rendered quite uncertain the course which China was ultimately destined to take. As we have seen, a Government, composed of a bloc of the military, the plutocracy and the rural gentry, held with some security the cities and commercial centres. But in many parts of the countryside it confronted either open or potential revolt. Moreover, there was division within the Government itself on personal grounds but also between the faction standing for military and semi-fascist government and the faction standing for a more liberal development.

The policy of General Chiang Kai-shek, of basing the unity of China on his personal authority, was, successful though it had been to date, a source of weakness; for though China in the brief span of ten years had made great progress in modernizing its government, and though public opinion stood for the unity of the country, that unity was a tender plant. For unity to be consolidated other than in the figure of Chiang himself, it seemed to China-watchers that the country needed twenty years of peace during which the new institutions could take root and a system might be perfected by which political power could be shared or transferred without domestic combat or violence. The position thus appeared far too delicate for the Government to enter a foreign war except as a last resort. The patience of Nanking; its willingness to make concessions; its anxiety – in spite of a very real patriotism and a determination to recover lost territory in the future – to find some *modus vivendi* with Japan; its politic readiness – in spite of its own sincere anti-Japanese sentiment – to suppress the manifestation of it by its citizens; all of these impulses for some years seemed to westerners not only comprehensible but wise and prudent. Eventually, however, pressure for change became irresistible.

While Chiang Kai-shek's best forces were employed in the war against the communists, a very brief and humiliating campaign took place in which Japan conquered the province of Jehol, which was part of Inner Mongolia, and incorporated it into Manchukuo. This mopping-up operation was conducted by the Kwantung Army. The Japanese Cabinet in Tokyo, the Army General Staff and even the Emperor attempted to frustrate it but to little avail. Jehol was historically of interest as it had been a vast hunting preserve of the Manchu princes when these ruled in Mukden. After the Japanese invasion had breached the Great Wall itself, an armistice known as the Tangku Truce was concluded between China itself and Japan on 31 May 1933. Among its provisions was an agreement to establish a 5,000-square-mile demilitarized zone within the adjacent province of Hopei, ending at the Great Wall. Chinese forces eventually withdrew even from the vicinity of Tientsin, the Shanghai of the north and gateway to Peking. The principal benefit of the Tangku Truce for China was that it enabled the Kuomintang to strengthen its hold upon the nation as a whole. The Truce itself did not address the question of the status of Manchukuo nor its relations with the northern lands which still maintained an allegiance to China.

Nevertheless, the Tangku Truce laid the groundwork for Japanese agents to foster autonomy movements throughout the whole of North China, not merely among the Mongols of Chahar, Suiyuan and Ningsia along the borderlands north of the Wall but in the northern provinces of China Proper, including Hopei, Shansi and even Shantung. One reason for these preparations was to secure the Japanese rear in Manchuria against a Chinese surprise attack in the event of serious trouble with the Soviet Union. Another reason was that the Kwantung Army was eager to exploit the 'inexhaustible' iron and coal reserves of Shansi.

If we dilly-dally, these resources will end up in British or American hands. If we keep saying this and that about so-called international ethics, and if we yield the road to others by saying 'after you, after you', the one who will be left holding the bag is Japan. Therefore, while Europe and America are preoccupied with situations in their own countries, and while their circumstances are such that they cannot interfere with the Orient, it is of vast importance and a very good opportunity to get North China into the hands of Japan.*

Exhilarated by their unbroken string of successes, the Kwantung Army was not immune from the temptation to extend their imperium as far as lay within their power. Peking itself, the historic capital of the Middle Kingdom, was now within their sights. The dangers were obvious.

*

* *Harada-Saionji Memoirs*, 23 June 1935, recording report from Sakatani Kiichi about the views of Itagaki Seishirō and other leading figures in the Kwantung Army.

During the two years that followed the Tangku Truce, the Chinese gave way to further demands imposed by the Kwantung Army while Tokyo ran hot and cold. In an address to the Imperial Diet on 22 January 1934, Foreign Minister Hirota Kōki proclaimed a Japanese Monroe Doctrine in East Asia: 'Japan, serving as the only cornerstone for the edifice of peace in East Asia, bears the entire responsibility. It is in this important position and vast responsibility that our foreign diplomacy and national defence are rooted.' In remarks to the foreign press on 17 April 1934, the Head of the Foreign Ministry Information Bureau, Amō Eiji, repeated the substance of Hirota's words and indicated that Japan had no intention of tolerating foreign interference in the bilateral relations between China and Japan. While Hirota's statement had passed off without much comment, western governments, driven by public outrage, responded to the Amō Declaration with howls of protest. Hirota's attempt to pour oil over these troubled waters proved unconvincing.

In July 1934 a 72-year-old admiral, Okada Keisuke, replaced the even more venerable Viscount Admiral Saitō Makoto as Prime Minister of Japan. Saitō himself arranged the succession to signify his Cabinet's united distaste and alarm over the Japanese Army's unchecked activities on the continent. There was an obvious continuity between the two Cabinets: the War, Navy and Foreign Ministers were all retained and Saitō's Minister of Agriculture and Forestry was elevated to the portfolio of Home Affairs with all of its police and public order functions. Nevertheless, the new Cabinet, like its predecessor, felt obliged to support the *faits accomplis* of the Japanese Army in China as well as in Manchuria. Foreign Minister Hirota, indeed, pursued diplomatic initiatives which closely dovetailed into the efforts of the Army to consolidate its gains in the region. In March 1935 the Soviet Union finally sold its Chinese Eastern (Trans-Manchurian) Railway to 'Manchukuo' after two years of haggling with Hirota over the price. *Pace* Clausewitz, this was (aggressive) war by other means. It also struck a responsive chord in the Manchurian popular memory, for as recently as 1929 Marshal Chang Hsueh-liang had tried to wrest the C E R from its Russian railway guards, lost an ensuing campaign when the Soviet Union dispatched an expeditionary force into northern Manchuria, and been forced to abandon his pretensions in exchange for the withdrawal of the Soviet troops. Ever since the Japanese military conquest of the whole of Manchuria, however, Russian control over the C E R had become untenable. The sale of the C E R marked the end of an era.

Then in June 1935, following the murder of two pro-Japanese Chinese journalists, General Ho Ying-ch'in, Head of the Peking Military Command, yielded to grotesquely disproportionate demands pressed upon him by the Commander of the Japanese North China Garrison in Tientsin, Lieutenant-General Umezu Yoshijirō, and endorsed the secret Ho–Umezu Agreement promising to evacuate Kuomintang troops and abandon all political activity in the province of Hopei. The Japanese Government in Tokyo was unaware until late in the day how far Umezu had exceeded his authority, but there was considerable satisfaction at the outcome once the crisis had passed. By degrees, the Chinese were learning the Japanese definition of 'cooperation'.

At almost the same time, another trifling incident took place in Chahar during which four Japanese soldiers were held at gunpoint for four or five hours by Chinese troops. Former War Minister General Minami Jirō, now Commander of the Kwantung Army, ordered the head of his Special Services Agency, Colonel Doihara Kenji, to negotiate a settlement of the incident that would satisfy the honour of Japan. Late in June 1935 the outcome, known as the Ching–Doihara Agreement, spoke volumes concerning the nature of the pressures which the Japanese were ready to impose. Unable to appease the Japanese by a token punishment of the Chinese officers responsible, General Ching Teh-ch'un, the Chinese Army commander in Chahar, unwillingly evacuated his military forces from the province, agreed that all political activity by the Kuomintang within the province should cease forthwith, prohibited further Chinese immigration into northern Chahar, and banned all anti-Japanese activities within the province.

Within two months of the Ho–Umezu and Ching–Doihara Agreements, Prince Teh, a Mongolian chieftain who had striven for some time to carve out an autonomous government north of the Great Wall, overcame his apparent reluctance to accept Japanese assistance. General Minami promised him money and lent him two battalions of cavalry to help the Prince extend his control from Suiyuan province into northern Chahar.

On 5 August 1935 Foreign Minister Hirota advanced several general guidelines which he believed should govern Japan's relations with her continental neighbours. He lost no opportunity to repeat these 'Three Principles' in the months that followed: first, the Kuomintang must suppress all anti-Japanese pronouncements and activities, end China's subservience to European and American interests, and take positive steps towards friendship and cooperation with Japan; second, China must accept Japan's special relationship with Manchukuo, cooperate with Manchukuo in economic and cultural relations, and, ultimately, grant formal diplomatic recognition to the independence of Manchukuo; third, China must collaborate with Japan in Chahar and adjacent territories to obliterate communist influence in areas bordering Outer Mongolia. At the time, Japanese military factions and business circles were obsessed by the fear that Communism might spread from Russia to China. There was some foundation for these fears, given the close connection between the Chinese communist movement and the spread of 'anti-Japanism' across the length and breadth of China.

A Five Ministers' Conference of the Japanese inner Cabinet (chaired by Prime Minister Okada and attended by his War, Navy, Finance, Foreign and Home Affairs Ministers) reviewed the situation and reached the conclusion that Japan should give strong support to other autonomy movements in North China, thus progressively undermining the Kuomintang's efforts to unify the whole country. Three days later the midwives of the Kwantung Army attended to the birth of the East Hopei Anti-Communist Autonomy Council within the demilitarized districts defined by the Tangku Truce of 1933. In early December the Kuomintang responded by establishing the Hopei–Chahar Political Council, headed by General Sung Che-yuan, who undertook the thankless task of attempting to effect a reconciliation. Contrary to the expectations of the Kwantung Army, Sung successfully steered a middle course between this Scylla and Charybdis.

In January 1936 the Commander of Japan's North China Garrison Army was instructed by his military superiors in Tokyo on how to deal with the situation in his area. A summary of those instructions, cabled by Foreign Minister Hirota to Ariyoshi Akira, Japan's first fully-fledged Ambassador to China in the modern era, accurately shows how naked self-interest tends to masquerade in altruistic clothes in such circumstances:

The principal objects to be borne in mind in dealing with the North China area are to assist the Chinese people in realizing a self-government in North China by themselves, and thus to let the people enjoy their lives and jobs peacefully; also to let them adjust their relations with Japan and Manchukuo, and thus promote the mutual welfare of these three nations . . .

Territorially speaking, the five provinces of North China will be made the object of that self-government, but we must be careful not to be too eager to embrace the entire area all at once. On the contrary, we should first aim at a gradual realization of self-government in Hopei and Chahar as well as in the Peking and Tientsin conurbations and we should aim at inducing the remaining three provinces to join with the other two voluntarily. Our advice and guidance to the Hopei–Chahar Political Council should be given through Sung Che-yuan for the time being, and self-government movements by the people should be encouraged in so far as they remain fair and just, and should make use of them in gradually realizing an actual self-government among the people of those two provinces, thus laying firmly the foundation of eventual self-government for all five provinces in North China . . .

With regard to the extent of that self-government, it would, of course, be better to let the people have as much liberty as possible, but for the present, we should aim at and endeavour for the realization of such a state as will leave no room for the Nanking Government [of Chiang Kai-shek] to carry out anti-Japanese and anti-Manchukuo policies, and by leaving the rest for gradual achievement in future, we should avoid too hasty a desire for an acquisition of independent powers.

With regard to the guidance to be given by us, we should endeavour principally to guide in the economic field, especially in finance, and also in military affairs, along with the education and guidance of the general populace; and in doing so, we should confine our guidance to the general line, leaving, as much as possible, the details to the task and responsibility of the Chinese people.*

The document goes on to explain these policies at greater length and to establish the importance of seeking cooperation from the Kwantung Army and close contact with Japanese military attachés, diplomats and naval officials stationed in China. Other messages, much more aggressive in expression, were to follow in the months ahead. More importantly, internecine political struggles and civil/military conflict once again rocked Japan. In North China, however, peace of a kind was maintained, uneasily, until July 1937.

Although it was not immediately apparent, a turning-point had been reached several months earlier in December 1936. The Young Marshal Chang Hsueh-liang, driven into a bitter exile from Manchuria, had found Chiang Kai-shek utterly unwilling to embark upon major operations designed to expel the Japanese from Manchuria and North China. On the contrary, Chiang attempted to pit the Young Marshal against the communist forces that had regrouped in Shensi. It was widely believed that Chiang confidently expected both sides to be badly mauled. In any event, the Young Marshal was appointed commander of the 'North-western Bandit-Suppression Forces'. His Manchurians, numbering 130,000 troops assisted by 40,000 local militia, were deployed across the central and southern areas of Shensi and Kansu provinces, showed themselves half-hearted against the communists, who operated from the more northerly districts. The campaign began well enough but soon began to run out of steam. The morale of Chang Hsueh-liang's forces drained away: two of his best divisions defected to the communists, weary of the

---

* Pritchard and Zaide, op. cit., 2, pp. 2721–6 [PX 215]. The text given here slightly rephrases the English translation admitted at the Tokyo Trial.

Chinese civil war, desiring only to push the Japanese out of Manchuria. The campaign ground slowly to a halt. By degrees, in the summer and autumn of 1936, the two sides found they had reached a common understanding and mutual respect. In June 1936 Chang met with an exceptionally astute young communist leader named Chou En-lai, one of Mao Tse-tung's most trusted lieutenants. It seemed pointless to fight one another: the time had come for all Chinese guns to turn against their common enemy. Chang did everything within his power to persuade Chiang Kai-shek to move in the same direction.

Chang Hsueh-liang made two fruitless journeys to Nanking simply to press his case. At the end of November, he wrote eloquently to Chairman Chiang:

For the period of nearly half a year, I have continuously laid before Your Excellency my principle and program of struggle against Japanese imperialism for national salvation . . . Now the war against Japanese imperialism is beginning . . . I have therefore waited patiently for Your Excellency's order of mobilization. To my greatest disappointment, I have so far received no such order at all . . . Pressed by the zealous sentiments of my troops and urged on by my personal convictions, I ventured to present my recent appeals, but Your Excellency instructed me to wait for an opportunity . . . In order to control our troops, we should keep our promise to them that whenever the chance comes they should be allowed to carry out their desire of fighting against the enemy. Otherwise, they will regard not only myself but also Your Excellency as impostors, and will no longer obey us. Now is exactly the right time. Please give us the order to mobilize . . .*

It was all in vain. Chiang was unmoved by the Young Marshal's pleas and warnings.

The tension came to a head in December 1936. Chiang flew to inspect the Manchurian troops at the Young Marshal's headquarters in Sian, the provincial capital of Shensi, accompanied by a large entourage and eighty bomber aircraft to see why no progress was being made in the 'bandit-suppression' campaign and to read the riot act.

From Chairman Chiang's point of view, the quality of the troops and their record as fighting men were both rather poor, and their employment had been a problem. Blockading is a tedious duty: the soldiers and officers felt themselves in a strange land; they desired only to be led back to their homes. So disgruntled were they that they fell easy victims to propaganda by the communists, whom they were supposed to be cutting off from all communications with the outside world. Rumour of this had reached

---

* Text released at Sian on 2 January 1937 following collapse of the mutiny: cited in T. A. Bisson, *Japan in China*, Macmillan, London, 1938, p. 162.

Chiang, but he did not realize how deeply the rot went. It is very strange that he should have ventured among such disaffected troops with no proper bodyguard. Not for the first or last time in his career, the secret police and Intelligence services, who were a major factor in his Government, failed him. He visited Chang Hsueh-liang twice at his headquarters in Sian, and on his second visit, on the first night, he was surprised while in a bungalow by a rising of the Manchurian officers. He managed to escape in the darkness and crawl up the garden, but he had hurt his back in getting away, and after a few hours he was discovered.

The Young Marshal had learned of the appointment of another general to take direct charge of the operations, and it was this which finally led him to break with Chiang, side with the communists and unexpectedly place Chairman Chiang and his entire entourage under arrest. Chang Hsueh-liang sent telegrams to Nanking. A period of suspense followed news of the kidnapping. The mutineers tried to negotiate Chiang's release in return for an undertaking that he would declare war on Japan. Chiang refused absolutely to enter into negotiations with them, and tried, though power was all on their side and he was isolated and defenceless, to over-awe them and compel them by superior strength of will to set him free. Chang Hsueh-liang appeared quite prepared to kill Chiang in the event of any attempt by the Kuomintang to mount an expedition to rescue their national leader. Afterwards it emerged that Chiang's life was spared mainly through the intercession of Chou En-lai, a man of great patience, tact and persuasion. Chiang, too, impressed his captor, who eventually wilted under Chiang's rebukes, and who, in consequence, became his protector against some of the more extreme officers, who would have shot him on the spot. Whatever may have been felt later about Chiang, his bearing among his captors compels admiration.

In the outer world, the Government in Nanking was extremely bewildered. There were signs of a break-up, and some of the key personalities began to prepare for a struggle for the post which Chiang seemed to be about to vacate. In Tokyo, too, the Government had no plans for such an unexpected contingency. Britain and America likewise waited, consulting their runes.

The people with resolution were on the one side Chiang's dynamic and opinionated wife and his brother-in-law, T. V. Soong: and on the other side the leaders of the communists, who were only a few miles away. After Chiang's captors had drawn a blank in their efforts at compelling him to negotiate, they sent for Chou En-lai and the political officers of the communists. It has never been cleared up whether the communists had known beforehand of the plot. One view is that, immediately after the kidnapping, Moscow had taken a hand in the direction of events. There was radio communication between them and Yenan, the capital of the communists in Shensi province; and the policy of Moscow, which was itself under menace from Japan, had been to preserve, at whatever sacrifice this might be to ideological sense, Chiang Kai-shek alive as the most useful and strongest ally against Japan. The kidnapping threatened this policy, and the interests of the USSR. Simultaneously, Madame Chiang and her brother flew to Sian. By acting whilst others talked, they had intervened to prevent the Nanking Government from using its planes to bomb the mutineers. Such an action might have seemed justified, but it would probably have resulted in Chiang's immediate execution. His death might have suited the ambitions of some of the higher officers of the Nanking régime.

There were confused and secret deliberations at Sian. In the end the communists returned home, apparently convinced that Chiang would call off another large-scale offensive against their position in Shensi, which had been planned for the immediate future: and they seem to have been given some assurance that he would in future carry on a more lively defence against the Japanese. The communists were to be autonomous in the areas, not very extensive, which they actively held, and an attempt was to be made at associating a few communist dignitaries in the central Government of the Kuomintang. Chiang flew back to Nanking on Christmas Day, a free man, and accompanying him was Chang Hsueh-liang, who said that he repented of his mutiny and desired to make restitution. Certainly Chang seemed to have neglected to obtain reliable guarantees of his treatment, for on arrival at Nanking he was promptly tried and imprisoned for a ten-year term. But this was nothing more than a gesture to demonstrate the authority of the National Government, and the Young Marshal was granted a free pardon almost immediately afterwards.

It took several months before the significance of these confusing events could be understood, months during which the central political authorities met to consider the situation. The Chinese communists put forward a programme calling for an end to the civil war; the introduction of freedom of speech, assembly, organization, etc., and the release of all political prisoners; the convening of a national congress representing all parties, factions, military groups and organizations, to serve as a focal point for national talents in the interests of national salvation; the initiation of preparations for a war of national resistance against Japan, and amelioration of the living conditions of the Chinese people as a whole. In exchange for these the communists declared that they would abandon their attempts to overthrow the Kuomintang by force of arms; transform their so-called 'Soviet Government of China' and 'Red Army' into a loyal 'Government of the Special Region of the Republic of China' and a 'National Revolutionary Army' subject to direct control by the Chinese central authorities; accept a democratic system of universal suffrage within the 'Special Region'; end the expropriation of landlords, and commit the communist movement to the service of the anti-Japanese united front.

The Government and the Kuomintang's political leadership, however, threw out the proposals put to them by Chang Hsueh-liang and the communists. Communists and their collaborators were declared to be anathema to the state. There could be no compromise with those who spread communist subversion, nor with any group whose activities undermined national unity. The Sian rebels had engaged in treasonable sedition; their resort to force nullified the terms which Chiang Kai-shek had been obliged to accept during his captivity. The Young Marshal, indeed, seemed to have struck the death knell of the 'common front' strategy. One foreign observer, listening perhaps too much to the opinions of well-connected Chinese politicians and bureaucrats, wrote at the time that the Young Marshal's 'foolhardy action . . . called down upon him the wrath of the vast majority of the Chinese people and robbed him of what little prestige he still possessed'.* Following his pardon, Chang retired to Fenghua in Chekiang province south-east of Nanking: far from Chang's Manchurian homeland but near to where Chiang Kai-shek was recovering from his injuries at his home outside Ningpo. The Young Marshal's disaffected troops were transferred to the provinces of Honan, Anhwei and Kiangsu, where they were integrated into the forces of the Central Government but retained their own officers. There they were kept out of trouble, and were well positioned to move forward against any attempt by the hated Japanese to seize control of Shantung or Shanghai.

The Sian Incident had been dramatic: and was also fateful. It might as easily have ended in an opposite way. Chiang Kai-shek might have been executed by the communists or his captors: the history of Sino-Japanese relations would in that case certainly have developed in a different way. It throws light on the intelligent and subtle mind of the communists, whose roughness of manner had hidden their talent for diplomacy. They must have calculated that Chiang alone could lead China into war: and they were content to use him, and the huge and growing armies of the Kuomintang, for this purpose. Ostensibly Chiang agreed to this; he accepted

---

* F 2835/829/10, Record of Leading Personalities in China, by B. E. F. Gage on behalf of Sir Hughe Knatchbull-Hugessen, 7 April 1937, FO 371/20999, British Public Record Office, Kew.

THE RESURGENCE OF MILITANT CHINESE COMMUNISM
Field Armies and Areas of Operations
1931—49

U S S R

MONGOLIA

HEILUNGKIANG

Harbin

④

Changchun

KIRIN

Mukden

LIAONING

KOREA

INNER MONGOLIA

HOPEI

Peking

Tientsin

⑤

Yinchuan

SHANSI
Taiyuan

Tsinan
SHANTUNG

NINGHSIA

Hsining

Lanchow

CHINGHAI

Chengchou

Sian
SHENSI

HONAN

KIANGSI
Nanking

①

SZECHWAN

Chengtu

HUPEI

②

Hofei

Wuhan

ANHWEI

Shanghai

Hangchow

③

CHEKIANG

Yangtze Kiang

Nanchang

Changsha

HUNAN

KIANGSI

Foochow

KWEICHOW

②

Kweiyang

④

FUKIEN

Kunming

Kiang

KWEICHOW

KWANGTUNG

YUNNAN

Nanning

Canton

Communist base areas during the
China Incident

② Areas of operation during the
Civil War

BURMA

VIETNAM

Haikou

═ ═ ═ 1   1st Field Army movement

SIAM
(THAILAND)

(INDO-CHINA)

LAOS

▬▬▬ 2   2nd Field Army movement

▬▪▪▬ 3   3rd Field Army movement

══ 4   4rd Field Army movement

that it was allegedly the national decision to respond to Japanese aggression by making war. One of the great curiosities of the next four decades was the fact that Chou En-lai, in no small measure the saviour of Chiang Kai-shek's life, was to devote the remainder of his own life and statesmanship to the extermination of Chiang's régime and reputation.

In reality Chiang fought still to temporize, to procrastinate, to trip up the persons who were relentlessly pressing him forward, to complicate the issues, to drag new considerations to the front. In any case time was needed to make dispositions for war. He was the Reluctant Dragon – dragon because all Chinese emperors (and Chiang was virtually an emperor) are thought of as dragons – reluctant because he was warned by his sure political instinct that his position – and much else besides – would not survive the war.

But in July 1937 the Japanese attacked, and Chiang had to accept their challenge. The assessment which he made, and which forced his hand, was probably as follows.

The students, and the university professors, so vastly influential in the China of that day, so exaggeratedly more important than their numbers or physical power made credible, were, with few exceptions, for resisting. They compelled the country as a whole to take a stiff line, beyond what it would otherwise have thought possible. Also, for an end to patience – though it was hard to speak of a solid voice of such a disparate class, and one not used to having its views considered – were the army officers as a whole, underneath the top commanders. They were variously derived: many were corrupt; but the national spirit was apparent, in varying degrees, in most of them. The same was less true, as Chiang knew well, of some of the senior commanders, who were exposed to the blandishments of the Japanese, whose attitude changed from time to time according to the inducements offered to them, and who did not constitute an inspiring leadership. However, in 1937, most were willing to fight. The landed gentry, while not exactly enthusiasts for resistance, reflected the mood of China: their patience was strained beyond endurance.

Of the true middle class – the native bankers and money-lenders, the petty manufacturers, the craftsmen, the minor civil servants – the disposition was fairly solidly nationalist, and ready to oppose Japan. Some sections were less forward than others; there was always the contradiction between defence of their commercial or other advantage, and the gratification of feeling: none of them could have felt that war would bring them benefits. But they also felt, obscurely perhaps, that they were instruments in a conflict, and it was not in their power to stand aside. They may have deplored their fate, but most of them, while privately desiring to be left in peace, were ready to follow the national path. The merchant guilds, which played a considerable part in the organization of economic life, had been very prominent in the organization of the resistance in Shanghai in 1931. It was indicative of the part which national sentiment was to play in the organization of the people in the Chinese war effort.

More individualist and more cynical was the attitude of the great bankers and financial magnates of the Treaty Ports. Some of them, indeed, were with the war party: many had greater political regard for the security of their possessions.

The masses of people – the poor peasantry, the unskilled workers of the towns – the people who were to bear the main burden of the war in hardship and toll of life – were not consulted, and their opinions would have been taken as being of little weight. But among these, so far as they were informed, the temper was apt to be nationalist, and strongly nationalist. In the Asia of the past generation, it was always remarkable how news circulated, and how accurate the reports tended to be which circulated in the back streets and urban slums. The temper of the vast anonymous mass could not be overlooked.

CHAPTER 8
Japan: Internal Revolutions and Foreign Policy

THESE years, 1931–6, had been, for Japan also, a period of relentless pressure towards a formal war with China, which had come to be regarded as inevitable. Japan's descent into Avernus, during the six brief years since the Manchurian Incident, and the corruption of its political system were rapid. Most of what happened prepared Japan for the part it was later to play. In this time Japan took, with great speed, a series of plunges which ensured that, when the Pacific War came, it was fought in a spirit that surprised the world by its barbarity.

Historians often despair at the fact that close examination of the web of historical events reveals it to be both intricate and seamless. Convention and the need for coherence force us to impose conceptual frameworks which assist us, imperfectly, in our efforts to describe the processes and events that form part of the history we seek to define. It is as well to recognize, however, that some of our conventional ideas concerning the Manchurian Incident, the China Incident and the Pacific War are hopelessly inadequate. As Ienaga Saburō, a distinguished and controversial Japanese who has had a profound effect upon Japanese historiography concerning 'Japan's Last War', writes:

The six years of intermittent military action and political intrigue after the Manchurian Incident suggest that 1937 marked a new phase of a war already well underway. It is impossible to delineate the major 'incidents' as separate crises; in fact, it is probably more accurate to treat events from 1931 on as a single conflict.*

A rapid deterioration set in among most of the national institutions. It had the obvious effect of easing the path to war, and it harmed the spirit of the country profoundly. When there was a lull in the development of external events, the crisis deepened internally. The process can be traced from point to point. In Manchuria, in 1931, the decision to act had been made by the Japanese Army. It dragged the civilian Government in the wake of its *fait accompli*. The precedent was alarming, and was regularly

---

* Ienaga Saburō, *Japan's Last War: World War II and the Japanese, 1931–1945*, Blackwell, Oxford, 1979, p. 70.

acted upon by the Army in the years which followed, and accepted by the nation. No successful revolution took place, and no change of institutions was necessary: the civil service continued to operate, and remained comparatively unpurged. But in the Government of the day, with a constitution all too precise, it was enough that one of the controlling forces should shift the balance of power in the administration for the whole nature of government to change. The civil authority from time to time ceased to intervene in matters which were properly its concern, and left these to the Army. It was a species of anarchy.

This uneasiness, vague but pervasive, increased the danger of war. Many Japanese, fearful that the military, which they felt was already beyond control, might now move towards the acceptance of all kinds of radicalism in Japanese internal affairs, thought that its giddy mind would best be occupied by foreign quarrels. Many voices were raised in open opposition to this trend, but gradually, by the Kwantung Army's successive *faits accomplis*, the critics were overborne.

Following hard on the success of the Kwantung Army in establishing its ascendancy throughout Manchuria in the years 1931–4, as we have seen, there was but a short step to its covert involvement in the political affairs of the buffer zone comprising Hopei, Chahar and even North China itself. In the end, this involvement became increasingly open, and Japan found itself with no option but to continue with its expansion in China, by peaceful or other means, despite the obvious inconsistencies in pursuing an aggressive foreign policy while complaining of Japan's isolation in foreign affairs. At the same time, having announced its withdrawal from the League of Nations, Japan now felt itself even more vulnerable than before to the constant and predictable winds of international disapproval for her actions and policies.

In these years there also took place a distinct shift in the religious life of the country. Attention was less on the compassionate, often intellectually subtle, religion of Buddhism; more emphasis was given to the religion which had co-existed with Buddhism for many centuries – Shintō, superficially a rather simple form of animism and worship of the symbols of state. Some of its adherents were inclined to take its cosmogony literally. Others found it more satisfactory as an extended metaphor. A Japanese scholar has noted that 'The myth is essentially beyond science.'* Many western observers, who knew next to nothing about Shintōism, believed that it had no intellectual corpus to it. It certainly is true that it was

---

* Anzu Motohiko, quoted in Jean Herbert, *Shintō: At the Fountain-Head of Japan*, Allen & Unwin, London, 1967, p. 230.

neither readily perceptible nor translatable into Aristotelian terms. Like the Japanese language itself, it was highly symbolic and ambiguous, even vague. It must not be thought of as having no substance, however, for its efficacy can be seen from its social impact, from its political achievements. That these were purposeful, however, is doubtful, nor was it by accident that the circumspect authors of the Meiji Constitution had regarded Shintōism as an unsatisfactory organizing principle for modern Japan but borrowed some of its underlying assumptions.

In some ways it became ill-advised for a Japanese to diverge by however little from the norm in behaviour, sentiment or thought. Japan had never been kind to the pronounced individual and Japanese society had eyed any departure from conformity with uneasiness. (Only those cases where experimentalism had been backed up by a reputation of extreme religiosity were exempted.) The increasing tension in political life made the Japanese dislike eccentricity even more severely. In the years preceding the end of the Japanese military venture, there was an increasing anarchy in Japanese literature and in all departments of creative life. Older generations of Japanese deplored the enthusiasm with which the youth of the country embraced alien imports such as baseball, football, golf, the cinema, jazz and ballroom dancing, all of which seemed to break down traditional Japanese cultural values. These, however, were fads, group obsessions, and they reflected a widespread sense of material well-being. Of true individualism, of the man with the social courage to stand up and denounce what society was doing, or the innovator who worked under the pressure of his *daimon* and ignored the praise or censure of the world, there was strikingly too much evidence.

All of this reinforced the desire of the Japanese to promote the cherished plurality of Japanese society, *Musubi* – a dynamic, vitalizing process in which all things bind themselves together. Strangeness and conflict were no enemies here: they could be utilized, not merely tolerated, by finding every manifestation a proper place and limited function, harmoniously helping to create and define the larger purposes of the whole community and nation. All of this is, of course, an extended image, a descriptive representation of birth and growth itself. Above all it depends upon constructs of compartmentalization, boundaries, and life-giving power. This concept, one of the basic concepts of Shintōism, had a strong grip on the people of Japan.

It is scarcely surprising, therefore, that people from all walks of life wanted the sublime reassurance that came from submitting themselves to what they perceived was a universal community of place and purpose under a truly all-encompassing organizing principle, the sacred Imperial

Will, made manifest in the *Kokutai* to which we have already alluded. This process, although it had formed the basis of the consolidation of political authority following the Meiji Restoration, itself involved a suspension of critical faculties, a febrile casuistry which, during periods of internal crisis, interfered with political judgement and made any exercise of political leadership objectively irrational. Japan had been saved from the dictation of a ruthless and flamboyant figure only because no such figure had the ability to seize the Government. The tradition of Japan was against individual leadership. Even in times of great crisis it required that revolutionaries should act in committees. But the spectacle of the administration of a great empire ceasing altogether for a few days, and great offices of state being hawked round by captains and majors, caused all lookers-on to marvel and to shudder.

The national temper began to be touched, but only touched, by hysteria. Thought control, imposed by the Government, meant the virtual interruption of all forms of rational thinking. An official version of Japanese history, drawing on fairy stories and full of absurdity, was made to prevail: it became dangerous to publish more serious matter. Dr Minobe Tatsukichi, the much respected Japanese professor, had been hounded from his job in 1935 because radical circles found it unforgivable that he had stated in a book on political science that the Japanese Emperor was an organ of the constitution. The Emperor was too sacred to be defined. The deification of the Emperor, which had been resurrected from the Japanese past, grew now to absurd proportions, and was especially ironical because it was known to be distasteful to the Emperor himself.

Nevertheless, consider these manifestations of the country's malaise within some sense of proportion. Whatever the tendency of certain factions and special interest groups to pursue courses of action which were fundamentally irrational, and whatever the temptations of hindsight to perceive the national life itself as ineluctably hysterical in the years which we know ended in the catastrophic disintegration of the Japanese Empire, the Land of the Rising Sun was not without subjectively reassuring features that eased the political and moral transitions through which the country passed. As the distinguished Israeli historian Ben Ami Shillony, an acknowledged authority on the development of Japanese extremism and political terrorism, has observed:

Throughout the decade Japan remained a land of law and order, despite the eruption of occasional 'incidents'. It was governed by its constitutional institutions: the Emperor, the Cabinet, the civilian bureaucracy and the military high command. There were constant frictions among them and periodic outbursts from below, but the system did not break. *Gekokujō*, or the rule of the higher by the lower, was a popular phrase with writers, but it very rarely materialised in reality. The special blend of pragmatism and fanaticism, which had characterised Japan in former times, continued to characterise her in the 1930s.*

Indeed, one may go even further: the same qualities that led Japan into the Greater East Asia and Pacific Conflict were to sustain it through the years of travail that followed, and were to prove receptive to the adaptations imposed upon Japan during the Allied Occupation in the post-war period.

The number of terrorist incidents multiplied. Some were simply lunatic in conception and execution, such as the assassination of Prime Minister Hamaguchi Osachi by Sagoya Tomeo at Tokyo Central Railway Station in 1930. Sagoya was a member of the 'Blood Brotherhood', one of many right-wing jingoistic associations, clubs and societies that proliferated in Japan. It is ironic that these organizations were bitterly divided, for one idea shared by most of them was the notion that the entire Japanese people were an extended family. Elaborate schemes were concocted in attempts to establish common ground between them. These efforts generally collapsed, abandoned because of the paranoia and testiness of their respective leaders. This in turn left a legacy of failure, disappointment, recrimination and even fratricide.

A growing number of prominent political and military figures became involved. The so-called March Incident of 1931 was, in Professor Maruyama's pregnant phrase, 'born in the dark and buried in the dark'. It was the product of a conspiracy in which prominent members of the *Tōseiha* (of which more anon), notably Lieutenant-General Ninomiya Harushige, Vice-Chief of the Army General Staff, Major-General Koiso Kuniaki, the powerful Chief of the Military Affairs Bureau at the War Ministry, possibly Colonel Nagata Tetsuzan, Chief of the Army Affairs Section under Koiso, and certainly Major-General Tatekawa Yoshitsugu, Chief of the Intelligence Division, were all deeply involved. Tatekawa was the general whom we find stumbling drunkenly outside on the night of the Mukden Incident six months later. Individuals such as these – and many of the junior officers who called upon them to rise up in the name of national integrity – were genuinely talented and privileged. They were motivated not so much by further personal ambition as by alarm at the drift of national policy and discontent over the quality of Japan's civil administration.

They fell under the influence of disaffected officers who belonged to the *Sakura-kai*, the radical 'Cherry Blossom Society', a secret fraternity of

* Ben Ami Shillony, 'Myth and Reality in Japan of the 1930s', in *Modern Japan: Aspects of History, Literature and Society*, ed. W. G. Beasley, Allen & Unwin, London, 1975, p. 88.

fewer than one hundred junior officers, none over the rank of Lieutenant-Colonel, formed in September 1930 by the notorious Lieutenant-Colonel Hashimoto Kingorō, a gunnery officer, then serving as Head of the Russian Desk at the Army General Staff after his return from an overseas posting as Military Attaché in Turkey, determined to model his activities upon those of Kemal Atatürk. The *Sakura-kai* was created as a 'discussion group' for the furtherance of his brand of crypto-fascist radicalism, identified more broadly as the *Seigunha* or Army Purification Faction. The *Sakura-kai* was his own personal instrument: it had no rulebook or membership fees. His recruits were drawn from the War Ministry, the Army General Staff and from military training establishments and forces garrisoned within the vicinity of metropolitan Tokyo. Hashimoto's plan called for close collaboration with a similar secret society of Navy officers, the *Seiyō-kai* (Stars and Ocean Society). He also sought and won the support of that indefatigable propagandist, Professor Ōkawa Shūmei, whose acquaintance we have already made.* War Minister Ugaki Kazushige, too, was tainted by the affair, although his real attitude towards it, like that of Nagata, remains obscure.

At a restaurant in Tokyo, Dr Ōkawa concocted a plan for a mass public rally to be held outside the Imperial Diet building in protest against anti-labour legislation. Amid ugly scenes, the Diet would come under a mock attack. Troops would rush to the scene, seal off the building and restore 'order'. The Cabinet would be compelled to resign. War Minister Ugaki would be called upon to form a reform Cabinet, sweeping away the corrupt party political machines. Hashimoto expressed enthusiasm for this plan, provided Ōkawa obtained Ugaki's personal blessing. Later that night, Ōkawa reported that Ugaki was willing to take part. He asked Hashimoto to obtain a supply of practice grenades to add convincing sound-effects during the disturbances which were to lead to the military coup. Hashimoto encountered difficulty in obtaining these and approached Major-General Tatekawa, until recently his immediate superior, who gave Hashimoto a letter of introduction to the Commandant of the Army Infantry School which overcame all obstacles. He in turn handed the grenades over to Major-General Koiso, who took them away for safekeeping. When Dr Ōkawa was put on trial in 1934 on charges of sedition, he testified that 'Koiso, taking charge of everything, told me that since there would be the danger of being discovered if too many fussed about it, we should pretend to have suspended it on the surface, and that I should represent the civilians and that he would represent the Army.'

* See p. 657.

Ugaki, however, evidently had second thoughts, the ever-vigilant *Kenpeitai* stood by, and the March Incident was nipped in the bud.

Seven months later, just a few weeks after the Manchurian Incident began, Lieutenant-Colonel Hashimoto went a step further. He had begun to feel that if civilians were involved, leaks would inevitably occur that would frustrate any attempt to overthrow the existing order. Together with one of his friends, Captain Chō Isamu, and Major Nemoto Hiroshi, Head of the China Desk at the Army General Staff, Hashimoto plotted a *coup d'état* known to history as the October Incident. Ostensibly they acted to prevent the Government from restraining the Kwantung Army's rampage through Manchuria. Nevertheless, there is evidence that at the time Hashimoto had neither met nor established any liaison with Itagaki, Doihara, Ishiwara or the other Kwantung Army officers principally involved in the outbreak of the Manchurian Incident. In any event Hashimoto was conscious that there were good grounds for supposing that a harmony of views existed between them. Hashimoto's plans began to assume fantastically grandiose proportions. The number of individuals involved rapidly increased. The plotters made preparations for mobilization of the First and Third Infantry Regiments of the Imperial Guards Division. The headquarters of the Army General Staff and the War Ministry were to be surrounded. Senior officers were to be coerced into declaring martial law. Naval aircraft from Kasumigaura Naval Air Training Centre would launch bombing attacks against key targets. A coordinated assault would be mounted against the Prime Minister's official residence during a meeting of his Cabinet with the intention of murdering all those in attendance.

Although there are conflicting accounts about what happened next, it appears that War Minister Minami and Vice-Minister of War Sugiyama learned of the plot about a week before it was due to take place. They were unable to bring the insurgents to their senses. The two then turned to Lieutenant-General Araki Sadao, a former President of the Army Staff College whom the rebels admired as 'a man of unimpeachable character'. Hashimoto and his conspirators regarded Araki as a model soldier and wanted to install him as Prime Minister. Minami and Sugiyama now asked him to sort out the mess. Araki's response was somewhat ambiguous: he, too, was deeply enmeshed in factional politics within the Army (as we shall see), and Hashimoto's plans caused him no little embarrassment. Minami asked the *Kenpeitai* to step in before the incident could take place. This time, however, the potato was too hot to handle. The forces of law and order achieved what must have seemed to be the best outcome to which they could aspire under the prevailing circumstances.

Those at the heart of the dispute were placed in protective custody for a short time. They were not charged with the commission of any offence, nor were the careers of most of them blighted (although Hashimoto himself, promoted to full colonel in 1934, was relegated to the reserves and never rose higher in the next eleven years of peace and Total War). Inconceivable as it may seem, there was scarcely any serious criticism of the idealistic patriotic fervour which had impelled the rebels to resort to force. Fainthearts and realists alike were fatally compromised. In a footnote to this incident, Hashimoto, Chō and their *Seigunha*, having been inspired by General Araki's eloquence in the past, now began slowly to turn against him, regarding him as a charlatan. Over the course of the next two years, there would gradually emerge a new, loose coalition of interests, bound together only in its opposition to Araki's *Kōdōha* group. It would absorb the *Seigunha* and become known to its enemies as the *Tōseiha*, or Control Faction.

Meanwhile the politics of terror, born out of despair but nurtured by success, continued to enjoy a vogue among radical groups. In December 1931 the charismatic General Araki was promoted to War Minister in a shrewd manoeuvre to bring order to the Army. Araki succeeded in this and then went on to dominate the Cabinet.

Araki's popularity among many junior Army officers remained high, and they were anxious to do nothing that might spoil his hopes of bringing about the political reforms they wanted by peaceful means. Their counterparts in the Navy, however, had never felt inclined to regard Araki as a national saviour. Despite opposition from the young Army officers, the Navy group decided to go ahead with a plan to kill a considerable number of leading statesmen and business magnates.

Inoue Nisshō, a half-crazed Nichiren monk, who prior to taking up holy orders had spent years in Manchuria as a secret agent of the Japanese Army, led a clandestine civilian gang that called itself the *Ketsumeidan* (the 'Blood Brotherhood', or 'Dare-Devil Bunch') and provided its members with what passed as spiritual guidance. He allied his movement with that of the young naval officers and even lent the conspirators his temple for an arsenal. In February 1932, Araki, who had been kept informed of developments, prevailed upon the young Army officers to have nothing to do with the plan. He did nothing to denounce the plot but the Naval General Staff caught wind of it and appeared to have averted it by a timely transfer of certain naval officers to sea duty. Unfortunately, this failed to prevent others from attempting to carry out the plan. Nineteen thirty-two became known as 'The Year of Assassinations'.

The 'Blood Brotherhood' Incident of early February 1932 was a lineal descendant of Sagoya's actions two years before. Inoue decided to act independently of both services. He selected a hit-list of twenty victims. His followers simply drew lots, a different assassin for each target. The first to be slain was Inoue Junnosuke (no relation to the turbulent priest), a former Finance Minister known to be strongly opposed to the Manchurian Incident. His death was followed by the murder of Baron Dan Takuma, Managing Director of the Mitsui business empire. Following police investigations, Inoue Nisshō and the other main culprits in the 'Blood Brotherhood' gang were soon arrested. After a trial they were convicted and Inoue himself was sentenced to life imprisonment; he was subsequently freed in 1940 as part of a general amnesty and later resumed an active political life with the help of his old disciples after the withdrawal of the Allied Occupation in 1952.

By tradition, Japanese Cabinets governed as long as they retained the confidence of their two armed services Ministers. The resignation of an unhappy War Minister or his Navy counterpart could force the downfall of a Cabinet. Civilian Ministers, however, could do the same. The most telling case was that of an ambitious Minister for Home Affairs, Adachi Kenzō, who in December 1931 compelled the Wakatsuki Cabinet to resign by refusing either to attend the Cabinet or to resign his office. Adachi had wanted to promote a Government of all the talents, modelled perhaps on Ramsay MacDonald's National Government in Britain and led, he evidently hoped, by himself. His own ambitions foundered, but his actions led directly to the first minority Government ever to be formed in Japan since Prince Saionji's introduction of party politics into National Government shortly after the turn of the century.

The new Prime Minister was Inukai Tsuyoshi, 75-year-old leader of the opposition *Seiyūkai*, who rejected calls for the formation of a Cabinet of National Unity in which both parties might participate. Inukai did not lack courage, and he took to heart the Emperor's injunction to resist the military's interference in Japan's domestic and international affairs. Five months later, he was dead, assassinated by another cabal of radical officers who carried out the 15 May Incident.

The terrorists had struck again, after a brief pause, mounting their unsuccessful *coup d'état* on 15 May 1932. This time it was the turn of the junior naval officers, who joined forces with an even more feckless band of radical Army cadets that had fallen under the influence of civilian ultranationalists including Dr Ōkawa and Tachibana Kosaburō. The naval officers and the Army cadets kept a Sunday rendezvous at the Yasukuni shrine, embarked in a pair of taxis to the official residence of Prime

Minister Inukai Tsuyoshi, and simply walked in unchallenged. The operation was bungled, the intruders lost their way, but they finally found and murdered the 77-year-old Premier. Leaving the building, the terrorists killed two guards. They made their way to the *Kenpeitai* Headquarters and gave themselves up. In the confusion, the remainder of the Cabinet had escaped harm. Meanwhile, a second squad of naval officers threw grenades at the house of Count Makino, the Lord Keeper of the Privy Seal. Makino himself may have been warned of the attack by Ōkawa, who regarded the old man with affection and even had hopes that Makino could be prevailed upon to be Prime Minister after the revolution. In any event, this attack caused no fatalities. A third group lobbed bombs at the Metropolitan Police Headquarters, again to little effect. Tachibana and his agrarian reformists carried out an elaborate attempt to black out Tokyo's electric power supply system but their bombs failed to wreck their targets. Finally, one of the Army's leading young radicals was shot and wounded by one of Tachibana's supporters for having been instrumental in withdrawing support for the plot six months before: it was a breathtakingly ill-conceived revenge attack which further cemented relations between the Army Young Officer movement and the Army top brass at the expense of future collaboration between the extremist factions of the two armed services. Once again, the leaders identified by the authorities were handled with kid gloves and respect for their lofty motives. The murderers of Premier Inukai declared at their trial that their motive had been to protest against the Japanese ratification of the London naval agreement which the Japanese Government had incurred much displeasure by accepting. It was to be the last constructive agreement for peace that a Japanese Government was to be allowed by public opinion to make. War Minister Araki issued a public statement proclaiming:

We cannot restrain our tears when we consider the mentality expressed in the actions of these pure and naïve young men. They are not actions for fame, or personal gain, nor are they traitorous. They were performed in the sincere belief that they were for the benefit of Imperial Japan. Therefore, in dealing with this Incident, it will not do to dispose of it in a routine manner according to short-sighted conceptions.*

Well may we marvel at his words. With the passing of time, however, opinion within the Young Officer movement was gradually hardening in its appreciation that Araki was too moderate for their taste, and began to think in terms of even more independent action.

* Maruyama Masao, *Thought and Behaviour in Modern Japanese Politics*, Oxford University Press, London, 1963, p. 67.

The culprits showed no remorse for their actions. They had every reason to believe that the reactions of their superiors to the March and October Incidents of 1931 had indicated that direct action was a not unwelcome response to civil corruption and indolence. The cynical opportunism of senior officers was an important element in creating a climate in which mass terrorism by young officers could flourish. The mechanism was a well-established Japanese tradition, one to which we have already referred in passing, known as *Gekokujō*, that phenomenon involving the subordination of senior officers by junior officers – the tail wagging the dog. It is not, perhaps, the frequency of its occurrence which is important. What is more significant is the fact that it led to very widespread displacements of authority and political judgement when it did occur. The same process had manifested itself in the development of the Manchurian Incident.

Following the 15 May Incident, those apprehended by the authorities were arraigned on a variety of charges including murder and sedition. The proceedings were held in public and received unprecedented publicity. Although Japan was by no means given to civil liberty and to the unfettered freedom of the press, on this occasion no attempt was made to impose either effective state censorship or any discernible self-restraint by the news media.

The rebels took full advantage of the occasion to proclaim the righteousness of their cause. Their patriotic motives elicited popular sympathy. The country was in a political ferment. None of those found guilty were executed. The penal sentences imposed by the courts were, under the circumstances, exceptionally mild. The leader of the Army Cadet group, Gotō Terunori, together with his ten military co-defendants, was court-martialled. They each received four-year prison terms. They were freed on parole within the year and were pardoned soon afterwards. Koga Kiyoshi and Mikami Taku, the two principal ringleaders of the naval faction, were sentenced by a naval court martial to fifteen years' imprisonment. Their followers received sentences of thirteen, ten, two and one year's imprisonment respectively. Pardons were granted to all of them by 1940. The civilians involved in the Incident were treated more severely by the civil courts. Tachibana Kōsaburō was singled out and sentenced to a term of life imprisonment. In Hugh Byas's evocative phrase, the 15 May Incident had been carried out by 'adolescents straying in a pink mist'. That mist was no more remarkable than the corrosive fog which enveloped the due processes of law and order.

In the following year, there was another hare-brained plot, known as the *Shinpei-tai Jiken*, or 'Heaven-Sent Troops' Incident. It was concocted by the Patriotic Labour Party and the Great Japan Production Party, both right-wing labour organizations which had links with the russo-phobic Amur River Society. This plot had no direct links with the Young Officer movement, but among the ringleaders were an Army Lieutenant-Colonel and a Navy Commander by the name of Yamaguchi Saburō. The idea was that on the morning of 7 July 1933, Yamaguchi, a naval pilot, would take off in his aircraft, bomb the Cabinet at the official residence of the Prime Minister, blow up the residence of the Lord Privy Seal, Count Makino, and then attack the Headquarters of the Metropolitan Police. He would then land in front of the Imperial Palace. At that point a mob of 3,600 men, having converged seemingly out of nowhere, would assault the Metropolitan Police Headquarters. A handpicked group of men would then rush away to attack the Prime Minister's residence and assassinate any Cabinet Minister who might have survived the initial air attack. Other units would attack the homes of the presidents of the two main parliamentary parties, the residence of the Lord Privy Seal, the Japan Industrial Club (where it was hoped to kill a few *zaibatsu*), the head-quarters of the left-wing Social Masses Party and a list of other hated targets. Still more units would smash their way into certain armouries to seize weapons and ammunition. The focus of the rebels would then shift to the Headquarters of the Industrial Bank of Japan where they planned to barricade themselves for a bloody last-ditch stand against the entire might of the Metropolitan Police. Evidently there was some thought that they might spark off a wider insurrection leading to Emperor Hirohito's replacement by his brother Prince Chichibu and the establishment of a new Government under Prince Higashikuni. There is not a lot that one can say about this plan except that the police arrested a number of the conspirators in time to prevent the Incident from occurring. Neverthe-less, there is some significance in the fact that the plot would have involved the assassination of War Minister Araki as well as his other Cabinet colleagues, and this lends some credence to suggestions that his opponents were also aware of the plan, hoped to use it as a pretext to seize power, and may even have intended to provide the conspirators with arms.

After the murder of Inukai in 1932, no other political party leader was to become Prime Minister until the defeat of Japan. It was not immediately apparent, but the mould of Japanese party government had been shattered – and the fault lay not so much with the terrorists (although they were a proximate cause) but mainly with the parties themselves, together with the local regional political machines upon whom they relied for support.

It is notable that neither of the two mainstream political parties sought mass political support from the general public as a means of bolstering its claim to authority over its opponents. The system was corrupt, and looked it. Indeed, the political parties never truly reflected the aspirations and concerns of the Japanese public at large. The parties served to legitimize the views of élites more interested in power and patronage than in democratic values.

Paradoxically, the political parties were intended to provide a vehicle for national opinion. Constitutionally, the elected House of Representatives in the Imperial Diet was not designed to be a powerful branch of government. The Meiji oligarchs had confined its purpose to the expression of popular sentiment. It was not an instrument for actively governing the country. It could obstruct the imposition of unpopular laws, and it could initiate legislation of its own devising, but its will could be thwarted by the inactivity of the House of Peers or by a vote of the Privy Council. It lacked any real power to control the budget.

Moreover, the political parties were perceived by many circles in Japan as divisive, alien structures, incompatible with traditional Japanese values and above all inimical to the neo-Confucian harmony and benevolence that ought to extend from the Emperor to all of his subjects. As long as Japanese security was seen to depend upon a more or less cooperative relationship with the Western Powers, as had seemed to exist throughout most of the years between the Anglo-Japanese Alliance and the late 1920s, more reactionary forces were held at bay notwithstanding the enmity that existed between the political parties. During this period, indeed, the political parties between them not only gained real control in the House of Representatives but selected successive Prime Ministers, determined the composition of their Cabinets and exercised a commanding influence over government policies on most issues. From thence the power of the political parties was extended into the House of Peers, determined the composition and attitudes of the Privy Council, intimidated the civil service, and established uneasy partnerships with factions in big business, in the armed forces and even in the Imperial Court itself. All of this seemed to represent a new kind of stability quite different from the clan-based oligarchic factions of previous decades. None of this had any natural place in the Meiji Constitution.

In the end, the party politicians lost whatever credibility they pretended to have. They seemed to be yesterday's men. Few could command general respect. None appeared to have the vitality, imagination and flair that people trusted in old war horses like Admiral Saitō Makoto, Admiral Okada Keisuke and General Hayashi Senjurō, or figures such as the

veteran Ambassador Hirota Kōki (a commoner) and the sophisticated
Prince Konoye Fuminaro, last of the noble Fujiwara line: each of these
men became Prime Minister, handpicked by the wily old democratic
Genrō, Prince Saionji Kinmochi, who himself bitterly regretted the eclipse
of the party system which he personally had introduced into Japanese
society in the early years of the century. Now even Saionji appreciated
that the leadership of the two great political parties of the mid-thirties was
bereft of talent, criss-crossed with factionalism, utterly unfit for the
daunting task of restoring a national consensus. The fact that after 1932
both main political parties – the *Minseitō* and the *Seiyūkai* – were committed to Japanese recognition of the puppet state of Manchukuo did
nothing to relieve the anxieties of Saionji, who fervently hoped that the
men he selected as Prime Ministers over the next few years had the strength
of character and moral toughness necessary either to withstand the temptations of overseas expansion or, when that failed, to bring the political
ambitions of the Army under control. If that strategy should fail, Saionji
appreciated, then Japan was set on a course leading directly to its own
ruination through economic collapse or through a collision with the Western Powers. Unhappily, the instruments through which Saionji attempted
to manipulate the policies of the nation were unequal to his purposes.

Following the murder of Prime Minister Inukai in May 1932, Saitō
Makoto was selected by Prince Saionji to take the dead man's place. He
had been a full admiral since 1916, had served as former naval attaché to
the United States before the turn of the century and then, as Vice-Minister
of the Navy for seven years between 1898 and 1906, had been largely
responsible for building the Navy which was to defeat the Russians in the
Russo-Japanese War. He then had served as Navy Minister for a period
of eight years until the beginning of the First World War. After the war
he emerged from a period of retirement to serve as Governor-General of
Japan between August 1919 and December 1927. He was very nearly the
victim of a terrorist bomb thrown at his carriage, shortly after taking up
that appointment but, undeterred, dedicated himself to the transformation
of the Japanese colonial government from a military occupation to a civil
administration. After attending the Geneva Disarmament Conference as
a plenipotentiary in 1927, he took a well-earned rest. He was clearly a
man of personal courage, and he later returned to Korea for a second
stint as Governor-General between 1929 and June 1931 (a period when
radical elements in the Korean Army were kept well under control). As
one of Japan's most distinguished elder soldier-statesmen, he was a man
of proven ability and experience; he had a reputation for being relatively
liberal by Japanese standards; and he had shown phenomenal staying-

power in the face of adversity. As Prime Minister, he also briefly reserved for himself the portfolios of Foreign Affairs (until July 1932) and Education (after March 1934). Nevertheless, the old man was tired. Two other figures, War Minister Araki Sadao and his Inspector-General of Military Education (Mazaki Jinzaburō), both leading figures in the Imperial Way Faction of the Army, dominated the policies of the Saitō Cabinet and were greatly esteemed by the same radical groups of Young Officers from whom the most recent crop of assassins had emerged. After presiding over Japan's recognition of Manchukuo, rejection of the Lytton Report, withdrawal from the League of Nations, and the approval of a huge arms procurement programme for the Navy as well as the Army, Saitō had proved a great disappointment to Saionji and the moderate elements in the country. In the end, however, Saitō only felt obliged to resign from office in July 1934 after his Finance Minister (former Prime Minister Takahashi Korekiyo), other members of his Cabinet and senior officials in the Finance Ministry were implicated in a sleazy bribes scandal involving the sale of stocks in a rayon company. His successor was another admiral, Okada Keisuke, who more or less unwillingly followed down the same path of compromise that Saitō had been forced to tread. A year later, Saitō himself was appointed Lord Keeper of the Privy Seal as a mark of the Emperor's affection, but the fire had gone out of his soul.

It should be said that corruption for some time had become much more blatant than before. Election fraud in particular had become a regular feature of Japanese political life, as had 'pork barrel' largesse and the sale of political offices to the highest bidder at local, regional and even national levels. The political parties did not exercise power autocratically, nor by means of any direct appeal for public support. Their authority survived only as long as they retained the allegiance of local political bosses at subordinate levels. This in turn meant that the political parties blocked efforts by the central bureaucracy to extend their power into local affairs.

Indeed, many bureaucrats found themselves unable to function at local or regional levels without surrendering their political initiative to the whims and personal interests of the local party bosses. As a result, discontent with the political parties spread laterally throughout the professional civil service apparatus as well as in the élite circles of the House of Peers (where political cant had begun to disrupt the clubby atmosphere of former times).

The whole system came crashing down under the weight of the Manchurian Incident and the international condemnation and isolation of

Japan which became a permanent feature of the nation's political life from 1932 until the end of the Pacific War. During this period, Japan turned gradually towards the military and civil bureaucracies to survive what was regarded universally as a period of national emergency surpassing anything in the country's previous history. The fact that both of these groups could claim legitimacy under the Constitution as mere servants of the Imperial Will also gave them authority as the constitutional embodiment and voice of that national essence, *Kokutai*, to which reference has already been made in Chapter 3. Added to that was the evidence, borne out in the years of maladministration, corruption and the demonstrable incompetence of many members of the Imperial Diet, that modern government was no place for bumbling amateurs: the reins of power should be in the hands of those best equipped by intelligence, training and experience to perform the functions of their offices. As the reputations of the political parties diminished, so did the ability of those parties to attract into their ranks men of experience and probity who might have led them through successive crises.

Parallel with the eclipse of the political parties and the rising importance of the military and civilian bureaucracies in the domestic as well as in the overseas affairs of Japan during the thirties, there took place in Japan an ideological splintering of the Army and the Navy but more especially of the Army. Although the situation was often more complicated, as we have already intimated, the factionalization of the Japanese Army officer corps is generally perceived as a struggle between two major ideological groups, each of which dispensed patronage and found outside supporters. The efforts of these groups to achieve supremacy in Japan shook the nation to its core.

The *Kōdō* group stressed obedience to the divine Imperial Will and sought to emancipate Emperor Hirohito from the baleful influence of effete, liberal-minded palace officials, the corrupt, materialistic accretions of twentieth-century parliamentarianism, and the bureaucratic and capitalistic opportunists who used the state to further their selfish interests. They yearned for a 'Shōwa Restoration' to usher in a new age of Imperial splendour. They saw themselves as the natural successors to the Samurai clansmen who had carried out the 'Meiji Restoration' in the previous century. Their vision of life in that future age was obscured by the misfortunes, maladministration and structures of the modern era. Only when all that was swept away would the one true path forward stand revealed in crystal clarity. Thus, so said one adherent of the Imperial Way: 'The punishment of evil men and the Restoration are the same thing.'* In terms of foreign affairs and military policy, however, the *Kōdōha* regarded war against the Soviet Union as inevitable and imminent. At all events it became a fixed star towards which all *Kōdōha* sought to steer Japan. From this phobic obsession with the Soviet Union (and the Comintern) sprang the demand of the Young Officer movement, with which the *Kōdōha* were allied, for the immediate spiritual reformation of Japan. At the moment, by contrast, it seemed prudent to avoid any military adventure against China. This consideration proceeded partly from the fact that the difficulties of overcoming Chinese resistance were regarded as considerable, and partly from a sense of kinship with the Chinese which members of the *Kōdōha* imagined the Chinese might be taught to reciprocate. By one means or other, however, the Imperial Way planned to embrace the Middle Kingdom: contrary to what is often supposed, the policy of restraint towards China was by no means unconditional. And when Kita Ikki, the most important ideologist associated with the movement, looked further into his crystal ball, he foresaw Japanese expansion beyond, as far as eastern Siberia and even, in due time, *Australia*.

Against the *Kōdōha* were ranged a number of groups which the *Kōdōha* tended to lump together under a pejorative label, the *Tōseiha* (Control Faction), in which a number of the elder generation of senior officers were allied to some of the young technocrats and brighter staff officers. Many of them rejected the spiritual mumbo-jumbo and traditional values promoted by General Araki and his cronies. Others felt that it compromised efforts to mechanize and introduce other technical innovations into the Army. The fixation of the *Kōdōha* about the Soviet Union worried those who wanted time to develop the economic infrastructure of Manchukuo rather than waste resources in a war for which they believed the nation would remain ill-prepared for a considerable period. Thus the *Kōdōha* harkened back to a mythical past but wanted radical changes overnight. The *Tōseiha*, arguably the more dangerous of the two groups in the long run, looked forward to a different kind of war, where all the resources of the modern state would be harnessed under unified direction: in two words, Total War.

The rapid eclipse of the *Kōdōha* began in 1934, when Araki resigned as War Minister, ostensibly due to ill-health but mindful of the animosity that he had generated within the senior ranks of the Army. As a naval Intelligence report on the Army, prepared within the Naval General Staff, observed rather drily:

* Muranaka Kōji, cited in Maruyama Masao, op. cit., p. 55.

While chanting effortlessly that he must promptly invest the Emperor's Army with integrity and abolish all cliques from the Army, War Minister Araki, in fact, built up his own large faction. The Imperial Army is not so generous as to permit this deed.*

In the aftermath of Araki's departure, the Vice-Chief of the Army General Staff, Lieutenant-General Ueda Kenkichi, had links with the Control Faction. Prince Kan'in Kotohito, the Chief of the Army General Staff, was personally rather favourable to it, too, while Major-General Nagata Tetsuzan, regarded as the 'brains' of the *Tōseiha*, now returned to the centre of power as Chief of the Military Affairs Bureau at the War Ministry after having being pushed out for a period by one of Araki's favourites to serve as a brigade commander. Nagata had first risen to prominence as the protégé of War Minister Ugaki in the ill-starred Cabinet of Hamaguchi during the great London Naval Conference controversy. He was an early advocate of Army modernization, the development of mechanized forces and research into biological and chemical weapons systems. He was dynamic, brilliant and thoroughly efficient. Araki's successor as War Minister, General Hayashi Senjurō, was greatly influenced by Nagata, who had set himself the task of rooting out adherents of the *Kōdōha* from all positions of influence in the Japanese Army. However, since Nagata himself had been implicated in the October Incident of 1931, it was a case of poacher-turned-gamekeeper. The main obstacle in Nagata's path was Mazaki, Ueda's predecessor as Vice-Chief of the Army General Staff and presently Inspector-General of Military Education. Mazaki was regarded as a lion by the Young Officer movement and the Imperial Way Faction. Nagata's schemes reached fruition, however, and Mazaki was forced to resign much against his will.

This signed Nagata's own death warrant. A lieutenant-colonel by the name of Aizawa Saburō decided that Nagata's actions in this and other matters had put him beyond the pale. He came up to Tokyo, made his way into Nagata's office, and murdered him with his sabre. The ensuing trial of the malefactor put Tokyo on tenterhooks. The defence used the occasion to ventilate the frustrations of the *Kōdōha* and to malign the reputation, and personal reputations of leading members, of the *Tōseiha*. Aizawa himself said that his sole regret was that he had failed to slay Nagata with a single blow of his sabre. For its part, the Control Faction, turning on those in the Imperial Way Faction whom they had recently

* Naval General Staff, Intelligence Report on the Military, 8 February 1934, cited in J. B. Crowley, *Japan's Quest for Autonomy: National Security and Foreign Policy, 1930–1938*, op. cit., p. 206.

been squeezing but had previously tolerated, determined to thwart further outrages by dispatching known *Kōdōha* troublemakers to the outer reaches of the Empire and beyond. Amid a general expectation of further outbreaks of violence, it had gradually become clear that the forces of discontent centred upon the First Division, which had been stationed in Tokyo for longer than scarcely anyone could remember. To defuse the situation, the First Division was ordered to proceed to Manchukuo. These steps, however, convinced leading elements within the *Kōdōha* that they must act in haste before the *Tōseiha* plans could be implemented and while the daily reports surrounding the public court martial of Aizawa still excited widespread national sympathy for the defendant.

In February 1936 the turbulence of the new Army reached its peak. There took place then an incident which embodied all the trends to violence of the time, and all the flouting of established political conduct. A plot was made by the younger officers in some of the most respected regiments. Plots, it will be gathered, were nothing new: it was the scope and audacity of this particular one which were original. The conspiracy was to murder the leaders of the Cabinet and the most respected elder statesmen who advised the throne. They intended to slaughter seven prominent individuals whom they regarded as representative of the reactionary elements of the country. These included the old Genrō, Prince Saionji (subsequently removed from the slate of intended victims); Prime Minister Okada; Finance Minister Takahashi; the Lord Keeper of the Privy Seal, Viscount Saitō; his predecessor, Count Makino; the Grand Chamberlain, Admiral Suzuki, and Mazaki's replacement as Inspector-General of Military Education, General Watanabe Jōtarō. A second deathlist was prepared in case any opportunities presented themselves during subsequent phases of the uprising. This list included the names of five individuals who were implicated in the terrorist plots of 1931 and the outbreak of the Manchurian Incident: War Minister Hayashi, Lieutenant-Colonel Mutō Akira, Lieutenant-Colonel Nemoto Hiroshi, Major Katakura Tadashi and Colonel Ishiwara Kanji. Then, as an act of unheard-of impiety, the conspirators planned to give an ultimatum to the Emperor for the appointment of a particular kind of Cabinet.

The disaffected troops finally mutinied on 26 February 1936, when they carried elements of the Imperial Guards Division with them. The usual mishaps and bloodthirsty scenes occurred, and it was notable that both the Metropolitan Police and the *Kenpeitai* were conspicuous by their absence in the opening hours of the Incident. The rebels occupied key positions in the city, including the Metropolitan Police Headquarters, the Ministry for Home Affairs and the War Ministry, holding them for several

days. The death toll was far less than might have been expected. The
number of troops deployed by the rebels was far greater than had taken
part in any previous rebellion on Japanese soil since the Great Saigō
had been put down by the forces of the Emperor Meiji. The terrorists
who conceived the incident failed because their plot was prepared inadequately, and because some of the leading figures escaped their
would-be assassins. But for some days the politics of Tokyo, which at
the time was snow-covered, was divided between a barracks, which
housed the rebellious officers who were waiting for high personages
such as their erstwhile spiritual mentor Araki Sadao to throw in their
lot with them, and the rest of the metropolis, variously (and nonetheless
entirely accurately) described as strangely apathetic, quiet or stunned
by the enormity of what had been done.

No attempt was made to inform, much less to appeal, to public opinion
about what was happening in the early stages of the uprising. The rebel
troops even failed to take the elementary precaution of seizing control of
the national broadcasting system or mounting any other kind of propaganda. Their civilian supporters printed a couple of hundred copies of
two or three bulletins which they composed during the first two days of
the uprising, then, with breathtaking fecklessness, contented themselves
with posting these to their supporters. Accordingly, the disturbances did
not spread beyond Tokyo. Apart from what little the people of Tokyo
garnered from rumours about the horrific series of murders at the beginning of the Incident, all that was visible was an unnatural calm and the
sight of troops occupying key positions near the Imperial Palace, Government buildings and the like in the centre of Tokyo. While the rebels and
the rest of the Army sought to find some peaceful solution to the crisis,
the rebels felt that it would be only a question of time before their coup
would receive the Emperor's own blessing. For some time Japanese troops
outside Tokyo remained calm and obedient to military discipline.

Gradually, the assembled forces of the Government took stock of their
position. Although the attitude of the bulk of the First Division remained
unclear, the other division stationed in Tokyo, the Imperial Guards
Division, largely remained in safe hands. Outside the metropolis, other
commanders were very much opposed to the uprising. The factionalism
with which the Japanese Army was riven made that certain. The struggle
was not between military moderates and radicals. Many of those most
keen to crush the rebellion had defied the central authorities when it had
suited them: they included General Tatekawa Yoshitsugu, who now
commanded the Fourth Division in Osaka, General Minami Jirō, now
Commander-in-Chief of the Kwantung Army, and Colonel Ishiwara

Kanji, who was appointed to head the Operations and Communications Sections of the Martial Law Headquarters in Tokyo.

The Emperor himself was powerless during the crisis. His initial reaction was one of undisguised outrage at the actions taken by the rebels. He subsequently told his chief aide-de-camp, General Honjō Shigeru: 'They have killed my advisers and are now trying to pull a silk rope over my neck ... I shall never forgive them, no matter what their motives are.'*

Having commanded his War Minister to smash the revolt without delay, the Emperor was at a loss to understand why his instructions were not carried out without further parleying. On the second day of the rebellion, the Emperor went further and told Honjō that unless the Army proceeded at once to end the mutiny, he himself would take personal command of the Imperial Guards and crush it. There seems little reason to doubt his resolve to carry out that threat if necessary. He and his palace advisers were also determined to oppose mounting pressures for the installation of a new Cabinet that might open the way for the rebels to achieve their aims. When the surviving members of Admiral Okada's Cabinet sent Home Affairs Minister Gotō Fumio to the Palace to suggest an interim Prime Minister, the Emperor appointed Gotō as Acting Prime Minister instead. Later, when Gotō returned to submit the collective resignations of himself and his colleagues, Emperor Hirohito informed Gotō that he would decline to permit any change in Government until his orders to end the uprising were carried out. News of this development finally reached the rebels on the night of 27 February, where it came as a shock. They had believed that they had hit upon a winning formula to achieve their demands by agreeing to return to their barracks if General Mazaki were to be appointed Prime Minister. The Emperor's opposition, in the end, sealed the fate of their fanciful Shōwa Restoration.

The decisive step, however, may have been the landing of strong contingents of marines backed up by the guns of some forty ships, which sailed into Tokyo Bay on 27 February, obedient to orders issued by moderate leaders of the Navy who were appalled at the gravity of the rebellion, concerned for the safety of the Imperial Court and incensed at the reported murder of two admirals (the Prime Minister, Okada Keisuke, and the Lord Keeper of the Privy Seal, Saitō Makoto) and the severe injuries sustained by a third (Suzuki Kantarō). Both the Army and the Navy shied away from an open confrontation, but the Navy was instrumental in forcing the military authorities to take positive action.

Finally the rebels recognized that their tide had run out. Their officers

* Shillony, op. cit., p. 173.

sent word that they would surrender their commands and commit suicide if ordered to do so by an Imperial Messenger. Hirohito, not wishing to dignify their actions, merely responded that if the rebels wanted to commit suicide then that was for them to decide. Stung by this rebuke, the mutineers decided to go down fighting. At the same time, the Cabinet, the General Staff and the Emperor were all determined that the rebel positions must be taken by storm. Throughout 28 and 29 February, military reinforcements poured into Tokyo from further afield. The city was cut off from the rest of the country. Civilians were evacuated from forward areas. Bombarded by Government leaflets, radio broadcasts and even an advertisement suspended from a tethered balloon, the rebels offered no resistance as the Army's tanks moved forward. Their morale utterly broken, the mutiny simply collapsed as the rebels came out, surrendered and returned to their barracks.

After all 1,483 surviving participants in the rebellion were interrogated, civilian as well as military, 124 were prosecuted. These included all nineteen of the surviving officers (two others had committed suicide), seventy-three of the ninety-one non-commissioned officers, nineteen of the 1,358 common soldiers, and a sorry lot of ten civilians. The remainder were set free on the grounds that they had done no more than to obey the orders of their superiors. The majority were returned to active service with the First Division and transported in disgrace to the outer reaches of Manchuria. The trials, held in camera, were conducted in an atmosphere of severity in great contrast to the trials of previous terrorists. There was no popular support for the accused, and senior officers who had felt some sympathy for their aims now kept their own heads down. The rumours that surrounded them added to public confusion and a pervasive sense of interlocking and countervailing conspiracies. After a considerable delay, there were some exemplary executions. Thirteen rebel officers and four of the civilians accused of major responsibility for the 26 February Incident were stood before firing squads. Five officers were sentenced to life imprisonment, another received four years, while forty-four NCOs, four common soldiers and one other civilian found guilty were sent to prison for varying terms. In subsequent proceedings against persons accused of collaboration with the active conspirators, the authorities managed to protect a number of influential individuals who had been favourable to the rebel cause. The natural tendencies of mainstream politicians to seek the support of influential cliques now led to the serious embarrassment of the *Seiyūkai*. The same tendencies had tempted large and vulnerable financial conglomerates to curry the favour of military or political circles, and many well-connected *zaibatsu* were implicated, notably Ikeda Seihin (the *de facto* head in the vast Mitsui empire, who was tipped off in time to escape the assassins on 26 February), Kuhara Fusanosuke (founder of the Kuhara Mining Company, partner and brother-in-law to Ayukawa Gisuke of Nissan and a man whose reputation abroad was thoroughly unsavoury)* and Ishihara Kōichirō (the President of the Ishihara Industries and Marine Transportation Company, who made his personal fortune as an importer of Malayan rubber and iron ore). Each of them attracted the unwelcome attentions of the police: Kuhara and Ishihara spent a period in protective custody. Ishihara was charged with conspiracy but was acquitted by the courts.

In the Army there were many leading figures, including some who harboured an honourable detestation of the wheeling and dealing that characterized the political and social life of Japan, who suddenly found themselves out of favour. Some of them retained sufficient influence to escape prosecution. General Mazaki Jinzaburō, who as Inspector-General of Military Education had been instrumental in exposing the leading rebels to the ideas for which they risked everything, was involved in the conspiracy up to his neck. He was indicted but won an acquittal. Retired General Saitō Ryū, who served as a middle-man between the *zaibatsu* and the plotters, was sentenced to five years' imprisonment. Other active sympathizers who were treated lightly included former War Minister Araki Sadao; General Kashii Kōhei, who commanded the Tokyo Garrison and was put in charge of the Martial Law Headquarters established to deal with the crisis; General Yanagawa Heisuke, Commander of the First Division until the eve of the Incident; General Hori Takeo, his successor; Major-General Yamashita Tomoyuki, Chief of the Research Bureau at the War Ministry, and General Murakami Keisaku, Chief of the Military Affairs Section of the Military Affairs Bureau, all of whom wriggled free. So, too, did War Minister Kawashima Yoshiyuki, who dithered throughout the crisis but at one point took the suggestion of Araki and other proactive generals and agreed to issue an official declaration supporting the aims of the rebels. Prince Chichibu, the Emperor's brother, had close ties with several of the leading Young Officers in the conspiracy, but by common consent the authorities turned a blind eye to his true role in the crisis. One disgusted onlooker, General Ugaki Kazushige, then Governor-General of Korea and one of the intended victims of the most recent crop of conspirators, remarked in his diary: 'How

---

* Kuhara's entry in the annual 'Report on Leading Personalities in Japan', compiled by the British Embassy in Tokyo, ends with the words 'He is an ambitious and unscrupulous person . . . a pure gangster and personally responsible for more than one murder.' F 4913/4913/23, Report by Sir R. L. Craigie, 2 April 1938, FO 371/22192.

disgusting it is to watch these rascals, holding in one hand the matches and in the other one the water hose, setting fire and putting it out at the same time, inciting the Young Officers, pleading their cause and then claiming credit for having put them down.'*

By contrast the authorities did not spare two of Japan's most notorious radical right-wing renovationists. The first was Kita Ikki, a one-eyed ascetic, fire-eating socialist turned Nichiren monk, whose most famous work, *An Outline Plan for the Reorganization of Japan*, banned in its unexpurgated form by the censor, called for the foundation of a revolutionary empire and was found among the personal effects of the rebels. The second was his disciple, Nishida Zei, once a promising young officer who had abandoned his career to pursue Kita's mystical vision of national and East Asian upheaval and reform. The evidence against them was weak and entirely circumstantial. It was afterwards revealed that their judges, however, decided to condemn them to death by firing squad in spite of the fact that the guilt of these two accused was not proven. Both men had been closely associated with Ōkawa Shūmei for many years.

This abortive revolution, by its radicalism, led to a realization that the Japanese Army, or part of it, was ceasing to be a conservator of the state. One of its causes was said to be the unfamiliar outbreak of political discussion among junior officers. This was partly the result of their becoming affected by Japan's economic problems. They were seeking solutions; they did not mind if these were radical. Hitherto the Army, to the comfort of the better-off classes of the Japanese, had seemed to connote safety, conservatism, stability. But they had to recast their thoughts towards what in Japan had been regarded as dangerous ideas. Some reflective onlookers noticed that, if the Army should turn towards Communism in its new adventurousness, it would have a good chance of putting the whole country on a communist footing. Japan, with its heavy industry, with its huge industrial population which was accustomed to strict discipline, and its underlying taste for violence, would be admirable material for a communist dictatorship to work on. The same was observed in the attractions which European fascism held for many Army officers.

The forces in opposition to the *Kōdōha* showed more diversity than might be supposed, especially in the period which followed the 26 February Incident of 1936. After the failure of that uprising, the influence of the *Kōdōha* simply collapsed. The surviving leaders of the faction

* Ugaki Kazushige, *Ugaki Nikki*, Asahi Shinbunsha, Tokyo, 1954, pp. 217–18, cited in Shillony, p. 203.

were isolated, consigned to the Reserves or sent off to remote corners of the Empire and Manchukuo. Generals Araki, Mazaki, Yanagawa, Obata and the rest simply ceased to exercise a dominant role. In their place Generals Umezu, Tōjō, Sugiyama and Koiso took control, and under the guise of protecting the nation from right-wing populist radicalism, they insisted upon taking steps which ensured that liberalism, too, would gain no headway.

The resurgence of the Control Faction after the 26 February Incident was coupled with a drawing together of the military, court administrators, civil bureaucrats and *zaibatsu*. The agrarian and social reformist impulses of the *Tōseiha* yielded to what was regarded by the established forces as a perfectly prudent concentration of the nation's resources on satisfying the requirements of the military. The Army leadership played upon the fears of the establishment, dwelling on their own alleged inability to restrain the *Kōdō* faction if progressively more militaristic policies were not adapted. In this way the *Tōseiha* did indeed become a controlling faction in the political affairs of the state, far beyond their ostensible constitutional responsibilities, especially in the realms of industrial development, fuel policy, labour, wage and price controls, financial policy, and the formulation of foreign policy. Heavy-handed legislation was passed concerning thought control, and jingoistic measures were introduced to ensure that militaristic values were inculcated in all sectors of education. The military utilized their power to select and replace Ministers at will, regulated only by their own sense of national priorities, collectivism, bureaucratic conceits and the inter-service rivalry between the Army and the Navy.

The outcome of the uprising therefore did nothing to restore a sense of balance to Japan. It frankly did not matter that only six days before the Incident, a national election had been held which had returned a liberal *Minseitō* majority to the Imperial Diet. It is a measure of the rebels' disinterest in any popular mandate that they acted before the outcome was even known. It is a measure of the *Tōseiha*'s victory that the outcome was irrelevant. After the incident, Hirota Kōki was selected as Prime Minister and General Terauchi Hisashi was chosen to be his War Minister. The new Finance Minister, Baba Eiichi, submitted a greatly inflationary budget and the Government set its sights on the national mobilization of heavy industry. Ten months later the uneasy working relationships in the Government came unstuck. War Minister Terauchi took offence when a member of the Imperial Diet, Hamada Kunimatsu, accused the Army of seeking to establish a dictatorship in Japan. Terauchi, enraged by this slur, required Prime Minister Hirota to prorogue the

Diet. Hirota refused on the grounds that the outcome of another election was uncertain. Terauchi promptly resigned, and the Army ensured that no other suitable candidate could be appointed. The Government thereupon fell from power, more or less bearing out Hamada's prophecy.

A further period of instability followed. The Emperor invited General Ugaki Kazushige to form a new Government only to find that Ugaki was blocked by the 'Three Chiefs Council' of the Army (the War Minister, the Chief of the Army General Staff and the Inspector-General of Military Education), who felt quite rightly that he was determined to put a brake upon the rapid expansion to which they were becoming accustomed. Since the Hirota Cabinet had bowed to Terauchi's demand for the reinstatement of a once-discarded provision of the Meiji Constitution that War Ministers must be selected from general officers on the active service list, the Prime Minister-designate effectively depended upon the grace and favour of the Army (and indeed the Navy) to fill his Cabinet. Ugaki had no choice but to return his mandate to the Emperor.

Instead, former War Minister Hayashi Senjurō formed a new Government in early February 1937. Two months later, seeking a popular mandate for a pattern of non-party government which he sought to legitimize, Hayashi called a snap election, the fourth since 1930. He abandoned any attempt to woo the political bosses and their party machines. Instead he offered the electorate a new party, the *Shōwa-kai*. His bombastic, barrack-square behaviour did not go down well, however, and the election gave the two main political parties a massive vote of confidence against the militaristic Hayashi. The two regular parties won 359 seats in the Diet with a tally of more than 7 million votes. The *Shōwa-kai*, by contrast, won nineteen seats with just over 400,000 votes, and another splinter party also backed by the Army, the *Kokumin Dōmei*, fared even more poorly. Thus the democratic instincts of the people (or the effectiveness of the party machines) remained surprisingly undimmed throughout the turbulent years that were to culminate in the outbreak of the China Incident in July 1937. Nevertheless, despite very outspoken criticism by members of the Imperial Diet concerning the drift of the nation towards militarism, the increasingly jingoistic and reactionary tenor of Japanese Governments was echoed in the mass media and, inevitably, was soon reflected by the general population.

On the whole, the Japanese showed little aptitude in their propaganda, particularly where it was intended for foreign parts. In great contrast to the Chinese, they not infrequently created greater misunderstanding and hostility towards themselves than had they left well alone. It was not a new problem: the Japanese had lost even the propaganda war with Tsarist Russia during the appeal to foreign opinion in the run-up to the Treaty of Portsmouth. In October 1934 the Japanese War Minister produced a famous pamphlet urging the creation of a centralized organ responsible for the dissemination of information and propaganda. One result of such pressure was the creation of the *Dōmei Tsūshinsha* (the United Press Agency) in June 1936 followed a month later by the establishment of a Cabinet Information Board, which was succeeded in turn by a Cabinet Information Division in September 1937 and upgraded to a Cabinet Information Bureau one year before Pearl Harbor. Whatever its name, these Cabinet organs were intended to manipulate the news and gradually fell under the control of military censors. At the same time the news apparatus became increasingly cumbersome, unreliable and an exasperation to foreign correspondents, who learned to place no reliance upon the factual accuracy of Japanese official statements as the years passed. Japanese goodwill missions likewise failed to achieve the positive impact upon foreign countries which exponents of these missions desired. Cultural exchanges often proved only slightly less counter-productive in the short term, and by the late 1930s only the short term mattered.

Public awareness of the irresponsibility of Japan's continental adventure was less pronounced in Japan than it was abroad. In part this was due to the imposition of censorship involving all forms of press and broadcasting media. Even Japanese street theatre, notably *Kamishibai*, or picture-postcard theatre productions akin to Punch and Judy shows, were subject to close examination by thought control police and so, like the cinema, played safe. There were other factors, too, such as the Army's step-by-step extension of the military training and indoctrination into Japanese schools, universities and factories. Then there was the matter of the economy.

Elated by the successes of the Japanese Armies, first in Manchuria and afterwards in Inner Mongolia and North China, initial worries in Japan about foreign reactions gradually subsided into mixed resentment and indifference when the West failed to take effective action. Industrial production in Japan by 1932 had returned to 98 per cent of its 1929 record, compared with corresponding figures of 84 per cent for the United Kingdom, 72 per cent for France, 67 per cent for Mussolini's Italy, 53 per cent for Germany on the eve of Hitler's accession to power, and 53 per cent for the United States at the commencement of the Roosevelt years. By 1933, therefore, the Japanese, buoyed up by defence expenditure, could regard the depression as a thing of the past. The illusion persisted for a surprisingly long period of time. Eventually the Ministry of Finance, excusing its own failure to operate within prudent monetary practices, as time wore on adopted the phrase 'quasi-war economy' to express the higher priority given to the development of Japanese military preparations for war rather than the demands of the civilian economy. In essence, the Japanese gradually were forced to recognize that what their British counterparts characterized as 'the Fourth Arm of Defence', financial stability, was something that Japan could not afford, and this added point to the importance of seeking concrete economic benefits from Japan's dependencies on the Asian mainland. As the country ground through its gears towards Total War, the mobilization of the Japanese economy was plain to see, together with the cracks caused by its disfunctioning. The mortal danger to which this exposed Japan was well understood. Japan's reliance upon the West for more than 90 per cent of its petroleum supplies meant that the liberty of Japan to wage war on the continent or anywhere else was subject to the goodwill of the United States and its friends, as the following table of Japanese petroleum imports in 1936 demonstrates:

Source	1,000 tons	%
United States	3,043	65.79
Netherlands East Indies	991	21.43
British North Borneo	301	6.51
Manchukuo	73	1.58
North Sakhalin	26	0.56
Others	191	4.13
Total	4,625	100*

Nevertheless, Japanese public opinion gradually appreciated that Japan was caught in an international crisis from which there could be no escape, and even began to develop a fatalistic sense, shared with many abroad, that war with the West as well as China might be unavoidable.

It was a world in which rearmament was becoming the order of the day. Recognizing the danger of a naval arms race against the combined strength of Britain and the United States, Japan demanded parity with each of them, with the object of making it impossible for the Anglo-Saxon countries to blackmail Japan. Thus the hard evidence of Japan's irremediable dependence upon foreign imports of strategical raw materials was ignored by the Japanese during what were to become their last naval

* Adapted from Hosoya Chihiro, 'Miscalculations in Deterrent Policy: Japanese–U.S. Relations, 1938–1941', *Journal of Peace Research*, V:2, 1968, p. 114.

arms limitation discussions prior to the Pacific War. Their demands were thwarted, however, and in a major miscalculation by its Navy, Tokyo thereupon closed its eyes to the factors which had impelled Japan to accept previous humiliations, and withdrew from the 1935–6 London Naval Conference. The Army and the Navy, with a carelessness born of distraction, drove along through the night, mechanized now, on the road to Total War.

CHAPTER 9

The War Resumed: The Outbreak
of the China Incident

THE second phase of the war began in an obscure skirmish between Japanese and Chinese troops at Lukouchiao, 'Black Moat Bridge', a site not far from Peking, better known in the West as the Marco Polo Bridge, after the Venetian explorer who had regarded it as one of the most beautiful in the world. During the night of 7 July 1937 some of the 15,000 Chinese troops in the region of Peking exchanged rifle-fire with a portion of the 550-strong Japanese garrison at Fengtai, which was carrying out night manoeuvres in open territory north of the bridge, an area long favoured for such purposes by the foreign garrisons guarding their respective legations in Peking under the terms of the Boxer Protocols. The Japanese reported the incident to the mayor of Peking, General Ching Teh-chun, at around midnight and expressed particular concern about the fate of one Japanese soldier who appeared to be missing and was presumed to have been taken captive.

Formal permission was requested for a company of Japanese troops to conduct a search for the missing man in the little fortified town of Wanping, which was also an important railway junction on the main line to Paoting and Hankow (and thus to Central China). Ching, however, denied this request and offered instead to send a joint investigating commission into Wanping to make any necessary inquiries. This was agreeable to the Japanese and suitable arrangements were made. In the meanwhile, Ching took the precaution of ordering the Chinese Army town commander at Wanping to repel any Japanese troops who might attempt to take matters into their own hands. These precautions were well-taken, for eight truckloads of Japanese troops turned up outside Wanping at 3.30 a.m. in an effort to enter the town and were forcibly repelled by the Chinese. While these events were in progress, it is said that the missing man, whose fate was ostensibly the main source of concern, added to the embarrassment of the Japanese by turning up at his unit two hours after his absence was first discovered, apparently having been led astray that night by nothing more than his sexual desire.

In response to the fighting at Wanping, however, each side rushed a battalion of reinforcements to the scene. The Japanese reinforcements, only a few hundred men strong, came not from Tientsin, fifty miles away, where the main elements of the Japanese North China Garrison Army were based, but like the Japanese troops already on the scene, were drawn instead from the 450-man Japanese Legation Guard, which was the only other Japanese force in the Peking area apart from the battalion based at Fengtai. All parties concerned recognized the gravity of the situation, which threatened to erupt into another Manchurian Incident.

The Japanese were in a particularly vulnerable position: virtually the whole of the North China Garrison Army, which altogether comprised little more than a single infantry brigade, had been deployed away from their various depots in field exercises ever since 6 June and was therefore in no immediate position to render practical assistance to the detachment at Wanping. Moreover, the asthmatic Commander-in-Chief of the North China Garrison, General Tashiro Kan'ichirō, had fallen victim to a serious heart-attack a fortnight before (from which he died on 16 July). In Tashiro's absence, his Chief of Staff, General Hashimoto Gun, exercised effective control of the North China Garrison and gave clear instructions to Major Ichiki, the battalion commander sent to Wanping, that no action must be taken pending a thorough review of the situation. Hashimoto also made it known that he intended to seek a peaceful resolution of the matter without delay.

And as hindsight soon overlaid the confusing reports issued at the time, the myth grew that the China Incident, as it came to be called, was the product of the same kind of conspiracy as had provoked the Manchurian Incident six years before. On the contrary, Japanese policy on the eve of the China Incident had been in a state of flux. Even the Kwantung Army was hesitant at taking action in China Proper, for as the Chief of Staff of that Army, one Tōjō Hideki, advised Vice-Minister of War Umezu Yoshijirō and Vice-Chief of the Army General Staff Imai Kiyoshi in June 1937, the Japanese Army's greatest concern remained Russia, not China:

Judging the present situation in China from the point of view of military preparations against the Soviet Union, I am convinced that if our military power permits it, we should deliver a blow first of all upon the Nanking régime to get rid of the menace at our back.

If our military power will not permit us to take such a step, I think it proper that we keep a strict watch on the Chinese Government that they do not lay a single hand on our present undertakings in China until our national defence system is completed. We will thus wait for the Chinese Government to reconsider.

We should not take the initiative to become friendly with the Nanking Government, which has no intention whatsoever of adjusting diplomatic relations with Japan, for, judging from their national characteristics, such a step will only aggravate their disdainful attitude towards Japan.*

The Chinese, in fact, desired peace no less than did the Japanese but were determined to resist any further Japanese aggression on a major scale, and on 8 July Chiang Kai-shek ordered four Nationalist divisions into the area. Although the evidence suggests that this move was probably designed as a precautionary step, it was regarded by the local Japanese commander at Wanping as highly provocative. Unfortunately, despite efforts by the Japanese representative on the *ad hoc* Sino-Japanese joint commission to restrain him, Ichiki threw caution to the winds and committed his battalion to a charge against the Chinese positions on 9 July. The attack failed. Three days later, six Kuomintang divisions were moving northwards. The situation was complicated by the fact that under the Ching–Doihara Agreement reached with Japan in June 1935, no troops under Kuomintang command were supposed to be in the North China provinces of Hopei and Chahar, which formed an autonomous buffer between Manchuria and the Nationalist Chinese further south.

Although Japan had intended for some years to establish political control or at least economic hegemony in North China, neither the Japanese military command in China nor the authorities in Tokyo were intent on seeking any trouble at that moment. The Japanese Government in Tokyo and Japanese military commanders in China made herculean efforts to isolate the conflict and avoid further provocations. Meanwhile, cool heads prevailed elsewhere. Hashimoto himself ordered his top aides to open negotiations with senior Chinese officials in Peking and flew there himself the next day, determined to put an end to the trouble. The Army General Staff in Tokyo backed up Hashimoto with orders to settle the matter; agreement was reached by bureau chiefs from the Navy, War and Foreign Ministries on the policy to be adopted in handling the dispute; and the recommendations made by these bureau chiefs were approved by the Japanese Cabinet as early as 8 July. On that basis the Chinese and Japanese negotiators soon achieved an interim local truce agreement.

Troops from other Japanese garrisons in North China, including every available man at Tientsin, were brought into the area, but rumours of major reinforcements from Japan's Kwantung and Korean Armies were

---

* I M T F E, P X 672, Telegram 670, marked Ultra Secret, Urgent, from Tōjō to Umezu and Imai, 9 June 1937. Taking the document out of its full context, the Prosecution at the Tokyo War Trial read only the first paragraph into the *Record of the Proceedings*: see Pritchard and Zaide, op. cit., 4, pp. 7336–7.

without foundation. On 11 July the Japanese Cabinet announced the mobilization of three divisions in response to Chinese troop movements, but late that evening the plan was cancelled when news came of Hashimoto's satisfactory agreement with Ching. For the next month the Japanese sent no fresh troops into the area from outside China. But a stalemate developed in negotiations for a withdrawal, and matters were not helped by Chiang Kai-shek's 'Kuling Declaration' on 16 July, in which he effectively tore up the Ching–Doihara Agreement and proclaimed his determination to re-establish China's historic territorial unity and sovereign rights. The thousands of Japanese troops and civilians legally present in China under existing treaties were at risk of being massacred by the many times more numerous Chinese regular and militia forces moving forward.

In 'efforts to save the situation', another far-reaching agreement was hammered out between the Head of the Japanese Foreign Ministry's East Asiatic Affairs Bureau, the Chief of the War Ministry's Military Affairs Bureau and the Navy Ministry's Chief of the Naval Affairs Bureau on 23 July. Like other documentary evidence from the period, it puts paid to the suspicion of onlookers that Japan's string of military victories in the early stages of the China Incident stemmed from a well-laid plot to take over the whole of China in one fell swoop:

1. As long as there is no big change in the situation, we stick to our policy of settling the incident on the spot and of non-expanding the incident, and stop further sending of troops.
2. To voluntarily and speedily evacuate our reinforced troops out of the Great Wall when we see for sure the possible conclusion of a local agreement and feel safe.
   Remark: We consider we can be sure of the possible carrying out of the local agreement when the forces of Feng Chi-an [a local Chinese commander] have completely been moved to Paoting.
3. To declare the purport of No. 1 and No. 2 at a good opportunity.
4. To begin negotiations with the Nanking Government for adjusting our relations with China immediately after the time for evacuating our troops is fixed.
5. In the negotiation for adjusting the relations of both countries, matters will not be biased by past circumstances, and these matters should be rapidly considered by the three ministers [Foreign, War and Navy Ministries] to work out a good plan.*

---

* IMTFE, PD 1634–L, *Aide-mémoire*, 23 July 1937. This Prosecution document was not tendered in evidence at the Tokyo War Trial.

Unfortunately, even these extraordinary efforts were unavailing. By late July further incidents were occurring with increasing frequency and seriousness. In many of these exchanges, the Japanese came out much the worse for wear. Within the space of a few weeks, at first sporadic, later general, fighting spread through all North China, and reached Shanghai. As far as can be discovered, none of the main Japanese generals, and certainly not Chiang Kai-shek, wanted war at this particular moment: and peace efforts were made constantly. But the situation was out of hand. The Chinese communists, who were now formally reconciled with the Kuomintang, used every opportunity to drive their allies on to war. The decision was forced by relatively junior officers in command in the field. The situation became virtually irretrievable after 25 July, when the Chinese, manning the ancient defences of Peking, trapped three hundred Japanese troops as they passed between the inner and outer gates of the city while returning from Fengtai to the Japanese Legation in the city: some of the Chinese guarding the gates found the temptation irresistible, swung the gates shut behind the Japanese, and raked their victims with withering grenade and mortar fire. Order was soon restored and the surviving Japanese were permitted to continue on their way, but this incident naturally provoked further outrages on both sides. Three days later, the Japanese Forces at Fengtai exacted their revenge, marched into Peking and made short work of Chinese resistance. Compulsively the fighting spread. The top commanders on both sides saw this and made futile efforts to check it, and excused themselves from all responsibility.

The situation became so tense by early August that the Japanese Cabinet agreed to take the precaution of sending an expeditionary force into China with the intention of protecting Japanese property and covering the withdrawal of Japanese civilians. It must be stressed that Japan did not intend to open a larger campaign at this stage, although obviously these reinforcements would be essential if Japan should find itself at war with the much larger forces that China was now bringing forward. Nevertheless, Japan's reinforcements had an electrifying effect on the Chinese, who were enraged at what they understandably interpreted as a Japanese design to extend the conflict. Too many Chinese and Japanese preferred to go to war rather than endure insults to their respective national honour.

The two years which followed were the chief phase of slaughter in the war between China and Japan: then came a renewed period of lull. The conflict was still separate from the Armageddon which was being prepared in the West, and at first remained a separate war when the explosion

AN OVERVIEW OF THE CHINA INCIDENT 1931–45

OPERATIONS ALONG THE NORTHERN SECTION OF THE PEKING-TIENTSIN, PEKING-HANKOW, TIENTSIN-PUKOW, RAILWAYS, AND THE PEKING-SUIYUAN RAILWAY

PRELIMINARY OPERATIONS

N

Changchun
Kailu
Szeping
Chihfeng
Mukden
Chengteh
Lingyuan
Haicheng
Chinchow
Linyu
Pailingmiao
Chining
Chang-yuan
Kupeiko
Peking
Lengko
Paotow
Kueisui
Tatung
Wei
Laiyuan
Tientsin
Tangku
Dairen
PortArthur
Pienkuan
Su
Yenmen-kuan
Wutaishan
Paoting
BATTLE OF TAIYUAN
Yulin
Niangtze-kuan
Shihchiachuang
Taiyuan
Changtien
Chiehsin
Linching
Tsinan
Yenan
Anyang
Taian
Hsintai
Tsingtai
BATTLE OF EASTERN & NORTHERN HONAN
BATTLE OF SOUTHERN SHANSI
Hwang-ho
Hotse
Langfeng
Linyi
Yungchi
Tungkuan
Loning
Kaifeng
Shangchiu
Tsuchow
Taierhchuang
Funing
BATTLE OF HSUCHOW
Sian
Lushih
Nanyang
Fuyang
Huaiyin
Pangpu
Chenchiang
Chiangyin
BATTLE OF SHANGHAI
BATTLE OF CENTRAL HONAN
Neihsing
Suiping
Kushih
Nanking
Shanghai
BATTLE OF SUITSAO
BATTLE OF TSAOYI
BATTLE OF SOUTHERN HONAN
BATTLE OF WESTERN HONAN
BATTLE OF NORTHERN HUPEI
Tungpo
Hsinyang
Huangchua
Hofei
Soochow
Sungchiang
Sui
Laohoko
BATTLE OF WUHAN
Ichang
Hankow
Hangyang
Wuchang
Hsu
Hangchow
Ningpo
BATTLE OF WESTERN HUPEI
BATTLE OF CHANGTEH
Kungan
Shihmen
Kiuchiang
Hukou
Fuliang
Chinhua
Chuchow
BATTLE OF CHEKIANG-KIANGSI
Shihmen
Yueyang
Tungshan
Tungcheng
Hsiushui
Nanchang
Shangyao
THREE BATTLES OF CHANGSHA
Changsha
Chuchow
Shangkao
Chienyang
BATTLE OF WESTERN HUNAN
Hsinhua
Pinghsiang
BATTLE OF NANCHANG-SHANGKAO
Chenyuan
Wukang
Hengyang
Foochow
Kweiyang
Tuyun
BATTLE OF CHANGSHA-HENGYANG
Sanchiang
Chuan
Laiyang
Taipei
Tushun
BATTLE OF KWEILIN AND LIUCHOW AND COUNTER-OFFENSIVE OPERATIONS
Kweilin
Kukong
Amoy
Taiwan
Liuchow
Tientung
Nanning
Si-kiang
Sanshui
Canton
Swatow
Lungmu
Chin
BATTLE OF SOUTHERN KWANGSI
Hong Kong
VIETNAM
Haikang
BATTLE OF HUNAN-KWANGTUNG-KIANGSI BORDER AREAS
INDO-CHINA
Chingshan
Hainan Island

INDIA
Expeditionary Force
Myityina
Operations clearing China-India Road
BURMA
Mongyu
VIET-NAM
Link-up of Chinese Forces in India and the Expeditionary Forces at Mongyu
LAOS
THAILAND

occurred in Europe. Naturally both sides followed with care the events in Europe, and at times they adjusted their policies accordingly. But the two wars were not to merge until December 1941. There were four years to go before that.

The history of these first years of fighting is fairly simple. As was expected, Japan quickly overcame the organized resistance in the north, and occupied the railway lines and the cities. Following a separate incident at Shanghai on 9 August, when two Japanese marines were shot and killed by a Chinese sentry, the Japanese and Chinese both sent in reinforcements to support their existing garrisons, and the history of the landing there after the Mukden Incident was repeated. In Shanghai itself, the Chinese resisted for seven weeks, and there was jubilation in China. The stakes were high: Shanghai, the largest city in China with a population in excess of 3½ million people in normal times, was swollen with refugees. Overhead the two sides waged the first air war on a major scale that had taken place since the First World War (although the effects of Italian aerial attacks on Abyssinian tribesmen had already been observed and the destructive power of air bombardment on undefended civilian targets had been proved by German aviators at Guernica as recently as April 1937). The lessons of this air war were watched keenly by occidental observers in China with less than dispassionate detachment: their general attitude was voiced by a senior British naval officer at the scene whose own personal association with China went back to his birth in Shanghai as the son of a British physician:

We on the spot share the disgust with which all the foreign inhabitants view the Chinese and Japanese for fighting their main battle here.

It is humiliating for the white man not to have the power to prevent these inferior yellow races from damaging and making use of the fine city which he, and most especially the British, have laboriously built up and which is such an asset to the Far East. There are signs, however, that both sides have attempted to spare foreign property. On the other hand, both use the [International] Settlement as a 'base of operations'.*

---

* China General Letter 16, Observations on the Sino-Japanese Conflict by Vice-Admiral Sir Charles Little, Commander-in-Chief, China Station, 14 September 1937, Adm. 116/3682, British Public Record Office, Kew. As a young midshipman, Little was present in Hong Kong when the Chinese leased the New Territories there to the British Crown. Later, as a captain, while still in his thirties, he was a member of the British delegation at the Washington Naval Conference in 1921–2. Notwithstanding the bluntly racialist tone of his remarks, his sentimental attachment to China continued unabated, and his home in Sussex was filled with Chinese art antiquities to the end of his days. His loathing and contempt for the Japanese were boundless.

At this point the undeclared hostilities suddenly exploded into a Total War of appalling ferocity. By the end of the month, Japanese armies began pouring into China, smashing the inefficient and often corrupt Chinese forces. Gradually the truth about the Chinese Armies became known in the outer world, which had at first been inclined to credit that China had become better organized than it was in fact. The Chinese command organization went to pieces. Soldiers went into battle as part of a modern military formation, but this usually broke under strain, and they became pockets of fighting men. Hence came much of the nightmare quality which made this one of the most awful periods of China's recent black record. Administration was primitive, corruption was extreme and pervasive. Army medical services and hospitals scarcely existed, and soldiers who were only slightly wounded usually perished. Volunteer medical aid began to appear from the sympathetic countries of the West, but all that its doctors could do was to add to the swelling chorus of lamentation.

Improvising a guerrilla warfare, the Chinese discovered in one or two isolated battles a military prowess which China's friends afterwards took too much for granted. But at Shanghai, on breaking through in the end to open country in early November, the Japanese advanced rapidly up the Yangtze River Valley and converged upon Nanking, 200 miles to the west. Swinging southward, they captured the important river port of Wuhu, fifty miles upstream. On 13 December they occupied the Chinese capital without difficulty.

Chiang Kai-shek and his Government had withdrawn to Hankow. In the last fortnight of December 1937, after they had lost Nanking, the slaughter and atrocities were far worse than in 1931. It was the history of an earlier time, of the Mongol ravages of Asia, of Timur and the cold terror he spread – a horror which his name can even now evoke in Central Asia. There are lurid tales of Timur sacking a city. If an army dared to oppose him, Timur built up a pyramid of skulls of those he slaughtered. He camped in a tent of scarlet canvas outside the towns he besieged, thus symbolizing the massacres he intended to carry out. The ferocity of the Japanese likewise amazed the world. The massacre was done for the most part by Japanese conscripts, unfamiliar with war, perhaps neurotically working out of their system the extreme repressions in which they had passed so much of their lives. Some Japanese officers in other centres wept with shame and indignation when they heard details of the carnage.

Chinese burial parties afterwards counted upwards of a quarter of a million dead: some of the dead may have been tallied more than once, and more accurate estimates, if indeed they do exist, are no less subject to controversy. In any case, the burial rolls that were compiled are a sufficient measure of the extent of the catastrophe. There were many eye-witnesses who survived: against all odds, there generally are survivors of such events. They told of scenes of systematic arson, of looting on an unbelievable scale, of mass rapes in hospitals, in exclusive Chinese women's colleges, in many of the twenty-five refugee camps dotted round the city, in residential districts. And there was worse, as Captain Liang Ling-fang of the Chinese Army Medical Corps, for instance, was to testify at the Tokyo War Crimes Tribunal after the surrender of Japan:

We were given orders to stay in Nanking and take care of the Chinese wounded, and stay there after the Japanese took the city. We found that the Red Cross was no protection, and therefore dressed in civilian clothes, and we were in a refugee camp when the Japanese took the city. On the sixteenth, we were ordered by the Japanese to proceed to Shsia Kwan, on the bank of the River Yangtze, in Nanking. I estimate there were above 5,000 who were marched four abreast, and the line was a ¾ of a mile long. When we arrived there we were placed in a line near the River, and on either side of the line there formed and in front of [the] line were machineguns and Japanese soldiers, with the machineguns pointing at the line. There were two trucks carrying rope, and men were tied five in a group with their wrists tied below their backs, and I saw the first men who were shot by rifles in such groups and who were then thrown in the river by the Japanese. There were about 800 Japanese present, including officers, some of whom were in sedan automobiles . . . We [had] started from the refugee camp about five o'clock in the evening, arrived at the bank of the River about seven o'clock, and the binding of the prisoners and shooting kept up until two o'clock [in the morning].*

Liang's body still bore the marks of his ordeal; his testimony was corroborated by other witnesses. The episode that he described was by no means an isolated occurrence. In post-war Japan, there has been an observable tendency to regard tales such as Captain Liang's as exceptional or exaggerated. At the time, Japanese who were there had no such illusions.

The effect was profound in other countries of the world. At first the news of the outrage was censored, but ultimately it got into the world's press. Anxious though they were to avert their gaze from Asia, because of their preoccupations in Europe, the countries of the West found themselves distracted first by Shanghai, then by the events at Nanking, and were appalled by seeing a foretaste of what might soon be everywhere. From then on, the Japanese Army was held to be uncivilized, savage and terrible. The incident became known as the Rape of Nanking, and frenzied

* Pritchard and Zaide, op. cit., 2, pp. 3369–75 [PX 250, Sworn Statement by Captain Liang, dated 7 April 1946].

atrocities which the Japanese Army committed there, although no different in kind from what was to happen elsewhere, were on a scale quite unmatched anywhere else during the Greater East Asia and Pacific Conflict.

World opinion had favoured the Chinese side from the beginning of the war, but even those who most admired China or most despised Japan came to wonder how long China could endure the Japanese onslaught. Foreign condemnation was ineffectual in these early years, however. Without the benefits of Germany's substantial military mission and supply programme to China, and without Britain's amorphous but indispensable economic empire within China, which provided, respectively, the basis of Chinese defence and financial stability in the early years of the war, there seems little doubt that Japan would have won the China Incident absolutely.

The Japanese Cabinet itself was bitterly divided over future policy almost from the very beginning: there were suddenly vast new territories to administer, a frightening financial outlook, and a war which patently neither the War Ministry nor the Army General Staff could control. In a sense Japan's policy-making machinery went to war with itself. The Army repeatedly promised the Cabinet and the Emperor that the military advance would halt at one specified objective after another. Each time it was found that additional territory was desired to protect previous gains, and each time it was clear that immoderate elements within the Army were set to act as they themselves determined.

The Japanese certainly believed that they gave China generous opportunities to negotiate a peace settlement. The war was nearly six months old before the Government in Tokyo abandoned the limited aims which they had held when the fighting had started. A considerable number of peace feelers were extended either directly to China or indirectly through serious approaches to Germany, Britain and America. The Americans showed a marked reluctance to become involved, but the British, and more especially the Germans, took their opportunities far more seriously. Even Italy and France occasionally served as intermediaries in the furtherance of peace negotiations. But if Japan was eager to conclude a peace settlement, its leaders were rarely prepared to offer genuinely conciliatory terms to the Chinese once Japan's ascendency in the war became clear. The often hamfisted quality of the Japanese proposals was itself a product of the political turmoil that existed within the upper reaches of the Japanese military and political leadership: those who offered such proposals not only had a natural tendency to adopt positions which would be acceptable to most of the Japanese policy-making élites but also had to take account of the damage which any offer of over-generous concessions would do to their continuing political influence at home.

While the frustrations experienced by the Japanese began to manifest themselves in an increasing unwillingness to treat with the Nanking Government at all, the Japanese began to explore the possibility of linking the Japanese and Korean domestic economies with those of Occupied China and Manchukuo. On 22 December 1938 Prime Minister Konoye Fumimaro made a major radio broadcast to the world in which he proclaimed Japan's determination to create a 'New Order in East Asia': 'The spirit of renaissance is now sweeping over all parts of China and enthusiasm for reconstruction is mounting ever higher,' he declared, and he went on to urge the people of China to embrace a three-fold programme based upon 'neighbourly amity, common defence against communism, and economic co-operation'. He utterly failed to anticipate that in demanding the right to station Japanese troops at predetermined places throughout China and in the designation of Inner Mongolia as 'a special anti-communist area', the Chinese understood that he intended nothing less than the complete domination of China. One must appreciate the elements of continuity that existed between this manifesto and the historical trends of Japanese military campaigns and political schemes north of the Great Wall prior to the outbreak of the China Incident. Not for the first time was the Japanese definition of 'cooperation' profoundly different from the meaning which other countries ascribed to the word. Most foreigners – including the Chinese – were utterly amazed that the Japanese Prime Minister could close such a speech with what appeared to be sentiments of either unsurpassed self-delusion or unmitigated hypocrisy:

If the object of Japan in conducting the present vast military campaign be fully understood, it will be plain that what she seeks is neither territory nor indemnity for the costs of military operations. Japan demands only the minimum guarantee needed for the execution by China of her function as a participant in the establishment of the new order.

Japan not only respects the sovereignty of China, but she is prepared to give positive consideration to the questions of the abolition of extraterritoriality and of the rendition of the concessions and settlements matters which are necessary for the full independence of China.*

Yet in efforts to explain his motives to American interrogators after the Pacific War, Prince Konoye insisted that he had intended his speech as a genuine contribution to mutual understanding and goodwill: it was *not* Japan's purpose to annex China. Japan, as the stronger economic, military and even political power, naturally expected 'to take leadership

---

* Joyce C. Lebra, *Japan's Greater East Asia Co-Prosperity Sphere in World War II*, Oxford University Press, Kuala Lumpur, 1975, pp. 68–70.

in the development of a unified Far East'. But that was not regarded by the Japanese as tantamount to the destruction of Chinese sovereignty. His broadcast had been intended as no more than an enunciation of moral or political principles. The objectives set out in his speech could have been achieved with goodwill and good faith on both sides through cultural and economic ties rather than by armed conquest. In the end, he declared, the high principles underlying his speech were betrayed firstly by his own military, which corrupted his benevolent political aims by means of military force, and secondly by the Government of Chiang Kai-shek, which proved equally unresponsive to his overtures. Whether this rather confused but popular Prime Minister ever truly expected anything less, however, must remain something of an enigma. What is clear is that Konoye's 'New Order in East Asia' projected nothing less than the alignment of the entire political and economic resources of China in support of the domestic and international aspirations of Japan. Expressed in terms of Total War, that could have provided Japan with an incalculable increase in strength against any of her potential adversaries.

China managed, just barely, to withstand wave after wave of Japanese attacks during the first two years of the China Incident. Despite losing her principal cities, rivers and thousands of miles of territory, China survived. As each successive catastrophe was endured, China's self-confidence in itself emerged to strengthen China's historic contempt for its barbarian invaders. The few Chinese voices raised in support of a negotiated settlement with Japan found precious little favour. They were either eased out of positions of authority or isolated by Chiang Kai-shek. By the end of 1937 there was no possibility of a return to the *status quo ante bellum*: the human cost of the fighting had become too terrible for that. It became evident that the very success of the Japanese armed forces was acting as an impediment to peace. When Prince Konoye, the unhappy Japanese Prime Minister, decided in January 1938 to offer no more peace compromises after the collapse of a particularly important German mediation attempt, he laid particular stress on the bitterness which the Chinese must feel after having lost 700–800,000 soldiers in barely six months of war. Japan's own war dead were thought to number only 50,000. This may have been an over-estimate of the losses of the one, and an under-estimate of the other. Yet there was a great gap between the losses on both sides. Later Prince Konoye, one of the most remarkable ditherers ever to hold the premiership of Japan in the twentieth century, changed his mind several times and made further peace efforts, but he and other Japanese leaders remained anxious about the effects which possible peace negotiations would have on Japanese Army and civilian morale: with an Army

Paotow
Peking
Tientsin
Taiyuan
Tsinan   Tsingtao
Chengchow   Taierhchwang
Sian   Loyang
Nanking
Ichang   Hankow   Shanghai
Chungking   Anking   Hangchow
Ningpo
Changsha   Nanchang
Hengyang   Foochow
Kweiyang
Liuchow   Canton   Amoy
Nanning   Wuchow   Swatow
Hainan
1937 — 8

Paotow
Peking
Hankow   Shanghai
Changsha
Canton   Amoy
1938 — 9

CHINA FIGHTS ALONE 1937—41

Paotow
Peking
Ichang   Hankow   Shanghai
Changsha
Canton   Amoy
Swatow
Nanning
1939—40

Paotow
Peking
Ichang   Hankow   Shanghai
Changsha
Foochow
Canton   Amoy
Swatow
1940—41

of 1,600,000 men fighting on behalf of the Emperor, it was argued that the nation had an obligation to the tens of thousands of Japanese war dead, who would never rest until Japan gained victory. Moreover, so far as Prince Konoye and his intimates were concerned, offering to come to terms would only be interpreted as an admission of Japan's underlying weakness which would create financial panic in the Japanese money markets and would inflict a major blow to Japanese morale. To this argument Prince Chichibu, the Emperor's younger brother, retorted, 'How much longer do they think that Japan's financial strength will last anyway?'*

The death toll grew, and the Chinese continued to lose many times the number of casualties that the Japanese suffered. Looking back, the British Embassy in China observed in an annual report: 'Measured in terms of human anguish, there has probably never been, even in the long history of Chinese suffering, such a year as 1938.'† The spirit of China was transformed in the process; an angry and increasingly resolute China faced Japan with implacable hatred.

Worries about the threat of Soviet mischief-making on the northern frontier, concern about Japan's relations with the Western Powers (and particularly Britain), and mounting evidence that the military and economic strength of Japan was unequal to the conquest of Chinese resistance all brought home to most members of the Government, to virtually the whole of the General Staff and to the War Minister, as it did to other influential circles such as the *zaibatsu*, that some kind of rapid settlement of the China Incident was imperative for Japan's well-being. But it did not happen. Chiang had set his face against peace; he was prepared to endure a long war because he and his supporters could have survived nothing shorter, and so the war dragged on. The American Ambassador in Tokyo, Joseph Grew, likened Japan's war with China to the fable of Brer Rabbit's struggle with the Tar Baby: the more fiercely the Japanese forces thrashed the Chinese, the more firmly the Japanese attached themselves to their victim, and when the Japanese did try to disengage themselves, they found themselves ensnared, stuck firmly to the Chinese.

In 1938 there was much fighting in North and Central China. The fighting tended to concentrate along the main arteries of the country, which were its railways, rivers and canals. China possessed 225,000 miles of canals, and as one well-qualified western scholar observed in the

---

* *Harada-Saionji Memoirs*, Part XIV, Chapter 260.
† F3662/53/10, Annual Report on China for 1938 by Archibald Clark Kerr, 28 February 1939, FO 371/23443.

mid-thirties: 'If forty canals were dug across the United States from east to west, and sixty from north to south, their total mileage would be less than that of the canals in China.'* In the spring, in an effort to halt the Japanese advance, Chiang ordered the breaching of the Yellow River dykes. This slowed but failed to halt them, but it was estimated that a million peasants drowned in the flood which resulted. It began to be clear what torment had been let loose on the world. There was heavy fighting: the Chinese engaged in positional warfare, and did not use guerrilla tactics.

Some divisions showed the result of their having received German training from Chiang Kai-shek's German advisers. In the Battle of Taierchwang, near the border between Kiangsu and Shantung Provinces, the Chinese won a temporary triumph in April which purchased a six-week delay in the advance of the Japanese upon Hsuchow, the junction of the important two Tientsin–Pukow and Lunghai railways, but the moral and strategic effect of this solitary victory were minor in comparison with the fighting that began to distract the world in the next few months at Changkufeng against the Russians. While fighting raged at Changkufeng, the Japanese advance through Wuhan Province in Central China slowed down but did not falter. After the Changkufeng Incident came to an end, Japanese reinforcements hastened to the Central China front, and the Japanese juggernaut, to no one's surprise, once more picked up speed.

In October, the Japanese, in the south, took Canton and its hinterland. Canton was the original base of the Kuomintang; its capture was significant, as it seemed to symbolize striking at the root of the Kuomintang. It also left the Japanese in possession of the hinterland surrounding Hong Kong, hitherto the principal avenue for German and other western arms imports intended for the Chinese Republic.

In the same month the Japanese, advancing up the Yangtze, had taken Hankow, last of the fabled Three Cities of Wu. This was not an easy victory, as many successes had been. Chiang Kai-shek's administration, with all the impedimenta of government, was forced to withdraw once more. This time, having learned something at least, the Kuomintang moved a thousand miles up the Yangtze to Chungking, the principal town (though not the capital) of the remote province of Szechwan, which bordered on Tibet, and which since 1935 had been prepared by Chiang as the national capital in an emergency. Chiang was now following what proved to be his masterplan for the war: to trade space for time; to care little for losses of territory (or manpower) provided the centre of resistance remained intact; to put faith in the huge distances and population of

* Scherer, op. cit., p. 14.

China, and to hang on in spite of defeats (and administrative incompetence or malfeasance).

Chungking was well beyond the gorges in the Yangtze, which are one of the beauty spots of China. To attack Chungking was to involve the Japanese in such problems of logistics that Chiang was safe there. The Japanese did not follow him further.

A very long pause set in. Japanese communications and supply lines grew lengthy and cumbersome. The prospect of a stalemate once again brought fear to the Japanese. There were few signs of public discontent, and official misgivings were muted. Despite deep gloom in Japan's Imperial Household and the Ministries of Finance and Foreign Affairs, ways seemed to be found to avoid the great threats of bankruptcy and international economic or armed intervention in the war by outside Powers. Senior naval officers, especially Navy Minister Yonai Mitsumasa and Navy Vice-Minister Yamamoto Isoroku, had opposed the war from the beginning and were unflagging in their efforts to moderate excessive Army demands for the commitment of more and more of the nation's resources to the military conquest of Chinese resistance. But beneath this thin crust of sensibility lay a core of middle-ranking naval officers who had control of the Naval General Staff and who were altogether too eager to exploit the war in China through a desire to support their common cause with their counterparts in the Army and through a wild ambition to 'facilitate future air-raids' against Hong Kong and other bastions of western power in East Asia. Even the Japanese Army found these Navy hotheads somewhat frightening and recognized that such men might bring the Army into conflict with Britain and America as well as the Army's traditional foes, China and Russia. A compromise was reached. Thus far the Army had been successful on the battlefield even if victory proved ever elusive. So long as naval appropriations suffered no harm, the senior naval leadership of Japan tolerated the maintenance of the Japanese Army's war in China until such a time as a truly favourable opportunity to end it might appear.

Japan took stock of what it had gained. After only a few months of war, the Japanese had captured most of the important river systems which formed China's economic arteries. By the end of 1938 they also possessed nine-tenths of the Chinese railway system and controlled the entire coastline of China under a tight blockade. In a technical sense little remained of China worth conquering by Japan at the end of 1938. Such heavy fighting was not to happen again, even when this war was eventually swallowed up in the Second World War, and when China's weapons were much strengthened by aid from its allies, mostly flown over 'the hump' of northern Burma. All the important battles appeared to have been fought and won. Japan could be content with consolidating her position and mopping up isolated pockets of resistance. Japanese morale predictably reached dizzying heights, and so did Japanese political ambition.

Superficially Japan had conquered territory which contained 170 million people. China had lost its principal seaports, the Chinese Navy had ceased to exist, and the Japanese mounted very effective naval patrols round the entire seaboard of the country from Manchukuo to French Indo-China. China depended henceforward for foreign supplies on two routes. The first was an earth road from Russia through the huge province of Sinkiang (Chinese Turkestan), which had been used for centuries as part of the ancient Silk Route linking China with Central Asia; in more recent times it had been used by the bandits of Sinkiang, a no man's land, and by Chinese communists as their back alley to the Soviet Union. The other was a new road, 350 miles long and completed only in 1938 by 200,000 coolies, from the city of Kunming (formerly Yunnanfu), provincial capital of Yunnan and the communications hub of south-west China, to the south, where it ended at Lashio in northern Burma, providing access to roads leading south to the Bay of Bengal at Rangoon. Both roads were very long, poorly constructed, virtually impassable by motor vehicles during the rainy season between June and November, and liable to traffic blocks at the best of times. The difficulties of the logistics and terrain were formidable. When pack animals instead of motor vehicles were used, it took about sixty days to transport military supplies from Rangoon to Kunming via the Burma Road. For a time China had been able to use the port of Haiphong, in Indo-China, but the French authorities ran hot and cold depending upon the attentions of the Japanese, and the bridges were destroyed which carried the French-owned railway line linking this port with its terminus 550 miles away at Kunming, where it connected with roads and canals to Chungking and the whole of South and Central China.

Unfortunately for the Japanese, the stalemate in China which had emerged in late 1938 grew more serious during the next year as the Nationalist régime continued to survive. By 1939 Japanese military forces seemed to have reached the limits of their power in China. No appreciable advances were made in the central regions of China, and events on the periphery had a significance far larger than the war against the Nationalists. Hainan Island was taken after an unopposed invasion on 10 February, which frightened the French into reducing the trickle of war supplies which flowed north from Haiphong in Indo-China to Kwangsi

Province in Free China. A larger expedition all but completed this object in November after landing north-west of Hainan on the Chinese mainland at Pakhoi and easily advancing north to Nanning. Neither of these campaigns materially advanced Japanese efforts to end the war in China, but the seizure of Hainan marked an important step towards the Pacific War. It was occupied in the vain hope of satisfying the ambitions of activists in the Japanese Naval General Staff who wanted to wrest control of the South China Seas from the British and so pluck from European hands the fabulous riches of Malaya, the Netherlands East Indies and French Indo-China. Thus the move into Hainan revealed how far the authority of moderate, pro-western senior leaders of the Japanese Navy had slipped. The advocates of Japan's 'Southern Advance' wanted to secure Asia's back door against the West, but in pursuing that strategy the Japanese invited more trouble than they could handle.

The notorious arrogance of Japanese soldiers, while often not much greater towards foreigners in China than towards Japanese civilians at home, inevitably led to international incidents. As Japanese casualties in China reached approximately half a million men during 1939, scapegoats were sought. Although Japanese officials never ceased to bicker among themselves, they found common cause in blaming Britain, France and the United States for Japan's failure to achieve victory in China. The expeditions to Hainan and Pakhoi reflected this general tendency, and so did crude reprisals against western property and commercial interests in Occupied China. These measures were effective locally but encouraged Britain and the United States at least to resist further encroachments on their treaty rights in China. There were frequent incidents on the Yangtze River involving confrontations between Japanese and western gunboats, and a particularly alarming confrontation occurred at the International Settlement on Kulangsu, an island lying off Amoy in the vicinity of Formosa. Japanese troops landed there on 23 May 1939 in search of Chinese terrorists. This resulted in a rapid concentration of British, American and French warships at Amoy, and all three countries promptly landed separate shore parties each equal in size to the Japanese contingent. Tension lessened only when the British and French forces withdrew at the outbreak of the European War. The Japanese and Americans then negotiated a mutual withdrawal of their marines in mid-October.

Notwithstanding the Kulangsu Incident and provocations on the Yangtze, Japan discounted the danger of armed intervention by the West. Indeed, the Japanese Army had developed no contingency plans for war against either Britain or the United States at this time, and the Japanese Navy had no detailed plan, yet, for war against an Anglo-American coalition. The Japanese had the satisfaction of believing they knew how Britain and America would react in the event of a war. The Japanese Embassy in Washington, DC, had secured a copy of War Plan Orange, the United States contingency plan for a war against Japan, and the Japanese Government knew the substance of British naval war plans, which had been obvious in general outline ever since construction of the Singapore Naval Base had begun in the aftermath of the First World War. Japanese cryptographers had cracked the British diplomatic codes and had the benefit of monitoring, among other things, how far apart the British and Americans were.

So long as Japan left Hong Kong to the British and avoided all but the occasional outrage against British or American nationals in China, the Anglo-Saxon Powers seemed unlikely and indeed unprepared to mount the kind of combined effort necessary to impose their will by naval means against Japan. Short of a world war, the Japanese Navy was capable of defending Japanese interests and even extending Japanese influence in the waters of the Western Pacific Ocean and South Seas. The China Incident did not adversely affect Japan's naval strength in the Western Pacific. On the contrary the training received by Japanese naval airmen under combat conditions in China was invaluable and allowed the Japanese to improve their aircraft far more rapidly than would have been possible in peacetime. Likewise, the war in China gave Japan the opportunity to develop amphibious operations into a new art several years ahead of any other nation. In traditional areas of naval construction, Japanese naval architects had managed to evade the restrictions of the Washington and London naval limitations treaties, which expired in 1936, and by means of four naval replenishment plans kept pace qualitatively, as well as quantitatively, with rapid British and American naval expansion programmes. The result was that by 1939 Japan was impervious to either (but not both) of the British or the United States navies in the Western Pacific and most of the China Seas.

Nevertheless, Japan had a well-justified fear of Anglo-American economic encirclement. There was disturbing evidence very early during the China Incident that Britain wanted American support for a programme to impose an early end to the war at Japanese expense through joint economic countermeasures against Japan. Later, strong pressure groups in the United States lobbied for similar ideas. Tokyo could not hope to resist such a programme for long.

Over 40 per cent of Japanese exports and more than half her imports were with the United States. Japan's balance of payments' situation was precarious, and her financial future was a hostage to the vagaries of

American public policy. Although Government controls in Japan succeeded in limiting Japanese imports to essential materials, the trend over the first two and a half years of the China Incident was for Japanese exports to fall sharply while imports from the United States continued to rise. Traditionally, Japan had been dependent upon the British Empire and the United States for vital strategical raw materials ranging from tin, nickel and zinc to oil, iron and steel. The British calculated that a bilateral embargo on Anglo-Japanese trade would hurt the British Empire more than Japan, but it was evident to all that confiscation of Britain's considerable assets in Japan would not begin to compensate Japan for the losses that Japan would suffer if Britain and America both imposed sanctions against the Japanese economy. This difficulty for Japan increased substantially when the European War began in September 1939: alternative sources of supply for some strategical goods vanished along with an important segment of the Japanese export market. Meanwhile, Yen-bloc countries such as Formosa, Korea and Manchuria absorbed an increasingly high proportion of Japanese industrial output while contributing a disappointingly low proportion of Japanese war production requirements. Self-sacrifice by Japanese consumers permitted the war to continue indefinitely, but it was universally accepted that Japan had no margin of safety against the firm application of Anglo-American economic sanctions.

Within China Proper, however, there was no more large-scale fighting of transcontinental dimensions for five years. For much of that time it might have been supposed that the war had petered out. Yet a staggering 40 to 50 per cent of Japan's entire national budget was appropriated for defence purposes, and the nation was resolved to fight for victory.

Japan suffered its first reverses in the occupied districts in the north. Its control of the railways and towns did not give it control of the rural areas. It began to feel severely the effects of communist guerrilla warfare. At first the Japanese generals had supposed that they had the measures for repressing the communists, and, for a time, little was heard about the communist armies. This was to the dismay of the friends of China who had built up extravagant hopes on the reconciliation between Chiang and the communists. Eventually, though, the stubborn resistance of the communists began to take a toll. To have overcome it, to have attempted a stricter control which would have eliminated this, would have cost many millions of troops, which the Japanese could not afford. China had begun to draw the advantages from one of its assets, size. Because the Japanese could not pacify the vast area of Hopei, Shantung and Shensi provinces, which they had overrun, they constituted themselves as a target for guerrilla action.

Chiang Kai-shek sat in his fortress at Chungking and waited. The city, though not beautiful like Chengtu, the capital of Szechuan, was fitted for its purpose. Rainfall was heavy, and the clouds which overhung it for weeks on end, together with surrounding mountains which made it difficult to approach, prevented it from being an easy target of attacks from the air. It was bombed heavily for a time, but later was left in peace. The city was large, and had once been affluent. Chiang's task was to keep his Government in existence, to survive the plots against him, to plot against others – to continue to be regarded as the symbol of nationalism. Alas, though wartime propaganda made the reputation of Chungking as a heroic centre of resistance, a long, slow demoralization set in among the Kuomintang establishment, the inevitable result among an army and bureaucracy condemned to too much idleness, and this proved in the long run too much for Chiang Kai-shek to combat. The Chinese of the Kuomintang and the Army staff were a different people from the particularist Szechuanese, who resented their impact on their ancient provincial culture. Relations between them and the local people deteriorated steadily. 'Down-river gangsters' was the term used for Kuomintang officials by the Szechuanese people. Internal rot was the price the Kuomintang paid for the tactics of masterly inactivity.

Chiang Kai-shek was resting his hopes, not on the Kuomintang Army, but chiefly on foreign aid, principally American aid, which his diplomats in the United States tirelessly sought. Certainly there was abundant American goodwill to China, based chiefly on the vast American missionary enterprise there. It seemed that China, before the war, had been willing to reconstruct its society according to American ideas, and this seemed to impose on the United States the obligation of protecting it internationally.

As far as China was concerned, Japan for a time now turned its back on battles and daring campaigns, and engaged in political warfare and in political intrigue. The only military action was a single attempt in June 1940 to force the Yangtse gorges, which ended at Ichang. Japan decided that to carry on the war was to bring complication after complication, and, from now on, explored ways to end it. From this time, 1939–40, the Japanese Army sought peace in China as constantly and assiduously (though maladroitly) as it had once welcomed war. It was out of the question to arrange to annex the vast territory it had overrun, and to rule it directly as the British used to rule India. The need for civil servants would be immense, beyond anything which Japan could supply. It turned in consequence to indirect rule, to organizing North China as a puppet state (similar in general shape to Manchukuo), which would be under the rule of a single man or body of men upon whose loyalty they could rely, because it would be clear that, with Japanese aid removed, they would collapse.

Their first thought was to use Chiang Kai-shek himself. If they could have detached him from his nationalism, and made it worth his while, Chiang would have proved an excellent puppet. He would have had a full and apparently contented life hunting down communists. Realizing how greatly an alliance with Chiang would serve them, understanding that this was indeed the crisis of the war, the Japanese used the utmost finesse to bring it about. But neither the secret emissaries whom they sent tirelessly to visit him, nor the German and British Ambassadors who proposed mediation, brought the Japanese any hopeful news. Chiang had little room to manoeuvre in. He had made his way to the top of the Kuomintang, but he had become a prisoner of the national movement, which would have broken him if he had sought to betray it. Chiang, who knew the dark corners of China's political life, and availed himself of the services of its inhabitants, knew well what agents it would employ.

Furthermore Generalissimo Chiang Kai-shek, who was the heart and soul of Chinese unity against Japan, probably never expected any peace to emerge from these discussions. Chiang demanded nothing less than Japan's unconditional withdrawal from China: he only departed from this basic position when he evidently hoped to throw Tokyo off course while Japanese armies were sweeping towards one particularly important objective or another. For the most part, Chiang disdainfully rejected Japan's efforts to seek a compromise based on present realities, and he made use of western good offices to further China's international propaganda campaign rather than to achieve a negotiated end to the war. Not only did the Chinese mistrust the Japanese peace offers but they had also come to regard resistance to Japan as a necessary precondition for the survival of Chinese nationalism. In addition, the Japanese terms were often poorly expressed due partly to the vagaries of the Japanese language and partly to fears that enemy morale might recover if it became known beforehand how small were Japan's fundamental desiderata.

Reluctantly the Japanese decided on alternative plans. After several experiments with Chinese puppet régimes of little significance, they set themselves to persuade certain respected nationalists, who were opposed to Chiang Kai-shek, to form a Government which had all the outward shape of the Kuomintang, and which the Japanese could substitute for the official Kuomintang. They had resort to one of the most distinguished members of the Kuomintang, who had been almost a founding father of the party.

This man, Wang Ching-wei, one time Vice-President of the Kuomintang republic, had previously built a career on the leadership of the left wing. He had never exhausted the fame which he had gained by being involved in a plot in the days of the Empire to murder a Manchu grandee. In private, his views were anything but radical and he had married a very wealthy wife, who came from a family of Singapore millionaires. But his political talents had been acceptable to the revolutionary branch of the Kuomintang. After the fall of Canton and Hankow he seems to have accepted the Japanese argument that further resistance was useless, and to have argued that China, by recasting its foreign policy, could still come to terms with Japan which would be mutually advantageous. At Chungking, he conferred at length with Chiang Kai-shek. Though no record exists of their conversation, it is known that the two men debated in full the Japanese peace offer.

In December 1939 he recognized his failure, and left the capital. The Japanese were willing to see in him the best substitute head of a cooperative Chinese Government. He had the aura of a major politician. He had the record of being a persistent rival of Chiang Kai-shek. Mostly Chiang had succeeded in keeping him out of office, and, when Wang Ching-wei had manoeuvred so that he compelled Chiang to share power with him, Chiang was suspected of a hand in the mysterious shooting which had removed him from office. The Japanese acted with resolution. Wang's name, the prestige of Nanking city, the attraction of the Kuomintang – renamed by Wang the Reformed Kuomintang – all these were used to give the new Government such prestige as it could have in a Nanking which remembered vividly what it had been made to suffer.

The Government came into being in 1940. A fairly long list of land-holders, industrialists, former officials, diplomats out of employment, politicians who had ruined their prospects with the official Kuomintang, came to see if the vistas opened up under the new administration appeared brighter for them. Many were recruited for the régime. Many of the more or less respectable Chinese nationalists had begun to find the régime of the Reformed Kuomintang very beguiling, especially since it reconciled nationalism with the prospect of opting out of the war. Wang Ching-wei's Government was a copy of the genuine Kuomintang. Its constitution was much the same; it contained the complications and intricacies which had puzzled all those who tried to follow Chinese politics. Its methods of administration were much the same.

In administration the régime was slightly less corrupt than had been expected. It did little that was outwardly disgraceful. As the head of a puppet Government, camouflaged for the general public in the colours of nationalism, Wang Ching-wei did neither more nor less than was expected of him: he fought for China's interests while being ready in the last resort to yield to Japan's superior strength. In China he played the same part as Marshal Pétain in France. But Wang's Government never succeeded in living down the sense of national shame in which it was born; never managed to take independent life; it remained a creature of the Japanese; it never became a serious body internationally. From the point of view of a historian detached from these events, the chief points worth under-scoring are that the Japanese did put a great deal of energy into cultivating local régimes as part of their search for a peaceful solution to the China Incident; that Free China's sole unifying force in local as in national government was Chiang Kai-shek's personality cult, and yet that there were many Chinese who took immense risks to seek some kind of com-promise based upon a mixture of *realpolitik*, personal ambition and their sense of Pan-Asian brotherhood.

Meanwhile the pretence that the war was a joint one, of the Kuo-mintang and the communists against Japan, was wearing thin. The Chinese communists, in the regions which they had overrun in the north, maintained a lively propaganda against the Japanese. Guerrilla warfare was their special art. There was also activity by guerrilla bands who fought in the name of the Kuomintang. But the pretence, which had been built up immediately after the Sian Incident, that the armies of the communists were to be fused with the armies of the Kuomintang under some kind of common command, never became a reality. The communists had no intention of surrendering the sole command of their Army. That was their most effective instrument in Chinese politics, and they would hold on to it. The communists relied on their Army to win them new territory, and to retain what they had; and they could scarcely trust their old enemy, the Kuomintang, with any recognized power to dispose of this force.

A subtle, concealed, very bitter struggle was resumed between the Kuomintang and the communists. Everybody who was interested in Chinese politics saw the danger of revived civil war taking shape. The Kuomintang, without entirely dropping the mask of the common front, was alert to the spread of communist power, and tried to guard against it by maintaining, as far as it could, an inner blockade of the regions which the communists ruled, including an embargo on all medical supplies. The most competent and orderly section of the Kuomintang Army was in fact left permanently at Sian, where its sole duty was to watch and over-awe the communists. The communists directed their fire equally against the Kuomintang and the Japanese.

Sometimes the struggle became too obvious for decency between apparent allies. Each side had its own territory. Sometimes the communists would move into a Kuomintang region: the Kuomintang would drive them out by force. At such times the hollowness of the partnership became plain. There was a particularly flagrant example of this in 1941 when the communist Fourth Route Army was ambushed by patent treachery, and fighting flared up on a large scale. The communists lost several generals in the course of this affair. But even at such times both the communists and the Kuomintang tried to put limits to hostilities. An important part in keeping peace at least formally was played by the communist representative at Chungking, who was Chou En-lai, saviour of Chiang, destined in the next decade to become Prime Minister of China. A competition was being fought out between the two Governments, to determine which of them, in the harsh conditions of war, had the better spirit to endure. The war was proving a hothouse, and had brought on the decision which otherwise might have taken half a century to deliver. All the data were to the discomfiture of the Kuomintang. The communists, who began as very much the weaker, became a steadily greater force.

Meanwhile a part of the horrors which had overtaken the Chinese people became known to the West – to a West which was bracing itself to face its own agony. The full terrors of war broke over the Chinese towns and countryside. They had gradually become accustomed to civil war during the thirty years of breakdown of ordered government. In much of the country, the old magistrates had left. The armies of the war-lords had harried the villages, seized their grain, and sometimes carried off the young men and women. But all this was as nothing compared with what befell in the years after 1936. One estimate puts the number uprooted from their homes by the war as 50 million. The Chinese are as a rule greatly attached to their villages, and will not forsake a home which contains the graves of their ancestors. Many of the cherished customs of the village – the sweeping of the family graves, ceremonial meals eaten over the tombs – are connected with tomb-rites. Now a great wrench had loosened the population from its hold. China dissolved from people living in orderly, extremely conservative patterns of life, into a maze of people wandering aimlessly from village to village. They sought food, protection, shelter. All China seemed to be restlessly on the move. Any representation of its people at this time shows them trudging from place to place, carrying their belongings with them. (A similar nightmare befell persons who were compelled to see the sights in post-war Germany.) How many perished in this time will never be known. Their plight made them powerless to escape the scourge of famine and the scourge of the other terror of the

Chinese countryside, flood. One by one, the very ancient annual ceremonies in the villages, which gave Chinese life its admirable quality and
its deep sense of continuity, were given up. Life became especially hard
for the old, the class which Chinese civilization was notorious for
revering.

Colour, richness and elegance disappeared from China. Everywhere
people went dressed in simple cotton clothes, either because they had been
impoverished, or because the slightest display of luxury was an invitation
to plunder. The pleasantness and decorum of the life of the Chinese upper
classes, which had already been much shaken for a hundred years by the
impact of the West, descended to a new calamitous level, as society gradually disintegrated. Only in such protected centres as Chungking was the
attempt made to live in accustomed Chinese style.

A similar break-up of society had taken place in France at the end of
the Hundred Years War, and in Germany during the Thirty Years War.

Early on in this period there had taken place one of the most unlooked-
for emigrations in history. As we have seen, the universities of China had
a precocious development. In wealth, in their standing in society, by the
personal eminence of their staff, both Chinese and also the core of expatriate foreigners, they were ahead of the standards which universities
might have been expected to reach in the country, and were suited for a
society such as China might have evolved two or three generations later.
In consequence of this, much of the most advanced, the purest, and
certainly the most disinterested nationalism of the day was nursed to life
within their walls.

Most of the universities were on the seaboard in the path of the Japanese
invasion. They were one of its special targets, because the Japanese, being
themselves an East Asian people, understood (though Japan did not share
this characteristic) the extraordinary influence which the Chinese intelligentsia had over the rulers of the nation. The Chinese student was alone
among the student class of the world in not feeling, or feeling much less,
an acute sense of frustration. Why should he? The nation hung on his
moods, was willing to follow him in his attitudes to Ministers and public
affairs. Since he was so influential, the student buoyed himself up: and
the conditions he put up with in student life, the squalid poverty, were
felt to be the necessary price of privilege. Besides it was spread equally
over the whole student body. Let them reduce the pride and aspiration of
the intelligentsia, the Japanese told themselves, and they would have gone
a long way in subduing Chinese nationalism. Under Japanese domination,
the universities knew that they would face a purge, and the conditions of

the new life would be quite intolerable to them. Rather than suffer it, many of the university communities moved off by spontaneous resolution, and trekked from the coasts to new sites far in the interior.

Chinese learning was pulling up its stakes and seeking out a territory where it might exist in freedom; and, as the price to be paid for this, live a life less gilded than before. The professors and their assistants, the student body, and university servants, all sought a home where they could continue their life with less harassment. Previously, Chinese scholars had not taken kindly to manual work; now they voluntarily undertook the hardship of the journey, the uncertainties of what awaited them, and a life of toil. It was the more surprising because these learned societies had to leave palatial premises, which had been given them by millionaires and foreign philanthropists, and had to fit their academic life into camps which had been made available to them as exiles. Throughout their vicissitudes they had safeguarded their libraries and the equipment of their scientific laboratories. Many of them transported these across the rivers and mountains of inland China.

During the war years the Chinese intelligentsia continued their studies diligently. In view of the way in which learning was regarded this turned out to be the most useful thing which they could contribute to China's war effort. They had firmly aligned themselves with the decision to resist Japan, and by their action in seeking voluntary exile they increased their prestige in the eyes of the people. The scholars and the mass of common people came closer together.

The universities, in deciding on their odysseys, were influenced by the example of the Chinese communists on the Long March. From this time there began to grow up the great sympathy of the Chinese scholar class for the communists. The scholars felt themselves being blown along by the same hurricane which had swept together the communist insurgents throughout China: and as the leadership of the Kuomintang began to falter, they began to look to the communists for an alternative. They did so with more eagerness because when they had migrated in the cause of freedom, they found that, when they eventually reached the security of the interior, they were regarded with suspicion by the Kuomintang, and that their freedom was interfered with by an irksome secret police. The campus was invaded by an army of spies.

The reliance on the secret police by Chiang Kai-shek to maintain his exaggerated political role was a departure from Chinese tradition. Before Chiang, China had known periods of despotism; but the despot had, to a remarkable degree, avoided the organization of a secret police as the instrument of tyranny. Even in the last years of the Manchus the

Government, though repressive, had avoided the creation of an organ specially for Intelligence and coercion. Therefore the collisions which now became frequent between the literati and the secret police offered the more provocation because the Chinese had not been accustomed in the past to think of the police as a necessary evil.

The writings of Chinese academics became full of woe; they had exchanged the persecution of the Japanese for the supervision of the police. It was less efficient, less rigorous, but it was deeply offensive. The grievances thus sown were to bear fruit at the end of the war. Without the moral approval of the scholar class, the Chinese communists would never have been able to impose themselves so successfully on the Chinese nation.

CHAPTER 10

International Alarums: Japan and Appeasement

'A war postponed may be a war averted!'* – Anthony Eden

BETWEEN 1931 and 1939, while facing military aggression committed or threatened by Germany, Italy and Japan, the foreign policy options of the western democracies were reduced to a choice between three dangerous strategies – or traditions – each with historical roots: 'Appeasement', 'Resistance' and 'Isolation'. The British tended to favour the well-trodden pathway of Appeasement, a policy based upon 'moderation' and conciliation which had served Britain's perfectly respectable selfish aims throughout most of the preceding century or more. By concessions to the territorial, economic or even ideological ambitions and conceits of powerful potential enemies, Britain hoped to lead their governments away from 'gangsterism' (to borrow Anthony Eden's word for it) and back into the modalities of peaceful international relations which so favoured British ascendency in the world.

'Resistance', a policy superficially opposite to 'Appeasement', involving steadfast confrontation against aggression, was favoured by France and some elements in the United States throughout most of the inter-war years (although practised more in the breach than in the observance). While Resistance may take 'peaceful' forms (for example, economic sanctions or non-recognition of territorial or political change), it carries with it an implication that war (for which France and the United States, as well as Britain, were generally unprepared) is preferable to surrender in matters of immutable principle. Lacking sufficient strength to defeat the forces ranged against them, any policy of British, French and even American resistance to German, Italian or Japanese aggression had to be predicated upon effective rearmament or, at the very least, upon the acquisition of powerful, dependable allies. Failing that, as Prime Minister Neville Chamberlain

---

* Quoted in K. Feiling, *The Life of Neville Chamberlain*, Macmillan, London, 1947, p. 320, or, as Winston Churchill wrote in his final volume of *The World Crisis* in 1931, 'A war postponed is a war prevented', cited in M. Gilbert, *The Roots of Appeasement*, Weidenfeld & Nicolson, London, 1966, p. 155.

avowed as late as January 1939, 'In the absence of any powerful ally, and until our armaments are completed, we must adjust our foreign policy to our circumstances.'* Unfortunately, there were practical difficulties which undermined British and French attempts to rearm or to attract the kind of allies they required: as the British Chiefs of Staff warned their political superiors in December 1937, more than three years after the rearmament programme began and while the greatest crises were yet to befall, it was the risk of a two- or three-enemy war which was of prime concern:

The outstanding feature of the present situation is the increasing probability that a war started in any one of these three areas may extend to one or both of the other two. Without overlooking the assistance which we would hope to obtain from France and possibly other allies, we cannot foresee the time when our defence forces will be strong enough to safeguard our trade, territory and vital interests against Germany, Italy and Japan at the same time ... they could not exaggerate the importance from the point of view of Imperial Defence of any political or international action which could be taken to reduce the number of our potential enemies and to gain the support of powerful allies.†

The underlying difficulty was that by the time the western democracies awoke to the challenge of Japanese aggression in Manchuria during 1931, neither Britain nor France had sufficient means to defend their respective vital interests and the United States plainly lacked the political will to do so. The effects of the economic depression placed severe limitations on the ability of any of the three to make good their military deficiencies. Too little rearmament would be ineffective; too much (or even enough) would bankrupt the soundest European economy. Prominent among the circumstances of the western democracies which differed from those of Germany, Italy and Japan was that the latter were intent upon drawing upon the resources of neighbouring economies through aggression (as in fact occurred in Manchuria, China, Austria, Czechoslovakia, Poland, France, the Netherlands and so forth). If they could be prevented from achieving their objectives, however, the economies of Germany, Italy and Japan were more vulnerable than the better balanced economies of the western democracies. The problem was that an *unanswerable* rearmament programme (that is, any programme which potential enemies could not match, step by step) would require *time* – purchased at great expense by international concessions or ignored only at great economic, political or military peril.

* Letter to Mrs Morton Prince, 16 January 1939, cited by Feiling, p. 324.
† CID 1366-B, Report by the Chiefs of Staff entitled 'The Strength of Great Britain Compared with Certain Other Nations as at 1 January 1938', 12 November 1937, CAB 4/26, British Public Record Office, Kew.

Even if governments did their sums correctly, an adequate scale of rearmament, if produced too soon, would doom a nation's armed forces to obsolescence in time of war. If, contrariwise, rearmament proceeded at an inadequate level or set out to achieve its designed results over too long a period, a crisis might occur or a war indeed might be lost before deficiencies could be overcome. As General Maxime Weygand, Inspector General of the French Army, declared in a review of French defence policy in mid-January 1933, less than a fortnight before Hitler swept to power in the German polls:

If we leave questions of this magnitude without examining or solving them, we shall be led inexorably day by day, under the pressure of budgetary necessities, political influences or international blackmail, to take measures which will gradually drain our national forces of their substance. They will become merely a façade and will not be in a condition to fulfil their mission at the hour of danger.*

In Britain, rearmament received its initial impetus first from the Manchurian Incident. Only later, after Hitler's rise to power, did attention begin to shift towards regarding Germany as the greater peril. In the process, time was lost. Yet the arguments in favour of limiting defence expenditure in the midst of a worldwide economic depression were plain enough, and so it took both the unbridled exercise of Japanese military might in Manchuria and the political changes in Germany to force the British Government to abandon the principle of Winston Churchill's 'Ten-Year Rule', imposed by him as Chancellor of the Exchequer in 1928, 'That it would be assumed for the purpose of framing the Estimates of the Fighting Services, that at any given date there will be no major war for ten years.'† Thus while French politicians, who were deaf to the sound of battle on the Asiatic mainland and responded to the economic crisis by actually *cutting* French expenditure on rearmament, the British authorities took the first steps in the opposite direction, although the faith of the British Treasury in orthodox economic doctrine severely limited the scale of what London attempted. In both countries, resources of skilled manpower, productive capacity and their ability to maintain financial credit abroad were crucial. Throughout the 1930s the French economy teetered on the brink of insolvency while at the same time the intense pacifism of the French public and the volatility of French domestic politics made a nonsense of long-range economic planning and rearmament policy.

* A. Adamthwaite, *The Making of the Second World War*, Allen & Unwin, London, 1974, doc. 2.
† N. H. Gibbs, *Grand Strategy* vol. I: *Rearmament Policy*, HMSO, London, 1976, pp. 55–64.

The importance of preserving Britain's purchasing power played a vital role in a country completely dependent upon overseas supplies for its survival: as Sir Warren Fisher, the immensely powerful Permanent Under-Secretary of the Treasury (and Head of the Civil Service), pointed out in a paper circulated to the Cabinet with the first Report of the Defence Requirements Committee in April 1934, raw materials and food 'are only produced within this country in negligible quantities and therefore have to be secured from other countries who will not, of course, give us them, and, when our international purchasing power is exhausted, will not continue indefinite credits to us'.*

Judged by orthodox economic standards, not only were financial strength and economic stability seen to be essential in peacetime economic recovery from the great depression but in time of war they would assume even greater significance – as what the British Treasury and strategical authorities termed 'the fourth arm in defence', no less important than the three fighting services and 'without which purely military effort would be of no avail'.† Although Britain and France felt they had little chance of coming out victorious in a short, sharp war, they believed they stood an excellent chance of eventual success against the military strength (and economic vulnerability) of their potential enemies in a long war. The point was put well by Sir Thomas Inskip, Minister for the Co-ordination of Defence, in December 1937:

The maintenance of credit facilities and our general balance of trade are of vital importance, not merely from the view of our strength in peacetime, but equally for purposes of war. This country cannot hope to win a war against a major power by a sudden knock-out blow; on the contrary, for success we must contemplate a long war, in the course of which we should have to mobilize all our resources and those of the Dominions and other countries overseas . . . We must therefore confront our potential enemies with the risks of a long war, which they cannot face.‡

Against Japan, particularly, Britain's economic advantages were believed for many years to be decisive. With time, however, these 'advantages' seemed less obvious and Britain became more and more stretched by the effort to establish the means to defend the Empire against the

---

* M. Howard, *The Continental Commitment*, Temple Smith, London, 1972, p. 135. See also G. C. Peden, *British Rearmament and the Treasury, 1932–1939*, Scottish Academic Press, Edinburgh, 1977, p. 91; D. C. Watt, *Too Serious a Business*, Temple Smith, London, 1975.
† CP 316(37), 'Defence Expenditure in Future Years: Interim Report by the Minister for Co-ordination of Defence', 15 December 1937.
‡ Ibid.

combination of enemies confronting it. In practice, the arguments in
favour of seeking coercion by the application of economic measures short
of war were never as attractive as some of its advocates supposed. There
were times when the British Foreign Office was inclined towards sanctions,
but in general most professional observers shared the view expressed by
one in relation to Japanese aggression at the outbreak of the China Incident in 1937, that 'the principle to be applied to the whole problem is
essentially simple: half-measures are far worse than useless and full
measures mean war'.* Equally, a strategy based upon deterrence – involving the threat rather than the use of force – had little to recommend
itself to the British or the French if their adversaries were demonstrably
better disposed to deter them from using it.

Both the British and French Governments during the 1930s aimed in
very different ways to establish adequate defences at what they regarded
as the highest level which could be maintained indefinitely. Added to the
costs of constructing modern armaments were enormous costs of maintenance, training and manning them. To turn resources of manpower and
production towards military ends too soon would adversely affect the
reconstruction of national prosperity, social welfare, and all manner of
foreign confidence and domestic support. All across the British political
spectrum, responsible leaders shared these sources of concern, differing
only by degree.

It bears emphasis that in so far as the international alarms of the day
were concerned, and Britain's capacity to respond, the whole machinery
of government was held together by finely interlocking networks of
committees through which a mere handful of brilliant civil servants and
their military counterparts worked hard to educate Ministers and formulate national policy. The British Civil Service and especially its most
senior officials, was much better informed than Government Ministers,
backbench Members of Parliament, the public and even the press. For the
most part, Ministers soon fell in step with their professional advisers in
their individual respective Government departments. Above all, however,
British military and foreign policy-making initiatives generated within
separate departments were filtered and refined by their passage through a
structure known as the Committee of Imperial Defence. Underneath the
Committee itself were more than a hundred inter-departmental sub-
committees of greater or lesser importance or duration, and the membership of most of these sub-committees was composed of officials who
genuinely shared a desire to work harmoniously with their opposite

* F 8142/6799/10, Minute by Gladwyn Jebb, 8 October 1937, FO 371/21015.

numbers in their sister departments or services. Thus debate, obstructiveness and paper-pushing made it almost impossible for solitary Ministers to carry out measures that lacked the collective support of the system. On the other hand, when there was a common purpose (and reaching that often involved a great deal of personal energy from its contributors as well as a readiness to compromise) the collective efforts that could be harnessed by this system made it the most efficient, although not necessarily the swiftest, governmental powerplant in the world. The significance of this cannot be overstated, for it gave to British policy-making a semblance of rational coherence and intelligence that was missing in other countries. In particular it provided a great contrast with the anarchy that prevailed in dictatorships like Germany or Italy where competing chiefs scrambled to catch their leader's eye and favours, and it also was the envy of popular democracies like that of the United States where institutionalized 'checks and balances' between the executive branch and Congress were an encouragement to continuous guerrilla warfare between independent-minded government departments who were only too eager to 'leak' sensitive information that would embarrass one another.

In any event, the personalities who dominated the British political scene during the years leading up to the Second World War did agree, in the words of a warning given the British Cabinet and Committee of Imperial Defence by the Chiefs of Staff, uttered in their 1933 Annual Review of Imperial Defence and repeated at regular intervals thereafter, 'The accumulation of deficiencies . . . is very heavy, and if we are to be ready for grave emergencies, a steady increase in certain of our estimates over a number of years is essential.'* The will was there. The two questions of unlimited complexity were What could be done? and Would it be effective?

Not until the late 1930s, with the shock of successive international crises and a growing appreciation of Keynesian theory, did the idea of public borrowing for rearmament gradually become respectable in the absence of viable alternatives: when as British Chancellor of the Exchequer Neville Chamberlain first suggested the idea of a 'National Defence Contribution' scheme in his budget speech of April 1937, there was enormous public outcry against this 'tax on recovery', and as the value of the French franc and of sterling plummeted, Parliament forced him to abandon the idea on 1 June, only five days after he had become Prime

* CTD 113–B, Chiefs of Staff Review of Imperial Defence, 12 October 1933, CAB 4/22.

Minister. While subsequent efforts to employ deficit financing proved more successful, the vulnerability of the British and French economies to financial panic fully vindicated their Governments' concern about financial stability: during the fifteen months between the Austrian Anschluss and the Tientsin crisis in June 1939, more than £300 million worth of gold – 40 per cent of Britain's total reserves – was lost, and Britain's balance of trade went into a steep decline as 25–30 per cent of the raw materials imported by the country were diverted to arms production rather than for exports.

By this time the point had been reached where Britain genuinely could do no more: as the First Lord of the Admiralty, Sir Roger Backhouse, wrote in November 1938, 'The trouble is . . . that we are now trying to take on more than we are really able to . . . and we simply cannot produce more than we are doing.'* Britain's arms factories were working to full capacity, but Treasury comparisons with the national debts per head of population in various countries at July 1939 gave equal cause for concern:†

	£s
United Kingdom	172
United States	64
France	57
Italy	52
Germany	33
Japan	11

As the Treasury informed the Cabinet, 'unless, when the time comes, the United States are prepared either to lend or to give us money as required, the prospects of a long war are becoming exceedingly grim'.‡ When the growing weakness of the nation's financial position was explained to the Cabinet, Oliver Stanley, the President of the Board of Trade, remarked to his colleagues that 'There would, therefore, come a moment which, on a balance of our financial strength and our strength in armaments, was the best time for war to break out.'§

From that point of view it was fortunate that war broke out in August 1939. A few months later, at about the turn of the year, the precarious balance between the nation's impending insolvency and the demands of

---

* Backhouse to Sir Percy Noble, 14 November 1938, Adm. 205/3, cited in Peden, op cit., p. 152.

† T 175/115, Internal Treasury Memorandum, cited in Peden, p. 192.

‡ CP 149(39), Cabinet Memorandum by the Treasury, CAB 24/287, cited in R. P. Shay, *British Rearmament in the Thirties: Politics and Profits*, Princeton University Press, Princeton 1977, pp. 279–80.

§ CC 36(39)2, Cabinet Minutes, 7 May 1939, CAB 23/100, cited in Shay, op. cit., p. 280.

rearmament was acknowledged by no less an authority than Keynes himself, the very apostle of 'deficit financing'. Writing from his chambers in Cambridge University at the invitation of the British Government in December 1939, he warned that unless the United States could be persuaded to back the British war effort not with loans but with outright grants, the United Kingdom would be bankrupt within six months. His letter was intended to galvanize the Americans into taking action to rescue Britain, but it provides stark and unequivocal evidence that the financial control and rearmament programmes of Britain in the pre-war period were by no means so mismanaged, inadequate, ill-conceived or unsophisticated as the majority of the critics of 'Appeasement' generally suppose. In time the United States came to underwrite the expenses of British rearmament (although this was accompanied by a liquidation of British investments in the United States). Yet the pre-war administrations of Baldwin and Chamberlain had never been in a position to request, much less to expect, such help from their most powerful potential ally. It was, indeed, by no means facile of the Committee of Imperial Defence to expect that Britain would have to pay its way, and that the maintenance of the financial strength of the Empire was an essential defence requirement.

Constraints upon British and French budgets and rearmament were thus governing factors in their foreign and defence policies which, even divorced (as they could not be) from isolationist sentiment and widespread resolve 'never to go to war again', would have made military intervention abroad a lunacy for France after 1936 and a reckless course for Britain before the end of 1939. As Chamberlain's successor at the Exchequer, Sir John Simon (who had been Foreign Secretary during the Manchurian Incident) summed up Britain's dilemma a few days after the Anschluss in March 1938:

At the present moment we are in the position of a runner in a race who wants to reserve his sprint for the right time, but does not know where the finishing tape is. The danger is that we might knock our finance to pieces prematurely.*

This brings us to the question of France's conception of her potential enemies, for we must remind ourselves that France considered herself as a European rather than as an essentially inter-continental imperial power. Home defence against Germany was her paramount concern in the face of which other considerations such as the defence of her overseas territories paled into insignificance. France's interest was to maintain the somewhat artificially contrived position of French dominance in Europe

---

* CC 13(38)3, Cabinet Minutes, 14 March 1938, CAB 23/92, cited in Peden, op. cit., p. 66.

with which she had been left at the end of the First World War. French hatred and suspicion of Germany, compounded by the failure of the Treaty of Versailles to quell her fears of German resurgence once the United States had withdrawn from active participation in continental European affairs, led France to strive to throttle German aspirations towards the revision or revocation of the most draconian measures embodied in the Versailles *Dictat*. France therefore adopted every measure it could in resistance to German economic, military and political recovery, and in doing so frantically negotiated mutual reinsurance treaties with most of Germany's continental neighbours. Ultimately this policy fell in a shambles as the French Foreign Minister was forced to appreciate that

such a policy is not practicable, for it assumes first of all that the participants are, in fact, all allied among themselves. The result of the present situation is not only weakness. It also results in the concentration on France of any attempt made against peace [*sic*, by Germany only!], France being – and how inadequately – the only link between countries which would be inclined to oppose such an attempt.*

A permanent alliance with Britain – or one with the United States – would have provided the basis for a different policy where trust and mutual respect could have been allowed to develop, but neither of these potential allies was prepared to underwrite French paranoia against Germany no matter how well-grounded it might have been in past experience. Locarno was briefly regarded as a satisfactory first step, but when Britain's reluctance to commit herself further became clearer, France considered her next best course to be a negotiated marriage of convenience with Mussolini since, without Britain, the French Government believed that the only way to cope with Germany was to gain Italian backing, or at any rate a sufficient improvement in Franco-Italian affairs to permit French military might to focus its undivided attention upon the frontier of Germany. In pursuing this relatively short-lived courtship of Italy, French diplomats found themselves at odds with the British over Abyssinia *and* unable to prevent Il Duce from listening to Hitler's sweet nothings. Italy scooped up Abyssinia, and Hitler in turn seized his moment – and the Rhineland – while France remained unprepared, irresolute and isolated. In the same way, France tried to avoid involvement in the Manchurian Incident (leaving Britain to shoulder the burden of any action taken by the League of Nations), the Spanish Civil War (where even Leon

* *Documents diplomatiques français, 1932–1939*, 2nd series, *1936–1939*, vol. II, Paris, 1964, doc. 372, transl. in Anthony P. Adamthwaite, op. cit., doc. 34.

Blum's Popular Front Government refused to be drawn into open conflict with Franco), the China Incident (during which the French often echoed the protests of Britain and the United States in Tokyo against Japanese actions but nevertheless successfully dissociated themselves from the two Anglo-Saxon Powers), and the Italian conquest of Albania (which occurred in the immediate aftermath of the German occupation of Prague in the spring of 1939). All these were for France merely distractions from the central issue which was her powerlessness to resist German aggression but her humiliating inability to tolerate it.

In contrast with France, Britain saw herself as the island anchor of a global empire, perhaps the only truly 'world power' and certainly unique in placing her 'imperial interests' above all others. When the Manchurian Incident broke, the British Chiefs of Staff were joined by the Treasury and senior diplomats in warning Ministers against becoming involved. The British Ambassador in Tokyo cabled that 'Tension here is so great that a false step might cause the Japanese to take some action which would render war with the Powers almost inevitable.'* The Chiefs of Staff painted a grim picture of the Empire's vulnerability to Japanese attack, suggesting that 'the political reaction in India and the various colonies' should give pause for thought, and quoting with approval the Ambassador's view that reaching an accommodation with Japan 'may well entail ... fewer military commitments than thwarting her'.† The Treasury declared 'that in present circumstances we are no more in a position financially and economically to engage in a major war in the Far East than we are militarily'.‡ Under these pressures, it is not surprising that the British Government did no more than lend its moral support to the Lytton Report.

When the shock of these events pushed Britain into rearmament, the nation's strategical authorities naturally concentrated upon the danger of war with Japan, the only first-class military power then threatening Britain's imperial survival. As technical experts pondered how to deal with Japan, they gradually found themselves forced to consider the question of Germany. By 1934, although still working from the premise of the Chiefs of Staff (as expressed in their annual Reviews of Imperial Defence) that 'the defence of possessions and interests in the Far East' continued to come before 'European commitments' and 'the defence of India' in terms of the balance of strategical risks, the British defence establishment as a whole (in which Treasury and Foreign Office interests

* Cited in Howard, op. cit., p. 97.
† ibid.
‡ ibid.

were strongly represented alongside their Army, Navy and Air Force counterparts) formally recognized that the danger posed by German rearmament would eventually surpass that of Japan.

The combination of these two potential enemies was so grave that the British Government's professional defence advisers vehemently opposed making any defence preparations whatever against Italy: there was no way in which Britain and her likely allies were in a position to cope with three enemies at once. Yet no sooner had this doctrine been accepted by the Cabinet than the Abyssinian crisis caught Britain by surprise and brought Italy and the United Kingdom to the brink of war. This, then, formed the background to the Hoare–Laval Pact aimed at nipping the crisis in the bud, and it greatly limited the ability of the British Government to give full vent to the nation's growing sense of outrage by formulating a programme of economic sanctions or military reprisals against Mussolini's antics whether in response to the Abyssinian campaign, the operation of Italian 'pirate' submarines during the Spanish Civil War in 1937, or the Italian conquest of Albania.

As the Chiefs of Staff warned in 1937 and constantly reminded Ministers thereafter:

The chief danger which imperial defence has to face at the moment is that we are in the position of having threats at both ends of the Empire from strong military powers, i.e., Germany and Japan, while in the centre we have lost our traditional security in the Mediterranean owing to the rise of an aggressive spirit in Italy accompanied by an increase in her military strength. So long as that position remains unresolved diplomatically, only very great military and financial strength can give the Empire security.*

The situation worsened rather than improved. Naturally, the three fighting services vied with one another for the resources which the country could spare on rearmament, and attempts were made to cut through the nation's tangled defence requirements by applying Occam's razor: 'Are we to put Germany or the Far East first?' wrote the British Air Minister privately to the Minister for Co-ordination of Defence as late as October 1937:

I assume finance precludes our taking both in our stride. No doubt production does, too. It is for the Cabinet to lay down where the great danger lies and where we should concentrate. This of course directly affects both the Admiralty and the Air Ministry. If we have to make provision for the Far East that means

---

* COS 560, Chiefs of Staff Review of Imperial Defence, 22 February 1937, CAB 53/30, cited in Pritchard, *Far Eastern Influences*, op. cit., p. 8.

a great increase in the fleet. It also means aircraft, which can only be provided in the fairly near future to the detriment of the home position.*

Yet the principal difficulty facing British Ministers and their professional defence advisers was that they simply could not ignore the threat to their imperial security from Japan while dealing with events nearer to the United Kingdom. Much was done to rearm, but the military strength of the British Empire was dissipated by the nation's inability to focus upon a single potential adversary. Viewed from London, the rearmament efforts of those enemies seemed to outpace those of the British Empire. The leadership of Britain's potential enemies faced similar difficulties but not over such extended lines of communication.

Underpinning and foreshadowing the foreign policies pursued by the Chamberlain Government during the closing years of the decade lay a revised list of strategical priorities prepared by the Chiefs of Staff in February 1937, and these were scarcely modified before the outbreak of the Second World War: in place of the three-fold liabilities outlined previously, five critical objectives were itemized and ranked in their importance: (i) the maintenance of imperial communications (and that implied good relations with the Dominions as well as a high regard for the welfare of the Colonial Empire); (ii) security of the United Kingdom against German aggression (a modification of Britain's traditional opposition to the hegemony of any one power in Western Europe); (iii) the protection of imperial interests in East Asia (where concern about Japan's encroachments had now completely supplanted the worries about Chinese jingoism which had been expressed by British officials in earlier decades); (iv) the stability of the Mediterranean and Middle East (made more difficult first by the expansion of Italian power and more recently by the outbreak of the Spanish Civil War), and (v) the Russian threat to India. In hindsight some of these contingencies appear far-fetched or fantastic. At the time, however, they crippled Britain's sense of initiative and self-possession.

In the view of His Majesty's Government, involvement in any other issues could only be risked in the knowledge that it would diminish the nation's ability to respond or to survive threats to Britain's vital imperial interests. 'The broad principles on which our Empire strategy has always been based should not be forgotten,' warned the Chiefs of Staff (whose expertise no Government could ignore without running appalling risks), 'nor should the lessons of history be overlooked. The greater

---

* Uncirculated Note concerning DP(P)12, October 1937, RAF Expansion Scheme file, Wier 19/18, Wier Papers, Churchill College, Cambridge, cited in Pritchard, *Far Eastern Influences*, op. cit., p. 48.

our commitments to Europe, the less will be our ability to secure our Empire and its communications.'*

It is scarcely surprising, therefore, that formal military pacts and other alliances were often considered but generally ruled out by Britain's policy-makers, who regarded most such treaties as inflammatory or self-deluding. In the British view, states should be expected to act in their own self-interest. The need was to find the common denominator of self-interest with potential allies that would make formal pacts unnecessary. In the absence of a common basis for such understandings, the prospect of concluding empty alliances with weak and unavailing allies held no charm for the United Kingdom, for while some outsiders saw only the benefits of 'collective security', the British Government appreciated only too well that there was rarely security in the collective. Meanwhile the self-governing British Dominions, whose role and influence tends to be underrated, expressed strong and vocal opposition in public as well as in private against any moves which might involve them in another European holocaust. The security of the greater part of the Empire as well as of the majority of the Dominions was threatened more directly by Japanese expansionism than by German or Italian adventurism.

The only potential ally strong enough to warrant Britain adopting a policy of 'Resistance' against Japanese aggression, the United States, ex-hibited a marked unwillingness to take a full share of the risks. Although sympathetic to Britain's plight, the United States had no wish to become involved in war unnecessarily. Notwithstanding public statements to the contrary, dating from posturing by the American Secretary of State at the time of the Manchurian Incident, Henry L. Stimson, right up to the period of the Munich Agreement and on to the outbreak of the European War in September 1939, the United States privately rebuffed repeated British overtures for consultation and collaboration against all three of the main potential enemies facing the British Empire. While Roosevelt used various incidents as a means of 'educating public opinion' to their common danger, Chamberlain's gradual appreciation that 'it is best to count upon nothing from the Americans but words' expressed only the simple truth.† On the other hand, as the Chiefs of Staff forecast in February 1939, in the kind of three-enemy war which by then looked the most likely prospect,

The British Empire would be threatened simultaneously in Europe, the Medi-terranean and the Far East by an immense aggregate of armed force, which neither our present nor our projected strength is designed to meet, with France as

* C P 218(36), Cabinet Memorandum by the Chiefs of Staff, cited in Howard, op. cit., p. 102.
† Feiling, op. cit., p. 324.

89   The *Panay* Incident, 12
December 1937 *Top*: The 450-
ton, 191-foot gunboat USS
Panay settles into the waters
of the Yangtze after being
bombed and strafed by four
Japanese naval aircraft

90   *Centre*: The passengers
and crew of the USS *Panay*
abandon ship and take to the
gunboat's motor launch

91   *Bottom*: HMS *Ladybird*
and the USS *Oahu* arrive at
Shanghai with the USS *Panay*
survivors and the bodies of
those who had been killed in
the attack

92 'Britain possesses what
Japan wants and what no
other country has – a
dominating position in China'
Top: With government
encouragement wall posters
appeared during the Tientsin
Incident in the summer of
1939

93 *Centre*: H·M·S *Ladybird*
lies in dry dock at Shanghai
after bombardment by Colonel
Hashimoto Kingoro's artillery
in December 1937

94 *Bottom*: The Tientsin
Incident, June–August 1939

95 *Top*: A band of Chinese
communist partisans, fleeing
from Kuomintang 'Bandit
Suppression' campaigns, trek
over a pass on the Long
March in search of refuge

96 *Bottom*: Four major
leaders of the Chinese
Communist Party:
Mao Tse-tung, Chou En-lai,
Po Ku and Chu Teh

97 *Top left*: A Japanese
political cartoon

98 *Top right*: Chinese troops
display German light machine-
guns against the backdrop of a
Chinese communist flag

99 *Bottom*: Marshal Chu
Teh, greatest military genius
of the Chinese Communist
Party, poses at the door of an
ambulance donated by the
Chinese Laundry Workers of
New York

100 *Top*: A camel train,
following the ancient Silk
Road to China, carries across
Sinkiang supplies sent through
Soviet Central Asia

101 *Bottom*: Russian tank
troops rest during a lull in the
fight against the Japanese at
Nomonhan, May–September
1939

102 *Top left*: The Sino-American-built Ledo Road links India, across the southern slopes of the Himalayan mountains and dense jungles, with the Sino-British-built Burma Road to China

103 *Top right*: The US Army and Chinese coolies, often working in difficult terrain without mechanized vehicles, construct the Ledo Road

104 *Bottom*: A convoy of Chevrolet trucks, carrying British markings, stands against the backdrop of a Hindu temple in Rangoon

105 A caterpillar tractor of
the US Army Engineering
Corps clears the way for a
convoy of supply trucks
travelling on the Ledo Road

106   *Top*: Chinese troops
disembark from an American
transport aircraft at Myitkyina
Airfield in northern Burma

107   *Bottom*: War-torn
Chungking, capital of Chiang
Kai-shek's régime

our only major ally. *The outcome of the war would be likely to depend on our ability to hold on to our key positions and upon other powers, particularly the United States, coming to our aid.**

Under the circumstances, the thought was harrowing.

If Japan was isolated economically, diplomatically and militarily during the first two and a half years of the Sino-Japanese War, the position of the British Empire was scarcely more enviable. Unlike the United States, the British had vital interests in the Far East. Those interests stood directly in the path of Japanese expansion. Japan could not hope to operate in China without appropriating the use of British-owned railway stock, interfering with British control over Chinese maritime customs and the salt gabelle, upsetting British merchant trading monopolies, and in many other ways disturbing Britain's nearly 50 per cent share in Chinese commercial affairs, a level of investment worth perhaps £500 million at 1937 prices.

Meanwhile Japan had been making itself conspicuously disliked by the classes which had no interest at all in residing in East Asia, but made their living at home in trade. For them, Japan mattered simply because of its commercial policy. In the thirties, this became increasingly competitive. To avoid its national destitution and starvation, Japan balked at nothing in efforts to increase its exports. Under this compulsion, it became notorious as the country hunting for markets, successfully snapping up the old markets of older countries, ruthlessly underbidding, successfully dumping.

Japan, in short, was feared and disliked by everybody in an established position in world trade, who saw its activities with dread. This dislike of Japan for commercial reasons was carried over into an irrational anti-Japanese prejudice. Feeling tilted over and became pro-China and anti-Japan; it was reinforced by a modish fashion among the intelligentsia for all things Chinese. Nevertheless, commercial competition was at the root of the sentiment.

Though feeling was shifting among even local businessmen from being pro-Japanese to being pro-Chinese, the British were resolved to go to great lengths to preserve their formal neutrality. All eyes in Britain were on the European continent. Through it all, however, as we have seen, there remained a constant and interdependent preoccupation in the cloisters of Whitehall with the strategic threat posed by all three of Britain's potential enemies: Germany, Italy and Japan. Their hesitations

---

* D P(P)44, Defence Plans (Policy) Committee Memorandum by the Chiefs of Staff: European Appreciation, 1939–40, 20 February 1939, CAB 16/183A, cited in Pritchard, *Far Eastern Influences*, op. cit., p. 138.

and preoccupations were rooted in an understanding of the world as it was, which was not the world that impatient amateur strategists and wishful thinkers thought it ought to have been.

The day was long past when Britain could afford to defend all her territorial and commercial outposts, and now for the first time in their history the British were confronted by a first-class threat to the eastern half of their Empire, while facing a similar threat in Europe. British defence experts had long anticipated that, in the absence of a two-hemisphere fleet, the next world war could bring about the downfall of the British Commonwealth of Nations at the hands of Japan and Germany: 'Australia, New Zealand, India, Burma, the rich colonies east of Suez and a vast trade would be at their mercy, and the eastern half of the British Empire might well be doomed,' predicted the Defence Requirements Committee.* Since Britain could not afford to build the forces required to give her real protection, it followed that unless sufficient allied support could be found, Britain would have to reach some kind of settlement with Germany or Japan. It was argued at the time that more economies in defence expenditure could be made by adjustments with Germany than with Japan; successful appeasement of Germany would do much to solve Britain's Far Eastern crisis.

Britain's peril in the Far East was one of diplomatic as well as strategical isolation. During July and August 1937 the State Department excused itself from participating in British initiatives to mediate the Sino-Japanese conflict and offered the lame excuse that it did not want the Japanese to feel 'that there is any form of collusion' between the British and Americans. The British wanted something far more definite: a commitment on the part of the United States to share all the risks of a firm policy in the Far East.† At first the British toyed with the idea of imposing sanctions against Japan in the early days of the war, but Chamberlain came to regard sanctions with deep loathing: in view of Japan's unbroken string of victories, 'economic sanctions are not likely to be effective in time to stop the war, and the experience of the Abyssinian affair shows that if unsuccessful they would leave behind them an evil legacy of ill-will and suspicion', he wrote in October. Suppose that Britain, America and the Netherlands East Indies imposed sanctions: 'If the sanctions seemed likely to become really effective Japan

---

* DRC 37, Third Report of the Defence Requirements Committee, 21 November 1935, CAB 16/112, British Public Record Office, Kew.

† The discussion which follows is based largely upon Pritchard, *Far Eastern Influences*, op. cit., pp. 69–91.

would be rendered desperate. Suppose she then made a sudden or unexpected attack on the possessions of one of the three sanctionist countries?' Were the other two Powers likely to defend the nation which was attacked? Chamberlain had his doubts, since on 5 October 1937, the very day of Roosevelt's famous Quarantine Speech calling for the isolation of aggressors, Under-Secretary of State Sumner Welles had informed the British that 'this country intends not to be drawn into any armed conflict'.

Chamberlain was convinced that 'the only way in which the war could certainly be brought to a close at once would be by the expressed determination on the part of . . . the U.S.A. and H.M.G. to use an overwhelming force to bring compulsion on Japan'. Since the United States specifically rejected all offers to bring Japan to her senses by 'superior sea force', Chamberlain reluctantly concluded that Britain could take no risks on the strength of Roosevelt's rhetoric alone: 'In the present state of European affairs with two dictators in a thoroughly nasty temper, we simply cannot afford to quarrel with Japan, and I very much fear, therefore, that after a lot of ballyhoo the Americans will somehow fade out and leave us to carry all the blame and the odium.' The Government's chief advisers in the departments concerned were agreed on this point. The Foreign Office, for instance, described British efforts to build an Anglo-American front as a 'sorry failure'; the defence departments had no confidence in Britain's ability to impose sanctions against Japan at a time of great European uncertainty and no assurances of American support; the Treasury view was summed up tersely by its permanent head, Sir Warren Fisher, who remarked: 'However much we denuded European waters our fleet could not hope to defeat Japan in her waters. And we should be at mercy in Europe. The U.S.A. would fail us at the critical moment even in the Far East. Still more would she fail us in our consequential danger in Europe.'

Although tempted time and again to dispatch the British battlefleet to Singapore, on each occasion Britain backed down because American support could not be secured and Britain could not afford to present Japan with any economic or naval challenge that might involve Britain in a single-handed naval war. The strafing of the British Ambassador in China, Sir Hughe Knatchbull-Hugessen, in August 1937; the repeated aerial and artillery bombardment suffered by British enclaves in China; Japanese abuse of British property and interference with trade: all of these created a succession of nasty but minor incidents. Similarly, there were incidents between the Americans and the Japanese, which stirred up the blood of the Americans and the hopes of the Chinese. The war was fought at Shanghai in a vastly overcrowded place, and inevitably the bystanders were hit. But the Americans, the British and the French in the area were divided about their policy, and nothing much was done.

Then in mid-December 1937, Japanese Army and naval forces attacked five western warships on the Yangtze: the HMS *Ladybird* and HMS *Bee* were damaged and the USS *Panay* was sunk. That rogue Japanese Army artillery officer, Colonel Hashimotō Kingorō, whom we have already encountered and who was now in charge of the invasion forces at Wuhu, had ordered his guns to open fire on the two British gunboats passing upstream: long afterwards it was confirmed at the Tokyo War Crimes Trial that his intention was to provoke a war with Britain that would lead to the eradication of British influence from China. On the very afternoon of Hashimoto's initiative, the USS *Panay*, an American gunboat, was bombed and sunk after successive attacks carried out by nine Japanese naval fighter aircraft, twelve dive bombers and three high-level bombers. Whether some of the Japanese commanders desired to frighten the United States away, or whether the bombing was a mistake, remains a matter of historical controversy. Those aboard the *Panay* were convinced that the identity of their vessel was clear to the attacking aircraft; however, the attack was carried out by three inexperienced group commanders who had arrived from Japan only eight days before. According to a post-war account by one of the attack leaders, the *Panay* Incident was simply a blunder from start to finish, one which horrified all the Japanese concerned when the facts became known. Reports from the survivors suggested that far from trying to render assistance, the Japanese made every attempt to hunt down and destroy those who had escaped from the vessel, who underwent a harrowing ordeal before they finally reached safety. In the same incident, moreover, two other British gunboats had also been attacked from the air but fortunately had escaped injury. The Japanese forces involved had exhibited great persistence in following up all of these attacks, and the *Ladybird*, the *Bee* and the other two British gunboats were fortunate to escape the fate of the *Panay*.

The British Government, like the American, was infuriated by the affair. At first, Prime Minister Neville Chamberlain was prepared to take any action – including a resort to force if necessary – to halt further Japanese erosion of western interests in China. Despite the risk that such an act might precipitate a pre-emptive strike by Japan, the British battlefleet was prepared to depart for Singapore. The United States Navy was in a war fever after the *Panay* affair, but American policy was in disarray. Roosevelt refused to take any parallel or identical action with Britain which would involve the threat or use of naval power, and he unilaterally accepted Japan's formal apologies and a $2 million indemnity without prior consultation with Britain. Taken by surprise, there was hardly anything that the British could do in the circumstances.

The Americans, however, were not insensible to the need for some sort of collaboration if events like these were to continue. The Incident gave ammunition to those in the United States Navy who wanted to develop Anglo-American naval collaboration against the Japanese, and so Roosevelt, who fondly recollected his own part in such contacts during the First World War, had a few private words with the British Ambassador at the White House, accepted a long-standing offer by the British, and sent Captain Royal Ingersoll of the United States Navy War Plans Division to London for clandestine naval staff talks at the beginning of the new year. These discussions provided an opportunity for the two navies to do little more than exchange opinions rather than to coordinate policies because the Americans divulged little information and refused to make any strategical commitments of any kind. The tone of the conversations was tentative and speculative; as the British had expected, the Americans were friendly but finally had to admit that the United States Navy was not nearly so ready for war as the Royal Navy: the most that the Americans could offer at this stage was to consider the possibility of cooperating in a long-distance naval blockade of Japan to take place after the next incident. Early action, in short, was ruled out, although these conversations were to become only the first of many.

Meanwhile, the American public watched newsreel footage of the attack on the *Panay*, taken by a camera team aboard the gunboat while the Japanese aircraft had pressed home their attack, and as details of the Incident emerged and the findings of the US Naval Court of Enquiry were reported in the press, these powerful graphic images became firmly linked in the public mind with the outrages against the Chinese civil population at Nanking. The Americans were confirmed in their anti-Japanese frame of mind. The tide was running in support of the China lobby which was made up of businessmen, scholars, philanthropists, former missionaries, and other specialists on Asia. Eventually the China lobby was to become one of the powers in the land, but that time had not yet arrived.

The next incident happened sooner than anyone expected. Before Ingersoll could return to Washington, DC, two British policemen were murdered by Japanese soldiers at Shanghai in early January 1938. Once again, Britain, with an irate Neville Chamberlain at the helm, went to the brink of war: the fleet might have been dispatched to the Far East within days, and for a brief moment the will to take such drastic action was manifest. Washington was contacted again. But the Americans, as before, declined to advance one step or give any assurances: indeed, they suggested rather archly that Britain would do well to concentrate on dangers nearer to English shores. Pricked, nay, deflated, by this rebuff and afterwards distracted by the steady increase in European tension in the nine months preceding the Munich Conference at the end of September 1938, the British lost heart. Apart from an ill-judged intervention by Foreign Secretary Anthony Eden (the balance of whose mind was deeply disturbed for some weeks prior to his resignation on doctor's orders in February 1938), the British made no more serious efforts to attract American support against Japan prior to the outbreak of the European War. Confrontations between Japan and the Occidental Powers emerged during 1938 at Shanghai, Tientsin and along the Yangtze, not to mention the Changkufeng Incident on the Korean border with the Soviet Union, but it was evident that the Konoye Cabinet in Tokyo, then preoccupied with the prosecution of its war in China, was doing its best not to antagonize any of the third Powers unnecessarily. The only development that was particularly dangerous occurred when Japanese troops seized Canton in October 1938, following a timetable which the British had known about several weeks before Munich. At this point there was a grave risk that a war might have started through the injudiciousness of local Japanese commanders on the doorstep of Hong Kong. But the Japanese were careful, and the British, who recognized that they stood no chance whatever of rescuing the fabulously wealthy Crown Colony by any defence measures they might take in the event of hostilities, were no longer prepared to respond to anything less than extreme provocation. Without American cooperation, Britain felt powerless against the two most aggressive nations of the world.

The United Kingdom Government also explored the possibility of gaining assistance from the only other make-weight power who might have supplemented rather than dissipated Britain's ability to resist aggression in Europe and East Asia: the Soviet Union. When the Manchurian Incident took place, Soviet land and air forces were the most powerful in the world and were generally regarded as unified and well-commanded. At that time, however, it was unimaginable that the United Kingdom would ever welcome Soviet assistance in establishing a common defence against Germany. The prospect of Soviet naval assistance in enforcing sanctions against Japan was equally uninviting. Politically unreliable and even hostile, the Soviet Union made no secret of its ambition to export the Bolshevik Revolution abroad, and that was reason enough to avoid taking Moscow into British confidence on military as well as on political matters, particularly when the consequences of any collaboration between the two powers would be bound to heighten international tension and war fever. Britain's potential enemies were already aware, after all, that they were liable to a Soviet attack if their backs were turned; clear evidence of British complicity in a policy of 'encirclement' would have forced Britain's enemies to attack or face destruction. By the time Britain was morally certain that she was unlikely to be able to avoid war within the more or less immediate future, Stalin's great military purges were believed – almost certainly rightly – to have disembowelled the Soviet armed forces. From the end of 1936, therefore, Britain could not anticipate any help from the Soviet Union in the struggles ahead, although London was quite prepared to welcome whatever help Moscow might provide of Russia's own accord after the outbreak of hostilities.

As for an alliance with France, during most of the 1930s the general opinion in Whitehall regarded that prospect as having little to recommend it. A few francophiles, notably within the Foreign Office and War Office, took exception to this view, but on the whole the cost of a 'Continental Commitment', which would have been the inevitable consequence of any meaningful alliance with France, was not regarded as commensurate with imperial self-preservation at a time when the globe was dominated by a loose alignment of great potential enemies. Even before the advent of Hitler to power, that commitment would have required of Britain the creation of an army incomparably larger than what those responsible for Britain's defence believed the nation could afford at a time when Britain already was fully stretched to meet what experts in Whitehall regarded as the Empire's minimum requirements in naval and air forces. London's objective in Europe as in East Asia was rather to foster international economic development and peaceful political evolution. Should Britain find itself at war with Germany, no one believed that France would stand aside. Just as Britain did not expect to dictate to the French how to deploy their huge land forces and whatever small British contingent might join them, so the British did not accept that the French would have any choice but to accept British direction when it came to war at sea. Premature disclosure to Paris about British naval war plans would only shock the French (and possibly lead to leaks of information) after the French appreciated Britain's resolve to abandon the naval defence of the Mediterranean to the French in order to dispatch the British fleet to the Pacific if Japan joined in the fighting as Britain expected. In maintaining her freedom of action for as long as possible, Britain gained rather more than she lost by delaying prior consultation with France about the forging of some kind of common strategy. Imperial defence had to come first. In fact, what the newly appointed Deputy-Chief of the Naval Staff, Admiral Cunningham, found to his amazement just after Munich was that apart from war plans against Japan, 'there were no naval plans at all'!*

The French, however keen to make an alliance with Britain, saw British imperialism as an obstruction to the development of a postive programme of opposition to German aggressive designs. At best the French regarded Britain's imperial defence priorities as a flimsy excuse for inactivity which had the effect of feeding Germany's boundless appetite and development while abandoning the possibility of playing any constructive role in policing the peace of Europe (although not the world) in support of France: as Edouard Daladier, the French Prime Minister at the time of Munich, confided several months afterwards to the American Ambassador in Paris, 'England had become so feeble and senile that the British would give away every possession of their friends rather than stand up to Germany and Italy.'† By contrast France, as the sympathetic contemporary historian Arnold Wolfers wrote in 1940,

may initially have acted only from fear of another German invasion, [but] her policy of security had led her to become the champion of the *status quo* and of the entire order of Central as well as of Western Europe. Her anxiety was, therefore, that of a nation with responsibilities truly continental in character and extent.‡

When in December 1938 the French looked round and counted the divisions which Appeasement had 'lost' to them (or so they felt) in Central Europe, they derided Britain's precious forces and demanded of her '*un effort du sang*'.§ Shamed and made desperate by events, Britain soon obliged. France did not.

The setting in of the war in earnest brought a decisive change in the attitude of the westerners. Sentiment, which among some classes in Britain, for example, had for some time been anti-Japanese, hardened; and it spread throughout most sections of the people, at least of those, admittedly a minority, who thought it necessary to take a view about such a distant part of the world.

The change was marked in the early period of the China Incident.

* Cunningham of Hyndhope, *A Sailor's Odyssey*, Hutchinson, London, 1951, p. 195.
† Adamthwaite, op. cit., doc. 67.
‡ A. Wolfers, *Britain and France between Two Wars*, Norton, New York, 1966 (reprint), p. 20.
§ Howard, op. cit., p. 126; Peden, op. cit., p. 182.

Westerners with foreign contacts, especially the businessmen resident in the Far East, had on the whole been well disposed to Japan. Japan professed to be the champion of foreign business interests. It claimed to be taking steps – in putting down bandits, in removing the Chinese officials who were the bane of traders – which the other countries had taken it upon themselves to do from time to time in the past and which they would have continued to do had they the resolution to stand up for their interests without regard for distractions elsewhere. Chinese xenophobia was the enemy of all who had to do with China. And, for a long while, Japanese action received a great deal of sympathy from certain sections of westerners.

This view continued to be held, at least until the China Incident merged with the Second World War. Not only a section of the business world but many of their diplomatic and military counterparts maintained their regard for Japan. They became progressively smaller in number as the years passed, but they still remained powerful in influence. They thought that no comparison was possible between the Japanese – clever, energetic, industrious, above all disciplined and punctual – and the Chinese, who, if they were clever, had all the faults which went with political impotence; who were corruptible, were voluble in justifying the inexcusable, were argumentative without being convincing to many of the western representatives whose opinions mattered in the propounding of their respective national responses to the developing East Asian Conflict. These westerners, from the less admirable specimens to some very astute observers indeed, liked the Japanese way of life, Japanese discipline and Japanese customs: though it should be noted that most of the things they admired were regarded by educated Japanese, who had continued to revere many standards from their past, as vulgar. They liked the solidity of the buildings in western style which the Japanese had put up. Some of the westerners even felt that the Japanese had very sensible ideas about the status of women. A few of its would-be admirers understood the genius of Japan to be aesthetic, non-intellectual, and non-acquisitive, were inclined to excuse the dramatic passions within Japanese society as but redeemable manifestations of temporary enthusiasms, and, taking the culture as a whole, saw that while it cultivated the art-forms of force it strove to avoid the necessity of any resort to arms. These considerations, however, were merely the contentious reflections of the few, and were of no concern to pragmatists.

Of great significance was the fact that the admirers of Japan were not unchallenged among the guardians of western interests in the East. A rival section of western residents in Treaty Ports had backed the rise of the new China. From among these there was, it is true, not at first a strong condemnation of Japan. Most of these people felt, secretly if not openly, that China had been moving too fast and too far, and that chastisement by Japan would bring it to reason. A series of murders and outrages had occurred in previous years: and Nanking did its cause no good by obvious deception and the pretence that it could not unravel the circumstances.

Western businessmen were less far-sighted, less impersonal than their Governments. They had also a sense of racial superiority, although some had abandoned it in the case of Japan, since the Japanese had demonstrated that they could not be pushed around. Business was conscious of the great advantage of living in concessions under an extra-territorial régime. It lamented the fact that negotiation had begun for their abolition, and that many concessions had already been surrendered: it saw itself vitally threatened. There were some men of vision among them, who looked ahead and saw the future; but these men were rare. American businessmen in spite of their general liberalism and of the pro-Chinese sentiment of many of their countrymen, were endowed with more than their share of the same temper as their European counterparts.

However, as the great offensive of the Japanese began to take shape and its direction passed from the Japanese civilian, whom the western businessmen used to know, into the hands of arrogant generals, with whom they did not feel at home, they began more and more to change their minds. The fear grew that it was the Japanese, not the Chinese, who would chase them out of the concessions. Japan was spending its blood and treasure to make China into a place fit for a person to live in; but the Japanese intended that it was to be a Japanese businessman, an agent of the Mitsui and the Mitsubishi, not the foreigner – whom the Japanese regarded as more undesirable than the Chinese. The western traders or industrialists saw that if they lost the protection under which they were living, they would not have a very long tenure of life. By controls, by subsidies, by taxation, by withholding permits to move their capital and profits out of the country, Japan would be able to drive them away in a brief time, and in less than ten years, perhaps, the concessions would be no more.

Thus the change of attitude had become almost universal, and the businessmen of the West who regarded the East were as anxious as the Chinese when in July 1937 the fighting began in earnest. At least they could console themselves that there was an end for the time being to the negotiations for the return of the concessions. The Chinese defence of Shanghai happened before their eyes, and the destruction which the Sino-Japanese conflict threatened to bring upon that city outraged more than it terrified westerners who witnessed it. An epitome of western reactions to this earliest phase of the war can be found in a succession of reports sent to London by the Commander-in-Chief of the China Station, Vice-Admiral Sir Charles Little, who watched the battle from his flagship. Reviewing the harrowing events of October 1937, he wrote of 'inexcusable carelessness and lack of control of subordinates, the use of modern weapons which have outstripped in their rapid evolution the until recently medieval brains that try to control them'.* A month later, as the Japanese moved forward to lay siege to Nanking, Sir Charles remained preoccupied by the lessons of the battle at Shanghai:

Depressing and nerve-wracking as the active military operations carried on round the defence perimeter . . . have been for the British community at Shanghai, they have always clung to the idea, fostered by the events of 1927 and 1932, that as soon as the 'cease fire' was sounded, somehow or other 'business as usual' would be the order of the day.

Of course there are exceptions and far-seeing people realise, as I am afraid it is the regrettable truth, that with Japanese domination, added to the blocking of the Yangtse and the reduction of trade at all the 'Treaty' ports, the troubles of Shanghai are only really commencing. It is already evident that with their narrow-minded, petty-fogging ideas, the Japanese mean to assert their rights, qua rights, in the Settlement, to possess themselves of everything they possibly can Chinese or destroy it and to squeeze and hinder the Foreigner.

With a broader outlook on the future and a magnanimous policy towards Foreign interests the Japanese are in a position to gain for themselves the respect and almost the gratitude of Foreigners, to their ultimate great advantage. For the Japanese though, such a far-sighted course is impossible!†

The Chinese did not lose hope of entangling foreign powers, including Britain, in the war as it moved through its successive stages. In August 1937, as the events took place that Sir Charles Little witnessed, two Japanese aircraft, perhaps unaware of who was their prey, machine-gunned from the air a motor car on the way from Shanghai to Nanking. In it was Sir Hughe Knatchbull-Hugessen, known as 'Snatch', the then British Ambassador in China. He was seriously wounded, and for a few days this nearly fatal accident, to which we have already alluded, caused an electric tension. But the British could do little more than protest, given that the Japanese military and civil authorities were plainly horror-struck by the event (and that none concerned was as keen to report the

* China General Letter 18, Report of Proceedings of the Commander-in-Chief, China, for the period 4–31 October 1937, 15 November 1937, Adm. 116/3683.
† China General Letter 19, Report of Proceedings of the Commander-in-Chief, China, for the period 1–30 November 1937, 14 December 1937, Adm. 116/3683.

circumstances of the 'accident' as eagerly as they were prepared to offer the British financial compensation for it). The incident was closed by an exchange of notes that were meant to save everybody's face. (Sir Hughe thus goes down in history as a diplomat who was nearly murdered and started a war. 'Snatch' is remembered also as the Ambassador in Turkey who had the plans of the Second Front filched by his valet who gave them to the Germans. Fortunately, the Germans could not credit their good fortune and assumed that false information was being planted on them.)

Moreover, that succession of incidents to which we have already referred involving Japanese attacks pressed home against western gunboats on the Yangtze, followed by the Rape of Nanking after barely six months of warfare, raised western discomfort to an acute level, purging for a time whatever cynicism the western businessman and his guardians might have striven to cultivate.

Western military and diplomatic observers nonetheless never lacked confidence in their ability to act far more objectively than their business compatriots in dealing with the Chinese and Japanese. The great western financial and commercial houses of the East, together with their trading associations and other pressure groups, ceaselessly plied their Government contacts with local tittle-tattle, opinions and representations. This certainly helped to condition the attitudes of western consular staff towards individual Chinese and Japanese personalities with whom they came into contact. The indomitable moral and physical courage of these merchant princes in the face of Japanese discrimination, persecution and threats cannot but excite one's admiration, and their correspondence, preserved in the records of the China Association, the Swire Archives and elsewhere, like the Fugger newsletters of the sixteenth century, offer historians useful insights into the local conditions experienced by agents of the various companies. Broadly speaking, the foreign tycoons in China showed far more fortitude than, say, the British community in Malaya or Burma. But western businessmen, like their missionary counterparts, had a negligible influence upon the course of the evolving western strategical relationship with Japan and China during these years.

The British Ambassador in Tokyo, Sir Robert Craigie, fought out a battle on what should be British policy towards the war with Sir Archibald John Kerr Clark Kerr, the successor to Knatchbull-Hugessen in China. Clark Kerr had spent most of his career in the Middle East, North Africa and in a cluster of South American banana republics. He was what can be delicately described as an acquired taste. He also had pronounced leftwing views, which were in favour of Britain supporting China on grounds of plain international morality. China was weak, was being bullied, and, he thought, should be protected. On this, at least, he had the advantage of reflecting the sentimentality of most of the western democratic nations of the day.

Craigie, in Tokyo, possessed one of the keenest intellects in the British diplomatic service of his day. He was fully convinced of the benefits which Britain had derived from the Anglo-Japanese Alliance, as long as this had existed. He saw the best hope in working for a revival of the spirit of Anglo-Japanese friendship which had marked the period of that Alliance. He was to a great extent conditioned by his lifelong knowledge of naval affairs (his father and both grandfathers had been admirals in the Royal Navy). His expertise in British naval arms control policy formulation was unsurpassed: he had been involved with the subject ever since attending the Washington Naval Conference, and he knew that throughout the years since the First World War its ultimate success or failure had always turned upon the (in)security of the various powers in the Pacific region. Moreover, he came to his duties in Tokyo after having served with distinction as Head of the American Bureau of the Foreign Office: he knew the political temperature of Washington, better than almost anyone in Whitehall, and his career was strongly influenced by his marriage to a Southern belle. He had also spent a sufficient period of service in the British Department of Overseas Trade to have reinforced his better than average sensitivity to Britain's commercial interests abroad. Although a man of his calibre would have made quite an impact upon the relation of the British Empire to the China Incident in any event, he was able to give effective voice to the pro-Japanese views of the British Embassy.

Unfortunately for Craigie, his critics made capital of the extent to which he made use of contacts served up to him by his military attaché, Major-General F. S. G. Piggott: Whitehall wits coined the word 'Piggottry' to describe those who shared the general's peculiarly romantic view of Japanese history. There is no doubt that Piggott's uncritical adulation of Japanese militarism did much to undermine his Ambassador's effectiveness at home.

The divergent views of the two British representatives, at Chungking and at Tokyo, inevitably clashed with vigour in the telegrams and reports. Those who took part in this conflict were convinced that the issue was of first importance. They did not fail to recognize that the attention of London was often otherwise engaged, and that their respective views were not treated very seriously within the Foreign Office. Yet in higher circles still, within the apparatus of the Committee of Imperial Defence and the Cabinet itself, the views of both men, but especially of Craigie, commanded attention. Time after time, however, they mainly contributed to a palpable sense of unease, malaise and vacillation: and so for the most part the voice of one or the other was used to nullify that of his opposite number.

Although Britain continued to adopt a policy considerably stiffer in the Far East than in Europe, there were major attempts to reach a limited understanding between Britain and Japan in the summer of 1938. In part these discussions, which were held in Tokyo between Ambassador Sir Robert Craigie and Foreign Minister Ugaki Kazushige, dealt with a formidable list of outstanding claims and complaints against Japanese behaviour detrimental to British interests in China. The Japanese countered this list with a demand that Britain should cease to support Chiang Kai-shek and should 'cooperate' with Japan in developing China. The British flatly refused to accept these suggestions, and the talks led to no significant improvements in the situation. Failure to reach an agreement led to an undermining of moderate elements in the Japanese Cabinet and the fall of Foreign Minister Ugaki, a man genuinely well disposed towards the Western Powers.

By 1939, as the clouds of war darkened steadily over Europe, many businessmen in East Asia recognized that their bright day was over: and that, once the Treaty Port system was disbanded, it would not be set up again. In this year there was a humiliation of occidental businessmen and other residents in Tientsin which profoundly affected the climate of official opinion in western capital cities. The European War was about to begin, although there were hopes in many quarters that Hitler as well as Mussolini could be deterred from further aggression. The British Government seemed preoccupied with that, and so far as the ever-speculative press reports of the day could discern, there was little faith or hope that the British authorities were prepared to do much for their countrymen in Shanghai or Tientsin.

In fact, however, the long-standing friction between the Japanese and the British at Tientsin escalated into a major international incident. To some extent the French Concession in the city was also drawn into the affair. Over the past few years, the diplomatic storm created during the Tientsin Crisis has become recognized as an important development in the breakdown of order that accompanied the China Incident and preceded the European War. Between June and August 1939 it even threatened to become the proximate cause of the next world war. From the perspective of Anglo-Japanese relations, the Tientsin affair was regarded – by all of the countries concerned – as far more serious than the machine-gunning of the hapless British Ambassador to China at the outbreak of the China Incident, or even the Japanese air attacks and artillery bombardments directed against British gunboats on the Yangtze in December 1937. Indeed, the only Anglo-Japanese confrontation during the China Incident which really compares with that at Tientsin was the Burma Road dispute in the darkest days of 1940 (to which we shall return in due course). Nevertheless, its peaceful outcome, coupled with the outbreak of the European War only a week and a half after pressure upon the British and French Concessions at Tientsin was relaxed by the Japanese, has led many historians to overlook or to doubt that both Britain and Japan had been determined to stand fast if the diplomatic negotiations failed or in case a direct military clash had ensued. In particular, Japanese commanders at Tientsin, as well as military and civilian leaders in Tokyo, assumed that London was bluffing in issuing warnings that the British fleet – or at any rate a major part of it – might depart for the Pacific if the situation deteriorated. A closer examination of the evidence, however, leads to completely different conclusions. So important are the wider implications of this struggle that it is worth examining in some detail.

First, the reader must appreciate that the whole issue pivots around what Britain planned to do in case of war. As is now widely known, Britain's contingency plans long envisaged the immediate dispatch of the main fleet to Singapore in the event of hostilities against Japan. The risks attendant in actually taking such a step were self-evident, and it is a common error to conclude that there was never much danger that the British Government would ever have been willing to take such a course, unilaterally, whatever the provocation. In the end, private reservations within the minds of military planners may exert a powerful and perhaps decisive influence in the formulation and execution of national defence and foreign policy. There is some truth, after all, in the cynical view that the art of contingency planning – in which the defence services contrive to establish plausible justifications for the construction of the most formidable forces which they feel their political masters can be persuaded to underwrite – is altogether a different matter from putting into execution operations which planners privately regard as wholly unrealistic. Not surprisingly, there were acrimonious differences of opinion within the British Foreign Office, the War Office, and – most importantly of all – the Admiralty during the period that culminated in the Tientsin Crisis. During the eight months between Munich and the unexpected eruption of the Tientsin dispute in June 1939, there occurred two 'palace revolutions' within the Admiralty. The importance and depth of these 'revolutions' and their effect upon British strategical policy towards Japan during the

Tientsin affair are comparable in significance to the eclipse of the *Kōdō* Group in Japan on the eve of the China Incident.

The two bodies that actually made Britain's war plans, the Chiefs of Staff and their Joint Planning Sub-Committee, began a sweeping re-evaluation of their strategical assumptions shortly after Munich. The basic assumption underlying their traditional 'Appreciation' of what to expect in case Britain became involved in hostilities in East Asia was no longer remotely tenable – that is, the idea that 'The European situation makes us entirely confident that European Powers will remain strictly neutral, and will not take advantage of our commitments in the Far East to prejudice our interests in other parts of the world.'*

Certainly the Admiralty needed no prompting by anyone before re-considering Britain's basic naval strategy. Admiral Chatfield, Britain's Chief of Naval Staff from the beginning of the decade, had never wavered in his determination to protect the East Asian half of the Empire with the main fleet in any war against Japan. However, he lost most of his influence over the Admiralty when he replaced the unfortunate Sir Thomas Inskip as Minister for the Co-ordination of Defence after Munich. The new Chief of Naval Staff, Sir Roger Backhouse, wasted no time in clearing the Admiralty of his predecessor's predilections by reorganizing key Admiralty departments. The Plans Department he left intact, but he invited Admiral Drax, the brilliant and acerbic former Commander-in-Chief, Plymouth, to advise the Admiralty on war plans as an independent voice before moving on to be principal A D C to the King (Backhouse's own previous posting). Drax shared the rising discontent of many senior line officers and relished his new appointment. Within a short period, he effectively smashed axioms which had governed naval policy for many years. Writing in mid-January 1939, Drax observed:

In our war plans, so far as I can ascertain, no details have been worked out for any offensive operations of major importance either by the Home or Medi-terranean fleets ... I venture the opinion that, if Japan joins our enemies, we should incur very great risks to the heart of our Empire if we dispatch our fleet too early to the Far East. The only hope for the Far East is, not to get active help from America (that, alas, is asking too much) but at least to persuade the U S A to move their whole fleet to the Pacific in order to 'keep the Japs guessing' and delay their entry into the war.†

* D P(P)S, 14 June 1937, C A B 16/182, British Public Record Office, Kew. The importance and context of the Tientsin dispute are discussed at greater length in Pritchard, *Far Eastern Influences*, op. cit., pp. 127–68, from which the following discussion borrows freely.

† Memorandum by Admiral Sir Reginald A. R. Plunkett-Ernle-Erle Drax, 20 January 1939, Drax 2/19, Drax Papers, Churchill College Archives, Cambridge.

These views coincided with Backhouse's own. The new Chief of Naval Staff thought the Japanese fleet was too powerful to oppose while Britain was refitting her older vessels and behind schedule in building new ones, particularly if Britain should have to fight Italy as well as Germany in the West. That seems plain enough to us, but it was a radical notion at a time when Britain's Navy was the strongest afloat. With the significant exception of the Director of Plans, Captain Danckwerts, who clung to Britain's traditional policies and was roundly rebuked by his superiors, sentiment within the Admiralty shifted behind the First Sea Lord in opposing the dispatch of the fleet to the Far East.

Meanwhile, higher authorities dealt with the implications of Far Eastern naval strategy. They met to consider a new appraisal prepared by the Joint Planning Committee (including the errant Captain Danckwerts) on behalf of the Chiefs of Staff Committee (including Admiral Backhouse). The document was called the 1939/40 European Appreciation.

In late February 1939 the Chiefs of Staff endorsed the Joint Planning Sub-Committee's draft. When it reached the Committee of Imperial Defence (on which Ministers sat with the most senior officials responsible for the Empire's security), the Ministers were stunned. For the first time, the strategical authorities had provided the Government with a grand review of a war against Japan, Germany and Italy in combination, no holds barred. The distinction which hitherto had existed between a European War and a Far Eastern War was blurred to an extent which was quite novel. Even were peace between Britain and Japan maintained, British interests in East Asia would soon wither away during a general European War. If Japan stayed out, the force of Anglo-French naval and economic power would be superior to that of Germany and Italy, but enemy army and air forces would surpass those of the Allies. Even so, once any European War began, a significant proportion of Britain's military and air strength would have to be diverted immediately to the Pacific and to staging points along the route there as a precaution against Japanese attack. Moreover, as the Chiefs of Staff already were aware, air squadrons in the East must have the latest types of aircraft: notwithstanding critical shortages of modern aircraft in Britain's metropolitan forces, nothing less would suffice against Japan.

If Japan formally entered the war alongside Italy or Germany, a British fleet strong enough to hold Japan must proceed to East Asian waters at once: again, no half-measures would contain the Japanese. This finding, too, coincided with what the Chiefs of Staff themselves had declared in recent advice to an Expert Committee on the Defence of India (which

Chatfield had chaired): 'We feel it right to point out that, while by force of circumstances we are bound to take risks in assessing the minimum defence requirements in certain parts of the Empire, we should not be justified in doing so at Singapore.'* It followed that in the light of more recent developments, including the Japanese occupation of Hainan and the Canton area of South-East China (surrounding Hong Kong), 'any alteration to our general naval plan of operations is unlikely. Far from any probability that naval dispositions can enable us to dispense with the military and air force requirements [in Malaya], their presence becomes all the more essential.'† Nevertheless, once the fleet departed for the Pacific, Anglo-French control in the Mediterranean could be expected to vanish after a short struggle. German and Italian influence over South-East Europe would mushroom. Enemy access to oil and other essential supplies in the western theatre would be greatly facilitated. The Middle East would tumble into the Axis camp. Thus the attitude of Japan would determine the degree of British ascendency or retreat throughout the Mediterranean and Middle East. If the war escalated into a three-enemy rather than a two-enemy conflict, then Anglo-French forces, alone, stood no reasonable hope of victory without the intervention of other Powers, particularly the United States.

When the Committee of Imperial Defence considered the European Appreciation in late February 1939, the First Lord of the Admiralty, Lord Stanhope, revealed the first signs of the change of heart in naval circles by suggesting that perhaps one or two capital ships would be enough to deter Japan from any adventure against British territory, considering Japan's own fear of attack by Russia or the United States. Prime Minister Chamberlain hesitated. Chatfield managed to stave off changes in policy for the moment. A select Strategical Appreciation Committee (SAC) was established to examine the Appreciation further.

From the first meeting of the SAC, an open feud existed between Backhouse and Chatfield. Chatfield argued that Britain's position had not deteriorated so much that it was impossible to protect the East Asian interests of the Empire. True, Italy was now regarded as a probable enemy in addition to Japan and Germany, but that was less important. Admiral Backhouse, however, thought that this made a tremendous difference. Britain's modernization was lagging. The Japanese fleet was fully modernized. Would any squadron that Britain might send be 'capable of acting as a deterrent'? Backhouse now called into ques-

---

* COS 805, 14 December 1938, CAB 53/42, British Public Record Office, Kew.
† ibid.

tion the very idea of a Far Eastern squadron, but Chatfield remained adamant: even if Britain found herself at war against all three potential enemies, 'We should have to send a fleet to the Far East ... If we sent seven [capital] ships, that would still leave us with six at home, which, with the seven French capital ships, would be a reasonable force. We must do this, or risk the Empire.' *

At this point, William Strang, representing the Foreign Office at the SAC, interjected that France had not yet heard officially of Britain's intention to send any fleet to the Pacific in certain eventualities. On the contrary, France had been told that Britain's contribution to the common cause would be mostly by air and sea. In French eyes the decisive theatre was Europe. Backhouse seized upon this as an additional reason for trying to knock Italy out of the war at the start, a complete reversal of previous strategy. This tipped the balance. The War Office and Air Ministry were enchanted by the prospect of an easy victory over Italy, and the SAC agreed that the French should be told that in the event of war an early offensive was envisaged by Britain against Italy with French cooperation. The SAC also decided 'that it is undesirable, if it can be avoided, to make any further communications to the Dominions as to the limitation in the size of the fleet' that might be sent to the East in case of trouble with Japan. These recommendations were condemned by Chatfield, who continued to demand political solutions that would avoid war against all three enemies at once. But if world war was inevitable, then he would prefer to abandon the Mediterranean rather than Britain's imperial obligations in East Asia: 'It would be better to lose the Empire by fighting than by default,' he said grimly. 'In the first case it would be an honourable defeat; in the second case it would be a disgrace.' †

As Minister for the Co-ordination of Defence, Chatfield ordered the Admiralty to present their views in writing to the SAC. This formal demand caused uneasiness in the Admiralty: they were uncertain what the SAC – and particularly Chatfield with his formidable mastery of naval affairs and political infighting – would do with the Admiralty's reply. Backhouse's new Deputy Chief of Naval Staff, Sir Andrew Cunningham, therefore emphasized that strategical circumstances could change rapidly: it might not be wise to commit the Admiralty to any specific policy 'until we are able to judge how the war is going'.‡

---

* SAC 4, 28 February 1939; SAC 1(39)1, 1 March 1939; SAC 2(39)2, 13 March 1939, all in CAB 16/209, British Public Record Office, Kew.
† ibid., SAC 2(39)2.
‡ Backhouse to Stanhope, 30 March 1939, Adm. 1/9897, British Public Record Office, Kew.

Taking a less cautious view, one in keeping with his maverick position, Admiral Drax wrote a detailed account of measures which he believed met the twin threats of war in Europe and in East Asia. Although he expressed a willingness to send a small detachment of ships to the Pacific at the outbreak of hostilities against Japan, he set two tests to establish whether any major transfer of forces should take place:

(a) that our main fleet in the Far East can do more towards rapidly winning the war than if it is kept in Europe;

(b) that the 'holding force' we have sent East is failing to maintain its object, and therefore there is real danger that the Japanese may shortly do us some vital damage.*

In Admiral Drax's estimation, neither precondition was liable to occur within the first six months of war. He closed with an emphatic warning: Britain's unconditional policy to send the main fleet to the Pacific in the event of a conflict with Japan 'constitutes a grave danger to the Empire and might easily lead to its complete ruin'.†

Drax's memorandum did impress the Admiralty: that much is clear. His detailed but bold proposals encouraged the First Lord to complain that the nominal Director of Plans, Captain Danckwerts, 'seems to afford the Navy no opportunity of helping to win the war and to be purely defensive'.‡ Backhouse himself went so far as to write in an internal Admiralty minute that 'It would certainly be very serious if Singapore fell to the Japanese but it would not necessarily mean, in my opinion, the loss of our Eastern Empire for all time.'§ He preferred to stress the shattering effect which the loss of Egypt and Suez would have upon British prestige round the world. Backhouse's thoughts and those of the new men he had brought into power with him departed so radically from Britain's traditional naval strategy that the Admiralty decided to return the vaguest possible written answers to Chatfield and the SAC. It was an old and favourite tactic of the Admiralty when faced with outside threats to its authority. Even Lord Chatfield found himself unable to grapple with a policy which was so non-committal. In oral explanations, the Admiralty convinced the SAC – and more importantly convinced Neville Chamberlain – that it was time to abandon in all but name Britain's long-standing guarantees of naval protection to the Pacific Dominions against Japan.

* Memorandum by Drax, 16 March 1939, Adm. 1/9897.
† ibid.
‡ Minute by Stanhope, 2 April 1939, Adm. 1/9897.
§ M.01188/39, Minute by Backhouse, 24 March 1939/Adm. 1/9909.

It should not be supposed, however, that the victory of Backhouse's men in this, the first of our two 'palace revolutions', was totally convincing. A gulf continued to exist between the Admiralty and the Far Eastern experts at the Foreign Office, where G. G. Fitzmaurice (an admiral's son) complained that the Admiralty displayed 'such a fatuous degree of complacency and ignorance of Far Eastern realities that sometimes I think we ought to let them know'.* The Permanent Under-Secretary at the Foreign Office, Sir Alexander Cadogan, privately called Admiral Cunningham 'King Half-wit' and Stanhope an 'exhibit'.†

The War Office, too, raised doubts about the new course set by the Admiralty, criticizing a recent paper from the Admiralty which suggested that Japan would rather bide her time and digest China than launch an unprovoked war against Britain. The War Office disagreed: 'Japan has been led on politically by her expanding military objectives until she is uncertain where to stop both politically and militarily. It is not certain what the extent of her present object is, as the Japanese are themselves uncertain how far to go.' ‡ Notwithstanding the recent recommendations by the S A C, the War Office insisted that 'Our general policy is already fixed – to retain our hold on Singapore at all costs and to do what is possible to protect our interests in China. This should be a sufficient guide to our actions whatever course Japan may adopt.' § Clearly, remarks such as these demonstrate something of the extent of the residual influence of the Chatfield or Far Eastern school. The revival of that faction a month later, therefore, may seem less surprising in view of the fact that in the Foreign Office, in the War Office, and even in planning circles at the Admiralty itself, there remained a well of sentiment throughout this period which tapped a sense that Britain had to defend imperial interests in East Asia more or less irrespective of dangers elsewhere.

Meanwhile, the extra naval power which it was now policy to use in Europe, once the Committee of Imperial Defence and the S A C had agreed to ignore the risks of war against Japan, momentarily appeared to offer a chance for changing the European strategical balance. Against Italy, in particular, the fleet might enable Britain to deal Mussolini such devastating blows that he could not survive. Before this prospect was recognized as an illusion, British defence planning grew increasingly muddled during the spring and summer of 1939, and Ministers took

* F 2798/471/61, Minute by G. G. Fitzmaurice, 28 March 1939, F O 371/23544.
† D. Dilks (ed.), *The Diaries of Sir Alexander Cadogan*, Cassell, London, 1971, pp. 169, 176.
‡ War Office Memorandum regarding J P 415, unsigned, 22 May 1939, W O 106/131.
§ ibid.

political decisions, such as Britain's new commitments to states already on the brink of collapse in Central Europe and the Balkans, without the benefit of sound strategical advice.

These new undertakings seriously compromised Britain's already weak position in East Asia. While attention remained focused upon Europe, Britain's newly revised global strategy – which depended upon an ability to maintain a naval offensive in the Mediterranean from the outbreak of war – began to fail its first major trial at Tientsin.

Although Britain and France had squabbled with Japan over complex local difficulties at Tientsin almost since the start of the China Incident in July 1937, the situation had remained deadlocked due to gross mishandling by both sides. To bring further pressure upon Britain (and, indirectly, France), the Japanese had imposed a makeshift blockade in mid-December 1938, curtailing entry and exit and restricting commercial traffic between the British Concession and the outside. These measures continued until General Kuwaki, the Japanese Army commander at Tientsin, was replaced by the relatively pro-British Lieutenant-General Honma Masaharu, who had been the Japanese military attaché in London at the height of the Manchurian Incident. In early February 1939 Honma temporarily relaxed the controls, much to the relief of the British.

Then, in the first week of March, Honma's soldiers began erecting barricades and live-wire entanglements, completely surrounding the British and French Concessions. Ostensibly this was in self-defence, counteracting the activities of 'anti-Japanese' elements operating from the relative safety of the Concessions. The British and French troops were brought to combat readiness.

Although weak in military terms, morale remained high in the British Concession. Evidently the French garrison was equally resolute. Brigadier A. H. Hopwood, Officer Commanding the British Forces in Tientsin, tried to improve the static defences of the British Concession and was determined to stand fast over British rights no matter what consequences might ensue. The War Office was sympathetic to Hopwood's stance and – astonishingly – derived some comfort from the view that 'What will weigh with the Japanese . . . is not the degree of strength of the local garrison but the fact that if they start a fight it means war.'

If Honma was proving an unpredictable quantity in his new role as commander of the Japanese Garrison at Tientsin, so were his two immediate superiors. It was more than coincidental that the original blockade in December 1938 had occurred as General Sugiyama Hajime became Commander-in-Chief of the North China Area Army in place of General

Terauchi (who went back to Tokyo to rusticate as a 'Supreme War Councillor'). Sugiyama's second-in-command, Major-General Yamashita Tomoyuki, likewise, had been appointed Chief of Staff of the North China Area Army only recently, and in high Japanese circles it was known that he had little care whether war with Britain resulted or not. This uncompromising attitude, in fact, was welcomed by the War Ministry and by the Army General Staff in Tokyo, who reasoned that Britain would try to avoid war but in any event posed no serious obstacle to Japan. At worst, war with Britain would align Japan with Germany at a moment when a European War already seemed imminent.

The next stage occurred when the manager of the Japanese-sponsored Federal Reserve Bank at Tientsin, who had just been appointed Superintendent of Customs, was assassinated by a Chinese terrorist. After being invited by the municipal authorities to assist, the Japanese helped to conduct a series of searches throughout the Concession. A number of arrests were made, and it was in the course of these that four Chinese detained by the British were accused by the Japanese of complicity in the deaths of three Japanese soldiers. Without conclusive proof to substantiate these charges, the matter languished until June, by which time Honma had grown weary of Britain's failure to comply with Japanese demands. The Japanese insisted that all four of the suspected terrorists should be surrendered to them. The Japanese also required that the British should hand over the precious silver reserves which the canny Kuomintang Government had deposited in British banks within the Concession: acceding to this Japanese demand not only could be expected to demoralize the morale of Chiang Kai-shek's supporters but might also have precipitated a catastrophic collapse in the value of his régime's currency and a strengthening of the Japanese puppet régime headed by Wang Ching-wei. Pressed to accept these and other radical demands, the British, perhaps predictably, refused: and in consequence the Japanese imposed a close blockade of the British Concession on 14 June 1939. People still went in and out but at the cost of an exhausting wait and a humiliating body search of men – and women – by the Japanese Army. A smile of appreciation went through Asia, even in countries which approved of China and were against Japanese militarism. The Japanese, it seemed, were effectively putting down the mighty from their seats, and scattering the proud. The Taipans, as the heads of firms were called, could not see their way ahead through the gloom. Perishable food stocks fell to 10 per cent of normal supplies, and rice disappeared altogether. At the same time, the Japanese Foreign Ministry demanded a reversal of key British policies concerning the China Incident as Japan's price for lifting the blockade. Ugly anti-British demonstrations were staged in Tokyo with official approval and with the active connivance of the Metropolitan Police (acting on instructions from the powerful Japanese Ministry for Home Affairs). Reports reaching London suggested that the police might allow the British Embassy to be stormed by mobs. Even moderate organs such as the *Oriental Economist* abruptly reflected this darkening mood. London was unclear whether those orchestrating these events wished to force Britain into war or merely into a humiliating loss of prestige (on the evidence of Baron Harada Kumao and Marquis Kido Koichi, it appears that Japanese honour would have been satisfied by minor British compromises in June but that a month later the situation was too exacerbated to allow for any simple resolution of the crisis).

Britain responded to the Tientsin Crisis in three ways. First, diplomatic exchanges were begun at Tientsin, later extended to formal exchanges between Ambassador Sir Robert Craigie and Foreign Minister Arita Hachirō. Eventually these conversations covered all major points of friction between the two countries. Second, to the despair of Britain's strategical advisers, the issue of commercial and financial reprisals against Japan was reopened in Whitehall. Third, the Tientsin Crisis made a nonsense of Britain's recent changes in defence strategy, which, as has been seen, were predicated upon the assumption, now, that war would begin in Europe and then spread to East Asia rather than the other way round.

Although Japanese policy was not as monolithic and unambiguous as London supposed, Britain's first reactions to Honma's blockade verged upon panic. 'Pug' Ismay, Secretary to the Committee of Imperial Defence, privately informed Lord Hankey's son, Robin, at the overwrought British Embassy in Warsaw, that 'For the moment all our eyes are on Tientsin instead of Danzig.'* The Foreign Secretary, Lord Halifax, closeted himself with his advisers: 'Had to spend half the day holding H[alifax]'s hand,' wrote Cadogan in his diary on 15 June.† When Halifax emerged, he met with Prime Minister Chamberlain and Lord Chatfield to discuss the question of retaliation and dispatching a battle squadron to the Pacific. The Commander-in-Chief, China Fleet, had cabled that 'Tientsin may develop into a case of giving in to such an extent that we virtually lose the Concession or of making a *casus belli*. I have never before suggested I required reinforcements but am reluctantly forced to the conclusion.' He asked for 'a squadron of two or three capital ships accompanied by

---

* Private Letter, Ismay to Robin Hankey, 16 June 1939, Ismay IV/Han/20, Ismay Papers, King's College [London] Centre for Military Archives.
† Dilks, op. cit., pp.186–8.

a cruiser squadron and a destroyer flotilla' to augment his slender forces.*

The Cabinet Committee on Foreign Policy was advised by the Foreign Secretary that

the present situation at Tientsin has revealed the policy of the Japanese to eliminate or vastly diminish British interests and prestige in China as a means to the attainment of her long-term objective of establishing her control over the whole of East Asia and the formation of a closed economic bloc between Japan, China and Manchuria, which would in turn place her in a position at some later stage to pursue ambitions to southward at the expense of the British Empire.†

Lord Halifax went on to inform his ministerial colleagues that 'the situation with which we are faced has reached an acute stage, and whereas up to date we have been able to allow our future course of action to wait upon events, the necessity to do something to counter the Japanese plan has now become imperative'.‡ Oddly enough, the Foreign Office rejected a policy of inaction on the grounds that it would weaken Britain's political position relative to Germany and Italy as well as against Japan.

At the behest of the Prime Minister, Chatfield asked the Chiefs of Staff for advice, admitting that 'we can only strengthen our position in the Far East by weakening our position in Europe and therefore the main decision is a political one'.§

At first sight, it might appear that the answers to Chatfield's questions were plain enough after the Government's recent acceptance of the naval strategy promoted by Backhouse and Cunningham. However, at the beginning of June, before the arrival of the warnings from the Commander-in-Chief, China Fleet, there began another major shift of power in the Admiralty which had the effect of enhancing the influence of the Admiralty's Plans Division. Now gravely ill, Backhouse retired in June as First Sea Lord and was replaced by the more traditionalist Sir Dudley Pound, while Admiral Tom Phillips, a former Director of Plans and an adherent of the Far Eastern School, became Deputy Chief of Naval Staff, relieving Admiral Cunningham, who went out to take Pound's place as Commander-in-Chief of the Mediterranean Fleet. Significantly, Danckwerts remained Director of Plans, and Drax, who had left the

---

* F 5800/176/23, C-in-C, China Fleet, to Admiralty, 13 June 1939, FO 371/23556, British Public Record Office, Kew.
† FP (36)95, 16 June 1939, CAB 27/627, British Public Record Office, Kew.
‡ ibid.
§ COS 300(39)1, 16 June 1939, CAB 53/11, British Public Record Office, Kew.

Admiralty to become ADC to the King at the beginning of April, no longer counter-balanced the orthodoxy of the Plans Division. All of this meant that difficulties which Chatfield had encountered with his immediate successors at the Admiralty might now be overborne. Certainly Chamberlain himself did not now regard the case against dispatching the fleet as unanswerable. The lesson to be derived from this is that policies cannot be divorced from personalities.

Haltingly, over the next few weeks, the issues became clear: the Tientsin Crisis threatened the very survival of British influence in East Asia; the Empire could not abandon its position there; only the dispatch of naval reinforcements to the Pacific would deter the Japanese; any fleet sent to the Pacific must be able to accept a main fleet action against the whole Japanese fleet if pressed; the dispatch of such a battlefleet to the East would involve the abandonment of Britain's naval control in the Mediterranean. No efforts must be spared to reach a compromise with the Japanese in the Craigie–Arita talks, but orders were issued that the fleet must be ready for immediate service in August in case events turned for the worse.

There were soon indications that Hitler might be taking advantage of the Tientsin Crisis. Henry Pownall, the War Office's chief planning officer, recorded in his diary, 'Things are beginning to thicken at Danzig. Rather earlier than we thought, but it may be that the Tientsin affair has caused Hitler to accelerate his tempo.'* It was also clear that the Germans were seizing upon the propaganda value of the Tientsin dispute in efforts to persuade the Japanese Government to conclude a military alliance with Germany, and there were reports from Egypt that the Germans were interpreting the incident 'to show that Orientals can insult Englishmen with impunity and that the British Empire is too enfeebled to react. Effect on Oriental mind is most damaging.'†

In the weeks after suggestions voiced by Admiral Pound opened the way to a reconsideration of a large fleet movement to the Pacific in the event that the negotiations with Japan failed to produce a satisfactory result, the second tide of changes continued to roll through the Admiralty in the wake of Admiral Backhouse's departure. The new Deputy Chief of the Naval Staff, Tom Phillips, used his influence in efforts to sweep away Admiral Drax's formulations. Drax's genius and daring earns our respect, and he had a natural flair for battle action. Tom Phillips, although perhaps equally gifted, was a complete contrast: a thorough master of detailed

---

* H. Pownall, *Chief of Staff*, vol. I: *1933–1940*, Leo Cooper, London, 1972, p. 209.

† Alexandria Telegram 397, 26 June 1939, copied to the War Office in WO 106/126, British Public Record Office, Kew.

staff-work, who, in between appointments in the Admiralty's Plans Division during 1930–32 and 1935–8, had served as Chief of Staff and Flag Captain to the Commander-in-Chief, East Indies, during 1932–5, where the prime mission had always been to move out to Singapore in case of trouble with Japan. It is hardly surprising, therefore, that Phillips now maintained that the Tientsin emergency proved the importance of re-articulating key elements in Britain's traditional naval strategy:

1. Make it clear that we cannot have three fleets.
2. Point out that Home Waters are vital and a sufficient force must always remain there.
3. If a fleet is sent to the East, it must be of sufficient strength.
4. As a corollary to the above, if the situation arises, HMG will have to choose between the Far East and the Eastern Mediterranean – this choice must depend upon circumstances and the progress of the war and must be made at the time, e.g., is Singapore invested, etc.
5. All references to a 'flying squadron' in the East to be omitted.*

One might recall these words when the time comes to consider the fate of the singularly unfortunate detachment of two battleships that Phillips was destined to command in December 1941, sunk by the Japanese off the coast of Malaya only two days after the outbreak of the War in the Pacific.

Throughout July came conflicting reports on the advantages or not of taking retaliatory steps against Japan. The British Senior Naval Officer at Tientsin told London that he wished to mount armed guards with Lewis guns aboard all British vessels in his area, with authority for 'forcibly preventing stopping and boarding'. He remarked, 'Armed conflict might result from [the] above, but it is considered that opposition would not be serious and that incidents would remain local.'† The British military, naval and air attachés in Tokyo, however, were far better informed. They strongly opposed provoking even slight clashes during this sensitive period, and in a joint message to London they agreed

In the event of our inability to meet Japanese desires at forthcoming conference resulting in increased Japanese pressure and further inimical action against our interests in the Far East, we are convinced that Japanese military and naval confidence, reinforced by present exacerbated state of public opinion, is such that retaliatory action on our part is more likely to act as an incentive to open hostilities on their part, than as a deterrent.‡

* M.06226/39, Minute by Phillips, 5 July 1939, Adm. 1/9767, British Public Record Office, Kew.
† Senior Naval Officer, Tientsin, to Commander-in-Chief, China Station, 20 July 1939 WO 106/128, British Public Record Office, Kew.
‡ ibid., Military Attaché, Tokyo, to War Office, 15 July 1939.

With such reports in mind, London came under great pressure to in-crease British land and air forces in the Far East. The Chairman of the Chiefs of Staff, Sir Cyril Newall, indicated that his Committee now 'were mainly exercised about the situation in the Far East. The prospect of a successful outcome to the [Craigie–Arita] negotiations did not appear very hopeful.'* In the end, combined pressure by the Chiefs of Staff, Admiral Chatfield in his capacity as Minister for the Co-ordination of Defence, and Sir Robert Vansittart as a spokesman for the Foreign Office, proved irresistible: the Committee of Imperial Defence voted to give Malaya two squadrons from Metropolitan Bomber Command, two further RAF squadrons from India, together with an Indian Army infantry brigade and support units.

On 24 July Neville Chamberlain announced in the House of Commons that Craigie and Arita had reached a formula which might lead to improved understanding with Japan and thus permit the two countries to negotiate a settlement of the Tientsin dispute. At once, it is true, these negotiations eased what the Prime Minister called 'the stripping, searching and slapping' of British residents in Tientsin, but even he recognized that 'The attitude of the military in China itself, especially at Tientsin, Peking and Shanghai, remains intolerable, provocative and offensive.'† The anti-British demonstrations in Tokyo showed signs of abating somewhat, but no one could predict what changes might lie in store should the pace of negotiations falter and so exasperate the Japanese even more.

The ensuing suspense grew so palpable that on 2 August 1939 the British Chiefs of Staff discussed whether full war precautionary measures should be taken. They finally decided that further reinforcements should be sent to East Asia without delay if conditions deteriorated – but not yet. Much would depend upon whether the reinforcements had to meet the demands of a Far Eastern emergency or to act as a barrier against the spread eastwards of tension now arising in Europe. Either way, the next few weeks might prove critical.

Across Whitehall on 2 August, Lord Halifax was informing the Cabinet that 'the situation in the Far East was now causing him more anxiety than the position in any other part of the world'.‡ When one considers that Britain was then only one month away from war against Germany, the Foreign Secretary's remarks gives one pause for thought. Halifax ex-plained that Japan insisted that general policy matters concerning the

---

* CID 367(39)1 [DP(P)], 21 July 1939, CAB 2/9, British Public Record Office, Kew.
† NC 18/1110, Neville Chamberlain to Hilda Chamberlain, 30 July 1939, Chamberlain Papers, Birmingham University Library.
‡ CC 40(39)4, 2 August 1939, CAB 24/100, British Public Record Office, Kew.

whole gamut of Anglo-Japanese affairs should be reviewed during the Tokyo conversations about Tientsin. These wider issues, originally excluded at Britain's request, might lead to an open breach in relations between the two countries. Since Sir George Sansom, in whose wisdom Halifax placed complete confidence, counselled that Japan merely wished to extort the best possible terms from Britain at the Conference, the Foreign Secretary suggested that Britain could afford to harden her approach to the Japanese. If relations continued to worsen so that further action became necessary, then Britain should denounce her commercial treaty with Japan – as America had done when the Craigie–Arita formula was announced. This would allow Britain and Japan to conduct further negotiations over a twelve-month period of grace and, in the Foreign Secretary's estimation, would be less likely to provoke military reprisals than an embargo (which would probably evolve into a naval blockade). Two days later, speaking in the Commons, Neville Chamberlain warned the world not to assume that Britain was incapable of establishing decisive naval superiority over Japan in the Pacific: 'we have such a fleet here, and in certain circumstances we might feel it necessary to send the fleet out there. I hope no one will think that it is absolutely out of the question for such circumstances to arise.' One can make of these words what one will. Not surprisingly, the mood in the Foreign Office verged on black despair: a member of the over-worked Far Eastern Department recalled afterwards that several of his colleagues collapsed under the strain. As far as the British Government was concerned, the outcome of the Tientsin Crisis, whether compromise or Pacific War, was up to Tokyo: in the face of Japanese blustering, the British Government had decided to stand fast. Nevertheless, judged by their own usual assumptions, normally cautious figures in the British Government responded to the threat of war in 1939 with apparent irrationality, a predisposition to bring matters to a head regardless of consequences. Although the country was better armed now than at any time since the end of the First World War, the international situation was virtually beyond hope of repair, and the dread prospect of a three-enemy war loomed dead ahead. In contrast to the winter of 1938–9, the later summer of 1939 was remarkably devoid of useful speculation about the strategical consequences of Britain's perilous course. The defence authorities, particularly the Admiralty, nevertheless remained worried about what effect the Tientsin Crisis might have upon the European situation. New operations plans written following Britain's strategical shifts in the spring of 1939 had not been received by British commands overseas when the Tientsin Crisis first blossomed in June. Out

of necessity, the Navy temporarily suspended their new operations plans
and returned to their earlier war plans for the fleet (based largely upon
the 1937 Far East Appreciation by the Chiefs of Staff, which had been
discarded as obsolete by the country's strategical and political authorities
in the spring of 1939). While high-level policy concerning the future dispositions of the fleet remained undecided, up-to-date amendments to the
Naval War Memorandum (Eastern) were not even sent to the Commander-in-Chief, China Station, until 15 June (the day after the Tientsin
blockade was imposed by the Japanese) – and even then these were suspended for a day on 20 June while the policy questions hung in the balance.
Relevant modifications to the Naval War Memorandum (European) were
sent to naval commanders abroad only on 4 August. Therefore the actual
fleet instructions in the hands of Britain's naval commanders overseas
during most of the summer of 1939 remained predicated upon a task
which the Admiralty wanted to abandon as hopeless only a few months
before – the dispatch of the fleet to Singapore in the event of a conflict
with Japan.

Finally, on Friday, 4 August 1939, British naval commanders
worldwide were told how the Admiralty planned to distribute British
naval forces if Japan joined the Axis in a world war against Britain and
France. In essential respects, Britain's new plan conformed to suggestions
which Chatfield had made at the worst of the initial Tientsin war scare.
Indeed, it departed little from Admiral Pound's reaction to Chatfield's
criticisms of the position taken by the Chiefs of Staff at the beginning of
the crisis. In short, it meant a return to Britain's traditional posture, since
it envisaged that control of the Mediterranean by the Royal Navy might
be sacrificed in order to send the main fleet to Singapore while retaining a
smaller force of six capital ships in Home Waters to contain the Germans.
The new plans stopped short, however, of reviving one vital doctrine
which the Chiefs of Staff had led the Government to abandon in the
spring, namely, that there must be no hesitation in reinforcing Britain's
imperial position in East Asia at full strength to the detriment of Britain's
position in the Mediterranean. The ultimate strength of Britain's Far East
Fleet would depend upon political decisions that Ministers could take only
after war was joined.

As it happened, these developments during the China Incident forced
London to choose either to accept the risk of Japanese belligerency against
the British Empire without making proper provision for it, so that Britain
could wage an intensive war against Italy with no immediate regard for
the consequences in East Asia and the Pacific, or, alternatively, to reserve
the forces believed necessary to resist Japan, renewing efforts to ensure

that Italy was kept out of the German camp permanently. Notwithstanding ominous news that German-Italian Naval Staff talks were taking place throughout the summer, the grave crisis at Tientsin forced the British to adopt the second course. After having dallied with the idea of pre-emptive action against Italy in the event of war against Germany, London now chose appeasement rather than confrontation with Italy. This attitude persisted beyond the Tientsin Crisis because the success of the policy could be seen. A result was that upon the outbreak of war against Germany, the British Government's latest thinking on the future distribution of British naval forces worldwide showed the degree to which strength in the Mediterranean had been reduced to skeletal proportions compared to the size of battlefleet once contemplated for a Mediterranean offensive.

The two power-shifts, or 'palace revolutions', in the British Admiralty during 1939 demonstrate beyond peradventure that, at least in relation to the threat of war against Japan, national policy evolved around the actual strength of Britain's defence system and the views of Britain's strategical authorities. These same two revolutions also show the limits of the influence of strictly military factors: outside developments in Europe, especially the Nazi-Soviet Pact and the crisis over Danzig, ultimately proved far more important and seem to have developed without too central a regard in London for Britain's imperial defence liabilities in East Asia and the Pacific.

By the end of August 1939, international conditions had undergone a complete transformation, and Tokyo was reeling in confusion. The Japanese Foreign Minister, Arita Hachirō, was ready to reach a limited agreement with Britain despite the power of the Army, but on 21 August the Craigie–Arita Conversations were suspended at Britain's request. Britain's resolute defiance of Japan might have uncovered the instability and weakness of Japan in any event, and it is worthwhile remembering that Japan had to consider the consequences of Roosevelt's decision to abrogate the Japan–US Treaty of Commerce and Navigation at the height of the Tientsin Crisis, a matter which was reason enough to make Japan pause. As it happened, both of these events occurred while Japan was suffering serious military reverses in its major border conflict with the Soviet Union at Nomonhan, and thus the startling announcement of the Nazi-Soviet Pact on 23 August, which completely undercut the foundations of the Anti-Comintern Pact, constituted a final blow which no government in Japan could have survived. Under this succession of shocks, the Hiranuma Cabinet fell in Japan, and both the immediate danger of an Anglo-Japanese War and the prospect of substantial gains for Japan from the European crisis abruptly receded.

Nevertheless, the Tientsin affair is immensely important in the story of the approach of the Pacific War, for it marked the end of two centuries of British dominance in East Asia. Above all, the Tientsin Crisis was the last time Britain independently defied Japan without the clear prospect of active American intervention. An Anglo-Japanese war was averted only narrowly in 1939 – and perhaps only by the coincidence of outside events. Never again did Britain maintain any illusions about exerting decisive influence in East Asia. With the outbreak of war in Europe, western authority passed irretrievably from Britain to the United States. In some ways Tientsin was an embarrassing hiccup in Britain's imperial responsibilities, which Britain did try to ignore after the spring of 1939. Ultimately, Britain did concentrate upon Europe rather than upon the Far East. Yet it is important to establish that Britain, however muddled, was neither bluffing nor blustering at Tientsin, and that the momentous collapse of British influence in East Asia which followed the outbreak of war in Europe was nothing short of cataclysmic, even if the effects of that cataclysm could not be assessed fully until the summer of 1940.

Before leaving the Tientsin Crisis behind, one should appreciate the restraint shown by the Japanese Garrison at Tientsin. In the last analysis, they could have seized the British and French Concessions at Tientsin at any time. It must have been tempting. The consequences of such a simple step hardly bear thinking about.

CHAPTER 11

India and the Conflict

A T the time of the clash between China and Japan, the surprising fact in the rest of Asia was that most of it was under western government. Much of India, for example, had been under British rule for 150 years. Nearly all the rest of the region had also passed into the empires, or spheres of interest, of one European Power or another. Two ancient, but comparatively small, countries, Persia and Thailand, were the only exceptions. They owed their preservation to uncommon adroitness, aided by the fact that in each case two foreign Powers were competing for dominance over their territories.

From the beginning of the 1920s India, the heart and core of this series of subject countries, had made a resolute and persevering effort to throw off western rule. It was a fair deduction that, if it succeeded, an end would be put to the lesser imperialisms of Europe in Asia. Their circumstances were in some respects dissimilar: their end would be the same. All Asia would be free. Moreover India had so central a position in Asia, was a country with such prestige and resources, that the way in which it reacted to the issues of the time would have the deepest consequences for its neighbours. An account of the war requires therefore that the affairs of India should be followed, that its quarrel with Britain should be recorded, that the degree at different times of its pro-Japanese sentiment should be remarked, and its role in Japanese strategy examined. It demands also an inquiry into the different quality of British imperialism from Japanese which made the British Empire, even in its decay, by contrast so durable.

The major part of India was conquered by Britain between 1757 and 1820. The form of conquest was straightforward military annexation, but of a somewhat unusual kind. The conquest was not premeditated by Britain. A British trading company, the Honourable East India Company, had begun to trade peaceably in India. It was sucked into intervening in the management of Indian affairs by the anarchy which followed the downfall in the eighteenth century of the Moghul Empire. Out of its activities, the British Government, which had gradually assumed control of the political responsibilities of the Company, eventually found itself the master of a great military empire.

The British Raj was unique in having been set up by a people which used no large standing army of its own countrymen for the purpose. Alone among governments which pursued an active imperialist role Britain operated with such a small army of its own that its aims seemed derisory. It was much too small for Britain to have played any notable part on the continent of Europe, and it might have seemed too small to undertake operations on other continents. The Empire was won, not by British forces in the main, but by dexterous political manoeuvre, and by the Indian forces who chose to fight on the British side in a situation where there were several claimants for their arms. The East India Company, which was in India for trade, became, to all intents and purposes, one of the native powers between which India was divided; and from being one of these native powers it became gradually the paramount native state. It raised and paid for native armies which won for it territories for which it had to provide an administration: and this, though informed by British concepts, continued in many respects the traditional administration. The predominance of the Company was due primarily to the coherent political organization which it imported into India. It was also due, initially, to superior military technique, but when other native powers through foreign advisers imported the technology, it was due to superior discipline and organization.

Those statesmen of the Company who had conceived the policy, and saw where it tended, had usually to draw along their reluctant colleagues, who were always saying that a trading company had no right to be considering policies which would thrust upon it unwelcome political re-sponsibilities. Nevertheless the bolder spirits prevailed, and they succeeded in their manoeuvres with startling ease. Thus Britain, which was five thousand miles away, found itself with an Empire which it had never, in its deliberate moments, set itself to acquire. It had gained it with the minimum military force; and it held it by the stiffening effect of a garrison of British troops which, in normal circumstances, amounted to no more than 60,000 men. It would have been impossible with such a puny force to have held down a genuine national movement, and to have ruled India by the sword. British Government thus rested, in the deepest sense, upon the consent of the people to be governed. Its continuance depended on the tacit ballot that this government afforded benefits which the majority of the people accepted, either from apathy or from general appreciation of it.

The reason why the British had made such an easy conquest of the country was that for the most part a stubborn defence was never en-countered. The country changed hands while the peasantry, from which a popular army would have had to be recruited, looked on. This followed an old tradition of India. Observers of the country from earliest historical times had often exclaimed with wonder at the detached attitude of the peasantry, who went on with agricultural tasks, ignoring a pitched battle of their betters which might be taking place a few hundred yards from them, and on which their destiny depended. Not all the conquests were as easy as this. The East India Company had to fight hard, for instance, against the Marathas and Sikhs, who both had organized military kingdoms of a formidable nature. But even with them, the kingdoms were the armies: once these were defeated the East India Company had no more to do: there was no great popular resistance to wear down. Popular feeling against the foreigner interfering in the political affairs of the country is mainly a product of the twentieth century.

In this take-over of India there was no intention on the part of the British to produce a social transformation. As regards forms of society, the British were willing to leave things put. This was in some part due to the fascination and esteem which Indian life, in all its astonishing variety, exercises over the spirits of those who encounter it. It was also due to the realization that any interference with existing customs was likely to cause trouble. For example, the British were at first reluctant to give any countenance to Christian missionaries. Later, with the growth of evangelism in the nineteenth century in England the resistance to missionaries was partly eroded; but the mutiny of 1857, which stemmed from the mistaken belief of Indian soldiers that the British intended to force Christianity upon them, demonstrated the wisdom of non-interference. Thereafter social change was on the whole carefully refrained from. Profound social changes did, in fact, take place, but these were the inevitable result of the impact of a modern, highly industrialized society, such as Britain became, on an archaic, predominantly agrarian one. They were part of a world-wide trend, and not peculiar to the relations of Britain and India.

It was in the sphere of politics and administration that the struggle for sovereignty developed in India, and it was here that interesting forms were evolved. Nearly all the strains of thought in political philosophy in Britain during a century and a half found at one time or another reflection in the institutions of India. At the end of the eighteenth century the main preoccupation was to protect the individual citizen against arbitrary power, and to put government in the shackles of regular procedure controlled by courts. Then for a while the dominant interest was the philosophy of utilitarianism. One Governor General, Lord William Bentinck, was a close disciple of Bentham, and for forty years James Mill, and his son

John Stuart Mill, held key positions in the office of the East India Company. Certain questions were endlessly discussed, for instance, the case for direct administration by the British and the case for indirect administration; the duty of the government to promote change, and its duty to shield people against too rapid change; the virtues of control from above and the virtues of self-government; and the discussion resulted in action, or in some cases inaction – for instance, after the mutiny of 1857 there was no extension of direct British rule. Some of the shrewdest minds in Britain, from Victorian times to the late 1930s, found the Indian Government more malleable to ideas than society in the West. A philosophically inclined visitor to India towards the end of the nineteenth century said that a trip there was like re-living his life as a student of politics at Oxford.

The civil service in British India became remarkable for its quality. In the kingdoms and empires of the sub-continent in the past, the central governments found it traditionally very hard to get anything done. Their acts might be sporadically vigorous and imaginative, but the sum total of their deeds was slight: it disappeared quickly in sand. The Indian Civil Service, first instituted by the British, and then increasingly operated by both British and Indians, gave India for the first time an instrument by whose means government could carry out reforms which were pushed through to the end. Such was the prestige, the intelligence, and the standard of service to the community of this body of men that, even when the freedom struggle was at its height, distinguished Indian families, including the Nehrus, sent some of their sons into government service while others were operating in the opposition movement. The ideal of the Indian Civil Service was to gain willing acceptance of the policies and actions of the Government. To be compelled to use force at all was, therefore, regarded as a mark of failure; and its excessive use was rarely forgiven. This was a reflection of the fact that from the beginning of the Raj the number of Englishmen in India was far too small for them to govern the country arbitrarily and with incessant use of force. In the last years of British rule the British members of the administrative class of the civil service numbered less than a thousand, and in the subordinate services they hardly existed, whereas the population of India by the beginning of the war had swollen to 350 million, or one sixth of the population of the world.

Although, through the British period, government was carried on chiefly by the civil service, India was also by stages equipped with free institutions. Because Britain, in the grip of nineteenth-century liberal ideas, knew only one way of being politically constructive, it instinctively introduced into India representative councils and assemblies and the whole apparatus of liberal democracy. At the beginning these councils were largely consultative, but they contained seeds which grew, and which decided that the struggle for freedom in India would take the form of a demand for parliamentary rule.

Constitutional reforms in India were partly a response to, and partly they stimulated, the Indian national movement. That the transition from subjection to independence in India came in the end with such remarkable ease and restraint on both sides was due chiefly to three things: the liberal institutions set up in India by the British; the genius of Mahatma Gandhi, for many years the leader of the national freedom movement; and the quickening of a new age in Asia, and new ideas and a new type of British personality in India, as a direct result of the Japanese War.

On the Indian side, a vital factor in the struggle for independence was the emergence of a new Indian middle class. This class adopted English as its language, and owed its existence to the mass of institutions which the Raj fostered. Some members of it adapted themselves so phenomenally well to English culture that they became, to all intents and purposes, Englishmen. They lived in English style. They spoke English in their homes. Perhaps there is no comparable case in modern history of a class taking over so completely and with such ease the culture and language of another people: the parallel in the past is the assimilation of Latin culture by the provincials of the Roman Empire. Not that these families lost all touch with India; the women especially carried on the old Indian tradition, and in the deeper layers of the mind, the Indian structure persisted. But in practical action most of the men thought, felt, acted like Englishmen, and made very much the same value judgements. This victory of an alien personality was seen at times as a doubtful advantage to India; its psychological effects were frequently lamented by the social group in which it took place; but in the long run such fusions of culture are prized by the countries in which they occur, provided the assimilation is complete. The most surprising instance of this deep westernization is usually masked. Gandhi, the man under whose leadership the independence of India was achieved, a man who always stressed that he was a Hindu, the heir of the Hindu tradition; who wore Indian clothes, or very few clothes at all in the manner of Indian holy men, was nevertheless profoundly influenced by ideas from Britain. Equality of citizens, non-doctrinaire socialism, his apotheosis of the individual conscience, his social experimentation, prohibition, feminism, nationalism itself – this was the British tradition, not perhaps of government, but of radical non-conformism. Here, it might be said, was an example rare in history, of Rome making Greece its captive, not vice versa.

This westernized Indian middle class, though numerically very small, became immensely important, and in the eyes of the rest of the world, it *was* Indian, spoke for India, represented India. As it matured, it inevitably took to nationalism, and the Indian patriot became the most typical example of the nationalist in his time. He was the most eloquent in denouncing imperialism – often in admirable English prose. He demanded the most fiercely to be liberated. He was the most confident, and with reason, of being able to operate by himself the institutions amongst which he had passed his life. Some years before the First World War, Indian nationalism was already vigorous. At first the nationalists had been divided between revolutionaries and constitutionalists. The revolutionaries, who carried on old Indian traditions of romantic protest, wanted root and branch overthrow of British rule, and terrorism seemed to be their best instrument. By contrast, the constitutionalists did not expect to end British rule by a lightning stroke; but by forming political parties, by entering the representative assemblies, by propaganda, and by accepting and operating the political systems which Britain had set up, they expected to be able to bring enough pressure to bear on the Government to make their voice felt in its decisions. They were buoyed up and encouraged by the support which they received from radicals in Britain. This active lobby in Britain for Indian independence was an important factor convincing Indian nationalism that constitutionalism would give results. After a time, terrorism lost its glamour, and the majority of nationalists opted for constitutional action, or only mildly unconstitutional action; and, with aberrations at times when crises came to a head, they remained faithful to this course.

On the British side there were, at times, explosive strains. There were, occasionally, violent men in the civil service and in the Army, and until the end the danger existed below the surface that in an emergency they might react brutally. Once violence had started it would have grown by its own momentum and both sides might have drifted into open war. An outrage occurred shortly after the First World War in the massacre at Amritsar. This town in the Punjab was the scene of demonstrations in which mobs got control of the city and martial law was proclaimed in the area. An Indian assembly convened in defiance of an order, was caught in a walled space, with inadequate exits, and a British general, General Dyer, ordered troops to open fire. As a result, nearly four hundred unarmed people were killed. That this atrocity should have taken place, and even been approved by a section of British opinion, was a shock to Indian leaders. But there were denunciations in London; those in Parliament were led with much force by Winston Churchill. The repudiation by the British Government of General Dyer was one of the factors which strengthened Indian nationalism in its belief that it could win freedom by relatively restrained means.

The chief organ of the freedom movement, the Indian National Congress, was led during the crucial years by one of the most extraordinary figures of history, Mahatma Gandhi. Gandhi's outstanding qualities were a combination of a peculiar gentleness with inflexible determination; his religious temperament, natural in an Indian, was allied with a practical ability, unusual in seers, to shape events to some extent in the light of his understanding. Gandhi made Indian nationalism self-confident; he fed it with imaginative ideas and moral fire. Avoiding the dreary tactics of terrorism and guerrilla warfare, he perfected the weapons of civil disobedience and non-violent resistance. Some of his methods, at first, struck his lieutenants in Congress as too ingenuous; for instance, Gandhi proposed a famous march to the sea, to defy the law and make salt, on which there was a very light tax. Congress regarded it as a useless demonstration and agreed to it only in order to humour him. But it set India alight, and demonstrated a method of inducing popular uprisings which was to be of first importance to Congress in their later campaigns. He pursued his ends undeviatingly, but discriminated about means; thus, in the greatest of human traditions, he made politics a branch of ethics. The moral reason for all his major decisions was clearly laid in view, and even if a sophisticated onlooker might sometimes have thought that he deceived himself, and that the moral judgements on which he based his actions were sometimes the flexible handmaids of political experimentation, his concern with principle was authentic, never hypocritical, and it affected those who dealt with him. An English judge, sentencing him on one occasion to a prison term 'for sedition', addressed Gandhi, as he stood before him in the dock, in words which illustrate the effect he had on his political opponents:

It would be impossible to ignore the fact that in the eyes of millions of your countrymen you are a great patriot and a great leader. Even those who differ from you in politics look on you as a man of high ideals and of noble and even saintly life . . .*

The whole character of Indian history in this period is the collusion, unspoken and hardly admitted, between the British power and Gandhi. For thirty years they fought each other, but cooperated tacitly in preventing the fight from getting out of hand. Both acted as if guided by the maxim of Machiavelli that you should treat your enemy as if he may one day become your friend. Because of the phenomenon of Gandhi's

* B. R. Nanda, *Mahatma Gandhi*, Allen & Unwin, London, 1958.

personality, a momentous struggle for freedom was fought, resolutely on
both sides, but with an almost cheerful cordiality on both sides, and in a
way which enabled both sides to be reconciled and to cooperate when it
was over.

The climax of the struggle before the war was the civil disobedience
campaign of Congress in 1930. Civil disobedience covered a variety of
activities aimed at bringing government to a standstill – strikes, boycotts
of British goods and services, and especially of foreign cloth, non-payment
of taxes, and massive demonstrations, which were remarkably non-violent
in the main, but on a scale large enough to alarm the authorities. The
police took prisoners on a large scale: the prisons were overflowing,
and special camps had to be organized. By these means the British
Government in India felt that it had been able to prevent revolution and
to maintain its power. But the years 1931–2 marked a watershed. The
Government realized that although a rebellion had been broken, it could
not repeat the operation, and that, if it tried to do so, it would strain too
far the allegiance of the Indians in the civil service and the police. The
issue from this period became the timing of the programme for self-
government. While some of the diehards among the British held back on
grounds of prestige, in other quarters in England and in British India
there was anxiety on the more reasonable grounds that India was full of
centrifugal and communal strains, and too hasty a withdrawal might lead
to breakdown of government.

Congress, on the other hand, regarded the Government of India Act of
1935 as insufficient, although they were about to give it a trial. This Act
had been thrashed out in a series of monumental deliberations in London,
in which Mahatma Gandhi had taken part as the representative of Congress. It provided for parliamentary government and democratically
elected Indian Ministers both in the central government at Delhi, and in
the provinces. It retained, however, a British authoritarian element in two
vital subjects: foreign affairs and defence. The demand of Congress at this
time was for full Dominion status.

On 3 September 1939 the war began between Britain and Germany,
and India was declared by the British Government to be also at war. It
had no adequate cause of dispute with Germany to justify this declaration,
and the Indian leaders said so forcibly. Nehru, it was true, and the more
liberal leaders of Congress, shared the sense of outrage at Nazi misdeeds
which was experienced by similar leaders in Europe. Nehru, while visiting
England in the previous year, had written in the *Manchester Guardian*
criticizing the policy of appeasement towards Germany. Gandhi, writing

in his own newspaper, *Harijan*, after war broke out, expressed condemnation of Hitler and moral support for Britain and France, although as a pacifist he also condemned the fighting. The more reactionary Indian leaders were indifferent: not that they would have condoned Germany's brutalities had they credited them, they wrote them off as inventions of British propaganda. But since no attempt had been made to consult Indian opinion through any representative institutions, how, asked the Indians, could there be any sincere talk of a war for democracy when the war was begun in such an undemocratic way? As a result, the Congress Party resigned from the Government, withdrew from the eight provincial Ministries which it held, and recorded its extreme disapproval of all the acts of British officialdom.

Yet India did not protest very effectively against the German War. Several divisions of its Army fought in the Middle East, gaining battle honours of which even Indian nationalists were, paradoxically, rather proud. In one province of India the war was genuinely popular. This was in the Punjab, which was traditionally the chief recruiting ground for soldiers, and where the provincial government had not considered resigning. The Punjab actively demonstrated in favour of the war, and regarded as enemies those who were lukewarm in its service. Surprisingly accurate knowledge of the ups and downs of war strategy began to circulate in Punjab villages. Elsewhere the war, simply as war, began to appeal to the so-called martial classes. Anything to do with it – news about it, the social and economic changes consequent on it – interested them as trenching on their monopoly in life.

But by the rest of India the war was treated with indifference: with neither the excitement caused by the sense of genuine change in the air, nor with the alarm caused by the knowledge that India was compassed about by real dangers, some of which might soon hit India very hard. The fact that the war was to be enlarged, that a new enemy was at hand by means of whom the war would be transformed, that through no initiative of its own India was to be placed in its vanguard, and that invasion was to be a very near possibility, would jerk it out of its previous apathy. It would go to bed at night and get up in the morning with war at its elbow, instead of viewing it academically at a safe remove. The extension of the war would be the signal for a new phase of the freedom struggle to begin.

CHAPTER 12

The Magnetic North

THUS far the war had chiefly concerned China and Japan. Japan was aggressive towards China; considerations of how far this affected Japan's relations with other countries were peripheral. But from this time onwards, Japan's relations with the Great Powers became the prime concern of its Government. The war between China and Japan became increasingly difficult to limit to a private war; Japan was faced with problems, rising out of this war, each one of which caused it to consider afresh its policy towards other Powers. Sometimes it experimentally remoulded its policies towards them, only to change them again, with all the repercussions which such instability led to. Japan's policies became very uncertain. No settled principles guided its action.

Actually, since the days of the Anglo-Japanese Alliance, Japan had pursued a wavering foreign policy, spreading everywhere a diffuse suspicion. It had no sure base in a firm agreement with a greater Power. But until a late period, it seemed that its special, inexorable opponent was Russia. Suspicion of and hostility towards Russia governed its designs. One product of this attitude of mind had been the signing by Japan of the Anti-Comintern Pact with Germany in 1936. This was an alliance which somewhat nebulously pledged the partners to resist the infiltrations of Communism, and, in a secret clause, bound them to withhold aid from Russia should either party be involved in hostilities with the USSR.

As we have seen, there was special meaning in Japan regarding Russia as its hereditary enemy. Russia, as the perpetual threat, had penetrated into the folklore of the people even before Commodore Perry's expedition in 1853 signalled the opening of Japan's modern period of history. Ever since the end of the nineteenth century, Japan had regarded Russia as the Great Power against which it was destined to fight for survival. In 1904–5 it had fought the first round; it was convinced that it would have to fight again. The Siberian Intervention not only reinforced that conviction but also demonstrated the rapidity with which Japan could and often did find itself isolated and abandoned by its erstwhile allies. The serious strains which developed between the Army and the civil Government as a result of that crisis were to recur in the future, but this time the civilian Government, using one of the anti-imperialist swings in public opinion which at the time alternated with moods of aggressive nationalism, had prevailed in restraining the military. The Army felt that it had been ordered to drop its legitimate prey when it had been certain of it, and the sense that the civilian Government could not be trusted continued to weigh with it.

After Manchukuo came into being in 1932, Japan stationed there a large part of the Japanese Army. This did not disguise the fact that the eyes of the Japanese Army were focused upon Russia. Much of its training and manoeuvres were made with Russia as the ultimate adversary. Preparations were made to meet the danger of a full-scale Russian invasion; even more elaborate contingency plans were devised for a repeat performance of the Siberian Intervention, this time to be a wholly Japanese offensive against the Soviet Union. Russian belligerency was no less marked, and the exchanges between the two countries became increasingly explosive.

By 1938 2,800 separate armed clashes between the Russians and Japanese had been recorded and their successive repercussions provided the General Staffs of both countries with a perennial headache from which they had no relief in the years leading up to the wider conflict which engulfed the whole of East Asia and the Pacific. Since the rivalry between Russia and Japan is in many ways as important as the struggle between China and Japan in the tragic sequence of events that ended with the defeat of Japan in 1945, we must not overlook the significance of this interminable tension and succession of military clashes. Each was a cautionary tale. If details of most of them are unmemorable, their continuity was not. Three of the incidents had particular significance: the Amur River Incident, the Changkufeng Incident and the Nomonhan Incident. They foreshadowed special features about Total War which affected the perceptions and expectations of all the Powers in the Second World War.

During late June to early July 1937, on the eve of the great Sino-Japanese war that we call the China Incident, Japan and Russia fought the 185th in their series of inconclusive Manchurian border clashes at a site seventy miles down the Amur River from Khabarovsk. This is roughly the same area over which the Russians and the People's Republic of China fought similar actions decades afterwards. The Amur River Incident with which we are concerned, however, exposed serious Russian weaknesses in the wake of the first Red Army purges to affect East Asia. The Incident began when Russian troops landed on several disputed islets lying in the middle of the Amur River and took off a few Manchurian gold miners whom they accused of trespassing. Soviet gunboats then exchanged fire with nearby

U S S R

Trans-Siberian Railway

Komsomol'sk

Blagoveshchensk

Khingan Mts

Sovetskaya

KUANGFENGTAO
October 1944

Khabarovsk

Sungari

KANCHATZU
June 1937

Ussuri

HUTOU (Hulin)
Dec. 1944

CHINGCHANGKOU
June 1936

KANHSIATUN
August 1945

Mutankiang

YANGMULINTUN
June 1935

Nikolsk
(Ussuriski)

CHANGLINGTZU
March 1936

WUCHIATZU
July 1944

Vladivostok

Rashin
(Najin)

CHANGKUFENG
(Khasan) July-Aug. 1938

SEA   OF

Seishin
(Chongjin)

JAPAN

Kankō
(Hamhung)

J APAN

**MAJOR BORDER CLASHES BETWEEN JAPAN
AND THE SOVIET UNION 1935—45**

0   500 km
0   300 miles

elements of the Manchukuoan Army. The Kwantung Army, with the approval of the Army General Staff in Tokyo, ordered the First (Tokyo) Division to respond. This division had been exiled in this remote hinterland for taking a leading role in the 26 February Incident of 1936. Before anything could come of this, more Soviet gunboats steamed to the scene and a number of Red Army regular divisions were put on a war footing. At this point the Army and Naval General Staffs in Tokyo lost their nerve and ordered the Kwantung Army and Japanese naval air and river patrol units in the vicinity to restrain themselves pending a peaceful resolution of the crisis. Elements within the First Division turned a blind eye to these instructions, opened fire on the Soviet gunboats and sank one of them. The Soviets were outraged by this development but with some alacrity agreed to a mutual withdrawal from the disputed points. After the Red Army retired, the Japanese reoccupied the territory.

Western observers, ever keen to extrapolate from such engagements some estimate of the attitude and military efficiency of the Soviet Union in the event of a European war, were unimpressed by the performance of either party in this incident. On the whole it was regarded as 'somewhat puzzling'. A senior member of the Far Eastern Department in the British Foreign Office put his finger on the problem: 'This sort of thing would be very serious indeed in almost any other part of the world, but such queer things happen almost every day on the Manchu-Siberian frontier that the sequel to the incident may be no more than some mudslinging by the press of Russia and Japan and an exchange of a few rude notes.' It was generally concluded that neither country was prepared to adopt extreme measures, nor was it likely that either would gain the upper hand. Thus while the scale of the fighting was considerable, the world was not alarmed. Such indifference seems the more remarkable now given the juxtaposition of the Amur River Incident and the China Incident.

Less significant border clashes flared up between Japan and the Soviet Union during the remainder of 1937 with no sign that either Power was disposed to settle these affairs once and for all. Diplomatically, the Soviets made faces at Japan, concluding a non-aggression pact with Chiang Kaishek's Kuomintang in August 1937. *Pravda* advertised that agreement as 'collective security', but the plain fact was that Russia had to contend with the animosity of Germany, too, and showed only token defiance of Japan. Indeed, the British Foreign Office advised Prime Minister Neville Chamberlain that 'one small ray of comfort to be found is the extreme and expressed reluctance of the USSR to allow themselves to get mixed up in the [Sino-Japanese] dispute. This allows us to hope that the dispute, if it develops, will be confined to China and Japan and that other Powers will not be dragged in.'*

As Japan sent more and more troops deep into China, the Soviet Union read the handwriting on the wall and began to reinforce its military forces in the East. The West privately counted this a blessing. It ought to make the Japanese more circumspect. There would be no need to encourage this development: Russia would strengthen her defence lines in her own interests, not because it might gain Moscow new friends. British air Intelligence experts – who in retrospect proved more perceptive (except in relation to Japan) than critics have credited – put Soviet front-line air strength at 4,000 aircraft, but 75 per cent of those aircraft reportedly were obsolescent. Soviet aircrews were regarded as badly trained, inefficient and very poorly led. No evidence could be found that Russia then believed that air bombardment of Japanese cities was practicable, although it was generally observed that 'the threat, slight as it is in reality, has altered the whole of Japan's strategical outlook and has created a most powerful deterrent to a Japanese attack on any part of Soviet Russia'.† On the eve of a European weekend crisis during mid-May 1938, French Intelligence suggested that Soviet pilots sent into action at Hankow and elsewhere in Central China were winning a string of victories against the Japanese. The British, however, discounted such reports. The difference in viewpoint between the two Powers in East Asia mirrored their respective (dis)inclination to welcome offers of Soviet air support for Czechoslovakia. In terms of what the Soviet Union could do to help preserve British, French and American interests in East Asia, London, at least, took the attitude that there were no significant developments up to the first anniversary of the birth of the China Incident. The French, who had less at stake anyway, remained slightly more hopeful if not optimistic. Both Powers, like the United States, recognized that for the time being the Japanese were in a position to do more or less as they liked in China although not, perhaps, further afield.

Then, late in July and throughout most of August 1938, a major battle erupted at Changkufeng, on the banks of the Tumen River west of Lake Khasan at a spot where the frontiers of Korea, the USSR and Manchuria meet some seventy miles south-west of Vladivostok. Changkufeng was

---

* Unnumbered FO note for Chamberlain, 10 August 1937, Premier 1/314, British Public Record Office, Kew, cited in Pritchard, *Far Eastern Influences*, op. cit. p. 93.
† File II A/1/37, item 37/12, Report by Squadron Leader Pelly (A.1.2.c), 4 November 1937, AIR 9/23, British Public Record Office, Kew.

one of the highest in a range of ancient volcanic peaks. It was possible to peer from its summit across intervening marshlands to Posyet Bay, fifteen miles distant, where the Soviet Union had begun constructing new submarine pens and air bases at the port of Novokievsk (Kraskino). Southwest of Changkufeng, about eleven miles away, lay the Japanese port of Rashin (Rajin), where transport vessels unloaded troops and supplies bound for the northern frontiers of the Japanese Empire. The railways, and the port of Rashin as well, were within sight of the ridge of the Changkufeng Hills. Observers there would encounter no difficulty in monitoring the bulk of Japanese railway traffic to the north. There were other vantage points from which the two sides could scrutinize each other. Changkufeng was not unique. However, possession of these crests affected the security of adjacent promontories which the two sides occupied along the same frontier.

Historians and political scientists have made much of this border incident. They have linked it to the great Soviet purges and the efficiency of the Red Banner Front armies. They have drawn conflicting conclusions about how it fits in with what are surmised to have been Soviet and Japanese intentions before, during and after it took place. They have argued over the manner in which the campaign was conducted and the scale of forces employed on both sides. They have inferred contradictory conclusions about the peace negotiations which followed in its wake. They have suggested that it demonstrated the ability or the inability of Japanese authorities in Tokyo and in the field to control the activities of their forces. They have even used it to advance various theories about wider conspiracies to wage aggressive war.

Almost everything about the Changkufeng Incident has been shrouded in mystery. The incident has long been appreciated as an event ranking in importance with, say, the far better known incidents of the German march into the Rhineland, the Italian conquest of Ethiopia, the American occupation of Iceland, or the Japanese advance into Indo-China with the acquiescence of the Vichy régime. Like each of those affairs, the Changkufeng Incident gave rise to accusations that one side or the other was guilty of systematic aggression.

The Soviet purges had decimated the Russian officer corps by the summer of 1938. Russian commanders everywhere were jittery. The initial Soviet occupation of the Changkufeng heights may have been prompted by the defection to Japan of General G. S. Lyushkov, the Commissar of the NKVD (Stalin's dread secret police) responsible for the whole of Soviet East Asia. In mid-June, Lyushkov's dramatic escape across the Manchurian frontier in full-dress military uniform, replete with medals,

Disputed boundaries in the Changkufeng area

Paksikori

Kucheng
Yangkuanping
Shachaofeng
L. Khasan
Changkufeng
Fangchuanting
82-metre Hill
52-metre Hill
82-metre Hill
L. Doritsine
Tumen
Podgornaya

Ⓐ Border line based on Hunchun Border Pact, 1886
Ⓑ Border line based on map by Chinese Army Survey Bureau, 1915—20
Ⓒ Border line based on maps by Russian General Staff, 1911, and Chinese Army, 1909

DISPOSITION OF FORCES EVENING, 30 JULY 1938

N

MANCHUKUO (MANCHURIA)

Tumen

KOREN (CHŌSEN)

U S S R

Huichungyuan

Paksikori

Kucheng

Yangkuanpi

Ushidana

Matsuotsuho

Fangchuanting

Podgornaya

Sozan
ShoSozan
Hongui

Ryukem

DISPOSITION OF FORCES NOON, 11 AUG. 1938 (Ceasefire)

xx	Division
iii	Regiment
ii	Battalion
i	Coy/Battery
···	Platoon

Tumen

U S S R

Huichungyuan

KOREA (CHŌSEN)

Paksikori

Shikai

Kucheng

Yangkuanpu

Matsuotsuho

Fanchuanting

Ushidana

Sozan
ShoSozan
Hongui

Podgornaya

Ryuken

32 Bn HQ
73 Regt
11 Regt
75 Regt
76 Regt
8GU
25 MT
19

THE CHANGKUFENG INCIDENT JULY—AUGUST 1938

☐ Japanese units
▭ Soviet units
Japanese forward positions
Soviet forward positions

JAPANESE STRENGTH
Infantry: 12 battalions, Artillery: 33 pieces
Aircraft: less than 30? (grounded)

SOVIET STRENGTH (estimated)
Infantry: 27 battalions
Artillery: 100–150 pieces
Tanks: 200–510
Aircraft: 120–150

0 1 2 3 4 5 km
0 1 2 3 miles

forced the Soviets to effect a thorough reorganization of their forces and a tightening of their border security arrangements. Within weeks the Kwantung Army's ever-vigilant signals Intelligence monitors were to intercept and decode Russian military communications that provided the Japanese with an inkling of the trouble ahead. Shortly thereafter, the Soviets began to construct fixed defensive lines and reconnaissance positions on Changkufeng.

As the area formed a sector of the Manchukuoan frontier, it was only natural that the Kwantung Army should take a keen interest in its defence. However, local features of the terrain, better lines of communication and the fact that four out of every five inhabitants were Korean (and thus regarded as Japanese rather than Manchukuoan subjects) dictated that defence of the area should fall within the jurisdiction of Japan's Korean Army, whose major responsibility was the preservation of civil order in Korea. At first the Korean Army was inclined to adopt a watchful but undemonstrative attitude towards the Russian moves. Subjected to ridicule and accused of timidity by the Kwantung Army, the Korean Army Staff wired Tokyo that while the Russian action was clearly illegal, it had little immediate bearing upon offensive operations which Japan was preparing against Hankow and elsewhere. It would not be prudent to conduct a precipitate counter-attack while the China Incident was in full flood: 'This Army is thinking of reasoning with the Soviets and requesting it to pull back, directly on the spot . . . In case the Russians do not accede in the long run, we intend to drive the Soviet soldiers out of the area east of Khasan firmly by use of force.'

Imperial General Headquarters in Tokyo considered the matter calmly. It agreed with the Korean Army that the border should be kept under close surveillance and that no hasty action should be taken. If attacked, however, the Korean Army was to press forward at once, seize control of the disputed territory and on no account cross beyond what Japan recognized as the legal frontier. There was no policy of subterfuge or aggressive intent in this: the purposes of the Japanese high command were clearly unprovocative and as moderate as any self-respecting nation could permit itself. Through spontaneous impatience or unendurable provocation, however, Japanese officers at the scene sent out an unauthorized 're-connaissance force' which resulted in a pitched battle for possession of the heights. The Japanese prevailed. In the weeks that followed, the Russians vainly attempted to re-establish themselves on the hills. The struggle intensified, but each successive Russian onslaught failed.

The emergency had arisen while the Korean Army was unusually weak. It normally comprised only two infantry divisions, but prior to the

Changkufeng Incident one of these, the Twentieth Division, had gone to take part in the China operation (leaving only a skeletal force at its depot in Korea). Fortunately, Lieutenant-General Suetaka Kamezō, commander of the remaining Nineteenth Division, giving vent to his mortification at long being held in reserve, had imposed an exceptionally arduous training regimen upon his troops that already had earned his division a reputation as one of the crack forces of the Japanese Empire. On the other hand, there was virtually no armour in Korea and only two air regiments (fewer than a hundred aircraft) in the entire country. Japan's experience in Manchuria and China had shown that any attempt to bring up reinforcements during a conflict was likely to lead to a mutual escalation of the fighting and to a vitiation of efforts to produce a negotiated settlement. The outlook was bad.

Once fighting developed, the world was confused by the evident scarcity of trustworthy reports from the battle zone. There was open disbelief about the veracity of information dispensed by Moscow and Tokyo. Western sentiments were summed up in a note which circulated in the British Foreign Office while the struggle was continuing: 'both Russians and Japanese are such accomplished liars and so addicted to all forms of bluff and bluster that one can be sure of nothing in this strange affair.' One curious difference was repeatedly remarked upon. The Soviet press was increasingly hysterical. The Japanese, in great contrast, took pains to underplay the strategical importance of the dispute. Each side, however, claimed to have suffered early setbacks followed by victory against almost overwhelming odds. British and American editors simply printed opposing accounts side by side under sensational headlines. The *New York Times* commented:

It isn't easy to guess what is going on. It is still more difficult to guess why it is going on ... In all the mystery and madness only one thing is clear from this distance. What takes place in the Manchurian frontier is not a mere border incident. It fits somehow into the great pattern of irrational forces moving behind events that involve Europe and Asia in an 'indivisible' struggle.

The little war of Changkufeng was no skirmish. Cramped within a radius of little more than one mile, an élite division of Japanese infantry, backed by a growing volume of artillery support but lacking any air or armour protection, was committed against a force three times as large and comprising no fewer than twenty-seven battalions of Soviet troops, 120–150 aircraft, 100–150 batteries of mostly heavy artillery, and massed tank assaults, often employing waves of 50–60 tanks, from Soviet armoured forces variously estimated at 200–500 tanks. Japanese military planners had long anticipated that in any war against the Soviet Union they would have to overcome odds of three to one. They expected to win. Here was a test case. Suetaka's under-strength division of barely 7,000 men faced the cream of the Soviet Far East Army, reputed to be a cut above the standard of the Red Army's European forces. By the time the guns were stilled, more than 40,000 men had been deployed by the two sides either directly in the fighting or acting in support. The intensity of the struggle can be gauged by measuring these numbers against the 70,000 troops which the Japanese would commit to the entire Malayan campaign and the roughly 43,000 utilized in the capture of the Philippines in 1941–2. Nevertheless, even experienced observers generally had no clear idea as to who started or even won the battle.

The truth was that both sides were badly mauled. The number of tanks, guns and aircraft which the Russians committed to the battle awed the Japanese but revealed a lack of imagination and common sense in terms of tactics and results. The performance of the Soviet infantry showed up badly against the initiative, efficiency and tenacity displayed by the Japanese. The effectiveness of the Red Army's artillery, although more impressive, by no means matched the standards set by the Japanese. Only 3 per cent of Japanese casualties were victims of aerial bombing compared to 37 per cent hit by shellfire. A neutral war correspondent at the scene who had fought on the Western Front in the First World War remarked that 'the Russian Army do not appear to have learnt anything of the art of war'.

The Japanese, who won the ground and held it, also had reason to be frightened. Although jubilant at their military victory, they knew how narrowly defeat had been averted. They were appalled not only by the rapidity with which the incident had developed but also by its sacrificial cost. The Japanese Army air force was not yet the superbly balanced instrument that it was to become in future. It was in no position to conduct air operations simultaneously in China and Manchuria. The Korean Army was desperately short of aircraft and first-class fliers, and Japan could not afford to be drawn into an air war that would prejudice the struggle underway in China. Military prudence as well as the political will to avoid any general escalation of the fighting compelled the Japanese to keep their own aircraft out of the skies and at airfields far from the scene. The Japanese gunners at Changkufeng, although able to engage the enemy at up to point-blank range, were seriously outnumbered and came perilously close to complete exhaustion of their ammunition. In these circumstances their technical superiority to the much-vaunted Russian artillery was scant comfort. The infantrymen fared little better:

their officers suffered exceptionally high losses and the exertions of the Nineteenth Division left it a spent force. The Japanese logistical system had repeatedly broken down, unequal to the demands placed upon it. This was serious. The main railway line between the port of Rashin and Hsinking (the imperial capital of Manchukuo and northern terminus of the South Manchurian Railway) ran within two or three miles of the battle line. In normal times troops embarked at Tsuruga on the west coast of Japan could cross the Sea of Japan and arrive at Hsinking via that railway within seventy-two hours. The Changkufeng Incident therefore exposed fundamental weaknesses in Japan's strategical position against the Soviet Union.

Fighting in such a confined space as Changkufeng and in such large numbers produced heavy casualties on both sides. The Japanese lost more than 500 dead and nearly 1,000 wounded. Although the Russians failed to overrun the Japanese positions on the eastern banks of the Tumen River and the absolute physical annihilation of the Nineteenth Division was narrowly averted, the human energies and material resources available to the Korean Army were all but consumed by the conflict. Estimates of Soviet casualties vary wildly, but the best guess is that the Russians suffered perhaps as many as 1,200 dead and more than 4,000 wounded. The Japanese set a pattern for the future by taking no prisoners. The casualties which each side suffered, while deeply disturbing to both, were minuscule compared to what Russia and Japan would lose when next they met on the battlefields of Asia.

The Changkufeng dispute was not settled by force of arms alone. Emperor Hirohito himself had already taken steps to express his unmistakable desire to see the Incident brought to a close and had insisted from the beginning that the forces committed to the battle must not advance into Russian territory. He had administered a strong rebuke to his War Minister, Lieutenant-General Itagaki Seishirō (the same man who had been one of the architects of the Manchurian Incident), and the Army Chief of Staff, the venerable old Prince Kan'in Kotohito, for seeking imperial authority to permit the Nineteenth Division and several divisions of the Kwantung Army to commence offensive operations against the Soviet Union if that perchance should seem appropriate to the Army General Staff. This was more than the Emperor was prepared to tolerate, and knowing that the Army's demands likewise were regarded as absurdly dangerous by Foreign Minister Ugaki Kazushige (himself a retired full general) and by the Navy Ministry and Naval General Staff, the Emperor forcefully expressed his abomination of the Army's propensity for embroiling itself in such incidents. From the

Army's point of view, the approach to the throne was therefore not only ill-conceived and ill-timed but heaped shame upon Japan's Imperial General Headquarters. Kan'in and Itagaki left the imperial presence completely shaken, convinced that their careers were in tatters and reflecting that they might have to atone for their misconduct by forfeiting their lives. In typically Japanese fashion, however, the Emperor sent word after them to say that he was content to retain them in the positions that they had so abused: divine benevolence could extend to those who saw the error of their ways.

Under the circumstances, the only way out was for the Japanese to abandon the field to the Russians or face the possibility of repeated counter-attacks by ever larger Russian forces. The Japanese Ambassador in Moscow, Shigemitsu Mamoru, was instructed to seek an immediate end to the conflict. The Russians seemed remarkably indifferent to his pleas, adding to the concern felt by the Japanese side. Any faint-heartedness felt by the Russians during the Amur River Incident was dispelled at Changkufeng by battlefield Intelligence coupled with high-level information acquired by Richard Sorge from a member of his spy ring who was a confidant of Prime Minister Konoye Fumimaro and in a position to observe the deliberations of the Cabinet close at hand. The certainty of the Russians that the Japanese authorities in the field and at Tokyo were determined to reach a rapid settlement of the incident at virtually any price laid the groundwork for the transformation of a military defeat into a Russian political triumph.

In the end, Ambassador Shigemitsu, with the full support of Foreign Minister Ugaki, agreed to surrender all of Japan's tactical gains. That, and the ability of the Japanese central authorities to control their troops on this occasion, impressed military planners, diplomats and their political masters abroad, who evaluated the slender information which had filtered through to them from the Changkufeng Incident. Many drew the ill-founded conclusion that Japan's wayward field commanders were only given their head when it suited the military authorities in Tokyo. In fact, the truth was almost precisely the opposite.

Odd though it may seem today, one theory which gained currency in Britain and elsewhere at the time was that the Japanese had bowed to German pressure in acquiescing to the only terms that Russia was prepared to accept: it was believed that the German Government had been so intent on resolving the Sudeten problem in Czechoslovakia that they had exerted all their influence upon Japan's military leaders to persuade them that it would be most unwise of Japan to start another major war prematurely. There was very little substance in this: Germany had no such influence over

Japan. Rather more accurately, Western doubts about the Soviet Union's military capabilities were abundantly confirmed by the events at Changkufeng. The tactical victory of the Korean Army showed that Japanese soldiers were just as able to stop a European Power (at least in a strictly limited war) as they had been in 1904–5. However the strategical lessons learnt from Russia's massive build-up during the fighting were that Japan could ill-afford to embark upon such adventures lightly and that Japan must liquidate the China Incident with all possible speed. Nearly everyone was convinced that Japan would scarcely be so foolhardy as to attempt any major offensive against the Soviet Union as matters stood. That being so, Russia might safely take a greater interest in European power politics for as long as Japan remained preoccupied in China. In each of these ways, then, the Changkufeng Incident provided a classic example of how events in East Asia were seen by the West to have a profound influence upon the stability of Europe.

Meanwhile, the Soviet Union gnawed its wounds. The celebrated and experienced Marshal Vasilii Konstantinovich Blyukher, who had risen from being a common soldier in the First World War to the command of the Red Army forces that had come to prominence during the Russian Civil War, and who afterwards had seen the Japanese out of Vladivostok in 1922, was obliged for the second time to bathe in the poisoned political waters of military defeat. In the mid-1920s he had been lent as a military adviser to Sun Yat-sen's young Chinese Republic. Under his tutelage, Chaing Kai-shek had embarked upon the northern campaign that had taken the Nationalist Armies to the gates of Manchuria. But when Chiang had turned against the communists, the man whom the Chinese had known by the name of 'General Galen' had been forced to flee. Afterwards, he had become virtually count palatine of Eastern Siberia. Now, having taken personal charge of the Red Army's operations at Changkufeng, Marshal Blyukher's second disaster proved fatal. Removed from command, he was executed by 9 November 1938. He had been living on borrowed time. General Lyushkov had given his Japanese and German interrogators information which linked Blyukher with anti-Stalinist circles within the Soviet Union. This Intelligence was fed back to Moscow by Richard Sorge in late October or early November 1938. Whether Blyukher would have survived the purges anyway is doubtful. More reliable and even more distinguished soldiers than he had perished in that lunatic bloodletting.

After the defeat of Japan in the Pacific War, fresh evidence concerning the operations at Changkufeng was put forward at the Tokyo War Trial by Soviet prosecutors. A parade of eye-witnesses, some lavishly decorated as 'Heroes of the Soviet Union' for their part in the action, tendered what purported to be incontrovertible proof that the Japanese first began the incident, were repulsed with heavy losses, thereafter continued to attack Soviet defensive positions along the disputed frontier, and treacherously took command of the heights only after a ceasefire had come into effect. The stories told by these Soviet affidavits and witnesses dovetailed together. They were packed with lies, but the Defence failed to rise to the challenge of producing evidence which would refute the Soviet claims. Due to lack of initiative and possibly lack of information such as a larger defence team might have amassed, the Tokyo Trial proceedings bogged down over the issue of conflicting Chinese and Imperial Russian versions of maps which neither side convincingly authenticated. In fact, the area had always been a no man's land, dotted with a few scattered Korean hamlets whose inhabitants cared nothing for frontiers and who had conducted seasonal religious sacrifices atop Changkufeng for centuries. The wooden stakes marking the original border had mostly rotted away long since, or been scavenged for firewood or been re-sited any number of times by over-zealous border guards. By 1938 there reportedly remained an average of one undisturbed marker for every twenty-five miles of frontier along a meandering line roughly 400 miles long. There were no markers at all within miles of Changkufeng. That was a suitably anonymous pretext for what is now seen as one of the classic limited wars of modern times. It was an archetypal antithesis, perhaps, to Total War, and yet nations stood eager to apply its lessons, imperfectly, on an unimaginably larger scale.

The following year, there was yet another of these incidents. The young turks of the Japanese Army believed that Japan was progressing. The Kwantung Army, recalling the imagined loss of face which it had endured when forced by Tokyo to restrain its subordinate units at the time of the Amur River Incident, distanced itself even further than before from the cautious policies promoted by the Japanese Government and the Imperial General Headquarters. Moreover, after analysing the Changkufeng Incident, Kwantung Army Headquarters was convinced that the Korean Army had bungled the affair and had been insufficiently aggressive from the start. So far as the bright sparks of the Kwantung Army were concerned, the only proper way to respond to Russian incursions was by the application of overwhelming force. Interrestingly enough, the Russians had come to much the same conclusions about the Japanese.

The Soviet Union laid a trap for the Japanese, a trap which seems to have been intended from the outset to teach the Japanese a punishing lesson. This incident occurred 700 miles away on the fringes of Outer Mongolia, where in the spring of 1939 a series of border incursions by cavalry units of the puppet Mongolian People's Republic culminated in an attack on 11 May 1939 by a force of seventy or eighty troops who crossed the Halha River and clashed with a Manchurian Army garrison a few miles to the north-east, at the Manchurian town of Nomonhan. The Kwantung Army, chafing at restraints imposed upon it by the General Staff in Tokyo ever since the Amur River Incident, was restless. In April 1939 the Commander-in-Chief of the Kwantung Army, General Ueda Kenkichi, had assembled his corps commanders to inform them that henceforward 'where the border lines are indistinct, the defence commander shall determine a boundary on his own'. As far as he was concerned, they could feel at liberty 'to invade Soviet territory temporarily, or to decoy Soviet soldiers and get them into Manchukuoan territory'.* It is unclear whether the trespass on 11 May 1939 stemmed from these instructions (which directly contradicted standing orders of Imperial General Headquarters). In the event, the local divisional commander ordered a Kwantung Army cavalry regiment to support the local Manchukuoan forces. When the Mongolian horsemen withdrew across the Halha, the Kwantung Army ordered its own cavalry to pursue and destroy them. A thousand infantrymen from the Kwantung Army's Sixty-fourth Infantry Regiment were dispatched to back up the cavalry. The trap claimed its first victims. The Japanese cavalry regiment was all but destroyed and the Japanese infantrymen narrowly avoided the same fate. Enveloped by Mongolian tanks and artillery before they had moved away from the river crossing, the Sixty-fourth Infantry Regiment were routed. This defeat was regarded by the Japanese as humiliating in the extreme, but no immediate steps were taken to avenge their defeat. For their part, the Russians issued an official warning that, by virtue of its defence treaty with Mongolia, Moscow would treat any further incidents on the Mongolian frontier as direct aggression against the Soviet Union.

By 18 June reports were received which indicated that Soviet forces had advanced once more across the frontier, driven back the Manchukuoan garrison forces (which may indeed have provoked them), and had bombed three major defensive positions to the rear. Within the Kwantung Army, a debate ensued during which it emerged that some staff officers were

---

* Cited by I. Hata in J. M. Morley (ed.), *Deterrent Diplomacy: Japan, Germany and the USSR, 1935–1940*, Columbia University Press, New York, 1976, p. 159.

inclined to take no action pending the outcome of Anglo-Japanese diplomatic conversations that were attempting to resolve the Tientsin Crisis and other outstanding sources of friction between Britain and Japan. Other voices, however, were raised in favour of inflicting an immediate blow against the Soviet Union sufficient to teach the Kremlin to avoid any further trouble with the Kwantung Army. The hotheads prevailed.

The Russians were far from blind to what the Japanese wanted to achieve at Nomonhan. Master spy Richard Sorge's top Japanese agent remained privy to the Japanese Cabinet's fervent desire to avoid war against the Soviet Union at virtually any price. The same agent also acquired detailed information from the South Manchurian Railway concerning the size and order of battle of the forces available to the Kwantung Army. Another Japanese in Sorge's employment toured the battlefront as a press correspondent, interviewed top-ranking Japanese military commanders at the scene, outlined the limited objectives of the Japanese forces and reported upon the numerical strength and types of Japanese aircraft and armoured fighting vehicles which had reached Nomonhan. Still other agents in Sorge's network passed on information about Japanese troop movements, the mobilization and state of readiness of Japanese air and armoured formations, and the strength of every unit which either had been committed to the battle or which might be in a position to take part in any full-scale offensive. Sorge himself learned from his contact with German military attachés and others that the Japanese had no intention of using the Incident as a pretext for a general invasion of the Soviet Union. The Kremlin may simply have chosen to disbelieve or to discount Sorge's Intelligence on this occasion. Moscow may have feared that the Nomonhan dispute was bound to escalate into a wider conflict unless drastic counter-measures were undertaken. On the other hand, the dispute provided a tempting opportunity to pay off a few old scores.

Kwantung Army Headquarters resolved to administer a crushing defeat upon the Russian and Mongolian forces by utilizing virtually all the rapid deployment forces of the Kwantung Army: the Twenty-third Infantry Division, nearly the whole of the Second Air Group, two regiments of light and medium tanks, a regiment of mechanized artillery, and an infantry regiment borrowed from the Seventh Division. This produced a force of some 15,000 men comprising three infantry battalions, 120 antitank guns, 70 tanks, 400 vehicles and 180 aircraft, leaving elsewhere only sufficient strength to safeguard the remainder of Manchuria. At this point the Soviet and Mongolian forces in the vicinity of Nomonhan were only less numerous than the Japanese, disposing of 12,500 men, 23 anti-tank weapons, 186 tanks and 266 armoured cars. Recalling recent experience and the Kwantung Army's formidable reputation as Japan's most battle-hungry military command, the odds appeared to be stacked heavily in favour of the Japanese. The War Ministry in Tokyo did hesitate to sanction an adventure which could contribute nothing to the China Incident (which was continuing to sap the nation's military and economic strength), but the Army General Staff felt justified in giving General Ueda its full support for the operation. War Minister Itagaki, who had retained a fondness for the 'forward policies' of the Kwantung Army ever since he had joined the conspiracy to assassinate Chang Tso-lin in 1928 and went on to engineer the Manchurian Incident in 1931, now decided to override the objections of his ministerial staff and gave his approval to the plans submitted by the Commander-in-Chief of the Kwantung Army. Significantly, however, General Ueda felt obliged to conceal his intention to open the campaign with an air offensive against the Russians: he was not the kind of man to shrink from the fact that a major air offensive, even if justified as a pre-emptive strike, was bound to provoke the Russians beyond measure. His worry was that revelation of his intentions would heighten the concern of those in Tokyo who wanted to avoid any serious escalation of the conflict: premature disclosure might prompt even the hawkish Army General Staff to abort the whole affair. When news of Ueda's secret intentions did come to the notice of Tokyo, his worst fears were abundantly fulfilled. A telegram was sent to Ueda ordering him to stay his hand pending the arrival of an emissary from the Army General Staff.

After considering the matter, the Kwantung Army staff responded by resorting to a trick which had served them well in early stages of the Manchurian and China Incidents: they advanced the date of their operations and pounded the Russian air base of Tamsagbulag before Tokyo could stop them. The returning pilots jubilantly claimed to have destroyed ninety-nine enemy aircraft in aerial combat and a further twenty-five on the ground. Tokyo was faced with yet another *fait accompli*.

Imperial General Headquarters in Tokyo was outraged by this latest example of the Kwantung Army's irresponsible and insubordinate attitude. The Emperor, too, was infuriated and demanded that General Ueda, if no one else, should be brought to book. Kwantung Army Headquarters, unrepentant, politely invited Tokyo to leave the fighting to the men at the scene. The Army General Staff and political authorities in Tokyo could do little else. They did force the Kwantung Army to suspend attacks against the Russian air bases, but air combat missions continued over the war zone. At the beginning of July, the Kwantung Army's Twenty-third Infantry Division crossed into Outer Mongolia. They were met by several hundred Russian tanks. At first the Japanese seemed destined to repeat their performance at Changkufeng. More than a hundred enemy tanks were set ablaze. But the Russians held, forcing the Japanese to withdraw across the river after less than two days of combat. Meanwhile, further south, a Japanese tank offensive was launched across the Halha River. After losing forty tanks, the momentum of the attack faltered and the Japanese again had no option but to withdraw. By this time more than half of the tanks deployed by each side had been put out of action after only a few days of combat. The Japanese were in a far worse position than the Russians to sustain such crippling losses. Moreover, the Japanese were alarmed to find that their own medium tanks were easily penetrated by Russian anti-tank guns and that Russian armour was proof against cannonfire from Japanese tanks. Most of the Russian tank losses to date had been due to grenade attacks pressed home by Japanese infantrymen who lacked effective artillery support. In an effort to remedy this imbalance, the Kwantung Army scoured its depots across the length and breadth of Manchuria and managed to gather together nearly a hundred heavy guns to bear upon the Russians. Their gunners laid down a barrage of some 15,000 shells a day and another Japanese offensive began.

The Russians replied with even heavier counter-fire. The Kwantung Army once again had to break off the engagement. The Army General Staff in Tokyo was ready to concede the victory to the Russians then and there, but the Kwantung Army was determined to continue. Then, unexpectedly, the Russians sent their bombers 200 miles deep into Manchuria. The Kwantung Army redoubled their efforts to raise the ban imposed by Tokyo on air strikes upon the Russian air bases. Imperial General Headquarters, however, flatly refused and intimated that the Kwantung Army was reaping a harvest which it richly deserved.

The Chief of Staff of the Kwantung Army, Lieutenant-General Isogai Rensuke, was summoned to Tokyo and on 20 July was told in no uncertain terms that the Kwantung Army must do everything within its power to bring the Incident to an end. If it should prove impossible to resolve the dispute by diplomatic means, then Tokyo would have to order the Kwantung Army to withdraw beyond the boundary now claimed by the Soviet Union. General Isogai was incensed by these instructions, flatly refusing to consent to them. In the end, however, he grimly agreed to convey the wishes of Imperial General Headquarters back to his Army Headquarters in Manchuria (where they were ignored).

By 21 July Japanese Intelligence reports were accurately predicting that the Russians would open their own offensive in a month's time. The Japanese anticipated, however, that the Kwantung Army could absorb whatever punishment that the Russian and Mongolian side might inflict. The military and political authorities in Tokyo remained as disturbed as formerly at the capricious behaviour of the Kwantung Army, and this certainly contributed towards their unwillingness to reinforce the units already engaged in the campaign. One trainload after another ferried fresh Soviet troops and up-to-date weaponry along the Trans-Siberian Railway. They disembarked and moved up to their assembly points beyond the Halha. In the early part of August, Tokyo reluctantly consented to a lifting of the ban upon air operations over Outer Mongolia: it was a purely precautionary measure, not an escalation of the conflict. News of this soon reached Marshal Zhukov. Then bad weather obscured Japanese aerial reconnaissance over the battlezone for a fortnight. The Russian commander seized his opportunity. The trap was sprung.

Rank upon rank of armoured vehicles backed by massed infantry and coupled with close air support (now far more effective than at Changkufeng) churned through the Japanese and Manchurian lines. Only when the weather began to clear did the Japanese discover to their horror that they were caught in a pincer movement by three infantry divisions and five tank brigades while Zhukov held two further divisions in reserve. This was four or five times the numerical strength of the faltering Japanese and Manchurian forces who were powerless to resist the Russian and Mongolian onslaught. The Japanese lines simply crumpled beneath the weight of the enemy attack. Within little more than the span of a week the remnants of the Japanese and Manchurian forces fled back across the Halha and beyond until they reached what was indisputably Manchurian soil. The Russo-Mongolian forces did not yield to any temptation to follow in hot pursuit. They settled down along the line of what they asserted to be the proper frontiers of the People's Republic of Mongolia and began to fortify it. This was Changkufeng turned upside down.

Deluded by the thought that Japanese divisional and company commanders at the scene had shown insufficient initiative, that courageous individual actions by common soldiers had somehow parried the Russo-Mongolian forces which (by this reckoning) must have lost any stomach for further fighting, Kwantung Army Headquarters decided to risk everything on an immediate, all-out riposte. Four more divisions as well as all the heavy artillery and quick-firing weaponry left in Manchuria were to be thrust into a counter-attack which was planned to open with a week of relentless night attacks from 10 September. The purpose of this whole operation was not merely to erase the Soviet gains by driving back the Russian and Mongolian armies. That was merely a preliminary objective. It was to be expected that military operations would have to break off for a season of suspended animation in the winter months, but Kwantung Army Headquarters planned its autumn offensive to herald nothing less than the opening of a general war against the Soviet Union in the following spring. Understandably enough, Imperial General Headquarters in Tokyo blenched. It was a perfectly ludicrous scheme. The Kwantung Army was told to abandon it at once.

Many considerations affected the outcome. Events were moving swiftly in international affairs and the chronic internal wrangling of Army politics grew if anything more important. War in Europe was imminent. Hitler's preparations for the attack on Poland, completed since June, had been suspended while the Russo-Japanese conflict at Nomonhan developed. Then, just as the Soviets launched their offensive against the Kwantung and Manchurian Armies, news came of the Nazi-Soviet Pact. The groundwork for that had been well prepared months before, but the Japanese had been duped by the Germans into discounting evidence of what was afoot. The threat of a Russo-German War now abruptly receded, leaving the Japanese completely isolated and exposed. No Japanese Cabinet could have survived such a shock. The Hiranuma Cabinet duly fell on 29 August 1939.

War Minister Itagaki was replaced by the less mercurial General Hata Shunroku, who had last fought the Russians during the Russo-Japanese War of 1904–5. Hata knew what kind of difficulties would confront Japan in its efforts to seek a negotiated settlement of the dispute: he had taken an active role in negotiating the Russo-Japanese Convention of 1925 by which Japan and the Soviet Union first established normal diplomatic relations in the aftermath of the Siberian Intervention. Furthermore Hata, who had been Commander-in-Chief of the Japanese Expeditionary Forces in Central China in the wake of General Matsui's disgrace after the Rape of Nanking, was acutely conscious of the quagmire into which the Japanese had slipped in China, and as if that were not enough to make him more cautious than Itagaki as War Minister, Hata had been engaged as Chief ADC to the Emperor in May 1939 on the eve of the Nomonhan Incident and thus knew the earnestness with which Hirohito yearned for peace.

However well suited Hata may have been for the onerous tasks which lay before him, neither his appointment as War Minister nor General Abe Nobuyuki's selection as Prime Minister could be made without the endorsement of the Army General Staff. That approval was willingly granted, thus setting the seal upon the realignment of national politics that now took shape. The Army General Staff appeared to have taken to heart the painful lessons administered by Zhukov's battalions, and Japan emerged from the Nomonhan Incident with a consensus between Imperial General Headquarters and the Government which had been conspicuously absent in the recent past. General Abe and his Cabinet were committed to ending the war as soon as possible, and on 2 September, as early news of the German invasion of Poland reached Japan, the Japanese Army General Staff decided to wait no longer but to break off the Nomonhan Incident by effecting a unilateral withdrawal.

The peace negotiations for which neither Japan nor the Soviet Union had shown enthusiasm between mid-July and late August, were rekindled by the Abe Government in early September. On 16 September an armistice was signed, sparing the Japanese Army General Staff the embarrassment of having to implement its decision of 2 September. All concerned recognized that the ceasefire confirmed the comprehensiveness of the Kwantung Army's military defeat. Detailed discussions held over the months which followed led step by step to further concessions by the Japanese, who finally yielded to the Russians virtually every bone of contention. The end result was marked by a formal accord signed on 18 July 1940: the Japanese diplomats, as usual, were obliged to accept the obloquy of a defeat which quite properly should have been reserved for the military alone.

The military, meanwhile, found other scapegoats, too. Matters were patched up so as to disturb the system as little as possible. Nothing like the great debate over the Washington Treaty System was to be allowed to fragment the Japanese military and political establishment. General Ueda Kenkichi, the ill-fated Commander of the Kwantung Army, and his Chief of Staff, General Isogai Rensuke, were simply replaced by less volatile men. Ueda was never again to be re-employed by the Army. He was so well buried that when he re-surfaced to give evidence at the Tokyo War Trial after the war, nobody even remembered to ask him about what he might recollect of the Nomonhan Incident. General Isogai, after years of disgrace, had the dubious honour to be resurrected as Governor-General of Hong Kong from January 1942 until the war was all but over. He, too, excited no curiosity from either side at the Tokyo Trial: the Nomonhan Incident was a chapter which both sides wanted to forget, except in abstract formulations, and yet it had been one of the most significant armed clashes in the modern history of East Asia.

In geographical terms, the Nomonhan Incident had covered a far wider front than the Amur River and Changkufeng Incidents: it had spread out over an area roughly forty miles wide and eighteen or twenty miles deep. That scarcely accounts for its true significance. It is conventional to judge the relative importance of armed conflicts in terms of their human and material costs. Altogether the Kwantung Army and its protégé, the Manchurian Army, sent 56,000 troops into battle at Nomonhan. It cost Japan and Manchuria 8,440 dead and 8,766 wounded, a devastating 32 per cent casualty rate. The veteran Twenty-third Infantry Division, which had borne the brunt of the fighting, suffered 11,000 casualties, three quarters of its original strength. One can only guess at the strength of the Soviet-Mongolian side but certainly after the opening rounds it was both qualitatively and numerically superior to the forces disposed by the Japanese. It is said that the Russians and Mongolians sustained about 9,000 casualties. Moscow never disclosed the true figures. The real significance of the Nomonhan Incident, however, extends beyond its human and material balance-sheet. To a great extent it was to determine the shape of the Total War that was yet to come.

From this point onwards the Kwantung Army, although previously regarded as the toughest and most audacious military force in East Asia, simply ceased to exert any decisive influence upon history. To all intents and purposes, it suffered a paralysing stroke at Nomonhan. It withered away and, by 1945, survived only in a twilight of senility which left it incapable of resistance when the Russians came to bludgeon their way across Manchuria. In a larger sense, the Nomonhan Incident provides us with a salutary demonstration of how limited military operations can affect the overall strategical balance between rival nations. It forced the Imperial Japanese Army to abandon any further serious design to mount a northern offensive to secure control over Eastern Siberia. The more bold and radical elements within the Army began to consider the merits of a southern advance instead. That was a strategy dear to certain middle-ranking cliques in the Imperial Navy with whom they were in contact. It was regarded by the Navy's more level-headed upper echelons as pie-in-the-sky, a mere nostrum that admittedly had served to justify ever-greater naval expansion over the years and in the past had helped to curb the hotheads who up to now had wanted to swarm across the Russian frontier. However cynically the Navy's most senior commanders may have paid lip-service to the southern advance idea in the past, it had been merely as a theoretical framework rather than as a blueprint for aggression. Now they and their civilian counterparts found themselves unwillingly drawn along by impatient junior officers who demanded deeds and despised masterly inactivity.

The lull in the north lengthened. The Kwantung Army and the Russians continued to probe each other, but the frontier gradually fell quiet. The small-scale incidents, the constant shooting and skirmishes, the espionage and incitements, which had from the start seemed natural to the relationship between these two Powers, dwindled. That is not to say that either side knew peace. At the Tokyo War Trial, Soviet Prosecutors would accuse the Japanese of having violated the frontiers of the Soviet Union on 49 occasions in 1940, 136 in 1941, 229 in 1942 and 414 in 1943. The Soviets would also charge the Japanese with having flown over Soviet territory on 56 occasions in 1940, 61 in 1941, 82 in 1942 and 119 in 1943. In reply, the Japanese would claim that the Soviets had violated the frontiers of Manchuria on 151 occasions in 1940, 98 occasions in 1942 and so on. Whatever the accuracy of these figures (and they cannot be said to be reliable), we must not doubt that these borders remained exceedingly sensitive. There was plenty of rumour, and the outbreak of war on the frontier was still regarded as a very natural possibility by the Japanese. The psychology had not changed: Japan remained malevolent and insecure towards Russia. Russia was still regarded, with deadly cold hostility, as a national enemy, in a way in which China, even at the height of the war between the two Governments, was not. But it became clear that in one way Japan had changed its behaviour. Unless attacked in Manchuria, it was content to do no attacking. More importantly, a powerful current began to pull Japan towards some kind of détente with the Soviet Union. Some Army circles even spoke up in favour of an alliance between Germany, Japan and the Soviet Union. It was an absurdly unrealistic idea. A non-aggression pact between Japan and the Soviet Union, however, was a practical proposition. It came to pass in April 1941, by which time Japan was well on her way towards the Pacific War.

Although one cannot say that peace subsisted between Japan and the Soviet Union after Nomonhan, an unnatural silence descended upon their common frontiers while, in other parts of the world, fighting broke out with great savageness.

Part II

OCEAN CLASH

CHAPTER 13

The War Changes Its Character

THE key to Japan's policy was still the China Incident. With this uppermost in mind, Japan approached the matter of its relations with the western countries in the war which was beginning in Europe.

When the Japanese found that Chungking would not make peace with them, they became convinced that it was enabled to continue fighting, and was encouraged to keep up a hopeless resistance, because of the aid given to it by the Western Powers. In fact, China was complaining desperately at the shortage of war supplies. The aid that it received from the western democracies was a trickle, which the Japanese greatly exaggerated. They professed to be convinced, however, that only the severance of China's link with the democratic Powers would bring an end to the China adventure. The war was telling upon the Japanese, and most groups were anxious to be free of it. Some of them had begun to think that it had been too lightly embarked upon.

The outbreak of the war in Europe in 1939 seemed to give Japan its opportunity to bring pressure to bear upon the countries which persisted in maintaining relations with China. Japan, on the world stage, found itself in much the same position as it had been in the war of 1914–18. To the average citizen reading his daily newspaper in London, Berlin or New York, the direction which Japan might take had suddenly magnified its value greatly: to the guardians of his country's security and foreign policies, the onset of hostilities in the West by contrast actually diminished the regard which European nations were disposed to give to events in East Asia. The experts agreed that for Britain, especially, whether Japan remained strictly neutral or sided with the Axis Powers remained a life or death matter but there was precious little that the British Empire could do to affect Japan's determination of its course. Nevertheless, Japan saw that a new bargaining opportunity had opened up. There was an unfamiliar flexibility in its international relations. Out of the international situation, by blackmail or cajolery, Japan could expect to bend the attitude of other Powers in such a way as to place the whole of East Asia under firm Japanese hegemony.

Already from 1938 Japan, partly under the impetus of patriotic parties which increasingly dictated its policies, partly because of the weakening position of its rivals in East Asia, drifted into a steady widening of its powers in the region. The stage was being set for its collision with the United States. It became convinced that it was practicable to clear East Asia of American as well as of European influences. The United States, while avoiding territorial aggressiveness, had no intention of vacating its position and rights.

First, however, Japan sought to apply its growing power to complete the isolation of China, and thus to compel it to bring the China Incident to an end. Japan's force had, as its immediate objective, the task of cutting off the links which enabled China, though beaten in the field, to refuse peace.

Chiang Kai-shek, in his retreat to Chungking in far-off Szechuan Province, had two lifelines to the West. There was a road through north-west China, occupied by the Chinese communists, down which filtered a little oil from Russia, a quantity of obsolescent weaponry and some Soviet personnel. The Soviet Union's most important contribution to the defence of Free China was a programme intended to build up the Chinese air forces. The first Russian airmen and ground mechanics had begun to arrive at the end of October or the beginning of November 1937. The Soviets evidently had agreed to sell the Chinese about 300 aircraft immediately and to keep about 200 in flying condition thereafter. It is difficult to put this into proportion, but British air Intelligence experts reckoned that this was about the same order of magnitude as the entire strength of the Czech Air Force, which was then judged to be a fairly formidable force: despite the vast differences in the size of Czechoslovakia and China, air operations over China tended to be concentrated in relatively small zones so the comparison is not unreasonable. In any event, the Soviets continued to maintain a steady supply of about forty aircraft per month to China, and the total number of aircraft supplied had reached around 500 at the first anniversary of the China Incident. At that time, the Soviet air mission in China was estimated by foreign Intelligence experts to include about 150 airmen and 300 ground staff. In combat and in training they suffered heavy losses. Two flying schools were established at Hankow and Lanchow early on, with about 100 aircraft and fifty Soviet instructors. Due to the low efficiency reached by the Chinese trainees, however, the Soviets tended to pilot their own aircraft in special-purpose squadrons, except during the Battle for Hankow and over neighbouring frontline areas where Chinese pilots were preferred.

All in all, the effectiveness of the Soviet aid to China is easy to exaggerate although the size of the Soviet commitment was substantial. Looking on the positive side, French Intelligence reports early on suggested that the Soviet airmen were very accomplished fliers and had proved themselves blindly obedient to orders whatever the consequences. Other western Intelligence officers, however, suggested that the true picture was far from rosy: the officer corps of Soviet air forces as a whole showed a notorious lack of initiative, employed wasteful, inefficient tactics, and disgraced the high morale and fair skill displayed by individual Soviet pilots. The performance of the Soviet air forces at Nomonhan in 1939 had surprised the Japanese. Yet by 1940 reports reaching western air staffs spoke of the uneasy state of relations between Chinese air officers and their propagandizing Soviet 'friends'. Americans who had seen the Soviet pilots took note of their unclean, unkempt appearance, their now poor flying skills, their obsolete aircraft, their high rates of attrition and their reluctance to press home any attacks against the Japanese. The same American observers were highly impressed by the skill of the Japanese, their discipline and their fighting spirit.

But it was clear to anyone who was at Chungking at this time that, following the collapse of German military assistance to China, the channels of communication which were valued most highly were those of the Anglo-Saxon Powers. It was on these – first on a railway through French Indo-China which had its outlet at Hanoi, and later, after it was wrecked by bombing and by Japanese intimidation of the Vichy French régime, on an earth road through Burma, and still later on an air lift from Calcutta direct to Chungking – that Kuomintang eyes were riveted. The Japanese were right in supposing that as long as these remained open China would feel that it was not cut off from support from the West. However little was flowing at the moment, as long as the communication remained open, the hope endured in China that more might be made to flow. But always the hinge of China's fate depended upon these communications remaining open. (There were still one or two other avenues, too, such as minute quantities of weapons smuggled out of Hong Kong to guerrilla forces operating within Japanese-occupied territories, but these, although much appreciated, were far less important.)

Japan was well aware that the most immediate way to force an end to the war lay in interrupting these tenuous lines of communication. The Japanese put their trust in a turn in events making it appear more a matter of material interest to the West that the western goverments should extinguish their foreign aid to China. The disastrous defeats suffered by France and Great Britain in the spring campaigns of 1940 appeared to give Japan its opportunity.

In the middle of 1940, after the fall of France, when Britain was in its most desperate condition, Japan demanded that Britain should close the Burma Road. Given the European situation, Britain was in no condition to refuse. Churchill demurred but in the end gave way. At the time, expert opinion was divided as to whether Japan would seize upon the issue as a pretext to open hostilities against Britain's imperial outposts in East Asia. Through well-judged crisis management all that Britain lost and Japan gained was a modicum of prestige, and even that was soon reversed to the discomfiture of the Japanese: the British agreed to suspend traffic on the Burma Road for an indefinite time, then re-opened it after the elapse of only three months, a period which (as British diplomats then lost no opportunity of recounting to the amusement of others round the world) happened to coincide with the monsoon season during which the Road was impassable anyway. After that, the aid again flowed, though scarcely more than a trickle. It was enough to give China hope and helped to restore flagging American confidence in the determination of the British Empire to continue to do its utmost to resist Japanese aggression. As Lieutenant-Colonel Harry Creswell, the long-serving United States Military Attaché in Tokyo, reported in October 1940:

In a practical sense it is difficult to determine how important the Burma Road is to China and whether any large bulk of supplies is being moved over that route. This aside from the fact that it is the last Chinese outlet except through Soviet Russia.

From the Japanese standpoint, however, the road has become the symbol of foreign opposition to the success of Japanese operations in China, and as such has taken on an importance in their eyes at least as great as whatever real value it may have as a source of supply to China.

As in the case of many controversies which were formerly more or less limited to the Orient, since the start of the European War and the alignment of Japan with the totalitarian Axis, the Burma Road issue has become more directly linked with the larger issues involved in that struggle . . . From this standpoint, what may be the Japanese reaction to a re-opening of this road is difficult to foretell at this time. That it will only serve to worsen both Anglo-Japanese and American-Japanese relations, should both nations use the road for supplying the Chinese, is too trite to deserve mention.*

Emperor Hirohito, indeed, had been deeply pessimistic about the outcome of the Burma Road Incident even as the crisis was coming to a head. The British announcement of the suspension of traffic on the Road surprised him. On 11 July, a week before, he gloomily told Marquis Kido Kōichi, Lord Keeper of the Privy Seal, 'I am inclined to think that Britain will

---

* MID 2063–357/37, Comments on Current Events No. 36, by Military Attaché, Japan, Report No. 10216, 7 October 1940, by Lieutenant-Colonel Harry I. T. Creswell, MA, RG 165, Modern Military Archives, Modern Military Branch, US National Archives, Washington, DC.

reject our proposal for closing the "Aid-Chiang Route". In such case, will not the occupation of Hong Kong become necessary, and result in the declaration of war? If so, the USA would probably resort at least to embargo measures.' Both of them worried lest unrest within the Army should 'stir up unpleasant incidents'.* In the Emperor's eyes, at least, the British position in East Asia thus far continued to command respect.

This seems, in fact, an appropriate place to observe that Britain's paramount position in China until the Second World War has been forgotten by the British public – and never was properly appreciated by the American people at large. The Japanese, however, knew of its importance as well as did the Chinese. It is easy to be more impressed by memory of the decline of British influence than by an appreciation of its long persistence.

It is commonly believed that Britain was caught lamentably off-guard by the Japanese attack in Malaya and Hong Kong at the close of 1941. That, however, is simply untrue. The Japanese threat was taken extremely seriously by the British Empire throughout the inter-war years, and until 1939 the position of Singapore was regarded as one of the two keystones upon which the survival of the Empire depended (the other being neither Suez nor Gibraltar but nothing less than the security of the United Kingdom itself). Britain's system of imperial defence planning, preparations and precautions continued to be as exemplary during the European War as it had been beforehand. The Royal Navy, as it existed at the outbreak of the European War, however, had been designed to fight the Japanese while containing the German fleet. There were no margins for error: until war actually broke out, the best professional advice was that the country could afford nothing more. If the generals and airmen grumbled, it was in part because huge sums of money had been spent on the Navy rather than reserved for ground or air forces. If the Japanese threat could have been ignored, all three of Britain's fighting services would have been constructed along very different lines. As it was, the British fleet in September 1939 continued to be the largest in the world, as it had been for longer than anyone cared to remember. The war against Germany and Italy made offensive action against Japan impossible throughout most of the Second World War. The loss of Malaya and Singapore, the obliteration of Britain's naval forces on the China Station, and the sinking of the *Prince of Wales* and *Repulse* within a week of the outbreak of the Pacific War may have been events which were still to come but they were not unexpected by Britain's admirals. They had always warned that the survival of Britain's defensive position in the East depended upon the

---

* PD 1632 QQ, Entry from Kido Diary, 11 July 1940, IMTFE Prosecution Documents.

immediate dispatch of Britain's main fleet to Singapore at the outset of hostilities – and that if the fleet that could be spared should prove unequal to its task, the British Empire would wither away. That is not to say that the United Kingdon always shrank away from war against the Japanese. There had been times – notably in December 1937, January 1938 and during the development of the Tientsin Crisis in the summer of 1939 – when Britain was exceedingly truculent and came within a hair's breadth of responding to Japanese provocations by sending out the fleet, even though knowing full well that such a step would commit Britain to war.

On the whole, however, the general tendencies of British policy in the East throughout this period remained as they had been since the beginning of the China Incident. In his epigrammatic way, Sir Robert Vansittart, the former Permanent Under-Secretary for Foreign Affairs, had voiced one strand of opinion quite succinctly in those days: 'Our policy', he said, 'is to let the Chinese win the war for us, but without our help.' To this the Deputy Director of Military Intelligence at the War Office had retorted, with some truth:

It would be more accurate probably to say, 'let the Chinese prevent Japan from winning the war'. While this policy appears to have more chance of success than one of making an arrangement with Japan, it will invariably result, I should say, in our becoming heartily disliked by both parties.*

The Burma Road affair was an occasion during which, in contrast to its handling of the Tientsin Dispute only a year before, Britain lacked any military means to act unilaterally in opposing the will of Japan. Britain's resort to nothing more than parlour tricks in order to regain the upper hand on the Burma Road issue was admired, and it did gain Britain sufficient time to adjust to the calamitous events which had just taken place in Europe. But the Burma Road Crisis, and the stepped-up American economic pressure upon Japan which counterpointed it, also served notice upon the Government and people of the United States – and Japan – that prime responsibility for the continued maintenance of western influence in East Asia had now passed irretrievably to America.

Throughout these years, indeed, Japan had come increasingly to collide with the other Anglo-Saxon Power, the United States. The clash with the United States, which at first had seemed a passing incident of its China

* MI2/379, Jap IV, 3.B(a), Minute by Deputy Director of Military Intelligence, 25 June 1938, to Director of Military Operations and Intelligence (through Deputy Director of Military Operations), covering copy of Foreign Office Despatch 305 [F4462/71/23] to Tokyo, 17 May 1938, WO 106/5469, British Public Record Office, Kew.

policy, swelled up until it came to dominate all Japan's foreign relations. The need to free itself from American pressure in its plans for the future of East Asia became an obsession with Japan.

Japanese relations with the United States had been worsening for years. They had taken a steady decline from the days of the Russo-Japanese War, at which time the United States had been very sympathetic towards Japan, and relations had been cordial. In those distant days the United States had the characteristic of not always appearing to base its sentiments in foreign relations so solidly on self-interest as did the other Great Powers. It gave more play to national feelings in favouring and disfavouring countries. America was temperamentally drawn to the underdog; Japan seemed to be a small Goliath.

Afterwards, as we have seen, the relations became less good as Japan became a great naval Power and a target as well as an apparent threat to the United States Navy and those sectors of the American public which sought to extend American domination across the whole of the Pacific. Simultaneously, the American enactment of the Japanese Exclusion Act of 1924, which forbade Japanese emigration to the United States, pursued with the maximum resolution and the minimum regard to sparing Japan's feelings, made Japan reconsider its sentiments towards the United States. To Japan, the United States had become the most insulting and insensitive of Great Powers, blocking Japan's path to progress and compelling the country to devote exceptional energies to its effort to escape the forces which seemed to be propelling her towards a collision against twin millstones of American naval and economic might.

When the Manchurian Incident had occurred, the United States had quickly disclosed a policy which it was to follow with remarkable consistency (although the executive branch of the United States Government was not entirely able to overcome temptations to do otherwise). It would have nothing to do with the League of Nations or – except at a uselessly superficial level – with collective attempts at restraining Japan as an aggressor. That was ruled out by the overwhelming strength of American isolation and by the notorious clumsiness of American policy-making machinery. American opinion was behind isolation as the only way of preserving the United States from involvement in war: and it was fondly believed by many that in isolating itself, the United States was cutting itself off from the possibility of influencing the course of world affairs. Many enlightened Americans chafed at this and, often at cross-purposes with one another, involved themselves in international conversations which hopelessly confused and exasperated foreign governments. But it was accepted by most realist Americans that the United States had no alternative in the state to which it had been brought by the many-sided propaganda to which it was subjected.

The United States was unwilling to draw the conclusion from its in-activity that it would acquiesce in the map of the world being redrawn by force. It declared that it would never recognize changes which were being brought about by aggression. There was, it must be admitted, something slightly ridiculous in the spectacle of the United States refusing to rec-ognize the facts brought about by war, but declining to do anything to prevent these changes. It was living in a fool's paradise. But the policy was calculated to bear fruit in the future. By persistently refusing to re-cognize Japan's coups in defiance of international law, but obstinately declining to regard Japan as ever succeeding in closing a door, by leaving open every issue for regulation in the future, and by resisting all efforts made by Japan to equate its actions with those which had been taken by other Powers, including the United States only a few decades before, the United States managed to undermine, with surprising success, Japan's various steps at building its Empire and establishing its hegemony in adjacent territories.

The United States, however, was peculiarly self-distrustful. It had had, in the First World War, the experience of being drawn into the fighting partly, as it decided afterwards, against its better judgement. Probably, when the war was over, a majority of the people, if their opinion had been tested in a plebiscite, would have opined that the First World War was a mistake. If they had had a second chance, they would have kept out. They believed that America had been over-persuaded by subtle propaganda. And unmindful as they were of the difficult economic circumstances which afflicted their erstwhile allies, the Americans were deeply offended by the reluctance or refusal of those allies to repay wartime loans granted by American institutions and taxpayers. There was more than one way to become victimized by scheming foreigners. There were many in the United States who became intent on warning their fellow countrymen to beware of all plots to make America go further than the American people meant.

So, when the Second World War broke out, most Americans, though their sympathies were for the most part engaged against Hitler and his supporters, were firmly against American participation in the war. They were bent on saving the United States from itself. Just because they wished for Hitler's defeat, they were suspicious that the United States would come under pressure to depart from its neutrality: they therefore sought to provide against American force being employed in his over-throw, and urged that the United States should not be officially engaged in war. They went to extraordinary lengths in devising laws which would tie up the American executive, and prevent it from drifting into war. Of the fetters by which the United States bound itself, the most remarkable were the successive Neutrality Acts: laws which aimed at prohibiting the United States from engaging in commerce with either of the belligerents which might involve the country in warlike attitudes. The Neutrality Acts had been passed by successive sessions of the United States Congress in the teeth of opposition by the administration. It was made possible by the American Constitution, which sharply separates the powers and responsibilities of the legislative and executive branches of the United States Government.

Because of this resolution to maintain the peace, because of the peculiar institutions by which the American resolve was enforced, Japan was for some years protected to a large extent from the consequences of its actions. The Neutrality Act was a product of the fear of war with Germany, but Japan derived benefit from it. There had never before in world history been such a strange case of a Great Power deliberately tying itself up, and ensuring that in no circumstances should it act as it would have been natural for it to do. The consequences, the ways that the United States responded to pressure from Japan, were curious. True, it was possible for the American administration to thwart in various ways the intentions of the American Congress, but the laws were rigid, and there were limits to the degree to which they could be transgressed.

One must not forget, however, that few modern nations are as politically volatile as the United States. Its elected officials are quick to follow the whims and fashions of a free but often xenophobic press, which itself is conscious of its need to balance its duty to inform an unsophisticated electorate with its duty to satisfy its advertisers and investors. In this government of the people, by the people and for the people, charismatic national figures with little knowledge of foreign affairs and party hacks with an inadequate grasp of the history of events, wield an uncommon control over generals, admirals and career civil servants, a control which is often undeflected by the weight of professional advice or experience. Given the extraordinary responsiveness of the United States Government to the political will of its people, it may have been as well that by passing the Neutrality Acts the American people effectively curbed for some years their own susceptibility to wild changes of mood and unproductive swings of political direction.

Throughout that time, some powerful American personalities and groups were warning the country that Japan on the march was a threat to the security of the United States. Each Japanese thrust – the rape of Manchuria, the rupture with the League of Nations, the war with China which had spread far and wide since 1937, the blowing of the wind in Japan of a revolutionary assertiveness – caused the warning to be louder. American opinion became troubled. It had reacted with little force to the beginning of the crisis in 1931 when Japan had seized Manchuria; ten years later, Japan's moves were followed with tense interest by many people in the United States. At first the concern over Japan was largely regional, being found especially on the West Coast, which had trading connections with Asia. Eye-witness reports also began to filter back home from missionaries who told of their first-hand experience of the horrors of life in the Chinese war zones. Gradually concern became more wide-spread.

Fortifying this group of people who would have liked the United States to take an active role in Asia was the China lobby. This became for some years an influential pressure group in American politics. The active and practical minded found themselves in an open conspiracy to bring pressure to bear in Congress upon all matters in which Chinese interests were engaged. The curious thing was that in the United States this group was so intent and generated so much emotion. Other countries, Britain for example, had had sectional groups which, by the accident of their history, had been equally exposed to the lure of Chinese civilization, a force which habitually proved attractive to minds of a certain type. But a Chinese lobby, in the sense in which it was known in the United States, never operated in British politics.

Japan doubtless failed to give due weight to the importance of the China lobby in the United States. It always mistook American politics: that was one of its features. Japan had, it is true, some experts on the United States who were well-informed: but they were not attended to. Some Japanese, including men of considerable influence among those who made Japanese policies, believed, and acted on the principle, that the United States, whose soul was given up to commerce, could not prevail over a nation of Samurai warriors, whatever material advantages it seemed to possess. They misread American history. They took no account of the fact that, after the compromises and the prevarication of the democratic system, the United States had shown itself able to go to war, and to wage it with an obsessive stubbornness until its objectives were achieved.

As German soldiers posed for triumphant photographs in occupied Norway, Denmark, the Netherlands, Belgium and France (not to mention countries facing east), there seemed little chance that Hitler's invasion of Britain would be long delayed. Clear-sighted observers tended to regard his complete conquest of the United Kingdom as a foregone conclusion.

Matsuoka Yōsuke was then the Foreign Minister of Japan. It was a critical period in Japan's foreign relations; and he was a new and unusual man to handle them. He came from a different background from those who were normally appointed to that office. As an impressionable child of thirteen, he had emigrated to the United States with his family in 1893, when American prejudice against the yellow man was near its height. Seven years later, he graduated from the University of Oregon Law School as the twentieth century dawned. Within twenty years, he had returned to Japan and had risen to become secretary to the Prime Minister of his native land. Afterwards, he had made his reputation as a business executive, working for the South Manchurian Railway. He became a director of the Railway in 1920 and its Vice-President by 1927. In 1930 he had resigned from the Railway to enter a controversial period as the head of the Japanese delegation to the League of Nations. That culminated in the storm which erupted as he led his people out of the League during its condemnation of Japan over the Manchurian Incident. He returned to Japan where he basked in his national popularity and enjoyed a prosperous life as President of the South Manchurian Railway between 1935–9. Never one to shirk his duty as he saw it, however, he accepted Prince Konoye Fumimaro's offer of the portfolio of Foreign Affairs in September 1940. It was a fateful decision.

By temperament Matsuoka was rather like the type of man who, in an earlier generation, had made the Meiji Restoration. He was abrupt, conceited, gauche, and impatient of the respect for old men which Japanese civilization, being partly Confucian, has usually shown. He was exaggeratedly westernized, or at least he had adopted wholeheartedly the characteristics which he and other Japanese thought to be the essence of western culture. At the same time, in keeping with his life-long love-hate relationship with the English-speaking world of his youth, he was exaggeratedly xenophobic, and opposed to the limit what he saw as an increasingly dangerous Anglo-American conspiracy to encircle Japan as a step towards the consolidation of Anglo-American hegemony in East Asia.

He began his ministerial career by negotiating Japan's adherence to a Triple Alliance with Germany and Italy. The Treaty, signed in September 1940, was subtly conceived. It was primarily directed against the United States: it was intended chiefly to immobilize the United States and to deter it from too active intervention in East Asia and in Germany's wars in Europe. It stipulated that if any Power – and the United States was particularly intended – attacked one of the three signatories or, by giving economic aid, should threaten to affect adversely to them the conflict then taking place, the other two should come to its aid. The

United States rightly interpreted this as an attempt to put fetters upon its freedom of action, and a Japanese withdrawal from the Pact became one of its demands upon Japan. Superficially, to the western democracies, the pact was aggressive: but on the whole, it was intended by the Japanese Government and the European Axis as a means to prevent the spread of war. In that sense, the Japanese and their European Allies regarded the Tripartite Agreement as defensive: it was therefore consistent with that view that Matsuoka and his followers interpreted the vociferous American condemnation of the pact as a proof that the ultimate purpose of United States policy was nothing less than to overthrow the New Orders in East Asia and in Europe by force of arms at a favourable opportunity.

Matsuoka conducted his foreign policy on the principle of *sacro egoismo*. In the spring of 1941, filled with this spirit, he made a tour of Italy, Germany and the Soviet Union. Before he went he had been in favour of committing Japan up to the hilt for Germany, giving it his warm support and leading it to suppose that it would have Japan's military backing if it attacked Russia. He was convinced that Germany was the winning Power, and that only by being among Germany's associates would Japan gain in the eventual share-out of the world at a peace settlement. He was restlessly aware that Japan could pluck great profit from the disorders of the world, and he feared that if it sat still it might fail to gain them. The world would have shaken itself to pieces – to no avail, if Japan did not set itself to win advantage from the outcome.

In his travels, Matsuoka was reassured by the Germans that Hitler harboured no intentions of attacking the Soviet Union: Berlin was not in the habit of confiding its innermost thoughts to its friends. When Matsuoka afterwards arrived in Moscow, therefore, the natural cynicism of this archetypal capitalist found the cynicism of Stalin irresistibly congenial. Conversation with him left Matsuoka convinced that Stalin was the wily man who would sit by Hitler's grave, and was the statesman whose combinations of policy were the most impressive he had met. (Unfortunately, the extraordinary lengths to which Shigemitsu Mamoru, his sagacious Ambassador in London, went in efforts to persuade Matsuoka to visit Winston Churchill in war-torn Britain on the eve of the trip to Moscow were unavailing.) The meetings of Matsuoka and Stalin were especially fateful. They resulted in a genuine change of policy by Japan, one of the Great Powers of the world. Matsuoka, behind his front of self-assurance, proved more volatile than is usually the case with foreign ministers; and he was able to communicate his erratic intentions to the Japanese state. So impressed was Matsuoka with what he deemed to be Stalin's superior power that he proposed that Japan and Russia should sign a Non-Aggression Treaty. Stalin, who was already alarmed at German intentions towards himself, and would in the coming days find Japanese neutrality a pearl beyond price, was much gratified, and closed with the offer at once: through his highly placed agents in Japan, Stalin knew that he could count upon the Japanese to keep their promises to him (as indeed they did). Matsuoka, for his part, chose to ignore the fact that the record of the Russians in keeping to treaties was somewhat poor.

Stalin played on the rather crude imagination of this brash man. When Matsuoka left Moscow, Stalin the oriental potentate surprised everyone by coming to the railway station to take farewell of him. Stalin hugged him, and used a phrase about their both being Asian which was taken to mean that, as a result of the western countries' collective suicide in the war, the future hegemony, at least in Asia, belonged to Japan and Russia. Matsuoka was flattered.

The Non-Aggression Pact signed by Japan and Russia on 14 April 1941 caused surprise. It was one of the sensational events of the war. The Japanese Government, confronted with this astonishing decision by its Foreign Minister, had to take stock of the new position. Events – the dying down of tension on the Russo-Japanese border – had, it is true, been running in this direction; but it was a different matter for the Japanese Government to recognize that its antagonism to Russia, the most cherished and traditional part of its foreign policy, should be formally suspended. Previous diplomatic negotiations between Russia and Japan had been characterized by nit-picking over fine details, demands and counter-demands. There had been Russian claims concerning Sakhalin, disputes over offshore fishing rights, arguments over the boundaries of Mongolia. All of that was swept under the carpet: the Pact covered only the broadest of issues. In a joint declaration appended to the Treaty, the two countries even guaranteed to protect the status quo in Manchukuo and the People's Republic of Mongolia. And most curious of all, no reference was made to the continuance or otherwise of Soviet aid to China. None of the real differences between the two countries had been resolved. Under these circumstances, the durability of this Treaty was probably understood by both sides to be less important than its general tone and moral effect. The truth of the matter is that the Russo-Japanese Non-Aggression Pact had no real foundation except in mutual expedience.

There are in existence the minutes of the Liaison Conferences and the Imperial Conferences held during 1941, at which the new situation was exhaustively debated. These conferences were a unique feature of the Japanese Constitution. The Japanese Government had been so much split up, particularly the Service Ministries which had been freed from civilian control, that special conferences were needed to achieve the unanimity of conclusions which alone made the Japanese mode of government possible. The Liaison Conferences became the centre at which the vital decisions of policy were made: representing the Cabinet there were present the Prime Minister, the Foreign Minister, the Service Ministers and sometimes other key Ministers such as the Finance Minister and the Director of the Cabinet Planning Board; the fighting services were represented by the Chiefs and Vice-Chiefs of Staff of the Army and Navy. In support of them the Chief Secretary of the Cabinet, together with the Chiefs of the Military and Naval Affairs Bureaux of the respective defence ministries, acted as secretaries and 'explainers'. General Mutō Akira, an enlightened and rather virtuous Chief of the Military Affairs Bureau whose ultimate fate was to be hanged as a war criminal by the International Military Tribunal for the Far East, struggled to convey to that court some impression of what the Liaison Conferences were like: he spoke of the harmony that these comparatively informal meetings were expected to produce. After frank exchanges of views, compromises would be agreed so that both the rational development of government policy and the independent operational control of the services could be accommodated without any impairment caused by misunderstanding or crossed purposes. Mutō recalled that members sat in a circle around the Prime Minister:

There was no presiding officer, and every member spoke freely. And, therefore, at times there might be occasions when two men would start talking at the same time, for one member to be whispering to another while another one was speaking. Secretaries were constantly leaving and entering the room on such business as making telephone calls, to call in explainers, or to bring in documents.*

The Imperial Conferences, which were held more rarely, were much more formal meetings of the Liaison Conference in the presence of the Emperor and the President of the Privy Council (who acted as a moderator): these were held when especially momentous decisions were being placed on record. The Emperor sat enthroned upon a dais in front of a gold screen while below him, ranged round a rectangular brocade-covered table, the members sat facing one another: the Prime Minister, followed in turn by the Foreign Minister, the War and Navy Ministers, other Cabinet Ministers in attendance, and then the Chiefs of Staff, would each read prepared statements. The President of the Privy Council would then direct questions to individual members.

---

* Pritchard and Zaide, op. cit., vol. 13, pp. 30618–19; vol. 14, p. 33270.

[Each member] speaking at the Conference stood up in front of his chair and spoke, after bowing to His Majesty. During the Conference no one would enter or leave the conference room. Conferences were held in a very solemn manner.*

The Emperor normally remained silent throughout the proceedings and afterwards gave its conclusions his sanction, which were tantamount to inscribing the outcome on tablets of stone, once and for all.

The notes of these meetings during 1941 are fascinating to read. They show the bewilderment of high Japanese officials at Matsuoka's radical new policy – which was the virtual designation of Japan's hereditary enemy, Russia, as the successor of Britain as the traditional friend of Japan. They show their constant confusion in the kaleidoscope of the contemporary world, always casting round for a dependable ally, always disappointed in the search. They reveal their experimentalism, which is very Japanese. The discussions took place under the urgent sense that at the time the world map was being re-made, and that a golden opportunity had arisen for Japan to share in the general loot – an opportunity which Japan, by its ineptitude, might lose.

The sense is conveyed that the Japanese were out of their depth (in fairness one must add that so were all the other great nations of the world, truth to tell). Here are generals, admirals and high diplomats ruthlessly planning how to further Japan's interests at the expense of the rest of the world: and, though later it was found that this ruthlessness could bear heavy consequences, their deliberations occasionally seem oddly light-weight. The Governments of most other countries, however, fare no better when the records of their inner councils are examined under the historian's microscope.

For the immediate period, the main preoccupation of the Japanese Government was to get rid of Matsuoka. Clearly some Ministers and officials felt embarrassed by this colleague, who spoke with such un-accustomed and uncomfortable directness, not taking advantage of the ambiguities and vagueness of the Japanese language. The Japanese are accustomed to convey their meaning by indirect hints and innuendoes, and the whole of life is in consequence strangely inexact, not as if they did not dare to face the truth but rather that they appreciated that life itself, whether a bed of roses or weeds, is far from cut and dried. In the case of Matsuoka, the Japanese dignitaries, already thinking of an enterprise which was so audacious that they hardly dared acknowledge it, were constantly embarrassed by a Foreign Minister who called a spade a spade.

This is not to imply that Matsuoka's colleagues were reluctant to cut

* ibid., vol. 14, pp. 33269–70.

him to ribbons, even to the point of excoriating his recommendations in front of the Emperor: listen to what Hara Yoshimichi, President of the Privy Council, for instance, had to say on 19 September 1940, when Matsuoka sought approval from an Imperial Conference concerning the Tripartite Alliance which he had negotiated with Germany and Italy:

This Pact is a treaty of alliance with the United States as its target. Germany and Italy hope to prevent American entry into the European War by making this Pact public. Recently the United States had been acting as a watchdog in Eastern Asia in place of Great Britain. She had applied pressure to Japan, but she has probably been restraining herself in order to prevent Japan from joining Germany and Italy. But when Japan's position becomes clear with the announcement of this Pact, she will greatly increase her pressure on us, she will greatly step up her aid to Chiang, and she will obstruct Japan's war effort. I assume that the United States, which has not declared war on Germany and Italy, will put economic pressure on Japan without declaring war on us. She will probably ban the export of oil and iron, and will refuse to purchase goods from us. She will attempt to weaken us over the long term so that we will not be able to endure war. The Director of the [Cabinet] Planning Board has said that all available steps will be taken to obtain iron and oil, but the results are uncertain. Also, the Foreign Minister's statement shows that we cannot obtain iron and oil right away, and that in any case the amount will be restricted. You cannot carry on a war without oil. The capital in Netherlands East Indies oil is British and American, and the Dutch Government has fled to England, so I think it will be impossible to obtain oil from the Netherlands East Indies by peaceful means. I would like to hear the Government's views on this.*

In reply, of course, Matsuoka robustly defended his policy. But the criticism which he endured made no difference anyway, for at the close of the Conference Hara was obliged by custom to give Matsuoka the ceremonial approval which was required.

So we see that Japan's policy to ensure the neutrality of the United States and to end the China Incident on acceptable terms had two legs while Matsuoka directed the Japanese Foreign Ministry: the Tripartite Alliance and the Russo-Japanese Non-Aggression Pact which closed the back door to Japan. It was therefore inevitable that Matsuoka's days in office were numbered once the Germans attacked the Soviet Union in June 1941. In the end, to get rid of him, the Prime Minister Prince Konoye, and the whole Cabinet, had to resign; and it was thus reformed in July 1941 without him, but with a Foreign Minister who spoke the diplomatic language, and rescued his colleagues from contemplating

---

* I. Nobutaka, *Japan's Decision for War: Records of the 1941 Policy Conferences,* Stanford University Press, Stanford, 1967, pp. 9–10: Imperial Conference, 19 September 1940.

ing too directly the stark realities of the world as it was being made by their policy. More significantly, it was hoped that the new man would give Japan a better chance of success in negotiating a successful compromise in the diplomatic negotiations underway with the United States.

During Matsuoka's tenure as Foreign Minister, Japan had decisively altered course and set sail towards the Pacific War. Yet while the Tripartite Pact of September 1940 was his initiative and creation, the fundamental changes of direction sprang from circumstances that Japan either had nothing to do with or policies which it seemed only prudent to take in Japan's self-interest. Among the most influential of the external factors affecting Japan's perceptions of its opportunities was the success of the German spring offensive in 1940 leading to German mastery over the whole of Western Europe from Norway to the Pyrenees. And among the objectives which it seemed thoroughly rational for the Japanese Army to take at this juncture were the efforts which were made to establish Japanese military strength in French Indo-China so that Japan would be enabled to cut the Burma Road by force if necessary at the end of the Burma Road Agreement. Similar efforts were made by the Japanese Navy to ensure access to the natural resources of the South Seas. All of these objectives were supported by a wide cross-section of opinion in Japan.

By the summer of 1941, opinion in Japan had veered round to the view that Japan should strike south. No Japanese leader, military or civilian, truly believed that Japan could withstand a prolonged attack by the combined might of the British Empire and the United States, far less achieve total victory over the Allies in a struggle to the death. But the Japanese Government and people felt that they had little option but to take whatever steps were necessary to force the great Western democracies to accept the wisdom of leaving East Asia to attend to itself. Almost by definition that meant that sooner or later – and well-informed Japanese fervently hoped it would be sooner – Japan and the Western Powers would have to reach a negotiated settlement which would re-shape the political map of Greater East Asia and the Western Pacific. These ideas were by no means incompatible with Japan's progressive steps towards a Southern Advance.

To the south lay the vastly rich resources of oil, tin, rubber and other valuable commodities. This was the area of colonies: British, Dutch, French and American. If it seized them, Japan could hope for three results. First, it would free itself from the economic pressure of the western countries, which had shown themselves ready to threaten Japan with strangulation by economic sanctions intended to control Japanese expansion.

JAPANESE PLANS AND THE 'SOUTHERN ADVANCE,' November 1941

1000   2000 km
500   1000 miles

160°E
100°E
130°E
60°N

U S S R

Attu I.

MONGOLIA

KWANGTUNG
ARMY

Kuril Is

40°N

KOREAN
ARMY

Approximate limit
of Japanese
Objective Area

CHINA
EXPEDITIONARY
ARMY

GENERAL
DEFENCE
COMMAND
(Homeland and
adjacent islands)

CHINA

J A P A N

Ryukyu Is

Formosa

BURMA

20°N

Hong Kong

Wake I.

FR. INDOCHINA

THAILAND

Luzon

SOUTHERN ARMY

14th Army — *to Philippines*
15th Army — *to Thailand*
16th Army — *to East Indies*
25th Army — *to Malay States*

PHILIPPINE
ISLANDS

Guam

MARSHALL IS

Palau Is

Truk Is

MALAY STATES

CAROLINE ISLANDS

0°

DUTCH EAST INDIES

Bismarck
Arch.

GILBERT IS

SOLOMON
IS

N

20°S

AUSTRALIA

Second, by making deadly war on these Powers, if that became necessary, it would crush the last hopes of Chungking and make it sue for peace. And finally, if Japan's western adversaries could be brought by successive shocks to acknowledge that the pursuit of victory over Japan made no sense in terms of western values, the Japanese would build up a new Greater Asia, a solid overseas buttress to the Japanese Empire which would guarantee future Japanese security and become the principal monument of the war. And there was the added advantage that Japan would no longer have to take account of the feeling of its Allies in Europe, whose influences had dangerously distorted the development of Japanese domestic politics over the years.

The birth of these new conceptions about Japan's Southern Advance was guided by the plan being presented, not as a military operation or crude imperialist activity, but as being a beneficent, world-regenerating liberating force in the East which was to be called 'The Greater East Asia Co-Prosperity Sphere'. It was to be a great enterprise, summoning under the protection of Japan the people of South-East Asia and of China, in which justice would reign and the needs of each would be promoted by what was done for the whole. The pride of Japan, the welfare of the world, would be satisfied in equal measure. The mixture of moral ideas, reinforced by a popular Confucianism, made a powerful appeal to the Japanese mood of the hour.

These ideas had been for some time in parturition. As early as 1938, as we have seen, Prince Konoye had proclaimed solemnly that the aim of the China Incident was not to conquer China but to win its cooperation. Looking at East Asia, seeing it threatened by Communism, he said that Japan hankered after a 'New Era' in the territory: a 'New Order' marked by harmony, universal cooperation, and, it was taken for granted, by the benevolent, organizing presence of Japan. Individualism, materialism, the power struggle, everything to do with Communism, were to be ruled out.

The ideas fructified in the next years: and as European imperial Powers all appeared to be toppling one by one, Japanese ideologues, economists and military strategists adapted, and came to apply, the ideas to a steadily widening territory. The 'New Order' was enlarged into the 'Greater East Asia Co-Prosperity Sphere'. In this the countries of Asia would re-orientate, even reconstruct, their economic relationships for their common good, escape from western domination, and be governed by what were thought of as essentially the ideas of eastern civilization. This meant an end to the long night in Asia during which western ideas had prevailed. It meant that an end would be put especially to everything which favoured

Anglo-American ideas and the British and American business presence. Reflecting as it did the aspirations of all the peoples of East Asia for independence from the West, it was to be an essentially cooperative movement. Naturally, given the circumstances of the day, East Asia would find itself for an indefinite period of time under strong Japanese leadership if not hegemony, perhaps in a closely linked federation of East Asian states; and everyone who accepted the 'New Order' more or less accepted this. It was marked by a recognition of the arrangements which Japan had organized, such as the quasi-state of Manchukuo, and the special zone of close Sino-Japanese collaboration.

One of the fascinating things learnt about the war by inquiries afterwards is the butterfly-mindedness of many of the imperialists in Tokyo. They were not dogged, implacable men, tied down to a single idea. They were resilient and receptive. Contrary to the general opinion, they did not make their plans far ahead, and in pursuit of short-term gains they were not unwilling to shift the immediate object of their enterprises and to change the details. So, in 1941, there took place the great movement which determined the course of the war: the shift of mental concentration from a land campaign against Russia, with armies locked together to see which would prevail, to a sea strategy, a joint operation of Army and Navy, which should have as its object the putting of western imperialism to its death, and which would be directed against the Anglo-Saxon Powers, not against the Soviet Union.

In 1941 the decision was not taken: what had happened was that the willingness had appeared to take a decision when a great crisis should happen. A great mental revolution was lived through. New possibilities were envisaged and welcomed by many but not by all. Emperor Hirohito summed up his understanding of the deep divisions of opinion that existed within the Government and Japanese High Command:

Premier Konoye seems to consider that the China Incident will not be settled easily, and favours advancing to the South at the cost of [a] reduction of the occupation area of China. In other words, he seems to be trying to divert the people's dissatisfaction, arising from the unsuccessful China Incident, to the South. The Army seems intending to advance to the South upon a good opportunity, leaving the China Incident as it is now. The Navy's opinion seems to be that unless the China Incident is settled first, we should not resort to force in the South.*

In the end the Government dithered but more or less came down on the side of the Army.

* P D 1632 R R, Entry from Kido Diary, 30 July 1940, I M T F E Prosecution Documents.

The Japanese people responded to this policy. Quite honestly and sincerely, many saw themselves, in opposing western activity in Asia, as emancipators fighting a battle against the dead hand of old-fashioned imperialism. They genuinely believed that the Japanese Government was altruistic, and that the Asian people, who objected to being saved by Japan, were simply misguided. There was little need for propaganda to prepare Japan for the war which it was risking with the United States. If ever a people has gone to war thinking it a just war, if ever a war has been thoroughly popular, so it was to be in 1941. There was little trace of an elaborate misleading of the people, save in estimations of Japan's slim chances of victory. In this, as in so much else, there were parallels between the thoughts of those who held power in London, in Paris and in Tokyo.

Having taken for granted the addition of Manchukuo and China Proper within its compass, which already stretched from Korea and Karafuto to Taiwan, the next territory which Japan was tempted to bring in to the Co-Prosperity Sphere was Indo-China. Its Government had been left helpless by the collapse of France. The only Power to which it could have looked for aid was Britain, but Britain, especially since Dakar, had become the enemy of France. Siam, now called Thailand by the Pan-Asian zealots who seized power there from elements who had been well disposed towards western countries, was incited to present ultimatums to France. Throughout 1940 and 1941, Japan was able to extract larger and larger concessions from French Indo-China for not swallowing it up entirely. By 1941 it had reduced the northern part of Indo-China to a protectorate; presently Japanese garrisons were admitted to the key areas further south; they came to occupy the centres from which they could strike at Malaya, Borneo and the Philippines.

Japan pressed on with this new policy regardless of the fact that on 22 June 1941 a separate war started between Russia and Germany. The German attack on Russia certainly did not take Japan completely by surprise; but Germany, in this as in several other matters of great consequence to Japan, acted without any consultation with the country which, since signing the German-Japanese Anti-Comintern Pact in 1936 and the Tripartite Pact of September 1940, was formally its ally. Seldom had an alliance been operated by a country with quite such painful, humiliating lack of confidential deliberation (although in fact Germany's disdainful treatment of Italy was just as bad). Apart from the psychological and political shock which news of Germany's invasion of the Soviet Union produced in Japan, the Japanese had not made sufficient military provision to enable them to enter such a war at that time. Proper mobilization against the Soviet Union would have taken time and, as Kido Kōichi pointedly told American interrogators after the war, 'if these preparations built up to a certain necessary point, it would [have] become a winter campaign for which Japan was not prepared'. Moreover, there was some doubt as to whether there was anything to be gained by redeploying Japanese forces for an offensive against the Soviet Union: 'The Germans were constantly informing the people here that the war against Russia could be completed within a very short time – a matter of three months or so.' *

Germany now began to press Japan to throw in its forces against the Soviet Union. It had previously indicated to Japanese diplomats, in boastful language, that should it at any time attack the Soviet Union, the campaign would be largely a police operation since Russian resistance would be swiftly overcome. The Japanese Government was inclined now to wait and see. The Kwantung Army, bogged down in China, was not in a mood to venture further afield without the prospect of specific advantage in the overriding aim of bringing China to its knees. Moreover, the pull of the Asian Co-Prosperity Sphere was now being strongly felt. In South Asia its opportunity and its natural sphere seemed to lie.

* USBSS No. 308, Interrogation of Marquis Kido Kōichi by the United States Strategic Bombing Survey, 10 November 1945, RG 343, Modern Military Archives, Modern Military Branch, United States National Archives, Washington, DC.

CHAPTER 14

The Negotiation preceding War

In December 1940, the United States Government, disturbed by the increasingly belligerent tone of the Japanese, had imposed an embargo on the sale of scrap iron and war materials to Japan. Hitherto it had put no hindrance in the way of trade with Japan, and China was able to argue, with reason, that Japan's operations, in the first three years of its warfare, had been made possible economically because of United States policy. The American Government took advantage of the rising temper of the US to act resolutely, but it still had to move cautiously. Its action was an attempt to halt Japan's military activity against China.

A new way of conducting diplomacy was being tried out: the method of using economic pressure to effect political ends. Ever since the covenant of the League of Nations was drafted, the efficiency of economic sanctions had been in dispute. They were tried out against Italy, unsuccessfully, and deliberately with so many imperfections that they were bound to fail (because that was the intention of some of the Great Powers which had been coerced by pressure of their electorates into taking part in the operation) at the Abyssinian Crisis. But, as enforced against Japan, in the peculiar conditions of the time, they had an indisputable effect. They suggested to President Roosevelt the line of government action which, because of the caution of public opinion, he would not have dared to propose that America should take by more political means.

Over 40 per cent of Japanese exports and more than half her imports were with the United States. Japan's balance of payments situation was precarious, and her financial future was in American hands. Although government controls in Japan succeeded in limiting Japanese imports to essential materials, the trend over the first two and a half years of the China Incident was for Japanese exports to fall sharply while imports from the United States continued to rise. Traditionally, Japan had been dependent upon the British Empire and the United States for vital strategical raw materials ranging from tin, nickel and zinc to oil, iron and steel. The British calculated that a mutual British-Japanese trade embargo would hurt the British Empire more than Japan, but it was evident to all that confiscation of Britain's considerable assets in Japan would not begin to compensate for the losses Japan must suffer in the event of joint

Anglo-American sanctions. This difficulty for Japan increased substantially when the European War began in September 1939: alternative sources of supply for some strategical materials vanished along with an important segment of the Japanese export market. Meanwhile, yen-bloc countries such as Formosa, Korea and Manchuria absorbed an increasing proportion of Japanese industrial production while contributing a disappointingly low proportion of Japanese war requirements. Self-sacrifice by Japanese consumers permitted the war to continue indefinitely, but it was universally accepted that Japan had no margin of safety against firm Anglo-American economic sanctions.

In July 1941 the Japanese extended their political control of Indo-China from the north to the south. Their motive was plain: the places Japan had demanded to occupy were those which the military experts regarded as essential for an operation to reduce South-East Asia. Japan had seized the opportunity of the desperate situation of the French in Indo-China, and of the inability of France, following its collapse, to give the local French Government any decisive aid. The American press digested the facts, debated them, and had seen that the damage, which might or must result to the security of the United States, was put before the American public. Even now the American will to peace, and the concern over its neutrality sentiment, remained strong. Its propagandists continued to warn that the United States was being led along the path to war by appeal to fear and sympathy. Many of them feared that the United States was being led by the back door of war with Japan into the war which they feared and opposed: war with Germany. In spite of the alarm which they expressed, President Roosevelt responded firmly in the crisis over Indo-China. He tightened very greatly the economic war which he had begun against Japan. He froze Japanese assets. He proclaimed what amounted to an embargo on Japanese trade in oil and steel, and in the next few months he issued executive orders which extended that embargo to cover scores of other commodities ranging from metals, chemicals and plastics to machinery, hides, skins, leather goods, vegetable fibres and manufactures, even wool.

This was a vital stage in the development of the crisis. The American Government had suddenly stiffened its policy. It did so to the surprise of many of the parties concerned, including the Japanese. It had moved somewhat in advance of the change in the mood of the country. It had taken steps which it knew to be desperately inimical to Japan.

The effects on Japan were immediate. It was especially susceptible to pressure from the oil sanctions. Japan had stored enough oil for two years of war. Denied the opportunity of replenishing these stores from the United

States, it had to recognize in the circumstances of the time that it could not gain oil from alternative sources of supply. The United States was immediately followed in its embargo by the British Empire and the Dutch in Indonesia: Japan discovered that there was no possibility of driving a wedge between them. Each month brought the prospect of the exhaustion of its supplies that much nearer. It knew that its aggressive policies, and Japan itself, must wither away when the time limit arrived – because the vital commodities which sustained them would no longer flow.

The United States during these months was in an extraordinary state. Roosevelt steered it resolutely on a course of economic strangulation so intense and so aggressive that it must result in war or the abject surrender of Japan to America's implacable demands. But Roosevelt did not make the decision publicly: and the majority of the American public, though more deeply stirred by Japan than in previous years, still wanted peace, not war. A certain amount of the exchange of views with Japan was behind the scenes: but much of it leaked to the public. In the last period before the final catastrophe American feeling had moved towards greater caution, so that an impartial observer, if he believed that the great decisions followed the popular will, would have said that the chances of the United States going to war were lessening, not increasing. But the country had the sense that it was in the grip of uncontrollable necessity. Like a sleepwalker, it moved towards war.

The President, though he believed that war was perhaps inevitable, was willing to test the possibility of curbing Japanese expansion without fighting: he would have abandoned larger projects if he could have gained acceptable guarantees of a reversal of Japan's policies in China and Asia generally. Such a degree of unreality has seldom been equalled by a Great Power. The outcome of American economic pressure was not certain. The United States might indeed have forced Japan into belligerent action, but against the British in Malaya and the Dutch in the Netherlands East Indies, not against the United States itself. The American Administration, handcuffed by the Neutrality Act, might have been helpless while its Allies in South-East Asia went down before Japanese attack.

By the later part of 1940 Prince Konoye's Government in Japan had already come to believe that a political settlement of the China Incident was possible only through American mediation, and it was for that reason as well as in response to the direct American economic pressure upon Japan that his Government began to send out signals indicating its desire to open the bilateral negotiations with the United States which finally began in the spring of 1941. After the war, American investigators asked Konoye to explain why Japan had not deployed against China the tremendous military power she was to display at the outbreak of the Pacific War. He replied that the Japanese had come to the conclusion that 'it was almost impossible to gain a decisive victory over China' and that Japan must commit itself to the real possibility of achieving a political settlement.

When Japan proposed a final effort to come to terms which would make the impending Pacific War unnecessary, Roosevelt, and his closest advisers, entered with some hopefulness on the negotiations. They did so with the more readiness because they knew (and nobody else then knew) that they had the great advantage of seeing into the mind of their adversary. The United States had got possession of Japanese ciphers (one of the most notable feats of code-breaking in history), and during these weeks no communications passed between the Japanese Embassy in Washington and its home base in Tokyo without the US Government being aware of it. The putting of the Japanese war machine into readiness, its dispatch into action, all took place under the eyes of the American Government, which knew that it was provoking Japan unendurably.

Unhappily, so highly did the Americans value this means of overhearing the conversation of its adversaries, so resolute was it to defend the secrecy of its knowledge, that the circulation of this Intelligence was rigidly circumscribed. Extremely few men were privy to it – President Roosevelt, Secretary of State Cordell Hull, Secretary of War Henry Stimson, Chief of Staff General George Marshall, and barely a handful of others – and all of them, to guard the secrecy, read the messages and destroyed them on the spot within sight of the bearer. They called it 'Magic'. Whether adequate advantage was taken of this unique knowledge at this stage of events is questionable. Undoubtedly intense precautions to guard security prevented it from being properly digested, and opportunities were missed. Later, after March 1942, summaries of 'Magic' intercepts were prepared and circulated together with background information to an ever-widening circle of Allied officers after the outbreak of the Pacific Conflict, and in terms of their sophistication, general strategical utility and extensive circulation, these summaries came to have immense practical usefulness in the overall conduct of war operations in terms of Total War. In this respect 'Magic' eventually had far more influence on Allied policy formulation than the famous 'Ultra' messages decoded by British cryptographers at Bletchley Park, which were made available in undigestible form as raw intercepts, never enjoyed a wide circulation and remained chiefly of tactical assistance.

In the conduct of the pre-war diplomatic negotiations with Japan, the United States rightly perceived that the interests of friendly Powers with East Asian and Western Pacific involvements were engaged. It informed

Britain, in particular, step by step of their progress. Churchill, for his part, offered no resistance, encouraged the United States to persevere, and blocked those within the British Government who wished to urge the United States into considering alternative policies towards Japan. Churchill, indeed, was less than clear-sighted about Japan. He tended to discount the conviction shared by many people in Washington – and London – that war was imminent. To the last, rather like Secretary of War Stimson, Churchill believed that Japan would probably back down: it must be said that the Greater East Asia and Pacific War surprised both men. Churchill, indeed, culpably neglected the defence of Britain's Eastern Empire prior to the outbreak of war in the East, even wilfully preferring to reinforce the air strength of the Soviet Union than to fulfil the sacred trust of self-defence. His crony, the newspaper magnate Lord Beaverbrook, persuaded Churchill that national prestige was better served by diverting Hurricane and Spitfire fighters to Russia than in shipping them to Malaya: the British Government then persuaded the United States that some of the obsolescent American Brewster Buffalo fighter aircraft which the United States had earmarked for the reinforcement of the Soviet Union ought to be sufficient to meet Britain's imperial air defence requirements in East Asia. It was important for the world to appreciate that Britain, too, was a first-class Power capable of making a significant contribution to the Great Patriotic War of the Soviet Union against their common foe in Europe. Not for the first time, nor for the last, Great Men, with their grand sense of occasion, refused to listen to the wise counsel of their aghast but too timorous professional advisers. Air Chief Marshall Sir Robert Brooke-Popham, then British Commander-in-Chief, Far East, whose Intelligence left much to be desired, said he was satisfied that the Buffaloes would prevail against the Japanese.

The vital negotiations were started through the initiative of some bumbling but well-intentioned amateurs of diplomacy, the clerics of the Catholic mission in East Asia known as the Maryknoll Fathers. Their intervention is an interesting story. On the one side they misunderstood and immensely over-simplified the complexity of the issues dividing Japan and the United States. They viewed the imminence of war with horror, and were convinced that, by taking diplomacy out of its accustomed rut, they could give men of goodwill on both sides the opportunity to turn their natural benevolence to useful account. In their opinion, in the new atmosphere which they tried to generate, matters which had appeared as great obstacles, matters which had in them the seed of war, would be found unexpectedly tractable and would shrivel away.

On the other side, their over-simplification of the issues, which they minimized for lack of adequate appreciation of them, led in the long run to increased confusion, and had the effect of making agreement harder to reach. They roused hopes on both sides by deliberately misrepresenting the exact nature of the demands being made. Thus they stirred up the expectations of a settlement which was found impossible when the exact terms of the other side were clarified. The possibility of an accord receded. It left disillusionment, and made the situation seem more hopeless than before.

The contribution which amateurs can make in complicated dealings between Great Powers is always apt to run into this difficulty. The work of experts is written off, and it is assumed that a fresh approach by fresh minds is likely to succeed: in the end it so often is found that the expert has the dreary and hard truth on his side. In the present case, the Maryknoll Fathers undoubtedly for a time raised hope in certain quarters in the United States and in Japan also, of being able to draft a kind of Monroe Doctrine for the Far East which would be acceptable to those circles in the United States which were anxious before all to secure peace. Determined men in Japan seized on this – in the Army and Navy as well as in court and diplomatic circles – and translated it into a draft agreement between the two Powers, which they sought constantly to put forward as the basis of negotiation. But their draft treaty revealed the insubstantial basis on which they proceeded. They would have been better advised to realize that in seeking an agreement of this kind they were bashing their heads against a stone wall.

The enterprise of the Maryknoll Fathers was a little like that of Swedish philanthropic interlopers who tried to come between Germany and the West in the years before the European War. They were prompted by goodwill: but their initiative did not achieve much.

The Maryknoll negotiations led on to official negotiations which began in July 1941. By November they had reached their climax.

Japan had begun them out of desperation, but it hoped little from them. The sanctions were pressing hard. It is true that there were powerful influences in Japanese Government circles which dreaded war, which were opposed to all the least fortunate tendencies which Japanese foreign policy had given rise to, and which snatched at Japan's peril to recommend that safety lay in retreat: these men, including high-ranking soldiers, sailors, diplomats, economists and courtiers, were quite sincere in wanting a rapprochement with the United States. But Japanese foreign policy was made now chiefly by generals and admirals who had come to the con-

108 *Top*: 'Morning exercises on board troopship': green troops *en route* from Australia to Singapore in the midsummer of 1941

109 *Bottom*: Sturdy but obsolete Brewster Buffalo aircraft, with RAF markings, were sent to defend Malaya during 1941 by the United States

110   *Top*: A Japanese
propaganda cartoon

111   *Bottom*: Japanese troops,
supported by light tanks,
storm across the Johore
Causeway leading to
Singapore Island

112 *Top*: The battleship
HMS *Prince of Wales*, the
most modern capital ship in
the Royal Navy, and the old
battlecruiser HMS *Repulse*
(obscured) reach Singapore on
2 December 1941

113 *Bottom*: The survivors of
the sinking battleship *Prince of
Wales* clamber over the side,
rescued by the destroyer HMS
Express

114 *Top*: Bicycle troops: the
Japanese intention was that all
Japanese troops without
mechanized transport would
travel by bicycle

115 *Bottom*: The turret of
one of the 15-inch naval guns
at Singapore, photographed
during the war by an
Australian prisoner of war

116 *Top*: Under a flag of truce the GOC, Malaya, Lieutenant-General Arthur Percival (*right*), goes to surrender his remaining troops to General Yamashita Tomoyuki, the 'Tiger of Malaya', on 15 February 1942

117 *Centre*: The waterfront of Keppel Harbour, looking back at the General Post Office, the morning after Singapore surrendered and shortly before Japanese occupation forces arrived to take charge of the city

118 *Bottom*: The first Japanese occupation forces march into Singapore: in front of the General Post Office, 16 February 1942

119 *Top*: The heavy cruiser
HMS *Cornwall* sinks after an
attack by Japanese carrier-
borne aircraft off Ceylon,
April 1942

120 *Bottom*: Operation
'Ironclad', a British invasion
of Vichy-controlled
Madagascar in May 1942, was
intended to deny the island's
use to the Japanese Navy

121 *Top*: An American B17 bomber burns after a Japanese air raid on Bandung Airfield in Java

122 *Centre*: Australian troops advance to recover Buna during the two-year New Guinea Campaign

123 *Bottom*: Strongly influenced by contact with Allied forces, bizarre 'cargo cults' were to spread among aboriginal tribesmen in many parts of Papua, New Guinea and nearby islands

124 *Top*: F-Force assembles
at Selarang Barracks, Changi,
before leaving for work on the
Burma–Siam railway

125 *Bottom*: Conditions in
Japanese prisoner-of-war
camps varied from bad to
atrocious during the Pacific
War. Here Dutch prisoners of
war 'take a day off work'
during the construction of an
Indonesian railway

clusion that war was the only policy which could effect sufficient change to offer hope of an acceptable negotiated settlement. They were being egged on by their exchanges of view with Germany, which in these months was urgent that they should embarrass Britain by attacking Singapore, and which supplied all kinds of information about how easy Japan might find this adventure to be. Contrary to the judgements of war crimes courts after the war, such men were not wicked or bloodthirsty. With troubled minds but the clearest of consciences they merely judged that sooner or later war would be inevitable, and that Japan stood a better chance by having the war then rather than later.

Many others in Japan took a contrary view, feeling that widening the East Asian War until it covered the whole of the Western Pacific and South-East Asia offered Japan no hope of victory, but that the United States might be brought to its senses, especially if Germany won the European War. Others were apprehensive that the Soviet Union posed a much clearer danger to Japanese security and believed that the survival of the Japanese Empire depended upon Japan's withdrawal from China as well as Indo-China. Scarcely anyone, however, believed that it would be realistic for Japan to abandon what were regarded as its responsibilities in Manchuria.

By November the United States was satisfied that general talks were fruitless. In this perception the United States Government was almost certainly wrong and, as British, Dutch and many individual American diplomats appreciated, the course which the American Administration pursued was singularly ill-conceived. However, the negotiations with Japan had been interrupted by a government crisis in Tokyo: the resignation of the sometimes moderate but hopelessly vacillating Prince Konoye, and his replacement in October 1941 by his own War Minister, General Tōjō Hideki.

No one believed that Japan was capable of winning a war outright against the United States: the purpose of any resort to arms would be to create the conditions which would permit Japan to extricate itself from the China Incident without submitting to American hegemony in East Asia. The Japanese Government had more or less lost its way. At an Imperial Conference held on 6 September, the Chief of the Army General Staff, General Sugiyama Hajime, recommended that Japan should go to war by mid-October if the outcome of the negotiations with the United States did not appear to be favourable. Tōjō took the same view. The Chief of the Navy General Staff, Admiral Nagano Osami, remarked that 'We can successfully oppose the United States in war for a period of two years. Any longer conflict would tend to be unprofitable for Japan.' The

Emperor himself emphasized his own hope that his Government would pursue peaceful negotiations energetically. His Government tried and failed. Now it was Tōjō's turn.

Tōjō was a military man, not in the highest position of control of the Japanese Army but a product of fashion, diligence and rather fine staff work. He had no special political ideas or standing, but represented in general certain unfortunate attitudes which were common among Army officers who had spent their careers engaged in Japan's military adventures on the Asiatic mainland: contempt for Britain and the United States, faith in what he regarded as the superior qualities of his native culture, willingness to take extreme risks against appalling odds, ignorance of the politics of the world. But Tōjō was also astute enough to recognize the underlying volatility of Japanese domestic politics and knew from personal experience the realities of Japan's predicament in China. He had been active in the Manchurian Incident but had done his level best to prevent the outbreak of the China Incident. His concern about the danger of war against the Soviet Union was acute. The Government which he led was serious in its aim to achieve a breakthrough in its negotiations with the United States, but Tōjō and his supporters were determined to end the policies of drift which had characterized the interplay between Japanese domestic political factions and had been manifest in the country's foreign relations with potential friends and foes for many years. Tōjō had acquired a well-deserved reputation for decisiveness. He also believed that only the manifestation of firmness on the part of Japan stood any chance of motivating the United States Government to seek a just resolution of the China Incident and any other disputes at issue with Japan.

Accordingly, Tōjō and his Cabinet more or less resolved in principle to go to war against the combined forces of the United States and its Allies; his Government nevertheless was ready to see whether anything would be offered by the United States which would make war unnecessary. Twice a deadline for a breakdown of the negotiations was fixed and later postponed. The absolute decision for war was not made until very late in the day. Even then, and until the end, the fleet, which was to deliver the first blow, was ordered to leave room for calling off its operations, so that it could return to Japan with peace preserved.

The Japanese did not seek to rely in their negotiations upon tactical threats or bluff: the negotiations begun by the second and third Konoye Governments and continued by Tōjō's Government were no idle game and the Japanese understood that oriental subtlety was wasted upon the kind of American gangbusters and coarse political hacks who did as much as America's career diplomats and xenophobic military advisers to influence the American President's conduct of American foreign policy. The negotiations were conducted in Washington, DC, because the Americans wanted it that way.

To lead the Japanese team, Admiral Nomura Kichisaburō, once a leading moderate in the inner counsels of the Navy, then called briefly from retirement to be Foreign Minister of Japan during the difficult months that followed the outbreak of the European War in September 1939, was chosen to be the Japanese Ambassador to the United States in January 1941. His appointment was meant to provide reassurance to the United States that the Japanese Navy itself fully supported the efforts of Japan's diplomatic corps to restore satisfactory relations between Japan and the United States. Recognizing his own limitations in the field of diplomacy, however, Nomura sought to obtain the assistance of a first-class professional Ambassador to provide him with help, someone who could guide him through the treacherous waters of diplomacy up the Potomac. The seriousness of the situation was so evident to the authorities in Tokyo that they sent him Ambassador Kurusu Saburō, formerly a Japanese consul in Chicago, later an Ambassador to Belgium (1937–9) and to Germany (1939–40). Kurusu seemed to be an ideal Special Envoy. He knew and liked America, he had an American wife, and, as the man who had signed the Tripartite Pact in Berlin on behalf of Japan, he could indicate to the Americans how truly insubstantial Japan's relations were with the European Axis Powers. A rather slick but well-intentioned banker named Ikawa Tadao, a crony of Prime Minister Konoye, who knew the United States well, was added to the team as an 'unofficial' participant. And backing up Nomura, Kurusu and Ikawa was a Japanese Army colonel, Iwakuro Hideo, who was sent in response to Nomura's request for a military aide who could advise him concerning the actual state of affairs in the China Incident. Iwakuro had been at the Army Affairs Section of the War Ministry's Military Affairs Bureau since 1938 and had headed it for the past couple of years. He had a reputation for excellent staff work, an even temperament and honesty. He had an intimate understanding about how the Army authorities viewed the history of the China Incident, but just as importantly he was chosen for secondment to the Japanese Embassy because he enjoyed the full confidence of Major General Mutō Akira, Chief of the Military Affairs Bureau, and Tōjō himself (who continued to hold the portfolio of War Minister after becoming Prime Minister).

Both Governments, however, handled the negotiations badly from start to finish. Neither Nomura nor Iwakuro recognized that their unofficial intermediaries had no standing with either the President or his Secretary of Staff. Nomura's command of English may not have been as poor as the Americans believed, but he certainly appeared to be exceptionally slow to grasp points of substance as well as of detail, and in any case he found particular difficulty in penetrating Secretary of State Hull's Tennessee accent and speech defects. Worse still, Nomura failed to keep his Foreign Ministry informed concerning precisely what Hull had to say regarding the manner in which the United States was prepared to receive the proposals being bandied about. Apparently he regarded Foreign Minister Matsuoka Yōsuke as so inimical to the peace negotiations that he deliberately sought to isolate the Foreign Ministry and win the general support of his Government by appealing to the Navy Minister and the Chief of the Naval General Staff. In this he did achieve considerable success, for Matsuoka was becoming such an embarrassment that he was ditched from power in July 1941. His replacement, Admiral Toyoda Teijirō, was another amateur in diplomatic affairs but was also one of Nomura's long-standing allies. Long before then, however, matters had become so confused by Nomura's unorthodox and selective reportage that the Japanese Government was heartened by the impression that a draft understanding largely composed by Iwakuro was in fact an American initiative and that the encouraging Japanese response which eventually emerged in reply to that supposed initiative was regarded in Washington as Japan's first official proposals. Cordell Hull took the view that

As the document stood, it offered little basis for an agreement, unless we were willing to sacrifice some of our most basic principles, which we were not. Nevertheless, it was a formal and detailed proposal from Japan. To have rejected it outright would have meant throwing away the only real chance we had had in many months to enter with Japan into a fundamental discussion of all the questions outstanding between us . . .

Consequently, we decided to go forward on the basis of the Japanese proposals and seek to argue Japan into modifying here, eliminating there, and inserting elsewhere, until we might reach an accord we could both sign with mutual good will.*

Everything now began to go utterly haywire as the Japanese gained the misimpression that the United States had been acting in bad faith all along. That misimpression was never corrected. Eventually a critical stage was reached during July 1941, after the Japanese had decided to occupy

* C. Hull, *The Memoirs of Cordell Hull*, vol. II, Hodder & Stoughton, London, 1948, p. 1001, cited by R. Butow, 'The Hull–Nomura Conversations: A Fundamental Misconception', *American Historical Review*, 65:4 (1960), p. 834.

the southern half of French Indo-China – but before the Americans imposed a freezing order on all Japanese assets within the United States – when for a period Hull refused to have anything to do with Nomura. All of this had serious consequences in terms of Japan's continuous monitoring of the prospect of a favourable outcome to the discussions. Equally unfortunately, Nomura himself seems to have believed that failure of the negotiations would produce nothing more catastrophic than a break in diplomatic relations between Japan and the United States. He apparently remained utterly unaware that his Government was finding itself driven to the point of having no alternative but to initiate an all-out attack upon the United States and its British and Dutch handmaidens.

Believing, rather like the Japanese, that their adversaries understood only the meaning of force, the Americans anyway were unusually inflexible in their approach to the negotiations and failed to appreciate the extent to which the Japanese yearned for a reasonable compromise. Though preparing for war, the Government of the United States had scant regard for the military resilience of the Japanese and accordingly did not expect to suffer any mortal injuries or even unduly serious consequences from any miscalculations which might lead to war. America went through the motions of manoeuvring for peace, knowing full well that Allied sanctions would become progressively more debilitating for the Japanese. At the end of the day, however, the United States decided to offer Japan a final 'bargain'. The embargoes on oil, steel and long lists of other commodities, which threatened to cut not only Japan's freedom of action on the Asiatic mainland but its very independence as a nation, were to be lifted: in return, Japan would need to give territorial guarantees. But what? Over this there was a great deal of debate: and the United States consulted its friends abroad.

The first attitude was to let Japan down lightly. Withdrawal from Indo-China would suffice. It was hoped that this would lead on to a general withdrawal from the Asiatic mainland: but this was not to be rushed, and was not to be included in the immediate terms.

But here came in the China lobby. Chiang Kai-shek had been informed of what was to be offered. He was indignant: he reported it as unlikely that China would be able to continue to fight Japan. He telegraphed London and, as an unlikely partner, he enlisted Churchill in representations. Churchill, ever conscious of the importance of the American deterrent to Japanese aggression against the territorial and commercial interests of the British Empire, mildly suggested to President Roosevelt that the proposed *modus vivendi* seemed to offer Chiang 'a rather thin diet'. Meanwhile, all the China lobby was turned on to the

President and Cordell Hull, a cantankerous and notably inflexible Secretary of State. In the result they stiffened the terms and called on the
Japanese to evacuate not only Indo-China, but the whole of China as well,
including Manchuria. In return for this, the United States would rescind
its oil embargo.

In the negotiations, Hull took a stiffer line than Roosevelt. The President
had been willing to accept an invitation from the Japanese Prime Minister,
Prince Konoye, while he was still in power, to negotiate personally. In an
unprecedented step for a Japanese Prime Minister, Konoye offered to
meet the President in Hawaii, risking everything (including the probable
loss of his own life at the hands of Japanese political extremists) on the
outcome. Remembering the fate of those who had aroused the fury of
Japanese radical elements during the Washington and London Treaty
negotiations, Konoye's proposal, which was evidently entirely his own
although warmly welcomed by his Cabinet and Emperor, was exceptionally courageous. One wishes that it could counteract the unfortunate
impression made by Konoye's otherwise rather uneven contributions to
his country's political welfare, but alas it seems only to confirm the rather
manic-depressive tendencies that we can discern in Konoye's behaviour.
This, after all, was a man who was subject to extremes: when the political
parties of Japan were troublesome because of the China Incident, he had
abolished them at a stroke and created a peculiar non-party apparatus
headed by something which he called the Imperial Rule Assistance Association. He was always starting balls rolling and then backing away. This
time, however, Konoye would have had no chance to back away. It was a
marvellous opportunity. Cordell Hull intervened, however, and killed
Konoye's initiative stone dead. Konoye had gone so far as to propose that
the two leaders should make a preliminary temporary pact under which
Japan would agree not to make war on the United States even if American
activities led to war with Germany in the Atlantic Ocean. This meant that
Japan was prepared to repudiate its Tripartite Alliance with Germany
and Italy. The purpose of that Alliance had been to deter the United
States from intervention in the German War by the threat of collision
with Japan. Konoye's offer demonstrates the extent to which Japanese
high officials recognized that their association with the European Axis
Powers had been a grievous miscalculation. Apparently Secretary of State
Hull, however, felt that Konoye was offering an engagement which he
would not be permitted to fulfil. It would appear that Hull also feared that
President Roosevelt would give away too much to the Japanese.

Once the United States Administration had responded to the China
lobby and Churchill's remarks, the possibility of any real *modus vivendi*

receded to vanishing point. The Japanese, their backs to the wall, recognized the utter futility of any further talk. President Roosevelt made what appeared to be a final attempt at peace by appealing over the heads of politicians to the Japanese Emperor. But this action, though it may have been meant as a serious contribution to world peace, probably sprang more from the President's self-interested desire to go down well in the history books. Whether or not his motives were misunderstood, the President's final message to the Emperor was scorned and resented by the Japanese.

On 7 December Japan sent a note which recognized that the negotiations had failed. By the time it was delivered, the consequences of the recognition were also clear: the Japanese were bombarding Pearl Harbor, which they had decided to do if the negotiations ended in deadlock. It is interesting to find that the US Army Chief of Staff General George C. Marshall, when news of the bombardment was first given to him, is reported to have said incredulously that it must be mistaken: Japan would have bombarded Singapore, not American territory. This is unlikely to be a measure of the failure of the Japanese to wring final advantage out of the preoccupation of the American public with remaining neutral. It is merely consistent with the certain knowledge shared by those privy to the most secret British and American Intelligence that a major Japanese task force had been shadowed on its way towards the Malayan coast for days. Above all, it must be stressed that the inevitable consequence of the economic pressures imposed by the United States upon Japan, and of America's failure to pursue its diplomatic negotiations with appropriate vigour, flexibility and imagination, was that Japan finally had no alternative to the Pacific War other than submission to abject surrender. The fact of the matter is that it lay within the power of the United States and the United Kingdom to adopt policies towards Japan which might have avoided that war.

CHAPTER 15
The Bombardment of Pearl Harbor

JAPAN, goaded into decisive action, was unleashing against the world its other major force, its Navy. Hitherto Japan's Army had been the agent of its dynamism: it was the Army which Japan's neighbours feared, and it was the influence of the Army upon the Japanese Government that kept the world in anxiety. The Navy, which by tradition was preponderantly officered by men whose Samurai origin lay in clans different from those which were powerful in the Army, was highly conspiratorial: it had tended to deplore the rashness of the Army, and to favour much more cautious policies. It was conservative: it did not feel the same desire to intervene over the whole range of government: it had less connection, though it had some, with patriotic societies. In the Navy, the old feeling in favour of the Anglo-Japanese Alliance lingered on, and there was a nostalgic sentiment in favour of the older basis of Japan's foreign policy.

But the Navy, like all other institutions in Japan, was divided by factions. One faction had been captivated by the vision of the economic adventure in the South Seas, and by the Empire which it felt lay open for Japan, open to the touch of the Japanese fleet. This section began to think of a war with the British Empire, which it would have to overthrow, as inevitable. It thought, too, that a collision with the United States was certain, for the United States also was likely to block Japanese expansion in this direction. The Navy, or this section of it, gradually came to regard the Anglo-Saxon Powers as the inevitable enemy, against whom war was to be prepared.

This faction identified itself in the vital years with the 'Go South' movement. It naturally saw in this an opportunity to reinstate itself with the Army in the public esteem, and to clip the Army's wings as the instrument of expansion *par excellence*. The prevailing war, an Army-led war, between Japan and China, would be transformed and eclipsed by being converted into a predominantly naval war, fought by the Navy chiefly instead of the land forces, and with the adversary changed. The war would be in a different terrain, would involve huge distances, vast oceans, distant islands – in all of which, the Navy, and not the Army, would shine.

In calling into action the second of the great weapons of Imperial Japan, the Japanese Government was employing an instrument which had been untested for thirty-five years. The Japanese Navy had won its greatest triumph as long ago as 1905, and had, since then, not fought a serious action. As long as the Washington Naval Limitation Treaty had been in force, the West had been able to inform itself of Japanese naval construction: and Britain, making use of old ties, had kept abreast of Japanese naval thinking. But the link had been severed in 1935: the American and British navies felt themselves incompetent at assembling information about interesting new developments in Japanese naval construction: in 1941, it was a matter of speculation how the Japanese Navy would fare if pitted against those of the other Great Powers. A great spurt in construction of big ships had taken place at the end of the 1930s.

In the twenties and early thirties, while contact lasted, the Japanese Navy had maintained a large battle fleet. It possessed ten large battleships: it was known to have built four more subsequently, though the West was without knowledge of their details. In addition the Navy, from the beginning of the 1920s, had been interested in the air, and had built aircraft-carriers. This was the speciality, not of the Navy as a whole, but of a clique in it, whose most forceful member was a Japanese naval officer, Yamamoto Isoroku, who early on had been attracted by theories of air power. He was openly sceptical about the usefulness of battleships: he thought their value was chiefly prestige, and he compared them to the ancestral scrolls which were hung upon the wall of Japanese houses, proving the piety of their upkeep but not able to guarantee much to the present prosperity of the family.

Yamamoto had, however, a very difficult time in propagating his views. Most Japanese admirals regarded his insistence on air power much as British military officers regarded the use of the machine-gun before the First World War. Some made it a point of honour never to fly in an aeroplane themselves, and to discourage flying by their officers. Yamamoto got his way, largely by becoming commandant of a naval school which trained a considerable number of naval pilots: they were to be the heroes of the coming war. By a characteristically Japanese compromise Yamamoto secured, not the replacement of the existing Japanese Navy by one which was governed by his ideas, but the organization of a separate fleet, which was geared to the air, in addition to the orthodox battle fleet. There was no stringent testing of naval construction in Japan by political commissions from the Imperial Diet, which might have subjected this settlement to criticism on grounds of economy, and the debate over the strategical and financial questions which were at issue took place within much the same channels as we have examined in connection with the related problems of international naval arms limitation.

The air development of the Japanese Navy was one of the things grossly underestimated by the Intelligence of the Anglo-Saxon countries. In 1938 aeroplanes which had bombed Shanghai had flown direct from Kyushu in southern Japan and had returned without refuelling. In spite of the stir which this made at the time, the official judgement in England and the United States continued to be that Japan had made little progress in turning out skilled naval pilots.

Admiral Yamamoto, it should be noted, was not a firebrand. He knew and respected the West, its navies and its statesmen. For many years he had been pivotal within the moderate group, a true disciple of Admiral Katō Tomosaburō, and he had risked assassination in consequence. Yamamoto had risen high in the Navy, by great industry fortified by originality of ideas. He became Vice-Minister of the Navy and exercised a powerful influence towards moderation in the mid-1930s. In the middle of 1939 he was made Commander-in-Chief of the Combined Fleet, which removed him from the political centre of civil-military controversies, reduced the likelihood of his assassination, but confirmed his position as one of the three or four men who were responsible for planning naval operations. As relations with the United States worsened, he became convinced that, in the event of Japan being forced into war by the United States – as the Japanese thought – Japan should begin operations with a surprise attack on the US Pacific Fleet, which was stationed at Pearl Harbor. By doing so, the Navy would be repeating its attack, before the outbreak of war, on the Russian fleet at Port Arthur in 1904. Yamamoto had himself been present at that famous action, and had lost two fingers. The American plans for war were known to be that, upon its declaration, the United States Fleet should advance westwards from Pearl Harbor, and that the war would take the form of great naval engagements with the Japanese fleet in the Western Pacific. Yamamoto's plan was to make this impossible by destroying the American fleet, by surprise, before it could sail. As a professional sailor charged with advising his Government on great matters, he recommended it to borrow from Japan's mode of action in the past, and to deal a lightning blow. His advocacy of his bold plan was conditional upon the Japanese Government concluding that no means other than war was open to it. It was to be the desperate means for a desperate situation.

For the attack on Pearl Harbor, Yamamoto proposed to use his aircraft-carriers, and to carry out the destruction from the air. No coup of such magnitude had as yet been carried out: it was its boldness which surprised the world. A relatively small operation of the kind had been executed by the British when they had bombed Taranto with twenty-three planes: their success undoubtedly encouraged Yamamoto to proceed. He had the operation studied minutely, and torpedoes were manufactured which were suitable for attacking in shallow waters: the depth of water at Pearl Harbor was little deeper than it had been at Taranto although the speed, height, bombs, torpedo weights and number of aircraft which he would employ made the puny Taranto raid look primitive by comparison. The Pearl Harbor attack plan was conceived in January 1941. Detailed planning of the action to be taken began in June 1941. Yamamoto had the greatest difficulty in getting the consent of the very few naval colleagues whom he had to consult, but whose number was rigidly limited by the need for entire secrecy. An appreciation by the Naval General Staff was that success would depend on surprise, and that the chances of sailing a task force within reach of Pearl Harbor undetected were negligible.

Yamamoto, however, was finally permitted to proceed. His skill in advocacy was great, and it was one of the qualities which made him so conspicuous in the war and in the years beforehand. He assembled a task force of twenty-three surface warships (which included six carriers, two battleships and nine cruisers), a considerable supply force and twenty-seven submarines. In the middle of November, one month before the actual bombardment, this force sailed from Japan to Tankan Bay in the Kurile Islands; from there they approached Hawaii from the north, arriving within 220 miles of it on the night of 6–7 December. Though Yamamoto had supervised in detail the planning and rehearsal of the expedition, he did not accompany it, but remained at his post of command near Tokyo.

It was understood that the issue of success and of disgraceful and humiliating failure turned upon secrecy. The United States had been warned many times that the Japanese did not exclude an attack on Pearl Harbor. It was not supposed that the Americans were likely to be as extraordinarily negligent as proved in fact to be the case. The idea that the Japanese attacks on 7–8 December 1941 were dastardly acts should be laid to rest: the notion of a Japanese 'Day of Infamy' has outlived its usefulness. Surprise attacks, as we have seen, has been the customary practice of states throughout modern times: they were not the exception, but the general rule.

Japan took a formidable risk in relying on the friendless and empty seas of the North Pacific to protect its fleet from discovery. In other ways it had taken security devices which had in some measure deceived the Americans, and were an essential part of the operation. When its fleet sailed from Japan, the fact had been camouflaged by setting up a system of fake radio messages which stilled any American suspicions that ships were on the move. After some time, however, some of the American monitors realized that calls to and from the aircraft-carriers, specifically, had unaccountably ceased. They accepted that the carriers had been moved, but made the wrong deduction that they had been sent south.

The Americans were already aware, from their interception of the code messages between Tokyo and the Japanese Embassy in Washington, that the Japanese were preparing for war in case the vital negotiations with the United States ended in deadlock; and they assumed that the operations would, in the first case, be directed only against Malaya, the Netherlands East Indies, or the Philippines. With this inference, the assumption that the disappearance of the aircraft-carriers meant a concentration of force in the South Seas fitted excellently. That the concentration was at that moment directed against Pearl Harbor never seemed to have crossed the mind of anyone in authority.

In the summer and autumn months of 1941, both the Army and Navy refrained from informing their commanders in Hawaii of vital information affecting the likelihood of a Japanese surprise attack. It has been suggested that President Roosevelt and his most senior military and naval advisers were so involved in a gigantic attempt to lure the Japanese into an attack on the United States, using the US Pacific Fleet as an opening gambit, that they were ready to risk the consequences of 'surprise' at Pearl Harbor rather than lose this opportunity to bring America into the Second World War on the side of the British Empire. These are serious charges and thus far the evidence offered in support of this conspiracy theory is exceedingly flimsy. The simplest explanation for the lapses that occurred is that many individuals in the American forces at the time were accustomed to sloppy, unprofessional staff work because the approved administrative procedures were cumbersome, irksome and often unworkable: supervision was capricious and poor. Officials tended to try to avoid taking personal responsibility whenever possible. Record-keeping was often haphazard. The fighting services were expanding rapidly and evolving. When pressure mounted so did inefficiency.

What is certain is that there was no shortage of Intelligence information about Japan's intentions. Much of the documentary evidence concerning that information has since disappeared. It is charitable but probably safe to assume that misguided efforts by individuals or by their departments to cover up embarrassing omissions or misperceptions have lent undue credence to those who promote the idea that the Federal Administration was involved in treacherous activities.

Shortly after the Pearl Harbor Strike Force sailed from Japan, two experienced radio operators aboard the Matson liner SS *Lurline* intercepted and logged a stream of radio traffic which they convinced themselves must have been exchanges between a Japanese fleet and Tokyo between 1 and 3 December. War was in the air, and the operators were naturally jittery. Upon docking at Honolulu, however, they immediately took their suspicions and radio log-book information to US Navy Intelligence. No action appears to have been taken.

Far away on the coast of California, an Intelligence officer working on routine Intelligence activities at the 12th Naval District in San Francisco learned that unusual radio transmissions were emanating from west of Hawaii. He telephoned contacts at the wire services and major shipping companies and from these contacts he and a young seaman were able to establish the approximate location of the mysterious signals. They then continued to monitor the position of the transmissions as its source, which they assumed to be a Japanese fishing fleet, continued on its course. It was actually Nagumo's carrier fleet. By the evening of 6 December the Americans had tracked it to a position only 400 miles north-west by north of Oahu, the Hawaiian island which contains Pearl Harbor. They speculated that if the force was the Japanese fleet, it would attack Pearl Harbor early the following morning. They were content to pass along the information to their Chief of Intelligence, an officer who, according to office chit-chat, knew President Roosevelt well enough to alert him personally and save the country. It was a plan of breathtaking naïvety. In any case, it is difficult to know how to regard these two stories: according to Japanese sources, Admiral Nagumo's forces maintained radio silence while on their way to Pearl Harbor.

On 2 December 1941 a Dutch Assistant Naval Attaché in Washington, in the course of a routine visit to the Office of Naval Intelligence, was shown a map plotting a Japanese fleet sailing west of Manila on its way down the South China Sea to the Gulf of Siam. Noting that two Japanese carriers were shown at a position half-way to Hawaii, he expressed his surprise. Four days later, on returning to ONI, he asked where the carriers had gone and was shown a position some 300–400 miles north-west of Pearl Harbor. He recorded this in his diary, reported it to his Ambassador and sent word to the Netherlands Government-in-Exile in London.

Dutch cryptographers, meanwhile, working with primitive resources in Bandung, Java, had managed to crack one of the Japanese consular codes. On 2 December they intercepted a message advising the Japanese Ambassador in Bangkok that Japanese surprise attacks on Hawaii, the Philippines, Malaya and Thailand were imminent and informing him of the famous 'Winds' signals giving notification of the attack. Upon receiving this information, the Commander-in-Chief of the Royal Dutch Netherlands East Indian Army, General Hein Ter Poorten, delivered the message, personally, to the head of the American military mission in Java, Brigadier-General Elliott Thorpe, who managed to cable the news to Washington through the senior US Naval Attaché, Commander Paul Sidney Slawson, and the American Consul-General in the Dutch East Indies, Dr Walter Foote, so as to arouse no suspicion from Japanese monitoring the air waves:

When crisis leading to worst arises, following will be broadcast at end weather reports:
    1. East wind, rain, war with United States.
    2. North wind, cloudy, war with Russia.
    3. West wind, clear, war with Britain, including attack on Thailand or Malaya and Dutch East Indies.

The messages were duly acknowledged by Washington, where no notice was taken. Meanwhile, General Ter Poorten had asked the Dutch Military Attaché in Washington to convey the message directly to General Marshall, the US Army Chief of Staff, who dismissed the report out of hand. When the 'East wind, rain' message was transmitted, it was remarked upon; but the machinery for bringing this information to the attention of American military and naval commanders round the globe was tied up with red tape.

The British authorities, too, had learned of the impending attack. They had been informed by the Dutch Government-in-Exile, who had passed it on to the British Embassy in Washington. Although other hard evidence is lacking, it seems inconceivable that the British would have failed to bring the news to the attention of United States authorities at the highest level. There is, however, no hint of this in the public records, despite the fact that there is an abundance of documentation showing the flow of information between the two Governments concerning the Japanese convoy steaming down the South China Seas on its way to Malaya. The British Cabinet records for the period show that Britain's uncertainty about whether the Americans would become involved continued to exist right up to the eve of Pearl Harbor. Despite months, indeed years, of effort by the British and Dutch to secure a definite commitment by the Americans to join forces in war against Japan in the event of an attack confined to European possessions in the East, Roosevelt continued to be evasive to the last. To some extent his reluctance was explained by his concern that any such commitment might be leaked prematurely in the American press with dire political consequences. However, at the root of his concern was his apparent and possibly genuine inability to forecast how American sentiment and Congressional opinion would respond to such a guarantee:

it is now generally accepted that for some considerable time Roosevelt had lagged behind American public opinion as his country drifted into war. Prime Minister Churchill together with President Roosevelt had become fixed in his belief that only a policy of Anglo-American firmness towards Tokyo could deter Japan from embarking on a Pacific War. Both men recognized, however, that it was one thing to utter warlike cries to undermine the confidence of a potential enemy, quite another thing to plunge blindly into war.

On Friday, 5 December, a United States naval patrol vessel on station north of Hawaii lay in the path of the Japanese fleet. According to evidence put before the subsequent US Congressional inquiry into the Pearl Harbor Attack, the patrol ship unaccountably disappeared from naval records of ship movements and locations the next day: no explanations were given.

On Saturday, 6 December, after having lost contact with the Japanese convoy north-west of Malaya in the fog where the waters of the South China Sea merge with the Gulf of Siam, British reconnaissance aircraft reported elements of the Japanese fleet off the coast of Thailand. The force reportedly included thirty-five transports accompanied by eight cruisers and twenty destroyers: it actually comprised two battleships, eight cruisers and fourteen destroyers backing up a flotilla of nineteen transports carrying troops who had embarked at Hainan only two days before. The Commander of the British Far East Fleet, Vice-Admiral Sir Tom Phillips, who had played such a prominent role in the pre-war naval planning and war preparations of the British Admiralty, was then in Manila for consultations with General MacArthur and the Commander of the American Asiatic Fleet, Admiral Thomas Hart. Upon hearing this latest news, Phillips immediately flew back to Singapore to rejoin his fleet.

Half-way across the globe, the senior United States Army observer in Cairo was informed by Air Marshal Sir Arthur Tedder, Air Officer Commander-in-Chief of the Royal Air Force Middle Eastern Command, that there were firm indications that the United States would be attacked within twenty-four hours. Meanwhile, out in the Aleutians and Hawaii, word came that the reconnaissance flights of the Catalina PBYs were to be relaxed, allowing their crews a much needed rest after an exhausting period of high alert. The dawn patrols in the morning were reduced. According to testimony before the Roberts Commission, at the time of the attack only three Oahu-based naval patrol aircraft were in the air out of a total available strength of around fifty long-range naval reconnaissance aircraft.

The American monitors intercepted wireless messages between some

USSR

Kuril Islands

Etorofu

Tankan Bay (Hitokappu Wan)

HOKKAIDO

Rendezvous 22 Nov.
Sortie 26 Nov.

43°N
159° 30' E

PEARL HARBOR STRIKE FORCE
Air Attack Force : 6 fleet a/c carriers
Screen : 9 destroyers, 1 light cruisers
Support Force : 2 battleships, 2 heavy cruisers
Ship Lane Patrol : 3 submarines
Midway Neutralization Unit : 2 destroyers
Fleet Train : 8 tankers and supply ships

J A P A N

H O N S H U

Tokyo
Yokosuka
Kure Kobe

P A C I F I C

Bonin Is

21°N, 141°E

21–23 Dec.

Wake Island

Mariana Is

Attacked 8–11 Dec. by 4th Fleet, based on Truk,
from Kwajalein ; air strikes 12–19 Dec. by land-
based aircraft ; invaded by Japanese marines
from Kwajalein after renewed naval and air
bombardment 21–23 Dec.

0   500   1000 km
0   500 miles

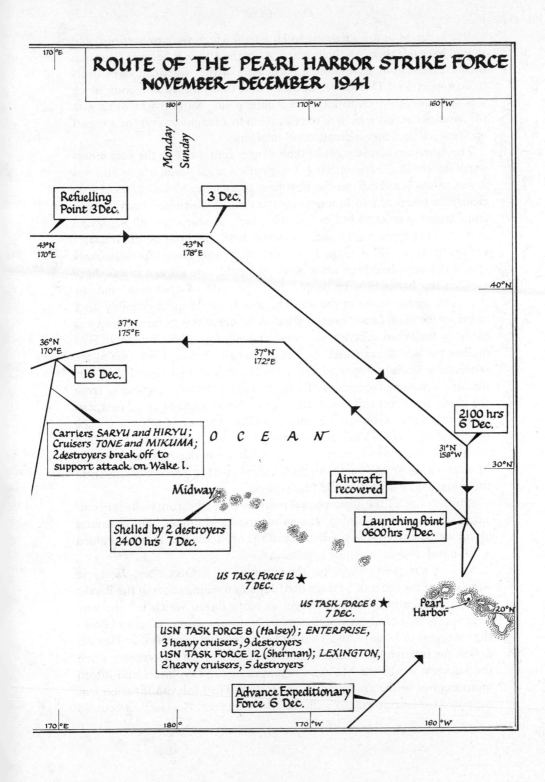

ROUTE OF THE PEARL HARBOR STRIKE FORCE
NOVEMBER–DECEMBER 1941

170°E

180°

170°W

160°W

Monday
Sunday

Refuelling
Point 3 Dec.

3 Dec.

43°N
170°E

43°N
178°E

40°N

37°N
175°E

36°N
170°E

37°N
172°E

16 Dec.

2100 hrs
6 Dec.

Carriers SARYU and HIRYU;
Cruisers TONE and MIKUMA;
2 destroyers break off to
support attack on Wake I.

O C E A N

31°N
158°W

30°N

Aircraft
recovered

Midway

Launching Point
0600 hrs 7 Dec.

Shelled by 2 destroyers
2400 hrs 7 Dec.

US TASK FORCE 12 ★
7 DEC.

US TASK FORCE 8 ★
7 DEC.

Pearl
Harbor

20°N

USN TASK FORCE 8 (Halsey); ENTERPRISE,
3 heavy cruisers, 9 destroyers
USN TASK FORCE 12 (Sherman); LEXINGTON,
2 heavy cruisers, 5 destroyers

Advance Expeditionary
Force 6 Dec.

170°E

180°

170°W

160°W

source in Japan and a Japanese in Honolulu which were mysterious, and should have put them on their guard. After the attack it became clear that these conversations gave minute particulars of the American ships likely to be in port on 7 December. But they were thinly veiled in a code which was subsequently seen to have been quite plain. All that was done with the messages at this time was to refer them to a language unit for a report on them without any indication of emergency.

The American carelessness of their danger continued on the very morning of the attack. Three outlying Army mobile radar units, whose business it was to track aircraft on the northern approaches to Oahu, picked up clearly the traces of two Japanese spotter aircraft which had been sent out from Japanese cruisers just before the attack, to search for all American carriers. They came on the radar screen at 6.45, one hour before the start of the attack. At that time the Japanese aircraft were some fifty miles away and, if this alert had been acted upon, it would, late though it was, have enabled the battleships to be put in some state of readiness, and the American planes to be in the air. The attack would quite possibly have failed, or the main havoc been averted. A report of this radar sighting was made to the Army aircraft warning service information centre at Fort Shafter but was disregarded. At 7.02 a.m., half an hour later, one of the same three stations reported from Opana that it had found and was tracking a massive formation of aircraft 130 miles away, coming in from the north. But when this radar station, which was manned by an inexperienced but enthusiastic trainee, informed Fort Shafter of what had been observed, he was told not to be alarmed. It was assumed that the unit must have detected reconnaissance aircraft from the American carrier force at sea, or an incoming American flight of B17s which was due from the mainland in transit to the Philippines.

Similarly one of the Japanese submarines entered through the harbour gates at 4.50 in the morning. It was reported and hunted: but a general alarm was not given; the significance of the news, the fact that it heralded a full naval assault, was not appreciated.

At 1.15 a.m. local time, on the morning of 8 December, Japanese warships off the coast of Malaya fired Japan's opening shots of the Pacific War in a preliminary bombardment at Kota Bharu which left the way clear for the first of seven landings made by Japanese troops up and down the east coast of Malaya and Thailand over the next two days. In Hawaii, east of the International Date Line, it was 5.45 a.m. on 7 December when the Japanese struck the Malayan Peninsula, a full two hours and fifteen minutes prior to the attack on Pearl Harbor. The Malayan invasion was supposed to coincide exactly with the attack on Pearl Harbor, but because

ROUTE OF THE MALAYAN CONVOY

BURMA

FRENCH

HAINAN

Samah

Invasion convoy
leaves Samah
0600 hrs 4 Dec.
1941

THAILAND
(SIAM)

INDO-

20°N

15°N

Bangkok

CHINA

Cam Ranh
Bay

Air strike force
leaves 0600 hrs
10 Dec.

Gulf of Siam

Saigon

10°N

Phu Quok

1200 hrs
7 Dec.

Cape Cambodia

0700 hrs
5 Dec.

0030 hrs
8 Dec.

No. 2 Route

Intended route
of British Vessels

1940 hrs
5 Dec.

Singora

Patani

0300 hrs
6 Dec.

Alor Star

Kota Bharu

Destroyer TENEDOS ordered
to Singapore

Sungei Patani

Midnight
7/8 Dec.

Sighting reported by Japanese
submarines 1400 hrs 9 Dec.

5°N

Butterworth

MALAY

Natuna Is

STATES

Kuantan

Kuala Lumpur

REPULSE sunk
1235 hrs 10 Dec.
PRINCE OF WALES
sunk 1320 hrs 10 Dec.

Destroyer TENEDOS bombed
0950–1020 hrs 10 Dec.

SUMATRA

Singapore

PRINCE OF WALES,
REPULSE, 4 destroyers
sailed 1735 hrs 8 Dec.

BORNEO

of an officer's error it took place ahead of schedule. There was no real harm done by this mistake: Britain and America were expecting the blow. The authorities in Hawaii, however, evidently remained unaware that the outbreak of hostilities in Malaya had occurred and took no special precautionary measures.

Later that morning, a dispatch rider, carrying a detailed warning from General Marshall in Washington to General Short's Headquarters Command in Hawaii – a warning that had taken an unaccountable time to transmit on the telegraph – was forced to take shelter in a ditch while the raid on Pearl Harbor, which was accurately forecast in the document which he carried, was taking place round him. The warning never reached the authorities who, had it been brought to their attention a few hours earlier, could have taken effective action.

So the evidence, and plenty was at hand, of a coming coup at Pearl Harbor was allowed to pile up, and no counter-measures were taken. The United States was amply served by an acute Intelligence force and given warnings by its Allies. But what is the use of Intelligence if there is negligence and incompetence of mind-boggling proportions over its use and interpretation? What was necessary was that Admiral Husband E. Kimmel, who was in command at Pearl Harbor, and General Walter C. Short, who was responsible for the Hawaiian Defence Command, should have instituted air reconnaissance of all the seas around them: but this, after weighing the advice, and with the assent of their staff, they neglected to do. They believed that it was unnecessary. For nothing was done to alert them to the fact that conditions had reached a more critical stage than ever before. On the contrary, they knew nothing about the Purple codes and had been desensitized over a period of months by a long succession of warnings that Japan was seriously preparing for war. Afterwards, the two men were made scapegoats for the failure of others in Washington who were never court-martialled or punished.

Thus secrecy was maintained: the Japanese triumph was assured. To do Yamamoto justice, he had doubts about the propriety of what he was doing, and stipulated that the attack should not be made until thirty minutes after Japan had informed the United States that it considered the peace negotiations at an end. Thereby a punctilious correctness would be observed, even though by a hair's breadth. Actually the attack, when it came, preceded the notification, and to the outraged Americans it appeared as perfidious as Admiral Tōgō's assault had seemed to the Russians in 1904. But the Japanese had in fact tried to observe the conventions as well as the customary usages of war. The notification was in a bulky 5,000-word message which it took the Embassy much longer to decipher than had been foreseen in Tokyo. The US Navy codebreakers on Constitution Avenue had cracked the message five hours ahead of the Japanese Embassy staff. It was in a way symbolical of how often the actions of the Japanese authorities were ruined by slovenly or incompetent work in their execution. It was Ambassador Kurusu, the professional diplomat, not Admiral Nomura, the amateur, who insisted on correcting the typing and wording of the Final Note, which in appreciation of its special secrecy was typed up by the Embassy's First Secretary, who was an inept typist, with the assistance at the eleventh hour of an equally inept translator. When the note was delivered, the blow had already been struck.

In the early hours of Sunday, 7 December, a last radio instruction came from Tokyo. By a quarter past six, the first wave of aircraft left the carriers. The flagship hoisted a flag reminiscent of the signal which Admiral Tōgō had carried thirty-six years before in his victory over the Tsar. The operation was the more hazardous because the Japanese possessed very sketchy information about the forces they were about to assail. It is a myth that they were well supplied by their Intelligence organizations about the American defences. They were uncertain to the end, for example, about whether the Americans had torpedo nets to protect their ships. They only had information, which they themselves mistrusted, about exactly what ships they were to encounter. One of their agents in Honolulu had warned them that the four aircraft-carriers which were normally with the Pacific Fleet were away from port that weekend. To catch the carriers was a vital objective. They had had in consequence serious thoughts of calling off the entire adventure at the last moment, or of postponing it indefinitely. Many of the decisions were made by guesswork.

The air attack force which the Japanese let loose was divided into groups of fighter planes, high-level bombers, torpedo-bombers and dive-bombers. Commander Fuchida Mitsuo, who led the first wave of the attack at the head of the torpedo-bombers, has put on record the sight which met him. It is quoted in John Deane Potter's book, *Admiral of the Pacific*:

Below me lay the whole US Pacific Fleet in a formation I would not have dared to dream of in my most optimistic dreams. I have seen all the German ships assembled in Kiel Harbour. I have also seen the French battleships in Brest. And finally I have frequently seen our warships assembled for review before the Emperor, but I have never seen ships, even in the deepest deep, anchored at a distance of 500–1,000 yards from each other. A war fleet must always be on the alert, since surprise attacks can never be fully ruled out. But this picture down there was hard to comprehend. Had these Americans never heard of Port Arthur?*

* Quoted by J. D. Potter, *Admiral of the Pacific*, Heinemann, London, 1965, p. 98.

OAHU: ROUTES OF ATTACKING
JAPANESE AIRCRAFT OVER
HAWAII, 7 DECEMBER 1941

FIRST ATTACK
0740 Deploy

SECOND ATTACK
0850 Deploy

0750 Attack
run ordered

0855 Attack
run ordered

Kahuku Pt.

Kahuku

Kaena Pt.

Mokuleia
Field

Waialua

Haleiwa Field

FIGHTERS

FIGHTERS

Waianae Range

Koolau Range

Wheeler Field

DIVE
BOMBERS

DIVE BOMBERS

Nanakuli

TORPEDO BOMBERS

HORIZONTAL BOMBERS

MCAS EWA

Pearl Harbor

Hickam
Field

Honolulu

Waikiki Beach

Diamond Head

HORIZONTAL   BOMBERS

NAS
Kaneohe

Kaneohe Bay

Bellows Field

Manana I.
Makapuu Pt.

Actually the mooring of the ships was culpably unsafe. It was odd that their radar protection did not afford more effective safety.

The attack lasted two hours. In this short time the Americans had suffered loss or damage to eighteen battleships and auxiliaries, the destruction or damage of 349 aircraft, and had 2,345 sailors, soldiers and marines killed, 1,247 wounded and 103 civilians killed or wounded. By mid-morning the vast and impressive naval base, which had filled the United States with such confidence, was transformed into a huge ruin with flaming ships, a decimated garrison, and a monumental disorganization. The base from which the United States had counted on directing the war was a chaos enveloped in smoke. The Japanese were amazed at the extent of their success and at their enemy's unpreparedness. Nevertheless, they also noted with concern and respect the speed with which the Americans responded to the attack once it was underway. The second wave encountered very stiff and determined anti-aircraft fire.

To effect this slaughter, the Japanese had used 353 carrier-borne aircraft and the two cruiser-borne reconnaissance aircraft launched earlier. They lost fifteen dive-bombers and high-level bombers, nine fighter planes, and five torpedo-planes in combat, 8 per cent of their total strength, a figure which was surprisingly similar to average losses then being inflicted upon air raiding aircraft by alert defence forces in Europe. In addition a number of other aircraft were badly damaged or crashed on returning to their carriers, and more than twenty aircraft of these had to be written off. The total loss in Japanese naval personnel was fifty-five officers and men. The statistics, however, do not convey the full sense of shock which was felt throughout the world by news of the Pearl Harbor attack. It was the most spectacular triumph of the war. The Americans in Hawaii remained unaware throughout of the source of their attack, and the entire fleet sailed back in safety to Japan.

Impressive as were the results of the raid, humiliating as it proved to be for the American Navy, Japan fell just short of making it the crushing success it was meant to be. The Japanese, inexplicably, did not destroy the vast oil stocks and fleet repair facilities on Hawaii, or, at that stage, seriously consider whether it could seize them. America began the war with oil reserves at Hawaii which were almost equal to the entire supplies of Japan. Japan had them at its mercy: why they neglected to fire them remains inadequately explained. At one stage it had, it is true, been the Japanese intention to try to seize Oahu, and in that case the oil would have passed into Japan's hands. But this part of the plan had been quickly

PEARL HARBOR
7 DECEMBER 1941

AIEA

East Loch

PEARL CITY
Pan-American
Airways Landing

3

4

5

BLUE

PHOENIX

6

DETROIT

SOLACE
ALLAN
CHEW

1

2
MEDUSA

RALEIGH

CURTISS

UTAH

Middle Loch

TANGIER

Beckoning Point

FORD
ISLAND

NEVADA

ARIZONA
IVESTAL
TENNESSEE
W. VIRGINIA
MARYLAND
OKLAHOMA

NEOSHO

CALIFORNIA

AVOCET

ARGONNE 8 SACRAMENTO

PELIAS

CINCPAC

OGLALA
HELENA
CACHALOT
VFD-2 PENNSYLVANIA

RAMAPO
NEW ORLEANS
SAN FRANCISCO
HONOLULU
BAGLEY
ST. LOUIS

Signal
Station

9

South-east
Loch

7

SUMNER

CASTOR
Merry Point

Tank
Farm

SHAW
Dry docks
CASSEN
DOWNES

Naval
Hospital

U S Naval Station

10

Tank Farms

U S
Naval
Reservation

West
Loch

Hickam Field
U S Air Base

1 Destroyer-minecraft
RAMSAY, GAMBLE,
MONTGOMERY
2 Destroyer-minecraft
TREVER, BREESE, ZANE,
PERRY, WASMUTH
3 Destroyers MONAGHAN,
FARRAGUT, DALE, AYLWIN
4 Destroyers HENLEY
PATTERSON, RALPH TALBOT
5 Destroyers SELFRIDGE, CASE,
TUCKER, REID, CONYNGHAM;
tender WHITNEY
6 Destroyers PHELPS,
MACDONOUGH, WORDEN,
DEWEY, HULL;
tender DOBBIN
7 Submarines NARWHAL,
DOLPHIN, TALITOG; seaplane
tenders, THORNTON, HULBERT
8 Destroyers JARVIS, MUGFORD
(inside ARGONNE and
SACRAMENTO)
9 Destroyer CUMMINGS;
dest.-minelayers PREBLE, TRACY
PRUITT, SICARD; destroyer
SCHLEY; minesweeper GREBE
10 Minesweepers BOBOLINK,
VIREO, TURKEY, RAIL, TERN

Other auxiliaries, not shown,
were moored up West Loch.
There were also several tugs
and yard-craft, not shown,
in the area of the chart.

This key reads NW to SE
through the nests of ships.

Salt
Works

Anti-torpedo
and boat nets

XXXX XXXXXXXXXXX
XXXX XXXXXXXXXX

U S Army Reservation

Fort
Kemenamena

given up as, among other reasons, it would have demanded troop transports and landing craft which were needed for the operation beginning at the same time in the South Seas. To have made the operation one which would really have altered the fundamental position of both sides, the Japanese would have needed not only to destroy ships but to have seized territory in the middle of the Pacific Ocean.

Japan did not include among its victims any one of the four major American aircraft carriers which were attached to the Pacific Fleet. These were to prove the decisive weapon in the subsequent struggle in the Pacific, as was well understood by Admiral Yamamoto. Fortunate accidents led to one aircraft carrier being away delivering some planes to Midway Island; to another delivering planes to Guam; another being under repair on the American Pacific coast. The fourth was, as was found out later, trailed for some hours by a large Japanese submarine, but, in the eventual contest with this, the submarine was sunk.

Pearl Harbor contained also one failure of the Japanese which was little noted at the time but which was to have a decisive effect. The plan of Yamamoto had included a submarine attack as well as one from the air: but this was as uniformly a failure as the attack from the air was a success. A special Japanese invention, the midget submarine, a minute submarine operated by a crew of two, was to be let loose inside the harbour among the battleships, and to work what havoc it could. Five of these submarines, which were transported by huge 2,000-ton ocean-going submarines, were inserted through the harbour gates: this was, to all intents and purposes, a suicide mission, for the chances of the crews being picked up again were, though it was just possible, exceedingly slight. In fact all the five midget submarines were destroyed and only one member of the crews survived, falling prisoner to the Americans. (Like most Japanese taken prisoner, he proved singularly talkative, and he disclosed useful information to the Americans.) In the subsequent share-out of the honours for the raid, the submarine commanders felt themselves neglected, and all the credit fell to the airmen. Subsequently, the submarine service was at a discount in Japanese eyes. No further plans were drawn up which devolved any great responsibility on it. Though attention had previously been given to the production of the midget, Japanese inventiveness swung away from the submarine and concentrated on other matters. Japan had begun the war with several very large and technically efficient submarines; they were subsequently engaged on colourful, hazardous action on the American coast and in the fighting at Guadalcanal; but they failed to keep their hold on the imagination of the public, which was fixed upon its navy pilots. So, in war, the issues can be decided by irrational judgement and politics. An unfair inference was that the Japanese Navy, though it possessed an incontestable genius in Yamamoto, did not have staff officers who were capable of recognizing that Japan possessed an asset which it was wasting; who were capable of evolving a strategy which would make use of this instrument; and who simultaneously had the ability to force their views on the attention of the faction-riddled Japanese High Command. What Yamamoto had done for naval aircraft, nobody seemed able to do for the submarine.

Was Pearl Harbor therefore really a success for the Japanese? Taking into account the whole course of the war, this has been doubted. The far from dispassionate or even-handed American naval historian, S. E. Morison, doubted this. He summed up the situation by saying that Pearl Harbor, for all the destruction which it achieved, was really an empty triumph. Looking at the careful Japanese plan which had been evolved for dealing with the expected offensive by the United States Pacific fleet advancing in the Pacific, he speculated that Japan would have done more wisely if it had waited for the attack, and contained it somewhere in the Marshall or Caroline Islands. By fleet action on these lines, Japan would have gained the best chance of surviving. Morison, in other words, believed that the war operations plan to which the Japanese Navy had adhered for twenty years until January 1941 was far more sound than Admiral Yamamoto's plans for the Pearl Harbor attack operation, which superseded it. Such a view may be hard to credit. Put at the most down-to-earth estimate, Yamamoto had gained eighteen months', or two years', respite for Japan, and, though the long-term prospects remained exceedingly black, he had insured that the typhoon should rage over Japan in two years' time, not rage at once. He gave the opportunity to his own war schemes, and to any others which Japan might produce, or, better still, to her diplomats and statesmen in their ability to work out a peaceable solution, to find a way of averting ultimate catastrophe. Here he felt there were genuine opportunities, making the mistake of assuming that his enemies still preferred peace to war. As for his own side, a close examination of the facts leaves one in no doubt that the Japanese recognized their mortal danger. One perceptive young Japanese historian has gone so far to argue that 'Not a single Japanese leader, either military man or civilian, believed that Japan could hold out against an Anglo-American combined attack for long, let alone achieve a sweeping victory over the Allies.' *

* Satō Ryozō, 'Japan's Entry into the Pacific War: A Reconsideration', *Senshū Jinmon Ronshū* (Collected Essays on Special Subjects in the Humanities), No. 30, Tokyo, March 1983, pp. 74–5.

One peculiar circumstance aided Japan at Pearl Harbor. It was to continue in some form throughout the war, and was to handicap American arrangements repeatedly. This was that the High Commands of the US Navy and Army at home were scarcely on speaking terms. The degree of discord varied from place to place, and depended in part on the accident of personalities engaged. But the tension was often an important fact of the situation: as it had been at Pearl Harbor, where there was the minimum cooperation between the Air Force, which in the United States was part of the Army, and the Navy. Much of the responsibility for friction lay with the Navy. The United States Navy existed in peculiar isolation from American society. It was self-sufficient and self-contained. It had its own politics, outlook, ethos. In war as in peace it was apt to think that its chief enemy was at home, in the rival services which entrenched upon its own liberty of action. The result was peculiarly catastrophic. Due to this self-imposed remoteness, the defence machinery creaked badly. Yet the United States Navy and its subordinate marine command was the country's only fully efficient fighting service at the outbreak of the war. Its training, weaponry and establishment were all capable of performing the tasks required of it. By comparison, the United States Army was clumsy, out-of-date, ill-equipped, under-strength and lack-lustre. It was scarcely surprising that the Navy regarded the Army with contempt – and preferred to rely upon its own people and their friends in Washington as well as overseas.

There were other defects in the American defence machine. All these stood out clearly at Pearl Harbor. The extension of peacetime bureaucratic controls went so far that the anti-aircraft batteries were obliged to indent for every shell which was fired. As the American wartime machine swung slowly into action, a great many blunders were discovered which had their source in this over-meticulousness of civilian control. It was the natural consequence of a long period of peace – and it was by no means peculiar to the United States.

If the sights are lifted beyond this war, it must be recorded that, by the shrewd blow delivered to the United States (which was so much larger than Japan) and by the superb secrecy which had been preserved in organizing such a complex operation, Yamamoto and Nagumo had given a boost to Japanese self-esteem, which would buoy the people up in future periods of national calamity. One day the Japanese triumph at Pearl Harbor will be regarded in a different light from that in which it was inevitably seen by the opposite side at the time; the memory of treachery will fade: it will stand out as a most memorable feat of arms.

CHAPTER 16
The War after Pearl Harbor

A N Imperial Rescript – the manifesto which is issued at great decisions of the Government – accompanied Japan's declaration of war, and read as follows:

> We hereby declare war on the United States of America and the British Empire ... It has been truly unavoidable ... More than four years have passed since China, failing to understand the true intentions of our empire, disturbed the peace of Asia. Although there has been re-established the National Government of China with which Japan has effected neighbourly intercourse and cooperation, the régime which has survived at Chungking, relying upon American and British protection, still continues its fratricidal opposition. Eager for the realization of their inordinate ambition to dominate the Orient, both America and Britain, giving support to the Chungking régime, have aggravated the disturbances of East Asia. Moreover these two powers, inducing other countries to follow suit, have increased military preparations on all sides of our empire to challenge us. They have obstructed by every means our peaceful commerce and finally have resorted to a direct severance of economic relations thereby gravely menacing the existence of our empire ... This trend of affairs would, if left unchecked, endanger the very existence of our nation. The situation being such as it is, our empire, for its existence and self-defence, has no other recourse but to appeal to arms and to crush every obstacle on its path.*

Except for the blame it casts on China for the convulsion, this is an accurate statement of why Japan went to war. Japan states that it enlarged the war because it believed that only by doing so was it possible to wind up a smaller war with China. Its intervention in Indo-China, to which America had reacted so stiffly, had been undertaken for the same reasons.

War on such a scale as Japan now embarked on had come out of the inability of the Japanese Government to find any other means of dealing with a situation which had passed out of its control. It was due in the last resort to a failure of ingenuity. The war was not preceded by elaborate planning. There was no systematic scheme of operations against the United States and Britain, which laid down a timetable for successive undertakings. British and American war planners and Intelligence experts,

---

* This is the translation introduced into evidence by the Prosecution at the Tokyo War Trial: see Pritchard and Zaide, *Transcript of the Proceedings*, op. cit., 5 [PX 1240], pp. 10686–9.

considering their prospects in the eventuality of a war against Japan, had been virtually unanimous in affirming their belief that while the Japanese were meticulous in their staff work, their gifts of improvisation were of a low order. That was to prove another failure by the West to know their enemy. All the evidence which was to become available to the Western Allies at the end of the hostilities confirms that the war was a desperate venture, hastily decided upon: that it was conducted by a series of improvisations, however brilliant some of these were: that no elaborate plans were made of the assets, military and economic, of the Western Allies, and that no intelligent scheme existed for eroding them: that Japan was, quite literally, taking a great leap in the dark, and casting its faith into the keeping of a veiled Providence, which it had no reason to think would be kind.

Admiral Yamamoto, accomplished gambler and the architect of Pearl Harbor, summed up the attitude of those who took the decision to go to war:

What a strange position I find myself in now – having to make a decision diametrically opposed to my own personal opinion, with no choice but to push full-speed in pursuance of that decision. Is that, too, fate?*

To his sister, he wrote, 'Well, war has begun at last. But in spite of all the clamour that is going on, we could lose it. I can only do my best.'† And to a fellow admiral he wrote:

This war will give us much trouble in the future. The fact that we have had a small success at Pearl Harbor is nothing. The fact that we have succeeded so easily has pleased people. Personally I do not think it is a good thing to whip up propaganda to encourage the nation. People should think things over and realize how serious the situation is.‡

He had, at Pearl Harbor, fought a successful holding operation, which had bought time. But he knew, as well as anybody, that this time would pass, and that, if at the end of it Japan – and its ally Germany – had not found a way to peace, Japan would be ruined. He had said repeatedly that it was easier to start a war than finish one. However much territory the Japanese took, however many American battleships they sank, final victory almost certainly would elude them.

One way only seemed to offer hope. Japanese strategy should be to win, by the impetus of surprise, as much as it possibly could in the first six

* J. D. Potter, *Admiral of the Pacific*, op. cit.
† ibid.
‡ ibid.

months of the war. The only chance of a satisfactory peace would be to follow up Pearl Harbor by sinking the American aircraft-carriers: and then, from the triumphal height of that moment, to persuade the United States to negotiate peace. It might hope that Japan would seem to be in such a commanding position that its Anglo-Saxon enemies would be cast down by the difficulty of dislodging it. Though Japan's occidental enemies had potentially invincible power, they would be unwilling to make the exertion of mobilizing it, the more so since they would have been worn out by the war effort they were making against Germany and Italy. Japan, it should be remembered, occupied a naval position of great strength strategically. After the war of 1914–18, it had inherited from Germany the Caroline and Marshall Islands in the Pacific which, if thoroughly fortified (as they were to become), interposed a screen which would hamper the Americans in defending the Philippines or in advancing westwards towards the Japanese homeland. And in the South Pacific there were other considerations.

The Japanese, linked by blood to Polynesia as well as to Mongolia, Korea and China, have always exhibited a degree of interest in the South Seas and in that concept of manifest destiny which they called the 'Southern Advance'. The South Seas Mandated Islands, wrested by Japan from Germany during the First World War and conceded to Japanese control by the League of Nations, were a source of national pride as well as being a focus for economic exploitation. From a naval point of view, the strategical importance of the islands was immense. It was the view of the Naval Affairs Bureau that:

the South Sea Islands were so situated geographically as to constitute the bulwark of sea defence for Japan and hence we termed it the first line of defence for our country. We felt that if these islands fell into the hands of an enemy it would have meant certain defeat for Japan. Hence it was but natural that the Navy was desirous of installing on these islands or some of them such military defensive measures as would satisfy our need for security. Were it not for treaty restrictions we would have carried out defensive constructions on these islands with no hesitation.*

In the Covenant of the League of Nations there was a general prohibition against the establishment of permanent defences on mandated territories. The award to Japan of the islands formerly possessed by Germany in the South Pacific was contingent upon additional assurances that it would respect that prohibition. That the Japanese eventually broke these promises is not in dispute and, since the United States never joined the League of

---

* Pritchard and Zaide, op. cit., 11, pp. 26468–9: Affidavit [D X 2990] and Testimony by Captain Yoshida Hidemi, I J N.

Nations, has little significance in itself. A nation's self-defence was regarded as its paramount obligation and inalienable right. It was, however, important that in several treaties concluded during the Washington Conference in 1922, the Japanese repeated their categorical assurances that the Japanese Mandated Islands would not be fortified although, of course, it was plain that their freedom of action (like that of their rivals) would be restored whenever the agreements finally terminated.

Long before the expiration of the Washington Treaties, the British and Americans convinced themselves that the Japanese were in breach of their undertakings. Their evidence for this was merely that the Japanese declared the Mandated Islands off-limits to foreigners and strictly enforced the rule. The rest was rumour and speculation. Subsequently it emerged that the civil administration of the islands had been put into the hands of naval officers. They thoroughly surveyed the defence potential of each one, naval manoeuvres were periodically conducted there, and a number of facilities were erected which, strictly speaking, were not proscribed by the Treaties but might have raised a hair on an international lawyer's eyebrow: these included some rudimentary air strips, light harbour facilities and modest fuel storage tanks – all ostensibly for civil use in the economic exploitation of the islands though with their potential conversion to military use clearly in mind. None of these constructions nor a few temporary buildings built there constituted the kind of defended bases and fixed artillery emplacements proscribed by the Treaties. Even the limited development that did take place on the Mandated Islands prior to the outbreak of the Pacific War occurred only after the demise of the Washington Treaty System, and the contrast between what was built before the war and the defence installations installed there after Pearl Harbor provides some measure of the Japanese Navy's attempt to uphold its Treaty obligations.

The suspicions of the Western Powers were in fact groundless although understandable. The matter was explored by both sides at the time of the Japanese war crimes trials, and notwithstanding the International Tribunal's characteristically one-sided judgement to the contrary, the evidence produced by the Defence seems far more convincing than the case for the Prosecution. The myths and legends persist, but the formidable defence works constructed on these islands during the war itself should be regarded as a memorial to Japanese forward planning, engineering skill and efficiency, not to duplicity. Indeed it is clear that the policy of successive Japanese Governments and of the Japanese fighting services was to conform to Japan's undertaking not to fortify the islands, until a surprisingly late stage. It is a point worth setting straight, and the Summation by the Defence at the Tokyo Trial puts the issue squarely:

It was frankly admitted that after November 1941 the Navy decided for the first time to carry out the construction of defence works on the Mandated Islands. But it was not until after the middle of November that the construction corps left Japan for some of the islands. But this was only after conditions between the Western Powers and Japan had come to the danger point of explosion and it would have been militarily ridiculous for the Japanese Navy to have sat back quietly with folded hands.*

The Japanese defences in their Mandated Islands do merit comparison with the poor state of readiness that existed in British, American, Australian and Dutch island possessions in the Pacific in the years between the termination of the Treaties and the outbreak of war in the Pacific. The economic parsimony of the western democracies was responsible for the fact that they achieved less where development was permitted. The Defence, however, made another cogent point as well in summing up:

If Japan had entertained the thought of aggressive war against the United States, Great Britain or the other countries, surely [it] would not have waited until this desperately late day to begin such military construction on the life-line of Japan.†

The vast depths of the Pacific Ocean were in themselves a very strong defence. Japan could argue that the United States, confronted with the possibility of either a prolonged, arduous counter-assault, or with a generous peace offer by Japan – generous in the sense that it would not be against the United States' interest in any part of the world except East Asia – would choose the path of peace.

Of the chances of their ally Germany – who was little more, either then or later, than their nominal ally – they took a rather similar view: Gemany's long-term prospects were black, but it might find salvation in the war-weariness of the Western Allies. In this titanic world contest, one of the most curious things was the failure of Japan and Germany to cooperate. Their relations throughout were scarcely more than the conventional ones of peacetime association. Their relations were conducted by Ambassadors. The joint planning which essentially made up Anglo-American cooperation was almost totally absent in the wartime partnership of their rivals. There were joint commissions which Japan and Germany established to help coordinate their policies, but these were largely empty shells without much vital substance. When diligent spying

---

* ibid., 17, pp. 43209–10.
† ibid., p. 43210.

failed to discover any joint war plans by Germany and Japan, it was assumed at first that an unusually opaque veil had been woven to hide them. Not until much later did the real and simple truth become credible. No such plans had been brought into being.

Japan, unlike Germany, had no well-considered long-term war aims. In contrast to what Germany planned for Europe, Japan invested little effort in its projects for the Greater East Asia Co-Prosperity Sphere. The direction of the war on the Japanese side was too widely diffused among different hands for a clear national policy to become plain. Japan, even though it had hopes of limiting the war, was easily diverted away from the idea of a defensive war. By Pearl Harbor and Japan's initial victories, a situation had been created which made prudence difficult, and lured the Japanese on. It was as impossible to restrain its generals and admirals from further adventures as it is to prevent bulls from charging in a bull-ring.

In general, Japan followed a strategy remarkably close to that by which Mr Micawber governed his life. It was to take violent action, and then to hope that something or other would turn up, enabling it to escape disaster and to re-establish peace.

Japan had committed the error of all military Powers in dealing with the United States. It underrated grossly the willingness of the United States to bear the adversities of war. It despised it; and continued to do so throughout the war. Because in the course of every war the United States armies had begun badly, because its democratic institutions encouraged crude criticism and loose talk, because its people were not ashamed to harp upon considerations of material interest, the Japanese, like Hohenzollern Germany before them, too easily expected the United States to give up. They scoffed at the American commercial instinct, and they predicted that, in the grim struggle of war, this could never survive against the Samurai tradition.

But the nature of Anglo-Saxon democracy has often been its tenacity. This the Americans, and the British, have demonstrated clearly in chapters of their history. Confront them wth a desperate situation, give them disastrous leaders, let their economic policies be deplorable, saddle their public life with a rising rate of casualties; and they have generally become more stubborn. They can be implacable, and seemingly their pocket is limitless. They become pitiless and merciless, both to their enemies and to the civilian minorities among them who protest against a transfiguration of the values of life by the stubborn resolve to continue war. Passchendaele and the battlefields of the American Civil War are a terrible warning, which naturally militant people, but those untouched by the

traditions of Anglo-Saxon democracy, have never taken to heart. Once it
has taken up arms, and has suffered the blood-letting which warms its
temper, the democracy long ceases to understand the virtues of a peace
which is negotiated, and is satisfied only with the barren conclusion
spreading bitterness everywhere, of absolute victory. There have been
exceptions – the history of the Vietnam War was one, the adventures of
the United States in Mexico and elsewhere in Latin America have been
others – when public opinion has cast a decisive vote against foreign wars.
Britain, too, had her Boer War, and her scuttle from African and East
Asian conflicts after the Second World War may count as much the same.
Yet generally the Anglo-American democracies at war set aside all rules,
and, with a mood created by the tempest of the hour, work simply and
mechanically, grinding their way to victory. This was the tempest which
Japan was bringing down upon itself: more awful than any of its feared
typhoons.

It was to discover later that, terrible as a victorious democracy may be,
it has at least the virtue of quickly changing its temper when the goad of
war is removed. The resolution and implacability, which thrive during war,
are dissolved after a year or so of peace. Hence Japan, if it had dwelt on
past history, need not have been so miserably cast down by its total defeat.

If the Japanese despised the United States, Americans no less misunderstood the Japanese. Their mutual incomprehension is one of the
facts, tragic and at times comic, of the war. Throughout its course, anyone
visiting the United States was at once made conscious of the passionate
contempt, originally based on resentment, which was felt for the Japanese.
All the discreditable facts about them were remembered. All that made
Japanese civilization interesting was, as by system, forgotten. All Japanese
were lumped together as a misshapen, ugly, stupid, dwarf people. They
were like nothing so much as Mr Tolkien's orcs in *The Lord of the Rings*,
creations of a people of sheer malevolence and hideousness. One discreditable consequence of this racialist response was the public hysteria
which quickly developed on the West Coast of the United States for the
forcible internment of Americans of Japanese extraction.

Many Americans of a more reflective turn of mind were dismayed by
this outrage, but they were powerless in the face of the sensationalist press
and radio coverage which pandered to the prejudices of the majority.
With strong backing from local congressmen and other public figures,
notably from State Attorney General Earl Warren, who was then campaigning for the governorship of California which he won in 1943 (he
went on to earn a place in history as a Chief Justice of the United States
Supreme Court renowned for his then less than popular advancement of

the civil liberties of other minority groups), sufficient pressure was put upon officials in Washington, DC, to produce results. At first the Japanese-Americans were subjected to abuse, harassment and worse as individual American citizens 'took matters into their own hands'. Soon various curfews were imposed and Japanese-Americans were excluded from specified 'prohibited zones', which grew in number or extent over the first few months after Pearl Harbor until these unfortunates were barred altogether from the western third of Washington and Oregon, the western half of California and the southern quarter of Arizona. Then in June 1942, orders were given that led to further controls which effectively deprived all Americans of Japanese extraction of their liberty within any part of those four states.

Eventually, 119,000 were taken away to be concentrated at ten internment camps established for that purpose at remote, inhospitable sites (where they lived in terrible hardship and a significant number died from their privations). Forced to abandon their property and personal possessions or to dispose of their homes, businesses and smallholdings at giveaway prices, there was to be no restitution of their property after the war. No real steps were taken by the United States Government to compensate Japanese-Americans for their losses until the early 1980s.

The supposed threat which was allegedly posed by these Americans to the national security of the United States was almost entirely imaginary – and was recognized as such by many of those who carried out the exercise: in that most sensitive of military districts, Hawaii, fewer than 500 persons of Japanese extraction were interned. Despite intensive surveillance by vigilant citizens, local police forces, the FBI and the Intelligence agencies of the defence services, not one Japanese-American was ever charged with the commission of an act of sabotage within the continental limits of the United States or Hawaii (although General John L. DeWitt, Commanding General of the Western Defense Command, who showed a keen interest in tightening his grip on the Japanese-Americans until their pips squeaked, remarked, 'The very fact that no sabotage has taken place to date is a disturbing and confirming indication that such action will be taken').* No similar measures were taken against the Italo-American or German-American ethnic communities in the United States or its overseas territories.

The British reacted in a no less extreme way. On going to war, Churchill wrote a quite sentimental letter to the Japanese Ambassador, but generally

---

* Cited by D. Swain Thomas and R. S. Nishimoto, *The Spoilage: Japanese-American Evacuation and Resettlement during World War II*, University of California Press, Berkeley, 1946, p. 5.

he shared the prejudices of his countrymen and of his American cousins. The stream of American feeling did not sweep the British along with it; the British had their emotions concentrated on the Nazis, and, except where they had powerful reasons for hatred from personal experience of Japanese camps or other atrocities, regarded the Japanese as a provoking irrelevance. These were differences of cultural styles, not of perception.

By its fateful decision Japan altogether changed the character of the war.

China, which until then had preserved the fiction that its war was no war but merely an incident, declared war on Japan on 9 December. It rejoiced in the United States being committed and saw the prospect of its operation being enlarged by American aid. All would have been denied to China by the isolationists of America had China declared war before America itself was committed to the struggle. So the declaration was a voluntary act by China. Events might have taken a different course if China had not thus regularized its American alliance. Similarly, on the same day that it declared war on Japan it declared war on Germany.

Why it did so is not clear. As Germany was under no obligation to declare war on the United States, and did so against its interests, so China was under no obligation to declare war on Germany. Apparently it did so out of a kind of contagion. It might be assumed that the countries were beset by madness.

From this time onwards, the direst and chiefly decisive part of the war was waged on sea and in the air. In fact the Japanese sea and air operations were probably the most spectacular in human history. It is true that the war with China continued desultorily, but the problems which compelled the attention of the wartime Japanese Governments had very little relation to those of the earlier period. Pearl Harbor meant a huge increase in Japan's enemies. It had against it the British Empire, in those days still a Super-power, as well as the United States. It had defied a great part of the world, and though it had at first won prodigious successes, the precariousness of its position was always plain, even to the Japanese man in the street.

In the whole of the latter part of the war, in the struggle of Japan with the Western Powers, Japan was by conviction as well as by circumstance compelled to appear as the liberator of the orient against occidental control. The role of the emancipator, which nationalists everywhere had first hopefully seen Japan as fulfilling in its victory against Russia in 1905, was now firmly wished upon it by the exigencies of the time. In India, in Indo-China, in Indonesia, in Burma, a tide was started which, if the Japanese had rightly worked with it, might have proved irresistible. In this new illumination the presence of the white man in Asia seemed a ghastly insult to the rights of Asian peoples. Even classes of people who had formerly been contented to work with the West hailed the new prospect of building the future of Asia upon Asian foundations.

The history of the war was to some extent a chronicle of Japan's lost opportunities: of a crusade which never got started; of a Japan which was so hampered by inner contradictions and by lack of a systematic blueprint that it was unsuccessful in rising to the occasion. As the war went on, many Japanese allowed it to become plain that they, at least, were bent on a simple predatory enterprise of the kind which had been supposed to have gone out of fashion with the passing of the nineteenth century. They failed to disguise in a plausible way that their interest was no higher than the transfer to Japan of the benefits enjoyed by western countries in the South Seas and in Asia. The ideology of the Greater East Asia Co-Prosperity Sphere, with its picture of an eastern world finding harmony under the protection of the Japanese armies, was far from being perfunctory for those who strove for it mightily. Yet for others it remained unconvincing amid the turmoil and the temptations of conquest which beggared the imagination of an island people. Opportunism, where it occurred, often overlay a deep-seated belief in *Hakkō Ichiu* (all-the-eight-corners-of-the-world-under-one-roof) rather than vice versa.

In three years, Japan, by a series of blunders, disappointed the hopes of Asia that it was the liberator. By extraordinarily insensitive action, hardline Japanese convinced Asian nationalists that so long as the war continued Japan could or would offer little or nothing to the peoples struggling to be free; and satisfied the national leaders that more was to be had from the European Imperial Powers – or from the United States – than from the victory of Japan. For this result, a part of the responsibility was due to the misconduct, repeated blunders, arrogance and stupidity, of the Japanese Army. Japan's imperial adventure was always associated with the Japanese Army: Japanese diplomats, civilians and captains of industry were of secondary importance. For reasons, one must look to the very sources of the Japanese Army's strength – to the social background, educational system, internal discipline and ascetic values of the Imperial Japanese Army, described earlier. The opportunities for a genuine new era in the region, which were made available by the daring and glittering achievements of Japanese arms, were flung away because the Japanese Army acted in the teeth of the inhabitants of the region, and came to be hated throughout Asia. It was defeated by Anglo-Saxon powers in military combat, but when this came about, few tears were shed by Asian nationalists at the result.

After Pearl Harbor, the war, or the China Incident and the European War, broadened out, and became a world war, in which nearly every country was engaged. It was more universal than the First World War had been. The greater part of the civilized world was drawn in.

There is a distinction, of kind as well as of degree, between a local war and a universal one. In a local war, there are boundaries to the general savagery. In general men can opt out of it: they, or at least some, can go to neutral territory. In a universal explosion, war is everywhere. The shortage of neutrals leaves man without refuge.

Ruskin, in a passage from *Praeterita*, describes the difference between a local war and a war which had got out of hand and swept the world: that of Napoleon. Of this war, Ruskin says that:

death was of another range and power; more terrible a thousand-fold in its merely physical grasp and grief; more terrible, incalculably, in its mystery and shame. What were the robber's casual pang, or the range of the flying skirmish, compared to the work of the axe, and the sword, and the famine, which was done at this time in all the hills and plains of the Christian earth, from Moscow to Gibraltar ... Look on the map of Europe, and count the bloodstains on it, between Arcola and Waterloo.

So with this later convulsion; only the scientific progress with weapons of destruction made the havoc worse. What, in other ages, armies could bring about in a dozen years, they had now the capacity to do in a dozen days, or even hours.

The greater part of the civilized world was at war: little by little, in almost every country of the world, in great cities, and in most of the accessible villages, the sights and sounds of war were to become the commonplace of the age. In North America, in the Asian countries, in Australia, and in North Africa, the progress of the war became a grand preoccupation. In all too many centres of ordered life, centres which for more than a century had been famous for commerce or culture, the distant hum of conflict turned abruptly into the clash and commotion of sudden battle, to be followed often by the long tedium and horror of military occupation by an alien power. In all the world, only Central Africa and South America were relatively undisturbed.

The whole world moved senselessly in one direction or another, suffered and died in great swaths. Peasants and citizens of the huge Asian towns were caught alike. Many more perished from famine and disease than were killed by the armies.

This huge populace was informed about what was happening chiefly by local newspapers. Other media of communication scarcely touched it. Beyond Japan Proper and the Philippines, only the rare Asian village was, at the time, equipped with radio. For the townsmen, the radio set poured out propaganda, but in the towns the people largely discounted this, and put more faith in the printed word. From newspapers, and still more by word of mouth, word was spread, without which the Asian peoples would have supposed that there was no rhyme or reason in the convulsion of the world. It is hard enough to see how these instruments were sufficient for their purpose. Even though newspapers made their way into most of the villages, even remote ones in China and India, the number of people who could read them was very restricted. The war which had engulfed the governments had drawn in a mass of illiterate peasants. Those who could read found their talent even more highly regarded than in the past. They read in their newspaper and told the rest of the people what it contained. They and their village councils and headmen were the agents of the increasing self-awareness of the peoples of Asia during this time. But it is unlikely that many of them came to any conclusion about the events they contemplated more perceptive than that of little Peterkin on the battle of Blenheim two and a half centuries earlier:

> But what they fought each other for
> I could not well make out.

Part III
THE HIGH TIDE OF WAR

CHAPTER 17

Japan's Hundred Days

HONG KONG

JAPAN, following its brilliant start in the new theatres of war, had the limelight in the times which succeeded. For the next three months it held the initiative in many different sectors. It concentrated on dealing with its new enemies, especially the United States and Britain, and it enjoyed a dashing period of cheaply won triumphs, rolling up the long established positions and colonial territories of the Western Powers in Asia. Its record was of almost unbroken success in the first hundred days of this war. This was to be a bitter recollection in Japan when its record ceased to be one of uninterrupted conquest, and the country faced the experience of endless decline.

Its first conquests were the remaining outposts of the western empires and of the United States in China. In some places, the defenders escaped into the interior or were evacuated by sea. Others were not so lucky. At news of the Japanese attack on Pearl Harbor, the Japanese demanded surrender of the British gunboat HMS *Peterel* at Shanghai. The British refused, and as the Japanese launch drew away Japanese troops along the Bund opened fire with small arms and artillery. The attack was soon over. The British ship caught fire and sank; its dead and dying crew were swept downstream in the retreating tide. A few survivors were rescued. The only remaining enemy warship, an American gunboat riding at anchor in the roadstead, lowered its colours and quietly surrendered without a fight. It was the end of an era.

Hong Kong fell almost immediately. A very small offshore island of China, useful for trade and for political action, Hong Kong had never been seriously prepared by the British for standing a prolonged siege, even in recent years when the situation looked threatening. It was ringed by Japan's armies and its fleet; it was without a hinterland of more than a few miles; its water supply was easily vulnerable; it was too far from a British base for there to be any possibility of reinforcing it. It never had a chance to survive, it was not expected to do so and it was surprising that it held out for as long as thirteen days.

The main feature of its siege was the confusion among the population, which was overwhelmingly Chinese. Many, though loyal inhabitants of

THE JAPANESE OFFENSIVE
DECEMBER 1941 — MAY 1942

Operation, December 1941
Operation, January—February 1942
Limit of Advance, May 1942

IS

Iwo Jima

SOUTH SEAS DETACHMENT

Mariana Islands

Wake I.

Saipan

P A C I F I C   O C E A N

Guam

Truk Is

Ponape

Elements 14th & 16th ARMIES

Palau I.

C a r o l i n e   I s l a n d s

Halmahera

Sorong

Manakwari

Admiralty Is

Hollandia

Kavieng

New Ireland

Babo

Bismarck Archipelago

Amboina

NEW GUINEA

New Britain

Solomon Is

Timor I.

Port Moresby

Guadalcanal

AUSTRALIA

the colony, had dual nationality with China, or else were moved by strong Chinese sentiments. These had for the most part been loyal to the Chungking Government, and its most active and enterprising members, who in consequence had become marked men to Japan, succeeded in escaping to mainland China; as also did the Chinese politicians who, because they found it safer to operate beyond reach of the Kuomintang, resided in Hong Kong. Many civilians in Hong Kong responded to the call for at least a token resistance. The Japanese, in the use of their political warfare techniques, attempted to set off the Scots in the garrison against the English. Pamphlets were dropped which were full of Scottish sentiment, invoked the memories of Loch Lomond, and inquired whether the Scots were willing to be sacrificed in an English quarrel.

The siege was ended on 19 December when the guns were silenced. There was heartening drama at the finish when some of the spirited young men of the colony, together with a one-legged Chinese admiral who gave a foretaste of the astonishing toughness which the Chinese today display, but did so seldom at that period, got clean through the blockading Japanese, and escaped up country to Chungking. Politically the forfeiture of Hong Kong was a blow to the British; but strategically it was inevitable. It had been foreseen and, privately, had been regarded by successive British governments as a foregone conclusion.

A serious loss at Hong Kong was of several of the Far Eastern experts which the British Army possessed at the start of the war. The number of these was appallingly scanty: the army authorities had caused surprisingly few of its officers to learn Chinese and Japanese at a time when trouble was evidently brewing in this part of the world. Of Chinese-speaking officers, many had been posted in Hong Kong, since naturally it was desired to employ them where their talents could be most immediately used. Apparently nobody foresaw that they would pass, after a few days, into captivity. The Army, for example in India, would be crying out bitterly against the famine of China experts, for the interrogation of prisoners, the reading of documents, or for the countless ways in which expertise in language is required in warfare.

THE PHILIPPINES

On the same day that they attacked Pearl Harbor, Japan had made a similar raid on Clark Field, the key to the defences of the Philippine Islands. This was an American possession which linked the United States with the imperial systems maintained by the European Powers. However, several years before the United States Government and key Congressmen had entertained serious doubts about whether or not the Islands were defensible or whether the Philippines should be granted 'Independence' merely in order to be 'neutralized'. Thus, effectively, the Philippines had been abandoned to their own devices rather than remaining a costly political and military encumbrance to the United States. As the risks from this process of estrangement mounted, leading Filipino politicians began to look elsewhere for defence guarantees, and the President of the Philippine Commonwealth, Manuel Quezon, sent feelers to the British Government in London offering to join the British Commonwealth and Empire in exchange for British protection. The British weighed up the risks involved and then secretly informed the Americans of what was afoot. By 1941, however, the American mood had changed and the United States was expected to defend it tenaciously. Although the real determination to hold fast in the Philippines came late in the day, the Philippine Commonwealth was not, like Hong Kong, regarded as expendable. With this attack, Japan launched upon the serious task of driving the white invader from the soil of Asia.

The Philippines are an island group off South-East Asia which for three hundred years had been the empire of Spain in this part of the world. They had passed into American possession – assisted in no small measure by a home-grown Filipino guerrilla rebellion against the Spanish crown – when the United States had defeated Spain in the Spanish-American War of 1898. It was a war which it was hard to justify: at first it seemed to show that the United States had given up its traditional stand against imperialism and was about to start on the acquisition of colonies. Its heart, however, was never in empire. No American literature had grown up around the Philippines; no class of Americans (except small groups of teachers, missionaries, West Point Army officers, businessmen, educators and planters) could claim to have the Philippines in their bones.

Thus it had been easy for Americans to compromise when they found that, among their new subject peoples, the Europeanized middle class of Manila was becoming inspired by the nationalism of the day. Americans had engendered no professional imperialists, in their adventure with ruling subject peoples. They could therefore readily conceive a constitution, which was a replica of the United States one, and could foresee that the Filipinos would make a success of this, and of governing their country without disaster.

By the time that Japan attacked, as a legacy of the period of doubts which Americans had held about the value of the Philippines in the past, the United States was already so well ahead with grooming the Philippines for liberation that all conceded that the Americans would not, after all,

115° E
120° E
125° E
20°N

8 Dec.
Batan

Luzon Strait

10 Dec.
Comiguin
11 Dec.
Aparri
PACIFIC
21 Dec.
Vigan
S.36
OCEAN
Lingayan
Gulf
San Fernando
LUZON
15°N
Ft Statsenberg
Clark Field
24 Dec.
Manila
Nielson Field
11 Dec.
Bataan
Nichols
Cavite
Field
Lamon Bay
Legaspi
San Bernardino
Strait
MINDORO
S.3900
South
SAMAR

China

PANAY
NEGROS
Leyte Gulf

Sea
USS HOUSTON
10°N
Palawan
8 Dec.

Sulu Sea
MINDANAO
Davao
Moro Gulf
17 Dec.
Jolo
Brunei
25 Dec.
20 Dec.
5°N
Tawitawi
Miri
Celebes Sea

Tarakan

BORNEO
THE JAPANESE INVASION OF
THE PHILIPPINE ISLANDS, DEC. 1941
☐   US operational airfields
➤   Japanese attacks December 1942
‒ ‒ ‒ Route of USS HOUSTON
500 km
14 Dec.
0   300 miles
Balikpapan Bay

renege on their promises. Japan did not find in it a representative of imperialism at its most stubborn. More than six years before it struck, the United States had already passed a law which set a timetable for Filipino emancipation. This envisaged, however, that there would be a treaty between itself and the Philippines, regulating their defence.

By this treaty, the United States was to keep a moderately powerful Air Force, stationed at Clark Field. The rather sketchy chain of airfields throughout the islands was to be at its disposal. The United States also maintained a weak garrison of soldiers. When the war began, the defences were out of date; in part that was yet another legacy of the ill-fated Washington Treaty System which had expired in 1936. The communications between the islands were especially poor. The native Filipino Army, which was being trained by the United States, was only half ready.

The Japanese bombed Clark Field some hours after they attacked Pearl Harbor. Reports of what was happening there had reached the Philippines by radio. On receipt of the news, the Air Force – thirty-five bombers and seventy-two fighters – was alerted and had taken to the air. But the Japanese attack was delayed by dense morning fog. At lunch-time nearly all the American planes were grounded. While they were being serviced, lined up, while the pilots were being fed, the Japanese struck. Nearly a hundred American aircraft were destroyed in the air or on the ground.

Thus the war in the Philippines began with recrimination over an unnecessary loss. The American habit of concentrating its aeroplanes in formations which made the perfect targets had before this caused anxiety. Before the War against Japan, Duff Cooper, who had been appointed a few weeks before as Resident Minister in the British Administration of Singapore, was horrified at seeing them parked wing by wing at Clark Field and had pointed out to the Americans what a temptation they might be to the Japanese. Lest the apparent alarm of this former First Lord of the Admiralty and ex-Minister of War be mistaken for a general British reaction, it must be said that the reports of British air attachés exuded confidence in what they saw as General Douglas MacArthur's strategical understanding of East Asian defence problems and the American's willingness to learn from Britain's experience regarding the handling and deployment of aircraft. On the whole, British visitors to MacArthur's domain came away feeling that the defence of the Philippines was being far better attended to than they had previously supposed. The loss sustained in the Philippines, when it occurred, was anyway nowhere near as fatal as that at Pearl Harbor. Obviously the disaster had no deep influence on what followed. But the disgrace and the material damage had a very discouraging effect.

The raid was followed up by a landing of the Japanese Army. It came from Formosa, and the troops had been embarked some days previously. At first there was doubt as to whether the Filipinos, under American command, would resist the Japanese armies, which proclaimed they were bringing freedom. But this doubt was quickly dispelled.

The command in the Philippines was in the hands of General MacArthur. He was thenceforward to play the most conspicuous part of any commander in the Pacific War. A rather older man than most of his contemporaries, a general with an outstanding record in the First World War, a former Chief of Staff of the United States Army, he had been loaned by the United States Government to the Filipino Service to organize the future armies of the free Philippines. He entered with enthusiasm on this task. His father had been the first military governor in the American rule of the island. The relation of trust between him as generous patron of the Filipinos, and the Filipinos as loyal and grateful clients, caught his imagination. He believed that he had the knack and principle to do what other western soldiers and administrators had failed to do: to win the attachment of an oriental people. He was enabled to stand to his own Government in the position of a semi-independent power rather than a subordinate servant, a relation which suited him much better than a more regular one.

At the time when the Japanese struck, he had completed six years of a planned ten-year period on this task, and the Filipino Army had been brought to a stage of fair competency. Its worst impediment had been the multitude of languages and dialects which were spoken by the soldiers, which made it difficult for them to be organized under a single command. In the months preceding the war, it was, as part of the rather belated American preparation against the Japanese threat, reincorporated in the US Army. But when the invasion came, the plans, such as they were, for the defence of the Philippines were sketchy and completely shattered by the events of Pearl Harbor. The American intentions had proceeded from the axiom that the United States Pacific Fleet and Asiatic squadron would be intact, and would, at least within months, be able to come to the rescue.

MacArthur quickly appreciated that he could not check the Japanese landings. He met them with a scheme which had something of surprise. He gathered together his force, and withdrew into the historic fortress of Corregidor, on an island in Manila Bay, and into the peninsula of Bataan, on the northern side of the bay. Corregidor was one of the famous strong points in the East. It had first been built by Spaniards in the early years of their rule in the seventeenth century, and was heavy with history. But, though extremely picturesque – like Cyprus in the wars against the Turks or like a Crusader's castle – it had had nothing done to it in modern times to make it suitable for modern war. On the other hand Bataan was more serviceable. It was a strip of country covered by jungle and had been prepared by MacArthur for its role by the installation of concealed factories, supply depots and hospitals. In these two centres MacArthur had more than 50,000 troops (of whom only 6,000 men were of the regular American Army). He planned to withstand a siege by a Japanese Army numbered about 200,000.

MacArthur was at first optimistic that he would be relieved. Apparently, for a senior officer of the US Army, he was singularly out of touch with the ways in which the US General Staff thought in time of emergency. The explanation is simply that MacArthur had left Washington years before under something of a cloud. His prima donna behaviour, his fondness for the field marshal's baton that his appointment in the Philippines had brought him, did nothing to endear him to the American military and political authorities in the United States. He reckoned in terms of a six months' siege, for which he had stored ammunition, though his supplies of food were far less satisfactory. He refused to admit that the United States had been robbed by Pearl Harbor of all powers to relieve and reinforce its protégé. The United States might have lost its battleship fleet, but a great deal could be contrived with cruisers, destroyers and submarines. These ships remained in existence: they might have been used in relation to the Philippines. Actually the American Navy fought actively for the next few years in the Pacific without receiving any large new ships. But the will and dash had departed temporarily from the Navy. MacArthur, isolated in beleaguered Corregidor, did not grasp this fact. He adapted tactics of strategic defence when they were in fact pointless because the defence, however resolute, could look for no eventual reward in the early restoration of communications with the United States.

When MacArthur in the end faced the facts as they were, he seriously planned that the entire Bataan garrison should attempt a break-out, and should then filter away to southern Luzon, where they should wage guerrilla warfare. But the scheme, transmitted to Washington, was coolly regarded, and was never sanctioned.

The Japanese began their serious offensive against MacArthur on 29 December, when they let loose their aircraft against Corregidor. Surprisingly, both Corregidor and Bataan held out. The Japanese met their first check of the war. The resistance, unexpectedly prolonged, began to upset the larger Japanese plan. They had calculated that their forces would be quickly disengaged from the Philippines, and would be free to

Subic
Bay

·3052

B

.3500
Manila
Bay

·Mt Natib
4422

Mt Silanganan

11 CORPS
6 Jan.

A

Moron
1 CORPS
6 Jan.

14°40'N

·1220

Y

Bagac
1 CORPS
26 Jan.

1920·

Orion

11 CORPS
26 Jan.

A

SOUTH

4193·
·3144

4220·
4660
·4305

Mariveles Mts

14°30'N

CHINA

Anyasia R.
Salaiim R.

Quinauan Pt
23 Jan.

·1026

Z

SEA

Longoskawayan Pt
23 Jan.

Mariveles

Corregidor I.

Caballo I.

14°20'N

BATAAN, JAN. 1942

Fil./American defence lines
Japanese thrusts

0   5   10 km
0   5 miles

120° 20'E   120° 30'E

move on to the belt of coral islands which lay along the northern coast of Australia. From these they would be able to prepare for the invasion of Australia, and the cutting-off of its communications with the United States.

Their delay continued. At one time the Japanese were so badly placed – stricken with dysentery, beri-beri and other tropical diseases – that the Americans and the Filipinos, had they been able to launch an offensive, could have retaken Manila. But this did not put hope into the Philippine President, Mañuel Quezon. On 8 February he sent a telegram to Washington saying that the Filipinos were nearly exhausted, and proposing that, as the United States had been unable to fulfil its pledges of protection, it should immediately declare the Philippines independent, the islands neutralized, and the American and Filipino armies disbanded. Quezon, though mercurial and vain, probably regarded himself as personally loyal to the United States (for lack of any satisfactory alternative). Now, however, he judged it possible for the Philippines to take refuge in neutrality.

At the end of January the Japanese troops were heavily reinforced. Two extra divisions were moved in, together with heavy artillery groups. The Japanese offensive continued. It was marked by none of the brilliant improvisation which the Japanese were showing in Malaya, but the geographical circumstances and the calibre of their enemy commanders were vastly different.

On 22 February, the President of the United States sent a telegram to MacArthur, ordering him to leave the Philippines and to go to Australia to organize the war from there. He went unwillingly, half under the delusion, as is plain from the documents of the time, that he would be put in command of a mighty Army with which he would return to the Philippines. From this time onwards he developed a monomania about return. 'I will return' were his last words in transferring his Filipino command to General Wainwright.

The United States Navy had kept four speedboats intact. MacArthur had sent Quezon, the Filipino President, to Australia in a submarine, but preferred to travel in a motor torpedo boat. On the night of 11 March this little flotilla ran the Japanese blockade. The sea is vast; it is surprising how many times a blockade has been successfully broken. The speedboat in which MacArthur sat found itself at one stage in the shadow of a Japanese battleship, but in the darkness it failed to be aware of its prize. Certainly Japan would have done well to have intercepted this general, who, once away, responded, as if to a magnet, to the powerful drawing force of Japan. But when he returned it would be with an army.

With MacArthur gone, the Filipinos carried on their resistance for a month longer, but the spirit passed out of it. It was one thing to resist under MacArthur's command, and another under General Jonathan Wainwright. Although Wainwright was a valiant soldier, the American and Filipino defenders were conscious that they had been left in the lurch. On 9 April Bataan surrendered; on 6 May Corregidor. The defenders, the majority of them of the Filipino Army, were still a large force, and, as Japan was in future to show, a Japanese garrison would have been disinclined to surrender. But resistance seemed pointless when the Filipinos heard on the American radio that the United States was putting its energies first into the German War; and that, for the time being, it had written off the Philippines. The Filipino Army had fought with distinction when there was still reason for fighting and, with that reason gone, was entitled by all the conventions of war to surrender.

The garrison of Bataan and Corregidor met with a terrible fate for having been the first to throw the Japanese timetable out of date. They were shepherded into captivity in a march which earned the grim name of 'the Death March'. Most of the victims passed into the hands of the Japanese military police, the Kempeitai.

The other American island possessions in the Pacific had been able to offer very much less resistance. Guam was taken on 10 December after a spirited defence. Wake Island held out gallantly, but succumbed on 23 December.

MALAYA

Two and a half years before Japan attacked Pearl Harbor it began its assault on Malaya. This was to be one of the principal theatres of the war, the scene of what was probably its most brilliant campaign, and of disaster and disgrace for Britain which was to bring about the twilight of the British in Asia.

Malaya was a peninsula inhabited by Malay sultanates. Great Britain had extended its colonial rule over them in the nineteenth century while leaving formally intact the machinery of the sultanates; and the territory, with the great importance of its rubber, had become a major part of the British colonial empire. The rich and peaceful country had attracted the Chinese, who became a very large minority.

Malaya had a special significance for all the Western Powers with territorial possessions in the East. At the southernmost tip of the peninsula is the island of Singapore, the size of the Isle of Wight. In the early 1920s, with the ending of the Anglo-Japanese Alliance, Britain had determined to build up Singapore into a great naval fortress, and to make Malaya the vital centre of British power in the Far East. Singapore was to be a dockyard, a naval base, barracks and communications centre. It was to safeguard the communications with Australia and was the base from which the British Navy would operate to ensure that the Indian Ocean continued to be a British lake. The British, having decided to rely in the Far East on steel and reinforced concrete instead of on diplomacy, spent £60 million, which at that time was a very large sum, on the fortification of the base. When finished, it was regarded as one of the four greatest sea-fortresses in the world (the others being Pearl Harbor, Malta and Gibraltar). As we have seen, it was also regarded by British defence planners as one of the two keystones of British imperial defence (the other being metropolitan Britain) upon whose security the very existence of the British Empire depended. It would have such obvious military might that, while it stood, it would provide a guarantee of the continuity of British power and thus it would be looked to by all other British territories in Asia; nor was it without significance for France and Holland for the security of their empires in South-East Asia.

The plan was carried through. Singapore was completed. It seemed to double-lock the gateway of the Empire so that it was useless for an unfriendly rival Power, such as Japan, to dream of forcing an entrance. Japan might have been expected to be daunted by such prestige, and to avoid a direct attack on such an invincible place. It was to prove, however, that the complacency and false security which were generated about Singapore told against drawing up plans for a modernized, flexible defence of the system in case it should ever be challenged.

Almost unbelievably, a totally false estimate of its strength became general. It proceeded from an erroneous view of military reality, which was to prove so eminently disastrous that it is inconceivable how it could ever have been formed, or that, once it had come to determine the fixed lines of policy, it was allowed to continue for nearly twenty years unchallenged. There were two delusions. The first was that, as Singapore lay at the southern extension of 200 miles of jungle, it was militarily impregnable to land attack. Without any serious tests having been made in time, and as it turned out without any basis in reason, this fortress was given the certificate of virtual invulnerability. It was taken for granted that no enemy could carry on tank warfare in the hinterland of rubber plantations, and it was thought to be impassable, a region exempt from the manoeuvres of modern armies. The actual arrangements for the defence of Singapore were made from this misreading of fact. The rubber jungle was left undefended by human arts. Efforts made by the chief engineer of Malay Command, Brigadier Ivan Simson, to erect fixed defences, blow up bridges and lay down minefields were resisted by General Arthur Percival, his commander, who regarded such steps as these – and the civil defence efforts which were also Simson's responsibility – as counterproductive and bad for the morale of British troops, local politicians and the native races of Malaya. From over-confidence, the garrison of Singapore was lamentably inadequate; the roads were poor; no network of airfields was made which would have been adequate for a great Air Force; no great Air Force had ever operated from the Malayan Peninsula.

The second fatal miscalculation was that, as Singapore was to be a naval base, it would be threatened only in a great naval war. Singapore was envisaged as the centre of a titanic naval struggle, with a large fleet occupying her to capacity. The eyes of the world would always be on her, and those eyes would always look seawards. All the guns of Singapore would point seawards also. It was prepared with the most modern artillery which money could buy; but the guns were never in a position to fire effectively at an adversary who came by land.

Alas, it was never to play its part in a great war of the seas; its guns necessarily remained silent, for they were not the mobile things of a hundred years before. They were built in concrete and could not in a matter of days or weeks be re-adapted to a new kind of war. The traversing mechanisms of electrically fired long-range guns of the period were fitted with stops to prevent their crews fouling control cables or damaging adjacent batteries and other installations by the effects of the blast cones of these devastating weapons. Nevertheless, in the final days of the siege at Singapore, one or two of the guns were modified so as to fire above Singapore town at the Japanese on the Malayan mainland. In any case, the effect of fifteen-inch A P (armour-piercing) naval shells on moist jungle was less than edifying. Had these guns been equipped with HE (high explosive) shells or proximity fuses, they would have wrought terrible carnage upon the Japanese. Money spent on Singapore was largely useless, for the same reason as was the treasure of France which had been squandered on the Maginot Line; they succeeded in deterring one form of attack, and greatly reduced the danger of a surprise attack, but the generals whose duty it was to integrate these magnificent fixed defences into an overall flexible response to invading forces elsewhere proved unequal to the challenge of war.

In the opening years of the war – before Japan suddenly made its nature real and alarming to them – British people living in Singapore had had time to digest how deadly was their peril. Most of them did not do so. The old myths bore them up. They were cheered by the belief that the British Navy, though it was away in other waters, had power to neutralize the Japanese. They could still see the apparent strength of Singapore, which they thought would house its Navy, and did not grasp its essential weakness.

Only a few British soldiers during this time saw the ominous cracks appearing. One was Colonel Stewart, the commanding officer of a battalion of the Argyll and Sutherland Highlanders, who refused to accept the conventions which govern the training of garrison troops. Day after day the soldiers under his command spent their time in jungle training. The Argylls were considered eccentric; but in the end, Colonel Stewart formed the view that Singapore was not in fact surrounded on the north and east by a vast and easily defensible belt of jungle. It was possible for an invading Army to use tanks in the jungle; and in a short time the Japanese Army, made formidable by all the instruments of modern war, would be at its doors. This was the uncomfortable message which he preached, but virtually nobody attended to him.

It happens that one of the Japanese officers concerned with preparing the Japanese offensive has left a full account of the processes involved (*Singapore – the Japanese Version*, by Colonel Tsuji Masanobu). It was conceived as a rescue operation to free the inhabitants from British imperialism. It was not planned years ahead, and in great detail, as was wrongly supposed by the British Government. The expedition was improvised, and planned on a shoestring. The serious preparation and advance studies began only eleven months before the actual attack, in January 1941, at the same time as Admiral Yamamoto set to work on the plans to attack Pearl Harbor, and had started with a monthly budget of no more than 20,000 yen (or less than £2,000). The initial planning was carried out in Formosa, which was then a firm part of the Japanese Empire, and it was rehearsed on Hainan Island, which had been annexed to the Japanese Empire in February 1939. The Japanese forces were able to use a mass of photographs and other data which its enthusiastic agents had been busy gathering, partly as a matter of habit and by voluntary initiative. Every town and village had had its Japanese businessmen, Japanese doctors and Japanese dentists, and these were now revealed as the advance guard of the invasion that was being launched; but it is surprising how sketchy was much of the information. It was discovered that for their coastal operation the Japanese had to rely upon the data furnished by a single master mariner, who had collected the facts for years in case they should come in useful.

The invasion did not begin with a surprise massive Japanese attack from the air, similar to that on Pearl Harbor and the Philippines. The war started with the transport of two divisions of Japanese soldiers from Indo-China, and the overcoming of the weak coastal defences in northern Malaya. At first, the Japanese were too distant from Singapore to make effective use of the air; today it is overlooked how comparatively limited the range of massive air operations still was. The Japanese landing in the north did not take the British by surprise. It had clearly been a possibility ever since the Japanese took Indo-China, and plans had been worked out, which were in fact forestalled by the Japanese, for a possible seizure of a part of southern Thailand, as a defensive move. The British were, however, outmanoeuvred by the speed and resiliency of the Japanese in moving from their bridgeheads to a lightning drive on the south.

In the first two days of the war the British commanders at Singapore disposed of two major warships, the *Prince of Wales* and the *Repulse*, which the Government at home, as the skies blackened in the days before Pearl Harbor, had been persuaded to detach from other operations and to spare for the East. These were a powerful reinforcement: with them, Singapore appeared to be about to play the part intended for it by British planning. In theory, at least, they would restore mobility to British arms. They were meant to insure the safety of Malaya, in case the Japanese struck out during the negotiations at Washington. The battleship and battle-cruiser would enable Britain to strike at great distances. With sea power, Britain could exercise what Bacon had described as its natural advantage in all its wars: to take as much or as little of the war as it desired.

Yet the voyage of these two ships was a perilous excursion into the unknown, and filled those who ordered it with great alarm. They moved northward from Singapore with the intention of disrupting the landing of the Japanese forces and their supplies. It was a sound objective and it might have altered the course of the war. They were moving against forces which they could not compute. The Japanese had a history of waiting for, and dealing with, naval units sent out from European waters to alter the balance of force in the East. Admiral Rozhdestvensky had sailed a fleet half-way round the world in 1905 to be destroyed at the battle of the Japan Sea. In like manner, the *Prince of Wales* and the *Repulse* were to be the victims, not it is true of a waiting Japanese Navy, but of the new Japanese Fleet Air Arm which sank the two warships on the second day of the war. The commander of the two capital ships, Admiral Tom Phillips, had been confident of air support from local R A F units, but, disgracefully, that support never materialized and this was, perhaps, the main cause for the disaster that occurred.

With these warships swept from the chess board, the Japanese advance

GUARDS DIVN
from Thailand

5th DIVN, MAIN STRENGTH 8 DEC.

18th DIVN, MAIN STRENGTH
23 JAN.

5th DIVN,
ANDO DETACHMENT,
8 DEC.

THE MALAYAN
CAMPAIGN, 25th ARMY
DEC. 1941 — FEB. 1942

Singora

Patani

18th DIVN, KOBA
DETACHMENT 28 DEC.

500 km

300 miles

Jitra
12 DEC.

Alor Star

18th DIVN, TAKUMI
DETACHMENT
8 DEC.

Kota Bharu

Gurun

PENANG
19 DEC.

Gong Kedah

C. Trengganu

South

China

Sea

Taiping

Kuala Kangsar

Ipoh

Kampar
3 DEC. — 2 JAN.

Kelantan

Perak

Telok Anson

Slim River

Tanjong Malim

TAKUMI DETACHMENT

Kuantan
31 DEC. — 3 JAN.

Pahang

Selangor

Kuala Lumpur

Kajang

KOBA DETACHMENT

Port Swettenham

Gemas
15 — 19 JAN.

Endau

Mersing
26 JAN.

Malacca

Muar

SUMATRA

Bakri
19 — 20 JAN.

SAEKI DET.

Kluang

Batu Pahat

Johore Bahru

Singapore

18th
DIVN

Skudai

5th
DIVN

GUARDS DIVN

Imperial
Palace

Naval Base

NIGHT
7

Johore Bahru

28th
INDIAN BGDE

27th AUSTRALIAN
BGDE

55th
BGDE

Ubin I.

THE CAPTURE OF
SINGAPORE, FEB. 1942

British Forces:

NIGHT 8

22nd
AUST.
BGDE

Sembawang
Airfield

Seletar
Airfield

54th
BGDE

Artillery

Airfield

Counter Attacks

Mandai
Village

NIGHT
10

EVNG
15

Changi

22nd MALAYA BGDE

Japanese Forces:

Tengah
Airfield
EVNG 9

Bukit Timah
EVNG 11 &
NIGHT, 8—9

EVNG
15

FORTRESS
TROOPS

Artillery

Headquarters

EVNG 11

EVNG 15

Kallang Airfield

City of
Singapore

Divisional Areas

Keppel Harbour

10 km

5 miles

down the peninsula to Singapore could go forward unimpeded. Troops came in by transport from Indo-China, and nothing availed to stop them; more alarmingly, they were accompanied by tanks, which against forecasts, overcame the natural barriers of the jungle. They advanced south with surprising speed. A clear picture of the Japanese strategy began to show itself. The British Army, heavily burdened with its impedimenta, untrained for jungle warfare, resisted as hard as it could by throwing up positions across the roads. Meeting their challenge, the Japanese forsook the main road, advanced through the allegedly impenetrable jungle, and took the British in the rear. The jungle betrayed the British; the jungle which had been in their possession for eighty years and whose possibilities for war they had never learned. By these means, repeated so often that they became monotonous, the Japanese came on, and within six weeks were within sight of Singapore.

The achievement of the Japanese has been glossed over. It was remarkable. The Japanese Army had until now acquired its battle experience in China, a terrain vastly different from Malaya: and its battle training had been almost exclusively the steppe country of Manchuria. Its performance in the tropics showed an adaptability and resourcefulness in the Japanese officers, and endurance by the Japanese soldiers, which had been insufficiently recognized. Though the imaginative qualities of the Japanese Army were not afterwards always apparent, they shone in this campaign.

The manner of fighting by the Japanese surprised their antagonists. They showed none of the preference for long-range combat, such as most of the other civilized combatants exhibited. They seemed to exult in struggle body to body. They produced gestures of defiance and glee and also of fear which, by most other soldiers, were regarded as childish. A skirmish was accompanied by grunts, gasps and blood-curdling yells. Later, when Japanese films became popular in the West, it was seen that the Japanese soldier had fought very much as Japanese actors traditionally represented him as doing. It made him a surprising and alarming adversary.

As the Japanese assault on Malaya intensified, it was noticed that the Japanese had a string of successes in air raids upon British aircraft. Time and again the British were caught on the ground. Japan's aircraft appeared in great force just when the British were getting ready to take to the air. Finally one reason for this striking good fortune of the Japanese came to light. An officer in the R A F, a citizen of southern Ireland, was pursuing his country's feud of twenty years back with the British Government, and was detected signalling to the Japanese. This affair was kept secret. It accounted for an unfortunate part of the air losses in the early stages of the campaign.

*

In the confused ill-temper of the retreat – and it was always retreat, without one solid success to restore self-respect – there was recrimination between the British commanders, and the commander of the large force of Australians which had been a part of the Allied garrison and who had shared in the defence. It was reflected in the lower ranks. Many of the Australians had been stationed in the Middle East before they fought the Japanese. As this was largely a time of defeat they had formed a disgruntled view of British competence. Their transfer back to the defence of the region where Australian interests were more vitally at stake had been agreed to with a rather ill grace by Churchill; this put the Australians in the mood to be touchy partners. By ill fortune they were under a general, Gordon Bennett, who, though a rather dashing soldier, had in addition qualities which hardly endeared him to the usual type of British officers. He was not of a modest nature, he did not minimize any affronts shown to him, he did not agree with those people who saw virtue in silence.

To the necessary disgraces which afflicted the beaten Army, there was thus added the scandal of a dangerous difference of opinion between England and one of the Dominions, which at bottom had always been loyal to it, and whose feelings were the more ruffled because they had been so warm. The quarrel threatened to widen out into a dispute which uncovered a diversity in war aims. Australia was left with the feeling that it had been betrayed. Its interests were treated as of slight concern. It seemed that England would unfeelingly sacrifice Australian soldiers for its own advantage. It was the type of ill-feeling which sooner or later was bound to cloud the cooperation of England and the Dominions. A considerable effort was needed to overcome the bitterness: Britain was too occupied for the diplomacy needed. Singapore, which was becoming a curse to the Empire which it had been called into being to serve, merely added to its demerits that, in the turmoil of this period, it caused London and Canberra to be for some weeks estranged.

In the long retreat through Malaya, the British had suffered much more than a great military reverse. For the first time their administrative system in oriental countries had been exposed, and was reduced to ridicule. They, the masters of political craft in conciliating the oriental, found that they had used up all their reserves of prestige, and had no comfort anywhere. In Penang, in Kuala Lumpur, in all the centres of administration, the events were disastrous. The institutions built up over decades, the loyalties so laboriously produced, the habits which the British had so complacently regarded as fixed and permanent – all were swept away. The British were not regarded with fear or hatred: had that been so, they would not have been so quickly written off. Their day was regarded as closed. The local Malay population (not the Chinese), giving a lead to other colonial communities of the Empire, regarded it as politic to transfer their loyalties as quickly as possible to the Japanese.

When the backward movement of the British began, it was supposed by home public opinion that, with the example of a scorched earth policy in Russia before them, arrangements would be made for the Japanese to meet with a similar bleak reception. But in almost all cases, the Government lacked the nerve to demand the sacrifice from the local people, or, more rarely, the demand was made, generally too late in the day, and the people refused to cooperate. The British efforts to build up a resistance behind the rear of the Japanese Army, and to create an adequate spying and Intelligence system were at first unsuccessful. Later on in the war, when the Japanese had made themselves detested, SOE and other similar organizations were to begin to function effectively: but this was to be in the future.

It must not be supposed that the psychological atmosphere changed abruptly to contempt or hostility towards the British. There were many warm and compassionate acts of loyalty and friendship by the Malays and the very mixed population of this cosmopolitan peninsula. The British, in defeat and disillusion, often found unexpected shelter.

How news of great and dramatic events transmits itself in Asia, by what means it travels to remote valleys and distant villages, is not clear. At this time there were very few radio sets outside the larger towns. But in these months a great sensation was felt throughout Asia. The British Empire was dying. It had been overturned in Malaya, and was found to have rotten roots. Soon it would be treated in the same way in the other countries, and in all parts of Asia where the union flag still flew, Britain never recovered from the deplorable events of these few weeks. The happenings in one small section of its Empire were enough to destroy its prestige everywhere: and the life and soul of the British Empire had consisted of prestige, which is almost indistinguishable from the oriental concept of 'Face'.

While Singapore was in its death throes, the British committed one more egregious mistake. Large reinforcements of British troops, complete with equipment, had been spared from the war in Europe and ordered to Malaya. These arrived off Singapore when the siege of the fortress was about to begin. With remarkable folly, and in the belief that there would be a final effort to redeem the fortress by undertaking a siege, they were disembarked instead of sailing away to India or Burma where they were urgently needed, as quickly as they could. These troops, with all their artillery and stores, were put ashore, never to fire a shot, and were to enter on the long martyrdom of Japanese imprisonment.

On 31 January 1942, the British and Commonwealth forces, defeated, bewildered and demoralized, re-entered Singapore. Their rear-guard was led across the causeway which connected Singapore with Johore by the remnants of the pipe band of the Argylls.

The final defence lasted fifteen days. Singapore surrendered on 15 February. It gave in because its defences crumbled; because its water supply passed out of its control; because the Japanese, again falsifying expectation, managed to infiltrate the island's defences at all points, and, within a week of crossing, were seen to be everywhere; because the troops were disorganized, and no pattern of defence established itself; because it was clear that the civilian population in the city had been paralysed and most of it, lacking training or proper organization, did not commit itself to self-defence; because the enemy, which had penned them up in the fortress, had swollen in their imagination to such a size by a unique series of triumphs that further resistance was not really thinkable. He had sunk two battleships which the English had naïvely supposed would have over-awed him; at Pearl Harbor he had struck away the Navy that would have made the Americans an effective ally; he had demonstrated that the jungle, that was feared by all other armies, could be treated as the home of the Japanese, from which Japan could draw strength. When this Japanese Army began to follow the British into Singapore, and to infiltrate over the island, the British recognized that the battle for South-East Asia had gone against them. By a local decision the fact was recognized: and Sing-apore was Japan's.

Yet it remained true that the Army in Singapore was twice as large as the besieging force, and, in theory at least, a prolonged resistance would have been possible. Even the fact of the non-existence of prepared defences did not cancel out the fact of the great British superiority in manpower. There have been famous sieges in history that have been carried on long enough to embarrass the besiegers and which have been begun in circum-stances as disastrous as those in Singapore. Exactly a year later, Singapore was to be followed in the news interest of the world by Stalingrad, and its defenders were not moved by the civilized sentiments of those who had to make the decision at Singapore. It is true that the defenders, unlike those of Stalingrad, could not have cut their way out to safety: but, in theory at least, they could have put up a notable resistance. The defeat was not gilded by any valiant enterprise, such as the rescue of the British troops at Dunkirk, which in after days made Dunkirk a stirring myth, instead of one of the worst reverses to British arms on the continent. In fact it became known later that General Yamashita Tomoyuki, the rather eccentric commander of the Japanese, had outrun his supplies. He would have been in no position to support the troops which he had filtered through to the island; they must have fallen back if the garrison had made the determined counter-attack of which it was capable. Thus, to other humiliations, the British added that of being bluffed.

To one man, the decision was particularly unwelcome, to the British Prime Minister. It is a little hard to say how at any one moment the events of the war in the Far East affected him. On the whole they were always secondary to affairs in Europe. It would seem that throughout the brilliant first hundred days of Japan he never succeeded in getting a grip of what was happening. Before the Japanese attack, he had continually underrated the chances of Japanese intervention. He did not equal the grasp which he had on the war in the Middle East. His speeches and his writings about it have a faint note of unreality, of a theatre of war where his views are not translated into action. The impression is dreamlike, of playing with vast conceptions which are fatally unrelated to fact; there is the occasional tumble into an abyss, which he must have foreseen but could not be reconciled to. Lieutenant-General Arthur Percival's decision to surrender at Singapore had been approved by General Sir Archibald Wavell, who only two days before, had ordered the landing of the Eighteenth Australian Division at Singapore against the advice of Auchinleck. Percival, the man on the spot after all, evidently convinced Wavell, who paid him a flying visit on 10–11 February, that the battle was lost. Percival took the view that the soldiers had done all that could be expected of them, and that further resistance would have been a pointless waste of life. Wavell went off to Java after trying to salvage what he could from the disaster. In Churchill's distrust of Wavell, which was to become so painfully obvious, perhaps there was an element of resentment for his part in the capitulation.

Churchill's speeches at this juncture are very curious. They are the comment of a detached observer rather than of a committed politician who had to explain the disaster which had befallen one of his projects. The British had surrendered Singapore: that was the bare fact, which people in Britain must stomach, and which they could not be expected to dwell on with satisfaction.

There departed into Japanese captivity a large British force and most of the civilian staff who had passed their lifetime in the administration of Malaya. They had little further part to play in the war, though the suffering of the prisoners was very great and was periodically used by the

British Ministry of Information to stir up public effort, and to keep the people resolute on their liberation. Given the chance to resist, these same prisoners, many of whom died before they could be released, might have preferred to be sacrificed in making the end of Singapore a little more creditable than it was.

The Japanese rejoiced, and not without cause. They looked almost incredulously at the size of their forces, and what they had achieved against much larger British forces. Usually the attacking force has to be considerably greater than the defenders if it is to have any chance of success; in the Malaya campaign this was reversed. The Japanese losses had been extravagantly small. From the time of their first landing to their occupying the Johore causeway and beginning the assault on Singapore their casualties were, according to Japanese official information which need not in this case be disbelieved, 1,793 killed and 2,772 wounded. They had deployed a force at Singapore not greater than 35,000 men, leaving another 35,000 or so men up country in Malaya. From information afterwards obtained, they found that the defending force numbered 85,000 out of an original strength of 139,000 British, Australian, Indian and local volunteer forces. In the actual assault on Singapore they lost a further 1,714 men killed, and 3,378 wounded. The Japanese claim that not a single Japanese soldier was captured. Certainly it would appear that none of those who did, lived to tell the tale: at least five wounded Japanese prisoners were among those murdered by rampaging Japanese troops at the Alexandra Hospital in Singapore following the British surrender. The myth has grown up that the Japanese troops were helped by having a corps of men trained in Malayan affairs. This is quite false. The number of Malayan experts in Japanese service was less than ten.

During 1940 and 1941 Germany had discussed with the Japanese from time to time the possibility of an attack on Singapore. But the German estimate was that the initial campaign would last one and a half years and would need five and a half divisions. Actually Japan required fifty-five days and only two divisions. At the outset of the campaign, Yamashita had been offered a third division but had declined it. His employment of the forces he had, and their logistical support, was masterful.

Japanese publications since the war have shown a high, rather theatrical morale among Japanese troops. The telegrams are still extant which Japanese generals sent to one another; their style is extremely patriotic, conventionally moralistic, reasonably free of the rivalries between officers and between services which were so common later in the war. One of the ceremonial acts which the Japanese performed after their victory was to build a tower which was dedicated to holding Buddhist requiem masses for the British killed in the campaign.

The Japanese, perhaps because they had taken Singapore with such an inadequate force, established there an occupation régime which governed it with extreme strictness, and rather purposeless brutality. They felt uneasy. Soon reports began to circulate of extraordinary Japanese measures against any suspected organization. Singapore was principally inhabited by Chinese, and the Kuomintang had used its citizens to extract funds for the Chinese Government. They were determined to stop this. The Chinese, in general, were irreconcilable; some had the reputation of being extremely radical in politics, which Japan also feared. The existence, in a peculiarly ramifying form, of the Chinese secret society, was another thing which provoked them. So, from the earliest days of their triumph, ugly tales of police terror and torture were mingled with a great victory. In the first days of the occupation of the city, they compiled a list of hundreds of Chinese and arrested them *en masse*. The beaches near the centre of the city became execution grounds by night where the *Kenpeitai* – the Japanese military police – took their preventive action. Altogether more than 5,000 Chinese were massacred at Singapore by the Japanese as a matter of policy in those few days.

BORNEO

With the sinking of the *Prince of Wales* and *Repulse*, the last obstacle was removed from the advance of the Japanese into Borneo. This thinly inhabited island, the third largest in the world, at 260,000 square miles the size of Texas and two and a half times the area of the United Kingdom, holds a central position from which it is possible to dominate the sea lanes to Singapore and to threaten Java, Sumatra, the Celebes, Malaya, Indo-China and the southern Philippines. It was, indeed, the security of Borneo that led Britain to consider, however briefly, proposals that emanated from President Quezon of the American Commonwealth of the Philippines in the mid-thirties for Britain to take possession of the Philippines in order to guarantee its defence against Japan in the event of an American withdrawal. Now, as dawn broke on 13 December, three days after the extinction of British naval power in the East, an absurdly small force of three destroyers, a sub chaser and ten transport vessels set sail from Camranh Bay in French Indo-China and put out to sea, bound for Borneo. Shortly afterwards, it was reinforced by a more substantial force of three cruisers, a further pair of destroyers and a solitary seaplane tender. The operation was regarded as a necessary adjunct to the Malayan campaign. With British forces fully occupied in the defence of Malaya, the Japanese were quick to exploit their opportunities. It was, by all accounts, a relatively laid-back invasion. Thanks to the Dutch, two Japanese destroyers and two transports were sunk and a further three other transports were damaged. The Anglo-Dutch oil denial schemes in Miri and elsewhere operated relatively smoothly. Nevertheless, the outcome of the campaign was never in doubt: the bulk of the British defence forces fled across the border into the Netherlands East Indies and on 19 January the remaining British forces on Borneo surrendered.

BURMA

In Burma, the history of the Malayan campaign repeated itself. The Japanese Army invaded it on 11 December from Thailand.

Burma, one of the smaller countries of the British Empire, had had, in the half century of its membership, a comparatively uneventful history. Now it became lurid in the extreme. In the minds of most English people, Burma became known, no longer as an oriental paradise inhabited by a merry, picturesque people, but as a fated, evil country, the arena – from no fault of its own, it is true – for some of the most horrible fighting of the war. It was not simply to flare into prominence by the brief experience of being overrun. It was to remain a contested land until the end of the war.

Burma had formerly been attached to India. It had been annexed to it as the result of three wars in the nineteenth century. It was an act of convenience for Britain; by no shadow of claims could it be regarded as an Indian land. Its majority people, the Burmese, were one of the Asian peoples with the clearest national consciousness; their economy was not inevitably linked with the Indian; their language and script had only a distant connection with Sanskrit; their religion, to which they were peculiarly devoted, was the Hinayana form of Buddhism, which ultimately derived from India, but which had practically died out there. Hinduism, which Buddhism had once rivalled in India, had revived there powerfully, and had overtaken Buddhism in the sub-continent. But in neighbouring Burma, Buddhism had no competitors, and flourished mightily. This rendered Burmese culture different from Indian.

The unnatural union of Burma with India was resented by the Burmese. Their desire for freedom was two-fold, freedom from Britain and freedom from India. This second freedom they won at the time of the great political recasting inaugurated by the Government of India Act of 1935. It was perceived that to continue to enforce the unity of the two countries would impose an unnecessary strain on the problematical machinery of government devised for India. Burma was allowed to settle its own destiny, and the Burmese legislature voted to go its own way. It had a constitution which half met Burma's growing demand for complete freedom. Its Government had the same liberties as a provincial government in India under the Act of 1935. But what in India were to be the federal powers of government were in Burma controlled by the British.

In the days of the union between India and Burma, the British had neglected to build up communications between the two countries. A railway was planned, chiefly for military reasons, but was never made. Its absence was to have a powerful effect on the shape of the fighting now to break out. Shipping interests, powerful with the Government, saw in it a threat to their monopoly of traffic with Rangoon, and successfully opposed the scheme.

In the years just before the war, political life developed rapidly. The professional and commercial classes were organized in orthodox political parties, which were willing to pursue their national aims through non-revolutionary means and within the framework of the institutions already conceded. But the desire for independence was greater, perhaps, than it was in India, though it was not taken as seriously. Moreover there were revolutionary parties, notably the Thakins, which meant the party of the 'masters' or 'gentlemen', which were ready to seek any aid, and do any-thing, which would bring about the end of British rule. These parties, which stirred up political consciousness in Burma, had a growing clientèle among students, and among people who had no limiting restrictions placed on their political activity by economic considerations.

Japan found the political situation in Burma more suited to its inter-vention than in any other country. Moreover Burma, through the exist-ence of the Burma Road, had become a major preoccupation of Japanese strategic plans.

Japan had prepared its action in Burma for several years, and more carefully than in most other centres. It had sent there a naval officer who, disguised as a trader, had made the first contact with Burmese politicians. The results were so promising that a Japanese consul was instructed to build up a pro-Japanese network. This, however, had brought the Japanese Ministry of Foreign Affairs into the picture. Fearful of angering the British unnecessarily, the Ministry demanded extreme caution.

Progress came, not from persons engaged in this part of the enterprise, but from the coming to Burma of a Japanese Army officer, Colonel Suzuki Keiji, who was a natural genius at all kinds of espionage and subversion. He modelled himself on Lawrence of Arabia. Until 1939 he had had a career as a regular combat officer; it ended with Suzuki under a somewhat mysterious cloud, brought about by an incident in 1939 in the war with China. Thenceforward he was a spy. He chose Burma as his field of activity, and he was as little subjected to control in what he did there as was Doihara, a much more celebrated agent and planner of subversive action in Manchuria and China. Officers like him were given much latitude by Japan. They might create a situation which the Japanese Army would be free, when the time came, to manipulate or to ignore, as circumstances decided.

Disguised as a mild-mannered newspaper reporter for the *Yomiuri Shinbun*, Suzuki explored Burma for a year and a half, concentrating upon gaining an understanding of its political and ethnic divisions. He decided that the Thakins offered promising material with which to work. He was a curious man; he was genuinely interested in promoting the movements of Asian peoples to be free; he took seriously the claims of Japanese propaganda that Japan supported all movements for independence; he was regarded with suspicion and as a nuisance by the more orthodox Japanese, who had no intention of conquering large parts of Asia, and simply transferring them to native hands. In Japanese service, he was advancing views and actions which were not at all favoured. He has been described as a rebel by temperament, a conformist by upbringing. His conversation fascinated the Burmese with whom he came into contact. He would tell them to insist on being independent. If, after the Japanese conquered their country, they refused to grant independence, the Burmese ought to shoot back.

Suzuki and his handful of associates set themselves to form the nucleus of a Burmese independent Army, which could be extended as soon as a Japanese Army crossed the borders. He calculated that a Burmese force would prove a valuable auxiliary for bringing about the discomfiture of the British, whether in harrying them politically, in forming a link with the Burmese population, or in straightforward military operations. In 1940 he began to select likely young revolutionaries from the class of political adventurers and arranged for thirty of them to be sent over to Formosa for military training in Japanese schools. The thirty Thakins received this education partly in Formosa, partly in Hainan Island; Suzuki had them well grounded, by strict Japanese discipline, in combat tactics, in methods of civilian cooperation with the Japanese Army, and in all ancillary methods. It is clear that he had some difficulty in getting these young men accepted in the various training camps, for he acted as a lone wolf, and had not fully emerged from the disaster which had temporarily blocked his military career. The Thakins, for their part, objected to the strenuous quality of their training, and contemplated desertion. They had actually got control of a small sailing ship with which they proposed to sail for home. On their fate depended much of the modern history of Burma. The accident of who was chosen among the thirty Thakins, the founder members of the Burma Independence Army, governed the course of Burmese politics down to the present day. Because of personality difficulties, the Thakins tended to fall into factional groups, which were reflected for long after, quite irrationally, in Burmese politics.

Suzuki, together with a staff of adventurous Japanese who were looked at rather askance by the Japanese Army, transported his thirty Thakins to join the two divisions of Japanese troops waiting to invade Burma. By a shrewd move to catch the Burmese imagination, he gave each of the Thakins a new name from Burmese folklore, which was peculiarly rich in such things. He devised ceremonial oaths to link them together. And he revived the old Burmese legend that they had discovered ancient charms which brought them invulnerability. This, which was traditionally affected by Burmese insurrectionists, and had been the sustaining weapon of the peasant leader, Saya Sen, in a rebellion in 1930, was obstinately believed by the Burmese populace. It was to support the Thakins handsomely. The atmosphere in their camp was that of a boy scout jamboree, the same vague high-mindedness, the same enjoyment in devising ruses, rather the same kind of humour. The Thakins, half in terrified awe of Suzuki, half in naïve enthusiasm for him, admired the way he genuinely fought for their interests with his orthodox Japanese colleagues.

This Japanese dealing with Burmese politicians was to have interesting consequences as the history of Burma unfolded. But, in the actual conquest, the principal agent was the Japanese Army. This fought the battles, and defeated the British. The British were embarrassed by the Burma Independence Army, but it only contributed marginally to their downfall. They complained of the treachery of the population, the clamour against them by the Pongyis (Burmese monks), the betrayal of their movements to the Japanese, and the false Intelligence often given to the Army by the villagers. For all these things, the Burma Independence Army, playing the part of aide to the Japanese, was partly responsible. Their experience permanently soured the British troops, and gave Burma a bad reputation as a country to fight in. Anything to do with Burma was thought to be unlucky, and the country filled the Army with great apprehension.

However, for their rout, the British had to blame the Japanese directly. They had invaded at the start with two divisions with which they overran the south and took Rangoon, the capital. As in Malaya, the British had placed their confidence in the natural obstacles to troop movements in the rugged, jungle country of the border. Again it had become axiomatic that tanks could not penetrate this, and again the fact had not been tested. They quickly found out that they had deceived themselves. Unlike Malaya, the country was held by too few troops, badly trained, with a defective Air Force. From the start, the British were too unevenly matched to have any chance of holding the Japanese advance. After Singapore fell, the Japanese were reinforced by another two divisions, which had been campaigning there, and they advanced to the north, pushing back the British before them.

The British accepted the offer of Chiang Kai-shek to send a Chinese Army to assist in the defence. They did so reluctantly because, through awareness of maps which were being published in Chungking, they had reason to suspect that Chiang had designs on the Burma frontier, and that, once they were in, the Chinese troops would be hard to evict. Japan, however, prevented this danger by driving them back into China. On the borderland some of the Chinese were broken up, and also suffered a great defeat.

By the end of April, the British were expelled from the country. They were pushed right out of Burma. Eventually the greater part of their forces escaped into India, marching out through the trackless jungle land which intervened between Burma and India. Only a part of the far north remained out of Japanese hands. It was inhabited by Chins and Kachins with whom British rule was unfamiliarly popular, being, like all British administration of the jungle fringes of their Empire, so light as hardly to be noticed. This territory was held by a body of irregular troops, recruited chiefly from the Chins, which was raised by British anthropologists. The exploits of this force, the intelligence and devotion of the Chin people, are one of the subjects which has escaped narration.

The same incidents marked the Japanese advance as had happened in Malaya. The civil government collapsed. It showed itself again and again to be extremely incompetent, its officers were lazy, its resolution was contemptible, its planning was certain to be based on faulty information, its complacency was unlimited. Its poor showing did not come altogether as a surprise. Before the war, the British administration in Burma had been notorious for delays and muddle. When it was put to the test, it perished with the same sense of scandal as the administration in Malaya. The machine of government had been allowed to rust, and its levers broke in the hand when pulled. It was unfortunate because the British could not rely upon any machine of popular government to provide a link with the people, or to rouse any enthusiasm on the Government

THE CHINA–BURMA–INDIA THEATRE 1942-5

DEVELOPING LINES OF COMMUNICATION TO NORTH-EAST FRONTIER OF INDIA AND BURMA 1944-5

- ■ Allweather RAF/USAAF airfields
- ○ Fairweather RAF/USAAF airfields
- ┼┼┼ Railways   ┼┼┼ Narrow gauge
- ─── Roads
- ─── 4" pipeline   ----- 6" pipeline

```
0        100        200        300 km
0             100            200 miles
```

LINES OF COMMUNICATION IN NORTHERN INDIA AND BURMA 1942

- ┼┼┼ Railways
- ━━ Barge routes
- ===== Proposed Ledo road

```
0        500        1000        1500 km
0              500             1000 miles
```

Bay of
Bengal

3 Jan.

Akyab

Myebon

12
Jan.

21
Jan.

Kyaukpyu

25 Jan.

Kamree I.

Cheduba I.

330 miles

160 miles

260 miles

380 miles

460 miles

➤ British Seaborne
Assaults

side for the war. Shortly before the start of the war, the Prime Minister of Burma, U Saw, who had been on a visit to London, was detected while returning home in making contacts with the Japanese. He was arrested and interned in the Seychelles, but although U Saw was made harmless, the episode did little good to the British sense of security, and brought little change among the politicians who replaced him. (U Saw, a turbulent figure, was the powerful opposition leader in post-war Burma. He came to world notoriety in 1947, when he organized the assassination of U Aung San and half the Burmese Cabinet. For this he was hanged.)

The growth of the Burma Independence Army took place as Suzuki had foreseen. By the time that they were able to parade in liberated Rangoon, they numbered 5,000 men, and claimed to number 10,000. Their appeal had been great. But their methods of recruitment were deplorable. The Burmese villages, partly because of the peculiarly rapid tendency of the Burmese to resort to violence, had always had a higher proportion of criminal types than was usual in the East. As the Burma Independence Army advanced through the country it proved to be irresistibly attractive to this sort of recruit. An armed force, with licence to rob and pillage, provided the ideal shelter behind which it was possible to hold the whole country to ransom. The Army spread a reign of terror behind the Japanese advance. Its original Thakin leaders found that the control of their troops was passing out of their hands. For seventy-five years Burma had experienced deep and unfamiliar peace in its rural life. The exploits of the Burma Independence Army abruptly destroyed this peace, and, to Burma's cost, it was to prove impossible to restore peace in this or the next generation.

The population of Burma consisted of a Burmese majority, and many non-Burmese people, organized with different customs and religions. Under the long British peace, these had relaxed their suspicions; the different peoples had mellowed, and their government had seemed easy. But the exploits of the Burma Independence Army stirred up the feeling of the Burmese that they ought by right to be dominant, and raised a consequent feeling among the minorities of great insecurity. In panic, the minorities organized for self-protection: where a minority possessed the remains of tribal life, its institutions were rapidly brought into play. In no time, civil war was provoked and was spreading, especially between the Burmese and the Karens, the Burmese and the very large Indian minority, and the Burmese and the hill people, the Kachins. As a result, there took place a terrified mass migration to India, and it is estimated that India, in the midst of war, had to receive half a million refugees. For

every refugee to cross the Indian frontier, there were several others who
starved and died on the way.

The Japanese became aware of the chaos which was being provoked.
Having driven out the British from the whole country, except for a comparatively small corner which was inhabited by Chins, they were looked to by
the law-abiding part of the population as the only power able to secure
basic order in the country. They had been manoeuvred by Suzuki into
giving countenance to Burmese revolution, but it had served its term, and
they had really no sympathy with its explosive purposes. Japan, whatever
its propaganda might declare, was never a revolutionary power, and generally was on the side of property and privilege. In the middle of June it
applied itself to the problem of providing a Government for the country.
It was not willing to proclaim Burma's independence, but established a
provisional Government, made up of politicians of the orthodox parties.
The Burmese Cabinet could only rule the country through the civil service
structure of the British, and this the Japanese sought to preserve. Burmese
civil servants were promoted to take the place of British officials.

Stability, however, could not be expected as long as the Burma Independence Army was allowed to roam the country, doing its will by sheer force.
The decision was therefore arrived at to suppress the Army. Colonel
Suzuki was to return home to Japan. He sought to stay, claiming that as
he held a commission for what he had had done from Prince Kan'in
Kotohiko, who had been Chief of the Imperial General Staff until 1940,
his orders had therefore come directly from the imperial house, of which
Prince Kan'in was a member. Suzuki asserted that this freed him from
control by the Japanese Army. It was a variant of an old theme tune
played by generations of swashbuckling Japanese military officers, who
trumpeted the doctrine of their superior allegiance to the Emperor as a
means of sidestepping restraints imposed on them by their military commanders. But Suzuki argued in vain. In place of the Burma Independence
Army, a new force was raised, much more regular in its structure, more
firmly under the control of the new Government.

This was a natural, merely prudent step of the Japanese Government. It
was a decision which any responsible government was bound to take: the
Burma Independence Army had stirred up so much feeling that any
orderly administration was really impossible so long as it persisted. But
the apparent repudiation of Burmese revolutionary nationalism by the
Japanese was held by nationalists all over Asia to be difficult to square
with Japanese propaganda claims; the more so since the Japanese were at
first unwilling to satisfy the Burmese with any talk of independence. In
Burma it caused the start of a long-drawn-out quarrel between the

THE BATTLE OF THE JAVA SEA

FIRST PHASE 27 FEBRUARY 1942
1525 – 1650 hrs

SECOND PHASE 27 FEBRUARY 1942
1650 – 1720 hrs

THIRD PHASE 27 FEBRUARY 1942
1720 – 1750 hrs

Japanese and Burmese nationalism, which was to play a part in the Japanese downfall at the end of the war.

THE NETHERLANDS EAST INDIES

The fate of the Dutch Empire was the same. Because of oil, the territory was especially attractive to Japan. The first Japanese landing in Indonesia had taken place on 6 January. On 6 March, Batavia, its capital, fell. A large-scale naval battle had been fought between 27 and 29 February and resulted in the destruction of five Dutch cruisers, and of the few British cruisers which were still afloat in these waters. By April the fighting was at an end.

The experience of the Dutch was generally similar to that of the British. They had a considerable Army in Indonesia; 98,000 men surrendered, almost without fighting, and were interned. Apparently the Dutch could not rely sufficiently on their Indonesian troops to risk combat. A feature of Dutch colonialism was the far greater number of Dutch residents in their colonial territories. The number of civilian internees was therefore greater.

The impressions formed by the Dutch of the victorious Japanese Army were interesting, since they come from people who formerly had less to do with the Japanese than the British or Chinese. Their first feeling was one of unwilling admiration. The Japanese marched in, in perfect discipline. For whatever reasons, the disorders of the Japanese occupation, which had been reported in the Philippines, Malaya and Burma, were avoided. There was no deliberate relaxing of discipline while the troops ran wild. Plundering and unlawful high-handedness by the soldiers were prevented. Before long, these first impressions were found to have been much too favourable but in the early days were unquestionably widespread.

The Dutch noticed that the Japanese carried very little impedimenta, and went without demur wherever their officers ordered them. It is usually reckoned that, in modern armies of the West, for every fighting man there are eight supporting soldiers; among the Japanese the ratio was said to be as low as one to one. The Japanese continually demonstrated before the eyes of the Dutch that no obstacle could deter them. And there was no sign that the Japanese private soldier, or junior officer, murmured against the savage discipline which was used against them.

With these conquests, there came to an end the extraordinary hundred days of Japan. The Army and Navy had raced ahead, and, after a period of rattling and shaking down the Empires of Britain, the Netherlands and the United States, they needed time to rest, and to make new plans. The extent of the territory which had fallen into their hands bewildered, while

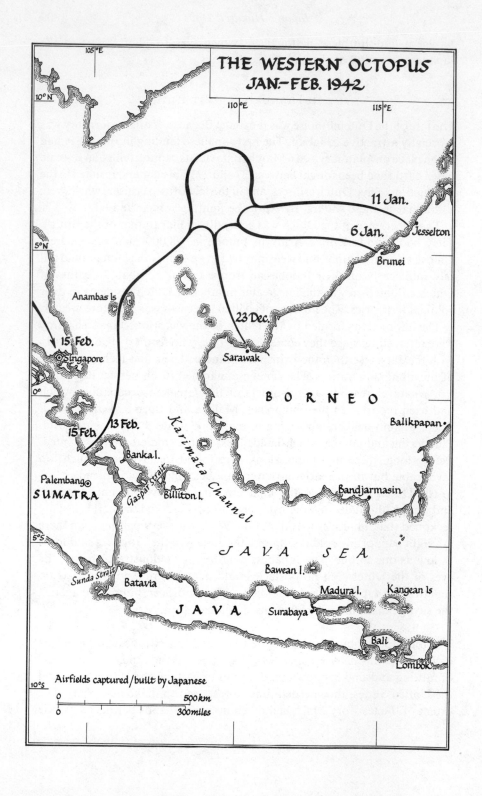

THE WESTERN OCTOPUS
JAN.-FEB. 1942

10°N   105°E

110°E   115°E

11 Jan.

6 Jan.   Jesselton

5°N

Brunei

Anambas Is

23 Dec.

Sarawak

15 Feb.
Singapore

0°

B O R N E O

Balikpapan·

13 Feb.

15 Feb.

Banka I.

Palembang⊙

SUMATRA

Gaspar Strait

Billiton I.

Karimata Channel

Bandjarmasin

5°S

J A V A   S E A

Bawean I.

Sunda Strait

Batavia

Madura I.   Kangean Is

J A V A   Surabaya

Bali

Lombok

10°S

Airfields captured/built by Japanese

0   500 km
0   300 miles

THE EASTERN OCTOPUS
JAN.–FEB. 1942

10°N

125°E

120°E

MINDANAO

Davao

Jesselton

5°N

Sulu Archipelago

Tarakan
10 Jan.

11 Jan.

BORNEO

Menado

0°

M
a
k
a
s
s
a
r

S
t
r
a
i
t

Balikpapan
24 Jan.

Adang

CELEBES

Soela Is.

30 Jan.

Molucca

Bandjarmasin

24 Jan.

Sea

Boeroe

Ambon

16 Feb.

5°S

Kendari

Makassar

9 Feb.

Flores   Sea

Wetar

20 Feb.

19 Feb.

Paternoster Is.

Bali

Dili

Baduıng
Str.

Lombok   Soembawa

Flores

Timor

10°S

Soemba

20 Feb.

Kupang

0   500 km
0   300 miles

it excited them. They had to provide for its administration. They had also to fill out the contents of the extremely vague and propagandist plans for the Greater East Asia Co-Prosperity Sphere, which had come into being long before it was planned as a reality.

Meanwhile the Japanese population would have been more than human if it had not given itself up for the time to the spectacle which was fed to it by all the propaganda machines of the modern state and was meant to generate a profound mood of self-wonder. The streak of exhilaration came after a long and anxious period which preceded Pearl Harbor, a period of grave economic anxiety, of regrets over the interminable war with China, of fears that Japan was getting out of its depth in international relations, and of perplexity over the disorders in its political life.

The great outburst of Japanese victories had lifted the reputation of the Japanese soldier to unexampled heights. He was suddenly regarded as superhuman and invincible: his military virtues were so stupendous that it seemed astonishing that they had not been noticed adequately before. It seemed to be useless to struggle against them: they had eclipsed the virtues of the white man, until then incontestably the most formidable in the imagination of the Orient. As the Japanese Army went to war in 1941 it sang a song called 'Umi Yukaba'. One of its verses, in translation, goes as follows:

> Across the sea,
> Corpses in the water;
> Across the mountain,
> Corpses heaped upon the field;
> I shall die only for the Emperor,
> I shall never look back.

No British or American troops ever sang such lugubrious or unsophisticated words. But the Japanese sentiment was precisely that of the song. It epitomises the difference in attitude to the war between the western world and Japan; Japan found it hard to understand the cryptic, quizzical, and somewhat ambiguous songs of the Western Allies: the simplicity of the Japanese view gave them strength.

The downward turn in Japan's war fortunes set in in the autumn of 1942, and thereafter its way was steadily towards disaster. Day after day there was only bad and worsening news; nowhere, either in its own fortunes or by rescue through possible triumphs of its European Allies, did there appear any rift in the clouds.

Meanwhile, in the brief moment of joy in Japan, it is vain to look for any lasting monument of Japanese achievement in art, music or letters.

The Japanese spirit remained strangely barren. No works of poetry, philosophy, architecture or painting during this time have come to the notice of the international world of cognoscenti, or have won sympathy for the civilization which was about to endure such ravage and destruction. No sounds of natural gaiety appeared to come from Japan: it seemed a world now devoted to material advance: devoid of lightness, wit, romantic lyricism, the cultivated intelligence of women. In politics there was no originality: in science, having borrowed from abroad, Japan was ingeniously adaptive, but was without a creative impulse; in sociology, it was unimaginative. The Japanese pursued their war in a grey atmosphere of the human spirit.

CHAPTER 18
The Storm in India

WITH Singapore and Burma lost, the storm was breaking on the edge of India. There the consequence was not at first military action, but an intensification of the political crisis which had lasted thirty years and which was compendiously called the freedom struggle.

A great excitement swept India. The British in India had the mortification of being made to realize that the military crisis did not signify for most people there a time of mortal danger, but was a time of opportunity and interesting uncertainty. The news of the rout in South-East Asia had the inevitable effect. Britain imposed only a very slight censorship on news, and it was in consequence possible to form a clear idea of Japan's military prowess. Under the influence of this situation the Indian political situation changed rapidly. The war, and its consequences, was suddenly at its gates: India was no longer to be the distant spectator of events: they were at hand.

By the time of the outbreak of war, it had been obvious, to all who chose to look, that India was nearing a period of deep change. Delhi, its capital, at this time was a place of unusual interest. The last days of the old order were bathed in a rather unreal light. They were touched by a sunset. This revealed possibilities and beauties of the scene which had never been noticed before. The British, who were about to put up the shutters on their period in India, suddenly discovered, as they were on the edge of terminating their role, the enchantment of the country, which most of them had ignored as long as they were in secure occupation. India was in the condition typical of countries which are approaching revolution. Only the first rustling of the storm could be heard. It was not yet disturbing because the politics were still interesting and had not yet become lethal.

New Delhi, built chiefly by Lutyens, was then at the height of its brief but real beauty. It had matured and had been sufficiently lived in to have the atmosphere of a city rather than a camp, as it had been only a short time before; but it had not been sufficiently encroached upon by planless building to be spoilt as it is today. Unlike most capitals which have played a part in this chronicle, it had remained outwardly at peace. It was full of talk, and uniforms, and war; but it remained unravaged. The war had brought a flood of new men to the city for the first time, especially young Englishmen of the citizen army of the war years: these were often intelligently attentive to the qualities of Indian life, and they refused to be bound by the restrictions of the colour bar – that fatal barrier which had done so much harm to race relations in the past, and also cut across the natural enjoyment of the country by British visitors. Though there was more political controversy than ever, there was a distinct thaw in the relations of the British and Indians. The old barriers were falling one by one. Life in the capital, though not in the backwoods, became more normal, relations more relaxed. Even while they were engaged in hot dispute, Indians and British alike began insensibly to sun themselves in the climate of emotional debate, which they enjoyed as the most engaging pastime in the world.

In the political arena war speeded up the struggle of Indian Nationalism against the British. But the war had the effect of inflaming even more intensely the divisions within Indian Nationalism: between Hindu Nationalism, which stood for a united India, and Moslem Nationalism, which envisaged a British withdrawal from the continent leaving the predominantly Moslem part to become the independent state of Pakistan. The Hindu–Moslem crisis was the heart of political India. In the critical war years, politics turned chiefly on this, and it was the key to almost everything which happened.

The issue between Hindus and Moslems was relatively simple. Over a part of North India, the Moslems, chiefly as a result of past invasions, were in a majority. This was limited to certain regions: over the country as a whole, the Hindus were in a substantial majority. They were, moreover, the more advanced community in political activity.

When Hindus raised the cry of Indian independence, they had assumed that the Moslems would support them, as following the most advanced political leadership, and, at the start of the national movement, most Moslems had done so. At this period, those Moslems who were politically interested, had been attracted by the parties, which, though predominantly Hindu, claimed to be national, transcending both Hindu and Moslem. But, as politics set light to ever-widening circles of people, the Moslems began to draw apart, and to question whether they would have any benefit from independence, if it were won by Hindus.

The issues thus opened up were plain. Could Hindus and Moslems, by a compact between them, still agree on a common plan? Or, when independence came, should there not more properly be an independence for a Hindu India, and another independence, involving the creation of a new state, for a Moslem India? It took time for this conception to spread among the Moslems, but when it had taken root, it was plain that from the Moslems would come a fierce demand for secession. The Congress claims for independence, which the Moslems represented as a plan for transferring British sovereignty over India into Hindu sovereignty over Moslems, lost its shine and became a matter for controversy.

The Moslem community was at first widely regarded as more backward than the Hindus. At first the Moslems had not taken the same advantage as the Hindus of the opportunities of adopting modern-style institutions. This was partly because the collapse of the Moghul power at the time when the British first arrived in India was a psychological blow from which it took the Moslem upper classes a long time to recover. Initially they had stood stubbornly aside from innovations and educational opportunities offered by the new Raj which, they felt, had displaced them. There was also the fact that Islam half a century ago was opposed to modern education: Moslems were more shackled by their faith at this time than were Hindus. The simplicity of the Moslem outlook commended itself to some temperaments among the British, who were mystified and repelled by the more subtle and exotic Hindu character: but some people sensed in the Moslem mind a greater confusion in the response to the modern world than was to be found among Hindus. The Moslem who fell back on Moslem traditions for guidance in the maze of the modern world often found himself afraid. The Islamic institutions were inadequate; they could not be brought up to date. Moslems tended to live in a world of the past, and, being called on to live in the present, were left with ways uncharted and with reactions for which there was no precedent. The Moslem response to the new life was often unpredictable, unreasonable, and, too often, violent.

The question turned on whether the Moslems were right in declaring themselves to be a separate nation from the Hindus, or whether both were fundamentally Indian, divided only by religion. Both Hindus and Moslems had shared a common Indian state for many centuries: at times the Hindus were dominant, at times the Moslems. Was religion alone sufficient to turn them into irreconcilables?

The Moslems argued that it was emphatically so. No common life for the two peoples was really possible; to hold them together was too artificial. Each community, though they had been joined under foreign rule, lived in isolation from the other. Each had a separate law, its own customs, wore its own clothes, had its own literature, preserved its own way of eating. Sometimes, after prolonged periods of ordered government, they would somewhat unbend and lower their guard. The natural affinities of neighbourliness would prevail to a limited degree over the divisiveness of religion. The common language would inevitably bear some influence in mingling the two peoples. But of a genuine merger of the two societies, there was no sign. Cases of intermarriage between the two communities were very rare, and free intermarriage is the best sign of the fraternization of communities.

The Hindus replied that this was a gross misrepresentation of the position. They could argue that in previous generations the Hindus and the Moslems had felt no such separateness, and automatically regarded themselves as forming a single people. Most Hindus were willing to concede that in recent years the relationship of Hindus and Moslems had often been bad, but this they attributed to the deliberate attempt of the Government to play off one community against the other. To divide and rule was, they held, the first principle of the administration. They argued too that the difference between the communities was largely one of economics, and that, if the economic processes were given free play, these would be enough to break down the communal differences and mould the peoples into a single great society.

As the political situation became more fluid, with signs from the British that they would contemplate withdrawal, there was deadlock between the two sides. The arguments of both appeared to be conclusive. Attempts at mediation proved always in vain.

The coming of wartime tension gave a great impetus to the deterioration. The Moslems, in the fevered atmosphere of the times, set themselves, under the lead of their principal Nationalist Party, the Moslem League, to mobilize their forces. In all the provinces of North India they agitated formidably, concentrating on drawing back all the Moslems who still supported the Nationalist Congress Party. With an ever-increasing show of force, they intimated that they would resort to civil war if any attempt were made to surrender British power to Hindu hands.

The achievements of the Moslem League at this time are due chiefly to a single man, Muhammad Ali Jinnah. He had two distinct careers. Before 1930 he was an all-India leader of the Congress. The interest of Indian Nationalism possessed him and the interest of the Moslem community seemed to be reconcilable with the ascendancy of Congress. In other words, he, though personally a Moslem, was very much like Motilal Nehru, the father of Jawaharlal Nehru, who, though a Hindu, assumed that Hindu interests would always be subordinate to Indian nationalism. In the beginning of the thirties, he had retired to England for some years, where he had a flourishing legal practice. During this time he reflected, brooded, thought about his previous career and meditated on the ways that his willingness to subordinate specific Moslem interests to national interests had not been met by a similar disposition in Hindu leaders. He returned to India, broke entirely with the old all-India ideas, and ceased to be in any sense a co-worker with the Congress leaders. Instead he challenged them, and on the whole out-witted and out-manoeuvred them. He denied their right to speak at all for the Moslems; his first major enterprise was to dislodge the Hindus from the foothold they had obtained in the Moslem community. Next he built up the Moslems as a formidable striking force which demanded a state for its expression and existence.

His achievement was to inform it with something like the questing assertive feeling of the Poles when for more than a century they had been deprived of a state. Eventually, in 1919, the Poles succeeded in breaking through, and forced themselves onto the map of Europe. In the same way the Jews, deprived of a state for many centuries, at last completed its reconstitution. Similarly the Indian Moslems had the will, at the time still partly subconscious, to carve out for themselves an independent state in the Indian sub-continent. Jinnah's contribution to history was to recognize the will in advance of anyone else, and to place himself in its service.

All his successes Jinnah won by the force of his character, by his iron will, and by his clearly marked intellectual superiority. He came to his ascendancy late in life. He had been obscurely born – he was a dentist's son in Karachi – and had had the handicap that he was hardly a true Moslem at all, but, according to local gossip, was the grandson of a converted Hindu. Gradually he made his career, and owed very little to any help which he received from any quarter. The unemotional single-mindedness of his character did not go with any of the amiable qualities which make a man the darling of the crowd. Nevertheless, his way forward was made in full view of the world. There were no secrets in his career: it could be discussed, analysed, appraised, and judiciously respected.

It was characteristic of the Moslem community that his worldly success won him solid esteem; as much as did Gandhi's unworldly conduct prevail with the Hindus.

At the beginning of the second chapter of his life history, his phase as leader of the Moslems, he began by taking over the leadership of a weak party, with a very vague ideology, representing every section of a deeply riven society. He hammered it together into an exceedingly effective political instrument, to which he then, relying for persuasion on intellectual power, dictated policy. He was the new force of Islam incarnate.

As such he was indisputably one of the great actors of the time in the war years. He was one of the few individual architects of the great changes which were coming about.

With the Japanese at the gates of India the British Government felt that something must be done to rally the country to its own defence. The Labour Party had at this time increasing influence on the policy of the British Government towards India, and they succeeded in persuading the Cabinet that the wisest course was to renew its attempt at conciliating Congress. The principal author of this policy was Sir Stafford Cripps. In the high tide of 'Appeasement', this left-wing firebrand had toured armaments factories in England and implored workers to 'refuse to make armaments; refuse to make war'. Later, in 1940, he had meddled in Anglo-Chinese relations and created a certain amount of mischief through the compound of his appalling reductionism and erratic energies. He was a peculiarly able lawyer, a masterly advocate, and firmly convinced of the benefits of democracy, which, he believed, was a suitable government for any territory, whatever might be its circumstances. He had devoted himself to the study of Indian problems. He was convinced that, if Congress demands were satisfied, it would be ready to take its share in the conduct of the war, and that, by a kind of political miracle, the Indian scene would be transformed.

Cripps was a busybody, mistrusted by Whitehall mandarins as well as by British diplomats and officials overseas. The more conservative influences in London believed that, in spite of the evidently superior quality of his mind, his judgement of reality was less than shrewd. They were convinced that his appreciation of India was wrong. The situation in India could not be transformed by eloquent appeal to Congress leaders; Congress support, they knew, might be bought at a price, but at a price which would worsen the situation, since it would bring about a revolt by the Moslem population, and would cause such chaos in India that it would be useless for the prosecution of the war and would drain off large forces of troops from elsewhere for internal pacification. At the same time Congress, if it were won round, could make no difference to the military circumstances. If Congress were given a free hand in war administration, it would, argued these critics, mismanage it. By its participation it would alienate a large part of India which, as the result of various appeals, was showing wartime zeal. There was a strong likelihood that Congress, having made a deal, would take the first opportunity of leading India out of the war altogether.

In spite of these doubts, Cripps was personally entrusted with the mission to conciliate Congress. The situation for Britain was at the time so bleak, and the Cabinet was so preoccupied with other matters, that his confidence that he could reason with the Indian leaders was contagious, and his offer to go out to see what he could do was welcomed. On 11 March 1942 he arrived and spent three weeks in the country, as a kind of Ambassador from Britain.

Cripps, as the chief motive of his tour, carried with him a specific offer to Congress from the British Cabinet. It proposed as the long-term part of the scheme, that at the end of the war a constituent assembly should draft a constitution for India, and no limitation should be put upon its work. Though it was hoped that India would stay inside the Commonwealth, it would be free to secede from it.

To most people in London, it had seemed that Congress could scarcely have asked for anything more complete or more explicit. Next, as a short-term measure, as something on account, Congress was offered immediate admission to the Indian Central Government, but on terms. The Government would be a diarchy, partly British controlled, partly Indian Nationalist in composition. It would continue to be under the chairmanship of the Viceroy. On its side Congress was to approve the war effort.

Bargaining on these terms had been what Congress had had in mind, when, in advance of the Cripps mission, it let it be known that the Labour Party pressure for a new initiative was welcome to it. But politics had moved a long way since the world had been at peace in 1939. In India they had become purely communal: the conflict between Hindu and Moslem, Congress and the League, had put all else, even the conflict between Nationalist India and the British, in the shade. The Cripps offer, being drafted in part by civil servants in London, had included matter to conciliate the Moslem League as well as Congress. A sense of realism dictated this. It would have been folly to win over the Hindus at the cost of causing inflexible hostility from the Moslems. In the midst of war, the British Government could do nothing which would provoke a civil war in India. Nor could it overlook the fact that a high percentage of the Indian Army was Moslem, and, in event of a Moslem rebellion, would have dissolved in its hands.

This explains why Cripps was equipped with a fatal document that came to be known as the 'Cripps Offer'. In the eyes of the Hindus, the proposals had the mortal defect that they were conciliatory to the Moslem League demand for Pakistan. The Cripps Offer included a provision that, if the Moslem parts of India declared their firm intention to be separate – by a plebiscite in the areas concerned – they should be permitted to secede and to form their own constituent assembly. This was a permissive clause, not a definite award; what was to be decided in fact was to remain open until the war was over. But though the plan was hedged round with limitations, and was only to be looked on as one among several possibilities, its proposal was a bitter shock to the Indian Nationalists, who had not yet been taught by frustration, disappointed hopes, and blows of fate, to adjust themselves to reality.

This was the point of major controversy. It was the reason why the Hindus felt they had nothing to gain from the offer. They could not bring themselves to complicate negotiations with Britain over what they considered the national demands of India by introducing a solution, if only tentative, of the Moslem problem; the more so because of their suspicion that the problem had been distorted by the British as a device to counter the national movement.

This was the reason for the breakdown of negotiations for long-term settlement. No less completely did Congress reject the short-term offer by which this was accompanied; this was the invitation to join the Central Government at once. Congress could argue, with some reason, that its Ministers, if it had supplied them, would have been installed in a subordinate position in the Central Government, from which they might have been again ejected; and, for this, they were asked, for the first time in history, for a solemn undertaking that, if the Moslems persisted in their demands, Pakistan would be conceded to them. Congress was quite sure that the Moslems would persist if they were encouraged to do so by the attitude taken up by Britain.

The Congress decision was not as unreasonable as it appeared at the time in London. The negotiations were not entirely straightforward. For tactical reasons, Congress preferred that the break with Cripps should come about over the powers which were to be offered to Congress Ministers if India threw in its lot with the war effort. These were to be limited in the Army itself to various matters of administration and supply, which the Government felt it would be safe to delegate; and it was made woundingly clear that in matters of the higher direction of the war, allied strategy and the organization of Intelligence, the Indian leaders would continue to be excluded. Nehru, after an exploratory session with Cripps, said that the offer boiled down to Indian Ministers being given control of the Army stationery and of canteens. In spite of exaggeration, there was some truth in this.

An American attempt to mediate in the negotiations was unsuccessful. The United States had become deeply disturbed at the situation. It saw a real danger that nationalist India would secede from the war, and, for military reasons, greatly feared the loss of Indian territory as a base. It feared also the effects upon its ally, China. Most Americans regarded India as unfathomable, a mysterious land full of magic, strife, heat, filth and teeming multitudes. Paradoxically, few Americans had ever even seen an Indian – or wished any acquaintance with one. They understood neither the complexity of Indian problems, nor the reasons which prompted the policies of the British Government. However much the British Raj excited their imagination, it did so only at a distance. At any closer examination, India – and the British connection with it – seemed to the Americans distasteful in the extreme. The British were kith and kin. The Indians emphatically were not. For others the situation in India was viewed simply as a repetition of the American War of Independence, and naturally their sympathies were strongly on the Indian side. The United States was embarrassed that, in a war which it increasingly advertised as a war for democracy and freedom, it should be tied in alliance with Britain, whose past role in India ran so counter to the principles of the Atlantic Charter. It therefore regarded itself as vitally interested in the outcome of Cripps's negotiations. But its endeavours to help them on, and to ease out difficulty, did not achieve their purpose.

Yet it was Gandhi who was ultimately responsible for Congress rejecting the British offer. Gandhi was still in effective command of Congress when Cripps came to India. Nominally he had for a long while stood aside from holding office in Congress. But in fact, as Congress adviser, he had the overriding – though never quite uncontested – influence on Congress decisions.

This was understood by the British. Cripps knew that he must convince Gandhi before anyone else. He had long interviews with him. At the end of one of them, it happened that Sardar K. M. Panikkar, an extremely able politician of the Indian princely states, was seen to be going from the sweepers' colony, where Gandhi was staying, on his way to report to his masters, some of the Indian princes whom the excitement of the times had brought to Delhi. He was asked what view Gandhi took of the Cripps Offer. Actually, Panikkar did not know: his visit had not been directly to Gandhi. But from a knowledge of Gandhi's mind, he was certain, and he expressed the opinion in an epigram which has the accent of the Mahatma. It was, he said, a post-dated cheque on a failing bank.

Gandhi later repudiated the latter part of the epigram; he said that he in no wise wished to impute failure to Britain in the war, or success to Britain's enemies. On the other hand, it was clear that his attitude towards

the waging of war differed from that of the belligerents. He proposed that
resistance to the Japanese on Indian soil should be non-violent. In a letter
written to one of his followers in 1942 (quoted by Shri B. R. Nanda in his
book on Mahatma Gandhi) he said:

> Remember that our attitude is that of complete non-cooperation with the
> Japanese Army . . . If the people have not the courage to resist (non-violently) the
> Japanese unto death and not the courage or the capacity to evacuate the portion
> invaded by the Japanese, they will do the best they can. One thing they should
> never do − to yield willing submission to the Japanese.*

However, Gandhi realized that the British in India, and a large element
in Congress, had it been brought to cooperate with the British by ironing-
out their political differences, would not employ non-violent tactics in
resisting Japan. He had, therefore, no wish to see a compromise between
Britain and the Congress which involved the issue of waging war. He
was, furthermore, possessed by the idea that if the British left India,
Japan would then leave India alone, and it would be spared the fate of
Burma and Malaya. Accordingly, his influence was thrown against the
Cripps Offer, and, in the circumstances of the time, was strong enough
to kill it.

In April, soon after Cripps had failed, Gandhi, by one of the daring
simplifications of issues which were a part of his strength, began to use the
slogan 'Quit India'. The precipitating cause of his decision was his foreboding of a coming crisis, should the Government take steps to compel
the peasantry to adopt a scorched earth policy in the case of an invasion.
Gandhi said that it was one thing for the Russians to adopt this policy
voluntarily; it was another for a Government to impose it on a confused
people, too poor to endure it.

The British protested that, as politically responsible beings, they
could not, in the middle of war, walk out of India, without making
arrangements for the orderly transfer of British power. The suggestion
that they should go seemed self-evidently absurd, and the fact that it
was made seemed to the local administration either to reflect on the
political sense of the opposition, or to suggest that the demand was
made for the purpose of whipping up national feeling, and was not
expected to be considered seriously. The British had been willing to
promise, in a series of policy statements, which gradually eroded their
position, that British power should eventually be wound up. Most of

* B. R. Nanda, op. cit.

these were sincere. They felt injured when Congress doubted their word. They argued that they must have time: essentially it was impossible to set about the hazardous political experiment in wartime. The British side, although under pressure of the social radicalism which was mounting at home – increasingly liberal in statements and assurances about long-term intentions – remained adamant against immediate radical changes until they judged that the war had been won. The day-to-day pressure of wartime events at home was too great to permit the liberal forces in the Westminster Parliament to give their undivided attention to events in India. It was upon the constant distraction of the British Government in London that British bureaucrats in India chiefly relied; it saved them from having their hands tied.

Congress, in facing a renewed rebellion, had the experience of its two major collisions with the British to work upon. It had learned much in these. In 1942 Congress was better organized than it had been ten years earlier.

The traditional Congress means of working against the Government was to use the method of 'open conspiracy'. That it conspired could not be doubted: but it avoided anything in the nature of a secret plot, since by doing so it strengthened its moral force. Politicians who plotted secretly drew on themselves some of the odium that terrorists are never entirely free from, even when the Government, as in India, was unpopular. Congress seldom made any secret of its plans; it carried them out in daylight.

Thus, when Gandhi turned from patient agitation and persuasion to direct action, he openly proclaimed it. Success in what he intended would depend on the willing cooperation of masses of the people. Therefore, after giving his ultimatum in late May, all through June and July he worked up the feeling of the country by explaining in every possible way what Congress, under Gandhi's direction, meant to do. He hoped, by summoning the people, to induce so many men at all levels to withdraw their support from the Government – while taking care to be non-violent – that the business of carrying on the Government would become impossible, and the British would evacuate. The Army would have a large number of deserters; so would the police; the workers in the towns, by going on strike, would halt the production of war materials; chaos would set in in the civil administration. And all would be done without violence. Gandhi, even at a great crisis, was enough of a lawyer to frame his own statements, and to persuade most of his colleagues to do the same, in such a way as to ensure that this point was clearly made.

Gandhi was waging a war of nerves. The British were bent on giving no provocation. Their interest was to prevent matters going to extremities. Though by the mid-summer, Japan had passed the peak of its war, though the battle of Midway Island was recognized by experts as having been a decisive test of strength, though Japan's *élan* was slightly drooping, the British Government had still only a very slight margin of safety to play with. The danger of invasion was still very real, and a Congress rebellion would be found to add to the emergency of the war; it would threaten the Allied use of India, which, geographically, seemed likely at this stage, before subsequent successes of the United States in the Pacific, to play a major part. To contain the outbreak of national feeling, which Gandhi knew he could command, required great coolness and discrimination on the part of the Government in deciding the precise moment for contending it.

The man who had to contend with Gandhi, and who at this stage flared into prominence, was Victor Alexander John Hope, Lord Linlithgow. He had been Viceroy for five years. On the whole he had not had an impressive term of office. He had arrived with the reputation of being an expert on agriculture, having been chairman of a commission which was expected to do something about this flagging but vital Indian industry; but he had totally disappointed the country by taking no initiative. By the time of the war he had shown that he entirely lacked the common touch, the ability to communicate with the masses, and, if he was sympathetic with anybody, it was with the bureaucrats. He may have been unlucky in this. His reports to London did little to inspire civil servants or Ministers, who regarded him as tiresome and a second-rate intellect. Although there were men who affected to find human feeling in him, few if any of the politicians ever established rapport with him. He had neither an evident enjoyment in the discharge of his great office nor a knack of handling the politicians of varying and often irreconcilable opinions who were his necessary acquaintances. He seemed totally to want imagination, and could not fire others with a vision of the importance of what he had to do. He had great industry without a capacity to turn this to account in ways which caught the imagination, considerable public spirit without it being able to gild any of his actions. Politically his main task had been to preside over the constitutional reforms which were meant to convert India into a Federation and to bring the Government of India Act of 1935 into operation; but in this also he failed to achieve anything. The Federation never got off the ground, and it was widely believed that its failure was partly due to Lord Linlithgow's willingness to let matters drift. He had allowed himself to be weighed down by the Indian realities and concluded, on seeing them at close quarters, that the proposed constitution was not really prudent.

There is no need to see Lord Linlithgow as an essentially fascist type, as was apt to be supposed by some Congressmen. In calmer times he would have been perfectly happy in presiding over a democratic and constitutional India; he was not a permanent adversary of liberalism. But in the conditions of war, he judged it clearly crazy to hand over political responsibility, even in part, to politicians who were untested, and whose statements had aroused a strong suspicion that they were opposed to the war. Lord Linlithgow's view was that of British common sense at the time. He had the strength of seeing India in the same nineteenth-century light as Churchill, whose stand against the 1935 Government of India Act had been recklessly anachronistic and ill-advised. The majority of Churchill's Cabinet during the war were not the kind of men to defy their master's voice on a matter so close to his heart. Linlithgow therefore was given their confidence in taking the steps which he proposed. One needed to be a man of exceptional political vision to see that Indian national feeling might still be enlisted for the war, and that political boldness might still achieve what it set out to do.

Lord Linlithgow's lack of imagination had allowed the initiative to pass to Gandhi. The Government only prevaricated and played for time; Gandhi promised action. Now Gandhi was about to use his opportunity, to take the steps which many men feared to tread but which their mood would support, and to commit Congress to the greatest gamble of its career. The expectation of action set in strongly among the people, so that Congress, though the organizers of the mood, found themselves finally swept along by it. Linlithgow had cool nerves. That which made him incapable of giving creative leadership and made him dull to the distressed conditions of all around him, served him well in this crisis.

In the first week of August, Gandhi summoned the Working Committee of Congress to Bombay. He made no secret of the fact that his intention was to speak the words which would set in motion a new civil disobedience movement on a grand scale.

Late at night the police pounced and arrested Gandhi and all the Congress leaders. They were transported to carefully arranged and not uncomfortable prisons. Gandhi himself was interned in a requisitioned palace of the Aga Khan. The operation had been carefully planned, and, unlike most actions of the Indian Government at that time, had been kept carefully secret. The success with which it was executed helped to restore the self-respect of the Government.

*

For the rest of the war, Congress was inactive. Most of its leaders continued to be in prison. The Government, which had been anxious about the extent of their popular support, discovered that this had been exaggerated; but exercised a perhaps understandable prudence in detaining the leaders until Hitler was defeated.

The continuing incarceration of the Congress leaders left the way clear for Moslem agitation. By the time that Congress orators were once again free, they found that the Moslem leaders had organized the Moslem community fairly solidly, and that Congress opposition counted for little. One of the unforeseen consequences of Gandhi's 'open revolt' had been to let in Pakistan.

The British authorities were relieved at the passing of a crisis. But, though they might have been expected to revise their general attitudes in the light of a proven weakness of Congress, they did not do so. Their policy followed very closely the official and unofficial statements of it. This was that time was nearly up for the British in India, and that at the end of the war Britain would do exactly what it had said it would do: make a sincere attempt to set up a Government, or Governments, in India and leave the sub-continent. Most of the politicians in England, even the less enlightened ones, and most civil servants in India, even the more elderly ones, were in agreement about this. For the present India's war-effort was still needed, and nothing would be done to rock the boat. But as the war went on, the Government gradually ceased to have the feel of certainty and stability, and took on the style and temper of a provisional Government. From London a strong breath of discouragement was blown at anyone who played with other concepts of the future.

Gandhi, the man of peace, who had been obliged by political circumstances to play such a large part in wartime politics, ceased to be a determining figure of the war. Indeed, never again was he to have the personal dictatorship which he had had of the opinion and actions of Congress. His decisions in 1942 marked his passage from supreme authority. After the war, though he had great influence, and though for a time a great deference was paid to him by all who sought to mould events in India, new forces had appeared, and he had to bend before these.

Gandhi's eclipse for the rest of the war, and the eclipse of Congress, removed from India the feature of its politics which had made India fascinating for so many. In a world given up to the contest for brute power, and, worse still, for military power, the claim of Congress that it was striving for higher things was refreshing. Congress politics were intensely histrionic; drama was the essence of them. They were also steeped in arguments over political and secular morality. It was breathtaking to find Congress, in the middle of the war, calmly demanding on moral grounds concessions which no Government could have made, least of all a Government which possessed a still unbeaten Army; yet it had the authority to compel the rational discussion of its demands. All this was now given up. The politics of India were deflated; they followed more practical, limited, lesser ends; greater vision had been dispersed by contact with reality. Yet never again were Indian affairs to be felt to touch the heart of humanity as they were when their arch prophet was moving around with his strange entourage which recalled, in manners and circumstances, that of St Francis of Assisi and the other compelling figures of the past.

Gandhi's adversary, Lord Linlithgow, also stalked out of the picture. Immensely tall, gaunt, awkward, he had been out of place in Hindu India, which liked to discuss with passion those ideas which seemed to mean little to Linlithgow. His final actions were not much to his credit. In the summer of 1943 there took place a frightful famine in Bengal. For the first time for thirty-five years this dreaded event had recurred in India. It was an ugly fact that this spectre, to exorcise which had been one of the claims made for British rule, had again appeared. This particular famine was man-made. Throughout the episode there was no actual shortage of food supplies in India. But these were allowed to remain hoarded because the railways, under pressure of wartime operations, had broken down, and because the civil servants, also under wartime pressure, realized too late what was happening. It did not adapt the famine code, which kept the country from starving in normal times, to the changed circumstances of war. It was too much harried by urgent and unfamiliar problems of administration.

In Bengal a great exodus took place from the countryside to the town, in the opposite direction to the population flow of the previous year when the panic set in that India was to be bombed. More and more frightful tales began to circulate of a population driven by hunger to roam until they fell dead from emaciation. The streets of the great modern city of Calcutta were strewn with corpses, and such sights began to appear there of the juxtaposition of extreme wealth and of stark hunger as had before the war been notorious of eastern metropolises such as Shanghai. Another blow had been dealt to the credit of the British Government in Asia.

As reports of what was happening began to come out of Bengal people expected that the Viceroy would tour the famine area, to bring what help was possible, to be seen communing with the people, and to inquire into

126 The Pearl Harbor attack,
7 December 1941 *Top*: The
battleship *West Virginia* sinks
alongside the *Tennessee*. A
survivor is pulled from the
water by a motor sailing
launch

127 *Bottom*: A scene of
general devastation

128 *Top*: US Army B25 aircraft fly off the USS *Hornet* on the first American air raid against the Japanese mainland; they are led by former test-pilot Colonel 'Jimmy' Doolittle

129 *Bottom*: Loss of the aircraft carrier USS *Lexington*, following the Battle of the Coral Sea, 8 May 1942

130 *Top*: A Japanese
propaganda photograph shows
two exultant children cheering
'Banzai'. Note their civil
defence gear

131 *Bottom*: A column of
battleships steams in line: the
most technologically
sophisticated, complex and
expensive machines of any
description ever made by man
before the Russo-American
space race

132   *Top*: The Japanese heavy
cruiser *Mikuma* lies dead in
the water and sinking, during
the Battle of Midway, June
1942. Over a thousand sailors
perished with her

133   *Bottom*: A US B25
medium bomber flies a sortie
over Wotje island in the
north-eastern Marshall Islands

134 *Top*: On Guadalcanal four of the US Marines who captured the island wade to their tents through knee-deep water

135 *Bottom*: Many Japanese naval experts regard the loss of Rabaul as the decisive turning-point after which the defeat of Japan was inevitable

136 *Top*: The Japanese
battleship *Yamato* undergoes
sea trials in October 1941. The
Yamato was the largest and
most powerful battleship ever
built

137 *Bottom*: The American
Resurrection. The Stars and
Stripes unfurls above the
parade ground at Topside,
Corregidor, on the return of
the Americans, 22 February
1945

138 *Top left*: This Pulitzer Prize-winning photograph, shows the Stars and Stripes being raised above Mount Suribachi on Iwo Jima in February 1945 and had a powerful effect on the American public

139 *Top right*: A Japanese kamikaze aircraft attacks the *Missouri* on VE Day, the last day of the European war: months later the surrender of Japan was signed on the *Missouri's* main deck

140 *Bottom*: US Marines wade ashore at Tinian Beach, August 1944

141 *Top*: Empty oildrums litter a beachhead established by US Marines on Okinawa in April 1945, evidence of the vehicles that have moved inland with the support of an armada of 1,300 ships

142 *Bottom*: The face of battle: three US Marines crouch under fire on Leyte Island in the Philippines in October 1944

what was evidently a failure of administration. To visit the scene of disaster was a tradition of the Viceroy. But, inexplicably, Linlithgow on this occasion departed from tradition. Week after week went by, and he spent the last days of his term of office in Delhi and Simla.

His successor, the new Viceroy, promptly reversed this behaviour. The solid benefit which by his immediate visit he was able to do the administration struck the country as a rebuke to his predecessor. It was evident that more could have been done by energy, imagination and improvisation. Field Marshal Lord Wavell called in the Army to relieve the miseries of the people, and for a period this enjoyed a very real and unusual popularity.

Yet Lord Linlithgow, reluctantly though he may be praised, played a great part in guiding Indian affairs so that events took one shape and not another. He was given much latitude by the Home Government. After the failure of Cripps, his judgement prevailed on most matters. He handled the open rebellion of Congress almost under the eyes of the would-be invader. That so few lives were lost, and that India continued belligerent, was due to his calm and to a sense of proper timing that actually belonged to his staff but has been credited to him.

CHAPTER 19
Four Loose Threads

JIMMY DOOLITTLE'S AIR RAID AND ITS AFTERMATH

FOR the dark months that followed Pearl Harbor, there were few military initiatives that America could take. In March 1942, at a time when the fall of the Philippines was imminent, President Roosevelt authorized a spectacular air raid upon Tokyo, primarily intended to lift morale in the United States. The raid, child of the fertile brain of Admiral Ernest J. King, Commander-in-Chief of the United States Fleet, and his senior operations officer, was not planned as more than a token gesture of defiance. Strictly speaking, it would serve no useful military purpose. Lieutenant-Colonel James H. Doolittle, a former stunt pilot, a qualified aeronautical engineer with a doctorate from MIT, and an outstanding aviator with a string of record-breaking aerial accomplishments to his credit, was selected to head a handpicked team of Army airmen whom he trained in less than a month to fly their specially adapted land-based aircraft off a tiny patch of runway intended to simulate a naval flight deck.

In April sixteen twin-engined B25s of the United States Army Air Force were loaded aboard the USS *Hornet* and, collecting an escort which included four cruisers, eight destroyers and an air umbrella provided by the USS *Enterprise*, they advanced into the Western Pacific. In the absence of radar, Yamamoto Isoruku had taken the precaution of stationing a line of picket-boats in a great arc, more than seven hundred miles out to sea east of the Japanese mainland, to provide early warning of any carrier-borne attack. The approaching task force spotted four of these boats, two of which flashed the news to Tokyo. The Japanese did not expect the Americans to launch long-range land-based aircraft from the decks of ships or at such a distance as to make their recovery aboard impossible. Having lost hope of nearing Japan undetected, however, Doolittle and Admiral 'Bull' Halsey, commander of the naval task force, decided that it would be too dangerous for the ships to venture closer or to linger within easy range of Japanese land-based aircraft. They agreed that the B25s should be launched without delay, correctly anticipating that Japanese misjudgement of the raiders' time of arrival would outweigh the risk that the aircraft were likely to run out of fuel before they could reach the safety of air bases in unoccupied China. It was a bold stroke and achieved effective surprise.

A solitary Japanese patrol aircraft six hundred miles out to sea had reported seeing one of the bombers heading westwards. Its warning was not heeded: the American carrier raid was expected to materialize on the morrow. Following the first signals from Yamamoto's picket ships, Japanese Naval Air Headquarters had ordered ninety fighters and 116 bombers to prepare for the contest at first light. Six heavy cruisers and ten destroyers set out at full steam to intercept the American warships. It was all in vain.

One of the American aircraft released a ton of incendiaries over Nagoya, while another hit Kobe and a third, originally scheduled for Osaka, bombed the Yokosuka Naval Yard and Yokohama instead. Twelve others headed straight for the heart of Tokyo, arriving from all points of the compass just as a full-scale mock air raid by Japanese aircraft was ending, throwing the Japanese air controllers into confusion. Tōjō himself, coming in to land at Tokyo in an Army transport aircraft following an inspection of troops outside the capital, was passed by one of the incoming B25s. The Americans encountered increasingly heavy anti-aircraft fire over Tokyo but released their bomb loads of incendiaries and high explosives unscathed. The sixteenth aircraft of the squadron, beset with fuel supply problems on its route to Japan, veered away from the Japanese mainland and headed alone for Vladivostok, where the Russians seized it and interned its crew. All of the other aircraft eluded pursuit and flew on to reach China, assisted by unexpectedly favourable tail winds. Their target landing fields were 1,500 miles beyond Tokyo. It had been hoped that any surviving aircraft would join Major-General Claire Chennault's hard-pressed air forces. None of them did so. Several flew directly over their intended landing field at Chuchow, but the Chinese, who had not been told that the Americans were heading there, mistook the planes for Japanese and switched off their field lights upon detecting the approaching aircraft. Four of the fifteen crash-landed when they ran out of fuel before reaching safety. The other eleven crews finally took to their parachutes, abandoning their aircraft in mid-air.

The raid shocked and mortified the Japanese nation and its leadership. There is no reason to doubt the genuine sense of moral outrage expressed by the Japanese, who had managed to suppress any twinges of conscience that some of them felt for the plight of the Chinese, Filipino and other civilian populations bombed so recklessly by Japanese aircraft earlier in this fifteen-year war. There is a great difference between those who give and those who receive the punishment of aerial bombardment.

The number of persons actually killed by Jimmy Doolittle's Raid was small, something like fifty people. Ninety buildings including a number of private homes were bombed and, in what appears to have been a tragic mistake, at least one of the aircraft attacked a school full of children, cutting down a number of teachers and their pupils by machine-gun fire. Tōjō and his Cabinet reacted strongly, issuing retroactive regulations condemning indiscriminate air attacks upon non-military objectives, private property or common civilians. These offences, as well as other serious infractions of the international laws of war, would now be treated as criminal acts punishable under Japanese military law. Captured enemy airmen convicted under these new regulations would be liable to a term of imprisonment of not less than ten years and could forfeit their lives.

The four-man crews from two of the Doolittle aircraft were taken captive by Japanese occupation forces in China and were paraded through the streets of Shanghai and Nanking respectively. They were subjected to torture in efforts to discover how they had made their way to Tokyo and where they had intended to land. The Japanese were briefly confused by the fact that the B25s and their crews belonged to the US Army Air Force, not the Navy. How had they reached Tokyo? The naval carriers, so it was believed, had sailed off as soon as their distance and bearing had become known. President Roosevelt's one-line jest that the aircraft had come from 'Shangrila' cut no ice. Bit by bit the Japanese soon pieced together more or less the whole story.

In due course exceptional pressure was imposed upon General Hata Shunroku, Supreme Commander of the Japanese Expeditionary Forces in China, to haul the captured fliers before a court-martial at which they were given no opportunity to defend themselves. The result was a foregone conclusion. Hata himself seems to have resisted the duties that he was required to perform, but in the end he had no choice but to carry out his instructions as directed. All eight airmen were condemned to death on 20 August 1942. Afterwards Tōjō commuted five of the sentences to life imprisonment as a practical demonstration of the Emperor's divine benevolence, but the remaining three prisoners were executed on 10 October 1942. All but one of the others miraculously survived the war and lived to tell their tale.

That the trial and punishment of the Doolittle fliers was a mockery of due process cannot be disputed, and it proved to be merely the beginning of what became the policy of the Japanese to execute Allied bomber crews taken captive by the Japanese. After the war Tōjō told the Tokyo War Crimes Tribunal that he had enacted the new Army regulations mainly to deter the Allied Powers from undertaking similar terrorist raids in future.

So far as the Japanese were concerned, these unfortunates were nothing less than war criminals, not entitled to protection as prisoners of war.

It is difficult to read the 1907 Rules of The Hague Convention (IV) on Land Warfare and the 1923 Hague Air Warfare Rules (although the latter document, commissioned by Britain, the United States, France, Italy and Japan in 1922, does not have the sanctity of a formal treaty) without feeling that the Japanese had a valid complaint. The declarations of statesmen, judgements of legal tribunals and unanimous resolutions of the League of Nations during the years before the war showed a well-nigh universal condemnation of aerial warfare directed against civilian population centres. Japan herself had declared as early as 1937 that in the conduct of the war in China she would abide by the 1923 Hague Air Warfare Rules. It was the common practice of all belligerents in the Second World War to ignore these provisions. Yet even though the experience of that conflagration confirmed in so many ways that nations tend to resort to the most fiendish means of war that they can devise except when deterred by their vulnerability to reprisals, most people on our planet today would still agree that any resort to indiscriminate attacks upon civilian targets is – or ought to be – in breach of the basic principles of international law. Indeed, the distinguished jurist Sir Hersch Lauterpacht, although cautiously sensing his way in the immediate aftermath of that war, goes much further:

These new problems raised by air warfare cannot be deemed to have affected the validity of the general principle of immunity of non-combatants from direct attack. They are not such as to provide a legal justification for offensive action which, although disguised under the cloak of attack upon a military objective or as a measure of reprisals, is directed in fact exclusively and deliberately against the civilian population. Non-combatants are not, under existing International Law, a legitimate military objective . . . International Law protects non-combatants from deliberate bombardment from the air directed primarily against them for the purpose of instilling terror or for similar reasons; recourse to such bombardment is unlawful.*

Nevertheless, the Japanese case was entirely vitiated by their own past violations of the same rules and by their callous disregard for just about every other international law of war on the books. Moreover, one of the other immediate consequences of the Doolittle Raid was that the Japanese launched a systematic counter-offensive of terror and punitive raids in the provinces of Chekiang and Kiangsi where all but one of the Doolittle aircraft had come down.

* L. Oppenheim, *International Law: A Treatise*, vol. II, *Disputes, War and Neutrality*, 7th edn, ed. by H. Lauterpacht, Longmans, Green & Co., London, 1952, pp. 516–30, especially p. 525.

JAPAN'S CHEKIANG–KIANGSI OFFENSIVE
MAY–SEPTEMBER 1942

Shanghai

Yupan Sea

Hangchow

2nd LINE ARMY

116D
Yuhang   32D
          Fuyang

Hsiaoshan
15D

Linpu

192D 0107
0707   Hsincheng
0715 192D
0518
0719   88C   1 BRIGADE
      Tunglu   Wangchensi
0521   0517
25D Chienteh   Chuchi
Yanghsi 60D
40D   Puchiang
146D 0528
Shouchang
Tatung   Chukeh
Kaihua   Lanhsi
26C   63D
86C   Yang- 05z Chinhua N21D
Huafu   Lumayu Fu   Hsiaoshan
0609 0606 052
Chaohsien   Tanghsi   Kufang
Chuchow 0606   0523
145D   0830
0823 Changshan   Tachow
0609 40C
Chiangshan   Huangtan Lingshan
0611 79C 105D Hushanchen
Hsiakou   0807
0819   Huichang Peichieh
0807 Paoan   0923
0808 Hsienhsia
0809 105D Sungyang
Pinhsi   79D
              Yunho
Pucheng

0521
Anhua
88C

0521
Yiwu   0521 Chienshan
Tungyang
Anwen
0520
0520 Yungkang
T9C
Hsuanping
0930
T9C T9C
0624
0828 Lishui
Pihu
0709
0729
Chingtien T33D
0711
0815
Wenchow
88C
Juian
0712

Shaohsing Shanyu
32D
KONO BRIGADE
Tangpu

Cheng
0313

Hsinchang

Chenshan

Hsiaoshan

Tientai

Ningpo

70D
Fenghua

Luchao

Chenchao

10 + GUNBOATS
1000 + MARINES

Just as Chiang Kai-shek had feared from the moment he became aware of the American plan to bomb Japan and fly on to China, the Japanese moved swiftly to avenge themselves. Imperial General Headquarters ordered the Japanese Expeditionary Forces in China to suspend operations elsewhere and concentrate their energies upon the seizure of the Chinese airfields in Chekiang while inflicting massive reprisals upon the Chinese. General Hata amassed more than 100,000 troops, more than nine divisions, and began to advance in mid-May. In a campaign reminiscent of Sherman's march through Georgia in the American Civil War, the Japanese first cleared the Chekiang–Kiangsi Railway and then systematically set about smashing the Chinese airfields, dismantling the railway itself and plundering the entire area. Characteristically, the Kuomintang régime's official history of the war heaps praise upon Chiang Kai-shek for his 'complete grasp of the overall situation':

Knowing the enemy and ourselves, Generalissimo Chiang resolutely ordered the 3rd War Area to avoid a decisive engagement ... Thus our forces were able to conserve our strength and continued to harass the enemy, forcing him to fall back to his original position. Generalissimo Chiang's decision was outstanding, as he caused the enemy to waste strength and time and enabled our forces to tide themselves over the most difficult period.*

The truth is that it was a military disaster, and a quarter of a million Chinese were butchered as a direct result of the Doolittle Raid. These appalling outrages by Hata's forces bear comparison with the notorious Rape of Nanking, and this loss of life must be added to the scales when considering the supposed impact of the Doolittle Raid upon Japanese morale.

The Americans greatly exaggerated the extent to which Japanese public support for the war would be undermined by the Doolittle Raid: it simply had no discernible effect upon morale except to harden the resolve of the nation to resist the 'hairy barbarian' hordes from across the seas. It did not even produce fundamental changes in Japanese civil defence and air raid precautions. For another year or so the Japanese authorities and public alike deluded themselves with the thought that the Doolittle Raid provided an accurate indication of the probable scale of damage and disruption that would follow in the wake of any resumption of American air operations over Japan. Local fighter defences were strengthened to guard against further attacks, and it is true that this diversion of Japanese

---

* Hsu Long-hsuen, Chang Ming-kai *et al.*, *History of the Sino-Japanese War (1937–1945)*, Chung Wu, Taipei, 2nd edn, 1972, pp. 379–90, especially p. 390.

air strength seriously undermined the ability of the Japanese Army Air Force to send badly needed air reinforcements to support frontline troops elsewhere. In truth, however, the number of aircraft and crews recalled from the Chinese mainland to the home defence of Japan was of little consequence when measured against the ever-accelerating disparity between the air resources of the Allied Powers and Japanese. The Doolittle Raid did boost the morale of the American people which the President had wanted so badly after the string of defeats that American arms had sustained in the war thus far. More significantly still, it forced the Japanese Naval General Staff to abandon its opposition to Admiral Yamamoto's ill-fated plan for another great strategic riposte: the battle for Midway, which meant the ruination of Japan's best chances to secure the capture of Port Moresby and was the first great turning point of the Pacific War.

INDIAN OCEAN EXCURSIONS LIMITED

Though the attention of the Western Allies was fixed uneasily upon the territorial gains of the Japanese, that of the most influential Japanese strategists continued to concentrate upon the war at sea. It was to be the greatest naval war in history. The great prize of war would be the mastery of the Pacific Ocean, and this would go to whichever Navy proved to be the stronger. The Japanese war planners, in the months after Pearl Harbor, had kept a very flexible outlook. Some favoured a blow in the Indian Ocean, which would open the way to military operations in the region. There was even talk of a naval sweep of the Indian Ocean, which would end with the Japanese making contact at Suez with the victorious German armies. Others wanted an attack in the South Pacific which would isolate Australia; others a renewal of the attack on Hawaii which Pearl Harbor had begun.

Nearly all sections agreed that Japan must continue to be aggressive. Only by exploiting the impetus gained by Pearl Harbor could Japan even seem to prosper. The long-term odds against Japan were so desperate that the conversion of the war into a defensive one would have been half to admit defeat. The best course lay in a constant series of surprises, which would divert attention from the sombre reality of Japan's true position.

During all this period, the Japanese Army showed little willingness to embark on joint plans with the Navy. At this time the situation and prospects of Germany were very uncertain: it was in the middle of its great adventure against Russia, which, if successful, would have altered the complexion of the war; the Japanese Army was therefore anxious to keep its hands free, so that it could be ready to strike whenever this might, by the unfolding of events, become desirable. Although, by its southward move, Japan had turned its back upon Russia, and was genuinely anxious to make its Non-Aggression Pact with Russia a reality, it could not ignore the fact that Russia was reeling. If it were to be defeated, or to be in obvious danger of defeat, a new situation would come into being, and Japan would be driven to interfere in Siberia. Its divided attention during these months probably accounts for the salvation of India, and perhaps of Australia, from invasion.

The centre of initiative in the months between Pearl Harbor and June 1942 was the brain of Admiral Yamamoto Isoroku. It is true that, as Commander-in-Chief of the Combined Fleet, he remained technically subordinate to the Naval General Staff. But he was regarded by everyone as the author of the victory at Pearl Harbor, and he used the prestige which this gave him to impose his concepts upon more conservative Japanese admirals. In Yamamoto, Japan had produced one of its undisputed geniuses of the war: a man whose ideas gave a new turn to naval strategy, and who had the capacity to translate the ideas into action.

As a next move, Japan sent a fleet of five aircraft carriers and four battleships, one light and two heavy cruisers and eleven destroyers, into the Pacific Ocean in the direction of Ceylon. It was a superbly well-balanced fleet, incomparably stronger and more efficient than any other then afloat. It was under the command of Admiral Nagumo Chūichi, who had had the operational command at Pearl Harbor. It was a task force very similar to that which had raided Pearl Harbor, and its objective was to bomb Colombo and a naval base at Trincomalee in the same manner, though of course it could not hope for the same element of surprise. It was seeking out the Eastern Fleet of the British Royal Navy, and would try to put it out of action in the Far East by dealing it the same crippling blow that had been inflicted on the American Pacific Fleet. In support of Nagumo, and to throw the enemy into confusion, a Second Expeditionary Fleet, called Malay Force, raided shipping and attacked shore installations along the east coast of India. This Fleet was split into three divisions covered by a screening force. Altogether this meant that Nagumo's Striking Force effectively was augmented by the *Ryūjō* (a light carrier carrying forty-eight aircraft), three heavy cruisers, two light cruisers and fifteen destroyers. The Japanese operations in the Indian Ocean were destined to be short-lived, but their formidable nature is self-evident from the size of the forces which the Japanese devoted to the accomplishment of their objectives.

This was a foreshortened version of the plan first prepared by Yamamoto's Combined Fleet Staff. They had wanted the Army to contribute an expeditionary force of five divisions, far larger than the forces employed in Malaya or the Philippines, to occupy the entire island of Ceylon. This in turn was to be the precursor of a grand plan to link up with German forces advancing from the Caucasus through the Middle East. The Army, owing to its preoccupations with the magnetic north, refused to take part in the plan.

On 1 April 1942 the British Admiral, Sir James Somerville, was alerted to the presence of Nagumo's fleet, and concentrated his available force to meet him. Somerville had a fairly large fleet, five battleships, five light and two heavy cruisers, three aircraft-carriers and fourteen destroyers; but only one of his lumbering battleships, HMS *Warspite*, was modernized. All five of his capital ships were fatigued, having begun their active service in the midst of the First World War, a quarter century before. Somerville's two fleet carriers, HMS *Indomitable* and HMS *Formidable*, were of the latest British designs and carried thirty-five to forty aircraft. His only other carrier, tiny HMS *Hermes*, the British first ship ever designed and built as an aircraft carrier, normally carried a complement of only nine obsolete swordfish torpedo-bomber/reconnaissance aircraft but could squeeze in half a dozen extra aircraft at a cost of seriously reduced ship efficiency. All these vessels were thoroughly outclassed by the fighting ships of Nagumo's Carrier Strike Force, which deployed more than 360 aircraft. On the other hand, Somerville had the enormous advantage that he held the Japanese naval cipher; and the Japanese did not suspect this. No major shift took place in the Japanese disposition but he was aware of it as soon as it happened. The eyes which this gave him were probably decisive in the action which followed.

On 4 April the Japanese made what was intended to be a major air strike at Colombo. They found the British alert to the attack; no warship was in harbour; the British air forces were already in the air, and gave the Japanese a fair fight. The Japanese, denied the advantage of surprise, broke off the attack to bomb, and sink, two British heavy cruisers, which had approached dangerously near to the Japanese aircraft-carriers from which the bombing planes had come.

Somerville had in the meanwhile discovered that Nagumo's force was larger than he had at first supposed. He recognized that he was hopelessly outclassed; his old and very slow battleships were no match for the enemy. He was therefore forced to take evasive action by day, and attempt to engage the Japanese at night, although in fact no naval engagement took place. On 9 April Nagumo made an air strike at Trincomalee, the British

JAPANESE ATTACKS ON CEYLON & BAY OF BENGAL, 31 MARCH – 5 APRIL 1942

———— British Eastern Fleet (Admiral Sir J. Somerville)
—·—·— Fast Division (2 fleet carriers, 1 battleship, 2 light cruisers, 6 destroyers)
    arrived Addu Atoll 1200 hrs 4 April, sailed 0015 hrs 5 April
- - - - - Slow Division (Vice-Admiral A.U. Willis)
    4 R-class battleships, 3 light cruisers, 5 destroyers arrived
    Addu Atoll 1200 hrs 4 April, sailed 0700 hrs 5 April
··········· Ships from Ceylon ———— Japanese Striking Force (Nagumo)
— — — Japanese Malaya Force (Ozawa) —··—··— Units of Japanese Malaya Force
   All times shown are −6 hrs GMT

Arabian Sea

INDIA

Bay

1100 hrs

Vizagapatam

Coconada 0600 hrs 6 April

1020 hrs 6 Apr.

Madras

70°E   80°E

10°N

Cochin

Trincomalee 0900 hrs 9 Apr.

1055 hrs 9 Apr. HERMES sunk

CEYLON

Colombo

Maldive Islands

1600 hrs 5 Apr.
2 carriers
5 unknown
reported 1817 hrs

Dondra Head

Area of operations of Eastern Fleet 31 Mar–2 Apr.

0700 hrs 7 Apr. 0200 hrs 7 Apr. 0900 hrs 5 Apr.

1845 hrs 5 Apr.
2 battleships
3 cruisers reported by British A/c

1115 hrs 6 Apr.

Veimandu Channel

0700 hrs 6 Apr. 1800 hrs 6 Apr. 1355 hrs 5 Dec. DORSETSHIRE & CORNWALL sunk

1355 hrs 5 Apr. R/v 1726 hrs 5 Apr.

1843 hrs 5 Apr.

Addu Atoll

0600 hrs 4 Apr.
large enemy forces
reported by Br. A/c

0900 hrs 6 Apr.

0°

0   500 km
0   300 miles

70°E   80°E

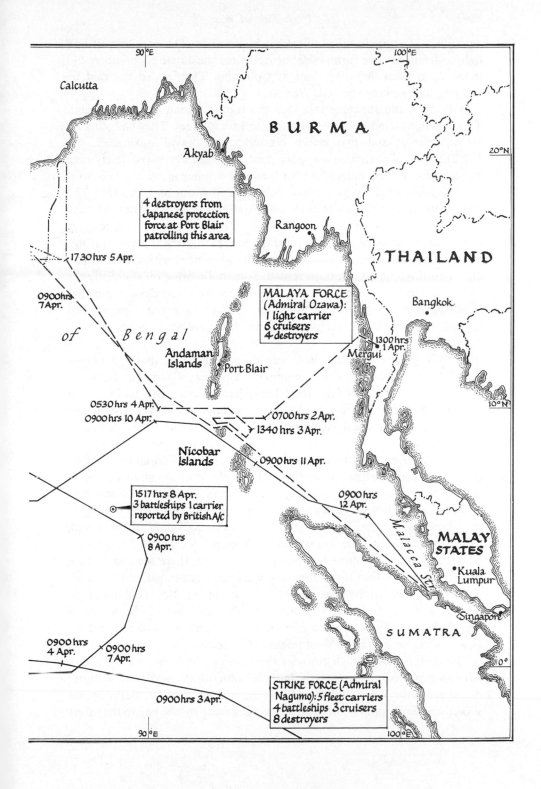

Calcutta

B U R M A

Akyab

20°N

4 destroyers from
Japanese protection
force at Port Blair
patrolling this area

Rangoon

THAILAND

1730 hrs 5 Apr.

0900 hrs
7 Apr.

MALAYA FORCE
(Admiral Ozawa):
1 light carrier
6 cruisers
4 destroyers

Bangkok

of   Bengal

1300 hrs
1 Apr.

Andaman
Islands

Port Blair

Mergui

10°N

0530 hrs 4 Apr.

0700 hrs 2 Apr.

0900 hrs 10 Apr.

1340 hrs 3 Apr.

Nicobar
Islands

0900 hrs 11 Apr.

1517 hrs 8 Apr.
3 battleships 1 carrier
reported by British A/C

0900 hrs
12 Apr.

0900 hrs
8 Apr.

MALAY
STATES

Kuala
Lumpur

Malacca Str.

0900 hrs
4 Apr.

0900 hrs
7 Apr.

Singapore

S U M A T R A

10°

STRIKE FORCE (Admiral
Nagumo): 5 fleet carriers
4 battleships 3 cruisers
8 destroyers

0900 hrs 3 Apr.

90°E

100°E

naval base, but again failed to take it by surprise. The anti-aircraft and fighter defences were formidable: nevertheless the Japanese bombers did more harm than they had done at Colombo. They ended the raid by locating and sinking the little *Hermes*.

With that, the Japanese raid into the Indian Ocean came to an end. Their total loss had been five bombers and six fighters. They had sunk an aircraft-carrier and two heavy cruisers, with naval auxiliaries and 112,312 tons of merchant shipping, and they had destroyed thirty-nine British aircraft. This coincided with Japanese submarine raids off the west coast of India which sent five more ships of 32,404 tons to the bottom. The combined effect of these operations was that military and merchant ship-ping traffic on both sides of the Indian sub-continent was thoroughly disrupted. In conjunction with the Japanese casualties at Pearl Harbor, their losses were absurdly low from this initial combat with the American and the British navies. In ships traded, Somerville came off decidedly the worse. But he had saved the bulk of his fleet from the destruction that might have overtaken it from the Japanese aircraft-carriers, and for this he had to thank Allied decipherers of the Japanese naval codes.

By this time, the British had convinced themselves that a Japanese attack upon Madagascar was imminent. This was a familiar theme: as early as November 1940 the Joint Intelligence Committee had received information indicating that the Vichy Government of France had yielded to German pressure and were prepared to accept Japanese occupation of the entire island. Following on the recent example of French Indo-China, it seemed exceptionally unlikely that the Vichy colonial administration on the island would refuse to permit the Japanese to establish at least sub-marine berths and depot facilities there. The establishment of Japanese air bases on the island was a distinct possibility, and there were even fears that Japanese cruisers might find shelter in the harbours of the island. Thus, even prior to the mutilation of Admiral Sir James Somerville's Eastern Fleet by Admiral Nagumo's five carriers, there seemed to be a considerable risk that if the Japanese were not forestalled, Britain's im-perial lifeline round the Cape to India, Australia and New Zealand might be severed; South Africa, together with the coastline of the whole of British East Africa, might be exposed to an effective blockade and the flow of Persian oil to the West might suffer serious disruption.

The British also had to consider the views of their Allies. The South African Prime Minister, General Jan Christian Smuts, never one to mince his words with Winston Churchill, made no secret of his desire to see something done quickly: he regarded Madagascar as 'the key to the safety of the Indian Ocean'. The Americans were inclined to agree: they encouraged the British to take the matter in hand. General Charles de Gaulle, likewise, fancied his own chances at capturing the whole island for the Free French, provided that the British gave him the necessary air and naval cooperation. Neither the British nor the South Africans were willing to risk another joint venture with de Gaulle's forces after the débâcle at Dakar.

Churchill and his advisers mulled over these ideas for several months. Ultimately, the Prime Minister brushed aside doubts expressed by the Chief of the Imperial General Staff and the objections of his Director of Military Operations to 'Bonus', a plan to invade Madagascar. 'We are not setting out to subjugate Madagascar but rather to establish ourselves in key positions to deny it to a far-flung Japanese attack,' he reminded the Chiefs of Staff. The War Cabinet, as usual, gave the Prime Minister what he wanted. Smuts and Roosevelt were informed; de Gaulle was not.

The forces required for the operation, renamed 'Ironclad', interspersed themselves in the stream of reinforcements bound for India and Ceylon. They assembled in Cape Town at the end of April and then moved on to Durban a few days later before setting sail for the short voyage to Madagascar. The attack on 5 May was spearheaded by Force 121, a commando and three brigades of Royal Marines led by Major-General R. C. Sturges, R M, supported by air and naval gun protection afforded by a considerable task force comprising two British aircraft-carriers, the venerable dreadnought H M S *Ramillies*, two cruisers, eleven destroyers and thirty other vessels. It was the first large-scale amphibious operation conducted by British forces since Churchill's Dardanelles campaign of the First World War. Nevertheless, Madagascar is an island larger than metropolitan France and more than twice the size of the United Kingdom. The plan was predicated upon a hope that the French colonial governor would offer no more than token resistance. The French garrison was believed to number only 6,000 troops, mostly African, and a few ragtail aircraft. The two initial objectives therefore were confined to storming of the outstanding natural harbour at Diego Suarez on the northern tip of the island and seizure of an airfield five miles to the south. Against all odds, the French stoutly resisted, however, and Churchill finally ordered the overall commander of the task force, Vice-Admiral Sir Neville Syret, to break off the attack in order to give the French Governor-General of Madagascar, Armand Annet, time to reconsider his predicament.

Meanwhile, at the end of April, five fleet submarines of the Japanese Fourth Submarine Flotilla had proceeded from Penang across the Indian Ocean towards East Africa on the first of two special missions by such

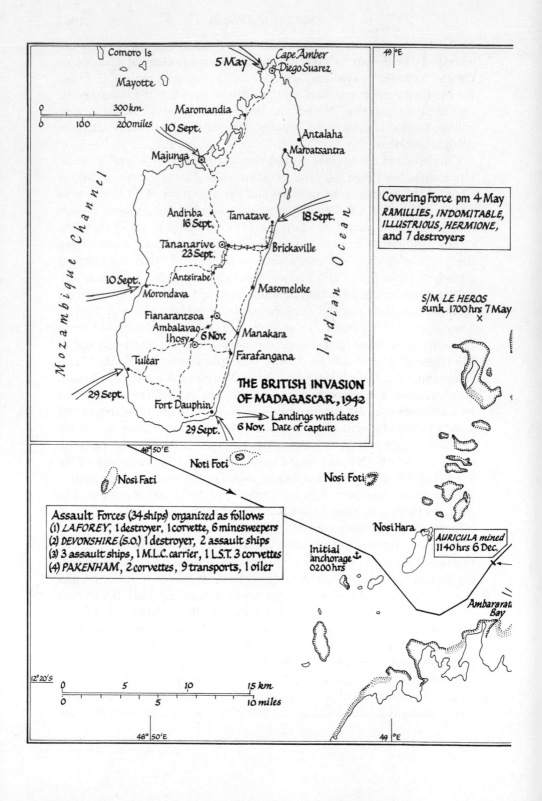

Comoro Is
Mayotte
5 May
Cape Amber
Diego Suarez
Maromandia
10 Sept.
Antalaha
Maroatsantra
Majunga
Andriba
16 Sept.
Tamatave
18 Sept.
Tananarive
23 Sept.
Brickaville
10 Sept.
Antsirabe
Morondava
Masomeloke
Fianarantsoa
Ambalavao
Ihosy
6 Nov.
Manakara
Tuléar
Farafangana
29 Sept.
Fort Dauphin
29 Sept.

Mozambique Channel

Indian Ocean

300 km
100   200 miles

**THE BRITISH INVASION
OF MADAGASCAR, 1942**

⟹ Landings with dates
6 Nov.   Date of capture

Covering Force pm 4 May
*RAMILLIES, INDOMITABLE,
ILLUSTRIOUS, HERMIONE,*
and 7 destroyers

S/M *LE HEROS*
sunk 1700 hrs 7 May
×

Noti Foti
Nosi Fati
Nosi Foti

Nosi Hara
AURICULA mined
1140 hrs 6 Dec.
×

Initial
anchorage
0200 hrs

Ambararat
Bay

Assault Forces (34 ships) organized as follows
(1) *LAFOREY*, 1 destroyer, 1 corvette, 6 minesweepers
(2) *DEVONSHIRE* (S.O.) 1 destroyer, 2 assault ships
(3) 3 assault ships, 1 M.L.C. carrier, 1 L.S.T. 3 corvettes
(4) *PAKENHAM*, 2 corvettes, 9 transports, 1 oiler

12°20'S
0   5   10   15 km
0   5   10 miles

48°50'E   49°E

48°50'E   49°E

THE BRITISH ASSAULT ON DIEGO SUAREZ 1942

Cape Amber

49° 10'E

49° 20'E

12° S

12° 10'S

Assault landings
1630 hrs 5 Dec.

Courrier Bay

Main Anchorage

No. 5 Commando

Assault landings
1630 hrs 5 Dec.

Ambararata

Main axis of army advance

Diego Suarez

Andrakaka Peninsula

Antsirane

ANTHONY lands marines 2050 hrs 6 Dec.

Main defence position

Diego Suarez Bay

Oronjia Pass

Bombardment by *RAMILLIES* 1040 hrs 7 Dec.

⊙Airfields

12° 20'S

49° 10'E

49° 20'E

forces intended to distract Allied commanders from the forthcoming Midway and Aleutians campaign. Refuelled by two supply vessels which sailed with them, the little hunting pack soon reached its target zone. Floatplanes catapulted from the decks of the 2,400-ton headquarters submarine *I-10* and at least one scouting submarine searched in vain for enemy warships in the ports of East Africa from as early as the first week of May. They only narrowly missed finding the British task force at Durban by four days. The Japanese then headed north towards the commotion at Diego Suarez. During a reconnaissance flight over the British invasion force after nightfall on 29 May, one of the Japanese floatplanes was spotted by the British, who opened fire without result. The British forces were alerted but to no avail. On the next night, at a distance of about ten miles from the harbour entrance, two midget submarines of the same class as those launched prior to the Pearl Harbor attack were released from their mother ships, the *I-16* and *I-20* attack submarines. Penetrating the British defensive screen, they entered the harbour, sank a tanker and badly damaged H M S *Ramillies*. Only luck and efficient damage control saved the battleship from total loss.

It was an effective reminder of that vulnerability which the British had every reason to fear in eastern waters, and it scuppered any remaining hopes that the desultory armistice negotiations then underway with Annet would lead to any early solution. As these negotiations dragged on without result, British patience waned. The Chiefs of Staff in London, concerned at recent reverses in the Middle East and worried at the possibility of a Japanese invasion of India, ruled out any resumption of the offensive on Madagascar until the broader strategic picture looked more favourable. As the summer drew to a close, a fresh East African brigade and a brigade of South African troops arrived in September to assist one of the brigades that had taken part in the initial landings and between them they mopped up what remained of the Vichy forces on the island. Two months later, the French governor finally surrendered in November after it had become abundantly clear that his position was untenable.

All but a remnant of the marines employed in the initial assault had re-embarked and sailed for India as soon as Diego Suarez itself was secured. Most of the naval support ships also quickly resumed their normal work. However the campaign as a whole was far more protracted than the British had anticipated. While the casualties sustained in the fighting had been light, malaria had cut a swath through the British troops during their cat and mouse game with the French after the initial struggle. Plans to reinforce frontline troops in India utilizing the forces engaged in this part of the Madagascan operation suffered setbacks and, according to the

British official history of the war against Japan, this in turn was to have a considerable effect upon Wavell's plans in the following months. This, like much of the Madagascan operation, remains a somewhat contentious point.

Ironically, the Japanese never had any intention of using Diego Suarez for themselves. Even Hitler recognized that the Vichy authorities would not have agreed to such a suggestion. The Japanese Navy regarded the Indian Ocean as a comparative backwater. They had missed a few opportunities yet they could look with satisfaction upon the whole Madagascan campaign as a fine short-term success.

Their next blow was another feint by submarines, this time delivered against Sydney Harbour in New South Wales. It was more or less intended as a carbon copy of the East African raid. Twenty-four hours after the attack on the British at Diego Suarez, a submarine-borne scout plane reconnoitred the harbour and escaped detection. On the following night four other submarines launched their midget submarines. The raiders sank one vessel of no military significance and failed to hit a nearby American heavy cruiser anchored in the harbour. The attack produced fright and pandemonium locally but had no greater result. Allied cryptanalysts had begun to unmask the true objectives of Yamamoto's main forces. Although it is tempting to compare the tip-and-run tactics of the Doolittle raiders and those of the Japanese submariners, their consequences were altogether dissimilar.

In May 1942 the United States became aware of the fact that the Japanese were concentrating massive land, sea and air forces in the Japanese Mandated Islands in preparation for another major offensive. At this point it was not clear where the Japanese intended to strike. For a time Admiral Nimitz, as Commander-in-Chief of the Pacific Fleet (CINCPAC), was advised by his cryptanalysts and radio traffic analysts that the next move of the enemy might well be to enlarge the Coral Sea operation into the maelstrom of a final main fleet action fought between the two sides. As early as 6 May, however, CINCPAC correctly revised this estimate and observed that the Japanese might move into the Central and North Pacific areas. The Navy Department's own cryptographic team in Washington, DC, Op20G, worked on similar material but still believed that the Japanese were intent on moving south. General MacArthur's people supplied him with information which supported his demands for 1,000 more aircraft, 100,000 fresh troops and two carriers of his own to add to his existing strength in the South-West Pacific: he anticipated that the Japanese intended to complete their conquest of New Guinea and

KOREA

120° E

140° E

Tokyo

HONSHŪ

to Etorofu 26/27 Nov.

18 Apr.

KYŪSHŪ

JAPAN

Planes launched
for Tokyo air-raids

CHINA

4 Mar.
Attack

FORMOSA

20° N

Marianas

PHILIPPINE
ISLANDS

Saipan

Guam

Palau Is

Truk Is
14 Jan.

C a r o l i n e   I s l a n d

Halmahera Is

BORNEO

0°

Rabaul

23 Jan.

Boetoeng
26 Mar.

NEW GUINEA

Celebes

Solomon
Islands

10 Mar.
Attack

Pt Moresby

Coral Sea

11 Mar.

9 Mar.

28 Feb.

JAPANESE & AMERICAN CARRIER
OPERATIONS, DEC. 1941 – JUNE 1942

1 Mar.

12 Mar.

13 Mar.

Movements of US carrier forces

Movements of Japanese carrier forces

13 Mar   Positions at noon

0   500   1000   1500 km

0   500   1000 miles

AUSTRALIA

then catapult themselves on to the Australian mainland. Meanwhile the United States Army's Air Intelligence experts were advising the head of the Army Air Corps, General Henry Arnold, that the Japanese were preparing to mount an assault on the American West Coast. The Chief of Staff of the United States Army, however, withstood pleas for any massive reinforcement of the American position in the Pacific. The 'Europe First' strategy agreed with the British was in safe hands.

Whether that was the wisest course will always be a subject for debate. Franklin Roosevelt himself had his doubts. Public opinion, although unaware that any formal decision had been reached, was deeply divided over the issue. The American public's thirst for a campaign of revenge against the architects of the Pearl Harbor attack was unslakable. There was also the thought so bitterly expressed by President Mañuel Quezon of the Philippine Commonwealth as his life ebbed away during his unequal struggle with tuberculosis: 'I cannot stand this constant reference to England, to Europe . . . How typically American to writhe in anguish at the fate of a distant cousin while a daughter is being raped in the back room!' Nevertheless, the political centre of gravity in the United States remained on the East Coast, where concern about the spread of Nazi influence across the European continent and over the United Kingdom outweighed all countervailing considerations. Moreover, the Third Reich was incomparably stronger than the Japanese Empire. Most Americans regarded themselves as merely temporary foster parents of the Philippines but as the sons and daughters of European cultures that Hitler and Mussolini seemed determined to brutalize or obliterate. Europe came first.

THE CORAL SEA

In the spring of 1942, flushed with the success that they had achieved at the outbreak of the Pacific War, the Japanese embarked upon an ambitious new campaign. It was called Operation *Mo*, and it envisaged an extension of the Japanese defensive perimeter across the length and breadth of the South-West Pacific. It all stemmed from events that had taken place back in January, when the Japanese Navy seized Rabaul in the New Hebrides virtually unopposed and quickly transformed it into a major fleet base. Now protection of that base had to be given a high priority.

Port Moresby lies on the southern coast of New Guinea, near the northernmost tip of Australia. From its occupation Japan counted on being able to menace Australian ports and airfields (where they knew the Americans were busy sorting themselves out for a counter-offensive). It would open the way for a Japanese conquest of New Caledonia and that, in turn, might enable Japan to cut off the vital movement of military equipment and personnel already beginning to flow westwards from North America to Australia. Indeed the capture of Port Moresby, as some optimistic Japanese Army appreciation asserted, might even force Australia out of the war. The naval force needed for this operation appeared to be so small that, for once, the Army had the ready cooperation of the Navy, which, in a revival of a Japanese inter-service tradition going back hundreds of years, consented to convoy a Japanese Army landing-force. The Americans and the British agreed with the Japanese appreciation, and decided that, though still far from ready to offer serious opposition to the Japanese, the operation must be resisted.

It was several months after the Japanese took Rabaul when Imperial General Headquarters resolved to capture Port Moresby by a naval *coup de main*. This attack was scheduled for March. Then Japanese Intelligence reported that the Allied Powers were amassing forces to counter just such a move. Yamamoto ordered the operation to be delayed until early May. The Japanese then assembled a veritable armada of seventy ships, including two attack carriers detached from Admiral Nagumo's force on their way back to Japan after the Indian Ocean campaign. An additional light carrier, the little 12,000-ton converted submarine tender *Shōhō*, was ordered to join the force. The fleet also included a seaplane tender, half a dozen heavy cruisers, three light cruisers, fifteen destroyers and fourteen Army troop transports.

To meet this formidable threat, the Allied Powers hurriedly assembled a scratch fleet comparable in size, including two American attack carriers, the *Yorktown* and the *Lexington*, together with a British battleship, two American battleships, four heavy cruisers, four light cruisers and seventeen destroyers.

Yamamoto split his forces in the South-West Pacific Operation into seven parts under the operational command of Admiral Inoue Shigeyoshi at Rabaul. The Port Moresby Transport Force, led by Rear-Admiral Abe Kōsō and consisting of twelve Army and Marine troop transports, a mine-layer and a number of supply vessels, was earmarked for the occupation of Port Moresby. It would be escorted by Rear-Admiral Kajioka Sadamichi's small Port Moresby Attack Force of a light cruiser, five destroyers, a patrol boat and some other auxiliaries. Rear-Admiral Marumo Kuniori's Close Cover Force, comprising two light cruisers, a seaplane carrier and three gunboats, would help protect the landing operations where required. The more powerful elements of Inoue's fleet were divided into Vice-Admiral Takagi Takeo's Carrier Strike Force, comprising two heavy carriers, the *Zuikaku* and *Shōkaku*, escorted by two

heavy cruisers and six destroyers, and two support forces, both commanded by Rear-Admiral Gotō Aritomo, the first of which was designated
as a Close Support Force and consisted of a light carrier accompanied by
a single destroyer, and the Main Body Support Force, a powerful squadron of four heavy cruisers. The remaining section of the fleet was the
Tulagi Invasion Force under Rear-Admiral Shima Kiyohide, consisting
of two destroyers, two mine-layers, a troop transport and some auxiliary
craft. Each of these forces was given a separate mission to accomplish in
Yamamoto's complicated plan, which relied upon precision timing and
the convergence of sections from various points of the compass.

Knowing the main features of the Japanese plans – and that, of course,
made all the difference – the USS *Yorktown* and the *Lexington* hoped to
join forces in the New Hebrides, far to the south-east, and then to jump
the Japanese at Rabaul as soon as the enemy's attack developed. A mixed
cruiser squadron of two Australian cruisers and the USS *Chicago*, under
the command of Rear-Admiral J. G. Crace of the British Royal Navy,
would rendezvous with the two American carriers as they joined forces
to surprise the Japanese. The only other American carriers in the Pacific
were on their way home to Pearl Harbor after having taken part in
Jimmy Doolittle's Raid over the Japanese mainland: ordered to the South
Seas as soon as they refuelled, they arrived too late to take part in the
action which followed.

In April 1942 Japanese assault forces opened Operation *Mo* with the
subsidiary attack on Tulagi, an insignificant speck of land off the coast of
Florida Island in the mid-Solomons, just twenty miles off a far larger
island that was due to assume a greater significance in the months ahead:
Guadalcanal. Acting on information derived from 'Magic' intercepts and
augmented by the efficient 'Coastwatcher' bush-telegraph network organized by European and Australian planters and native islanders, the Australian garrison at Tulagi had been prudently withdrawn from the island
before it could be overwhelmed. The Japanese saw nothing suspicious in
this. They were intent upon their objective, which would soon be achieved,
of transforming the island into a major seaplane base to protect the
bastion which the Japanese were fast establishing at Rabaul, 600 miles to
the north-west, and the eastern flank of the Japanese forces then fighting
their way across New Guinea.

Confident of success, the Japanese anticipated that their next move
would be to utilize the Tulagi Invasion Force to block off the back alley
to their new property by taking Nauru Island and Ocean Island, 600 and
800 miles to the north-east. Then, secure in their new domains, the
Japanese would be well placed to dispose of any forces sent out to dislodge

them. Meanwhile, the assault on Port Moresby could be expected to entice the United States Pacific Fleet within range before it could recover from the losses it had sustained at Pearl Harbor. With good fortune, this might lead to the destruction of what remained of America's offensive capabilities at sea. It was just possible that the Midway Operation might prove to be unnecessary.

The Japanese believed that they could rely upon speed to achieve their objectives before the arrival of any Allied counterstroke. The Midway Operation was already scheduled to take place in June, and Admiral Yamamoto Isoruku, a master at poker as well as at other games of chance, anticipated that he would need to place nearly the whole resources of the Imperial Navy in the stakes at Midway if his gamble there were to succeed.

The Japanese plan began to unravel almost at once. On 4 May the Port Moresby Transport Force and the Close Cover Force were in the Louisades, expecting to rendezvous with the Port Moresby Attack Force before rounding the tip of New Guinea on their way to Port Moresby (which was already under attack by a naval air fleet operating out of Rabaul). To the north, off New Georgia Island, lurked the Distant Cover Force which would have to protect the Japanese flanks during both the Tulagi and Port Moresby invasions. Having approached the Solomons from the north, the Japanese Carrier Attack Force shortly moved south-easterly to skirt the islands on a course which was to take it round San Cristobal. At this moment aircraft from the USS *Yorktown* intercepted the Tulagi Invasion Force and broke its back. The *Yorktown*, acting completely independently, hared off alone to the doorstep of Tulagi when a reconnaissance aircraft from Australia reported that the Japanese were busy disembarking their forces there. This seemed too good an opportunity to be missed. On this occasion it might have been better to wait.

Swathed in a protective blanket of cloud and closing upon their enemy at 27 knots, the *Yorktown* and her destroyer escort neared the mid-Solomons and in a series of three strikes delivered by *Yorktown*'s aircraft in rapid succession, the Americans created havoc in the harbour area. But the light force of Rear-Admiral Shima's ships covering the Japanese landing were scarcely worth the effort. About half of that force was sunk, the seaplanes were cut to ribbons, and most of Shima's other vessels sustained heavy damage. But this sally by the *Yorktown* had deprived the Americans both of surprise and of the significant trophies that would have justified the effort. Up to this point, the Japanese had been completely ignorant of the fact that there were any American carriers in the vicinity. The Japanese landing force was evacuated, apart from a small

Kavieng

Bismarck

New
Ireland Arch.

Bismarck Sea

Rabaul

5°S

New Britain

NEW GUINEA

INVASION FORCE
Transports & Des-
troyers from Rabaul
1800 hrs 4 May

PAPUA

Huon Gulf

S o l o m o n

Joined by units
from Tulagi invasion
force, midnt 5/6 May

Gulf of
Papua

Triobrand Is.

Woodlark I.

0800 hrs
6 May

Port Moresby

10°S

Bombed by carrier
Force, 5 May

1030 hrs 6 May
Aust. based B-17s
bomb SHŌHŌ

0800 hrs 7 May.
Invasion force
retires

×

SHŌHŌ bombed
again and sunk
1135 hrs 7 May

Milne
Bay

Louisiade Arch.

0800 hrs 8 May

Under heavy air attack
from shore-based aircraft
1400-1445 hrs 7 May

1425 hrs
7 May

Attack groups
launched 1000 hrs 7 May

2000 hrs 7 May

1358 hrs 7 May
air attack fails

2000 hrs
7 May

0800
7 May

2000 hrs 8 May

SUPPORT GROUP (Crace)
AUSTRALIA HOBART
CHICAGO 2 destroyers

2000 hrs 9 May

15°S

Attack groups launched
0900 hrs 8 May against
SHOKAKU and ZUIKAKU

QUEENSLAND

C O R A L

AUSTRALIA

145°E

150°E

155°

THE BATTLE OF THE CORAL SEA, MAY 1942

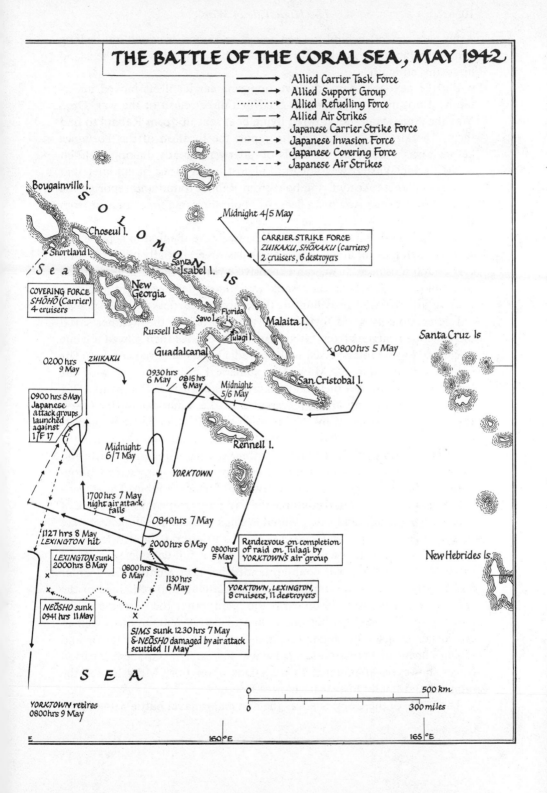

→ Allied Carrier Task Force
--→ Allied Support Group
····→ Allied Refuelling Force
–·–→ Allied Air Strikes
→ Japanese Carrier Strike Force
---→ Japanese Invasion Force
–··–→ Japanese Covering Force
- - -→ Japanese Air Strikes

Bougainville I.

SOLOMON

Choseul I.

Shortland I.

Santa
Isabel I.

Sea

New
Georgia

Russell Is.

Savo I.

Florida
I.

Tulagi I.

Guadalcanal

San Cristobal I.

Midnight 4/5 May

CARRIER STRIKE FORCE
ZUIKAKU, SHOKAKU (carriers)
2 cruisers, 6 destroyers

COVERING FORCE
SHŌHŌ (Carrier)
4 cruisers

Malaita I.

Santa Cruz Is

0800 hrs 5 May

0200 hrs
9 May

ZUIKAKU

0930 hrs
6 May

0815
8 May

Midnight
5/6 May

0900 hrs 8 May
Japanese
attack groups
launched
against
TF 17

Midnight
6/7 May

Rennell I.

YORKTOWN

1700 hrs 7 May
night air attack
fails

0840 hrs 7 May

1127 hrs 8 May
LEXINGTON hit

2000 hrs 6 May

0800 hrs
5 May

Rendezvous on completion
of raid on Tulagi by
YORKTOWN'S air group

New Hebrides Is

LEXINGTON sunk
2000 hrs 8 May

0800 hrs
6 May

1130 hrs
6 May

YORKTOWN, LEXINGTON,
8 cruisers, 11 destroyers

NEŌSHO sunk
0941 hrs 11 May

SIMS sunk 12.30 hrs 7 May
& NEŌSHO damaged by air attack
scuttled 11 May

SEA

YORKTOWN retires
0800 hrs 9 May

0   500 km

0   300 miles

160°E

165°E

Army garrison left behind to keep an eye on things. It would not be long before the Japanese would return to re-establish themselves on the island in greater strength.

For the next two days, the two opposing carrier fleets moved uncertainly, if not nervously, towards their first direct clash of the war. On 5 May the Americans shot down a flying boat sent up from Rabaul to find them. The aircraft had no time to report the location of the *Yorktown* before it was intercepted: the effect of radar was already making itself felt in the Pacific War. It was not until almost twenty-four hours later that another Japanese Army flying boat from Rabaul found and reported the whereabouts of the American fleet. At about the same time, aircraft from the two fleets spotted their enemy's vessels.

Shortly after dawn on 7 May the Japanese were the first to achieve any success when they hit an oil tanker and a destroyer, initially mistaken for a carrier and a cruiser. It was an expensive error, for in the general mêlée that followed, the Americans sank the almost defenceless little *Shōhō* while its aircraft were away hunting the American carriers without success: only exceptionally good fortune and the vagaries of the weather saved the American carriers from discovery. The two sides then played a game of cat and mouse interspersed with sporadic bursts of aerial combat. The fighting continued on 8 May. The numerical advantage lay with the American airmen, and their odds improved still further thanks to a 2:1 superiority in the anti-aircraft firepower of the American surface fleet. However, this was offset by the far superior skill, discipline and aircraft of the Japanese. The *Shōkaku* sustained severe damage. Her sister ship, the *Zuikaku*, was untouched. The USS *Lexington* sank, a lingering death, and the *Yorktown* suffered bomb damage, only narrowly escaping serious harm.

Both sides then began to limp away from further trouble. The Americans were in no position to continue the battle without running the risk of losing the *Yorktown* and other valuable ships as well. The Japanese were in a stronger position: the *Zuikaku*, thanks to aircraft landed from the *Shōkaku* as well as its own squadrons, carried a full complement of aircraft. Yamamoto, indeed, countermanded his fleet commander's order and angrily signalled the Japanese to annihilate all that remained of the enemy force. His intervention came too late to alter the outcome of the battle. It produced no result other than to betray Yamamoto's lack of confidence in his subordinate commanders and to delay the repair and replenishment of his battle-scarred naval forces. The Japanese invasion forces, however, abandoned their designs upon Port Moresby for the moment and finally lost their chances for good.

The Battle of the Coral Sea was the first major naval battle between the two opposing sides to demonstrate the strengths and weaknesses which were to affect the future course of the war. It was a conflict entirely different in character from what had occurred before.

By standards of subsequent phases of the Pacific War, the Battle of the Coral Sea was amateurish and not particularly costly. The Americans and Crace's forces had lost sixty-six aircraft, 543 dead, the 42,000-ton USS *Lexington*, a single destroyer and a fleet oiler as well as the damage sustained by their only other carrier in the engagement, the USS *Yorktown*. The Japanese lost seventy-seven aircraft, 1,074 dead, the 12,000-ton carrier *Shōhō*, a destroyer and three auxiliary vessels. Strictly speaking, the Japanese had won the engagement but at a higher price than was immediately evident. Both of their other carriers in the engagement had been crippled. The two heavy aircraft-carriers returned safely to Japan, but in a condition which put them out of use for several months while undergoing repairs and the training of new flight crews. The absence of these two ships in the impending engagements was probably of decisive consequence.

There were lessons to absorb. The rival forces had never sailed within sight of one another, and the battle had resolved itself into a hunt for one another by their aircraft. It was the first naval battle in history to be decided by a struggle for air supremacy. The surface ships engaged in the action never exchanged fire.

The Japanese regarded the Battle of the Coral Sea as a success, although one costly enough to remind them of the possibilities of defeat. Tactically speaking, it was a Pyrrhic victory for the Japanese. In a wider context, the result was something of a draw. Japanese plotting officers and air controllers had proved themselves far superior to their enemy in the course of the battle, but Japanese combat communications and the coordination of their surface vessels had proved clumsy and unresponsive to the demands of a modern, highly mobile and rather confused mêlée. Beneath the unedifying and exaggerated claims and counter-claims made by the two sides, the *élan* of the Japanese naval command never recovered.

The Americans, though they were concerned about the eventual loss of the *Lexington*, were not entirely displeased at the result of the battle, which had brought to an end the run of easy and almost insolent successes by the Japanese. As a result of the air battles, the Americans drew various tactical conclusions and strengthened the force of fighter aircraft on their carriers. Yamamoto, it began to be whispered abroad, had allowed his methods of warfare to outstrip the personnel which would have made these decisive. Against this, the hit-rate of the Japanese aircraft against the enemy warships had achieved a remarkable 58 per cent, confounding pre-war estimates where figures as low as 3 per cent had been bandied about.

Although the Battle of the Coral Sea weakened both sides on what was to be the eve of the Battle of Midway, the really important fact that would become apparent only in retrospect was that the Battle of the Coral Sea thwarted the Japanese attack on Port Moresby and with it their advance towards the northern approaches of Australia. This was to prove of great significance for the future development of the war.

After the Coral Sea campaign, the Japanese Army wanted to mount another attack on Port Moresby, this time by an overland assault. Once that objective had fallen into Japanese hands, the Army hoped to cross the Coral Sea and invade northern Australia in order to counter the forces which MacArthur was building up for the re-conquest of the Southern Regions. The Naval General Staff, in their turn, was anxious to sever the long line of communications between North America and Australia by seizing New Caledonia, Samoa and the Fiji Islands. This scheme was abandoned when Admiral Yamamoto's Midway Island Campaign was adopted.

THE BATTLE OF MIDWAY

These two operations strengthened Yamamoto in his belief that the further acquisition of territory was not of consequence, and that any action which distracted Japanese power from its main preoccupations was dangerous. At his insistence, it was decided that Japan must concentrate its efforts on the destruction of what was left of the sea power of the Western Allies, especially of the American Pacific Fleet. He, who had inspired the raid on Pearl Harbor, was under no illusion about Japan's hopeless position if the war was prolonged, or until Japan had gained the full advantage which had been hoped for in that bombardment. At the moment when Japan at home was still exulting in the mastery of the lands in the South Seas, he saw only the danger preparing for it in the American dockyards. If the United States had the time to bring its economic strength into play, and to translate this into warships, the United States would be irresistible. Japan could find safety only by striking again, and at once.

Yamamoto had his mind set upon enticing the United States Pacific Fleet out to its destruction by his numerically superior forces. He had little option but to attempt this. His defensive line, 3,000 miles long, was in no sense a barrier impervious to enemy task forces advancing westwards across the Pacific. United States naval operations in the Atlantic and in the Caribbean had deprived the US Pacific Fleet of the superior numerical strength that had figured so largely in pre-war calculations. Nevertheless, United States task forces could be expected to penetrate the Japanese perimeter soon and at any point. Only a dynamic, not static, defence stood any chance of victory in the Pacific. Yamamoto perceived that the only hope of the Imperial Navy lay in luring those task forces into well-laid traps. To that end he formulated a masterful plan. It would incorporate features of Japan's traditional naval strategy, rehearsed a thousand times in Japanese blackboard and table-top exercises, a strategy based upon an attrition of the enemy by auxiliary forces prior to a main engagement from which there would be no escape. It would manifest all the intricacy and counterpoint that the Japanese had learnt from Chinese classical studies of the art of war. The rather simpler and more hidebound dogmas of Admiral Alfred Thayer Mahan and the strictures of Admiral Sir Herbert Richmond, although understood and appreciated by the Japanese, would be expected to limit the initiative of the Americans, who would find themselves mystified, befuddled and demoralized by the dazzling synchronization and complexity that the Japanese attack would display. It was to be an operation, then, well worthy of this historic occasion in the destiny of nations.

Yamamoto urged, and after strong dissent from the Naval General Staff had it accepted, that Japan's next move should be a conquest of Midway, a small coral outcrop composed of two tiny islands less than 1,200 acres in size, linked together to form a circular atoll located near the geographical centre of the North Pacific, where the prevailing oceanic currents sweep 1,100 miles west by north-west of Pearl Harbor along the arc of the Hawaiian Islands. The Doolittle Raid, quite apart from its other consequences, had convinced the Japanese Government and High Command that Yamamoto had been right all along in advocating the importance of depriving the United States of its commanding position in Hawaii.

Hawaii, then, as recent scholarship now shows, was the ultimate objective of the great strategical game that ended in disaster for Japan at Midway. In any event, there were other sufficiently compelling reasons for the Japanese to regard the capture of Midway as a major prize worthy of the risks and expense involved in the operation. If Midway fell into Japan's hands, it would be ideal for mounting Japanese raids against the Pacific coast of America. Yamamoto counted on the United States accepting that its defence was of vital interest, and that it would bring out what was left of the American Navy in its defence. In the battle which would result, he reckoned on sinking the American carriers; and this was the main objective of the expedition. The force which chance had put beyond Japan's reach at Pearl Harbor he would now succeed in driving into action.

Another motive which also weighed with him was to deprive America of the possible use of Midway Island as the airfield for the bombardment of Japan. Though Midway Island had played no part in the recent Doolittle air raid, Midway was only 2,500 miles from Tokyo. Yamamoto felt himself heavily burdened by the duty of protecting the capital of his lord the Emperor from the indignity of bombardment. Everything pointed to Midway Island as the next target at which he should strike. Yamamoto hoped that if the Combined Fleet decisively won the Battle of Midway, as he expected, he could ride the crest of his personal popularity to induce Prime Minister Tōjō to offer the United States a generous peace on terms that the United States could not afford to refuse. Yamamoto's plan involved the extension of Japan's defensive perimeter 2,000 miles into the Pacific through a balletic sequence of offensives executed by half a dozen task forces.

The United States had been in occupation of Midway Island since as long ago as 1867; but it was only in 1938, two years after the expiration of the Washington Treaty limitations, that it recognized its importance. It began to spend large sums of money in fortifying it as a kind of outpost of Pearl Harbor. It was to prove one of the chief theatres of the Pacific War. It was a small coral atoll; the colours, in the dazzling sunshine, were so bright and assertive that they wearied the eye. In the years just before the war, the Americans had built a small but very up-to-date hotel. Its public rooms had, uncannily, the feeling of mountain hotels in, say, Austria; it was strange because the nearest mountains were thousands of miles away; the illusion was heightened because the views from the hotel rooms might have been alpine. The vivid white of the ubiquitous coral might have been snow. The strangest phenomenon of the island was its prehistoric appearance. On all sides were small, gnarled, dried-up, gaunt trees, of stilted and incredible shape, looking like fossils. The whole place was unnaturally silent. There were noises of traffic and motor cars; but behind this a great hush prevailed. The impression was unreal and nightmarish. This was now to be the scenery for one of the greatest battles of the war.

The Japanese assembled a huge fleet. It included eight aircraft-carriers of which four were very large, eleven battleships, twenty-two cruisers, sixty-five destroyers and twenty-one submarines. It was the greatest fleet concentration which had been known in the history of the Pacific. The 145 ships in the fleet were divided into no less than sixteen divisions under four separate commands each assigned a role in Yamamoto's grand strategy to envelop the American fleet. Admiral Nagumo's First Carrier Striking Force, in which were four aircraft-carriers, two battleships, one heavy cruiser, one light cruiser and eleven destroyers, was to make for Midway. They would operate in close support of Vice-Admiral Kondō's Midway Invasion Force, consisting of two battleships, one light carrier, two seaplane carriers, eight heavy cruisers, two light cruisers, twenty-one destroyers and one patrol boat. Under the shadow of Kondō's formidable gunnery was a convoy of fifteen transports under Rear-Admiral Tanaka Raizō carrying an Army regimental force of 3,000 troops and two battalions of marines to form the necessary landing party. Following this, 300 miles in the rear, lurked an even more powerful surface fleet, designated Main Force. It comprised seven battleships, one light carrier, two seaplane carriers (one loaded with midget submarines), three light cruisers and twenty-one destroyers. Very oddly, Yamamoto, who this time did not confine himself to making the general plan of action and supervising it from his headquarters in Japan, placed himself aboard the 72,000-ton monster battleship *Yamato* in command of this section. It was held in reserve to take whatever action might be required after the invasion of Midway, but its intended role was to spring the trap when the United States main battlefleet emerged from its lair at Pearl Harbor to break up the landings. The fourth section of the Japanese fleet, Northern Force, commanded by Vice-Admiral Hosogaya and grouped round two carriers supported by three heavy cruisers, three light cruisers, an armed merchant cruiser, twelve destroyers and three troop transports, was to detach itself from the main body and to move up to the Aleutian Islands, attacking and landing on some selected places three days before the invasion of Midway. This was included in the general plan as the complication and the feint which nearly all Japanese plans contained. The concept was that the United States would divide whatever forces were available to it, and one force would sail for the North Pacific in search of this decoy.

The plan as a whole was a re-run of the Battle of Jutland, in which the stage encompassed the whole of the mid-Pacific rather than the confines of the North Sea. As in the classical, time-honoured battle plan upon which Japan had relied prior to 1941, an advance screen of Japanese submarines, spread across the line of the American advance, would weaken and demoralize the American main fleet as it sailed towards its obliteration in a final duel to the death. Any misjudgement of the American response on the part of Yamamoto and his commanders, however, would doom the Japanese fleet to the destruction of its widely dispersed divisions. It was a calculated risk which went contrary to Admiral Mahan's injunction against divisions into inferior fleets. It ignored Admiral Richmond's reminders that larger capital ships and carriers were not necessarily more capable of performing their mission than smaller ones. It was, however, a gamble worthy of the player, and it went wrong.

From the start there were grave doubts about the expedition among the Japanese Naval Staff, as indeed there were, privately, in the upper echelons of the Combined Fleet. There was anxiety about the deficient preparation of officers, about their inadequate briefing, about the speed with which the expedition was launched, about the lack of time for adequate digestion of the lessons of the Battle of the Coral Sea, about the wisdom of the tactics which had been used in that, about the security which had been observed, even about the morale of some of the fleet. The senior officers were despondent at the boasting and indiscipline of some of the younger men. The Navy pilots, whom Yamamoto had trained, were held in suspicion by the rest of the Navy, and this was not relieved by their tendency to regard themselves as a race apart. Especially by the more responsible officers, Yamamoto was criticized for the speed which he demanded. This meant that the two powerful aircraft-carriers which had been badly damaged in the Battle of the Coral Sea could not take part; they had to be in dock under repair for several months. Their absence was severely felt. So was the fact that the remaining carriers and their crews, worked to the limits of their endurance since 7 December, were sorely in need of extensive refurbishment and rest. But Yamamoto felt that the political situation required immediate action, and everything was subordinated to this.

The sailing of the fleet from Hashira through the Bungo Channel on 21 May for two days of fleet exercises was one of the most spectacular sights in any country during the war years. There were cheers and enthusiasm from the considerable crowd who witnessed it. The Japanese, though they lived with extreme frugality on all their expeditions, contrasting spectacularly in this with the standards of well-being required by British and American forces, observed ritual and ceremony for commemorating the start of a major operation. On their return to their anchorages on 25 May, Yamamoto gathered together his senior commanders to issue them with final instructions. On 27 May, Navy Day, celebrations were held in harbour to mark the anniversary of Admiral Tōgō's victory over the Russians at Tsushima. All present were conscious that the destiny of Japan now lay with them. The sailing of a fleet which was intended to complete the work of Pearl Harbor and to destroy the capacity of the American Navy to restrain Japan in Asia, was blessed by all the forms of Shinto, the Japanese state religion, and also, though less wholeheartedly, by Buddhism. Cups of sake were drunk which were a present from the

Japanese Emperor. Early on the morning of 28 May, the first elements of Yamamoto's forces weighed anchor, sailing away from Hashira and from other harbours for their appointed positions. For two days, other ships followed at pre-set intervals. The weather was fair, and along the shores, where people once more gathered to watch in awe as the ships departed, it was widely rumoured that the destination of the fleet was Midway. Yamamoto, however, hoped that the complexity of his plan would disguise his ultimate objective. He knew from intercepted radio transmissions that American submarines reported his departure. Western scholars, reading of these scenes, may remember the account by Thucydides of the sailing of another fleet on what was meant to be the culminating operation of a war 2,300 years before:

The ships being now manned, and everything with which they meant to sail being put on board, the trumpet commanded silence, and the prayers customary before putting out to sea were offered, not in each ship by itself, but by all together to the voice of the herald; and bowls of wine were mixed through all the armament, and libations made by the soldiers and their officers in gold and silver goblets. In their prayers joined also the crowds on shore, the citizens and all others that wished them well. The hymns sung and the libations finished, they put out to sea, and sang. The first ships then raced each other in columns as far as Aegina.

The battle came on 4 June 1942. The Americans had been better informed than Japanese Intelligence allowed for, and had again been admirably served by what they were able to learn from cracking the Japanese naval codes. On 1 April the Japanese Naval General Staff had taken the precaution of distributing new codes to the fleet, but the United States Navy had recovered a set of codebooks and cipher tables from a Japanese fleet submarine sunk in shallow waters off the coast of Australia in January. This, together with the activities of a United States Navy codebreaking team based in Hawaii, had enabled the Americans to unravel vital naval ciphers that had previously eluded them. Problems in distributing the new codebooks led the Japanese to delay their introduction until 1 June. By then it was too late. The broad outlines of the Japanese plans were known (although it would take the Americans months to adapt to the new codes afterwards).

We may pause to marvel at the fact that on the other side of the globe German naval Intelligence had come to believe that the Japanese naval ciphers were being read by the Allied Powers. Their long-standing suspicions had been confirmed by documentary evidence acquired after the German surface raider *Thor* intercepted the Australian steamer *Nankin* in the Indian Ocean on its way from Sydney to Colombo on 10 May 1942: mail bags found aboard the vessel included Intelligence summaries prepared by the Combined Operations Intelligence Centre at Wellington. In spite of this hard information, the Germans remained silent, doing nothing to alert the Japanese. It was a decision which speaks volumes about the contemptuous disregard of the Germans for their most powerful ally, and it was a disastrous misjudgement.

The Americans, then, and their British Allies were aware of what Japan had gone to ingenious lengths to hide: that Yamamoto's main objective was Midway, and that the assault on the Aleutians was a diversion. Yamamoto was right in supposing that the Americans would fight, even though their Navy had not yet recovered from Pearl Harbor, and was manifestly not ready; he was wrong in thinking that they would divide their inadequate fleet, and would send a part to hunt for the raiders in the Aleutians. The Americans could assemble on the spot three aircraft-carriers: in the whole American Navy at this time there were seven. One of these carriers was the *Yorktown*, which had been so heavily damaged in the Coral Sea that the Japanese believed it sunk, and had accredited themselves with a groundless victory. In fact it escaped to Hawaii, and, while the Japanese ships in a similar plight had entered the Japanese shipyards for thorough repairs, and were out of action for some months, the Hawaiian shipyards, under pressure of the news about Midway, made the *Yorktown* fit for fighting again in three days, though their first estimate had been that it would take three months: 1,400 men worked on her round the clock. The Americans also assembled eight cruisers and fifteen destroyers. The Japanese had therefore a more formidable resistance to overcome than they had thought it possible for the United States to assemble, especially as they also underestimated the American strength in aircraft and troops on Midway.

The poor state of Japanese naval Intelligence at Midway is illustrated by an expectation at the Imperial General Headquarters that the Invasion Force would have to overcome 750 American troops and 60 land-based enemy aircraft. It was anticipated that the 5,000 Japanese marines and close to 234 operational Japanese naval aircraft available to cover them would quickly overwhelm the defenders. In fact, however, Midway was protected by a battalion of more than 3,000 marines and 126 aircraft, and since the 230 aircraft in the combined task forces of Rear-Admiral Raymond Spruance and Rear Admiral Frank Jack Fletcher were lying in wait for the Japanese to strike, the odds were stacked heavily against the success of the invasion.

Bad preliminary Intelligence on the Japanese side was compounded by haphazard fleet reconnaissance during the operation. The over-confidence felt by the Japanese naval forces affected every aspect of the battle in its initial phases. Luck favoured the Americans as it had at the Battle of the Coral Sea. Ever since March, Kawanishi flying boats based in the Marshall Islands had flown periodic night-time reconnaissance missions over Pearl Harbor, hazardous undertakings made possible only by refuelling from big I-class submarines at an isolated anchorage known as French Frigate Shoals. Between 27–30 May, however, while the USS *Yorktown* was under repair at Pearl Harbor, the submarines signalled Tokyo that a tanker, two American destroyers and two flying boats were patrolling the reef where the rendezvous was expected to take place: the Americans, having discovered what the Japanese were doing, were determined to put a stop to it. On 30 May the Naval General Staff ordered the flights suspended. Unaccountably, the Japanese had failed to provide a fall-back plan and no attempt was made to divert the submarine to nearby Necker Island where refuelling could have taken place. Had a flight been possible on the following day, the Japanese would have found Pearl Harbor empty: the hunted had turned hunters. Meanwhile Yamamoto had sent out thirteen I-class submarines to form a picket line between Pearl Harbor and Midway. They were intended to detect the approach of the American fleet and then to attack it. They arrived too late: the Americans were already in the vicinity of Midway. Although Yamamoto had not expected to surprise the Americans at Midway, the Japanese Fleet continued to remain in the dark concerning the size and location of the US Pacific Fleet.

The Japanese Navy had no radar. That Japan, and that Admiral Yamamoto, who had espoused everything to do with the air, had neglected to acquaint himself with this invention, is astonishing. The fact must detract something from Yamamoto's reputation for alertness. Radar had already been widely used in Britain for more than two years, and a form of it was also known in Germany. The Germans sent the Japanese two radar sets by submarine, but either they did not send technicians with the apparatus, or these made no impression upon the Japanese. This incident, together with the Germans' failure to advise the Japanese about the insecurity of the Japanese ciphers, shows how slight and ineffective was much of the technical cooperation of the two Powers. In the present case the deficiencies of Intelligence, working without adequate equipment, was to exact a price.

As the two American task forces awaited the approaching Japanese, a US Navy Catalina PBY flying boat, only thirty miles within the extreme range of his aircraft, early on the morning of 3 June located Rear-Admiral

THE BATTLE OF MIDWAY, 5 JUNE 1942

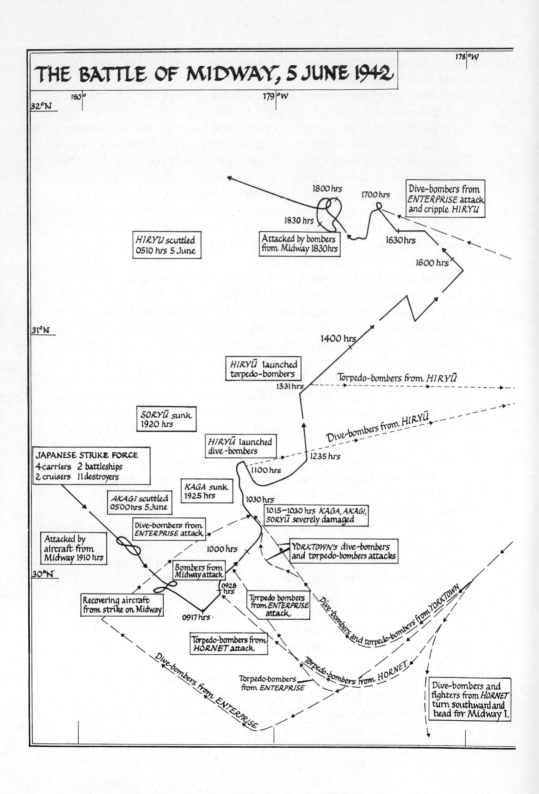

32°N

180°

179°W

178°W

1800 hrs

1700 hrs

Dive-bombers from *ENTERPRISE* attack and cripple *HIRYU*

1830 hrs

1630 hrs

HIRYU scuttled 0510 hrs 5 June

Attacked by bombers from Midway 1830hrs

1600 hrs

31°N

1400 hrs

HIRYŪ launched torpedo-bombers

Torpedo-bombers from *HIRYŪ*

1331 hrs

SORYŪ sunk 1920 hrs

Dive-bombers from *HIRYŪ*

HIRYŪ launched dive-bombers

1235 hrs

JAPANESE STRIKE FORCE
4 carriers   2 battleships
2 cruisers   11 destroyers

1100 hrs

KAGA sunk 1925 hrs

1030 hrs

1015–1030 hrs *KAGA, AKAGI, SORYŪ* severely damaged

AKAGI scuttled 0500 hrs 5 June

Dive-bombers from *ENTERPRISE* attack

YORKTOWN's dive-bombers and torpedo-bombers attacks

Attacked by aircraft from Midway 1910 hrs

1000 hrs

30°N

Bombers from Midway attack

0928 hrs

Dive-bombers and torpedo-bombers from *YORKTOWN*

Recovering aircraft from strike on Midway

0917 hrs

Torpedo-bombers from *ENTERPRISE* attack

Torpedo-bombers from *HORNET* attack

Torpedo-bombers from *HORNET*

Dive-bombers from *ENTERPRISE*

Torpedo-bombers from *ENTERPRISE*

Dive-bombers and fighters from *HORNET* turn southward and head for Midway I.

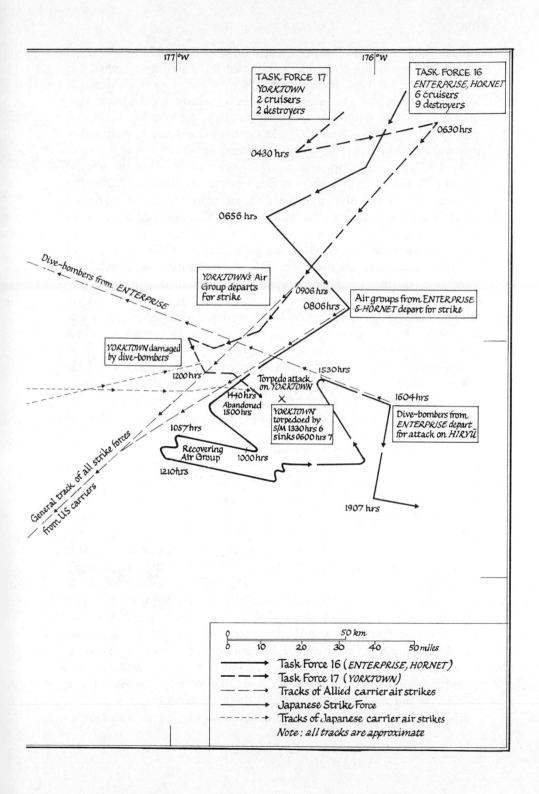

177°W   176°W

TASK FORCE 17
YORKTOWN
2 cruisers
2 destroyers

TASK FORCE 16
ENTERPRISE, HORNET
6 cruisers
9 destroyers

0630 hrs

0430 hrs

0656 hrs

Dive-bombers from *ENTERPRISE*

YORKTOWN's Air Group departs for strike

0906 hrs

0806 hrs

Air groups from *ENTERPRISE* & *HORNET* depart for strike

YORKTOWN damaged by dive-bombers

1200 hrs

1530 hrs

Torpedo attack on *YORKTOWN*

1140 hrs
Abandoned
1500 hrs

1604 hrs

Dive-bombers from *ENTERPRISE* depart for attack on *HIRYU*

YORKTOWN torpedoed by S/M 1330 hrs 6 sinks 0600 hrs 7

1057 hrs

Recovering Air Group

1000 hrs

1210 hrs

1907 hrs

General track of all strike forces from U.S. carriers

0   50 km

0   10   20   30   40   50 miles

⟶ Task Force 16 (*ENTERPRISE, HORNET*)

⟶ Task Force 17 (*YORKTOWN*)

⟶ Tracks of Allied carrier air strikes

⟶ Japanese Strike Force

⟶ Tracks of Japanese carrier air strikes

Note: all tracks are approximate

Tanaka Raizō's Second Fleet Occupation Escort Force 670 miles west of Midway. A few hours later, nine land-based B17 bombers attacked this force, scoring no hits. Before the B17s returned, four Catalinas left Midway in search of the same targets. In a moonlit night attack, they torpedoed a tanker and raked one of Tanaka's fifteen troop transports with machine-gun fire. As the Catalina crews neared home, their radios reported that Midway itself was under enemy air attack.

At 4.30 a.m., 108 Japanese aircraft prepared for take-off aboard Admiral Nagumo's four carriers in fine weather and calm seas 220 miles west of Midway. Within a quarter of an hour, 36 Aichi high-level bombers and 36 Nakajima torpedo bombers accompanied by 36 Zero fighters were airborne. Half an hour later, a Catalina reconnaissance aircraft sighted the *Akagi* and flashed its location to Midway. The USS *Enterprise* overheard the exchange and passed the message to the USS *Yorktown*. Another Catalina reported sighting the incoming enemy aircraft heading for Midway at a distance of 150 miles from the atoll. Within minutes radar installations on Midway began tracking the Japanese aircraft. At 5.53 a.m. every American aircraft on Midway capable of flight was ordered into the air to meet the enemy.

A motley collection of 6 Navy Avenger torpedo bombers, 16 Marine Corps Dauntless dive bombers, 16 Army B17s and 4 strange torpedo-carrying B26s left Midway in a splendidly brave but vain effort to destroy Nagumo's Carrier Strike Force. They caused little direct damage. Few of them survived.

The air raid on Midway went ahead at 6.34 a.m. In the one-sided aerial combat that ensued, 17 of the 27 hopelessly outdated Buffaloes and Wildcat fighter aircraft flown by US Marine Corps airmen perished. Of the remaining 10, 7 sustained such severe damage that they would never fly again. None of the Japanese aircraft fell victim to the American fliers, a tribute to the skills of the Japanese and to the performance of the latest Japanese Zeke fighters (which were incomparably superior to the Zeros that had proved so successful in the opening days of the Pacific War). Nevertheless, exceptionally accurate anti-aircraft fire took a toll of 38 Japanese aircraft and disabled a further 29. That left Nagumo with only 167 aircraft to match against the 230 of the American carriers. The advantages of experience and better aircraft still lay with the Japanese, but it was apparent that Admiral Yamamoto had been unfortunate in frittering away a third of his total air combat forces by detaching the *Ryūjō* and *Junyō* to the Aleutian Campaign, the *Hōshō* to his Main Force battleships and the *Zuiho* to Admiral Kondō's Second Fleet.

The first that the Japanese admiral commanding the aircraft-carrier, who was again Nagumo, knew of the proximity of the Americans was when, about 9 a.m. on 4 June, he was surprised by an American raid when he had his aircraft assembled on deck for a raid on Midway, but when they had not yet taken off. As it appeared afterwards, the fate of the mighty armada, of the Midway expedition, and of the possibility of a future descent on the American coast, was decided in five minutes. Nagumo's carrier was torpedoed at this time, and three of the four carriers in his Strike Force were mortally struck. The battle continued all that day, very similar to the Coral Sea, with the two navies out of sight of each other; this time the Japanese pilots, in contrast to the Americans, proved definitely inferior. The action was a confused affair of aircraft from each side which savagely attacked the others, and then pounced on each other's carriers when they were inadequately guarded.

The Japanese had more than their share of misfortune. Radio messages were received five minutes too late; cloud movements happened in such a way as just to obscure the movements of the enemy. But in all the confusion, it is clear that on this occasion the high commanders, and the Japanese Navy as a whole, did not display the professionalism, the power of rapid adaptation, the coolness amid the horrors of air combat at sea, which were necessary to bring victory in this kind of action.

Apart from the deficiencies in their communications equipment, the defects in the Japanese Fleet were personal rather than mechanical. Japan did not lose the battle because of the engineering superiority of the United States. In the actual fighting, the Japanese aircraft, the Zeke fighter, which was first tried out at Midway, was the best plane on either side.

Skilful shiphandling by the Japanese, far superior skill by the Japanese pilots in their even more superior aircraft – all of this was set at nought by reconnaissance failures and errors in judgement of Admiral Yamamoto, Admiral Nagumo and their subordinate commanders. Yamamoto himself cannot escape blame for his failure to obtain reliable Intelligence confirming his assumptions that the *Yorktown* had perished in the Coral Sea and that the *Hornet* and *Enterprise* had remained in the South-West Pacific. Equally, he alone had the responsibility of determining the moment when the screen of submarines should take their appointed place in the line: it is difficult to fathom why he failed to dispatch them earlier. These errors were compounded by his inability to change the plan once it was set in motion. He and his subordinate commanders were handicapped by a completely inadequate radio communications system. Even after his forces were detected, Yamamoto imposed a radio silence throughout the battle; he was virtually a spectator of the action. Thus Yamamoto, his fleets widely and needlessly dispersed, condemned himself to impotence in the kind of battle which he had for so long preached as inevitable at the stage which naval strategy had reached at the time.

The American fleet, as it appeared later, did not realize for some time how complete and profound their victory had been. In the confusion of the conflict, they assumed for some time that two of the carriers, which had in fact been sunk, had escaped and were on their way back to Japan. Ultimately the facts were established and they were these. Within the space of twenty-four hours, Japan had lost all four of its largest aircraft-carriers (the fourth sank later in the day) and a heavy cruiser. Another heavy cruiser suffered serious damage, two destroyers were disabled, and three further vessels including a battleship were slightly damaged. The Japanese had lost a total of 332 aircraft, including 10 flying boats, 6 aircraft shot down by anti-aircraft fire during the Midway air strike, 12 fighters that failed to return from combat air patrol, 24 aircraft lost in attacking the American carriers, and another 280 (including 70 partially dismantled fighter aircraft which the carriers were ferrying to Midway) that went down when their carriers sank. A total of 3,500 Japanese sailors lost their lives.

By contrast, the American losses were the *Yorktown*, which was finally sunk, a destroyer, 38 shore-based aircraft, 109 carrier-based aircraft, and 307 lives. A number of ground installations on Midway were destroyed and others were temporarily put out of action.

The nature and source of the losses reveals the scale of the Japanese misfortune. The Imperial Navy lost a high percentage of its best pilots not in air combat (where they continued to excel) but aboard the carriers where the Americans caught them rearming their aircraft. Others dropped one by one into the sea when their fuel supplies were exhausted and there was nowhere else left to land. These airmen, many veterans of the China Incident and years of training, were irreplaceable. Midway marked a turning-point in the fortunes of the Pacific War, and the Japanese Navy never again fought from a position of strength.

Admiral Yamamoto, with the Main Force of battleships, made some effort at retrieving the disaster. He ordered Vice-Admiral Tanaka's Invasion Force back to Japan before it had even attempted to storm the Island of Midway. He recalled the aircraft-carriers which had been sent to the Aleutians, and resumed the hunt for the American carriers, which had destroyed his own fleet. But, in the end, he broke off the battle, partly, it seems, because he felt he could no longer rely on Japanese Intelligence, and because he wisely decided not to risk his battleships further. He brought the Combined Fleet home to Japan, reorganized it, and with an oddly disembodied sense of purpose, laid plans for what should be done next.

Only the Alaskan venture went ahead to achieve a modest success before it petered out in aimless sailings. An American weather station, fuel dumps, a handful of vessels and a few aircraft were attacked at Dutch Harbor on the eastern end of the Aleutians. Japanese troops made unopposed landings on Attu and Kiska at the extreme western end of the island chain and thereby had the distinction of becoming the only enemy garrisons ever to establish themselves on the soil of the Western Hemisphere at any time during the Second World War. Without the strength of the Combined Fleet to give it support, it was to be only a question of time before it would wither on the vine. It was a thoroughly bad detachment. Eventually the Americans were sufficiently distracted by the bait to tie up tens of thousands of troops and considerable naval forces in what became a protracted effort to recapture the two islands. But from the Japanese point of view it became costly to maintain the garrisons, which anyway suffered excruciating hardships. Any small gains produced by their fortitude and endurance, however, were as nothing compared to the importance of the losses sustained by the Japanese at Midway.

The Japanese Government, very prudently, did not allow the shock of the defeat and the collapse of hopes to become public. Its first aim was to hush up the defeat. Admiral Kondō Nobutake, to whom Yamamoto had handed command of Admiral Nagumo's carriers after the latter's disgrace, said: 'Our forces suffered a reverse so decisive and so grave that details of it were kept as a secret to all but a limited circle, even within the Japanese Navy. Even after the war, few among high ranking officers were familiar with the details of the Midway operation.'* A Japanese naval captain complained of the way that the returning sailors were held incommunicado. The wounded were brought ashore after dark, and taken to hospital through the rear entrances. He was himself among those who suffered. The experience is described in *Midway: The Battle that Doomed Japan* by Fuchida and Okumiya.† 'My room was in complete isolation,' he says. 'No nurses or medical attendants were allowed in, and I could not communicate with the world outside. All the wounded from Midway were treated like this. It was like being a prisoner of war among your own people.' After the Japanese surrender in 1945, all the papers that the Japanese authorities could

* John Deane Potter, op. cit.
† Fuchida and Okumiya, *Midway: The Battle that Doomed Japan*, US Naval Institute, Hutchinson, London, 1957.

find about the defeat, classified as top secret, were burned. The extent and gravity of the disaster which Japan had suffered did not become plain to the Japanese public until publication of accounts of the battle by survivors in the course of the 1950s.

The long run of sensational Japanese victories, bought at such little cost, had come finally to an end. The crippling of the U S Pacific Fleet at Pearl Harbor, and the blows at the Royal Navy, had all been made at the ridiculously small expense of the loss of four destroyers. This period was over. At Midway a technically smaller American fleet had challenged the passage of the Japanese Imperial Navy, had defeated it, had turned it back. It had lost prestige hopelessly, it had lost the *élan* of victory, and the margin of its losses turned decisively against it. It had forfeited its ability to strike where it chose, and to govern the course of the war. Having lost this initiative, it had condemned Japan to convert the war into a holding operation – this, as Admiral Yamamoto had warned, condemned Japan to defeat by the United States as soon as the American economic mobilization was complete.

CHAPTER 20

MacArthur in the Pacific

THE naval war between Japan and the United States was to be waged henceforward with the utmost ferocity in the crucial theatre of the South-West Pacific. Japan had not foreseen that its action there would become so critical for its fate: but it had lost the freedom of action at the Battle of Midway Island. The United States set itself to wrest the South-West Pacific from its hold, and Japan, which had committed itself heavily in the region, set itself doggedly to oppose it, first of all trying to enlarge its position, and later selling its territory inch by inch, and with such grimness that it hoped that the United States would become tired of the enterprise.

As the fighting grew in intensity, it gradually became plain that, in this Pacific theatre, the war against Japan could be won. The Pacific offered the path to Tokyo. Interest fell away from the other theatres and other activities, from India and from China, and was concentrated on two American commanders, General Douglas MacArthur and Admiral Chester Nimitz, who shared the direction of events in this region.

General MacArthur, in whom burned most clearly the determination to restore the United States' position, and whose skill, confidence and military genius were thought to have made him the most effective commander for the purpose, had in March 1942 been ordered to withdraw from the fighting in the Philippines. He began his duel with Japan under something of a cloud. His withdrawal from the Philippines, though it had been ordered by Roosevelt, and though it was common sense, had, in the hectic atmosphere of the time, been criticized by the American Army, especially by the troops he had left behind. MacArthur was a general whose behaviour often flouted the conventions of the day. In the Philippines he had won disapproval by insisting that his wife and family should remain with him: he was able to do so because he had been under Filipino regulations and was free of American Army discipline. This singular man was to impose himself on the American and Australian Armies, who were almost fanatical in their dislike of privilege, and to make himself respected by virtue of his cult of personality if not superiority.

On his escape from Manila in a speedboat, he had had an adventurous voyage to the southern tip of the Philippines. When he got there, he found difficulty in going further. Rivalry between the American services made the American admiral in command in the region unwilling to spare any aircraft for his rescue. Application had to be made over his head through Washington to transport MacArthur to Australia.

It had been agreed between President Roosevelt and Churchill that operations in Australia should be under an American command, and to this post MacArthur was designated. The Australian forces, many of them battle-trained in the Middle East, passed under his control. On taking over, MacArthur found the Australians thinking in terms of defence. Their morale had been shattered by the events in Singapore, which they had been accustomed to thinking of as a guarantee of Australian security, and they did not quickly adapt themselves to its overthrow. Psychologically they were in the position of France after the loss of the Maginot Line. The Japanese appeared to be unstoppable, and were heading for Sydney and Melbourne; and the Australians looked round in despondency for a remedy. They aimed at holding the southern part of the continent on a line which passed through Brisbane. That portion to the north of this they had virtually reconciled themselves to losing when the Japanese invasion, which was expected in a matter of weeks, should begin.

MacArthur's initial success was to change this attitude. He infused the Australians with confidence, and with the offensive spirit. His command was extremely short in manpower: it was poorly equipped, and its air power was deficient. But within three months the counter-offensive started.

The area which was the scene of the fighting was a chain of coral islands which lies to the north of Australia and curls around to the northeast. The pressure of the original Japanese offensive had nearly carried them to this region. But it had begun to flag before Japan had occupied the whole system. If Japan had overrun the islands, it would have been able to set up bases there from which it could have interrupted communications between Australian ports. The chain of islands was half-held by the Japanese, but their firm occupation came to an end in the Solomon Islands, and did not extend to the New Hebrides or New Caledonia. The objective of their next offensive, with a dangerously extended line of communication, was the Australian outpost of Port Moresby in the south of Papua, which was the Australian extension of New Guinea. This lay just to the south of the islands occupied by Japan and well within range of their new stronghold at Rabaul, a superb natural harbour in New Britain, easily captured from the Australians in January and then quickly transformed into an impressive fleet base surrounded by a cluster of airfields and military installations.

It was a matter of urgency to scatter the Japanese forces, which were preparing to take Port Moresby. The first engagement was the drawn naval battle between American and Japanese aircraft-carriers off the coast of Papua at the beginning of May 1942: the Battle of the Coral Sea. It was said to be drawn because losses on both sides had been roughly equal; but the Japanese had been convoying troops, which were intended for a *coup de main* against Port Moresby, and these were turned back and never came again. Thus the issue of the battle in truth favoured the Allies.

The Japanese were, however, favourably placed. From their bases they bombed Port Darwin, on the Australian coast, and severely damaged it. Having abandoned their hopes of taking Port Moresby by a frontal assault from the sea, the Japanese Army landed the first of 15,000 troops on the northern coast of Papua on 21 July 1942 with the intention of advancing overland across the Owen Stanley Range to take Port Moresby from the rear. MacArthur moved to counter the attack, inadequate though his force was. Three weeks after the Japanese landing, MacArthur sent reinforcements to New Guinea with orders to wrest Papua from the Japanese. At first the Japanese pushed the Australians southward until, suffering from severe malnutrition, dysentery and food poisoning – all of which affected both sides – the Japanese advance ground to a halt barely thirty miles from Port Moresby in mid-September. By that time MacArthur had assembled two Australian divisions (less one brigade) and leading elements of a United States Army division which was on its way. They could call on no effective naval support and their air support was supplied by a hodge-podge of aircraft of indeterminate vintage. On 23 September MacArthur handed over the counter-offensive to General Sir Thomas Blamey, the Australian Commander-in-Chief for Allied Land Forces in the South-West Pacific. In a painful struggle which took a further four months under appalling conditions, they prevailed. The struggle ended in January 1943 when the few surviving Japanese were no longer capable of organized resistance.

The backbone of the force was the Seventh Australian Division, veterans of the Middle East who had been among the Australian forces originally sent out as a rag-tag force, under-equipped and under-trained, to Palestine, then ordered to Greece, but diverted first to the Western Desert and back to Palestine whence it earned its spurs in a difficult but forgotten campaign in Lebanon and Syria against the Vichy French. With the collapse of British resistance in Malaya, the Seventh had been pulled out of the Middle East as part of the forces shifted to defend Australia.

Wavell, with Churchill's support, had wanted them in Burma and tried to hijack them when they reached Ceylon, but the Australian Prime Minister insisted they proceed to Java, which was how they came to be in Papua. Gripped by political and strategical forces beyond its ability to influence, the Division's history of irritating administrative confusion and muddle was perhaps no more than characteristic of army life. The fighting in Papua well suited the individual qualities of the men of the Seventh.

It was largely a series of savage hand-to-hand conflicts, and there was less skill in manoeuvre than was to be usual in the campaigns designed by MacArthur. It was, however, notable for the skilful use of aircraft, themselves largely improvised for supplying troops (as in Burma later). It was also remarkable for the endurance of the troops, and for their overcoming mountainous jungles in conditions of equatorial heat, humidity and mud that make the area one of the most unhealthy and exhausting climates in the world.

It was a battle on a scale smaller than many, yet the maniacal tenacity of the Japanese which was to be a feature of the entire campaign is summed up in the final tally of human lives: of 13,000 Japanese losses in action in the final stage, only thirty-eight men were taken prisoner. The Australians lost 5,700 men, the Americans a further 2,800.

This operation in eastern New Guinea was quite a small one, and, with so much happening in the rest of the world, not very much noticed. But in the record of the whole war, it was significant. It marked the end of the Japanese offensive. It was the start of expeditions, desperately hard-fought but in the end universally successful, to force Japan back across the sea which it had sailed out to dominate so spectacularly. But MacArthur, surveying the tasks which still lay before him, was painfully aware of the difficulties which lay ahead.

He was fighting over a vast area, large parts of which were still unmapped. This was a handicap which has been little recognized, but was very grave indeed. For an American general to plan a troop landing in Europe with maps and charts showing the tidal movements was one thing: to plan the same operation for coral islands, where all that was available was native guess-work, was quite another. He was short of ships; he was given only medium-range bomber aircraft when he needed essentially long-range bombers; everywhere he went, airfields had to be constructed, often hacked out of the jungle by indigenous labour. For his supplies he had to compete with seven or eight rival theatres of war, and, as it seemed to him, invariably came out worst. Disease, especially malaria, was a still more deadly enemy than the Japanese, and the means of overcoming it could only be found by experimenting – and by exposing his armies at first to its ravages.

Nevertheless, from Port Moresby and the operations which he conducted for its relief in the encircling Owen Stanley Mountains, he was led on to the steps which, laborious operation after perilous initiative, in the end resulted in the reconquest of all New Guinea from the Japanese. From this position, he prepared to leap ahead, to wreak havoc among the forces guarding the Japanese Empire.

As the campaign in Papua was coming to a close, in the first part of 1943 the Ninth Australian Division, which had displayed superb fighting qualities against Field Marshal Erwin Rommel's forces at the Battle of Alamein, was returned to Australia for a much-needed period of recovery. After training in jungle warfare in Australia, the Ninth was dispatched to help four other Australian divisions and several American regiments to expel the Japanese from the Huon Peninsula, the area of the New Guinea mandate nearest to New Britain (and therefore Rabaul). The Japanese had taken control of the whole of the Peninsula and its southern approaches in March 1942 and had utilized their year of grace to construct airstrips and well-prepared fixed defences. The whole operation took a year to complete between early 1943 and the first few months of 1944. The vast difficulties of nature took its toll as it had elsewhere in New Guinea and the lesser islands nearby, where American forces were also overwhelming the Japanese defenders. Lieutenant-General R. L. Eichelberger, Commander of the Thirty-second US Army Division in Papua, painted the scene:

It was about one part fighting to three parts sheer misery of physical environment. It was climbing up one hill and down another, and then, when breath was short, fording streams with weapons held aloft or wading through swamps. It was sweat and then chill; it was a weariness of body and spirit; and once again tropical illness was a greater foe than enemy bullets.*

The eventual victory of the Allied forces, costly though it was, had never been in doubt. MacArthur was not a sporting man, and he used his superior numerical strength to advantage. The Huon Peninsula campaign, however, is interesting from another point of view as well: in the event, it was to be the last major campaign involving Australian Army forces in the Second World War.

In retrospect, it is plain that the Japanese, from the point of view of their long-term interests, would have done well to limit their offensive; to avoid overlong lines of communication; to have declined combat when

* R. L. Eichelberger, *Jungle Road to Tokyo*, Odhams Press, London, 1951, p. 109.

1078   *The High Tide of War*

this could be avoided; above all, not to have been lured into a contest for
the possession of islands, which could only be of marginal use to them.
This was the view of many of the Japanese generals, and if it had prevailed
in shaping the strategy would have greatly increased the difficulty of the
Americans in coming to grips with the Japanese Empire. But the Japanese
Navy, still determined to conduct the Pacific War as a naval war, still
over-confident in spite of the Battle of Midway, still with an abundance
of battleships and cruisers which it could safely risk, overruled the Japanese Armies. Little by little the scope of the war enlarged, and eventually
spread through all the intricate chain of coral islands in the Pacific. There
was little rational planning behind the operations.

From the start the Americans had had a second headquarters command
in the Pacific Ocean. In March 1942 the Pacific, by a decision of President
Roosevelt, ratified perforce by the British, Australians and Dutch, was
divided formally between General MacArthur and Admiral Nimitz.
MacArthur's command included Australia, the Philippines, the Solomons,
and most of the Dutch East Indies. The rest of the Pacific fell to Nimitz.
But it was not a clear-cut geographical division of responsibility. Each of
these officers was entrusted formally with the command of all armed
forces in his area, whether on land, sea or in the air; but, by the instrument
providing for the division between the commands, it was provided that
Admiral Nimitz should have general control of all amphibious operations,
whether these took place in his own zone or MacArthur's.

This rather peculiar division caused trouble about the demarcation. It
was against logic, and ran counter to the teaching of experience in other
theatres of war. MacArthur wrote:

Of all the faulty decisions of the war, perhaps the most inexpressible one was the
failure to unify the command in the Pacific ... It resulted in divided effort, the
waste of diffusion and duplication of force, and undue extension of war with
added casualties and cost.*

The division was difficult to maintain. For example, MacArthur's operations in clearing the menacing Japanese from Port Moresby were on
various occasions more amphibious than military, but he succeeded in
keeping the campaign to himself. MacArthur wrote with a personal interest about the danger of divided aims. It galled him that it was freely
suggested that he, though he was celebrated for his caution, could not be
trusted with the safety of the Navy's precious ships. A further limitation

* C. Willoughby and J. Chamberlain: *MacArthur 1941–51*, McGraw-Hill, New York,
  1954.

on him was that the charter setting up the respective commands laid down that Nimitz was from the start to be offensive in his operations; MacArthur, by contrast, was to fight defensively. This grudging attitude was to run, as a discordant thread, throughout the early years of the American counter-attack.

In this issue, MacArthur set himself, not for the only time in his career, to oppose the general political plan of Washington, on which the plan of campaign eventually depended. The Navy had for long looked forward to a war with Japan. War in the Pacific must essentially be a naval one; the principal interest with which it was fought must be the aircraft-carriers and battleships and the commander of these must be an admiral. The plans according to which it was fought had for two or three generations been the basic manuals for American naval training. This was the prevailing conception among the service chiefs in Washington; MacArthur was a general, and that was fatal to him. American naval officers form a curious, exclusive caste in American society; the war was an opportunity for this caste which it could not neglect. It is true that in the European War the Navy took second place; circumstances had taken charge and had directed a land strategy. It seemed only compensating justice that in the East Asian and Pacific Conflict, where geography restored primacy to the sea, the Navy and its traditional ancillary arm, the Marines, should be the main protagonists.

The arrangement of the two commands had further consequences. It had been agreed between Roosevelt and Churchill that the United States should have a large measure of independent initiative in the organization of military affairs in the Pacific. As Britain had the lion's share of the initiative in the Middle East and in the Indian Ocean, so did the United States rule the Pacific War. This was in contrast to the convention operating in Europe and the Atlantic, where the planning was a matter of joint British and American responsibility; in the Pacific, any British initiative came to be headed off. By this process, the United States to some extent evaded the general directive, laid down very soon after Pearl Harbor, that the war in the Pacific was to take second place to the war in Europe. In 1942 the Americans systematically built up their war-making capacity in the Pacific through the sympathetic connivance of the Chiefs of Staff in Washington. MacArthur might groan that he still had ridiculously inadequate supplies, but they were very much larger than had been envisaged by the directive. Twice as many supplies were sent across the Pacific in the first six months of March 1942 as were sent to the European theatre of war. By the end of 1942, the United States had reinforced its stations in the Pacific by a total of 15,000 troops more than had been originally intended.

In August 1942 the Navy had its first chance to take charge of amphibious operations on a large scale. These were in Guadalcanal, a tiny island in the Solomons: it was in MacArthur's command area, but the campaign there was directed by the Naval Chiefs of Staff and played little part in his biography. Once more, the area of combat was in the disputed coral islands which ringed Australia. Guadalcanal was very little known or explored; before its conquest by Japan, it had been a British colony; the local people were extremely primitive; a few traders were like characters from a novel by Joseph Conrad. The colony, which is only ninety miles long and twenty-five miles broad, is the epitome of a tropical island. Along its sandy beaches are coconut palms; abruptly behind them there rise jungly mountains and extinct volcanoes to a height of seven thousand feet. The flat ground is dark, steamy, rotting jungle, the perfect terrain for breeding the malaria mosquito.

The Japanese nearly beat the Americans to possession of it. They had occupied it with a skeleton force, and American air reconnaissance showed that they were building an airfield on it. They were interrupted by a counter-invasion: the Americans landed a force of 11,000 men. At first, both sides supposed that the fate of Guadalcanal would be settled within a week. Actually a savage and terrible struggle developed there which lasted until February 1943, when the Japanese decided to release their grip. The Americans had discovered what war in the Pacific amounted to, and had done so at horrendous cost. There had been no such gruelling campaigns before in the history of the war. The victory won by the Americans eliminated a threat to the Allied supply lines and provided the United States forces with a valuable forward airbase.

The battle cost the Americans six major naval engagements, and a heavy toll of shipping. Both sides lost an equal number of warships (twenty-four of all classes), though Japanese losses in supporting ships, such as transports, were much heavier. The Japanese dead among the ground troops numbered 24,000: American losses were lighter, but by a remarkable feint the Japanese managed to rescue 12,000 of their soldiers. The Japanese troop commander killed himself as the final troops were withdrawn.

This savage battle marked out the pattern of operations which was to be repeated again and again in the Pacific during the next few years. Careful and skilful preparation by the American staff had been the main factor in the American victory; and so it was to be at Tarawa, in the Gilbert Islands, at Kwajalein and Eniwetok and Bougainville Island. The Navy concentrated upon the islands and pushed the Japanese relentlessly back. This strategy was a head-on assault. It was effective, and remorseless; but it was not very imaginative.

As the Nimitz campaign developed, General MacArthur was simultaneously attacking in his corner of the Pacific and the strategy of the two campaigns inevitably invited comparisons. Both showed undoubted successes. From September 1942 down to the middle of 1944, MacArthur was employed in re-occupying New Guinea. It was not the extent of the land occupied which was significant; MacArthur had overcome the arts of the Japanese in defensive warfare, in territory very favourable to them, and he had inflicted enormous losses of manpower on them.

Nimitz's war machine had rolled over the Gilbert Islands and the Marshalls. Little by little the Japanese gave way at the edges of the vast Empire they had seized; but Nimitz gained his successes by weight of assault and as a result of the endurance of his troops. His casualties were usually considerable. The American troops who were flung into action were for the most part a civilian Army. Many of them had, however, been harshly prepared in the rather barbaric training grounds of the United States Marines in the Carolinas. Stories of these which seeped out during the war seem to have been well founded. Some troops had been less well prepared, and this accounted for some of the reverses which the Americans suffered in this campaign, which was the most sanguinary of any which were fought during the war. The American advance proceeded atoll by atoll. It was a war fought among tropical islands, with the same unreal beauty as a background, the same refusal to surrender among the Japanese, the same monotony of desperate attack and desperate defence. It became taken for granted that the Japanese did not surrender, but were killed. Often the sites which occasioned the worst slaughter were incredibly small. MacArthur, on the other hand, won his battles by sheer artistry. No other captain of the war based his strategy so consistently on principles. He commanded with style. He was conscious of history, and of the examples of other generals. The ghosts of all the battles of the world stalked the combats for which he was responsible. In the map rooms of his headquarters there was an atmosphere of erudition which was unfamiliar in the war. The bloody patterns of assault on these remote coral reefs were studiously compared with Napoleon's famous victories, and even on one occasion with the victory of Hannibal at Cannae in 204 B.C. He also had a self-conscious, narcissistic regard for his own place among the pantheon of American military giants.

MacArthur despised brute strength. He sought, in a way which was rather like the principle on which the Japanese system of judo is based, to bring his force to bear on the enemy in places and at times that would find his opponent off balance. In this way he could hope to succeed with weaker strength, which was usually the position in which he found himself,

ALLIED OPERATIONS IN THE SW PACIFIC JUNE 1942 — MAY 1944

ALLIED AMPHIBIOUS OPERATIONS TO REGAIN CONTROL OF THE SOLOMONS

Green I.

15 Feb. 1944
NZ 3rd Divn

BUKA

Buka • Bonis

BOUGAINVILLE

• Tenekan

• Kieta

'BLISSFULL' 28 Oct.1943
Landing 2nd Marine
Para Battalion

Bougainville Strait

CHOISEUL

'CHERRY BLOSSOM'
1 Nov. 1943
Landing by 1st Marine
Amphibious Corps

Shortland Is.

D.G

VELLIA
LAVILLA

KOLOMBANGARA

'TOENAILS' 5 July
Landing by 43rd
Infantry Divn

'GOODTIME' 27 Oct.1943
Landing by 8th NZ
Brigade Group

NEW
GEORGIA

THE TIDE TURNS

— Japanese National Defence Zone boundary
······ Limit of Japanese advance in 1942
← Allied gains to December 1943

GANONGGA

5 Aug.1943 US
forces take Munda

Viru

Segi

RENDOVA

Tetipati

JAPAN

CHINA

Bonin Is.

Midway I. ○

2–5 July 1943 landing
by 168 and 172
Infantry Regiments

Mariana Is.

Philippine
Is

Guam

Wake I. ○

Truk Is.

Marshall Is

Caroline Island

Gilbert Is

Solomon Is.

New Guinea

Ellice Is

1000   2000 km
0
1000 miles

New Hebrides

♂ Fiji Is

AUSTRALIA

Admiralty Is.

NEW IRELAND

0   100   200 km
0   100 miles

29 Feb. 1944 1st, 7th,
8th and 12th Cavalry
Divisions land

Japanese Eighth Area
Army HQ (Imamura)

Rabaul

Link-up
March 1944

NEW BRITAIN

Madang

Umboi

N E W

Arawe
Is.

15 Dec. 1943
diversionary attack

New Guinea
Infantry lands

Jan.-Feb. 1944
US and Aust.
landings

Lae

26 Dec. 1943 1st Marine
Division lands

GUINEA

Trobriand or
Kiriwina Is.

Woodlark I

Japanese advance
Jan.-July 1942

Buna (taken
2 Jan. 1943)

30 June 1943 158th
Infantry landing

Port Moresby

US & Australian
attacks Dec. 42

D'Entrecasteaux Is.

30 June 1943
112th Cav. Regt

23 Sept. 1942 Aust.
25th Bde attacks
Japanese positions

Milne Bay

SANTA ISABEL

'THE SLOT'
(New Georgia Sound)

Indispensable Strait

21 June 1943 Landing by
4th Marine Raider Batt.
Viru Harbour taken 1 July

MALAITA

FLORIDA
IS.

BANIKA Savo
PAVAVU

Iron Bottom Sound

'CLEANSLATE' 25 Feb. 1943
Landing by US Army and
Marine Battalions

Honaira   Henderson Field

GUADALCANAL

SAN CRISTOBAL

0   100   200 km
0   100 miles

and with minimum loss. In this island warfare he eschewed the practice of Admiral Nimitz of reducing the Japanese strong-points one by one. Nimitz modified these tactics as time went on, and employed a limited plan of by-passing small islands which would have made an inconvenient defence. MacArthur, on the other hand, practised a strategy of envelopment. He refused to assail the Japanese head-on in one of their prepared fortresses, and thought out ways of isolating it by operating upon its exposed line of communication. The by-passed stronghold proved in the end to be his victim, but it had been left to 'die upon the vine'. General MacArthur then shifted his base forwards by some hundreds of miles, when the process was repeated with care never to expose his forces beyond the reach of protective air cover. He described as follows the system which he pursued:

> The system is as old as war itself. It is merely a new name dictated by new conditions given to the ancient principle of envelopment. It was the first time that the area of combat embraced land and water in such relative proportions. Hereto-fore, either the one or the other was predominant in the campaign. But in this area the presence of transportation of ground troops by ships as well as land transport seemed to conceal the fact that the system was merely that of envelopment applied to a new type of battle area. It has always proved the ideal method for success by inferior in number but faster-moving forces. Immediately upon my arrival in Australia and learning the resources at my command, I determined that such a plan of action was the sole chance of fulfilling my mission.*

The concept that success lay with a commander who best cooperated with nature was ever-present to him. One of his maxims was: 'Nature is neutral in war, but if you beat it and the enemy does not, it becomes a powerful ally.' A part of his success was due to the United States Army becoming more at home in the coral islands than the Japanese: which reversed the experience of the Japanese and of the British Army in the Malayan jungle at the start of the war.

In his campaigns, MacArthur relied to an exceptional extent on spying. He was fortunate enough to discover an Australian, Commander Long, with a great gift for attracting information and for sifting it. This was a new art in Australia, and Long organized a service which was free of the traits – the elaborate games and the affectation of policy making – which proved so constricting in other countries. The most valuable information was given by a force called the 'coast watchers of the islands'. These were a fifth column which had been left behind in the islands when they were overrun by the Japanese. They consisted of British and Australian civil

---

* Willoughby and Chamberlain, op. cit.

servants, anthropologists, telegraph operators, traders: and they were admirably served by bands of local natives. They were able to communicate by wireless with MacArthur's headquarters. In war of unorthodox character, this kind information about Japanese strong-points and the distribution of Japanese manpower was often worth a whole division of troops. The exploits of these men are one of the most exciting chapters of war history; and it is very extraordinary that they have not become part of the folklore of the war.

To MacArthur's military tasks were added the military and diplomatic ones of welding Australia and the United States in a close alliance. The Australians, in spite of their many positive qualities, were at this period notoriously hard to deal with: they were touchy, quick to take offence where none was intended, hypercritical as a kind of self-defence. In spite of a grotesque side to his character – which was self-assertive and boastful and which went with genuine confidence and did not mask self-distrust – MacArthur actually made himself liked, and won the confidence of Australia. He esteemed and got along well with Curtin, the Australian Prime Minister, and the two of them often collaborated in opposing Washington or London. He took an interest in preparing the reorganization of the Australian supplies so that by re-orienting Australian industry his armies actually received from Australia itself a much larger proportion of its needs than had been supposed possible.

In playing this role, MacArthur was much helped by accidents in his previous career which had detached him from the ordinary life of an American soldier. In his service as military adviser to the Philippine Government, he had come to conduct himself with an unusual detachment from the American military machine. This, combined with a natural tendency to a certain Caesarism in politics, had brought it about that in his Pacific command he was often handled by the American Government as if he were an independent political power and not a subordinate officer. His relation to the American authorities was like that of a much-prized condottiere to an Italian city state. The legend of MacArthur as the great American pro-consul was enhanced by the fact that when the war began he had not been back in America for years, nor was he to return until 1951. Though MacArthur undoubtedly gained from this position, he had as a rule to forgo the ability to influence the military planners by personal knowledge of the officers concerned. A remoteness from understanding American politics complicated his career. Piercing political insight into fundamentals was combined with a pathetic political incompetence in day-to-day matters.

Throughout this fatal combat in which Americans were locked with

Japanese in a contest from which neither side could free itself, one single fact stood out. The war was waged with the utmost ferocity, but often under the eyes of relatively idle armies who were obliged to remain spectators of what was going on. Of the vast number of men mobilized for the war, the greater part were destined never to come into combat. Japan had an Army of fifty-one divisions: until the very end of the war, forty of these divisions were either occupied in China, which for most of this period had a totally inactive front, or were employed in guarding the frontier with Russia. And on the American side the number of troops employed in the actual offensive by MacArthur, and later in the reduction of the Pacific islands, was very small indeed in comparison with the vast army which the United States had concentrated for war in the Far East. (Similarly in this Far Eastern War the British troops who had actual combat experience were limited to the four or five divisions in Burma.) The Western Allies could not make use of a larger force. They had chosen to fight the Japanese on narrow fronts – in New Guinea and in the Pacific islands – and the circumstances of the war were such that there was no room for a great concourse of troops. Thus the war came to resemble the war at Troy. The serried ranks stood and watched the combat fought between the heroes. Their fate was decided in battles in which they had no part.

In this desperate fighting in the Pacific, Admiral Yamamoto, still the central figure and imaginative genius at war whom the Japanese, with their great military gifts, had contributed to that conflict, was taken out of the picture. His death was plotted in Washington. It was brought about by arranging an ambush by American fighter aircraft which fell on him in great strength as he was flying on a tour of inspection to one of the Pacific bases held by Japan. This was in April 1943, soon after the Japanese withdrawal from Guadalcanal. The details of his flight, the precise time of arrival, were all obtained by intercepting cipher messages which could be read. Yamamoto was always punctual to the moment: the surprise depended on the ambushing aircraft being able to count to the minute upon his presence at the destined place of encounter. Yamamoto went to his death with a punctuality that was a rare virtue among orientals, even among commanding officers. His end was like the death of Hector who was similarly taken at a disadvantage by a force of Achilles' myrmidons:

> Look Hector how the sun begins to set
> How ugly night comes breathing at his heels
> Even with the veil and darkling of the sun
> To close the day up, Hector's life is done.

The American Admiral, having plotted his overthrow, could find no more fitting words to announce it than the following telegram to the exterminators: 'Congratulations Major Mitchell and his hunters; sounds as though one of the ducks in their bag was a peacock.' Democracies have curious lapses of taste when they go to war. At the press conference to celebrate the success of the plan, the same Admiral observed: 'I had hoped to lead that scoundrel up Pennsylvania Avenue in chains with the rest of you kicking him where it would do the most good.' It is said that the audience whooped and applauded.

By July 1943 the American planners were already satisfied that they had chosen the right road. They lifted their sights, and began to consider what they should do when they drew near to Japan. Could intense air bombardment, from Chinese airfields and from their great aircraft-carriers, and unremitting submarine warfare, really reduce this proud people, or would the unemployed army of over a million be ready to dispute their way? Would an invasion be necessary; and, if so, would the history of the fanatical defence of small atolls be lived through once again, this time in the island centre of the terrible and warlike race?

MacArthur and Nimitz were the two American personalities who dominated the Pacific. They had taken up the initiative when it had been dashed from the Japanese by the Battle of Midway Island. They had begun to attack, and had succeeded in their campaigns ever since. To halt them began to appear as being beyond Japan's capacity: the only doubt was how long they would take to cross the Pacific, and to make war on Japan at its gateway.

Part IV

THE DEFEAT OF JAPAN

CHAPTER 21

Mid-1943

IN the middle of 1943 the war had resolved itself into a defensive struggle by the Japanese to hold the vast territory which they had overrun, for such little loss, in the hectic days early in 1942. With the crippling loss of their Navy at Midway Island, their drive outwards had lost its impetus; it had failed in its purpose of gaining for them a rapid peace. But the Japanese were left in possession of a vast territory, economically very rich; and the operations of MacArthur and of Nimitz had only begun to win this back.

They held, and preparations had hardly begun to expel them from, a line behind which were included Burma, Thailand, Malaya and the Dutch East Indies; and it extended far out across the Pacific. Behind this line they had obtained 80 per cent of the world's rubber, 54 per cent of its tin, 19 per cent of its tungsten, the oil wells of the Dutch East Indies with a huge reserve, and large supplies of manganese and iron ore. The map and economic Intelligence suggested that Japan, if it showed the administrative competence to organize these assets, could, with some equanimity, face a prolonged war. It need have no panic, at least for the time being, before the very heavy counter-attack which America, now at last fully mobilizing for war, was mounting against it.

By 1943, however, it began to become plain that Japan, as an adversary of the United States, was outdated by two or three generations. In the organization for war, the contest was between the Americans – a nation of businessmen, amateurs in war but bringing to it all the skill learned in a century and a half of fierce capitalist struggle, in which lack of imagination and foresight exacted disaster and retirement – and the Japanese, who still regarded American business as vulgar, and who sought to combat it by an economy held together on a basis of command. Japan still thought of war in strictly military terms. Its eyes were fixed on territory which had to be held, on the battles which were taking place, and on the tactics to be used. The fact that the war was to be won or lost in the nation's factories and workshops had never clearly established itself in the mind of the Japanese Supreme Command. Japan had, it is true, passed a law even before Pearl Harbor, which gave the Government totalitarian powers to regulate the economy; but the economy, under war conditions, exhibited nothing like the transformation which the United States and Britain underwent in similar circumstances.

Even after it had staked everything on the action at Pearl Harbor, Japan failed to give top economic priority to building aircraft, warships and submarines upon which the defence of the Empire it had won must eventually depend. The Japanese had the initial advantage that they began the war with aircraft which surprised their antagonists by their performance. But the Japanese unaccountably failed to exploit this superiority. Japanese aircraft production in 1943, though it had tripled since 1941, was very much less than it might have been. In 1943 it was in fact only one fifth of the total American output. And, even for the use of its restricted air forces, Japan failed to mobilize anything approaching the manpower which was needed. The skill and audacity of the pilots at Pearl Harbor, and the extreme popularity which the flying service enjoyed, showed that Japan was not wanting in resource to organize its Air Force adequately. Moreover, until the end of the war, Japanese aircraft designers went on improving the standard fighters and bombers. But there was a failure of liaison: the Army and Navy were unwilling to make their wants clear, and to transmit these to the planners of the Japanese war effort. And even more than aircraft, a territory such as the Japanese had to defend, required warships and submarines. Here, also, the Japanese record is hardly comprehensible. In the months when America was turning out a prodigious number of aircraft-carriers – twenty-two were under construction in 1943 – Japan, which by the action of Pearl Harbor had shown itself to be a pioneer of naval air strength, was content to build only three new carriers. The disparity was greater still in cruisers and destroyers. The Japanese Naval Staff had apparently reverted to an older view, recoiled from reading the lessons which they had themselves demonstrated, and put their faith in battleship construction. They did not seem to realize, for example, how fatal it was to be outrun in submarine production. They had begun the war with high-quality submarines, but this arm never played the defensive role which might have been expected in a campaign fought among countless islands.

For Japan to realize the advantages of the economic riches of its Empire, a vast, flexible Merchant Navy was necessary. In scarcely any other department of war was Japanese planning so inefficient. It began the war without a realistic or adequate appreciation of the demands which were likely to be made upon its merchant shipping. In 1941, it possessed 5.3 million tons of shipping; about 35 per cent of Japanese trade had been carried in foreign vessels. The greater part of this fleet was at once requisitioned for service use, 1.2 million tons for the Army and 1.4 million tons for the Navy; and a large part of this was squandered by the wasteful operations in the Solomon Islands. In 1942 the Japanese lost over a million tons of shipping, and by 1943, the shortage had become acute, and the estimates and forecasts of the Japanese Planning Board had been exposed. The losses, by submarine warfare, by mines, and by air attack, were such as to make ridiculous the attempt to weld together the Japanese territories in a single viable Empire. Faced with this challenge, Japan made no adequate response: there were no interesting tactics, no system of convoys, no asdic, no radar. By 1943 they were forced to replace their dwindling merchant fleet with wooden ships, but these boats were terribly slow, and also vulnerable. Worse, they had neglected their shipyards, which were ill equipped and antiquated, and these were clogged, in the middle of 1943, by a fifth of the entire merchant marine undergoing repair.

These weaknesses must in the first place be put down to unimaginative planning by the Japanese Command, and the fact that civilian Ministries were instinctively held in contempt by Service Ministries. At joint conferences the requests of civilians for allocations of manpower and materials tended to be overruled, even though the end product might be one of which the Services were badly in need. For such reasons as these Japan was never able to utilize its huge economic assets. Japan had risked war for the sake of obtaining raw materials under its flag; but, when this was brought about, it could not transport them. It had the intense mortification of being in possession in the South Seas of one of the richest economic units in the world, but of being unable to enjoy its usufruct. The iron, the coal, the bauxite, nickel, tin, manganese, lead, salt, graphite, potash, all the vital materials for war, were all of them technically Japanese, guarded by Japanese troops, but they lay as useless to Japan as though they were in the hands of the enemy, because they could not be transported. They were a kind of fairy gold. Japan's plight is vividly shown by one figure. In 1940, before the war, it bought and imported three million tons of iron ore from the Philippines and Malaya. By 1942, though its troops had absolute control over the iron mines, it managed to carry just over 100,000 tons of iron ore from these territories to Japan.

The most acute famine was in oil. This had been foreseen, and the need for oil was the basic reason for Japan's going to war. But the oil had remained elusive. The wells of the Dutch East Indies produced an abundant supply, but it could only be transported in tankers, which were an easy target for the aircraft of the Western Allies and for their submarines. The shutting down of one economic activity after another in Japan was the consequence of this very real blockade. First civilian transportation was hit: then production in one industry after another. Already, by 1943, the oil shortages hampered the operations of the Navy and grounded many of Japan's aircraft.

The weakness of the Japanese defensive structure was, then, economic. The Japanese waged a war against the most effective economic organization of history, and waged it with totally inadequate resources. In vain did they put their trust in reeking tube and iron shard, when even their ability to manufacture tubes and shards was being limited. But, though the nemesis worked itself out in an economic form, the weakness was not really economic, but one of Intelligence. The Japanese civil service, Japanese planners, the Supreme Command, failed their country. The economic resources had been there, and they could not be used, because the Japanese Empire failed to remain linked together. Given flexibility and foresight, this weakness might have been overcome. A different organization of their supplies, more local initiative, more skilful prevention of submarine warfare, better use of the submarine and the aeroplane in striving to solve the economic problems – any of these might have availed to forestall the end, which already, in mid-1943, was becoming certain to those who possessed the economic Intelligence to see where war was leading Japan.

It is not surprising that Japan did not make more rapid progress with economic planning. In 1942 the Cabinet had established a Greater East Asian Ministry which took upon itself the functions of the 'Overseas Affairs Ministry' (more accurately known as the 'Colonial Affairs Ministry') and the old 'Asian Development Board', the *Kōa-in* (sometimes called the 'China Affairs Board': the Japanese language can be uncomfortably ambivalent to a western mind). The new Ministry was handed the formidable task of reconciling national policy decisions with the dictates of local military administration in areas under Japanese sway. It was a Ministry for coordination, touching every level of government. Such Ministries always walk a tightrope. Their enemies are invariably numerous, powerful and well-entrenched. In this case Prime Minister Tōjō Hideki appointed as his Greater East Asia Minister an able economist, former Minister of Finance and ex-President of the Cabinet Planning Board who until recently had served as Supreme Adviser to the Japanese puppet régime of Wang Ching-wei in Nanking. His name was Aoki Kazuo, and he left his mark on the tightrope before he and the Tōjō Cabinet toppled from power together.

Aoki was not without physical and moral courage. As a senior official in the Finance Ministry in 1933, he had gone to Manchuria and withstood threats of physical violence from Kwantung Army hotheads; he won his way then and did so again in 1940, after a fight with the Japanese Expeditionary Forces in China to uphold the integrity of the currency system established within Occupied China: that time he even extracted an apology from the then overall Chief of Staff of the Japanese Expeditionary Forces on the mainland, the mercurial Lieutenant-General Itagaki Seishirō. On another occasion, as head of a Cabinet Planning Board sub-committee in 1938, he had reported that even if the Japanese Army and Navy won the war in China and then seized the rich prize of the Southern Regions, they would remain incapable of sustaining a long war due to their reliance upon the resources of the United States and the British Empire; in this instance the Cabinet had accepted that unpalatable truth despite strenuous objections from the Vice-Minister of War. Clearly, then, this man knew how to work with the Army and was no lightweight. If anyone could have succeeded as Greater East Asia Minister, Aoki would have done so.

Aoki's new remit included the preparation of vast political and economic schemes. But no programme was published, and there were no elaborate accompanying sets of statistics. The Government hoped that the Greater East Asia Co-Prosperity Sphere would form a regional economic and political bloc. The Greater East Asia Ministry was intended to operate as a counter-weight to the pervasive influences of western capitalism and imperialism on the one hand and the Japanese military machine on the other. Aoki believed that the strength of any self-contained economic sphere was determined by three parameters: its natural resources, scientific knowledge and technical development, and manpower. The job of the Greater East Asia Ministry was to make this cumbersome system work harmoniously. Judged objectively, and notwithstanding Aoki's considerable skills, the Greater East Asia Ministry was a flop. Nevertheless, it was a very considerable attempt to come to terms both with Total War and with its expected aftermath.

From its very inception there was a good deal of conflict in Tokyo about this Ministry. Some civilians, especially those in the Foreign Ministry, feared that it would be regarded as provocative in South-East Asia: it would unmask a determination of the Government to plan the life of the region, and would be counter to the policy of granting independence. After some initial equivocation, Prime Minister Tōjō Hideki became adamant in its favour. The decision, however, cost him the resignation of his able Foreign Minister, Tōgō Shigenori, in protest at the setting-up of such a Ministry and its diminution of the traditional role of the diplomatic service.

Advocates of the Greater East Asia Ministry intended that 'pure diplomacy' (whatever that meant) should remain the exclusive prerogative of the Japanese Minister for Foreign Affairs. The fact remained that the creation of the new Ministry effectively separated the conduct of Japan's diplomatic relations with East Asian countries from that of the rest of the outside world. This had been one of the less attractive and unsuccessful features of the *Kōa-in*, and Tōgō was not alone in anticipating that an extension of that scheme to the whole region would prove equally un-workable. Tōjō's own response was that the countries of East Asia should be treated differently: they were Japan's kith and kin. Most of the other Ministers also positively welcomed the creation of the new Ministry. They anticipated that the new arrangements would give the Army and the Navy greater scope to carry out their wartime responsibilities without having to endure the constant aggravation of interference from Japanese diplomats accredited to local governments. Tōgō, however, was prepared to bring down the entire Cabinet over the issue. It must be remembered that Japanese Cabinet decisions had to be carried unanimously. Failure to reach agreement on a matter of such importance would inevitably lead to the resignation of Tōjō and his Cabinet *en masse*. The crisis came to a head at a Cabinet meeting on 1 September 1942. Tōgō refused to alter his position. The meeting broke up in disarray. Afterwards, efforts to per-suade Tōgō to reconsider his position proved unavailing. The Foreign Ministry itself was united behind him. Then Tōgō learned that the Em-peror wanted a compromise: this was no moment for a change in Cabinet. Hours later Tōgō resigned, Tōjō himself temporarily took control of the Foreign Ministry, and the final obstructions to the creation of the Greater East Asia Ministry were overcome at a stroke.

At this point it is relevant to digress for a moment to consider where the Greater East Asia Co-Prosperity Sphere fits within the general develop-ment of Japanese imperialism. Japan, it will be recalled, had emerged in the late nineteenth century from a long period of isolation and had found itself in a quasi-colonial economic and political relationship with the United States and the European Powers. From thence it had moved with remarkable speed to become the dominant Power in East Asia. It had been a late developer on the imperial scene, and it could not replace, resist or reject the Treaty Port system and the trading barriers imposed by 'most favoured nations' upon other states. Accordingly, the only course open to Japan was to join the system as it existed at the time (in the 1880s) and as it developed and flowered.

By the 1920s, as Japan's strength had increased, Japan faced two alternatives if it wished to advance further: it could champion the Treaty Port system and seek to make it work better for Japan than it did for other countries. This, in a nutshell, was the Shidehara Policy. Otherwise, Japan could devise a completely different system more suitable to its own needs. This, in fact, is the line which led to the Greater East Asia Co-Prosperity Sphere.

The concept of the Greater East Asia Co-Prosperity Sphere emerged from the First World War. Like 'imperialism', it was a term that enjoyed a wide currency and, as Professor Beasley has suggested, it had a wide range of connotations rather than denotations, and it developed specifically in relation to China and nowhere else.* It depended on an unequal technological relationship, and was characterized by the provision of management skills and trade in finished or semi-finished goods exchanged for raw materials. During the closing years of the First World War, Nishihara had attempted to forge not simply common links between Japanese industry and Chinese raw materials but a new, united common market. This, it must be said, was intended to be nothing less than a form of economic imperialism, established and kept in place by means of loans and other incentives. The scheme failed, largely for political reasons, but it was a purely Japanese idea, and it was quite contrary to the Treaty Port system.

By the 1920s, however, Japan was examining its position from a fresh point of view. It was seeking to optimize the necessary balance between the strategical materials required for war and those required by industry. Two of the figures most closely associated with this idea were Ishiwara Kanji and Nagata Tetsuzan, both of whom we have previously encountered. Japan's foremost problem, as they perceived, was that most well-developed Imperial Powers had large resources of coal, iron ore and other strategical materials at home. Japan, however, had to look abroad for these things, and therefore had to regard them as a legitimate strategical objective. It was this which supplied the driving-force for the creation of a bloc economy. It was a process accomplished by degrees and accompanied by slogans: the New Order in East Asia in 1937, the Greater East Asia Co-Prosperity Sphere in 1941.

From 1941 this form of Japanese economic imperialism followed no preconceived political pattern: that was purely *ad hoc*. Economically, and indeed geographically, however, it was more defined. In the old area of the Japanese Empire (Japan Proper, Korea, Taiwan and Karafuto), there was already a close integration between the four Japanese home islands and its dependencies. To this area was added Japan's new interests in

* See, for instance, W.G. Beasley, 'Japan and Pan-Asianism: Problems of Definition', in J. Hunter (ed.), *Aspects of Pan-Asianisn,* Suntory-Toyota International Centre for Economics and Related Disciplines, London, 1987, pp. 1–16.

Manchuria and North China. In time this became a written plan and was therefore identifiably and specifically Japanese. The rest of the Greater East Asia Co-Prosperity Sphere, however, was treated on an *ad hoc* basis, although generally with a greater stress than the Western Powers would have put on strategical materials. Once again, a distinction has to be made between an early version (which was refined in the Cabinet Planning Board during 1939–40 as a contribution towards a national defence strategy, against the background of the European War but prior to the breakdown of Japanese economic relations with the West) and a later version (which was a direct product of the Pacific War).

In the initial phase, the Japanese sought to reach agreements with the Imperial Powers and their local administrators. Their objectives were to negotiate guaranteed export quotas; free access to business investment and trade; special credit terms and rates of exchange; special powers over the supervision of communications, and the secondment of Japanese advisers to local colonial governments. All of this was essentially an extension to South-East Asia of a Japanese version of the old Treaty Port system, and it was very similar to the arrangements that already existed in North China and Manchuria.

In the second phase, a product of the Pacific War itself, many more *ad hoc* arrangements were envisaged, and even in principle these were not very closely worked out in advance. The objectives remained the same, but there was great uncertainty as to how Japan should achieve those objectives. In reality, the decision-making process devolved upon the military authorities, not the Japanese Foreign Ministry nor even the new Greater East Asia Ministry. What did emerge was direct Japanese control of trade with Japan, direct Japanese financial investment in the countries concerned, and Japanese provision of shipping services. There were specific restrictions on local industries that might compete with Japanese targets and home industries. Resources 'liberated' by these measures were redirected into other areas of commercial activity. Specific attempts were made to modify local economies to make them self-sufficient in terms of fuel requirements. These provided the local economies with a relatively wide base: only exceptionally was one geographical area to be dependent for food or transport on another area. It is impossible to know with certainty what success this phase would have enjoyed, given the opportunity, for Japan of course lost the war. Nevertheless, again according to Professor Beasley's reading of the facts, it would probably have proved too ambitious for Japan's resources in terms of technology, manpower and finance. In the event, the most interesting aspect of this issue is the clear, racialist distinction that the Japanese made between their treatment of the peoples of North-East Asia and South-East Asia. Their aim in North-East Asia was to provide Japanese leadership in advance of a kind of self-determination and self-sufficiency that would benefit Japan. In the Southern Regions, however, the Japanese inherited the White Man's Burden and contempt for the native populations. Notwithstanding the efforts of a few individuals to the contrary, there was no general desire by the Japanese Government or its administrators to encourage those countries to progress towards quasi-independence.

A vast reorganization of the Japanese Government was necessary to accommodate this remarkable attempt to rationalize the administration of Japan's relations with her satellite states in a huge area extending from the frozen waters of the Amur River to the tropics of the south. In the process 170,000 government bureaucrats were transferred from agency to agency. Thirty-one bureaux and twelve departments were abolished or absorbed. That alone may convey a sense of the confusion and dislocations that the creation of this Ministry brought with it. Nevertheless, something had to be done. Thirty thousand technical experts and officials were wanted in the southern areas alone: they would have to come from somewhere and be responsible to someone. In the event, Tōgō's fears proved amply justified. The Greater East Asia Ministry was rather successful in its sponsorship of cultural exchanges and studentships, but in virtually every other aspect of its function the Ministry had little power to restrain the Japanese military or naval governors of the occupied territories. The devastation and disruption of the war years made much more than that impracticable and unrealistic.

No attempt by a nominally civilian Ministry within a largely military Cabinet in Tokyo could hope to thwart or interfere with the pragmatic military administration of Japanese-occupied territories threatened by counter-invasion and subversion. It is doubtful whether more could have been done than the Japanese succeeded in doing in transporting economic resources, machinery, know-how and finished goods across seas infested with enemy submarines and swarming with Allied aircraft. The plain fact is that the Allied blockades were savagely effective. Once the spoils and stores of pre-war days had dwindled, far too little could be found or made to replace them.

The desperate reality was, however, still unclear to most people. It was to be found only in economic statistics, which were a military secret. One of the undeniable successes of the Japanese military was in concealing the weakness of its Intelligence alike from the enemy, from its colleagues in the Government of Japan, and from its own people. It was the consequence of the rigid drill in security which had been practised at least since

1930. Let nobody decry the effects of such a tight anti-espionage system. The consequence was that, in 1943, Japan, though already toppling on its feet of clay, was able to deny this knowledge to a large part of the world, including the Intelligence services of the Western Allies. They saw the advantages which Japan possessed, its still formidable Army, only a small part of which had so far been engaged in battle, and its tremendous morale. They were impressed by the fact that no rumours of mutiny ever reached them, and that there were no strikes or signs of civilian unrest in Japan. They were conscious too of the very great disadvantages under which they had to carry on the offensive against Japan. Japan held the inner lines, and could transport a stiffening of defence forces wherever these were threatened. The Japanese themselves were conscious of the immense handicap of enormous distance: the handicap that weapons, fuel, ammunition, cement and road materials, were being shot out in an unending flow, and vanishing across the Pacific Ocean. It needed a calm judgement in their adversaries to realize that this would tell against them, and that, sooner or later, the inherent deficiencies of the Japanese would force them to the huge convulsion of surrender.

Many of the lands taken over by the Japanese, and included in their fortress area, were the homes of nationalist movements which had come near erupting against their former white imperialist rulers. Japan, in letting loose its campaign against the Western Powers, had expressed its natural sympathies with Asian aspiration. The pricking of the balloon of western prestige, and the surprising ease with which the West was put to rout, had had a profound effect on everybody's mind; though Japanese sympathy was largely propagandist, many Japanese themselves were sincerely committed to its aims. The campaigns thus had had the effect of intensifying the nationalist resolve. In some cases, Japanese propaganda had led the people of these South-East Asian countries to believe that Japanese conquests would automatically bring them independence. But time was lost by the Japanese in fulfilling these hopes. Had the peoples of South-East Asia merely exchanged white imperialism to pass under the rule of a Japanese Empire?

The territories occupied by Japan were at different stages of political development. In most of them, the British or American influence was strong. They had accepted the way of parliamentary democracy as holding out the best prospects of obtaining their independence, and since both the United States and Britain could apparently not envisage any other course of progress, they had accepted constitutions of a more or less truncated form of Westminster or Washington democracy. That the Asian nationalists had allowed themselves to be directed along these lines is one of the astonishing facts of the time. It is a sign of the political vitality in Asia of western ideas, which remained very vigorous in spite of the inefficiency which had been revealed by the western systems administratively. Japan, as was natural, was more open-minded about the forms of government which should ultimately prevail; it was inclined to be suspicious of all forms of democracy, as being intrusions by the West into the East, and seemed to favour instead the forms which emerged from fascism (though these were as much of western origin), but it recognized that, in the storm of war, it was in no position to apply itself to political experiment in South-East Asia. It preferred to leave this for the years of peace which it hoped would follow, and for the time being to make do with provisional, make-shift forms of government. The régimes which Japan set up in the areas under its control usually took the form of a committee of the existing political parties, relieved of control by parliaments, which it declared abolished. The Governments themselves used most of the institutions with which they were already familiar. The Japanese, as has been noted here, were fond of regarding their activities as an asiatic adaptation of the Monroe Doctrine, and to a dispassionate observer it must be said that in their applications of that concept they tended to treat the countries of the southern regions like various species of transplanted Latin American banana republics.

In Burma the new Government was set up by a brief decree. In the Philippines, a Philippine Executive Commission, consisting of seven well-known politicians, took over the Government. In Malaya, which was more backward politically, the Japanese were content to preserve the forms of government through the sultanates. It is illuminating to see how, in the more developed countries – Burma and the Philippines – the tracks which they had been following before the war still governed their minds and set the tone of their political life.

The fate of Burma in these years is especially worthy of study. U Ba Maw, a lawyer, a party leader and former Prime Minister under the British, was designated by the Japanese as national leader in 1942. He later published a book, *Breakthrough in Burma*, which gives a clear picture of Burma under the Japanese. At first there was confusion. Japan raised the Burmese Independence Army, which has already been described, to harry the British, but this, attracting the elements normally associated with banditry, grew out of hand; it was liable, from the first, to turn upon the Japanese. Ba Maw, once appointed by the Japanese, had as his first mission the task of restoring order in Burma, on which he worked closely with the Japanese.

There was a period of euphoria, a festival of feeling Asian. Ba Maw describes in his book how

... on both sides we believed in an ultimate Axis victory, which would wipe out the western empires in Asia for ever. This lasted for several months, during which the leaders of the various political and communal groups went out to the districts in mixed teams on a 'trust Japan' campaign. The Japanese on their part reciprocated by giving the Central Government as much independence as their notion of independence would allow, and also by supplying us with most of the essential commodities and services we lacked and needed. This was the Asian relationship between the two sides in the first months of our administration.*

Ba Maw recognized that tension rose because of the different aims and interests of the Japanese and the Burmese.

The Japanese wanted the Burmese to put victory in the larger world war before their own limited political objectives in Burma, whereas the Burmese wanted to gain those objectives first and at once. Thus a basic contradiction which already existed when our administration was formed now began to harden and divide the two peoples. My view about this matter is that the blame lay with both sides, but more with the Japanese. They were a far more immature people in that they proved to be so devoid of judgement in their dealings with others, so domineering and blinded by delusions of their own racial grandeur and Asian destiny when it was most clearly in their interests to move with history by getting rid of all such racial nonsense. They could have achieved so much more if they could only have shown a spirit of true Asian fellowship and equality with the other peoples in Asia instead of claiming, in defiance of the clear world trends, to be 'more equal' than the others. This happened not only in Burma but all over South-East Asia.†

In spite of this, Ba Maw's personal relations with many Japanese continued to be good. It is true that he had continual difficulty with the more brutal type of officer, and claims that he was constantly in conflict with them for the protection of the Burmese people. He condemns utterly the soldiers brought in from China, who had been hardened by long experience of occupying that country of hostile people. He gives details of the Japanese mania for slapping people, and of their insensitiveness to Burmese custom and convention. But the Japanese at the top make a very different impression. Of Lieutenant-General Iida Shōjirō, the Commander-in-Chief in Burma, he says:

I found him to be the best type of Japanese soldier, human, fatherly, and very understanding, a militarist on the surface, but not altogether so deeper down; at least he always tried to see things your way too, which was what made him

* Ba Maw, *Breakthough in Burma*, Yale University Press, New Haven and London, 1968, pp. 283–4.
† ibid., p. 274.

different from the other militarists. It gave him a good deal of inner perception, particularly of the fact that a war can be won or lost in many ways and for many reasons, one of the surest ways to lose it being to rouse the hostility and resistance of a whole people.*

And of Field Marshal Terauchi Hisaichi, who was the Supreme Commander of all the Japanese forces in South-East Asia, he says:

As a person I found him to be really remarkable, a handsome, princely figure, out of a long and mellow feudal past, and yet belonging very much to the present in Japan. I had thought that as the chief of the conquering Japanese army he would most incarnate the dizzy reflexes of the conquest, but I was completely wrong. It may have been because I had least expected to find it in him, but the quality which struck me particularly was his essential humanity. Unlike most other militarists, this consummate war lord was not afraid to show that he was also human, and precisely because of this he understood us better than many around him.†

Even General Tōjō Hideki, the Japanese Prime Minister who had unleashed the Pacific War which had enveloped Burma, gets a good report from Ba Maw.

National relations, as distinct from personal ones, however, continued to be bad. The Japanese Army continued to insist that the Burmese puppet Government was ultimately responsible to it. It continued to make demands on the Burmese civil servants which outraged them; and continued to produce a type of myopic and over-confident officer who angered the Burmese by racial arrogance. They were notorious for seizing the crops and carts of the peasantry; for insisting on forced labour, for intervening everywhere.

Relations became so strained that ultimately the Government in Tokyo felt that it must make a great effort at their improvement. Early in 1943 General Tōjō announced in the Japanese Diet that Burma would be declared to be independent within a year. Japan had grasped that independence was the deep longing in the soul of the peoples of South-East Asia, and that, if this were granted, Japan could continue in fact to direct their policies. There followed some hard bargaining over the exact form of their future relationship, in which the Japanese Army endeavoured to stipulate that it should have the legal right to intervene if the Burmese Government departed from agreed principles. In the face of Burmese opposition, it accepted instead a treaty of alliance between the two countries, in which they simply pledged their cooperation for the

* ibid., p. 264.
† ibid., p. 308

self-determined development of all the countries of South-East Asia. These negotiations were completed by August 1943, and the declaration of Burma's complete freedom was made in conditions of apparent reconciliation and confidence. Japan had certainly made an effort at overcoming hostility. But Ba Maw concludes on a disillusioned note:

> On the Japanese side, many militarists went back to their old ways again. They could never remember for long that the Burmese were now a free people. I have already mentioned their charge against me that I took our independence too seriously. The cause of the mischief was that they wanted it both ways; they wanted the Burmese to fight the war as people defending their own independence and yet in other matters they were to behave as if they were not independent. The militarists merely changed their argument; previously they had tried to impose their will upon us in the name of military administration, and now it was in the name of military necessity without bothering to convince us that there was really any necessity at all; and as the pressures increased they refused even to argue about the necessities, but treated them as Japanese imperatives which ruled out all argument. Knowing how critical the situation had become we tried to go along some of the way with them, but they wanted us to go the whole way, which was clearly impossible unless we were convinced of the need for doing so. Thereupon these little war lords accused me of trying to subvert their war effort; and so we drifted further apart.*

At the end of the same year, 1943, Japan made a further effort at demonstrating that it was really in earnest in seeking, by the gift of independence, to gain the friendship of Asia. It convened a conference in Tokyo between Japan and five Governments, those of Burma, the Philippines, Thailand, Manchukuo, and of the anti-Chiang segments of China. It also invited the Indian refugee leader, Subhas Chandra Bose.

The Dutch East Indies had been omitted from the countries invited to take part, being barred from any prospect of regional independence. The Japanese attitude towards this territory was always peculiar. The nationalist movement there was as strong as, or stronger than, that in Burma; and the national parties had made it plain that they desired the same coveted gift of independence. Japan, however, was not so understanding in their case. The Supreme Command firmly refused to allow Japan to commit itself on its post-war status, either because it was so rich economically that it was unwilling for Japan to forgo the possibility of annexing it and retaining it as a prize of war, or because it wished to keep it as something to bargain over with the Western Allies at the eventual peace settlement. In the meantime, the Dutch East Indies were governed by the Japanese military, tempered by local councils. Some of the Japanese

* ibid., p. 331.

Ministers thought that this was a mistake, and would have been very willing to buy amity at the price of eventual independence; but, at an Imperial Conference in May 1943, the views of the Supreme Command had prevailed. They had not changed by the time of the East Asia Conference in November.

The Conference met for two days at the beginning of November. Opportunity was given for the oratory of several eloquent statesmen; their speeches were widely reported; some of them took the chance of ingratiating themselves with the Japanese. Most of those who took part, and the Japanese, felt that the Conference had been helpful to them. At its end a joint declaration was issued, which pledged everybody concerned to work for Asian independence – which had become the fixed idea of all the lesser countries of Asia – and to support each other in the cause. In many respects it was gloriously visionary and spiritually uplifting.

More than this was hardly to be expected of a political conference which had been called to demonstrate happiness and unity, not to discuss differences. The final resolution spoke, it is true, of economic cooperation. Japan had been pressing the idea of the economic interdependence of the region, and of the benefit, for all the countries of the area, of economic connection with Japan. The concept was a kind of Asian Common Market linked to that old familiar idea of a Japanese Monroe Doctrine.

One purpose of that Conference had apparently been to embarrass the Western Allies and, by demonstrating that total independence had become the political currency in Japanese Asia, to deter them from pressing on with plans for its reconquest. A rather more subtle aim may have been to cause dissension between Great Britain and the United States. Japan was aware of the American criticism of Great Britain for its tardiness in meeting the demands of nationalism, and it counted on causing further disputes between the Allies if it stirred up the nationalist claims still more. The difference in outlook towards nationalism between Britain and America was, in this and many other matters, the chink in their armour which Japan tried to exploit. At the same time Japanese propaganda had attempted to persuade the Australians that the eruptions of American influences in Australia were incompatible with the national independence of the Antipodean Dominions. Japan had attempted to convince the people of South-East Asia that it was the sincere friend of the independence of their national units. At the same time Japan, by its action, demonstrated that it was establishing a new Empire in place of the one which had been overthrown.

Similar experiences to those of Ba Maw with the Japanese were repeated

again and again by other peoples of South-East Asia. Everywhere at first
their expectations had been favourably aroused; the Japanese arrived to
general acclamation; their victories gave them glory; they strode over the
vanishing West with pleasure. The *mise en scène* was admirably contrived
for Japanese achievement. Restraint, moderation, modesty would have
paid them huge dividends. But instead of even pretending to live up to
their propaganda about the new age of Asian brotherliness, with which
they flooded the countries taken over, most Japanese, and especially the
Army, made no secret of the fact that they considered that they had won
an Empire, and were intent on enjoying it. Nearly all instruments of the
Japanese state were under the firm control of the Supreme Command,
and this was determined not to release any prize which Japanese arms had
gained. Those people in South-East Asia with a sophisticated understanding of the ways of government could see the callous, and more or
less disguised, ways in which the Japanese economic and political instruments set about exploiting them; those who relied upon their eyes for
information saw the Japanese, with a naïve disregard of consequence,
humiliating the people, insulting their customs, not bothering to learn
their languages, and enjoying the confusion.

There were certainly many Japanese, even many Japanese generals
and high officers, who, traditionally civilized, understood the sensibili-
ties of subject peoples. The Japanese Foreign Ministry, some Japanese
politicians and some businessmen struggled hard to get official sanction
for more generous policies. Many of them genuinely believed that the
future of the Greater East Asia Co-Prosperity Sphere depended upon
efforts to cultivate mutual respect and amity between its constituent
nations. As Tōgō Shigenori foresaw, his dream that 'Japan, as an
advanced nation of East Asia, was to assist in the development of the
other nations and the territory of this area, thereby bringing about
through peaceful means the prosperity of all' was a vision of 'mutual
assistance' which 'left no room for any thought of control by military
force'. Tōgō and others like him were not blind to the writing on the
wall in South-East Asia, and understood the strength of national feeling. That Japan was as receptive as it was, and that, at the top level, it
was willing to meet Ba Maw and the other nationalists half way, says
much for the quiet pertinacity with which they struggled. This (and the
worsening position of Japan in the war) brought Independence for the
Philippines in September 1943 in the same way that it had come in
Burma. But it bore the same sense of sham and unreality as long as the
Japanese Army and the much more dreaded military police were there
and took the law into their hands. The milder Japanese were terrorized

into acquiescence by the general will of the Japanese Army which was to plunder and oppress. In face of the mass descent on to South-East Asia of the military machine, in face of the reality of Japanese extortion, brutality and incompetence, Japanese good intentions were advertised in vain. In a very short time, their Empire had exhausted its credit, and the Japanese uniform had made itself detested.

In mid-1943 the British reorganized their command system in Asia. They recognized that Delhi was no longer the ideal centre for the head-quarters of the military. It was too heavy with history, and had too many historic distractions. Essentially it was the base of the Indian Army; and this was not suited for a war such as the present one, involving amphibious operations and regional East Asian diplomacy. The eyes of a General Staff in India were apt to fix on India's North-West Frontier, and on the Middle East. Only by constant effort could they be prevailed upon to study the Burma frontier, and to give due weight to new Allies and friends, the hard-pressed Chinese and peoples of South-East Asia. It appeared best to wrench the command away from its old associations, and to locate it at some centre where it could achieve a more correct view of the war. New men were to be brought in, to operate from a new centre. It would be one in which more attention was paid to voices which went unheeded in Delhi. The command was in fact divided: Delhi continued to be responsible for the Indian Army in its home organization; the new command was to be responsible for mobilizing and directing all forces involved in the attack against Japan in the East. It would include all three services, Army, Navy and Air Force.

At the Quebec Conference of the Allied Powers in 1944, it was decided that the new command should be located at Colombo. It was to be under Vice-Admiral Lord Louis Mountbatten. He was a cousin of King George VI, and it was felt that royal status would give him additional prestige in dealing with Britain's Allies, and discharging the political duties which it was clear the post would involve. It was to be international; Mountbatten was to be equally responsible to the British Prime Minister and to the American President. Undoubtedly the arrangement was well conceived; it gave a new tone to the British war effort in the Indian Ocean: it created a new race of military planners who were free from traditional concerns.

A further ingenious tie-up of the command was made by appointing General 'Vinegar Joe' Stilwell as the deputy of the Supreme Commander. He was the American general who was simultaneously acting as a ranking general of the Chinese Nationalist Army. His aims and objects had diverged greatly from those of the British, of whose military achievements he thought meanly. By this provision, he, and the Chinese, secured a share in the command; at the same time it proved easier to control him.

Mountbatten proved a less heavy-weight figure than is sometimes supposed but an ample complement to General MacArthur and to Admiral Nimitz as a member of the triumvirate by which the rest of the war was directed. He was a scientifically minded commander, and many first-rate scientists from England appeared on his staff at Colombo: a happening which in Delhi would have been thought eccentric. He was not the most able of military commanders but he more than made up for that with a gift for public relations which he used, among other ends, for establishing a rapport with the troops, many of whom had been dangerously demoralized when Mountbatten was appointed. He had in fact something of the personal glamour of the filmstar, which the public, as the war progressed, increasingly demanded of troop commanders. In a word, he had style, and he was well loved.

With these developments, there faded out one of the most impressive commanders of the war, Archibald Wavell. It is true that Field Marshal Lord Wavell continued for a time as Commander-in-Chief in India, and that in the summer of 1943 he was made Viceroy of India; as such he enjoyed political power. But as a maker of war strategy his role was finished. He had played an original, if an inadequately appreciated, part. As Commander in the Middle East in the early part of the war he had borne the brunt of the early attacks by the Italians. He had been starved of resources, and, by bluff and intellectual ability, he had won successes against immense odds. At the beginning of the Japanese War, he had been appointed to Supreme Command of the troops in Malaya and in the Dutch East Indies, in addition to India, in the hope that, with his quite inadequate force, he might work the same miracle that he had done in the Middle East. The task was a hopeless one; Wavell, also, was a tired man by this time, and had lost a part of his cunning. By temperament an intellectual who combined reflection, and a strange kind of mysticism, with a life of action, a natural scholar whose career had been among soldiers, he failed to achieve recognition among the politicians who mattered because of an inability – or rather an unwillingness – to instil among his colleagues and subordinates a cult based on nothing more substantial than his own personality.

The creation of the Colombo Command put new energy into the conduct of British propaganda. It began to be classed as one of the major instruments of war.

Propaganda work had begun before Pearl Harbor. It had been centred in Singapore in an office called the Bureau of the British Ministry of Information, and had operated through the information sections of different British missions in the Far East, such as the British consulate in Shanghai. The early network, which thus came into existence, was disrupted when the Japanese captured most of these places, including Singapore. They were especially severe on prisoners who had any connection with this organization. This was not because they realized the latent power of propaganda, but because they assumed – not without reason – that a Bureau of Information must be concerned with espionage, of which they were particularly afraid. Certainly the Bureau of Information had three functions: it collected intelligence, distributed it throughout the information-hungry channels of the Empire, and performed valuable propaganda fuctions too. The officer who was Director General of the Bureau, Robert Scott, formerly in the Consular Service in China, had first-hand experience of the Japanese which encompassed a period of service in Manchuria between October 1931 and February 1932, during the initial Japanese onslaught there. He had also been the Acting Commercial Counsellor at Shanghai in the first three months of the China Incident. Now he had a very grim experience during the years of captivity. The Japanese had a curious respect for legality, and were unwilling to execute their victims unless they had made a confession. Time and again, in an effort to extort this confession, they imposed savage tortures on him. He refused to confess, and therefore survived: but when he came out of prison he weighed only 70 pounds.

With Singapore lost, an organization had to be built afresh. It was centred on Delhi; and soon a staff with a highly international flavour was put together – Chinese, Indonesians, Dutch, Frenchmen, Greeks, Hungarians – all the cosmopolitan elements which had escaped from Shanghai and Hong Kong and had taken refuge in India. Some of them were journalists or writers, some were businessmen, a few had been politicians. Their collective knowledge of the Far East was variegated and extensive. The predominant personality was the gifted and imaginative Director of Broadcasting, John Galvin. He was an Irish Australian who, in a crowded life, seemed to have prepared himself for the role he now had to play. He had a vision of Asia as a force to be reckoned with in the world of the future, when the Japanese should have been thrown back to their own shores. He could appeal to intelligent nationalist sentiment in the occupied territories because of the genuinely democratic quality of his own outlook; upon the organization of propaganda he brought to bear original talents, and extraordinary energy and resourcefulness.

By all the regular methods of propaganda, by broadcasts from a radio station set up by Galvin in New Delhi, by pamphlets and books, by the organization of a news-reporting service which was accurate about defeat and could be trusted in accounts of victory, little by little the British version of the war was radiated out. The propagandists in New Delhi exposed the falseness of the Japanese claim for a Greater East Asia Co-Prosperity Sphere. They stripped Japan of the claim to be anything but an old-fashioned imperialist Power. They gave to the Asian world the lively sense that western power still existed, was preparing for a riposte, and had good hopes of a future in which men could live at liberty and peace. They transformed the image of India from being a country in collapse to being a power house in which returning armies were girding on invincible force.

Of the powerful effect of this invisible arm of the British Army there can be little doubt. Ba Maw speaks in his memoirs of the disquieting effect in Burma of British propaganda and the British agent on the minds of a rather mercurial population. The sense that the British were gone was undermined by the awareness that British eyes were still upon them, and that the slightest and most intimate details of the Burmese districts were being discussed in London and Delhi.

The propaganda had more effect on the peoples who were subordinate, and rather unruly, allies of Japan than on Japan itself. Showers of propaganda burst unavailingly on the granite of Japanese civilian morale, and the Japanese Army was never known to have lost a battle, to have flagged in any way, or to have been at all diverted from its purposes by any of the wiles of psychological warfare.

It was proof against American propaganda no less than against British. A most effective instrument at the United States' disposal was a broadcasting station at San Francisco beamed at Japan. Propaganda was backed up by the useful research done in numerous centres. On the whole, however, American arms gained little support from the labour of American propagandists against the apparently monolithic Japanese.

On the other side, only perfunctory use of propaganda was made by the Japanese. Indeed, both Japanese and Chinese seemed to pay only a perfunctory regard to the possibilities of propaganda until the very end of the war. No Japanese figure rose to play anything like the same part as Dr Goebbels, Minister of Enlightenment in Nazi Germany. Japanese propaganda was directed chiefly towards the people of the countries that it occupied, or planned to attack. The media which it used were the same as those employed by its adversary, predominantly the wireless and the printed word. But there is little to be said of this side of Japan's war effort. On the whole it was parched for lack of imagination.

Thus all the eastern world resounded, both with explosives and with the monotonous exchange of propaganda. *Inter arma silent leges*: but the media of mass communications were busier than ever. Every nation talked with every other; to argue with it, to inform or mislead about the direction of hostilities. America spoke to Japan. Japan spoke to South-East Asia. Britain spoke through numerous languages on the Delhi wireless. In this general post there was one notable exception. Britain did not speak to India. The British political warfare executives operated from Indian soil, and used Indian facilities, but in return for this the British Government had given an undertaking that radio propaganda would be directed outwardly, and that it would not use these instruments for arguing with Indian public opinion.

The Indian Government had its own propaganda organization. This, though partly operated by British staff, conceived its task rather differently from the outward-directed political warfare. Its task was limited to explaining to the people of India the motives of the Government of India in fighting the war, and to demonstrating the progress it was making. It was not to debate with Indians the rights and wrongs of their differences with the British. From this use of the radio, the British barred themselves. They accepted the limitation formally; and investigation shows that on the whole they stuck by this agreement. The British never, for example, put over to Indian opinion its own case on Indian constitutional developments, as it stated this in broadcasts to America. The motive was that the British feared to aggravate India the more by supplying its own commentary on events. As was usual, it put its confidence in bland silence; which of course in the end was the more provoking.

The Allies announced, at the Cairo Conference of the United States, Britain and China, in November 1943, the severe peace terms which they proposed to exact from Japan. They were not put forward as opening the way to peace, as a bait to negotiation: the Allies intended them as declaring their programme of action, and as an encouragement to China, and as a persuasion of China to remain in the war. Japan's overseas Empire was to be forfeit; it must surrender unconditionally. At first, this declaration did not have the deflationary effect on Japanese morale which had been hoped for. Japan, which privately had already begun to envisage the possibility of defeat, was, however, optimistic that it could avoid the worst consequences. It knew the very great defensive strength of its position, due to geography. It was confident that the United States and Britain would not be unmindful of the vast losses in manpower which they would

1112 The Defeat of Japan

have to incur in the last stages of the war if it came to a struggle to land in Japan itself. The United States and Britain would, it was sure, snatch at the possibility of a reasonable negotiation, in which much of what Japan judged to be indispensable could be preserved.

Therefore Japan interpreted the menacing words from Cairo as being a good deal less than their face value. They were reassured also by the absence of a Russian signature to them. Russia, though it was allied to the US and Britain, was active only in the German War, and had not committed itself to the eastern conflict. The Conference at Cairo had been designed to take place without the Soviet Union being represented, since Soviet Russia was unwilling to compromise its neutrality in the Pacific. Japan saw this and was deeply relieved. If Russia was firmly attached to neutrality in 1943, what might be its position in a year or two, when its experience with its Western Allies had further frayed its nerves? Besides, was it in the real interests of any of the Great Powers to destroy Japan as an organized force, and open the way to another Power to occupy the vacuum? Did the United States or Britain desire to make a ruin there in which Communism could flourish? Japan still had sufficient reason for not regarding the Cairo Declaration as an accurate forecast of history.

Moreover Japan was to nurse, until the very end, false comfort from its long immunity from occupation. Japan, alone of Asian countries, had never known the tramp of invading armies. It had come to believe that it was especially protected by the gods from the hand of war. For a warlike people, the Japanese had been singularly little affected by threats from abroad. Only twice, in the thirteenth century, had Japan itself been in danger from invasion by foreign soldiers. In the time of Kubla Khan, in 1274 and again in 1281, great Mongol armadas had set sail to conquer the small island empire, and annex it as a tributary. They were seemingly irresistible; Japan seemed done for; it quaked with terror, while it began to defend every inch of the way against those troops who had managed to land. But on each occasion great storms scattered and wrecked the mighty fleets, and the invaders stood no chance. These events became a part of the national memory. The *kamikaze* or 'divine wind' which had saved Japan in the thirteenth century was expected, until the very end, to blow again, or the divine protection would manifest itself in some other guise.

The wind was not to blow. Russia entered the war, America put its trust in an army of occupation to avert Communism. The eventual peace was almost identical with the terms of the Cairo Conference. But no American or British life was lost storming the beaches of Honshu.

CHAPTER 22

Two Indian Armies

THE Japanese, after overrunning Burma, had been content for two years to remain on the defensive. They had repelled the attack organized by General Wavell from India in the autumn of 1942, against Arakan. The operation, which was encouraged from London in the hopes that it would repair British prestige, was premature and was made with inadequate force and troops insufficiently trained; the Japanese were never embarrassed by it – except that it restricted a move which they had been intending to make at the same time into North India – and, by outmanoeuvring and outflanking the British, they compelled the British to retreat.

The country between India and Burma was peculiarly difficult; communications almost did not exist; the disease-infestations required that armies, if they were to operate with any degree of efficiency, should be remarkably well organized with medical and sanitation services, which in many areas they were not until 1944. These facts, as much as any other, kept the British and Japanese apart, though great pressure was brought on British troops by Churchill to go on the offensive. In fact, the Japanese had acted on the principle that geography had contrived to give Burma the perfect scientific frontier, and calculated that they would do enough if they posted troops to guard the few practicable approaches from India.

In 1943 the adventure of General Orde Wingate in Burma took place. This strange, eccentric soldier, who had formed his ideas in Palestine and Abyssinia, and who took T. E. Lawrence and the Arab revolt in the First World War as his model, was confident that Burma would make an ideal field for guerrilla war. If it was hard for armies to make contact, he suggested that guerrillas should do their work for them; and that, once these had made a long-range penetration behind the Japanese lines, they could, by superior mobility and surprise, produce as much havoc as would be caused by a successful army invasion.

Wingate convinced the Indian Army with great difficulty, and made an expedition with just over three thousand men. The higher Japanese officers regarded him without anxiety, and said that he must starve in the jungle; the more junior officers were shocked by the boldness of his strategy, and by their inability to hunt him down. The advance of Wingate upon T. E. Lawrence was in the use of wireless and of aircraft. Wingate lost a thousand men, one third of his force, and put a Burmese railway temporarily out of action. Whether his guerrilla successes came near justifying his theory was an open question; a much larger operation, employing aircraft, was planned for the next year, but it met with disaster at the outset, Wingate being killed on taking off. He is a hard man to assess. England, for prestige reasons, urgently needed a success, and it possessed at this time a propaganda machine, which could create heroes overnight. Wingate's personality and achievement were written up and blazed across the world. It may be that Wingate demonstrated not the success of his own guerrilla strategy but the success of British propaganda. He supplied to the waiting and idle troops of the British Army, in the tedious interval of training and before they were offensively engaged, the spectacle of exciting warfare and of individual performance. Wingate believed himself to be a man of destiny and that the situation was also one of destiny.

A far more orthodox, and forceful, attack was intended by the British in the spring of 1944. The Fourth Army Corps was preparing it, using the small town of Imphal in North-East India as its base. The Japanese, who had two divisions in the region, had Intelligence that it was coming, and resolved to strike first.

The campaign inside the borders of India which resulted was interesting partly because, in it, Japan again put to the test its claim that it was fighting, not simply for itself, but for the freedom of the Asian peoples. It is true that the organized forces of allegedly 'free India', which it had among its troops, played only a minor part; the campaign was so interesting, so stubborn, so terrible, and the 'free Indians' played such a small role in it, that the history of it, and its narration by the Japanese, might well overlook their presence. Yet, symbolically, the event is important, and was certainly seen to be so by the people of India and South-East Asia. Japan had announced that it had opted out of the circle of imperial predatory powers, and that it could rightly claim to be the patron of free Asia. It had not, until this time, done anything very striking to show that it was living up to this claim. In Japan, all attention was given to the gallantry of the Japanese forces. The average Japanese subjects scarcely thought of their army as fighting Asian battles, or that their Asian Allies could be of much worth to them. The opportunity had come to show that this was a mistaken view.

Chance presented itself in the shape of the Indian leader Subhas Chandra Bose. He played at this stage an extraordinarily decisive part. By accident, and by seizing an exceptional opportunity, he was able to cut a figure which made him outstanding among the comparatively small number of men who influenced the course of the war by their individual qualities. He chanced to be available to the Japanese to lead a movement to free India, and, in retrospect, it appears that this was the last chance of saving itself with which Japan was presented.

Bose was a Bengali, the son of a comparatively high civil servant who became a judge. Bengal had a special place in the history of Indian nationalism. It stood by itself culturally, and bred a type which was peculiar in being the exponent of a classical strain of regional loyalty. Bengali patriotism was deeply devotional: it was less associated than in other parts of India with day-to-day economic interests: the Bengali really believed the singularly powerful oratory which surged over the province especially after 1905. The passionate quality of Bengali nationalism, monomaniac, hot, somnambulist, is rather like that of the Sinn Fein patriot who is heard, off-stage, as a repeated theme in Sean O'Casey's play, *Red Roses for You*, repeating his hypnotic oratory. This nationalism expressed itself, to a degree quite unknown in other parts of India, in a fascination with violence and in a cult of terrorism. The typical Bengali nationalist was quite carried away, renounced his home and the ties of ordinary business, and plunged into secret conspiratorial activity in a way which horrified the rest of India as being extravagant and an affront to domestic obligation.

Bengal differed so much in temperament from the other parts of India that political cooperation with it was not easy. Bose became a leader of Bengali nationalism, and was so powerful a personality that his shadow fell over the rest of India. He was in the recognizable succession to the Bengal leaders of his youth who used to be carried away by the poetical implications of 'mother India', Hinduism, and Indian uniqueness. Always, Bose saw himself, and conducted himself, as a man of destiny. He had a great appeal to youth, frustrated, very poor but very proud, liking rhetorical leadership, always responding enthusiastically to the idea of a solution through some act of violence. He sought to turn Indian nationalism into the kind of movement which grew in Bengal.

As a young man, Bose, who was born in 1897, had been sent by his family to England, where he studied so diligently at Cambridge that he passed the entrance examination into the Indian Civil Service. This still enjoyed so much prestige in India that a lifetime spent in it, or a resignation from it, produced equal *réclame*. Bose chose the latter course. By resigning even before he had been posted to any particular duty, he gained a flying start in the Bengal Congress Party. Two decades of serious attachment to Congress, and a spell of office as Mayor of Calcutta, brought him, after a term of imprisonment which he spent in Mandalay Fort in Burma, to the presidency of the All-India Congress in 1938. Though the inner springs of his being may have been poetical, he developed, during his time as Mayor, a businesslike aptitude, which won recognition from British officers.

This proved to be a parting of the ways with his non-Bengali Congress colleagues. In his struggle with them, and partly because of his temperament, he moved sharply to the left, though for him there was no special attraction in socialism, and he was not moved by the conflict between this and free enterprise. The left meant simply extremism, more determined personalities, a more congenial emotional atmosphere. He advocated ever more extreme Congress policies: and in particular he opposed Gandhi's stubbornly held advocacy of non-violence. In this contest, Gandhi faced the blind emotional forces of Bengali nationalism, which repudiated Gandhi's homespun philosophy of the spinning wheel and of the virtues of simple peasant life. A religious preoccupation such as Gandhi's – a religion which dwelt on the virtues of the Sermon on the Mount which Gandhi had taken over in his version of Hinduism – was alien to Bose. Bose's passion was summed up in his favourite slogan: 'Give me blood and I promise you freedom.'

The year of his final breach with Gandhi was also the year of the outbreak of the war in Europe. Bose was not inclined to sit still among such events. For the attitude of Gandhi and Vallabhai Patel, the men he was opposing, it is possible to feel much admiration. They were realists, as intransigently opposed to the British as he was himself. But they accepted that military action was not the way to strike at them. They were organizing a vast, poor, ignorant, apathetic nation in the only way it could be mobilized. A military adventure was just the kind of thing the British would expect and would know how to deal with. They were helpless against this unspeakable groundswell. Subhas Bose was simply too impatient for this Himalayan wisdom.

Bose thought otherwise. The world was being changed by armies, and he was impatient to have an Indian Army. His agitation grew unrestrained of bounds. He was arrested, rather oddly for a seditious speech in connection with the agitation for the removal of a memorial to the victims of the Black Hole of Calcutta, which was thought to be hurtful to national sentiment. In prison he meditated upon the progress of the war, on the might of Germany, on the great opportunities for Indian freedom which he felt that Gandhi, with a senile attachment to non-violence (as it appeared to Bose) was at this time allowing to pass by. He was distracted when he thought of what he might be able to effect if he was at liberty. He procured his temporary release by beginning a hunger strike, and ensured that he would not thereafter be restored to jail by absconding from his home in Calcutta early on a January morning of 1941, disguised as an elderly Moslem mullah.

By a daring journey he made his way across India, through Afghanistan and through the Soviet Union, into Germany. There he found his spiritual home, and probably would have done better if he had stayed there instead of answering the call of Japan. He had alway been attracted by Germany. His temperament was Wagnerian: the Nazi grandees proved attractive personally. The colourful side of Nazism appealed to him profoundly. The heroics, the mythology, the dangerous and insidious concepts, the affected contempt for weakness and pity, the invocation of history, all seemed congenial to him. Bengali culture is strongly patriarchal, and the Nazi concept of the placc of women in the warrior's life appealed to one who, till he went to Germany and married a German, had apparently been indifferent to women. In the Siegfried cult and the heroic life, he saw a model which he found admirable. He was deficient in the sense of humour that was the best preservative against Nazi fantasy; and his Hindu education had given him a natural tendency towards a narrow concentration on whatever happened to appeal to him for intellectual reasons. Even the Nazi brutality he found brisk, salubrious and invigorating.

In politics he found the Nazi form of state entirely congenial. The rule by the Nazi Party, and the authoritarian rule of the party by a small caucus of leaders, seemed to him to provide India with a model form of government. Discipline, before all else, was what India seemed to need for overcoming its problems of the division into separate castes and communities, and for dealing with its great economic problem of poverty. The democratic type of government which it might imitate from Great Britain had the fatal weakness of permitting so much liberty that the state might fall in pieces. New vistas opened for an Indian Government which would be equipped with a Gestapo, concentration camps and an SS. On the precise details of the policy he would pursue if the war should bring him to power, he was vague. It was enough that he should proclaim the bracing virtues of authoritarianism.

Bose therefore found the situation promising. He was satisfied with his personal reception. The Germans invited him to take charge of organizing the rebellious Indians in their hands into a body which might be useful for war purposes. He was given access to the Indian prisoners captured by the Germans in North Africa. He broadcast to India over the German radio; and he took part in the controversy over the Cripps mission to India. Volunteers began to come forward to form an Indian Legion, and about two thousand men were enlisted for training. There was much ceremonial feasting and mutual compliment.

Spiritually this was probably the happiest part of Bose's somewhat neurotic life. But after some months Bose had to recognize that his German friends had not acknowledged him as the head of an Indian Government-in-Exile. Perhaps this was due, as was explained to him, to the fact that they could as yet, while Russia remained undefeated, have brought no effective aid to an Indian rebel government; perhaps it was because Hitler could not bring himself to recognize that Indians would be equal citizens in the post-war world which he was planning. Hitler, if Germany won the war, intended to dispose of India by a diplomacy in which Indians would play no part.

Whatever the reason, the Germans put no obstacles in Bose's way when an invitation reached him from the Indians in South-East Asia to transfer himself to this new sphere, and to take charge of the Free India movement which was being organized by the Japanese. His imagination, the dramatic part he might play, the appeal of the idea of Pan-Asianism, his calculation of how India, or at least Bengal, might respond to new situations, all impelled him to accept.

Bose sailed from Keil in a German U-boat in February 1943. He left behind some lieutenants to continue the work of organizing the available Indians, though he had failed to come to an agreement with the Nazis on precisely how they were to be used. The U-boat sailed to Madagascar, and there, off shore, it made a rendezvous with a Japanese submarine which carried him for the last half of his journey. He reached Tokyo on 13 June, after a voyage of thirteen weeks. That he was permitted to be so slow may suggest that the Japanese, at least at this time, did not found great hopes on the plan for which he had been imported.

Indeed they had been making half-hearted bids at raising the Indians in revolt against the British ever since the first days of the war; and they had suffered a series of disappointments. At first the project had been entrusted to a man named Major Fujiwara Iwaichi, of the Army General Staff, who appears to have been of some probity, with an understanding of what would appeal to Indians. He was fortunate in lighting, in the first days of the war, on a sick prisoner, Captain Mohan Singh. Singh was a man of character; he was a cousin of the Maharaja of Patiala, a great prince of the Punjab; he was a capable professional soldier, and he had become, apparently without the knowledge of the Indian Army, a convinced nationalist. With the backing of Fujiwara, and the financial aid of some of the leaders of the 800,000 Indians resident in Malaya, he undertook to raise from the Indian prisoners of war a force which might prove useful to the Japanese.

Of the total of 115,000 men who surrendered during the whole of the Malayan Campaign, Indians made up a very large number. Though at first a near-blind confidence was put in their loyalty by the Indian Government, this had an unenviable, if amiable, record, of being deceived. The inquiries which followed the Indian Mutiny of 1857, had shown that an almost insane trust had been placed in troops which had given every sign that they were preparing for rebellion.

Certainly the experience of some of the troops, in the months immediately before the surrender of Singapore, had not been such as to ensure their fidelity. Malaya was in many ways the weakest link in the British imperial chain. Among other disservices, it brought about the demoralization of many of those who served the Raj in the Indian Army. The culture and atmosphere of Malaya has been described very exactly in the stories of Somerset Maugham, and this society did not seem to most Indians as one worth dying for. Near Singapore there was a very luxurious country club with a much sought-after swimming pool. In the six months before the war, it became known in Singapore that the wives of the planters and of local white businessmen had objected to the swimming pool being used by Indian officers. British officers from the same regiments were eagerly invited, solicitously treated, and competed for assiduously. The Indians were dismayed when this action of the club was officially condoned: at least no protest against it was made from the Government or from the military command. This insult, casually offered by the Tanglin Club, did more than many other graver measures to undermine the British Empire in Asia. A dispassionate observer, surveying what was done, must have decided that the English, and especially their wives, were mad. It is not politic to insult a man mortally who is about to defend you.

The Japanese attempts at subverting the loyalty of the prisoners had as their background this resentment at the arrogance of the white society of Malaya. In spite of this preparation of the soil, the first attempts of Fujiwara and of Mohan Singh to set up the Indian National Army, which was inaugurated at Singapore on 12 February 1942, had only limited success. True, they had much to offer the Indian captives – immediate freedom, good wages, the resumption of their military careers, an apparently bright political prospect, exemption from the dreadful forced labour squads, for which Japanese prison camps soon became notorious. Yet the response was poor and Mohan Singh proved anything but an obedient tool. He laid down conditions that the Japanese were unwilling to accept; he stated plainly that if the Japanese aimed at replacing the British in India, they would, after a short time, have to face the aroused opposition of Indian nationalism. In December 1942 Mohan Singh resigned from his position and was arrested by the Japanese, and the first stage of the Japanese experiment at collaboration with Indian nationalism was over.

The Japanese had been handicapped in their efforts because of a deep-seated contempt which they had for prisoners of war, and, still more, for prisoners who were willing to be untrue to their oath of service. Nothing struck them as so contemptible as disloyalty, and they were unable to hide this. Simple-mindedly they judged their prisoners by the same exacting standards which they would have applied to their own people. This made them maladroit in the project of raising an army out of defaulters and deserters.

The decision was, however, taken to persevere in this venture. It was resolved to see whether better results could be obtained from enlisting a politician of standing to head the movement, instead of working exclusively through military men. Subhas Bose, whose mission in Germany had been favourably reported on by the Japanese Military Attaché there, seemed to be well qualified for this role.

Bose, on returning to Asia, threw himself energetically into organizing the Indian movement, and, in a short time, he gave it a life of its own, irrespective of the intentions of its Japanese sponsors. Bose was a different type from the sycophants and commercial adventurers who were usually available to support the Japanese enterprises. The qualities of action he had once displayed as Mayor of Calcutta were now directed to the preparation of a Government-in-Exile, which should be ready to replace the existing Government of India. On 23 October 1943 the Provisional Government of Free India (Azad Hind) was set up in Singapore with Bose at its head. He bled the Indian businessmen white for funds for his enterprise, being given by the Japanese the power to levy taxes on them, and having acquired in the service of Congress the right combination of contempt for millionaires and of businesslike respect for money. Bose worked under the great handicap that adequate human material for forming a provisional administration was absent. In spite of this, the sketchy organization of Azad Hind was set up.

Though Bose, between June and October, had transformed the position of the Indians in South-East Asia, and had built them into one of the forces which had to be taken account of, yet he had not succeeded in getting Japan to the point of recognizing a full-fledged Government-in-Exile. The most that he gained was an invitation to take part as an observer, along with the puppet Governments of the Japanese system, in the Greater East Asia Conference in November 1943, although his status was certainly inflated by the oratory of those present; Japan also declared its readiness to hand over the Andaman and Nicobar Islands in the

Indian Ocean to Bose's administration. But as his organization grew in effective power, the relation with local Japanese officials deteriorated. All the vexations which Ba Maw had had to endure, also faced Subhas Bose. The Japanese Army was aware of the nuisance which an opinionated exiled government could make, and, deeply suspicious, was anxious to thwart it. However, the Japanese commanders agreed to test out what effect the Indians could bring upon a battle; and Bose glowed at the opportunity.

In the meanwhile the Japanese had made their plans for an offensive from Burma which was to be directed against India. Their position was gradually growing dangerous. Large forces were being prepared against them – potentially fourteen divisions from China in the north, three or possibly six divisions from India in the west. In the spring the Japanese in Burma were reinforced, and the decision was made. Basically, the Japanese attack on India was intended to forestall an ultimate offensive against themselves by striking at once and dispersing the gathering British force. The conception was sound, if somewhat optimistic. The Japanese threw into disorder the aggressive plans on the British side.

First the Japanese hoped to overrun the British in Arakan, and then to advance into India, taking in the Assamese towns of Imphal and Kohima. From there they would move into Bengal, though probably they intended no larger action which would have taken them beyond that province. They affected, however, to fall in with Bose's plans for the general invasion of India, as they made stirring material for propaganda. In March 1944 they began their attack and crossed the Indian frontier. The Japanese Army employed three divisions.

Bose was determined that they should be accompanied by regiments of the Indian National Army. His Provisional Government had been transferred to Burma in January 1944. He is described by Ba Maw at the time as a 'bold, khaki-clad figure, carrying with him everywhere the aura of his vast, fabulous country'. In what followed, Bose's sense of reality, his strong point compared with the Indian leaders on the British side of the dividing line, deserted him. He proclaimed the slogan 'Chalo Delhi'. ('On to Delhi'). Its Red Fort, the ancient citadel built by Shah Jahan, hypnotized him, and its occupation became an obsession. In his elation, he foresaw himself sweeping on, made master of the country by a popular upsurge; able, with the strength which this would bring him, to dictate terms to the surrendering British, and to ensure that the Japanese did not misuse their victory, or ride roughshod over the country. He calculated that a Japanese invasion of India would create a very divided feeling among

Indians, and might even, the reputation of Japan being what it was, bring a mass of them to the side of the British; but the appearance on Indian soil of an Indian army of liberation would have the most rousing effect all over the country. The world would hear for the first time of the Indian National Army, and thousands of Indians would surge to it. It is strange to find a politician as practical as Bose nursing such illusions. The conversations at this time between Bose and his captains in the Indian National Army, the records of which have survived, are the proofs of his misconception.

The Japanese took a cooler view of his prospects. They wanted to divide the INA (Indian National Army) up into units of 250 men, who would act as liaison troops, guides and spies, and who would each be attached to a Japanese force. In the end a compromise was arrived at. The INA had three organized divisions in the expedition, each of two thousand men. The remainder moved as auxiliaries. It became known that the Japanese Army had reserved for itself the right of gaining the first victory on Indian soil, and looked forward to offering Imphal as a birthday present to the Emperor, which would be the more welcome because the war was going badly on other fronts.

The Army against which it moved, the Fourteenth Army, was, like the armies in the Middle East, a joint Anglo-Indian one. Battalions were either British, Indian or Gurkha, but the battalions were mixed up, and the brigade, and still more the division, were heterogeneous. Throughout the war, there was general good feeling and cooperation between the British and Indians. Whatever the grievances, they did not show themselves on the battlefield. This Army, by the reorganization of command which took place in 1943, had passed under the supreme direction of Lord Louis Mountbatten, Commander-in-Chief in South-East Asia, with the ultimate command post at Colombo.

The Army which was about to receive its first campaigning experience represented, at least in part, a new kind of India in arms. Its old pre-war armies had been drawn from a relatively few districts and, among Hindus, from a few chosen castes. Now, under wartime necessity, the Army had very much widened its intake of recruits: and with surprising results. For example, Madrasis, who had formed an important part of the armies of Lord Wellesley at the Battle of Assaye, had not been recruited for many years. Now they were offered employment, and the Madrasis celebrated their readmission by supplying the most decorated Air Force pilots that came from any region of India.

The Army undoubtedly gained from opening its ranks; and in so doing the Government met a long-standing grievance of the people. The economic benefits of supplying troops were very considerable, and these accounted in part for the prosperity of such regions as the Punjab. It had seemed unjust to favour some parts of the country and to withhold benefits from the others. The lot was cast by a theory, largely arbitrary and false, that some of the people were naturally martial, others not; in fact the distinction dated from the Indian Mutiny, and it operated chiefly on the principle of rewarding the classes which had not joined the Mutiny and of discriminating against those which had. At last the Army shook itself free from baleful memories, and thereafter it recruited itself on a more national basis.

This new Army began to reflect the new interests of India. Whereas the old Army had been entirely non-political, the new entries inevitably brought in with them something of their political interests. The attempt to debar contacts with political leaders had to be given up: the brightest of the recruits, especially for the officer corps, were the most political: the pride in being above politics had to give way. These new recruits thought it unnatural and absurd to volunteer their lives for use in a war in which they had no say. The mess rooms became forums where every aspect of the world and of government action was under constant scrutiny. This was reflected in the concern of the Government in seeing that the reading rooms of the Army were well stocked with propaganda. The older generation of thoroughly professional Army officers and of Indian NCOs looked on disapprovingly, but they could do nothing to stem this constant debate. Increasingly the Government was compelled to open the barrack-room gates, so the Army became less cloistered. In these months of the war, the old life of India was talked away in the heroic and mock bravura of undergraduate politics conducted by an Army of civilians in uniform.

In the campaign which was about to begin, many of the regular Indian officers, whose admission to the Army had been the great event in its history during the 1930s, were to be for the first time in action. Soldiers who afterwards became well-known, such as Ayub Khan, later to become President of Pakistan, were tested in this fighting.

About the British soldiers in this Army, the main fact was that they began the campaign by being war-weary. They had many of them been on duty for a long time, in an unhealthy climate. They were unsettled by the separation from their families. They were bored by inactivity. They, too, regarded themselves as true professional soldiers, but they complained – with some reason – that they were the 'forgotten Army': an Army which had lain in preparation too long and had not the bracing experience of coming into action. It did not take to the poisonous atmosphere of the country it was to fight in, to the jungles and the eerie silences, to the leeches and snakes: its medical services were inadequate, and, before the introduction of mepacrin, it was always decimated by malaria.

The Japanese advance became bogged down in the siege of Imphal. For over eight weeks, beginning on 8 March 1944, a terrible contest, perhaps the most primitive of the war with the exception of the struggle for the Pacific atolls, took place for the possession of the city: there was resolute hand-to-hand fighting.

At the beginning of the siege, the Japanese, at the start of their offensive, looked very likely to succeed. But the expedition was doomed when the Japanese found it impossible, because of the nature of the country and the blockage of supply routes from the air, to reinforce it with men and materials to overcome the defence. For days the Japanese were convinced that a final effort by them would deliver the city into their hands: but always they were disappointed. They beat off British and Indian sorties, but their own attacks were repulsed. There was great carnage, the more intense because the Japanese had to be killed at their posts, in the bunkers and wherever they had found cover. A similar struggle took place a little to the north of Imphal for Kohima, where a gigantic battle was waged over the possession of a tennis-court in the garden of the Commissioner's house.

A tactical innovation which deprived the Japanese of one of their habitual means of securing advantage was made during the campaign. In their drive through Malaya and Burma two years before, they had, using their superior mobility, habitually surrounded British forces; and, when this took place, the British habitually withdrew. This time the British did not retreat; and, though surrounded, relied on being supplied by air. An elaborate organization of the RAF flew in large amounts of food and ammunition. Without this airlift Imphal would have fallen. This change in tactics, which was due to the improved strength of the RAF in the area, changed the situation. The Japanese plans went awry when the troops, whom they thought they had trapped, stayed to fight it out instead of retiring in disorder. They misjudged profoundly the quality of the troops they opposed. They had formed so low an opinion of the British in the Malayan fighting that this betrayed them; the extent to which British troops under British command were underrated turned out to be one of their principal assets.

Another important, significant, hopeful change was that, for the first time in the war the Japanese began to surrender. Not in large numbers: the majority were still faithful to the idea that defeated Japanese are killed or commit suicide. But that some at least, when wounded, depressed, cut

143 *Top*: An American
bulldozer scoops out a mass
grave for some 2,000 Japanese
killed in Saipan during a final
'Banzai' charge on 7 July
1945.

144 *Bottom*: A prisoner-of-
war stockade holds some 300
Japanese who surrendered to
US Marines during the last
twenty-four hours of fighting
on Okinawa

9621 GENERAL VIEW OF POW STOCKADE FILLED WITH SOME OF 300 JAPANESE PRISONERS WHO CAM

145 *Top*: Air reconnaissance of Tokyo, along the Sumida river, shows the effect of firestorms caused by a US Army Air Force B29 incendiary-bomb attack on 13 September 1945

146 *Bottom*: After the first firestorm in Tokyo, caused by the Allies, Emperor Hirohito walks through the same district as the ruins smoulder

147 *Top*: The small-parts
assembly line of the Mitsubishi
aircraft works at Nagoya after
air raids by B29
superfortresses based in the
Marianas

148 *Bottom*: Central
Hiroshima at the very moment
of its destruction by an atomic
bomb, 6 August 1945. The
building on the right, an
astronomical observatory, was
one of the few buildings to
survive. It became a memorial

149 *Top*: A panorama of Hiroshima half a mile west of ground zero, looking away from ground zero. Everything within a radius of 4.4 miles has been burned out

150 *Centre and bottom*: After a Japanese military arsenal at Kokura was obscured by haze, Nagasaki became the second city to fall victim to an atomic bomb on 9 August 1945

151 *Top*: The Kwantung
Army's main bacteriological
warfare complex at Pingfan,
Manchuria

152 *Bottom left*: Japanese
subjects bow in reverence on a
bridge over the moat of the
Imperial Palace in Tokyo as
the Shōwa Emperor
broadcasts the surrender of
Japan on 15 August 1945

153 *Bottom right*: The
Japanese regarded the Allied
policy of mass destruction of
enemy cities as criminal. Here
a convicted Australian airman
is beheaded at Fukuoka
Prison immediately after the
Emperor announced the
surrender of Japan

154 *Top*: Scene of the surrender of Japanese forces in China at Tsingtao Race Course

155 *Bottom*: US Marines in post-war China: the First Marine Division occupies Tientsin, 1 October 1945

156 *Top*: The courtroom of the International Military Tribunal for the Far East

157 *Centre*: Lieutenant-General Fukuei Shinpei, formerly officer in command of the Japanese prisoner-of-war camps in Singapore and Malaya, is executed by a British firing squad in April 1946

158 *Bottom*: Japanese prisoners of war stacking shell casings after defusing and removing their powder charges following the surrender of Japan

159 *Top*: The Emperor
promulgates the new post-war
Constitution of Japan in
ceremonies before the Imperial
Diet

160 *Bottom*: Part of the US
Navy's 'mothball' fleet
anchored at the Eleventh
Naval District, San Diego,
California

THE BATTLE OF IMPHAL

THE JAPANESE IMPHAL OFFENSIVE MARCH 1944

- (23) Areas held during battle
- (23) Areas vacated during the withdrawal
- ★ IV Corps Headquarters
- Line of Advance of Japanese divisions
- Allweather roads
- Fairweather roads
- Tracks

Kohima Phakekedzumi Jessami

Maram 31 Layshi 31

Somra Tamanthi

Fort Keary

Kangpokpi Ukhrul Para Bde

Kanglatongbi Mollen Homalin

0   20 km
0   10 miles 15 31

IMPHAL 23 (1st & 4th), part of 5

17 & Humine
Para (2nd) Thanan Chindwin

Bishenpur Wangjing

23 (3rd) Palel Thaungdut

Torbung 20 (2nd) 15

Churachandpur Shorganu Iamu

33 Mombi Y Sittaung 20 (1st)

Hengtam Y

23 (2nd) Yuwa

Y Mawlaik

Tongzang 33

33 17 (1st) Zazagyo

Tiddim Fort White

33 Kalewa

Kalemyo

THE BRITISH COUNTER-OFFENSIVE AT IMPHAL JUNE–JULY 1944

- Line of advance of British divisions
- Position and line of retreat of Japanese divisions
- Position and line of retreat of Yamamoto detachment
- Allweather roads
- Fairweather roads
- Tracks

0   30 km
0   20 km

Kohima 31 23 LRP
2 114 Bde 161 Bde of 5
31 Mao Jessami
7 23 LRP
35 Bde Somra

Kangpokpi 7 Ukhrul 7 BURMA
2 31 INDIA

Kanglatongbi 5 20 31

IMPHAL 15, 31
15 Humine
Bishenpur 17 15
33 5 Palel Sita
Torbung 268 Bde 23 Thaungdut
Shuganu Mintha
Y 2/3
33 Tamu 6/1
Sittaung 15, 31

off and cold, acted as other soldiers similarly placed were accustomed to do, was a cheering fact.

The action took place in the country of the Nagas. Some spectacular achievements brought the Naga tribesmen into the light of world publicity. Much more has happened since to these attractive people. Their activities in Intelligence, and as porters, played an unexpected part. A monument erected on the battlefield recalls how two Nagas, disguised as mess servants, stole the Japanese plans of their future lines of advance, passed these to the British, and enabled them to be frustrated.

One Japanese newspaper reporter wrote: 'These fierce battles are comparable with Verdun in the last war.' Finally, logistics were decisive. There was an utter failure of communications, and the Japanese Air Force was too weak to emulate the British in air transport. The Japanese could bring in neither rice, nor medical supplies, nor essential equipment. The Japanese, who always travelled light, had relied on capturing stores and living on stocks of rice which they might seize; but in this they had failed. The Japanese troop commander issued the following order: 'A decisive battle is the only battle known to a Japanese soldier, or fitting to the Japanese spirit, but now other methods may have to be adopted.' By this he meant a strategic withdrawal. On 4 July the Japanese lifted the siege, and, on their way back, their retreat became a disaster.

They began the campaign with an army of 85,000 men; in it they lost 53,000. British and Indian casualties amounted to 16,700. The result of the campaign was a terrible, wasteful, ignominious defeat. It was one of the worst disasters that the Japanese Army suffered in the whole war; comparable in disgrace, if not in magnitude, to that of the Japanese Navy at the Battle of Midway Island. Primarily, when all due allowance had been made for the performance of the Fourteenth Army, it had been due to ineffective staff work by an Army which was not familiar with campaigning in the tropics. It must be remembered that the war in Malaya had been before this the only large-scale operation of this kind which the Japanese Army had fought, and, on balance, its training was still for temperate climates. The higher officers would not cooperate with one another. Perhaps because of this, the Japanese GHQ demanded a rigid obedience to orders and thus checked initiative from the officers in the field, which could often have turned defeat into victory. Another cause of the rout was the numerical weakness of the Japanese Army Air Force.

But that the Japanese soldiers had fought like tigers cannot be denied. A quotation may be given from the book on the campaign by Colonel Barker entitled *The March on Delhi*:

Recruits in the Japanese Army were subjected to an intense three-month course of indoctrination which changed them into fanatics, ready to die for their Emperor, their country and the honour of their regiments. The slogan 'Our highest hope is to die for the Emperor' was chanted until it became a positive obsession. The indoctrination of their families was not forgotten either; soon after the new recruit was called up, his relatives received a letter from his commanding officer asking them to be careful not to block his road to an honourable death. The effectiveness of the propaganda may be judged from the fact that there were cases of wives killing their children and committing suicide so that their husbands would not be reluctant to die. Many officers and men even had their funeral rites performed before leaving for the front to show their intention of dying for their country . . .*

Yet, impressive as their military behaviour was, it was undoubtedly an aberration. There was madness in it, as well as remarkable self-discipline. For, as the war dragged on to its close, and as the Japanese position grew steadily worse, so did the Japanese military behaviour become more ferocious. Its extreme cult of death was a new thing of this century, as least in the form which it took at the time. Early in this century, the Russo-Japanese War had not been particularly savage. And the new sternness was only to be found in the Japanese overseas. As long as they were in the homeland, they did not seem to be possessed, as were the troops in Burma, in the Philippines and in China. It was as if the Japanese Army, once it had had battle experience, succeeded in passing its *furor Japonicus* to all the reinforcements which came to it from Japan. The madness came out in some of the battle orders which were captured:

You men have got to be fully in the picture as to what the present position is. Regarding death as something lighter than a feather you men must tackle the task of capturing Imphal. You must accept that the division will be almost annihilated. I have confidence in your courage but should any delinquency occur, I shall take the necessary action. In order to keep the honour of his unit bright, a commander may have to use his sword as a weapon of punishment, shameful though it is to have to shed one's own soldiers' blood on the battlefield.†

Some of the men who were the victims of this military discipline, some of the officers who enforced it, are now living quietly in Japan, and they must look back on their wartime experience with surprise and almost with disbelief.

The news of the defeat on 4 July arrived in Tokyo at the same time as the news of the loss of Paris by Germany. It was hard to say which of them

* A. J. Barker, *The March on Delhi*, Faber, London, 1963.
† ibid.

faced the blacker prospects, Germany or Japan. The disaster increased the bad relations between the Army and the Navy: this came, said the Navy, of the Army 'taking walks' in Asia, and entering on unnecessary adventures instead of concentrating on the problems of the defence of the homeland.

The adventures were nearly at an end. The Army would be needed in the Japanese islands. This campaign was nearly the finish of the Japanese in Burma. For a time they were saved from effective pursuit by the monsoon, which put an end to all war. But when the monsoon ended, the Fourteenth Army moved forward. The offensive had already been joined by a bitterly fought advance of Americans and American-trained Chinese troops (who had fallen back on India in 1942) led by General Stilwell; a thrust from Arakan for which the prelude was the taking of Akyab from the sea; and by four Chinese divisions reluctantly introduced by Chiang Kai-shek from Yunnan. This time the offensive progressed. The Allies had clear air supremacy, and this was decisive, particularly because it enabled them to keep their armies fully supplied. The Japanese had stirred up opposition from all corners of the world; they must however have felt somewhat surprised at finding among their pursuers divisions of West African and East African troops. They had been raised by the British, and the war in Burma in tropical conditions offered them appropriate employment. That the African people had no quarrel with Japan, that Japan had no significance to them except as the exporter of textiles which were prized by them, did not seem to cause any comment.

As the British slowly reoccupied Burma, they felt the imperial itch reviving. An Imperial Army in advance bred different sentiments from an Imperial Army in retreat. 'By English bones the English flag is stayed.' This old line of poetry took on a new meaning.

By April 1945 Rangoon had fallen. It fell actually to the advance from Akyab, which beat by a few hours the advance from the north. The Japanese soldiers continued to fight savagely, but they were the victims of the bad strategy of their generals. Soon all Burma was clear. The end was made more certain because most of the Burmese Army, which had been raised and trained by the Japanese, revolted and changed sides at a critical moment.

In the course of this campaign, there had taken place a sharp revision of the complacency of the Japanese about the demerits of the British soldier. Soon after the start of the war, the Japanese had met with such success, and the morale of the white troops they had encountered had been so low that they had supposed that the prestige the British had enjoyed during the previous century had been the result of a confidence trick. Caution towards the British was succeeded by extreme scorn. They could not have held them in lower esteem, and this probably accounted for their over-confidence in the Kohima operations, which otherwise appeared light-headed. They preferred to have British troops to deal with rather than Indian, since, in the new reckoning of the Japanese Army, white troops were less tenacious than Asian troops. In the vicissitudes of this campaign, however, they learnt, very expensively, that they had made a wrong assessment. The British troops put on their laurels again, and their recent campaign gave the Japanese new respect for their adversary.

In the battle, the Indian National Army had proved useless. In nearly all the fighting, it had disgraced itself. Its largest losses were from desertion. Its heart was not in combat with the Government to which it had formerly owed allegiance. Its performance had a depressing effect on the hopes of seeing the war turn into an Asian defensive operation against the western counter-attack. Subhas Chandra Bose sustained himself in his disappointment, and against the contempt which the Japanese military did not bother to hide, by putting out an account of near-treachery by the Japanese. Imphal, according to him, had been helpless before the Indo-Japanese force, but the Japanese had held back the Indian advance which would have taken it. They were unwilling that the Indians should have the great prize of the campaign; they wished to present Imphal as a Japanese conquest to the Emperor on his birthday. An Indian governor had been ready to take possession, but the Indian troops were forestalled from inducting him.

The tale was too inaccurate to be effective. Subhas Bose lost nearly all his magical appeal. In despair, he turned away from his concern with the Indian National Army to the political regimentation of the million Indians living in South-East Asia. But his fortunes sank with those of the Japanese. When these were finally overwhelmed, and had surrendered, he prevailed on a local officer to let him try to escape by air to Russia. It was a move consonant with his daring and his obstinate opportunism. He foresaw that relations between the West and Russia would be bad, and hoped that Moscow would see the opportunity of letting him set up in Russia his provisional Government of India. But the aeroplane in which he was flying crashed on the way to Formosa, on 18 August 1945, and Bose ended his melodramatic life. In spite of his failure, he had, by his daring, so much caught the imagination of the Indians who had been in touch with him, that they refused to believe that he had really been killed. The rumour spread that he had gone underground and had become a Sadhu (there is some evidence that some of the defeated rebels did this in 1858 after the failure of the Indian Mutiny), and that he would emerge again to lead a triumphant rising against the British. The legend was firmly believed in by his brother, Sarat Chandra Bose, a leading, and apparently hard-headed, Congressman of Bengal.

Bose's idea of corrupting the Indian Army, and of leading it back in triumph against the British in Delhi, though it turned out to be a fiasco, could have been a formidable threat to Britain. Its concept was sound: it was fortunate for Britain that the morale of the INA was such as to make the plan unworkable. For months the news of the INA caused very deep anxiety among the Army Staff and the informed civilians in Delhi, and their failure in action was received with intense relief. The enterprise had been kept reasonably secret from the public in India. It was not entirely unknown, for the information about it was contained in the monitoring report which had a fairly wide circulation; moreover, Bose's radio was listened to fairly extensively. But the public was surprised when it learned later from the press how wide the conspiracy had been.

Of 70,000 Indians who had been captives, over half resisted all the lures to serve either Japan direct or else rebel India. They had nothing very much to induce them to remain loyal beyond their oath of service and their regimental pride. These ties held; and their strength was an important factor in determining the history of the war in Asia. For this the main credit goes to the regimental commanders of the previous two or three generations who, by and large, were trusted by their men to stand up for their interests, for fair treatment, and for an honourable status. These men built up the ties which between 1942 and 1945 bore the great strain.

This left the problem of what to do with the soldiers who had been less loyal. Most of those who had enlisted in the INA had passed into British hands, and for the second time had become prisoners of war. Technically they were all of them guilty of an internationally agreed crime of the darkest nature. For desertion, treason, rebellion and levying war against the King, a harsh penalty was likely to be exacted. Actually, no drumhead court-martials were held on any of the prisoners upon capture. They were kept in captivity, and what to do about them became a political case which was hotly debated.

It was not decided until the war ended. The Congress leaders, on coming out of their own wartime captivity, saw in it an ideal means of attacking the Government. The INA were presented as the true heroes of the Indian nation, and, if harshly dealt with, would become revered martyrs. The British were impressed by this danger. They were inclined to act in the spirit of Winston Churchill, who advising clemency on another occasion, had said: 'The grass grows quickly over the battlefield. Over the scaffold, never.' They decided to release the undistinguished mass of the prisoners. But they hesitated at the ring-leaders, and those who, in the course of the campaign, had been guilty of war crimes, or had tortured their former comrades because these had stood firm against the allurements of the Japanese. They had to keep it in mind that those who felt most bitterly against the Indian National Army were the officers and men of the Indian Army who had remained loyal. For the sake of the morale of this Army, it was scarcely possible to release without some punishment at least the more spectacular of the prisoners. Therefore, after much indecision, and much discussion which became involved with the renewed negotiations between the Government and Congress, the decision was made to limit prosecution to a few cases, ultimately restricted to three.

The trials were held in the Red Fort of Delhi in 1946. A more peculiarly inept setting could not have been chosen. The Red Fort had become, in Indian national mythology, the shrine of Indian national hopes. It had been built as a citadel and palace by the Moghul Emperors, and symbolized the time before the British conquest, when all that Britain meant had been individual merchants coming to beg for patronage from the great ones of India. The trials gave so much publicity to the Congress lawyers, who were able to defend the prisoners, and to Jawaharhal Nehru who, having once been a barrister, could appear before the courts, that the Government was glad to call them off quickly. It was content with the simple dismissal from further service of the great majority of officers and men. Such dismissal was punishment in itself, since service in the Army brought with it economic privilege; and, by confiscating this advantage from the disaffected, it was thought that the loyal part of the Indian Army would be at ease.

Burma had been freed as the result of a sustained thrust of the British and the Americans against the Japanese Army, which had worn itself out by the offensive at Imphal and Kohima. From recovered Burma, the victors prepared to move afresh. Singapore and Malaya were the next targets: and Japan had there, and elsewhere in South-East Asia, a very large Army, as yet unscathed, its morale untouched by Allied propaganda, with vast supplies of arms and ammunition. The prospect which this opened up, and the length of time which would be taken in ejecting Japan from one well-defended post to another, caused a great upsurge of criticism of British strategy. Had the drive on Burma, even though it was ultimately successful, really been justified? Were there not better ways of using British power than in following the withdrawal of Japan? Could

Britain, using its recovered naval supremacy, not strike at some vital ports, less protected?

There is a notable passage in Tolstoy's *War and Peace* describing men's behaviour on the battlefield. When he is stricken on the field of Austerlitz, Prince Andrei sees two opposing men, French and Russian, both seizing hold of a ramrod, and struggling for its possession. Each would have done better to release his hold of it, and to free himself to use his musket. But they were too much hypnotized by the struggle to let go. So they continued to tussle. In the circumstances of the war in Asia, it was asked whether the British and Japanese really did any good for themselves, or brought the war nearer to an end, by remaining locked in conflict.

In fact, the decisive fighting was going on in the Pacific. Britain was denied a role in this: it could supply no adequate force, and the American commanders were under pressure to distance themselves from allies who put their cause in such an imperialist colour. Keeping the British at arm's length was held to improve the American image with the national parties of South Asia. The future of that part of the world was held to lie with them.

CHAPTER 23

China 1942–4

BEFORE describing the end of Japan, and the breakthrough of the American ships from the Pacific, it is necessary to review the fate of China up to this point. After all, China had been one of the principal causes of the war in the Far East. This conflict, which had spread so widely, had begun as the result of the refusal by Chiang Kai-shek to come to terms with Japan. China had not ceased to count. But, after the intervention of the United States, it had taken a relatively minor part in the military affairs of the nations.

Before the conflict was enlarged, Chiang had calculated that, if he held out, sooner or later Japan would come into collision with other Powers. He had resolved, and it was more or less public knowledge, that, when this time came, China, which for four years had borne the fury of the Japanese offensive, would retire from the actual fighting, and would leave it to the fresher forces which should become engaged to complete the wearing down of Japan, of which China felt that it had done enough. Without fighting further, Chiang Kai-shek counted on being able to join in the eventual share-out of territory, and in the other benefits, when the world was rearranged at the general peace. In this, events had gone more or less as Chiang expected. Chiang, the simple and, in the eyes of the sophisticated statesmen of the West, rather primitive soldier, seemed at the time to have his judgement vindicated, his diplomacy confirmed.

It appeared to the Americans that China, poor in resources for making war, now held the best cards. The United States had chosen to take up the challenge of Japan. But it had handicapped itself by the decision to concentrate on fighting Germany first, Japan afterwards. In the interval before it could concentrate its whole attention on Japan, allies in the East seemed likely to be of greater moment to the United States than the United States was to them. It became a major preoccupation with it to keep China in the war, at the cost of offering it all possible inducement to stay. China could have all that it asked, in exchange for its willingness that the total commitment of American force in the Far East should be delayed. In the long run, the United States believed that the use of Chinese territory was indispensable for making it geographically possible for the

Allies to defeat Japan; it had no confidence that Russia, which also had a land army able to get to grips with Japan, would ever, in the way that events were shaping themselves, break its neutrality with Japan. For the United States, China represented the corridor along which their armies might eventually proceed, and get at Japan on level terms. In the meanwhile, China was to be the subject of a holding operation: to be kept in the war at all costs. For this the Americans were prepared to pay a great deal, and they had insufficient regard for the fact that the Chinese were accustomed to considering long-term as well as the short-term interests of their country. Chiang Kai-shek and his supporters could read their balance sheets and were masters at calculating profit and loss.

The impediment lay chiefly in geography. With the fall of Burma, the precarious link with Chungking along the Burma Road was interrupted. China was cut off. Between it and the Americans there was the enormous barrier of the Himalayas. To keep China in the war, the Americans, with ingenuity, tried by every means to circumvent the obstacle. They organized an airlift to China over the mountain ranges from India; they sent American officers to re-train the Chinese Army; they put continual pressure upon India to demonstrate that China might eventually find aid there. In immediate aid, China was given a large Anglo-American loan: America subscribed $500 million and Britain £50 million: this relieved its immediate financial problems.

This aid the Allies intended for China as a whole. It was directed to whoever in China would fight Japan. Chiang Kai-shek's aim was to engross it all for himself. It was to ensure that his hold over the country was continuously and decisively strengthened; it was to deny aid to those who might threaten it. In his thinking at that time dollars counted for more than morale in the upkeep of government. He saw danger principally in one fact – that the communists, the party of revolution, might obtain the economic backing which would transform the situation, and put them on equal terms with the Government. In a China in which the ferment of revolution was working ever more actively, in which communism had already mastered the circumstances of the war, it was essential that the communists should be denied their share of foreign aid, even at the cost of their military efficiency as allies against Japan. Technically, the Kuomintang and the communists were still allies; they were pledged together to fight Japan; the American aid, on a reading of the military situation, should have been divided between them. That it should not became the governing aim of Chiang's policy. He was still the embodiment of Chinese nationalism, but he was first and always a warlord.

At first, the prospects appeared bright for Chiang. His more distant ambitions, of being the supreme force in Asia at the end of the war, buoyed him up when his Government, as the result of the intensification of the blockade, suffered blow upon blow. Chiang was sanguine: this perhaps explains why he took phlegmatically even the worst of news. Both his enemies, Japan and Chinese Communism, were being trampled into ruin by the United States. His long-term prospects were heady. His standing in Washington mattered more to him than military realities in the Far East. In this he was served zealously, alike by plausible Chinese and by foreigners over whom China had cast its spell.

Chiang, in order apparently to gratify his sense of importance, struck out in directions which caused surprise, and ways which were unwelcome to his allies. He had insisted on visiting India, in February 1942, and seeing Indian affairs for himself. He could urge that India had suddenly become vitally important for China, both as a base, and as transit territory for American supplies. The bad relations between the Government of India and Indian nationalists were a menace to China, because they could result in a situation which interrupted communication. Chiang insisted on studying matters for himself, and tried, by personal diplomacy with the Viceroy and Indian leaders, to bridge the gap between them.

The British were annoyed. They found Chiang extremely ill-informed, and privately judged that, in the guise of a mediator, he was prospecting the ground for Chinese intervention in case the military necessity in Europe should compel a British withdrawal from India. They objected to the need for providing Chiang and his wife with banquets at the moment when, too late in the judgement of many observers, they had become conscious of their desperate state. Especially, though, they demurred at the increased prestige which his interest brought to the Indian Congress in its duel with the Viceroy.

Chiang Kai-shek could not blame the Indian Administration for a failure to back him. This somewhat lethargic Government went out of its way to provide, with energy and great speed, the institutions which were needed to bind the two Governments together in their war effort. On the Indian side, a China Relations Department was brought into being, to whose good offices a thousand things were owing: the Department did everything, from supply to strengthening military cooperation. It was efficient, it was prompt, it cut through delays. It was so much out of character for the Government of India that it quite astonished the Chinese.

In spite of these inducements to be up and doing, China remained more or less militarily inactive. The performance of Chinese troops, in the rare

Paotow   Peking

Shanghai

Ichang   Hankow

Changsha

Foochow

Amoy

Canton

1941 — 2

Paotow   Peking

Shanghai

Ichang   Hankow

Changsha

Foochow

Amoy

Canton

Swatow

1942 — 3

1943 — 5

Paotow

Peking

Tientsin

Taiyuan

Tsinan   Tsingtao

Sian   Loyang

Taierhchwang

Nanking

Ichang   Hankow   Shanghai

Anking   Hangchow

Chungking   Ningpo

Nanchang

Changsha

Hengyang

Myitkyina   Kweiyang

Tengyueh   Kunming   Foochow

Bhamo

Liuchow   Amoy

Canton   Swatow

Mandalay   Nanning   Wuchow

BURMA   FRENCH   INDO-

THAILAND   CHINA

'BRER RABBIT & THE TAR BABY':
THE CHINA STALEMATE
CONTINUES 1941—5

actions in which they were engaged, was unmemorable. Nor was this surprising. Their armies were shockingly organized; relations between officers and men were deplorable. The officers were increasingly arrogant and corrupt; they embezzled the wages of the soldiers; they were often brutal and ignorant. The soldiers either were separated for many years from their families, or, if they had news of them, were rightly disturbed at the news of worsened conditions in the countryside. The rank and file had nothing to fight for.

Chiang Kai-shek chose, in March 1943, to publish under his name a highly controversial book. It was written in Chinese. The book was called *China's Destiny*. It contained the familiar story of the unjust dealings with China by the Great Powers, the unequal treaties, the shearing away from China of her dependencies. Thus it revealed that China still nursed her grievances when it might have seemed better policy to have concealed them. The Powers which had done China its past wrongs had now shown a willingness to repair the damage, and the exposure of China's wound could only damage their cooperation. The effect of its publication was to cause mistrust, rouse suspicion, and generate bad blood. Madame Chiang Kai-shek shrewdly advised against an English translation: this did not appear therefore until 1947. The book, however, had come to the attention of the West's China hands when it first appeared in Chinese, and therefore it had precisely the effect which Chiang wanted to produce.

Chiang, in his relations with his Allies, followed the tactics of 'threatening to fall'. He advertised that his position was calamitous. The weaker he was, the more anxious the Americans were for him, and the greater the efforts which they were willing to make on his behalf. Naturally he led them on; and he was helped by the chance that President Roosevelt revealed, from the United States' entry into the war until his death in 1945, an extraordinary partiality for China. The accidents of personality played here a fateful part. Roosevelt, active in Washington, had an even greater influence on events by the climate of opinion which he germinated, than by the measures he took as head of the American Government. He was himself endowed with no special perspicacity, but he did surround himself with able men who dwelt much on the shape which the world must take as a result of the war; and he became convinced that, round a firm Sino-American axis, the Asian countries were destined to revolve. American aid would supply strength to China; China would revert to its traditional art of radiating its great civilizing influence out across its borders.

Roosevelt saw rightly that the crisis in East Asia was due ultimately to the collapse of the political power of China. The United States would restore it. This time there would be no imperialists to undermine it again; President Roosevelt was satisfied that the eastern role of Britain and other colonial Powers was coming to an end and he had a curious blind spot in relation to the Soviet Union's inheritance of Imperial Russian pretensions in world politics. Asia would be safe again, except from its own dissension, and what power would thrive better in this atmosphere than China. He gained comfort from the signs that China's appetite for its historic greatness was beginning to recover. He became convinced that he was serving alike the interests of the United States and also all the world by throwing his mantle over China.

Roosevelt had an extraordinary power of communicating his vision to the public. In this case, however, he preached mostly to the converted. The United States' attitude towards China in the later stages of the war was rather unbalanced. If one nation can be said to adopt another, the United States adopted China. The United States has been liable to periodical phases of extreme partiality to certain foreign countries; in its fervent feeling towards China at this time, it outdid itself. The United States was hallucinated; like Titania by Bottom the Weaver. The reality was that the United States became enthusiastic for the tyranny of the Kuomintang, which was passing increasingly into the most reactionary hands; the Americans saw it, not as it was, but as a democratic party full of vigour and promise. In place of a military rabble, the United States saw in the Chinese Army an inspiring force, which was a mixture of a romanticized version of the American armies of the Revolution and the Civil War. Where there was evident and apparently irreparable economic ruin, it saw lively economic promise. China's intellectual and artistic life, which, to the trained eye, was in the ruins of a great cultural past, appeared to the USA to be full of a fresh, imaginative view of the world. China appeared as nearly a new Utopia. The United States of course produced its realists, who protested against its romantic illusions, but they could scarcely make themselves heard against the newspapers and radio, which almost all of them followed the fashion.

Roosevelt's policies, the American hallucination, the realities of geography and of logistics in the East, produced, between them, a mood of accommodation to China which bewildered the rest of the world. China was pitied, but the United States postponed coming to its aid with immediate and effective military succour. It was encouraged by the United States to pass its time in discussing its growing ambition. American patronage ensured that China's claims were not regarded as simply ludicrous. Men like Winston Churchill took a sceptical view, but it was hardly worth their while to oppose the United States over this. In war, naked strength is in the last resort the thing which counts; but prestige may be manufactured by handfuls of dedicated officials and the few statesmen who matter, and may, in the short run, pass for strength. China was in this condition, and advanced by several degrees in the world's esteem.

All the while that this was happening, the Chinese press, which was of course under strong Government influence, had, as was natural in the relations between states, been biting the hand which fed it. The newspapers were full of articles which attacked the United States very bitterly. They made use of the stale propaganda methods of the Nazis early in the war in Europe. They claimed that the United States would fight until the last Chinaman; they envisaged that China, having made great sacrifices for democracy, would be a certain loser at the peace, and would itself be sacrificed. They painted a picture of the riotous life lived by Americans in luxurious camps in the midst of the poverty of China. This mood, when it became known in the United States, took a little of the glow out of the American feeling for China. But the work of the China lobby had been very far-reaching, and the suspicion that the Chinese were ungrateful was lightly borne by American philanthropy.

Although there was much criticism of Chiang Kai-shek by some Americans with a clearer vision, too much can be made of occasional Sino-American friction. In particular, the incompetence and bad morale of the Chinese were probably overrated by some American experts. There was no real likelihood of China making a separate peace. Chiang Kai-shek had steered China's policy since the earliest years of the conflict, but, by the latest years, China had probably steered itself. The muddle, constant criticism, and apathy misled the United States. China, though it detested war, was averse to surrender. It would have opposed Chiang if he had wished to make a dishonourable peace with nearly as much compulsive force as it had done when it suspected him in 1937. China's mood was frightening. It had not the least enthusiasm for the war; it was profoundly weary of it; but it was determined to continue to resist. If ever a war had in fact been a 'people's war', this was one, even though there were large and respectable elements of the population who were cooperating with the Japanese. The Government was forbidden by the nation to make peace: by a nation which, by all reasonable arguments, yearned for peace. The war seemed likely to continue indefinitely.

It was the Americans who had to serve in China who were naturally less affected by the pronounced American enthusiasm for all things

1140   *The Defeat of Japan*

Chinese. Their position was extremely difficult; they suffered much less from the delusions which were making American policy, but they were expected to act as if they did so. The attitude of the much-tried American General Joseph Stilwell deserves study. His mishaps are part of the misunderstandings of the time.

He was a naturally bilious man aptly nicknamed 'Vinegar Joe': he was extraordinarily suspicious of everyone, especially of Americans who fawned on Chinese; of all British, with whom he had to be in alliance but whom he suspected of outwitting the United States, and of the Chinese, above all of Chiang Kai-shek, whom he saw playing a gigantic confidence trick on the United States. The irony was that he, who had few illusions, was inclined to be grimly friendly towards China, and, in a professional manner, to defend its interests.

After Pearl Harbor, when American aid began to pour into China, it was clearly desirable to appoint someone to be responsible on the spot for its distribution. A commander was needed for the American personnel who were militarily active in or near China. A military expert was also necessary to work out joint military plans with the Chinese. Stilwell, as a person of unquestionable experience, and available immediately, was appointed. He had spent most of his career in China, with some dedication had studied the Chinese language since 1919 (when he had been appointed the first Chinese language officer in the history of the US Army), and had served for many years in a quasi-diplomatic status in the American Embassy. At Roosevelt's insistence, in his instinct to mix up America's affairs with those of its Allies, Stilwell was given by Chiang Kai-shek the Chinese rank of his Chief-of-Staff.

When, as described earlier, the British formed their South-East Asia Command in 1943, Stilwell was appointed as the deputy of Mountbatten. From a comparatively minor position, he had accumulated appointments, all of which gave him authority. Few men in the war were in a position of such power.

The multitude of functions was a mistake. With such divergent pressures upon him, no man could have made a success of being a loyal servant of the United States and China. For a joint post to be workable, there must be coincidence of interests between the countries to which a man is jointly responsible. Stilwell, in serving Roosevelt and Chiang, had an impossible task. Much as Roosevelt respected the role that China was destined to play, the interests of the United States and China were different. Stilwell had decided that he would be through and through American: he would serve the United States and would correct Roosevelt's rather eccentric judgement.

The difficulty was increased because Stilwell's own judgement was defective. He did not see that, for the issue of the war, it really was unnecessary for Chiang to fight much more. Roosevelt himself had probably glimpsed this truth. But Roosevelt erred because he supposed that it was necessary for the United States to make strenuous efforts to keep China in the war. China would have remained belligerent in any circumstances, and its real interests, which Chiang saw very clearly, were all against making a separate peace. Having won credit with the Western Allies, China would have been suicidal to fling it away by becoming a renegade towards the end of the war, in which the difficult part had been the beginning. Nor would it have gained any advantage by doing so. The United States and Britain were satisfied as long as China remained formally at war, and turned a blind eye to the reality of much of China's wartime record.

Stilwell, however, did not perceive this. He had a mania to drive China back to war: both its bureaucrats living in comfort in Chungking, and its wretched conscripts herded to war by force. Chinese guile, Chinese pretence that it was doing much more than it was, he exposed with relish. Stilwell obtained Chinese agreement that thirty Chinese divisions should be allotted for cooperation with the British from India for the operations in Burma and to reconquer South-East Asia. To facilitate these operations, the Ledo Road was constructed across the southern slopes of the Himalayan mountains through dense jungles.

It linked the Calcutta-Dimapur-Ledo rail line up the North-East Frontier of India (in Assam) with a south-easterly cross-country track right across North Burma via Myitkyina and Bhamo until it joined the route of the original Sino-British Burma Road, north of Lashio, to Kunming and Chungking. The Ledo Road was one of the major engineering enterprises of the war.

Stilwell, and the toadies who clustered round him on his American staff, made no secret of the fact that they greatly desired that American and Chinese forces should get into many of these regions in advance of the British, and they wished to eradicate British influence where it still survived. They considered the British Empire obsolete and effete, and they had no desire to see it re-established. They counted on a peace settlement which would create an Asia of self-determining nation-states, always the American ideal, as 1919 had shown in Europe. For this, they considered it of first-class importance that they should end the war in military possession of disputed territory. But the thirty Chinese divisions proved to be a paper force. Only a fraction was ever available. For Stilwell's aim, there was to be no Chinese manpower.

Stilwell, in his vigour for the war, could get little response from the Kuomintang officials, and from Chiang Kai-shek personally. He became increasingly obsessed with the fact that Chiang was employing 200,000 of his best troops for cordoning off the area that was occupied by the Red Army; and that this Army, alone of China's military forces, had proved that it was anxious to fight, and had shown the value of its guerrilla strategy against the Japanese. But it was prevented by the Kuomintang from playing its part in the war. Chiang, in his fear that substantial economic aid would reach the communists, and would make them dangerous to him, blockaded them shamelessly.

Stilwell denounced him to the Americans as a bad ally: Chiang complained that he could have no confidence in such a Chief-of-Staff. To do him justice, he could say that Stilwell had not grasped the fact that the civil war in China was continuing. The merger of the armies, which was to have taken place by the pact which Chiang made with the communists and the Young Marshal of Manchuria at the time of the Sian kidnapping, had never been carried out. The communists had laid down their own strategy in their war with Japan, and, as by their guerrilla methods of war they penned Japan more and more to the towns, they continually occupied a larger and larger area of the country. All the while the communists were consolidating their hold. Was Chiang to assist them by removing his forces which kept them under surveillance?

The problem was difficult; Chiang was notable for his obstinacy, which had established him where he was; Stilwell was notorious for pertinacity and for courting disfavour. With Stilwell's agreement, a whitewashing of the communists took place in America. The news about them was surprising, and cheered an America which was hungry for hopeful news. It was said that they were not real communists at all; they were Jeffersonian democrats, simple rural reformers, who desired only to fight for their country, and they were held back by Chiang Kai-shek, the real nature of whose Government had by this time become plain. They were a brand-new and unexpected ally, waiting to be used against the Japanese if the United States would sanction it. Chiang Kai-shek, treating this as a threat of American repudiation of him, fulminated, and put the blame on Stilwell. He supposed him responsible for the agitation in the press.

By the autumn of 1944 the breach between Chiang and Stilwell had become wider, beyond reconciliation. Chiang officially demanded that Roosevelt should dismiss Stilwell. Roosevelt, though his confidence in Chiang had been half-changed by Stilwell – but not his confidence in China – consented.

With the fall of Stilwell there vanished a plan which had been dear both to him and to Roosevelt. This was for the re-training and modernization by American officers of the entire Chinese Army. The United States was characteristically ready to take responsibility for this gigantic task; but it required Chinese consent to the appointment of Stilwell as Chief-of-Staff, and Chiang would not trust such authority to any foreigner.

Admittedly it would have been difficult; there would have been storms, and, whilst Stilwell's attitude to the communists was at best ambiguous in the view of Chiang Kai-shek, it was clear that there were many fundamental principles on which the two men were divided in any reform. Stilwell would certainly have wanted to incorporate part of the Red Army, and much of its system of command and administration. Neither of them would compromise. But Chiang, in winning his point that there should be no foreign command in his Army, sacrificed the possibility of ending the war with a re-born, reliable, modernized force.

The war was very depressing when seen in these years from Chungking. Air raids, which had been plentiful, had died down, and had become rare. But with this there had come hunger and a dreadful boredom with nothing to distract people from being conscious of their extreme discomfort. The city was overcrowded: it was full of refugees. The lives of most people had become a nightmare because of inflation; it was still under a semblance of control; it was to reach fantastic proportions, as in Germany during the period at the end of the First World War, only when the war was over; but already inflation in China cast very deep shadows, and it had become the main impediment in life.

The extent of the inflation was a novelty in human history. In Chungking, prices rose by two hundred and fifty times in the two years 1942–4. The price index of goods, quoted at 100 in 1937, was 125,000 by 1945. How to cope, how to find money, became the overriding concern of everyone, including all the Army officers, and the events of the war sank a long way behind. Another stunning blow had been dealt at human society, seen from a Chinese perspective, and strong suspicions grew up as to whether life could ever be normal again, even if peace was restored. It was the classical effect of an uncontrolled inflation. 'If you wish to make a revolution,' Lenin had said, 'first debauch the currency.'

In spite of this, many people were growing very rich out of wartime enterprises and profiteering, but they hid themselves, and no bright plumage lit up the drab scene. Only gossip and scandal circulated wildly. The inflation had the usual effects in disintegrating the society. The corruption became impudent. One day, when a general of the Indian Army was paying a visit to the city, a cousin of the Chinese Finance Minister called on him by night, and outlined a plan of partnership by which the two could make a fortune. All that was necessary was the use of the general's means of transport, and of his prestige to keep official interference at arm's length.

To keep their armies in the field, the Chinese had to make more and more use of conscription. It was an ordinary sight to see in the country-side, even close to Chungking, squads of soldiers being deported to fighting areas; the soldiers were all chained together. Across the length of the huge country, there was constant, small-scale, sporadic action, which, though of little military consequence, did much material damage. The Japanese occupying the cities were harried, and in many parts of the country could not venture, except in great force, into the countryside; they raided and massacred sporadically. Insecurity was constant; the war had apparently ceased to have a reason and the possibility of an end.

In parts of the country, however, the war seemed to have run its course, to be exhausted, and to have fought itself out. It was succeeded by the armed forces on both sides following the age-old instincts for trade. The armies became trading organizations. Trading is a passion with the Chinese; with the Japanese it is familiar. As soon as the armies stood still, the Chinese put out their feelers, and the Japanese, who were not paid very highly and welcomed some supplement to their wages, responded. The metamorphosis of the barbaric Japanese conquerors into the scheming Japanese traders was curious to watch. The attempts by high Japanese officers to restrict the trade were in vain. The Japanese generals, even at the highest level of direction of the Japanese Armies, were too deeply engaged. China, by the action not of its Government or of its soldiers but by the private enterprise of its merchants, had woven a web of commerce. Within a month or so of conquest it snared the Japanese as well as their opposite numbers and bound them in all sorts of ways to courses of action which aimed at the satisfaction of private wants rather than the advancement of Japan's public enterprise of subjugation. And so it was to continue until the end of the war. The spectacle is of exuberant trade springing up and flourishing wherever the two belligerents came in contact. Patrolling warships operated most. The Japanese Navy was par-ticularly notorious for doing traffic with the Chinese. This was very well attested by watchers in Hong Kong in the months before the island was invaded.

Stilwell's fall in 1944 coincided with the last great military effort in China by the Japanese. During 1943 and the first part of 1944, the Ameri-cans had built up a new war machine on Chinese soil with which they had at last succeeded in reaching the heart of the Japanese war effort, and which held out hopes of being deadly. This they did by expanding greatly the activities of General Claire Lee Chennault. This man had begun by recruiting a private air force, mercenaries, drawn from the staff of American airlines and college youths. They were known as Chennault's Flying Tigers. In the summer of 1941, while the United States was still neutral, this force, put at the service of the Kuomintang, proved itself indispensable for the air defence of Chungking. Later, when the United States entered the war, it was incorporated in the United States Army, and Chennault also returned to it. In the course of time he established airfields in South-East China, and from there B29 bombers began the first systematic bombardments that the Japanese had had to endure. By prodigious efforts, huge stockpiles of munitions, fuel and other supplies were flown over the 'hump' of the Himalayas to the new forward airfields which 300,000 Chinese coolies had built under American direction. It was exceptionally costly in terms of time, manpower, airlifting capacity and expense, and it proved to be an almost entirely unproductive diversion from more useful enterprises.

The Japanese were not inclined to wait while America surmounted the technical challenges involved in carrying out very long-range strategic bombing raids over the Japanese home islands. Spurred on by the early bombing runs, Japan decided that it was necessary to renew their military effort against China. They had halted large-scale military campaigning at the end of 1938, and, during the years since then, it had seemed that they were best served by letting time work for them. They hoped that the discomfort, and the upset from the perpetual strain of trying to appease the communists, would in the end induce Chiang Kai-shek to submit his stubborn neck to peace negotiations. They could place their trust in Chinese racial dislike of the country's Western Allies. During this period, the Japanese were satisfied with the steady stream of defections from the Kuomintang to the side of the Wang Ching-sei Government and its Japanese guardians of law and order. It occurred as a natural by-product of fraternization, propaganda, a desire for greater material comfort and an interest in self-preservation. By 1942, the communists estimated, and published with some smugness, that twenty-seven Kuomintang generals had gone over.

Times had changed. In 1944 the Japanese Army in China gathered itself together and commenced an offensive which they named *Ichi-Gō* (literally, 'Operation Number One'). It was an exceptionally ambitious plan designed to extend Japanese control deep into the interior of China and possibly to open the way for yet another attempt to seek a negotiated peace with Chiang Kai-shek or his forces. The campaign was in part prompted by the need to establish secure overland communications extending from Manchuria and North China right the way through to

SHANSI

SHENSI

Yuanchu
Mienchih
Langpao · Loyang · Mihsien · Chengchow
Chungmou
Hwang-ho

Sian

H O N A N

Nanyang · Siping · Chumatien

SZECHWAN

·Chengtu

HUPEH

Sinyang

Ichang
Toushih

Chungking

Yangtze-kiang

(Wuhan) · Hankow
Hanyang · Wuching

Ansiang

Changteh

Xiyang

Shaoyang · Siangtan · Changsha · Kukang

KWEICHOW

HUNAN

KIANGSI

Kweiyang

Hengyang

Leiyang

Tuyun
Tuhsha

Lingling

Nantan
Hochih

Kweilin

Linchow

Wuchow

KWANGTUNG

Pinyang
Nanning · Kweiping
Si-kiang

Canton

Lungchow

KWANGSI

N

VIETNAM

Hong Kong

Hanoi

0   100   200   300 km
0   100   200 miles

**THE ICHI-GŌ OFFENSIVE
1944**

Japan's forces in Occupied South-East Asia. This need sprang from the fact that Allied attacks had decimated Japanese merchant shipping. One of the main purposes of the whole campaign, however, was to capture and dismantle the American air bases on Chinese soil.

The first phase of *Ichi-Gō* opened with an onslaught to clear out the Chinese nationalist forces from northern Honan which had concentrated on the plains of central Honan. For some time these had remained undisturbed along the Japanese flanks south of the Yellow River and north of the Yangtze, where thus far the southernmost sector of the Peking–Hankow Railway had lain beyond the limits of the Japanese occupation zone. If any of the Chinese armies were to stand fast, they were simply to be minced. And so the Japanese plan was put into effect.

The new Japanese offensive burst upon China like a thunderclap. Lieutenant-General Okamura Yasuji (Neiji), who had distinguished himself in the Japanese campaign against Hankow in 1938 but who had languished since then as the Japanese Army Commander-in-Chief within the comparative backwater of North China, was given his big chance. At the head of 150,000 troops drawn from his forces in North China and from far-off Manchuria (where they had passed the war in idleness, watching Russia), his powerful forces swarmed across central Honan. There was far more devastation than had occurred in the bad old days of Chiang Kai-shek's bandit-suppression campaigns. The Japanese Army found in its renewal of the Chinese war an opportunity to work out its feeling of frustration. The new divisions roared through the seaboard of Central China and cut a broad swath further inland, not meeting any Chinese Army able to stand up to them in pitched battles. Where there was a struggle, as in Hunan, the Chinese, when they were eventually broken, were set on by an enraged population, who blamed them for having disturbed the unofficial armistice. To such a squalid end had the Chinese Army's defence of the country been reduced.

Thirty-four Chinese divisions simply evaporated into thin air. As the Chinese nationalist armies melted away, the Japanese winkled out scattered pockets of resistance. In the next phase of the campaign, however, the Japanese planned to adopt even more extreme measures. The pressure upon the Chinese air bases became too perilous for the Americans to endure. They had to abandon one airfield after another across the whole of South-East China. Priceless equipment and supplies had to be destroyed in the path of the Japanese offensive.

The loss of General Chennault's airfields drew the world's attention once more to China's weakness. It settled a controversy which had been going on among strategists. One side had taken the view that Chennault had proved that land operations were unnecessary: it was enough to build airfields in distant places, lightly protected by guerrilla operations, and leave the air forces to carry on the war. The other side had argued that, without a properly equipped and efficient army, airfields were entirely vulnerable. The latter view proved correct; and it was found that the Chinese armies were inadequate to safeguard them.

The American advance across the Pacific, however, now provided the long-range bombers with safer havens. By mid-September 1944 orders were given to withdraw the last of the B29 bombers from China to the relative safety of the Mariana Islands. Two months later, they began to operate in earnest. But the usefulness and importance of China to the Western Allies had changed sharply.

The beginning of 1943 had seen the last great western incentive offered to the Chinese. In that year, the West (following the diplomatic precedent already set by Japan) had made the gesture of terminating their right to maintain Treaty Ports in China. The largest tool of imperialism was renounced. The Japanese renunciation of extra-territorial rights had been hemmed in by restricitive conditions. The Allies led by the United States were now far more ready to sacrifice commercial interests to suit their broader political objectives. The negotiations, which the Western Powers had pursued desultorily since the 1920s, were accelerated, and agreement was reached. If the war had ultimately grown out of China's endeavour to extirpate these foreign footholds in China, it had, by this decision of the Allies, been won. Later in the year, Roosevelt had secured an Allied statement of the intention to associate China as an equal Power with themselves in remoulding the pattern of the world at the peace conferences. Other countries may have had their tongue in the cheek at this, but Roosevelt had his way.

Nevertheless the period of excessive complacency towards Chiang Kai-shek was immediately after this brought to an end, or was very much qualified, by the events of the Teheran Conference in November 1943. Just before had come the high point of Chiang Kai-shek's apotheosis. At the conference at Cairo of Roosevelt and Churchill, which Chiang Kai-shek had attended – but Stalin, because of his neutrality towards Japan, did not – Chiang had reached the peak of his fortunes. He received a pledge from the Allies that Manchuria, Formosa and the Pescadores would be returned to China at the peace.

On leaving Cairo, Churchill and Roosevelt went to Teheran for a meeting with Stalin. They were told for the first time that Russia had begun to make troop dispositions to enter the war against Japan as soon as Germany was defeated.

This changed the picture of the war. China would no longer be indispensable to the Allies. Japan could be reached in other ways; all attention was now focused on obtaining Russia's eventual permission to operate from Russian bases in the Maritime Provinces. The huge new factor of the Red Army operating against the Japanese in Manchukuo had to be digested. From that time on, China was no longer treated with such careful solicitude as it had been hitherto, though it was not solely the reason for the change of attitude. China still enjoyed the delusive grandeur which had been built up in President Roosevelt's time, and communicated by him to the public, but this was a wasting asset.

China, as an object of strategic concern, became of secondary importance. Chiang Kai-shek, his suspicions and ambitions, no longer held the centre of the picture. The war, which had originated in the crisis in China, was to come to an end with the fate of China of apparently small concern to the Great Powers, which now pressed on towards the final kill.

In the course of the war, a profound change had, however, come over the prestige of the Kuomintang and of the communists. They had both of them engaged in warfare, which they had fought by different means using different arms. They had been in competition with each other. The upshot, though it was not yet definite, was that, in the judgement of the various important groups of Chinese society, the communists had shown themselves more durable than the Kuomintang. True, the Kuomintang was, technically, to be one of the victorious powers. But the Kuomintang had lost face irrevocably.

It was not so much that the communists had shining victories to their credit. They had latterly fought very little. But their Government survived the war with an infinitely better morale than the Kuomintang.

Soon after the war, the two Governments would come into open conflict. Support would vanish away from the Kuomintang. It would transfer itself to the communists.

The Kuomintang had plenty of opportunity to see how unpopular its régime was becoming, and plenty of opportunity to take up some more popular course. But it kept obstinately on its disastrous career. As it became manifest that China, thanks to its Allies, was to be on the winning side in the war, there grew up naturally a discussion about the form that post-war politics was to take. Similarly the Kuomintang could have met the public half way, and announced the approaching end of its party dictatorship. But its reply, as the demand for this grew, was to increase the size of the secret police. Its activities became intolerable. The Kuomintang gave every indication that it would continue unreformed.

CHAPTER 24

Twilight

THE attention now turns to the American offensive, far across the Pacific, and it turns away from all the other theatres of the Asian War. Fighting still continued in these, but it became obvious that it was irrelevant. The turmoil in the Pacific dwarfed all other, and this became increasingly so until the end.

In the middle of June 1944, the Americans invaded Saipan in the Mariana Islands. This island, 1,350 miles from Tokyo, was the most vital point in the outer defences of Japan. It had become strongly fortified, so strongly that even the naval experts believed it to be impregnable. Its strategic importance was appreciated; from Saipan, the Americans would be able to bomb Tokyo; they could also disrupt the communications of the remaining forward posts in the Pacific with Japan. Its loss would breach what was called in Japanese 'the absolute zone of national defences'.

The Americans had assembled huge forces. They had an escort fleet, for the troop transports for the invasion, of 7 battleships, 12 escort carriers, 11 cruisers and 91 destroyers. It took only half an hour for the assault forces to get ashore at Saipan, but it still remained to be captured. At once the Japanese assembled their still very formidable fleet, and sought a decisive battle. They had foreseen the American moves and were not taken by surprise; they had ample strength in Guam and in the islands of the Philippines. The battle which resulted was the fourth large-scale naval combat of the war. The sense of occasion was in the message of the Japanese admiral to the fleet before the action began: 'The fate of the Empire rests on this one battle.'

The result was entirely disastrous to Japan. The successive strikes by Japanese aircraft were beaten off, and in the whole battle Japan lost nearly four hundred aircraft. The destruction of these, and the repelling of the Japanese attacks, were more spectacular than the loss of ships, though the operation cost the Japanese two battleships and an aircraft-carrier; two other carriers were disabled. This was far beyond the capacity of the Japanese shipyards, at this stage of the war, to make good. The American damage was very slight.

As was usual, the Japanese Navy silenced the news of the defeat. Even high officials of the Foreign Office remained without knowledge of what had been happening. They were especially confused because, after the defeat, they were invited by naval officers to banquets to celebrate a great Japanese triumph.

Admiral Toyoda Soemu, die-hard Commander-in-Chief of the Combined Fleet from May 1944 to May 1945 and Chief of the Naval General Staff during the last five months of the war, told investigators of the United States Strategic Bombing Survey that retrospectively he believed at the beginning of the Pacific Conflict that American submarines had posed a greater danger to Japan than any other enemy weapon system. Nevertheless, he stressed, the principal threat to Japan throughout virtually the whole Greater East Asia War had come from the depredations of US Navy surface forces. The other forces of the United States and their Allies were of far less importance. The critical factor was oil. Japanese fuel shortages had become serious as early as Midway, when fleet oil usage had far exceeded expectation. This had a knock-on effect felt in all subsequent operations. The real turning-point, however, was the loss of Japanese control in the Philippines, for thereafter American air and naval control over South China was secure and Japanese shipping lanes to the south were completely cut off: 'By the time of the Saipan operations, the greatest hindrance to the drafting of the operations plans was the fact that we did not have sufficient tankers to support it.'

The fall of Saipan could not, however, be hidden. The news began to circulate in the middle of July 1944. To most people it came as an entire shock, and for the first time the average Japanese, without any such information as had been weighing on the experts, began to surmise that Japan was in fact losing the war. Saipan had fallen with such ease; the Americans were ahead of their timetable. An evident *frisson* went through the nation, well disciplined though it continued to be.

A result was the resignation of General Tōjō, who had remained not only the Prime Minister but Minister of War, Minister of Munitions and Chief of the Army General Staff. He fell, now, after a complicated intrigue of the politicians. This was the first sign of serious political malaise which had come from Japan during the war; and it was received with relief by those watching among its enemies. The actual procedures by which government changes were brought about in Japan were as a rule more convoluted and dynamic than the dry official processes engraved on the marble cornerstone of the Japanese Constitution. In this instance, a group of high civilian and Army officers, especially those who had formerly held official positions, began to agitate more strongly for what they had long wanted in their hearts: that General Tōjō's Cabinet should resign. Saipan had caused them to open their eyes, and to press their arguments as a matter of life or death. Their dissensions were heard at high level, and they arranged that they should be transmitted to the throne.

A great agitation was set afoot among a large circle of those holding the various offices of importance. Tōjō, who, a week earlier had apparently been completely safe, suddenly found the ground trembling under his feet. He sought to appease his critics by yielding to one of their demands, and proposed that he should no longer combine the posts of Prime Minister, War Minister and Chief of the Army Staff. The arrangements were made for General Umezu Yoshijirō to become Minister of War. But by this time, the opinion of the inner circle had moved on, and it could be satisfied with nothing less than the resignation of Tōjō as Prime Minister. He demurred, and argued in vain. On the day of the announcement of the loss of Saipan, on 18 July 1944, his resignation from all his duties was in the hands of the Emperor.

The choice of a successor to the premiership fell to a formal group of seven elder statesmen, the *Jūshin*, all former prime ministers themselves. This body was unknown to the written constitution; it had in consequence no rights, such as access to government papers; it came, however, to exercise great power. It had an influence like that of the Genrō, or elder statesmen, though the power of the Genrō had been openly recognized. The re-entry to Japanese politics of such an influence was important. It was the more so at this period because the Jūshin had tended, with some exceptions, to work for peace. Most of them thought that the war was irrevocably lost, that the leaders knew this well, but that, floundering and indecisive, they saw no means of terminating it.

Their deliberations about Tōjō's replacement appear to have been unsubtle. All they could do was to agree on the nomination of General Koiso Kuniaki, an Army officer who had a bad reputation from the days of terrorism in the thirties when the Army was promoting a series of crises with the civilian Ministers in order to advance its claims of controlling the Government.

At the outbreak of the Manchurian Incident, Koiso had been Chief of the powerful Military Affairs Bureau in the War Ministry, one of the big 'Three Chiefs'. When the Japanese Army's conquest of Manchuria was secure, he was promoted to Vice-Minister of War. Shortly after the establishment of Manchukuo, he was then sent to serve as Chief of Staff of the Kwantung Army and as head of the Japanese Army's secret service there in the critical period between August 1932 and March 1934. A year and a half later, he became Commander-in-Chief of the Korean Army and held that position until he temporarily fell from grace at the outbreak of the Changkufeng Incident in July 1938. From then on, he was to make his mark as a reliable manager in Japan's exploitation of its occupied territories: he served two terms as Minister of Overseas (Colonial) Affairs, firstly in the six months which led up to the outbreak of the European War, and then during the first six months of 1940. When the China War spilled out into the Pacific, Koiso was on the sidelines. So long as General Tōjō was in power, Koiso was kept well away from duties which might undermine Tōjō's influence. At the time of General Koiso's recall to Tokyo to take up the premiership of Japan, He had been Governor-General of Korea since the middle of 1942. He had a track record as a competent administrator, someone who could make sense of civil/military relations. The Emperor, however, appointed him as Prime Minister simply beause he had been recommended by the Jūshin: it was the established way. The thing was done properly.

It was a choice which was apparently made under the compulsion of avoiding events such as those which had happened a year earlier in Italy. The elder statesmen judged it necessary to avoid nominating a man who might play in Japan the same part as General Badoglio. The extent to which Badoglio had captured the mind of Japan is curious. It showed perhaps how much the Japanese desired a Badoglio, and for how long they found it imperative not to disclose this.

Kase Toshikazu, a senior Foreign Ministry official, has described these confused and rather dark transactions. He himself belonged to the 'pro-British, pro-American' circles. His book, *Eclipse of the Rising Sun*, is useful in showing how many of these men had continued thoughout the war to hold high position in the Foreign Office, in certain Ministries, at the imperial court. They had been inactive from prudence: from the fall of Saipan, however, they began to work for peace. They had still to be very cautious, for they would have been rendered helpless if it had become known how specific, and actively specific, were their intentions. By their sympathies becoming known they would at best have made themselves ineffective: at the worst they would have been assassinated. And there were of course many who, when the war was over, claimed to have been pro-Ally, but whose memory may have exaggerated its degree.

At the end of 1944, Kase Toshikazu wrote in his diary the following:

Defeat now stares us stark in the face. There is only one question left: how can we avert the chaos attendant upon a disastrous defeat? The preservation of my fatherland, that is a paramount task assigned to me by fate. The hostile attack is developing so surprisingly swiftly that it may be that diplomacy cannot intervene before it is too late. I must redouble my efforts to expedite the restoration of peace. For that purpose I shall secure friends in the army who will collaborate with me secretly, and enlighten public opinion through wider exchanges of view with politicians, publicists and press representatives. The chances are that the re-orientation of our policy is yet feasible. If so the nation will escape annihilation. Even so, it will probably be accompanied by civil disturbances. Much blood will flow – and who knows that mine, too, will not be spilt? . . . This, in short, is my New Year's Day prayer.*

This sums up very well the feeling of the small class of clear-sighted, non-fanatical men. But a difficult task lay ahead for them. Kase Toshikazu and his friends had to convert a sufficient number of patriotic Japanese to enable them to shift the vital balance against the fanatical, the deluded and the ignorant. They had to do this with the certain knowledge that charges of treason might well be brought against them, and would be paid for either with execution or else by the familiar old Japanese resort to private violence.

The American drive from the Pacific continued. After Saipan, the strongly fortified positions of Tinian and Guam were captured in August 1944. These were also considerable victories, made possible only by mobilization of resources, and their concentration upon tiny islands, which were possibly unique in military history. A feature of all these operations was the disparity of the losses. The Americans should in theory, being attackers, have suffered at least three to one more heavily than the Japanese. But, in all three operations, the American dead numbered just over 5,000, while the Japanese lost 42,000. On Guam, for the first time, there had been a dent in Japanese morale: over 12,000 prisoners were taken. Usually these island defences ended in a great *banzai* charge of the remaining garrison, who plunged to death, rather like the death charge of the chivalry among the Rajputs of medieval India, who vowed themselves thus to self-destruction. The generals on both Saipan and Guam committed ceremonial seppaku.

In October, General MacArthur, in the South-West Pacific, made his expected attack on the Philippines. He was still under the disadvantage of the somewhat complicated command arrangements which shared between him and Admiral Nimitz the control of operations in his area. He could count upon a powerful fleet detached from the Central Pacific. Japan chose to regard his attack as a crisis of the war. Its generals recognized that, if the Philippines were occupied by the Americans, the supply lines of the Japanese Empire would be fatally obstructed. Therefore Japan stated that, on its ability to defend the Philippines, the issue of the war would depend.

* K. Toshikazu, *Eclipse of the Rising Sun*, Jonathan Cape, London, 1951.

Such repeated pronouncements were foolish, and, in making them, the Japanese generals should have had in mind their grave embarrassment if their defence proved ineffective. They would be in the position of carrying on the war even while admitting that the war was a lost cause. That they permitted themselves so talk so rashly was the best proof that the morale of the Japanese General Staff was beginning to fail even though the Japanese soldiers fought as tenaciously as before.

The Japanese lived up to the words of their military leaders. They gathered their Navy, which was still very powerful in surface ships – only in the loss of the aircraft-carriers had it been gravely weakened – and sought, by putting all their effort into a single decisive blow, to turn their great danger into a decisive victory. And circumstances played into their hands. It had been calculated that the local airfields would be operational for the landings, but the rainy season broke, and they were flooded. The Japanese had a period of air superiority, flying in from Samar. For a few days it was touch and go whether the American advance would be disastrously defeated.

MacArthur's invasion force, which landed on 20 October 1944 on the shores of the Gulf of Leyte which is a central island of the Philippines, had the protection of very powerful warships. The Japanese sought to lure this naval force away by sending a decoy fleet, and then, with a much larger fleet, aimed to sink the American transports, and to destroy MacArthur's Army, which was to be taken at a disadvantage while they were still engaged in disembarkation. The Japanese placed their confidence in the battle upon the greater fire power of the Japanese Navy; the days of attacking by waves of aircraft from carriers was over, since the Japanese naval air force had been virtually eliminated. The Navy was back to reliance upon its battleship fleet, and among this it included the battleship, *Yamato*, which had been built free of the former limitations on the size of battleships. It was the most formidable ship in the world, well-protected and mounting eighteen-inch guns which fired 3,220 lb (1460 kg) projectiles to a range of up to twenty-six miles (41.4 km).

If they had succeeded in their plan, the Japanese would have achieved a second Pearl Harbor, this time destroying the American Army in Asia as formerly they had annihilated the American Pacific Fleet. Even so, the United States, with its economic might only just beginning to operate at its full strength, could, in all reasonable probability, have regarded a defeat as a temporary setback, and the inevitable conclusion of the war would have been merely postponed by a year or so. But, though this possibility must have been clear to the Japanese admirals, an interruption of the continuous American advance would have been dear to them. They rejoiced in the likelihood of a pause in the war: Japanese optimism would have taken on new life: victory would have set alive again Japanese hopes that their staying power might outlast America's. Nobody can foresee all the unexpected circumstances which might happen in war. Given time, Japan could begin to hope that the germs of a negotiated peace might sprout.

MacArthur's moves had therefore created a situation more fraught with consequence than even he, with his flair for reading the Japanese mind, at first realized. His landing had created a profound stir, alike in America and throughout Asia. He had chosen the elements of drama. He was not far from the point from which he had made his take-off in his direct contact with the Japanese in 1942, and, as he had promised to do, he had returned. But at once the Japanese Navy pounced, and dreamed of plucking from this nettle, danger, the flower, which might be the checking of the American guillotine as it was about to fall, the dismantling of the instrument, and the creation of the necessity to rebuild it if the war were to continue. Its ships, some from Borneo, some from Formosa and Japan itself, converged upon the Gulf of Leyte.

The officer in command of the Japanese fleet was Admiral Toyoda Soemu. There is no doubt of the merit of his overall plan, which he directed at long range from Tokyo. The ships from Japan he formed into a decoy force, with which he aimed at dividing the Americans from their protective force of battleships and aircraft-carriers, which were commanded by Admiral W. F. Halsey. This force included what remained of Japan's once formidable fleet of aircraft-carriers; it was less strong than it seemed for, as was discovered afterwards, the Japanese carriers sailed empty of planes. Japan had used up its planes and pilots, many of the last batch of these at the futile battle of Guam, and oil was running desperately short. Nevertheless, the manoeuvre was successful. Admiral Halsey went in pursuit, and left MacArthur dangerously exposed.

With two forces of battleships which were held in readiness in Borneo, Toyoda planned to attack the American transport fleet as soon as it was deprived of much of its protective escort. The first of these forces was exceptionally powerful; it contained five battleships, all of them larger and faster than any which they were still liable to meet. Toyoda gambled on these making unimpeded contact with the enemy, free from the diversion of air attack – which was reasonably certain, as the American transport fleet was beyond the range of land-based aeroplanes – and, by superior fire power, sinking it.

Against reasonable expectation, however, both the Japanese fleets failed in their objects. The lesser of the two was ambushed by what had been left behind of the American fleet, which was rather larger than was foreseen by Japanese Intelligence, and was completely annihilated except for one destroyer. The Japanese had the mortification of seeing their ships sunk by ships which were technically inferior to their own. Ironically, in this action, the Americans employed battleships which were obsolete, had already been once sunk by the Japanese – at Pearl Harbor – and which had been dredged up from the mud of the sea bed. The larger Japanese fleet, though it was engaged and disorganized earlier on, got through the American defences, and for a time, if it had but known this, had the American transports at its mercy, but because of muddle, of being let down by other ships, and because of deep misunderstanding of what was being done by the American ships, the Japanese Admiral did not bombard but sailed away inexplicably. His losses had been heavy; his actual gains were very slight; his potential gains, those which he had unaccountably let slip through his fingers, made this, their final battle of the war, very poignant to the Japanese Navy.

Among the warships employed, the Japanese decoy force from the north alone avoided heavy losses. It retired in good order. Similarly Admiral Halsey's powerful battleships, which had been the main concern of the Japanese, were never in serious action throughout. They steamed 300 miles to the north, and when, as was afterwards discovered, they were within forty miles of the decoy force, they steamed 300 miles south. Upon their arrival, they found that the battle of Leyte was over. Admiral Halsey was much criticized for having made so powerful a fleet ineffective in the action, but, given the system of communication prevailing among warships, he could hardly have done other than he did.

For the Japanese defeat, the same forces seemed to operate as before in the melancholy history of this Navy. Bad Intelligence work, bad coordination between commanders, the scarcely trained generation of naval fliers, and an inability of the Japanese commanders to retrieve disaster and to provide a new plan: these, which had dogged the Navy since the battle of Midway, continued to do so until the death of the Navy at Leyte.

The principal defect was in the quality of the command. The Japanese admirals and captains had been too old for their work. They were too fearful of risking their ships; they were certainly brave, and reasonably competent, but they creaked in manoeuvring a modern fleet, which was beyond their capacity. No common doctrine of strategy or tactics united them, and they were handicapped by the failure of Japanese engineers to provide for the Navy some of the devices which had become common among other belligerents. Above all, it had turned out that, where the Japanese had been forced to make an innovation in the arts of naval

JAPANESE AND ALLIED FLEET MOVEMENTS
CULMINATING IN THE BATTLE FOR
LEYTE GULF, OCTOBER 1944

0 ————————— 500km
0 ————————— 300 miles

CHINA

25°N
115 °E
120 °E
125 °E
20°N
15°N
10°N
50°N

FORMOSA

Luzon Strait

Cape Engamo

LUZON

Lingayen Gulf

Manila

BATAAN
Corregidor

Mindoro Str.

South

China

Sea

Sulu Sea

PALAWAN

NEGROS

PANAY

LEYTE

MINDANAO

NORTH BORNEO

Brunei Bay

Sulu Archipelago

Celebes
Sea

MOROTAI

UNITED STATES
Fast Carrier Task Group (T.F. 38)
Task Groups
Detached Forces
JAPAN
Northern Force (Ozawa)
Centre Force (Kurita)
Van of Southern Force (Nishimura)
Rear of Southern Force (Shima)
Detached Squadron

Rear of Southern
Force (Shima)

Heavy air attacks
on Centre Force
from Fast Carrier
Task Group

1800 hrs
23 Oct.

Departed
0200 24 Oct.

0600 hrs
24 Oct.

DACE (Sub)
DARTER
MAYA
ATAGO
0600 hrs 23

Van of Southern Force
(NISHIMURA)
Departed Brunei Bay
1500 hrs 22 May

Bombed
0918 hrs 24

1800 hrs
22 Oct.

Centre Force (Kurita): 5 battleships,
9 cruisers, 13 destroyers

0822hrs
22 Oct.

MUSASHI

2100 hrs
23 Oct.

San Bernardino Str.

Rendezvous of
Task Force

2000 hrs

Task Group
38-3 Sherman

PRINCETON
1800 hrs
24 Oct.

0800 hrs 24

Battle of
Samar

Leyte
Gulf

2000 hrs 24 May

Battle of
Surigao

Task Group
38-2 (Bogan)

Task Group
38-4 (Davison)

Midnt 24/25

1445 hrs
25 Oct.

Halsey forms
battleship force

1st strike force
flown

0550 hrs

2020 hrs

1115
hrs

Battleship force and
TG 38-2 despatched to
San Bernardino Strait

Midnt 24/25

Detached
Squadron

0630
hrs

1030 hrs
24 Oct.

1430
hrs

1630 hrs

Midnt 25/26 May

Detached cruiser force

1900 hrs

ZUIHO
ZUIKAKU
CHIYODA
CHITOSE

Midnt 24/25 Oct.

1800 hrs 25 Oct.

Northern Force
(Ozawa)

0100 hrs 24 Oct.

Midnt
25/26 May

TALLAO (Sub)
TAMA
2310 hrs 25 Oct.

THE BATTLES OF SAMAR AND
SURIGAO STRAIT, 24–25 Oct.1944

→ Main units of US Seventh Fleet
--→ General track of escort carrier groups
→ General track of Japanese Centre and
    Southern Forces
--→ General track of rear of Japanese
    Southern Forces

0   50   100 km
0   50 miles

124°E   125°E   126°E

L U Z O N

13°N

2100 hrs 24 Oct.

Midnt 25th

San Bernardino Strait

2130 hrs
25th Oct.

1800 hrs 25 Oct.

KURITA's force at
midnight 24/25
4 battleships, 8 cruisers
11 destroyers

12°N

S A M A R

Visayan
Sea

0700 hrs

0800 hrs 25 Oct

0700 hrs 25

CAF
SPRAGUE'S
Task
Group

SUZUYA

1230 hrs

GAMBIER BAY ✕

0700 hrs
25

0920 hrs

CHŌKAI ✕
CHIKUMA ✕
✕ ST LO

0925 hrs

STUMPS
Task Group

11°N

L E Y T E

Transport
Anchorage

Leyte
Gulf

1050 hrs 24 Oct.

☉ SULUAN

Night of 24/25

OLDENDORF'S Force
6 battleships, 8 cruisers
28 destroyers

MASHIRO ✕

✕ FUSO

Surigao Strait

D I N A G A T

T.L.SPRAGUE'S
Task Group

10°N

First Attack
by PT boats

1030 hrs
24 Oct.

0700 hrs
25 Oct.

NISHIMURA's Force
YAMASHIRŌ, FUSO,
MOGAMI, 4 destroyers

✕ 1300 hrs
25 Oct.

✕ MOGAMI
0900–1000 hrs 25 Oct.

SHIMA's Force
NACHI, ASHIGARA,
ABUKUMA, 4 destroyers

M I N D A N A O

warfare – in combining naval and air power – this advantage had not been sustained. Yamamoto, whose ideas had first prevailed, had not succeeded in training up a younger section of the Navy with ideas similar to his own, and Yamamoto's death at Bougainville on 18 April 1943 ended the innovation. The pilots, who should have become principal commanders, and who had had battle experience, had all of them met their premature death in the Pacific Ocean, and the direction of new recruits was left to men who had never been converts to Yamamoto's ideas, and had seen his successes with a certain amount of envy and scepticism. Especially, the tactics of Yamamoto required an expert and highly trained personnel; he had begun the war with an inadequate supply; it had continued lacking; nobody had come to prominence as a gifted air trainer. The dash, the precision, and the brilliance of his fliers at Pearl Harbor lingered in the memory and were gone.

In January 1945 General MacArthur, thus surviving his most perilous passage in the history of the war, overcame the Japanese resistance on Luzon. From there he moved to Mindanao, the main island, and carried through land operations, which followed the same pattern and had the same results as the events in New Guinea. It turned out that the Japanese Army, in spite of its emphasizing that the fighting would be decisive, had been unable to assemble a land force strong enough to make the resistance as tenacious as that of the Pacific Islands.

This ended the war for MacArthur. He did no more fighting, though after the war's end, another great historic role fell to him as Supreme Commander for Allied Powers, with chief responsibility for the occupation of Japan. For the present, MacArthur wore the laurels of having been the most spectacular commander of the Allied side, in both the Pacific and the European theatres of war. His victories, usually gained with forces which were in the minority, were due to remarkable imagination; and they were made possible by an extreme cult of efficiency by his staff. For the time, MacArthur busied himself with the preparation for the projected Allied offensive against Japan itself, which was to have begun with a landing on Kyushu Island; not expected, however, before 1 December. For this projected operation, the command arrangements were changed. MacArthur was given command of all the Army throughout the Pacific (with important exceptions); but the American Navy was still strong enough to oppose a unified command of all the sea forces.

For the first assault, 5 million men would have been employed. It is notable that they would for the most part have been American; though American Allies begged a place in the operation, room was found for only a token force of three divisions from the Commonwealth. The war was coming to an end in a very different way from the war in Europe. The invasion of Normandy and the campaigns in France and Germany had been genuinely joint enterprises: there was not even the pretence of such in Japan.

As the end of the European War approached, the British Chiefs of Staff were keen to restore Britain to a position of genuine partnership alongside the United States in the Pacific. The difficulty was in finding a credible way to do that. Somewhat diffidently Prime Minister Churchill approached President Roosevelt with an offer of help in the summer of 1944. By the end of that year, a new British Pacific Fleet was more or less in being, although it was not pitted against serious opposition at the time. As a prelude, elements of the new force sailed away under Rear Admiral Sir Philip Vian to attack the oilfields of Sumatra. They struck at Belawan Deli and Palembang and overcame intense ground-based defences. At Palembang the Japanese had the two largest oil refineries in South-East Asia: it was estimated that together they could meet three-quarters of the aviation fuel requirements of the Japanese Empire. The raids succeeded beyond the hopes of the Royal Navy. One of the refineries was all but destroyed and the other one was so seriously damaged that three months afterwards the combined facilities were producing no more than a third of their previous output. Vian's force retired without much loss and linked up with other units to complete the formation of the new fleet. The command of the British Pacific Fleet was placed in the hands of Admiral Sir Bruce Fraser, who previously had been engaged in shepherding arctic convoys that carried supplies to the Soviet Union. He now had the delicate task of reconciling his responsibilities to the British Admiralty for the safety and handling of his fleet and its supplies, not only with the demands pressed upon him by the Australian and New Zealand authorities (although they were difficult to appease) but also with the subordination of his force to operational orders given to him by the Americans.

At first General MacArthur and Admiral Nimitz argued over who should be placed in overall operational command of the British Pacific Fleet. MacArthur wanted to use it in the reconquest of the Philippines which was still underway, and Nimitz wanted to use it in support of the planned invasion of Okinawa. Nimitz won and, in the closing months of the war, first he and then Admiral 'Bull' Halsey, the two successive Commanders-in-Chief of the United States Pacific Fleet, employed the British as a flexible, self-contained reserve. It was from the British Pacific Fleet's subordination to CINCPAC that its fleet train became known as Task Force 112 and its main force of 4 aircraft carriers, 2 battleships, 5 cruisers and 14 destroyers was named Task Force 113. Together they soon became known as Task Force 57. In fact, when the B P F sailed off to fight the Japanese, under the tactical comand of Vice-Admiral Sir Bernard Rawlings, his force consisted of nearly the whole of the frontline strength of the Royal Navy. It was more powerful and larger than any other assemblage of British and Commonwealth fighting ships brought together in the Second World War. However, the expansion of the United States Navy after the Pearl Harbor attack had been so huge that the British Pacific Fleet was only equivalent in strength to a 'task force' within the United States Fifth Fleet. The Americans cordially welcomed 'the British Carrier Task Force and attached units', respected its efficiency and gave it considerable tactical independence. But naturally from fleet admirals down to swabbies, the men of the United States Navy made it their business to put the sailors of the Royal Navy in their proper place. The days of naval parity were long since over. In the war in the Pacific in the later stages America had become very conscious that the United States was first, the Allies nowhere. In the conquest of Japan the fact was to be rubbed in. The United States welcomed this sign that European imperialism had little part to play in the new Asia.

The way to final assault had been opened by the success of the United States' other campaign which advanced from the Central Pacific to the entrances of Tokyo Bay. The fall of Saipan had been an important stage in this advance; it marked a change in Japanese defensive tactics. Hitherto the Japanese had sought to repel American invaders by making mass charges on them as they landed. But at Iwojima, the next island to be attacked after Saipan, the Japanese fought in prepared positions, inflicting great damage on the Americans before they were overwhelmed in March 1945. The island had to be wrenched from them, trench by trench. The Japanese losses were 20,000: the American Marines lost 26,000 killed, and the US Navy nearly 900 killed or missing and about 2,000 wounded.

From Iwojima, Nimitz had first intended to make his main target Formosa. He changed his plan, and launched his attack on Okinawa, a heavily fortified island, forty miles long, in the Ryukyu Islands, 500 miles from Japan Proper. On 1 April 1945 the Americans landed, and at first met with almost no opposition. But they were in an enormous ambush: they realized suddenly that the northern part of the island was alive with troops, all of them skilfully hidden. A feature of the resistance was their use of light artillery, among the most effective of the war. While the Americans were meeting deadly resistance from the north, their plans were disordered by the Japanese use of Kamikaze aircraft. These were manned by volunteer squads of suicide pilots, who flew their planes to crash on the decks of ships and there explode. The Kamikaze, who were first used by the Japanese in the Battle of Leyte, had by now been incorporated in the general plan for the defence of Japan. The Kamikaze were genuinely volunteers; the Americans were unwilling to believe that such a corps could be formed on a free-will basis, but their efforts to find that they had been conscripted were in vain. By the ferocity of their action, by the unreason of their suicidal intentions, they struck the Americans with peculiar horror. The Kamikaze fought with a peculiar exaltation, they appeared insanely exhilarated, and they went to their death as though to a fascinating ceremony. It was the eschatology of war. In the battle for Iwojima they did very great damage. On one day they sank twenty-four ships. But they could not alter the fact that the number of aeroplanes, as also the number of pilots, was shrinking fast, and would presently be used up.

The battle for Okinawa changed rapidly into nightmare. It progressed like a surrealist film. On the sixth day, 6 April, the Japanese dispatched from the Inland Sea their huge battleship, the *Yamato*. It was a huge Kamikaze. Its mission was to wreak as much havoc as possible: it carried only enough oil for a one-way trip, and was meant for destruction. In fact it was engaged by American aircraft, and was sunk before it could do much damage. But the madness of the sacrifice in such a way of the world's largest battleship convinced Japan's antagonist that the Japanese staff was near the end of its judgement.

The battle lasted until 21 June. It ended in scenes of horror. The Japanese commander and his deputy both committed ceremonial seppaku. Over a hundred thousand Japanese were dead. A very small number survived as prisoners.

The Americans were satisfied that a weighty section of the Japanese command, both in the Navy and the Army, now saw no chance of success in war, and no opportunity of gaining even a temporary respite, and would be glad to make peace. The war might have ended then. But how were these high officers to terminate it? They were afraid of being assassinated if they made any move: the mass of the Army and Navy was still able to fight, and there was still a minority of the more senior officers who were willing to fight on to the end. No mutinies or outbreaks of any kind took place among the forces.

The difficulty for the United States was that it lacked the means of making contact with the politically reasonable sections in Japanese life. The attempt to signal to the East that the United States would respond favourably to any bid for surrender was made again and again, usually by cryptic speech on the American broadcasting stations; but they met with no reply from any who could speak responsibly in Japan. Still the war went on, and no peace was yet possible, though the majority of all classes of Japan desired it greatly. The civil servants, the industrialists and bankers, the trade union leaders, the considerable classes of the intelligentsia – all despaired of war, and regarded with frenzy the piece by piece destruction worked on them by the American aircraft. But the intransigent section of the military, who had gained control of the direction of Japan ten years before, could not be set aside. The Americans persuaded themselves and the British that a dramatic and novel development in the art of war was necessary for this.

A picture of the Japanese Empire in twilight, and approaching dissolution, is given by the puppet Prime Minister, Ba Maw. Ba Maw, as has been seen, had had his quarrels with the Japanese, and, though he had made his position tolerable, he had hardly cause to love them. The more remarkable is his sober account of the way in which they faced defeat and international disgrace. He was invited to Japan in November 1944, just as the systematic bombing of Japan's home islands was beginning, in an endeavour to organize Asian support for the tottering Japanese imperial structure. Ba Maw owed his eminence to the Japanese, and knew that he must fall with them. This is the general impression which he describes:

Tokyo and its people had changed since I had seen them a year ago, visibly subdued and disillusioned by events, but most of them as determined and defiant as ever. They were now a people in the grip of the biggest crisis in all their history and grimly waiting for the worst. But they were facing the situation wonderfully and revealing their latent racial qualities, their almost inexhaustible capacity to take whatever should come, to endure and survive and wait and even hope. They were more or less the same outwardly, but in the course of a long quiet talk they could not help but betray their true thoughts and fears. Unlike before, they now spoke mainly of the Kamikazes, thus showing that they were placing most of their hopes on something which was really an act of desperation. The people were living with a new terror, the threat of American mass air bombing; they knew that they had no real way to protect their millions of paper and bamboo houses; not even, as it turned out, the Imperial Palace.*

The topic of chief concern was the air bombardment, and the damage which that was able to do, especially on the morale of the population. This is what Ba Maw says of this:

One of the worst incendiary bombings of Tokyo occurred when I was there near the end of November 1944. The result was quite literally a holocaust, a mass

* Ba Maw, *Breakthrough in Burma*, op. cit., p. 374.

burning of one of the densest areas of the city. I saw the ghastly devastation the next morning. But there was no panic or self-pity or even audible complaint among the huge mass of victims. In fact some of them were able to express their happiness that the Imperial Palace had escaped. It was a heart-breaking sight but it also lifted one's heart immensely to see so much human endurance and strength of character displayed in so dark an hour.*

Ba Maw was taken round the headquarters of the Japanese Army. The Kamikaze were exhibited to him as a kind of Japanese secret weapon. He met Koiso, the Japanese Prime Minister, and General Sugiyama, the War Minister, who was soon to play a decisive part. He took every opportunity of discussing with the Japanese commanders their defence tactics, and represented that a scorched earth policy would be intolerable to the Burmese as was also the plan of using the Burmese forces to fight the rear-guard action against the British. Ba Maw had the satisfaction of saving the Shwe Dagon Pagoda from being incorporated in the Japanese defence perimeter. At least he gives himself the credit of having achieved it by the negotiations of his visit.

* ibid.

CHAPTER 25

The End

THE war had entered its final stage. Japan still battled on, but its position was hopeless. The United States, still arming, poured out its fleet and aircraft across the Pacific, and was preparing the great offensive against the sacred Japanese homeland. The expectation was that the American war machine, which had swallowed up so many Pacific islands, would in the long run devour Japan Proper. The economic might of the United States must finally prevail. The war machine moved on, and the only uncertainty was the length of time it would take to complete the process. Japan, as Germany before it, was given no time to summon up its resources and to organize them for the optimum defence of its own country.

Japan, in its final phase, was like Macbeth cooped up in Dunsinane, without any rational hope of a happy issue from his adversities, mechanically wound up to continue to shout defiance at the armies investing him.

> Some say he's mad: others that lesser hate him
> Do call it valiant fury: but, for certain,
> He cannot buckle his distemper'd cause
> Within the belt of rule.
> ANGUS: Now does he feel
> His secret murders sticking on his hands; . . .
> Those he commands move only in command,
> Nothing in love; now does he feel his title
> Hang loose about him, like a giant's robe
> Upon a dwarfish thief.

One hope alone sustained Japan. The Soviet Union had not renounced the Non-Aggression Treaty which Matsuoka Yōsuke, Japan's Foreign Minister, had been able to negotiate with it in 1941. In spite of the bad blood between them five years earlier, this treaty, to the surprise of on-lookers, had kept the peace between the apparently predestined enemies, though war had raged universally elsewhere. Japan could reckon that peace in Europe would bring to a head the issues between Russia and the United States. Was it too much to expect that Russia, threatened and thwarted by the United States, might see that its true interest lay in accepting the partnership of Japan? Japan could claim that it had already shown, by refraining from striking at Russia when Hitler was at the doors of Moscow in 1941, that no insuperable cause of conflict lay between it and the Soviet Union. It could represent that, in spite of the severe destruction which it had suffered, it still possessed an army which was one of the key pieces on the board internationally. The Japanese Army still had fighting spirit, still had ammunition, and could hope to take an immense toll from a threatened invasion. It boasted that to overrun Japan, when all its natural advantages of defence were taken into review, the United States would need a force of 10 million men, a force which it could not hope to transport. If the United States came to be at loggerheads with Russia, it was unlikely that it would willingly force through the attack on Japan to its conclusion, which would be frightful carnage.

In 1945, as the Japanese position grew evidently more desperate, Russia began to unmask its intentions. At the Yalta Conference in February, Roosevelt offered Russia a larger bait to enter the war against Japan. He unilaterally raised the stakes. Confident of Churchill's support, he promised their recognition of the Russian protectorate in Outer Mongolia and, much more importantly, their support for the reversion to the Soviet Union of 'the former rights of Russia violated by the treacherous attack of Japan in 1904'. By this formula the Treaty of Portsmouth, a treaty for which another American President had been happy to accept responsibility, would be set aside. Southern Sakhalin (Karafuto) would be returned to the Soviet Union, the 'pre-eminent interests of the Soviet Union' in the commercial port of Dairen would be 'safeguarded', the Russian leasehold over ice-free Port Arthur would be restored, Russia's claims to the Kurile Island chain would be upheld, and the Russians would once again assume the same rights and interests over the South Manchurian Railway and the Chinese Eastern Railway that Japan had enjoyed at the height of its power. In exchange Stalin promised Churchill and Roosevelt that he would enter the war against Japan within two or three months after the surrender of Germany. It was an ominous, although secret, bargain, one which was scarcely affected by the agreement between the three leaders that Chinese concurrence would be sought in matters affecting their historic suzerainty over the whole of Manchuria and Mongolia. Roosevelt, by negotiating on these lines, had taken upon himself to re-make history. With Churchill's acquiescence, he had behaved in a very cavalier fashion in disposing of huge 'Chinese' assets and settling vast issues in disregard of wholly legitimate Chinese claims. To be perfectly plain, the Yalta trade-off was no more legitimate and no less aggressive than the offensive behaviour of the Japanese against which the world had complained for half a century.

In April, at the time of the attack on Okinawa, the Soviet Government announced that it would not renew the Russo-Japanese Non-Aggression Pact, which was due to expire one year hence. When the Japanese made proposals about the possibility of a new agreement (and offered terms that were very much like those conceded by Britain and America at Yalta), the Russian Ambassador was ominously evasive. Russia gave every sign that it was preparing for war with Japan. Thus its final hope was nearly extinguished. 'Despair thy charm' seemed to cry out the omens for Japan.

In the light of what is now known, it seems probable that Japanese Intelligence had heard of Stalin's information to Churchill and Roosevelt at the Teheran Conference: Russia was preparing for war with Japan as soon as Germany was defeated. Confirmation of this should have come easily to Japanese spies, although there seem to have been no figures in Japan's employment comparable to Richard Sorge, the Russian agent, who, in the critical phase before Pearl Harbor, had spied on Japan for the USSR. He had been able to reassure Russia that Japan had decided not to hasten to the aid of Germany, and refused to attack Russia as Germany wished.

It is a canard that there is no record of Japan having been well-served by Intelligence. On the contrary, the Japanese networks learned a great deal. Unfortunately for Japan, there was no effective mechanism for ensuring that information acquired by the Intelligence apparatus would affect the Government's basic strategy or perceptions. Throughout these years of Total War, the Japanese were handicapped by having by far the most cumbersome policy-making and policy-review machinery of any belligerent in the conflict, worse even than that of Germany and not a patch on the brilliant system for strategical coordination that the British pioneered and which the Americans copied.

Japan was of course under the handicap that, if it employed men of its own nation as agents, they were more conspicuous than others. Japanese could hardly wear the appearance of blank anonymity which is essential to espionage. The same is broadly true of western spies in an eastern country. They may succeed, by exceptional audacity, in exceptional circumstances, as Sorge was able to do, or as the West's and China's Korean agents did at lower levels in Japanese-occupied territories. But in a war between East and West, where racialism and jingoism are harnessed together, espionage is likely to play less part than in a war in which the contestants share a similar racial background. As it happens, the Japanese did cultivate White Russian émigrés and European Jewish refugees with an eye on their utility in espionage: the results of this collaboration remain obscure, although the size of the networks involved tens of thousands of people directly or indirectly. In any event, the Japanese Government's Russian experts warned that the Soviet Union was girding itself for war, and they were mocked for their pains by the same adventurers whose singularly misconceived optimism had carried havoc into every other corner of East Asia.

Espionage, likewise, paid the British and Americans only very mean dividends. British SOE operations in South-East Asia do not appear to have affected the outcome of the war in any significant way, but the quality of Intelligence produced at great personal risks and sacrifices by the agents involved deserves our respect and appreciation. In Japan Proper, however, the situation was otherwise, and it would appear that little information of value was gained by the use of secret agents. In pre-war days, British and American language officers were seconded on a regular basis to Japanese regiments, training establishments and man-oeuvres. The military, naval and air attachés of the western democracies were restricted in their freedom of movement, but they nevertheless displayed a marvellous capacity to mislead their Governments about the quality of Japanese weaponry and technological sophistication. It is worthwhile recollecting that the Japanese Zero, which made its first appearance in the China theatre on April Fool's Day 1939, made no significant impression upon those whose job it was to keep up to date on the capabilities of potential enemies. In a word, the quality of Allied military Intelligence about Japan prior to Pearl Harbor was abysmal. It was a commonplace assumption almost everywhere in the West during the years leading up to the Pacific War that the Japanese were master copycats who possessed little native ingenuity. There was, for instance, a British air attaché who reported that the Japanese held 2:1 reserves of spare engines for their frontline aircraft, from which he deduced that the Japanese, with their well-known mechanical incompetence, were obliged to throw away faulty or damaged engines rather than repair them! This is about on a par with the other hoary chestnut that most Japanese made poor pilots because they nearly all wore glasses and suffered from vertigo. The patent absurdity of such things is self-evident, but the magnitude of the miscalculations was not. Even to this day, many people who lived through the war still believe that the Japanese never displayed any orig-inality in their weapons development. In fact, as we now know, the

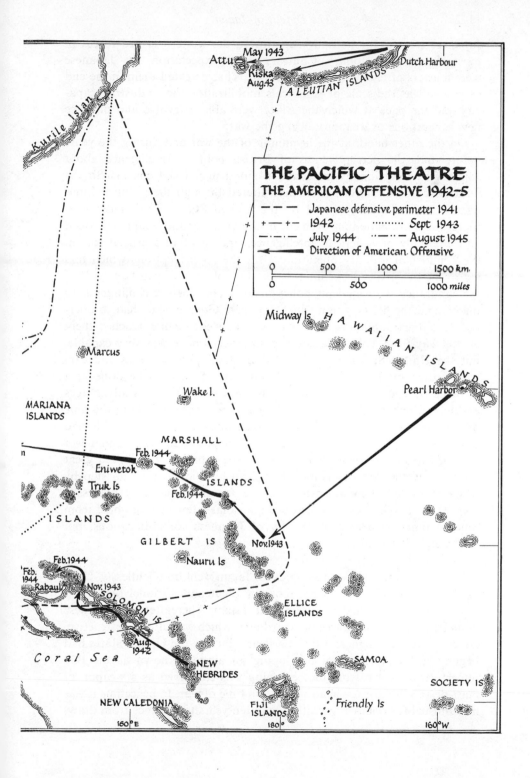

Attu May 1943
Kiska Aug. 43
Dutch Harbour
ALEUTIAN ISLANDS
Kurile Island

THE PACIFIC THEATRE
THE AMERICAN OFFENSIVE 1942–5
- - - - - Japanese defensive perimeter 1941
+ — + — 1942   .... Sept 1943
— · — · July 1944   — ·· — ·· August 1945
━━━◀ Direction of American Offensive

0   500   1000   1500 km.
0   500   1000 miles

Midway Is   HAWAIIAN ISLANDS
Pearl Harbor

Marcus
Wake I.
MARIANA ISLANDS
MARSHALL
Feb. 1944
Eniwetok
Truk Is   ISLANDS
Feb. 1944
ISLANDS
GILBERT IS   Nov. 1943
Nauru Is
Feb. 1944
Feb. 1944
Rabaul   Nov. 1943
SOLOMON Is
ELLICE ISLANDS
Aug. 1942
Coral Sea
NEW HEBRIDES
SAMOA
NEW CALEDONIA
FIJI ISLANDS
Friendly Is
SOCIETY IS
160° E   180°   160° W

Japanese were technologically superior to the western armed forces in most classes of weaponry. Contrary to all expectation, the Japanese were masters of technical improvisation. What defeated them in the end of course was the scale of America's mobilization, her industrial capacity and the pace at which the Allies were able to evolve and produce new generations of weapons during the war.

On the other hand, at the beginning of the war and during the years beforehand, the perceptiveness of British political Intelligence about Japan was exceptionally high, and it stood in marked contrast to the inadequacy of the information that filtered through the political Intelligence about Japan gathered by the United States. During the war, there was a dramatic improvement in the quantity and quality of Allied and especially of American Intelligence, and this had a crucial role in the conduct of military operations. But the misperceptions which had led to the outbreak of hostilities in the first place stemmed largely from the ignorance of American policy-makers and their unwillingness to understand the limits within which Japanese Governments had to operate. It is remarkable how little was the knowledge which reached them in this way from Tokyo. Japanese counter-espionage was very capable, but the United States had succeeded in developing the eyes and ears which pried on Japanese moves, though this tended to be done at a distance by code-breaking, and not by means of spies. Its advantages and limitations in this have already been noted, for example at the time of the negotiations before Pearl Harbor, and in naval battles; it had continued to read the Japanese codes throughout the war, and never betrayed to the Japanese that it was in fact doing so. It required great restraint by the Americans and their British Allies to take no step by which it should become obvious to the Japanese that they possessed the secret. It is, in fact, recorded in Japan that a few men doubted from time to time the degree of security of Japanese communications, but they were not attended to.

Meanwhile the American air raids on Japan went on relentlessly. Until 1944 American aircraft, except those in Lieutenant-Colonel Doolittle's adventure in 1942, had not been over Japan. Thereafter the Japanese homeland was subjected to a bombardment which was utterly destructive. Even before the Japanese attack on Pearl Harbor, the United States had begun the long process of developing an aircraft known as the B29 Superfortress which from the beginning was conceived as a weapon of mass destruction for use against Japan in time of war. In peacetime it was not unusual for bomber aircraft to take ten years to advance from draw-

ing-board to full production, and the B29 was perhaps the most complicated and sophisticated bomber aircraft of its generation. Not surprisingly, it experienced teething problems. Gradually, however, everything
moved into place. To utilize this special weapon, General 'Hap' Arnold,
Commanding General of the United States Army Air Force, took over
executive control of a unique B29 bomber command, responsible only to
the Joint Chiefs of Staff and the President. President Roosevelt, after
considering the advantages of deploying the B29s from bases in Ceylon,
India and Australia, chose to use them in support of China.

Before leaving India to establish themselves at the new Chinese air
bases, the B29 crews carried out the first of a series of raids on relatively
soft targets to gain experience. On 5 June 1944 ninety-eight B29s set
off to bomb Bangkok. The raid was thoroughly bungled. Ten days later,
ninety-two of the aircraft left for Chengtu, in Szechuan, on their way
to attack the Imperial Iron and Steel Works at Yawata on Kyushu,
their first attack against a Japanese city. Only one bomb hit the plant,
but the Japanese, as we have seen, received the message. In the months
that followed, four other raids on Kyushu and others against targets in
Manchuria and Sumatra were scarcely more successful. The Japanese,
in their Ichi-Go campaign, fared rather better.

Driven out of China, the B29s gradually established themselves in the
Marianas. Progress, if it is right to use such a word, was slow. On 12
October 1944 the first B29 raid on Tokyo took off from Tinian. It achieved
nothing. A raid by a hundred massed aircraft attacked the Okayama
aircraft assembly plant on Taiwan in November 1944. It, too, was ineffective. The US Army Air Force found its exalted expectations regarding
the performance of the Superfortresses plunging as rapidly as their payloads towards the ground. No less than eight attempts were made between
late November 1944 and early March 1945 in an extended effort to destroy
the Nakajima factory on the outskirts of Tokyo by high-level bombing
runs. All of these raids were unavailing, even humiliating. The failure of
the strategic bombing campaign stood out in marked contrast to the
successes which rival services were clocking up against the Japanese at sea
and in the Philippines.

Thirty-eight-year-old General Curtis H. Le May was brought in to
direct the United States strategic bombing operations against Japan. He
was a skilled technician, with experience of the air war against Germany.
Fresh from his 'successful' destruction of Hamburg, he soon chafed with
frustration. His superiors wanted results, certainly, but many felt qualms
of conscience about resorting to the indiscriminate use of fire bombs. In
December 1944, however, a number of B29s had attacked Japanese-

occupied Hankow with incendiaries, reducing much of that city to ashes. On 23 February 1945 Le May ordered a daylight attack upon Tokyo by 130 aircraft loaded with incendiaries. It produced only 640 casualties but destroyed 25,000 buildings. This whetted the appetite of the Americans. Arnold authorized Le May to conduct a series of large-scale fire-bomb attacks upon Tokyo, Nagoya, Osaka and Kobe, targeted upon selected blocks of twelve square miles in which there was a population density calculated at the time as in excess of 128,000 per square mile.

What followed was sheer, unadulterated murder. It was also the greatest air offensive in history. No one believed that the horrors about to be inflicted upon Japanese civilians would suddenly melt Japanese resistance or produce a wave of popular rebellion against the Japanese Government. But it was nonetheless an effort designed to undermine Japanese morale and came as the Japanese were emerging from a particularly hard winter exacerbated by acute food and fuel shortages. The United States Army Air Force generals hoped to inflict such great punishment that the Japanese would learn respect for the power and relentless determination of the United States in a manner reminiscent of the determination of Kaiser Wilhelm's men to 'educate' the Chinese by inflicting upon them punitive demonstrations of German savagery after the Boxer Rebellion: as the creatures of the observant American humorist Finley Peter Dunne had commented then:

> ' 'Twill civilize th' Chinnymen,' said Mr Hennessy,
> ' 'Twill civilize thim stiff,' said Mr Dooley.*

On the night of 9–10 March 1945 General Le May launched his first full-scale incendiary attack against Tokyo. A huge force of 334 big four-engined B29 Superfortresses rose up from the new American runways on Guam, Tinian and Saipan in a strike at the heart of the Japanese Empire. It took two and a half hours for the planes to assemble in their formations. Desirous of increasing their bomb payloads, and confident of encountering little resistance, the American aircraft had been stripped of all their ammunition and defensive armament except what they carried in their tail-turrets. Le May's bombers flew abnormally low that night: this was a protection against anti-aircraft guns, which were abundant in Tokyo. The Japanese, even as late as this, did not have their guns adjusted to radar: they were operated manually, and they were made largely ineffective by Le May's strategy. There was no attempt to single out military

---

* 'The Future of China (On German Intervention in China)', in *Mr Dooley's Philosophy*, R. H. Russell, New York, 1900.

targets, nor was this raid in reprisal for any specific Japanese breaches of international law. It was deliberate, indiscriminate mass murder, centred upon the *shitamachi* (downtown) district of southern Tokyo, the most heavily populated urban quarter on earth, where actually upwards of a million people were packed in an area four miles by three to a density of 103,000 per square mile. The Japanese in their flimsy wooden buildings and narrow back streets had no advance warning before the bombs began to fall at a quarter past midnight. The raid lasted two and a half hours. There was very little flak and negligible fighter opposition. The fires spread well beyond the target zone. Somewhere between 70,000 and 140,000 people died. The injuries suffered by many of the survivors were nightmarish. Nearly a million people were left homeless: 267,000 buildings were destroyed. All of this cost the United States Army Air Force a mere 2,000 tons of incendiaries and the loss of fifteen B29 aircraft. It was to be only the first of such raids, but its effects were by far the most catastrophic of all the Allied 'conventional' air stikes against the Japanese in terms of human mortality.

Individual instances of courage or resourcefulness counted for very little in the firestorm that began fifteen minutes after the first bombs fell. The intensity of the flames within the conflagration exceeded 1800°F. They generated a holocaust which surpassed even the horrors of Dresden and Hamburg: much more damage could be done to Japanese cities by fire bombs because of the light structure of most buildings; the same weight of explosives led to much more destruction. It was the most destructive man-made fire in recorded history, and the loss in terms of human lives was of a similar order of magnitude to the toll which was to be exacted by the atomic bomb blasts at Hiroshima or Nagasaki. Japanese not immediately caught by the flames are said to have stood musing at the terrible hypnotic beauty of the spectacle. This was Total War at its most awful. With unspeakable grief, the Emperor, accompanied by his Lord Privy Seal and Grand Chamberlain, went on foot to tour the smoking remains of the worst-hit areas of the *shitamachi*. The ordeal cannot fail to have made a huge impression upon them. It would take twenty days to bury the dead, many of whom were committed to mass graves.

Meanwhile, less than thirty hours after the first great Tokyo firestorm, three square miles of Nagoya were subjected to a concentrated attack by 317 B29s. Eight square miles of the industrial heartland of Osaka were laid waste in a three-hour raid on 13 March. Kobe suffered the same fate on 16 March. Then Nagoya was hit again. Assessing the results at the end of this ten-day experiment, the United States Army Air Force examined its balance sheet. It had expended 10,000 tons of bombs in a total of 1,600 sorties and sustained a loss of less than 1 per cent of its striking force. In the months that followed, the campaign of destruction spread out in all directions. Le May's strike force grew until it reached nearly 600 aircraft. Nearly every conurbation in Japan came under brutal attack. At the peak of the bombing campaign, Le May's B29s dropped 40,000 tons of bombs on Japan in a single month.

In the B29 campaign, Total War nurtured one of the most revolting monsters ever conceived by modern technology. These grim tactics, operated with the thoroughness of General Le May, were new, and marked a change in air warfare. In the aftermath of such a development, it is appropiate to feel an abiding revulsion. Yet it must be said that there is no evidence to suggest that the Japanese would have shirked from utilizing such fearful weaponry had they themselves been able to do so. The overwhelming consensus among Americans was that the mass murders being carried out in their name were justified. They felt that the havoc wrought by the B29s would bring a rapid end to the war. After the war, Prince Konoye recalled that the B29 raids were responsible for hardening the determination of the Japanese Government to make peace. More than that, however, the American people regarded the bombings as a fitting punishment to inflict upon the Japanese people. Here was no fine distinction between an enemy Government and its people. Both were to be execrated. Americans reminded each other that in the aerial bombardment of Chinese cities, beginning in August 1937, Japan had been the first nation since the First World War to adopt a programme of systematic terror and mass destruction against densely populated conurbations. And so the Americans rededicated themselves to their grim task and felt little remorse. Indeed, few foreigners at the time were inclined to share in the grief of the Emperor for the wretched sufferings of his subjects.

The Japanese authorities tried to rise to the occasion, and ambitious schemes were put forward to counter or at least to mitigate any repetition of such horrors. Japanese schools had already closed throughout the capital. By March 1945 1.7 million people had been evacuated from Tokyo, but 6 million still remained huddled in the city. Now the mass evacuation of Tokyo became uncontrollable. Like much of the Japanese civil defence effort, chaos and confusion prevailed. The air-raid shelters, fire precautions, provisions for medical services and preparations for the maintenance of public order were hopelessly inadequate, primitive and anyway came far too late to cope with dangers for which the Japanese authorities had ample forewarning. The evacuation had always lacked that systematic planning and administrative coordination which had characterized the precautions taken by the British in the early days of the war and during the perils of the Blitz. Now as many Japanese fled their great cities in blind panic and descended upon ill-prepared and starving surrounding country districts like locusts, many of those left behind went into an almost catatonic state of shock. The uncharacteristic despair of the Japanese people was nowhere more clearly exemplified than by the fact that after the raids Japanese civil defence training was all but abandoned. Japanese medical and fire services for a time simply disintegrated. These terrible months had their counterparts in the European War, but running throughout the whole of the Second World War was a curious inability of either hemisphere to learn from what was happening on the opposite side of the globe.

The economic consequences were devastating. At first the destruction, as was the case in Germany, had less effect on industrial production than might have been supposed, but, as it became more wholesale, and surpassed the war damage in Europe, so its effects became harder to circumvent. The Japanese Government took more sweeping powers to direct the economy of the country; but where was the economy left to direct? The food supplies began to fall dangerously, and could not be distributed because of the destruction of the railways and the breakdown of commercial organization. The description of the life of the Japanese worker at this stage of the war, underfed, harried to inhuman extremes by the Government, lacking the elementary comforts of a safe home, must touch even the reader who knows something of the terrors endured by the German population. A great flight began from the towns to the countryside.

For the first time the civilian part of the nation began to turn against the military. In parts of the country it became positively dangerous to wear uniform. Such aberrant behaviour shook deeply the Army General Staff.

Japanese experts at the time said that the Japanese standard of nutrition in the towns in the last year was below that of Germans in the fateful winter of hunger after the end of the first European War. Even the Army, which was the last to be affected, was put on short supplies. The soldiers were found to be bartering military equipment for the scanty food supplies which filtered through to private hands. In spite of all this, both the civilian and military morale remained astonishingly high. There were no food riots in the Japanese towns, such as were already causing great concern in Germany in the First World War as early as 1916. It may be that the Japanese were less shocked by this adversity than were European populations, because they had been inured to it. Twenty years before, the people of Tokyo had experienced similar devastation in their capital city; that time from the horrors of the Tokyo earthquake.

In April 1945 the Prime Minister, Koiso Kuniaki, fell from office. He had engaged in negotiations with questionable Chinese emissaries, by which he had intended to split the Chinese and the Western Allies. They were of course secret, but when they failed, they leaked out and he was dismissed. His years of intrigue and adventurism had come full circle. Mistrusting the services and skills of diplomats, he held himself out as an astute judge of men, expert in negotiations. Koiso believed the assurances of his Chinese contacts that he could detach China from the war by signing a truce agreeing to the abandonment of the puppet régime of Wang Ching-wei and the withdrawal of all Japanese forces from China. In exchange, or so Koiso believed, Chiang Kai-shek would guarantee to prevent American forces from landing in China. The Supreme War Council regarded the whole idea as fatuous. There were, however, other factors, equally important. Koiso had shown himself unable to hold himself apart from the myopic propaganda issued for public consumption by the Army. He took so little trouble to establish the truth that he succeeded in embarrassing the Supreme Command as well as appalling those who knew that the time had come to seek peace on whatever terms the Allied Powers would accept. The Palace and Government bureaucrats had expected Koiso to work closely with Admiral Yonai Mitsumasa, a perceptive and highly personable former Prime Minister, a man known to be committed to the search for peace, who was entrusted by the Emperor to act as Koiso's Deputy Premier and served concurrently as Navy Minister. Yonai did not lack bravery, and his personal views were unequivocal: in May 1945, indeed, he went as far as declaring, 'If we can just protect the Imperial family, that will be sufficient. Even if it means the Empire is reduced to the four home islands, we'll have to do it.'* Unfortunately, as a Japanese diplomat with some knowledge of the facts wrote afterwards with uncharacteristic bluntness:

Koiso was utterly ignorant of the realities of the military situation. It was thus impossible to get him to work for a termination of the war. Yonai told me he was

* Quoted by I. Saburō in *Japan's Last War*, Blackwell, Oxford, 1979, pp. 230–31, citing the private records of Rear-Admiral Takagi Sōkichi, one of Yonai's closest confidants, a brilliant man who had been deeply involved in a secret conspiracy to find a suitable formula for the surrender of Japan ever since heading a Navy research team that had investigated America's productive capacity at the beginning of the war.

surprised to discover that Koiso had come from Korea with a ready-made list of cabinet members, mostly names of his old henchmen and cronies in Korea. These men were entirely unacquainted with the difficulties then confronting the country. They were popularly dubbed the 'Korean Cabinet' in contrast with Tōjō's 'Manchurian Cabinet'. Yonai gave what advice he decently could under the circumstances but it remained for the most part unheeded. The Koiso Cabinet was clearly a severe disillusionment to him and his friends. There was little opportunity left for Yonai to work for peace.

While the Emperor desired to see the new Cabinet operated on the basis of a close working partnership of Koiso and Yonai, actually Yonai thought, or preferred to think, that his responsibility as Koiso's partner ended with the formation of the Cabinet. After that, he was a mere Navy Minister and, as such, he did not like to interfere with what Koiso did as Prime Minister.*

Long before the failure of the Chinese negotiations, therefore, the Jūshin had come to recognize the country's urgent need for a change of premier. Within the Daihon'ei he was regarded with derision as 'a snobbish, senile general on the reserve list without any influence whatever in the Army'.† The public, dismayed by what news filtered through to them about the disasters in the field, also seemed to appreciate that the Prime Minister was out of touch with reality. As American forces stormed ashore on Okinawa, Koiso conceived the fantastic idea that he might ride out the crisis and consolidate his authority by returning to active military service and taking on additional responsibilities as Minister for War in addition to his responsibilities as Premier. The Army refused. Only then did Koiso accept his humiliation, bow to the inevitable and resign.

Baron Suzuki Kantarō, a retired admiral, succeeded him. It was remarked that he was sworn in on the day after the loss of Japan's prize battleship, the *Yamato*: it seemed as though Japan had turned to the Navy for its Prime Minister just at the time that it had lost its fleet. He had a good record, having been a target of the military conspirators of February 1936, by whom he was badly wounded. He was an aged hero of the Russo-Japanese War. He had a likeable, rather enigmatic, personality, and was almost universally popular – a rare thing in Japan. From experience, he believed that the scope for personal intervention in public affairs was limited, and he was apt to preside benignly over them, and, like many Japanese, to acquiesce philosophically in what came to pass. In fact there was, in Suzuki, a touch of Tolstoy's Kutuzov: the much respected figure, clothed with glory from the past, who is wise enough to collaborate with events, rather than to withstand them – or even to attempt to understand them.

* K. Toshikazu, *Eclipse of the Rising Sun*, Jonathan Cape, London, 1951, pp. 86–7.
† ibid., p. 106.

But he was eighty years old: too venerable to be effective, even by roundabout means. Having the virtue of open-mindedness, he lacked the decisiveness, the singlemindedness, which were essential qualities in a Prime Minister in such a crisis. The choice of Suzuki, however, was a sign that the peace party was gradually prevailing. He was not a born leader, did not aspire to the office thrust upon him, and did not incarnate the fabled Japanese desire to go down fighting. Intellectually, he needed no convincing that Japan had lost the war; he was himself more than ready for peace. But he moved too slowly to be able to save Japan. The peace party, backed by the Imperial Court and by responsible members of that solid corps of professional bureaucrats that is the repository of common sense in most countries, was looking for a totem, was ready to be rallied, and to assert itself, but it was beyond Suzuki to provide this.

In the next month, May, Japan lost its ally, Germany. The Supreme War Council met and approved the decision to carry on the war notwithstanding. It declared, however, that Japan was released from the provisions of the Tripartite Pact (which was somewhat overdue and rather went without saying). Japan had now to face the switch of the Allied forces engaged in the European War, and their addition to the force already employed against Japan in the East; it had also to meet the possible use against it of the Russian Army, now disengaged.

In the summer of 1945, Prime Minister Suzuki, his Foreign Minister and the two Service Ministers decided to send Prince Konoye Fumimaro to Moscow as head of a peace delegation, provided he proved acceptable to the Soviets. This decision may have reached the Moscow Embassy only after Molotov had departed for the Potsdam Conference. Konoye, thrice Prime Minister, remained in favour as a man behind whom the whole country could feel a sense of unity in adversity. In any event, the Soviet Union made no reply. Then came news of the Potsdam Declaration, which fell upon the Japanese leadership like a thunderclap. Obviously something had to be done. Several Cabinet meetings were held to decide how to proceed: these broke up in confusion and despair.

An outside chance for Japan lay in the complications set up by the death of Roosevelt on 12 April, and his succession by Vice-President Harry Truman. But to have used these to advantage, to have extricated Japan from the net which was closing in, would have required a very flexible diplomacy. Flexibility was never a strong point with the Japanese and the number of neutral centres where Japan could operate, and from which it could obtain its Intelligence, had, to the advantage of the United States, become very small.

In spite of their Yalta agreement with the Russians, which had been so dearly purchased, the Americans, and to a large extent the British, continued to be profoundly distressed by the memory of the savage Japanese defence of the Coral Islands. The ferocity of their resistance in the homeland was expected to be as formidable. Nothing like the same internal collapse was foreseen as followed the death of Hitler in Germany. The war might continue for as much as a year, and with what was foreseen as the mounting strain of tension with Russia, in spite of the glitter of the terms of Yalta, the upshot was not clear.

In the meanwhile it became known that the Japanese General Staff was pressing on with plans for a fanatical defence of the Japanese islands. Rightly it was supposed that the principal American blow would be directed at Honshu. To deal with this it could assemble two and a half million troops in the home islands. Tales arrived to the effect that a vast underground headquarters was being dug out at Tokyo. The Japanese Army was said to be gambling on the blind determination which would halt the Americans on landing. Clearly the Americans had still much effort before them.

But very shortly after, a great change came over the situation. It was brought about by the completion of the atom bomb. Partly this was the result of German-Jewish genius, which, barred from Germany by racial madness, had been mobilized in the invention of this device of war, which had been meant in the first place for the overthow of the Nazi system. Part of the early work was done in England: and, when it was concentrated in the United States, British scientists participated. The war against Germany had come to an end in May 1945, with the bomb still a project, and not realized in fact: but by June it was clear that it was about to become operational. The news that it was to be so, and would be available for use against Japan, had already been grasped by the very small circle in which, at this stage of the war, had been concentrated the making of American policy. Its immense, hardly credible, destructive power could quench the continuing flame of Japanese fanaticism. With its finality there could be no discussion.

By this trick of fate, the need to cajole and coax Russia, the need for Russian complicity and Russian power, were all removed.

By the summer of 1945 it was stated that American policy would be revised: Russian aid was now no longer so necessary for bringing to an end the war with Japan. The United States had initially perceived that through the possible intervention of Russia it could go ahead without perpetually needing to keep China contented, and now it saw that it would be able to discard Russia in its turn.

In fact America was by this time as zealous to deter Russia from entering the war as before it had been to bring Russia in. Truman had succeeded Roosevelt; his period was from the start different from the period of Roosevelt. Other considerations apart, Truman was less inclined to exert himself to maintain good relations with Russia. He was less of a historian. He was less inclined, especially at this point of his career, to look into the future, and to adjust his actions accordingly. Instinctively, Truman was thinking in terms of the containment of Russia, and he was anxious that in East Asia as elsewhere, Russia should make as little headway as possible. If Russia once went to war and invaded Manchuria, there would be little chance of keeping it out of Port Arthur and Dairen (which it had already been promised at Yalta). Even though Truman, who was new to these issues of foreign policy, did not himself stress all these points, he was more available than Roosevelt had been to advisers who suggested a frankly anti-Russian policy. None of the advisers knew, but Truman did, that the atom bomb would be available for putting Japan out of the war. For the time being he was satisfied that Russian demands would not be extravagant. If the effects of the bomb were to be as he was advised, a Power without the bomb could not argue aggressively with the Power which possessed it.

The condition of Japan continued to deteriorate. It was uncertain that the bomb would ever be required. General Le May was claiming that his air bombardment had totally paralysed life in sixty major cities. He claimed that Japan was being driven back to the stone age. The Joint Chiefs of Staff reported at the beginning of July: 'Japan will become a nation without cities, with her transportation disrupted, and will have tremendous difficulty in holding her people together for continued resistance.' By March 1945 Japan had lost 88 per cent of the merchant fleet tonnage with which it had begun the war, and it had become almost impossible to import any goods, even the most essential. The Service departments of the Government cried out for the punishment of those engaged in the economic administration; but this could do no good. American Intelligence was, however, rather less optimistic. It gave due allowance to the putting out of action of much of Japanese heavy industry by the blockade and through air bombardment. But it reported that the Japanese output of combat aircraft was still between 1,200 and 1,500 a month (as compared with a peak production of 2,300 reached late in

1944). The greatest shortage was of fuel oil, which was bringing orthodox air operations to a standstill. On the other hand Japan had little to worry about in its stock of ammunition. The Intelligence Committee still thought that the highly trained Japanese Army, the greater part of which had as yet never been in action, was a formidable fighting force. It reckoned that it would probably take another twelve months to subdue it. It made its report, it must be noticed, without knowledge of the bomb.

At the Potsdam Conference in July, when the three masters of the world met face to face, Truman, with careful premeditation and calculated misdirection, told Stalin, apparently in passing, that the Allies had in their hands a more powerful bomb than any previously used. No word was said about the bomb being nuclear, or about the transformation of the war by its invention. Churchill, who knew the true facts, and who watched Stalin carefully, agreed that he had not suspected the truth behind Truman's apparently routine information. He took it as an announcement that the United States had been able to charge its bomb with a heavier load of dynamite. There is drama in the spectacle of these two men, the pillars of the western world, systematically observing the demeanour of a man whom they both regarded as their potential enemy, while in public they played on him something which resembled a confidence trick. The drama is heightened because Stalin had in his pocket, in the communist offensive which he knew he could release in Europe, something like an atom bomb in politics.

A race, in which one of the partners, Stalin, was in darkness about the true facts and about their urgency, then took place between the Americans, who were about to explode the bomb, and the Russians, who were in the last stages of the preparation to attack in Manchuria. Russia had become aware of the change of attitude by the United States, of the desire that it should not participate, though it may have been partly puzzled about the reason. The United States rushed the preparations. At one time the bomb was to have been used on 1 August. Last-minute delays in completing its manufacture put this back a few days. Further delay came because the weather made it almost impossible to raid Japan accurately.

During the Potsdam Conference it was learnt that Japan had requested Swedish mediation in working out surrender terms. It was plain that peace could not be far off. The United States, however, showed surprisingly little zeal in developing this initiative.

The United States made at this time the decision to exclude Russians as members of an occupation force in Japan. The plans for occupying Japan were made surprisingly late. Their details were all improvised. For example, the decision to divide the occupation of Korea and to fix the boundary between the American zone and the Russian zone at the thirty-eighth parallel, was made between an American captain and a Russian major. Thus, casually, there came into being a frontier problem which subsequently divided the world. The Americans and the British were informed by Molotov about the repeated, almost frenzied, attempts by Japan to enlist the support of Russia as a mediator. They were being rebuffed by Russia. It was clear that Russia was not going to back Japan as a move in the war that had already begun between it and its Allies.

At Potsdam, on 26 July 1945, the Allies had issued a final and solemn summons to Japan to surrender. Its terms were broadcast over the wireless. They were that those Japanese who had been responsible for the policies which had led to war were to be forever eliminated; that Japan must renounce all its overseas empire; that war criminals must be punished; that Japan should be occupied. As had become the habit of the United States with beaten adversaries, Japan was required to surrender unconditionally. These demands, though exceedingly radical, were not entirely rejected by Japan, so desperate had its position become.

An answer was understood to have been given in a press conference on 30 July by the Japanese Prime Minister, Admiral Suzuki, at which he spoke in Japanese. It was, as might have been expected from an old man, doubtful, temporizing and ambiguous. Apparently he had meant to say that he withheld comment. The Allies interpreted the Japanese word he used as meaning that Japan not only would not comment, but would treat the summons with contempt. This was taken by the handful of Americans who knew what was intended as the signal for dropping the bomb. Actually it has been suggested since that a word was mistranslated, and meant much less than was supposed, signifying merely that Japan's first reaction to the summons was not being published. The subsequent controversy about what really happened has been inconclusive. That the confusion in fact occurred, is typical of the Japanese language, one of the most involved and ambiguous languages of the world, and the reader must not be astonished that it should have betrayed Japan towards its disaster.

The bomb was dropped on Hiroshima, the chosen target, on 6 August 1945. The attack was made from Tinian, not far from Guam, which had been taken in the previous year. The plane, a B29 bomber, had been blessed for its mission by a Roman Catholic priest. The havoc made was as great as was forecast. It was clear that the war could not be pursued when America could drop bombs of this kind. Within three days a second bomb, of a different and even more deadly type, was dropped on the civilian port of Nagasaki. It did slightly less damage, because Nagasaki had better air-raid precautions and because the bomb did not set off a fire-storm; but its blast was greater than that at Hiroshima. This time, to signalize the joint responsibility of the United States and Britain, the death plane was accompanied by a plane carrying British observers, Dr W. Penney, the physicist, and Wing Commander L. Cheshire, who, by one of the ironies of these events, was later to win celebrity in Britain as the leader of one of the most inspired missions of the day, that of bringing comfort and the opportunity of decent existence to the incurably disabled. With the bomb at Nagasaki, there was released a manifesto to a top Japanese physicist, addressed to him by his American colleagues and explaining some of the details of the bomb. It urged him to enlighten the Japanese Government.

Ironically, Nagasaki was one of the parts of Japan which had the connections of longest duration with the West. It was founded in the sixteenth century by a feudal lord who was a Christian, and who wanted the trade between Japan and the Christian world to be based on it. For a time the port was actually ceded to the Jesuit missionaries, who organized its administration. It was subsequently the centre of persecution of Japanese Christians when the Japanese Government become alarmed by their number.

The dropping of the atom bomb was so dramatic, the awed shock it provoked throughout the world was so final, and the sense that it was, in President Truman's phrase, 'the greatest thing in history', seemed so incontestable that there was a general instinct to think that it had brought to an end one phase of human affairs. From then onwards everything would be dwarfed by events. But the appalling news of the disaster produced by atomic radiation, the vaporizing and burning of human beings, the whole vast panorama of unutterable suffering, somehow failed to register with most people who lived through those days. Even the horrible details, published some months afterwards and set out with all the technical skill of American publicity, were too terrible for belief. The mind set up impediments to taking in such information. There was born at that time an uneasiness which has affected a whole age.

The Americans had thus won the race. They had set themselves against Russia; but it was virtually a dead heat because on the next day, before Japan had had time to surrender, the Russians crossed the frontier of Manchuria. By a four-pronged offensive, Russia overran the country as neatly as Germany had picked off countries earlier in the war. Though the fate of Hiroshima has stuck in the world's memory and though it has been regarded as the final cause of Japan's capitulation, the Russian invasion shares in the distinction of having tilted the Japanese over to put an end to the war.

The effects of the atom bomb and the grim finality of its consequences were not immediately clear. Among most people outside Hiroshima itself, even among those in Tokyo, there was doubt about what had really happened. A great bomb had fallen; terrible destruction had been wrought; but Japan had become thoroughly used to such calamities. Actually the loss of life in the atomic phase, though it was rendered peculiarly horrible by atomic radiation, was less than that in the great B29 raids, to which Japan had been subjected since March 1945. Prince Konoye afterwards told American investigators that Japan's greatest fear of the Soviet Union in the closing stages of the war had been this psychological fear, especially after the Soviet Union's renunciation of the Russo–Japanese Non-Aggression Pact. But all Japan knew the significance of the dreaded invasion of Manchuria, the advent of the Russian hordes, the coming into reality of that threat which had, as long as man could remember, been the governing fact in Japan's foreign policy. Japan could not face war with another Great Power. It was this which made it 'despair its charm', and accept the facts.

The history of the way Japan surrendered is dramatic, and even today, has probably been only partly told. At least, new accounts are constantly appearing in Japan with new details, which, true or false, require the narrative of events to be considered afresh.

A new personality in Japan played a large part at the conclusion. This was the most august person in the land. Hitherto he had been content to be a spectator of the great events, but now he entered the arena. This was the Japanese Emperor.

He was a virtuous prince. The irony is that such dark proceedings had been allowed to happen under his aegis. In the whole range of personalities who held positions of distinction in the war, whether of actual power or of decorativeness, he, and the English monarch, George VI, were the only ones without serious blemish. Like George VI he had a stammer; like him, he held in reality very little political power. It must have been discouraging for this young man, entering on his life's career, that he succeeded his father, who had been deranged during almost the whole of his reign. Yet that fact had not compromised the monarchy, and this speaks highly of the reserves of credit which the institution enjoyed. In one respect the Emperor was ahead of George VI. He had strong intellectual interests, though these were concentrated on a single subject, marine biology. The corollary of the secure eminence of the Japanese Emperor was that ordinarily public opinion severely restricted the range of his activities; he was expected to do almost nothing because his role was almost deified. And Hirohito could not be said to have contributed anything remarkable to the political debates of his time. From the day he ascended his throne in 1926, to the day when he nearly lost it at the time of Japan's defeat, he did what was expected of him. He was reliable; he was thoroughly constitutional; he gave no trouble to the politicians by threatening to use the stored-up prestige of the Japanese monarchy to embarrass them. The inner circle of Japanese with knowledge of what went on behind the façade of public life knew that the course of Japan's affairs – the autonomy of the military, and a foreign policy which brought it into collision with the United States and Britain – was profoundly antipathetic to him. But beyond asking the occasional awkward question at imperial conferences, or confiding his anxieties to those few who had audiences with him on rare occasions, he gave no sign of his continual vexation.

However, at the crisis of Japan, he acted with much common sense. He borrowed from the Confucian philosophy of China the maxim by which he governed his actions. The Confucian wisdom was not to stand up like an oak tree before a raging tempest: in a storm, the oak tree is uprooted and perishes. The willow tree has the better chance of survival; it bends before the wind, but, when the hurricane is over, its root is unsnapped, and it stands up once again by its own resilience. Thus, before the storm of the Japanese military, which was to blow away many persons in its time, the Emperor bowed, and was inconspicuous. Now the storm was nearly blown out, and the opportunity came for the reassertion of the powers of the monarchy, which were real and legitimate even if they had been so long unused. He was guided, in the crucial days when he felt that his personal intervention was timely, that in fact the spirit of the Japanese constitution called for it, by a suave and subtle sense of correct timing. He was capable of choosing the right men to collaborate with – or he was very lucky in these being available, and in offering their services. His conduct at the time suggests that this marine biologist had developed a political instinct during the years of inoffensive constitutional practice.

Throughout July the conviction of defeat had been gripping one person after another and one institution after another. In the past year the fortunes of the civilian elements of government in their control of the military had begun to revive. In the complex balance of forces which made up Japanese politics, the centre of authority began to pass a little away from the soldiers and towards the civilians.

But the services, both the Army and Navy, were obdurate for continuing war: and the senior officers, even if compelled by reason to admit the hopelessness of their case, could point out that they were powerless to assent to peace. They would have been assassinated. The spirit of the nation had passed into the custody of the patriotic societies which would have employed the sanction of murder against anyone who dared to speak of surrender. Both the Jūshin, and the more reasonable service officers, had to mask their intention, to carry on their intrigue behind walls of extreme secrecy, and had to say one thing while in fact strenuously doing another. As a result, Japan's resolution to fight on appeared undented. It had become as good as impossible for it to capitulate. Japan, having made a cult of the principle that no Japanese ever surrendered to the enemy, now found it impossible to accept the findings of common sense.

Behind the scenes, however, and with every secrecy, Japan had been sounding the possibilities of an honourable peace; and peace, with honour that would satisfy Japan meant, in effect, a peace on the simple condition that Japan was allowed to keep its Emperor. In every other respect Japan was ready, except for the irreconcilables in the Army, to surrender unconditionally; with the Emperor's position guaranteed, the Japanese would sigh with relief and cease their hopeless resistance. There is undeniable pathos about these last days of Japanese agony. Japan was willing to trade the entire substance of capitulation for this one concession to a principle which, to its western conquerors, appeared perverted and of no worth. To the West, attachment to an Emperor was sentimental; a defeated Japan must eventually have a chief executive, and the title he would use of himself was no matter. But to the Japanese it was beyond price. Even so, some of the Jūshin were frankly disposed to sacrifice the Emperor, if peace could be gained by this.

President Truman had to take account of the fact that feeling against the monarchy was strong in the United States. Those in favour of tolerating it were accused of being appeasers. Truman himself, backed by Henry L. Stimson, the Secretary for War, was in favour of accepting the Japanese terms on this point. They were influenced by the argument that the American occupying force would find it much simpler to do its work if it had the Japanese Emperor on its side. His prestige was so immense that he would, as it were, legitimize the occupation in Japan's eyes. Also, an American commander, able to speak through him, would be able to gain control of the surrendering Japanese armies; which, otherwise, would have presented a problem. Truman did not directly meet the Japanese condition. But he drafted the American reply in terms that, while avoiding all mention of the Emperor problem, conveyed the general sense that the Emperor would be kept.

These exchanges came between two vital meetings in Tokyo, the first on 13 August, between the Japanese Emperor and the Supreme Command, the committee of which directed the war; the second on the next day, a conference of the Emperor with the Japanese Cabinet. The meetings were held in a dug-out in the imperial palace. In spite of the belligerent circumstances, a certain formality was observed. All those taking part wore full dress uniform, or morning dress; the long table at which they sat was covered with a precious gold brocade. But the Emperor himself, appearing unshaven, increased the general sense of gloom. At the first meeting, no decision was reached: the case for further resistance, the case for immediate capitulation, were fully argued. But the Prime Minister, Admiral Suzuki, succeeded in getting agreement that the Emperor should be asked to decide personally what should be done. To follow such a procedure was revolutionary in Japan: the convention was that he should never be embarrassed by having to give instructions to his Ministers. At the second meeting, after those present had again expressed their views, and the American attitude towards the Emperor had been weighed up, the decision was taken by the Emperor. 'The unendurable must be endured', was the imperial pronouncement which terminated the war. It was a conscious echo of Hirohito's grandfather's remarks at the end of another great humiliation of Japan, and it therefore was understood to contain elements of continuity and regeneration as well as of despair and resolution.

With the last military hope gone, with the Red Army pouring into Manchuria, and with further air attacks expected, which nobody had the remotest idea of how to resist, the Japanese Emperor, in form using the procedure with which he had committed Japan to the calamity of Pearl Harbor, but in fact having taken on himself the personal responsibility for what was now done, gave instructions that hostilities were to cease and, on 14 August Japan replied, accepting the Potsdam declaration.

Until the last moment, it continued to be uncertain if even the intervention of the Emperor would succeed. The military, which had made the war, would not lightly abdicate. It was one thing for the Emperor to forbid further war; it was another for him, great though the Imperial prestige was, to be obeyed. Moreover the United States, in refusing all bargaining, had not satisfied the Army that it stood to gain nothing by forcing American troops to fight their way ashore in Japan. Action was precipitated because a fairly accurate account of the peace negotiations had leaked to the Army. On the night after the decision to end the war was taken, a melodrama took place in Tokyo which was equal to any of the sensational passages in the history of conspiracy. It recalls Hitler's night of the long knives, in which there culminated the feud between him and the SA leaders; St Bartholomew's Eve in Paris four centuries earlier; the fight, again at Paris, on the night of Robespierre's fall, between the moderate politicians and those who wanted the Terror to continue. A group of young, well-connected, passionately unappeasable officers tried to halt the negotiations, make a coup, and seize the sacred person of the Emperor.

To succeed, they needed the support of three or four generals, who were in key positions in Tokyo. Their plot began in the office of the general commanding the First Imperial Guards Division, which was garrisoning the imperial palace. For hours they pleaded with him: then, their tempers breaking, and pressed for time, they abruptly murdered him. In these bloody proceedings, there is an odd atmosphere of a family quarrel which had passed out of control and become terribly serious. Many of the officers were related to the generals with whom they were pleading. One of them was the son-in-law of General Tōjō Hideki, the former Prime Minister. Another was the brother-in-law of General Anami Korechika, the War Minister.

The officers went to the part of the palace where the Emperor was. Comedy then took over. On the evening before, the Emperor was known to have recorded a wireless address, which would be broadcast to the people of Japan on the next morning, 15 August, and in which he had declared the Japanese decision to surrender. When it was once played on the air, the act would be irrevocable; it was therefore vital to the officers to seize the record and destroy it. It was known to be present in the palace until it was needed for broadcasting, and the soldiers in the plot spent some hours searching for it in vain. Some of those taking part, with the curious detached Japanese aestheticism, remarked on the great beauty of the night, the uncanny and eerie moonlight which provided a backcloth of deep peace for these disordered events. The Emperor, the occasion of this wild conspiracy, was sleeping peacefully, a few yards away, and when it came to the point nobody would commit the impiety of waking him. In a cellar, directly underneath, the Lord Keeper of the Privy Seal, Marquis Kido Kōichi, who was deeply committed to the peace negotiations, was quaking for his life, for, if the officers had discovered him, they would certainly have slaughtered him. Some radio officials, who had played a part in manufacturing the record, were rounded up and kept prisoner for a while. Their lives were also in danger.

The conspiracy ended because, with the passage of time, the officers began to ask themselves whether they were not going too far. Sake flowed; but this did not avail to stifle doubt. The failure to find the gramophone record put a lesion on the unfolding of the plot. Resolution drained away, and the band dispersed. Fake orders, which they had issued to the Guards division to rise and seize the place, were intercepted. They did not dispose of a sufficient body of rank and file troops.

As a result of this sacrilege of Army officers in seizing the imperial palace, the War Minister committed seppaku. He had been on the verge of this supreme act as a gesture of atonement for the behaviour of the Japanese Army in losing the war; the night's doings probably overcame his natural hesitancy, and made death the way out of a situation which had become unbearable to him. In the ministerial debates of the previous days he was one of those whose opinion was most consulted, and had been the most vacillating. He had readily agreed that the military situation was hopeless; but he had been withheld from advising surrender as the only rational course by doubts over what the Americans intended to do about the Emperor. Now he was for capitulation, now he veered towards those who suggested that Japan should try again to save itself by force. His attitude, even towards those who attempted the military coup, was ambiguous. He was not taken by surprise; for days he had known that something was afoot. He had said to those around him that a coup would be impious and impossible; but, at the same time, he had shown marked favour to the more irresponsible officers. He summed up in himself the weakness that was general in the higher ranks of Japanese officer considered from the point of view of their reliability to the state. He took it as axiomatic that a general need not in all cases obey instructions which reached him, but should be free to connive at gangsterism when the situation required. It was clear that his heart yearned for a coup: and his head only partially restrained him from siding with the young officers. Very distressingly, and rather characteristically, he bungled his suicide, and lived in great agony until the following day.

In the anti-climax which followed these exciting events, the rumours of which began to get about, Hirohito's speech was played over to the Japanese people. It was still touch and go how the speech would be received. In fact, the speech was not generally or at least clearly understood, and that for a very curious reason. The Japanese Emperor spoke the language of the court, very flowery, with a strange lilt, which it was hard for modern Japanese to grasp, at least auditorily. This, and the uncharacteristically high pitch of his voice which came from his nervousness on this occasion, combined with sentiments so unexpected – to the uninformed – coming from such a source, produced at first a general bewilderment.

Meetings of colonels and majors were taking place the whole time in all parts of Japan. The plan for a final national effort by Air Force pilots who had sworn themselves to act as suicide squads was nearly put into effect. The proposal was to bomb the United States warship, the *Missouri*, which was steaming into Tokyo Bay, to accept the Japanese surrender. This was narrowly averted. Hirohito's speech contained a notable sentence, probably inserted on the Emperor's own responsibility, which may have irritated American and British listeners, but which represented the Emperor's own, perhaps naïve, views. He said:

We declared war on America and Britain out of our sincere desire to ensure Japan's self-preservation and the stabilization of South-East Asia, it being far from our thought either to infringe upon the sovereignty of other nations or to embark upon territorial aggrandizement.

He continued with a statement of the incontrovertible fact of Japan's utter helplessness, and the lunacy of continuing the war. He was aware of the danger of seeming to break faith with those who had been killed, but the plight of those still alive required peace absolutely.

The Japanese people wept tears of disbelief and shame, but also of relief, when the imperial message at last sank home. The long nightmare of hypnosis under which they had been held by the military at last was shaken off. With the disciplined self-control of their race, which usually succeeded in clamping down upon their very volcanic emotion – which always so surprised the onlookers – they switched their behaviour overnight, and became the welcoming hosts to the advancing wave of American occupiers. By one of the psychological swings, irrational and extraordinary, which are evident among people under severe strain, the Japanese passed abruptly from regarding the Americans as barbarians, who were contemptible and to be treated with unappeasable hostility, to accepting them as a people who had incontestably proved their superiority by victory, and who had earned their consequent respect. Peace had come partly because of the effort, at the risk of their lives, of the peace party, and, when they had succeeded, it was plain that it had the support of the majority of the people. But this mass had, to the very end, remained completely unorganized. Peace was brought about with the Japanese public still as spectators of the event. They contributed nothing to it.

Everywhere the Japanese Empire surrendered, or crashed. In Burma it was already a memory, and the Japanese were gone. In Indonesia they had delayed too long to proclaim independence under Japanese auspices. This move, which was calculated to earn them plaudits in defeat, had been sabotaged by the Japanese Army, which had no confidence in the return which could be gained by apparently serving the Asian cause. On 17 August 1945, the impatient leaders of the Indonesian National Party declared independence for themselves, thus forestalling the return of the Dutch. They persuaded Sukarno, the apparently fiery but in reality circumspect principal leader of the revolution, to read out the document which, in Indonesia ever since, has been famous. Sukarno's courage had failed him at the last moment, but his confederates held him to his task, and induced him, at pistol point, to go through with his broadcast statement. Thus a national leader was compelled to go through a historic act for which he must have been very grateful ever afterwards. Soon British troops would arrive to supervise the Japanese surrender, and soon their relation with the Indonesian nationalists would deteriorate. Within a matter of days an action would take place between the Indonesians and the Japanese, who were fighting under the command of British officers. To such a topsy-turvy condition had affairs been brought in that country.

In Manchukuo the Russians streamed in. Under the direction of Marshal Vassilievsky, the Russians attacked in a four-pronged offensive. One huge Army of Soviet troops commanded by General Meretskov had assembled in the region of Vladivostok. On 9 August it advanced swiftly across the Ussuri River into northern Korea and eastern Manchukuo, crushing all opposition in its path. At the same time, a second Army under General Purkayev rolled forward, crossed the Amur River and spread across northern Manchukuo. A third Russian Army, largest of the three and led by Marshal Malinovsky, struck the north-west sector of Manchukuo. On his southern flank, the Army of the (Outer) Mongolian People's Republic sliced through Chahar and Jehol. Stalin afterwards boasted that the combined strength of these forces amounted to seventy divisions. The Japanese, who may have had forty, stood no chance. It was an awful invasion, one of terrible massacre, incredible speed, confusion and panic. The way in which the Soviets sacked Manchuria, their revenge upon the White Russians and small colonies of East European refugees, the plight of defenceless Japanese, Korean and Manchurian non-combatants and local militia caught up in the destruction, the disintegration of the Kwantung and Korean Armies (shells of their former selves, long ago stripped of seasoned warriors to stiffen the far-flung Japanese forces where mettle might prevail), the fate of those taken as prisoners of war – slave labour – by the Red Army and its political commissars, all of these things should be remembered and unforgiven, but here the details must be left to the imagination.

Nicolayevsk

U S S R

Komsomol'sk

Trans-Siberian Railway

Amur

Blagoveshchensk

SECOND FAR-EASTERN FRONT

14th

Sunwu

Khabarovsk

Sovetskaya

Khingan Mts

Fuchin

K U O

(A)

Sungari

Chiamussu

134 DIV.

5th ARMY

Iman

FIRST FAR-EASTERN FRONT

Maritime Province

14th

Mutanchiang

Suifenho

Yehho

14th

Tungning

ARMY

1st AREA

14th

Tumen

Vladivostok

Yenchi

SEA OF
JAPAN

Rashin(Najin)

10th

14th

Seishin Ranan
(Chongjin)

13th

JAPAN

ARMY

Kankō
(Hamhung)

A

THE SOVIET INVASION OF MANCHUKUO
AND THE JAPANESE EMPIRE, AUG.1945

0   500 km

0   300 miles

The administrative structure erected by the Japanese in Manchukuo vanished in a flash. Their puppet Manchu Emperor, Pu-Yi, has recorded the final scene which took place in his capital at Changchun:

My brother, sisters, brothers-in-law and nephews were already at the railway station, and, of my entire family, only I and two of my wives were left in the palace. Yoshioka addressed me and the servants who were still with me in a peremptory tone:

'Whether we walk or go in automobiles, the sacred objects to be carried by Hashimoto Toranosuke will go in front. If anyone passes the sacred vessels they must make a ninety-degree bow.'

I stood respectfully and watched Hashimoto, the President of the Bureau of Worship, carry the bundle containing the sacred Shinto objects to the first car. I got into the second and, as we left the palace, I looked around and saw flames rising above the National Foundation Shrine.*

Pu-Yi set off to make his way to Japan. He was informed that the American Government had left Hirohito on his throne. He sank to his knees, and kow-towed to him, expressing his relief at the news. He hoped to find safety under his wing. But at Mukden he was arrested by the Russians.

The airfield reverberated to the sound of aircraft engines as Soviet planes landed. Soviet troops holding sub-machine guns poured out of the planes and immediately disarmed all the Japanese soldiers on the airfield, which was soon covered with Soviet troops.†

Pu-Yi remained for five years the captive of the Russians. He was then handed over to the Chinese communists for 'brainwashing'. It took time, but eventually the Chinese were satisfied that he was in a desirable state of mind. From 1959, until his death in 1967, he was in Peking, employed as a gardener in the former imperial gardens of the city and was a striking national monument. Mao Tse-tung seems to have regarded him with a curious affection mixed with respect and looked after him with some benevolence. Thereafter he was forgotten by the human race until Bernardo Bertolucci brought to our screens the tragical history of this curious 'Last Emperor'.

In the defeat of Japan lay some of the seeds of the Cold War in Asia. Nowhere is this more evident than in the controversies surrounding the possession and use of the atomic bomb. The horrific consequences of the atomic explosions on the civilian populations of Hiroshima and Nagasaki

---

* Pu-Yi, *From Emperor to Citizen: the Autobiography of Aisin-Gioro Pu-Yi,* Foreign Language Press, Peking, 1965 (OUP, 1987).
† ibid.

may have killed fewer people than conventional bombs had done but nevertheless created an entirely new arms race and balance of terror. At the same time, but covertly, the efforts made by the United States, Britain, China and the Soviet Union to acquire what the Japanese had learned from its practice of biological warfare and human experimentation undoubtedly contributed to the poisoning of relations between the 'Great Powers' (a phrase rather out of fashion after 1945) in the post-war era. There were other ways, too, in which the very collapse of Japan hastened the breakdown of the wartime Alliance.

It is abundantly clear that the Japanese themselves often took a more important part in this than is generally appreciated. Late in the war, Japanese administrators in Indonesia, Indo-China, Burma and elsewhere helped to nurture militant nationalist movements which often had a communist taint. With the defeat of Japan in prospect, the Japanese hoped that they could produce conditions which would poison the European imperial administrations about to return. At some time in the future, so these Japanese dreamt, their actions might create favourable opportunities for Japan to rise again and lead independent Asian nations in a crusade for a second Greater East Asia Co-Prosperity Sphere. These were not merely spoiling operations. They were consistent with the sense of guardianship that so many Japanese truly believed they would exercise towards their Asian brethren. In the end, Pan-Asianism failed to have the impact its adherents devoutly wished. It was vitiated not by the efforts of the Allied Powers but rather by the nationalist passions unloosed during the war within each of the countries occupied by the Japanese. This is scarcely to be wondered at: European, South American and more recently African and Arabic regional solidarity have foundered upon the same rock.

Individual Japanese took other employment which had a subsequent bearing on the development of the Cold War in Asia. Many took positions as valued military advisers to the contending forces in the Chinese Civil War, chiefly on the side of the Kuomintang. Others, particularly former Intelligence officers, helped General MacArthur and his Occupationaires to fathom the complex military and political conditions of areas such as Manchuria and Korea which had lain under the exclusive control of Japan, or adjacent areas under communist control which had been more closely and systematically observed for many years by the Japanese than by the Western Powers. The Japanese Research Division, established under the wing of Military Intelligence within MacArthur's Far East Command, commissioned former Japanese military and naval officers to prepare nearly two hundred monographs on their observations and experiences for information and guidance. With time, it was discovered that many of these monographs were unreliable. Intensive research was conducted to make them more accurate and comprehensive: the unit, having accomplished its work, was disbanded only in 1960. Meanwhile, as late as the early fifties, Japanese airmen were flying covert reconnaissance missions over North Korea, North China, Manchuria and as far away as the Soviet Union. Japanese minesweepers secretly helped to clear the way for United Nations landings on the North Korean coasts: their availability and undoubted familiarity with these waters outweighed the risk of political repercussions. Japanese factories were used to repair damaged American tanks sent back into action in Korea. All of these instances suggest that at least some Japanese know-how was used with effect by the Americans and Japanese preconceptions gained during the years of Total War slowly percolated into the American military establishment in Japan during the years which followed the termination of hostilities. Although there are indications that the Soviets were no less eager to make use of their former enemies, it would appear that the exclusion of the Soviet Union from the occupation of Hokkaido, or indeed from the administration of any Japanese territory not overrun by Red Army troops, was of more consequence in the refrigeration of politics in East Asia (and in the national salvation of post-war Japan).

Power was everywhere passing away from those who had held it, and a new world was being created. It was the same in those parts of Asia which were, at least formally, on the victors' side. In India the negotiations were beginning which resulted in its complete emancipation within two years.

The war was at an end, and no further attempt will be made to trace the history of the countries, or to examine the effects of the rewards and penalties which they incurred. It is arbitrary to mark a divide anywhere in history, and the new age in Asia which began in 1945 is really the pendant of Asia at war, and is inseparably connected with that. It would take decades to work out the consequences of the great struggle. But the history of the world must be chopped into comprehensible lengths. For the purpose of this book the dropping of the bomb is the terminus.

By dropping the atom bomb the British and Americans had done much more than put an end to the war with Japan. They had put an end to a chapter of human history, and had transformed the nature of war. In the future neither governments nor people would enter on a war as lightly as the Japanese had done. The interest of the historian lies in the question of what induced the British and Americans to take the responsibility of dropping it.

Why did the two great Allies, who had it in their power to terminate the war by simply notifying Japan of the terrible effectiveness of the new weapon which had come into their hands, go to the lengths of actually dropping it? Why did they not content themselves with one bomb, but in a matter of hours, and without waiting to see the consequences of Hiroshima, drop the second bomb on Nagasaki?

The answer to these questions is, and is likely to remain, the greatest single matter of controversy of the war. The documents do not clarify the reasons. Churchill, for instance, is hardly enlightening. In his memoirs, he says, quite simply:

> The historic fact remained, and must be judged in the after time, that the decision whether or not to use the atomic bomb to compel the surrender of Japan was never even an issue. There was unanimous, automatic, unquestioning agreement around our [Council] table.

The Allies were nearly as well aware as Japan of the desperation of the Japanese.

American cryptographers had continued to listen in on exchanges of information between the Japanese Government, its outposts, and its agents and diplomats abroad. The Americans, who had been quick to appreciate the fact that they were overwhelmed by the sheer quantity of Intelligence they had been receiving from deciphered Japanese Purple code transmissions since 1940, had taken steps to put this information into an appropriate context shortly after the lessons of Pearl Harbor had been studied. Thereafter, daily summaries were prepared from these exchanges, known as Magic. These were remarkable in their clarity of analysis and were valued by those privileged enough to receive them.

Magic circulated among the highest echelons of Allied policymakers and field commanders. In contrast with the British Ultra code-breaking operation, the Magic Summaries, prepared by the Special Branch of the U S Army's Military Intelligence Branch, were circulated with background notes and a sophisticated commentary on the strategical implications of the information contained within the intercepted Japanese code transmissions. As time passed, other agencies, British as well as American, had fed Special Branch with additional information that became interwoven into the summaries. Now, as the war was drawing to a close, Magic took on a new significance. The horror of the B29 raids was unmistakable. The upheaval in Europe made its mark, and the disintegration of Germany took place in full view of the Japanese. Soviet interference with Japanese diplomatic pouches now seemed dangerous, not simply irksome. The Japanese said farewell to Germany and stood alone against the might of the western democracies. Soviet reinforcements sped to the East: the Japanese watched them go. Reports came through from Berne on talks with Allen Dulles of the prospects for peace negotiations. Other transmissions between Stockholm and Tokyo expressed the same desire for peace. The evacuation of Japanese families from China began in earnest. Food shortages grew worse. Fuel was unobtainable. There were strikes at currency printing plants in Shanghai. Civil unrest grew in North China and Inner Mongolia. The despondency of Tokyo and of Japanese diplomats and espionage agents abroad became increasingly clear and rapidly translated into straightforward defeatism. The reports filed from Tokyo left the recipients in no doubt about the frantic efforts of the Japanese to seek an early peace. There was no determination to fight the war to the last Japanese. On the contrary, the importance which the Japanese attached to the good offices of the Soviet Union was unmistakable. As the summer of 1945 drew on, the Japanese missions in foreign countries gradually closed down, and their agents, one by one, twinkled out like little stars. Reading the Magic Summaries today is a strangely moving experience, for together with our relief at the imminent termination of hostilities, it involves us in a strong sense of tragedy as well. The Summaries continued throughout the days and the weeks that followed Hiroshima, the Soviet invasion of Manchuria and Korea, Nagasaki, the death of Bose, the disintegration of Ba Maw's Government, the end of the Nanking Government, the possible abdication of Hirohito, exchanges on the treatment of Wainwright, and on to the end of radio communications in early November 1945, a full two months after the Japanese surrender. The Summaries, trusted by those fortunate few who read them day by day, must have given their readers much pause for thought. And through it all the question persists: Why the Bomb? Why twice?

In Japanese prisoner-of-war and civilian internment camps they had answers to those questions. So did those who worked in the secret chambers of Anglo-American technical Intelligence. There were reports of a Japanese atomic bomb, and there was an abundance of information about the mad, super-scientific world of Japanese chemical and biological warfare.

Orders had already been issued instructing the prison camp commanders to annihilate all prisoners in certain eventualities. Many of the prisoners had seen the elaborate preparations that had been made. Some were told by horror-struck guards or outside Intelligence agents. The orders themselves survived and were introduced in evidence at post-war trials of Japanese war criminals. The Allied Powers prepared plans to take the camps by storm. The Bomb, it is said, saved the lives of these prisoners. But it is more accurate to suggest that luck, the Emperor's broadcast, and the arrival of Allied relief teams at a time when prison camp guards were still in a state of shock at the end of the war, all played contributory parts. The peaceful liberation of the camps, in scenes repeated all over East Asia, resulted from the fact that The War Had Ended. It is quite illogical to suppose that the lives of these hostages to fortune were saved through any fine appreciation by the Japanese authorities that, a fortnight ago, their barbarous enemies had compounded the offences perpetrated by the B29 incendiary raids and had rejoiced in two further massacres of hundreds of thousands of innocent Japanese noncombatants in contravention of every recognized conventional law of war or principle of humanity.

The Japanese also possessed their own weapons of mass destruction, and they were not averse to using them where it seemed profitable to do so. Japanese employment of chemical and biological warfare (and Japanese research involving the vivisection of thousands of prisoners of war in CBW experiments) has become a matter of great public concern in Japan today. Western text-books have been mute on the issue, doubtless accepting British and American official denials of accusations dismissed as blatant and groundless communist propaganda in the late 1940s and early 1950s. More than forty years after the end of hostilities, however, fresh documentary evidence from British and American official sources, amounting to thousands of pages concerning this highly sensitive area, has come to light. Disclosure of this information has been somewhat piecemeal until recently, but those examining the totality of what is now known on the subject are bound to question the probity and integrity of their wartime Governments to a degree matched only by the controversy surrounding the use of the atomic bomb on Hiroshima and Nagasaki.

Briefly, the story of Japanese biological warfare implicates more than half the persons tried by the International Military Tribunal for the Far East, and more than 5,000 others who worked on the BW programme in some capacity. It involved a genuine conspiracy of silence that began soon after the Japanese occupation of Manchuria and spread its tentacles throughout all Japanese occupied territories during the Greater East Asian War. Thousands of people were butchered in the name of science and for the sake of war technology in experiments conducted by a secret network of research establishments. The first of these was established in 1932 in Manchuria, where others followed. A detachment spirited off victims for experimentation on the outskirts of Nanking in 1937. That detachment became a major research institute in its own right. University medical faculties on the Japanese mainland were headhunted for the brightest and

LUZON inset map:

Baguio (4)
Bayambang
Cabanatuan
Manila (31)
Pasay
Mutinlupa
Tagavtav
Tayabas
Los Baños
Lipa
Batangas
Tarlac
O'Donnell
Clark Field
BATAAN
Limaye
Corregidor
Ft Hughes
Ft Drum
Nasugbu

100km
50 miles

NEW IRELAND
Kavieng

NEW BRITAIN
Bita Paka
Kokupo, Rabaul

NEW GUINEA
(4)
Windehsi
Manokwari
Wiringg

Haroekoe
Ambon

DILL
TIMOR
Alamboe
Oespa Besar
Maumere
Ampenan
Kesilur
Tegalsanggar
Banjoewangi (4)
Blambangan
Malang
Makoronem
Pare Pare
Kapang
Makassar

Menado

POSO

CELEBES

Balikpapan

BORNEO

Jesselton

Sandakan

PALAWAN
Puert
Princessa

Cuyo I
Manamoc I.
Iloilo City
Cebu City
Bacolod
Zamboanga

MINDANAO
Tagbilaran
Lasang
Davao
Samal I.
Matina
Sasa
Malabalay
Tacloban
LEYTE

PHILIPPINE ISLANDS

LUZON
Baguio
Manila
Paracale
Corregidor

South China Sea

THAILAND (SIAM)
Sukhotai
Missoth
Savannaket
Hindat
Ubon
Bawa Sane
3 Pagodas Pass
Sor. Naung Lu
Tha Thonza, Tuang
Bangkok
Ban Pong
Saigon
Cholon
Mytho
Battambang
CAMBODIA
Phnom Penh.
Thanbyuzayat
Moulmein
Ye
Zai Yok
Tavoy
Rataburi
Prochaburi
Mergui
Ross I.
BURMA
RAILWAY

Victoria Point

Songkla
Yala
Jitra
AlorStar
Penang
Taiping
Ipoh
Koetatjane
Belewan
Galang
Medan
Tandjong Balai
Port Swettenham
Serenban
Malacca
Muar
Sikarakara
Kebondoerian
Rantauparapat
Pakoe
Pakanbang
Padang

Kuala Kangsar
Kuala Lumpur (5)
Endau
MALAYA
Kota Bharu
Trang

Singapore (30)
Bintan Is.

Bangkal Pinang

Kuching
Pontin

Djambi
Loeboekrama
Talang Semot
Palembang

Djakarta (8)
(Batavia)
Serang
Soerakaboem
Tandjong Priok
Cheribon
Bandung (1)
Kartus
TjimaPoerwokert
Poerwokerto
Ambarawa
Mageland
Moethan
Djogjakarta
Banteu
Soerang
Vredenburg
Surabaya (4)
Pamekssan
Pamekssan

JAVA

500 km
300 miles

Muar
Ayer Hitam
Batu Pahat
Kluang
Kota Tinggi
Johore Bahru
Singapore (30)

500 km
300 miles

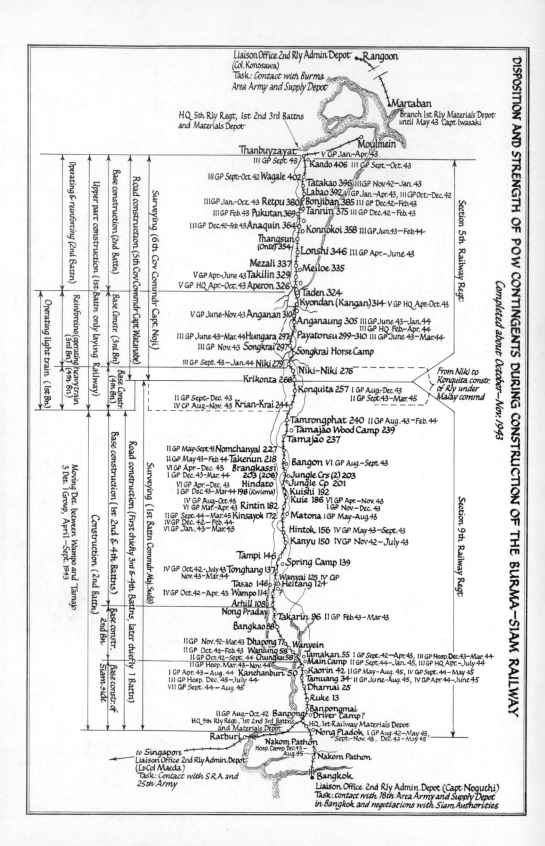

DISPOSITION AND STRENGTH OF POW CONTINGENTS DURING CONSTRUCTION OF THE BURMA–SIAM RAILWAY

Completed about October–Nov. 1943

Liaison Office 2nd Rly Admin Depot • Rangoon
(Col. Konosawa)
Task: Contact with Burma
Area Army and Supply Depot

Martaban
Branch 1st Rly Materials Depot
until May 43 Capt Iwasaki

HQ 5th Rly Regt, 1st 2nd 3rd Battns • Moulmein
and Materials Depot

Thanbuyzayat   V GP Jan.–Apr. 43
III GP Sept 43   Kando 406   III GP Sept.–Oct. 43
III GP Sept.–Oct. 42 Wagale 402
                     Tatakao 396 III GP Nov. 42–Jan. 43
                     Labao 392 V GP Jan.–Apr. 43, III GP Oct.–Dec. 42
III GP Jan.–Oct. 43 Retpu 380   Bonjiban 385 III GP Dec. 42–Feb. 43
III GP Feb. 43 Pukutan 369   Tannin 375 III GP Dec. 42–Feb. 43
III GP Dec. 42–Feb. 43 Anaquin 364   to Konnokoi 358 III GP Jun. 43–Feb. 44
Thangsun   Lonshi 346 III GP Apr.–June 43
(Onte) 354
Mezali 337   Meiloe 335
V GP Apr.–June 43 Takilin 329
V GP HQ Apr.–Oct. 43 Aperon 326
                Taden 324
                Kyondan (Kangan) 314 V GP HQ Apr.–Oct. 43
V GP June–Nov. 43 Anganan 310
                Anganaung 305 III GP June 43–Jan. 44
                Payatonsu 299–310 III GP HQ Feb.–Apr. 44
                                   III GP June 43–Mar. 44
III GP June 43–Mar. 44 Hungara 297½
III GP Nov. 43 Songkrai 297½   Songkrai Horse Camp
III GP Sept. 43–Jan. 44 Niki 279
                Niki–Niki 276
Krikonta 268   From Niki to
                Konquita 257 I GP Aug.–Dec. 43   Konquita constr.
II GP Sept.–Dec. 43   II GP Sept. 43–Mar. 45   of Rly under
IV CP Aug.–Nov. 43 Krian–Krai 244   Malay commd

                Tamrongphat 240 II GP Aug. 43–Feb. 44
                Tamajão Wood Camp 239
                Tamajão 237
II GP May–Sept. 43 Nomchanyal 227
II GP May 43–Feb. 44 Takenun 218
VI GP Apr.–Dec. 43 Brangkassi
I GP Dec. 43–Mar. 44   203 (208)   Jungle Crs (2) 203
VI GP Apr.–Dec. 43 Hindato   Jungle Cp 201
I GP Dec. 43–Mar 44 198 (Kwiema) Kuishi 192
IV GP Aug.–Oct. 43   Kuie 186 VI GP Apr.–Nov. 43
VI GP Mar.–Apr. 43 Rintin 182   I GP Nov.–Dec. 43
II GP Sept. 44–Mar. 45 Kinsayok 172 Matona I GP May–Aug. 43
II GP Dec. 43–Feb. 44
VI GP Jan. 43–Mar. 43   Hintok 156 IV GP May 43–Sept. 43
                Kanyu 150 IV GP Nov. 42–July 43
Tampi 146
                Spring Camp 139
IV GP Oct. 42–July 43 Tonghang 137
Nov. 43–Mar. 44   Wanyai 125 IV GP
Tasao 146   Heitang 124
IV GP Oct. 42–Apr. 43 Wampo 114
Arhill 108
Nong Praday   Takarin 96 II GP Feb. 43–Mar. 43
Bangkao 88
II GP Nov. 42–Mar. 43 Dhapong 77 Wanyein
II GP Oct. 42–Feb. 43 Wanlung 58   Tamakan 55 I GP Sept. 42–Apr. 43, III GP Hosp. Dec. 43–Mar. 44
II GP Oct. 42–Sept. 44 Chungkai 58 Main Camp II GP Sept. 44–Jan. 45, III GP HQ Apr.–July 44
II GP Hosp. Mar. 43–Nov. 44   50
I GP Apr. 43–Aug. 44 Kanchanburi 50   Kaorin 42 II GP May–Aug. 45, IV GP Sept. 44–May 45
III GP Hosp. Dec. 43–July 44   Tamuang 34 II GP June–Aug. 45, IV GP Apr. 44–June 45
VII GP Sept. 44–Aug. 45   Dharnai 25
                Ruke 13
                Banpongmai
II GP Aug.–Oct. 42 Banpong   Driver Camp?
HQ 9th Rly Regt, 1st 2nd 3rd Battns   HQ 1st Railway Materials Depot
and Materials Depot   Nong Pladok I GP Aug. 42–May 43,
Ratburi   Sept.–Nov. 43, Dec. 43–May 45
        Nakom Pathon
to Singapore   Hosp. Camp Dec. 43–
Liaison Office 2nd Rly Admin. Depot   Aug. 45   Nakom Pathon
(Lt Col. Maeda)
Task: Contact with S.R.A. and   Bangkok
25th Army   Liaison Office 2nd Rly Admin. Depot (Capt Noguchi)
                Task: contact with 18th Area Army and Supply Depot
                in Bangkok and negotiations with Siam Authorities

Section 5th Railway Regt
Section 9th Railway Regt

Operating & reinforcing (2nd Battn)
Upper part construction (1st Battn)
Road construction (5th Gov Commndr Capt Watanabe)
Surveying (6th Gov Commndr Capt. Noji)
Operating (light train) (1st Bn.)
Reinforcing (operating heavy train 3rd Bn.) (4th Bn.)
Base construction (2nd Battn)
Base Constr. (3rd Bn)
Base Constr. (4th Bn.)
Road construction (First chiefly 3rd & 4th Battns, later chiefly Suidc)
Surveying (1st Battn Commndr Maj. Suidc)
Base construction (1st 2nd & 4th Battns)
Construction (2nd Battn)
Moving Det. between Wampo and Tamajo
3 Det. 1 Group, April–Sept. 1943
Base constr. 2nd Bn
Base constr. of Siam-side
Base constr (Siam side 1 Battn)

best biochemists and physiologists the Japanese Army could buy or conscript, and university medical laboratories in Tokyo, Osaka, Kyoto and a number of other places were utilized in the research and experimentation. Delivery systems were refined, vast quantities of bacteria were produced. Thousands of cultivators grew so much bacteria that at full capacity the monthly output of germ-laden froth could be measured in tonnes.

Field trials of Army biological munitions were conducted, first in Manchuria and then in China Proper. Attacks were made at Ningpo in 1940, at Changteh in 1941, in the Chekiang offensive of 1942 (in the revenge attacks that followed the Doolittle raid), and elsewhere. Early (and as it happens exceptionally accurate) Chinese medical and Intelligence reports were brought to the personal attention of President Roosevelt and Prime Minister Churchill: their experts found them unconvincing. Later the mad Japanese medical scientists operated in Burma, Malaya, French Indo-China, Thailand, the Netherlands East Indies and New Guinea. They applied their skills at Nomonhan against the Russians and sent saboteurs across the Soviet Union itself in a succession of secret missions carried out over a number of years, allegedly in response to Russian biological warfare attacks carried out against the Japanese in China and Manchuria. A ship carrying a biological warfare assault team was dispatched to Saipan to slow down the American advance: it was sunk *en route* by an American submarine. Funds amounting to a ten million yen annual budget were allocated for offensive BW research as the B29 raids on Japan intensified. The money, as always, was channelled through the Kwantung Army. Production facilities increased more or less continuously: three million rats were to be ready for use by September 1945; storage of the food to sustain them required a four-storey building. A proposal to employ BW following the defeat of Japanese forces on Iwojima was only turned down on the grounds that it would have no effect on the outcome of the Pacific War. *

Allied prosecutors from half a dozen countries affected by the issue remained silent at the Tokyo War Crimes Trial about what they knew. The scientists and technicians who were involved in these, the most ghastly atrocities of the Eastern War, were granted immunity from prosecution by General MacArthur with the blessing of the United States Government, with at least the tacit consent if not complicity of the British Government and the acquiescence of the Chinese. The British and Americans pooled what they knew. This was a standing measure of their technical collaboration, but there were practical benefits to both sides. Porton

* D. Wallace and P. Williams, *Unit 731: Secret of Secrets*, Hodder & Stoughton, London, 1989.

Down's scientists were regarded as a cut above their American counterparts; the Americans had systematically assembled a vast amount of information from their Intelligence during the latter stages of the war and
during their early days in Japan. Meanwhile, in Singapore, the Central
Pathology Laboratory of Lord Mountbatten's forces had occupied the
only Japanese BW laboratory now known to have remained operational
following the surrender of Japan: records concerning what happened next
are unavailable. The Chinese, whose own knowledge about the Japanese
use of BW was quite extensive (as appears not only from the quality of
their wartime reports but also from information which they shared with
Allied prosecutors on the eve of the Tokyo Trial), must have lived in hope
of gaining some kind of a quid pro quo for their silence during the Court
proceedings. The Russian authorities, who sought to raise the matter at
Tokyo, allowed themselves to be silenced. The French and the Dutch
Governments, on whose territories in Indo-China and the East Indies
human experimentation also took place, were kept in the dark by the British
and Americans but may have learned of what had happened by other means.
    What seems quite incredible is that the cover-up conspiracy – for it is
by no means a demonological exaggeration to speak of it as a conspiracy
– was maintained throughout the three years which elapsed between the
Japanese defeat and the conclusion of the Tokyo Trial and that, apart
from mischief-making communist mudslinging, this conspiracy was
sustained for so long afterwards. The conspiracy extended into the post-
war period of Anglo-American weapons research, surfaced again during
the Korean War, and is rumoured to have carried on beyond. Much more
research needs to be done to complete our understanding of this astonishing story, but what is already known makes chilling reading.
    The decision to use the atomic bomb to terminate the war involved no
fine calculations, however, and it seems to have been taken without any
special regard for the dangers of a last-minute BW offensive. Japan
virtually had conceded defeat at the end of July, and had put out peace
feelers, first asking the Russians to act as mediators, and, on finding them
unobliging, had approached the Swedish Government. Anyone with experience of diplomacy could perceive that the upshot, after a few days'
natural hesitation, must be the surrender so much desired. In the days of
decision during the Potsdam Conference anything like a sustained
Japanese defence, from strong defensive positions, had clearly become
impossible. By ending the war in a ghastly and fearful massacre, the
British and Americans cast over their triumph a dark shadow, and one
which may, as is the way in great historical transactions, return to haunt
the doers in the future.

After the bomb had been exploded, Russian policy became, for the time being, very conciliatory. It was in this period that Truman announced his recent decision that the Occupation of Japan should fall exclusively to the Americans. The details of the Occupation of Germany had been discussed inexhaustibly, and continued to be a major issue among the Allies: by contrast, the Occupation of Japan seemed to have been arranged at very short notice, and by the United States alone. Great Britain made no demur at the American decision. Russia limited its protests to a proposal that the surrender on the battleship, the *Missouri*, should have its counterpart on Hokkaido with a ceremony of the surrender of the Kwantung Army to Russia. This was rejected. Probably the existence of the bomb frustrated Russian plans for insisting on a joint occupation of Japan, and the consequences of this were incalculable. It avoided endless intrigue, and conflict of puppet parties; probably it saved Japan from a great deal of hardship and made the return to normal life in Japan much quicker. By taking out Japan as a major question of dispute, it probably made the relations of Russia and the United States by that much easier to handle. It may even have kept them from war. It was perhaps the only good thing which came out of the dropping of the bomb.

The fateful decision to drop the bomb was made within a matter of days. Most of the men who were responsible for Japan's policy had not known a fortnight before that the atom bomb was in existence. Even General MacArthur, who, more than any other man, was responsible for the overthrow of Japan, was given the information only a very brief time before the bomb was due. He had said that he deplored it, but he had no time to make his protest effective. Admiral William D. Leahy, the Chief of Staff of the President, was consulted in advance and said, bluntly, that he thought that the use of the bomb was brutal, and served no rational end. It is possible that President Truman, whose subsequent decisions about the bomb were on the whole sober and responsible as, for example, during the later Korean War, may have acted in these days very much in the dark; and it is at least charitable to suppose that he did so. Churchill remarked that, as soon as the news of successful tests arrived, the President seemed to be determined to use it. Churchill judged it useless to press for discussion. All these statesmen suddenly found the bomb at their disposal, and they had no reasonable opportunity to think out the implications of atomic warfare, nor, it seemed, was the phenomenon of fall-out clear in their minds. The real essential difference between an atom bomb and a larger conventional weapon had not been grasped. Most Americans supposed, like Stalin, that it was simply a bigger and more lethal weapon. The discovery of atomic power required that men of exceptional vision and judgement should have been in power, who could see the consequences of the action they took then upon the politics of the next half century or longer. Those men were hardly likely to have been thrown up by the circumstances of directing the war.

There is a misperception, finally, that commonly surrounds Japan's 'unconditional surrender', and it serves no purpose today to ignore it. The fact is that the Japanese surrender was *not* unconditional (although at the time it was regarded as such by most Japanese themselves). Under the terms of the Potsdam Declaration, the Imperial Rescript ending the war, the Instrument of Surrender, etc., the Japanese *armed forces* surrendered unconditionally. But the Japanese Government retained its *civil* powers. Indeed, under the terms of the surrender, the Japanese Government was obliged to exert those powers in order to ensure compliance with the terms of the Potsdam Declaration. Accordingly, many of the steps taken by General Douglas MacArthur and his forces to impose their will upon the civil Government of Japan amounted to a usurpation of authority which breached the terms of the surrender. In no places were this more evident than in the establishment of the International Military Tribunal for the Far East and in the great purges and blacklists imposed upon the Japanese by MacArthurian *Diktat*. In short, the differences between 210,288 individual Allied Occupation of Germany and that of Japan deserve attention: the former occurred as a result of the Allied conquest of German territory and its sub-division by the occupying Powers. But the war against Japan ended as a result of a contract between the two sides, and while the Japanese civil power was clearly in no position to contest the issue, the fact remains that the Occupationaires grossly exceeded the terms of that contract. American defence attorneys challenged the International Military Tribunal on this basis (and on other grounds), and they were ruled out of order. Nevertheless, the truth of the matter is perfectly clear and is a subject of some controversy in Japan in our own day. Unfortunately, it has the effect of diminishing still further the gulf which was once believed to exist between the capricious and arrogant abuse of power by the Japanese armed forces in Occupied East Asia and the self-righteous morality of the Allied Powers who brought them down.

Epilogue

IT may have been useful to tell the facts of this conflict. There can seldom have been fought a war which engaged so much of the attention of so many Powers, the details of which have so rapidly been allowed to become vague. Within a generation the dramatic events of Japan's surrender, the particulars of the relations between Japan and China, the great struggle at Imphal, the island-hopping across the Pacific by the United States, the great naval battles, have all begun to be touched by the waters of Lethe. Even Pearl Harbor, which has naturally entered into the folklore of the USA, today appears far-off, and what happened there is only vaguely understood.

The Eastern War was inevitably overshadowed by Hitler's War in Europe. It was interdependent with it, and its events criss-crossed with those of the western conflict. But, in retrospect, they have seemed to some to assume a subordinate part. The events of the European War stand out clearly; they are remembered sharply; the events of the war in the East are, by contrast, hazy in the public memory, and are heaped together in a certain confusion. Ask any young man born at or after the dropping of the bomb at Hiroshima, be he of Asian or European origin, to outline the events which led up to the fearsome drama, and you will be surprised to find what lacunae lie in his narrative.

And yet the events which had to be settled by arms, and by the atom bomb, were as great as the issues in Europe, the suffering was as widespread, the events spread over as many continents, involved more civilizations, and left as large a dent in the history of world culture. For this reason, it has seemed to be worthwhile seeking to protest a little at the progress of the waters sweeping away the recollection of those years – even if the waters are fundamentally healthful, doing the saving work of washing away the memories of brutality and the hatred of nations for one another, and other things which are best forgotten. The famous feats of endurance of the peoples, the daring projects of the national leaders, may, with justice, be offered up as alms to oblivion; yet no people can afford to neglect the history which has made them what they are.

The war, for all the damage it had done, was not, by the standards of past wars, a particularly long one. Three series of wars, which were needed to settle the opposition of deeply conflicting forces, and which turned upside down the affairs of all the participants, took somewhat longer. One was the Thirty Years War between Protestant and Catholic Europe: its historians are quick to point out that its protagonists and allegiances changed as it progressed through a succession of phases linked only by opportunism, cause and effect, rather than by a single national will. Another, the Peloponnesian Wars, which checked finally the Athenian attempt at imperialism, lasted nineteen years: it had the same elements of fundamentalist irrationality, hysteria and total commitment that we have traced throughout the conflict that subsumed East Asia and the Pacific. The wars which rose out of the French Revolution ran a course which ended at the Battle of Waterloo, and covered twenty-three years: like the Japanese war(s) of the twentieth century, they brought together unlikely coalitions of Allies, all with different aims and mutual mistrust, linked only in their abiding determination to rid the world of a peculiarly blood-thirsty Empire. The present war, from the time that the fighting commenced in earnest on the Asiatic mainland in 1931, and excluding the opening skirmishes between China, Korea and Japan, was over in fifteen years.

The War in the East can be addressed by many names. The Japanese wartime censor regarded it as 'The Greater East Asia War'. His successors in the (mainly American) Allied Occupation Forces banned that phrase and substituted 'The Pacific War'. Can it really be regarded as 'The Second World War in the Pacific', bearing in mind that the China Incident preceded the outbreak of the European War by two years and only ended with the Japanese surrender to the Allied Powers in 1945? Surely the Japanese experience of Total War really began with the Manchurian Incident in 1931, and what of the mental and physical resources expended on the inevitable clash over the preceding decades? The trend in Japan today is to call it 'The Fifteen-Year War', a somewhat unsatisfying and curiously anonymous sobriquet if ever there was one: it does not seem likely to find favour in the United States or in British countries. 'The Far East War' offends some people not only because it is Eurocentric in its geographical conception but because that conception involves an ineluctable sense of isolation and irrelevance. 'The War against Japan' is revealing but one-sided: the war also involved the positive aspirations of dozens of racial and national groups. In the end, we have to come to terms with the war's ambivalence, its complexity and, above all, its size. If it must be known and remembered in a single evocative phrase, let us simply call it 'The East Asian and Pacific Conflict'.

The great modern wars have reflected the deadly nature of modern armaments, and international efforts to control their spread and influence. The causes nevertheless have been weighty and complex. Economic issues contributed to the struggle but did not, perhaps, outweigh the conceits and misperceptions of individual men acting collectively. The issue of the strife in Asia settled a number of conflicts which, but for the war, might have dragged on for years, causing constant unrest, and keeping the region in continual uncertainty. It settled which of various trends were to continue, and which, among those which had seemed strong and flourishing a few years before, were either to stop abruptly or else to fade away.

The decision was sharpest for Japan. The attempt to maintain Japan's unnatural pre-eminence in East Asia, and to spread it over the lands to the south and west, had failed. Japan's Empire was dissolved. A relatively small country in relation to its dependencies and enemies (although larger than Britain, metropolitan France or Germany), its principal assets were the ardent will of its citizens and their regimentation. It had had the temerity to challenge three quarters of the world to come against it in arms; and had shaken the established order of the earth more than many had thought possible. Yet the war did not spring from a foolish intent by the Japanese to conquer the globe, to bring, as the ancient Japanese phrase has it, 'all the eight corners of the world under one roof'. The American Ambassador to Japan, Joseph Grew, distinguished Bostonian though he was, found illumination in comparing Japan to the Uncle Remus story of Brer Rabbit, who attacked a tar baby for spite, and other fatuous reasons, and then found himself stuck to it ever more thoroughly as he struggled to break free from his ill-advised entanglement. The image works well, and is worth remembering.

It is also important to bear in mind that the history of the 'East Asian and Pacific Conflict' is not a sequence of events between the Japanese attack on Pearl Harbor and the surrender aboard the battleship *Missouri* which can properly be isolated from the previous half-century of conflict on the Asiatic continent. The titanic and enduring contest between Russia and Japan for domination of North-East Asia changed the political map of the world early in the twentieth century as it did again in August 1945: the latter-day changes were not merely echoes but the extension of the former. The tug-of-war between the Japanese, local upstart bullies as they were, and the imperialists of faraway Europe, took place over the recumbent body of China. Japan emerged from that a monster, conscious of its feats of strength and daring, aware of past humiliations and foreign contempt, determined to establish an area of peace and security, governing by means of what it chose to name 'cooperation', hoping for what it called 'co-prosperity' in regions and markets that suited it. The

Manchurian Incident and the transformation of Manchukuo into a dependency of the Japanese Empire form an inseparable part of the Greater East Asian War and therefore of the 'East Asian and Pacific Conflict' as a whole: it was a hinge, a fulcrum around which turned the histories of China, Japan and the West.

The Japanese of that generation had passed through a strange phase of their national history. In the past, there had been little to single them out for particular reprobation. They were always very vigorous, usually artistic, often somewhat muddled intellectually, which was apparently due to the imprecision of their language. They were also perhaps outstanding for an exaggerated conformism, though they expressed this in an unusual manner by extending the pale of conformism to include those whose vision of the national future was grander, and who dared to call for radical change. Traditionally also the Japanese relaxed the tyranny of society over the older members of the community, and gave them a licence to do and say what they pleased. All of this gave colour to a land where the vigilance of thought police was well developed. And always, as with any generalization about an entire people, one is conscious at once of many eccentric members of the community for whom the general rule did not apply.

The main fact in the twentieth century is the acute military phase that the Japanese lived through. It was an aberration. It was not really traditional. It may be that Japanese society has a Samurai streak, and a prolonged feudal period had left it too ready to respond to the call of arms. Many of its ways of thought were military in origin. But, if one looks back on Japanese history, the Japanese do not appear to have been an unduly military people. At one period they were predominantly artists, and would not allow matters of soldierly concern to interfere with the artistic life. In the great Heian period, which is perhaps the outstanding example in history of a leisured class giving up all its time to artistic living, there was once a complaint that the imperial bodyguard could not be properly maintained. The soldiers could not ride horses: they constantly fell off them. The detailed history of the society of this time is full of anecdotes of the extreme lengths to which Japanese aestheticism would go. The men of the Heian period are strange ancestors of the Japanese who took Singapore.

The Japanese of recent generations were conditioned by the institutions of their society to offer themselves in the bid to establish a Japanese imperialism. These institutions, most of them borrowed from the West though given a peculiar slant in their development, are the monument of the Meiji Restoration. Gradually they induced in the mass of the people the willingness to support a more and more aggressive national policy. The institutions took on a life of their own. In the end, they carried the Japanese people into a great war, and brought down half a continent.

The prime evil of Japan was certainly the ascendancy of the military. This led, in time of war, to the Supreme Command conducting the war as a state secret from the civilian parts of the Japanese administration. Whatever else may be said of such a system, it proved to be most incompetent militarily. Thus Japanese militarism held within it the seeds of its own defeat. It was unable to organize Japanese society so that in modern warfare it could compete with the Powers which were organized to be more flexible.

The same militarism, as far as it was able to prevail in making Japanese foreign policy, was responsible for the basic error which brought about Japan's downfall. This was to found Japan's policy on fear of the outside world, and to meet this by seeking to spread a counter-fear of Japan. Because Japan was in a difficult position internationally, because it was vulnerable, because its economic position required that it should have unimpeded access to imports and a constantly growing market overseas for its exports, and because it feared that these might be interrupted by force by an unfriendly Power, it counted that prudence required it to be ever on its guard, to arm and show its teeth in a way that would fend off dangerous intentions in its rivals. There were Japanese voices which protested at such a policy, and pointed, rightly, to the inevitable end; but they were not attended to. The result was a long period of tension, culminating in a war in which Japan lost everything, a war which could not possibly have safeguarded the things which Japan had armed itself to save.

The contradictions of Japan's foreign policy are stated compendiously by the Foreign Ministry official, Kase Toshikazu, who played such a useful part as intermediary of the court circles in bringing the war to an end. 'For a poor country like Japan,' he said,

the construction of costly warships meant a crushing burden upon the national treasury. And yet we built a good number of them. We also maintained a vast Army and an ever expanding Air Force. In the end we became like the mammoth whose tusk, growing ever bigger, finally unbalanced its bodily structure. As everything went to support the huge tusks, very little was left to sustain the rest of the body. The mammoth finally became extinct.

Why did the mammoth arm itself with weapons such as ultimately to bring about its own destruction? Because it was apprehensive. In its desire to defend itself against external enemies the poor creature forgot the very fact that its tusks were its own mortal enemy! Why did Japan arm herself to the teeth? Because she was apprehensive. Why was she apprehensive? Because she had enemies. Why were there enemies? Because her aggressive policy excited suspicion in others. Rather than abandon the objectionable policy she augmented her armaments. But armaments are a relative affair. There is no end to an armament race.*

The men who served ruthless, imperialist Japan were not by nature particularly ruthless or imperialist. They bore no signs of predestination, and there was nothing about them which marked them as enemies of the human race. The Japanese generals, though superficially they might seem to conform to a rather brutal and disgusting pattern, were often men of singular eccentricity. In other circumstances, they might have appeared as rather engaging. Many of them had a vivid and vigorous interior life, and the most varied traits of personality. Some of them practised Japanese archery and fencing each day, not for athletic reasons but for the self-control which these disciplines induced, and for greater proficiency in the art of meditation. They were an interesting contrast to the British Army, much more emotional, much more given to adjusting their philosophy and their actions. The contrast between them and the commanders of the Anglo-Saxon forces was often richly comical. Rigid behaviour patterns in their native environment made them what they were and, uprooted from this environment, their behaviour was unpredictable. It could, of course, be terrible; occasionally, however, it was the reverse.

The behaviour of the Japanese soldiers, and their cult of non-surrender, may have seemed to those fighting them to mark them out as an especially desperate, unreformable species of military man. This, too, is only an example of the lengths to which institutions may go in marking their victims. Biologically similar young men, transported to another society and brought up under other institutions, turned out to be enthusiastic liberals or democrats, and found reprehensible the Japanese cult of military national aggrandizement and the pursuit of death.

The Japanese, in the last war, were shocked at finding a most rigid refusal to respond to the call of their country and race on the part of the *Nisei*, the children of the Japanese emigrants to America, who had most of them continued to marry with Japanese. In this they were much disappointed: they had counted on being able to convert this class, and if they had succeeded, would have disposed a valuable ally for their war-making. The Nisei had some reason to attend to their call, for the United States was less than generous in its treatment of them, and did not hide its suspicion. The deportation or preventive confinement of the large masses of Americans of Japanese origin, who had given no reason for doubting their loyalty, was one of the blots on wartime American government. But

*K. Toshikazu, *Eclipse of the Rising Sun*, op. cit.

the Nisei almost without exception, refused the appeal of their blood relations, and were almost fanatical in their devotion to the new institutions among which they had been brought up.

The Nisei show that there is no such thing as a militarist through and through, made such by his physical make-up, and a stranger to civilization because of the military activities of his ancestors.

Most significant of all, the Japanese, since their surrender, have undergone a thorough change of heart. In no country in the world is militarism so thoroughly reprobated. All Japan's energies are now concentrated on remaining a friendly civilian state. Possibly the very completeness of the emotional swing is suspicious. What is today so violently renounced may tomorrow be once more violently espoused. But all the signs are that the world has, as the result of the war, gained a new Japan.

At the end of the war an international tribunal was set up by the Allies in order to put on trial a representative group of those who had allegedly been responsible for crimes against peace and other war crimes. The Japanese had wished to reserve a trial of war prisoners to themselves as a condition of Japanese surrender, but that had been denied to them by the Allied Powers. At the major War Crimes Tribunal in Tokyo, twenty-five Japanese leaders were sentenced, seven of them to death, others to life imprisonment: among these were General Tōjō Hideki, the Prime Minister; General Koiso Kuniaki, his successor; the wily court chamberlain, Marquis Kido Kōichi, who played so large a part in bringing about Japan's surrender; Tōgō Shigenori, the Foreign Minister who had showed a most un-Japanese independence of judgement; and Hirota Kōki, another former Prime Minister. The conveners even proposed trying Prince Konoye Fumimaro, but he evaded arrest by poisoning himself. These doubtful proceedings went like a swath through all those who had been in any way prominent in Japanese politics of the period. The biographical footnotes of a book on Japanese history at this time make heavy reading because of the end of many of the characters. The major good that came out of these proceedings at Tokyo was that they are the most complete, exhaustive account of Japanese politics in the militarist period.

Other war crimes trials were held in Hong Kong, Singapore, Borneo and elsewhere in the recent Japanese Empire. Detainees were arraigned for cruelty towards local populations and prisoners of war, and over 900 were executed. Thoughts of these melancholy figures, and the deeds which in many cases preceded this toll of life, lead to the reflection that had the war had a different result, the subsequent years might have been the age of Japanese Imperialism. Asia has been spared that. The war, with all its horrors, had achieved this positive good. A reluctant admiration for

Japan's military feats must not block out the consciousness of the sinister shadow which for a time hung over the eastern world.

Search the record how one will, it is almost impossible to find anything good to say of the Japanese Empire. Its liquidation was an unqualified benefit to the world. In the years before the conflict, Japan had had its opportunity to develop its Empire in miniature – in Korea, in Formosa, and in the parts of China which it came to dominate – and in this exhibition of the Japanese spirit it failed to show many virtues. An empire, which by its definition is a political structure housing peoples of different cultures and languages, is different from the nation-state, which is the most approved political form in the twentieth century. Nations object to being included in an empire. Empires are out-of-fashion. But some empires are more tolerable than others. They may have qualities which actively catch the imagination of their people. In the case of a very few, their peoples will actually be willing to die in their defence, though instances of this have become increasingly rare. The classic case, in comparison with which other empires may be judged, was the Rome of antiquity. That Empire seems to have offered a wider life, richer opportunities, a larger destiny, than could be looked for within the confines of small states.

The Japanese Empire, if it is judged from its beginnings, was not at all likely to develop into one of these rarer structures. In its origin it was essentially primitive and of petty conception. It was put together by conquest, and its prime aim was to plunder the subjected peoples for the benefit of the Japanese. The Empire offered hardly anything to its citizens which led them to take pride in membership of it beyond a pride in being Asian. This should not be neglected. The Japanese made considerable play of Pan-Asianism. The contemporary writing is all about the joy of being Asian. It was the outstanding fact of the time. But it was not long before the contrast between Japanese idealism and Japanese practice took away this enthusiasm.

The Japanese system was founded on no great code of law. In its organization it embodied no exhilarating concepts such as have led men elsewhere into giving their loyalty, even if divided – concepts such as liberty, equality and fraternity; the career open to talents; the greatest good of the greatest number or restraint of the evil of exploitation. The Japanese Empire signified no large cult of reason, a defective vision, few distinctive habits of thought or behaviour, a strange corpus of books by which to set the tone of people's thought, a pattern of individual behaviour which gave few people a liberating vision. It was the starting place of no system of philosophy which was likely to appeal to men of all races and different cultures: in other words, it lacked the universalist appeal. The most to which it invited its citizens was to the enjoyment of Japanese culture, and there the difficulty was that, though this culture is not inferior, it is one which most Asians find uncongenial and it is at best provincial and not a universal civilization. In particular, the Japanese language was unsuited as a medium of communication for holding the political machinery together. It seemed scarcely imaginable that anyone talked Japanese as a form of intellectual pleasure, as the subjects of the French Empire often spoke French: the language was thought to be muzzy and imprecise.

Japanese culture is especially strong in the inculcation of the correct attitudes for aesthetic appreciation: but aesthetics has never been strong enough to hold an empire together. Besides, this quality of mind was often considered out-of-date or parochial in Japan itself.

Calling on the people of its Empire to share Japanese culture was summoning them to a Barmecide feast. Responding to the call, the Chinese felt themselves (not for the first or last time) sitting with more primitive people than themselves. They found that Japanese culture was a tiresome and constricting limitation on their minds.

A peculiarly evil feature of the system was that it would endure only as long as Japanese military power lasted: it was sustained by that and by that alone. It invited head-on collision with all the emerging forces of Asia, and if it had not been destroyed in war, it would sooner or later have led to bloody wars of liberation.

When the war was over, when Japan had given up the pretence at founding a new political order, and gave free play to its natural talents, the Japanese surprised the world, and themselves, by solving their problems by simple hard work, and without any use of force or creation of grandiose political structures. With western help (and spared most of the expense of defence), they recovered economically in the minimum of time; they rapidly became a beacon-light in Asia; they proved – as to be fair they had always promised – that an Asian people could save itself by its own exertions. And all this without even the dream of empire. Energy, skill in planning, imagination in enterprise, ability in the application of techniques to the economic processes proved enough to get Japan over all its obstacles; and Japan has discovered the political advantages in having a foreign policy which is audacious by reason of its modesty. Socially, too, the war and its aftermath helped to emancipate many underprivileged elements in Japanese society. One thinks of the story of a young naval officer – now a distinguished professor of economics but then a Kamikaze pilot awaiting his turn to die – who sat in his bath, facing the setting sun, when news was brought to him of the surrender of Japan. As he arose, his batman reached forward to dry his back. The young officer, his eyes blazing with intensity turned on him and said, 'The war is over: don't you ever wash another man's back again.' It was the end of an era.

The war – or more precisely Japan – also precipitated everywhere the demise of western power in Asia. The Western Powers withdrew from China. The Treaty Port system was at an end: also the rights of extra-territoriality. Within two years Britain withdrew from India. This was a change which plainly doomed the French Empire in Indo-China, and the Dutch in Indonesia. Within ten years, they had each of them passed away. They did not go voluntarily, or reluctantly, as did the British Empire in India; they attempted to stay, and they were willing to go to war against the national parties which rose up to extrude them. But they were too weak to prevail. Moreover they were too much concerned with their problems in Europe to be able to give the war their whole-hearted attention.

The Japanese Empire having been destroyed and the Western empires put down, a power vacuum existed which only the nationalist organizations could fill. These were left to organize most of Asia in the pattern they desired. The West, including the United States, tried to influence them in one way or another, using their economic power to make their will effective, and in the case of Britain and the United States their armaments when the situation did not respond to economic manipulation. By indirect means they hoped to prevail as effectively as in the days when they sat with political power in Delhi and in the eastern capitals. This was the phase of neo-colonialism, and the emancipated countries of Asia have been on their guard against it and have sought to render themselves really free even at the expense of neighbouring territories.

China, released from the incubus of an Imperial Japan, has been free to develop as the inward forces in the country directed. Within four years of the ending of the war China became communist. The excessive corruption, the paralysis of will and venal incompetence of the later years of the Kuomintang were increased by its unnatural isolation from the rest of the country. Once this was removed its downfall was inevitable.

The prolonged agony which had been suffered by the Chinese people as the twentieth century wore on, opened the way to a violent remedy. The chief leaders of the Kuomintang escaped the vengeance of the opposing party by retiring, with vast fortunes, to the island of Formosa whence they kept up, under an American umbrella, a somewhat ludicrous show of still exercising an influence in world affairs. In the first flood of revenge, many of the landlords, who had lived for so long in the sun of prosperity in China, were violently put down, with sufferings as cruel as any which they had, by past insensibility and negligence, occasioned among the poor. Later, 're-education' was the term used to describe the method by which the bourgeoisie were broken in. The mass of the people were liberated into a new life of undreamed-of sufficiency in living standards and educational opportunity: as against this, freedom for the individual – of thought or self-direction – was largely absent. In foreign relations, communist China's extreme isolationism, and the mutual suspicions between it and the United States, have kept the world on edge, but from time to time have shown signs of relaxing. There is no doubt of the greatly recovered prestige of China since the war or its eventual re-emergence as a major Power in Asia.

What had been the effects in India? Great though the upheaval had been in India's domestic life, the war affected the pace of the development of its history, and accelerated the divorce of India and Britain: it did not necessarily give events an essentially new turn. Many who looked with the eye of history on India from 1930 onwards foresaw that the end of the British Raj was approaching. Others looked forward to India's elevation to full status as a self-governing Dominion at some faraway, indeterminate time. Even perceptive young revolutionaries elsewhere in the British Empire, like Jomo Kenyatta in East Africa, scarcely dreamt that they would ever see the independence of India within their lifetimes, much less the decolonization of Africa and beyond. They, at least, credit Japan with having shown the fragility of far-flung imperial bonds – and with having been the direct cause of the disintegration of the British, Dutch, French and Portuguese Empires east of Suez.

Yet in one fateful respect the war gave an unexpected twist to the long process of the freedom struggle by the Indian Congress. In the circumstances of wartime politics, a sudden and accelerated growth took place in the Moslem League. It had been provoked by the Congress success; it was already apparent before the war; but the war acted like a hot-house in compressing into a few years the development which might otherwise have been spread over decades. The Moslem League, which increased in strength so radically, was emboldened to press for the creation of the Moslem state of Pakistan.

After the Greater East Asia War, that state came into being and eventually led to the creation of a second independent nation, Bangladesh. These were, when still united, an exceptional creation which reminds us of the continuing force of religion in politics. Religion was the driving

force in making for the existence of this state. As such, the creation of
Pakistan seems to be a digression from the ideas of the Enlightenment,
and a return to the Middle Ages. Its establishment was accompanied by
forebodings and very great reluctance on the part of the British Government. If independence had come in 1937, instead of 1947, it would
undoubtedly have been given to a united India. The intensity of the great
religious divide between Hindu and Moslem did not appear until later:
they only manifested themselves in their full significance during the war
years. But an undivided India would not have held together. The Hindu–
Moslem cleavage would have declared itself under the strain of self-
government. Sooner or later, unified government would have been made
impossible: communal tension, and eventually communal civil war, would
have brought it to a standstill.

It is easy to forget how at the end of the war the decision to partition
the sub-continent was on a knife edge. Without the war, the British would
hardly have considered the creation of Pakistan as a necessary act. The
state of Pakistan is therefore one of the monuments to the war with
Japan. It is an unlikely one: few today see any special connection between
its history and that of Japan, yet the two are causally linked as is the
enventual emergence of Bangladesh, and the vituperation that continues
to exist between all three nations of the Indian sub-continent.

For the United States the war was an incident in its rise to be one of the
two greatest Powers in the world. It received its baptism of fire. For many
years before 1941, America had distorted the natural play of international affairs by utterly refusing to act the part of a Great Power. Its
people, in general and except at certain conjunctures, appeared to be
without the political instincts of the citizens of a major state. Because of
their unique behaviour, and of the influence of this upon the official
conduct of the American Government, the United States, at a time when
fate and its economic power called upon it to exert tremendous influence,
limited its voice in world affairs to be hardly of more account than that of
a third-class European state. Doubtless the reasons for this lay far back in
American history, and touch on George Washington, the fear of 'entangling Alliances' and the belief that foreign governments were very wily
and would inevitably bamboozle an American Government which was
rash enough to negotiate with them. But the United States had been in the
First World War; its reaction to this experience and withdrawal into
isolation had been a setback to normal growth. When Pearl Harbor
happened, the United States, in a world at war, still had an army of about
the same size as Sweden's; it still made the gestures, to which it had

accustomed itself before its entry in 1917 into the First World War, of being 'too proud to fight'. It is true that American ideas and American business influence were very prevalent, as also was the uncontrollable propulsive power of American culture. But the American state did not set itself to propagate them.

In the course of the war, the United States developed amazingly. It grew with the alarming speed of Alice when she ate a small cake marked 'Eat me'. It began the war with organs and ministries for taking part in foreign affairs which seem like toys. But, with the creative wind of improvisation which swept through America, the institutions developed rapidly. Simultaneously its public opinion, and the institutions by which this was made effective, grew in self-confidence. By the end of the war, the United States was moving in international affairs with professionalism and boldness.

American democracy was to show that while it was surprisingly persevering as long as the war lasted, it was, once peace was restored, capable of a rapid, revolutionary change of mood. The fires died as swiftly as they had blazed fiercely. Within seven years America had come to feel towards Japan as towards its protégé: and had transferred to Japan some of the abnormally cordial feeling which it had held towards China, until China became communist.

Finally, this was probably the last major war which Great Britain took part in as a world Power, certainly an Asian Power. For the last time Britain manoeuvred as a government with interest and concern in every part of the world, especially in Asia. It ended its Asian history with panache. It was nevertheless an end, and the speed with which it was accomplished left men to ponder whether Britain's departure represented a policy of grace or scuttle. Either way, it was certainly an inevitable consequence of the economic exhaustion brought about by Total War and by the failure of Appeasement. Within two years of the dropping of the bomb on Hiroshima, Britain ended its responsibility for India. Although it took some time to work out the details, by this one act it terminated its Empire everywhere in Asia; for a British Empire in Asia which excluded India was not really a possibility.

Great Britain, at that time, was more than a small country, with a restricted part to play, as seemed to befit one of a cluster of West European islands. By the accident of history, by the energy of its peoples it had, for the previous two centuries, been shot out of its natural sphere. It had risen to a height of power and prestige which obviously it could not retain but to which people in Britain had become accustomed. The leaders of institutional life had risen to their opportunity, and for some decades this had been reflected in politics. These seemed to have an influence totally out of the proportion which would naturally be expected of such a numerically small people. Living in Britain at this time had a magnifying effect, so that what was done seemed to be done with a deep sense of responsibility. The proceedings of the Parliament at Westminster were gazed at by so many people that those who took part in it had the uneasy sense of acting on a great stage of the world, and being the cynosure of the world's eyes. This sense was often embarrassing. It often invested relatively trivial affairs with a false glamour. It would have been healthier if they had been dealt with without these overtones. Even so, thought in Britian was still apt to be large; small conceptions were still at a discount. It was this quality which perhaps most separates the Britain of those days from what it has become.

Within ten years of Indian Independence, Britain had liquidated practically all that was left of its Asian Empire. Ceylon, Malaya, Burma: it let them all go. It was not a matter of no longer discouraging their instinct to break away from the Empire which had once been thought of as a supra-national organization, a house where all the rising nationalisms of the Empire might, of their own free will, find asylum. They were positively conducted to the door. They were given a golden handshake – financially a rather mean one – and were sped into independence with expressions of goodwill.

Britain, which had enjoyed in Asia the great romantic period of its history, turned back, as a result of the war, and after an interval for readjustment, to the more sober task of discovering the contrast between being a world Power and being a small country off the north-west corner coast of continental Europe. It became preoccupied with the total revolution which should adapt Britain for its new role; with anxious debate as to whether it should think once more to become a European Power as it had been under its Angevin monarchs, or whether it could exist as a small island alone.

It is irony that, at the end, Britain finds itself in very similar circumstances to those which worried Japan at the start of this history. Transpose the islands off the north coast of Asia to the islands off the north-west of Europe, and the parallel, often remarked, is strangely apt. Its history, as Dean Acheson rightly diagnosed – only to be the object of bitter vituperation by people in Britain – was that it had lost an empire and not found a new part to play. The British may count themselves fortunate that the public opinion of the world has moved on, and it is unlikely that Britain will be tempted to try and solve its problems in a similar way to Japan.

*

And the human side? What of the war of the Little Peterkins of Asia?

The conflict had a recognizable pattern, though there were so many confusing cross-currents. One purpose of this book has been to trace it out. It settled the influences which were to be dominant in the lives of people for the next generation or so – until new pressures meet new obstacles, and all is again in the melting pot, the issue having again to be settled by conflict. For this last great cataclysm, the price paid in human life and suffering was truly prodigious. The numbers of those killed in the war on all fronts have been analysed. Of two of the great Asian families of people engaged, the Chinese casualties, difficult to estimate, have been given by Chiang Kai-shek in his book, *A Summing-Up at Seventy*, as over 3 million. 'These figures,' he says, 'do not include the heavy losses in life and property sustained by the people in general.'* Japanese losses in battle and air-attack have been estimated at around 2.3 million. Of the people elsewhere in Asia, by far the largest proportion had no wish to take part in the quarrel. They neither understood, nor cared for, nor were consulted about, the objects of conflict. From first to last they viewed the war as a fact of destructive nature, which everyone in his senses sought to evade, but which was fated to make enormous waves. Those who voluntarily went to war, or felt passionately about the issues to the extent of being genuinely willing to die for them, were very few. Submitting to the economic inducements because of poverty and destitution was the nearest that most combatants came to acting by a reasonable decision. The only Asian people of whom this was not really true were the fatally indoctrinated Japanese.

It is, however, economic pressure alone which interests nine tenths of the population of Asia. It is idle to think that people living in conditions of Asian poverty, and with so much mass illiteracy, can be capable of acting in any other way. Any system of government which offers them the prospects of seeing a barely tolerable life, barely tolerable though it be, for six months ahead, will be more than welcome. Frills of government, freedom, choice, are suspect to them. Those combatants who came from a society in which the compulsion of hunger was less present were swept together by conscription, and had even less say in their destiny.

The war was probably the last major conflict which will be fought in Asia in which all the Asian antagonists except Japan were predominantly agrarian. This gave the war its peculiar, and rather antiquarian flavour. Time will ensure that, before another great contest can happen, larger segments of society will have become heavily industrialized, and, with

---

*Chiang Kai-shek, *A Summing-Up at Seventy*, Harrap, London, 1957.

industrialization, will have come the special type of social organization which renders society so different in behaviour from that which was traditional.

Even the very few of the educated classes – the Chinese university professors, the Japanese, the Indian leisured upper classes – who had the inclination and the ability to trace out the pattern of events behind the confusion, to understand the whys and wherefores, derived little consolation, when they were compelled to live among a collapsing economy and the dangers of loot and arson, from the fact that to them was vouchsafed some understanding of what the war was all about.

It is clear that, to the many millions who fought and suffered unvocally, to the ignorant armies clashing by night, unselfconsciously, those who survived owe an inexpiable debt. It seems at some points in history, that only through a convulsion involving millions is understanding painfully acquired. 'The cut worm forgives the plough', said the poet Blake. By invoking this kind of charity, there can perhaps be forgiveness for the ungovernable fury of the instruments by which history is made.

Afterword

We are left, as we began, lingering over thoughts collected by Sun Tzu twenty-three and a half centuries ago:

While an angered man may again be happy, and a resentful man again be pleased, a state that has perished cannot be restored, nor can the dead be brought back to life. Therefore, the enlightened ruler is prudent and the good general is warned against rash action. Thus the state is kept secure and the army preserved.

Chronological Skeleton

1937

July 7   Japanese attack Chinese at Marco Polo Bridge

Dec. 14   Fall of Nanking to the Japanese

1938

July 11   Japanese-Soviet battle of Chang-kufeng

Oct.   Chiang Kai-shek's Government withdraws to Chungking

Oct. 21   Fall of Canton to the Japanese

Oct. 25   Fall of Hankow to the Japanese

Nov. 5   Prince Konoye declares 'New Order' in Asia

1939

May– Sept   Battle of Nomonhan between Japan and USSR

Sept. 1   Germans invade Poland

Sept. 3   Great Britain and France declare war

Sept. 17   USSR invades Poland

1939

Oct.   USSR exacts mutual assistance treaties from Estonia, Latvia and Lithuania

Nov. 30 USSR invades Finland

Dec. 17 *Graf Spee* scuttled

1940

Mar. 12 Finland capitulates

Mar. 30 Setting up of Wang Ching-wei's puppet Government at Nanking

Apr. 9 Germans invade Denmark and Norway

May   British occupy Iceland

May 10 Germans invade Low Countries and France. Churchill Prime Minister

May 15 Dutch lay down arms

May 20 Germans reach English Channel

May 28	Belgium capitulates	
May 27–June 4	Dunkirk	
June 10	Italy declares war	
June 14	Germans enter Paris	
June 22	France signs armistice	
July 3	British action against French fleet at Mers-el-Kebir	
July 10–Sept. 15	Battle of Britain	
		July–Oct. Closing of the Burma Road
Aug. 4	Italians invade British and French Somaliland	
Sept. 3	Anglo-US bases destroyers deal	
Sept. 14	Italians invade Egypt	
		Sept. 27 Tripartite Pact between Japan, Germany and Italy
Oct.	Hitler confers with Mussolini (4), Franco (23), Pétain (24)	
Oct. 28	Italians invade Greece	
Nov. 5	Roosevelt re-elected President	
		Nov. Hungary, Rumania and Slovakia brought into Tripartite Pact
Nov. 11	British attack Italian fleet at Taranto	

1940

	Dec.	British offensive in North Africa captures Tobruk (Jan. 22) and Benghazi (Feb. 7) 1941	Dec.	American embargo on sales of scrap iron and war material to Japan

1941

Mar. 11	Lend-Lease Act signed		
		Mar. 1	Bulgaria joins Tripartite Pact
		Mar. 27	Simovic coup: Yugoslavia refuses to join Tripartite Pact
		Mar. 28	Battle of Cape Matapan
		Mar. 31	First German offensive in North Africa: takes Benghazi and invests Tobruk
Apr.	US occupies Greenland	Apr. 6	Germans invade Yugoslavia and Greece
			Apr. 13 Non-Aggression Pact signed between Japan and Russia
		May 2	British invade Iraq
		May 20– June 2	Germans take Crete
May 27	*Bismarck* sunk		

June 8   British defeat Vichy French in Syria and Lebanon

June 22   Germans invade USSR

July   US joins occupation of Iceland

July 2   Japan decides on extensive moves into Indo-China

July 12   Anglo-Soviet Treaty of Mutual Assistance

July 28 and 29   US, British and Dutch East Indies impose embargoes on the sale of oil and steel to Japan

Aug. 14   Roosevelt–Churchill conference, Placentia Bay: Atlantic Charter

Aug. 17   Fall of Kiev

Aug. 25   Anglo-Russian occupation of Iran

Sept.   US 'shoot at sight' order

Sept. 8   Leningrad invested

1941

Oct. 17 General Tōjō replaces Konoye as Prime Minister of Japan

Oct. 30 Sebastopol invested. German thrust for Moscow

Dec. 1 Russian counter-attack

Dec. 7 Japan sends a declaration of war to the US

Dec. 7 Japan attacks Pearl Harbor, the Philippines, Hong Kong and Malaya

Dec. 8 US and Great Britain declare war on Japan

Dec. 9 China officially declares war on Japan and Germany

Dec. 10 Japanese sink the *Prince of Wales* and the *Repulse*

Dec. 10 Japan captures Guam

Dec. 11 Japan attacks Burma

Dec. 11 Germany and Italy declare war on US

Dec. 23 Fall of Wake Island

Dec. 24 British re-capture Benghazi

1942

Jan.	28	Germans re-capture Benghazi
Mar.		Bomber Command raids Baltic towns
Apr.		German 'Baedeker' raids
May	30	'1,000-bomber' raid on Cologne

Jan.	11	Japan attacks the Dutch East Indies
Feb.	8	Fall of Rangoon
Feb.	15	Fall of Singapore
Feb.	19	Japanese bomb Port Darwin in Australia
Feb.	27–29	Battle of the Java Sea
Mar.	2	Fall of Batavia
Mar.	11	Cripps mission to India
Apr.	4–9	Japanese raid into the Indian Ocean, bombing Ceylon
Apr.	9	US surrender of Bataan
Apr.	18	US air raid on Tokyo
May	1	Surrender of Mandalay
May	6	Surrender of Corregidor
May	6–8	Battle of the Coral Sea

1942

June — Destruction of PQ 17	July 3 — Fall of Sebastopol	June 4 — Battle of Midway Island
		June 4 — Japanese attack on the Aleutian Islands
July — Regular raids on Ruhr and Hamburg begin		Aug. 7 — US landings on the Solomon Islands
		Aug. 9 — Civil disobedience campaign announced in India
Aug. 12–15 — Stalin–Churchill meeting in Moscow	Aug. 12–15 — Stalin–Churchill meeting in Moscow	
Aug. 17 — First US raid on Germany		
Aug. 19 — Dieppe raid		
Aug. 31 — Battle of Alam el Halfa: German–Italian advance stayed		
Sept. 13 — Battles for Stalingrad begin	Sept. 13 — Battles for Stalingrad begin	
		Sept. 21 — Opening of the Arakan offensive under Wavell
		Sept. 21 — Opening of US offensive in New Guinea

Nov.	Record months for sinking by U-boats	
Nov.	Regular raids on Berlin begin	
Oct. 23	Battle of Alamein	
Nov. 8	Allied landings in Morocco and Algeria	
Nov. 11	Germans occupy southern France and Tunisia	

1943

Jan. 14–24	Casablanca Conference	
Jan.	German retreat from Caucasus	
Jan. 11		Treaty relinquishing extra-territorial rights between the US, Britain and China
Feb. 2	German surrender at Stalingrad. Russians recover Kursk (8) and Rostov (14)	
Feb. 8		Wingate's expedition into Burma
Mar. 2		Battle of the Bismarck Sea
Mar. 29	Battle of the Mareth	
Apr. 18		Death of Admiral Yamamoto, at Bougainville
Apr. 19–May 16	Rising and extinction of Warsaw Ghetto	

1943

May 11   US begin to liberate Aleutian Islands

May 12   German-Italian surrender in Tunisia

May 17   Attack on Ruhr dams

May 26   Discovery of Katyn massacre and severance of Russo-Polish relations

June 29   US landings in New Guinea

July 5–Aug. 6   Battles in the Kursk salient and Russian recovery of Orel and Belgorod

July 10   Invasion of Sicily

July 25   Dismissal of Mussolini

Aug. 17   US daylight raids on Regensburg and Schweinfurt

Aug. 17   Quebec Conference: setting up of South-East Asia Command, under Mountbatten

Aug. 23   Russians recover Kharkov

Sept.   Russians recover Novorossisk and Smolensk (25)

Sept. 3   Invasion of Calabria and signing of Italian surrender

Sept. 9   Landings at Salerno

Sept. 12   Rescue of Mussolini

1943		
Oct. 13 — Italy declares war on Germany	Oct. — Russians recover Zaporozhe (14) and Dnepropetrovsk (25)	Nov. 5–6 — Greater East Asia Conference held in Tokyo
	Nov. 6 — Russians recover Kiev	Nov. — US landings in the Gilbert Islands
		Nov. 22–26 — Cairo Conference: unconditional surrender demanded of Japan
Nov. 28–Dec. 1 — Teheran Conference		Dec. — Opening of the assault on the Marshall Islands
1944		
Jan. 12 — Landings at Anzio	Jan. 27 — Leningrad relieved	Feb.–Mar. — Beginning of Japanese offensive on borders of India, siege of Imphal and Kohima
Feb. 15 — Bombing of Monte Cassino	Apr. 2 — Russians enter Rumania	Apr. 17 — Renewed Japanese offensive in China
		Apr.–July — US advances through Dutch New Guinea

1944

June 6 Invasion of Normandy
June 12 First V1s hit London

July 20 Attempt on Hitler's life

May 17 Germans evacuate Monte Cassino
June 4 Americans enter Rome

May Russians recover Sebastopol and Crimea

June 23–July 3 Russians recover Byelorussia

July 23 Russians take Lublin and establish Polish Committee of National Liberation

June 15 Americans invade Saipan
June 15 First B29 raid on Japan

July 4 Japanese defeated at Imphal
July 9 Fall of Saipan
July 18 Resignation of General Tōjō

Aug. 15	Allied landings in southern France
Aug. 17	Final victories in Normandy. Paris rises
Aug. 24	Leclercq enters Paris
Sept. 3	Brussels liberated
Sept. 8	First V2s hit London
Sept. 17–30	Arnhem operations fail
Dec. 16	German offensive in the Ardennes

Aug.	Kesselring mans the Gothic Line
Aug. 1– Oct. 2	Warsaw rising against the Germans
Sept. 5	USSR declares war on Bulgaria
Sept. 12	Rumania signs armistice
Sept. 19	Finland signs armistice
Oct. 20	Partisans and Russians enter Belgrade

Aug.	US recovery of Tinian and Guam
Sept.	Allied counter-offensive in Burma, under Mountbatten
Oct. 20	US landings in the Philippines
Oct. 25	Battle of Leyte Gulf
Nov.	Beginning of systematic US bombing of Japan

1945

Jan.	9	US landings on Luzon
Jan.	12	General Russian offensive begins
Jan.	17	Russians enter Warsaw
Feb.	4–12	Yalta Conference
Feb.	13	Surrender of Budapest
Feb.	13–14	Dresden raids
Mar.	7	Americans cross the Rhine at Remagen
Apr.	1	US landings on Okinawa
Apr.	4	Japanese Prime Minister Koiso resigns and is replaced by Suzuki
Apr.	12	Death of Roosevelt
Apr.	13	Russians enter Vienna
Apr.	16	Last Russian offensive begins
Apr.		Russia refuses to renew her non-aggression pact with Japan
Apr.	28	Death of Mussolini
Apr.	30	Death of Hitler
May	2	Berlin in Russian hands. Germans in Italy capitulate
May	3	Japanese surrender Rangoon

May 7 Germans surrender at Rheims

July 17 Potsdam Conference

May 5 Prague rises

May 9 Russians enter Prague

July 26 Allies at Potsdam call on Japan to surrender

Aug. 6 Hiroshima

Aug. 8 Russia declares war on Japan

Aug. 9 Nagasaki

Aug. 14 Japan capitulates

Sept. 2 Japanese surrender signed

Books: The Western Hemisphere

Books on the Second World War are legion. The lists which follow embrace only a small proportion. By and large they contain books written in or translated into English but this is not a rigid rule.

The contribution of official historiography is itself substantial both in the number of books published, and their bulk and importance. The forbidding nature of official histories should not be allowed to obscure the fact that they contain numerous volumes that are uncommonly good and as readable as they are scholarly. The British official History of the Second World War runs to more than eighty volumes divided between Military, Civil and Medical series. The US collection is longer still; its volumes on the US Army alone almost equal the entire British *oeuvre*. Other English-language collections – Canadian, Australian, New Zealand, Indian, South African – are commensurately weighty. Their subject matter ranges from Grand Strategy and Foreign Policy to particular topics and services such as Merchant Shipping, Manpower, Civil Defence. The lists below do not include these official publications.

ORIGINS

(i) *General Surveys*

Christopher Thorne, *The Approach of War 1938–39* (1967); A. J. P. Taylor, *The Origins of the Second World War* (1961, reprinted with new introduction 1963); Elizabeth Wiskemann, *Europe of the Dictators* (1966), *Czechs and Germans* (1967); D. C. Watt, *Too Serious a Business: European Armed Forces and the Approach to the Second World War* (1967); A. Adamthwaite, *The Making of the Second World War* (1977).

(ii) *British Policies*

Michael Howard, *The Continental Commitment: The Dilemma of British Defence Policy in the Era of Two World Wars* (1972); C. G. Peden, *British Rearmament and the Treasury 1932–39* (1979); L. R. Pratt, *East of Malta, West of Suez: Britain's Mediterranean Crisis 1936–39* (1975); R. P. Shay, *British Rearmament in the Thirties: Politics and Profits* (1977); S. W. Roskill, *Naval Policy between the Wars*, vol. 2: *The period of Reluctant Rearmament 1930–39* (1936), *Hankey,*

Man of Secrets, vol. 2: *1919–31* (1972), vol. 3: *1931–63* (1974); Lt-Gen. Sir H. R. Pownall, *Chief of Staff: The Diaries of Lt-Gen. Sir Henry R. Pownall* (ed. B. Bond, vol. 1: *1933–40*, 1972, and vol. 2: *1940–44*, 1974); T. Jones, *A Diary with Letters 1931–50* (1954).

(iii) *Appeasement and Munich*

M. Gilbert, *The Roots of Appeasement* (1966); C. A. Macdonald, *The United States, Britain and Appeasement* (1981); A. A. Offner, *American Appeasement: U.S. Foreign Policy and Germany 1933–38* (1969); R. Ovendale, *Appeasement and the English-speaking World: Britain, the United States, the Dominions and the Policy of Appeasement* (1975); R. Parkinson, *Peace for Our Time: Munich to Dunkirk, the Inside Story* (1971); Telford Taylor, *Munich: The Price of Peace* (1967); K. Middlemas, *Diplomacy of Illusion: The British Government and Germany 1937–39* (1972); I. Colvin, *The Chamberlain Cabinet* (1971); J. A. Cross, *Sir Samuel Hoare: A Political Biography* (1977); S. K. Newman, *March 1939: The British Guarantee to Poland, a Study in the Continuity of British Foreign Policy* (1976); Sir A. M. Cadogan, *Diaries 1938–45* (ed. D. Dilks, 1971); R. G. Vansittart, *The Mist Procession* (1958); D. E. Kaiser, *Economic Diplomacy and the Origins of the Second World War* (1980); D. Calleo, *The German Problem Reconsidered: Germany and the World Order 1870 to the Present* (1978); G. Niedhart (ed.), *Kriegsbeginn 1939* (1976); M. Baumont, *Les Origines de la Seconde Guerre Mondiale* (1969; English trans. 1976); R. Douglas, *The Advent of War 1939–40* (1978); W. J. Mommsen and L. Kettenbacker (eds.), *The Fascist Challenge and the Policy of Appeasement* (1983).

HITLER, NAZISM, FASCISM, THE AXIS

(i) *Hitler and the Third Reich*

Adolf Hitler, *Mein Kampf* (17th edn 1939), first, abbreviated, English translation: *Mein Kampf* (1933); A. Bullock, *Hitler: A Study in Tyranny* (2nd edn 1965); J. P. Stern, *Hitler: The Führer and the People* (1975); J. F. C. Fest, *Hitler: Eine Biographie* (*1973*), English translation: *Hitler* (1974); N. Stone, *Hitler* (1980); W. Maser, *Adolf Hitler: Legende, Mythos, Wirklichkeit* (1972), English translation: *Hitler* (1973); F. Jetzinger, *Hitlers Jugend* (1956), English translation: *Hitler's Youth* (1958); A. Kubizek, *Adolf Hitler: Mein Jugendfreund* (1953), English translation: *Young Hitler* (1954); K. Heiden, *Hitler: A Biography* (1936); W. A. Jenks, *Vienna and the Young Hitler* (1960); E. Calic, *Ohne Maske* (1968), English translation: *Unmasked* (1971); H. Picker (ed.), *Hitlers Tischgespräche im Führerhauptquartier* (1951); H. Rauschning, *Conversations with Hitler* (1939); M. Domarus, *Hitler: Reden und Proklamationen 1932–45* (1953); H. R. Trevor-Roper, *The Last Days of Hitler* (4th edn 1971), *Hitler's War Directives 1939–45* (ed., 1964), *Hitler's Table Talk 1941–44* (ed., 1953); Maj.-Gen. J. M. Strawson, *Hitler as Military Commander* (1971); P. E. Schramm, *Hitler als militärische Führer* (1965); K. D. Bracher, *Die deutsche Diktatur* (1969), English translation: *The German Dictatorship* (1971); J. F. C. Fest, *Das Gesicht des Dritten Reiches* (1963), English translation: *The Face of the Third Reich* (1970); M. Broszat, *Der Nationalsozialismus* (1960), English translation: *German National Socialism* (1966); W. Shirer, *The Rise and Fall of the Third Reich* (1960); P. Ayçoberry, *La question nazi* (1979), English translation: *The Nazi Question: An Essay on the Interpretation of National Socialism 1922–1975* (1981); W. S. Allen, *The Nazi Seizure of Power: The Experience of a Single German Town 1930–35* (1966); J. Nyomarkay, *Charisma and Functionalism in the Nazi Party* (1967); H. Krausnick (ed.), *Anatomy of the SS State* (1968); G. H. Stein, *The Waffen SS* (1966); A. Speer, *Erinnerungen* (1969), English translation: *Inside the Third Reich* (1970); P. Schmidt, *Statist auf der diplomatischen Bühne* (1951), abbreviated English translation: *Hitler's Interpreter* (1951); H. B. Gisevius, *Bis zum bitteren Ende* (1946), English translation: *To the Bitter End* (1948); N. Rich, *Hitler's War Aims: Ideology, the Nazi State and the Course of Expansion* (1973); R. J. O'Neill, *The German Army and the Nazi Party 1923–39* (1966); Telford Taylor, *The Sword and the Swastika* (1952); F. L. Carsten, *Reichswehr and Politics 1918–1933* (1956); J. S. Conway, *The Nazi Persecution of the Churches 1939–45* (1958).

(ii) *Nazism and Fascism*

B. Moore, *The Social Origins of Dictatorship and Democracy* (1967); J. L. Talmon, *The Origins of Totalitarian Democracy* (1952); H. Arendt, *The Origins of Totalitarianism* (1958); F. Meinecke, *The German Catastrophe* (1950); E. Nolte, *Der Faschismus in seiner Epoche* (1963), English translation: *Three Faces of Fascism* (1965); H. Kohn, *The Mind of Germany* (1961); G. L. Mosse, *The Crisis of German Ideology* (1966), *Nazi Culture* (1966); D. Gasman, *The Scientific Origins of National Socialism* (1971); R. Butler, *The Roots of National Socialism* (1941); P. Gay, *Weimar Culture* (1969); A. J. Nichols, *Weimar and the Rise of Hitler* (1968); F. Neumann, *Behemoth: The Structure and Practice of National Socialism* (1942); B. Granzow, *A Mirror of Nazism* (1964); F. Chabod, *Storia del fascismo italiano* (1960), English translation: *A History of Italian Fascism* (1963); G. Carocci, *Storia del fascismo* (1972), English translation: *Italian Fascism* (1974); C. Seton-Watson, *Italy from Liberalism to Fascism* (1967); D. Mack Smith, *Mussolini* (1981); R. De Felice, *Mussolini il duce: gli anni del consenso* (1974); I. Kirkpatrick, *Mussolini: A Study of a Demagogue* (1964); C. Hibbert, *Benito Mussolini: The Rise and Fall of Il Duce* (1962); G. Ciano, *Diario 1937–43* (ed. R. De Felice, 1980), partial English translations: *Ciano's Diary 1937–38* (1952) and *Ciano's Diary 1939–43* (1947); E. Wiskemann, *Fascism in Italy: Its Development and Influence* (1969), *The Rome–Berlin Axis* (1949); M. Toscano, *Le origini diplomatiche del patto d'acciaio* (2nd edn 1956), English translation: *The Origins of the Pact of Steel* (1967); F. W. Deakin, *The Brutal Friendship: Mussolini, Hitler and the Fall of Italian Fascism* (1962); M. Knox, *Mussolini Unleashed 1939–41* (1982).

THE FRENCH COLLAPSE

M. Bloch, *L'étrange défaite* (1946); A. Beaufre, *Le drame de 1940* (1965), English translation: *1940: The Fall of France* (1967); A. Adamthwaite, *France and the Coming of the Second World War* (1977); G. Chapman, *Why France Fell* (1968); P. Stehlin, *Témoignage pour l'histoire* (1964); G. Warner, *Pierre Laval and the Eclipse of France* (1968); H. Cole, *Laval: A Biography* (1963); C. M. de la Gorce, *La république et son armée* (1963); R. T. Thomas, *British and Vichy: The Dilemma of Anglo-French Relations 1940–42* (1979).

AMERICAN POLICIES

C. C. Tansill, *Back Door to War: The Roosevelt Foreign Policy 1933–41* (1952); D. Drummond, *The Passing of American Neutrality* (1955); W. A. Williams, *The Tragedy of American Diplomacy* (1966); W. L. Langer and S. E. Gleason, *The Challenge to Isolation* (1952), *The Undeclared War* (1953); S. Friedlander, *Prelude to Disaster: Hitler and the United States* (1967); W. S. Cole, *Roosevelt and the Isolationists 1932–45* (1983); C. A. Beard, *President Roosevelt and the Coming of War* (1946); R. Dallek, *Franklin D. Roosevelt and American Foreign Policy 1932–45* (1979); G. C. Smith, *American Diplomacy during World War II* (1965); G. Kolko, *The Politics of War: Allied Diplomacy and the World Crisis of 1943–45* (1969); W. L. Langer, *Our Vichy Gamble* (1966); K. S. Davis, *The American Experience of War* (1970); B. J. Bernstein (ed.), *Towards a New Past* (1968); J. L. Gaddis, *The United States and the Origins of the Cold War 1941–47* (1972); R. A. Divine, *The Reluctant Belligerent: American Entry into World War II* (1965).

RUSSIAN RESISTANCE

N. A. Voznesensky, *The Economy of the USSR in the Period of the Patriotic War* (1948); V. Conolly, *Beyond the Urals* (1967); N. Jasny, *Soviet Industrialization 1928–52* (1961); A. G. Mazour, *Soviet Economic Development* (1968); M. Fainsod, *Smolensk under Soviet Rule* (1959); D. J. Dallin, *Soviet Foreign Policy 1939–42* (1945); E. H. Carr, *German–Soviet Relations between the Two World Wars* (1952); J. Erickson, *The Soviet High Command: A Military–Political History 1918–1941* (1962); R. Kolkowicz, *The Soviet Military and the Communist Party* (1967); A. Dallin, *German Rule in Russia 1941–45* (revd edn 1981); V. M. Mastny, *Russia's Road to the Cold War: Diplomacy, Warfare and the Politics of Communism 1941–45* (1979). And *see under* The Fighting.

GREAT BRITAIN AT WAR

There are numerous excellent volumes in the Civil series of the official History of the Second World War. In addition:

A. Bullock, *The Life and Times of Ernest Bevin*, vol. 2: *Minister of Labour 1940–45* (1967); A. Marwick, *Britain in the Century of Total War* (1968); A. S. Milward, *War, Economy and Society 1939–45* (1977); H. Pelling, *Britain and the Second World War* (1970); A. Calder, *The People's War: Britain 1939–45* (1971); P. Addison, *The Road to 1945: British Politics and the Second World War* (1975); A. J. Youngson, *The British Economy 1920–57* (1960); M. Bruce, *The Coming of the Welfare State* (1968).

THE FIGHTING

The campaigns are covered in detail in the various official histories. In addition:

(i) *General Surveys and Strategy*

B. H. Liddell Hart, *History of the Second World War* (1970); G. Wright, *The Ordeal of Total War 1939–45* (1968); H. Michel, *La seconde guerre mondiale*, 2 vols. (1968–9); S. E. Morison, *American Contributions to the Strategy of World War II* (1958), *Strategy and Compromise* (1968); A. J. Marder, *From the Dardanelles to Oran* (1974); M. Howard, *The Mediterranean in the Second World War* (1968); F. H. Hinsley, *Hitler's Strategy* (1951); K. R. Greenfield, *American Strategy in World War II: A Reconsideration* (1963); A. Bryant (ed.), *The Turn of the Tide* (1957), *Triumph in the West* (1958), extracts with commentary from Lord Alanbrooke's papers; C. Bekker, *The Luftwaffe War Diaries* (1967); General F. Halder, *Kriegstagebüch* (ed. H. A. Jacobsen, 1962–6); General W. Warlimont, *Im Hauptquartier der deutschen Wehrmacht 1939–45* (1962), English translation: *Inside the Führer's Headquarters* (1964).

(ii) *The First Year*

V. Tanner, *The Winter War* (1975, Finland); Maj.-Gen. J. L. Moulton, *The Norwegian Campaign of 1940* (1966); N. Harman, *Dunkirk, the Necessary Myth* (1980); W. Lord, *The Miracle of Dunkirk* (1983); Telford Taylor, *The March of Conquest* (1958), *The Breaking Wave* (1967); H. R. Allen, *Who Won the Battle of Britain?* (1974); R. Wright, *Dowding and the Battle of Britain* (1964); R. Wheatley, *Operation Sea Lion* (1958).

(iii) *The Mediterranean and North Africa*

D. Macintyre, *The Battle for the Mediterranean* (1964); B. Pitt, *The Crucible of War: The Western Desert* (1980); Maj.-Gen. J. M. Strawson, *The Battle for North Africa* (1965), *El Alamein: Desert Victory* (1981); Field-Marshal Lord Carver, *Tobruk* (1964), *El Alamein* (2nd edn 1979); Corelli Barnett, *The Desert Generals* (2nd edn 1983); I. M. G. Stewart, *The Struggle for Crete* (1966).

(iv) *The Atlantic*

P. Beesly, *Very Special Intelligence* (1977); Vice-Admiral Sir P. Gretton, *Convoy Escort Commander* (1964), *Crisis Convoy: The Story of HX231* (1974); Vice-Admiral B. B. Schofield, *The Arctic Convoys* (1977); J. Rohwer, *Geleitzug Schlachten in März 1943* (1975), English translation: *The Critical Convoy Battles of March 1943* (1977).

(v) *The Russian Fronts*

J. Erickson, *Stalin's War with Germany*, vol. 1: *The Road to Stalingrad* (1975), vol. 2: *The Road to Berlin* (1983); Col. A. Seaton, *The Battle for Moscow* (1971), *The Russo-German War* (1971); A. Werth, *Russia at War 1941–45* (1964); D. Irving, *Hitler's War* (1977); S. Bialer (ed.), *Stalin and His Generals: Soviet Military Memoirs of World War II* (1970); A. Clark, *Barbarossa* (1964); H. E. Salisbury, *The Siege of Leningrad* (1969); L. Goure, *The Siege of Leningrad* (1962); G. Jukes, *Kursk: The Clash of Armour* (1968); Marshal V. I. Chuikov, *The Beginning of the Road* (English translation 1963), *The End of the Third Reich* (English translation 1967); J. Thorwald, *Es begann an der Weichsel* and *Das Ende an der Elbe* (combined and abbreviated English translation: *Flight into the Winter*, 1953); F. W. Deakin and R. Storry, *The Case of Richard Sorge* (1966); R. Cecil, *Hitler's Decision to Invade Russia* (1975); B. A. Leach, *German Strategy against Russia 1939–41* (1973); G. C. Herring, *Aid to Russia 1941–46* (1973).

(vi) *Italy*

W. G. F. Jackson, *The War in Italy* (1967); G. A. Shepherd, *The Italian Campaign 1943–45* (1968); Janusz Piekalkiewicz, *Cassino* (1980); R. Trevelyan, *The Fortress: A Diary of Anzio and After* (1956); P. Verney, *Anzio: An Unexpected Fury* (1978); D. W. Orgill, *The Gothic Line* (1967); D. W. Elwood, *Italy 1943–45* (1985).

(vii) *The Last Year*

J. Keegan, *Six Armies in Normandy: From D-day to the Liberation of Paris* (1982); S. Westphal, *The German Army in the West* (1951); Forrest C. Pogue, *The Supreme Command* (1954); R. Lamb, *Montgomery in Europe* (1983); Carlo d'Este, *Decision in Normandy: The Unwritten Story of Montgomery and the Allied Campaign* (1983); C. Bauer, *The Battle of Arnhem* (1966); C. Hibbert, *The Battle of Arnhem* (1962); C. Ryan, *A Bridge Too Far* (1974); Maj.-Gen. J. M. Strawson, *The Battle for the Ardennes* (1972); C. B. McDonagh, *The Battle of the Bulge: The Definitive Account* (1984); H. Essame, *The Battle for Germany* (1969).

(viii) *Bombing and Countermeasures*

A. Verrier, *The Bomber Offensive* (1968); N. Frankland, *The Bombing Offensive against Germany* (1965); H. Rumpf, *The Bombing of Germany* (1963); R. V. Jones, *Most Secret War* (1978); M. Middlebrook, *The Peenemünde Raid* (1982), *The Nuremberg Raid of 30–31 March 1944* (1973); D. Irving, *The Destruction of Dresden* (2nd edn 1966); A. S. Milward, *The German Economy at War* (1965); M. Kaldor, 'The German War Economy' in *Essays in Economic Policy*, vol. 2 (1964); B. Klein, *Germany's Economic Preparations for War* (1959); A. Milward, *The German Economy at War* (1964).

OCCUPATION, COLLABORATION, RESISTANCE, REVOLUTION

A. M. Meerloo, *Total War and the Human Mind* (1944); M. R. D. Foot, *Resistance: An Analysis of European Resistance to Nazism 1940–45* (1976); E. H. Cookridge, *Inside SOE* (1967); Bradley F. Smith, *The Shadow Warriors: OSS and the Origins of the CIA* (1982); David Stafford, *Britain and the European Resistance 1940–45* (1980); P. Auty and R. Clogg (eds.), *British Policy towards the Wartime Resistance in Greece and Yugoslavia* (1975); Werner Rings, *Leben mit dem Feind* (1979), English translation: *Life with the Enemy* (1982); Henri Michel, *La guerre de l'ombre* (1970), English translation: *The Shadow War: Resistance in Europe 1939–45* (1972), *Paris allemand* (1981), *Les courants de la pensée dans la Résistance* (1962); Pierre Lorain, *Armement clandestin: SOE 1941–44 France* (1972), expanded English translation: *Secret Warfare: The Arms and the Techniques of the Resistance* (1984); C. Bellanger, *Presse clandestine 1940–44* (1961); P. Arnoult, *La France sous l'occupation* (1959); J. Kruuse, *Madness at Oradour* (1969); P. Novick, *The Resistance versus Vichy: The Purge of Collaborators in Liberated France* (1968); H. R. Lottmann, *The People's Anger: Justice and Revenge in Post-Liberation France* (1986); W. Warmbrunn, *The Dutch under German Occupation* (1963); W. B. Maass, *The Netherlands at War 1940–45* (1970); T. Bor-Komorowski, *The Secret Army* (1950); J. Gorlinski, *Poland, SOE and the Allies* (1969); V. M. Mastny, *The Czechs under Nazi Rule* (1971); Tore Gjelsvik, *Hjemmefronten* (1977), English translation: *Norwegian Resistance 1940–45* (1979); J. O. Thomas, *The Giant Killers: The Story of the Danish Resistance Movement 1940–45* (1975); J. Bennett, *British Broadcasting and the Danish Resistance Movement 1940–45* (1966); J. K. M. Hanson, *The Civilian Population and the Warsaw Uprising of 1944* (1982); Mark C. Wheeler, *Britain and the War for Yugoslavia* (1980); Jozo Tomasevich, *War and Revolution in Yugoslavia 1941–45* (1975); V. Dedijer, *Tito Speaks* (1953); E. W. Deakin, *The Embattled Mountain* (1971); C. F. Delzell, *Mussolini's Enemies: The Anti-Fascist Resistance* (1961); Roberto Battaglia, *Storia della Resistenza Italiana* (1953), abbreviated English translation: *The Story of the Italian Resistance* (1957); G. Bocca, *Storia dell'Italia partigiana* (1964); C. Amè, *La guerra segreta in Italia 1940–43* (1954); E. Schramm von Thadden, *Griechenland und die Grossmachte im zweiten Weltkrieg* (1955); C. M. Woodhouse, *Apple of Discord* (1948); D. G. Kousoulas, *Revolution and Defeat* (1965); D. Eudes, *Les Kapetianos* (1970), English translation: *The Kapetianos: Partisans and Civil War in Greece 1943–49* (1972); J. C. Loulis, *The Greek Communist Party* (1982); N. Hammond, *Venture into Greece: With the Guerrillas 1943–44* (1983); E. C. W. Myers, *Greek Entanglement* (1955); A. Dallin, *German Rule in Russia 1941–45* (revd edn 1981); J. A. Armstrong (ed.), *Soviet Partisans in World War II* (1964); A. Oras, *Baltic Eclipse* (1948); C. G. Cruickshank, *The German Occupation of the Channel Islands* (1975); A. Roberts (ed.), *The Strategy of Civilian Defence* (1967). Also the periodicals *Revue d'histoire de la deuxième guerre mondiale* and *Esprit de la Résistance*; *European Resistance Movements, 1939–45* (proceedings of the International Conferences on the History of the Resistance, Milan 1961 and Oxford 1962).

ANTI-NAZI GERMANS

H. Rothfels, *Die deutsche Opposition gegen Hitler* (1958), English translation: *The Secret Opposition to Hitler* (1962); C. Sykes, *Troubled Loyalty* (1968); G. Ritter, *Carl Goerdeler und die deutsche Widerstandsbewegung* (1954), English translation: *The German Resistance* (1958); F. von Schlabrendorff, *The Secret War against Hitler* (1966); W. Hoettl, *The Secret Front* (1954); M. Mourin, *Les complots contre Hitler* (1948); H. Höhne, *Canaris* (1976), English translation: *Canaris* (1979); T. Prittie, *Germans against Hitler* (1964); G. C. Zahn, *German Catholics and Hitler's War* (1963), *In Solitary Witness* (1964); G. Lewy, *The Catholic Church and Nazi Germany* (1964); A. Leber, *Das Gewissen steht auf* (1954); E. Kordt, *Nicht aus den Akten* (1950); V. von Hassell, *Vom anderen Deutschland: aus den nachgelassenen Tagebüchern 1938–44* (1946), abbreviated English translation: *The von Hassell Diaries 1938–44* (1948).

PSYCHOLOGICAL WARFARE, PROPAGANDA

E. K. Bramstedt, *Goebbels and National Socialist Propaganda 1925–45* (1965); Z. A. B. Zeman, *Nazi Propaganda* (1964), *Selling the War: Art and Propaganda in World War II* (1978); L. Fraser, *Propaganda* (1957); M. Mégret, *La guerre psychologique* (1963); D. Lerner (ed.), *Sykewar: Psychological War against Germany* (1949).

ANTI-SEMITISM, THE CAMPS, THE HOLOCAUST

M. A. Meyer, *The Origins of the Modern Jew* (1967); Gerald Fleming, *Hitler und die Endlösung* (1982); G. Reitlinger, *The Final Solution* (1953); N. Cohn, *Warrant for Genocide* (1967); L. Poliakoff, *Harvest of Hate* (1956); Reuben Ainsztein, *Jewish Resistance in Nazi-Occupied Eastern Europe* (1974); Lucy S. Davidowicz, *The War against the Jews 1933–45* (1975); Yisrael Gutman, *The Jews of Warsaw*

1939–43: Ghetto, Underground and Revolt (English translation from Hebrew, 1983); D. S. Wyman, *The Abandonment of the Jews: America and the Holocaust 1941–1945* (1984); Martin Gilbert, *Auschwitz and the Allies* (1981); A. D. Morse, *Why Six Million Died* (1968); S. Friedländer, *Pius XII and the Third Reich* (1968); P. E. Lapide, *The Last Three Popes and the Jews* (1967); C. Falconi, *The Silence of Pius XII* (1970); B. Wasserstein, *Britain and the Jews of Europe* (1975). Also: the series of Records and Documents of the Holy See relating to the Second World War in the course of publication.

AT THE TOP

H. Feis, *Churchill, Roosevelt and Stalin: The War They Waged and the Peace They Sought* (1967); W. H. MacNeill, *America, Britain and Russia: Their Co-operation and Conflict 1941–46* (1963); D. S. Clemens, *Yalta* (1971); A. Theoharis, *The Yalta Myths* (1971); J. M. Burns, *Roosevelt, the Soldier of Fortune 1940–45* (1971); R. A. Divine, *Roosevelt and World War II* (1970); R. Sherwood (ed.), *The White House Papers of Harry Hopkins* (1948); H. L. Stimson and McGeorge Bundy, *On Active Service in Peace and War* (1947); C. Hull, *The Memoirs of Cordell Hull* (1948); A. B. Ulam, *Stalin, the Man and His Era* (1973); Guy Hentsch, *Stalin négociateur: une diplomatie de guerre* (1967); Martin Gilbert, *Winston S. Churchill* (1979); E. Barker, *Churchill and Eden at War* (1978); C. de Gaulle, *Mémoires de guerre*, vol. 1: *1940–42*, vol. 2: *1942–44*, vol. 3: *1944–46* (1954–59), English translation: *War Memoirs* (1955–60); Stephen E. Ambrose, *Eisenhower: Soldier, General of the Army, President-Elect 1890–1952* (1984); N. Hamilton, *Monty*, vol. 1: *The Making of a General 1887–1942* (1981), vol. 2: *Master of the Battlefield 1943–44* (1983); R. Lewin, *The Chief: Field Marshal Lord Wavell, Commander-in-Chief and Viceroy 1939–47* (1980); K. Sainsbury, *The Turning Point: Roosevelt, Stalin and Churchill 1943* (1985); E. Barker, *British Policy in South-East Europe in the Second World War* (1976); F. Kersaudy, *Churchill and de Gaulle* (1981); M. Kitchen, *British Policy towards the Soviet Union during the Second World War* (1986); A. M. de Zayas, *Nemesis at Potsdam: The Anglo-Americans and the Expulsion of the Germans* (1979).

ON THE FRINGES

Urs Schwarz, *The Eye of the Hurricane: Switzerland in World War II* (1980); F. G. Weber, *The Evasive Neutral: Germany, Britain and the Quest for a Turkish Alliance* (1979); R. A. Humphreys, *Latin America in the Second World War*, vol. 1: *1939–42* (1981), vol. 2: *1942–45* (1982); C. Falconi, *Il silenzio di Pio XII* (1965), English translation: *The Silence of Pius XII* (1970); S. Friedländer, *Pius XII and the Third Reich* (1966); Geoffrey Warner, *Syria and Iraq 1941* (1974); Jean Stengers, *Léopold III et le gouvernement: les deux politiques belges de 1940* (1980); D. G. Anglin, *The St Pierre and Miquelon Affair of 1941* (1966).

ULTRA INTELLIGENCE

Peter Calvocoressi, *Top Secret Ultra* (1980); Patrick Beesly, *Very Special Intelligence: The Story of the Admiralty's Operational Intelligence Centre 1939–1945* (1977); J. Garlinski, *Intercept: The Enigma War* (1979); Gordon Welchman, *The Hut 6 Story* (1982); Ralph Bennett, *Ultra in the West* (1979); Aileen Clayton, *The Enemy is Listening: The Story of the Y Service* (1980); Andrew P. Hodges, *Alan Turing: The Enigma* (1983).

DECEPTION

C. G. Cruickshank, *Deception in World War II* (1979); David Mure, *Master of Deception* (1980); J. C. Masterman, *The Double-Cross System* (1971); E. Howe, *The Black Game* (1982).

NUREMBERG

Bradley F. Smith, *The Road to Nuremberg* (1980), *Reaching Judgement at Nuremberg* (1977); Anne and John Tusa, *The Nuremberg Trial* (1984); Robert E. Conot, *Justice at Nuremberg* (1983); Werner Maser, *Nuremberg: Tribunal der Sieger* (1977), English translation: *A Nation on Trial* (1979); Peter Calvocoressi, *Nuremberg: The Facts, the Law and the Consequences* (1947).

PERSONAL ANGLES

Christabel Bielenberg, *The Past is Myself* (1968); Ninetta Jucker, *Curfew in Paris* (1960); Gustav Herling, *A World Apart* (English translation from Polish 1951); Christopher Burney, *Solitary Confinement* (2nd edn 1984); Primo Levi, *La tregua* (1963), English translation: *The Truce* (1963), *The Periodic Table* (1984); Norman Lewis, *Naples '44* (1978); Curzio Malaparte, *La pelle* (1950), English translation: *The Skin* (1952); Goronwy Rees, *A Bundle of Sensations* (1960); M. Picard, *Hitler in uns selbst* (1946); S. Terkel, *'The Good War': An Oral History of World War II* (1984); E. Newby, *Life and War in the Apennines* (1983).

Books: the Greater East Asia and Pacific Conflict

The Second World War was the first truly global conflict in the history of mankind. The notion that it began with the German invasion of Poland in September 1939 is widely believed but is, in fact, absurdly parochial and unhistorical. It is always difficult to draw arbitrary distinctions between events, their causes and the causes of the causes. Any such attempt is bound to introduce subjective elements, distortions, illusions. Obviously, we gain a measure of understanding from making the attempt. When we look closely at the Thirty Years War that occurred between 1618 and 1648, we find a cluster of small wars, each of which lasted a few years and involved separate sets of belligerents. Together they changed the political geography and social fabric of the European continent. It is no use isolating one or other of those small wars without bearing in mind their relationship to each other; it is no less nonsensical to believe that the concatenation of these events produces a comprehensible, single, seamless progression of cause and effect: each of those small wars had special features which can be appreciated only when looked at individually, others which stand out only when looked at as part of a collective experience. And so it was with the Second World War. From a half-century of more remote events sprang a succession of wars that began in East Asia with the outbreak of the Manchurian Incident in September 1931 and continued with little interruption until the surrender of Japan in September 1945. As that succession of wars intertwined with the history of the European War of 1939–45, the combined conflict came to justify its epic description as a 'World War'. Those readers who wish to explore in greater detail some of the subjects this book has opened up may find useful the following suggestions for further reading.

PART I: ASIAN CONFLICT

General

A. P. Adamthwaite, *The Making of the Second World War* (London, 1977); G. C. Allen, *Western Enterprise in Far Eastern Economic Development: China and Japan* (London, 1954); W. G. Beasley, *Japanese Imperialism, 1894–1945* (Oxford, 1987), *The Modern History of Japan* (New York, 1963); C. Beaton, *Far East* (London, 1945); G. Bienstock, *The Struggle for the Pacific* (Port

Washington, NY, 1937); C. Browne, *Tōjō: The Last Banzai* (London, 1967); R. D. Burns and E. M. Bennett, *Diplomats in Crisis: United States-Chinese-Japanese Relations, 1919–1941* (Santa Barbara, 1974); C. A. Buss, *The Far East: A History of Recent and Contemporary International Relations in East Asia* (New York, 1955); W. H. Chamberlin, *Japan over Asia* (London, 1938); A. S. Cochran (ed.), *Magic: Diplomatic Summary*, 8 vols. (New York, 1980); B. Collier, *The Second World War: A Military History from Munich to Hiroshima* (Gloucester, Mass., 1967); W. F. Craven and J. L. Cates, *The Army Airforces in World War Two*, 7 vols. (Chicago, 1948–58); P. Darby, *Three Faces of Imperialism: British and American Approaches to Asia and Africa, 1870–1970* (New Haven, 1987); J. P. Davies, *Dragon by the Tail: American, British, Japanese, and Russian Encounters with China and One Another* (London, 1974); R. A. Dayer, *Bankers and Diplomats in China, 1917–1925: The Anglo-American Relationship* (Totowa, New Jersey, 1981); J. M. Dorwart, *Conflict of Duty: The US Navy's Intelligence Dilemma, 1919–1945* (Annapolis, 1983); J. W. Dower, *Empire and Aftermath: Yoshida Shigeru and the Japanese Experience, 1878–1954* (Cambridge, Mass., 1979); P. Einzig, *The Japanese 'New Order' in East Asia* (London, 1943); J. K. Fairbank *et al.*, *East Asia: The Modern Transformation* (Boston, 1965), and S. Y. Teng, *China's Response to the West* (Cambridge, 1954); J. Gunther, *Inside Asia* (New York, 1939); S. Henny and J.-P. Lehmann (eds.), *Themes and Theories in Modern Japanese History: Essays in Memory of Richard Storry* (London, 1988); E. P. Hoyt, *Japan's War: The Great Pacific Conflict, 1853–1952* (London, 1987); E. R. Hughes, *The Invasion of China by the Western World* (London, 1937); R. Hughes, *Foreign Devil: Thirty Years of Reporting in the Far East* (London, 1972); S. Ienaga, *Japan's Last War: World War II and the Japanese, 1931–1945* (New York, 1978); T. Ishimaru, *The Next World War* (London, 1937); D. Kahn, *The Codebreakers* (New York, 1968); M. Kennedy, *A History of Japan* (London, 1963); R. Lewin, *The American Magic: Codes, Ciphers and the Defeat of Japan* (New York, 1982); Sir B. H. Liddell Hart, *History of the Second World War* (London, 1970); H. Michel, *The Second World War* (London, 1975); H. B. Morse, *The International Relations of the Chinese Empire*, 3 vols. (London, 1910–18), and F. H. McNair, *Far Eastern International Relations* (Boston, 1931); I. H. Nish, *The Story of Japan* (London, 1968); Sir J. T. Pratt, *Before Pearl Harbour: A Study of the Historical Background to the War in the Pacific* (London, 1944); C. R. Shepherd, *The Case against Japan* (London, 1939); B. Smith, *The War's Long Shadow: The Second World War and its Aftermath: China, Russia, Britain, America* (London, 1986); R. H. Spector, *Eagle Against the Sun: The American War with Japan* (New York, 1985); G. R. Storry, *A History of Modern Japan* (London, 1960); J. Toland, *The Rising Sun: The Decline and Fall of the Japanese Empire, 1936–1945* (New York, 1970); T. Troy, *Donovan and the CIA: A History of the Establishment of the Central Intelligence Agency* (Frederick, Maryland, 1983); United States Army: Headquarters, Far East Command, Military History Section, Japanese Research Division, *Japanese Monographs*, 185 vols. (Tokyo and

Washington, DC, 1945–60); W. W. Willoughby, *Japan's Case Examined* (Baltimore, 1940).

The Sino-Japanese Conflict, 1894–1927

R. F. Hackett, *Yamagata Aritomo and the Rise of Modern Japan* (Cambridge, Mass., 1971); S. R. MacKinnon, *Power and Politics in Late Imperial China: Yuan Shi-kai in Beijing and Tianjin, 1905–1908* (Berkeley, 1980); H. B. Morse, *The International Relations of the Chinese Empire*, 3 vols. (London, 1910–18); M. Mutsu, *Kenkenroku: A Diplomatic Record of the Sino-Japanese War, 1894– 95* (Tokyo, 1982).

The Russo-Japanese War, 1904–5, and its Aftermath

K. Asakawa, *The Russo-Japanese Conflict: Its Causes and Issues* (London, 1904); M. Baring, *With the Russians in Manchuria* (London, 1905); R. V. C. Bodley, *Admiral Togo* (London, 1935); W. C. Braisted, *Report on the Japanese Naval, Medical and Sanitary Features of the Russo-Japanese War to the Surgeon General* (Washington, DC, 1906); Lord Brooke, *An Eye Witness in Manchuria* (London, 1905); R. Charques, *The Twilight of Imperial Russia* (London, 1958); E. L. V. Cordonnier, *The Japanese in Manchuria*, vols. I–II (London, 1912, 1914); R. Dua, *The Impact of the Russo-Japanese War on Indian Politics* (Delhi, 1966); T. E. Ewing, *Between the Hammer and the Anvil? Chinese and Russian Policies in Outer Mongolia, 1911–1921* (Bloomington, Indiana, 1980); E. A. Falk, *Togo and the Rise of Japanese Sea-Power* (London, 1936); Great Britain, Committee of Imperial Defence, *Official History (Naval and Military) of the Russo-Japanese War*, 3 vols (London, 1910, 1912, 1920); R. F. Hackett, *Yamagata Aritomo and the Rise of Modern Japan* (Cambridge, Mass., 1971); Sir I. Hamilton, *A Staff Officer's Scrap Book during the Russo-Japanese War*, 2 vols. (London, 1905, 1907); H. Hayashi, *The Secret Memoirs* (New York, 1915); R. Hough, *The Fleet that Had to Die* (London, 1958); D. James, *The Siege of Port Arthur* (London, 1905); A. Lloyd, *Admiral Togo* (Tokyo, 1905); A. Malazemoff, *Russian Far Eastern Policy, 1881–1904* (Berkeley, 1958); N. A. McCully, *The McCully Report: The Russo-Japanese War, 1904–05* (Annapolis, 1977); I. H. Nish, *The Anglo-Japanese Alliance: The Diplomacy of the Two Island Empires, 1894–1907* (London, 1966); B. W. Norregaard, *The Great Siege: The Investment and Fall of Port Arthur* (London, 1906); S. Okamoto, *The Japanese Oligarchy and the Russo-Japanese War* (New York, 1970); D. Walder, *The Short Victorious War: The Russo-Japanese Conflict, 1904–5* (London, 1973); J. M. Westwood, *Witnesses of Tsushima* (Tokyo, 1970); J. A. White, *The Diplomacy of the Russo-Japanese War* (Princeton, 1966).

Korea

G. A. Lenson, *Balance of Intrigue: International Rivalry in Korea and Manchuria,*

1884–1899, 2 vols. (Tallahassee, 1982); R. R. Swartout, *Mandarins, Gunboats, and Power Politics: Owen Nickerson Denny and the International Rivalries in Korea* (Honolulu, 1980).

The Post-War Settlement, Arms Limitation and Collective Security

R. L. Buell, *The Washington Conference* (New York, 1922); H. Bywater, *Sea-Power in the Pacific: A Study of the American-Japanese Naval Problem* (London, 1921); P. T. Etherton and H. H. Tiltman, *Japan: Mistress of the Pacific?* (London, 1933); A. Iriye, *After Imperialism: The Search for a New Order in the Far East, 1921–1931* (Cambridge, Mass., 1965); T. Ishimaru, *Japan Must Fight Britain* (London, 1936); T. F. Mayer-Oakes, *Fragile Victory: Prince Saionji and the 1930 London Treaty Issue from the Memoirs of Baron Harada Kumao* (Detroit, 1968); F. Moore, *America's Naval Challenge* (New York, 1929); S. E. Pelz, *Race to Pearl Harbor: The Failure of the Second London Naval Conference and the Onset of World War II* (Cambridge, Mass., 1974); E. S. Rubinow, *Sino-Japanese Warfare and the League of Nations* (Geneva, 1938); H. L. Stimson, *The Far Eastern Crisis: Recollections and Observations* (New York, 1936); G. E. Wheeler, *Prelude to Pearl Harbor: The United States Navy and the Far East, 1921–1931* (Columbia, Missouri, 1963); G. Woodcock, *The British in the Far East* (London, 1969).

Japan and Manchuria

R. Bassett, *Democracy and Foreign Policy: A Case History: The Sino-Japanese Dispute, 1931–1933* (London, 1952); J. D. Doenecke (ed.), *The Diplomacy of Frustration: The Manchurian Crisis of 1931–1933 as Revealed in the Papers of Stanley K. Hornbeck* (Stanford, 1981); F. C. Jones, *Manchuria since 1939* (London, 1949); League of Nations, *The Report of the Commission of Enquiry into the Sino-Japanese Dispute* (Tokyo, n.d.), *The Verdict of the League: China and Japan in Manchuria* (Boston, 1933); G. A. Lenson, *Balance of Intrigue: International Rivalry in Korea and Manchuria, 1884–1899*, 2 vols. (Tallahassee, 1982), *The Damned Inheritance: The Soviet Union and the Manchurian Crises, 1924–1935* (Tallahassee, 1974); G. McCormack, *Chang Tso-lin in Northeast China, 1911–1928: China, Japan and the Manchurian Idea* (Stanford, 1927); J. W. Morley ed., *Japan Erupts: The London Naval Conference and the Manchurian Incident, 1928–1932* (New York, 1984); S. N. Ogata, *Defiance in Manchuria: The Making of Japanese Foreign Policy, 1931–1932* (Berkeley, 1964); Y. P. Pickering, *Japan's Place in the Modern World* (London, 1936); H. Pu-Yi, *From Emperor to Citizen: The Autobiography of Aisin-Gioro Pu-Yi* (Peking, 1965; OUP, 1987); G. B. Rea, *The Case for Manchukuo* (New York, 1935); J. A. B. Scherer, *Manchukuo: A Bird's-Eye View* (Tokyo, 1933); E. B. Schumpeter et al., *The Industrialization of Japan and Manchukuo, 1930–1940* (New York, 1940); P. S. Tang, *Russia and Soviet Policy in Manchuria and Outer Mongolia, 1911–1931* (Durham,

North Carolina, 1959); C. Thorne, *The Limits of Foreign Policy: The West, the League and the Far Eastern Crisis of 1931–1933* (London, 1972); United States Army: Headquarters, Far East Command, Military History Section, Japanese Research Division, *Japanese Studies on Manchuria*, 13 vols. (Tokyo and Washington, DC, 1945–56); W. W. Willoughby, *The Sino-Japanese Controversy and the League of Nations* (Baltimore, 1935); T. Yoshihashi, *Conspiracy at Mukden: The Rise of the Japanese Military* (New Haven, 1963); C. W. Young, *Japan's Special Position in Manchuria: Its Assertion, Legal Interpretation and Present Meaning* (Baltimore, 1931).

Japanese Expansion in North China, 1934–7

China: Delegation to the League of Nations, *Japanese Aggression and World Opinion, July 7 to October 7, 1937* (Geneva, 1938); China: Delegation to the Nine-Power Conference, *Development of the Crisis in the Far East in the Last Six Years Brought About by Continuous Japanese Aggression against China* (Brussels, 1938); Foreign Affairs Association of Japan, *How the North China Affair Arose* (Tokyo, 1937); J. W. Morley, ed., *The China Quagmire: Japan's Expansion on the Asian Continent, 1933–1941* (New York, 1983).

Chinese Internal Revolutions and Foreign Policy

R. W. Barnett, *Economic Shanghai: Hostage to Politics, 1937–1941* (New York, 1941); S. de Beauvoir, *The Long March* (London, 1958); R. E. Bedeski, *State-Building in Modern China: The Kuomintang in the Prewar Period* (Berkeley, 1981); L. Bianco, *The Origins of the Chinese Revolution, 1915–1949* (London, 1971); C. Brandt, *Stalin's Failure in China, 1924–1927* (London, 1958); E. F. Carlson, *The Chinese Army: Its Organization and Military Efficiency* (New York, 1940); A. B. Chan, *Arming the Chinese: The Western Armaments Trade in Warlord China, 1920–1928* (Vancouver, 1982); K.-S. Chiang, *A Summing Up at Seventy* (London, 1957), *China's Destiny* (London, 1947); O. E. Chubb, *Twentieth Century China* (New York, 1966); L. E. Eastman, *Seeds of Destruction: Nationalist China in War and Revolution, 1937–1949* (Stanford, 1984); J. K. Fairbank (ed.), *The Cambridge History of China:* vol. XII, *Republican China, 1912–1949*, pt 1 (Cambridge, 1983), and A. Feuerwerker (eds.), *The Cambridge History of China:* vol. XIII, *Republican China, 1912–1949*, pt 2 (Cambridge, 1986); Great Britain: Admiralty, Naval Intelligence Division, *China Proper:* vol. II: *Modern History and Administration* (London, 1945); A. Isaac, *The Tragedy of the Chinese Revolution* (Stanford, 1938, 1951); F. C. Jones, *Shanghai and Tientsin: With Special Reference to Foreign Interests* (London, 1940); T. Kataoka, *Resistance and Revolution in China: The Communists and the Second United Front* (Berkeley, 1974); G. N. Kates, *The Years that were Fat: Peking, 1933–40* (New York, 1952); D. Lary, *Warlord Soldiers: Chinese Common Soldiers, 1911–1937* (Cambridge, 1985); 'G. E. Miller' [M. Fresco], *Shanghai:*

Paradise of Adventurers (New York, 1937); R. Pelissier, *Awakening of China, 1783–1949* (New York, 1967); M. N. Roy, *Revolution in China* (Calcutta, 1951); F. Schurmann and O. Schell (eds.), *Republican China: Nationalism, War and the Rise of Communism, 1911–1949* (New York, 1967); B. Schwarz, *Chinese Communism and the Rise of Mao* (Cambridge, Mass., 1952); E. Snow, *Red Star over China* (London, 1937); L. W. Snow, *Edgar Snow's China: A Personal Account of the Chinese Revolution, compiled from the Writings of Edgar Snow* (New York, 1981); A. N. Young, *China and the Helping Hand, 1937–1945* (Cambridge, Mass., 1963), *China's Wartime Finance and Inflation, 1937–1945* (Cambridge, Mass., 1965).

Japanese Internal Revolutions and Foreign Policy

G. C. Allen, *Japanese Industry: Its Recent Development and Present Condition* (New York, 1940); M. A. Barnhart, *Japan Prepares for Total War: The Search for Economic Security, 1919–1941* (Ithaca, 1987); W. G. Beasley, *Modern Japan: Aspects of History, Literature and Society* (London, 1975); G. M. Berger, *Parties out of Power in Japan, 1931–1941* (Princeton, 1977); H. Byas, *Government by Assassination* (New York, 1943); E. E. N. Causton, *Militarism and Foreign Policy in Japan* (London, 1936); K. W. Colegrove, *Militarism in Japan* (Boston, 1936); L. Connors, *The Emperor's Adviser: Saionji Kinmochi and Pre-war Japanese Politics* (London, 1987); J. B. Crowley, *Japan's Quest for Autonomy: National Security and Foreign Policy, 1930–1938* (Princeton, 1966); M. S. Farley, *The Problem of Japanese Trade Expansion in the Post-war Situation* (New York, 1940); W. Fleisher, *Volcanic Isle* (London, 1942); M. Hane, *Emperor Hirohito and his Chief Aide-de-Camp: The Honjo Diary, 1933–36* (Tokyo, 1982); K. Harada, *Saionji-Harada Memoirs* (Tokyo, 1945–6); J. A. Harrison, *Japan's Northern Frontier: A Preliminary Study in Colonization and Expansion with Special Reference to the Relation of Japan and Russia* (Gainsville, 1953); K. Haushofer, *Japan bout sein Rich* (Berlin, 1941); J. Herbert, *Shinto: The Fountainhead of Japan* (London, 1967); A. E. Hindmarsh, *The Basis of Japanese Foreign Policy* (Cambridge, Mass., 1930); S.-H. Hsu, *Japan and the Third Powers*, 4 vols. (Shanghai, 1941); T. Kase, *Journey to the Missouri* (New Haven, 1950); T. Kawai, *The Goal of Japanese Expansion* (London, 1938); K. K. Kawakami, *Japan in China: Her Motives and Aims* (London, 1938); Y. S. Kuno, *Japanese Expansion in the Asiatic Continent* (Berkeley, 1937); L. N. Kutakov, *Japanese Foreign Policy on the Eve of the Pacific War: A Soviet View* (Tallahassee, 1972); J. C. Lebra, *Japan's Greater East Asia Co-Prosperity Sphere in World War II: Selected Readings and Documents* (Kuala Lumpur, 1975); D. J. Lu, *From the Marco Polo Bridge to Pearl Harbor: Japan's Entry into World War II* (Washington, DC, 1961); J. M. Maki, *Government and Politics in Japan: The Road to Democracy* (London, 1962), *Japanese Militarism: Its Cause and Cure* (New York, 1945); M. Maruyama, *Thought and Behaviour in Modern Japanese Politics* (London, 1963); Y. C. Maxon, *Control of Japanese Foreign*

Policy: A Study in Civil-Military Rivalry, 1930–1945 (Berkeley, 1957); M. J. Mayo (ed.), *The Emergence of Imperial Japan: Self Defence or Calculated Aggression?* (New York, 1970); R. H. Mitchell, *Censorship in Imperial Japan* (Princeton, 1983), *Thought Control in Pre-war Japan* (Ithaca, 1976); J. W. Morley, *Dilemmas of Growth in Pre-war Japan* (Princeton, 1971), *The Fateful Choice: Japan's Advance into Southeast Asia, 1939–1941* (New York, 1980); W. F. Morton, *Tanaka Giichi and Japan's China Policy* (New York, 1980); T. Nakano, *The Ordinance Power of the Japanese Emperor* (Baltimore, 1923); I. H. Nish, *The Story of Japan* (London, 1968); I. Nitobe, *Bushido: The Soul of Japan* (Tokyo, 1969); R. A. Scalapino, *Democracy and the Party Movement in Pre-war Japan: The Failure of the First Attempt* (Berkeley, 1953); B.-A. Shillony, *Revolt in Japan: The Young Officers and the February 26, 1936, Incident* (Princeton, 1973); G. R. Storry, *The Double Patriots: A Study of Japanese Nationalism* (London, 1957), *A History of Modern Japan* (London, 1960); M. Shigemitsu, *Japan and her Destiny* (London, 1958); Takeuchi, *War and Diplomacy in the Japanese Empire* (Chicago, 1935); C. Thorne, *Allies of a Kind: the United States, Britain and the War against Japan, 1914–1945* (London, 1978); H. H. Tiltman, *The Far East Comes Nearer* (London, 1936); D. A. Titus, *Balance and Politics in Pre-war Japan* (New York, 1974); S. Togo, *The Cause of Japan* (New York, 1956); M. Tokayer and M. Swartz, *The Fugu Plan: The Untold Story of the Japanese and the Jews during World War II* (London, 1979); O. D. Tolischus, *Tokyo Record* (London, 1943); G. O. Totten, *The Social Democratic Movement in Pre-war Japan* (New Haven, 1966); T. Uyeda, *The Recent Development of Japanese Foreign Trade with Special Reference to Restriction Policies of Other Countries and Attempts at Trade Agreements* (Tokyo, 1936); W. W. Willoughby, *Japan's Case Examined* (Baltimore, 1940); A. M. Young, *Imperial Japan, 1926–1938* (New York, 1938).

The China Incident, 1937–45

H. Abend, *Chaos in Asia* (London, 1940); C. Boyd, *The Extraordinary Envoy: General Hiroshi Oshima and Diplomacy in the Third Reich, 1934–1939* (Washington, DC, 1980); J. H. Boyle, *China and Japan at War, 1937–1945: The Politics of Collaboration* (Stanford, 1972); G. E. Bunker, *The Peace Conspiracy: Wang Ching-wei and the China War, 1937–1941* (Cambridge, Mass., 1972); H.-S. Ch'i, *Nationalist China at War: Military Defeats and Political Collapse, 1937–1945* (Ann Arbor, 1982); China: Delegation to the League of Nations, *Japanese Aggression and World Opinion, July 7 to October 7, 1937* (Geneva, 1938); China: Delegation to the Nine-Power Conference, *Japanese Aggression and the Nine-Power Conference of Brussels*, 2 pts (Brussels, 1937); China Information Committee, *Organized Pillaging by Japanese* (Hankow, 1938), *Sino-Japanese Hostilities in North China: A Survey of the First Five Months of Armed Conflict North of the Yellow River* (Hankow, 1937); A. D. Coox, *Year of the Tiger* (Tokyo, 1964); D. S. Detwiler and C. B. Burdick, *War in Asia and the*

Pacific, 1937–1939: Japanese and Chinese Studies and Documents, 15 vols. (New York, 1980); E. M. Gunn, *Unwelcome Muse: Chinese Literature in Shanghai and Peking, 1937–1945* (New York, 1980); L.-h. Hsu *et al.*, *History of the Sino-Japanese War, 1937–1945* (Taipei, 1971); F. C. Jones, *Japan's New Order in East Asia: Its Rise and Fall, 1937–1945* (London, 1954), *Shanghai and Tientsin, with Special Reference to Foreign Interests* (London, 1940); L. Li, *The Japanese Army in North China, 1937–1941* (London, 1975); M. Lindsay, *The Unknown War: North China, 1937–1945* (London, 1975); K. Miki and K. Hosokawa, *Introductory Studies on the Sino-Japanese Conflict* (Tokyo, 1941); J. W. Morley ed., *The China Quagmire: Japan's Expansion on the Asian Continent, 1933–1941* (New York, 1983); K. Nichi, *Introductory Studies on the Sino-Japanese Conflict* (Tokyo, 1941); R. Payne, *Chungking Diary* (London, 1945); H. S. Quigley, *Far Eastern War, 1937–1941* (Boston, 1942); H. J. Timperley, *Japanese Terror in China* (Freeport, New York, 1938); F. Utley, *Japan's Gamble in China* (London, 1938); J. G. Utley, *Going to War with Japan, 1937–1941* (Knoxville, 1985); D. Wilson, *When Tigers Fight: The Story of the Sino-Japanese War, 1937–1945* (Viking, 1982).

British Commonwealth Interests and Policies in East Asia

H. T. V. Baker, *The New Zealand People at War* (Wellington, 1965); J. Bertram, *The Shadow of a War* (London, 1947); B. Bond (ed.), *Chief of Staff: The Diaries of Lt.-General Sir Henry Pownall*, 2 vols. (London, 1972, 1974); M. H. Brice, *The Royal Navy and the Sino-Japanese Incident, 1937–41* (London, 1973); H. Burton and B. R. Pearn, *The Far East, 1942–46* (London, 1955); R. A. Butler, *The Art of the Possible* (London, 1971); S. J. Butlin, *The War Economy, 1939–1942* (Canberra, 1955); Lord Casey, *Personal Experience, 1939–1946* (London, 1962); Lord Chatfield, *It Might Happen Again* (London, 1947); W. S. Churchill, *The Second World War*, 6 vols. (London, 1948–54); C. Clifford, *Retreat from China: British Policy in the Far East, 1937–1941* (London, 1967); C. Cooke, *The Life of Richard Stafford Cripps* (London, 1957); Sir R. L. Craigie, *Behind the Japanese Mask* (London, 1946); Lord Cunningham, *A Sailor's Odyssey* (London, 1951); H. Dalton, *Memoirs, 1931–1945: The Fateful Years* (London, 1957); A. L. P. Dennis, *The Anglo-Japanese Alliance* (Berkeley, 1923); D. Dilks (ed.), *The Diaries of Sir Alexander Cadogan, 1938–1945* (London, 1971); L. G. Elliott, *A Role of Honour: The Story of the Indian Army* (London, 1965); S. L. Endicott, *Diplomacy and Enterprise: British China Policy, 1933–1937* (Manchester, 1975); E. Estorick, *Stafford Cripps: A Biography* (London, 1949); H. V. Evatt, *Australia in World Affairs* (Sydney, 1946); K. Feiling, *The Life of Neville Chamberlain* (London, 1977); I. S. Friedman, *British Relations with China, 1931–1939* (New York, 1940); H. G. Gelber, *Problems of Australian Defence* (London, 1970); N. H. Gibbs *et al.*, *Grand Strategy*, 6 vols. (London, 1957–76); M. Gilbert, *The Roots of Appeasement* (London, 1966); A. Gilchrist, *Bangkok Top Secret* (London, 1970); P. Gore-Booth, *With Great Truth and Respect*

(London, 1974); E. M. Gull, *British Economic Interests in the Far East* (London, 1943); P. Haggie, *Britannia at Bay: The Defence of the British Empire against Japan, 1931–1941* (Oxford, 1981); J. Harvey (ed.), *The Diplomatic Diaries of Oliver Harvey, 1937–1940* (London, 1970); F. H. Hinsley *et al.*, *British Intelligence in the Second World War: Its Influence on Strategy and Operations*, 3 vols. (London, 1981–8); M. Howard, *The Continental Commitment* (London, 1972); Lord Ismay, *Memoirs* (London, 1960); M. D. Kennedy, *The Estrangement of Great Britain and Japan, 1917–1935* (Manchester, 1969); Sir H. Knatchbull-Hugessen, *Diplomat in Peace and War* (London, 1949); R. and N. Lapwood, *Through the Chinese Revolution* (London, 1954); B. A. Lee, *Britain and the Sino-Japanese War, 1937–1939* (London, 1973); R. Lewin, *The Other Ultra* (London, 1982); W. R. Louis, *British Strategy in the Far East, 1919–1939* (Oxford, 1971); P. Lowe, *Great Britain and the Origins of the Pacific War: A Study of British Policy in East Asia, 1937–1941* (Oxford, 1977); H. Macmillan, *The Blast of War, 1939–1945* (London, 1967), *Winds of Change, 1914–1939* (London, 1966); N. B. Mansergh, *Documents and Speeches on British Commonwealth Affairs, 1931–1952* (London, 1953), *Survey of British Commonwealth Affairs: Problems of External Policy, 1931–1939* (London, 1952), *Survey of British Commonwealth Affairs: Problems of Wartime Co-operation and Postwar Change, 1931–1952* (London, 1958); A. J. Marder, *Old Friends, New Enemies: The Royal Navy and the Imperial Japanese Navy: Strategic Illusions, 1936–1941* (Oxford, 1981); W. N. Medlicott, *The Economic Blockade*, 2 vols. (London, 1952, 1959); R. G. Menzies, *Afternoon Light* (London, 1967); P. Moon (ed.), *Wavell: The Viceroy's Journal* (London, 1973); I. Morrison, *Malayan Postscript* (London, 1942); I. H. Nish, *The Anglo-Japanese Alliance: The Diplomacy of the Two Island Empires, 1894–1907* (London, 1966), *Alliance in Decline* (London, 1972), (ed.) *Anglo-Japanese Alienation, 1919–1952: Papers of the Anglo-Japanese Conference on the History of the Second World War* (Cambridge, 1982); R. Ovendale, *'Appeasement' and the English-Speaking World* (Cardiff, 1975); G. C. Peden, *British Rearmament and the Treasury, 1932–1939* (Edinburgh, 1979); F. S. G. Piggott, *Broken Thread* (Aldershot, 1950); Sir J. Pratt, *War and Politics in China* (London, 1943); L. R. Pratt, *East of Malta, West of Suez: Britain's Mediterranean Crisis, 1936–1939* (Cambridge, 1975); R. J. Pritchard, *Far Eastern Influences upon British Strategy towards the Great Powers, 1937–1939* (New York, 1987); R. Roskill, *Hankey: Man of Secrets*, vol. III, *1931–1963* (London, 1974), *Naval Policy between the Wars*, 2 vols. (London, 1968, 1976); B. E. V. Sabine, *British Budgets in Peace and War, 1932–1945* (London, 1970); K. Sansom, *Sir George Sansom and Japan: A Memoir* (Tallahassee, 1972); A. Shai, *Origins of the War in the East: Britain, China and Japan, 1937–39* (London, 1976); R. P. Shay, *British Rearmament in the Thirties: Politics and Profits* (Princeton, 1977); Lord Strang, *At Home and Abroad* (London, 1956); C. Thorne, *Allies of a Kind: The United States, Britain and the War against Japan, 1914–1945* (London, 1978); A. Trotter, *Britain and East Asia, 1933–1937* (Cambridge, 1977); A. Watt, *Australian Diplomat* (Sydney, 1972), *The Evolution of Australian Foreign Policy* (Cambridge, 1967); D. C. Watt, *Personalities and Policies: Studies in the Formulation of British Policy in the Twentieth Century* (London, 1965), *Too Serious a Business* (London, 1975); G. Wint, *The British in Asia* (New York, 1954); A. Wolfers, *Britain and France between the Two Wars* (New York, 1966); S. Woodburn Kerby *et al.*, *The War Against Japan*, 5 vols. (London, 1957–69); Sir L. Woodward, *British Foreign Policy in the Second World War* (London, 1970–76).

German Interests and Policies in East Asia

K. Bloch, *German Interests and Policies in the Far East* (New York, 1940); H. von Dirksen, *Moscow, Tokyo, London* (London, 1951); J. P. Fox, *Germany and the Far Eastern Crisis, 1931–1938: A Study in Diplomacy and Ideology* (Oxford, 1982); F. W. Iklé, *German-Japanese Relations, 1936–1940* (New York, 1956); V. Issraeljan and L. Kutakov, *Diplomacy of Aggression: Berlin, Rome, Tokyo Axis: Its Rise and Fall* (Moscow, 1970); H.-h. Liang, *The Sino-German Connection: Alexander von Falkenhausen between China and Germany, 1900–1941* (Assen and Amsterdam, 1978); B. Martin, *Die Deutsche Beraterschaft in China, 1927–1938: Militär-Wirtschaft-Aussenpolitik* (Düsseldorf, 1981); J. M. M. Meskill, *Hitler and Japan: The Hollow Alliance* (New York, 1966); J. W. Morley *et al.*, *Deterrent Diplomacy: Japan, Germany, and the U.S.S.R., 1935–1940* (New York, 1976); E. L. Presseisen, *Germany and Japan: A Study in Totalitarian Democracy, 1933–1941* (The Hague, 1958); T. Sommer, *Deutschland und Japan zwischen den Machten, 1935–1940: von Anti-Kominternpakt zum Dreimächtepakt* (Tübingen, 1962).

French and Italian Interests and Policies in East Asia

J. Decoux, *A la barre de l'Indochine* (Paris, 1949); A. Hytier, *Two Years of French Foreign Policy: Vichy, 1940–1942* (Geneva, 1958); J. Legrand, *L'Indochine à l'heure japonaise* (Cannes, 1963); R. Levy *et al.*, *French Interests and Policies in the Far East* (New York, 1941); Marchand and Rollet, *L'Indochine en guerre* (Paris, 1954); Mordant, *Au service de la France en Indochine* (Saigon, 1950); G. Sabatier, *Le destin de l'Indochine* (Paris, 1952); F. Tamagna, *Italy's Interests and Policies in the Far East* (New York, 1941).

American Interests and Policies in East Asia

G. Alperovitz, *Atomic Diplomacy: Hiroshima and Potsdam* (London, 1966); C. A. Beard, *President Roosevelt and the Coming of the War, 1941: A Study of Appearances and Realities* (New Haven, 1945); T. A. Bisson, *American Policy in the Far East, 1931–1941* (New York, 1941); J. M. Blum, *From the Morgenthau Diaries*, 2 vols. (Boston, 1958, 1965); D. Borg, *Historians and American Far Eastern Policy* (New York, 1966), *The United States and the Far Eastern Crisis of 1933–1938: From the Manchurian Incident through the Initial Stage of the Undeclared*

Sino-Japanese War (Cambridge, Mass., 1964), and S. Okamoto (eds.), *Pearl Harbor as History: Japanese-American Relations* (New York, 1973); R. J. C. Butow, *Tōjō and the Coming of the War* (Stanford, 1961), *The John Doe Associates: Backdoor Diplomacy for Peace, 1941* (Stanford, 1974); J. F. Byrnes, *Speaking Frankly* (London, 1948); T. Campbell and G. Herring (eds.), *The Diaries of Edward R. Stettinius, Jr., 1943–1946* (New York, 1975); C. L. Chennault, *Way of a Fighter* (New York, 1949); J. W. Christopher, *Conflict in the Far East: American Diplomacy of China, 1928–33* (Leiden, 1950); S. Conn and B. Fairchild, *The Framework of Hemisphere Defence* (Washington, DC, 1960); R. Dallek, *Franklin Roosevelt and American Foreign Policy, 1932–1945* (London, 1979); R. A. Divine, *Roosevelt and World War II* (Baltimore, 1969); E. R. Drachman, *United States Policy toward Vietnam, 1940–1945* (Rutherford, New York, 1970); J. K. Emmerson, *The Japanese Thread: A Life in the US Foreign Service* (New York, 1978); M. S. Farley, *American Far Eastern Policy and the Sino-Japanese War* (New York, 1938); H. Feis, *The China Tangle: The American Effort in China from Pearl Harbor to the Marshall Mission* (Princeton, 1953), *The Road to Pearl Harbor: The Coming of the War between the United States and Japan* (Princeton, 1950); R. H. Fifield, *Southeast Asia in United States Policy* (New York, 1963); J. Forrestal, *The Forrestal Diaries* (New York, 1951); J. C. Grew, *Report from Tokyo: A Message to the American People* (New York, 1942), *Ten Years in Japan* (New York, 1944), *Turbulent Era: A Diplomatic Record of Forty Years, 1904–1945*, 2 vols. (Boston, 1952); A. W. Griswold, *The Far Eastern Policy of the United States* (New York, 1938); J. H. Herzog, *Closing the Open Door: American-Japanese Diplomatic Negotiations, 1936–1941* (Annapolis, 1973); S. K. Hornbeck, *The United States in the Far East* (Boston, 1942); C. Hull, *Memoirs*, 2 vols. (London, 1948); M. H. Hunt, *The Making of a Special Relationship: The United States and China to 1914* (New York, 1983); H. L. Ickes, *The Secret War Diary of Harold L. Ickes*, vol. III (London, 1955); A. Iriye, *Across the Pacific: An Inner History of American-East Asian Relations* (New York, 1967), *Mutual Images: Essays in American-Japanese Relations* (Cambridge, Mass., 1975), *Power and Culture* (Cambridge, Mass., 1981); E. J. King and W. Whitehill, *Fleet Admiral King* (London, 1953); R. Y. Koen, *The China Lobby in American Politics* (New York, 1974); W. Langer and S. E. Gleason, *The Challenge to Isolation, 1937–1940* (New York, 1952), *The Undeclared War, 1940–1941* (New York, 1953); D. W. Leahy, *I Was There: A Personal Story of the Chief of Staff to Presidents Roosevelt and Truman* (New York, 1950); J. Leutze (ed.), *The London Observer: The Journal of General Raymond E. Lee* (London, 1972); D. J. Lu, *From the Marco Polo Bridge to Pearl Harbor: Japan's Entry into World War II* (Washington, DC, 1961); D. MacArthur, *Reminiscences* (New York, 1964); M. Matloff, *Strategic Planning for Coalition Warfare, 1943–1944* (Washington, DC, 1959), and E. Snell, *Strategic Planning for Coalition Warfare, 1941–1942* (Washington, DC, 1953); H. Morgenthau, Jr, *Diary: China*, 2 vols. (Washington, DC, 1965); S. E. Morison, *American Contributions to the Strategy of World War Two* (London, 1958);

J. W. Morley (ed.), *The Final Confrontation: Japan's Negotiations with the United States, 1941* (New York, forthcoming, 1989); L. Morton, *Command Decisions: United States Army in World War Two* (Washington, DC, 1962), *Strategy and Command: The First Two Years* (Washington, DC, 1962); Y. Nagai and A. Iriye (eds.), *The Origins of the Cold War in Asia* (Tokyo, 1977); A. Offner, *American Appeasement* (Cambridge, Mass., 1969); R. Ovendale, *'Appeasement' and the English-Speaking World* (Cardiff, 1975); H. Perry, *The Panay Affair: Prelude to Pearl Harbor*, 8 vols. (New York, 1969); F. C. Pogue, *George C. Marshall*, 3 vols. (New York, 1964–73); W. D. Puleston, *The Armed Forces of the Pacific: A Comparison of the Military and Naval Power of the United States and Japan* (New Haven, 1941); A. Saxton, *The Indispensable Enemy: Labor and the Anti-Chinese Movement in California* (Berkeley, 1971); P. W. Schroeder, *The Axis Alliance and Japanese-American Relations, 1941* (Ithaca, 1958); J. S. Service, *The Amerasia Papers* (Berkeley, 1971); R. E. Sherwood, *Roosevelt and Hopkins: An Intimate History* (New York, 1948); K. E. Shewmaker, *Americans and Chinese Communists, 1927–1945* (Ithaca, 1971); D. M. Shoup, *The Marines in China, 1927–1928: A Contemporaneous Journal* (Hamden, Conn., 1987); G. Smith, *American Diplomacy during the Second World War* (New York, 1965); R. H. Spector, *Eagle against the Sun: The American War with Japan* (New York, 1985); H. L. Stimson, *Far Eastern Crisis: Recollections and Observations* (New York, 1936), and M. Bundy, *On Active Service in Peace and War* (New York, 1948); T. Tang, *America's Failure in China, 1941–50* (Chicago, 1962); J. C. Thomson *et al.*, *Sentimental Imperialists: The American Experience in East Asia* (New York, 1981); C. Thorne, *Allies of a Kind: The United States, Britain and the War against Japan, 1941–1945* (London, 1978); H. S. Truman, *Memoirs:* vol. 1, *Year of Decisions, 1945* (London, 1955); B. Tuchman, *Sand Against the Wind: Stilwell and the American Experience in China, 1911–45* (New York, 1970); T. V. Tuleja, *Statesmen and Admirals: Quest for a Far Eastern Naval Policy* (New York, 1963); United States: Department of State, *Foreign Relations of the United States: The Far East* [annual vols.] (Washington, DC), *Foreign Relations of the United States: Japan, 1931–1941*, 2 vols. (Washington, DC, 1943); P. Varg, *The Making of a Myth: The United States and China, 1897–1912* (East Lansing, 1968); M. S. Watson, *Chief of Staff: Prewar Plans and Preparations* (Washington, DC, 1950); S. Welles, *A Time for Decision* (London, 1944); R. D. Weston, *Racism in U.S. Imperialism* (Columbia, South Carolina, 1972); T. H. White (ed.), *The Stilwell Papers* (New York, 1948), and A. Jacoby, *Thunder out of China* (London, 1947); C. A. Willoughby and J. Chamberlain, *MacArthur, 1941–51* (New York, 1954); J. E. Wiltz, *From Isolation to War, 1931–1941* (London, 1969); R. Wohlstetter, *Pearl Harbor: Warning and Decision* (Stanford, 1962); E. M. Zacharias, *Secret Missions: The Story of an Intelligence Officer* (New York, 1946).

Soviet Interests and Policies in East Asia

M. Beloff, *Soviet Policy in the Far East*, 2 vols. (London, 1953); O. Braun, *A Comintern Agent in China, 1932–1939* (Stanford, 1982); O. E. Clubb, *China and Russia: The Great Game* (New York, 1971); A. D. Coox, *The Anatomy of a Small War: The Soviet-Japanese Struggle for Changkufeng/Khasan* (Westport, Conn., 1977), *Nomonhan: Japan against Russia, 1939*, 2 vols. (Stanford, 1985); J. Degras, *Soviet Documents on Foreign Policy*, 3 vols. (London, 1953); H. Feis, *Churchill, Roosevelt, Stalin* (Princeton, 1957); G. A. Lenson, *The Strange Neutrality: Soviet-Japanese Relations during the Second World War, 1941–1945* (Tallahassee, 1972); H. Lupke, *Japans Russlandpolitik von 1939 bis 1941* (Frankfurt, 1962); H. L. Moore, *Soviet Far Eastern Policy, 1931–1945* (Princeton, 1945); J. W. Morley, *The Japanese Thrust into Siberia, 1918* (New York, 1957), (ed.) *Deterrent Diplomacy: Japan, Germany, and the U.S.S.R., 1935–1940* (New York, 1976); G. D. R. Phillips, *Russia, Japan and Mongolia* (London, 1942); R. Swearington, *The Soviet Union and Japan* (Stanford, 1978); P. S. Tang, *Russia and Soviet Policy in Manchuria and Outer Mongolia, 1911–1931* (Durham, North Carolina, 1959).

Indian Nationalism

J. G. Elliott, *A Roll of Honour: The Story of the Indian Army, 1939–1945* (London, 1965); N. Mansergh *et al.*, *The Transfer of Power, 1942–1947*, 12 vols. (London, 1970–83); P. Morn, *Gandhi and Modern India* (London, 1968); B. R. Nanda, *Mahatma Gandhi* (London, 1958); B. N. Pandey, *The Break-Up of British India* (London, 1969); B. R. Tomlinson, *The Political Economy of the Raj, 1914–1947: The Economics of Decolonization in India* (London, 1979).

PART II: OCEAN CLASH

The Outbreak of the Pacific War

L. Allen, *Singapore, 1941–1942* (London, 1977); C. A. Beard, *President Roosevelt and the Coming of the War* (New Haven, 1948); T. Carew, *The Fall of Hong Kong* (London, 1960); S. Chapman, *The Jungle is Neutral* (London, 1949); D. Crisp, *Why We Lost Singapore* (Bombay, 1945); L. Falk, *Seventy Days to Singapore: The Malayan Campaign, 1941–1942* (London, 1975); S. Falk, *The March of Death* (New York, 1962); R. Grenfell, *Main Fleet to Singapore* (London, 1951); P. Herde, *Pearl Harbor, 7. Dezember 1941: Der Ausbruch des Krieges zwischen Japan und den Vereinigten Staaten und die Ausweitung des Europäischen Krieges zum Zweiten Weltkrieg* (Darmstadt, 1980); R. Hough, *The Hunting of Force Z* (London, 1963); N. Ike, *Japan's Decision for War: Records of the 1941 Policy Conferences* (Stanford, 1967); J. Leasor, *Singapore: The Battle that Changed the World* (London, 1968); W. Lord, *Day of Infamy* (London, 1957); G. Morgenstern, *Pearl Harbor: The Story of the Secret War*

(New York, 1947); I. Morrison, *Malayan Postscript* (London, 1942); L. Morton, *The Fall of the Philippines* (Washington, DC, 1952); A. E. Percival, *The War in Malaya* (London, 1949); G. W. Prange, *At Dawn We Slept* (New York, 1981); B. Rauch, *Roosevelt from Munich to Pearl Harbor* (New York, 1950); C. P. Romulo, *I Saw the Fall of the Philippines* (London, 1943); D. Russell-Roberts, *Spotlight on Singapore* (London, 1965); I. Simson, *Too Little, Too Late* (London, 1970); Sir J. Smith, *Percival and the Tragedy of Singapore* (London, 1971); J. Toland, *Infamy: Pearl Harbor and its Aftermath* (London, 1982); H. L. Trefousse, *What Happened at Pearl Harbor* (New York, 1958); M. Tsuji, *Singapore: The Japanese Version* (London, 1962); United States Congress: Joint Committee on the Investigation of the Pearl Harbor Attack, *Hearings* and *Report* (Washington, DC, 1946); H. Wallin, *Pearl Harbor: Why, How: Fleet Salvage and Final Appraisal* (Washington, DC, 1968); R. Wohlstetter, *Pearl Harbor: Warning and Decision* (New York, 1963); S. Woodburn Kirby, *Singapore: The Chain of Disaster* (London, 1971).

PARTS III–IV: THE GREATER EAST ASIA AND PACIFIC WAR

War Crimes and the Misconduct of War

J. and C. Blair, *Return from the River Kwai* (London, 1979); T. Bowden, *Changi Photographer: George Aspinall's Record of Captivity* (Sydney, 1984); R. Braddon, *The Naked Island* (London, 1952); Committee for the Compilation of Materials on Damage Caused by the Atomic Bombs in Hiroshima and Nagasaki, *Hiroshima and Nagasaki: The Physical, Medical and Social Effects of the Atomic Bombings* (London, 1981); H. Feis, *The Atom Bomb and the End of the War in the Pacific* (Princeton, 1961); J. Fletcher-Cooke, *The Emperor's Guest, 1942–45* (London, 1971); A. Girdner and A. Loftis, *The Great Betrayal: The Evacuation of the Japanese-Americans during World War II* (Toronto, 1969); C. V. Glines, *Doolittle's Tokyo Raiders* (Princeton, 1964); E. Gordon, *Miracle on the River Kwai* (London, 1963); L. Groves, *Now It Can Be Told* (New York, 1962); M. Hachiya, *Hiroshima Diary* (Chapel Hill, 1955); R. Hammond, *The Flame of Freedom* (London, 1988); Lord Hankey, *Politics, Trials and Errors* (Oxford, 1950); J. Hersey, *Hiroshima* (New York, 1946); B. Jeffrey, *White Coolies* (Sydney, 1954); J. Lane, *Summer Will Come Again: The Story of Australian POWS' Fight for Survival in Japan* (Fremantle, 1987); T. Lawson, *Thirty Seconds over Tokyo* (London, 1943); H. L. Leffelaar, *Through a Harsh Dawn: A Boy Grows Up in a Japanese Prison Camp* (Barre, Mass., 1963); C. Lemay, *Mission with Lemay* (Garden City, New York, 1966); C. Lucas, *Prisoners of Santo Tomas* (London, 1975); C. McCormac, *You'll Die in Singapore* (London, 1956); J. Miller, *Guadalcanal: The First Offensive* (Washington, DC, 1949); R. H. Minear, *Victors' Justice: The Tokyo War Crimes Trial* (Princeton, 1971); P. R. Piccigallo, *The Japanese on Trial: Allied War Crimes Operations in the East, 1945–1951* (Austin, 1979); Laurens van der Post, *The Night of the New Moon* (London, 1970); R. Prising, *Manila, Goodbye* (London, 1976); R. J.

Pritchard and S. M. Zaide (eds.), *The Tokyo War Crimes Trial: Index and Guide*, 5 vols. (New York, 1981–7), *The Tokyo War Crimes Trial: The Complete Proceedings of the International Military Tribunal for the Far East*, 22 vols. (New York, 1981); L. Rawlings and B. Duncan, *And the Dawn Came Up Like Thunder* (n.p., 1972); A. F. Reel, *The Trial of Yamashita* (Chicago, 1949); R. D. Rivett, *Behind Bamboo: An Inside Story of the Japanese Prison Camps* (Sydney, 1947); Lord Russell of Liverpool, *The Knights of Bushido* (London, 1958); C. Sleeman, *Trial of Gozawa Sadaiichi and Nine Others* (London, 1948), and S. C. Silkin, *The 'Double Tenth' Trial* (London, 1951); A. P. Staufer, *The Quartermaster Corps: Operations in the War against Japan* (Washington, DC, 1956); D. S. Thomas and R. S. Nishimoto, *The Spoilage: Japanese-American Evacuation and Resettlement during World War II* (Berkeley, 1946); J. Thomas, *Exile Within: The Schooling of Japanese Americans, 1942–1945* (Cambridge, Mass., 1987); Y. Uchida, *Desert Exile: The Uprooting of a Japanese American Family* (Seattle, 1982); USSR, *Materials on the Trial of Former Servicemen of the Japanese Army charged with Manufacturing and Employing Bacteriological Weapons* (Moscow, 1950); F. J. P. Veale, *Advance to Barbarism: The Development of Total Warfare from Sarajevo to Hiroshima* (New York, 1959); L. Warner and J. Sandilands, *Women Beyond the Wire* (London, 1982); P. Williams and D. Wallace, *Unit 731: The Japanese Army's Secret of Secrets* (London, 1989).

The War in the Pacific

H. Agawa, *The Reluctant Admiral: Yamamoto and the Imperial Navy* (Tokyo, 1979); R. Appleman *et al.*, *Okinawa: The Last Battle* (Washington, DC, 1948); H. H. Arnold, *Global Mission* (New York, 1949); D. E. Barbey, *MacArthur's Amphibious Navy* (Annapolis, 1969); J. H. and W. M. Belote, *Titans of the Seas: The Development and Operations of American Carrier Task Forces during World War II* (New York, 1975), *Typhoon of Steel: The Battle for Okinawa* (New York, 1969); C. Blair, *Silent Victory: The US Submarine War against Japan* (Philadelphia, 1975); T. E. Buell, *The Quiet Warrior: A Biography of Admiral Raymond Spruance* (Boston, 1974), *Master of Seapower: A Biography of Admiral Ernest J. King* (Boston, 1980); H. Cannon, *Leyte: The Return to the Philippines* (Washington, DC, 1954); R. W. Coakley and R. M. Leighton, *Global Logistics and Strategy*, 2 vols. (Washington, DC, 1955); R. H. Connery, *The Navy and the Industrial Mobilization in World War II* (Princeton, 1951); P. Crowl, *Campaign in the Marianas* (Washington, DC, 1960), and E. G. Lowe, *Seizure of the Gilberts and Marshalls* (Washington, DC, 1955); M. Dexter, *The New Guinea Offensives* (Canberra, 1961); P. S. Dull, *A Battle History of the Imperial Japanese Navy, 1941–1945* (Annapolis, 1978); G. C. Dyer, *The Amphibians Came to Conquer: The Story of Admiral Richmond Kelly Turner*, 2 vols. (Washington, DC, 1969); S. Falk, *Decision at Leyte* (New York, 1966); M. Fuchida and M. Okumiya, *Midway: The Battle that Doomed Japan* (Annapolis, 1955);

K. R. Greenfield (ed.), *Command Decisions* (Washington, DC, 1960); B. Greenhill *et al.*, *The Second World War in the Pacific: Plans and Reality* (London, 1974); S. Griffith, *The Battle for Guadalcanal* (New York, 1963); W. F. Halsey and J. Bryan, *Admiral Halsey's Story* (New York, 1947); M. Hashimoto, *Sunk: The Story of the Japanese Submarine Fleet* (New York, 1954); P. Hasluck, *The Government and the People, 1939–1941* (Canberra, 1956); S. Hayashi, with A. D. Coox, *Kōgun: The Japanese Army in the Pacific War* (Quantico, 1959); G. P. Hayes, *The Joint Chiefs of Staff and the War against Japan* (Annapolis, 1982); R. D. Heinl, *The Defense of Wake* (Washington, DC, 1947); W. Hoffman, *The Seizure of Tinian* (Washington, DC, 1950); C. W. Hoffmann, *Saipan: The Beginning of the End* (Washington, DC, 1950); W. J. Holmes, *Double-Edged Secrets* (Annapolis, 1979); A. Iriye, *Power and Culture: The Japanese-American War, 1941–1945* (Cambridge, Mass., 1981); J. A. Isely and P. A. Crowl, *The US Marines and Amphibious War* (Princeton, 1951); M. Ito, *The End of the Imperial Japanese Navy* (London, 1962); D. C. James, *The Years of MacArthur*, 2 vols. (New York, 1972, 1975); E. J. King and W. Whitehill, *Fleet Admiral King: A Naval Record* (New York, 1952); R. Leckie, *Strong Men Armed: The US Marines Against Japan* (New York, 1962); D. Lockwood, *Australia's Pearl Harbour: Darwin, 1942* (Sydney, 1967); W. Lord, *Incredible Victory* (London, 1968); J. B. Lundstrom, *The First South Pacific Campaign: Pacific Fleet Strategy, December 1941–June 1942* (Annapolis, 1976); W. Manchester, *American Caesar: Douglas MacArthur, 1880–1964* (Boston, 1978); S. Milner, *The War in the Pacific: Victory in Papua* (Washington, DC, 1957); S. E. Morison, [Official] *History of United States Naval Operations in World War II*, 15 vols. (Boston, 1947–62); R. Newcomb, *Iwojima* (New York, 1965); M. Nichols and H. Shaw, *Okinawa: Victory in the Pacific* (Washington, DC, 1948); G. Odgers, *The Air War against Japan, 1943–1945* (Canberra, 1957); M. Okumiya and J. Horikoshi, *Zero* (New York, 1956); C. M. Petillo, *Douglas MacArthur: The Philippine Years* (Bloomington, Indiana, 1981); F. C. Pogue, *George C. Marshall: Ordeal and Hope, 1939–1942* (London, 1968), *George C. Marshall: Organizer of Victory, 1943–1945* (New York, 1973); J. D. Potter, *Admiral of the Pacific: The Life of Yamamoto* (London, 1965), *Nimitz* (Annapolis, 1976); C. G. Reynolds, *The Fast Carriers: The Forging of an Air Navy* (New York, 1968); H. M. Smith and P. Finch, *Coral and Brass* (New York, 1949); R. R. Smith, *The Approach to the Philippines* (Washington, DC, 1953), *Triumph on the Philippines* (Washington, DC, 1963); S. Smith, *The Battle of Sawa* (New York, 1962); J. J. Stephen, *Hawaii under the Rising Sun: Japan's Plan for Conquest after Pearl Harbor* (Honolulu, 1984); R. W. Tregaskis, *Guadalcanal Diary* (New York, 1962); A. J. Watts and B. G. Gordon, *The Imperial Japanese Navy* (London, 1971); A. C. Wedemeyer, *Wedemeyer Reports!* (New York, 1958); L. Wigmore, *The Japanese Thrust: Australia in the War of 1939–1945* (Canberra, 1957); F. L. W. Wood, *The New Zealand People at War: Political and External Affairs* (Wellington, 1958); W. T. Y'Blood, *Red Sun Setting: The Battle of the Philippine Sea* (Annapolis, 1980); M. Yoshida, *Requiem for Battleship Yamato* (Seattle, 1985).

The War in South-East Asia

L. Allen, *Burma: The Longest War, 1941–45* (London, 1984); M. A. Aziz, *Japan's Colonialism and Indonesia* (The Hague, 1955); Ba Maw, *Breakthrough in Burma* (New Haven, 1968); A. J. Barker, *The March on Delhi* (London, 1963); H. Benda, *The Crescent and the Rising Sun: Indonesian Islam under Japanese Occupation* (New Haven, 1958); M. Collis, *First and Last in Burma, 1941–48* (London, 1956); E. R. Drachman, *United States Policy toward Vietnam, 1940– 1945* (Rutherford, New York, 1970); R. L. Eichelberger, *Our Jungle Road to Tokyo* (New York, 1950); F. Eldridge, *Wrath in Burma* (New York, 1946); W. H. Elsbree, *Japan's Role in Southeast Asian Nationalist Movements, 1940– 1945* (Cambridge, Mass., 1953); T. Friend, *Between Two Empires: The Ordeal of the Philippines* (New Haven, 1965); A. Gilchrist, *Bangkok, Top Secret* (London, 1970); L. E. Gleek, *General History of the Philippines:* V, vol. 1: *The American Half-Century, 1898–1946* (Manila, 1984); A. W. H. Harterdorp, *Japanese Occupation of the Philippines* (Manila, 1967); D. Jajanama, *Thailand im Zweiten Weltkrieg* (Hamburg, 1970); J. Keats, *They Fought Alone* (London, 1964); J. Legrand, *L'Indochine à l'heure japonaise* (Cannes, 1963); Marchand and Rollet, *L'Indochine en guerre* (Paris, 1954); J. Masters, *The Road Past Mandalay* (New York, 1961); H. J. van Mook, *The Netherlands Indies and Japan: Battle on Paper, 1940–41* (New York, 1944), *The Stakes of Democracy in South-East Asia* (London, 1950); Mordant, *Au service de la France en Indochine* (Saigon, 1950); Sir L. Mountbatten, *Report to the Combined Chiefs of Staff* (London, 1951); A. W. McCoy (ed.), *Southeast Asia under Japanese Occupation* (New Heaven, 1980); M. Murray, *Escape a Thousand Miles to Freedom* (Sydney, 1965); T. Nu, *Burma Under the Japanese* (London, 1954); T. O'Brien, *The Moonlight War: The Story of Clandestine Operations in South-East Asia, 1944–5* (London, 1987); C. Ogburn, *The Marauders* (London, 1960); W. Peers and D. Brelis, *Behind the Burma Road: The Story of America's Most Successful Guerrilla Force* (Boston, 1963); J. D. Potter, *A Soldier Must Hang: The Biography of an Oriental General* (London, 1963); B. Prasad (ed.), *Official History of the Indian Armed Forces in World War II: Defence of India: Policy and Plans* (n.p., 1963), *Indian War Economy: Supply, Industry and Finance* (n.p., 1962); G. Sabattier, *Le destin de l'Indochine* (Paris, 1952); W. Slim, *Defeat into Victory* (London, 1956); S. Woodburn Kirby, *The Reconquest of Burma*, 2 vols. (London, 1958, 1961).

The War in China

A. Chennault, *Chennault and the Flying Tigers* (New York, 1963); C. L. Chennault, *Way of a Fighter* (New York, 1949); J. W. Esherwick (ed.), *Lost Chance in China: The World War II Despatches of John S. Service* (New York, 1974); H. Feis, *The China Tangle: The American Effort in China from Pearl Harbor to the Marshall Mission* (Princeton, 1953); L. L. Liu, *A Military History of Modern*

China (Princeton, 1956); M. E. Miles, *A Different Kind of War: The Little Known Story of the Combined Guerilla Forces Created in China by the US Navy and the Chinese during World War II* (Garden City, New York, 1967); C. F. Romanus and R. Sunderland, *Stilwell's Mission to China, Stilwell's Command Problems* and *Time Runs Out in CBI* (Washington, DC, 1953, 1956, 1959); L. K. Rosinger, *China's Wartime Politics, 1937–1944* (Princeton, 1944); L. van Slyke (ed.), *The Chinese Communist Movement: A Report of the United States War Department, July 1945* (Stanford, 1968); J. W. Stilwell, *The Stilwell Papers* (London, 1949); G. Stuart and A. Levy, *Kind-Hearted Tiger* (London, 1965).

The War in Japan

E. J. Drea, *The 1942 Japanese General Election: Political Mobilization in Wartime Japan* (Lawrence, Kansas, 1979); G. K. Goodman (ed.), L. de Asis, *From Bataan to Tokyo: Diary of a Filipino Student in Wartime Japan, 1943–1944* (Lawrence, Kansas, 1979); B.-A. Shillony, *Politics and Culture in Wartime Japan* (Oxford, 1981); G. Terasaki, *Bridge to the Sun* (London, 1958).

Russo-Japanese Relations During the Second World War

J. W. M. Chapman, *The Sorge Cover-Up* (Brighton, 1980); F. W. Deakin and G. R. Storry, *The Case of Richard Sorge* (London, 1966); C. Johnson, *An Instance of Treason: The Story of the Tokyo Spy Ring* (Stanford, 1964); G. A. Lenson, *The Strange Neutrality: Soviet-Japanese Relations during the Second World War, 1941–1945* (Tallahassee, 1972); C. A. Willoughby, *Sorge: Soviet Master Spy* (London, 1952).

The Surrender of Japan

L. Allen, *The End of the War in Asia* (London, 1976); L. Brooks, *Behind Japan's Surrender: The Secret Struggle that Ended an Empire* (New York 1967); J. F. C. Butow, *Japan's Decision to Surrender* (Stanford, 1954); W. Craig, *The Fall of Japan* (New York, 1967); H. Feis, *Japan Subdued: The Atomic Bomb and the End of the War in the Pacific* (Princeton, 1961); T. Kase, *Journey to the Missouri* (New Haven, 1950).

The Aftermath of the War

E. A. Ackerman *et al.*, *Japan's Prospect* (Cambridge, Mass., 1946); J. E. Auer, *The Postwar Rearmament of Japanese Maritime Forces* (New York, 1973); H. Baerwald, *The Purge of Japanese Leaders under the Occupation* (Berkeley, 1959); T. A. Bisson, *Zaibatsu Dissolution in Japan* (Berkeley, 1954); R. Buckley, *Occupation Diplomacy: Britain, the United States and Japan, 1945–1952* (Cambridge, 1982); T. W. Burkman (ed.), *The Occupation of Japan: Education and Social Reform* (Norfolk, 1982), *The Occupation of Japan: The International Context* (Norfolk, 1982); J. F. Cady, P. G. Barnett and S. Jenkins, *The Development of Self-Rule in Burma, Malaya and the Philippines*, 3 vols. (New York, 1948); W. J. Coughlin, *Conquered Press: The MacArthur Era in Japanese Journalism* (1952); W. H. M. Creemers, *Shrine Shinto after World War II* (Leiden, 1968); R. Dingman, *Documents on New Zealand External Relations:* vol. II, *The Surrender and Occupation of Japan* (Wellington, 1982); F. S. V. Donnison, *British Military Administration in the Far East, 1943–46* (London, 1956); R. Drifte, *The Security Factor in Japan's Foreign Policy, 1945–52* (London, 1983); R. Fifield, *The Diplomacy of South-East Asia, 1945–1958* (New York, 1958); J. W. Gaddis, *Public Information in Japan under American Occupation* (Geneva, 1950); G. Goodman (ed.), *The American Occupation of Japan: A Retrospective View* (Lawrence, Kansas, 1968); E. M. Hadley, *Anti-Trust in Japan* (Princeton, 1970); R. K. Hall, *Shushin: The Ethics of a Defeated Nation* (New York, 1949); N. Ito, *New Japan: Six Years of Democratisation* (Tokyo, 1952); K. Kawai, *Japan's American Interlude* (Chicago, 1960); D. MacIsaac, *Strategic Bombing in World War II* (New York, 1976), *The United States Strategic Bombing Survey*, 10 vols. (New York, 1976); E. Martin, *The Allied Occupation of Japan* (Stanford, 1948); J. D. Montgomery, *Forced to be Free: The Artificial Revolution in Germany and Japan* (Chicago, 1957); Y. Nagai and A. Iriye (eds.), *The Origins of the Cold War in Asia* (Tokyo, 1977); I. Nish (ed.), *The British Commonwealth and the Occupation of Japan* (London, 1983), and C. Dunn (eds.), *European Studies on Japan* (Tenterden, Kent, 1979); T. Nishi, *Unconditional Democracy: Education and Politics in Occupied Japan, 1945–1952* (Stanford, 1982); E. W. Pauley, *Report on Japanese Reparations to the President of the US, November 1945 to April 1946* (Washington, DC, 1948); J. C. Perry, *Beneath the Eagle's Wings: Americans in Occupied Japan* (New York, 1980); L. H. Redford, *The Occupation and its Legacy to the Post-war World* (Norfolk, 1976); M. Schaller, *The American Occupation of Japan: The Origins of the Cold War in Asia* (London, 1985); W. Sebald with R. Brines, *With MacArthur in Japan: A Personal History of the Occupation* (New York, 1965); K. Tsurumi, *Social Change and the Individual: Japan Before and After Defeat in World War II* (Princeton, 1970); J. Williams, *Japan's Political Revolution under MacArthur: A Participant's Account* (Georgia, 1979); R. Wolfe (ed.), *Americans as Proconsuls: United States Military Government in Germany and Japan* (Carbondale, Illinois, 1984); W. P. Woodard, *The Allied Occupation of Japan, 1945–52 and Japanese Religions* (Leiden, 1972); S. Yoshida, *The Yoshida Memoirs: The Story of Japan in Crisis* (London, 1961); M. M. Yoshitsu, *Japan and the San Francisco Peace Settlement* (New York, 1982).

LIMITS OF GERMAN, JAPANESE AND ITALIAN
DOMINANCE 1934 - 1944

USSR

ALASKA

MONGOLIA

JAPAN

Tokyo

Pacific

San
Francisco

CHINA

Chungking

Shanghai

Midway Is

Karachi

INDIA

Hong Kong

Wake I

Pearl Harbor

Hawaiian Is

Calcutta

Philippine
Is.

Guam

Marshall
Is

Singapore

Caroline Is

Indian
Ocean

Ocean

DUTCH
EAST
INDIES

AUSTRALIA

Brisbane

Sydney

NEW ZEALAND

Aleutian Is

GREENLAND

ICELAND

Murmansk

SWEDEN

Leningrad

• Moscow

USSR

CANADA

Montreal

UNITED
KINGDOM

Stalingrad

UNITED
STATES

New York
Washington

Casablanca

IRAN
Basra

Atlantic

Cairo

MEXICO

WEST
INDIES

FRENCH
W. AFRICA

FR. EQ. AFRIC.

SUDAN

VEN.

GUIANAS

NIG.

COL.

EQUADOR

Accra

BELG.
CONG.

KENYA
TANGANYIKA

PERU

BRAZIL

Natal

BOL.

Ocean

ANGOLA

CHILE

Rio de Janeiro

S.W.
AFRICA

Madagascar

ARGENTINA

Buenos
Aires

Cape
Town

SOUTH
AFRICA

~ARTHUR BANKS~

WORLD POWER 1949

U S S R

MONGOLIA

TIBET

CHINA *(Communist)*

INDIA

JAPAN

Tokyo

TAIWAN *(Nationalist)*

Hong Kong

Singapore

Philippine Is

Caroline Is

NEW GUINEA

INDONESIA

Indian Ocean

ALASKA

C A

Aleutian Is

Pacific

Midway I

Hawaiian Is

Marshall Is

Ocean

AUSTRALIA

Sydney

NEW ZEALAND

GREENLAND

ICELAND

SWEDEN

USSR
Moscow

UNITED
KINGDOM

Berlin

CANADA

Montreal

IRAN

UNITED
STATES

New York
Washington

Atlantic

MOROCCO

ALGERIA LIBYA EGT.

MEXICO

WEST
INDIES

FRENCH
W. AFRICA

FR. EQ. AFRICA

SUDAN

VEN.
COL.

GUIANAS

NIG.

EQUADOR

PERU

BRAZIL

BELG.
CONG.

KENYA

TANGANYIKA

BOL.

Ocean

ANGOLA

RHO.

Madagascar

Rio de Janeiro

S.W.
AFRICA

CHILE
ARGENTINA

Buenos
Aires

Cape
Town

SOUTH
AFRICA

| | USA and allies (NATO and Japan). |
| | USSR and dependencies. |

~ARTHUR RANKS~

INDEX:
The Western Hemisphere

INDEX:
The Greater East Asia and Pacific Conflict